A Practical Guide to Solaris

A Practical Guide to Solaris

Mark G. Sobell

ADDISON–WESLEY

Boston • San Francisco • New York • Toronto • Montreal
London • Munich • Paris • Madrid
Capetown • Sydney • Tokyo • Singapore • Mexico City

The publisher offers discounts on this book when ordered in quantity for special sales. For more information, please contact:

Pearson Education Corporate Sales Division
One Lake Street
Upper Saddle River, NJ 07458
(800) 382-3419
corpsales@pearsontechgroup.com

Visit AW on the Web: www.awl.com/cseng/

Library of Congress Cataloging-in-Publication Data

Sobell, Mark G.
      A practical guide to Solaris / Mark G. Sobell.
            p.   cm.
      Includes bibliographical references.
      ISBN 0-201-89548-X
      1. Op.   I. Title.
    III. Series.
    TK5105.35.I24   1997
    004.6'—dc21   97-17977
                                                         CIP

ISBN 0-201-18461-3
Text printed on recycled paper
5 6 7 8 9 10—MA—0403020100
Fifth printing, September 2000

Trademark acknowledgments appear on page 1112, which is a continuation of this copyright page.

For my Wife Laura,
without whose untiring support
I would never have completed this book

BRIEF
CONTENTS

Brief Contents

Contents

PART I
<u>Introduction to Solaris</u>

x   Contents

CHAPTER 2
Getting Started 15

CHAPTER 3
The Solaris Utilities. 41

CHAPTER 4
The Solaris Filesystem 75

Chapter 5
The Shell I 103

PART II
<u>Intermediate/Advanced Solaris</u>

CHAPTER 6
Graphical User Interfaces 129

xvi   Contents

CHAPTER 8
The vi Editor 245

CHAPTER 9
The **emacs** Editor **291**

xxii   Contents

Chapter 10
The Shell II (sh) 347

CHAPTER 11
Bourne Shell Programming 393

CHAPTER 12
The C Shell 435

CHAPTER 13
The Korn Shell and Advanced Shell
Programming 479

CHAPTER 14
Programming Tools 547

CHAPTER 15
System Administration 591

PART III
The Solaris Utility Programs

APPENDIX A

Regular Expressions **953**

APPENDIX B

Help!. 963

APPENDIX C
Security 993

APPENDIX D
The POSIX Standards 1007

Preface

This book is *practical* because it uses tutorial examples that show you what you will see on your terminal, workstation, or terminal emulator screen each step of the way. It is a *guide* because it takes you from logging in on your system (Chapter 2) through writing complex shell programs (Chapters 11, 12, and 13), using sophisticated software development tools (Chapter 14), and administrating a system (Chapter 15). Part III is a *reference guide* to more than 90 Solaris utilities. This *Practical Guide* is intended for people with some computer experience but little or no experience with a Solaris/UNIX system. However, more experienced Solaris/UNIX system users will find Parts II and III to be useful sources of information on subjects such as GUIs, basic and advanced shell programming, editing, C programming, debugging, source code management, networks, the Internet, the World Wide Web, and Solaris system administration.

▲ Audience

This book appeals to a wide range of readers. As a minimum it assumes some experience with a PC or a Mac, but it does not require any programming experience. It is appropriate for

- Users of both single- and multiuser Solaris systems
- Students taking a class about Solaris
- Students taking any class in which they use Solaris
- Computer science students studying the Solaris Operating System
- People who want to run Solaris at home
- Professionals who want to use Solaris at work
- Programmers who need to understand the Solaris programming environment

▲ Benefits

You will come away from this book with a broad knowledge of Solaris and how to use it in day-to-day work. Whether you are a C or Shell programmer or a user who wants to run application programs, this book will give you the knowledge to proceed. *A Practical Guide to Solaris* gives you a broad understanding of Solaris, including how to administer, maintain, and update the system. It will remain a valuable reference tool for years to come.

▲ Scope of Coverage and Features

A Practical Guide to Solaris covers a wide range of topics, from writing simple shell scripts to recursive shell programming; from local email to using Netscape to browse the World Wide Web; from using simple utilities to source code management using SCCS; from using a system to administrating one. The following section highlights some of the features of this book and is followed by more in-depth discussions of some of these features.

▲▲ Features

- Full coverage of Sun's GUIs: Common Desktop Environment (CDE) and OpenLook Window Manager (**olwm**)
- Tutorials on key topics (**vi**, CDE editor, Netscape, and more)
- Discusses terminal emulation (logging in from a PC or other emulator)
- Appendixes covering
    - Regular expressions
    - Help: covers finding and downloading software, login information, basic GUI information
    - Security
    - POSIX
- Covers important GNU tools such as **gcc** and **gzip**
- Covers the **emacs** and **vi** editors (one complete chapter on each)
- Part III covers the use of over 90 utilities including many examples

▲▲ Solaris

- Compatible with all releases of Solaris 2.x through System 7 (Solaris 2.7)
- A complete discussion of the Solaris filesystem
- A discussion of the SPARC PROM Mode
- Coverage of both the Intel (x86) and SPARC versions of Solaris
- Discusses SPARC and x86 (Intel) Boot procedures
- Covers both the CDE and OpenLook GUI interfaces
- Covers AnswerBook2 including installation and running from the CDROM (System 7 only)

▲▲ Internet

- Broad Internet coverage including Netscape, **ftp**, downloading software and documentation using a search engine, and constructing a simple HTML page
- Complete instructions on obtaining and using free software: finding, downloading (using Netscape or **ftp**), decompressing, compiling, and installing software from the Internet
- Guidance on using **ping**, **whois**, **nslookup**, **traceroute**, and more
- Getting online documentation from many sources (local and Internet)

▲▲ Tutorials

- **vi** editor
- **dtmail** mail program (CDE)
- **mailtool** mail program (Open Look)
- **dtpad** text editor (CDE)
- **textedit** text editor (Open Look)
- **pine** as a mail program
- **pine** as a newsreader
- Netscape as browser
- Netscape as a newsreader
- How to use a search engine

▲▲ Assistance

- Many examples throughout
- Comprehensive index
- Caution boxes warn you of the consequences of taking certain actions
- Security boxes caution you where security may be breached
- Tip boxes give you helpful hints
- Appendix B, *Help!,* written in FAQ style covers (partial list):
    - Internet addresses of where you can obtain additional software (some free)
    - Downloading software from the Internet
    - Decompressing, compiling, and installing software obtained from the Internet
    - Basic login and GUI information to help you get started
    - Setting up special keyboard keys

▲▲ The Shells

- Thorough shell coverage including an introductory shell chapter as well as chapters on the Bourne Shell (**sh**), the C Shell (**csh**), and the Korn Shell (**ksh**). Coverage includes both interactive use of the shells and programming.

- Korn Shell coverage of the coprocess, with examples

▲▲ The X Window System

- Window managers

- Bringing up and shutting down the X Window System

- Setting X resources

- Using the X Window System

- Customizing the X Window System

- Remote Computing and Local Displays

▲▲ Common Desktop Environment (CDE) Desktop Manager

- Window Manager (**dtwm**)

- Creating and using Actions

- File Manager (**dtfile**)

- Front panel use and customization

- Editing (**dtpad**)

- Mail (**dtmail**)

- Building Menus (**dtwm**)

- Windows

- Terminal emulation

- Style Manager

- Login Manager

- Initialization files used to customize CDE

▲▲ OpenLook Window Manager (**olwm**)

- Workspace Menu

- File Manager

- Customizing the desktop
- Help viewer
- Customizing menus

▲▲ System Administration

- Using **pkginfo**, **pkgadd**, and **pkgrm** to add/remove software packages
- Adding and removing users
- Using **patchadd/installpatch** to install patches to the system
- Adding local and remote printers
- Installing AnswerBook2
- Using **admintool** for system administration
- Using **ufsdump** and **ufsrestore** to back up and restore files
- Sharing files with other machines (RFS, NFS)
- Coverage of ACL (Access Control List) permissions
- Security issues
- The PROCFS filesystem
- Configuring and booting the system (both SPARC and x86)
- Adding and removing devices and drivers
- Performing a reconfigure reboot
- Disk capacity planning and partitioning
- Setting up network files
- Running system reports (**sar**, **iostat**, **vmstat**, **netstat**, **mpstat**, **top**)

▲▲ Programming Environment

- Using SCCS (source code management)
- Using **make**
- Using the Sun C compiler (**cc**) as well as the GNU C compiler (**gcc**)
- Using both the **dbx** and **gdb** debuggers
- Using shared libraries

▲ Parts I, II, and III

A Practical Guide to Solaris shows you how to use Solaris from your terminal. Part I comprises Chapters 1 through 5, which introduce the new user to Solaris: introduction, getting started, basic utilities, filesystem structure, and the shell. Part I contains step-by-step tutorials covering the most important aspects of the Solaris operating system.

Part II comprises Chapters 6 through 15, which cover intermediate and advanced aspects of Solaris: GUI interfaces, networking, the **vi** and **emacs** editors, the Bourne, C, and Korn Shells and shell scripts, programming, and system administration.

Part III offers a comprehensive, detailed reference to more than 90 Solaris utilities, with numerous examples. If you are already familiar with the Solaris/UNIX system, this part of the book will be a valuable, easy-to-use reference. If you are not an experienced user, you will find Part III a useful supplement while you are mastering the subjects and tutorials in Parts I and II.

> If you have used a Solaris/UNIX system before, you may want to skim over Chapters 2 and 3 or even all of Part I.

The more advanced material in each chapter is presented in sections marked "Optional," which you are encouraged to return to after mastering the more basic material presented in the chapter. Review exercises are included at the end of each chapter for readers who want to hone their skills. Some of the exercises test the reader's understanding of material covered in the chapter, while others challenge the reader to go beyond the material presented to develop a more thorough understanding.

▲▲ Organizing Information

In Chapters 2, 3, and 4, you will learn how to create, delete, copy, move, and search for information using Solaris utilities. You will also learn how to use the Solaris file structure to organize the information you store on your computer.

▲▲ Electronic Mail and Telecommunications

Chapters 2 and 3 and Part III include information on how to use utilities (**pine**, **talk**, **write**, and the graphical mail programs **dtmail** and **mailtool**) to communicate with users on your system and other systems. Chapter 7 details how to address electronic mail to users on remote, networked systems.

▲▲ Using the Shell

Chapter 5 shows you how to redirect output from a program to the printer, to your terminal, or to a file—just by changing a command. You will also see how you can use pipes to combine utilities to solve problems right from the command line.

▲▲ Advanced Shell Coverage Including Shell Programming

Once you have mastered the basics of Solaris, you can use your knowledge to build more complex and specialized programs using a shell programming language (shell scripts). Chapter 10 picks up where Chapter 5 leaves off. It covers more advanced aspects of working with a shell, using the Bourne Shell for examples. Chapter 11 shows you how to use the Bourne Shell to write scripts composed of Solaris system commands. Chapter 12 covers the C Shell. Chapter 13 covers the Korn Shell, which combines many of the popular features of the C Shell (such as history and aliases) with a programming language similar to that of the Bourne Shell. This chapter also covers many concepts of advanced shell programming. The examples in Part III also demonstrate many features of the utilities you can use in shell scripts.

▲▲ Using Programming Tools

Chapter 14 introduces you to Solaris's exceptional programming environment. This chapter describes how to use some of the most useful software development tools: **cc** (Solaris C compiler), **gcc** (the GNU C compiler), **make**, the Source Code Control System (SCCS), and the **dbx** and **gdb** debuggers. The **make** utility automates much of the drudgery involved in ensuring that a program you compile contains the latest versions of all program modules. SCCS help you to track the versions of files involved in a project. The **dbx** and **gdb** debuggers help you get your programs running correctly.

▲▲ Networking, the Internet, and the World Wide Web

Chapter 7 explains what a network is, how it works, and how you can use it. It tells you about types of networks, various network implementations, distributed computing, how to use the network for communicating with other users, and using various networking utilities (such as **rcp**, **telnet**, **ftp**, **pine**, **nslookup**, and more). This chapter also discusses the use of the Internet and shows, with examples, how to use a browser (Netscape) and a search engine (AltaVista) and how to create a very simple page on the Web.

▲▲ Graphical User Interfaces (GUIs)

Chapter 6 discusses the X Window system, how to open and control windows, how to customize your X work environment, and how to use and customize the CDE and OpenLook window managers.

▲▲ The Korn Shell and Advanced Shell Programming

Chapter 13 covers many of the features of this powerful shell. It extends the concepts of shell programming introduced in Chapter 11 into more advanced areas, including more information on the locality of variables, recursion, and the coprocess.

▲▲ The **vi** Editor

The screen-oriented **vi** editor, which was originally a part of Berkeley UNIX, is still one of the most widely used text editors. Chapter 8 starts with a tutorial on **vi** and goes on to explain how to use many of the advanced features of **vi**, including special characters in search strings, the general-purpose and named buffers, parameters, markers, and executing commands from **vi**. The chapter concludes with a summary of **vi** commands.

▲▲ The **emacs** Editor

Produced and distributed (for minimal cost) by the Free Software Foundation, the GNU **emacs** editor has grown in popularity and is available for Solaris. Chapter 9 includes information on **emacs** versions 19 and above and the X Window System, allowing you to use a mouse and take advantage of X Window System features such as cut and paste with **emacs**. This chapter explains how to use many of the features of this versatile editor, from a basic orientation to the use of the META, ALT, and ESCAPE keys; key bindings, buffers, the concept of Point, the cursor, Mark, and Region, incremental and complete searching for both character strings and regular expressions; using the online help facilities, cutting and pasting (from the keyboard and with a mouse), and using multiple windows; and C Mode, which is designed to aid a programmer in writing and debugging C code. The chapter concludes with a summary of **emacs** commands.

▲▲ Job Control

The job control commands, which originated on Berkeley UNIX, allow a user to work on many jobs at once from a single window, and switch back and forth between the jobs as desired. Job control is available under the Job, C, and Korn Shells.

▲▲ Shell Functions

A feature of the Bourne and Korn Shells, shell functions enable you to write your own commands that are similar to the aliases provided by the C Shell, only more powerful.

▲▲ Source Code Management: SCCS

The Source Code Control System is a convenient set of tools that enables programmers to track multiple versions of files on a number of different types of projects.

▲▲ POSIX

The IEEE POSIX committees have developed standards for programming and user interfaces based on historical UNIX practice, and new standards are under development. Appendix D describes these standards and their direction and effect on the UNIX industry.

▲▲ System Administration

Chapter 15 explains the inner workings of the Solaris system. It details the responsibilities of the Superuser and explains how to bring up and shut down a Solaris system, add users to the system, back up files, set up new devices, check the integrity of a filesystem, and more. This chapter goes into detail about the structure of a filesystem and explains what administrative information is kept in the various files.

▲▲ Using Utilities

The Solaris system includes hundreds of utilities. Part III contains extensive examples of how to use many of these utilities to solve problems without resorting to programming in C (or another language). The example sections of **nawk** (over 20 pages, starting on page 820) and **sort** (page 891) give real-life examples that demonstrate how to use these utilities alone and with other utilities to generate reports, summarize data, and extract information.

▲▲ Regular Expressions

Many UNIX utilities allow you to use regular expressions to make your job easier. Appendix A explains how to use regular expressions, so that you can take advantage of some of the hidden power of your Solaris system.

▲ Supplements

The author's home page (**www.sobell.com**) contains downloadable listings of the longer programs from the book; current pointers to many interesting and useful Solaris sites on the World Wide Web; a list of corrections to the book; and a solicitation for corrections, comments, suggestions, and additional programs and exercises.

▲ Thanks

First of all a big thanks to Doug Hughes who gave me a big hand with the entire book and especially the parts on system administration, networks, the Internet, and programming. Doug is the Solaris Guru who takes care of everything computer at Auburn University College of Engineering.

Thanks also to the folks at AW who helped bring this book to life: My editor Carter Shanklin who put up with my procrastination and gave me the support and leeway I needed to get this book out; John Fuller who gave me guidance and much latitude in producing the book; and everyone else who worked behind the scenes to make this book happen.

Also, a big, "Thank You" to the folks who read through the drafts of the book and made comments that caused me to refocus parts of the book where things were not clear or were left out altogether. Thanks to Ronald Hiller, Graburn Technology, Inc., Charles A. Plater, Wayne State University, Kaowen Liu, Andy Spitzer, Bob Palowoda, Sun Microsystems, Rik Schneider, Tom Bialaski, Sun Microsystems, Roger Hartmuller, TIS Labs at Network Associates, Jesse St. Laurent, Steve Bellenot, Ray W. Hiltbrand, Jennifer Witham, Gert-Jan Hagenaars, and Casper Dik.

I am also indebted to Denis Howe who edits *The Free On-line Dictionary of Computing.* Dennis has graciously permitted me to use entries from his compilation. Be sure to look at the dictionary at **foldoc.doc.ic.ac.uk/foldoc**.

l Preface

A Practical Guide to Solaris is based in part on two of my previous UNIX books, *UNIX System V: A Practical Guide* and *A Practical Guide to Linux*. There were many people who helped me with those books and thanks is due them here: Thanks to Pat Parseghian, Dr. Kathleen Hemenway, and Brian LaRose; Byron A. Jeff, Clark Atlanta University; Charles Stross; Eric H. Herrin, II, University of Kentucky; Jeff Gitlin, Lucent Technologies; Kurt Hockenbury; Maury Bach, Intel Israel Ltd.; Peter H. Salus; Rahul Dave, University of Pennsylvania; Sean Walton, Intelligent Algorithmic Solutions; Tim Segall, Computer Sciences Corporation; Arnold Robbins, Georgia Tech. University; Behrouz Forouzan, DeAnza College; Mike Keenan, Virginia Polytechnic Institute and State University; Mike Johnson, Oregon State University; Jandelyn Plane, University of Maryland; Sathis Menon, Georgia Tech. University; Cliff Shaffer, Virginia Polytechnic Institute and State University; and Steven Stepanek, California State University, Northridge, for reviewing the book.

I also continue to be grateful to the many people who helped with the early editions of my UNIX books. Special thanks to Roger Sippl, Laura King, and Roy Harrington for introducing me to the UNIX system. My mother, Dr. Helen Sobell, provided invaluable comments on the original manuscript at several junctures. Also thanks to Isaac Rabinovitch, Professor Raphael Finkel, Professor Randolph Bentson, Bob Greenberg, Professor Udo Pooch, Judy Ross, Dr. Robert Veroff, Dr. Mike Denny, Joe DiMartino, Dr. John Mashey, Diane Schulz, Robert Jung, Charles Whitaker, Don Cragun, Brian Dougherty, Dr. Robert Fish, Guy Harris, Ping Liao, Gary Lindgren, Dr. Jarrett Rosenberg, Dr. Peter Smith, Bill Weber, Mike Bianchi, Scooter Morris, Clarke Echols, Oliver Grillmeyer, Dr. David Korn, Dr. Scott Weikart, and Dr. Richard Curtis.

Dr. Brian Kernighan and Rob Pike graciously allowed me to reprint the **bundle** script from their book, *The UNIX Programming Environment.*

Of course I take responsibility for any errors or omissions. If you find one or just have a comment, let me know (**mark@sobell.com**), and I'll fix it in the next printing. My home page (**www.sobell.com**) contains a list of all the errors found so far, and who found them. It also contains copies of the longer scripts from the book and pointers to many interesting Solaris pages.

Mark G. Sobell
Menlo Park, California

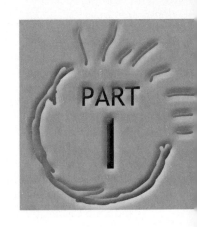

PART

1

Introduction
to Solaris

The Solaris Operating System

An operating system is a control program for a computer. It allocates computer resources and schedules tasks. Computer resources include all the hardware: The central processing unit, system memory, disk and tape storage, printers, terminals, modems, and anything else that is connected to or inside the computer. An operating system also provides an interface to the user—it gives the user a way to access the computer resources.

An operating system performs many varied functions almost simultaneously. It keeps track of filenames and where each file is located on the disk, and it monitors every keystroke on each of the terminals. Memory typically must be allocated so that only one task uses a given area of memory at a time. Other operating system functions include fulfilling requests made by users, running accounting programs that keep track of resource use, and executing backup and other maintenance utilities. An operating system schedules tasks so that a processor is working on only one task at a given moment, although the computer may appear to be running many programs at the same time.

The Solaris 2 operating system is based on UNIX System V Release 4 (SVR4) with a lot of additional work done by Sun. To understand Solaris 2 you must first understand some of the history of UNIX.

▲ The Heritage of UNIX

The UNIX system was developed by researchers who needed a set of modern computing tools to help them with their projects. The system allowed a group of people working together on a project to share selected data and programs while keeping other information private.

Universities and colleges played a major role in furthering the popularity of the UNIX operating system through the "four-year effect." When the UNIX operating system became widely available in 1975, Bell Labs offered it to educational institutions at nominal cost. The schools, in turn, used it in their computer science programs, ensuring that computer science students became familiar with it. Because UNIX is such an advanced development system, the students became acclimated to a sophisticated programming environment. As these students graduated and went into industry, they expected to work in a similarly advanced environ-

3

ment. As more of these students worked their way up in the commercial world, the UNIX operating system found its way into industry.

In addition to introducing students to the UNIX operating system, the Computer Systems Research Group (CSRG) at the University of California at Berkeley made significant additions and changes to it. They made so many popular changes that one of the two most prominent versions of the system in use today is called the Berkeley Software Distribution (BSD) of the UNIX system. The other major version is UNIX System V, which descended from versions developed and maintained by AT&T and UNIX System Laboratories.

▲ What's So Good about Solaris?

The Sun operating system was originally called SUNOS. When Sun bundled OpenWindows with SUNOS 4.1.2, they called the package Solaris 1.0. Solaris has evolved a great deal since that time, most notably with the introduction of Solaris 2. Solaris 2 has many features to its credit. This section lists some of the more important ones.

▲▲ System Features

The Solaris operating environment includes a 32-bit and 64-bit kernel, standards-based networking, support for both SPARC and Intel platforms, and Java technology support. The 64-bit computing environment, introduced as part of Solaris 7 (also known as Solaris 2.7) provides greater capacity, precision, and performance than earlier systems.

The symmetric multiprocessing (SMP) kernel allows Solaris to run on multiple-processor machines. In addition the web-based installation, GUI-based text/voice notes, and process manager make it easier to install and use Solaris software.

Solaris supports the Euro currency symbol, complex text formats for Arabic, Thai, and Hebrew languages, and development of multilanguage applications.

▲▲ Standards

Solaris supports the POSIX.1 (page 1007) and POSIX.2 (page 1009) standards. It also supports the X/Open Common Applications Environment (CAE), Portability Guide Issue 4 Version 2 (XPG4v2), and Networking Services Issue 4 (XNET4). Sun has cleverly set the system up so you can run POSIX-compliant utilities or the historical UNIX utilities (page 1013). Give the command **man xpg4** for more information (page 27).

▲▲ Binary Compatibility

One of the advantages of Solaris 2 is that it is scalable from a single-processor Intel or old SPARC1 machine up to a 64-processor supercomputer-class Ultra Enterprise 10,000 (Starfire) server cluster. Also, the entire SPARC line from the slowest machine up to the fastest multiprocessor machine is binary compatible (you can take the same program and run it on any of the machines—you cannot, however, run a SPARC binary on an Intel x86 machine, nor vice versa).

▲▲ The Standardization of UNIX

Individuals from companies throughout the industry have joined together to develop a standard named POSIX (Portable Operating System Interface for Computer Environments), which is largely based on the UNIX System V Interface Definition (SVID) and other earlier standardization efforts. These efforts have been spurred by the U.S. government, which needs a standard computing environment to minimize training and procurement costs. Now that these standards are gaining acceptance, software developers are able to develop applications that run on all conforming versions of UNIX, including Solaris. See Appendix D.

▲▲ How Can UNIX Run on Different Computers/Processors?

A *portable* operating system is one that can run on many different machines. More than 95 percent of the UNIX/Solaris operating system is written in the C programming language, and C is portable because it is written in a higher-level, machine-independent language. (Even the C compiler is written in C.) Just as UNIX is portable between different machines, Solaris runs on two different architectures.

▲▲▲ The C Programming Language

Ken Thompson originally wrote the UNIX operating system in 1969 in PDP-7 assembly language. Assembly language is machine-dependent: Programs written in assembly language work on only one machine or, at best, one family of machines. Therefore the original UNIX operating system could not easily be transported to run on other machines.

To make UNIX portable, Thompson developed the B programming language, a machine-independent language, from the BCPL language. Dennis Ritchie developed the C programming language by modifying B and, with Thompson, rewrote UNIX in C in 1973. After this rewrite the operating system could be transported more easily to run on other machines.

That was the start of C. You can see in its roots some of the reasons why it is such a powerful tool. C can be used to write machine-independent programs. A programmer who designs a program to be portable can easily move it to any computer that has a C compiler. C is also designed to compile into very efficient code. With the advent of C, a programmer no longer had to resort to assembly language to get code that would run well (that is, quickly—although hand-tuned assembly language will always generate more efficient code than a high-level language).

C is a modern systems language. You can write a compiler or an operating system in C. It is highly structured, but it is not necessarily a high-level language. C allows a programmer to manipulate bits and bytes, as is necessary when writing an operating system. But it also has high-level constructs that allow efficient, modular programming.

Like UNIX, C is popular because it is portable, standard, and powerful. It has high-level features for flexibility and can still be used for systems programming. These features make it both useful and usable. A standards organization, the American National Standards Institute (ANSI), defined a standard version of the C language in the late 1980s that is commonly referred to as *ANSI C*. The original version of the language is often referred to as *Kernighan & Ritchie* (or just *K&R*) C, named for the authors of the book that first described the C language. Another researcher at Bell Labs, Bjarne Stroustrup, created an object-oriented programming language named *C++*, which is built on the foundation of C. Because object-oriented programming is desired by many employers today, C++ is preferred over C in many environments.

▲ Overview of Solaris

As a version of UNIX, the Solaris operating system has many unique and powerful features. Like other operating systems, Solaris is a control program for computers. But it is also a well-thought-out family of utility programs (Figure 1-1) and a set of tools that allows users to connect and use these utilities to build systems and applications.

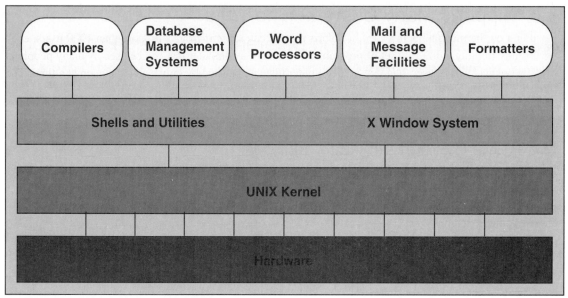

Figure 1-1   A layered view of the Solaris operating system

▲▲ Solaris Has a Kernel Programming Interface

The *kernel* is the heart of the Solaris operating system, responsible for controlling the computer's resources and scheduling user jobs so that each one gets its fair share of system resources, including access to the CPU and peripheral devices such as disk and CDROM storage, printers, and tape drives. Programs interact with the kernel through *system calls,* special functions with well-known names. A programmer can use a single system call to interact with many different kinds of devices. For example there is one **write** system call, not many device-specific ones. When a program issues a **write** request, the kernel interprets the context and passes the request along to the appropriate device. This flexibility allows old utilities to work with devices that did not exist when the utilities were originally written, and it makes it possible to move programs to new versions of the operating system without rewriting them (provided that the new version recognizes the same system calls).

▲▲ Supports Many Tasks at One Time

Solaris is a fully protected, multitasking operating system (unlike Windows 95). It allows each user to run more than one job at a time. While processes can communicate with each other, they are also fully protected from one another just as the kernel is protected from all processes. You can run several jobs in the background while giving all your attention to the job being displayed on your screen; you can even switch back and forth between jobs. If you are running the X Window System (page 10), you can run different programs in different windows on the same screen and watch all of them. With this capability users can be more productive.

▲▲ Supports Many Users at One Time

Depending on the machine being used, a Solaris system can support from 1 to more than 1000 users, each concurrently running a different set of programs. The cost of a computer that can be used by many people at the same time is less per user than that of a computer that can be used by only a single person at a time. The cost is less because one person cannot generally use all the resources a computer has to offer. No one can keep the printers going constantly, keep all the system memory in use, keep the disks busy reading and writing, keep the modems in use, and keep the terminals, workstations, and terminal emulators busy. A multiuser operating system allows many people to use all of the system resources almost simultaneously. Thus, use of costly resources can be maximized, and the cost per user can be minimized. These are the primary objectives of a multiuser operating system.

▲▲ Solaris Provides a Hierarchical Filesystem with Builtin Security

A *file* is a collection of information, such as text for a memo or report, an accumulation of sales figures, an image, or an executable program created by a compiler. Each file is stored under a unique name, usually on a disk storage device. The Solaris filesystem provides a structure where files are arranged under *directories,* which are like folders or boxes. Each directory has a name and can hold other files and directories. Directories in turn are arranged under other directories, and so forth, in a treelike organization. This structure assists users in keeping track of large numbers of files by enabling them to group related files into directories. Each user has one primary directory and as many subdirectories as required (Figure 1-2).

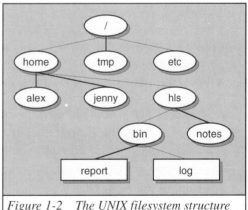

Figure 1-2   The UNIX filesystem structure

Another mechanism, *linking,* allows a given file to be accessed by means of two or more different names. The alternative names can be located in the same directory as the original file or in another directory. Links can be used to make the same file appear in several users' directories, enabling them to share the file easily.

Like most multiuser operating systems, Solaris allows users to protect their data from access by other users. Solaris also allows users to share selected data and programs with certain other users by means of a simple but effective protection scheme.

▲▲ The Shell Is a Command Interpreter and Programming Language

The shell is a command interpreter that acts as an interface between users and the operating system. When you enter a command, the shell interprets the command and calls the program you want. While there are a number of shells available for Solaris, some of the more popular ones are

- The Bourne Shell (**sh**), which is an enhanced version of the Bourne Shell, one of the original UNIX shells

- The C Shell (**csh**), which is an enhanced version of the C Shell, developed as part of Berkeley UNIX

- The Korn Shell (**ksh**), which incorporates features from a number of shells

Because users often prefer different shells, multiuser systems can have a number of different shells in use at any given time. The choice of shells demonstrates one of the powers of the Solaris operating system: The ability to provide a customized user interface.

Besides its function of interpreting commands from a terminal, terminal emulator, or workstation keyboard and sending them to the operating system, the shell can be used as a high-level programming language. Shell commands can be arranged in a file for later execution as a high-level program. This flexibility allows users to perform complex operations with relative ease, often with rather short commands, or to build elaborate programs that perform highly complex operations with surprisingly little effort.

▲▲▲ Filename Generation

When you are typing commands to be processed by the shell, you can construct patterns using special characters that have special meanings to the shell. These patterns are a kind of shorthand: Rather than typing in complete filenames, users can type in patterns, and the shell will expand them into matching filenames. A pattern can save you the effort of typing in a long filename or a long series of similar filenames. Patterns can also be useful when you know only part of a filename and when you cannot remember the exact spelling.

▲▲▲ Device-Independent Input and Output

Devices (such as a printer or terminal) and disk files all appear as files to Solaris programs. When you give the Solaris operating system a command, you can instruct it to send the output to any one of several devices or files. This diversion is called output *redirection*.

In a similar manner a program's input that normally comes from a user's keyboard can be redirected so that it comes from a disk file instead. Under the Solaris operating system, input and output are *device-independent;* they can be redirected to or from any appropriate device.

As an example, the **cat** utility normally displays the contents of a file on the screen. When you run a **cat** command, you can easily cause its output to go to a disk file instead of to the screen.

▲▲▲ Shell Functions

One of the most important features of the shell is that users can use it as a programming language. Because the shell is an interpreter, it does not compile programs written for it but interprets them each time they are loaded from the disk. Loading and interpreting programs can be time-consuming.

Many shells, including **sh** and **ksh**, allow you to write shell functions that the shell will hold in memory, so it does not have to read them from the disk each time you want to execute them. The shell also keeps functions in an internal format, so it does not have to spend as much time interpreting them. Refer to page 506 for more information about shell functions.

Although **csh** does not have a general-purpose function capability, it has a similar feature: *Aliases*. Aliases allow you to define new commands and to make standard utilities perform in nonstandard ways. The C Shell provides aliases but not shell functions; **ksh** provides both.

▲▲▲ Job Control

Job control is a feature of the shell that allows users to work on several jobs at once, switching back and forth between them as desired. Frequently when you start a job, it is in the foreground, so it is connected to your terminal or workstation. Using job control, you can move the job you are working with into the background and continue running it there while working on or observing another job in the foreground. If a background job needs your attention, you can move it into the foreground so it is once again attached to your terminal or workstation. The concept of job control originated with Berkeley UNIX, where it appeared in the C Shell.

▲▲ A Large Collection of Useful Utilities

Solaris includes a family of several hundred utility programs, often referred to as *commands*. These utilities perform functions that are universally required by users. An example is **sort**. The **sort** utility puts lists (or groups of lists) in order. It can put lists in alphabetical or numerical order and thus can be used to sort by part number, author, last name, city, zip code, telephone number, age, size, cost, and so forth. The **sort** utility is an important programming tool and is part of the standard Solaris system. Other utilities allow users to create, display, print, copy, search, and delete files. There are also text editing, formatting, and typesetting utilities. The **man** (for manual) utility provides online documentation of Solaris itself.

▲▲ Interprocess Communication

Solaris allows users to establish both pipes and filters on the command line. A *pipe* sends the output of one program to another program as input. A *filter* is a special form of a pipe. It is a program that processes a stream of input data to yield a stream of output data. Filters are often used between two pipes. A filter processes another program's output, altering it in some manner. The filter's output then becomes input to another program.

Pipes and filters frequently join utilities to perform a specific task. For example you can use a pipe to send the output of the **cat** utility to **sort**, a filter, and then use another pipe to send the output of **sort** to a third utility, **lp**, that sends the data to a printer. Thus in one command line you can use three utilities together to sort and print a file.

▲▲ System Administration

The system administrator has many responsibilities. The first responsibility may be to set up the system and install the software. Once the system is up and running, the system administrator is responsible for downloading and installing software (including upgrading the operating system), backing up and restoring files, and managing system facilities such as security, network setup and maintenance, printers, terminal ports, and remote logins via phone lines, the local area network, and the internet. The system administrator is also responsible for setting up accounts for new users (on a multiuser system), bringing the system up and down as needed, and taking care of any problems that arise. This book *does* cover post-installation system administration in Chapter 15 and throughout the book.

▲ Additional Features of Solaris

▲▲ Graphical User Interfaces

The X Window System, also called X, developed in part by researchers at MIT, provides the foundation for the graphical user interface (GUI) available with Solaris. Given a terminal or workstation screen that supports X, a user can interact with the computer through multiple windows on the screen; display graphical information; or use special-purpose applications to draw pictures, monitor processes, or preview typesetter output. X is an across-the-network protocol that allows a user to open a window on a workstation or computer system that is remote from the CPU generating the window.

A *window manager* is a program that runs under the X Window System and allows you to open and close windows, start programs running, and set up a mouse so it does different things depending on how and where you click. It is the window manager that gives your screen its personality. While Microsoft Windows allows you to change the color of key elements in a window, a window manager under X allows you to change the overall look and feel of your screen. It allows you to change the way a window looks and works (you can give a window different borders, buttons, and scroll bars), set up a virtual desktop, create mouse button menus, and more.

Solaris is shipped with three window managers. The ODT window manager (**dtwm**), the OpenLook window manager (**olwm**), and the Tab window manager (**twm**). You will probably use one of the first two.

▲▲ (Inter)networking Utilities

Solaris network support includes many valuable utilities that enable users to access remote systems over a variety of networks. Besides giving you the ability to send mail easily to users on other machines, you can access files on disks mounted on other computers as if they were located on your machine, make your files available to other computers in a similar manner, copy files back and forth, run programs on other machines while displaying the results back on your machine, and perform many other operations across local area networks (LANs) and wide area networks (WANs), including the Internet.

Layered on top of this network access is a wide range of application programs that extend the computer's resources around the globe. You can carry on conversations with people throughout the world, gather information on a wide variety of subjects, and download new software over the Internet quickly and reliably. Chapter 7 gives more information on how to use Solaris when connected to a network.

▲▲ Software Development

One of the strengths of Solaris is its rich software development environment. You can find compilers and interpreters for many computer languages. Besides C and C++, other languages that are available for Solaris include such standard languages as Ada, Fortran, Lisp, Pascal, and many others. The **yacc** utility generates parsing code that makes it easier to write programs to read input, whereas **lex** generates scanners, code that recognizes lexical patterns in text. Tools such as the **make** utility and GNU's automatic configuration utility (**configure**) make it easy to manage complex development projects, whereas source code management systems such as SCCS simplify version control. The **debugger** debugger can help in tracking down and repairing software defects. The **lint** program can perform extensive checking of C code that can make the code more portable and cut down on debugging time. These and other software development tools are discussed in Chapter 14 and are described in detail in Part II. In addition to the Solaris tools, GNU has a complete set of high-quality compilers, debuggers, and so forth that are available for free. See Appendix B.

▲▲ Screen-Oriented and Graphical Editors

Screen-oriented editors (for example **vi** and **emacs**) are an advance over their predecessors, line-oriented editors (**ed**, **teco**). A screen-oriented editor displays a context for editing: Where **ed** displayed a line at a time, **vi** displays a screenful of text. You can run a screen-oriented editor on a terminal or in a terminal emulator window on a graphical display.

An editor designed for a GUI can only run on a graphical display. Two graphical editors supplied with Solaris are OpenLook's **textedit** and CDE's **dtpad**. This book starts by teaching you to create and edit files using **dtpad** (page 30). Or you can read the tutorial on **textedit** (page 32) if you prefer. These editors are easier to learn than **vi** or **emacs**, so they allow you to work with files in the process of learning Solaris without getting bogged down in the specifics of a more complex editor. Chapter 8 explains how to use **vi** in stages, from a tutorial introduction (page 246) through "Advanced Editing Techniques" (page 277). Chapter 9 is dedicated to **emacs**, the do-everything editor written by Richard Stallman of the GNU/Free Software Foundation.

▲▲ Advanced Electronic Mail

Choosing a mail program is largely a matter of personal preference. Popular mail programs commonly used with Solaris include **dtmail**, **mailtool**, **mail**, **pine**, Netscape mail, **elm**, and mail through **emacs**. This book has tutorials on **dtmail** and **mailtool** (page 62), and **pine** (page 65) because of their popularity and availability. The **dtmail** program is often used from CDE, whereas **mailtool** is used from OpenLook. The Berkeley **Mail** program was the first mail utility with advanced features. Today any modern mail program allows you to

- Reply to a message, automatically addressing the reply to the person who sent the message.

- Use an editor (such as **vi** or **emacs**) to edit a piece of electronic mail while composing it. With a graphical mail program (**dtmail** and **mailtool**) you are using an editor while you compose your email.

- Provide a summary of all messages in your inbox when you call it up to read your mail.

- Automatically keep a copy of all electronic mail you send.

- Create aliases that make it easier to send mail to groups of people.

- Send and receive encoded binary messages, including compiled code, pictures, documents formatted by a word processor, and audio or visual information using the MIME (Multipurpose Internet Mail Extensions) standard.

- Customize features to suit your needs.

▲ GNU/FSF

The goal of the Free Software Foundation is to create a UNIX-like system, named HURD. Their project is known as GNU (which stands for GNUs Not UNIX). In the process of writing HURD, they have written many useful, highly portable versions of popular utilities (compilers, debuggers, editors, and so on). You can run many of the GNU tools (for example the GNU C compiler, **gcc**) under Solaris. These tools are available as source code, which you need to compile, and executable files that you can run immediately.

You can obtain GNU code at no cost over the Internet. You can obtain the same code via U.S. mail at a modest cost for materials and shipping. You can support the Free Software Foundation by buying the same (GNU) code in higher-priced packages.

GNU software is distributed under the terms of the GNU Public License Agreement (GPL). The GPL says that you have the right to copy, modify, and redistribute the code covered by the agreement, but that when you redistribute the code, you must also distribute the same license with the code, making the code and the license inseparable. If you get the source code for an accounting program that is under the GPL off the Internet and you modify it and redistribute an executable version of the program, you must also distribute the modified source code and the GPL agreement with it. Because this is the reverse of the way a normal copyright works (it gives rights instead of limiting them), it has been termed a *copyleft*. (This paragraph is not a legal interpretation of the GPL; it is here only to give you an idea of how it works. Refer to the GPL itself if you want to make use of it.)

Summary

Solaris grew out of the UNIX heritage to become a very popular operating system. Its availability on both Intel and Sun hardware means that it has a wide appeal. The Sun computers and operating system are known for networking superiority, which makes many system administrators' jobs easier. The excellent programming and development environment means that programmers as well as end users are more comfortable on it. These reasons and more make Solaris a viable version of UNIX.

Review Exercises

1. What is a multiuser system? Why are they successful?

2. Why is Solaris popular?

3. In what language is Solaris written? What does the language have to do with the success of UNIX?

4. What is a utility program?

5. What is a shell?

6. How can you use utility programs and a shell to create your own applications?

7. Why is the Solaris filesystem referred to as a *hierarchical* (or *treelike*) filesystem?

8. What is the difference between a multiprocessor and a multiprocessing system?

9. Give an example of when you would want to use a multiprocessing system.

10. How many people wrote UNIX (approximately)? Why is this unique?

11. Who owns the GNU **gcc** compiler? What are the key terms of the GNU Public License Agreement?

12. What does it mean to be POSIX-compliant?

13. Name three standards that Solaris supports.

14. What makes GNU an unusual acronym?

15. Why is it much more difficult to write a virus for UNIX than for DOS or Macintosh operating systems?

Advanced Review Exercises

16. What is a macro virus and what makes it so troublesome?

Getting Started

This chapter helps you get started using Solaris. Read this chapter in front of a Solaris system so you can experiment as you read. If you are familiar with the topics described in this paragraph, you may want to skip this chapter or just skim through it. This chapter discusses conventions used in this book and leads you through a brief session with your Solaris system. After showing you how to log in and out, it explains how to correct typing mistakes, abort program execution, and change your password. Next it covers two important utilities that you can use to get help with your system and commands: Answerbook2 and **man** (or **xman**), each of which displays online documentation. Finally it presents two tutorials: The **dtpad** editor and the **textedit** editor. Then it introduces some basic utilities that manipulate files. With these utilities you can obtain lists of filenames, display the contents of files, and delete files. For more help see Appendix B.

▲ Before You Start

The best way to learn is by doing. You can read and use Chapters 2 through 15 while you are sitting in front of a terminal, computer, or workstation. Learn about Solaris by running the examples in this book and by making up your own examples. Feel free to experiment with different utilities. The worst thing that you could do is erase one of the files that you have created, but because these are only practice files, you can easily create others.

Before you get started, you should know the answers to most of the following questions. If you do not, browse through the "Help!" appendix on the pages indicated in the following list.

- What is the name of the machine I will log in on (networked systems only)?   (page 988)
- What is my login name?   (page 988)
- What is my password?   (page 988)
- What is the termcap or terminfo name for my terminal, workstation, or terminal emulator?   (page 988)
- How do I specify my terminal type?   (page 987)
- Which shell am I using?   (page 989)

- How can I send files to a printer?   (page 988)
- Where can I find the Solaris documentation?   (page 963)

▲▲ Name and Version of the Operating System

The names of the releases of Solaris are confusing. The following may help to straighten things out.

- **Solaris 7** = Solaris 2.7 = SunOS 5.7
- **Solaris 2.6** = SunOS 5.6

This book is about *Solaris 2.x* (referred to as Solaris2) through *Solaris 7* and calls your attention to features that are new to *Solaris 7* or *Solaris 2.6*. There is no *Solaris 6*.

▲▲ Conventions

This book uses typographical conventions to make its explanations shorter and clearer. The following paragraphs describe these conventions.

▲▲▲ Keys and Characters

THIS FONT describes three kinds of items:

- important keys, such as the SPACE bar and the RETURN,[1] ESCAPE, and TAB keys

- the characters that keys generate, such as the SPACEs generated by the SPACE bar

- keys that you press with the CONTROL key, such as CONTROL-D (Even though D is shown as an uppercase letter, you do not have to press the SHIFT key; enter CONTROL-D by holding the CONTROL key down and pressing **d**.)

▲▲▲ Utility Names

Names of utilities are printed in this **bold**, **sans serif** typeface. Thus there are references to the **sort** utility and the **vi** editor.

---

1. Different keyboards use different keys to move the cursor to the beginning of the next line. This book always refers to the key that ends a line as the RETURN key. Your keyboard may have a RET, NEWLINE, Enter, RETURN, or other key. Some keyboards have a key with a bent arrow on it. (The key with the bent arrow is not an arrow key. Arrow keys have straight shafts.) Use the corresponding key on your keyboard each time this book tells you to press RETURN.

▲▲▲ Filenames

Filenames appear in the same font as the rest of the text, but in a **bold** typeface. Examples are **memo5**, **let-ter.1283**, and **reports**. Filenames may include upper- and lowercase letters; however, Solaris is *case sensitive* (it differentiates between upper- and lowercase letters), so **memo5**, **MEMO5**, and **Memo5** are three different files to Solaris (and UNIX in general).

▲▲▲ Shell and Builtin and Variable Names

This book covers three shells: the Bourne Shell, or **sh**; the C Shell, or **csh**; and the Korn shell, or **ksh**. It discusses shell builtin programs, shell variables, and shell functionality, each of which is specific to one or more of the three shells. Where appropriate each of these items is followed by a symbol such as $\frac{sh}{csh}$ or $\frac{sh}{ksh}$. This box lists the shells specific to the preceding item.

▲▲▲ Items You Enter

Everything that you enter at your keyboard is displayed in a bold typeface: Within the text, **this bold typeface** is used (the same as filenames in the text), and within examples and screens, `this one` is used.

This book refers to the **ls** utility, or just **ls**, but instructs you to enter **ls –a** on the keyboard. Thus a distinction is made in the text between utilities, which are programs, and the instructions you give the computer to invoke the utilities.

In the first line of Figure 2-1, for example, the word `login:` is printed in a nonbold typeface because Solaris displayed it. The word **jenny** is in a bold typeface to show that the user entered it; this word would appear as **jenny** within the text.

```
login: jenny
Password:
Last login: Sat Jul 29 10:33:11 from lightning
Sun Microsystems Inc.    SunOS 5.6        Generic August 1997
$
```

Figure 2-1   Logging in

▲▲▲ Prompts and RETURNS

Most examples include the *shell prompt*—the signal that Solaris is waiting for a command—as a dollar sign (**$**). Your prompt may differ—another common prompt is a percent sign (**%**). The prompt is printed in a nonbold typeface because you do not enter it. Do not enter the prompt on the keyboard when you are experimenting with examples from this book. If you do, the examples will not work.

Examples *omit* the RETURN keystroke that you must use to execute them. An example of a command line is

```
$ vi memo.1204
```

To use this example as a model for calling the **vi** editor, type **vi memo.1204** and then press the RETURN key. (Press **:q!** to get out of **vi**—Refer to "Starting vi" on page 246.) This convention makes the examples in the book match what appears on your screen.

▶ Start Optional

▲▲▲ Optional Information

Passages marked as optional are not central to the concepts presented in the chapter, and they often involve more challenging concepts. A good strategy when reading a chapter is to skip the optional sections and then return to them after you are comfortable with the main ideas presented in the chapter. This is an optional paragraph (and if you are not reading it, . . .).

▶ Stop Optional

▲▲▲ Solaris2 Designation

This book uses the terms *Solaris2* and *Solaris* without a *2* following it. Solaris1.0 was introduced with SunOS 4.1.2 as a way of naming the operating system bundled with OpenWindows. In practice almost no one refers to the moniker drafted by Sun marketing as it applies to the SunOS 4 operating system. These days the name Solaris generally refers to Solaris2 or above. Also see "Product Name" on page 592.

▲ Logging In

Now that you are acquainted with some of the special keyboard characters and the conventions this book uses, it will be easier to start using Solaris. This section leads you through a brief session, explaining how to log in and log out.

Chapter 15 Covers System Administration

If you are running on a system you are administrating, that is, if you are responsible for setting up users (such as yourself), a printer, and have other administration responsibilities, refer to Chapter 15. Specifically see "Day-to-Day System Administration" on page 625.

Because many people can use a single Solaris computer at the same time, the operating system must be able to differentiate between you and other users. You must identify yourself before Solaris processes your requests. On networked systems where you can potentially log in on a number of different systems, you must also make sure you identify yourself to the correct system. There are two ways to log in on your system: Using a character-based interface (Figure 2-1) or a graphical user interface (Figure 2-2). If you are using a character-based interface, skip the next section.

▲▲ Graphical User Interface (GUI)

Your system is probably set up so you can log directly in on a graphical user interface (GUI). If it is, your screen will look similar to the one in Figure 2-2. Enter your username, press **RETURN**, and enter your password before pressing **RETURN** again. Your password will not appear on the screen as you type. Once you have logged in, you will be presented with your graphical user interface (probably OpenLook or Common Desktop Environment [CDE]). For more information see "Logging In" on page 131.

*Figure 2-2   Logging in on a Solaris machine named **friday***

Start Optional

Even if your system supports a GUI, you do not have to log in as described here. You can always start the GUI after you have logged in. You may find it more convenient to log in on a character-based system. The Solaris GUI allows you to log in on either. You may have applications that work only in one environment or the other so it is useful to have access to both environments.

At the GUI login display, move the mouse pointer until it is over the **Options** box (Figure 6-3, page 131). Click and hold the left mouse button down and drag the arrow on the screen until it is over **Command Line Login**. Release the mouse button, wait a moment, and press **RETURN**. You will shortly see the login prompt described in the next section. If you do not log in promptly, the screen will revert to the GUI login display.

For more information see "Using a GUI" on page 130.

Stop Optional

▲▲ Character-Based Interface

(If you are using a GUI interface you can skip this section.) Figure 2-1 shows how a typical login procedure appears on a screen. Your login procedure may look different. If you are using a terminal that is directly connected (not some form of computer) and your screen does not display the word `login:`, check to see that the terminal is plugged in and turned on and then press the **RETURN** key a few times. If `login:` still does not appear, try pressing **CONTROL-Q**. If you are using a computer or workstation, make sure it is running. Run **telnet** (page 21) or whatever communications/emulation software you have to log in on the system.

You must end every message or command to the Solaris system by pressing the **RETURN** key. Pressing **RETURN** signals that you have completed giving an instruction and that you are ready for the operating system to execute the command or respond to the message.

```
SunOS 5.6

login: jenny
Password:
Last login: Wed Mar 25 10:46:27 from lightning
Sun Microsystems Inc.    SunOS 5.6        Generic August 1997
$
```

Figure 2-3   Logging in using a character-based interface

The first line of Figure 2-3 (following the minimal system identification) shows the Solaris `login:` prompt followed by the user's response. The user enters **jenny**, her *login name* (also called a *username*), followed by a **RETURN**. Try logging in, making sure that you enter your login name as you specified it when you set up your account—the routine that verifies the login name and password is case sensitive.

The next line of Figure 2-3 shows the `Password:` prompt.

Keep your password secure

For security reasons Solaris never displays a password. Enter your password in response to the `Password:` prompt, and then press **RETURN** as the user has done in the example. The characters you enter do not appear on the screen.

The third line gives you information about the last login on this account, showing when it took place and where it originated. In Figure 2-3 the last access came from a machine named **lightning**. You can use this information to see if anyone else has accessed this account since you last used it. If someone has, it might indicate that an unauthorized user has learned your password and has logged on as you. In the interest of security, advise your system administrator of the circumstances that made you suspicious. If you do not have a system administrator, or when your system administrator advises you to do so, change your password (page 24).

Next the *shell prompt* (or just *prompt*) appears, indicating that you have successfully logged in. The shell prompt line may be preceded by a short message or two. The first message, called the *message of the day,* or **motd** (page 612), generally identifies the version of Solaris that is running along with any local messages placed in the **/etc/motd** file. The second message comes from the **/etc/issue** file if it exists. The default prompt is a dollar sign (**$**) $_{\text{ksh}}^{\text{sh}}$ or a percent sign (**%**)$_{\text{csh}}$. These shell prompts are easy to change and frequently reflect your user and machine names. Each of these prompts indicates that the system is ready for you to give it a command.

▲▲▲ Incorrect Login

If you enter your name or password incorrectly, the **login** utility displays the following message after you finish entering both your login name *and* password:

```
Login incorrect
```

This message tells you that you have entered either the login name *or* password incorrectly or that they are not valid. The message does not differentiate between an unacceptable login name and an unacceptable password. This discourages unauthorized people from guessing names and passwords to gain access to the system.

Log In On the Right Machine

One reason the login/password combination may not be valid is because you are trying to log in on the wrong machine. If you are using a larger, networked system, you may have to specify the machine you want to connect to before you can log in. You can see a list of machines you can log in on or specify a machine from the GUI login screen. Move the arrow on the screen to the **Options** box and click and hold either mouse button. A menu will appear. Drag the arrow until it is over **Remote Login** and release the button. Move the arrow until it is over either **Enter Host Name ...** or **Choose Host From List ...** and click the left mouse button. Enter the name of the computer you want to connect to and press **RETURN**, or click on the computer you want to log in on to highlight it and then click on **OK**. Proceed to log in.

Make Sure Your Login Name Is Valid

Another reason the login/password combination may not be valid is because you have not been set up as a user. If you are administrating your machine, see "Adding and Removing Users" on page 625. Otherwise check with your system administrator.

▲▲▲ The Shell

Once you log in you are communicating with the command interpreter known as the *shell*. The shell plays an important part in all your communication with Solaris. When you enter a command at the keyboard (in response to the shell prompt on the screen), the shell interprets the command and initiates the appropriate action. This action may be executing your program, calling a standard program such as a compiler or a Solaris utility, or giving you an error message telling you that you have entered a command incorrectly.

Refer to "**passwd**: Changing Your Password" on page 24 if you want to change your password.

▲▲ Logging Out

Now try logging out and back in again. Using CDE, click the left mouse button on the **EXIT** button on the Control Panel. If you are using OpenLook, place the mouse pointer over a portion of the screen that is not covered by a window and press and hold the right mouse button. With the button still depressed, slide the mouse pointer until it is over **Exit...** and take your finger off the button. If you are using a character-based interface, press **CONTROL-D** in response to the shell prompt to log out. If **CONTROL-D** does not work, try giving the command **exit** or **logout**. The **logout** command is typically used with the C Shell (Chapter 12), whereas the Bourne Shell (Chapter 10) and the Korn Shell (Chapter 13) use **exit**. **CONTROL-D** works from all shells.

▲▲ Terminal Emulation and **telnet**

If you do not have your own workstation or X terminal, chances are you are connected to a Solaris machine using a terminal emulator. A terminal emulator is a piece of software that produces a window on your screen that looks and acts like a simple ASCII (character) terminal. Because a terminal uses a simple, basic interface (as opposed to a graphical user interface), terminal emulators have been written for almost all computers. The terminal emulator, running on your computer, connects to a Solaris machine via a network (Ethernet, asynchronous phone line, PPP, or any other type) and allows you to log in on the Solaris machine. The two most common places you will find terminal emulators is on Apple Macintosh machines and PCs running DOS or MS Windows. For more information see "Opening a Terminal Emulator Window" on page 140.

If you are logging in via a dialup line, the connection will be straightforward: When you instruct the emulator program to contact the computer, it dials the phone and you get a login prompt from the remote system. If you are logging in via a directly connected network, you will use **telnet** or **rlogin** to call the computer so you can log in. Like the terminal emulator, **telnet** is a program that has been implemented on many machines, not just UNIX systems. Most implementations of **telnet** include a terminal emulator. From your Macintosh, PC, or UNIX machine, give the command **telnet** followed by the name or IP address (a number that has four segments separated by periods; see "Host Addresses" on page 193) of the machine you want to connect to. Or click on the **telnet** icon to open a terminal emulator window. From that window you can usually connect to Solaris by using a menu. Once you are connected you will get a login prompt. For examples and more detail, see "**rlogin**, **telnet**: Access a Remote Computer" on page 203.

No matter how you connect, make sure you have your TERM variable set to the type of terminal your emulator is emulating. For more help see "How Do I Specify the Terminal I Am Using?" on page 987. If you see the following prompt:

```
Term = (unknown)
```

and press **RETURN**, the system will assume you have a dumb terminal and the emulator will not produce acceptable results when running programs (such as **vi**) that take advantage of full screen terminal capabilities such as arrow key movement. You need to enter a value (such as **vt100**—a common terminal to emulate) following the (unknown) prompt before you press **RETURN**. Most systems come with **vt100** terminal emulation patterned after the original DEC VT100 terminal.

▲▲ Superuser

While you are logged in as the user named *root,* you are referred to as *Superuser* and have extraordinary privileges. You can read from or write to any file on the system, you can execute programs that ordinary users cannot, and more. On a multiuser system you may not be permitted to know the **root** password. In this case there is someone, usually called the *system administrator,* who knows the **root** password and maintains the system. If you are running Solaris on your own computer, you will assign a password to **root** when you set your system up. Refer to "The System Administrator and Superuser" on page 592 for more information.

Do Not Experiment while You Are Superuser

Do not experiment with the system while you are logged in as **root**. Superuser *can* do a lot of damage quite quickly and easily with a Solaris (or any UNIX) system.

▲ Correcting Mistakes

This section explains how to correct typos and other errors you may make while you are logged in. Log in on your system, and try making and correcting mistakes as you read this section.

Because the shell and most other utilities do not interpret the command line (or other text) until after you press **RETURN**, you can correct typing mistakes before you press **RETURN**. There are several ways to correct typing mistakes: You can erase one character at a time, you can back up a word at a time, or you can back up to the beginning of the command line in one step. After you press **RETURN**, it is too late to correct a mistake; you can either wait for the command to run to completion or abort execution of the program (page 24).

> ### CONTROL-Z Will Stop Your Program
>
> Although not a way of correcting a mistake, you may press **CONTROL-Z** by mistake and wonder what happened (you will see a message containing the word `Stopped`). You have just stopped your job using job control (page 357). Give the command **fg** and you should be back to where you were before you pressed **CONTROL-Z**.

▲▲ Erasing a Character

While entering characters from the keyboard, you can back up and erase a mistake by pressing the *erase key* one time for each character you want to delete. The erase key backs over as many characters as you wish. It does not, in general, back up past the beginning of the line.

The default erase key is **BACKSPACE**. If this key does not work, try **Delete**. If these keys do not work, or if you would like to use another key as your erase key, give the following command in response to the shell prompt ($ or %):

```
stty erase key
```

In place of *key*, press the key or combination of keys you want to use as your erase key. Then press **RETURN**. Common choices are **BACKSPACE**, **CONTROL-H**, **Delete**, and **Del**. You can use any key you like, but some choices are more convenient than others. For more help see "Examples" on page 905.

▲▲ Deleting a Word

In many shells you can delete the word you are entering by pressing **CONTROL-W**. When you press **CONTROL-W**, the cursor moves left to the beginning of the current word, removing the word. A *word* is any sequence of nonblank characters (that is, a sequence of characters that does not contain a **SPACE** or **TAB**). If you press **CONTROL-W** while in the process of typing a word, the cursor moves to the beginning of the current word. If you press **CONTROL-W** after ending a word with a **SPACE** or **TAB** character, the cursor moves to the beginning of the previous word.

▲▲ Deleting a Line

You can delete a line you are entering any time before you press **RETURN** by pressing the *line kill* key (or just kill key). When you press this key, the cursor moves to the left, erasing characters as it goes, back to the beginning of the line. The default line kill key is **CONTROL-U**. If this key does not work, try **CONTROL-X**. If these keys do not work, or if you would like to use another key as your line kill key, follow the preceding instructions for changing the erase key, substituting the word `kill` for the word `erase`. For more help see "Examples" on page 905.

▲▲ Aborting Execution

Sometimes you may want to terminate a running program. A Solaris program may be performing a task that takes a long time, such as displaying the contents of a file that is several hundred pages or copying a file that is not the file you meant to copy.

To terminate a program press the interrupt key (**CONTROL-C** or sometimes **Delete** or **Del**). When you press this key, the Solaris operating system sends a terminal interrupt signal to the program you are running and to the shell. Exactly what effect this signal has depends on the program. Some programs stop execution immediately, whereas others ignore the signal. Some programs take other appropriate actions. When the shell receives a terminal interrupt signal, it displays a prompt and waits for another command. If these keys do not work, or if you would like to use another key as your interrupt key, follow the preceding instructions for changing the erase key, substituting the word `intr` (interrupt) for the word `erase`. For more help see "Examples" on page 905.

If these methods do not terminate the program, try stopping the program (**CONTROL-Z**), giving the **jobs** command to verify the job number of the program, and using **kill** to abort the program. The job number is the number within the brackets at the left end of the line that **jobs** displays (**[1]**). The **kill** command uses **–9** to send a KILL signal to the job specified by the job number, which is preceded by a percent sign (**%1**):

```
% bigjob
^Z
Stopped (user)
% jobs
[1]  + Stopped (user)        bigjob
% kill -9 %1
%
[1]    Killed                bigjob
```

The **kill** command returns a prompt; press **RETURN** again to see the confirmation message. For more information on job control, see the discussion on page 118.

▲ passwd: Changing Your Password

If you were assigned a password by someone other than yourself, it is a good idea to give yourself a new password. A good password is seven or eight characters long and contains a combination of numbers, upper- and lowercase letters, and punctuation characters. Avoid using control characters (such as **CONTROL-H**) because they may have a special meaning to the system, making it impossible for you to log in. Do not use names, words from English or other languages, or other familiar words that someone can guess easily.

```
$ passwd
passwd:  Changing password for jenny
Enter login password:
New password:
Re-enter new password:
passwd (SYSTEM): passwd successfully changed for jenny
$
```

*Figure 2-4   Using **passwd** to change your password*

Figure 2-4 shows the process of changing a password using the **passwd** utility. For security reasons none of the passwords that you enter is ever displayed by this or any other utility.

Give the command **passwd** (followed by a **RETURN)** in response to the shell prompt. This command causes the shell to execute the **passwd** utility. The first item **passwd** asks you for is your *old* password. The **passwd** utility verifies this password to ensure that an unauthorized user is not trying to alter your password. Next **passwd** requests the new password.

Your password should meet the following criteria to be relatively secure (only the first is mandatory):

- It must be at least six characters long (or longer if the system administrator sets it up that way).

- It should not be a word in a dictionary of any language, no matter how seemingly obscure.

- It should not be the name of a person, place, pet, or other thing that might be discovered easily.

- It should contain at least two letters and one digit.

- It should not be your login name, the reverse of your login name, or your login name shifted by one or more characters.

- If you are changing your password, the new password should differ from the old one by at least three characters. Changing the case of a character does not make it count as a different character.

After you enter your new password, **passwd** asks you to retype it to make sure you did not make a mistake when you entered it. If the new password is the same both times you enter it, your password is changed. If the passwords differ, it means that you made an error in one of them; **passwd** displays the following message:

```
passwd(SYSTEM): They don't match; try again.
New password:
Re-enter new password:
passwd (SYSTEM): passwd successfully changed for jenny
$
```

After you enter the new password, **passwd**—as it did before—asks you to reenter it. If your password is not long enough, **passwd** displays the following message:

```
passwd(SYSTEM): Password too short - must be at least 6 characters.
New password:
```

Enter a longer password in response to the `New password:` prompt.

When you successfully change your password, you change the way you log in. You must always enter your password *exactly* the way you created it. If you forget your password, Superuser can straighten things out. Although no one can determine what your password is, Superuser can change it and tell you your new password.

▲ Documentation

Online documentation has always been one of UNIX's strong points. The manual (or man) pages have been available (and still are) via the **man** utility since early releases. With Solaris2 and the advent of the Internet, the sources of documentation have expanded. Sun produced a graphical documentation package named AnswerBook which, in Solaris2, became HTML-based and was renamed AnswerBook2.

▲▲ AnswerBook2

The AnswerBook2 package is a network documentation server that talks to Web browsers, such as Netscape (page 234), as clients. In other words if one machine on a network runs AnswerBook2, all the other machines on the network can retrieve information from that instance of AnswerBook2 by using their Web browsers.

Solaris 2.6 and Solaris 2.7 come with AnswerBook2, which includes a lot of Solaris documentation. After you install AnswerBook2 locally (page 643), you will normally run the default database that Sun provides with AnswerBook2. You can expand the AnswerBook2 database to include whatever documentation you like. Sun provides a much expanded AnswerBook2 server on the Internet (Figure 2-5). On this server (**docs.sun.com**) Sun supplies hardware, software, system administration, programming language, and introductory information in English, Japanese, Spanish, French, German, Italian, and Swedish.

The AnswerBook2 software will run only on a Web browser such as HotJava or Netscape Navigator. There are several ways to start AnswerBook2: One way is by giving the command **answerbook2**. After your browser appears (AnswerBook2 launches the browser automatically) with the AnswerBook2 interface, enter one or two words that describe what you are looking for in the box in the upper-right corner of the screen to the right of the word `Search` (Figure 2-5). Then click on the displayed items that are of interest to you.

Searching for More Information

If you cannot find the information you need locally, use your browser to go to **http://docs.sun.com** and search there. Double-click on the underlined words that best match the item you are looking for and search as you would in your local AnswerBook2 database. For more help see "Tutorial: Using Netscape" on page 234.

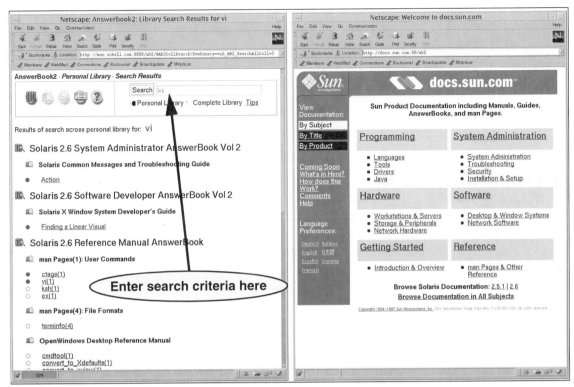

*Figure 2-5   AnswerBook2 on a local system (left) and the AnswerBook2 server at **docs.sun.com** (right)*

▲▲ man and xman: Displaying the System Manual

The **man** (manual) and **xman** (a version of **man** for the X Window System graphical user interface) utilities display pages, known as **man** pages, from the system documentation. This documentation is useful if you know what utility you want to use but have forgotten exactly how to use it. Because the descriptions in the system documentation are often quite terse, they are most helpful if you already understand basically what a utility does. If a utility is new to you, the descriptions provided in this book are typically easier to understand.

To find out more about a utility, including the **man** utility itself, give the command **man** followed by the name of the utility. For example, the following command displays information about the **who** utility:

```
$ man who
```

The **man** utility automatically sends the output through a *pager,* usually **more**. When you display a manual page in this way, **more** displays a prompt at the bottom of the screen after each screenful of text and waits for you to request another screenful. When you press the **SPACE** bar, you see a new screenful of information. Pressing **h** (help) displays a list of the **more** commands you can use. Pressing **q** (quit) stops **man** and gives you a shell prompt. If you want to change the directories that **man** looks in, see page 810.

Xman Sections
(1) User Commands
(1B) SunOS/BSD Compatibility Package Commands
(1C) Communication Commands
(1F) FMLI Commands
(1M) Maintenance Commands
(1S) SunOS Specific Commands
(2) System Calls
(3) C Library Functions
(3B) SunOS/BSD Compatibility Library Functions
(3C) C Library Functions
(3E) C Library Functions
(3G) C Library Functions

Figure 2-6   The Xman Sections menu

If you are using the X Window System, you can use **xman**, which provides a *point-and-click* interface (generally using a mouse to point and click) to the online manual pages.

To start **xman** on your system, give the command **xman** from a terminal emulation window. Or use **xman&** if you want **xman** to run in the background (page 116) so you can use the window while **xman** is running. Either way a small **xman** window appears (see the embedded figure to the right). When you move the mouse pointer and click on **Manual Page** at the bottom of the window, **xman** displays a larger window named **Manual Page** containing a description of how to use **xman**. See "How Do I Get Started with a Graphical User Interface (GUI)?" on page 989 for more information on using a mouse.

In the upper-left corner of the **Manual Page** window are the words **Options** and **Sections**. When you move the mouse pointer to **Sections** and click and hold the left mouse button, the **Xman Sections** menu appears (Figure 2-6 shows the top of this menu). Keep holding the mouse button down and drag the mouse pointer to select the submenu named **(1) User Commands**. Release the mouse button and this selection displays the next level of submenus: A list of Solaris user commands (Figure 2-7). The list is alphabetized from left to right, top to bottom. Use the scroll bar at the left of the window to view the entire list (see "Athena Scroll Bar" on page 143). Figure 2-8 shows the result of clicking on **man**—this is **xman** explaining how to use **man**.

The Solaris system manual (and the **man** pages) are divided into 9 sections (see the list on the following page). Each of the sections describes related tools. This layout closely mimics the way the set of UNIX/Solaris manuals has always been divided.

Manual Page
Options | Sections   The current manual page is: man.

```
imagetool      imake          mixdvfb
intro          ipcrm          ipcs
isalist        jar            java
javac          javadoc        javah
javakey        javald         javap
jdb            jobs           join
jre            jsh            kbd
kbd_mode       kcms_calibrate kcms_configure
kcms_server    kdestroy       kerberos
keylogin       keylogout      kill
kinit          klist          ksh
ksh93          ksrvtgt        last
lastcomm       ld             ld.so.1
ldd            let            lex
limit          line           listres
listusers      ln             loadfont
loadkeys       locale         locale_env
localedef      logger         login
logname        logout         look
lookbib        lorder         lp
lpstat         ls             m4
mach           machid         mail
mailcompat     mailp          mailprint
mailstats      mailtool       mailx
makebdf        makedepend     makepsres
man            mconnect       mcs
mesg           mkdir          mkdirhier
mkfontdir      mkmsgs         more
mp             msgfmt         mt
mv             native2ascii   navigator
nawk           neqn           newaliases
newform        newgrp         news
newsp          nice           nis
nis+           niscat         nischgrp
nischmod       nischown       nischttl
nisdefaults    niserror       nisgrep
nisgrpadm      nisln          nisls
nismatch       nismkdir       nispasswd
```

*Figure 2-7   A list of commands in Section 1 of the Solaris system manual displayed by **xman***

1. User Commands

2. System Calls

3. Library Functions

4. File Formats

5. Headers, Tables, and Macros

6. Demos

7. Device and Network Interfaces[2]

8. (None)

9. DDI and DKI[3]

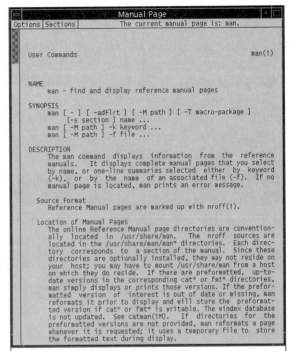

Figure 2-8   **xman** displaying information about **man**

Unless you specify a manual section, **man** displays the earliest occurrence in the manual of the word you specified on the command line. The **xman** utility requires that you specify the manual section you want to look in.

Most users find the information they need in section 1; programmers and system administrators frequently need to consult the other sections. In some cases there are manual entries for different tools with the same name. For example if you enter the following command, you see the manual page for the **write** utility (section 1), which is described in the next chapter:

```
$ man write
```

To see the manual page for the **write** system call from section 2, you would enter

```
$ man -s2 write
```

which instructs **man** to look only in section 2 for the manual page.

▲ Editing a File

A text file is a file that can contain alphabetic, numeric, punctuation, and control characters. The entire set of characters is defined as the ASCII character set (page 1026). You can use **cat**, **pg**, and **more** to view a text

---

2. Also special files

3. Device Driver Interface and Driver-Kernel Interface

file and an editor to create or modify one. The following tutorial sections explain how to get started using **dtpad**, the default CDE (Common Desktop Environment) graphical text editor, and **textedit**, the default OpenLook editor. If you are not using CDE or OpenLook, refer to Chapter 8 (page 246) for a tutorial on **vi** (a standard UNIX editor you can use with a graphical interface from a terminal emulation window or from a character terminal). Chapter 9 covers the **emacs** editor.

This book asks you to create and change files as you read along and practice with the examples. Any one of these editors, or another one, will allow you to work with files as used in this book.

▲▲ Tutorial: dtpad: Creating and Editing a File

When you use **dtpad** you may never see its name. It is simply called Text Editor in the menu you choose it from and at the top of the window you run it in. It is, nonetheless, the principal editor supplied with CDE.

Double-click (all mouse clicks in this discussion of **dtpad** are made with the left mouse button) on the pencil-and-paper icon (Figure 2-9) on the left side of the front panel to bring up the editor. You will see the window shown in Figure 2-10. This window represents a clean sheet of paper or an empty file you can write on with the editor.

Figure 2-9 The **dtpad** *icon on the CDE front panel*

Type whatever you like using the keyboard. Make sure the window is highlighted while you are typing or nothing will appear in the editor window. To highlight the window move the mouse pointer until it is on the window and click the left mouse button.

If you do not press **RETURN**, the text you type will keep flowing in one long line. The editor will scroll the text left so you can continue to see the point at which you are inserting text. You can use **RETURN** at the ends of your lines to keep the window from scrolling horizontally, or you can select **Wrap to Fit** from the **Options** menu at the top of the window. The **Wrap to Fit** option causes **dtpad** to wrap the line you are entering as it approaches the right side of the window.

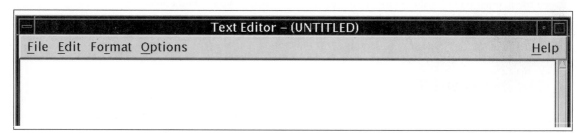

Figure 2-10 The **dtpad** *window*

▲▲▲ Correcting Mistakes

The **BACKSPACE** key erases the character you just entered (the one to the left of the cursor). The Delete and Del keys erase the character to the right of the cursor.

 Moving the Cursor

You can move the keyboard cursor (which indicates where the next character you type will appear) with the mouse by positioning the mouse pointer where you want the keyboard cursor to be and clicking the left mouse button. The keyboard cursor will jump to the location of the mouse pointer. You can also use the ARROW keys to move the keyboard cursor.

Highlighting Text

Click and drag the mouse pointer over the text you want to highlight. Double-click to highlight the word under the mouse pointer. Drag the mouse without releasing the mouse button to highlight additional words. Triple-click (and drag) to highlight lines of text.

Once you have highlighted text you can delete it (BACKSPACE or choose Delete from the Edit menu), replace it (just type the replacement text), or cut or copy it (Cut or Copy from the Edit menu). Position the keyboard cursor where you want to paste the cut or copied text and choose Paste from the Edit menu to insert the text.

Saving a File

The **dtpad** editor does not write anything to the hard disk until you tell it to save the file. When you choose Save[4] from the File menu (Figure 2-11) you will see the Save window shown in Figure 2-12. There are several ways to specify the filename you want to use. The easiest way is to save the file in the working directory (probably your home directory). Because **dtpad** chooses this directory by default, all you have to do is enter the filename in the box labeled Enter file name: and click on OK or press RETURN. In Figure 2-12 Alex has entered the name **testfile**.

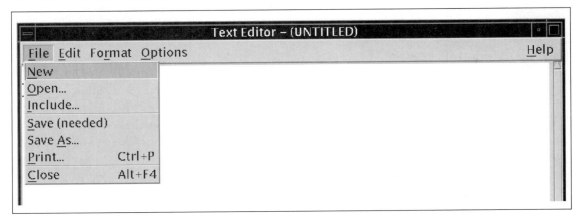

Figure 2-11   The File menu

---

4. If the file has been changed since you last saved it, **dtpad** puts the word (needed) after the Save selection in the File menu.

You can choose another directory (folder) to store the file in by entering the *pathname*[5] of the directory in the top box in the window or double-clicking on a directory in the scrolling list of directories in the box labeled **Folders**.

The default filter (shown in Figure 2-12) displays all file-names that do not begin with a period.

▲▲▲ Ending an Editing Session

Select **Close** from the **File** menu when you are done editing a file. If you have made changes since the last time you saved the file, **dtpad** will ask if you want to save the changes before closing the editor.

*Figure 2-12 The **dtpad** Save As window*

Figure 2-13   The Workspace menu and the Programs sub-menu

▲▲ Tutorial: textedit: Creating and Editing a File

The **textedit** editor is the standard editor for Sun's OpenLook window system. However there is nothing sacred about this relationship: You can use **textedit** in CDE and you can use **dtpad** in OpenLook.

▲▲▲ Getting Started

When you click the right mouse button while the mouse pointer is over the background and not over a window (called the *root window*), OpenLook displays the **Workspace** menu (Figure 2-13). (This is the only time you will use the right mouse button in this discussion of **textedit**. All other mouse clicks are made with the left mouse button.) Click on the triangle at the right of the word Programs to display the **Programs** menu (Figure 2-13). Then select **Text Editor** ... from the **Programs** menu. You will see the window shown in Figure 2-14. This window represents a clean sheet of paper or an empty file you can write on with the editor.

Type whatever you like using the keyboard. Make sure the window is highlighted while you are typing or nothing will appear in the editor window. To highlight the window move the mouse pointer until it is on the window and click the left mouse button. If the window is partially covered by another window, you can

---

5. A pathname is the name of a file, optionally preceded by the names of the directories that hold each other all the way to the file. The names of the directories and the file are separated from each other by a slash (/). DOS and MS Windows use the same type of pathname, only the slashes go the other way (\). See Chapter 4 for more information.

uncover it (bring it to the top) by clicking on the title bar (where it says Text Editor...)

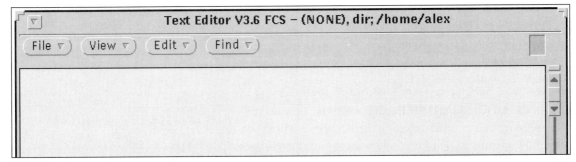

*Figure 2-14   The **textedit** window*

▲▲▲ Correcting Mistakes

The **BACKSPACE**, **DELETE**, and **DEL** keys erase the character you just entered (the one to the left of the cursor).

▲▲▲ Moving the Cursor

You can move the keyboard cursor (which indicates where the next character you type will appear) with the mouse by positioning the mouse pointer where you want the keyboard cursor to be and clicking the left mouse button. The keyboard cursor will jump to the location of the mouse pointer. You can also use the **LEFT** and **RIGHT ARROW** keys to move the keyboard cursor.

▲▲▲ Highlighting Text

Click and drag the mouse pointer over the text you want to highlight. Double-click to highlight the word under the mouse pointer. Drag the mouse without releasing the mouse button to highlight additional words. Triple-click (and drag) to highlight paragraphs of text.

Once you have highlighted text you can delete it (**BACKSPACE** or choose **Cut** from the **Edit** menu), replace it (just type the replacement text) or cut or copy it (**Cut** or **Copy** from the **Edit** menu). Position the keyboard cursor where you want to paste the cut or copied text and choose **Paste** from the **Edit** menu to insert the text.

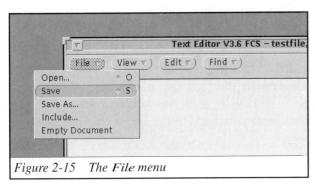

Figure 2-15   The File menu

▲▲▲ Saving a File

The **textedit** editor does not write anything to the hard disk until you tell it to save the file. When you choose **Save** from the **File** menu (Figure 2-15), you will see the Save window shown in Figure 2-16. There are several ways to specify the filename you want to use. The easiest way is to save the file in the working directory (probably your home directory). Because **textedit** chooses this directory by default, all you have to do is enter the filename after the word `Save:` and click on **Save** or press **RETURN**. In Figure 2-16 Alex has entered the name `testfile`.

You can choose another directory (folder) to store the file in by entering the pathname of the directory at the top of the window after the words `Go To:` or double-clicking on a directory in the scrolling list of directories.

▲▲▲ Ending an Editing Session

Click on the **Window** button (the downward pointing triangle just above the **File** menu button, at the left end of the title bar) to display the **Window** menu. Select **Quit** from the **Window** menu when you are done editing a file. If you have made changes since the last time you saved the file, **text-edit** will ask if you want to save the changes before closing the editor.

▲ Basic Utilities

One of the important advantages of Solaris and other UNIXs is that they come with several hundred utilities that perform many functions. You will use utilities every day you use Solaris, whether you use them directly by name or indirectly. Following are some of the most basic and important utilities you will need to know if you use utilities directly from the command line.

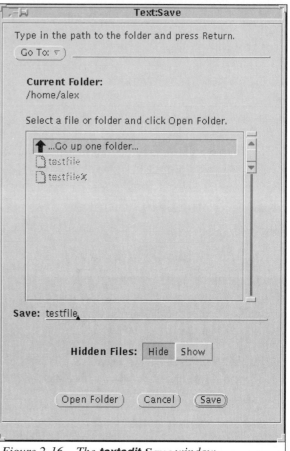

*Figure 2-16   The **textedit** Save window*

▲▲ ls: Listing the Contents of a Directory

Using the editor of your choice, create a small file named **practice** in your directory. After exiting from the editor, you can use the **ls** (list) utility to display a list of the names of the files in your directory. The first command in Figure 2-17 shows **ls** listing the name of the **practice** file. (You may also see files listed that were put there by your system administrator or created automatically by a program you ran.) Subsequent commands in Figure 2-17 display the contents of the file and remove the file. These commands are described next.

▲▲ cat: Displaying a Text File

The **cat** utility displays the contents of a text file. The name of the command is derived from *catenate*, which means to join together one after the other. Chapter 5 (page 110) shows how to use **cat** to string together the

```
$ ls
practice
$ cat practice
This is a small file that I created
with a text editor.
$ rm practice
$ ls
$ cat practice
cat: practice: No such file or directory
$
```

Figure 2-17   Using **ls**, *cat*, *and* **rm**

contents of more than one file. A convenient way to display the contents of a file to the screen is by giving the command **cat** followed by a SPACE and the name of a single file.

Figure 2-17 shows **cat** displaying the contents of **practice**. This figure shows the difference between the **ls** and **cat** utilities. The **ls** utility displays the *names* of the files in a directory, whereas **cat** displays the *contents* of a file.

▲▲ pg or more: Displaying a Long Text File

If you want to view a file that is longer than one screenful, you can use the **pg** (page) or **more** utility in place of **cat**. Each of these utilities pauses after displaying a screenful of text. Although they are very similar, there are subtle differences. For example **pg** waits for you to press RETURN before it displays another screenful, whereas **more** waits for you to press the SPACE bar. At the end of the file, **pg** displays an EOF (end of file) message and waits for you to press RETURN before returning you to the shell, whereas **more** returns you directly to the shell. Give the commands **pg practice** and **more practice** in place of the **cat** command in Figure 2-17 to see how these commands work. Use the command **pg /etc/termcap** instead if you want to experiment with a longer file. Refer to page 815 in Part III for more information on **more** and page 857 for **pg**.

▲▲ rm: Deleting a File

The **rm** (remove) utility deletes a file. Figure 2-17 shows **rm** deleting the **practice** file. After **rm** deletes the file, **ls** and **cat** show that **practice** is no longer in the directory. The **ls** utility does not list its filename, and **cat** says it cannot open the file. Use **rm** carefully.

A Safer Way of Removing Files

You can use the interactive form of **rm** to be sure you delete the file(s) you intend to delete. When you follow **rm** with SPACE, –**i**, SPACE and the name of the file you want to delete, **rm** displays the name of the file and asks you to respond with **y** (yes) or **n** (no) before it deletes the file. The –**i** is called an option. Your system may be set up to function like this automatically.

```
$ rm -i toollist
rm: remove toollist (yes/no)? y
```

▲▲ hostname: Displaying a Machine Name

The **hostname** command displays the name of the machine you are working on. Use it if you are not sure you are logged in on the right machine.

▲ Quoting Special Characters

Special characters, which have a special meaning to the shell, are discussed in Chapter 5. These characters are mentioned here so that you can avoid accidentally using them as regular characters until you understand how the shell interprets them. For example avoid using any of these characters in a filename (even though **emacs** and some other programs do) until you learn how to quote them (as discussed next). The standard special characters are

```
& ; | * ? ' " ` [ ] ( ) $ < > { } ^ # / \ % ! ~ +
```

Although not considered special characters, **RETURN**, **SPACE**, and **TAB** also have special meanings to the shell. **RETURN** usually ends a command line and initiates execution of a command. The **SPACE** and **TAB** characters separate elements on the command line and are collectively known as *whitespace* or *blanks*.

If you need to use one of the characters that has a special meaning to the shell as a regular character, you can *quote* (or *escape*) it. When you quote a special character, you keep the shell from giving it special meaning. The shell treats a quoted special character as a regular character.[6]

To quote, or escape, a character, precede it with a backslash (\). One backslash must precede each character that you are quoting. If you are using two or more special characters, you must precede each with a backslash (for example you must enter ****** as ******). You can quote a backslash just as you would quote any other special character—by preceding it with a backslash (\\).

Another way of quoting special characters is to enclose them between single quotation marks (as in '******'). You can quote many special and regular characters between a pair of single quotation marks (as in 'This is a special character: >'). The regular characters remain regular, and the shell also interprets the special characters as regular characters.

The only way to quote the erase character (**CONTROL-H**), the line kill character (**CONTROL-U**), and other control characters (try **CONTROL-M**) is by preceding any one with a **CONTROL-V**. Single quotation marks and backslashes do not work.

---

6. Except that a / is always a separator in a pathname, even if you quote it.

Summary

As with many operating systems, your access to the system is authorized when you log in. You enter your login name at the `login:` prompt, followed by a password. You can use the **passwd** utility to change your password at any time. Choose a password that is difficult to guess and that conforms to the criteria imposed by the **passwd** utility.

The system administrator is responsible for maintaining your system. On a single-user system, you are the system administrator. On a smaller multiuser system, you or another user is the system administrator, or this job may be shared. On a large multiuser system or network of systems, there is frequently a full-time system administrator. When extra privileges are required to perform certain system tasks, the system administrator logs on as the **root** user by entering the username **root** and the **root** password. While logged on in this manner, this user is called Superuser. On a multiuser system several trusted users may be given the **root** password.

A **RETURN** terminates the commands you enter at the keyboard. Until you press **RETURN**, you can make corrections to the command line by backing over typed characters with the erase key or deleting the entire line with the line kill key. You can usually delete the current word by pressing **CONTROL-W**.

The following list of keys includes control characters usually defined for correcting command-line mistakes, as well as some other useful control characters.

Key	Use
CONTROL-C	Frequently the interrupt key: It interrupts execution of the program you are running (page 24).
CONTROL-D, logout, or exit	Logs you off the system (page 21).
CONTROL-H or BACKSPACE	Frequently the erase key: It erases a character on the command line (page 23). (**BACKSPACE** *is* **CONTROL-H**.)
CONTROL-R or CONTROL-L	Refreshes the screen.
CONTROL-U	Frequently the line kill key: It deletes the entire command line (page 24).
CONTROL-W	Frequently the word erase key: It erases a word on the command line (page 23).

Once you press **RETURN** a program called the shell interprets the words of the command. Most people use the Bourne Shell (**sh**), the C Shell (**csh**), or the Korn Shell (**ksh**). The shell treats a few characters, called special characters, differently than regular characters; if you want one of these characters to represent itself, you must quote it. One way to quote a character is to precede it with a backslash (\).

You often use an editor to create a file in the Solaris filesystem. Among the editors available on Solaris systems are **dtpad** (page 30), **textedit** (page 32), **vi** (Chapter 8), and **emacs** (Chapter 9).

AnswerBook2 is Sun's online documentation system. If one computer on a network runs this utility, all the users on the network can access it through a Web browser. This utility is very helpful to new Solaris users, as well as to experienced users, who must often delve into the system documentation for information on the finer points of the system's structure or behavior. The **man** (or **xman**) utility also provides you with online documentation on system utilities.

   After reading this chapter and experimenting on your system, you should be comfortable using the following utilities.

Utility	Use
cat	Catenates the contents of files and displays them on the screen (page 34)
dtpad	Creates and edits text files (page 30)
ls	Displays a list of files (page 34)
man and xman	Displays pages from the online Solaris manual (page 27)
passwd	Changes your password (page 24)
pg and more	Displays the contents of a text file one screenful at a time (page 35)
rm	Deletes a file (page 35)
textedit	Creates and edits text files (page 32)

   Part III has more information on **pg**, **ls**, **rm**, **man**, and **cat**, and Appendix B has useful ideas and helpful information to use once you are logged in on your system.

Review Exercises

1. The following error message is displayed when you attempt to log in with either an incorrect username *or* an incorrect password:

   ```
   Login incorrect
   ```

   This message does not indicate whether your username, your password, or both are invalid. Why does it not tell you?

2. Give three examples of poor password choices. What is wrong with each? Include one that is too short. Give the error message displayed by the **passwd** utility.

3. Is `fido` an acceptable password? Why or why not (give several reasons)?

4. Using **dtpad**, **textedit**, or another editor, show how you would:

   a. Delete a line.

   b. Save the file you are working on.

   c. Insert some text.

   d. Leave the editor.

5. What are the differences between the **cat** and **ls** utilities? What are the differences between **pg** or **more** and **cat**?

6. What is special about the shell special characters? How can you cause the shell to treat them as regular characters?

7. Most **man** pages begin with the NAME and SYNOPSIS sections. List the other **man** page sections that are commonly used. (*Hint:* Look at several **man** pages; they will use different sections.)

8. Experiment with the **man** and **xman** utilities to answer the following questions:

   a. How many **man** pages are there in the `Special Files` section of the manual?

   b. What version of **xman** are you using?

   c. What happens if you request a **man** page that does not exist?

9. If you cannot find the answer to a question from AnswerBook2 or the **man** pages, where else can you look?

Advanced Review Exercises

10. Four of the following five filenames contain special characters:

    ```
    "\abc
    "abc"
    'abc'
    ab*c
    abc
    ```

    a. Show how to create files with these names.

    b. Give commands to remove the files

    ```
    "\abc
    "abc"
    ab*c
    'abc'
    ```

    leaving only **abc**.

11. You saw that **man** pages for **write** appear in sections 1 and 2 of the system manual. Explain how you can determine what sections of the system manual contain a manual page with a given name.

    a. using **man**

    b. using **xman**

    What are the advantages and disadvantages of using **man** or **xman** for this task?

12. How many **man** pages are there in the `Devices` subsection of the system manual? (`Devices` is a subsection of `Special Files`.)

The Solaris Utilities

Solaris utility programs allow you to work with Solaris and manipulate the files you create. Chapter 2 introduced the shell, the most important Solaris utility program, and **passwd**, the utility that allows you to change your password. It also introduced some of the utilities that you can use to create, view, and manipulate files: **vi**, **ls**, **cat**, **pg**, **more**, and **rm**. This chapter describes other file manipulation utilities, as well as utilities that allow you to find out who is logged in, communicate with other users, print files, compress and expand files, and unpack archived files. It provides many jumping off points in the form of page references for the curious or more advanced reader. Part III covers many of these utilities as well as others more concisely and completely.

▲ Working with Files

The following utilities perform various tasks involving files, including copying, moving, and printing them. If you want to download files from a remote location, see "How Do I Download gzip?" (page 976) and "Downloading a File Using a Browser (and Installing It)" (page 984).

▲▲ cp: Copy a File

The **cp** (copy) utility makes a copy of a file. It can copy any file, including text and executable program files. Using **cp** you can make a backup copy of a file or a copy to experiment with.

A **cp** command line specifies source and destination files with the following syntax:

cp ***source-file destination-file***

The ***source-file*** is the name of the existing file that **cp** is going to copy. The ***destination-file*** is the name that **cp** assigns to the resulting (new) copy of the file.

The command line shown in Figure 3-1 copies the file named **memo**. The copy is named **memo.copy**. The initial **ls** command shows that **memo** is the only file in the directory. After the **cp** command, the second **ls** shows both files, **memo** and **memo.copy**, in the directory.

```
$ ls
memo
$ cp memo memo.copy
$ ls
memo memo.copy
```

*Figure 3-1   Using **cp** to copy a file*

cp Can Destroy a File

If the *destination-file* exists *before* you give a **cp** command, **cp** overwrites it. Because **cp** overwrites (and destroys the contents of) an existing *destination-file* without warning, you must take care not to cause **cp** to overwrite a file that you need. It is a good idea to use the interactive (**–i**) option with **cp**; it checks with you before it overwrites a file. (To use this option, type **cp** SPACE **–i** SPACE before you give the rest of the command—options are discussed on page 104.)

Sometimes it is useful to incorporate the date in the name of a copy of a file. The following example includes the date, January 30 (0130). The period is part of the filename—just another character:

```
$ cp memo memo.0130
```

Although the date has no significance to the Solaris operating system, it can help you find a version of a file that you saved on a certain date. It can also help you avoid overwriting existing files by providing a unique filename each day. Refer to "Filenames" on page 77.

When you need to copy a file from one system to another on a common network, you can use **rcp** (remote copy [page 870]) or **ftp** (File Transfer Protocol [pages 207 and 765]).

▲▲ mv: Change the Name of a File

If you want to rename a file without making a duplicate (copy) of it, you can use the **mv** (move) utility. The **mv** command line specifies an existing file and a new filename with the following syntax:

*mv **existing-filename new-filename***

The command line in Figure 3-2 changes the name of the file **memo** to **memo.0130**. The initial **ls** command shows that **memo** is the only file in the directory. Following **mv**, **memo.0130** is the only file in the directory. Compare this with the earlier **cp** example.

```
$ ls
memo
$ mv memo memo.0130
$ ls
memo.0130
```

*Figure 3-2   Using **mv** to change the name of a file*

The **mv** utility can be used for more than changing the name of a file. Refer to "**mv**, **cp**: Move or Copy a File" on page 88.

▲▲ lp: Print a File

Because several people or jobs can use a single printer, Solaris provides a means for *queuing* printer output so that only one job gets printed at a time. The **lp** (line printer) utility places one or more files in the printer queue for printing. The following command line prints the file named **report** on the printer named **printer_1**, the default printer:

```
$ lp report
request id is printer_1-496 (1 file)
```

The Default Printer May Not Be the One You Think It Is

On a system or network with several printers, the *default* printer may not be the one that is physically closest to you. Do not assume that a print job that you send to the default printer will appear on the printer in your classroom, office, lab, or workroom. Find out the name of the closest printer and use the **–d** option as discussed in the following paragraph.

On machines with access to more than one printer, you can use the **–d** option to instruct **lp** to place the file in the queue for a specific printer, even if that printer is connected to another machine on the network. The next command line prints the same file on the printer named **mailroom**:

```
$ lp -dmailroom report
request id is mailroom-2788 (1 file)
```

You can see the printing jobs in the printer queue using the **lpstat** (line printer status) utility:

```
$ lpstat
printer_1-496        kudos!alex        136545   May 28 16:13
```

If **lpstat** does not work as shown, try **lpstat –o**. In this example Alex has a job that is currently being printed, and no other jobs are in the queue. Alex was logged in on the machine named **kudos** when he sent the job to the printer. The job number (`printer_1-496` in this case) can be used with the **cancel** utility to remove the job from the printer queue and stop it from printing:

```
$ cancel printer_1-496
     printer_1-496: canceled
```

You can send more than one file to the printer with a single command. The following command line prints three files on the printer named **laser1**:

```
$ lp -dlaser1 05.txt 108.txt 12.txt
request id is laser-5524 (3 files)
```

▲▲ grep: Find a String

The **grep** (global regular expression print) utility searches through one or more files to see if any contain a specified string of characters. This utility does not change the file it searches through but displays each line that contains the string.

The **grep** command in Figure 3-3 searches through the file **memo** for lines that contain the string credit and displays a single line.

```
$ cat memo

Helen:

In our meeting on June 6th we
discussed the issue of credit.
Have you had any further thoughts
about it?

                    Alex
$ grep 'credit' memo
discussed the issue of credit.
```

*Figure 3-3   Using **grep** to find a word in a file*

If **memo** contained words such as discredit, creditor, or accreditation, **grep** would have displayed those lines as well because they contain the string it was searching for. You do not need to enclose the string you are searching for in single quotation marks, but doing so allows you to put SPACEs and special characters in the search string.

The **grep** utility can do much more than search for a simple string in a single file. Refer to **grep** on page 777 in Part III and to Appendix A, "Regular Expressions," for more information.

▲▲ head: Display the Beginning of a File

The **head** utility displays the first ten lines of a file. You can use it to help you remember what a particular file contains. If you have a file named **months** that contains the 12 months of the year in order, one to a line, **head** displays Jan through Oct (Figure 3-4).

The **head** utility can display any number of lines, so you can use it to look at only the first line of a file or at a screenful or more. To specify the number of lines **head** displays, include a hyphen followed by the number of lines in the **head** command. For example the following command displays only the first line of **months**:

```
$ head -1 months
Jan
```

The **head** utility can also display parts of a file based on a count of blocks or characters rather than lines. Refer to page 784 in Part III for more information on **head**.

```
$ cat months
Jan
Feb
Mar
Apr
May
Jun
Jul
Aug
Sep
Oct
Nov
Dec
$ head months
Jan
Feb
Mar
Apr
May
Jun
Jul
Aug
Sep
Oct
```

*Figure 3-4   Using **head** to display the first ten lines of a file*

▲▲ tail: Display the End of a File

The **tail** utility is similar to **head**, except it displays the *last* ten lines of a file by default. Depending on how you invoke it, the **tail** utility can display fewer or more than ten lines, display parts of a file based on a count of blocks or characters rather than lines, and display lines being added to a file that is changing. The following command causes **tail** to display the last five lines, Aug through Dec, from the **months** file shown in Figure 3-4:

```
$ tail -5 months
Aug
Sep
Oct
Nov
Dec
```

The ability to display lines as they are added to the end of a file is a very useful feature of **tail**. If you have a log file or other growing file, you can monitor lines as they are added to the end of the file with the command:

```
$ tail -f logfile
```

where **logfile** is the name of the file you want to monitor. Press **CONTROL-C** to stop **tail** and return to the shell prompt. Refer to page 909 in Part III for more information on **tail**.

▲▲ sort: Display a File in Order

The **sort** utility displays the contents of a file in order by lines. It does not change the original file. If you have a file named **days** that contains the name of each of the days of the week on a separate line, **sort** displays the file in alphabetical order (Figure 3-5).

The **sort** utility is useful for putting lists in order. Within certain limits you can use **sort** to order a list of numbers. Refer to page 891 in Part III for more information on **sort**.

▲▲ uniq: Remove Duplicate Lines in a File

The **uniq** (unique) utility displays a file, skipping adjacent duplicate lines. It does not change the original file. If a file contains a list of names and has two successive entries for the same person, **uniq** skips the extra line.

```
$ cat dups
Cathy
Fred
Joe
John
Mary
Mary
Paula
```

```
$ cat days
Monday
Tuesday
Wednesday
Thursday
Friday
Saturday
Sunday
$ sort days
Friday
Monday
Saturday
Sunday
Thursday
Tuesday
Wednesday
```

*Figure 3-5   Using **sort** to put a list in alphabetical order*

```
$ uniq dups
Cathy
Fred
Joe
John
Mary
Paula
```

If a file is sorted before it is processed by **uniq**, **uniq** ensures that no two lines in the file are the same. Refer to page 940 in Part III for more information on **uniq**.

▲▲ diff: Compare Two Files

The **diff** (difference) utility compares two files and displays a list of the differences between them. This utility does not change either file; it just displays a list of the actions you need to take to convert one file into the other. This is useful if you want to compare two versions of a letter or report or two versions of the source code for a program.

The **diff** utility produces a series of lines containing instructions to add (**a**), delete (**d**), or change (**c**) followed by the lines that you need to add, delete, or change. If you have two files named **colors.1** and **colors.2** that contain names of colors, **diff** compares the two files and displays a list of their differences (Figure 3-6).

The **diff** utility assumes that you want to convert the first file (**colors.1**) into the second file (**colors.2**). The first line that **diff** displays (4d3) indicates that you need to delete the fourth line. (You can ignore the number following the **d** since it is only important if you want to convert the second file into the first.) The next line of the display shows the line to be deleted. The *less than* symbol (<) indicates that the line is from the first file; a *greater than* symbol (>) identifies lines that are from the second file. Refer to page 739 in Part III for more information on **diff**.

```
$ cat colors.1
red
blue
green
yellow
$ cat colors.2
red
blue
green
$ diff colors.1 colors.2
4d3
< yellow
```

*Figure 3-6   The **diff** utility*

▲▲ file: Test the Contents of a File

You can use the **file** utility to learn about the contents of any file on a Solaris system without having to open and examine the file yourself. In the following example **file** reports that **letter_e.Z** contains data that has been compressed in a particular way:

```
$ file letter_e.Z
letter_e.Z:          compressed data block compressed 16 bits
```

Refer to page 752 in Part III for more information on **file**.

▲▲ unix2dos: Convert Solaris Files to DOS/Windows Format

The **unix2dos** utility converts a Solaris text file so that it can be read by a DOS or MS Windows system. Give the following command to convert a file named **memo** (created with **dtpad**, **textedit**, **vi**, or another text editor) to a DOS format file named **memo.txt**:

```
$ unix2dos memo memo.txt
```

The original file is not changed. You can email the new file as an attachment to someone on an MS Windows system. Use **dos2unix** to convert DOS files so they can be read on a Solaris system.

▲ Three Useful Utilities

The **echo** and **date** utilities are two of the most frequently used from the large collection of Solaris utilities. The **script** utility helps you record part of a session on your computer.

▲▲ echo: Display Text

The **echo** utility copies anything you put on the command line after **echo** to your screen. Some examples are shown in Figure 3-7.

The **echo** utility is a good tool for learning about the shell and other Solaris programs. In Chapter 5 (page 120), **echo** is used to learn about special characters. In Chapter 10 (page 362), it is used to learn about shell variables and about how to send messages from a shell script to the screen.

```
$ echo Hi
Hi
$ echo This is a
sentence.
This is a sentence.
$ echo Good morning.
Good morning.
```

*Figure 3-7   The **echo** utility*

Builtin Commands

Some commands (also called utilities) are built directly into the shell. The **echo** $_{csh}^{sh~a}$ $_{ksh}$ utility discussed previously is a shell builtin. The shell always executes a shell builtin before it tries to find a command/utility with the same name in your search path.

a. A *builtin* command is built into and is part of the shells named within the shaded rectangle following its name ($_{csh}^{sh}$, page 17). Give the command **man shell_builtins** to see a list of builtins.

▲▲ date: Display the Time and Date

The **date** utility displays the current date and time. An example of **date** is:

```
$ date
Fri May 29 10:48:51 PDT 1998
```

▲▲ script: Record a Solaris Session

The **script** utility allows you to record part (or all) of a login session, including your input and the system's responses. It is only useful from character-based devices such as a terminal or a terminal emulator. It will capture commands you give the shell and the shell's responses just fine. It does capture a session with **vi**, but because **vi** uses control characters to position the cursor and display different typefaces (such as bold), it will be hard to read and may not be very useful. If you **cat** a file that has captured a **vi** session, you will see the session pass before your eyes in a great hurry. By default **script** captures the session in a file named **type-script**. To use a different filename, follow the script command with a SPACE and the filename you want to use. To append the file, use the **–a** option (after **script** but before any filename), otherwise **script** will overwrite an existing file. Following is a session being recorded by **script**.

```
$ script
Script started, file is typescript
$ date
Thu Oct 15 11:49:54 PDT 1998
$ who am i
alex        /dev/pts/4 Oct 15 11:49
$ apropos rwho
in.rwhod        in.rwhod (1m)    - system status server
rwho            rwho (1)         - who is logged in on local machines
rwhod           in.rwhod (1m)    - system status server
$ exit
Script done, file is typescript
$
```

Use the **exit** command to terminate a script session. You can view the file you created with **cat**, **pg**, **more**, or an editor. Following is the file that was created by the preceding **script** command.

```
$ cat typescript
Script started on Thu Oct 15 11:49:52 1998
$ date
Thu Oct 15 11:49:54 PDT 1998
$ who am i
alex        /dev/pts/4   Oct 15 11:49
$ apropos rwho
in.rwhod        in.rwhod (1m)    - system status server
rwho            rwho (1)         - who is logged in on local machines
rwhod           in.rwhod (1m)    - system status server
$ exit
script done on Thu Oct 15 11:50:07 1998
$
```

If you will be editing the file with the **vi** or **emacs** editor, process it with **dos2unix** to remove the ^M that appears at the end of each line (**newname** is the name of the processed file):

```
$ dos2unix typescript newname
```

▲ Compressing and Archiving Files

Compressing files (making them smaller) causes them to consume fewer resources such as disk space on the local machine and network bandwidth when they are sent to or received from a remote machine. An *archive* allows you to keep track of files that are not immediately needed but that must be easy to recreate on demand.

▲▲ compress: Shrink a File

Large files can use up a lot of disk space and take longer than smaller files to transfer from one system to another over a network. If you do not need to look at the contents of a large file very often, you may want to save it on a magnetic tape or removable disk and delete it from the hard disk. If you have a continuing need for the file, however, retrieving a copy from a tape or removable disk may be inconvenient. To reduce the amount of disk space you use without removing the file entirely, you can compress (shrink) the file without losing any of the information. Also, you will frequently get a compressed file when you download something from the Internet. The utilities described below allow you to compress and decompress files a couple of different ways.

The **compress** utility can shrink a file by analyzing it and recoding it more efficiently. The new version of the file looks completely different. In fact the new file contains many nonprinting characters, so you should not try to read it directly. The **compress** utility works particularly well on files with a lot of repeated information such as text and image data.

The following example shows a boring file. Each of the 8,000 lines of this file, named **letter_e**, contains 72 e's and a NEWLINE character marking the end of the line. The file occupies more than half a megabyte of disk storage.

```
$ ls -l
-rw-rw-r--  1 alex    speedy   584000 Jul 31 06:07 letter_e
```

The **–l** option causes **ls** to show more information about files. Above, it shows that **letter_e** is 584,000 bytes long.

The **–v** option below causes **compress** to report how much it was able to reduce the size of the file; in this case by more than 98 percent.

```
$ compress -v letter_e
letter_e: Compression: 98.24% -- replaced with letter_e.Z

$ ls -l
-rw-rw-r--  1 alex    speedy    10234 Jul 31 06:07 letter_e.Z
```

Now the file is only 10,234 bytes long. The **compress** utility also renamed the file—it appended **.Z** to the file's name. This naming convention helps to remind you that the file is compressed; you would not want to display or print it, for example, without first decompressing it. The **compress** utility does not change the modification date associated with the file, even though it completely changes the file's contents.

In the following more realistic example, the file **card2.bm** contains a complex computer graphics image. Here **compress** can reduce the disk storage for the file by only about 20 percent:

```
$ ls -l
-rw-rw-r--  1 jenny   speedy   131092 Jul 31 10:48 card2.bm
$ compress -v card2.bm
card2.bm:       19.7% -- replaced with card2.bm.Z
$ ls -l
-rw-rw-r--  1 jenny   speedy   105261 Jul 31 10:48 card2.bm.Z
```

Start Optional

The GNU project (page 12) offers a more effective pair of compression utilities: **gzip** and **gunzip** (GNU zip and GNU unzip [see page 781]). They work the same way as **compress** and **uncompress** but use a filename extension of **.gz** in place of **.Z** and tend to create smaller compressed files. The **gunzip** utility will even decompress files that were compressed with **compress**. Although Sun does not supply these utilities with Solaris, they are readily available and easy to download (page 976). Do not confuse these UNIX utilities with **zip** and **unzip**, which are frequently used with DOS and MS Windows (and are available starting with Solaris 2.6).

Stop Optional

▲▲ uncompress, zcat: Expand a File

You can use the **uncompress** utility to restore a file that has been shrunk with **compress**:

```
$ uncompress letter_e.Z
$ ls -l
-rw-rw-r--  1 alex    speedy  584000 Jul 31 06:07 letter_e
$ uncompress card2.bm.Z
$ ls -l
-rw-rw-r--  1 jenny   speedy  131092 Jul 31 10:48 card2.bm
```

The **zcat** utility allows you to view a file that has been compressed with **compress**. It is the equivalent of **cat** for **.Z** files; unlike **cat**, **zcat** interprets the compressed data and displays the contents of the file as though it were not compressed. The vertical bar (|), called a *pipe* (page 113), passes the output of **zcat** to **head** so you see only the first two lines of the file:

```
$ zcat letter_e.gz | head -2
eeeeeeeeeeeeeeeeeeeeeeeeeeeeeeeeeeeeeeeeeeeeeeeeeeeeeeeeeeeeeeeeeeeeee
eeeeeeeeeeeeeeeeeeeeeeeeeeeeeeeeeeeeeeeeeeeeeeeeeeeeeeeeeeeeeeeeeeeeee
```

After running **zcat**, the contents of **letter_e.Z** are unchanged—the file is still stored on the disk in compressed form.

▲▲ tar: Pack and Unpack a File

The **tar** utility is used for many things. Its name is short for *tape archive,* as its original function was to create and read archive and backup tapes. Today it is used to create single files that, when unpacked, create multiple files or a directory with any level of subdirectories and subfiles beneath it.

In the following example **ls** first shows the existence and sizes of the files **g**, **b**, and **d**. Next **tar** uses the **c** (create), **v** (verbose), and **f** (write to or read from a file) options[1] to create an archive in **all.tar** from

---

1. Although **tar** originally did not use a leading hyphen to indicate an option on the command line, it now accepts them. This book uses the hyphen for consistency with most other utilities.

these files. Each line of the output from **tar** starts with the letter a to indicate it is appending to the archive. This letter is followed by the name of the file and its size in kilobytes. The **tar** utility does add overhead when it creates an archive. The next command shows that the archive file, **all.tar**, is about 9,700 bytes whereas the sum of the sizes of the three files is about 6,000 bytes. This overhead is more appreciable on smaller files.

```
$ ls -l g b d
-rw-r--r--   1 jenny      jenny          1302 Aug 20 14:16 g
-rw-r--r--   1 jenny      other          1178 Aug 20 14:16 b
-rw-r--r--   1 jenny      jenny          3783 Aug 20 14:17 d
$ tar -cvf all.tar g b d
a g 2K
a b 2K
a d 4K
$ ls -l all.tar
-rw-r--r--   1 jenny      jenny          9728 Aug 20 14:17 all.tar
$ tar -tvf all.tar
tar: blocksize = 19
-rw-r--r-- jenny/jenny     1302 Aug 20 14:16 1998 g
-rw-r--r-- jenny/other     1178 Aug 20 14:16 1998 b
-rw-r--r-- jenny/jenny     3783 Aug 20 14:17 1998 d
```

The final command above uses the **–t** option to display a table of contents for the archive. Use **–x** in place of **–t** to extract files. Omit the **–v** option if you want **tar** to do its work silently.

You can use **compress** or **gzip** to shrink **tar** files and make them easier to store and handle. Many files you download from the Internet are in one of these formats. Files that have been processed by **tar** and compressed by **compress** frequently have a filename extension of **.tar.Z**. Those processed by **tar** and **gzip** use **.tgz** or **.tar.gz**. You can unpack a **tar**red and **gzip**ped file (if you have installed **gzip/gunzip**) in two steps (follow the same procedure if the file was compressed by **compress**, only use **uncompress** in place of **gunzip**).

The next example shows how to unpack the GNU **make** utility after it has been downloaded.

```
$ ls -l mak*
-rw-r--r--   1 mark       mark        634229 Oct 17 15:01 make-3.76.1.tar.gz
$ gunzip mak*
$ ls -l mak*
-rw-r--r--   1 mark       mark       2344960 Oct 17 15:01 make-3.76.1.tar
$ tar -xvf mak*
x make-3.76.1, 0 bytes, 0 tape blocks
x make-3.76.1/Makefile.in, 19129 bytes, 38 tape blocks
x make-3.76.1/AUTHORS, 1391 bytes, 3 tape blocks
.
.
.
x make-3.76.1/make.info-8, 42472 bytes, 83 tape blocks
x make-3.76.1/make.info-9, 10289 bytes, 21 tape blocks
$ ls -ld mak*
drwxr-xr-x   4 mark       mark          2048 Sep 19  1997 make-3.76.1
-rw-r--r--   1 mark       mark       2344960 Oct 17 15:01 make-3.76.1.tar
```

```
$ ls make-3.76.1
total 4196
-rw-r--r--   1 mark     mark        1391 Aug 27  1997 AUTHORS
-rw-r--r--   1 mark     mark       18043 Dec 10  1996 COPYING
-rw-r--r--   1 mark     mark      153710 Sep 19  1997 ChangeLog
.
.
.
-rw-r--r--   1 mark     mark        5586 Jul 25  1996 vmsfunctions.c
-rw-r--r--   1 mark     mark       15653 Aug 27  1997 vmsify.c
-rw-r--r--   1 mark     mark       16320 Aug 27  1997 vpath.c
drwxr-xr-x   5 mark     mark         512 Sep 19  1997 w32
```

The first command in the preceding example lists the downloaded **tar**red and **gzip**ped file: **make-3.76.1.tar.gz** (about 0.6 MB). The ✳ in the filename matches any characters in any filenames, so you end up with a list of files whose names begin with mak (page 120). The following **gunzip** command decompresses the file and yields **make-3.76.1.tar** (no **.gz** extension) which is about 2.3 MB. The **tar** command unpacks the files in **make-3.76.1.tar** into the working directory (usually). After tar unarchives the files, there are two files whose names start with mak in the working directory: **make-3.76.1.tar** and **make-3.76.1**. The **–d** option causes **ls** to display only file and directory names, not the contents of directories. The final **ls** shows the files and directories in the **make-3.76.1** directory.

tar: x Option May Extract Many Files

Some **tar** archives contain many files. Run **tar** with the **–t** option and the name of the **tar** file to list the files in the archive without unloading them. In some cases you may want to create a new directory (**mkdir** [page 78]), move the **tar** file into that directory, and expand it there. That way the unpacked files do not mingle with your existing files and there is no confusion. It also makes it easier to delete the unarchived files if you choose to do so.

Start Optional

If you want to take advantage of the power of UNIX, you can combine the **gunzip** and **tar** commands on one command line with a pipe (|), which passes the output of **gunzip** to **tar** so it can be unarchived:

```
$ gunzip -c make-3.76.1.tar.gz | tar -xvf -
```

The **–c** option causes **gunzip** to send its output through the pipe instead of creating a file. Refer to "Pipes" (page 113), **gzip** (page 781), and **tar** (page 912) for more information about how this command line works.

Stop Optional

▲ Locating Commands

The **whereis** and **apropos** utilities help you find a command whose name you have forgotten or whose location you do not know. In addition **which** can tell you which copy of a command you will run, and **whereis** can help you locate a file.

▲▲ which, whereis: Locate Utilities

When you type the name of a utility on the command line, the shell searches a list of directories for the program and runs it. This list of directories is called a *search path;* the chapters that describe each shell explain how to change it. If you do not change the search path, the shell searches only a standard set of directories and then stops searching. There are other directories on your system that contain useful utilities.

The **which** utility helps you locate commands by giving the full pathname to the file for the command. (Chapter 4 contains more information on pathnames and the structure of the Solaris filesystem.) There may be multiple commands on your system that have the same name. When you type the name of a command, the shell searches for the command in your search path and runs the first one it finds. You can find out which copy of the program the shell runs by using **which**. In the following example **which** reports the location of the **tar** command:

```
$ which tar
/usr/bin/tar
```

The **which** utility can be very helpful when a command seems to be working in unexpected ways. By running **which** you may discover that you are running a nonstandard version of a tool or a different one than you expected. For example if **tar** is not working properly and you find that you are running **/usr/local/bin/tar** instead of **/usr/bin/tar**, you might suspect that the local version is broken.

To locate a command try using **whereis**, which looks in a few standard locations instead of using your search path. For example you can find out the locations for versions of the **tar** command:

```
$ whereis tar
tar: /etc/tar /usr/bin/tar /usr/sbin/bin/tar /usr/include/tar.h /usr/man/man1/tar.1
```

This **whereis** command finds five references to **tar**. If the **whereis** utility can find any **man** pages for the utility, it lists those too. In this case the **whereis** utility has located three versions of **tar**, one tar header file, and one version of the **man** page.

> ### which versus whereis
>
> Give **which** the name of a program you want to run, and it will look through the directories in your search path, in order, and locate the program. If, in your search path, there is more than one program with the name you specify, **which** only displays the name of the first one (the one you will execute).
>
> Use **whereis** to locate a binary (executable) file, any manual pages, and source code for a program you specify. This utility looks through a list of standard directories and works independently of your search path.

---

which, whereis, and Builtin Commands

Both the **which** and **whereis** utilities report only the names for commands as they are found on disk and do not report shell builtins. If you try to find out where the **echo** command (which exists as both a utility program and a shell builtin) is using **whereis**, you will get the following:

```
$ whereis echo
echo: /usr/bin/echo /usr/ucb/echo /usr/man/man1/echo.1
/usr/man/man1b/echo.1b ...
```

You will not see the **echo** builtin. Even the **which** utility reports the wrong information.

```
$ which echo
/usr/bin/echo
```

As you read this book and learn new utilities, you may want to use **man** or AnswerBook2 to find out more about the utilities. Although you probably have access to a *hardcopy* (paper) Solaris manual, the electronic copies are generally more up to date. If you have the ability to print PostScript documents, you can print a manual page with the **man** utility using the **–t** option. Better yet use your browser to look at the documentation on **docs.sun.com**. Using your browser, you should be able to download and/or print the information from that site. For more information see the tip named "Searching for More Information" on page 26.

▲▲ apropos: Search for Keywords

If you do not know the name of the command you need to carry out a particular task, you can use a keyword and the **apropos**[2] utility to search for it. This utility searches for the keyword in, and displays, the short description lines[3] for all **man** pages that contain a match. The **man** utility, with the **–k** (keyword) option, gives you the same output as **apropos**.

Figure 3-8 shows the output of **apropos** when you call it with the sort keyword and pipe (page 113) the output through **sort** with the **–u** option, which yields a unique, sorted list. It includes the name of each command, the section of the manual that contains it, and the brief description from the top of the **man** page. This list includes the utility that you need (**sort**) and also identifies other related tools that you might find useful in the future.

---

2. The windex database has to be set up with **catman** in order for **apropos** to work. Refer to page 700 for more information on **catman**.

3. The top line on a **man** or **xman** page. See Figure 2-8 on page 29 in which man(1) is the short description line.

```
$ apropos sort | sort -u
Consortium       X (7)            - X Consortium information
Standards        X (7)            - X Consortium Standards
X                X (7)            - X Consortium Standards
X                X (7)            - X Consortium information
aclsort          aclsort (3)      - sort an ACL
alphasort        scandir (3b)     - scan a directory
bsearch          bsearch (3c)     - binary search a sorted table
disksort         disksort (9f)    - single direction elevator seek sort for buffers
look             look (1)         - find words in the system dictionary or lines in a sorted list
qsort            qsort (3c)       - quick sort
sort             sort (1)         - sort, merge, or sequence check text files
sortbib          sortbib (1)      - sort a bibliographic database
tsort            tsort (1)        - topological sort
$
```

Figure 3-8   The **apropos** *utility*

▲ Obtaining User and System Information

This section covers utilities that allow you to find out who is using the system and how it is running. If you are running Solaris on a workstation that is not connected to a network, you may want to skip the rest of this chapter (unless you are set up to send and receive electronic mail, in which case you may want to read "Electronic Mail" on page 61).

To find out who is using the computer system, you can use one of several utilities that vary in the details they provide and the options they support. The oldest utility, **who**, produces a short list of usernames along with the terminal connection each person is using and the time the person logged in.

Two newer utilities, **w** and **finger**, show more detail (such as each user's full name and the command line each user is running). The **finger** utility can also be used to retrieve information about users on remote systems if your computer is attached to a network (page 198).

▲▲ who: List Users on the System

The **who** utility displays a list of users who are currently logged in. In Figure 3-9 the first column of **who** shows that Alex and Jenny are logged in. (Alex is logged in twice.) The second column shows the designation of the terminal that each person is using. The third column shows the date and time the person logged in. The final column, when present, identifies the name of the remote computer where the person is logged in.

```
$ who
root      console    Mar 27 05:00    (:0)
alex      pts/4      Mar 27 12:23
alex      pts/5      Mar 27 12:33
jenny     pts/7      Mar 26 08:45    (bravo.tcorp.com)
```

Figure 3-9   The **who** *utility*

The information that **who** displays is useful if you want to communicate with someone at your installation. If the person is logged in, you can use **write** (page 58) or **talk** (page 59) to establish communication immediately. If **who** does not show that the person is logged in, or if you do not need to communicate immediately, you can send that person electronic mail (page 61).

If you are logged in on a machine that is on a local area network, you may want to use **rwho** (page 210) to see who is logged in on all the systems in your network. If the output scrolls off your screen, you can send the output through a pipe (l [page 113]) to **pg** (page 35) which allows you to look at the output one page at a time. You can also pipe the output through **grep** (page 43) to look for a specific name.

If you need to find out which terminal you are using or what time you logged in, you can use the command **who am i**:

```
$ who am i
alex       pts/5       Mar 27 12:33(:0.0)
```

▲▲ finger: List Users on the System

You can use **finger** to display a list of the people who are currently using the system. In addition to login names, **finger** supplies each user's full name, along with information about which terminal line the person is using, how recently the user typed something on the keyboard, when the user logged in, and information about where the user is located (if the terminal line appears in a system database). If the user has logged in over the network, the name of the remote system is shown as the user's location. For example in Figure 3-10, the user hls is logged in from the remote system named **bravo**. The asterisk (✳) in front of the name of Helen's terminal (TTY) line indicates that she has blocked others from sending messages directly to her terminal (see "mesg: Deny or Accept Messages" on page 60).

```
$ finger
Login      Name           TTY      Idle    When     Where
root       Super-User     console 1:35 Fri  5:00    :0
alex       Alex Watson    pts/4        Fri 12:23    :0.0
alex       Alex Watson    pts/5     19 Fri 12:33    :0.0
jenny      Jenny Chen     pts/7   2:24 Fri  8:45    (bravo.tcorp.com)
hls        Helen Simpson  *pts/11    2 Fri 12:23    (bravo.tcorp.com)
```

*Figure 3-10   The **finger** utility I*

```
$ finger alex
Login name: alex                     In real life: Alex Watson
Directory: /home/alex                Shell: /bin/ksh
On since Wed Aug  7 12:23  on pts4 from :0
20 minutes Idle Time
New mail received Wed Mar 27 11:31:45 1998
   unread since Wed Mar 25 19:51:02 1998
Plan:
I will be at a conference in Hawaii all next week.  If you need
to see me, contact Jenny Chen, x1693.
```

*Figure 3-11   The **finger** utility II*

You can also use **finger** to learn more about a particular individual by specifying more information on the command line. Figure 3-11 displays detailed information about the user named Alex. Alex is currently logged in and actively using his terminal (if he were not, **finger** would report how long he had been idle). You also learn from **finger** that if you want to set up a meeting with Alex, you should contact Jenny at extension 1693. Most of the information in Figure 3-11 was collected by **finger** from system files. The information shown after the heading `Plan:`, however, was supplied by Alex. The **finger** utility searched for a file named **.plan** in Alex's home directory and displayed its contents. You may find it helpful to create a **.plan** file for yourself; it can contain any information you choose, such as your typical schedule, interests, phone number, or address. In a similar manner **finger** displays the first line of the **.project** file in your home directory. If Alex had not been logged in, **finger** would have reported the last time he logged on, the last time he read his electronic mail, and his plan.

finger Can Be a Security Risk

On systems where security is a concern, the system administrator may disable **finger**. This utility can give a malicious user information that can help him/her break into the system.

If you do not know a person's login name, you can use the **finger** utility to learn it. For example you might know that Helen's last name is Simpson, but you might not guess that her login name is hls. The **finger** utility can also search for information on Helen using her first or last name. The following commands find the information you seek, along with information on other users on the system whose names are Helen or Simpson. The **finger** utility is not case sensitive.

```
$ finger HELEN
Login: hls                              Name: Helen Simpson.
.
.
.

$ finger simpson
Login: hls                              Name: Helen Simpson.
.
.
.
```

▲▲ w: List Users

The **w** utility displays a list of the users currently logged in. In Figure 3-12 the first column **w** displays shows that Alex, Jenny, and Scott are logged in. The second column shows the designation of the terminal that each person is using. The third column shows the time each person logged in. The fourth column indicates how long each person has been idle (that is, how much time has elapsed since a key on the keyboard was pressed). The next two columns give measures of how much computer processor time each person has used during the current login session and on the task that is currently running. The last column shows the command each person is currently running.

The first line that the **w** utility displays includes the current time of day, how long the computer has been running (in days, hours, and minutes), how many users are logged in, and how busy the system is (load average). The three load average numbers represent the number of jobs waiting to run, averaged over the past minute, 5 minutes, and 15 minutes.

```
$ w
  8:20am  up 4 days,  2:28,  3 users,  load average: 0.04, 0.04, 0.00
User     tty           login@ idle   JCPU   PCPU   what
alex     pts/4         5:55am 13:45                 w
alex     pts/5         5:55am   27   2:55    1     -ksh
jenny    pts/7         5:56am 13:44                 vi 36tmp.txt
scott    pts/12        7:17pm          1           run_budget
```

*Figure 3-12   The **w** utility*

The information that **w** displays is useful if you want to communicate with someone at your installation. If the person is logged in and recently active, you can use **write** or **talk** (discussed below) to establish communication immediately. If **w** does not show that the person is logged in, or if you do not need to communicate immediately, you can send that person electronic mail (page 61).

Feature	w	who	finger
User login name	x	x	x
Terminal identification (tty)	x	x	x
Login day and time	x		x
Login date and time		x	
Idle time	x		x
What program the user is executing	x		
Where the user logged in from		x	x
CPU time used		x	
Full name (or other information from /etc/passwd)			x
User-supplied vanity information			x
System up time and load average—use **uptime** for only this information	x		

▲ Communicating with Other Users

The utilities discussed in this section allow you to exchange messages and files with other users either interactively or through email.

▲▲ write: Send a Message

You can use the **write** utility to send a message to another user who is logged in. When the other user also uses **write** to send you a message, you establish two-way communication. Initially a **write** command (Figure 3-13) displays a banner on the other user's terminal saying that you are about to send a message.

The syntax of a **write** command line is

```
$ write alex
Hi Alex, are you there? o
```

Figure 3-13   Starting to **write** *to Alex*

write **destination-user** *[terminal]*

The **destination-user** is the login name of the user you want to communicate with. The **terminal** is the optional terminal name. You can discover the login and terminal names of the users who are logged in by using **who, w,** or **finger**.

To establish two-way communication with another user, you and the other user must each execute **write**, specifying the other's login name as the **destination-user**. The **write** utility then copies text, line by line, from one terminal to the other (Figure 3-14). Alex and Jenny have established a convention: Type o (for over) when you are ready for the other person to type, and type oo (for over and out) when you are ready to end the conversation. You can use this convention, another convention, or none at all. When you want to stop communicating with the other user, press **CONTROL-D** at the beginning of a line. Pressing **CONTROL-D** tells **write** to quit, displays EOF (end of file) on the other user's terminal, and returns you to the shell. The other user must do the same.

If the Message from ... banner appears on your screen and obscures something you are working on, press **CONTROL-L** or **CONTROL-R** to refresh the screen and remove the banner. Then you can clean up, exit from your work, and respond to the person who is writing you. You just have to remember who was writing you as the banner will no longer be on your screen.

```
$ write Alex
Hi Alex are you there? o
        Message from alex on Bravo (pts/4) [ Fri May 29 13:15:57 ] ...          Yes Jenny,
I'm here. o
```

Figure 3-14   Alex responding with **write**

▲▲ talk: Communicate with Another User

You can use the **talk** utility to carry on a two-way conversation with another person who is logged in on your system. If your system is connected to a network, you can also use **talk** to communicate with someone on a different computer (page 201). The **talk** utility splits your screen into two sections; once you establish contact with the other person, the messages you type appear in the top half of your screen, and the messages from the other person are displayed in the bottom half. In this example Alex needs some information from Jenny:

```
$ talk jenny
```

Alex's display is immediately split into two sections, and the following message appears at the top of his screen:

```
[Waiting for your party to respond]
```

Meanwhile the following message appears on Jenny's screen and she responds. If she was unable to respond immediately, she could use **CONTROL-L** or **CONTROL-R** to refresh her screen and remove the banner (see the preceding discussion of **talk**):

```
Message from Talk_Daemon@bravo at 9:22 ...
talk: connection requested by alex@bravo.
talk: respond with: talk alex@bravo
$ talk alex@bravo
```

Above, Alex and Jenny are both using a computer named **bravo**; **alex@bravo** is Alex's network address, which is described in more detail in Chapter 7. Figure 3-15 shows what Jenny's and Alex's screens look like as they type their messages.

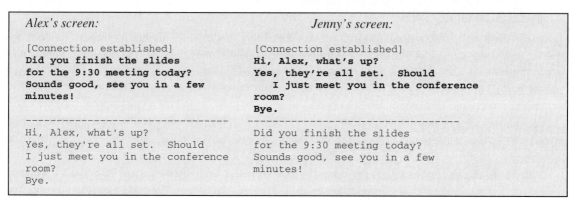

Alex's screen:

```
[Connection established]
Did you finish the slides
for the 9:30 meeting today?
Sounds good, see you in a few
minutes!

------------------------------

Hi, Alex, what's up?
Yes, they're all set.  Should
I just meet you in the conference
room?
Bye.
```

Jenny's screen:

```
[Connection established]
Hi, Alex, what's up?
Yes, they're all set.  Should
  I just meet you in the conference
room?
Bye.

------------------------------

Did you finish the slides
for the 9:30 meeting today?
Sounds good, see you in a few
minutes!
```

*Figure 3-15　The **talk** utility*

To end the **talk** session, one person interrupts by pressing CONTROL-C, and the following message appears before a new shell prompt is displayed:

```
[Connection closing. Exiting]
```

The other user must also press CONTROL-C to display a shell prompt. If you see the following message when you try to use **talk** to reach someone, the **mesg** command has been used to block interruptions (see the next section):

```
[Your party is refusing messages]
```

Before the **talk** utility was available, people used the **write** command to interact with each other on the same computer. The **talk** utility has a few advantages over **write**: With **talk** the other person's messages appear on your screen, letter by letter, as they are typed; **write**, on the other hand, sends only a whole line at a time. If you use **write**, sometimes you are not sure whether the person at the other end is disconnected or just a slow typist. Also, unlike **write**, **talk** has been extended to support communication over the network. Still if you need to exchange a quick message with another person logged in on your system, without disrupting your current screen display, you may want to use **write** instead.

▲▲ mesg: Deny or Accept Messages

If you do not want to receive messages from another user using **write** or **talk**, give the following command:

```
$ mesg n
```

If Alex had given this command before Jenny tried to send him a message, she would have seen the following:

```
$ write alex
Permission denied
```

You can allow messages again by entering **mesg y**.

If you want to know if someone can write to you, give the command **mesg** by itself. The **mesg** utility responds with is y (for yes, messages are allowed) or is n (for no, messages are *not* allowed).

▲▲ Electronic Mail

Electronic mail, or *email,* is similar to post office mail except that it is usually much quicker and does not involve any paper, stamps, or human intervention at various points along the way. You can use it to send and receive letters, memos, reminders, invitations, and even junk mail (unfortunately). It can also transmit binary data such as pictures or compiled code by including them as attachments. An *attachment* is a file that is attached to, but is not actually part of, a piece of electronic mail. Attachments are frequently opened by programs (including your Internet browser) that are called by your mail program so you may not be aware that they are not an integral part of an email message.

You can use electronic mail to communicate with users on your system and, if your installation is part of a network, with other users on the network. If you are connected to the Internet, you can communicate electronically with users around the world.

The email utilities differ from **write** (page 58) and **talk** (page 59) in that they allow you to send a message to a user whether or not that user is logged in on the system. The **talk** and **write** utilities allow you to send messages only if the user is logged on and willing to receive messages. The email utilities also allow you to send a message to more than one user at a time.

Solaris has several utilities you can use to send and receive electronic mail. These include **dtmail** (the CDE mailer), **mailtool** (Sun's OpenWindows interface for the mail program), **mail** (Berkeley mail), and **mailx** (System V mail). In addition there are many other mail programs available for Solaris including Netscape mail, **pine**, mail through **emacs**, and **xmh** (a graphical interface to the MH Message Handling System). This section describes **dtmail** and **mailtool**. Refer to page 65 for a tutorial on **pine** (not supplied with Solaris), which you can use from a character (nongraphic) terminal.

▲▲▲ Similarities between dtmail and mailtool

The **dtmail** and **mailtool** programs are similar in many respects as they are both graphical interfaces to mail programs, but they differ in style and details. You can run either program from CDE or OpenWindows, but each runs more naturally with the window manager for which it was designed.

When iconified (reduced to an icon), both programs show whether or not there is mail waiting for you; you do not have to open the program to find out (if you have mail). In addition **mailtool** shows you if you have new mail or just mail you have read already (Figure 3-16). Both programs open displaying a list of messages that are waiting to be read, marking new messages (**dtmail** uses an N for new and **mailtool** uses a U for unread) and allowing you to read, reply to, and/or dispose of messages as you choose. Each allows you to sort messages into folders so you can easily retrieve them.

Of course both programs allow you to compose and send new messages to one or more people on your system or on any system on the network you are connected to.

▲▲▲ Tutorial: Using **dtmail** or **mailtool** to Send and Receive Electronic Mail

The best way to learn about a mail program is to try out its various features until you are comfortable using them. To assist you in this process, **dtmail** provides help text for every screen. Refer to the **mailtool man** page if you want help with it. Netscape also has a mail client (a program that sends and receives email), but it is not covered in this book. To start double-click on the appropriate icon. Use the Mailer Control on the CDE Front Panel for **dtmail** or the **mailtool** icon[4] on the root (background) window (all in Figure 3-16).

▲▲▲▲ Reading Mail: As soon as either mail window opens, you will see a scrollable list of message headers including the sender's name and the subject, date, time, and size of the message. If you are using **dtmail**, the header of the first message will be highlighted and the corresponding message displayed in the lower portion of the window (Figure 3-17). The **mailtool** program draws a box around the header of the first unread message but does not display it. Double-click on the message header to cause **mailtool** to open another window that displays the message (also in Figure 3-17).

*Figure 3-16   Left are **dtmail** and right are **mailtool** icons; the first and second rows show empty and full mailboxes. The third **mailtool** icon indicates new mail.*

To display other messages click on the message header (once for **dtmail**, twice for **mailtool**). If the message is longer than the display window, use the scroll bar on the right to scroll through the message. For help on using the scroll bar, see "Scrolling Text" on page 142.

To learn more about **dtmail**, you can display the **Help** menu by clicking on the word Help at the top-right of the window (Figure 3-18). When you click on the On Item selection on the **Help** menu, **dtmail** changes the cursor to a large arrow and a question mark. Move this new cursor until it is over the item you want help with and click the mouse button; **dtmail** will open a help screen describing the item you clicked on.

---

4. If the **mailtool** icon is not visible on your desktop, bring up the **Workspace** menu (Figure 6-32 on page 178) by clicking and releasing the right mouse button while the mouse pointer is over the root (background) window. Move the mouse pointer until it is over the word Programs and click once more to display the **Programs** menu. Now move the mouse pointer until it is over the words Mail Tool... and click the mouse button once again. The **mailtool** icon will appear on the desktop.

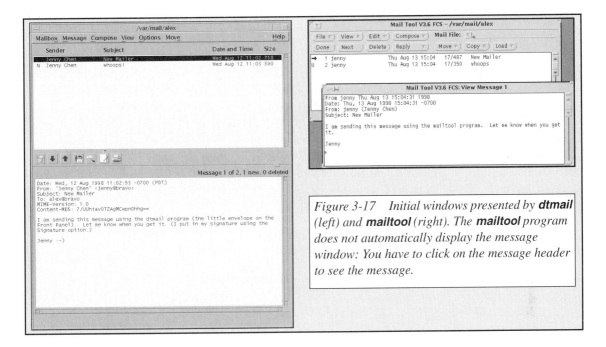

*Figure 3-17   Initial windows presented by **dtmail** (left) and **mailtool** (right). The **mailtool** program does not automatically display the message window: You have to click on the message header to see the message.*

▲▲▲▲ Sending Mail: Like other mail utilities, **dtmail** and **mailtool** have two distinct functions: Sending and receiving electronic mail. A good way to learn about a mailer is by sending mail to yourself.

To send mail to himself, Alex selects New (Message) from the **Compose** menu. A new window named **Compose Message** or **New Message** appears on the desktop. First Alex must fill in the first three lines, or header (Figure 3-19).

▲▲▲▲ Header: At a minimum you must specify the name (and address) of the user who is to receive the message. Both **dtmail** and **mailtool** allow you to specify three lines of header information. The three lines begin with: To:, Subject:, and Cc: (for carbon copy, left over from days of yore—and carbon paper). The To: and Cc: lines specify the recipients of the message. You can specify multiple names on either line, separating one recipient from the next with a **SPACE** or comma. When the message is delivered, the header will have many lines, two of which will be the To: and Cc: lines. Users you specified on the To: line will appear on the To: line, and those you specified on the Cc: line will appear on the Cc: line. The Subject: line contains a brief description of what the message is about and appears in the initial list of message headers you see when you open either mail program.

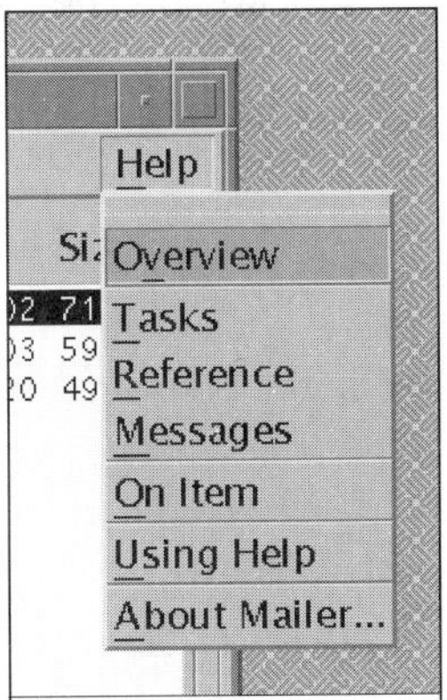

Because Alex is sending mail to himself, he types his login name after the To: prompt, followed by **RETURN** or **TAB**. To send the mail message to more than one user, Alex can enter additional login names following his own, each separated from the next by a **SPACE** or comma.

Figure 3-18   The Help menu

Alex can send mail to any user on his system by using that user's login name, but sending mail to users on other systems requires more complex (network) addresses. For more information see "Network Addresses" on page 70.

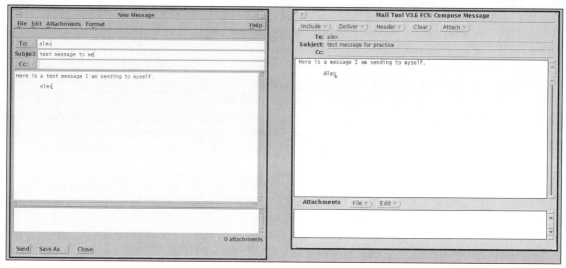

Figure 3-19   Composing an email message in **dtmail** *(left) and* **mailtool** *(right)*

The next line of the header contains the `Subject:` prompt. Alex types in the subject of his message and presses **RETURN**.

The cursor moves to the last line of the header, the `Cc:` line. Because Alex wants to send mail only to himself, he presses **RETURN** to move the cursor to the text area where he types the text of the message.

When he is finished typing his message, Alex clicks on **Send** at the lower left of the **dtmail** window to send it. To send a message from **mailtool**, click on **Deliver** at the top of the window and then select **Quit Window**.

Alias: An *alias* is a name you can use to refer to one or more addresses. You can reduce a hard-to-spell name or long Internet address to a simple one-syllable name using the alias feature of either **mailtool** or **dtmail**. Because both programs use the **.mailrc** file as a startup file, and because aliases are specified in that file, you can create and use aliases interchangeably between the programs.

An alias takes the form of:

```
alias lunch.buddies hls scott jenny
```

or

```
alias mark mark@sobell.com
```

The name or word on the left is the alias; the following **SPACE**-separated names or words are the addresses. When you ask the mail program to send a message to an alias, it substitutes the addresses. Using the preceding aliases as an example, when you send mail to `lunch.buddies` it automatically goes to `hls`, `scott`, and `jenny`.

To set up an alias from **dtmail**, click on Options and then Aliases.... From **mailtool** click on **Edit** and then Properties.... The **dtmail** program shows you the Alias window immediately, but **mailtool** requires another step: At the top-left of the Properties window is the word `Category:` with a raised box with a down-pointing triangle to its right. Move the mouse pointer and briefly click on the triangle. You will see a list of properties. Then move the mouse pointer and click on **Alias**.

With either program you will have two lines, one labeled `Alias` and the other labeled `Addressees`. There is also a larger box to hold the aliases once you create them. Fill in the `Alias` line with the name of the alias (`lunch.buddies`) and the `Addresses` line with the address(es) you want the mail program to substitute for the alias (`hls scott jenny`). When you are satisfied with the alias, click on **Add**. Close the window by double-clicking on the menu button (**dtmail**) or the pushpin (**mailtool**) in the upper-left of the window.

You can use other selections from the Options or Edit/Properties menus to further customize your mailer.

▲▲▲ Tutorial: Using pine to Send and Receive Electronic Mail

In 1989 a group of individuals at the University of Washington decided to write a UNIX mailer that was easy to learn and use, especially for beginners. They wanted to provide a mail utility to administrative staff at the university that had a clean and friendly interface and encouraged use without the risk of making serious and confusing errors. They named the mailer **pine**. The popularity of **pine** quickly extended beyond the boundaries of the University of Washington, and capabilities were added to meet the needs of the growing community of **pine** users. Since that time a number of advanced features have been added to **pine**, including a way to access Internet newsgroups, a mechanism for transmitting files containing any kind of data, and ways to tailor **pine**'s behavior to the individual user. Although still easy to use, **pine** is no longer geared to the beginner. Sun does not supply **pine**; see page 971 for information on where to obtain it.

▲▲▲▲ Getting Started: Try out the various features of **pine** until you are comfortable with them. To assist you in this process, help text is available for every screen. To start give the following command at the shell prompt (either from a terminal emulator window or from a character terminal):

$ **pine**

You will see a screen similar to Figure 3-20. The **pine** Main menu offers a choice of seven general **pine** commands in the middle portion of the screen. A letter representing each com-

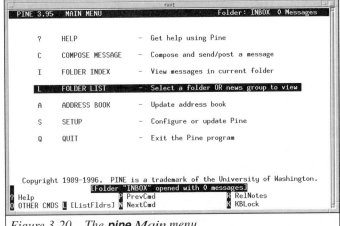

*Figure 3-20   The **pine** Main menu*

mand appears to its left. The **pine** mailer also displays a status line at the top of the screen and two more complete lines of commands at the bottom. The status line displays the version of **pine** you are using, the name of the currently active screen (**Main** menu), and some additional information about the program. The bottom two lines of the screen list all the commands defined for the **Main** menu, including the general **pine** commands. On the bottom two lines, each command is represented by a single highlighted character, displayed to the left of the command's name.

There are two ways to execute a **pine** command. You can always press the key corresponding to the character to the left of the command you want to execute. For the general commands appearing in the middle of the screen, you can also use the arrow keys (or **N** for Next and **P** for Previous) to position the cursor over the command you want and then press **RETURN** to execute the command.

Because the **Main** menu has too many commands to fit in the display at the bottom of the screen, the **O** (Other) command provides a way to view the additional ones. Enter **O** to view another two-line display. These two two-line displays comprise the full set of commands that are active for the **Main** menu; the next **O** command also takes you back to the original two-line display.

The basic format of the **Main** menu appears throughout the many **pine** screens: There is always a status line at the top and a two-line display at the bottom of the screen. The **O** command is available, if necessary, to view additional commands, and help text is available at strategic points along the way. In most screens the **M** command puts you back in the **Main** menu, and **Q** allows you to quit **pine**.

To learn more about **pine**, you can display the Help Screen for the **Main** menu by entering a question mark (**?**). The Help Screen displays general information about **pine** and a description of the commands available in the **Main** menu. As in all **pine** screens, the two-line display at the bottom of the Help Screen tells you what commands are currently active.

Another way to view help text from the **Main** menu is to highlight the general **pine** command Help using **N** and **P** or the arrow keys and then press **RETURN**. Selecting highlighted items with **RETURN** is a shortcut available in most of the **pine** screens; you will find it very useful as you become proficient in the use of **pine**.

When you start running **pine**, the general **pine** command Folder List is highlighted. Entering the command **N** or pressing **DOWN ARROW** highlights the next general **pine** command, and entering **P** or pressing **UP ARROW** highlights the previous one.

To get back to the shell prompt, enter **Q**. You are asked to confirm that you really want to quit **pine**, at which point entering **Y** causes **pine** to quit and returns you to the shell.

▲▲▲▲ Sending Mail: To learn about **pine** send mail to yourself. Use the example below as a guide, replacing **alex** with your login name.

To send mail to himself, Alex types **pine** to bring up the **Main** menu. He then chooses the general **pine** command Compose Message and presses **RETURN** (he could also have entered **C**) to put himself in the message composer. The name of the current screen, Compose Message, is shown in Figure 3-21. The line beginning with the To: prompt is highlighted. The mail header consists of the To: prompt and the next three lines.

The display at the bottom of the screen shows that all of the commands require you to use the **CONTROL** key; the command Get Help, for instance, is **CONTROL-G**. Using **CONTROL** keys for commands allows **pine** to distinguish commands from text that you type to fill in the header fields and the mail message itself. There are a few other places in **pine** where commands are control characters, such as when you edit the address book (see the **Main** menu Help Screen).

Because Alex is sending mail to himself, he types his login name after the `To:` prompt, followed by **RETURN**:

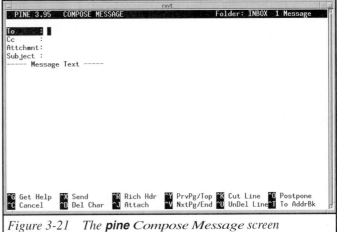

To: **alex**

As soon as Alex presses **RETURN**, **pine** replaces his login name with his full name and his actual email address (inside angle brackets):

To: alex watson <alex@speedy>

Alex's email address allows others to send him electronic mail. Alex can send mail to any user on his system by using that user's login name, but to send

*Figure 3-21   The **pine** Compose Message screen*

mail to users on other systems requires more complex addresses. If you press **CONTROL-G** when the `To:` prompt is highlighted, **pine** gives you help on addresses.

You can use the next line of the header, the `Cc:` line, to send copies of a message to other users. In response to this prompt, you can enter the login names of users whom you want to receive copies of the message. Separate the names in the list with commas and terminate the list with a **RETURN** or **DOWN ARROW**. Because Alex wants to send mail only to himself, he presses **RETURN** to highlight the next line of the header.

The third line displays the `Attchmnt:` (Attachment) prompt. In response to this prompt, you can give the name of a file or files (either text or binary) that you want attached to the mail message. Alex skips this line by pressing **RETURN**.

The last line of the header contains the `Subject:` prompt. Alex types in the subject of his message and presses **RETURN**:

Subject: **Test Message**

After typing in the subject, Alex types in a short message, ending each line with **RETURN**:

This is a test message that I am sending myself.
I am using Pine to write it and will use Pine to read it.

When he is finished typing his message, Alex presses **CONTROL-X** to send it. As with many **pine** commands, Alex is prompted to confirm his intention. After entering **y** for yes (or just pressing **RETURN**—yes is already highlighted), **pine** sends his message. Alex may remain in the mailer, perhaps to compose a message to someone else or to select another command from the **Main** menu. Because Alex is done for now, he enters **Q** to return to the shell.

Entering **pine** followed by an email address is a shortcut to the message composer. For example Alex could have entered the message composer directly from the shell with the following command:

$ **pine alex**

After sending a message using this shortcut, Alex would have been returned directly to the shell without having to enter **Q**.

▲▲▲▲ Receiving Mail: In order to read his mail, Alex starts **pine** by giving the following command to enter the **Main** menu:

$ **pine**

He selects the highlighted item **Folder List** for viewing a list of his Message Folders—files that **pine** uses to store mail messages. Alex gets a screen containing a list of three Message Folders with the first, **INBOX**, highlighted.

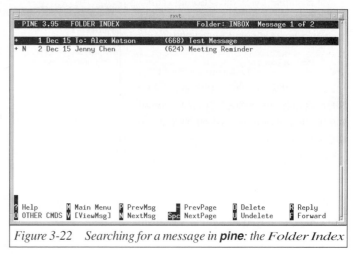

```
INBOX          sent-mail
saved-messages
```

Figure 3-22   Searching for a message in **pine***: the Folder Index*

The first time you run **pine**, the utility usually creates the folders **INBOX**, **sent-mail**, and **saved-messages**. **INBOX** stores messages before you read them and messages that you have read but have not removed. The **sent-mail** folder stores copies of all mail that you send to others, and the **saved-messages** folder (by default) stores messages that you want to save. You can also use **pine** to create folders, delete folders, transfer messages from one folder to another, and organize folders into collections of folders.

Because Alex wants to read his new mail messages, he presses **RETURN** and sees the screen shown in Figure 3-22. It contains a list of messages waiting for him. The list includes a header for each message, consisting of codes on the left, a message number, the name of the person who sent it, the date it was sent, its length in bytes (characters), and the subject of the message.

The code + means that the message was sent directly to Alex, not as part of a Cc:, for instance. The code N says that the message is new. Another common code is D, which means that the message has been marked for deletion.

Alex has two messages, the one he just sent and one from Jenny. The current message, the one he sent to himself, is highlighted. Alex presses **RETURN** to read the highlighted message, shown in Figure 3-23. The first four lines of the message are header lines. They list the date, the sender, the receiver, and the subject of the message.

Figure 3-23   Alex reading his message to himself

Alex has many choices at this point: He can enter **R** to reply to the message, **F** to forward the message to another person, **S** to save the message in a Message Folder, and **D** to mark the message for deletion. These commands and others are listed at the bottom of the screen (use the **O** command to view the **S** command). Alex enters **D** to mark the message for deletion.

Then using the **DOWN ARROW**, he highlights the second message, the one from Jenny, and presses **RETURN** (Figure 3-24). After reading this message, Alex presses **M** to return to the **Main** menu. The message remains in **INBOX**.

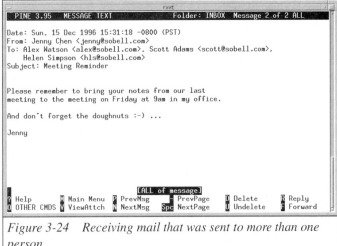

Figure 3-24   Receiving mail that was sent to more than one person

When Alex quits, **pine** asks if he wants to expunge the message marked for deletion from the Message Folder. The deletion of a mail message is a two-step process in **pine**—marking the message for deletion and expunging the message from the Message Folder. This gives you an opportunity to change your mind about deleting a message and also prevents you from inadvertently deleting a message. Alex enters **Y** and is returned to the shell.

Like composing mail messages, reading mail is such a common use of **pine** that there is a shortcut to enter the Folder Index screen from the command line:

```
$ pine -i
```

This command puts you directly into the Folder Index screen, where **pine** displays the list of messages in your default folder (**INBOX**). If you are already in the mailer and want to read the messages in your default folder, you can bypass the Folder List screen by selecting **Folder Index** from the **Main** menu.

▲▲▲▲ **Sending Mail to More Than One Person:**   You can send mail to more than one person at a time. Figure 3-24 shows a reminder that Jenny sent to Alex, Scott, and hls (Helen's login name).[5] To access the message composer directly, Jenny types the following command at the shell prompt:

```
$ pine alex scott hls
```

From within the message composer, Jenny could have just entered the three names in response to the To: prompt.

---

5. The characters **:-)** in the message portray a *smiley face* (look at it sideways). This *glyph* (a symbol that communicates a specific piece of information nonverbally), and many related ones, are also called smileys, smilies, and recently even emoticons **:-(**. Because it can be difficult to tell when the writer of an electronic message is saying something in jest or in seriousness, electronic mail users often use **:-)** to indicate humor. The two original smileys, designed by Scott Fahlman, were **:-)** and **:-(**.

▲▲▲ Network Addresses

If your system is part of a network, you can send mail to and receive mail from users on other systems if you know their addresses. All you generally need for people on systems on your local area network (LAN) is a login name and a machine name, separated by the @ character. For example if Alex has login accounts for the machines **speedy** and **bravo** on the local network, you can send mail to his account on **bravo** using the address: **alex@bravo**. Someone sending Alex email on the Internet would need to specify his domain name (page 217) along with his login name but probably would not need to specify his machine name (finding someone's machine name is usually taken care of locally by the program that receives the mail). So Alex's email address on the Internet might be **alex@tcorp.com**.

Use this address to send the author email: **mark@sobell.com**.

Summary

Chapters 2 and 3 introduced a small but powerful subset of Solaris utilities. Because you will be using them frequently and because they are integral to your understanding of the following chapters, it is important that you become comfortable using these utilities.

This chapter introduced some general file manipulation utilities that allow you to compress files and file archives, identify or locate utilities on the system, obtain information about other users, and communicate electronically with others.

▲▲ Utilities That Operate on Files

These utilities print, compare, manipulate, and display files.

Utility	Function
cancel	Removes a job from the printer queue (page 43)
cp	Makes a copy of a file or files (page 41)
diff	Displays the differences between two files (page 46)
dos2unix	Converts DOS/Windows files to Solaris format (page 46)
file	Displays information about the contents of a file (page 46)
grep	Searches a file for a string (page 43)
head	Displays the lines at the beginning of a file (page 44)
lp	Places a file or files in the printer queue (page 43)
lpstat	Displays a list of jobs in the printer queue (page 43)
mv	Renames a file, or moves files to another directory (page 42)
sort	Puts a file in order by lines (page 45)
tail	Displays the lines at the end of a file (page 45)

Utility	Function
uniq	Displays the contents of a file, skipping successive duplicate lines (page 45)
unix2dos	Converts Solaris files to DOS/Windows format (page 46)

▲▲ Frequently Used Utilities

The **echo** builtin is especially useful for learning about shell behavior; it is used in examples throughout this book.

Utility	Function
date	Displays the current date and time (page 47)
echo	Copies its arguments to the screen (page 47)

▲▲ Compression Utilities

To reduce the amount of disk space a file occupies, you can compress it with the **compress** utility. Compression works especially well on files that contain patterns, as do most text files, but reduces the size of almost all files. The inverse of **compress**—**uncompress**—restores a file to its original, decompressed form.

Utility	Function
compress	Compresses a file (but not as well as **gzip**) (page 49)
gzip/gunzip	Compresses/decompresses a file (page 50, a GNU utility not supplied with Solaris)
uncompress	Returns a **compress**ed file to its original size and format (page 50)
zcat	Displays a **compress**ed file (page 50)

▲▲ Archive Utility

An archive is a file, usually compressed, that contains a group of smaller, related files. The **tar** utility packs and unpacks archives. The filename extensions **.tar.gz** and **.tgz** identify **tar** archive files compressed by **gzip** and are often seen on software packages obtained over the Internet.

Utility	Function
tar	Creates or unloads an archive file (page 50)

▲▲ Locating Utilities

The following utilities determine the location of a command or utility on your system.

Utility	Function
apropos	Searches the **man** page one-line descriptions for a keyword (page 54)

Utility	Function
whereis	Displays the full pathnames of a utility, source code, or **man** page (page 53)
which	Displays the full pathname of a command you can run (page 53)

▲▲ User and System Information Utilities

Some utilities display information about other users. You can easily learn a user's full name, whether the user is logged in, the login shell of the user, and other items of information maintained by the system.

Utility	Function
finger	Displays information about users who are logged in, including full names (page 56)
w	Displays detailed information about users who are logged in (pages 55 and 57)
who	Displays information about users who are logged in (page 55)

▲▲ Communication Utilities

The following utilities enable communication with other users:

Utility	Function
dtmail	Sends and receives electronic mail (page 62)
mailtool	Sends and receives electronic mail (page 62)
mesg	Permits or denies messages sent by **write** or **talk** (page 60)
pine	Sends and receives electronic mail (page 65)
talk	Supports an online conversation with another user who is logged in (page 59)
write	Sends a message to another user who is logged in (page 58)

Review Exercises

1. What commands can you use to determine who is logged in on a specific terminal?

2. List some differences between **talk** and **write**. Why are three different communications utilities (**talk**, **write**, an email utility) useful on a Solaris system? Describe a situation where it makes sense to use:

   a. an email utility instead of **talk** or **write**.

   b. **talk** instead of **write**.

   c. **write** instead of **talk**.

3. Show how to use an email utility to send a single mail message to both **agnes** on the system named **cougar** and **jim** on **ucsf**. Assume your computer has network links to **cougar** and **ucsf**.

4. How can you keep other users from using **write** to communicate with you? Why would you want to?

5. What happens if you give the following commands when the file named **done** already exists?

   ```
   $ cp to_do done
   $ mv to_do done
   ```

6. What command sends the files **chapter1**, **chapter2**, and **chapter3** to the printer?

7. How can you find out which utilities are available on your system for editing files?

8. How can you find the phone number for Ace Electronics in a file named **phone** that contains a list of names and phone numbers? What command can you use to display the entire file in alphabetical order? How can you remove adjacent duplicate lines from the file?

9. What happens if you use **diff** to compare two binary files that are not identical? (You can use **compress** to create the binary files.) Explain why the **diff** output for binary files is different than the **diff** output for ASCII files.

10. Create a **.plan** file in your home directory. Does **finger** on your system display the contents of your **.plan** file?

11. What is the result of giving the **which** utility the name of a command that resides in a directory that is *not* in your search path?

12. Experiment by calling the **file** utility with names of files in **/usr/bin**. How many different types of files can you find there?

13. What command can you use to look at the first few lines of a file called **status.report**? What command can you use to look at the end of the file?

14. You will find the answers to the following questions in the **man** pages or in AnswerBook2.

    a. What do the **–n** and **–b** options to **cat** do? What is the difference between them?

    b. Which option to **rm** could you use to remove a directory and all files in it? Why is this not a good idea? How could you make it a safer process? (*Hint:* You need to combine two options.)

    c. What does the **–r** option to **ls** do? The **–F** option? When would each of these options be useful?

Advanced Review Exercises

15. Assume that in exercise 8 Ace Electronics and the phone number appear on adjacent lines. How can you find the phone number without using a program that displays a large chunk of the file (for example an editor, **more**, **pg**, **cat**, or **page**? (*Hint:* use **sed**.)

16. Try giving these two commands:

    ```
    $ echo cat
    $ cat echo
    ```

    Explain the differences between them.

17. Repeat exercise 8 using the file **phone.Z**, a compressed version of the list of names and phone numbers. Try to consider more than one approach to each question, and explain how you chose your answer.

18. Use the **pine** mailer to create a new folder named **tmp-mail**. Then describe how to move a message from the **sent-mail** folder to the **tmp-mail** folder.

19. Find an existing file, or create a file, that:

    a. **compress**es by more than 80 percent.

    b. **compress**es by less than 10 percent.

    c. gets larger when compressed with **compress**.

    Use **ls –l** to determine the sizes of the files in question. Can you characterize the files in parts a, b, and c?

20. Some mailers, particularly older ones, are not able to handle binary files. Suppose that you are mailing someone a file that has been compressed with **compress**, which produces a binary file, and you do not know what mailer the recipient is using. Refer to the **man** page on **uuencode**, which converts a binary file to ASCII. Learn about the utility and how to use it.

    a. Convert a compressed file to ASCII using **uuencode**. Is the encoded file bigger or smaller than the compressed file? Explain.

    b. Would it ever make sense to use **uuencode** on a file before compressing it? Explain.

The Solaris Filesystem

A *filesystem* is a data structure (a framework that holds data) that usually resides on part of a disk. This chapter discusses the organization and terminology of the Solaris filesystem. It defines ordinary and directory files and explains the rules for naming them. It shows how to create and delete directories, move through the filesystem, and use pathnames to access files in different directories. This chapter also covers file access permissions that allow you to share selected files with other users. The final section describes links, which can make a single file appear in more than one directory.

▲ The Hierarchical Filesystem

A *hierarchical* structure frequently takes the shape of a pyramid. One example of this type of structure is found by tracing a family's lineage: A couple has a child; that child may have several children; and each of those children may have more children. This hierarchical structure, shown in Figure 4-1, is called a *family tree*.

Like the family tree it resembles, the Solaris filesystem is also called a *tree*. It is composed of a set of connected files. This structure allows users to organize files so they can easily find any particular one. In a standard Solaris system, each user starts with one directory. From this single directory users can make as many subdirectories

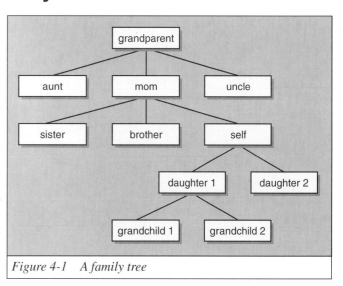

Figure 4-1   A family tree

as they like, dividing subdirectories into additional subdirectories. In this manner they can continue expanding the structure to any level according to their needs.

▲▲ Using the Hierarchical Filesystem

Typically each subdirectory is dedicated to a single subject. The subject dictates whether a subdirectory should be subdivided further. For instance Figure 4-2 shows a secretary's subdirectory named **correspond**. This directory contains three subdirectories: **business**, **memos**, and **personal**. The **business** directory contains files that store each letter the secretary types. If you expect many letters to go to one client (as is the case with **milk_co**), you can dedicate a subdirectory to that client.

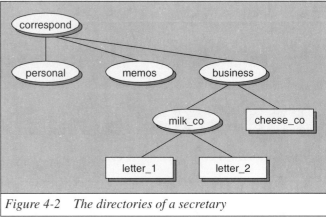

Figure 4-2   The directories of a secretary

One of the strengths of the Solaris filesystem is its ability to adapt to different users' needs. You can take advantage of this strength by strategically organizing your files so they are most convenient and useful for you.

▲ Directory and Ordinary Files

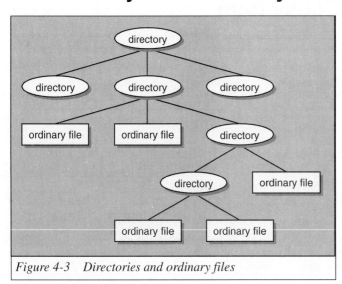

Figure 4-3   Directories and ordinary files

Like a family tree, the tree representing the filesystem is usually pictured upside down, with its *root* at the top. Figures 4-2 and 4-3 show that the tree "grows" downward from the root, with paths connecting the root to each of the other files. At the end of each path is either an ordinary file or a directory file. *Ordinary files,* frequently just called *files,* are at the ends of paths that cannot support other paths. *Directory files,* usually referred to as *directories,* are the points that other paths *can* branch off from. (Figures 4-2 and 4-3 show some empty directories.) When you refer to the tree, *up* is toward the root and *down* is away from the root. Directories directly connected by a path are called *parents* (closer to the root) and *children* (farther from the root). A *pathname* is a series of names that traces a path along branches from one file to another.

▲▲ Filenames

Every file has a *filename*. The maximum length of a filename varies with the type of filesystem; Solaris includes support for different types of filesystems. On most filesystems you can create files with names up to 255 characters long, but some filesystems may restrict you to 14-character names. Although you can use almost any character in a filename, you will avoid confusion if you choose characters from the following list:

- uppercase letters (A–Z)
- lowercase letters (a–z)
- numbers (0–9)
- underscore (_)
- period (.)
- comma (,)

The root directory is always named / (slash) and referred to by this single character. No other file can use this name (or have a / in its name).

Like children of one parent, no two files in the same directory can have the same name. (Parents give their children different names because it makes good sense, but Solaris requires it.) Files in different directories, like children of different parents, can have the same name.

The filenames you choose should mean something. Too often a directory is filled with important files with names such as **hold1**, **wombat**, and **junk** (not to mention **foo** and **foobar**). Names like these are poor choices because they do not help you recall what you stored in a file. The following filenames conform to the suggested syntax *and* convey information about the contents of the file:

- **correspond**
- **january**
- **davis**
- **reports**
- **2001**
- **acct_payable**

If you share your files with users on other UNIX systems, you may need to make long filenames differ within the first 14 characters. If you keep the filenames short, they are easy to type; later you can add extensions to them without exceeding the 14-character limit imposed by some filesystems. Of course the disadvantage of short filenames is that they are typically less descriptive than long filenames. If you share files with systems running DOS or older versions of MS Windows, you must respect the 8-character name length and 3-character filename extension length imposed by those systems.

Long filenames enable you to assign descriptive names to files. To help you select among files without typing entire filenames, some shells support filename completion. Refer to "Filename Completion" on page 453 (C Shell) or "Pathname Completion" on page 512 (Korn Shell).

You can use uppercase and/or lowercase letters within filenames. The Solaris operating system is case sensitive, thus files named **JANUARY**, **January**, and **january** represent three distinct files.

▲▲▲ Filename Extensions

In the filenames listed in the following table, filename extensions help describe the contents of the file. A *filename extension* is the part of the filename following an embedded period. Some programs, such as the C programming language compiler, depend on specific filename extensions. In most cases filename extensions are optional. Use extensions freely to make filenames easy to understand. If you like, you can use several periods within the same filename (for example **notes.4.10.97** or **files.t.Z**).

Filename	Meaning of Filename Extension
compute.c	A C programming language source file
compute.o	The object code for the program
compute	The same program as an executable file
memo.0410	A text file
memo.ps	A postscript file
memo.Z	A file compressed with **compress**; use **uncompress** (or **gunzip**) (page 50) to decompress
memo.tar.Z	A **tar** archive of files compressed with **compress** (page 50)
memo.gz	A file compressed with **gzip** (page 50); view with **zcat** I or decompress with **gunzip** (both on page 50)
memo.tgz or **memo.tar.gz**	A **tar** archive of files compressed with **gzip** (page 50)
memo.html	A file meant to be viewed using a browser such as Netscape
photo.jpg, **photo.gif**	A file containing graphical information such as a picture (also **.jpeg**)

▲▲▲ Invisible Filenames

A filename that begins with a period is called an *invisible filename* (or *invisible file* or sometimes *hidden file*) because **ls** does not normally display it. The command **ls –a** displays *all* filenames, even invisible ones. Startup files (page 81) are usually invisible so that they do not clutter a directory. The **.plan** file (page 57) is also invisible. Two special invisible entries, a single and double period (**.** and **..**), appear in every directory (page 83).

▲▲ mkdir: Create a Directory

The **mkdir** utility creates a directory. It does *not* change your association with the *working directory* (the name the **pwd** [print working directory] utility displays, see page 79). The *argument* (the word following the name of the command) to **mkdir** becomes the pathname of the new directory.

Figure 4-4 shows the directory structure that is developed in the following examples. The directories that are added are shaded and are connected by light lines.

Figure 4-5 uses **ls** to show the names of the files Alex has been working with in his home directory: **demo, names**, and **temp**. Then it shows **mkdir** creating a directory named **literature** as a child of the **/home/alex** directory. When you use **mkdir**, enter the pathname of *your* home directory in place of **/home/alex**. The second **ls** verifies the presence of the new directory.

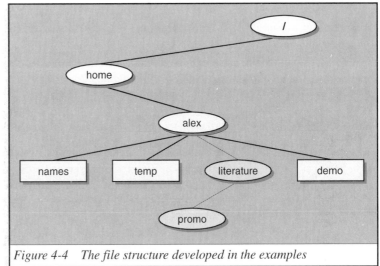

Figure 4-4   The file structure developed in the examples

```
$ ls
demo            names            temp
$ mkdir /home/alex/literature
$ ls
demo            literature    names       temp
$ ls -F
demo            literature/   names       temp
$ ls literature
$
```

*Figure 4-5   The **mkdir** utility*

You can use the **–F** option (options are discussed on page 104) with **ls** to display a slash after the name of each directory and an asterisk after each executable file. When you call **ls** with an argument that is the name of a directory, it lists the contents of the directory. If there are no files in the directory, **ls** does not display anything.

▲▲ cd: Change to Another Working Directory

The **cd** (change directory) command makes another directory the working directory—it does *not* change the contents of the working directory. In this context you can think of the working directory as a place marker. The first **cd** command in Figure 4-6 makes the **/home/alex/literature** directory the working directory, as verified by **pwd**.

Without an argument, **cd** makes your home directory the working directory, as it was when you first logged in. The second **cd** in Figure 4-6 does not have an argument and makes Alex's home directory the working directory.

```
$ cd /home/alex/literature
$ pwd
/home/alex/literature
$ cd
$ pwd
/home/alex
```

*Figure 4-6   The **cd** utility*

▲▲ The Working Directory

While you are logged in on a Solaris system, you are always associated with one directory or another. The directory you are associated with, or are working in, is called the *working directory* or the *current directory*. Sometimes this association is referred to in a physical sense: "You are *in* (or *working in*) the **jenny** directory." The **pwd** command displays the pathname of the working directory (Figure 4-7).

To access any file in the working directory, you do not need a pathname—just a simple filename. To access a file in another directory, you *must* use a pathname.

> ### The Working Directory versus the Home Directory
>
> The working directory is not the same as your home directory. Your home directory remains the same for the duration of your session and usually from session to session. Each time you log in, you are working in the same directory, and that directory is your home directory.
>
> Unlike your home directory, your working directory can change as often as you like. You have no set working directory. That is why some people refer to it as the *current directory*. When you log in and until you change directories (using **cd** [page 79]) your home directory is your working directory. If you were to change directories to Scott's home directory, then Scott's home directory would be your working directory.

▲▲▲ Significance of the Working Directory

Typing a long pathname is tedious and increases the chance of making a mistake. You can choose a working directory for any particular task to reduce the need for long pathnames. Your choice of a working directory does not allow you to do anything you could not do otherwise—it just makes some operations easier.

Files that are children of the working directory can be referenced by simple filenames. Grandchildren of the working directory can be referenced by relative pathnames, composed of two filenames separated by a slash. When you manipulate files in a large directory structure, short relative pathnames can save time and aggravation. If you choose a working directory that contains the files used most for a particular task, you need to use fewer long, cumbersome pathnames.

▲▲ Your Home Directory

When you first log in on a Solaris system, your working directory is your *home directory*. To display the absolute pathname of your home directory, use **pwd** just after you log in. Figure 4-7 shows Alex logging in and displaying the name of his home directory.

Without any arguments the **ls** utility displays a list of the files in the working

```
login: alex
Password:
Last login: Fri Mar 27 12:33:35 from :0.0
Sun Microsystems Inc.    SunOS 5.6        Generic
August 1997
You have mail.
$ pwd
/home/alex
```

Figure 4-7   Logging in

directory. Because your home directory has been the only working directory you have used so far, **ls** has always displayed a list of files in your home directory. (All the files you have created up to now were created in your home directory.)

▲▲▲ Startup Files

An important file that appears in your home directory is a *startup file*. It gives the shell specific information about you as a user. Frequently it tells the shell what kind of terminal you are using and executes the **stty** (set terminal) utility to establish your line kill and erase keys. Refer to page 902 in Part III for more information on **stty**.

Either you or the system administrator can put a startup file, containing shell commands, in your home directory. The shell executes the commands in the **.profile** $_{ksh}^{sh}$ or the **.cshrc** csh and **.login** csh files each time you log in. Although the C Shell only executes **.login** when you first log in, it executes **.cshrc** each time it starts up a new shell. The **.cshrc** file is frequently considered a startup file. Because the startup files have invisible filenames, you must use the **ls –a** command to see if one of these files is in your home directory. For more information on startup files and other files the shell executes automatically, refer to page 364 (Bourne Shell), page 437 (C Shell), or page 480 (Korn Shell). A graphical user interface has many startup files. Usually you do not have to work with these files directly but can control startup sequences using icons on your desktop. See page 163 for more information.

▲▲ Absolute Pathnames

Every file has a pathname. Figure 4-8 shows the pathnames of directories and ordinary files in part of a file-system hierarchy.

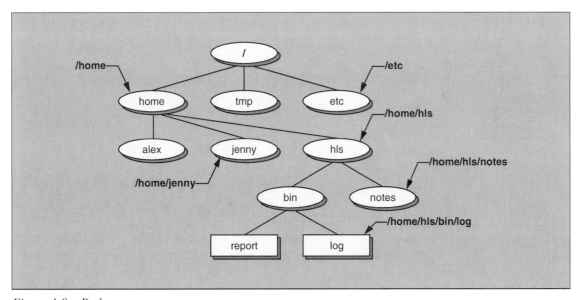

Figure 4-8   Pathnames

An absolute pathname always starts with a slash (/), the name of the root directory. You can build the absolute pathname of a file by tracing a path from the root directory, through all the intermediate directories, to the file. String all the filenames in the path together, separating each from the next with a slash (/) and preceding the group of filenames with a slash (/).

This path of filenames is called an *absolute pathname* because it locates a file absolutely, tracing a path from the root directory to the file. The part of a pathname following the final slash is called a *simple filename*, or just a *filename*.

Another form of absolute pathname, which the C Shell, Korn Shell, and some programs such as **vi** recognize, begins with a tilde (~), which represents a home directory. For more information see "Special Pathnames" on page 87.

▲▲ Relative Pathnames

A *relative pathname* traces a path from the working directory (see page 79) to a file. The pathname is *relative* to the working directory. Any pathname that does not begin with the root directory (/) or a tilde (~) is a relative pathname. Like absolute pathnames relative pathnames can describe a path through many directories.

Alex could have created the **literature** directory (Figure 4-5) more easily using a relative pathname.

```
$ pwd
/home/alex
$ mkdir literature
```

The **pwd** command shows that Alex's home directory (**/home/alex**) is still the working directory. The **mkdir** utility displays an error message if a directory or file named **literature** already exists—you cannot have two files or directories with the same name in one directory. The pathname used in this example is a simple filename. A simple filename is a kind of relative pathname that specifies a file in the working directory.

Know Your Working Directory When Using Relative Pathnames

Because the location of the file that you are accessing with a relative pathname is dependent on (relative to) the working directory, always make sure you know which is the working directory before using a relative pathname. Use **pwd** to verify the directory: If you are using **mkdir** and you are not where you think you are in the file hierarchy, the new directory will end up in an unexpected location.

It does not matter which directory is the working directory when you use an absolute pathname.

The following commands show two ways to create the **promo** directory as a child of the newly created **literature** directory. The first way assumes that **/home/alex** is the working directory and uses a relative pathname; the second way uses an absolute pathname.

```
$ pwd
/home/alex
$ mkdir literature/promo
```

or

```
$ mkdir /home/alex/literature/promo
```

▲▲▲ The . and .. Directory Entries

The **mkdir** utility automatically puts two entries in every directory you create: A single period and a double period, representing the directory itself and the parent directory, respectively. These entries are invisible because their filenames begin with periods.

Because **mkdir** automatically places these entries in every directory, you can rely on their presence. The . is synonymous with the pathname of the working directory and can be used in its place; .. is synonymous with the pathname of the parent of the working directory. The following example copies **file3** to the parent directory (**/home/alex**) using **..** and then lists the contents of the **/home/alex** directory from **/home/alex/literature**, again using **..** to represent the parent directory.

```
$ pwd
/home/alex/literature
$ cp file3 ..
$ ls ..
demo           file3         literature        names           temp
```

While working in his **promo** directory, Alex can use the following relative pathname to edit a file in his home directory. Before calling the editor Alex checks which directory he is in.

```
$ pwd
/home/alex/literature/promo
$ vi ../../names
```

Virtually anywhere that a utility program requires a filename or pathname, you can use an absolute or relative pathname or a simple filename. This holds true for **ls**, **vi**, **mkdir**, **rm**, and most other Solaris utilities.

▲▲ Important Standard Directories and Files

The Solaris file structure is set up according to a convention. Figure 4-9 shows the locations of some important directories and files. Give the command **man filesystem** for a more complete and detailed description of the filesystem. The significance of many of these directories will become clearer as you learn more about Solaris.

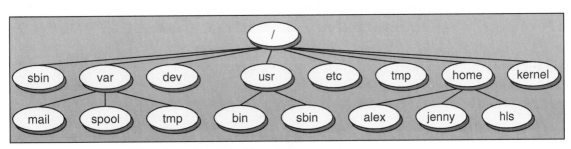

Figure 4-9   Part of a typical Solaris system file structure

The following list describes the directories shown in Figure 4-9 and some others. Also see page 608.

/
> **Root**   The root directory is present in all Solaris system file structures. It is the ancestor of all files in the filesystem.

/bin
> Symbolic link (page 96) to **/usr/bin**.

/dev
> **Device (special) files**   All files that represent peripheral devices, such as disk drives, terminals, and printers, are linked under this directory. The system builds device files to match the kernel and hardware of the system. Refer to "Device-Independent Input and Output" on page 8. Also see **/devices** below.

/devices
> **Device files**   All devices are represented as architecture specific links in this tree. How the device is represented depends on the hardware in use. Links in **/dev** point to files in this directory.

/etc
> **Machine-local system configuration**   Administrative, configuration, and other system files make up this directory; in a sense this directory defines the machine's identity. One of the most important files in this directory is **/etc/passwd**, which contains a list of all users who have permission to use the system. Chapter 15 discusses many of the files in the **/etc** directory, referred to as "e-t-c" or "et-cee."

/export
> **Exported files**   A machine that exports filesystems (such as root, swap,[1] and **/usr**) typically stores them in this directory. Frequently the importing machine requires these files because it has no disk.

/home
> **User directories**   Typically houses user's home directories (such as **/home/jenny**). On some systems the users' directories may not be in **/home** (that is, they might all be under **/inhouse**, or some might be under **/inhouse** and others under **/clients**). By default **automount** has control of **/home** (page 646).

/kernel
> **Kernel files**   This directory along with **/platform** and **/usr/kernel** holds the platform independent and generic parts of the Solaris2 kernel as well as the loadable modules and device drivers.

/lib
> Symbolic link to **/usr/lib**.

/opt
> **Optional packages**   Houses optional software packages such as Netscape, the GNU C compiler (**gcc**), or the Sun Workshop C compiler (**cc**). Also see **/usr/local** on the next page.

/platform
> See **/kernel**.

---

1. The *swap space* is the area of the disk that Solaris uses to hold a currently operating program when it is not in system memory (when it is "swapped out"). See pages 814, 1047, and 907 for more information on swap space.

/sbin   **Essential system binaries**   Utilities used for system administration are stored in **/sbin** and **/usr/sbin**. The **/sbin** directory houses utilities needed during the boot process, and **/usr/sbin** holds those utilities that are most useful after the system is up and running. In older versions of Solaris, many system administration utilities were scattered through several directories that often included other system files (**/etc**, **/usr/bin**, **/usr/adm**, **/usr/include**).

/tmp   **Temporary files**   Many programs use this directory to hold temporary files. It is cleared when the system is booted. The swap space (see footnote 1 on page 84) frequently resides on this filesystem.

/usr   **Second major hierarchy**   Houses subdirectories that contain information used by the system. Files in subdirectories do not change often and may be shared by multiple systems.

/usr/bin   **User commands**   Houses standard Solaris utility programs—binaries that are not needed in single-user mode (page 603).

/usr/ccs   **Software developer**   Houses files used for software development such as **make**, **sccs**, and **yacc**.

/usr/dt   **Desktop**   Files related to CDE.

/usr/include   **Header files**   Houses files included by C programs.

/usr/include/X11   Symbolic link to **/usr/openwin/include/X11**.

/usr/kernel   See **/kernel**.

/usr/lib   **Libraries and locales**   Houses shared libraries, static libraries, profiling libraries, and locale information (page 1010).

/usr/local   **Local hierarchy**   A holdover from earlier systems. If present, this directory houses locally important files and directories that are often added to Solaris. Subdirectories of **/usr/local** may include **bin**, **lib**, and **man**. This directory is sometimes a link to **/opt** (see the preceding page).

/usr/man   **Man pages**   Symbolic link to **/usr/share/man**.

/usr/openwin   **OpenWindows**   Files related to X, OpenLook, and CDE.

/usr/openwin/bin   **X Window System binaries**   Houses X executables (binaries) for desktop applications.

/usr/openwin/lib/X11   **Libraries**   X Window System libraries.

/usr/sadm   **System administration**   Houses system upgrade scripts, package maintenance binaries, and other files used in system administration. Also see **/var/sadm**.

/usr/sbin   **Nonvital system administration binaries**   See **/sbin**.

/usr/share/   **Shareable**   Shareable/common components such as manual pages, dictionaries, time zone information, and terminal types.

/usr/ucb	**BSD compatibility** Houses programs designed for compatibility with BSD operating system. Examples of programs that behave differently on Solaris and BSD are **mail**, **df**, **ls**, and **ps**.
/usr/X *or* **/usr/X11**	**X Window System** (only if installed).
/usr/xpg4	**Standards compliance** Houses binaries and libraries that conform to POSIX, XPG4, and other standards. Refer to the appropriate **man** page for differences between how these binaries and the corresponding Solaris binaries work. See the **man** page for **xpg4** for a complete list of standards supported by Solaris.
/var	**Variable data** Houses subdirectories containing files whose contents vary as the system runs. Some examples are temporary files, system log files, spooled files, and user mailbox files. Older versions of UNIX scattered such files through several subdirectories of **/usr** (**/usr/adm**, **/usr/mail**, **/usr/spool**, **/usr/tmp**).
/var/sadm	**System administration** Houses patches, OS level, install information, and information about what packages are currently installed.

▲ Working with Directories

This section covers deleting directories, copying and moving files between directories, and moving directories. It also describes how to use pathnames to make your work with Solaris easier.

▲▲ rmdir: Delete a Directory

The **rmdir** (remove directory) utility deletes a directory. You cannot delete the working directory or a directory that contains entries other than **.** and **..** If you need to delete a directory with files in it, first delete the files (using **rm**) and then delete the directory. You do not have to delete the **.** and **..** entries; **rmdir** removes them automatically. The following command deletes the directory that was created in Figure 4-5:

```
$ rmdir /home/alex/literature
```

The **rm** utility has a **–r** option (*rm –r filename*) that recursively deletes files (including directories) within a directory and also deletes the directory itself.

Use rm –r Carefully, if at All

Although **rm –r** is a handy command, you must use it carefully. Do not use it with an ambiguous file reference. It is quite easy to wipe out your entire home directory with a single, short command.

▲▲ Using Pathnames

The following example assumes that **/home/alex** is the working directory. It uses a relative pathname to copy the file **letter** to the directory named **/home/alex/literature/promo**. The copy of the file has the simple filename **letter.0610**. Use a text editor to create a file named **letter** if you want to experiment with the examples that follow.

```
$ cp letter literature/promo/letter.0610
```

Assuming that Alex has not changed to another directory, the following command allows him to edit the copy of the file he just made:

```
$ vi literature/promo/letter.0610
.
.
```

If Alex does not want to use a long pathname to specify the file, before using **vi** he can use **cd** to make the **promo** directory the working directory.

```
$ cd literature/promo
$ pwd
/home/alex/literature/promo
$ vi letter.0610
.
.
```

If Alex wants to make the parent of the working directory (named **/home/alex/literature**) the new working directory, he can give the following command, which takes advantage of the **..** directory entry:

```
$ cd ..
$ pwd
/home/alex/literature
```

Start Optional

▲▲▲ Special Pathnames

Two shells csh as well as some utilities such as **vi** also recognize a few shortcuts in pathnames to save typing. ksh The shell expands the characters ~/ (a tilde followed by a slash) at the start of a pathname into the pathname of your home directory, so you can examine your **.login** file with the following command no matter which directory is your working directory:

```
$ pg ~/.login
```

Using a tilde allows you to reference paths quickly, starting with your home directory. The shell expands a tilde followed by a login name at the beginning of a pathname into that user's home directory. Alex can examine Scott's **.login** file (assuming he has permission to do so) with:

```
$ pg ~scott/.login
```

Refer to "~: Tilde Expansion" on page 448 for a more thorough discussion of this topic.

Stop Optional

▲▲ mv, cp: Move or Copy a File

You can use the **mv** (move) utility to move files from one directory to another. Chapter 3 discussed the use of **mv** to rename files. However **mv** is actually more general than explained in Chapter 3—you can use it to change the pathname of a file as well as change the simple filename.

When used to move one or more files to a new directory, the syntax of the **mv** command is

mv **existing-file-list directory**

If the working directory is **/home/alex**, Alex can use the following command to move the files **names** and **temp** from the working directory to the **literature** directory:

$ `mv names temp literature`

This command changes the absolute pathname of **names** and **temp** from **/home/alex/names** and **/home/alex/temp** to **/home/alex/literature/names** and **/home/alex/literature/temp** (Figure 4-10).

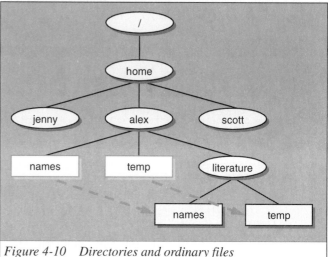

Figure 4-10   Directories and ordinary files

Like most other Solaris commands, **mv** accepts either absolute or relative pathnames.

The **cp** utility works the same way that **mv** does except it makes copies of the *existing-file-list* in the specified *directory*.

As you work with Solaris and create more and more files, you will need to create directories (using **mkdir**) to keep them organized. The **mv** utility is a useful tool for moving files from one directory to another as you develop your directory hierarchy.

▲▲ mv: Move a Directory

Just as **mv** moves ordinary files from one directory to another, it can also move directories. The syntax is similar except you specify one or more directories to move, not ordinary files.

mv **existing-directory-list new-directory**

If *new-directory* does not exist, the *existing-directory-list* must contain just one filename, which **mv** changes to *new-directory* (**mv** renames the directory). Although directories can be renamed using **mv**, their contents cannot be copied with **cp** (unless you use the **–r** option [page 719]). Refer to **tar** or **cpio** in Part III for other ways to copy/move directories.

▲ Access Permissions

Three types of users can access a file: The owner of the file (*owner*), a member of a group to which the owner belongs (*group;* see page 610 for more information on groups), and everyone else (*other*). A user can attempt to access an ordinary file in three ways: By trying to *read from, write to,* or *execute* it. Three types of users, each able to access a file in three ways, equal a total of nine possible ways to access an ordinary file.

▲▲ ls –l: Display Permissions

When you call **ls** with the **–l** (long) option and the name of an ordinary file, **ls** displays a line of information about the file. The following example displays information for two files. The file **letter.0610** contains the text of a letter, and **check_spell** contains a shell script (a program written in the high-level shell programming language).

```
$ ls -l letter.0610 check_spell
-rw-r--r-- 1 alex   pubs  3355  May  2 10:52 letter.0610
-rwxr-xr-x 2 alex   pubs   852  May  5 14:03 check_spell
```

From left to right, the lines contain the following information:

- the type of file (first character)
- the file's access permissions (the next nine characters)
- the number of links to the file (see page 92)
- the name of the owner of the file (usually the person who created the file)
- the name of the group that has group access to the file
- the size of the file in characters (bytes)
- the date and time the file was created or last modified
- the name of the file

The type of file (first column) for **letter.0610** is a hyphen (–) because it is an ordinary file (directory files have a **d** in this column).

The next three characters represent the access permissions for the owner of the file: **r** indicates that the owner has read permission, **w** indicates the owner has write permission, and the – in the next column indicates that the owner does *not* have execute permission (otherwise you would see an x here). Refer to the figure on page 793 that identifies the columns that **ls –l** displays.

In a similar manner the next three characters represent permissions for the group, and the final three characters in the access permissions represent permissions for everyone else. In the preceding example the owner of the file **letter.0610** can read from and write to it, whereas group and others can only read from the file, and no one is allowed to execute it. Although execute permission can be allowed for any file, it does not make sense to assign execute permission to a file that contains a document such as a letter. The **check_spell** file is an executable shell script, and execute permission is appropriate. (The owner, group, and others have execute access permission.)

With Solaris2.5, Sun introduced another, more refined file permission system that works in conjunction with the traditional permissions explained in the preceding paragraphs: ACL, or access control list. ACLs allow you more flexibility in setting up file permissions. For example with ACLs you can give more than one group access to a file or give access to a single file to a single user who is not the owner of the file and does not belong to the group the file is associated with. If a file has an ACL, you will see a plus sign at the end of the list of permissions output by **ls –l**:

```
$ ls -l report
-rwxr-----+  1 alex          0 Jun 19 21:34 report
```

For more information see "ACL (Access Control List)" on page 674.

▲▲ chmod: Change Access Permissions

The owner of a file controls which users have permission to access the file and how they can access it. If you own a file, you can use the **chmod** (change mode) utility to change access permissions for that file. In the following example **chmod** adds (**+**) read and write permission (**rw**) for all (**a**) users:

```
$ chmod a+rw letter.0610
$ ls -l letter.0610
-rw-rw-rw- 1 alex  pubs   3355  May  2 10:52 letter.0610
```

In the next example **chmod** removes (**–**) read and execute (**rx**) permissions for users other than Alex and members of the pubs group (**o**):

```
$ chmod o-rx check_spell
$ ls -l check_spell
-rwxr-x--- 2 alex  pubs    852  May  5 14:03 check_spell
```

In addition to **a** (for *all*) and **o** (for *other*), you can use **g** (for *group*) and **u** (for *user*, although user actually refers to the owner of the file, who may or may not be the user of the file at any given time) in the argument to **chmod**. Refer to pages 349 and 709 for more information on **chmod**.

> ### chmod: o for Other, u for Owner
> When using **chmod**, many people assume the **o** stands for *owner*; it does not. The **o** stands for *other*, whereas **u** stands for *owner* (*user*).

The Solaris file access permission scheme lets you give other users access to the files you want to share and keep your private files confidential. You can allow other users to read from *and* write to a file (you may be one of several people working on a joint project); only to read from a file (perhaps a project specification you are proposing); or only to write to a file (similar to an in-basket or mailbox, where you want others to be able to send you mail, but you do not want them to read your mail). Similarly you can protect entire directories from being scanned.

There is an exception to the access permissions described above. Anyone who knows the **root** password can log in as Superuser (page 592) and have full access to *all* files, regardless of owner or access permissions.

▲▲ Setuid and Setgid Permissions

When you execute a file that has setuid (set user ID) permission, the process executing the file takes on the privileges of the owner of the file. As a simple example, if you run a setuid program that removes all the files in a directory, you can remove files in any of the file owner's directories even if you do not normally have permission to do so. In a similar manner setgid (set group ID) permission means that the process executing the file takes on the privileges of the group the file belongs to. The **ls** utility shows setuid permission as an s in the owner's executable position and setgid as an s in the group's executable position:

```
$ ls -l program1
-rwxr-xr-x   1 alex      pubs        15828 Nov  5 06:28 program1
$ chmod u+s program1
$ ls -l program1
-rwsr-xr-x   1 alex      pubs        15828 Nov  5 06:28 program1
$ chmod g+s program1
$ ls -l program1
-rwsr-sr-x   1 alex      pubs        15828 Nov  5 06:28 program1
```

Security: Minimize Use of setuid and setgid Programs

Because of the power they hold and potential destruction they can do, avoid creating and using setuid and setgid programs indiscriminately. Because of the inherent dangers, many sites do not allow these programs on their machines at all. See page 593 for information on setuid and Superuser.

Security: Do Not Write setuid Shell Scripts

Never write shell scripts that are setuid. There are several well-known techniques for subverting them.

▲▲ Directory Access Permissions

Access permissions have slightly different meanings when used with directories. Although the three types of users can read from or write to a directory, the directory cannot be executed. Execute access permission is redefined for a directory: It means you can **cd** into the directory and/or examine files (that you have permission to read from) in the directory. It has nothing to do with executing a file.

If you have only execute permission for a directory, you can use **ls** to list a file in the directory if you know its name. You cannot use **ls** without an argument to list the contents of the directory. In the following exchange Jenny first verifies that she is logged on as herself. Then she checks the permissions on Alex's **info** directory and **cd**s into it. (You can view the access permissions associated with a directory by running **ls** with the **–d** [directory] and **–l** [long] options. The d at the left end of the line that **ls** displays indicates that **/home/alex/info** is a directory.) Because Jenny does not have read permission for the directory, the **ls –l** command without any arguments returns an error. The period (.) in the error message represents the working directory.

```
$ who am i
jenny      pts/7   Aug 21 10:02
$ ls -ld /home/alex/info
drwx-----x   2 alex      pubs          512 Aug 21 09:31 /home/alex/info
```

```
$ cd /home/alex/info
$ ls -l
.: Permission denied
total 2
```

When Jenny specifies the names of the files she wants information about, she is not reading new directory information, just searching for specific, which she is allowed to do with execute access to the directory. She cannot display **financial** because she does not have read access to it. She does have read access to **notes** so she has no problem using **cat** to display the file.

```
$ ls -l memo.1 memo.2 financial notes summary
-rw-------   1 alex      pubs             34 Aug 21 09:31 financial
-rw-r--r--   1 alex      pubs             21 Aug 21 09:31 memo.1
-rw-r--r--   1 alex      pubs             21 Aug 21 09:32 memo.2
-rw-r--r--   1 alex      pubs             30 Aug 21 09:32 notes
-rw-r--r--   1 alex      pubs             32 Aug 21 09:32 summary
$ cat financial
cat: cannot open financial
$ cat notes
This is the file named notes.
```

Now suppose Alex gives everyone read access to his **info** file with the following command:

```
$ chmod o+r /home/alex/info
```

Now when Jenny checks access permissions on **info** she finds that she has read access as well as execute access to the directory. Now **ls –l** works just fine without arguments, but she still cannot read **financial** (this is an issue of file permissions, not directory permissions). Finally she tries to create a file named **newfile** by redirecting output from **cat** (page 109). If Alex were to give her write permission to the **info** directory, she would be able to create new files in it.

```
$ ls -ld /home/alex/info
drwx---r-x   2 alex      pubs            512 Aug 21 09:31 /home/alex/info
$ ls -l
total 10
-rw-------   1 alex      pubs             34 Aug 21 09:31 financial
-rw-r--r--   1 alex      pubs             21 Aug 21 09:31 memo.1
-rw-r--r--   1 alex      pubs             21 Aug 21 09:32 memo.2
-rw-r--r--   1 alex      pubs             30 Aug 21 09:32 notes
-rw-r--r--   1 alex      pubs             32 Aug 21 09:32 summary
$ cat financial
cat: cannot open financial
$ cat > newfile
cat: permission denied
```

▲ Links

A *link* is a pointer to a file. Every time you create a file using **vi**, **cp**, or any other means, you are putting a pointer in a directory. This pointer associates a filename with a place on the disk. When you specify a filename in a command, you are pointing to the place on the disk where the information that you want is located.

Sharing files can be useful if two or more people are working on a project and need to share some information. You can make it easy for other users to access one of your files by creating additional links to the file.

To share a file with another user, you first give the user permission to read from and write to the file. (In addition you may have to use **chmod** to change the access permission of the parent directory of the file to give the user read, write, and/or execute permission.) Once the permissions are appropriately set, you allow the user to create a link to the file so that each of you can access the file from your separate directory hierarchies.

A link can also be useful to a single user with a large directory hierarchy. You can create links to cross-classify files in your directory hierarchy, using different classifications for different tasks. For example if your directory hierarchy is the one depicted in Figure 4-2, you might have a file named **to_do** in each of the subdirectories of the **correspond** directory—that is, in **personal**, **memos**, and **business**. Then if you find it hard to keep track of all the things you need to do, you can create a separate directory named **to_do** in the **correspond** directory and link each to-do list into that directory. For example you might link the file named **to_do** in the **memos** directory to a file named **memos** in the **to_do** directory. This set of links is shown in Figure 4-11.

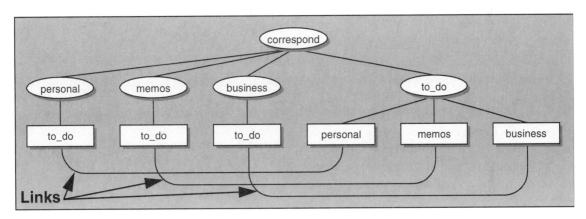

Figure 4-11   Cross-classification of files using links

Although this may sound complicated, this technique allows you to keep all of your to-do lists conveniently in one place. The appropriate list is also easily accessible in the task-related directory when you are busy composing letters, writing memos, or handling personal business.

About the Discussion of Hard Links

There are two kinds of links: Hard links and soft, or symbolic, links. Hard links, discussed first, are older and becoming dated. The section on hard links is marked optional; you can skip it, although it discusses inodes and gives you insight into how the filesystem is structured.

Start Optional

▲▲ In: Create a Link

The **In** (link) utility creates an additional link to an existing file. The new link appears as another file in the file structure. If the file appears in the same directory as the one the file is linked with, the links must have different filenames. This restriction does not apply if the linked file is in another directory. The syntax for **In** is:

In existing-file new-link

The following command makes the link shown in Figure 4-12 by creating a new link named **/home/alex/letter** to an existing file named **draft** in Jenny's home directory. It assumes that the working directory is **/home/jenny** and that Jenny is creating a link to the file named **draft**.

```
$ ln draft /home/alex/letter
```

The new link appears in the **/home/alex** directory with the filename **letter**. In practice it may be necessary for Alex to use **chmod**, as shown in the previous section, to give Jenny write and execute access permission to the **/home/alex** directory. Even though **/home/alex/letter** appears in Alex's directory, Jenny is the owner of the file.

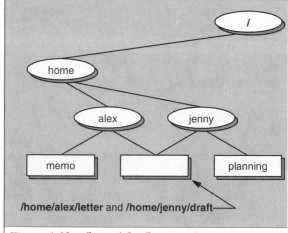

Figure 4-12   /home/alex/letter and /home/jenny/draft are two links to the same file

The **In** utility creates an additional pointer to an existing file. It does *not* make another copy of the file. Because there is only one file, the file status information (such as access permissions, owner, and the time the file was last modified) is the same for all links. Only the filenames differ.

▲▲▲ cp versus In

The following commands allow you to verify that **In** does not make an additional copy of a file: Create a file, use **In** to make an additional link to the file, change the contents of the file through one link, and verify the change through the other link:

```
$ cat file_a
This is file A.
$ ln file_a file_b
$ cat file_b
This is file A.
$ vi file_b
.
.
```

```
$ cat file_b
This is file B after the change.
$ cat file_a
This is file B after the change.
```

If you try the same experiment using **cp** instead of **ln** (and make a change to a *copy* of the file), the difference between the two utilities will become clearer. Once you change a *copy* of a file, the two files are different.

```
$ cat file_c
This is file C.
$ cp file_c file_d
$ cat file_d
This is file C.
$ vi file_d
.
.
.
$ cat file_d
This is file D after the change.
$ cat file_c
This is file C.
```

You can also use **ls** with the **–l** option, followed by the names of the files you want to compare, to see that the status information is the same for two links to a file and is different for files that are not linked. In the following example the **2** in the links field (just to the left of **alex**) shows there are two links to **file_a** and **file_b**:

```
$ ls -l file_a file_b file_c file_d
-rw-r--r-- 2 alex pubs 33  May 24 10:52 file_a
-rw-r--r-- 2 alex pubs 33  May 24 10:52 file_b
-rw-r--r-- 1 alex pubs 16  May 24 10:55 file_c
-rw-r--r-- 1 alex pubs 33  May 24 10:57 file_d
```

Although it is easy to guess which files are linked to one another in this example, **ls** does not explicitly tell you. If you use **ls** with the **–i** option, you can determine without a doubt which files are linked to each other. The **–i** option lists the *inode number* for each file. An *inode* is the control structure for a file. If the two filenames have the same inode number, then they share the control structure, and they are links to the same file. Conversely if two filenames have different inode numbers, they are different files. The following example shows that **file_a** and **file_b** have the same inode number and that **file_c** and **file_d** have different inode numbers:

```
$ ls -i file_a file_b file_c file_d
3534 file_a   3534 file_b   5800 file_c   7328 file_d
```

All links to a file are of equal value—the operating system cannot distinguish the order in which two links were made. If a file has two links, you can remove either one and still access the file through the remaining link. You can even remove the link used to create the file and, as long as there is a remaining link, still access the file through that link.

Stop Optional

▲▲ Symbolic Links

The links that are described in the preceding, optional section are *hard links*. In addition to hard links, Solaris supports links called *symbolic,* or *soft, links*. A hard link is a pointer to a file, and a symbolic link is an *indirect pointer* to a file. It is a directory entry that contains the pathname of the pointed-to file.

Symbolic links were developed because of the limitations of hard links. No user can create a hard link to a directory, but anyone can create a symbolic link to a directory. Also a symbolic link can link to any file, regardless of where it is located in the file structure, but all hard links to a file must be in the same filesystem. Often the Solaris file hierarchy is composed of several filesystems. Because each filesystem keeps separate control information (that is, separate inode tables) for the files it contains, it is not possible to create hard links between files in different filesystems. If you are creating links only among files in your own directories, you probably will not notice these limitations.

One of the big advantages a symbolic link has over a hard link is that it can point to a nonexistent file. This ability is useful if you need a link to a file that periodically gets removed and recreated. For example a symbolic link could point to a file that gets checked in and out under the Source Code Control System or a **.o** file that is recreated by the C compiler each time you run **make**.

Although symbolic links are more general than hard links, they have some disadvantages. Whereas all hard links to a file have equal status, symbolic links do not have the same status as hard links. When a file has multiple hard links, it is like a person having multiple, full legal names (as many married women do). In contrast symbolic links are like pseudonyms. Anyone can have one or more pseudonyms, but pseudonyms have a lesser status than legal names. Some of the peculiarities of symbolic links are described in the following sections.

▲▲▲ Creating a Symbolic Link

Use **ln** with the **–s** option to create a symbolic link. The following example creates a symbolic link, **/tmp/s3**, to the file **sum**. When you use the **ls –l** command to look at the symbolic link, **ls** displays the name of the link as well as the name of the file to which it is an indirect pointer. Also the first character of the listing shows **l** for link.

```
$ ln -s sum /tmp/s3
$ ls -l sum /tmp/s3
-rw-r--r-- 1    alex    pubs    981 May 24 10:55 sum
lrwxrwxrwx 1    alex    pubs      4 May 24 10:57 /tmp/s3 -> sum
```

The sizes and times of last modification of the two files are different. Unlike a hard link a symbolic link to a file does not have the same status information as the file itself.

You can also use a command such as the one above to create a symbolic link to a directory. When you use the **–s** option, **ln** does not care whether the file you are creating a link to is a regular file or a directory.

Start Optional

▲▲▲▲ Using Symbolic Links to Change Directories

When you use a symbolic link as an argument to **cd** to change directories, the results can be confusing, particularly if you did not realize you were using a symbolic link. Adding to the confusion is the fact that, when using **cd**, the Korn Shell handles symbolically linked directories differently than the Bourne and C Shells.

▲▲▲▲ Symbolically Linked Directories under the Bourne and C Shells: After

you use **cd** to change directories to a symbolic link to a directory, **pwd** displays the name of the original directory, not the linked directory.

```
$ ln -s /home/alex/grades /tmp/grades.old
$ pwd
/home/alex
$ cd /tmp/grades.old
$ pwd
/home/alex/grades
```

When you use **cd** to change your working directory to the parent directory, you end up in the parent of the original directory, not the parent of the linked directory.

```
$ cd ..
$ pwd
/home/alex
```

Because **pwd** does not identify the symbolic link, the C Shell provides the **cwd** (current working directory) variable that contains the name of the symbolic link (assuming you used a symbolic link to access the working directory). If you did not use a symbolic link to access the working directory, **cwd** contains the name of the hard link to the working directory. To display the value of the variable **cwd**, use **echo** followed by a SPACE and the variable name preceded by a dollar sign. Shell variables and the use of the dollar sign are explained in Chapters 10 through 13. The following example shows that **/usr/man** is a symbolic link to **/usr/share/man**. This relationship is confirmed by **ls** with the **–l** option.

```
% pwd
/usr/share/man
% echo $cwd
/usr/man
% ls -l /usr/man
lrwxrwxrwx   1 root      root          11 Apr 23 16:05 /usr/man -> ./share/man
```

▲▲▲▲ Symbolically Linked Directories under the Korn Shell: The Korn Shell keeps

track of the symbolic links when using **cd** to move into a symbolically linked directory and when moving back to the parent of that directory.

```
$ cd /tmp/grades.old
$ pwd
/tmp/grades.old
$ cd ..
$ pwd
/tmp
```

Stop Optional

▲▲ rm: Remove a Link

When you first create a file, there is one hard link to it. You can delete the file or, using UNIX terminology, remove the link with the **rm** utility. When you remove the last hard link to a file, you can no longer access the information stored in the file, and the operating system releases the space the file occupied on the disk for use by other files. The space is released even if there are remaining symbolic links. If there is more than one hard link to a file, you can remove a hard link and still access the file from any remaining link.

If you remove all the hard links to a file, you will not be able to access the file through a symbolic link. In the following example **cat** reports that the file **total** does not exist because it is a symbolic link to a file that has been removed:

```
$ ls -l sum
-rw-r--r-- 1 alex pubs 981  May 24 11:05 sum
$ ln -s sum total
$ rm sum
$ cat total
cat: cannot open total
$ ls -l total
lrwxrwxrwx 1 alex pubs 6  May 24 11:09 total -> sum
```

When you remove a file, be sure to remove all symbolic links to it. Remove a symbolic link in the same way you remove other files.

```
$ rm total
```

Summary

Solaris has a hierarchical, or treelike, file structure that makes it possible to organize files so that you can find them quickly and easily. The file structure contains directory files and ordinary files. Directories contain other files, including other directories, whereas ordinary files generally contain text, programs, or images. The ancestor of all files is the root directory named /.

Solaris, as well as most UNIX systems today, supports 255 character filenames. Nonetheless it is a good idea to keep filenames simple and intuitive. Filename extensions can help make filenames more meaningful.

An absolute pathname starts with the root directory and contains all the filenames that trace a path to a given file. Such a pathname starts with a slash representing the root directory and contains additional slashes between the other filenames in the path.

A relative pathname is similar to an absolute pathname, but the path it traces starts from the working directory. A simple filename is the last element of a pathname and is a form of a relative pathname.

When you are logged in, you are always associated with a working directory. Your home directory is your working directory from the time you first log in until you use **cd** to change directories.

There are many important directories in a Solaris filesystem, including **/usr/bin**, which stores most of the Solaris utility commands, and **/dev**, which stores device files, many of which represent a physical piece of hardware. An important standard file is the **/etc/passwd** file. It contains information about a user, such as the user's ID and full name.

Among the attributes associated with each file are access permissions. These determine who can access the file and the manner in which the file may be accessed. There are three groups of user(s) who can access the file: The owner, members of a group, and all other users. There are three ways to access a regular file: Read, write, and execute. The **ls** utility with the **–l** option displays these permissions. For directories, execute access is redefined to mean that the directory can be searched—that it can be used as part of a pathname.

The owner of a file (or Superuser) can use the **chmod** utility to change the access permissions of a file at any time. This utility allows you to define read, write, and execute permissions for the owner, the file's group, and all other users on the system.

A link is a pointer to a file. You can have several links to a single file, so that you can share the file with other users or have the file appear in more than one directory. Because there is only one copy of a file with multiple links, changing the file through any one link causes the changes to appear in all the links. Hard links cannot link directories nor span filesystems, but symbolic links can.

This chapter introduced the following utilities:

Utility	Function
cd	Associates you with another working directory (page 79)
chmod	Changes the access permissions on a file (page 90)
ln	Makes a link to an existing file (page 94)
mkdir	Creates a directory (page 78)
pwd	Displays the pathname of the working directory (page 79)
rmdir	Deletes a directory (page 86)

Review Exercises

1. How are directories different from ordinary files? How can they be distinguished using the **ls** utility?

2. Is each of the following an absolute pathname, a relative pathname, or a simple filename?

   a. **milk_co**

   b. **correspond/business/milk_co**

   c. **/home/alex**

   d. **/home/alex/literature/promo**

   e. **..**

   f. **letter.0610**

3. List the commands you can use to

   a. make your home directory the working directory

   b. identify the working directory

4. If your working directory is **/home/alex** with a subdirectory named **literature**, give three sets of commands that you can use to create a subdirectory under **literature** named **classics**. Also give several sets of commands that you can use to remove the **classics** directory and its contents.

5. The **ls –i** command displays a filename preceded by the inode number of the file (page 95). Write a command to output inode/filename pairs for the files in the working directory, sorted by inode number. (*Hint:* Use a pipe.)

6. The **df** utility displays all mounted filesystems along with information about each. Use the **df** utility to answer the following questions:

    a. How many filesystems are there on your Solaris system?

    b. What filesystem stores your home directory?

    c. Assuming that your answer to part a is two or greater, attempt to create a hard link to a file on another filesystem. What error message do you get? What happens if you attempt to create a symbolic link to the file instead?

7. You should have read permission for the **/etc/passwd** file. To answer the following questions, use **cat** or **pg** to display **/etc/passwd**. Look at the fields of information in **/etc/passwd** for the users on your system.

    a. What character is used to separate fields in **/etc/passwd**?

    b. How many fields are used to describe each user?

    c. How many users are on your system?

    d. How many different login shells are in use on your system? (*Hint:* Look at the last field.)

    e. The second field of **/etc/passwd** stores user passwords in encoded form. If the password field contains an x, then your system uses shadow passwords and stores the encoded passwords elsewhere. Does your system use shadow passwords?

8. If **/home/jenny/draft** and **/home/alex/letter** are links to the same file and the following sequence of events occurs, what will be the date in the opening of the letter?

    a. Alex gives the command **vi letter**.

    b. Jenny gives the command **vi draft**.

    c. Jenny changes the date in the opening of the letter to January 31, 1999, writes the file, and exits from **vi**.

    d. Alex changes the date to February 1, 1999, writes the file, and exits from **vi**.

    Suppose that you have a file that is linked to a file owned by another user. What can you do so that changes to the file are no longer shared?

9. Assume you are given the directory structure shown in Figure 4-2 and the following directory permissions:

```
d--x--x---   3 jenny    pubs        512 Mar 10 15:16 business
drwxr-xr-x   2 jenny    pubs        512 Mar 10 15:16 business/milk_co
```

For each category of permissions—owner, group, and other—what happens when you run each of the following commands? Assume that the working directory is the parent of **correspond** and that the file **cheese_co** is readable by everyone.

a. **cd correspond/business/milk_co**

b. **ls –l correspond/business**

c. **cat correspond/business/cheese_co**

10. Are there any subdirectories of the **root** directory that you cannot search? Are there any subdirectories of the **root** that you cannot read? Explain.

11. Suppose that a user belongs to a group that has all permissions on a file named **jobs_list**, but the user, as the owner of the file, has no permissions. Describe what operations, if any, the user can perform on **jobs_list**. What command that the user can give will grant the user all permissions on the file?

Advanced Review Exercises

12. Create a file named **–x** in an empty directory. Explain what happens when you try to rename it. How can you rename it?

13. Suppose that the working directory contains a single file named **andor**. What error message do you get when you run the following command line?

```
$ mv andor and\/or
```

Under what circumstances is it possible to run the command without producing an error?

14. Explain the error messages displayed in the following sequence of commands.

```
$ ls -l
total 1
drwxrwxr-x   2 alex     bravo      1024 Mar  2 17:57 dirtmp
$ ls dirtmp
$ rmdir dirtmp
rmdir: dirtmp: Directory not empty
$ rm dirtmp/*
rm: No match.
```

15. Do you think that the system administrator has access to a program to decode user passwords? Why or why not (see exercise 7 above)?

16. Is it possible to distinguish a file from a (hard) link to a file? That is, given a filename, can you tell if it was created using an **ln** command? Explain.

The Shell I

T his chapter takes a close look at the shell and explains how to use some of its features. It discusses command-line syntax and how the shell processes a command line and initiates execution of a command. The chapter shows how to redirect input to and output from a command, construct pipes and filters on the command line, and run a command as a background task. The final section covers filename expansion and explains how you can use this feature in your everyday work. Except as noted everything in this chapter applies to the Bourne, C, and Korn Shells. However this chapter uses the Bourne Shell for examples, so if you use another shell, the behavior of the shell or the exact format or wording of the shell output may differ from what you see here. Refer to Chapters 10 through 13 for shell-specific information and more on writing and executing shell scripts.

▲ The Command Line

The shell executes a program when you give it a command in response to its prompt. For example when you give the **ls** command, the shell executes the utility program named **ls**. You can cause the shell to execute other types of programs—such as shell scripts, application programs, and programs you have written—in the same way. The line that contains the command, including any arguments, is called the *command line*. In this book the term *command* refers to the characters you type on the command line as well as the program that action invokes.

▲▲ Syntax

Command-line syntax dictates the ordering and separation of the elements on a command line. When you press the **RETURN** key after entering a command, the shell scans the command line for proper syntax. The syntax for a basic command line is

> *command [arg1] [arg2] ... [argn]* **RETURN**

One or more **SPACE**s (or **TAB**s in some cases) must appear between elements on the command line. The **command** is the command name, **arg1** through **argn** are arguments, and **RETURN** is the keystroke that terminates all command lines. The arguments in the command-line syntax are enclosed in square brackets to show that

103

they are optional. Not all commands have arguments; some commands do not allow arguments; other commands allow a variable number of arguments; and others require a specific number of arguments. Options are a special kind of argument that are usually preceded by a hyphen (also called a dash or minus sign: **–**).

▲▲▲ Command Name

Some useful Solaris command lines consist only of the name of the command without any arguments. For example **ls** by itself lists the contents of the working directory. Most commands accept one or more arguments. Commands that require arguments typically give a short error message, called a *usage message,* when you use them without arguments.

▲▲▲ Arguments

An *argument* is a filename, string of text, number, or some other object that a command acts on. For example the argument to a **vi** command is the name of the file you want to edit.

The following command line shows **cp** copying the file named **temp** to **tempcopy**:

```
$ cp temp tempcopy
```

Arguments are numbered starting with the command itself as argument zero. In this example **cp** is argument zero, **temp** is argument one, and **tempcopy** is argument two. The **cp** utility requires two arguments (it can take more, but not fewer—see Part III) on the command line. Argument one is the name of an existing file, and argument two is the name of the file that **cp** is creating or overwriting. Here the arguments are not optional; both arguments must be present for the command to work. If you do not supply the right number or kind of arguments, **cp** displays a usage message. Try typing **cp** and then pressing RETURN.

▲▲▲▲ Options: An *option* is an argument that modifies the effects of a command. You can frequently specify more than one option, modifying the command in several different ways. Options are specific to and interpreted by the program that the command calls.

By convention options are separate arguments that follow the name of the command. Most utilities require you to prefix options with a hyphen. However this requirement is specific to the utility and not to the shell. GNU program options are frequently preceded by two hyphens in a row, with **––help** generating a (sometimes extensive) usage message.

Figure 5-1 first shows what happens when you give an **ls** command without any options. By default **ls** lists the directories in alphabetical order, vertically sorted in columns. Next you see that the **–r** (reverse order) option causes the **ls** utility to display the list of files in reverse alphabetical order (still sorted in columns). The **–x** option causes **ls** to display the list of files in horizontally sorted rows.

If you need to use several options, you can usually (but not always) group them into one argument that starts with a single hyphen; do not put SPACEs between the options. Specific rules for combining options depend on the program you are running. Figure 5-1 shows both the **–r** and **–x** options with the **ls** utility. Together these options generate a list of filenames in horizontally sorted columns, in reverse alphabetical order. Most utilities allow you to list options in any order; **ls –xr** produces the same results as **ls –rx**. The command **ls –x –r** also generates the same list. For more information see "Option Processing" on page 496.

```
$ ls
alex      house     mark      office    personal  test
hold      jenny     names     oldstuff  temp
$ ls -r
test      personal  office    mark      house     alex
temp      oldstuff  names     jenny     hold
$ ls -x
alex      hold      house     jenny     mark      names     office    oldstuff
personal  temp      test
$ ls -rx
test      temp      personal  oldstuff  office    names     mark      jenny
house     hold      alex
```

Figure 5-1   Using options

▲▲ Processing the Command Line

As you enter a command line, Solaris examines each character to see if it must take any action. When you press **CONTROL-H** (to erase a character) or **CONTROL-U** (to kill a line), the operating system immediately adjusts the command line as required; the shell never sees the character you erased or the line you killed. Often a similar adjustment occurs when you press **CONTROL-W** (to erase a word). If the character does not require immediate action, the operating system stores the character in a buffer and waits until it receives additional characters. When you press **RETURN**, the operating system passes the command line to the shell for processing.

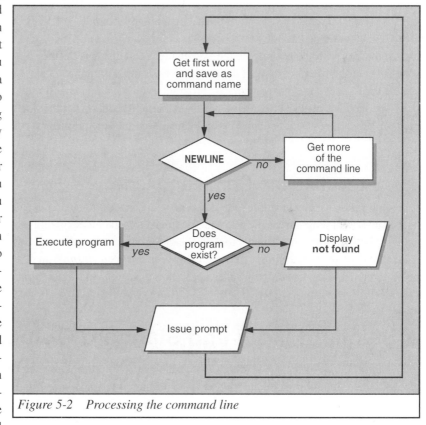

Figure 5-2   Processing the command line

When the shell processes a command line, it looks at the line as a whole and *parses* (breaks) it into its component parts (Figure 5-2). Next the shell looks for the name of the command. It usually assumes that the name of the command is the first thing on the command line after the prompt (argument zero), so it takes the first characters on the command line, up to the first blank (**TAB** or **SPACE**), and looks for a command with that name. On the command line each sequence of nonblank characters is referred to as a *token* or *word*. The command name (the first word) can be specified on the command line either as a simple filename or as a pathname. For example you can call the **ls** command in either of the following ways:

```
$ ls
$ /bin/ls
```

If you give an absolute pathname on the command line or a relative pathname that is not just a simple filename (that is, any pathname that includes at least one slash), the shell looks in the specified directory (**/bin** in this case) for a file that has the name **ls** and that you have permission to execute. If you do not give a pathname on the command line, the shell searches through a list of directories for a filename that matches the name you specified and that you have execute permission for. The shell does not look through all directories—it looks through only the directories specified by a *shell variable* named **PATH**. Refer to page 372 (Bourne Shell), page 461 (C Shell), or page 485 (Korn Shell) for more information on **PATH**. Also refer to the discussion of **which** and **whereis** on page 53.

If the Bourne Shell cannot find the executable file, it displays the message xx: not found, where xx is the name of the file (program). If the shell sh/csh/ksh[1] finds the program but cannot execute it (if you do not have execute access to the file that contains the program), you see a message similar to: xx: cannot execute.

The shell has no way of knowing whether a particular option or other argument is valid for a given program. Any error messages about options or arguments come from the program itself. Some utilities ignore bad options.

▲▲ Executing the Command Line

If the shell finds an executable file with the same name as the command, it starts a new process. A *process* is the execution of a program (page 360). The shell makes each command line argument, including options and the name of the command, available to the called program. While the command is executing, the shell waits, inactive, for the process to finish. The shell is in a state called *sleep*. When the program finishes execution, the shell returns to an active state (wakes up), issues a prompt, and waits for another command.

▲ Standard Input and Standard Output

The *standard output* is a place to which a program can send information such as text. The command never "knows" where the information it sends to standard output is going. The information can go to a printer, an ordinary file, or a screen. This section shows that the shell directs standard output from a command to the ter-

---

1. Refer to "Shell and Builtin and Variable Names" on page 17 for an explanation of the sh/csh/ksh symbol.

minal and describes how you can cause the shell to redirect this output to another file. It also explains how to redirect *standard input* to a command so that it comes from an ordinary file instead of the keyboard.

In addition to standard input and standard output, a running program normally has a place to send error messages: *standard error.* Refer to pages 355, 452, and 503 for more information on handling standard error under the different shells.

Running a Different Shell

The person who sets up your account determines which shell you will use when you first log in on the system (page 625). You can run any shell you like once you are logged in. Give the name of the shell you want to use (**sh**, **csh**, or **ksh**), press **RETURN**, and you are using the new shell. Experiment with the shell as you like and give the **exit** command to return to your previous shell. Because shells you call in this manner are nested (one runs on top of the other) you will not be able to log out from any but your original shell. If you have nested several shells, keep giving **exit** commands until you are back to your original shell. Then you will be able to log out.

Superuser can use **passwd –e *username*** (when using files or NIS) or **nispasswd –s *username*** (with NIS+) to permanently change the user's login shell.

▲▲ The Window/Terminal as a File

Chapter 4 introduced ordinary files, directory files, and hard and soft links. Solaris has an additional type of file, a *device file.* A device file resides in the Solaris file structure, usually in the **/dev** directory, and represents a peripheral device such as an emulator window, terminal, printer, or disk drive.

The device name that the **who** utility displays after your login name is the filename of your window/terminal. If **who** displays the device name **pts/4**, the pathname of your window/terminal is **/dev/pts/4**. You can also use the **tty** utility to display the name of the window/terminal you give the command from. Although you would not normally have occasion to, you could read from and write to this file as though it were a text file. Writing to it would display what you wrote on the screen, and reading from it would read what you entered on the keyboard.

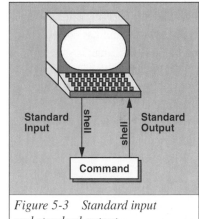

Figure 5-3   Standard input and standard output

▲▲ The Window/Terminal as Standard Input and Standard Output

When you first log in, the shell directs standard output of your commands to the device file that represents your window/terminal (Figure 5-3). Directing output in this manner causes it to appear on your screen. The shell also directs standard input to come from the same file, so that your commands receive anything you type on your keyboard as input.

The **cat** utility provides a good example of the way the terminal functions as standard input and standard output. When you use **cat**, it copies a file to standard output. Because the shell directs standard output to the terminal, **cat** displays the file on the screen.

Up to this point **cat** has taken its input from the filename (argument) you specified on the command line. If you do not give **cat** an argument (that is, if you give the command **cat** immediately followed by a RETURN), **cat** takes input from standard input.

The **cat** utility can now be described as a utility that, when called without an argument, copies standard input to standard output, one line at a time.

```
$ cat
This is a line of text.
This is a line of text.
Cat keeps copying lines of text
Cat keeps copying lines of text
until you press CONTROL-D at the beginning
until you press CONTROL-D at the beginning
of a line.
of a line.
CONTROL-D
$
```

*Figure 5-4   **cat** copies standard input to standard output*

To see how **cat** works, type **cat** and press RETURN in response to the shell prompt. Nothing happens. Enter a line of text and a RETURN. The same line appears just under the one you entered. The **cat** utility is working. What happened is that you typed a line of text using the keyboard, which the shell associated with **cat**'s standard input, and **cat** copied your line of text to standard output, which the shell also associated with the screen. This exchange is shown in Figure 5-4.

The **cat** utility keeps copying until you enter CONTROL-D on a line by itself. Pressing CONTROL-D sends an EOF (end of file) signal to **cat** that indicates it has reached the end of standard input and that there is no more text for it to copy. When you enter CONTROL-D, **cat** finishes execution and returns control to the shell, which gives you a prompt.

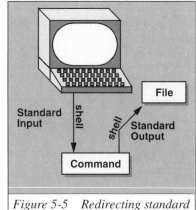

Figure 5-5   Redirecting standard output

▲ Redirection

The term *redirection* encompasses the various ways you can cause the shell to alter where standard input of a command comes from or where standard output goes to. As the previous section demonstrated, by default the shell associates the standard input and standard output of a command with the window/terminal. You can cause the shell to redirect standard input and/or standard output of any command by associating the input or output with a command or file other than the device file representing the terminal. This section demonstrates how to redirect output to and input from ordinary text files and utilities.

▲▲ Redirecting Standard Output

The *redirect output symbol* (>) instructs the shell to redirect the output of a command to the specified file instead of to the window/terminal (Figure 5-5). The format of a command line that redirects output is

command [arguments] > filename

where **command** is any executable program (such as an application program or a utility), **arguments** are optional arguments, and ***filename*** is the name of the ordinary file the shell redirects the output to.

> ### Redirecting Output Can Destroy a File I
>
> Use caution when you redirect output to a file. If the file already exists, the shell will overwrite it and destroy its contents. For more information see the Caution named "Redirecting Output Can Destroy a File II" on page 111.

In Figure 5-6 **cat** demonstrates output redirection. This figure contrasts with Figure 5-3, where both standard input *and* standard output were associated with the window/terminal. In Figure 5-6 only the input comes from the window/terminal. The redirect output symbol on the command line causes the shell to associate **cat**'s standard output with the file specified on the command line, **sample.txt**.

```
$ cat > sample.txt
This text is being entered at the keyboard.
Cat is copying it to a file.
Press CONTROL-D to indicate the
End of File.
CONTROL-D
$
```

*Figure 5-6   **cat** with its output redirected*

Now the file **sample.txt** contains the text you entered. You can use **cat** with an argument of **sample.txt** to display the file. The next section shows another way to use **cat** to display the file.

Figure 5-6 shows that redirecting the output from **cat** is a handy way to make a file without using an editor. Its drawback is that once you enter a line and press RETURN, you cannot edit the text. While you are entering a line, the erase and kill keys work to delete text. This procedure is useful for making short, simple files.

Figure 5-7 shows how to use **cat** and the redirect output symbol to *catenate* (join one after the other—this is the derivation of the name of the **cat** utility) several files into one larger file. The first three commands display the contents of three files: **stationery**, **tape**, and **pens**. The next command shows **cat** with three filenames as arguments. When you call **cat** with more than one filename, it copies the files, one at a time, to standard output. In this case standard output is redirected to the file **supply_orders**. The final **cat** command shows that **supply_orders** contains the contents of all three files.

```
$ cat stationery
2000 sheets letterhead ordered:      10/7/97
$ cat tape
1 box masking tape ordered:          10/14/97
5 boxes filament tape ordered:       10/28/97
$ cat pens
12 doz. black pens ordered:          10/4/97
$ cat stationery tape pens > supply_orders
$ cat supply_orders
2000 sheets letterhead ordered:      10/7/97
1 box masking tape ordered:          10/14/97
5 boxes filament tape ordered:       10/28/97
12 doz. black pens ordered:          10/4/97
$
```

*Figure 5-7   Using **cat** to catenate files*

▲▲ Redirecting Standard Input

Just as you can redirect standard output, you can redirect standard input. The *redirect input symbol* (<) instructs the shell to redirect a command's input from the specified file instead of the keyboard (Figure 5-8). The format of a command line that redirects input is

command [arguments] < filename

where **command** is any executable program (such as an application program or a utility), **arguments** are optional arguments, and **filename** is the name of the ordinary file the shell redirects the input from.

Figure 5-9 shows **cat** with its input redirected from the **supply_orders** file that was created in Figure 5-7 and standard output going to the window/terminal. This setup causes **cat** to display the sample file on the terminal. The system automatically supplies an EOF (end of file) signal at the end of an ordinary file, so no CONTROL-D is necessary.

Giving a **cat** command with input redirected from a file yields the same result as giving a **cat** command with the filename as an argument. The **cat** utility is a member of a class of Solaris utilities that function in this manner. Some of the other members of this class of utilities are **lp**, **sort**, and **grep**. These utilities first examine the command line you use to call them. If you include a

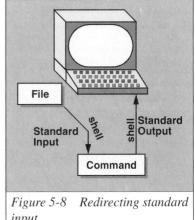

Figure 5-8   Redirecting standard input

filename on the command line, the utility takes its input from the file you specify. If you do not specify a filename, the utility takes its input from standard input. It is the utility or program, not the shell or the operating system, that functions in this manner.

The following example shows how you can use redirected input to send a file to another person with the **mail** utility (**mail** is used in place of **dtmail** here because **dtmail** is screen oriented and does not allow you to redirect standard input). Frequently you want to compose your thoughts in a file by using an editor before you send someone electronic mail. You can use **spell** to look for misspellings, **lp** to print the file, check that

```
$ cat < supply_orders
2000 sheets letterhead ordered:     10/7/97
1 box masking tape ordered:         10/14/97
5 boxes filament tape ordered:      10/28/97
12 doz. black pens ordered:         10/4/97
$
```

*Figure 5-9   **cat** with its input redirected*

it is correct, and send it at your leisure. The following command sends the contents of the file **memo.alex** to Alex, using **mail**. The redirect input symbol redirects standard input to **mail** so that it comes from **memo.alex** instead of the keyboard.

```
$ mail alex < memo.alex
```

Redirecting Output Can Destroy a File II

Depending on which shell you are using and how your environment has been set up, a command such as the following may give you undesired results:

```
$ cat orange pear >orange
cat: input/output files 'orange' identical
```

Although **cat** displays an error message, the shell goes ahead and destroys the contents of the existing **orange** file. If you give the command above, the new **orange** file will have the same contents as **pear**, because the first action the shell takes when it sees the redirection symbol (>) is to remove the contents of the original **orange** file. If you want to catenate two files into one, use **cat** to put the two files into a third, temporary file, and then use **mv** to rename the third file as you desire.

```
$ cat orange pear > temp
$ mv temp orange
```

What happens with the typo in the next example can be even worse. The user giving the command wants to search through files **a**, **b**, and **c** for the word `apple` and redirect the output from **grep** (page 43) to the file **a.output**. Instead the user enters the filename as **a output**, omitting the period and leaving a SPACE in its place. The shell obediently removes the contents of **a** and then calls **grep**. The error message takes a moment to appear, giving you a sense that the command is running correctly. Even after you see the error message, though, you may not know that you destroyed the contents of **a**.

```
$ grep apple a b c > a output
grep: can't open output
$
```

The shell provides a feature called **noclobber** csh (page 464) or **NO_CLOBBER** ksh (page 519) that stops you from inadvertently overwriting an existing file using redirection. If you enable this feature by setting the **noclobber** variable or the **NO_CLOBBER** option and you attempt to redirect output to an existing file, the shell presents an error message and does not execute the command. If the examples above result in a message such as `File exists`, then the noclobber feature is in effect.

▲▲ Appending Standard Output to a File

The *append output symbol* (**>>**) causes the shell to add new information to the end of a file, leaving intact any information that was already there. This symbol provides a convenient way of catenating two files into one. The following commands demonstrate the action of the double greater than signs. The second command accomplishes the catenation described in the preceding Caution:

```
$ cat orange
this is orange
$ cat pear >> orange
$ cat orange
this is orange
this is pear
```

First you see the contents of the **orange** file. Next the contents of the **pear** file is added on to the end of (catenated with) the **orange** file. The final **cat** shows the result.

Do Not Trust noclobber

This technique is simpler to use than the two-step procedure just described, but you must be careful to include both greater than signs. If you accidentally use only one and the noclobber feature is not on, you will overwrite the **orange** file. Generally even if you have the noclobber feature turned on, it is a good idea to keep backup copies of files you are manipulating in these ways in case you make a mistake.

Although noclobber protects you from making an erroneous redirection, it cannot stop you from overwriting an existing file using **cp** or **mv**. These utilities include the **−i** (interactive) options that protect you from this type of mistake by verifying your intentions if you try to overwrite a file. For more information see the Caution named "**cp** Can Destroy a File" on page 42. The **mv** utility also accepts the same option.

The example in Figure 5-10 shows how to create a file that contains the date and time (the output from the **date** utility) followed by a list of who is logged in (the output from **who**). The first line in Figure 5-10 redirects the output from **date** to the file named **whoson**. Then **cat** displays the file. Next the example appends the output from **who** to the **whoson** file. Finally **cat** displays the file containing the output of both utilities.

```
$ date >whoson
$ cat whoson
Sat Mar 27 14:31:18 PST 1999
$ who >>whoson
$ cat whoson
Sat Mar 27 14:31:18 PST 1999
root       console      Mar 27 05:00(:0)
alex       pts/4        Mar 27 12:23(:0.0)
alex       pts/5        Mar 27 12:33(:0.0)
jenny      pts/7        Mar 26 08:45 (bravo.tcorp.com)
$
```

Figure 5-10   Redirecting and appending output

▲▲ /dev/null

The **/dev/null** device, which is a data sink, commonly called a bit bucket, is a place you can redirect output that you do not want. The output disappears without a trace.

```
$ echo "hi there" > /dev/null
$
```

When you read from **/dev/null**, you get a null string. Give the following **cat** command to truncate a file named **messages** to zero length while preserving the ownership and permissions of the file.

```
$ ls -l messages
-rw-r--r--   1 alex      pubs         25315 Oct 24 10:55 messages
$ cat /dev/null > messages
$ ls -l messages
-rw-r--r--   1 alex      pubs             0 Oct 24 11:02 messages
```

▲ Pipes

The shell uses a *pipe* to connect standard output of one command directly to standard input of another command. A pipe (sometimes called a *pipeline*) has the same effect as redirecting standard output of one command to a file and then using that file as standard input to another command. It does away with separate commands and the intermediate file. The symbol for a pipe is a vertical bar (I). The syntax of a command line using a pipe is

command_a [arguments] I command_b [arguments]

This command line uses a pipe to generate the same result as the following group of command lines:

command_a [arguments] > temp
command_b [arguments] < temp
rm temp

The preceding sequence of commands first redirects standard output from **command_a** to an intermediate file named **temp**. Then it redirects standard input for **command_b** to come from **temp**. The final command line deletes **temp**. The command using the pipe is not only easier to type, it is generally more efficient than the sequence of three commands because it does not create a temporary file.

You can use a pipe with a member of the class of Solaris utilities that accepts input either from a file specified on the command line or from standard input. You can also use pipes with commands that accept input only from standard input. For example the **tr** (translate) utility takes its input only from standard input. In its simplest usage **tr** has the following format:

tr string1 string2

The **tr** utility accepts input from standard input and looks for characters that match one of the characters in **string1**. Finding a match, **tr** translates the matched character in **string1** to the corresponding character in **string2**. (The first character in **string1** translates into the first character in **string2**, and so forth.) In the following examples **tr** displays the contents of the **abstract** file with the letters **a**, **b**, and **c** translated into **A**, **B**, and **C**, respectively:

```
$ cat abstract | tr abc ABC
```

or

```
$ tr abc ABC < abstract
```

As with other Solaris filters (page 115), **tr** does not change the content of the original file. Refer to page 924 in Part III for more information on **tr**.

The **lp** (line printer) utility is among the utilities that accept input from either a file or standard input. When you follow **lp** with the name of a file, it places that file in the printer queue. If you do not specify a filename on the command line, **lp** takes input from standard input. This feature allows you to use a pipe to redirect input to **lp**. The first set of commands in Figure 5-11 shows how you can use **ls** and **lp**, with an intermediate file (**temp**), to send a list of the files in the working directory to the printer. If the **temp** file already exists, the first command overwrites its contents. The second set of commands sends the same list (with the exception of **temp**) to the printer using a pipe.

```
$ ls > temp
$ lp temp
$ rm temp

or

$ ls | lp
request id is printer_1-501 (1 file)
$
```

Figure 5-11   A pipe

The commands in Figure 5-12 redirect the output from the **who** utility to **temp** and then display this file in sorted order. The **sort** utility (page 45) takes its input from the file specified on the command line or, if a file is not specified, from standard input. It sends its output to standard output. The **sort** command line in Figure 5-12 takes its input from standard input, which is redirected (<) to come from **temp**. The output that **sort** sends to the terminal lists the users in sorted (alphabetical) order.

```
$ who >temp
$ sort < temp
alex       pts/4      Mar 27 12:23(:0.0)
alex       pts/5      Mar 27 12:33(:0.0)
jenny      pts/7      Mar 26 08:45 (bravo.tcorp.com)
root       console    Mar 27 05:00(:0)
$ rm temp
```

Figure 5-12   Using a temporary file to store intermediate results

Figure 5-13 achieves the same result without creating the **temp** file. Using a pipe, the shell directs the output from **who** to the input of **sort**. The **sort** utility takes input from standard input because no filename follows it on the command line.

```
$ who | sort
alex        pts/4       Mar 27 12:23(:0.0)
alex        pts/5       Mar 27 12:33(:0.0)
jenny       pts/7       Mar 26 08:45 (bravo.tcorp.com)
root        console     Mar 27 05:00(:0)
$
```

Figure 5-13   A pipe doing the work of a temporary file

If a lot of people are using the system and you want information about only one of them, you can send the output from **who** to **grep** (page 43) using a pipe. The **grep** utility displays the line containing the string you specify—root in the following example:

```
$ who | grep 'root'
root        console     Mar 27 05:00(:0)
```

Another way of handling output that is too long to fit on the screen, such as a list of files in a crowded directory, is to use a pipe to send the output through **pg** (or **more** [both on page 35]).

```
$ ls | pg
```

The **pg** utility allows you to view text a screenful at a time. To view another screenful press RETURN. To view one more line press **l** ("ell" for line) RETURN. Press **h** (and RETURN with **pg**) for help.

▲▲ Filters

A *filter* is a command that processes an input stream of data to produce an output stream of data. A command line that includes a filter uses a pipe to connect the filter's input to standard output of one command. Another pipe connects the filter's output to standard input of another command. Not all utilities can be used as filters.

In the following example **sort** is a filter, taking standard input from standard output of **who** and using a pipe to redirect standard output to standard input of **lp**. The command line sends the sorted output of **who** to the printer.

```
$ who | sort | lp
```

This example demonstrates the power of the shell combined with the versatility of Solaris utilities. The three utilities, **who**, **sort**, and **lp**, were not specifically designed to work with each other, but they all use standard input and standard output in the conventional way. By using the shell to handle input and output, you can piece standard utilities together on the command line to achieve the results you want.

▲▲ tee: Sending Output in Two Directions

You can use the **tee** utility in a pipe to send the output of a command to a file while also sending it to standard output. The utility is aptly named—it takes a single input and sends the output in two directions. In Figure 5-14 the output of **who** is sent via a pipe to standard input of **tee**. The **tee** utility saves a copy of standard input in a file named **who.out**, while it also sends a copy to standard output. Standard output of **tee** goes, via a pipe, to standard input of **grep**, which displays lines containing the string scott.

```
$ who | tee who.out | grep root
root         console     Mar 27 05:00(:0)
$ cat who.out
root         console     Mar 27 05:00(:0)
alex         pts/4       Mar 27 12:23(:0.0)
alex         pts/5       Mar 27 12:33(:0.0)
jenny        pts/7       Mar 26 08:45 (bravo.tcorp.com)
$
```

*Figure 5-14   Using **tee***

▲ Running a Program in the Background

In all the examples you have seen so far in this book, commands were run in the *foreground.* When you run a command in the foreground, the shell waits for it to finish before giving you another prompt and allowing you to continue. When you run a command in the *background,* you do not have to wait for the command to finish before you start running another command.

A *job* is a series of one or more commands connected by a pipe (|) or pipes. You can only have one foreground job in a window or on a terminal screen, but you can have many background jobs. By running more than one job at a time, you are using one of Solaris's important features: Multitasking. Running a command in the background can be useful if the command will be running a long time and does not need supervision. The window/terminal is free so you can use it for other work. Of course if you are using a graphical user interface (Solaris windows), you can just open another window to run another job.

To run a command in the background, type an ampersand (**&**) just before the **RETURN** that ends the command line. The shell assigns a small number to the job called a *job number* and displays it between brackets. Following the job number the shell displays the *process identification* (PID) number—a bigger number assigned by the operating system. Each of these numbers identifies the command running in the background. Then the shell gives you another prompt so you can enter another command. When the background job finishes running, the shell displays a message giving both the job number and the command line used to start the command.[2]

The following example runs a command line in the background. This and the examples that follow use the Job Shell; your output may look different with another shell. The command sends its output through a pipe

---

2. The C and Korn Shells have job control. The standard Bourne Shell does not have job control; however the Job Shell has job control and complete Bourne Shell features and syntax. The Job, C, and Korn Shells use and display both the job number and PID. (Give the command **jsh** to start using the Job Shell and the command **exit** to leave the Job Shell and return to your original shell.)

to **lp**, which sends it to the printer. (The prompt appears before the message from **lp**: Hit RETURN for another prompt.)

```
$ ls -l | lp &
[1] 22092
$ request id is printer_1-496 (standard input)
```

The [1] following the command line indicates that the shell has assigned job number 1 to this job. The 22092 is the PID number of the first command in the job (the C Shell shows PID numbers for all commands in the job). When this background job completes execution, you see the message

```
[1]+ Done            ls -l | lp
```

If you are running the Job, C, or Korn Shell you can stop a foreground job from running by pressing the suspend key, usually CONTROL-Z. The shell stops the process and disconnects standard input from the terminal keyboard. You can put the job in the background and start it running using the **bg** shell builtin[3] $\frac{jsh}{csh}$ followed by a percent sign and the job number. You do not need to use the job number if you have only one stopped job.

If a background task sends output to standard output and you do not redirect it, the output appears on your terminal, even if you are running another job. If a background task requests input from standard input and you have not redirected standard input, the shell stops the job and displays a message. The following example shows what happens when you start a program named **promptme**, which requires input from the keyboard, in the background under the C Shell:

```
% promptme &
[1]   + Stopped (tty input)   promptme
%
```

Only the foreground job can take input from the keyboard. To connect the keyboard to the program running in the background, you must bring it into the foreground using **fg** (followed by a percent sign and its job number if there is more than one job in the background). The shell displays the command you used to start the job, and you can enter the input the program requires to continue.

```
$ fg %1
[1] promptme
```

Redirect the output of a job you run in the background to keep it from interfering with whatever you are doing at the terminal. Refer to "Command Separation and Grouping" on page 351 for more detail about background tasks.

---

3. A *builtin* (page 47) is a command that is built into and is part of the shells named within the shaded rectangle following its name ($\frac{sh}{csh}$ [page 17]). All builtins available in **sh** are also available in **jsh**. Give the command **man shell_builtins** to see a list of builtins.

The interrupt key (usually **CONTROL-C**) cannot abort a process you are running in the background; you must use the **kill** (page 785) builtin ᶜˢʰₖₛₕ for this purpose. Follow **kill** on the command line with either the PID number of the process you want to abort or a percent sign (%) followed by the job number.

If you forget the PID number, you can use the **ps** (process status [page 361]) utility to display it. The following example (using the C Shell) runs a **tail –f outfile** command (the **–f** option causes **tail** to watch **outfile** and display any new lines that are written to it) as a background job, uses **ps** to display the PID number of the process, and aborts the job with **kill**. So that it does not interfere with anything on the screen, the message saying that the job is terminated does not appear until you press **RETURN** after the **RETURN** that ends the **kill** command.

```
% tail -f outfile &
[1] 22170
% ps | grep tail
22170 pts/7     0:00 tail
% kill 22170
% RETURN
[1]    Terminated        tail -f outfile
%
```

If you forget the job number, you can use the **jobs** shell builtin ᶜˢʰₖₛₕ to determine the job number of the background job. The following example is similar to the previous one but uses the job number in place of the PID number to kill the job:

```
% tail -f outfile &
[1] 3339
% bigjob &
[2] 3340
% jobs
[1]  - Running           tail -f outfile
[2]  + Running           bigjob
% kill %1
%RETURN
[1]    Terminated        tail -f outfile
%
```

▲ Filename Generation/Pathname Expansion

When you give the shell abbreviated filenames that contain special characters, or *metacharacters* (characters that have a special meaning to the shell), the shell can generate filenames that match the names of existing files. These special characters are also referred to as *wildcards* because they act as the jokers do in a deck of cards. When one of these special characters appears in an argument on the command line, the shell expands that argument (in sorted order, see "LC_COLLATE" on page 1010) into a list of filenames and passes the list to the program that the command line calls. Filenames that contain these special characters are called *ambiguous file references* because they do not refer to any one specific file. The process that the shell performs on these filenames is called *pathname expansion* or *globbing*.

Ambiguous file references allow you to reference a group of files with similar names quickly, saving you the effort of typing the names individually. They also allow you to reference a file whose name you do not remember in its entirety. If no filename matches the ambiguous file reference, the shell generally passes the unexpanded reference, special characters and all, to the command.

▲▲ The **?** Special Character

The question mark is a special character that causes the shell to generate filenames. It matches any single character in the name of an existing file. The following command uses this special character in an argument to the **lp** utility:

```
$ lp memo?
```

The shell expands the **memo?** argument and generates a list of the files in the working directory that have names composed of **memo** followed by any single character. The shell passes this list to **lp**. The **lp** utility never "knows" that the shell generated the filenames it was called with. If no filename matches the ambiguous file reference, the shell $_{csh}^{sh}$ passes the string itself (**memo?**) to **lp** or, if it is set up to do so, displays an error message $_{ksh}^{csh}$.

The following example uses **ls** first to display the names of all the files in the working directory and then to display the filenames that memo? matches:

```
$ ls
mem        memo12     memo9      memoalex   newmemo5
memo       memo5      memoa      memos
$ ls memo?
memo5   memo9   memoa   memos
```

The **memo?** ambiguous file reference does not match **mem, memo, memo12, memoalex**, or **newmemo5**. You can also use a question mark in the middle of an ambiguous file reference:

```
$ ls
7may4report     may14report     may4report.79   mayqreport
may.report      may4report      may_report      mayreport
$ ls may?report
may.report   may4report   may_report   mayqreport
```

To practice generating filenames you can use **echo** as well as **ls**; **echo** displays the arguments that the shell passes to it. Try giving the following command:

```
$ echo may?report
may.report   may4report   may_report   mayqreport
```

The shell expands the ambiguous file reference into a list of all files in the working directory that match the string may?report and passes this list to **echo**, as though you had entered the list of filenames as arguments to **echo**. The **echo** utility responds by displaying the list of filenames. A question mark does not match a leading period (one that indicates an invisible filename). If you want to match filenames that begin with a period, you must explicitly include the period in the ambiguous file reference.

▲▲ The * Special Character

The asterisk performs a function similar to that of the question mark, except that it matches any number of characters, *including zero characters,* in a filename. The following example shows all the files in the working directory and then shows three commands that display all the filenames that begin with the string **memo**, end with the string **mo**, and contain the string **alx**:

```
$ ls
amemo          memo          memoalx.0620  memosally     user.memo
mem            memo.0612     memoalx.keep  sallymemo
memalx         memoa         memorandum    typescript
$ echo memo*
memo memo.0612 memoa memoalx.0620 memoalx.keep memorandum memosally
$ echo *mo
amemo memo sallymemo user.memo
$ echo *alx*
memalx memoalx.0620 memoalx.keep
```

The ambiguous file reference **memo*** does not match **amemo**, **mem**, **sallymemo**, or **user.memo**. As with the question mark, an asterisk does not match a leading period in a filename.

The **–a** option causes **ls** to display invisible filenames. The command **echo *** does not display **.** (the working directory), **..** (the parent of the working directory), **.aaa**, or **.profile**. The command **echo .*** displays only those four names.

```
$ ls
aaa memo.0612 memo.sally report sally.0612 saturday thurs
$ ls -a
.   .aaa      aaa           memo.sally sally.0612 thurs
..  .profile memo.0612  report        saturday
$ echo *
aaa memo.0612 memo.sally report sally.0612 saturday thurs
$ echo .*
. .. .aaa .profile
```

In the following example **.p*** does not match **memo.0612**, **private**, **reminder**, or **report**. Following that the **ls .*** command causes **ls** to list **.private** and **.profile** in addition to the entire contents of the **.** directory (the working directory) and the **..** directory (the parent of the working directory).

```
$ ls -a
.          .private   memo.0612   reminder
..         .profile   private     report

$ echo .p*
.private .profile
$ ls .*
.private .profile

.:
memo.0612  private    reminder   report

..:
.
.
```

If you establish conventions for naming files, you can take advantage of ambiguous file references. For example if you end all your text filenames with **.txt**, you can reference that group of files with ***.txt**. Following this convention the next command sends all the text files in the working directory to the printer. The ampersand causes **lp** to run in the background.

```
$ lp *.txt &
```

▲▲ The [] Special Characters

A pair of square brackets surrounding a list of characters causes the shell to match filenames containing the individual characters. Whereas memo? matches **memo** followed by any character, memo[17a] is more restrictive—it matches only **memo1**, **memo7**, and **memoa**. The brackets define a *character class* that includes all the characters within the brackets. The shell expands an argument that includes a character-class definition, substituting each member of the character class, *one at a time*, in place of the brackets and their contents. The shell passes a list of matching filenames to the program it is calling.

Each character-class definition can replace only a single character within a filename. The brackets and their contents are like a question mark that substitutes only the members of the character class.

The first of the following commands lists the names of all the files in the working directory that begin with a, e, i, o, or u. The second command displays the contents of the files named **page2.txt**, **page4.txt**, **page6.txt**, and **page8.txt**.

```
$ echo [aeiou]*
.
.
.
$ cat page[2468].txt
.
.
.
```

Within square brackets a hyphen defines a range of characters within a character-class definition. For example **[6–9]** represents **[6789]**, **[a–z]** represents all lowercase letters in English, and **[a–zA–Z]** represents all letters, upper- and lowercase, in English.

The following command lines show three ways to print the files named **part0**, **part1**, **part2**, **part3**, and **part5**. Each of the command lines causes the shell to call **lp** with five filenames.

```
$ lp part0 part1 part2 part3 part5

$ lp part[01235]

$ lp part[0-35]
```

The first command line explicitly specifies the five filenames. The second and third command lines use ambiguous file references, incorporating character-class definitions. The shell expands the argument on the second command line to include all files that have names beginning with **part** and ending with any of the characters in the character class. The character class is explicitly defined as 0, 1, 2, 3, and 5. The third command line also uses a character-class definition, except it defines the character class to be all characters in the range from 0–3 and 5.

The following command line prints 39 files, **part0** through **part38**:

```
$ lp part[0-9] part[12][0-9] part3[0-8]
```

The following two examples list the names of some of the files in the working directory. The first lists the files whose names start with **a** through **m**. The second lists files whose names end with **x**, **y**, or **z**.

```
$ echo [a-m]*
.
.
.
$ echo *[x-z]
.
.
.
```

Start Optional

If an exclamation point (**!**) or a caret (**^**) immediately follows the opening bracket (**[**), then the string enclosed by the brackets matches any character not between the brackets, so that [**^ab**]* matches any filename that does not begin with **a** or **b**. You can match a hyphen (**–**) or a closing bracket (**]**) by placing it immediately before the final closing bracket.

Stop Optional

The Shell Expands Ambiguous File References

The shell does the expansion when it processes an ambiguous file reference, not the program that the shell runs. In the examples in this section, *the utilities (**ls**, **cat**, **echo**, **lp**) never see the ambiguous file references.* The shell expands the ambiguous file references and passes the utility a list of ordinary filenames.

The following example demonstrates that the **ls** utility has no ability to interpret ambiguous file references. First **ls** is called with an argument of ?old. The shell expands ?old into a matching filename, **hold**, and passes that name to **ls**. The second command is the same as the first, except the ? is quoted (page 36) so the shell does not recognize it as a special character and passes it on to **ls**. The **ls** utility generates an error message saying that it cannot find a file named **?old** (because there is no file named **?old**). Like **ls** most utilities and programs cannot interpret ambiguous file references; that work is left to the shell.

```
$ ls ?old
hold
$ ls \?old
?old: No such file or directory
```

Summary

The shell is the Solaris command interpreter. It scans the command line for proper syntax, picking out the command name and any arguments. The first argument is referred to as argument one, the second as argument two, and so on. The name of the command itself is sometimes referred to as argument zero. Many programs use options to modify the effects of a command. Most Solaris utilities identify an option by its leading hyphen.

When you give the shell a command, it tries to find an executable program with the same name as the command. If it does, it executes the program. If it does not, it tells you that it cannot find or execute the program. If the command is expressed as a simple filename, the shell searches the directories given in the variable **PATH** in an attempt to locate the command.

When the shell executes a command, it assigns a file to the command's standard input and standard output. By default the shell causes a command's standard input to come from the keyboard and standard output to go to the screen. You can instruct the shell to redirect a command's standard input from, or standard output to, any reasonable file or device. You can also connect standard output of one command to standard input of another using a pipe. A filter is a command that reads the standard output of one command (as its standard input) and writes its standard output to the standard input of another command.

When a command runs in the foreground, the shell waits for it to finish before it gives you another prompt and allows you to continue. If you put an ampersand (**&**) at the end of a command line, the shell executes the command in the background and gives you another prompt immediately. Put a command in the background when you think it may not execute quickly and you want to enter other commands at the shell prompt. The **jobs** builtin displays a list of background jobs and includes the job number of each.

The shell interprets shell special characters on a command line for filename generation. It uses a question mark to represent any single character and an asterisk to represent zero or more characters. A single character may also be represented by a character class—a list of characters within brackets. A reference that uses special characters to abbreviate a list of one or more filenames is called an ambiguous file reference.

This chapter covered the following commands:

Utility	Function
tr	Maps one string of characters into another (page 113)
tee	Sends standard input both to a file and to standard output (page 115)
bg	Moves a process to the background (page 117)
fg	Moves a process to the foreground (page 117)
jobs	Displays a list of currently running jobs (page 118)

Review Exercises

1. What does the shell ordinarily do while a command is executing? What should you do if you do not want to wait for a command to finish before running another command?

2. Rewrite the following sequence of commands using **sort** as a filter:

```
$ sort list > temp
$ lp temp
$ rm temp
```

3. Assume the following files are in the working directory:

```
$ ls
intro       notesb      ref2        section1    section3    section4b
notesa      ref1        ref3        section2    section4a   sentrev
```

Give commands for each of the following, using wildcards to express filenames with as few characters as possible.

a. List all files that begin with section.

b. List the **section1**, **section2**, and **section3** files only.

c. List the **intro** file only.

d. List the **section1**, **section3**, **ref1**, and **ref3** files.

4. Refer to the documentation of utilities in Part III or the **man** pages to determine what commands will do the following.

a. Output the number of lines in the standard input that contain the *word* a or A.

b. Output the names (only) of the files in the working directory that contain the pattern $ (.

c. List the files in the working directory in their reverse alphabetical order.

d. Send a list of files in the working directory to the printer, sorted by size.

5. Give a command to:

a. Redirect the standard output from a **sort** command into a file named **phone_list**. Assume the input file is named **numbers**.

b. Translate all occurrences of characters [and { to the character (, and all occurrences of the characters] and } to the character) in the file **permdemos.c**. (*Hint:* Refer to **tr** on page 924 in Part III.)

c. Create a file named **book** that contains the contents of two others files, **part1** and **part2**.

6. What is a PID number? Why are they useful when you run processes in the background?

7. The **lp** and **sort** utilities accept input either from a file named on the command line or from standard input.

a. Name two other utilities that function in a similar manner.

b. Name a utility that accepts its input only from standard input.

8. Give an example of a command that uses **grep**

a. with both input and output redirected.

b. with only input redirected.

c. with only output redirected.

d. within a pipe.

e. In which of the above is **grep** used as a filter?

9. Explain the following error message. What filenames would a subsequent **ls** display?

```
$ ls
abc   abd   abe   abf   abg   abh
$ rm abc ab*
rm: abc: No such file or directory
```

Advanced Review Exercises

10. When you use the redirect output symbol (>) with a command, the shell creates the output file immediately—before the command is executed. Demonstrate that this is true.

11. In experimenting with shell variables, Alex accidentally deletes his **PATH** variable. He decides he does not really need the **PATH** variable. Discuss some of the problems he may soon encounter and explain the reasons for these problems. How could he *easily* return **PATH** to its original value?

12. Assume that your permissions allow you to write to a file, but not to delete it.

a. Give a command to empty the file without invoking an editor.

b. Explain how you might have permission to modify a file that you cannot delete.

13. If you accidentally create a filename with a nonprinting character in it (such as a **CONTROL** character), how can you rename the file?

14. Why can the **noclobber** variable not protect you from overwriting an existing file with **cp** or **mv**?

15. Why do command names and filenames usually not have embedded **SPACE**s? If you wanted to create a filename containing a **SPACE**, how would you do it? How would you remove it? (This is a thought exercise—it is not a recommended practice.)

16. Create a file named **answers** and give the following command:

```
$ > answers.0197 < answers cat
```

Explain what the command does and why. What is a more conventional way of expressing this command?

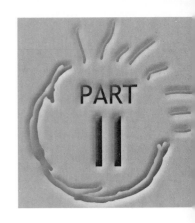

Intermediate/
Advanced Solaris

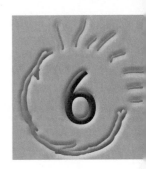

Graphical User Interfaces

Over the past decade it has become the norm to use a graphical user interface (GUI) to interact with a computer system. It is hard to imagine using a UNIX system that is not configured to take full advantage of the graphical displays and pointing devices that have become standard equipment.

This chapter begins by describing the common attributes of a graphical user interface (GUI) and providing a short background on the X Window System and how it works with Solaris. The chapter then describes how to use the X Window System with the Common Desktop Environment, or CDE (using **dtwm**), and the OpenLook Window Manager (**olwm**). Although you can configure X and the interfaces in complex ways, this chapter acquaints you with the basic terminology and operations. For clarity this chapter focuses on examples that are straightforward; it does not describe every method or shortcut available in X.

Because Motif is widely accepted throughout the UNIX community, you may want to use it on your Solaris system. Although Sun provides some Motif libraries with Solaris, it does not provide the Motif Window Manager (**mwm**), and this chapter does not cover Motif.

▲ What Is a GUI?

A user interface is the connection between the user and, in this case, the computer system. The user interface controls how the user interacts with the system. It used to be that the typical UNIX user interface was the command-line interface: In response to a shell prompt, you type a command line (ending with the RETURN key). For example to remove a file named **junkfile** you would type:

```
$ rm junkfile
```

One of the most common complaints about UNIX running a command-line interface is that the interface and command names are difficult to learn and use. To use a command you must know its exact name; most are abbreviated and not intuitive. For example if you are not familiar with UNIX, you might guess that the command to get rid of an old file would be Remove or Delete. You probably would not guess that the command is named **rm**.

129

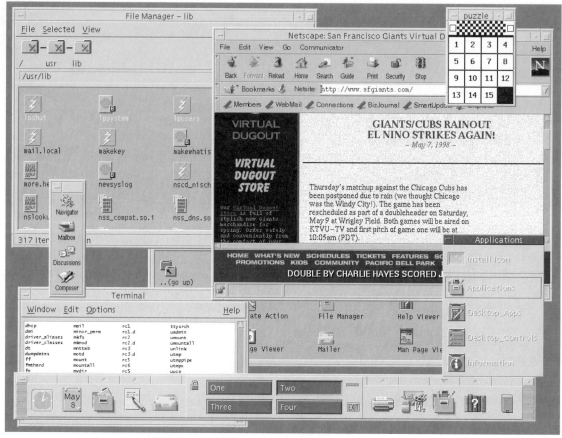

Figure 6-1 *The Common Desktop Environment desktop manager*

Contrast that with the Common Desktop Environment (CDE) graphical user interface on a machine running Solaris, which is designed so that you can communicate with the computer by manipulating pictures of objects on your screen (Figure 6-1). To get rid of an unwanted file on CDE, you highlight the picture of the file and drag it across the screen until it collides with a picture of a trash can. This approach is so straightforward that many people can begin to use CDE immediately, without being trained or reading instructions.

Once you are familiar with a system, however, a purely graphical interface can be tedious to use. Suppose you want to remove several files, named **junkfile1, junkfile2,** and **junkfile3.** Dragging a picture of each file into a trash can is time-consuming compared with the powerful shorthand of a command-line interface:

```
$ rm junkfile?
```

▲ Using a GUI

Before you continue, you should be familiar with the following components of a GUI. If you are not, read through the pertinent parts of the Help appendix starting on page 989.

- What Is a Window? (page 990)

- What Is the Root Window? (page 991)
- What Is a Title Bar? (page 991)
- What Is a Button? (page 991)
- What Is a Slider? (page 991)
- What Is a Scroll Bar? (page 992)
- What Is an Icon? (page 992)

▲▲ Logging In

Use the same login name and password to log in on a system with a graphical user interface as you would use to log in on a system with a command-line interface (page 988). Figure 6-2 shows the default Solaris login display.

Figure 6-2   The default Solaris login display

By selecting **Session** from the **Options** menu (Figure 6-3) and **Common Desktop Environment** (**CDE**) or **OpenWindows Desktop** from the **Session** menu, you can log in on the desktop/window manager of your choice. Normally the **User's Last Desktop** in the **Session** menu will be marked and you will not use **Options**. The **Failsafe Session** allows you to log in on a minimal desktop in case your standard login does not work well enough to allow you to log in to fix a login problem.

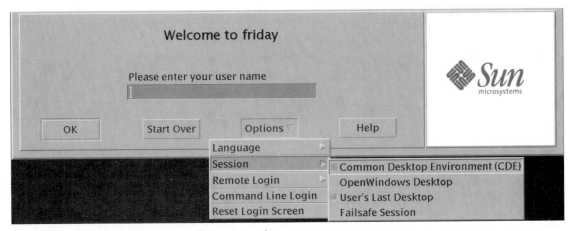

Figure 6-3   The Options menu and Session submenu

Once you log in on CDE you will see a window with the Front Panel at the bottom and one or more other windows (Figure 6-1).

▲▲ Menus

When you need to choose among several items, it is often easier to work with a list of options, called a *menu,* rather than an array of individual buttons. Instead of cluttering your screen, menus stay out of sight until you need to use them. One type of menu is a *pull-down menu,* such as the Netscape Communicator menu shown in Figure 6-4. To view a pull-down menu, click on a word or button displayed on your screen. In Figure 6-4 you click on the word **Communicator**. A pull-down menu usually stays attached to the word or button you clicked on to display it.

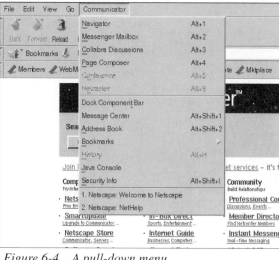

Figure 6-4   A pull-down menu

If you display the menu by clicking and releasing the mouse button (without moving the mouse), you can move the mouse pointer until it is over the item you want, and click again to select it. You can also click the mouse and drag the mouse pointer from the word or button that displays the menu to the menu item you want to select. Release the mouse button to select the item.

A *pop-up menu* is the menu that appears when you press a particular mouse button somewhere inside a larger region (such as inside a window or on its border). When you press the right mouse button while the mouse pointer is in the root window, CDE displays the **Workspace** menu. Everything about this menu can be modified so what you see may be different than what appears in Figure 6-5.

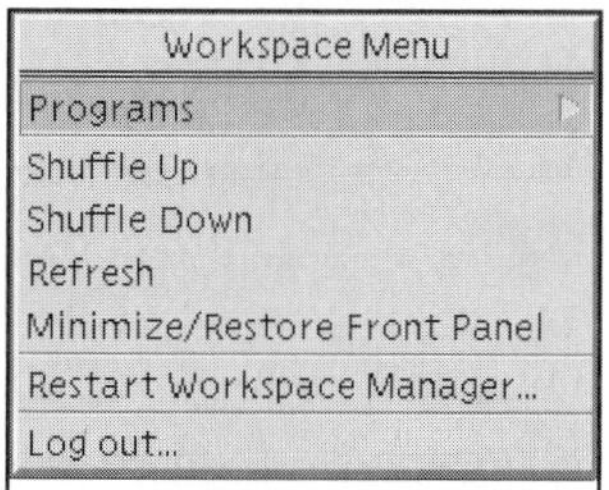

Display and select items from a pop-up menu just as you would from a pull-down menu. If a menu item does not make sense in a particular context (for example an option to expand a window that is already full-size), the text for that item is usually displayed in a lighter color or in broken text. By making the text hard to read, the system is giving you a cue that the option is not available or that choosing it will have no effect.

Figure 6-5   The Work-space menu

A menu that contains submenus is known as a *cascading menu.* Each item that contains a submenu is identified by a right arrow after the item name. The next menu level appears when you select this type of menu item (Figure 6-6).

▲▲ Dialog Boxes

A *dialog box* is a small window that appears when an application needs to notify you about something, such as a result or an error message (Figure 6-7), or when it needs to solicit a brief response from you. Like a regular window a dialog box has a title bar and some buttons, but there is little you can do with it. Typically the application expects you to acknowledge that you have read the message by clicking your mouse on a button drawn inside the box; after you have done so, the dialog box disappears from the screen.

You can experiment with dialog boxes with the **dterror.ds** utility. Give the following command from a terminal emulation window and you will see the dialog box shown in Figure 6-7. See the **dterror.ds man** page for details.

```
$ dterror.ds "You blew it\!" "Error Window" "Press RETURN or click\nhere and try again."
```

▲▲ Screen Layout

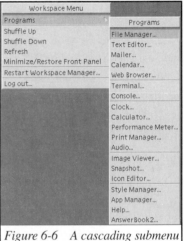

You can arrange the windows on your screen in many ways. Just as you might stack or overlap pieces of paper on your desk, you can position one window on top of another (as in Figure 6-1). The topmost window is fully visible, covering up pieces of the windows below. If you choose to overlap windows, it is a good idea not to cover the lower windows completely. It is easier to *raise* a window (bring it to the top of the stack) if you can position the mouse pointer somewhere on its border.

Another approach is to set up your windows so that there is no overlap, like floor tiles (called *tiling*). This arrangement is useful if you need to see the full contents of all your windows at the same time. Unfortunately the space on your screen is limited; one of the disadvantages of tiling is that if you need more than a few windows, you need to make each one quite small.

Figure 6-6   A cascading submenu

However you arrange your windows, you will need to be able to specify which window is to receive your keystrokes (or which window has the *input focus*). You do this by moving the mouse pointer into the window you want to work in; sometimes you need to click the right mouse button while the cursor is there, sometimes not. Refer to "Window Window" on page 165 for more information on input focus.

▲▲ Window Manager

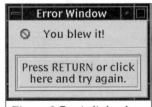

A *window manager* is the program that controls the look and feel of the basic graphical user interface. Window managers make it easier for a user to run programs on and work with Solaris. The window manager defines the appearance of the windows on your screen, as well as how you operate them: Opening, closing, moving, resizing, and so on. The window manager may also handle some session-management functions, such as how to pause, resume, restart, or end a windowing session. Refer to "X Window System Window Managers" on

Figure 6-7   A dialog box

page 154. See "Bringing Up the X Server" on page 156 if you want to see how your desktop would work without a window manager.

▲▲ Desktop Manager

A picture-oriented interface to common commands is often referred to as a *desktop manager*. A desktop manager allows you to copy, move, and delete files by manipulating icons instead of typing the corresponding commands to a shell. Using icons also makes it easier to run applications and utilities. Frequently a desktop manager will work in conjunction with a window manager (such as CDE and **dtwm**).

People who are unaccustomed to working with computers, or with a UNIX system, often feel more comfortable working with a desktop manager. Solaris is shipped with three desktop/window managers: CDE/**dtwm** (Common Desktop Environment/Desktop Window Manager), OpenLook/**olwm**, and **twm** (Tab Window Manager).

▲▲ Workspace Manager

If you are working in a complex environment, using many windows to run a variety of programs simultaneously, a *workspace manager* may help you organize and separate your tasks. Using a window system is like working on several terminals at the same time; using a workspace manager is like working with several windowing sessions at the same time. A workspace manager allows you to switch between multiple screen contexts. You can also think of a workspace manager as a *virtual desktop,* because it allows you to work with a single desktop as if it were many. The CDE Front Panel **Workspace Switch** allows you to push a button to select a workspace.

A system administrator, for example, might be working on several distinct activities, each of which involves more than one window. One workspace might consist of a series of windows set up to edit, compile, and debug software. In another workspace the task might be to locate and restore some lost user files. A third workspace might be dedicated to reading mail messages and news. The advantage of a workspace manager is the ease of switching between sets of tasks—without having to fuss with icons or reposition overlapping windows.

▲ CDE Desktop Manager

The Common Desktop Environment (CDE) desktop manager provides several advantages over other desktop managers and command-line interfaces. CDE

1. simplifies the Solaris command-line interface,

2. makes applications easier to use by providing a common look and feel,

3. makes use of desktop integration services (common interface for multiple applications running on local or remote machines, cut and paste between applications, communication with other CDE applications, and more), and

4. allows for personal preferences and cultural differences (fonts, colors, keyboard and mouse bindings, and locale-specific configuration files).

These sections describe how to manage an X session using CDE and **dtwm**. As with all X window managers, CDE/**dtwm** is highly configurable. This section describes common attributes of CDE/**dtwm**; see "Customizing CDE" on page 163 for customization information.

Where Are the X Utilities?

Most tools are not listed in CDE's menus. You will find X utilities and application programs in many locations on a Solaris system. Some of the most popular are in **/usr/dt/bin**, **/usr/openwin/bin**, **/usr/openwin/demo**, and **/usr/lib/ab2/bin**; look on your system to familiarize yourself with which tools are available. Read the manual pages for the tools you are not familiar with or just experiment with them. Some of the most useful X utilities are listed at the end of this chapter (page 181).

▲▲ Front Panel

After your name and password are accepted, CDE typically displays a screen showing the Front Panel (Figure 6-8) and possibly other windows. In most displays the Front Panel is key to getting your work done using

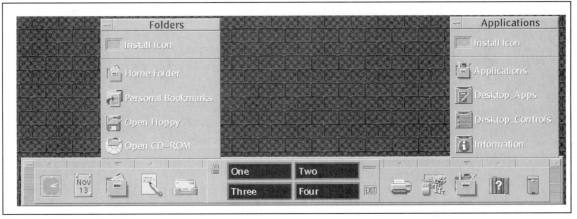

Figure 6-8   The CDE Front Panel with the Folders and Applications subpanels displayed

CDE. When you push one of the Front Panel **Workspace Switches** labeled **One**, **Two**, **Three**, or **Four**, CDE transports you to the specified workspace. It is as though you were using a different display, only the Front Panel stays the same. By default each of the workspaces uses a different *wallpaper* (background). The different patterns make it easier to recognize the different workspaces and to know when you have changed to another workspace.

A *control* is one of the items on the Front Panel such as the **Mailer**, **Clock**, or **Help Control** (Figure 6-9). Some controls, such as the **Help Control**, do something when you click on them, some, such as the **Clock Control**, are indicators that do nothing when you click on them, and some are both; the **Mailer Control** puts the front envelope in the icon at an angle when you have mail and allows you to read and send mail when you click on it. Some controls on the Front Panel, such as **Help**, have arrow buttons (pointing up) above them to indicate that the control has a subpanel. A subpanel is a menu of icons that allows you to perform (usually) related tasks. Click on the arrow button to display the subpanel (Figure 6-8 shows the Fold-

Figure 6-9   The Help Control

ers and **Applications** subpanels displayed). It will pop up and remain visible until you click on one of the icons on the subpanel or click on the arrow again (now a down arrow to indicate it will put the subpanel down). The **Install Icon** icon at the top of the subpanels allows you to add programs/actions to the subpanels (page 172).

The Front Panel	
Icon	**Action**
	Clock Control Displays the time of day based on the system clock. There is no action associated with the clock.
	Calendar Control Displays the month and day based on the system clock. Click on the calendar to start the Calendar Manager (**dtcm**).
	File Manager Starts and points the File Manager at your home directory showing you a list of the files therein and allowing you to work with them (page 145). The subpanel starts: • **Home Folder** Same as the File Manager, above. • **Personal Bookmarks** Starts and points the File Manager at the **.dt/bookmarks** directory under your home directory. • **Open Floppy** Starts and points the File Manager at the disk in the floppy drive. • **Open CD-ROM** Starts and points the File Manager at the CDROM.
	Text Editor Starts the graphical **dtpad** editor. The subpanel starts: • **Text Editor** Same as above. • **Terminal** Starts the **dtterm** terminal emulator. • **Web Browser** Starts the HotJava browser.
	Mail Program Shows when you have mail by putting some envelopes in the icon at an angle. Click on icon to run the **dtmail** program. Drag and drop an icon (representing a file) on the mail icon to create a new piece of email with the specified file attached to the email.
	Lock Screen Click on the lock to lock the screen. Unlock the screen with the same password you use to log on.
	Workspace Selection Click on One, Two, Three, or Four to display the corresponding workspace. Right click to add a new workspace, or delete or rename an existing one.

The Front Panel	
Icon	**Action**
EXIT	EXIT Click on EXIT to log out.
Busy Light	Busy Light Flashes when the computer is busy.
Default Printer	Default Printer Drag and drop a file on this icon to print it. The subpanel contains the **Print Manager**.
Style Manager	Style Manager Displays a window that lets you select keyboard, mouse, speaker, screen, window, and startup characteristics as well as colors, fonts, and backdrops.
Application Manager	Application Manager Gives you access to applications, tools, controls, system administration utilities, OpenWindows programs, and system information. The subpanel starts: • **Application Manager** Same as above. • **Desktop_Apps** Calendar, create action, image viewer, print manager, and more. • **Desktop_Controls** Keyboard enhancements for people with disabilities and Style Manager. • **Information** AnswerBook2, Solaris version information, and sample bookmarks.
Help Manager	Help Manager Displays the Help Manager in the Help Viewer. The subpanel starts: • **Help Manager** Same as above. • **Desktop Introduction** In the Help Viewer. • **Front Panel Help** In the Help Viewer. • **On Item Help** Turns the mouse pointer into a question mark with an arrow; click on the object you want help with. • **AnswerBook2**
Trash	Trash Drag and drop a file on this icon to move it to the **Trash Can**. Click on the icon to open (and optionally empty) the **Trash Can**.

For a complete explanation of the Front Panel, click on the arrow button above the **Help Control** and then on the Front Panel **Help** icon on the subpanel. To learn more about buttons and icons on the Front Panel, click on the **On Item Help** icon (also in the **Help Control** subpanel). When you click on this icon, the mouse pointer turns into a question mark with a down arrow built into it. Move this arrow and click on the part of the Front Panel you want to know more about. The **Workspace Manager Help** window will open to the subject you pointed to.

▲▲ Title Bar

Because the appearance of CDE is so easily changed (page 163), the sample screens in this chapter show a variety of styles. A standard setup of the CDE title bar includes three buttons, as shown in Figure 6-10 and in the figures throughout this chapter: a **Window menu** button, a **Minimize** button, and a **Maximize** button. The **Window**

Figure 6-10   The title bar

menu button contains a horizontal bar and appears at the left of the title bar. Clicking the left mouse button while pointing to the **Window menu** button brings up a list of operations you can perform on that window. See "Window Menu" below. It also associates the input focus with this window (makes it the active window). The **Maximize** button, which contains a large square or an up arrow, appears at the far right side of the title bar. Clicking on this button maximizes the size of the window (causes it to fill the whole screen). To the left of the **Maximize** button is the **Minimize** button, which contains a tiny square). Clicking on the **Minimize** button iconifies the window. In the middle of the title bar is the name of the window. Customized applications can rearrange, eliminate, and add title bar buttons.

▲▲ Common Operations—Menus

CDE provides menus to make it easier for you to work on the system. You generally call up the menus by clicking the mouse while the mouse pointer is in a given location. The items on the menu depend on the location of the mouse pointer (context) and any custom programming that has changed the CDE or application defaults.

▲▲▲ Window Menu

Most windows have a menu for performing both common and specific operations on the window. You display this menu, called the **Window** menu, by clicking the left mouse button while the mouse pointer is on the horizontal bar within a small box at the upper-left of most windows (at the left of the title bar in Figures 6-10 and 6-11). When the window is iconified, you display this menu by clicking anywhere on the icon. Inappropriate items appear in gray.

The specific or nonstandard item in the **Window** menu is **Toggle Menu Bar**. This item, available in a terminal emulator window, alternately displays and removes the menu bar, which contains menus of commands for the terminal emulator (see page 140).

The standard items in the menu shown in Figure 6-11 are listed in the following table:

		Terminal
Restore	Alt+F5	
Move	Alt+F7	
Size	Alt+F8	
Minimize	Alt+F9	
Maximize	Alt+F10	
Lower	Alt+F3	
Occupy Workspace...		
Occupy All Workspaces		
Unoccupy Workspace		
Close	Alt+F4	
Toggle Menu Bar		

```
91 bytes received in 0.058 seconds (1.52 Kk
ftp> exit
```

Figure 6-11   The Window menu

Menu Item	Function
Restore	Changes an icon (back) into a window
Move	Allows you to move the window to another location on the screen (page 141)
Size	Allows you to change the size of the window (page 141)
Minimize	Iconifies the window
Maximize	Enlarges the window to its maximum size
Lower	Moves the window behind any windows it overlaps.
Occupy Workspace...	Allows you to select which workspaces the window is to appear in
Occupy All Workspaces	Makes the window appear in all workspaces
Unoccupy Workspace	Removes the window from the current workspace
Close	Closes the window (also by double-clicking on the button that produced the Window menu)

▲▲▲ Workspace Menu

By default the Workspace menu (Figure 6-12) contains several useful items including Programs, Minimize/Restore Front Panel, and Log out.... You access this menu by clicking the right mouse button while the mouse pointer is positioned anywhere in the root window (background). Displaying the Workspace menu from the root window has no effect on the input focus.

▲▲▲ Logging Out

Click on the EXIT sign on the Front Panel or choose Log out... from the Workspace menu to end your session and display the login screen again.

▲▲ Working with Windows

This section describes how to open a terminal emulator window; close, move, resize, raise, and lower a window; and how to use a scroll bar to scroll text.

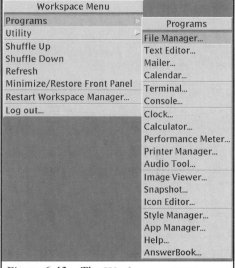

Figure 6-12   The Workspace menu

▲▲▲ Closing a Window

Just as there are several ways to open a window, you can use different methods to close a window. The two methods that are common to most CDE windows are to double-click on the Window menu button and to select Close from the Window menu. You can close a window running a shell by giving an **exit** command. This command terminates the shell and closes the window automatically. Individual applications may provide other ways to close their windows, such as a specialized Quit button or menu selection.

It is good practice to close all windows before exiting from an X session completely. Some applications may not shut down cleanly if you do not close windows first, while others may try to protect your work for you. For example if you try to close a text editor application (by closing its window *or* exiting from the application) without first saving changes to the file you were editing, most editors will prompt you to save your work before exiting.

▲▲▲ Opening a Terminal Emulator Window

A terminal emulator or terminal window is a window that you can interact with just as you would work at a regular character terminal (see Figures 6-11, 6-13, and the lower left of Figure 6-1). You see a shell prompt in the window and can run any Solaris command that you choose (Figure 6-13). Because this window looks like an ordinary character terminal to Solaris, you can run utilities, such as **vi**, that manipulate the display within that window. A terminal window may seem like a disap-

```
                                     Terminal
 Window  Edit  Options                                                    Help
$ ls -l /usr/dt
total 26
drwxrwxr-x   3 root      bin         512 Apr 23 16:03 app-defaults
drwxrwxr-x   9 root      bin         512 Apr 23 16:16 appconfig
lrwxrwxrwx   1 root      root         17 Apr 23 16:07 backdrops -> ./share/backdrops
drwxrwxr-x   2 root      bin        2048 Apr 30 10:07 bin
drwxrwxr-x  15 root      bin        1024 May 22 16:14 config
drwxrwxr-x   6 root      bin         512 Apr 23 16:06 dthelp
lrwxrwxrwx   1 root      root         16 Apr 23 16:04 examples -> ./share/examples
lrwxrwxrwx   1 root      root         15 Apr 23 16:01 include -> ./share/include
drwxrwxr-x   6 root      bin        1024 Apr 30 10:07 lib
lrwxrwxrwx   1 root      root         11 Apr 23 16:01 man -> ./share/man
lrwxrwxrwx   1 root      root         16 Apr 23 16:05 palettes -> ./share/palettes
drwxrwxr-x   7 root      bin         512 Apr 23 16:01 share
$ ▮
```

Figure 6-13   Terminal emulator window

pointing way to interact with a window system, because it is restricted to operating on characters (and not graphical objects). However a terminal window is a powerful tool because it allows you to run all the existing Solaris command-line programs, even if they have not been converted to run in a graphical environment. A terminal emulator also can save you from having to learn a program's new versions that were specifically designed to run with a graphical user interface.

There are two easy ways to open a terminal emulator window with the default CDE setup: From the **Workspace** menu (Figure 6-12) choose **Programs** and then **Terminal...** and from the Front Panel click on the arrow button above the **Text Editor Control** (the pencil and paper) and choose **Terminal**.

If you can interact with the shell in a window, you can open a new window by running an application by name. To open a new terminal emulator window in this fashion, type **xterm** or **dtterm** in response to a shell prompt; to start up a clock, type **xclock** (Figure 6-14). Start applications in the background so you can continue to interact with the shell in the original window.

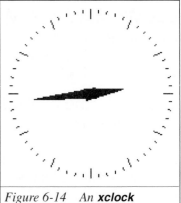

*Figure 6-14   An **xclock***

▲▲▲ Moving a Window

There are two common ways to move a window to another location on the desktop (root window). First you can click on **Move** on the **Window** menu; the mouse pointer changes from an arrow to a pair of crossed, double-ended arrows located in the center of the window (left), and the window moves as you move the mouse. Click a second time when the window is in the location you want. The mouse pointer will revert to an arrow, and the window will stay at its new location.

> ### Lose the Title Bar?
> If you inadvertently position a window so that its title bar is off the desktop, you can reposition it by choosing **Restart Workspace Manager...** from the **Workspace** menu.

The second way to move a window is to place the mouse pointer on the title bar and hold down the left mouse button. The mouse pointer changes to a pair of crossed, double-ended arrows located in the center of the window as you start to drag it. While keeping the mouse button depressed, slide the mouse around. As you move the mouse, you drag either an outline of the window or the whole window on the screen. When you have placed the outline or window where you want it, release the mouse button. The mouse pointer will revert to an arrow, and the window will remain at its current location.

▲▲▲ Resizing a Window

There are two common ways to resize a window. First you can click on **Size** on the **Window** menu; the mouse pointer changes from an arrow to a pair of crossed, double-ended arrows located in the center of the window. As you slide the mouse around, the first one or two sides of the window the mouse pointer bumps into stick to the mouse pointer, moving in and out or up and down as you move the mouse. Click a second time when the window is the size you want.

You can also use the mouse to resize a window by an arbitrary amount. To make a window larger or smaller, position the mouse pointer on one of the corners of the window border. The mouse pointer changes to an arrow pointing toward the inside of a right angle. (See figures embedded at the right above: Top is a window corner; bottom is a graphic of the arrow that appears.) To make the window larger, hold down the left mouse button and slide the mouse away from the window; to shrink the window slide the mouse toward the interior of the window. See Figure 6-15.

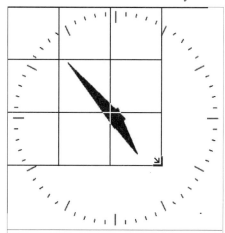

Figure 6-15   Resizing a window

You can also change the shape of the window along one side at a time by positioning the mouse pointer on one side of the window border. The mouse pointer changes to an arrow pointing toward a short line that sits next to the window border. Hold down the left mouse button and move the mouse up/down for a top/bottom side or left/right for a left/right side. As you move the mouse, you see an outline of the window change dimensions on your screen. Release the mouse button when the window is the size you want.

▲▲▲ Raising and Lowering Windows

As you position windows on the screen, chances are that some of them will overlap. Any window can be the active window (have the window focus), even one that is partially obscured, but it is usually easier to work with a window when you can see all of it. To raise a window to the top (so you can see it over all other windows), click anywhere on the window with the left mouse button. Raising a window also makes it the active window. You can lower a window by raising other windows on top of it. Many window operations, such as moving and resizing windows, have the side effect of raising the window.

You can think of the windows on the desktop as a *stack* of windows. Raising a window brings it to the *top* of the stack (where it is visible in its entirety); lowering it brings it to the *bottom* (where it may or may not be obscured). The **Workspace** menu has **Shuffle Up** and **Shuffle Down** items. These choices move the windows in the stack in order. **Shuffle Up** moves each window up one position (or layer) in the stack, wrapping the top window to the bottom of the stack. **Shuffle Down** works the opposite way.

▲▲▲ Scrolling Text

Figure 6-16
Motif scroll bar

If a scroll bar appears along one side of a window and there is more text[1] to be displayed than fits in that window, you can use the scroll bar to control which section of the text is visible in the window. The next sections describe three common types of scroll bars: The Motif scroll bar, the Athena scroll bar, and the OpenLook scroll bar. The application, not the window manager, determines which scroll bar a given application uses. All three scroll bars appear as skinny rectangles that a sliding object, called a *slider bar, thumb,* or *elevator,* moves up and down on. Despite the different implementations, all sliding objects have two things in common:

1. The position of the sliding object in the center portion of the scroll bar indicates the relative location of the visible text. If the section of text displayed in the window is near the end of what is available, the sliding object appears near the bottom of the scroll bar. Similarly if you scroll up to the beginning of the text, the sliding object moves to the top of the scroll bar. Understanding this relationship is very helpful when you want to find a particular section of text and you know approximately where that part is located (for example two-thirds of the way through the text).

_____

1. Although this section refers to *text,* you can just as easily scroll any type of image.

2. The size of the sliding object or the shadow around this object represents the proportion of the text that is displayed in the window in relation to the entire text available for viewing—a small sliding object or shadow indicates that only a small portion of the text is visible. If all the text is displayed, the sliding objects fills the area between the two ends of the scroll bar and you cannot scroll up or down (there is nothing else to see).

Motif Scroll Bar Commands		
Scroll	**Mouse Button**	**Click on**
One line	Any	Up arrow at top or down arrow at bottom of scroll bar
Continuously	Any	Up arrow at top or down arrow at bottom of scroll bar, keep mouse button depressed as long as you want to continue scrolling
One screenful	Left	Scroll bar between slider and up or down arrow
To a specific point	Right	Scroll bar between slider and down arrow or between slider and up arrow at location you want slider to move to
Drag	Any	Slider and drag up or down

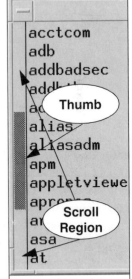

Figure 6-17   Athena scroll bar

▲▲▲▲▲ Motif Scroll Bar: A Motif scroll bar (Figure 6-16) uses a rectangular sliding object called a *slider bar* (page 991). There is an up arrow at the top and a down arrow at the bottom of the scroll bar. To move backward through the text, or to scroll up, use the left mouse button to click on the up-arrow button at the top of the scroll bar. Each time you click on the arrow, one more line is displayed at the top of the window. If you keep the mouse button depressed the text will scroll continuously. There are various ways to use a Motif scroll bar: Refer to the preceding table.

▲▲▲▲▲ Athena Scroll Bar: Prior to the development of the Motif and Tk widget sets, X applications used a scroll bar that differs in operation and appearance from the Motif scroll bar. The original Athena scroll bar, which is used by **xterm** and other standard X tools, derived its name because it was built with a library of X tools from Project Athena at the Massachusetts Institute of Technology (MIT; Figure 6-17). The Athena scroll bar uses a *thumb* in place of Motif's slider (they look very similar) but lacks the arrow buttons; whether you scroll up or down depends on which mouse button you apply in the scroll region.

As with Motif's slider bar, you can scroll through the text by dragging the thumb up or down; in contrast to Motif you must use the middle (or right) mouse button for this purpose. To scroll back through the text, hold down the middle mouse button and drag the thumb toward the top of the scroll bar; to scroll forward drag the thumb toward the bottom of the bar. Refer to the following table for a list of Athena scroll bar commands.

Athena Scroll Bar Commands		
Scroll	**Mouse Button**	**Click on**
One line	line right (up) or left (down)	Near top of scroll bar
Continuously	n/a	n/a
One screenful	One screenful right (up) or left (down)	Scroll bar between thumb and down arrow
To a specific point	Middle	Click on the location you want the thumb to move to
Drag	Middle	Click thumb and drag up or down

Use the following command to experiment with the Athena scroll bar. It sets up an **xterm** window with a scroll bar (**–sb**) that has no room for movement. Give the command **cat /etc/termcap** so that the window fills and the thumb shrinks. Then you can experiment with scrolling.

```
$ xterm -sb
```

Click the left mouse button while the mouse pointer is within the scroll bar, above or below the thumb, to scroll up or down a screenful at a time.

▲▲▲▲ OpenLook Scroll Bar: Although the Open-Look scroll bar (Figure 6-18) looks different from the other two scroll bars, it performs the same functions. Refer to Figure 6-31 to see this scroll bar in context. Instead of a thumb or slider bar, the OpenLook scroll bar has an *elevator*. The elevator houses up and down arrows as well as a *drag area*. Click and hold the drag area as you drag it up and down to manually scroll the text. The size of the elevator does not change, but the position of the elevator within a highlighted portion of the *cable* does. This relationship shows the relative location of the text you are viewing within the entire document. Click on the end box or the cable to jump to the beginning or end of the document.

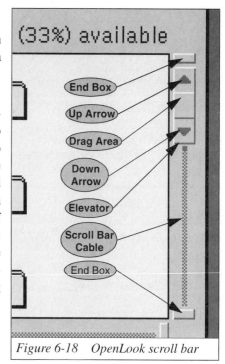

Figure 6-18   OpenLook scroll bar

OpenLook Scroll Bar Commands		
Scroll	**Mouse Button**	**Click on**
One line	Left	Up or down arrow on elevator
Continuously	Left	Up or down arrow on elevator, keep mouse button depressed as long as you want to continue scrolling. Click on cable to scroll continuously by pages
One screenful	Left	Cable
To a specific point		
Drag	Left	Drag area and drag up or down

▲▲ Using Icons

An *icon* is a small picture or a few words that represent a window. You can change a window into an icon and change the icon back into a window without affecting any programs that are running in the window. The terms *iconify* or *minimize* describe the process of changing a window into an icon. The term *restore* describes the process of turning an icon into a window.

To iconify a window click the left mouse button on the **Minimize** button (the button at the right end of the title bar with the very small square on it—just to the left of the button with the large square). If the system chooses an inconvenient location for the icon, you can move it by positioning the mouse pointer on the icon, holding down the left mouse button, and dragging the icon to a new location.

To restore the original window from the icon, position the mouse pointer on the icon and double-click on it with the left button. The window reappears exactly as it was before you iconified it: The contents of the window, as well as its size and original position on your screen, are restored. This is true even if you moved the icon from its original position. You can also click the right mouse button on an icon to display the **Window** menu of the iconified window. From that menu click on the **Restore** selection to restore the icon.

▲▲ File Manager

The File Manager (**dtfile** if you want to run it from the command line on a GUI) creates, finds, uses, and manipulates objects (files, folders, and applications) that appear within the **File Manager** window. For example the File Manager allows you to open, move, copy, or delete a file.

You can use either a keyboard or a mouse to command the File Manager to perform a given action. This book assumes that if you are running CDE you have a mouse and thus concentrates on the mouse commands. Click on the **File Manager** window **help** button if you want to read about how to control the File Manager solely from the keyboard.

Figure 6-19
File Manager icon

To open the File Manager, click once on the **File Manager** icon (Figure 6-19), located on the Front Panel. The File Manager displays the contents of your home directory (Figure 6-20), using icons to represent files much as **ls** displays filenames in a character-based environment.

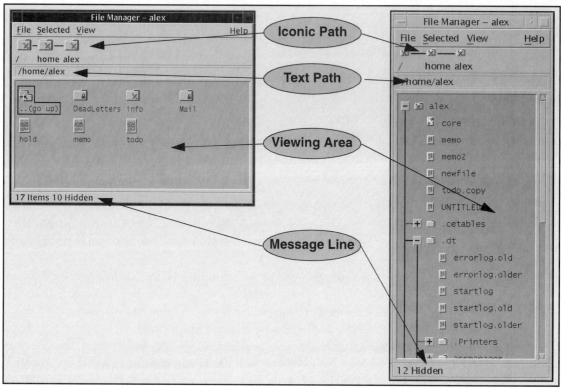

Figure 6-20   Two views of the File Manager

The File Manager creates, finds, uses, and manipulates objects that appear within the **File Manager** window.

Action	Command (using the left mouse button)
Select an icon	Click the mouse button once while the mouse pointer is on the icon, or click and hold the mouse button while the mouse pointer is outside of the icon and drag a box around the icon. The name of the selected icon is highlighted (usually dark letters on a light background).
Select multiple icons	Click once on the first icon (its name becomes highlighted), hold the **CONTROL** key down and click once on subsequent icons. (Each name becomes highlighted in addition to those already highlighted as you click on each icon.) Or click and hold the mouse button while the mouse pointer is outside of the icons; drag a box around all the icons you want to select. Each icon's name becomes highlighted as you drag/expand the box over it.

Action	Command (using the left mouse button)
Getting help	Click once while the mouse pointer is on the Help menu item at the top right of the File Manager window. Choose Using Help if you need further instruction on using Help, On Item to turn the mouse pointer into a question mark and arrow that you can click on the icon or other item that you need help with, or one of the other selections to get help with a specific topic.
Drag and drop	Move the mouse pointer so it is on the icon you want to drag. Click and hold the mouse button. Drag the icon to its new location, still holding the mouse button. Release the mouse button. To cancel a drag press ESCAPE before you release the mouse button. Common drag and drop tasks include: • Drop a file onto a folder icon or within an open folder's window (moves the file) • Drop a file onto the root window (the Workspace—makes a link to the file) • Drop a file onto the Printer control on the Front Panel (prints the file) • Drop a file or folder onto the trash can on the Front Panel (removes the file) To copy an object (leave the original in place and make a copy somewhere else) hold the CONTROL key down during a move. Make sure you press the CONTROL key before you depress the mouse button, and do not release it until after you have released the mouse button.
View a folder	There are several ways to open a folder icon so you can view its contents: • Double-click on the folder icon • Double-click on a folder in the iconic path (Figure 6-20) to replace the current view with that folder. • Select an icon and choose Open In Place or Open New View from the File Manager Selected menu or from the pop-up menu that appears when you click the right mouse button while the mouse pointer is over a selected icon.
View home folder	Select Go Home from the File Manager menu.
View parent folder	Double-click on the ..(go up) icon at the upper left of the File Manager window.
Open object	Double-click on an object to open it. Opening a file causes different things to happen, depending on the type of file. If you open an executable file such as Netscape, you will start Netscape. If you open a text file, you will open a text editor that displays and allows you to edit the file.
Open terminal window	Select Open Terminal from the File selection of the File Manager window menu. The terminal (emulator) you open has a working directory of the folder that was selected at the time you chose Open Terminal. It provides an easy way to give a command-line command that affects the files in the selected folder.
Open floppy	Opens a File Manager window with the disk in the floppy drive as the current folder.

Action	Command (using the left mouse button)
Open CD-ROM	Opens a File Manager window with the disk in the CDROM drive as the current folder.
Delete to trash	Select the icon(s) you want to delete and choose Put in Trash from the File Manager Selected menu or from the pop-up menu that appears when you click the right mouse button over a selected icon. Or drag and drop the icon to the trash can (usually) at the right end of the Front Panel or into the trash folder.
View trash	Click one time on the trash can (usually) at the right end of the Front Panel to open the trash folder.
Restore from trash	Select icon from trash folder and using the right-click menu or the File menu of the Trash Can, choose Put Back.
Shred	Select icon from trash folder and using the right-click menu or the File menu of the Trash Can, choose Shred.
Find	Select the icon(s) of one or more folders you want to search through or choose Select All from the Selected menu of the File Manager. Choose Find from the File menu. The Find window appears. Fill in either the File or Folder Name box (wildcards are okay) or the File Contents box (slower because it opens files), set Follow Links to On or Off, change the Search Folder if it is not correct, and click on the Start button at the lower left of the window. Find returns a scrollable list of files in the Files Found subwindow. Double-click on a filename or highlight the file and click on the Open Folder button just below the subwindow to view the file icon, selected, within its parent folder. Highlight the filename and click on Put In Workspace to make a link to the file in the root window (the Workspace).
Create bookmarks	Just as you can keep icons for files and folders in a folder, so you can keep icons for bookmarks. Bookmarks can point to files on your local machine, other machines on your LAN, or anywhere on the Internet. To create such an icon, put a URL (such as **www.sobell.com** [page 241]) in a text file and give it an appropriate name. Or drag a URL from a browser, such as Netscape, into a folder. The new icon will be given the name **Untitled.url**. Rename it appropriately. Open (double-click) on a bookmark made either way and you will open your browser to the bookmarked page.

▲▲▲ The View Menu

The **View** menu controls what you see in the **File Manager** window and what it looks like.

Action	Command
Set view options	See "The View/Set View Options Window" on page 149.
Save as default options	Saves the current File Manager options, window size, and filter list as the default that is used when you start the File Manager from the Front Panel.
Show hidden objects	Toggles the display of hidden objects as established by **Set Filter Options** (below).
Set filter options	The filter allows you to specify data types to hide or display. Choose **Hidden** or **Shown** from the **Select Datatypes to be:** menu. Select all data types you want to be **Hidden** or **Shown** from the horizontal scrolling list. Use the **Select All** or **Deselect All** buttons if that is what you desire. The default entry in the **Also hide (Optional):** field is **.***, indicating files with a name beginning with a period are not displayed. You can put whatever you want in this field; it accepts regular expressions (Appendix A). Click on **OK** to accept the changes you made and close the **Set Filter Options** window. Use **Apply** to accept the changes and leave the window open.

▲▲▲ The View/Set View Options Window

To change the way the File Manager displays folders and files, select **Set View Options** from the **View** menu in the **File Manager** window and make the changes you desire (Figure 6-21). The window is broken into sections, each of which is described in this table.

Figure 6-21   Set View Options window

Window Section	Effects
Headers	Click on the header checkmark boxes to indicate the types of headers you want (Iconic Path, Text Path, Message Line [Figure 6-20 on page 146]). Choose the Placement you want (not used with **Show By Tree**, below): **As Placed** leaves icons where you place them and **Rows and Columns** arranges icons in sorted order in rows and columns each time a change is made to the folder. The order is determined by **Order**, below.
Show	The **By Single Folder** selection displays the contents of the current folder (like the working directory in Figure 6-20 on the left), whereas the **By Tree** selection shows the contents of the current folder(s) in the form of a tree (Figure 6-20 on the right). Click on any directory, in any of the following modes, to open a new **File Manager** window that shows that directory.
	The nodes (directories, connecting points) of the tree appear as boxes with a plus (**+**) or minus (**–**) sign in each. When you click on a plus sign, the directory expands to show its contents and the plus sign turns into a minus sign. When you click on a minus sign, it turns into a plus sign, and the directory contracts to show only itself.
	The **Folders only** choice displays folders only; when you click on a plus sign, the folder expands to show only other folders, not any files. The **Folders, then Files** choice initially shows folders only. One click on a folder expands to show subfolders. A second click expands to show files. A third click contracts the directory. The **Folders and Files** choice shows both folders and files on the first click.
Representation	Specifies what information you want the **File Manager** to display about each file or folder. **By Name Only** displays only names, **By Large Icons** and **By Small Icons** display an icon for each file along with its name, and **By Name, date, size...** displays a listing that is similar to the output of **ls –l** (page 89).
Order	Determines the sort order of the files in the **File Manager** window: **Alphabetically**, **By File Type**, **By Date**, or **By Size**.
Direction	Specifies the direction of the sort: **Ascending** or **Descending**.

▲▲▲ Properties

You can view information about a file, such as ownership, permission, size, and so on, by selecting an icon and choosing Properties from the right mouse button menu or from the Selected menu. When the Properties window opens (Figure 6-22), you will see the Permissions information; click on the Information button to see additional information, and then click on Permissions to return to the initial display.

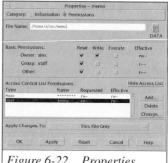

Figure 6-22   Properties window

Property	How to View
File Name	The simple filename is on the title bar, to the right of the word `Properties`. The complete pathname appears in the box near the top of the window. To the right of the filename is an icon with a word below it indicating the type of the file. In the figure at the start of this table, it is a DATA file.
Basic Permissions	The next section of the window displays the **Basic Permissions**. You can change these (assuming you have permission to do so) by adding and removing check marks (single-click adds or removes a check mark).
Access Control List (ACL)	Click on the **Show Access Control List** button to expand the window so that it looks similar to the figure at the start of this table. Clicking on a line in this subwindow highlights the line and turns on the **Add**, **Delete**, and **Change** buttons to the right. Change permissions as you wish and change the **Mask** as necessary to set up the ACL you need. For more information see "ACL (Access Control List)" on page 674.
Apply Changes To	Selects the files you want to apply your changes to. Select **This File Only**, **All Files in Parent Folder**, or **All Files in Parent Folder and its Subfolders**.
Action Buttons	**OK** applies changes and exits from the **Properties** window, whereas **Apply** applies changes without exiting.

▲▲ Copying and Pasting Text

Using the mouse, it is easy to copy text from one part of the screen and paste (insert) it in another location. This is useful when you want to move a block of text, not only within a particular window but also between windows. For example suppose you want to send email to the system administrator to find out more about an error message that appeared on your screen. Instead of retyping the message (and possibly introducing mistakes in the process), you can use the mouse to copy the text and insert it in a mail message (Figure 6-23).

First select the text to copy: Position the mouse pointer in front of the first character in the message, press and hold down the left mouse button, and drag the mouse pointer over the text you want to copy. If the message is long, you can continue dragging the mouse pointer over multiple lines. As you drag the mouse pointer over the text, the characters are highlighted. Release the mouse button when you have positioned the pointer after the last character you want to include. If you change your mind about the selection (for example you selected too little or too much), you can cancel it by clicking the left mouse button and starting over.

Next make a copy of the text. From a terminal emulator window the text is automatically copied when you select it. From most other windows select **Copy** from the **Edit** menu on the menu bar. Many windows provide a keyboard shortcut (such as **CONTROL-C** or **CONTROL-Insert**) to use in place of **Copy**. If the window you are using provides a shortcut, it will be listed to the right of the word **Copy** on the **Edit** menu. Choosing **Copy** from the **Edit** menu and pressing the shortcut keys perform exactly the same function.

Next paste the text: Move the mouse pointer to the new location for the text, which may be in another window, and press the middle or right mouse button from a terminal emulator window or select **Paste** from the **Edit** menu on the menu bar from another window. There may also be a keyboard shortcut—check the

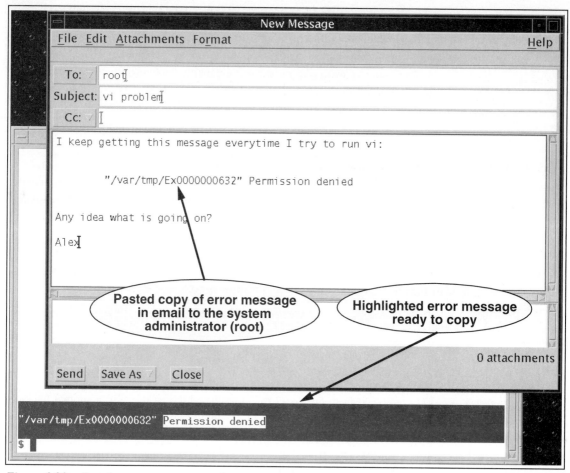

Figure 6-23   Copying an error message from one window and pasting it into another

Edit menu in the window you are pasting *to*. The text you have just pasted should appear on the screen at the location of the mouse pointer.

In addition to pressing the mouse button one time and dragging over single characters, some applications (terminal emulators) permit you to double- or triple-click the mouse button, holding it down and dragging it after the last click. The highlight sweeps over words (double-click) or lines (triple-click) as you move the mouse. Macintosh users will be right at home with this feature.

Another useful application for copying and pasting text is to run one or more commands without retyping them. You can use this method to run commands that are displayed anywhere on your screen—in a set of instructions displayed from a file, an email message, and so on: Select and copy the command, then, with the cursor at a prompt, paste the command (you may have to press **RETURN**).

Be Careful What You Paste

Be careful when copying and pasting text. If you paste text in a window running a shell (a terminal emulator window), any text you have copied is sent to the shell just as if you had typed it. This can produce exciting results as the shell tries to interpret the pasted text as commands.

▲ X Window System

The X Window System was created in 1984 at the Massachusetts Institute of Technology (MIT) by researchers working on a distributed computing project at the Laboratory for Computer Science and on a campuswide distributed environment, Project Athena, with support from Digital Equipment Corporation (DEC) and International Business Machines (IBM). It was not the first windowing software to run on a UNIX system, but it was the first to become widely available. In 1985 MIT released X (version 9) to the public, license free. Three years later a group of vendors formed the X Consortium to support the continued development of X, under the leadership of MIT. By 1998 the X Consortium had become part of the Open Group and released version 11, release 6.4 (commonly called X11R6.4). This release includes a few extensions and enhancements and is fully compatible with X11R6.

X was inspired by the ideas and features found in earlier proprietary window systems, but it is written to be portable and flexible. X is designed to run on a workstation, typically attached to a local area network. The designers built X with the network in mind. If you can communicate with a remote computer over a network, running an X application on that computer and sending the results to your local display is straightforward. The X Window System includes the X Toolkit, a library of powerful routines that handle common graphics operations. As a result, programmers need to know little about the low-level graphical display details and can develop portable applications more quickly.

Often developers provide collections of routines with more powerful interface components than found in the X Toolkit. These *widget sets,* as they are called, let application programmers quickly build sophisticated interfaces to their programs and enforce a uniform look and feel to all parts of the GUI. The X Window System comes with a simple widget set called the Athena widget set. Other popular widget sets available for use with UNIX/Solaris include an enhanced version of the Athena widget set that provides a three-dimensional (3D) appearance and the Motif and Tk widget sets. The Tk widget set was made to resemble the popular Motif widget set; they both give a similar look and feel to applications.

The popularity of X has extended outside the UNIX community and beyond the workstation class of computers it was conceived for. X is available for Macintosh computers, as well as for PCs running Microsoft Windows and Windows NT. It is also available on a special kind of display terminal, known as an *X terminal,* developed specifically to run X.

▲▲ X Window System Window Managers

There are many different window managers available for use with the X Window System, each with different characteristics. Choosing a window manager is largely a matter of individual taste; all window managers allow you to perform the basic operations described in this chapter, but how you perform them differs. You should be able to run any X application under any window manager.

The Motif Window Manager (**mwm**) is popular; it was developed by a consortium of leading computer manufacturers known as the Open Software Foundation (OSF). Motif was designed to be used with the X Window System. It was created using libraries developed by the manufacturers so that applications, including the window managers themselves, could have a consistent look and feel.

Sun ships Solaris2 with the **dtwm** (Solaris 2.5 and above), **olwm**, and **twm** X Window System window managers: The DeskTop Window Manager (**dtwm**) is based on Motif and is compatible with it on a functional level. It is also an integral part of CDE. It provides workspace management and starts many components through Front Panel commands. It also communicates with and facilitates access to other components in the environment.

The OpenLook Window Manager (**olwm**) is the standard window manager for Sun's OpenWindows product but also works in X. Because CDE/**dtwm** is a standard that is available from several manufacturers, many people are using it in place of the proprietary OpenWindows/**olwm**.

Using the standard X libraries, individual programmers have created window managers such as **twm** (Tab Window Manager), **vtwm** (Virtual Tab Window Manager), **gwm** (GNU Window Manager), **olvwm** (OpenLook Virtual Window Manager), **afterstep** (a NeXTStep clone), **xfce** (a CDE clone), and **fvwm** (Virtual Window Manager—the original meaning of the *f* seems to have been lost—feeble?). These window managers are readily available and are free of charge.

Some window managers include a virtual desktop feature, which permits you to have a workspace that is larger than your physical display. These window managers provide a way for you to move around in the larger workspace, controlling which portion of it is visible in full size on your physical display. A virtual desktop can be implemented in several ways. One method presents a small box, called a *panner,* that represents the entire workspace in one corner of the screen. Each window you open appears as a rectangle within this box. The second method, which **olvwm** and **fvwm** use, also presents a small box representing your virtual display in one corner of the screen. The box is subdivided into a grid of your chosen dimensions (2x2, 2x3, 2x4, 3x3, and so on). Each rectangle in the grid represents a virtual display. Clicking on one of the rectangles takes you to another display that has its own set of windows. There is no panner; you move between displays by clicking on the small window or using keyboard or mouse commands. CDE/**dtwm** uses buttons on the Front Panel to move between virtual displays (see Figure 6-8 on page 135 and "Workspace Selection" on page 136).

▲▲ X Window System and Solaris

When you start an X Window System session, you set up a *client-server environment.* One process, called the *X server,* runs on the same machine that displays the X windows. Each application program and utility that makes a request of the X server is a *client* of that server. Examples of X clients are **xterm**, **dtwm**, **olwm**, **xclock**, and so on. A typical request would be to display an image or open a window. An X client can run on the same machine as the server, or a machine halfway around the world.

The server also monitors keyboard and mouse actions (*events*) and passes these on to the appropriate clients. For example when you click on the border of a window, this event is sent by the server to the window manager client. Characters typed into a terminal emulation window are sent to that terminal emulation client. The client takes appropriate action upon receiving an event (makes a window active or displays the typed characters in the preceding examples).

Separating the physical control of the display (the server) from the processes needing access to the display (the client) makes it possible to run the server on one computer and client(s) on other(s). The following sections discuss running the X server and client applications on a single machine. Refer to "Remote Computing and Local Displays" on page 156 for more information about using X in a distributed environment.

Start Optional

You can run **xev** (X event) and watch the information flow from the client to the server and back again by giving the command **/usr/openwin/demo/xev**[2] from a terminal emulation window. This utility opens a window with a box in it and asks the X server to send it events each time anything happens (such as moving the mouse, clicking a mouse button, moving into the box, typing, resizing). Then **xev** displays information about each event in the window you called **xev** from. You can use **xev** as an educational tool: Start it and see how much information is being processed each time you move the mouse. Use CONTROL-C to exit from **xev**.

Stop Optional

When the X Window System creates a display, it assigns that display a locally unique identification string. The value of the **DISPLAY** environment variable contains the ID string for a display.

```
$ echo $DISPLAY
:0.0
```

The format of the complete (globally unique) ID string for a display is:

hostname:X-server:screen-number

where *hostname* is the name of the machine running the X server, *X-server* is the X server number and is 0 unless you are using virtual servers, and *screen-number* is 0 unless you have multiple displays. When you are working with a single physical screen, you can shorten the identification string to:

hostname:0

For example you can use **speedy:0.0** or **speedy:0** to identify the only physical display on the machine named **speedy**. If the X server and the X clients are running on the same machine, you can shorten this identification string even further to **:0.0** or even just **:0**.

---

2. **xev** is part of the SUNWxwdem package on the Solaris installation CD.

▲▲▲ Bringing Up the X Server

By default Solaris brings up **olwm** (OpenLook) or **dtwm** (CDE). If you want to bring up X by itself or in a simple configuration, you have to do so from a command-line prompt. To display a command-line login prompt, select **Command Line Login** from the **Options** menu (Figure 6-3) of the Login Screen. When you see a character-based interface on the screen, press **RETURN** to display a `login:` prompt. You have a limited time to respond to this prompt: If the GUI login screen appears, just repeat the process. Log in as usual and you will see a shell prompt. You can then start the X Window System server by setting the **PATH** variable and giving an **xinit** command:

```
$ PATH=$PATH:/usr/openwin/bin
$ xinit
```

First you will see the Solaris banner page, and after a few seconds the X server displays an **xterm** window on an X screen *without* a window manager (assuming you do not have an **.xinitrc** file; if you do, read on). Because you are running without a window manager, you cannot move or resize the **xterm** window, and the mouse buttons have no effect outside of the **xterm** window. If you create another **xterm** window (by giving an **xterm** command from the first window), the new window appears on top of the first. Because you cannot move the top window, you cannot use the first window until you exit from the second by giving an **exit** command.

xhost **Grants Access to a Display**

If you get an error message when you try to open a window on a remote display, you need to have the remote user run **xhost** to grant you access to the display. For example if you are logged in on a system named **kudos** and you want to create a window on Alex's display, Alex needs to run the following command:

```
$ xhost +kudos
```

If Alex wants to allow anyone to create windows on his display, the following command line grants access to all hosts:

```
$ xhost +
```

If you frequently work with others over a network, you may find it convenient to add an **xhost** line to your **.profile** or **.login** file. Be selective about granting access to your X display with **xhost**; if you allow another machine to access your display, you may find that your work is often interrupted by others.

▲▲ Remote Computing and Local Displays

Computer networks are central to the design of X. It is possible to run an application on one computer and display the results on a screen attached to a different computer; the ease with which this can be done distinguishes X from other window systems available today. Because X has this capability, a scientist can run a program on a powerful supercomputer in another building (or even another state) and view the results on a personal workstation.

There are two ways to identify the display that an X application should use. The most common method is by using the **DISPLAY** environment variable, which is set automatically when the X server starts up (Figure 6-24). You can also specify a display on the command line, using the **–display**

```
xterm
$ hostname
speedy
$ echo $DISPLAY
:0.0
xclock -display max:0.0 -hd white -bg white -fg black &
$
```

*Figure 6-24   Starting an **xclock** on remote display **max:0.0***

option. This option is useful if you want to override the default display (the display you are using or the one specified by **DISPLAY**).

Figure 6-25 shows display **:0.0** for a system named **max**, which includes the clock window that was opened remotely from the display **:0.0** on **speedy** (Figure 6-24).

▲▲▲▲ Local X Server, Remote Display: The screen created by a call to **xinit** has the default ID **:0.0**, as shown previously. If **DISPLAY** is empty or not set, then the process is not using an X display screen. Applications use the value of the **DISPLAY** variable to determine which display, keyboard, and mouse to use. If you want to run an X application (client) such as **xman** on your local computer but have it use the X Window System display (server) on a remote computer, you will need to change the value of the **DISPLAY** variable on your local computer to identify the remote X server:[3]

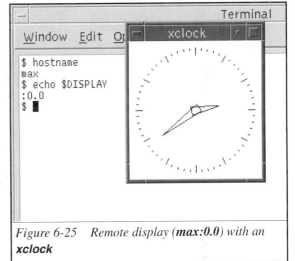

*Figure 6-25   Remote display (**max:0.0**) with an **xclock***

```
$ DISPLAY=bravo:0.0
$ export DISPLAY
$ xman &
```

The preceding example starts **xman** with the default X server running on the computer **bravo**. After giving **DISPLAY** the ID of the **bravo** server, all X programs you start will have their displays on **bravo**. If this is not what you want, you can specify the display you want to use on the command line.

```
$ xman -display bravo:0.0
```

Most X programs use the **–display** option. This option affects only the one command you use it with. All other X-related commands will have their displays on the display named in the **DISPLAY** variable.

---

3. If you get a refused/not authorized error, refer to the Tip named "**xhost** Grants Access to a Display" on page 156.

Security and xhost

Allowing a remote machine access to your display using **xhost** means that any user on the remote computer can watch everything you type in a terminal emulation window, including passwords. For this reason some software packages, such as the Tcl/Tk development system, restrict their own capabilities when **xhost** is used. If security is a concern to you, or if you want to take full advantage of systems such as Tcl/Tk, you should use a safer means of granting remote access to your X session. See the **xauth man** page for information about a more secure replacement for **xhost**.

Start Optional

▲▲▲▲▲ Local Display, Remote X Server: When you start the X server, it opens the display and executes any commands that are present in **.xinitrc**, the user's X initialization file. (As you saw earlier, if there is no **.xinitrc** file, X opens an **xterm** window only.) The X server executes these commands as if they had been typed at the shell prompt. This makes **.xinitrc** a convenient place to start commonly used applications and the window manager of your choice. For example if you use **twm** and want a clock and a terminal window present on your screen whenever you start X, you could use the following **.xinitrc** file:

```
$ cat .xinitrc
xclock &
xterm &
twm
```

The commands in the **.xinitrc** file are executed sequentially, as though you had entered them one at a time on the command line. Leaving the ampersand (**&**) off the **xclock** line would prevent the initialization of your X session from continuing past the display of the **xclock**, and the terminal emulator and **twm** would not start. For the same reason it is necessary to run **xterm** in the background.

.xinitrc and .xsessions Not Used by olwm and dtwm

The following **OPTIONAL** section *does not* pertain to systems running OpenWindows/**olwm** or CDE/**dtwm** desktop/window managers. These managers do not typically use the **.xinitrc** or **.xsession** files.

The last command is left as a foreground job because X quits and returns you to command-line mode when it has finished executing all the commands in **.xinitrc**. Usually you put the command for starting your window manager here. In the example above this is **twm**, but you can substitute **olwm** if you want to run OpenLook window manager. If you have purchased and installed the Motif Window Manager, you can substitute **mwm**. (Although you can bring up a window that looks like CDE by substituting **dtwm**, it will not function properly unless it has additional initialization files.)

You can customize how individual applications start up by specifying options on each command line in **.xinitrc**. In the **.xinitrc** file below, **xsetroot** paints the root window, or background, a solid steel blue. This command completes so quickly it does not need to be run in the background. The second line starts **xterm** as an icon; when you need it, you can "restore" it to full size. The third line starts another **xterm**, with a scroll bar and large type (font). The next line starts Netscape as an icon. (The first time you open Netscape you will have to deal with some other self-explanatory windows before it displays the icon.)

```
$ cat .xinitrc
xsetroot -solid SteelBlue
xterm -iconic &
xterm -sb -fn 10x20 &
netscape -iconic &
twm
```

Experiment with xsetroot from olwm

You cannot see the effects of **xsetroot** when you run it from a terminal emulator window in CDE. If you want to experiment with **xsetroot**, do so from OpenLook.

Stop Optional

▲▲ Stopping the X Server

How you terminate your window manager depends on which window manager you are running and how it is configured; with CDE click on the **Exit** button on the Front Panel (page 137) or choose **Log out** from the **Workspace** menu. With OpenLook choose **Exit** from the **Workspace** menu. If X is not responding, log in from another terminal or a remote system or use **telnet** to gain access to the system. Then **kill** the process running **Xsun**. Refer to "kill: Abort a Process" on page 508.

▲▲ Customizing Your X Work Environment

Chances are that your system administrator or vendor has configured your system so that working with CDE or OpenLook is quite straightforward. The following sections introduce some of the techniques you can use to configure applications to match your preferences, to control which applications run automatically whenever you start the window manager, and to change menu listings to meet your needs.

▲▲▲ Remapping Mouse Buttons

Throughout this chapter each description of a mouse click has referred to the button by its position (left, middle, or right) because the position of a mouse button is more intuitive than an arbitrary name. In X terminology the leftmost mouse button is named button 1, the middle one is button 2, and the right one is button 3.

If you are right-handed you can conveniently press the left mouse button with your index finger; X programs take advantage of this by relying on button 1 for the most common operations. If you are left-handed, your index finger rests most conveniently on button 3 (the right button).

If you are using CDE, you can use the **Style Manager/Mouse** (page 164) to change to a left- or right-handed mouse. From **olwm** choose the Properties option from the Workspace menu and select the Mouse categories display. See Figure 6-32 on page 178 and Figure 6-35 on page 180. Change the Mouse Button Order to MENU-ADJUST-SELECT for left-handed mouse operation. This preference is saved in the **.OWdefaults** file in your home directory under OpenWindows.PointerMapping as right or left.

You can also change how X interprets the mouse buttons by using **xmodmap**. If you are left-handed the following command causes X to interpret the right mouse button as button 1 and the left mouse button as button 3:

```
$ xmodmap -e 'pointer = 3 2 1'
```

Or with a two-button mouse:

```
$ xmodmap -e 'pointer = 2 1'
```

If you remap the mouse buttons, remember to reinterpret the descriptions in this chapter accordingly: When this chapter refers to the left button, you would use the right button instead.

▲▲▲ Customizing X Applications on the Command Line

The possibilities for customizing your environment can seem daunting. There are 40 pages in the **dtwm man** section, 50 in **mwm**, 18 in **dtterm**, and 30 in **xterm**. Before you try to customize a particular application, get some experience with its default performance. After you are familiar with an application, it is easier to read the manual page and explore the details of its features and how to use and change them. This chapter describes some of the basic methods that allow you to set up your X environment.

Each X client (application) understands certain attributes, or *resources,* such as typeface, font size, and color. There are several ways you can change the resources to match your preferences. One method is to specify options on the command line when you start an application. The following example invokes the scrolling feature in **xterm**, using the **–sb** (scroll bar) option, and saves the specified number of lines that have scrolled off the top of the screen using the **–sl** (save lines) option; if you do not change **xterm**'s default characteristics, it does not start up with a scroll bar and saves 64 lines:

```
$ xterm -sb -sl 200 &
```

If you are working at a color display, the following example starts a terminal window titled Hard to Read that presents characters in yellow (foreground) on a green background:

```
$ xterm -bg green -fg yellow -title "Hard to Read" &
```

You can also control where windows appear on the screen. You can control the placement (and size) of X applications with the **–geometry** option. The default size of an **xterm** window includes 24 lines of 80 characters each. The following line creates an **xterm** window that has 30 lines of 132 characters:

```
$ xterm -geometry 132x30 &
```

For most X applications the **–geometry** option recognizes pixels as the unit of size; for some applications, such as a terminal emulator, it is more natural to think in terms of rows and columns; the application is designed to interpret the values accordingly. The following line starts a clock that is 200 pixels wide by 200 high (larger than the default):

```
$ xclock -geometry 200x200 &
```

To place a window in a particular location on the screen, you must specify *x*- and *y*-axis offset values, where each unit represents one pixel. The following line places a terminal window 25 pixels in from the left edge of the screen and 15 pixels down from the top edge:

```
$ xterm -geometry +25+15 &
```

Positive offset values refer to the distance from the upper-left corner of the screen; negative values refer to the distance from the lower-right corner. Figure 6-26 summarizes the effects of the four possible window offset combinations. You can specify both the size and location of a window with one **–geometry** specification. The following command places a long terminal window toward the bottom right of the screen:

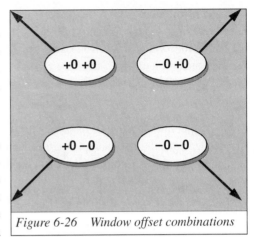

Figure 6-26   Window offset combinations

```
$ xterm -geometry 80x35-10-10 &
```

Although you probably find it awkward to estimate pixel offsets to place windows on your screen, you begin to develop a feeling for these values as you work with the window manager. When you move a window on your screen, the window manager displays a box that reports the approximate offset values (updating them as you drag the window around the screen). You can also use **xwininfo** to display properties associated with a particular window, including the offset values.

▲▲▲ Setting X Resources

Although it may be convenient to specify command-line attributes for a few applications, it is awkward to type complicated option specifications on a command line each time you start a new application during the course of your session. You may also find that you always want to run certain applications with particular options (such as **dtterm**'s scroll bar). To accomplish this you can store your preferences in a file in your home directory named **.Xdefaults**. Because this file is read by X, it works with both CDE and OpenLook. The format of a line in the **.Xdefaults** file is

name-of-application✳*name-of-resource: value*

For CDE the systemwide application defaults are controlled by files in the **/usr/dt/app-defaults/***lang* directory.[4] Refer to the **dtterm** and **dtwm** files in that directory for examples of X resource settings for the **dtterm** editor and **dtwm**. Any settings in your personal **.Xdefaults** file override the system default values. If

---

4. The *lang* element of the pathname describes the language you are using on your system. The default value of *lang* for a system with German-speaking users is **de**, French is **fr**, U.S. English is **en_US.UTF-8**, U.K. English is **en_UK**, Italian is **it**, Swedish is **sv**, and POSIX is **C**. You can obtain other values by looking in the **/usr/lib/locale** directory or giving the command **locale –a | pg**.

you specify different options on the command line when you start a new application, those values will override the settings in your **.Xdefaults** file.

The following entries in a **.Xdefaults** file start all **dtterm** windows with gray characters on a light blue background:

```
Dtterm*background:    lightblue
Dtterm*foreground:    gray22
```

If you omit the name of the application, the resources and values you list are used by all applications that recognize them. For example the following entries cause all windows to have a light blue background, with the exception of **xclock** (notice that both the X and C are capitalized), which has a turquoise background:

```
*background:         lightblue
XClock*background:   turquoise
```

The asterisk is a pattern that matches only the whole name of an application or resource component. A specification such as **XT*background** would apply to an application named **XT**, if one existed, and would have no effect on other applications with names that start with the letters **XT** (such as **xterm**). The following example includes some useful entries to guide you in setting up your own **.Xdefaults** file. You can include comments in the file by starting a line with an exclamation point (**!**).

```
$ cat .Xdefaults
! Resources for Xterm:
!
! Turn on the scroll bar.
XTerm*scrollBar:        True
! Use large font (10 pixels wide, 20 pixels high).
XTerm*Font:             10x20
! Retain more lines to scroll through.
XTerm*saveLines:        150
!
!
!
! Resources for the calculator
!
XCalc*Background:           slategray
XCalc*Foreground:           white
XCalc*screen.LCD.Background: lightgray
XCalc*screen.LCD.Foreground: black
!
! Set up Netscape resources
!
Netscape*Foreground:        White
Netscape*Background:        #B2B2B2
!
! Some defaults for all windows (including XTerms)
!
*highlight:             black
*borderColor:           black
*Foreground:            black
*Background:            bisque
```

When the X server starts it gathers information from many sources to create a resource database in the X server process. After merging system default information, the server typically merges information from your personal **.Xdefaults** file (if it exists in your home directory). An application that runs as a client to the X server may have its behavior or appearance adjusted by means of resources that you specify in **.Xdefaults**. These resources are application dependent and are usually listed in the **man** page for the application.

If you have accounts on multiple computers with different home directories, you can customize the resources for any application on a per host basis. For example if you set XTerm*background: blue in your **.Xdefaults** file on **bravo** and XTerm*background: black on **kudos**, the background color of the **dtterm** windows on your screen varies depending on whether you run **dtterm** on **bravo** or **kudos**. If your home directory is shared by many machines over a network filesystem, you can achieve the same effect by creating multiple **.Xdefaults** files in your home directory, each including the name of the host where it will be recognized. To extend the example above, files named **.Xdefaults-bravo** and **.Xdefaults-kudos** set the resources for applications started on those particular hosts.

You can apply resources consistently across multiple hosts by loading the configuration directly into the X server. Resources configured in the server take precedence over those specified in **.Xdefaults** files. By convention resources loaded into the server are typically stored in a file named **.Xresources**. To load these resources when starting X, add the following line near the beginning of your **.dtprofile** file:

```
xrdb $HOME/.Xresources
```

In this case you do not want to run the command in the background, as that could allow an application to start before **xrdb** has a chance to load that application's options from **.Xresources**. If you change your **.Xresources** file after starting the X Window System, you can load the new specifications immediately by typing the above command at a shell prompt. The **xrdb** utility loads **.Xdefaults** in the same manner.

▲ Customizing CDE

▲▲ Style Manager Tools

The Style Manager is available from the Front Panel—see the icon to the right and Figure 6-8 on page 135. Click on the **Style Manager** icon to open the **Style Manager** window. For help beyond what is covered in this section, click on **Help** at the top right of the **Style Manager** window and then click on **On Item**. The mouse pointer will turn into an arrow and question mark. Position the new mouse pointer until it is over the item in the **Style Manager** window that you want help with and click. The **Style Manager**  Help window will appear. Scroll through the text on the lower portion of the window, clicking on the hypertext links (the boxed and underlined words) you want more help with.

▲▲▲ Color Window

The **Color** window establishes a palette of colors for your desktop. These colors do not affect the programs you run and, within a window, can be overridden by the program using the window. Click on the **Color** icon in the Style Manager to display the **Color** window. Scroll to and click on an item (the name of a palette) from the scrolling menu to see what the palette looks like on your desktop. At this point you can make another selection, click on **Cancel** to close the **Color** window and revert to the palette you were using before you opened it, or click on **OK** to close the **Color** window and accept your choice of palettes. The **Modify...** and **Number Of Colors...** selections allow you to design a custom palette.

▲▲▲ Font Window

The **Font** window changes the size and style of type that is used by default in CDE windows. Click on the **Font** icon in the Style Manager. You can then make a selection from the **Size** box and/or add or delete a font group from the **Font Group** box. When you click on **Add...** in the **Font Group** box, CDE displays two windows each with a list of fonts. In the **System** window you select the font family you want the system to use for window titles, buttons, menus, and other text that the user cannot edit. The **User** window specifies the type for user-editable data. You can preview the fonts in the **Preview** window and you can view the attributes of the fonts by choosing the **Attributes...** selection.

Choose **OK** after you make the changes you selected or **Cancel** to close the **Font** window without making the changes.

▲▲▲ Backdrop Window

If you want to change the backdrop (the pattern/color on the root window), click on the **Backdrop** icon in the **Style Manager** window. As you scroll and click on menu selections to the right of the **Backdrop** window, you will see sample backdrops in a box to the left. Use the buttons at the bottom of the window as follows:

OK	Apply sample backdrop to entire screen and set as default. Close **Backdrop** window.
Apply	Apply sample backdrop to entire screen and set as default. Do not close **Backdrop** window.
Close	Do not apply sample backdrop. Close **Backdrop** window (and leave existing backdrop as it is).

Once you click on **Apply**, you cannot go back to the backdrop you had before you called the **Backdrop** window except by choosing that backdrop again—there is no cancel button.

▲▲▲ Keyboard Window

The **Keyboard** window allows you to control the loudness of the key click and turn on/off the keyboard autorepeat feature.

▲▲▲ Mouse Window

The **Mouse** window allows you to adjust mouse responses and test the double-click speed. Double-click on the picture of the mouse at the upper-left of the **Mouse** window. If the shading of the mouse changes, the system registered the double-click. Adjust the **Double-Click** slider if you want the system to recognize a faster or slower double-click. Use the **Acceleration** slider to change the speed that the mouse pointer moves in relation to the speed of the mouse. A value of 2 means the cursor moves twice as fast as the mouse. The **Threshold** determines how many pixels you need to move the mouse to get the cursor to move at its accelerated speed. If you are doing a lot of detailed graphics work, you may want to increase this number. **Handedness** changes the mouse to a right- or left-handed mouse. **Button 2**, which has no effect on two-button mice, determines what mouse button 2 (and therefore mouse button 1) does.

▲▲▲ Beep Window

The **Beep** window sets the volume, tone, and duration of the warning beep some programs use to get your attention.

▲▲▲ Screen Window

The **Screen** window controls the screen saver and screen lock features. The screen saver blanks the screen and displays a moving image after the number of minutes you set with the **Start Saver** slider. At the top of the window are **On** and **Off** buttons for the screen saver.

You can select one or more screen saver images from the scrolling list toward the top-left corner of the window. As you select each image, the Style Manager displays that image in a small window to the right of the list. Click on an image name a second time to deselect it. When you want to view several screen savers, you can set the **Time Per Saver** slider to control how long each will be displayed.

The **Screen Lock** feature blanks and locks the screen and keyboard after your terminal has not been used for **Start Lock** minutes. Use the **Screen Lock On** and **Off** buttons to turn this feature on or off.

▲▲▲ Window Window

When you type on the keyboard, the window manager needs to be able to direct the characters you are typing to the proper window. The active window (the window accepting input from the keyboard) is said to have the *input focus*. The **Window Behavior** box within the **Window** window allows you to choose one of two common ways to specify which window has the input focus.

Using the *focus-follows-mouse* method, you position the mouse pointer inside the window and keep it there, even though you use the keyboard, not the mouse, as you type characters. With this method if the pointer strays outside the window you are using, the characters you type are lost (if the pointer is positioned on the root window) or sent to another window unintentionally (if positioned on a different window).

Using the *explicit* or *click-to-focus* method, you select a window by clicking on it with the left mouse button; that window continues to accept input from your keyboard regardless of the position of the mouse pointer. With the click-to-focus method, the characters you type are sent to the input focus, even if you move the mouse pointer to another window (until you click the left mouse button).

You can tell which window has the input focus by comparing the window borders; the border of the active window is a different color than the others, or is darker on a monochrome display. Another indication that a window is active is a flashing keyboard cursor (it is steady solid in windows that are not active—you will see this most often in terminal emulator windows). Although clicking the middle or the right mouse button also activates a window, you should use only the left mouse button for this purpose; other mouse buttons may have unexpected effects if you use them to activate a window.

To tell which method your desktop is set up to use, position the mouse pointer in a window and click the left mouse button. Then move the mouse pointer over another window (do not click the mouse button). If that window becomes active (border changes color or brightness), then CDE is configured to use the focus-follows-mouse method. If the border of the window does not change, you are using the click-to-focus method to activate windows.

Just below a dividing line in the **Window Behavior** box are three checkboxes. You will normally check the **Raise Window When Made Active** box so that when you change the input focus to an obscured or partially obscured window CDE puts that window on top (so you can see and work with the entire window). When you check **Allow Primary Windows On Top** the initial, or primary, window can remain on top of others in its group. You should normally check this box also. A blank **Show Contents During Move** checkbox causes CDE to display an outline of a window as you drag it from one place to another on the desktop. This method of moving a window does not put much of a load on system resources, but it is not as pretty as displaying the window as you move it. Mark this checkbox to display a window as you move it.

The **Window Icons** box allows you to choose between gathering icons on the desktop within an **Icon** window or allowing them to remain anywhere on the desktop.

▲▲▲ Startup Window

This window controls what happens when you log in on and out of the system. The **At Login** box allows you to choose one of three radio buttons. **Resume Current Session** causes CDE to store the specifics of the current session so that you can pick up where you left off next time you log in. **Return to Home Session** causes CDE to bring up the same (home) session each time you log in, no matter how you left your desktop when you logged out. **Ask Me At Logout** allows you to make the choice when you log out. Information necessary to restore your home session is kept in the **.dt/sessions/home/dt.session** file in your home directory.

When **Logout Confirmation Dialog** is **On**, CDE verifies your intention when you log out. When it is **Off** CDE does not prompt you before logging you off. Click on **Set Home Session...** to establish the current session as your home session for use with the **Return to Home Session** choice in the **At Login** box.

You can customize the CDE window manager in many ways. You can change or add menus that you use to interact with CDE, change the actions tied to keys and mouse buttons, alter the size of the virtual desktop, and alter the look and feel of the interface.

▲▲ .dtprofile

Similar to the Style Manager tools discussed above, **.dtprofile** allows you to customize your work environment. This file does not provide the easy-to-use graphical interface of the Style Manager tools, yet it allows you to control many more features. Read each time you log in on CDE, **.dtprofile** provides a place for you to set or override environment variables for your CDE session. You can use either Bourne or Korn Shell syntax for commands in this file. Errors from this file, as well as **.profile** and **.login**, are sent to **startlog** in the **.dt** directory in your home directory (**$HOME/.dt/startlog**).

The **DTSOURCEPROFILE** variable is set on the last line of **.dtprofile** to cause **.profile** and **.login** to be read and executed when you start a shell. Put a pound sign (#) at the start of this line to comment it out and bypass these startup files.

Errors in **.dtprofile**

Be careful when experimenting with your **.dtprofile** file; if the file contains an error (for example leaving the **&** off a command line), the X server may not start up properly. If this happens, terminate the X server (or just the hung program) from another terminal/workstation and fix the problem.

▲▲ Building Menus

When you click the right mouse button while the mouse pointer is over the root window, CDE displays the Workspace menu, which contains submenus and commands (Figure 6-12, page 139). You can modify this menu, add a new submenu to it, or create your own menu by modifying the **dtwmrc** file that resides in the **.dt** directory in your home directory (**$HOME/.dt/dtwmrc**). By its name you can tell it is a startup (**rc**) file for the Desktop Window Manager (**dtwm**), which forms the foundation for CDE. If this file does not exist in your **.dt** directory, copy it by giving the following command (see footnote on page 161 for *lang*):

```
$ cp /usr/dt/config/lang/sys.dtwmrc $HOME/.dt/dtwmrc
```

Within **dtwmrc** a very simple menu that does nothing can appear as:

```
Menu Screenlock
{
# placeholder
}
```

The Menu keyword is followed immediately by the internal name for the menu and then by a structure that defines the menu. The internal name of the preceding menu is Screenlock—that is the name used to refer to this menu within **dtwmrc**; it does not appear in the window shown to the user. The body of the menu is delimited by braces. The word placeholder in the body of the menu is a taken as a comment because it is preceded by a pound sign (#).

The following example shows the source code for a menu that lets you start a number of useful utilities. Figure 6-27 shows the resulting cascading menu.

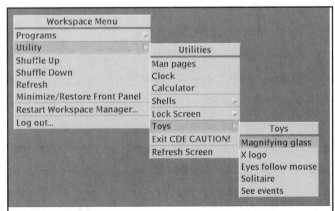

Figure 6-27   The cascading menus produced by the sample dtwmrc file

```
###
#
# Root Menu Description
#
###

Menu UtilityMenu
{
   # Set the title for the menu
   Utilities          f.title

   # These lines run some useful applications
   "Man pages"        f.exec /usr/openwin/bin/xman
   Clock              f.exec "oclock -transparent -fg red -bd red"
   Calculator         f.action Dtcalc

   # Skip a line in the menu
   no-label           f.separator

   # Access a submenu of terminal emulators for different shells
   Shells             f.menu Shells
   no-label           f.separator

   # Submenus of different screen locks and diversions
   "Lock Screen"      f.menu Screenlock
   "Toys"             f.menu Toys
   no-label           f.separator

   # Quit CDE (but not X)
   # Following closes the CDE window manager but not the X Window
   # System, yielding some strange results. Make sure you have an
   # xterm window opened before you give this command.  Use ps and
   # kill to Kill the xsession process and log off when you can do
   # nothing else.
   #
   "Exit CDE CAUTION!" f.quit_mwm
   no-label           f.separator

   # Redraw the screen to clean it up
   "Refresh Screen"   f.refresh
}

Menu Toys
{
   # Set the title for the menu
   Toys               f.title
   "Magnifying glass" f.exec /usr/openwin/bin/xmag
   "X logo"           f.exec /usr/openwin/bin/xlogo
   "Eyes follow mouse" f.exec /usr/openwin/demo/xeyes
   "Solitaire"        f.exec /usr/openwin/demo/xsol
   "See events"       f.exec "xterm -exec /usr/openwin/demo/xev"
}
Menu Screenlock
{
```

```
}

Menu Shells
{
}

Menu DtRootMenu
{
    "Workspace Menu"    f.title
    "Programs"          f.menu ProgramsMenu
    "Utility"           f.menu UtilityMenu
     no-label           f.separator
    "Shuffle Up"        f.circle_up
    "Shuffle Down"      f.circle_down
    "Refresh"           f.refresh
 .
 .
 .
```

Most lines that generate menu items have three fields. The first field is a label that identifies the menu item for the user. The second field contains the function associated with the menu item. The **f.exec** function runs the executable file named in the third field, and **f.action** runs an action (such as **/usr/dt/appconfig/app-manager/***lang***/Desktop_Apps/Dtmail** [see footnote on page 161 for *lang*]). Give the command **man –s4 dtwmrc** for a complete listing of these functions. The third field is the argument to the function given in the second field. The only arguments you can use with **f.exec** are programs that will run in the X environment; **vi** will not work, **dtterm** and **"dtterm vi"** will. The first line of the following example from **dtwmrc** causes CDE to display a horizontal rule (line) in the menu. You can use these lines to separate groups of related menu items. The label (no-label) has no meaning.

```
    no-label            f.separator

    # Redraw the screen to clean it up
    "Refresh Screen"    f.refresh
```

The third line of the preceding example, the one that begins with a pound sign (#), is a comment. The next line adds a menu item that invokes the **dtwm refresh** function. The label appearing with this menu item is Refresh Screen.

The first of the following mouse button bindings (from a **dtwmrc** file) binds the Utilities menu (with the internal name UtilityMenu) to the right mouse button (number 3, or 2 of a two-button mouse) when it is pressed together with the CONTROL key while the mouse pointer is in the root window.

```
Buttons DtButtonBindings
{
    Ctrl<Btn3Down>      root            f.menu   UtilityMenu
     <Btn1Down>         root            f.marquee_selection
     <Btn3Down>         root            f.menu   DtRootMenu
     <Btn1Down>         frame|icon      f.raise
 .
 .
```

With the commands described in this section, you can build a custom interface to the CDE/**dtwm** window manager. This makes it easy for you to design an interface that suits the way you want to use the X Window System. Refer to the **dtwm(1)** and **dtwmrc(4) man** pages to learn more about how to customize the **dtwmrc** file.

▲▲ Actions

An *action* provides a user interface for running applications, executing commands, printing, manipulating files and directories, and more. An *action icon* represents an action in a **File** or **Application Manager** window. Many action icons exist on the system: Any icon you double-click on to make something happen is an action icon. You can create additional action icons as needed.

To create an action icon, click on the **Desktop_Apps** in the **Applications** submenu in the control panel. Then click on the **Create Action** (action) icon (Figure 6-29) in the **Desktops_Apps** window. CDE will display the **Create Action** window (Figure 6-28). Enter an action name in the first field, find an icon (**Find Set...**) or edit an icon (**Edit icon...**), and choose an icon size by clicking on one of the sample sizes.

Next fill in the **Command When Action Is Opened** field. This can be as simple as a command that does not take any arguments (for example **who**), it can be the name of a shell script or executable file, and it can take one or more command-line arguments (which it prompts for). If your action is set up to accept an argument, you can also drop another, appropriate icon on the action icon instead of supplying an argument. Figure 6-28 uses the command **pg $1**, which takes an argument and displays it using **pg**.

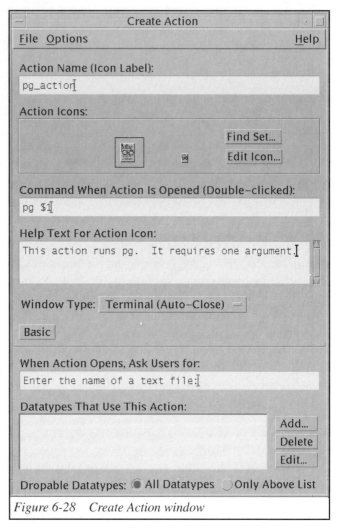

Figure 6-28   Create Action window

You can leave the **Help Text** field blank or enter whatever words you think may help a user. The user will see this text after selecting the action icon and choosing **Help** from the right-click menu.

Select the **Window Type** as follows:

- **Graphical (X-Window)**   Use for an application that creates its own X window and does not need the system to supply a terminal emulator window.

- **Terminal (Auto-Close)**   The system provides a character-based terminal emulation window. The window closes when the action finishes.

- **Terminal (Manual Close)**   The system provides a character-based terminal emulation window. The window remains open until you close it manually.

• **No Output** The action does not generate any output so it does not need a window.

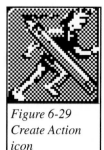

Figure 6-29
Create Action
icon

The sample **Create Action** window uses **Terminal (Auto-Close)** because **pg** requires a terminal emulation window to run (it does not create its own window) and because **pg** prompts you before ending (you need to press **q**) so the window will not close before you are done with **pg** (when you press **q**).

If you want the action to prompt the user for input, click on the **Advanced** button if it is visible. If the **Basic** button is visible, you are already in advanced mode. Enter the text that you want the action to use to prompt the user in the box under **When Action Opens, Ask Users for**. Although you can specify a data type to use this action, you can leave this section blank; make sure **All Datatypes** is selected (below the **Datatypes** subwindow).

Next select **Save** from the **File** menu and you are ready to test the new action. Double-click on the action in your home directory and see what happens. If you want to see the code for the action, look in **.dt/types** in your home directory. You will find a file with the action name and a filename extension of **.dt**. The filename for the action in Figure 6-28 is **pg_action.dt**. Following is a listing of the file:

```
$ cat pg_action.dt
######################################################################
#
#     Common Desktop Environment (CDE)
#
#     Action and DataType Definition File
#
#        Generated by the CreateAction tool
#
#        $Revision: 1.0
#
#        $KEY: 4279
#
######################################################################
#
#     WARNING:
#
#     This file was generated by the CDE CreateAction tool.
#     If this file is modified by some other tool, such as vi,
#     the CreateAction tool will no longer be able to load and
#     update this file.  For this reason, changes to this file
#     should be handled through CreateAction whenever possible.
#
######################################################################

ACTION pg_action
{
        LABEL          pg_action
        TYPE           COMMAND
        EXEC_STRING    pg %Arg_1"Enter the name of a text file:"%
        ICON           DtRdMe
        WINDOW_TYPE    TERMINAL
        DESCRIPTION    This action runs pg.  It requires one argument.
}
```

You can leave the action icon in your home directory, move it to another folder or to the desktop, or you can add it to the items you can select from the Front Panel (next section).

▲▲ Front Panel

You can modify the subpanels of the Front Panel (Figure 6-8 on page 135): Raise the subpanel you want to add an action to and drag and drop an action icon onto **Install Icon** at the top of the subpanel. That icon now appears and functions in that subpanel. If there is no subpanel associated with the control you want to add to, right click on the control and select **Add Subpanel**. The control will then have a subpanel and you can proceed as described above.

▲▲ Login Manager

The Login Manager is a server that displays a login screen, makes sure a user is allowed to log in, and starts a session once a user logs in. One instance of the Login Manager can perform these tasks for multiple graphical and character-based displays, both those that are directly attached to the machine the Login Manager is running on as well as X terminals and workstations anywhere on the network.

The **dtlogin** program is the Login Manager. You could run it as follows, but this is *not* recommended:

```
# /usr/dt/bin/dtlogin -daemon
```

Instead use the **dtconfig** script to set up and start **dtlogin** so it is run every time you boot the system. Without an argument **dtconfig** displays a list of its options and their functions. With the **–e** option it enables the desktop autostart feature. The Login Manager sends errors to **/var/dt/Xerrors** by default.

```
# /usr/dt/bin/dtconfig

Usage: Needs one argument

 CDE configuration utility

  /usr/dt/bin/dtconfig -d        (disable auto-start)
  /usr/dt/bin/dtconfig -e        (enable auto-start)
  /usr/dt/bin/dtconfig -kill     (kill dtlogin)
  /usr/dt/bin/dtconfig -reset    (reset dtlogin)
  /usr/dt/bin/dtconfig -p        (printer action update)
  /usr/dt/bin/dtconfig -inetd    (inetd.conf /usr/dt daemons)
  /usr/dt/bin/dtconfig -inetd.ow (inetd.conf /usr/openwin daemons)



# /usr/dt/bin/dtconfig -e
done
desktop auto-start enabled.
```

When you start **dtlogin** it runs the **Xsession** script, which runs, as its last action, the Session Manager (**dtsession**).

▲▲▲ Session Manager

The Session Manager starts the desktop and can automatically save (when you end a session) and restore (when you start a session) all the components of a desktop (running applications, fonts, colors, keyboard click, mouse behavior, and more). Also see "Startup Window" on page 166.

Altering X Resources

The **/usr/dt/config** directory contains files that you can use to customize the behavior of the Login Manager. Because a Solaris upgrade will overwrite files in this directory, you must make a copy of files you change to preserve them through an upgrade. The Login Manager gives priority to the files in the **/etc/dt/config** directory over those in the **/usr/dt/config** directory. To change a file in **/usr/dt/config**, first copy it to **/etc/dt/config** and then modify the copy: The system will use the modified copy, you will have the security of having a backup copy of the original file, and the modified copy will be preserved during an upgrade.

▲▲ Initialization Files

You can control almost every aspect of a user's experience of a CDE session. From logging in to logging out, from colors to fonts, from window behavior to menus, the system administrator can make the system easier to use for all different types of users. Many aspects of system behavior are controlled by initialization files. This section describes many of the initialization files you can use to customize a user's CDE environment.

▲▲▲ Login Screen

The Login Manager shows a login screen on a GUI display while waiting for someone to log in. You can alter the appearance of the login screen (color, fonts, logo, greeting, and more) by changing X resources in the **Xresources** file. After copying **/usr/dtconfig/*lang*/Xresources** to **/etc/dt/config/*lang*/Xresources**, you can edit the file.[5] (See footnote on page 161 for *lang*.)

While editing your *copy* of **Xresources**, look for the following lines:

```
!!###################################################################
!!
!!   GREETING
!!

!! Dtlogin*greeting.foreground:        black
!! Dtlogin*greeting.background:        #a8a8a8
!! Dtlogin*greeting.labelString:       Welcome to %LocalHost%
!! Dtlogin*greeting.persLabelString:   Welcome %s
!! Dtlogin*greeting.alignment:         ALIGNMENT_CENTER
```

---

5. There are two errors in the 12/1/95 version of the **Xresources** file: The paragraph just below the line that says DO NOT EDIT THIS FILE says to copy the file to an incorrect directory; use the directory name given above. It also says you must edit **Xconfig**; this is not so if you use the directories specified above.

To change the color of the login greeting, make a copy of the `Dtlogin*greeting.foreground` line and put it at the end of the file,[6] remove the leading exclamation points from the copied line, and change `black` to `red` (or any color you want to use). Save the file, log out, and you will see the new color on the login screen. You can change the values of other resources in this file in the same manner.

Any line that starts with an exclamation point is a comment: You must remove the exclamation points for the resource to take effect. For a list of available fonts, run the **xlsfonts** utility without any options (only from a GUI window).

▲▲▲ Issuing Commands before and after the Session

There are several scripts that CDE runs at different points both before the login screen appears and after you log off.

/usr/dt/config/Xsetup   Establishes the display setup. It is run with **root** privileges (make sure all utilities run from this script are secure) after the X server has started and before the login screen is presented to the user.

/usr/dt/config/Xstartup   Runs systemwide initialization commands. It is run with **root** privileges (make sure all utilities run from this script are secure) after the user has logged in but prior to the start of the user session.

/usr/dt/bin/Xsession   Starts a desktop session. When this Korn Shell script is run (with user privileges), it carries out the following steps (there are actually more steps, and some of the detail has been left out, refer to the **Xsession man** page and the **/usr/dt/bin/Xsession** file itself for more information), using the **source** or dot (**.**) builtin to execute all scripts in the same environment as the user's login shell:

- If **$HOME/.dtprofile** does not exist, then **Xsession** copies **/etc/dt/config/sys.dtprofile** if it exists or else **/usr/dt/config/sys.dtprofile** to **$HOME/.dtprofile**. Then it runs **$HOME/.dtprofile**.

- Runs all the scripts in the **/etc/dt/config/Xsession.d** directory, or if that directory does not exist, it runs the scripts in the **/usr/dt/config/Xsession.d** directory. The scripts in these directories set up search paths, temporary directories for users and sessions, a default environment, and more. Refer to **/usr/dt/config/Xsession.d/0010.dtpaths** for a sample file.

---

6. You do not *have* to make a copy of the line you want to change, it is just a good habit. Frequently you will want to refer back to the original line, and it is convenient to have it close at hand. This technique works even if the line you are copying is not commented out as the Login Manager will use the last value assigned to a resource.

- Displays a greeting (**usr/dt/config/***lang***/Xresources** [see footnote on page 161 for *lang*]). For more information see "Login Screen" on page 173.

- Calls **/usr/dt/bin/dtappgather** to establish search paths that the desktop will use.

- Runs the **.profile** and **.login** files from the home directory of the Korn and Bourne Shell user and **.cshrc** from the home of a user running the C Shell.

- Starts the **dtwm** (or another) workspace (or window) manager.

- As its last action, starts **/usr/dt/bin/dtsession**, which starts a window manager.

/usr/dt/config/Xfailsafe   Brings up a simple window manager (**dtsession**) and a terminal emulator (**dtterm**). Frequently you can use this minimal session to repair problems with your windowing system that may prevent you from logging on normally.

        To run a failsafe session, choose Failsafe from the Options menu on the login screen (page 131).

/usr/dt/config/Xreset   Lists commands to execute after the session ends.

▲▲▲ Session Setup

The scripts and programs in this section control many aspects of the login including appearance and network logins. Some are data files that contain information that can be useful to a system administrator.

/usr/dt/bin/dtlogin   Manages a login. The **dtlogin** utility runs **dtgreet** (below), allows a user to have access to a character-based terminal login from a GUI login screen, and starts a session. It is similar in function to **init**, **getty**, and **login** on character-based terminals. The **/etc/dt/config/Xconfig** or **/usr/dt/config/Xconfig** file controls the way this utility functions.

/usr/dt/bin/dtgreet   Used by **dtlogin** to display the greeting/login screen. This screen prompts you for a name and password and, upon verification, allows you to log in on the system. You cannot use **dtgreet** to customize the greeting/login screen; all customization is done from **dtlogin**.

/usr/dt/bin/dtchooser   Used by **dtlogin** to display a host chooser screen. The host chooser screen allows you to choose between one of several systems available on the network. You may not see this screen on your system. You cannot use **dtchooser** to customize the host chooser screen; all customization is done from **dtlogin**.

/usr/dt/config/Xconfig   Configures the login screen. This file controls behavior resources and locations of configuration files used by the Login Manager. In it you can specify the path, shell, time zone, as well as the location of configuration files including the **Xsetup**, **Xstartup**, and **Xsession** scripts. Copy to and edit as **/etc/dt/config/Xconfig**.

/usr/dt/config/Xservers   Provides a list of location(s) at which X server(s) need to be started. It specifies each location as local or remote and with or without a display. This file also identifies the display (as : 0 for the root for example) and whether to display a command-line login or a screen login. The Login Manager reads this list and starts X servers as needed. Copy to and edit as **/etc/dt/config/Xservers**.

/usr/dt/config/Xaccess	Describes access to the login server. Each machine named in the file can connect to the local machine. When a remote display (usually an X terminal or workstation) asks for a login, **dtlogin** consults this file to see if someone from that machine is allowed to log in on the local machine. Copy to and edit as **/etc/dt/config/Xaccess**.
/usr/dt/config/*lang***/ Xresources**	Controls login screen attributes. Refer to "Login Screen" on page 173. Copy to and edit as **/etc/dt/config/***lang***/Xconfig**. (See footnote on page 161 for *lang*.)
/var/dt/Xpid	Holds the Process ID of the login server.
/var/dt/Xerrors	Holds the error log of the login server.

▲ OpenLook Window Manager

The OpenLook Window Manager (**olwm**, Figure 6-30) implements part of Sun's OpenLook graphical user interface. It runs under Sun's OpenWindows and the X Window System. This window manager is flexible and powerful, but it is not standard across manufacturers as CDE is, so it is not as popular as CDE.

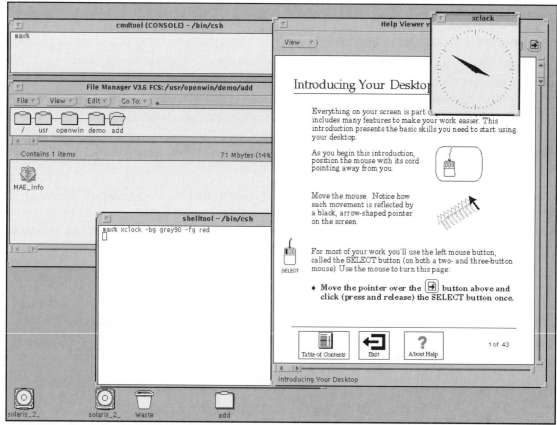

Figure 6-30   A sample OpenLook desktop

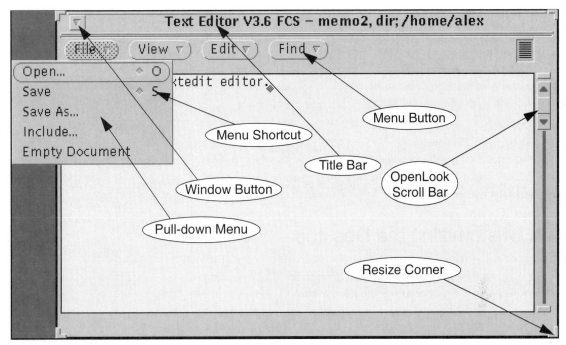

Figure 6-31   Components of an OpenLook window

To use OpenLook choose **OpenWindows Desktop** from the **Sessions** submenu of the **Options** menu on the login screen (Figure 6-3 on page 131). Then log in with your name and password. You will see various windows or maybe none at all on the desktop. Figure 6-31 shows important standard features of an OpenLook window.

There is a free implementation of XView toolkit for developing and supporting OpenLook applications at most major X archive sites (page 967). XView stands for X Window System based Visual/Integrated Environment for Workstations.

▲▲ Workspace Menu

As with CDE, there is a **Workspace** menu (click and release the right mouse button while the mouse pointer is over the root window). The **Workspace** menu allows you to select **Programs** and **Utilities** you want to run; interface **Properties** you want to change including display, mouse, keyboard, locale, and what appears on the **Programs** menu; **Workstation Information**; system **Help**; and **Exit** to log off. Slide the mouse pointer over one of the menu items and click to choose the item. Or you can just click on the root window again without choosing anything and the **Workspace** window will disappear.

In the upper-left corner of the **Workspace** window is a picture of a *pushpin*. Click on the pushpin to pin the window to the desktop. When you pin a menu, it will stay put even after you make a selection or click somewhere else. Figure 6-32 shows the **Workspace** and **Programs** menus pinned in place with pushpins. The way pushpins work is similar to the Motif concept of tear-off menus.

▲▲ File Manager

The OpenLook File Manager (Figure 6-33) looks and works very much like the CDE File Manager (Figure 6-20). You can drag a box around one or more icons to select one or more icons. Or you can single-click to select one icon, and hold the SHIFT key down while clicking on additional icons to select more than one icon. Figure 6-33 shows the **core** file selected.

There is no Selected menu as with CDE; you can take actions on the selected file(s) using the right mouse button and the File and Edit menus. Use File/Information to change permissions, ownership, and group of the selected file.

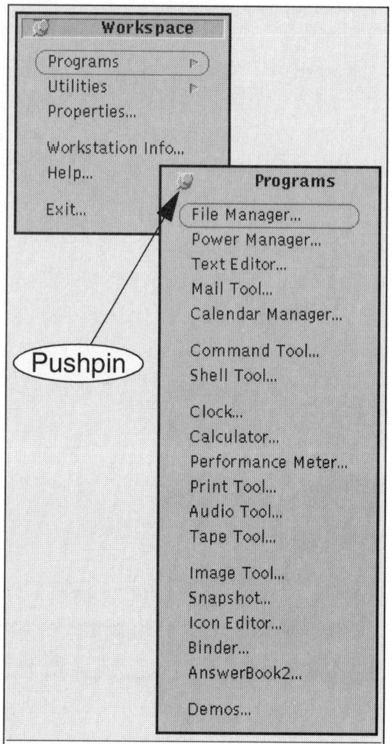

▲▲ Customizing the Desktop

When you select Properties from the Workspace menu, you will see the opening window of the Workspace Properties windows. This window displays the properties of the Color choice (shown in the upper-left of the window) that allows you to adjust the foreground and background colors of windows, data areas, and the workspace. Click on the ellipsis (. . .) following the name of the area whose color you want to change. The inset window at the bottom of this menu allows you to keep track of what your screen will look like as you change colors.

Select other property menus by clicking on the triangle pointing down within the box following Category: at the upper-left of the Workspace Properties menu and moving the mouse pointer to the selection you want be-fore you click again (Figure 6-34). Figure 6-35 shows the Locale window with Numeric Format selected. Here you can choose from several different ways of representing ten thousand point zero.

Figure 6-32   The Workspace menu and the Programs submenu

▲▲▲ Saving the Desktop

You can further customize your desktop by running programs, sizing and positioning their windows, and saving the result. For example you might want to run Calendar Manager each time you log in. To do so run Calendar Manager from the Workspace menu (under Programs); position and size it where you want.

Once the **olwm** desktop looks the way you want it to, with the windows you want in the correct locations, colors, mouse behavior, and so on, you can save the desktop by opening the Workspace menu, choosing Utilities, and then clicking on Save Workspace. The **olwm** utility will create two files in your home directory to save information about your custom desktop: **.openwin-init** and **.OWdefaults**.

Tools that do not understand the OpenLook method of positioning may not be in the same place the next time you log in. Commercial applications, such as Netscape, that are not written using the OpenLook widget set will still be started but may not look the same as when you saved your workspace.

▲▲▲ Help Viewer

The first time you log in using OpenLook, you will see the default desktop, which includes a Help Viewer, File Manager, and Command Tool. You can display the **Help Viewer** window (Figure 6-35) manually by choosing **Help** from the **Workspace** menu. The Help Viewer provides information about OpenLook and various tools you can use from OpenLook. In addition you can open AnswerBook2 for more general information by selecting **Programs** from the **Workspace** menu and then **answerbook2** from near the bottom of the menu.

▲▲▲ Customizing Menus

As with other Solaris customizable features, **olwm** first looks for **Workspace** menu files in your home directory. If it does not find any files, it looks in the default directory. The default menus are kept in files named **/usr/openwin/lib/openwin-menu***. If you want to create or customize **Workspace** menus, copy the appropriate file to your home directory, and precede its filename with a period. For example to modify the top-level **Workspace** **Properties** menu, copy **/usr/openwin/lib/openwin-menu** to **.open-win-menu** in your home directory and change the file to suit your needs. (You can also cus-

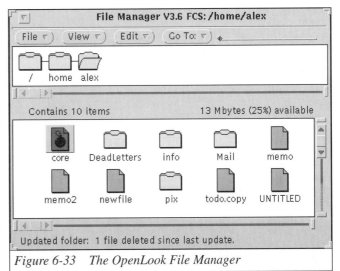

Figure 6-33   The OpenLook File Manager

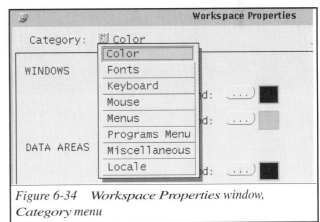

Figure 6-34   Workspace Properties window, Category menu

tomize the **Programs** submenu by using the **Workspace Properties** window.) Following is the default **openwin-menu** file:

```
$ cat /usr/openwin/lib/openwin-menu
#
# @(#)openwin-menu     23.18 93/01/11 openwin-menu
#
#        OpenWindows default root menu file - top level menu
#

"Workspace" TITLE

"Programs"      DEFAULT INCLUDE openwin-menu-programs

"Utilities"             INCLUDE openwin-menu-utilities
```

```
"Properties..."           PROPERTIES

SEPARATOR

"Workstation Info..." exec $OPENWINHOME/bin/wsinfo

"Help..."                 exec $OPENWINHOME/bin/helpopen handbooks/top.toc.handboo
k

SEPARATOR

"Exit..."                 EXIT
```

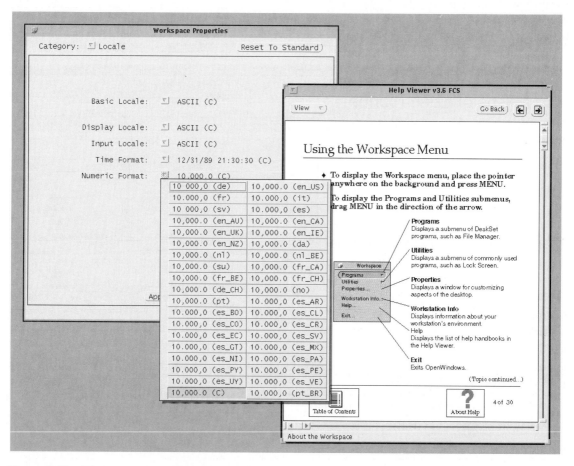

Figure 6-35   The Workspace Properties/Locale window and the Help Viewer window

There are only a few keywords you can use when configuring **olwm** menus. The **/usr/open-win/lib/openwin-menu-utilities** file is a good example of an **olwm** menu file as it uses many of the important keywords. Refer to the following table and the "MENU SPECIFICATION SYNTAX" section of the **olwm man** page for a discussion of the syntax of the commands used in the **openwin-menu** and related menu files.

Keyword	Meaning
"*text*"	Displays *text* literally in the menu (a label)
TITLE	Indicates that the preceding "text" is the title for a sub (cascading) menu
exec *pgm*	Executes *pgm* when the user selects the corresponding *text*
DEFAULT	Specifies the default menu selection
SEPARATOR	Separates groups of menu items
MENU	Indicates the beginning of a submenu
END	Indicates the end of a submenu
PIN	Allows a submenu to be pinned to the desktop (page 177)
EXIT	Exits **olwm** (and usually returns you to the login screen)

▲▲▲ Application Preferences

Most OpenLook tools (such as Mail Tool, Calendar Manager, File Manager, and Image Tool) have a Preferences choice under the Edit menu. Using Preferences, you can customize many internal aspects of these applications. The **olwm** utility stores the customization information in the **.desksetdefaults** file in your home directory.

▲ X Applications

If you are using X on Solaris, you can use many applications from a variety of sources: tools that are part of the standard distribution from the X Consortium, tools provided by Sun, software added by your Solaris distributor, other tools purchased from third-party suppliers, free applications that are publicly available, and perhaps some applications created locally. The table that follows lists a few of the tools that are distributed with Solaris. For detailed information consult the online **man** pages. For more information about tools that are not currently available on your system, visit the Internet sites that support Solaris and the X Window System. These sites also contain information about many more X applications that you might find useful. Chapter 7 explains more about searching the Internet (page 236). Also see Appendix B for more information.

Application	Function
appres	Lists resource values that apply to particular tools
bitmap	Builds small black-and-white bitmaps
calctool	Sun calculator
cm	Sun calendar manager
cmdtool	OpenLook terminal emulator
ddd*	Graphical front end for **gdb** debugger
dtcalc	CDE Calculator
dtcm	CDE Calendar Manager

Application	Function
gimp*	GNU Image Manipulation Program, painting and markup suite
gs*	GNU PostScript imaging engine, required by **ghostview** and **gv**
gv*	Updated and enhanced version of **ghostview**
ImageMagick*	Converts between different types of images and manipulates images
imagetool	OpenLook image viewer for PostScript, **gif**, **tiff**, **jpeg**, and other files
oclock	Displays a round (analog) clock
shelltool	Like **cmdtool**, but without a scroll bar
showrgb	Shows all the color names available with X
ups*	A very powerful GUI-only debugger
wish*	Tcl/Tk interactive windowing shell
workman*	Use your CDROM player to play music CDs
xcalc	Emulates a hand-held calculator
xclipboard	Stores and displays text cut or copied from other applications
xclock	Displays a running time-of-day clock
xdpyinfo	Lists information about an X server
xfontsel	Displays available fonts and font names
xhost	Controls access to an X display
xli*	Another image loader and manipulator
xload	Displays a running graph of how busy the system is
xlock	Keeps others from using your keyboard and display
xlsfonts	Lists names of available fonts
xlswins	Displays the window tree of parents and children
xmag	Displays a magnified image of part of the screen
xman	Browser interface to the online manual pages
xmodmap	Remaps mouse buttons and keyboard keys
xpdf*	Viewer for Portable Document Format (PDF or Acrobat) files
xpr	Prints an image created by **xwd**
xprop	Shows window and font properties
xrdb	Loads resource settings into the active database
xrn*	Reads USENET news
xset	Sets user preferences (display, keyboard, and mouse)
xsetroot	Changes appearance of the root window

Application	Function
xterm	Emulates a character terminal
xv*	Grabs, displays, and manipulates picture images
xvgr/xmgr	A window-oriented graph plotting program in OpenLook (**xvgr**) or Motif (**xmgr**)
xwd	Stores a screen image (window dump) in a file
xwininfo	Displays information about a particular window
*Not supplied with Solaris	

Summary

A graphical user interface lets you interact conveniently with many different applications and utilities by allowing you to open windows, each capable of running a different program. It also provides a way for you to work with pictures of objects and to select options from menus, an approach that many novice users prefer to the less intuitive command-line interface of the traditional shell. Most GUIs run on bitmapped displays and respond to input from a mouse. In addition to the various menu types, GUIs typically provide you with graphical aids such as scroll bars, buttons, and dialog boxes, each of which allows you to use the mouse to control some aspect of the application.

The X Window System GUI is portable and flexible and makes it easy to write applications that work on many different types of systems without having to know the low-level details about the individual systems. It can operate in a networked environment, allowing a user to run a program on a remote system and send the results to a local display. The concept of client and server is integral to the operation of the X Window System, with the X server responsible for fulfilling requests made of the X Window System applications, or clients. There are hundreds of clients that run under X, some of which are the OpenLook, CDE, and Motif window managers and the applications listed in the table on page 181. X Window System programmers can also write their own clients using tools such as the Tk and Athena widget sets.

The look and feel of an X graphical user interface is determined by an application program called a window manager. Window managers control the appearance and operation of windows, such as how to open, resize, move, and close them. Many X Window System managers have been written, and although they offer different styles of interaction, they have many features in common. Several window managers are available for Solaris systems, including CDE and OpenLook. They are popular because they are easy to use and support the features that most people need without requiring extensive customization.

Part of the power of the X Window System is that applications are independent of window managers; a window manager, such as CDE, is really just another application. As a result, you can run any X application with any window manager. An application does not inherit properties from the window manager. For example the Athena scroll bar used by the **xterm** terminal emulator appears and operates the same way under all window managers; it does not turn into a different style scroll bar when you invoke **xterm** while running a different window manager.

The window managers, and virtually all X applications, are designed to permit users to tailor their work environments in simple or complex ways. Users can designate applications that start automatically, set attributes such as colors and fonts, and even alter the way keyboard strokes and mouse button presses are interpreted. There are many ways to customize your work environment; you can specify desired attributes in your files run by the X server when it starts up, give options that control attributes on the command line starting an application, configure your window manager, and so on.

Review Exercises

1. What is a window manager? Name two X Window System managers, and describe how they differ.

2. What happens if you position the mouse pointer in an **xterm** window's scroll bar and click the middle button? The right button? The left button? Do these techniques work for all scroll bars?

3. Describe three ways to

   a. change the size of a window

   b. delete a window

   c. uncover a small window that is completely obscured by another, larger window

4. If the characters you type do not appear on the screen, what might be wrong? How can you fix it?

5. Given two computer systems that can communicate over a network, **bravo** and **kudos**, explain what the following command line does:

   ```
   bravo% xterm -sb -title bravo -display kudos:0.0 &
   ```

6. Many X applications use the **–fn** option to specify a font. Given that the following **.Xdefaults** entries exist on the system named **bravo** (but not on **kudos**),

   ```
   XTerm*saveLines: 100
   *Font: 10x20
   XTe*title: Terminal Emulator
   ```

   describe fully the characteristics of the **xterm** window that is opened by each of the following (on **bravo**):

   a. using the Xterm entry on the Utilities menu to open a new **xterm** window

   b. giving the command **xterm –sb &**

   c. giving the command **xterm –fn 5x8 &**

   d. giving the command **xterm –display kudos:0.0 &**

   On **kudos** what is the effect of the following command line:

   ```
   $ xterm -display bravo:0.0 &
   ```

7. Add the following customization: When you position the mouse pointer anywhere on the border of a window and press the middle mouse button, that window drops below any of the windows that overlap it.

Networking and the Internet

The communications facilities that link computers together are constantly improving, allowing faster and more economical connections. The earliest computers were stand-alone machines—not interconnected at all. To transfer information from one system to another, you had to store it in some form (usually magnetic tape or paper punch cards), carry it to a second, compatible system, and read it back in. It was a notable advance when computers began to exchange data over serial lines, though the transfer rate was slow (hundreds of bits per second). People quickly invented new ways to take advantage of this computing power, such as electronic mail, news retrieval, and bulletin-board services. With the speed of today's networks, it is normal for a piece of electronic mail to cross the country or even travel halfway around the world in a few seconds.

It would be hard to find a modern computer facility, with more than one computer, that does not include a local area network (LAN) to link the systems together. Solaris systems are typically attached to an Ethernet network. Large computer facilities usually maintain several networks, often of different types, and almost certainly have connections to larger networks (company- or campuswide, and beyond). The Internet is a loosely administered network of networks (an *internetwork*) that links computers on diverse local area networks around the globe. It is the Internet that makes it possible to send an electronic mail message to a colleague located thousands of miles away and receive a reply within minutes. A related term, *intranet* (following), refers to the networking infrastructure within a company or other institution. Intranets are usually private; access to them from external networks may be limited and carefully controlled, typically using firewalls.

A *firewall* prevents certain types of traffic from going in to or out of a network. The implementations of firewalls vary widely, from UNIX machines with two interfaces running custom software to a router with simple access lists to esoteric, vendor-supplied hardware. If your need for privacy is critical, you can meet with a consulting firm that will discuss your security strategy, produce a written implementation policy, and design a firewall for you from scratch. More on security in Appendix C.

You can also use an *extranet* (or *partner net*) to improve your security. A closely related term is virtual private network (VPN). These terms describe ways to connect remote sites securely to a local site. Typically this is done by using the public Internet as a carrier and using encryption as a means of protecting your data in transit. An abridged glossary of networking terms is provided in the following table.

Term	Definition
l2f	**layer 2 forwarding** Cisco's proprietary VPN solution.
bridge	A device for connecting networks at layer 2 (data link) of the Internet protocol model. (Refer to the paragraph following this table.)
extranet	A Web for some subset of users (such as students at a particular school, or engineers working for the same company), an extranet limits access to private information even though it travels on the public Internet.
firewall	A device for policy-based traffic management.
gateway	A generic device used to connect networks. It may be a router, bridge, switch, firewall, or other such device. The previous usage of gateway, to designate a router, is deprecated.
intranet	An inhouse web designed to serve a group of people such as a corporation or school. The general public on the Internet does not have access to the intranet.
internet	A large network that encompasses other, smaller networks.
Internet	The public network of networks.
ISP	**Internet service provider** Provides Internet access to its customers.
L2TP	**layer 2 tunneling protocol** Used for VPNs, an Internet Engineering Task Force (IETF) proposed standard based on PPTP (next).
PPTP	**point-to-point tunneling protocol** Used for setting up VPNs; developed by an industry consortium including Microsoft and 3COM.
router	A device for connecting networks at layer 3 (network) of the Internet protocol model. (Refer to the paragraph following this table.)
sneaker net	Using hand-carried magnetic media to transfer files between machines.
switch	A device for connecting networks at layer 2 or 3. Normally a switch is a special kind of bridge, but newer so-called layer 3 switches perform many of the functions of a router. (Refer to the paragraph following this table.)
VPN	**virtual private network** A private network that exists on a public network such as the Internet. A VPN is a less-expensive substitute for company-owned/leased lines and uses encryption (page 993) to ensure privacy. A nice side effect is that you can send non-Internet protocols such as Appletalk, IPX, or Netbios over the VPN connection by tunneling them through the VPN IP stream.

The Internet protocol model differs from the ISO seven-layer protocol model; it uses a simplified five-layer model that is categorized as follows:

1. The first layer, called the *physical layer,* represents the physical medium (copper, fiber) and the data encoding used to transmit signals on that medium (pulses of light or electrical waves for instance).

2. The second layer, called the *data link layer,* covers media access by network devices, a means of putting data into frames (packets), and error checking and retransmission of damaged frames. Ethernet is at this layer, as is token ring, and FDDI.

3. The third layer, called the *network layer,* frequently uses the IP protocol. It provides for host addressing and routing of packets.

4. The fourth layer, called the *transport layer,* is where the TCP protocol exists. It provides flow control, error detection and correction, and reliability. All packets transmitted at the transport layer are guaranteed to arrive without error and in the correct order.

Anything above this layer is the domain of the application. In the Internet model there is no distinction between application, presentation, and session layers as there is in the ISO model. All of the upper-layer characteristics such as character encoding, encryption, interface, and so on are part of the application.

Speed of throughput is very important to the proper functioning of the Internet. Some of the networks that form the backbone of the Internet have been upgraded in the past few years from 45 megabits per second to 155 or 622 megabits per second and even multiple gigabits (billion of bits) per second to accommodate the ever-increasing demand for network services.

▲ Network Services

Over the past decade many network services emerged and became standard. On Solaris systems, as on other UNIX systems, special processes called *daemons* run constantly to support such services by exchanging specialized messages with other systems over the network. Several software systems have been created to allow computers to share their filesystems with one another, making it appear to users as though remote files are actually stored on disks attached to their local computer. Sharing remote filesystems allows users to share information without knowing where the files physically reside, without making unnecessary copies, and without learning a new set of utilities to manipulate them. Because the files appear to be stored locally, you can use standard utilities (such as **cat**, **vi**, **lpr**, **mv**, or their graphical counterparts) to work with them.

To take advantage of the higher speeds available on computer networks, some new utilities have been created, and existing commands have been extended. The **rwho** utility provides status information about computers and users on a local area network. The **rlogin** and **telnet** utilities allow users to log in on remote computers on their local network or at a distant site through interconnected networks. Users rely on commands such as **rcp** and **ftp** to transfer files from one system to another across the network. Communication utilities, such as electronic mail utilities, **talk**, and Internet Relay Chat (IRC), have been adapted to understand remote network addresses and to set up the connections necessary to exchange information with a remote computer.

▲ Intranets

An *intranet* is a network that connects computing resources at a school, company, or other organization but, unlike the Internet, typically restricts access to those internal users. An intranet is very similar to a local area network, but it is based on Internet technology. It can provide database, email, and web page access to a limited group of people.

The fact that an intranet is able to connect dissimilar machines is one of its strengths. Think of all the machines that are on the Internet: Macs, Suns, PCs running Windows 95, PCs running Windows NT, PCs running UNIX (including Solaris), and so on. Each of these machines can communicate via IP (page 191), a common protocol. So it is with an intranet: Different machines can all talk to one another.

Another key difference between the Internet and an intranet is that the Internet will only transmit one protocol suite, the IP protocol suite. An intranet can be set up to use a number of different protocols such as IP, IPX, Appletalk, Decnet, XNS, or various other protocols developed by vendors over the years. Although these protocols cannot be transmitted directly over the Internet, you can set up special gateway boxes in remote sites that allow you to tunnel or encapsulate these protocols into IP packets in order to use them on the public network.

When Jenny was a student, she wanted feedback on an important paper before publishing it. She set up a web page on the university intranet, complete with illustrations, sound clips, hypertext links to references, and so on. Then Jenny put a note in the daily intranet-based newspaper asking for feedback and help with one of the illustrations. In addition she sent email to people who needed to see the paper. Jenny did all this without going public on the Internet with the paper. When it was time to put the work on the Internet, the document was in the right format, so moving it over was a snap.

As with the Internet, the communications potential of intranets is boundless. You can set up a private chat between people at remote locations, access a company database, see what is new at school, or read about the new university president. Companies that developed products for use on the Internet are investing more and more time and money developing intranet software applications as the intranet market explodes.

▲ Common Types of Networks

If a Solaris system is attached to a network today, it is most likely one of three types: Broadcast, token ring, or point-to-point link. On a broadcast network, such as Ethernet, any system attached to the network cable can send a message at any time; each system examines the address in every message and responds to the messages that are addressed to it. Because there are multiple systems on the cable and any one of them can send a message at any time, messages sometimes collide and become garbled. When that happens the sending systems notice the problem and resend, after waiting a short (but random) amount of time to try to avoid another collision. The extra network traffic that results from collisions can put quite a load on the network; if the collision rate gets too high, the retransmissions result in more collisions, and the network becomes unusable.

Token Ring was designed as an end station technology and popularized by IBM. On a token-based network, such as Fiber Distributed Data Interface (FDDI), only one system can send a message at any time. A token (a small, special message) is constantly being passed from one host to the next, around the ring. A system can send a message only if it currently has the token. This prevents the collision problems that are troublesome in broadcast networks, but it can have a serious impact on performance if the ring is large (a host may have to wait a long time before it gets the token that allows it to send a message). Another drawback is that if the ring breaks, the token passing is interrupted, and none of the systems can transmit a message.

It is because of the ring failure scenario that nodes are often connected to a central box called a concentrator. A concentrator acts much like a switch: If it detects that a segment of the ring has failed, it will pare off the bad part and reconstitute a whole ring. In this sense the ring is an artificial, logical construction only. If the token is lost in the process, each host engages in a special procedure to create a new token via a voting process. Another technique is to connect each host to the ring in a bidirectional manner. There are two rings, one with the token circulating in a clockwise manner, and the other in a counterclockwise manner. If one ring fails, the other one can keep operating. In these ways ring-based networks can be made more resilient.

A number of ring-based networks are in use today. The most popular of these are FDDI and Token Ring. FDDI specified a bandwidth of 100 megabits per second and fiber optic cable as the medium for connection to the ring. These specifications gained it wide popularity as a backbone technology but made it very expensive. FDDI did not become the popular network choice for many reasons, most relating to cost: Fiber optic cable is more expensive and difficult to work with than copper cable, and the computer interfaces that attach to the cable are also more expensive. FDDI has been largely supplanted by 100BaseT, although there are still sizable segments of FDDI in existence. Copper Distributed Data Interface (CDDI) was proposed as a means of running the FDDI protocols on copper cable, but it never prevailed.

Whereas FDDI was designed as a network backbone technology, Token Ring was designed as an end-station technology. Token Ring networks have recently undergone some evolutionary changes with the advent of switches and higher access speeds, but there are many fewer installations of Token Ring networks than Ethernet ones.

A point-to-point link does not seem like much of a network at all, because only two endpoints are involved. However most connections to wide area networks are through point-to-point links, using wire cable, radio, or satellite links. The advantage of a point-to-point link is that the traffic on the link is limited and well understood, because only two systems are involved. A disadvantage is that each system can typically be equipped for a small number of such links, and it is impractical and costly to establish point-to-point links that connect every computer to all the rest.

Point-to-point links often make use of serial lines and modems but can use personal computer parallel ports for faster links between Solaris systems. The use of a modem with a point-to-point link allows an isolated system to connect into a larger network inexpensively.

The most common types of point-to-point links are the ones used to connect to the Internet and to connect the Internet to itself. Serial lines such as T-1, T-3, ATM links, and ISDN are all point to point. Also in this category are new technologies such as the xDSL suite (ADSL, XDSL, SDSL, HDSL, and more).

▲▲ Local Area Networks (LANs)

Local area networks, as the name implies, are confined to a relatively small area—within a single computer facility, building, or campus. Today most LANs run over copper or fiber optic cable, but other technologies, such as infrared (similar to most television remote control devices) and radio wave, are also available.

▲▲▲ Ethernet

If a Solaris system is connected to a LAN today, that network is probably an Ethernet that can support rates from 10 megabits to 1 gigabit per second (with future speed enhancements planned). Due to computer load, competing network traffic, and networking overhead, file transfer rates on an Ethernet are always lower than the specified transfer rate.

Computers communicate over networks using unique addresses that are assigned by system software. A message sent by a computer, called a *packet, frame,* or *datagram,* includes the address of the destination computer (as well as the sender's return address). On an Ethernet each computer checks the destination address in every packet that is transmitted on that network. When a computer finds its own address as the destination, it processes that packet appropriately. If a packet's destination address is not on the local network, it must be passed on to another network by a router (see "Internetworking through Gateways and Routers" below). A router may be a general-purpose computer or a special-purpose device that is attached to multiple networks to act as a gateway among them.

The Ethernet network is typically composed of one of three types of copper cabling, though it is also possible to use fiberoptic (glass) cable with special equipment. In the original design each computer was attached to a thick coaxial cable (sometimes called *thicknet*) at tap points spaced at six-foot intervals along the cable. The thick cable was awkward to deal with, so other solutions were developed: A thinner coaxial cable known as *thinnet* or 10Base2, as well as devices to run Ethernet over unshielded twisted pair (referred to as UTP, Category 3, Category 5 [also cat 3 and cat 5], 10BaseT, or 100BaseT) wire—similar to the type of wire used for telephone lines and serial data communications. IBM even developed a standard to run Ethernet over shielded twisted pair cable (Type-1). Its use has gradually waned over the years as well. Newer specifications (cat 6 and cat 7) are being standardized for 100Mb/sec. and faster networking.

Ethernet technology continues to advance. One solution for improving the network throughput to individual computers uses a device known as an Ethernet switch. A computer attached to an unshared switched Ethernet segment can use the full 10 megabits of network bandwidth. With each computer isolated on its own network cable, the switch takes care of distributing data packets only to those segments with the hosts that should receive them. Full duplex Ethernet further improves things by eliminating collisions. Each host can transmit and receive simultaneously at 10Mb/sec. for an effective bandwidth between hosts of 20Mb/sec.

▲▲ Wide Area Networks (WANs)

As the name implies, a wide area network covers a large geographic area. The technologies used for local area networks (such as Ethernet or FDDI) were designed to work over limited distances and for a certain number of host connections. A WAN may span long distances over dedicated data lines (leased from a telephone company) or radio or satellite links. Wide area networks are often used to interconnect local area networks. Major Internet service providers rely on WANs to connect to customers within a country and around the globe.

Some networks do not fit into either the local or wide area network designation: A metropolitan area network (MAN) is one that is contained in a smaller geographic area, such as a city. Like wide area networks, MANs are typically used to interconnect local area networks.

▲▲ Internetworking through Gateways and Routers

A local area network connects to a wide area network through a *gateway*. A gateway is a generic term for a computer or another special device with multiple network connections. The purpose of the gateway is to convert the data traffic from the format used on the LAN to that used on the WAN. Data that crosses the country today from one Ethernet to another over a WAN, for example, is repackaged from the Ethernet format to a different format that can be processed by the communications equipment that makes up the WAN backbone. When it reaches the end of its journey over the WAN, another gateway converts the data to the format appropriate for the receiving network. For the most part these details are of concern only to the network administrators; the end user does not need to know anything about how the data transfer is carried out.

A *router* is the most common form of a gateway. Routers play an important role in internetworking. Just as you might study a map to plan your route when you need to drive to an unfamiliar place, a computer needs to know how to deliver a message to a system attached to a distant network by passing through intermediary systems and networks along the way. You can imagine using a giant network road map to choose the route that your data should follow, but a static map of computer routes is usually a poor choice for a large data network. Computers and networks along the route you choose may be overloaded or down, without providing a detour for your message. Routers communicate with one another dynamically, keeping each other informed about which routes are open for use. To extend the analogy this would be like heading out on your car trip without ever consulting a map; instead you would stop at one highway information center after another and get directions to find the next one. Although it would take a while to make the stops, each center would advise you of bad traffic, closed roads, and alternate routes. The stops the data makes are much quicker than those you would make in your car.

Figure 7-1 shows an example of how local area networks might be set up at three sites interconnected by a wide area network (Internet). In network diagrams such as this, rings are typically drawn as such; Ethernet LANs are usually drawn as straight lines, with devices attached at right angles; wide area networks are represented as clouds, indicating that the details have been left out. Modem connections are drawn as zigzag lines with breaks, indicating the connection may be intermittent. In Figure 7-1 a gateway or a router relays messages between each LAN and the Internet. Three of the routers in the Internet are shown (for example the one closest to each site). Site A has a server, a workstation, an X-terminal, and a PC sharing a single Ethernet. Site B has two LANs: One Ethernet, which serves a printer and three Solaris workstations, and one FDDI ring that includes two servers, two routers, and a workstation. One of the routers passes data between the Ethernet and the FDDI ring. At Site C are three LANs, linked by a single router. Site C's FDDI ring includes a server and two Solaris workstations. There are two Ethernet segments at site C, perhaps to reduce the traffic load that would result if they were combined or to keep workgroups or locations on separate networks. One Ethernet includes a printer, a PC, and a workstation; the other supports two Solaris workstations, a printer, and a terminal server. A terminal server is a device that attaches serial devices, such as modems and character-based terminals, to a network.

▲▲ Network Protocols

To exchange information over a network, computers must communicate using a common language called a *protocol*. The protocol determines the format of the message packet. The predominant network protocol used by UNIX/Solaris systems is TCP/IP, which is an abbreviation for Transmission Control Protocol/Internet Protocol. If you think of IP as the native language of the Internet, then TCP represents one of many specialized dialects. Network services that need highly reliable connections, such as **rlogin** and **rcp**, tend to use TCP/IP. Another protocol used for some system services is UDP, the User Datagram Protocol. Network services such as **rwho** tend to operate satisfactorily with the simpler UDP protocol.

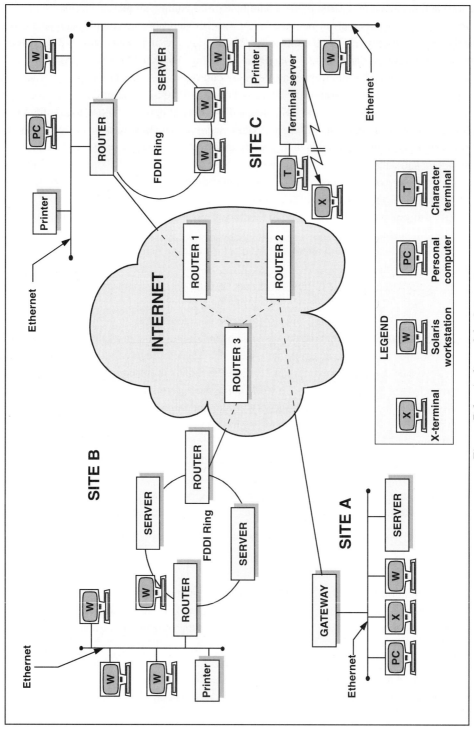

Figure 7-1   A slice of the Internet

Other network protocols you might use with Solaris are SLIP (Serial Line Internet Protocol) and PPP (Point-to-Point Protocol). SLIP and PPP both provide serial line point-to-point connections that support the standard Internet Protocol (IP). These protocols were designed to work efficiently over serial lines, in part by compressing/decompressing data to make the most of the limited bandwidth available on these lines. Because they were designed to support the Internet Protocol, any IP-based service runs successfully over these connections (such as TCP or UDP).

Two protocols that speed up work over serial lines are Xremote and LBX. Xremote compresses the X Window System protocol so that it is more efficient over slower serial lines. LBX (low bandwidth X) is based on the Xremote technology and is a part of the X Window System release X11R6.

▲▲ Host Addresses

Each computer interface is identified by a unique address, or host number, on its network. If a system is attached to more than one network, it has multiple interfaces, each with a unique address—one for each network.

Each packet of information that is broadcast over the network has a destination address. All hosts on the network must process each broadcast packet to see if it is addressed to that host.[1] If the packet is addressed to a given host, the host continues to process it. If not, the host ignores it.

The address you see on most Solaris systems is an IP (Internet Protocol) address, which is represented as one number broken into four segments separated by periods (for example **192.192.192.5**). The address assignments are handled by a central authority named the Network Information Center (NIC or InterNIC).[2] The NIC rarely gets involved in handing out addresses for individual host computers; instead when an organization registers with the NIC, it receives a block (range) of addresses that it can use as needed. An individual who connects a system to the Internet through a dialup link to a commercial service provider does not contact the NIC for an address but uses one assigned by the service provider. Often this address is dynamically assigned by the service provider on an as needed basis, which allows inactive addresses to be reused.

How a company uses IP addresses is determined by the system or network administrator. For example the leftmost two sets of numbers in an IP address might represent a large network (campus- or companywide); the third set could specify a subnetwork (perhaps a department or single floor in a building), and the rightmost number could identify an individual computer. The operating system uses the address in a different, lower-level form (converting it first to a binary equivalent, a series of 1s and 0s). See the following Optional section for more information.

---

1. Contrast broadcast packets to unicast packets: The Ethernet hardware filters out unicast packets that are not addressed to a given machine, and the operating system on that machine never even gets a chance to look at them.

2. The InterNIC (**www.internic.net**) is a cooperative activity between the U.S. Government and Network Solutions, Inc. (**www.netsol.com/nsi**).

Start Optional

If any of the following terms are not familiar to you, refer to the Glossary (page 1025) before reading this optional section: *broadcast address, IP multicast, netmask, network address, network segment, subnet, subnet address,* and *subnet mask.*

To facilitate routing on the Internet, IP addresses are divided into *classes.* Classes, labeled *class A* through *class E,* allow the Internet address space to be broken into blocks of small, medium, and large networks that can be assigned based on the number of hosts within a network.

When you need to send a message to an address outside your network, your system looks up the address block/class in its routing table and sends the message to the next router on the way to the final destination. Every router along the way does a similar lookup to forward the message. At the destination, local routers direct the message to the specific address. Without classes and blocks your host would have to know every network and subnetwork address on the Internet before it could send a message. This would be impractical because of the number of addresses on the Internet.

Each of the four numbers that make up the IP address is in the range of 0–255 because each segment of the IP address is represented by 8 bits (for a total of 32 bits), each capable of taking on two values, that is $2^8 = 256$. When you start counting at zero in place of one, the highest value is 255.[3] Each IP address is broken down into a net address (*netid*) portion (which is part of the class) and a host address (*hostid*) portion.

Class	Start Bits	Address Range	All Bits (including start bits) 0–7	8–15	16–23	24–31
Class A	0	001.000.000.000–126.000.000.000	0-**netid**	---------------------**hostid**-		
Class B	10	129.000.000.000–191.255.000.000	10--------**netid**--	----------**hostid**--		
Class C	110	192.000.000.000–223.255.255.000	110-----------------**netid**--	-**hostid**		
Class D (Multicast)	1110	224.000.000.000–239.255.255.000	1110			
Class E (Reserved)	11110	240.000.000.000–255.255.255.000	11110			

Figure 7-2   IP addresses: Ranges and classes

The first set of addresses, defining class A networks, is for extremely large corporations or ISPs, such as General Electric (3.0.0.0) and Hewlett-Packard (15.0.0.0). One start bit (0) in the first position designates

---

3. Internally the IP address is represented as a set of 4 unsigned 8-bit fields, or a 32-bit unsigned number depending on how programs are using it. The most common format in C is to represent it as a union of an unsigned 32-bit long integer, 4 unsigned chars, and 2 unsigned short integers.

a class A network, 7 bits hold the network portion of the address (netid), and 24 bits hold the host portion of the address (hostid, Figure 7-2). This means that GE can have 2^{24} or approximately 16 million hosts on its network. Subnets and unused address space lower this number quite a bit.

The 127.0.0.0 subnet is reserved (page 197) as are 128.0.0.0 and several others.

Two start bits (10) in the first two positions designate a class B network, 14 bits hold the network portion of the address (**netid**), and 16 bits hold the host portion of the address (**hostid**, Figure 7-2) for a potential total of 65,534 hosts. A class C network uses 3 start bits (110), 21 **netid** bits (2 million networks), and 8 **hostid** bits (254 hosts). Today a new large customer will not receive a class A or B network but is likely to receive a class C, or several (usually contiguous) class C networks if merited.

There are several other classes of networks too. Class D networks are reserved for multicast networks. If you run **netstat –nr** on your Solaris system, you will see that your machine is a member of a multicast network. The 224.0.0.0 in the `Destination` column that **netstat** displays is a class D, multicast address (Figure 7-2). A multicast is like a broadcast, but only hosts that subscribe to the multicast group receive the message. To use WWW terminology a broadcast is like a push. A host pushes a broadcast on the network and every host on the network must check every broadcast to see if it contains relevant data. A multicast is like a pull. A host will only see a multicast if it registers itself as subscribed to a multicast group or service and pulls the appropriate packets from the network.

Because a class B network uses 16 bits for the hostid, the total number of possible hosts should be 2^{16} (65,536) and not 65,534, as indicated earlier. In a similar manner Class C networks use 8 bits to determine the host, which should give you 256 hosts, not 254. With no subnets (see next section) in place, this is the maximum number of hosts that you can have on each of these types of networks. These values are two less than expected because the first and last addresses on any network are reserved. The 0 host address (for example 194.16.100.0 for a class C or 131.204.0.0 for a class B) is reserved as a designator for the network itself. Also there are several old operating systems that use this as a broadcast address. The 255 host address (for example, 194.16.100.255 for a class C or 131.204.255.255 for a class B) is reserved as the IP broadcast address. An IP *datagram* (packet) that is sent to this address is broadcast to all hosts on the network.

Figure 7-3 shows some of the computations for IP address 131.204.027.027. Each address in this figure is shown in decimal, hexadecimal, and binary. Binary is the easiest to work with for logical computations. The next three lines show the subnet mask in three formats. Next the IP address and the subnet mask are logically ANDed together to yield the subnet number (which is subsequently shown in three formats). The last three lines show the broadcast address which is computed by taking the subnet number and turning the hostid bits to 1s. The subnet number is the name/number of your local network. The subnet number and the subnet mask determine what range the IP address of your machine must be in. They are also used by routers to segment traffic (see *network segment* on page 1040). A broadcast on this network will go to all hosts in the range 131.204.27.1 through 131.204.27.254, but will be acted on only by hosts that have a use for it.

▲▲ Subnets

Each host on a network must process each broadcast to determine if the information in the broadcast packet is useful to that host. If there are a large number of hosts on a network, each host must process many packets. To maintain efficiency most networks, particularly shared media networks such as Ethernet, need to be split

	----------Class B-------		netid	hostid	
IP Address	131	.204	.027	.027	decimal
	8C	CC	1B	1B	hexadecimal
	1000 1100	1100 1100	0001 1011	0001 1011	binary
Subnet Mask	255	.255	.255	.000	decimal
	FF	FF	FF	00	hexadecimal
	1111 1111	1111 1111	1111 1111	0000 0000	binary
IP Address AND	1000 1100	1100 1100	0001 1011	0001 1011	decimal
Subnet Mask	1111 1111	1111 1111	1111 1111	0000 0000	hexadecimal
= Subnet Number	1000 1100	1100 1100	0001 1011	0000 0000	binary
Subnet Number	131	.204	.027	.000	decimal
	83	CC	1B	00	hexadecimal
	1000 0011	1100 1100	0001 1011	0000 0000	binary
Broadcast Address	131	.204	.27	.255	decimal
(Set host bits to 1)	83	CC	1B	FF	hexadecimal
	1000 0011	1100 1100	0001 1011	1111 1111	binary

Figure 7-3   Computations for IP address 131.204.027.027

into subnetworks (or *subnets*).[4] The more hosts on a network, the more dramatically network performance is impacted. You need to subnet (divide the network) into smaller networks to create self-contained broadcast domains.

A *subnet mask* (or *address mask*) is a bit mask that allows you to identify which parts of an IP address correspond to the network address and subnet portion of the address. This mask has 1s in positions corresponding to the network and subnet numbers and 0s in the host number positions. When you logically AND an IP address and a subnet mask (Figure 7-3), the result is an address that contains everything but the host address (hostid) portion.

---

4. This is also an issue with other protocols, particularly Appletalk.

There are several ways to represent a subnet mask: A class B network could have a subnet mask of 255.255.255.0 (decimal), FFFFFF00 (hexadecimal), or 8 (the number of bits used for the subnet mask, excluding the class B 16 bits). This yields $2^8 - 2$ ($256 - 2 = 254$) networks[5] with $2^8 - 2$ ($256 - 2 = 254$) hosts[6] on each network. If you do use a subnet mask, you need to add it to the **/etc/netmasks** file or the equivalent Network Information Service (NIS) or NIS+ database. Refer to the **netmasks man** page and example in the **/etc/netmasks** file.

For example when you divide the class C address 192.25.4.0 into 6 subnets, you get a subnet mask of 255.255.255.224, FFFFFFE0, or 3. The 6 resultant networks are (skip 192.25.4.0) 192.25.4.32, 192.25.4.64, 192.25.4.96, 192.25.4.128, 192.25.4.160, and 192.25.4.192 (skip 192.25.4.224). There is a Web-based subnet mask calculator that you can use to calculate subnet masks (page 968). To use this calculator to determine the preceding subnet mask, use an IP Host Address of 192.25.4.0 and set **Maximum Possible Subnets** to 6.

People generally find it easier to work with symbolic names rather than numbers, and Solaris systems provide several ways to associate hostnames with IP addresses. The oldest method is to consult a list of names and addresses that are stored in the **/etc/hosts** file.

```
$ cat /etc/hosts
127.0.0.1     localhost
130.128.52.1  gw-tcorp.tcorp.com gw-tcorp
130.128.52.2  bravo.tcorp.com bravo
130.128.52.3  hurrah.tcorp.com hurrah
130.128.52.4  kudos.tcorp.com kudos
```

The address 127.0.0.1 is reserved for the special hostname **localhost**, which serves as a hook for the system's networking software to operate on the local machine without actually going out onto a physical network. The names of the other systems are shown in two forms: First in a *fully qualified domain* format that is meant to be unique, and second as a nickname that is unique locally but is probably not unique over all the systems attached to the global Internet.

As more hosts joined networks, storing these name-to-address mappings in a regular text file (**/etc/hosts**) proved to be inefficient and inconvenient. The file grew ever larger and impossible to keep up to date. Solaris supports Network Information Service (NIS [page 218]) and NIS+, which were developed for use on Sun computers. Each of these network services stores information in a database. These solutions make it easier to find a specific address, but are only useful for host information within a single administrative domain. Hosts outside the domain cannot access the information. The most popular solution is the Domain Name Service (DNS [page 217]). The Domain Name Service effectively addresses the efficiency and update issues by arranging the entire network naming space as a hierarchy. Each domain in the DNS manages its own

---

5. The first and last networks are reserved in a manner similar to the first and last host, although the standard is flexible. You can configure your router(s) to reclaim the first and last networks in a subnet. Different routers have different techniques for reclaiming these networks.

6. Subtract 2 because the first and last host address on every network are reserved.

name space (addressing and name resolution), and each domain can easily query for any host or IP address by following the tree up or down the name space until the appropriate domain is found. By providing a hierarchical naming structure, DNS distributes name administration across the entire Internet.

The explosive growth of the Internet has uncovered deficiencies in the design of the current address plan. Over the next few years, a revised protocol will gradually be phased in. This protocol is named IPng (IP Next Generation) or IPv6 (IP version 6). This new scheme has been designed to overcome the major limitations of the current approach and can be phased in gradually, because it is compatible with the existing address usage. IPv6 makes it possible to assign many more unique Internet addresses and offers support for security and performance control features.

The Internet and its accompanying suite of protocols are described in standards and documents called RFCs (request for comments). Submitting an RFC, which describes the practical implementation aspects of the IP suite, is a way to publish a standard to the Internet community and get comments. Many, but not all, of the RFCs are full-fledged standards. The complete list of RFCs is available on the Internet (page 964).

▲ Communicating over the Network

Many commands that you can use to communicate with other users on a single computer system have been extended so that they work over the network. Three examples of extended utilities are electronic mail programs (such as **pine**), **finger**, and **talk** (introduced in Chapter 3). These utilities are each examples of the UNIX philosophy: Instead of creating a new, special-purpose tool, modify an existing one.

These utilities understand a common convention for the format of network addresses: **user@host** (often read as *user at host*). When you use an @ sign in an argument to one of these commands, the utility interprets the text that follows as the name of a remote host computer. When your command-line argument does not include an @ sign or hostname, it assumes that you are requesting information from or corresponding with someone on your local host (as shown in Chapter 3).

The prompts shown in the examples in this chapter differ from the simple prompts carried through the rest of this book in that they include the hostname of the machine you are using. If you frequently use more than one system over a network, you may find it hard to keep track of which system you are using at any particular moment. If you set your prompt to include the hostname of the current system, it will always be clear which system you are using. To identify the computer you are using, run **hostname** or **uname –a**.

```
% hostname
kudos
```

See pages 373 (**sh** and **ksh**) and 462 (**csh**) for information on how you can change your prompt when you use each of the shells.

▲▲ finger: Learn about Remote Users

The **finger** utility displays information about users on remote systems. It was originally designed for local use, but when networks became popular, it was obvious that **finger** should be enhanced to reach out and collect information remotely. In this example **finger** displays information about all the users logged in on the system named **bravo**:

```
kudos% finger @bravo
[bravo.tcorp.com]
Login     Name                TTY         Idle   When     Where
root      Super-User          console     1:35 Fri  5:00  :0
alex      Alex Watson         pts/4            Fri 12:23  kudos.tcorp.com
alex      Alex Watson         pts/5        19 Fri 12:33  :0.0
jenny     Jenny Chen          pts/7      2:24 Fri  8:45  :0.0
hls       Helen Simpson       pts/11        2 Fri 12:23  :0.0
```

A user's name (or login name) in front of the @ sign causes **finger** to retrieve the information from the remote system only for the user you have specified. If there are multiple matches for that name on the remote system, **finger** displays the results for all of them.

```
kudos% finger alex@bravo
[bravo.tcorp.com]
Login     Name                TTY         Idle   When     Where
alex      Alex Watson         pts/4            Fri 12:23  kudos.tcorp.com
alex      Alex Watson         pts/5        19 Fri 12:33  :0.0
```

The **finger** utility works by querying a standard network service, the **fingerd** daemon, that runs on the remote system. Although this service is supplied with Solaris, some sites choose not to run it to minimize load on their systems, reduce security risks, or maintain privacy. If you try to use **finger** to obtain information about someone at such a site, the result may be an error message or nothing at all. It is the remote **fingerd** daemon that determines how much information to share with your system and in what format. As a result, the report displayed for any given system may differ from the preceding examples.

The **fingerd** Daemon

The **finger** daemon (**fingerd**) gives away information about accounts on the system that can be used by would-be hackers. Some sites disable **finger** and randomize user account ids to make a hacker's job harder.

The information for remote **finger** looks much the same as it does when **finger** runs on your local system, with one difference: Before displaying the results **finger** reports the name of the remote system that answered the query (**bravo**, as shown in brackets in the preceding example). The name of the host that answers may be different from the system name you specified on the command line, depending on how the **finger** daemon service is configured at the remote end. In some cases several hostnames may be listed if one **finger** daemon contacts another to retrieve the information.

Some remote sites have special services that you can contact using **finger**. For example you can retrieve information about recent earthquakes from a system run by the U.S. Geological Survey. (The information is kept in the **.plan** file of the user **quake** at the specified location.)

```
$ finger quake@gldfs.cr.usgs.gov
[gldfs.cr.usgs.gov]
Login name: quake                    In real life: see Ray Buland
Directory: /home/quake               Shell: /home/quake/run_quake
Last login Mon Dec 21 12:40 on ttyp0 from mhagd.production
No unread mail
Plan:
The following near-real-time Earthquake Bulletin is provided by the National
Earthquake Information Service (NEIS) of the U. S. Geological Survey as part of
a cooperative project of the Council of the National Seismic System.  For
a description of the earthquake parameters listed below, the availability of
additional information, and our publication criteria, please finger
qk_info@gldfs.cr.usgs.gov.
Updated as of Wed Dec 23 13:47:10 MST 1998.


DATE-(UTC)-TIME     LAT     LON     DEP    MAG   Q   COMMENTS
yy/mm/dd hh:mm:ss   deg.    deg.    km
98/12/20 12:23:57   54.03N 168.14W 118.0  4.0Mb B   FOX ISLANDS, ALEUTIAN ISLANDS
98/12/20 20:51:53    4.85S 102.06E  33.0  5.3Mb C   SOUTHERN SUMATERA, INDONESIA
98/12/21 04:56:56   13.90N 145.43E 100.0  4.8Mb B   MARIANA ISLANDS
98/12/21 10:04:17   51.91N 179.52W 127.2  4.1Mb C   ANDREANOF ISL, ALEUTIAN IS.
98/12/21 13:10:57   51.24N 176.36W  33.0  3.9Mb C   ANDREANOF ISL, ALEUTIAN IS.
98/12/22 01:17:46   48.02N 115.23W  10.0  4.5Md A   MONTANA
98/12/22 01:49:06   24.32N 122.73E  61.6  4.8Mb B   TAIWAN REGION
98/12/22 02:24:45   35.92N  70.20E  90.8  5.1Mb B   HINDU KUSH REGION, AFGHANISTAN
98/12/22 04:51:14   35.91N  33.81E  25.0  4.4Ml     <GII> CYPRUS REGION
98/12/22 10:06:23   25.96S 176.24W  33.0  5.0Mb C   SOUTH OF FIJI ISLANDS
98/12/22 10:34:55   51.97N 176.58E  33.0  3.9Mb C   RAT ISLANDS, ALEUTIAN ISLANDS
98/12/22 12:28:12   52.83N 144.61W  10.0  4.2Mb A   SOUTH OF ALASKA
98/12/22 13:41:34   43.10N 126.75W  10.0  4.1Mb B   OFF COAST OF OREGON
98/12/22 17:04:33   80.08N  89.29W  10.0  4.4Mb B   QUEEN ELIZABETH ISL, CANADA
98/12/22 17:20:11    0.32S  99.27E  33.0  5.1Mb C   SOUTHERN SUMATERA, INDONESIA
98/12/22 22:07:52   25.02S 179.58E 495.0  5.0Mb B   SOUTH OF FIJI ISLANDS
98/12/23 04:51:04   34.20N  25.67E  33.0  4.3Ml B   CRETE
98/12/23 15:14:07   17.55N  94.52W 144.6  4.5Mb B   CHIAPAS, MEXICO
98/12/23 15:14:47   37.48N 118.81W   9.2  3.0Md     <GM> CALIFORNIA-NEVADA BDR RE
98/12/23 16:20:58   40.49N  42.70E  10.0  4.3Mb B   TURKEY
98/12/23 20:01:56   18.90S 169.12E 300.0  4.8Mb C   VANUATU ISLANDS
```

▲▲ Sending Mail to a Remote User

If you know a user's login name on a remote system and the name of the remote system or its domain, you can use an electronic mail program such as **dtmail** or **mailtool** (both on page 61) to send a message over the network or the Internet using the @ form of address as follows:

```
jenny@bravo
```

or

```
jenny@tcorp.com
```

▲▲ talk: with a Remote User

Similarly you can communicate interactively with a remote user over the network by using the **talk** utility (page 59).

```
kudos% talk jenny@bravo
```

Although the @ form of network address is recognized by many Solaris utilities, you may find that you can reach more remote computers with electronic mail than with the other networking utilities described in this chapter. The reason for this disparity is that the mail system can deliver a message to a host that does not run the Internet Protocol (IP), even though it appears to have an Internet address. The message may be routed over the network, for example, until it reaches a remote system that has a point-to-point, dialup connection to the destination system. Other utilities, such as **talk**, rely on the Internet Protocol, and operate only between networked hosts.

▲▲ Mailing List Servers

A mailing list server (listserv[7]) allows you to create, manage, and administrate an electronic mailing list. This type of mailing list provides a means for people interested in a topic to participate in an electronic discussion and for a person periodically to disseminate information to a potentially large mailing list. One of the most powerful features of most list servers is the ability to archive email postings to the list, create an archive index, and retrieve postings from the archive based on key words or discussion threads. Typically there is a means for you to subscribe and unsubscribe from the list with or without human intervention. The owner of the list can restrict who can subscribe, unsubscribe, and post messages to the list. Popular list servers include LIST-SERV, Majordomo, SmartList, Mailman, and ListProc. See page 966 or use a browser to search on each of these names for lists of lists and more information.

▲ Networking Utilities

To make use of a networked environment, it made sense to extend certain tools—some of which have already been described in this chapter. Networks also created a need for new utilities to control and monitor them and led to ideas for new tools that took advantage of their speed and connectivity. The commands described in this section were created for systems attached to a network; without a network connection they are of little use.

---

7. Although the term *listserv* is sometimes used generically to include many different list server programs, it is actually a specific product and a registered trademark of L-soft International, Inc.: LISTSERV (**www.l-soft.com**).

▲▲ ping: Test a Network Connection

The **ping** utility sends a particular kind of IP data packet to a remote computer that causes the remote system to send back a reply. This is a quick way to verify that a remote system is available, as well as to check how well the network is operating, such as how fast it is or whether it is dropping data packets. The protocol **ping** uses is ICMP (Internet Control Message Protocol). The name **ping** mimics the sound of a sonar burst used by submarines to identify and communicate with each other. Without any options **ping** tests the connection to the remote system once and reports back. With the **–s** option **ping** tests the connection once per second until you abort the execution with CONTROL-C.

```
kudos% /usr/sbin/ping tsx-11.mit.edu
tsx-11.mit.edu is alive
```

```
kudos% /usr/sbin/ping -s tsx-11.mit.edu
PING tsx-11.mit.edu: 56 data bytes
64 bytes from TSX-11.MIT.EDU (18.86.0.44): icmp_seq=0. time=128. ms
64 bytes from TSX-11.MIT.EDU (18.86.0.44): icmp_seq=1. time=117. ms
64 bytes from TSX-11.MIT.EDU (18.86.0.44): icmp_seq=2. time=117. ms
64 bytes from TSX-11.MIT.EDU (18.86.0.44): icmp_seq=3. time=115. ms
64 bytes from TSX-11.MIT.EDU (18.86.0.44): icmp_seq=4. time=121. ms
CONTROL-C
----tsx-11.mit.edu PING Statistics----
5 packets transmitted, 5 packets received, 0% packet loss
round-trip (ms)  min/avg/max = 115/119/128
kudos%
```

In these examples the remote system named **tsx-11.mit.edu** is up and available to you over the network.

By default **ping** sends packets containing 64 bytes (56 data bytes and 8 bytes of protocol header information). In the preceding example five packets were sent to the system **tsx-11.mit.edu** before the user interrupted **ping** by pressing CONTROL-C. The four-part number in parentheses on each line is the remote system's IP address. A packet sequence number is also given (called **icmp_seq**). If a packet is dropped, a gap occurs in the sequence numbers. The round-trip time is listed last, in milliseconds; this represents the time that elapsed from when the packet was sent from the local system to the remote system until the reply from the remote system was received by the local system. This time is affected by the distance between the two systems as well as by other network traffic and the load on both computers. Before it terminates **ping** summarizes the results—indicating how many packets were sent and received, as well as the minimum, average, and maximum round-trip delays it measured.

When ping Cannot Connect

If **ping** is unable to contact the remote system, and you are using the **–s** option, **ping** continues trying until you interrupt it with CONTROL-C. There may be several reasons why a system does not answer. For example the remote computer may be down, the network interface or some part of the network between your systems may be broken, or there may be a software failure.

▲▲ rlogin, telnet: Access a Remote Computer

If you have an account on a remote system, you can use the **rlogin** utility to connect to it over the network and log in. You might choose to use a remote system to access a special-purpose application or device that is available only on that system, or because you know that the remote system is faster or not as busy as your local computer. When you log out, your connection is broken and you can resume using your local computer. If you are using a window system on your local computer (Chapter 6), you can use many systems simultaneously by logging into each one through a different window.

To use **rlogin** (page 872) you must specify the name of the remote system you want to connect to:

```
kudos% rlogin bravo
Password:
Last login: Sat Sep 14 06:51:59 from kudos.tcorp.com
Sun Microsystems Inc.   SunOS 5.6      Generic August 1997
You have new mail.
bravo%
.
.
.
bravo% logout
rlogin: connection closed.
kudos%
```

You can also use **telnet** to interact with a remote computer. The **telnet** utility is similar to **rlogin**, but it will work in many places where **rlogin** is not available (there is more non-UNIX support for **telnet** access than there is for **rlogin** access).

```
bravo% telnet kudos
Trying 130.128.52.2...
Connected to kudos.tcorp.com
Escape character is '^]'.


SunOS 5.6

login: watson
Password:
Last login: Sat Sep 14 14:46:55 from bravo.tcorp.com
Sun Microsystems Inc.   SunOS 5.6      Generic August 1997
You have new mail.
kudos%
.
.
.
kudos% logout
Connection closed by foreign host.
bravo%
```

When you connect to a remote UNIX or Solaris system through **telnet**, you are presented with a regular `login:` prompt, whereas **rlogin** assumes that your login name on the remote system matches that on your local system. Because **telnet** is designed to work with non-UNIX systems, **telnet** does not make such assumptions. You can specify a different login name with **rlogin** by using the **–l** option:

telnet and rlogin Are Not Secure

Anytime you enter sensitive information, such as your password, while you are using **telnet** or **rlogin**, it can be read by someone who is "listening in" on the session. Refer to **ssh** and **STel** in "Login Security" on page 1002.

```
bravo% rlogin -l watson kudos
Password:
Last login: Sat Sep 14 14:52:06 from kudos.tcorp.com
Sun Microsystems Inc.   SunOS 5.6      Generic August 1997
You have new mail.

kudos% who am i
watson      pts/8         Sep 14 15:41     (bravo.tcorp.com)
kudos%
```

Another difference between these two utilities is that **telnet** allows you to configure many special parameters, such as how RETURNs or interrupts are processed. When using **telnet** between two UNIX/Solaris systems, you rarely need to access or change any parameters.

If you do not specify the name of a remote host on the command line, **telnet** runs in an interactive mode. The following example is equivalent to the previous **telnet** example:

```
bravo% telnet
telnet> open kudos
Trying 130.128.52.2...
Connected to kudos.
Escape character is '^]'.
    .
    .
    .
```

Before **telnet** connects you to a remote system, it tells you what your *escape character* is—in most cases, it is ^] (the ^ represents the CONTROL key on your keyboard). If you press CONTROL-] you escape to **telnet**'s interactive mode. Continuing the preceding example:

```
kudos% CONTROL-]
telnet> ?
```

(displays help information)

```
telnet> close
Connection closed by foreign host.
bravo%
```

When you enter a question mark in response to the telnet> prompt, **telnet** displays a help list of the commands it recognizes. The **close** command ends the current **telnet** session, returning you to your local sys-

tem. To get out of **telnet**'s interactive mode and resume communication with the remote system, press RETURN
in response to a prompt.

It is also possible to use **telnet** to access special remote services at sites that have chosen to make such
services available. For example you can use **telnet** to connect to the U.S. Library of Congress Information
System (LOCIS). The following example is abbreviated.

```
bravo% telnet locis.loc.gov
Trying 140.147.254.3...
Connected to locis.loc.gov.
Escape character is '^]'.
        L O C I S :  LIBRARY OF CONGRESS INFORMATION SYSTEM

          To make a choice: type a number, then press ENTER

    1   Library of Congress Catalog       4   Braille and Audio
    2   Federal Legislation               5   Foreign Law
    3   Copyright Information


        Choice:
1
                        LC CATALOG

CHOICE                                                    FILE
   1   BOOKS cataloged from 1898 to 1949                  LOC1
       (most older records are in PREM, option 4 below)
   2   BOOKS cataloged from 1950 to 1974                  LOC2
   3   BOOKS cataloged since 1975                         LOC3

        Choice:
3

WEDNESDAY, 12/23/98  05:18 P.M.
  TO BROWSE, USE FIRST WORDS OF:            EXAMPLES:
              subject ----------------->    b gardens
              author ------------------>    b faulkner, william
              title ------------------->    b hamlet
              partial LC call no. ----->    b call HB61
  TO SEARCH WORDS/PHRASES ANYWHERE --->     find parks
  TO SEARCH LC RECORD NO. IN LOC3 ---->     loc3 93-13841
    UPDATE:  Index terms are added and updated each night.
      HELP:  Enter HELP for LOC3 info, or HELP COMMANDS for command list.
    READY FOR NEW COMMAND:
sobell

To choose from list, see examples at bottom.          FILE: LOC3
Terms alphabetically close to:SOBELL

B06+Sobell, Linda C//(AUTH=5)
B07 Sobell, Mark B//(AUTH=5)
B08 Sobell, Mark G//(AUTH=10)
B09 Sobell, Morton--//(AUTH=1; SUBJ=3)
    READY:
b08
```

```
ITEMS 1-3 OF 10              SET 2: BRIEF DISPLAY              FILE: LOC3
                           (DESCENDING ORDER)
1. 98-5085: Sobell, Mark G.  Hands-on Linux : featuring Caldera Open Linux
     Lite, Netscape Navigator Gold, and Netscape FastTrack Server on two CDs /
     Reading, Mass. : Addison-Wesley, c1998.  xlviii, 1015 p. : ill. ; 24 cm. +
     1 computer laser optical disc (4 3/4 in.)
     LC CALL NUMBER: QA76.76.063 S5939 1998  <MRC>
2. 97-8248: Sobell, Mark G.  A practical guide to Linux /  Reading, Mass. :
     Addison Wesley, c1997.  xlvii, 1015 p. : ill. ; 24 cm.
     LC CALL NUMBER: QA76.76.063 S5948 1997


NEXT PAGE:          press transmit or enter key
SKIP AHEAD/BACK:    type any item# in set          Example--> 25
FULL DISPLAY:       type DISPLAY ITEM plus an item#  Example--> display item 2
READY:
 quit
bravo%
```

▲▲ Trusted Hosts and the .rhosts File

Some commands, including **rcp** and **rsh**, work only if the remote system trusts[8] your local computer (that is, it believes that your computer is not pretending to be a different system and that your login name on both systems is the same). The **/etc/hosts.equiv** file lists trusted systems; however, the Superuser account does not rely on this file to identify trusted Superusers from other systems.

If your login name is not the same on both systems or if your system is not listed in the remote **/etc/hosts.equiv** file, you can arrange for the remote system to trust you by creating a file named **.rhosts** in your home directory on the remote system. For security reasons the **.rhosts** file must be readable and writable only by the owner (mode 600). Suppose that Alex's login name on the local system, **kudos**, is **alex**; but on the remote system, **bravo**, his login is **watson**. A **.rhosts** file on **bravo** that contains the entry

```
kudos alex
```

allows Alex to use **rcp** to copy files from **kudos** to **bravo** by typing

```
kudos% rcp memo.921 watson@bravo:memos/memo.921
```

Similarly a **.rhosts** file on **kudos** that contains the entry

```
bravo watson
```

permits him to transfer files in the opposite direction.

---

8. Host-based trust is largely obsolete. Because there are many ways to subvert this sort of trust including subverting DNS systems and *spoofing* (where a host pretends to be another host), authentication based on IP address is widely regarded as insecure and obsolete. In a small homogeneous network of machines with local DNS control, it can be "good enough." The ease of use in these situations may outweigh the security concerns.

The system name you specify in **.rhosts** must match the name you see when you run **hostname**. That is, if **hostname** returns **bravo.tcorp.com**, then you must put the fully qualified name in your **.rhosts** file on the remote system.

Do Not Share Your Login Account

You can use a **.rhosts** file to allow another user to log in as you on a remote system without knowing your password. This is not recommended. Do not compromise the security of your files, or the entire system, by sharing your login account.

▲▲ rcp, ftp: Transfer Files over a Network

You can use the **rcp** (remote copy) utility to transfer files between two UNIX/Solaris computers attached to a network. The **rcp** utility works in the same manner as **cp**. In the following example Alex copies **memo.921** from the working directory on **kudos** (the local system) to his **memos** directory on **bravo**. It is assumed that Alex has an account on **bravo** and that a directory named **memos** exists in his home directory there:

```
kudos% rcp memo.921 bravo:memos/memo.921
```

As with **cp**, if Alex had not specified the filename on the remote system in the preceding example, the system would have used the original filename. That is, the following command line is equivalent to the preceding one. Refer to page 870 in Part III for more information on **rcp**.

```
kudos% rcp memo.921 watson@bravo:memos
```

You can also use the **ftp** (file transfer protocol) utility to transfer files between systems on a network. Unlike **rcp**, **ftp** is interactive—it allows you to browse through a directory on the remote system to identify files you may want to transfer. Instead of **rcp** Alex could have used **ftp** to transfer **memo.921** to **bravo**.

```
kudos% ftp bravo
Connected to bravo.tcorp.com.
220 bravo.tcorp.com FTP server (SunOS 5.6) ready.
Name (bravo:alex): watson
331 Password required for watson.
Password:
230 User watson logged in.
ftp> bin
200 Type set to I.
ftp> cd memos
250 CWD command successful.
ftp> put memo.921
200 PORT command successful.
150 Binary data connection for memo.921 (204.94.139.74,35216).
226 Transfer complete.
local: memo.921 remote: memo.921
2337 bytes sent in 0.00098 seconds (2328.80 Kbytes/s)
ftp> quit
221 Goodbye.
bravo%
```

The remote system prompts you for a login name and password. By default it expects that your login name is the same on both systems; just press **RETURN** if it is. In this case it is not, so Alex enters **watson** before pressing **RETURN**. Then he enters his password.

Alex gives a **bin** (binary) command as a matter of habit—he always establishes binary transfer mode as soon as he logs on. With **ftp** in binary mode you can transfer ASCII[9] and binary files. In ASCII mode (the Solaris default) you can only transfer ASCII files successfully.

Before transferring the file Alex uses **ftp**'s **cd** command to change directories *on the remote system* (use **lcd** to change directories on the local system). Then the **put** command followed by the filename transfers the file to the remote system in the remote working directory (**memos**).

Unlike **rcp** the **ftp** utility makes no assumptions about filesystem structure because you can use **ftp** to exchange files with non-UNIX/Solaris systems (whose filenaming conventions may be different).

For more information see "How Do I Use **ftp**?" on page 974.

▲▲▲ Anonymous ftp

Systems often provide **ftp** access to anyone on a network by providing a special login: **anonymous** (you can usually use the login name **ftp** in place of **anonymous**). The anonymous **ftp** user is usually restricted to looking only at a selected portion of a filesystem that has been set aside to hold files that the site administrator wants to share with users on other systems. For complete examples of anonymous **ftp** transfers, see "How Do I Download gzip?" on page 976, "How Do I Use **ftp**?" on page 974, and "Downloading Files" on page 237.

Traditionally any password was acceptable for anonymous **ftp**; by convention you are expected to give your email address. Some sites reject your connection if they cannot identify the name of your computer or if you supply a password that doesn't match up with the name of your site. In this case Alex entered **alex@tcorp.com** in response to the password prompt.

While using **ftp** you can type **help** at any `ftp>` prompt to see a list of commands. Refer to page 765 in Part III for more information on **ftp**.

▲▲ rsh: Run a Command Remotely

The **rsh** utility allows you to run a command on a remote system without logging in. If you need to run more than one command, it is usually easier to log in and run the commands on the remote machine. The next example runs **ls** on the **memos** directory on the remote system **kudos**. It assumes that the user running the command has a login on **kudos** and that **memos** is in the user's home directory on **kudos**.

---

9. Binary mode transfers an exact, byte-for-byte image of a file. ASCII mode performs end-of-line conversions between different systems and is consequently slower than binary mode. (DOS/MS Windows, Macintosh, and UNIX all use different characters to indicate the end of a line of text.) Unless you specifically need to convert the end-of-line characters, use binary mode.

```
bravo% rsh kudos ls memos
memos/memo.draft memos/memo.0921
```

Suppose that there is a file named **memo.new** on your local machine, and you cannot remember whether it contains certain changes to the memo you have been working on, or if you made these changes to the file named **memo.draft** on the system named **kudos**. You could copy **memo.draft** to your local system and run the **diff** utility on the two files, but then you would have three similar copies of the file spread across two systems. If you are not careful about removing the old copies when you are done, you may be confused again in a few days. Instead of copying the file, you can use **rsh**:

```
bravo% rsh kudos cat memos/memo.draft | diff memos.new -
```

When you run **rsh**, standard output of the command run on the remote machine is passed back to your local machine. Unless you quote characters that have special meaning to the shell, they are interpreted by the local machine. In this example the output of the **cat** command on **kudos** is sent through a pipe on **bravo** to **diff**, which compares the local file **memos.new** to standard input (–). The following command line has the same effect but causes the **diff** utility to run on the remote system instead:

```
bravo% cat memos.new | rsh kudos diff - memos/memo.draft
```

Standard output from **diff** on the remote system is sent back to the local system, which displays it on the screen (because it was not redirected).

The **rsh** and **rlogin** utilities are similar; both prompt you to enter a password if the remote system does not trust your local system. As with **rlogin**, **rsh** allows you to specify the login name you use on the remote system if it is different. The following command lists the files in Watson's home directory on **kudos**:

```
bravo% rsh kudos -l watson ls -l
```

If you do not specify a command line to run on the remote system, the **rsh** utility runs **rlogin** for you.

```
bravo% rsh -l watson kudos
Last login: Sat Sep 14 14:58:50 from bravo.tcorp.com
Sun Microsystems Inc.   SunOS 5.6      Generic August 1997
kudos%
```

▲▲ traceroute: Trace a Route over the Internet

The **traceroute** utility (supplied with Solaris 7; source code is available on the Internet for earlier versions of Solaris) traces the route an IP packet follows to its destination (the argument to **traceroute**—an Internet host). It displays a numbered list of host names, if available, and IP addresses together with the round-trip time it took for a packet to get to each router along the way and an acknowledgement to get back. You can put this information to good use if you are trying to determine where a network bottleneck is.

The **traceroute** utility can help you solve routing configuration problems and routing path failures. When you cannot reach a host, use **traceroute** to see what path the packet follows, how far it gets, and what the round trip delay is.

Following is the output of **traceroute** following a route from the local computer to **sun.com**. The first line tells you the IP address of the target, the maximum number of hops that will be traced, and the size of the packets that will be used. Each numbered line contains the name and IP address of the intermediate destination followed by the time it takes a packet to make a round trip to that destination and back. The **traceroute** utility sends three packets to each destination thus there are three times on each line. Line 1 shows the statistics when a packet is sent to the local gateway (under 1.5 ms). Between hops 7 and 8 the packet travels across the United States (San Francisco to Boston). By hop 10 the packet has found Sun, but not **sun.com**. Each asterisk on the eleventh line indicates that traceroute has waited three seconds without a response.

```
traceroute to sun.com (192.9.49.33), 30 hops max, 40 byte packets
 1  gw-localco (204.94.139.65)  1.424 ms  1.395 ms  1.378 ms
 2  localco-ascend (140.174.164.37)  30.883 ms  27.933 ms  27.764 ms
 3  gw.meer.net (140.174.164.1)  29.903 ms  30.596 ms  28.363 ms
 4  core2-serial4-5.mv.best.net (206.184.210.233)  32.404 ms core2-serial4 2.mv.best.net
(140.174.26.9)  56.999 ms  36.942 ms
 5  core1-fe11-0-0.mv.best.net (206.184.188.1)  38.459 ms  31.841 ms  31.695 ms
 6  core1-hssi11-1-0.san-francisco.best.net (206.86.228.90)  41.334 ms  38.734 ms 33.652 ms
 7  bordercore1-hssi0-0-0.SanFrancisco.cw.net (166.48.13.249)  38.177 ms  37.263 ms  43.549 ms
 8  core2.Boston.cw.net (204.70.4.237)  107.587 ms  104.497 ms  111.402 ms
 9  borderx1-fddi-1.Boston.cw.net (204.70.179.52)  104.263 ms  115.013 ms  110.212 ms
10  sun-micro-system.Boston.cw.net (204.70.179.102)  110.829 ms  146.064 ms  114.111 ms
11  * * *
```

▲▲ rwho: List Users on Remote Computers

The **rwho** utility reports the login names of users who are using remote systems. The information is presented in five columns: username, remote system name, the line the user is connected to, when the user logged in, and how long ago the user last typed on the keyboard. If the last column is blank, then the user is actively typing at the terminal. This information is especially useful when users work at individual Solaris workstations rather than on a central computer system; **rwho** is a **who** command that reports on a networkwide, rather than a computer-specific, basis.

```
kudos% rwho
alex      kudos:pts/4    Sep 19 10:54
jenny     bravo:pts/7    Sep 20 10:19    :01
roy       bravo:pts/8    Sep 20 14:24    :33
```

▲▲ nslookup: Query Internet Name Servers

The **nslookup** utility queries Internet domain name servers (DNS). When you start **nslookup**, and when you give it a command, it displays the name and IP address of the default name server that the system you are working on uses. This is where answers to your DNS questions to **nslookup** come from. The **nslookup** command below shows that you are using **mailhost.cs.upstate.edu** and gives its address.

```
$ nslookup

Default Server:  mailhost.cs.upstate.edu
Address:  131.301.89.13
```

The first command to **nslookup** requests the complete name and IP address of a machine named **strangelove**. This machine is on your LAN (its IP address differs from yours only by one). Searching for **strangelove.cs** gives you the same results.

```
> strangelove
Server:   mailhost.cs.upstate.edu
Address:   131.301.89.13

Name:     strangelove.cs.upstate.edu
Address:   131.301.89.12

> strangelove.cs
Server:   mailhost.cs.upstate.edu
Address:   131.301.89.13

Name:     strangelove.cs.upstate.edu
Address:   131.301.89.12
```

The next example shows how to give **nslookup** an IP address in order to look up the name of the machine that uses that address. In this case the address 131.301.89.11 is used by a machine named **darwin** on your LAN.

```
> 131.301.89.11
Server:   mailhost.cs.upstate.edu
Address:   131.301.89.13

Name:     darwin.cs.upstate.edu
Address:   131.301.89.11
```

Next is an example of how to perform a specific query using **nslookup**. Give the **set query** command, as shown, to get **nslookup** to display the MX (mail exchanger) record. The MX record, if present, specifies a mail address for the domain. You can see from the output that **cs.upstate.edu** has two MX records. The lower the preference value, the higher the priority (**dns.cs.upstate.edu** will always be tried before **wilbur**)

```
> set query=MX
> cs.upstate.edu

Server:   mailhost.cs.upstate.edu
Address:   131.301.89.13

cs.upstate.edu     preference = 20, mail exchanger = wilbur.cs.upstate.edu
cs.upstate.edu     preference = 9, mail exchanger = dns.cs.upstate.edu
cs.upstate.edu     nameserver = wilbur.cs.upstate.edu
cs.upstate.edu     nameserver = dns.upstate.edu
cs.upstate.edu     nameserver = dns.cs.upstate.edu
wilbur.cs.upstate.edu internet address = 131.301.110.10
dns.cs.upstate.edu    internet address = 131.301.10.13
dns.upstate.edu   internet address = 131.301.41.3
```

While using **nslookup** you can establish different types of queries. In the following example the first command sets the query type to NS (name server). When you query a domain, you get NS (name server) records. The output displays three name server records.

```
> set query=NS
> cs.upstate.edu
Server:  mailhost.cs.upstate.edu
Address:  131.301.89.13

cs.upstate.edu          nameserver = wilbur.cs.upstate.edu
cs.upstate.edu          nameserver = dns.upstate.edu
cs.upstate.edu          nameserver = dns.cs.upstate.edu
wilbur.cs.upstate.edu internet address = 131.301.110.10
dns.upstate.edu         internet address = 131.301.41.3
dns.cs.upstate.edu      internet address = 131.301.10.13
```

An NS type query is only meaningful when you query a domain. When you perform an NS query on a host, the output gives you basic SOA (start of authority—more on this in a few paragraphs) and A (address) records.

```
> strangelove
Server:  mailhost.cs.upstate.edu
Address:  131.301.89.13

cs.upstate.edu
   origin = dns.cs.upstate.edu
   mail addr = doug.cs.upstate.edu
   serial = 773
   refresh = 3600 (1 hour)
   retry  = 900 (15 mins)
   expire = 604800 (7 days)
   minimum ttl = 86400 (1 day)
```

There is one SOA (start of authority) for a given domain. The SOA:

- is the authoritative primary DNS (domain name server) for the domain
- defines who the point of contact is for the domain
- controls how long another name server will cache a record from the domain's name server
- controls how often another name server will retry the domain's name server
- controls when another name server will timeout when trying to contact the domain's name server

When one DNS server queries another for information (name, address, etc.), the SOA parameters and values are returned along with the results of the query. These parameters are used by other domain name servers to control caching, retries, and so on.

```
> set query=SOA
> cs.upstate.edu
Server:  mailhost.cs.upstate.edu
Address:  131.301.89.13

cs.upstate.edu
   origin = dns.cs.upstate.edu
   mail addr = doug.cs.upstate.edu
   serial = 773
```

```
    refresh = 3600 (1 hour)
    retry   = 900 (15 mins)
    expire  = 604800 (7 days)
    minimum ttl = 86400 (1 day)
cs.upstate.edu      nameserver = wilbur.cs.upstate.edu
cs.upstate.edu      nameserver = dns.upstate.edu
cs.upstate.edu      nameserver = dns.cs.upstate.edu
wilbur.cs.upstate.edu internet address = 131.301.110.10
dns.upstate.edu    internet address = 131.301.41.3
dns.cs.upstate.edu internet address = 131.301.10.13
```

▲▲ whois: Look Up a User on the Internet

The **whois** utility looks for an Internet directory entry that you specify. It returns site contact and InterNIC registry information that can help you track down the person responsible for a site—perhaps they are *spamming* (sending a lot of unwanted email to) your company. You can search by name (sobell) or handle (MS989). As you will see in the following examples, you will usually use the handle to narrow a search to a single entry. Although the syntax used by **whois** servers around the world differs, you can frequently distinguish a handle from a name by preceding it with an exclamation mark, escaped (quoted) as necessary. After the first command you can see that Mark Sobell has a handle of MS989. The second command searches for this handle.

```
$ whois sobell
Kramer, Mary J. (MJKXX)          sobell@XXXX.NET                XXX XXX XXXX
SOBELL, NINA (NSXXXXX)           sobell@XXXX.XXXX.EDU           (XXX) XXX.XXXX
Sobell Associates Inc (SOBELL-DOM)                              SOBELL.COM
Sobell Variety Islington Trust (XXXXXXXXXXX-DOM)                XXXXXXXXXX.ORG
Sobell, John (JSXXXXX)           aaaco@KSC15.TH.COM
                                      ((XXX) XXX.XXXX (FAX) (XXX) XXX.XXXX
Sobell, Mark (MS989)             sobell@MEER.NET

To single out one record, look it up with "!xxx", where xxx is the
handle, shown in parenthesis following the name, which comes first.

The InterNIC Registration Services database contains ONLY
non-military and non-US Government Domains and contacts.
Other associated whois servers:
    American Registry for Internet Numbers - whois.arin.net
    European IP Address Allocations        - whois.ripe.net
    Asia Pacific IP Address Allocations    - whois.apnic.net
    US Military                            - whois.nic.mil
    US Government                          - whois.nic.gov

$ whois \!MS989
Sobell, Mark (MS989)             sobell@MEER.NET
    Sobell Associates Inc
    PO Box 1089
    Menlo Park, CA 94026

    Record last updated on 24-Aug-95.
    Database last updated on 19-Nov-98 04:36:23 EST.
    .
    .
```

The **whois** utility is also capable of handling IP addresses. As an example, suppose you get spam from someone who has forged his domain name. You can use the IP address from the spam to track back to his real domain, and email the point of contact for the domain to complain about the breach. Suppose the spam came from 195.XX.174.18 (an IP address cannot contain letters, XX is used here to protect the innocent). You can use **whois** to query the North American Internet Registry for subnet 195.XX.174 with the following command:

```
$ whois -h whois.arin.net 195.XX.174
European Regional Internet Registry/RIPE NCC (NETBLK-RIPE-C)
These addresses have been further assigned to European users.
Contact information can be found in the RIPE database, via the
WHOIS and TELNET servers at whois.ripe.net, and at
http://www.ripe.net/db/whois.html

Netname: RIPE-CBLK3
Netblock: 195.0.0.0 - 195.255.255.0
Maintainer: RIPE

Coordinator:
RIPE Network Coordination Centre (RIPE-NCC-ARIN) nicdb@RIPE.NET
+31 20 535 4444
Fax- - +31 20 535 4445

Domain System inverse mapping provided by:

NS.RIPE.NET 193.0.0.193
NS.EU.NET 192.16.202.11
AUTH03.NS.UU.NET 198.6.1.83
NS2.NIC.FR 192.93.0.4
SUNIC.SUNET.SE 192.36.148.18
MUNNARI.OZ.AU 128.250.1.21
NS.APNIC.NET 203.37.255.97

To search on arbitrary strings, see the Database page on
the RIPE NCC web-site at http://www.ripe.net/db/

Record last updated on 16-Oct-98.
Database last updated on 24-Nov-98 16:11:15 EDT.

The ARIN Registration Services Host contains ONLY Internet
Network Information: Networks, ASN's, and related POC's.
Please use the whois server at rs.internic.net for DOMAIN related
Information and nic.mil for NIPRNET Information.
```

As you can see from the first paragraph of the output, the North American registry does not have an entry for this address, and you must contact the European registry for further information. You can either go to the Web site (**www.ripe.net/db**) and use **whois** there, or you can use **whois** locally to get the information via the command line. The Web page at **www.ripe.net/db/whois.html** has a lot of useful information about using **whois**. From this page click on `flags` to get the information you need to construct the following command-line query.

```
% whois -h whois.ripe.net '-T inetnum -r 195.XX.174'

% Rights restricted by copyright. See http://www.ripe.net/db/dbcopyright.html

inetnum: 195.XX.160.0 - 195.XX.191.255
netname: DE-INET-000000
descr: Provider Local Registry
country: DE
admin-c: AA000-RIPE
tech-c: AA000-RIPE
tech-c: AA000
status: ALLOCATED PA
mnt-by: RIPE-NCC-XX-MNT
source: RIPE
```

In this case the argument `'-T inetnum -r 195.XX.174'` is passed to the **ripe** net server which performs a database query based on the type **inetnum** (Internet number), **–r** (no recursion[10]), and the record (IP address) 195.XX.174. One of the technical contacts for this domain is AA000. You can query for more information about this contact by using the following command:

```
$ whois -h whois.ripe.net '-r AA000'

% Rights restricted by copyright. See http://www.ripe.net/db/dbcopyright.html

person: John Doe
address: Big Company GmbH
address: Wiesenhuettenplatz 145
address: D-60341 Frankfurt
address: Germany
phone: +49 69 XXX XX 0
fax-no: +49 69 XXX XX 444
e-mail: john@doe.com
nic-hdl: AA000
mnt-by: PT0000-MNT
source: RIPE
```

After several tries you have your point of contact to send email to complain about the spam.

There are several different top-level registries serving various regions of the world. The ones you are most likely to use are:

- North American Registry   **whois.arin.net**
- European Registry   **whois.ripe.net**

---

10. The **–r** option limits the search to the most specific record. Without this option **whois** returns the ISPs (Internet service providers) and these ISPs' ISPs, and so on. Once in a while this information is useful, but most of the time it is not.

- Asia-Pacific Registry   **whois.apnic.net**
- American Military   **whois.nic.mil**
- American Government   **whois.nic.gov**

▲ Distributed Computing

When there are many similar systems on a network, it is often desirable to share common files and utilities among them. For example a system administrator might choose to keep a copy of the system documentation on one computer's disk and to make those files available for all remote systems. In this case the system administrator would configure the files so that users who need to access the online documentation would not be aware that the files were actually stored on a remote system. This type of setup, which is an example of *distributed computing,* not only conserves disk space but also allows you to update only one central copy of the documentation rather than tracking down and updating copies scattered throughout the network on many different systems.

Figure 7-4 illustrates a *fileserver* that stores the system manual pages and users' home directories. With this arrangement a user's files are always available to that user—no matter which system the user is on. Each system's disk might contain a directory to hold temporary files, as well as a copy of the operating system. For more information refer to "Share Files with Other Machines" on page 646 and specifically see "Automatically Mount Filesystems" on page 649.

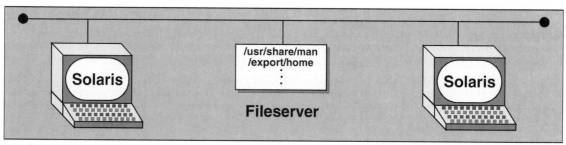

Figure 7-4   A fileserver

▲▲ The Client/Server Model

Although there are many ways to distribute computing tasks on hosts attached to a network, the client/server model dominates UNIX and Solaris system networking. A server system offers services to its clients and is usually a central resource. In Figure 7-4 the system that acts as the documentation repository is a server, and all the systems that contact it to display information are clients. Some servers are designed to interact with specific utilities, such as Web servers and browser clients. Other servers, such as those supporting the Domain Name Service (next section), communicate with one another in addition to answering queries from a variety of clients; in other words one server may query another as a client.

The client/server terminology also applies to processes (which may be running on one or more systems). A server process may control some central database, and client processes send queries to the server and collect replies. In this case the client and server processes may be running on the same computer. The client/server model underlies most of the network services described in this chapter.

▲▲ Overview of Domain Name Service (DNS)

The Domain Name Service (DNS) is a distributed service—name servers on thousands of machines around the world cooperate to keep the database up to date. The database itself, which contains the information that maps hundreds of thousands of alphanumeric hostnames into numeric IP addresses, does not exist in one place. That is, no system has a complete copy of the database. Instead each system that runs DNS knows about the hosts that are local to that site and how to contact other name servers to learn about other, nonlocal hosts.

Like the UNIX/Solaris filesystem, the DNS is organized hierarchically. Outside the United States each country uses its ISO (International Standards Organization) country code designation as its domain name (for example AU represents Australia, IL is Israel, JP is Japan). Although it might seem logical to represent the United States in the same way (US) and to use the standard two-letter Postal Service abbreviations to identify the next level of the domain, that is not how most of the name space is structured.

Following is a list of the six original, common, top-level domains in the United States:

- COM   Commercial enterprises
- EDU   Educational institutions
- GOV   Nonmilitary government agencies
- MIL   Military government agencies
- NET   Networking organizations
- ORG   Other (often nonprofit) organizations

More recently the following domain names have been proposed: WEB, SHOP, FIRM, INFO, ARTS, REC, and NOM.

As with Internet addresses, domain names are assigned by the Network Information Center (NIC [page 193]). A system's full name, referred to as its *fully qualified domain name,* is unambiguous in the way that a simple hostname cannot be. The system **okeeffe.berkeley.edu** at the University of California, Berkeley (Figure 7-5) is not the same as one named **okeeffe.moma.org**, which might represent a host at the Museum of Modern Art. Not only does the domain name tell you something about where the system is located, it adds enough diversity to the name space to avoid confusion when different sites choose similar names for their systems.

Unlike the filesystem hierarchy, the top-level domain name in the United States appears last (reading from left to right). Also, the DNS is not case sensitive. The names **okeeffe.berkeley.edu**, **okeeffe.Berkeley.edu**, and **okeeffe.Berkeley.EDU** refer to the same computer. Once a domain has been assigned, the local site is free to extend the hierarchy to meet local needs.

With DNS, mail addressed to **user@tcorp.com** can be delivered to the computer at **tcorp.com** that handles the corporate mail and knows how to forward messages to user mailboxes on individual machines. As the company grows, the site administrator might decide to create organizational or geographical subdomains. The

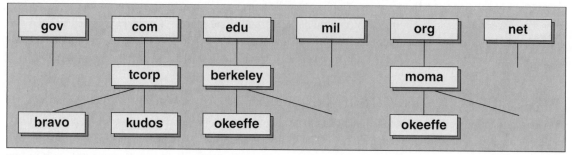

Figure 7-5   United States top-level domains

name **tcorp.ca.tcorp.com** might refer to a system that supports California offices, while **alpha.co.tcorp.com** is dedicated to Colorado. Functional subdomains might be another choice, with **tcorp.sales.tcorp.com** and **alpha.dev.tcorp.com** representing the sales and development divisions, respectively.

On Solaris systems the most common interface to the DNS is the Berkeley Internet Name Domain (BIND) software. BIND follows the client/server model. On any given local network, there may be one or more systems running a name server, supporting all the local hosts as clients. When a system wants to send a message to another host, it queries the nearest name server to learn the remote host's IP address. The client, called a *resolver,* may be a process running on the same computer as the name server, or it may pass the request over the network to reach a server. To reduce network traffic and accelerate name lookups, the local name server has some knowledge of distant hosts. If the local server has to contact a remote server to pick up an address, when the answer comes back, the local server adds that to its internal table and reuses it for a while. The name server deletes the nonlocal information before it can become outdated.

How the system translates symbolic hostnames into addresses is transparent to most users; only the system administrator of a networked system needs to be concerned with the details of name resolution. Systems that use DNS for name resolution are generally capable of communicating with the greatest number of hosts—more than it would be practical to maintain in an **/etc/hosts** file or private Network Information Service database.

Four common sources are used for host name resolution: NIS, NIS+, DNS, and system files (such as **/etc/hosts**). Solaris2 does not ask you to choose between these sources, rather, the **nsswitch.conf** file (page 612) allows you to choose any of these sources, in any combination, and in any order.

▲▲ Network Information Service (NIS)

The Network Information Service is another example of the client/server paradigm. Sun Microsystems developed NIS to simplify the administration of certain common administrative files by maintaining them in a central database and having clients contact the database server to retrieve information. Just as the DNS addressed the problem of keeping multiple copies of the **hosts** file up to date, NIS was created to keep system-independent configuration files current (such as **/etc/passwd**). Most networks today are *heterogeneous* (that is, they include systems supplied by many different manufacturers), and even though they run different varieties of UNIX or Solaris, they have certain common attributes (such as the **passwd** file).

NIS was formerly named the *Yellow Pages,* and many people still refer to it by this name. Sun renamed the service because another corporation holds the trademark to that name. The names of NIS utilities, however, are still reminiscent of the old name: **ypcat** (displays an NIS database), **ypmatch** (searches), and so on.

Consider the file **/etc/group**, which maps symbolic names to group ID numbers. If NIS is being used to administer this configuration file on your system, you might see the following single entry, instead of a list of group names and numbers:

```
$ cat /etc/group
+:*:*
$
```

When a utility needs to map a number to the corresponding group name, it encounters the plus sign (**+**) and knows to query the NIS server at that point for the answer. You can display the **group** database with the **ypcat** utility:

```
$ ypcat group
pubs::141:alex,jenny,scott,hls,barbara
  .
  .
  .
```

Or you can search for a particular group name using **ypmatch**:

```
$ ypmatch pubs group
pubs::141:alex,jenny,scott,hls,barbara
```

You can retrieve the same information by filtering the output of **ypcat** through **grep**, but **ypmatch** is more efficient because it searches the database directly, using a single process. The database name is not the full pathname of the file it replaces; the NIS database name is the same as the simple filename (**group**, not **/etc/group**). However **ypmatch** utility will only work on the key for the table (the group name). If you want to match on members of the group, the group number, or other fields of a map (such as the full name in the **passwd** map), you still need to use **grep** with **ypcat**.

As with the Domain Name Service, ordinary users need not be aware that NIS is managing system configuration files. Setting up and maintaining the NIS databases is a task for the system administrator; individual users and users on single-user Solaris systems rarely need to work directly with NIS.

▲▲ Network File System (NFS)

Using the Network File System (NFS), you can work locally with files that are stored on a remote computer system's disks. These files appear as if they were present on your own computer. The remote system acts as the fileserver; the local system is the client, making requests.

NFS is configured by the person responsible for the system. When you work with a file, you may not be aware of where the file is physically stored. In many computer facilities today, user files are commonly stored on a central fileserver equipped with many large-capacity disk drives and devices that easily make backup copies of the data. A Solaris system may be *diskless,* where a floppy disk is used to start Solaris and then load system software from another machine on the network (or from a CDROM). Another type of Solaris system is the *dataless* system, in which the client does have a disk, but no user data is stored on it (only the system software, Solaris, and the applications are kept on the disk).

The **df** utility with the **–k** option displays a list of the filesystems available on your system, along with the amount of disk space, free and used, on each. Filesystem names that are prepended with **hostname:** are available to you through NFS.

```
bravo% pwd
/kudos/home/jenny
bravo% df -v
Filesystem         kbytes       used      avail capacity    Mounted on
/dev/dsk/c0d0s0     59827      52406       1439     98%      /
/dev/dsk/c0d0s6    542995     409495      79201     84%      /usr
/proc                   0          0          0      0%      /proc
fd                      0          0          0      0%      /dev/fd
/dev/dsk/c0d0s1     29905      21658       5257     81%      /var
/dev/dsk/c0d0s7    694813     611782      27446     96%      /export/home
swap                19907        373      19534      2%      /tmp
/cdrom/sol         169783     169783          0    100%      /vol/dev/dsk/c0d1/solaris_2_...
kudos:/home        198275      68408     119621     36%      /kudos/home
kudos:/usr/X386    199271     125163      63817     66%      /usr/X386
kudos:/usr/share   640281     445399     161807     73%         /usr/share
```

In this example Jenny's home directory is actually stored on the remote system **kudos**. The **/home** filesystem on **kudos** is mounted on **bravo** using NFS; as a reminder of its physical location, the system administrator has made it available using a pathname that includes the remote server's name. (Refer to page 736 in Part III for more information on **df**.) Two other filesystems on **kudos** have been made available on **bravo**: the X Window System filesystem (**/usr/X386**) and **/usr/share**.

The physical location of your files should not matter to you; all the standard Solaris utilities work with NFS-remote files in the same way that they operate on files that are stored locally on your computer. At times, however, you may lose access to your files: Your computer may be up and running, but a network problem or a remote system crash may make your files temporarily unavailable. In this case when you try to access a file, you probably see an error message like NFS server kudos not responding. When your system can contact the remote server again, you see a message like NFS server kudos OK.

▲▲ automount: Automatic Filesystem Mounting

With distributed computing you can log in on any machine on the network, and all of your files, including startup scripts, will be easily available. In a distributed computing environment, it is common to have all machines able to mount all filesystems on all servers: Whatever machine you log in on, your home directory will be waiting for you.

Having all machines mount all servers all the time can be problematic. What if machine A mounts machine B for some filesystems and machine B mounts machine A for other filesystems? What happens if you have to bring one of these machines down for maintenance or one crashes? In what order do you reboot them when they depend on each other to be up? In a large network you can have a machine mounting tens or hundreds of others for software files and home directories.

One way around this problem is to mount filesystems only on demand. In Sun operating systems (going back to SunOS 4), demand mounting is handled by the **automountd** daemon. If you know that Alex has a home directory, you can issue the command **ls /home/alex**. This command causes **automountd** to go to work: It looks in the **auto_home** map, finds that **alex** is a key that says to mount **franklin:/export/homes/alex**, and mounts the remote filesystem.

Once the filesystem is mounted, **ls** displays the list of files you want to see. If, after this mounting sequence, you give the command **ls /home**, **ls** shows that **alex** is present within the **/home** directory. The **df** utility (previous section) shows that **alex** is mounted from **franklin**. The **automountd** daemon automatically unmounts this filesystem after five minutes (by default) of inactivity.

There are several default automount maps including the **/net** and **/home** (above) maps. You can use the **/net** mountpoint to generically access other hosts. It is similar in concept to the Windows 95 network neighborhood. If you know there are NFS servers named **franklin**, **adams**, and **madison**, you can see all the filesystems that are exported by each by using **ls** to display **/net/franklin**, **/net/adams**, and **/net/madison**. Once these filesystems are mounted, you can browse through them (assuming you have permission).

The **automount** facility of Solaris is very flexible and powerful. It is one of the features of Solaris that sets it above most other versions of UNIX. Refer to "Automatically Mount Filesystems" on page 649, the **automount man** page, and AnswerBook2 for more information.

Start Optional

▲ Network Services/Daemons

On Solaris systems network services are provided by daemons that run continuously or are automatically started by the system when a request comes in (see **inetd** in the following list). The network services that your system supports are listed in **/etc/rpc** and **/etc/inet/services**. There is a link to **services** that appears as **/etc/services**. The daemons (the executable files) are usually stored in **/usr/sbin**. By convention the names of most daemons end with the letter **d** to distinguish them from a utility. Daemon names often have a prefix of **in.** or **rpc.**.

As an example, when you run **rsh**, your local system contacts the **rsh** daemon (**in.rshd**) on the remote system to establish the connection. The two systems negotiate the connection according to a fixed protocol. Each system identifies itself to the other, and then they take turns asking each other specific questions and waiting for valid replies. Each network service follows its own protocol.

In addition to the daemons that support the utilities described up to this point, there are many other daemons that support system-level network services that you will not typically interact with. Some of these include:

automountd   **automatic mounting**   Handles RPC requests from the **autofs** service. Automatic mounting is a way of demand-mounting directories from remote hosts without having them hard-configured into **/etc/vfstab**. The **automountd** daemon makes administration of a group of machines easier. It is started by the **/etc/rc2.d/S74autofs** script.

cachefsd

cache filesystem   The cachefs filesystem caches network or CDROM file requests on a local filesystem. Where network bandwidth is limited, or for ease of administration, cachefs can be used to provide a local cache of frequently accessed files. For better performance cachefs should not be used on home directories or on other filesystems where there is a high ratio of writes to reads. Sun has a white paper on cachefs as well as lots of information in the manual pages and in AnswerBook2. The daemon is kept in **/usr/lib/fs/cachefs/cachefsd** and is launched by **inetd**.

cron

Used for periodic execution of tasks, this daemon looks at the files in the directories named **/var/spool/cron/crontabs** and **/var/spool/cron/atjobs**. When a task comes up for execution, **cron** executes it as the user owning the file in the corresponding directory. Cron is started by **/etc/rc2.d/S75cron**. Uncharacteristically the name of this daemon does not end in **d**.

dtspcd

desktop subprocess control   Used by CDE for remote execution, this daemon authenticates and provides variables for remotely executed processes. Launched by **inetd**.

in.comsat

Used by **biff**, a utility that notifies users of incoming mail. If the user is logged on and has run **biff y**, **in.comsat** sends a message to the user's shell saying that there is new mail (at appropriate times). Security-conscious sites may want to disable this service, as it has a history of security holes. Uncharacteristically the name of this daemon does not end in **d**. Launched by **inetd**.

in.dhcpd

dynamic host configuration protocol   Assigns Internet address, subnet mask, default gateway, DNS, and other information to hosts. This protocol answers DHCP requests and optionally BOOTP requests. The control script is **/etc/init.d/dhcp**. DHCP is only available if the SUNWdhcsr and SUWdhcsu packages are installed.

inetd

The Internet *superserver* listens for service requests on network connections and starts up the appropriate daemon to respond to any particular request. Because of **inetd**, your system does not need to have all the daemons running all the time in order to handle various network requests. The **inetd** daemon is started by the **/etc/rc2.d/S72inetsvc** script. The configuration file for **inetd** is **/etc/inet/inetd.conf** (with a link at **/etc/inetd.conf**). This file contains the list of servers that **inetd** invokes when it receives a request.

in.fingerd

finger   Handles requests for user information from the **finger** utility. Launched by **inetd**.

in.ftpd

file transfer protocol   Handles incoming requests for the Internet file transfer protocol (**ftp**). Launched by **inetd**.

in.lpd

line printer daemon   Solaris 2.6 introduced a new printing service that can replace the old **lp/lpsched** SYSV method of printing. The new SunSoft print client has direct support for network printers and uses a file named **/etc/printers.conf**. The daemon is kept in **/usr/lib/print/in.lpd** and is launched by **inetd** when printing requests come to the machine.

in.rarpd   **reverse address resolution protocol**   Used for address resolution. Some devices such as network printers, network probes, and X terminals use RARP to obtain their Internet addresses. A machine uses RARP to determine its address by sending out its Ethernet hardware address in a specially formatted packet. Any RARP servers that have a corresponding entry in their **/etc/ethers** file send back the appropriate IP address to the requesting machine. This service is run on startup on machines that have been set up as jumpstart (page 1036) servers.

in.rexecd   Allows remote users with a valid username and password to run programs on a machine. Its use is generally deprecated because of security, but certain programs, such as PC-based X servers, may still use it. Launched by **inetd**.

in.rlogind   **remote login**   Allows the users of a group of similarly administrated machines in a common domain to remotely log in to each other without giving a username or password. The **/etc/hosts.equiv** file controls which machines will be able to use **rlogin** without giving a username and password. Accounts on all machines should be synchronized either by having identical **/etc/passwd** files or by using a common network information service such as NIS or NIS+. Launched by **inetd**.

in.rshd   **remote shell**   Allows you to run a command on a remote machine without a password. Programs such as PC X servers make use of this daemon to launch X applications. Similar to **in.rlogind**, access is enabled in the **/etc/hosts.equiv** file. However there may also be a **.rhosts** file in the user's home directory that gives **rsh** access. Launched by **inetd**.

in.rwhod   **remote who**   Allows you to see who is logged in on other machines that are also running this daemon. The **in.rwhod** periodically broadcasts on the network. Any listening **in.rwhod** daemon picks up the broadcast and stores the information in the **/var/spool/rwho** directory. Programs such as **rusers**, **rwho**, and **ruptime** make use of **in.rwhod** and the data it keeps to display information about other machines and users on your local network. This service is usually run as a stand-alone daemon by **/etc/rc3.d/S50rwho**.

in.talkd   **talk**   Allows you to have a conversation with another user on the same or a remote machine. The **talk** daemon handles the connections between the machines. The **talk** utility on each machine contacts the **in.talkd** daemon on the other machine for a bidirectional conversation. Launched by **inetd**. See the tutorial on page 59.

in.telnetd   **telnet**   One of the original Internet remote access protocols. When you use **telnet** to access a machine, you follow the same login procedure that you would follow if you were logging in locally. Launched by **inetd**.

in.tftpd   **trivial file transfer protocol**   Used by certain machines to boot or get information from a network. Examples include X terminals, network computers, and some printers. Launched by **inetd**.

in.uucpd   **UNIX to UNIX Copy**   The **uucp** daemon has largely been supplanted by SMTP (simple mail transfer protocol). There are still pockets of UUCP on the Internet today where a remote site's only means of connection is a dialup link. Launched by **inetd**.

kerbd   Kerberos, developed at MIT, securely authenticates local and remote users. Once authenticated through Kerberos, you are given a *ticket*[11] that grants you access to certain hosts and services as configured in an administrative database. The **kerbd** daemon integrates a Kerberos environment and maps between Kerberos ids and local user ids and group ids. This daemon is started by the **/etc/rc2.d/S73nfs.client** script.

named   Supports the Domain Name Service (DNS), which has replaced the use of the **/etc/hosts** table on most networked UNIX systems today for hostname-to-IP address mappings.

nfsd, statd, lockd,   These five daemons operate together to handle NFS operations. The **nfsd** daemon
mountd, rquotad   handles file and directory requests. The **statd** and **lockd** daemons implement network file and record locking. The **mountd** daemon takes care of converting a filesystem name request from the **mount** utility into an NFS handle and checks access permissions. Finally if disk quotas are enabled, **rquotad** handles those. They can all be found in **/usr/lib/fs/nfs**.

nscd   **name service cache**   Caches name service request data obtained from the passwd, hosts, and group maps. This caching can improve efficiency on servers that have many users logging in or launching programs. Because of problems with the name resolver libraries in some versions of Solaris, some administrators disable host caching by changing the **S76nscd** startup file or changing the **/etc/nscd.conf** file. Launched by **inetd.**

powerd   **power**   Manages automatic and low-power shutdowns. Automatic shutdowns are configured in the **/etc/power.conf** files, and low-power shutdowns are only a consideration with machines that have batteries (such as portables running X86). The power management daemon is started up automatically in run level 2 by the **S85power** script. This feature was introduced in Solaris 2.6.

---

11. A Kerberos ticket is an authenticated sequence of bytes that network services examine to make sure you are who you say you are. It is like an all-day pass to use the network: Once the day is over, you need to get a new ticket.

rdisc	**router discovery service** This service runs if the machine has one interface and there is no **/etc/defaultrouter** file to configure a default route for the machine. It uses the Internet router discovery service to find suitable routers for traversing the local subnet.
routed	**route** The routing daemon manages the routing tables, so that your system knows where to send messages that are destined for distant networks. If your system has more than one network interface, **routed** is started automatically to listen to incoming routing messages as well as to advertise outgoing routes to other systems on your network. A newer daemon, the Gateway daemon (**gated**), offers enhanced configurability and support for more routing protocols. It is in the public domain.
rpcbind	The **rpcbind** service is an integral part of Solaris. It maps incoming requests for RPC service numbers to a TCP or UDP port number on the local machine. Also, whenever an RPC daemon starts, it registers itself with the **rpcbind** daemon, so it is critical that **rpcbind** is started before any of the other RPC daemons (and consequently before **inetd**). This daemon is started by the **/etc/rc2.d/S71rpc** script.
rpc.bootparamd	**jumpstart boot parameter** Used on systems with a jumpstart (page 1036) server, this service allows rapid installation of a new system by attaching the new system to the network and turning it on. See AnswerBook2 for more information on configuring jumpstart.
rpc.cmsd	Used by the deskset calendar tool (**cm** for OpenWindows, or **dtcm** for CDE), this daemon coordinates calendars that are distributed on a central host or remote hosts. It manages the calendar files by communicating with **dtcm** or **cm** directly, or with **rpc.cmsd** on another host. It is located in **/usr/openwin/bin**.
rpc.nisd	**NIS** Runs on NIS+ masters and handles requests for NIS+ databases such as passwd, netgroup, and group. NIS+ was developed as a more secure replacement for NIS/YP. It is started by **/etc/rc2.d/S71rpc** if NIS+ is configured.
rpc.rexd	If the **rpc.rexd** service is enabled in your **inetd.conf** file, immediately comment it out and restart **inetd**. This is an insecure and deprecated service. If exploited, any remote user can run any command on your machine as root.
rpc.rstatd	Collects information about the local system such as load average, paging, disk I/O, and interrupts for the OpenWindows **perfmeter** program. This service is launched by **inetd** on the target machine and is found in the **/usr/lib/netsvc/rstat** directory.
rpc.sprayd	Handles connections from the **spray** utility, which measures bandwidth between hosts. It is deprecated because it is not accurate and because malicious users can cause denials of service using this daemon. Launched by **inetd**.
rpc.ttdbserverd	Used by the ToolTalk (page 1048) services for inter-tool communication (for example drag-and-drop services). Launched by **inetd** and located in **/usr/openwin/bin**.

sendmail

The **sendmail** daemon came from Berkeley and has been available for a very long time. It is the de facto mail transfer program on the Internet. The **sendmail** daemon always listens on port 25 for incoming mail connections and then calls a local delivery agent such as **/usr/bin/mail** or **mail.local** to deliver to addresses that are local to the machine. Mail user agents such as **mailtool**, **mailx**, and **dtmail** typically use **sendmail** to deliver a mail message. It is started from **/etc/rc2.d/S88sendmail**.

syslogd

system log   The **syslog** utility transcribes important system events. It stores these events in files and/or forwards them to users or another host running the **syslogd** daemon. This daemon is started by **/etc/rc2.d/S74syslog** and is configured with **/etc/syslog.conf**.

utmpd

Keeps the **/etc/utmp** and **/var/adm/wtmp** files clean by updating them when a process terminates; required because some programs do not properly update these files upon exiting. Keeps programs such as **last**, **w**, and **who** informed about which users are logged on. Started by the **/etc/rc2.d/S88utmpd** script.

vold

volume management   Takes care of automatically mounting CDROMs, floppy disks, and other removable media. Started by the **/etc/rc2.d/S92volmgt** script.

walld

write all   Allows you to send messages to all users logged in on all machines on your network. When you enable this service in **inetd.conf**, all users receive messages generated by **wall** (page 679) in all of their shell windows. This daemon is located in **/usr/lib/netsvc/rwall**.

Xaserver

Xaudio server   The Xaudio service, an extension to the X Window System, plays sound over the network. Launched by **inetd**.

xntpd

network time protocol   The **xntpd** daemon synchronizes with a network time protocol server and keeps the clocks on a network of computers accurate and synchronized. Although free versions of **xntpd** have been available for years, Sun did not start shipping it until it released Solaris 2.6. Located in **/usr/lib/inet/xntpd**.

ypserv, ypxfrd, ypbind, rpc.yppasswdd

YP/NIS server   NIS is available as part of the SUNWypu, and SUNWnisu packages on the Solaris operating system CDROM. When the packages are installed, the NIS daemons are kept in **/usr/lib/netsvc/yp**. The **ypserv** and **ypxfrd** daemons are only run on NIS servers, and **ypbind** is run on every NIS client. NIS servers may also be running **rpc.yppasswdd**, used for changing passwords through NIS. NIS services are started from **/etc/rc2.d/S71rpc**.

Stop Optional

▲ USENET

One of the earliest information services available on the Internet, USENET, is like an electronic bulletin board that allows users with common interests to exchange information. See page 231 for information on the World Wide Web. USENET is an informal, loosely connected network of systems that exchange electronic mail and news items (commonly referred to as *netnews*). USENET was formed in the early 1980s when a few sites decided to share some software and information on topics of common interest. They agreed to contact one another and to pass the information along over dialup telephone lines (at that time running at 1200 baud at best) using UNIX's **uucp** utility (UNIX-to-UNIX copy program).

The popularity of USENET led to major changes in **uucp** to handle the ever-escalating volume of messages and sites. Today much of the news flows over network links using a sophisticated protocol designed especially for this purpose (Network News Transfer Protocol, or NNTP). The news messages are stored in a standard format, and there are many public domain programs available to let you read them. An old, simple interface is named **readnews**. Others, such as **rn** and its X Window System cousin **xrn**, have many features that help you browse through the articles that are available and reply to or create articles of your own. The USENET software has been ported to non-UNIX systems as well as UNIX systems, so the community of netnews users has grown more diverse. You can now choose from quite a few user interfaces to read news. The one you select is largely a matter of personal taste. Four popular interfaces are **tin**, **nn**, **xvnews**, and **xrn**. In addition Netscape includes a graphical interface that you can use to read news (Netscape News) as part of its Web browser.

In the UNIX tradition categories of netnews groups are structured hierarchically. The top level includes designations such as **comp** (computer-related), **misc** (miscellaneous), **rec** (recreational topics), **sci** (science), **soc** (social issues), and **talk** (ongoing discussions). There is usually at least one regional category at the top level, such as **ba** (San Francisco Bay Area), that includes information about local events, and there are many new categories constantly being added (there are more than 30,000 newsgroups). The names of newsgroups resemble domain names but read from left to right (like Solaris filenames): **comp.os.UNIX.misc**, **comp.lang.c**, **misc.jobs.offered**, **rec.skiing**, **sci.med**, **soc.singles**, **talk.politics**. The following article appeared in **comp.unix.solaris**:

```
XXX XXXXXXX (xxxxxx@xxx.uk) wrote:
> This may be a simple problem.
>
> When I log into my SPARC running Solaris 2.6, my .profile is not being
> run. Shows up when running up an xterm and all the settings in .profile
> have not be instigated. Odd.
>
> The home directory is auto-mounted and there does not seem to be a
> problem with the mounting. (i.e. I can get to all my ~/* files)
>
> Any ideas anyone?

What shell do you use? sh, ksh, bash, csh, tcsh? Only sh-compatible
shells will read .profile, and some of them only if the shell is login
shell (shell in xterm is not login shell) and/or if there is no shell
specific version of .profile (like in case of bash shell and
.bash_profile file).
```

```
--
Aleksandar Milivojevic | alex@srce.hr | http://jagor.srce.hr/~alex/
Opinions expressed herein are my own.
===============================oooooO=Ooooo===============================
Real Users never know what they want, but they always know when your
program doesn't deliver it.
```

A great deal of useful information is available on USENET, but you need patience and perseverance to find what you are looking for. You can ask a question, as the user did in the previous example, and someone from halfway around the world may answer it (Croatia, in this case). Before posing such a simple question and causing it to appear on thousands of systems around the world, ask yourself if there is a less invasive way to get help:

- Refer to the **man** pages and AnswerBook2.

- Ask your system administrator or another user for help.

- All of the popular newsgroups have FAQs (lists of frequently asked questions). Consult these lists of questions to see if it already has an answer corresponding to your question. FAQs are periodically posted to the newsgroups; in addition all of the FAQs are archived at sites around the Internet, including **rtfm.mit.edu**, **ftp.uu.net**, and in the USENET newsgroup **alt.answers**.

- Because someone has probably asked the same question before you, search the netnews archives for an answer: Try looking at **dejanews.com**, which has a very complete netnews archive. Also, many search engines, including AltaVista, allow you to use a Web browser to search on netnews archives.

- Contact a Solaris user's group.

Use the worldwide USENET community as a last resort. If you are stuck on a Solaris question and cannot find any other help, try submitting it to one of these Solaris newsgroups:

- **comp.unix.solaris**
- **alt.solaris.x86**
- **net.computers.os.unix.solaris**
- **comp.os.UNIX.help**
- **comp.sys.sun.admin**
- **comp.sys.sun.hardware**

One way to find out about new tools and services is to read the USENET news. The **comp.os.UNIX** hierarchy is of particular interest to UNIX users; for example news about newly released software for UNIX is posted to **comp.os.UNIX.announce**. People often announce the availability of free software there, along with instructions on how to get a copy for your own use (via anonymous **ftp** [page 208]). Other tools exist to help you find resources, both old and new, on the network; see Appendix B.

▲ Tutorial: Using pine as a Newsreader

The **pine** news interface resembles the **pine** mail interface (page 65), with as much consistency between commands, screen displays, and folder organization as possible. This consistency makes it easier for those used to the **pine** mailer to use **pine** as a newsreader. However if you are not using **pine** and you are using Netscape, you may prefer to use Netscape News (page 236).

In order to use **pine** as a newsreader (or to use any newsreader) you must have access to USENET news. Ask your Internet service provider or your system administrator for the address of your news server. If your site has no news server, you will not be able to read news.

Next start **pine** and select **Setup** from the **Main** menu. The **Main** menu will remain on the screen while **pine** prompts you for the setup task on the bottom lines. Enter **C** (Config) to cause **pine** to display the **Setup Configuration** screen, where you can view and modify many configurable aspects of **pine**'s behavior (Figure 7-6).

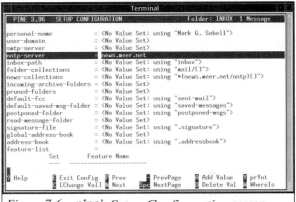

Figure 7-6   **pine**'s *Setup Configuration screen*

Highlight the **pine** variable **nntp-server**, select **A** (Add Value), and enter the name of the news server (unless it is already set).

In most cases this is all you need to do to start using **pine** as a newsreader. The next time you run **pine**, it will contact the news server on your behalf as you give commands to read and post news.

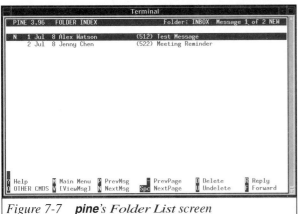

Figure 7-7   **pine**'s *Folder List screen*

You are probably accustomed to seeing the Folder List screen containing the mail folders **INBOX**, **sent-mail**, and **saved-messages**, and any other mail folders you have created. If this group, or *collection,* of folders is the only one defined, **pine** displays the individual folders within the collection when you select **Folder List**. Once you enable news, however, an additional collection—the **news-collection**—is automatically defined, and the **Folder List** screen changes to display a list of the two folder collections instead. Under the name identifying each collection is the line [Select Here to See Expanded List]. Highlighting this line makes the corresponding collection current. Highlight the line for the **news-collection** to tell **pine** that you plan to use the news feature (Figure 7-7). The command lines at the bottom of the screen show that the label for command **D** has changed from Delete to UnSbscrbe, and that the label for command **A** has changed from Add to Subscribe.

Within the news-collection a folder corresponds to a single newsgroup. If you want to see a list of your active newsgroups, highlight the news folder collection and press **RETURN** to expand it. If you do not yet subscribe to any newsgroups, you will see the message `empty list`. You can move among the newsgroups, or folders, in the usual way, and can select any one by pressing **x**.

▲▲ Subscribing to Newsgroups

The *news subscription file,* **.newsrc** in your home directory, is used by **pine** to keep track of your news subscriptions. It is in a standard format that can be used by most newsreaders. You may find this file in your home directory, initialized with a list of newsgroups deemed to be of general interest. If not, **pine** will create the file for you the first time you subscribe to a newsgroup.

A newsgroup that might be useful at this point is **comp.mail.pine**. To subscribe to this newsgroup, highlight the news folder collection in the Folder List screen, then enter **A** (Subscribe) followed by **comp.mail.pine** at the prompt. The new newsgroup will subsequently appear in the Folder List screen display.

If you want to find all the newsgroups that include the name `Solaris` in their titles, enter **∗Solaris∗** in response to the prompt you get when you give the **A** (Subscribe) command (Figure 7-8) shows the results of this query). If you want to see a list of all newsgroups, just press **RETURN** after you give the **A** command (the list is long).

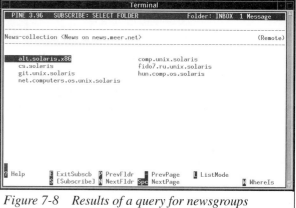

Figure 7-8   Results of a query for newsgroups containing `Solaris` *in their titles*

▲▲ Reading News

Because the **pine** newsreader is modeled after the **pine** mailer, most aspects of reading mail apply to reading news: You will see a numbered list of messages (*posts*) identified with dates, sender names, and subject lines. You can select messages that interest you, mark messages for deletion, export messages to files, and so on. When viewing a news message, you will see headers that resemble the headers used in **pine** mail messages. The fields `Date:`, `From:`, and `Subject:` appear in the four-line header, with similar meaning. To emphasize that recipients of news messages are newsgroups, the `To:` field is replaced with the `Newgroups:` field. This field lists the newsgroups receiving the post and may list one or more newsgroups.

Unlike many other newsreaders, **pine** does not automatically delete the news messages that you have read; you must explicitly mark news messages for deletion using the **D** command, as you do for **pine** mail messages. Because **pine** remembers which messages you have deleted between **pine** sessions, you can pick up where you left off the next time you run **pine** to read your news.

▲▲ Posting News

The commands to post news in **pine** are nearly identical to the commands to send **pine** mail. The main difference is that the list of recipients is comprised of newsgroup names, not the addresses of individual users.

This can be seen by comparing the `To:` line of a mail message header with the `Newsgroups:` line of a news message header. Like mail messages news messages may be sent to multiple recipients.

Use **R** With Care

If you enter **R** to reply to a news post, you will be asked if you want your message to be posted to all recipient newgroups. Enter **Y** (Yes) only with the greatest caution; your message will reach thousands of people. Unless you want your message to go to *all* the subscribers of *all* the newsgroups listed in the `Newsgroups:` field of the header, enter **N** (No) at this prompt. **N** causes your reply to be sent as an electronic mail message only to the individual who posted the original message.

▲▲ Unsubscribing from Newsgroups

If you decide that you do not wish to belong to a newsgroup, you can unsubscribe from the newsgroup. You will probably want to unsubscribe from many newsgroups if your **.newsrc** file was initialized for you; the list of such newsgroups is likely to be long and diverse.

To unsubscribe from a newsgroup, select news-collection from the Folder List screen, enter RETURN to expand the news-collection, highlight the newsgroup you want to unsubscribe from, and enter **D** (UnSbscrbe). Unsubscribing from a newsgroup does not remove the newsgroup from the **.newsrc** file; it simply tells **pine** not to include that newsgroup in the FOLDER LIST display. If you decide to subscribe to the same newsgroup again, **pine** will remember what messages you deleted, and you can resume reading the posts where you left off.

▲ Overview of the World Wide Web

The World Wide Web (WWW, W3, or Web) provides a unified, interconnected interface to the vast amount of information stored on computers around the world. The idea that created the World Wide Web came from the mind of Tim Berners-Lee of the European Particle Physics Laboratory (CERN) in response to a need to improve communications throughout the High Energy Physics community. The first generation was a notebook program called Enquire, short for "Enquire Within Upon Everything" (the name of a book from his childhood), that he created in 1980 and which provided for links to be made between named nodes. It was not until 1989 that the concept was proposed as a global hypertext project to be known as the World Wide Web. In 1990 Berners-Lee wrote a proposal for a HyperText project, which eventually produced HTML, HyperText Markup Language, the common language of the Web. The World Wide Web program became available on the Internet in the summer of 1991. By designing the tools to work with existing protocols such as **ftp** and **gopher**, the researchers who created the Web created a system that is generally useful for many types of information and across different types of hardware and operating systems.[12]

---

12. Thanks to Marcia Casey for this research.

The WWW is another example of the client/server paradigm that is common to most network services described in this chapter. You use a WWW client application, or *browser,* to display or retrieve information stored on a server that may be located anywhere on your local network or the global Internet. WWW clients can interact with many different types of servers; for example you can use a WWW client to contact a remote **ftp** server (page 237) and display the list of files it offers for anonymous **ftp** (page 208). Similarly you can use a WWW client to interact with a remote **gopher** server. Most commonly you use a WWW client to contact a WWW server, which offers support for the special features of the World Wide Web that are described in the remainder of this chapter.

The power of the Web is in its use of *hypertext,* a way to navigate through information by following cross-references (called *links*) from one piece of information to another. If this book were available as a hypertext document, you would have a convenient way to get more detail about some of the topics described here. Your hypertext client (browser) would highlight and/or underline certain terms that were links to servers that could provide additional information.

For example if the word CERN in the first paragraph of this section were a hypertext link and you selected it, your client would contact the appropriate server and display the results, which might be a page or two of information about the laboratory. Those pages might have additional links, providing more information, and so on.

To use the Web effectively, you need to be able to run interactive network applications. The first graphical user interface for browsing the Web was a tool named Mosaic, released in February 1993. It was designed at the National Center for Supercomputer Applications at the University of Illinois and sparked a dramatic increase in the number of users of the World Wide Web. Marc Andreessen, who participated in the Mosaic project at the University of Illinois, later cofounded Netscape Communications with the founder of Silicon Graphics, Jim Clark. They created Netscape Navigator, a Web client program that was designed to perform better and support more features than the Mosaic browser. Netscape Navigator has enjoyed immense success and has become a popular choice for users exploring the World Wide Web.

The Netscape Navigator[13] (Figure 7-9) provides a graphical user interface that allows you to listen to sounds, watch Web events or live news reports, and display pictures as well as text, giving you access to *hypermedia.* A picture on your screen may be a link to more detailed, nonverbal information such as a copy of the same picture at a higher resolution or a short animation. If you run Netscape on a system that is equipped for audio playback, you can to listen to audio clips that have been linked into a document. For example when you select a picture of a loudspeaker in the Web page shown in Figure 7-10 on page 235, you hear an audio clip about the discovery of the Dilophosaurus, narrated by one of the men who discovered the first specimen. All the underlined and highlighted words and phrases in the Web pages shown in Figures 7-9, 7-14, and 7-15, as well as the images with colored borders, are hypertext links. If you have a monochrome monitor, you only see the underlining.

---

13. Netscape only runs on a graphical user interface. If you are working on a character-based terminal or emulator, use **lynx** to access the Internet.

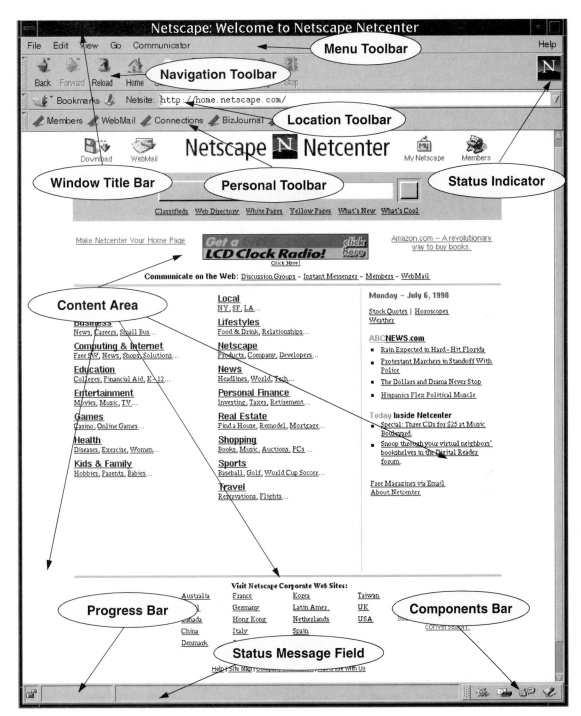

*Figure 7-9   The Netscape home page (**home.netscape.com**)*

▲ Tutorial: Using Netscape

The easiest way to learn about Netscape and the Web is to run Netscape and begin exploring. Most of your inter-action with Netscape involves pointing to an item and clicking the left mouse button. This point-and-click inter-face makes it easy to get around the Web and to learn quickly about the features Netscape has to offer.

Shortly after you start Netscape, you see a page on the screen that identifies Netscape and welcomes you. This special page is called a *home page;* Figure 7-9 shows a sample of Netscape's home page. (You can customize Netscape, so what you see and what is described in this text may not be exactly the same.) A home page is the starting point that visitors can use to begin exploring a particular site (similar to the table of con-tents for a book). A home page includes links that lead you to pages of related information. A Web site is typ-ically organized with the home page at the root of a tree, with links providing access to information located at various branches within the tree and on other trees. You follow a given link by moving the mouse pointer to the link and clicking the left mouse button.

▲▲ Screen Elements

The home page or other information you are viewing with the Netscape browser is displayed in the **Content** area. Figure 7-9 points out the **Content** area, as well as other areas of the Netscape browser window that are described in the following paragraphs.

At the top of the screen is the **Menu** toolbar, and at the right end of the **Menu** toolbar is the **Help** menu. Clicking on the word `Help` displays a popup menu of items that can help familiarize you with Netscape. View the interactive Netscape documentation by selecting **Help Contents** from this menu. On the left of the documentation window is a table of contents that gets more detailed as you click on each item. To the right is the documentation (with hyperlinks) that corresponds to the table of contents entry you have high-lighted. Each table of contents selection is actually a link to a page on a server at Netscape Communications Corporation; until you download it the page is not stored on your computer. The **Personal** toolbar gives you access to additional information about Netscape as well as several useful directories; it is a good place to begin exploring the Web.

Whenever a new page is transferred to the local client (your browser), the **Content** area changes to reflect the structure and content of the new page. The **Status** indicator in the upper-right portion of the screen moves while the information is being transferred to you. The **Progress** bar and the **Status Message** field, both to the lower-left of the Netscape window, provide details about the progress of the transfer. Because the local network load is generally greater during working hours and Web servers receive a large number of requests, transfers are often noticeably slower during these peak hours.

Every Web page has a URL (Uniform Resource Locator) that identifies the location of the document on the Internet in a form that both client and server can use. The **Goto** field[14] of the **Location** toolbar in the

---

14. Although it is referred to as the **Goto** field, the label for this field says **Netsite** when you are viewing a URL (Figure 7-10) and only says Goto as you enter the name of a URL you want to visit.

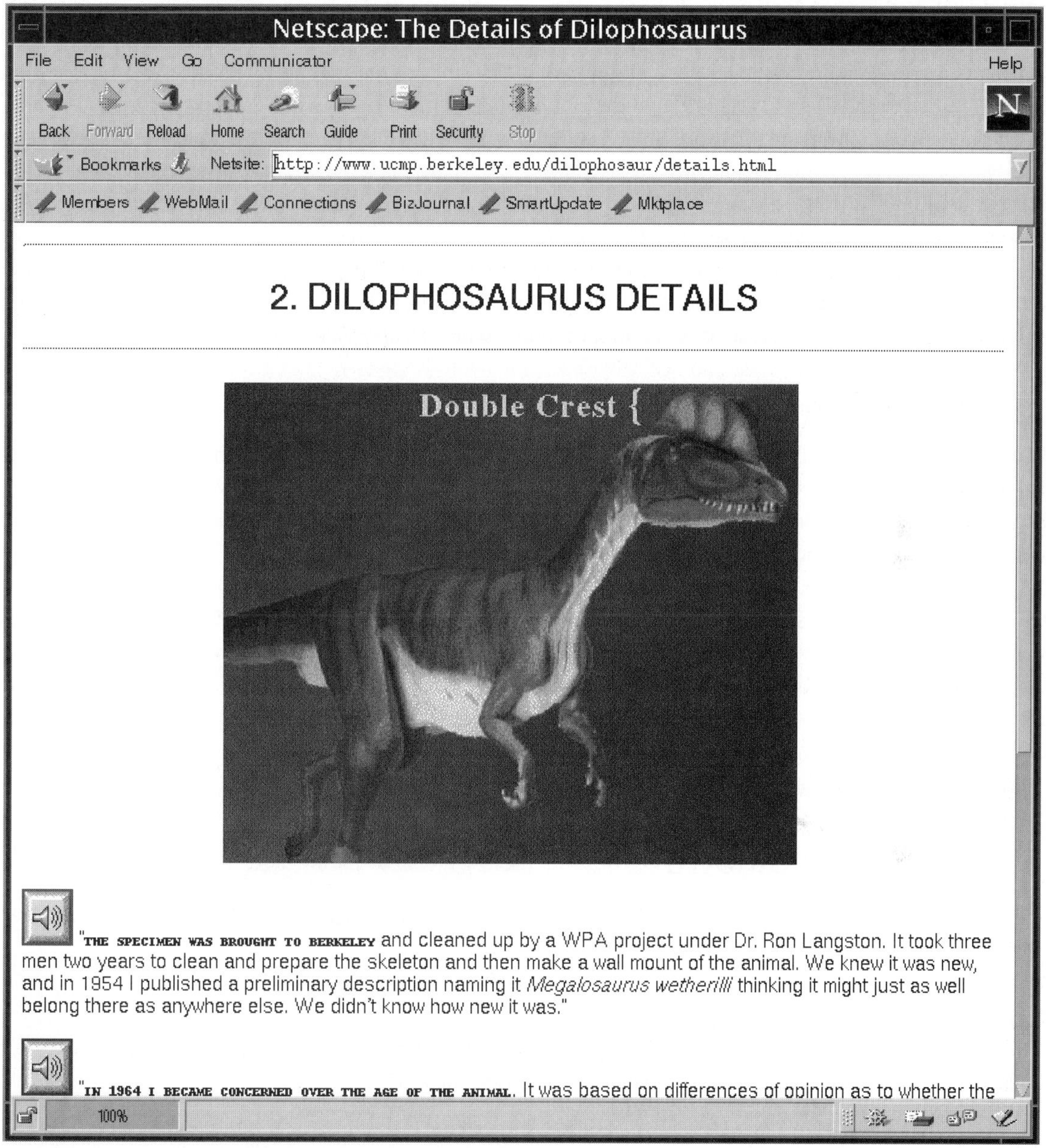
Netscape: The Details of Dilophosaurus
File Edit View Go Communicator Help
Back Forward Reload Home Search Guide Print Security Stop
Bookmarks Netsite: http://www.ucmp.berkeley.edu/dilophosaur/details.html
Members WebMail Connections BizJournal SmartUpdate Mktplace
2. DILOPHOSAURUS DETAILS
Double Crest {
"THE SPECIMEN WAS BROUGHT TO BERKELEY and cleaned up by a WPA project under Dr. Ron Langston. It took three men two years to clean and prepare the skeleton and then make a wall mount of the animal. We knew it was new, and in 1954 I published a preliminary description naming it Megalosaurus wetherilli thinking it might just as well belong there as anywhere else. We didn't know how new it was."
"IN 1964 I BECAME CONCERNED OVER THE AGE OF THE ANIMAL. It was based on differences of opinion as to whether the
100%

Figure 7-10 Dilophosaurus details

Netscape window displays the URL of the page currently displayed in the Content area or a URL you have typed in and want to visit. In Figure 7-10, the Goto field of the Location toolbar displays the URL **http://www.ucmp.berkeley.edu/dilophosaur/details.html**, whereas the Netscape home page in Figure 7-9 displays the URL **http://home.netscape.com**. Because you do not have to enter the `http://` when you enter a URL to display a Web page, these characters are often omitted when a URL is shown in print (as in this book). Another important item that appears on the **Menu** toolbar is the **File** menu. This menu includes items that let you print pages at your local printer and exit from Netscape. Below the Netscape **Menu** toolbar is the **Navigation** toolbar. Each button on the **Navigation** toolbar is associated with a particular function; buttons to move backward and forward in the list of recently visited Web pages make navigation much easier. You can use the **Stop** button (with a picture of a stoplight) on the **Navigation** toolbar to terminate a transfer at any time. Below the **Navigation** and **Location** toolbars is the **Personal** toolbar, which you can personalize to contain buttons pointing to any URL you like.

As you move the mouse pointer around the screen, it changes shape when it is on top of a hyperlink, and the **Status Message** field displays the link's URL. The URLs can represent different sections within a single file (document) or the locations of files at sites separated by thousands of miles.

▲▲ Navigating the Web

In addition to navigating through the Web by links, you can use a *search engine* to explore the Web. A search engine is an interface to a large database of resources available through the World Wide Web. Each search engine relies on its own database, which its creators have built up over time by using a program that wanders around the Web automatically and indexes the contents of all the pages it finds.

Clicking on the **Search** button on the **Navigation** toolbar presents you with a list of *search engines.* Click on a search engine, such as InfoSeek or Yahoo. Enter the string you want to search for in the small query window and press **RETURN**, or click on the button to the right of the query window; the engine searches its extensive database of URLs for the word(s) you specified and displays a list of sites that contain that word or words. Read through this list to see if a site interests you. Each of the names in this list is a hypertext link to the site identified by the name: Click on the name to visit the site.

For more information see "Using a Search Engine" on page 238.

▲▲ Reading Netnews

You can use Netscape to read netnews quite easily. As with any newsreader, you need to have access to, and know the address of, your news server before you start: Check with your Internet service provider (ISP). To set up Netscape to read netnews, first choose **Edit** from the **Menu** toolbar: Netscape displays a popup menu. Next select **Preferences** from the popup menu: Netscape displays a new window named **Preferences**, with a list of categories along the left side (Figure 7-11). Each of the major categories has subcategories that are visible when you expand the category. To expand a category click on the triangle to the left of a category name: You see the expanded category and the triangle points

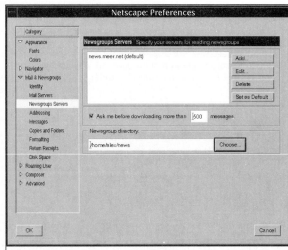

*Figure 7-11   Netscape **Edit/Preferences** window*

down. Click again to make the triangle point to the right and contract the list. Expand the **Mail & News-groups** category if it is not already expanded and click on the **Newsgroup Servers** subcategory (Figure 7-11). Click on **Add...** to the right of the **Newsgroup Servers** window to display another window. Enter the address of the news server you want to use and click on **OK** (you do not have to change any of the other items in this window. To start with leave **Ask me before downloading more than XXX messages.** checked and set to 500. If you have a slower Internet connection, you may want to lower this value in the future. In the **Newsgroup directory** subwindow, enter the name of the directory you want to store news items in (**~/news** works fine) or click on **Choose...** to search for a directory. Once you have made these entries, click on the **OK** box at the bottom of the form, and you are done with the setup.

Once you have set things up, select **Communicator** from the **Menu** toolbar, and then choose **Newsgroups**. The Message **Center** window will pop up and you will see a (possibly empty) list of mail folders. The news directory is generally at the bottom labeled with the name of your news server. To add newsgroups select **Subscribe** from the **Navigation** toolbar and enter or pick the groups you want to subscribe to. To read newsgroups expand the news directory by clicking on the plus sign (+) to the left of the news directory's name; double-click on the name of the newsgroup you want to visit, and you will see the window shown in Figure 7-12.

The upper portion of the **Content** area lists the postings (the newsgroup items), including the name of the sender and the subject. Click on a posting that interests you, and after a moment the item will appear in the lower portion of

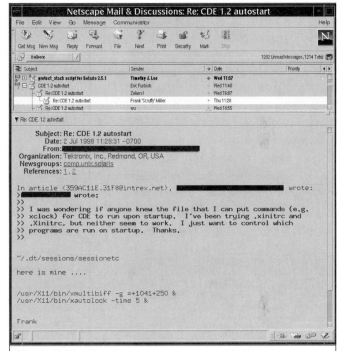

Figure 7-12   Reading a news posting with Netscape

the **News** window. You can read and reply to postings from this window. For more information on Netscape News, refer to the online Netscape documentation by selecting **Help** at the right end of the **Menu** toolbar.

▲▲ Downloading Files

You can use Netscape or another browser to look at and download files from an **ftp** or **html** site. Suppose you enter **ftp://sunsite.unc.edu** in the **Goto** field of the **Location** toolbar and press **RETURN**. After seeing the initial set of directories, click on **pub** (many sites give their public directory this name). The resulting display is shown in Figure 7-13. You can then click on any of the directories (try **solaris**) to view the available files. When you click on a file that is intended to be downloaded, Netscape will open a window asking you where to put the file on your system. For more information see "Downloading a File Using a Browser (and Installing It)" on page 984.

▲▲ Using Bookmarks

Netscape's bookmark feature enables you to save the names and URLs of Web pages that are of special interest to you or that you access frequently. Because it is nearly impossible to remember the sequence of links that led to a certain page of interest, and almost as difficult to remember many URLs, this feature can save a lot of time and frustration. Clicking on **Bookmarks** on the **Location** toolbar displays a list of bookmarks with a menu as the first three items on the list. Click on a bookmark to visit the location that bookmarks points to or select **Add** (to add the URL you are currently viewing as a bookmark), **File** (to file a bookmark in a bookmark folder/directory), or **Edit** (to edit bookmarks) from the menu at the top of

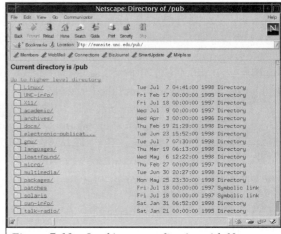

*Figure 7-13   Looking at an **ftp** site with Netscape*

the list. You can also choose **Bookmarks** from the **Communicator** popup menu (on the **Menu** toolbar) to browse through a hierarchical list of bookmarks.

Over time you will build a list of interesting Web pages; following are a few to get you started. Also see Appendix B.

URL	Contents
www.sun.com/solaris	The root of Sun's Solaris site
docs.sun.com	Sun documentation site
www.w3.org/pub/WWW	World Wide Web Consortium
www.yahoo.com	General-purpose hierarchical directory and search engine
home.netscape.com	The home of Netscape
www.sobell.com	The author's home page
www.cnn.com	CNN News
www.altavista.com	General-purpose hierarchical directory and search engine

▲▲ Using a Search Engine

Search engine is a name that applies to a group of hardware and software tools that helps you find sites on the World Wide Web that have the specific information you are looking for. A search engine relies on a database of information collected by a *Web crawler,* a program that regularly looks through the millions upon millions of pages that make up the World Wide Web. It also must have a way of collating the information the web crawler collects so you can access it quickly, easily, and in a manner that makes it most useful to you. This part of the search engine is called an *index*—it allows you to search for a word, a group of words, or a concept and returns the URLs of Web pages that pertain to what you are searching for.

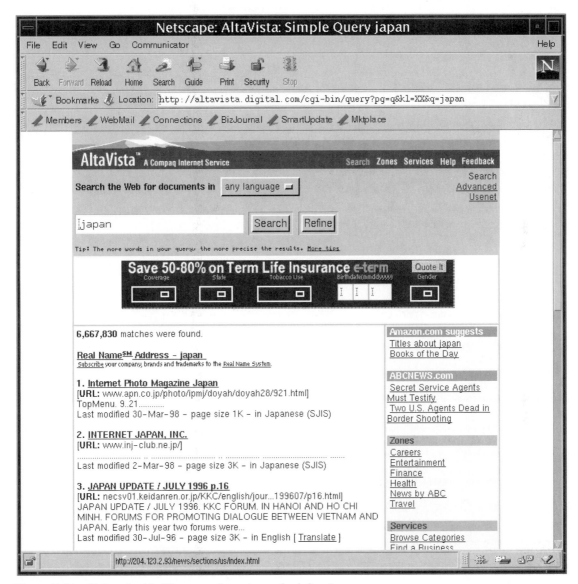

Figure 7-14   Using the AltaVista search engine to look for japan

There are many different types of search engines on the Internet. Each type of search engine has its own set of strengths and weaknesses. You can obtain a current list of search engines by going to the URL **home.netscape.com/escapes/internet_search.html** or by pressing the Search button on the Navigation toolbar. This section describes how to use AltaVista (**www.altavista.com**) to locate specific pages on the Web. Figure 7-14 shows the AltaVista Main Page. This is an HTML front end that allows you to query the index that the search engine has created. If you want more information about the hardware and software behind this site, click on the words About AltaVista at the bottom of the AltaVista home page.

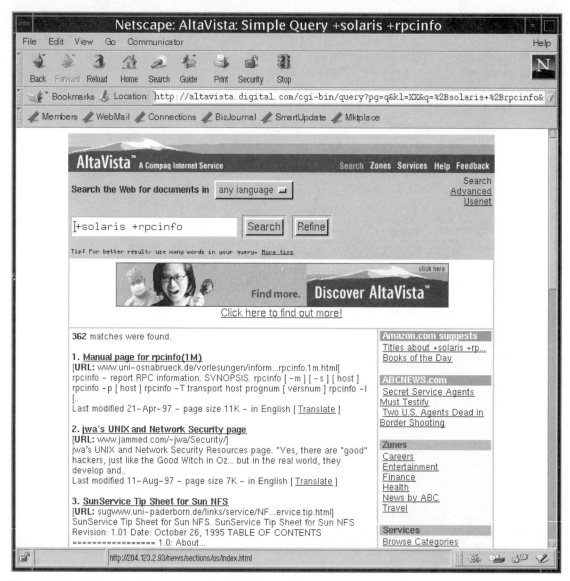

Figure 7-15   Using + to force a search to include words

To search the index type your query into the window that is just to the left of the **Search** button. For a simple search enter a single word such as solaris or dog or japan. A search on japan (Figure 7-14) returns almost seven million links. A more limiting search makes your job of searching through returned links much easier. If you are looking for information on the **rpcinfo** utility, you could enter `rpcinfo`. The search engine would return every site that has information on `rpcinfo`: SunOS `rpcinfo`, Ultrix `rpcinfo`, Unicos `rpcinfo`, Linux `rpcinfo`, VAX `rpcinfo`, and so on. If you just want to see sites that only cover Solaris **rpcinfo**, you can specify the search criteria as `solaris rpcinfo`. The **SPACE** between the words implies AND/OR, so that in addition to sites that have information on both words, the search also returns sites that have information only on Solaris or only on **rpcinfo**. You would get more sites than when you searched on **rpcinfo** alone. As Figure 7-15 shows, you can force the search engine to return only sites that contain a specific reference by putting a plus sign in front of the word. When you specify `+solaris +rpcinfo`, the search engine returns only sites that contain references to both Solaris and **rpcinfo**.

The preceding example returns sites that contain references to both Solaris and **rpcinfo** *anywhere in the document.* If you want to query for `red hat`, you would not use this technique. You actually want to find sites that have the two words next to each other. You do not want to find a story about a `red ball` and `green hat`. To find two words next to each other, you must enclose the words within double quotation marks (`"red hat"`).

Finally if you want the Red Hat version of **rpcinfo** for Linux, you can query for `+"red hat" +linux +rpcinfo`. You can also perform much more complex queries that include the NEAR, NOT, AND, *, and OR operators. Using AltaVista, click on **Help** to get information about how to construct a query. Click on **Advanced** to construct a more complex query. Most search engines include instructions for creating both simple and complex queries. If you are using a search engine other than AltaVista, the query syntax may be different.

▲ Other WWW Browsers

There are many Web browsers other than Netscape that you might want to consider using with your Solaris system. First is HotJava, a browser that comes with Solaris (this may not be your best choice as it will not be included with future versions of Solaris). If you do not use the X Window System, you may want to try a text browser such as **lynx**. Mosaic is still available for Solaris. Although each Web browser is unique, they all allow you to move about the Internet viewing HTML documents, listening to sounds, and retrieving files.

▲ More about URLs

Consider the following URL:

```
http://www.w3.org/pub/WWW
```

The first component in the URL indicates the type of resource, in this case, **http** (HyperText Transfer Protocol). There are other valid resource names, such as **https** (secure **http**), **ftp**, and **gopher**, that represent information available on the Web using other protocols. Next comes a colon and double slash (**://**). Frequently the `http://` string is omitted from a URL in print as you seldom need to enter them to get to the URL. Following this is the full name of the host that acts as the server for the information (**www.w3.org**). The rest of the URL is a relative pathname to the file that contains the information (**pub/www**). Although there is no suffix on this address, the implied suffix (or filename) is **index.html**. The implied filename suffix, **html**, indicates that its contents are expressed in HTML (HyperText Markup Language), which is the dominant language of the Web.

By convention many sites identify their WWW servers by prefixing a host or domain name with **www**. For example you can reach the Web server at the New Jersey Institute of Technology at **www.njit.edu**. When you use a browser to explore the World Wide Web, you may never need to use a URL directly. However as more information is published in hypertext form, you cannot help but find URLs everywhere—not just online in mail messages and USENET articles but also in newspapers, advertisements, and product labels.

If you know the URL of a resource on the Web, you can enter it in the Goto field of the Location tool-bar. Pressing RETURN loads that page into the Netscape window. Then you can click on links in the usual manner.

Start Optional

▲ Creating Your Own Web Page

Eventually you may want to create your own Web page. To do this it is useful to learn HyperText Markup Language (HTML). There are many HTML editors available for Solaris (such as the one built into Netscape) that enable you to view your Web page as you are constructing it. While HTML editors are easy to use, you can get started creating HTML files with a standard text editor, such as **dtpad** or **vi**.

Figure 7-16 shows a simple Web page displayed by Netscape Navigator and the source that created it. Web browsers, such as Netscape and Mosaic, read HTML documents and interpret tags in them that tell how to organize and display the information within the documents on the screen. Tags are enclosed in angle brackets and consist of one or more characters that tell the browser how to format a portion of text in the document, such as a title or heading. Other tags are used to identify a portion of text as a link to related information. Tags usually appear in pairs; for example <TITLE> precedes a title and </TITLE> follows it, signaling an end to the title formatting.

You can view the source for a Web page that is displayed in the Content area of your Navigator window by choosing the Document Source button in the top-level View menu.

Stop Optional

Summary

A Solaris system attached to a network is probably communicating on an Ethernet, which may be linked to other local area networks (LANs) and wide area networks (WANs). Communication between local area networks and wide area networks requires the use of gateways and routers. Gateways translate the local data to a format suitable for the wide area network, and routers make decisions about optimal routing of the data along the way. The most widely used network, by far, is the Internet.

Basic networking tools allow Solaris users to log in on remote systems (**rlogin**, **telnet**), run commands on remote systems (**rsh**), and copy files quickly from one system to another (**rcp**, **ftp**). Many tools that were originally designed to support communication on a single host computer (for example **finger**, **talk**, **pine**) have been extended to recognize network addresses, thus allowing users on different systems to interact with one another. Other features, such as the Network File System (NFS), were created to extend the basic UNIX model and to simplify information sharing.

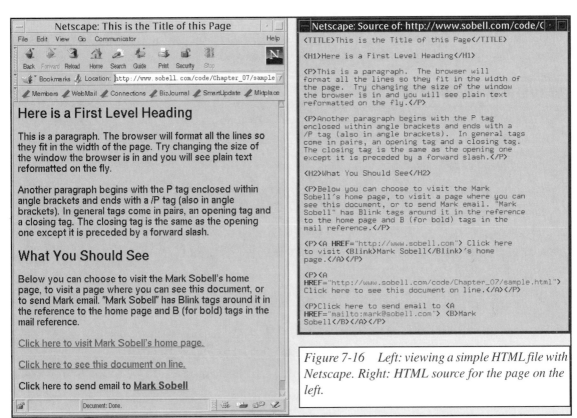

Figure 7-16   Left: viewing a simple HTML file with Netscape. Right: HTML source for the page on the left.

Two major advantages of computer networks over other ways of connecting computers are that they enable systems to communicate at high speeds and they require few physical interconnections (typically one per system, often on a shared cable). The Internet Protocol (IP), the universal language of the Internet, has made it possible for dissimilar computer systems around the world to communicate easily with one another. Technological advances continue to improve the performance of computer systems and the networks that link them together.

One way to gather information on the Internet is USENET news (netnews). Many Solaris users routinely read USENET news to learn about the latest resources available for their systems. USENET news is organized into newsgroups that cover a wide range of topics, computer-related and otherwise. To read USENET news you need to have access to a news server and the appropriate client software. Many modern mailers, such as **pine** and Netscape, are capable of reading netnews.

The rapid increase of network communication speeds in recent years has encouraged the development of many new applications and services. The World Wide Web provides access to vast information stores on the Internet and is noted for its extensive use of hypertext links to promote efficient searching through related documents. The World Wide Web adheres to the client/server model so pervasive in the UNIX and Solaris networked communities; typically the WWW client is local to a site or is made available through an Internet service provider. WWW servers are responsible for providing the information requested by their many clients.

The Netscape Navigator is a WWW client program that has enormous popular appeal. Netscape uses a graphical user interface to give you access to text, picture, and audio information. Netscape makes extensive use of these hypermedia to simplify access to and enhance the presentation of information.

Review Exercises

1. Describe the similarities and differences between these utilities:

   a. **rcp** and **ftp**

   b. **rlogin** and **telnet**

   c. **rsh** and **rlogin**

2. Suppose **rwho** is disabled on the systems on your local area network. Describe two ways to find out who is logged in on some of the other machines attached to your network.

3. Explain the client/server model, and give three examples of services that take advantage of this model on Solaris systems.

4. What is the difference between a diskless and a dataless workstation? Name some advantages and disadvantages of each approach.

5. An interesting language named Perl was developed for UNIX systems. It is in the public domain (free). How can you use the Internet to find a copy and download it to your system?

6. What is the difference between the World Wide Web and the Internet?

7. If you have access to the World Wide Web, answer the following:

   a. What browser do you use?

   b. What is the URL of the author's home page? How many links does it have?

   c. Does your browser allow you to create bookmarks? If so, how do you create a bookmark? How can you delete one?

8. Explain what happens if you transfer a binary file while running **ftp** in ASCII mode. What happens if you transfer an ASCII file in binary mode?

Advanced Review Exercises

9. Refer to the network shown in Figure 7-1. Someone at Site A sends a message to three users, one at each site. Each of the recipients is on a Solaris workstation that is attached to an Ethernet cable. Which message is likely to arrive first? Last? Explain your answer.

10. Suppose the link between routers 1 and 2 is down in the Internet shown in Figure 7-1. What happens if someone at Site C sends a message to a user on a workstation attached to the Ethernet cable at Site B? What happens if the router at Site B is down? What does this tell you about designing network configurations?

11. If you have a class B network and want to divide it into subnets, each with 126 hosts, what subnet mask should you use? How many networks will be available? What are the four addresses (broadcast and network number) for the network starting at 131.204.18.x?

The vi Editor

This chapter begins with a history and description of **vi**, a powerful, sometimes cryptic, interactive, visually oriented text editor. It continues with a tutorial that shows you how to use **vi** to create and edit a file. This chapter also goes into detail about many of the **vi** commands and explains the use of parameters for customizing **vi** to meet your needs. At the end of the chapter is a quick reference summary of **vi** commands.

Solaris2 includes an updated copy of the original version of **vi**, but there are also a number of alternative versions, or *clones*. The most popular **vi** clones are **elvis**, **nvi**, **vile**, and **vim**. All four clones offer additional features beyond those provided with the original **vi** but also may lack a few of the fringe features in some cases. The examples in this chapter are based on the standard Solaris **vi** installed on your system, which is based on the original source. If you use one of the other versions, you may notice slight differences from the examples used in this book.

▲ History

Before **vi** was developed the standard UNIX system editor was **ed**. The **ed** editor was line oriented, which made it difficult to see the context of your editing. Then **ex** came along—**ex** was a superset of **ed**. The most notable advantage that **ex** had over **ed** was a display editing facility that allowed users to work with a full screen of text instead of working with only a line at a time. While you were using **ex**, you could use the display editing facility by giving **ex** the command **vi** (for Visual Mode). People used the display editing facility of **ex** so extensively that the developers of **ex** made it possible to start the editor with the display editing facility already running, without having to start **ex** and give the **vi** command. Appropriately they named the program **vi**. You can still call the Visual Mode from **ex**, and you can go back to **ex** while you are using **vi**. Give **vi** a **Q** command to use **ex**, or give **ex** a **vi** command to switch to Visual Mode.

The **vi** editor is not a text formatting program. It does not justify margins, center titles, or provide the output formatting features of a sophisticated word processing system. It is a sophisticated text editor meant to be used to write code (C, HTML, and so on), short notes, and input to a text formatting system such as **troff**.

Because **vi** is so large and powerful, only some of its features are described here. Nonetheless if **vi** is completely new to you, you may find even the limited set of commands described in this chapter overwhelming. The **vi** editor provides a variety of different ways to accomplish any specified editing task. A useful strategy for learning **vi** is to begin by learning a subset of commands to accomplish basic editing tasks. Then as you become more comfortable with the editor, you can learn other commands that enable you to do things more quickly and efficiently. The following tutorial section introduces a very basic but useful set of **vi** commands and features that allow you to create and edit a file.

Many features described in this chapter, although easily accessible from **vi**, are **ex** commands. If you cannot find what you are looking for in the **vi man** page, look at the **ex man** page.

▲ Tutorial: Using vi to Create and Edit a File

This section is a tutorial introduction to **vi** that describes how to start **vi**, enter text, move the cursor, correct text, save the file to the disk, and exit from **vi**. It discusses two of the modes of operation of **vi** and how to go from one mode to the other. It lists commands you can use to create a file and store it on disk.

▲▲ Specifying a Terminal

Because **vi** takes advantage of features that are specific to various kinds of terminals, you must tell it what type of terminal or terminal emulator you are using. On many systems your terminal type is set for you automatically. If you need to specify your terminal type, see "How Do I Specify the Terminal I Am Using?" on page 987.

▲▲ Starting vi

Start **vi** with the following command line to bring **vi** up in Beginner Mode and create a file named **practice** (use **vi** in place of **vedit** to use **vi** in Normal Mode):

```
$ vedit practice
```

When you press **RETURN**, the command line disappears, and the terminal screen looks similar to the one shown in Figure 8-1.

```
    ~
    ~
    ~
    ~
    ~
    ~
    ~
    ~
    ~
"practice" [New File]
```

Figure 8-1   Starting **vi**

The tildes (~) indicate that the file is empty. They go away as you add lines of text to the file. If your screen looks like a distorted version of the one shown, your terminal type is probably not set correctly. If your screen looks similar to the one shown in Figure 8-2, your terminal type is not set at all.

```
$ vi practice
I don't know what kind of terminal you are on - all I have is 'unknown'.
[Using open mode]
"practice" [New File]
```

*Figure 8-2   Starting **vi** without your terminal type set correctly*

If you start **vi** with an incorrect terminal type, press ESCAPE and then give the following command to exit from **vi** and get the shell prompt back:

:q!

When you enter the colon (:), **vi** moves the cursor to the bottom line of the screen. The characters q! tell **vi** to quit without saving your work. (You will not ordinarily exit from **vi** in this way because you typically want to save your work.) You must press RETURN after you give this command. Once you get the shell prompt back, see "How Do I Specify the Terminal I Am Using?" on page 987, and then start **vi** again.

The **practice** file is new; there is no text in it yet. The **vi** editor displays a message similar to the one shown in Figure 8-1 on the status (bottom) line of the terminal to show that you are creating and editing a new file. Your version of **vi** may display a different message. When you edit an existing file, **vi** displays the first few lines of the file and gives status information about the file on the status line.

▲▲ Command and Input Modes

Two of the **vi** editor's modes of operation are *Command Mode* and *Input Mode* (Figure 8-3). While **vi** is in Command Mode, you can give **vi** commands. For example in Command Mode you can delete text or exit from **vi**. You can also command **vi** to enter Input Mode. In Input Mode **vi** accepts anything you enter as text and displays it on the screen. Press ESCAPE to return **vi** to Command Mode.

The **vi** editor does not normally keep you informed about which mode it is in. The following command causes **vi** to display the mode it is in while you are entering text or commands:

:set showmode

The colon (:) in this command puts **vi** into another mode, *Last Line Mode*. While in this mode, **vi** keeps the cursor on the bottom line of the screen. When you enter the colon, **vi** moves the cursor to the last

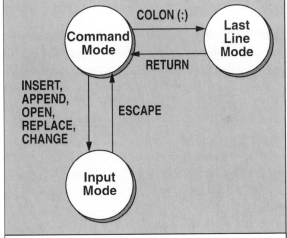

*Figure 8-3   Modes in **vi** (see page 251 for an explanation of Replace and Change)*

line. Finish the command by pressing RETURN. There are three types of Input Modes: OPEN, INSERT, and APPEND. Refer to "Show Mode" on page 275.

When you give **vi** a command, it is important to remember that the editor is case sensitive. The **vi** editor interprets the same letter as two different commands, depending on whether you enter an upper- or lowercase

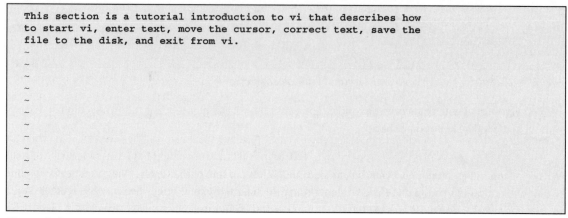

```
This section is a tutorial introduction to vi that describes how
to start vi, enter text, move the cursor, correct text, save the
file to the disk, and exit from vi.
~
~
~
~
~
~
~
~
~
~
~
~
~
```

Figure 8-4   Entering text with **vi**

character. Beware of the key that causes your keyboard to send only uppercase characters; it is typically labeled **CAPSLOCK** or **SHIFTLOCK**. If you set this key to enter uppercase text while you are in Input Mode and then exit to Command Mode, **vi** interprets your commands as uppercase letters. It can be very confusing when this happens because **vi** does not appear to be following the commands you are giving it.

▲▲ Entering Text

When you start a new session with **vi**, you must put it in Input Mode before you can enter text. To put **vi** in Input Mode, press the **i** key (insert before the cursor) or the **a** key (append after the cursor). If you have not set **showmode**, **vi** does not respond to let you know that it is in Input Mode.

If you are not sure whether **vi** is in Input Mode, press the **ESCAPE** key; **vi** returns to Command Mode if it was in Input Mode or beeps (some terminals flash) if it is already in Command Mode. You can put **vi** back in Input Mode by pressing the **i** key again.

While **vi** is in Input Mode, you can enter text by typing on the terminal. If the text does not appear on the screen as you type, you are not in Input Mode.

Enter the sample paragraph shown in Figure 8-4, pressing the **RETURN** key to end each line. If you do not press **RETURN** before the cursor reaches the right side of the screen or window, **vi** will wrap the text so that it appears to start a new line: Physical lines will not correspond to programmatic lines, and editing will become more difficult.

While you are using **vi**, you can always correct any typing mistakes you make. If you notice a mistake on the line you are entering, you can correct it before you continue. Refer to the following table. You can correct other mistakes later. When you finish entering the paragraph, press **ESCAPE** to return **vi** to Command Mode.

Correcting Text as You Insert It   The keys that allow you to back up and correct a shell command line serve the same functions when **vi** is in Input Mode. These keys include the erase, line kill, and word kill keys (usually **CONTROL-H**, **CONTROL-U**, and **CONTROL-W**). Although **vi** may not remove deleted text from the screen as you back up over it, **vi** removes it when you type over it or press **RETURN**.

There are two restrictions on the use of these correction keys. They allow you to back up only over text on the line you are entering (you cannot back up to a previous line), and they back up only over text that you just entered. As an example, assume that **vi** is in Input Mode, you are entering text, and you press the **ESCAPE** key to return **vi** to Command Mode. Then you give the **i** command to put **vi** back into Input Mode. Now you cannot back up over text you entered the first time you were in the Input Mode, even if the text is part of the line you are working on.

Moving the Cursor

When you are using **vi**, you need to move the cursor on the screen so that you can delete, insert, and correct text. While **vi** is in Command Mode, you can use the **RETURN** key, the **SPACE** bar, and the **ARROW** keys to move the cursor. If you prefer to keep your hand closer to the center of the keyboard, if your terminal does not have **ARROW** keys, or if the emulator you are using does not support them, you can use the **h**, **j**, **k**, and **l** (ell) keys to move the cursor left, down, up, and right, respectively.

Deleting Text

You can delete a single character by moving the cursor until it is over the character you want to delete and then giving the command **x**. You can delete a word by positioning the cursor on the first letter of the word and giving the command **dw** (delete word). You can delete a line of text by moving the cursor until it is anywhere on the line you want to delete and then giving the command **dd**.

The Undo Command

If you delete a character, line, or word by mistake, give the command **u** (undo) immediately after you give the Delete command; **vi** restores the deleted text. If you give the command **u** again immediately, **vi** undoes the Undo command, and the deleted text will be gone again. (In some **vi** clones this feature works differently, sometimes allowing you to back up over many of your actions.)

Inserting Additional Text

When you want to insert new text within text that you have already entered, move the cursor so that it is on the character that follows the new text you plan to enter. Then give the **i** (insert) command to put **vi** in Input Mode, enter the new text, and press **ESCAPE** to return **vi** to Command Mode. Or position the cursor on the character that precedes the new text and use the **a** (append) command.

To enter one or more lines, position the cursor on the line above where you want the new text to go. Give the command **o** (open). The **vi** editor opens a blank line, puts the cursor on it, and goes into Input Mode. Enter the new text, ending each line with a **RETURN**. When you are finished entering text, press **ESCAPE** to return **vi** to Command Mode.

Correcting Text

To correct text use **dd**, **dw**, or **x** to remove the incorrect text. Then use **i** or **o** to insert the correct text.

For example one way to change the word tutorial to section in Figure 8-4 is to use the **ARROW** keys to move the cursor until it is on top of the t in tutorial. Then give the command **dw** to delete the word tutorial. Put **vi** in Input Mode by giving an **i** command, enter the word section followed by a **SPACE**, and press **ESCAPE**. The word is changed, and **vi** is in Command Mode, waiting for another command. A shorthand for the two commands **dw** followed by the **i** command is **cw** (change word). The command **cw** automatically puts **vi** into Input Mode.

Page Breaks for the Printer

A **CONTROL-L** is a signal to a printer to skip to the top of the next page. You can enter this character anywhere in a document by simply pressing **CONTROL-L**. If a ^L does not appear, press **CONTROL-V** before **CONTROL-L**.

▲▲ Ending the Editing Session

While you are editing **vi** keeps the edited text in an area called the *Work Buffer*. When you finish editing, you must write out the contents of the Work Buffer to a disk file so that the edited text is saved and available when you next want it.

Make sure **vi** is in Command Mode, and use the **ZZ** command (you must use uppercase **Z**s) to write your newly entered text to the disk and end the editing session. After you give the **ZZ** command, **vi** returns control to the shell. You can exit with **:q!** if you do not want to save your work. Refer to page 284 for a summary of **vi** commands.

Do Not Confuse CONTROL-Z with ZZ

When you exit from **vi** with **ZZ**, make sure you use **ZZ** and not **CONTROL-Z**. If you are using a shell with job control, when you enter **CONTROL-Z vi** will disappear from your screen, almost as though you had exited from it. But **vi** will be running in the background with your file unsaved. See page 359 for more information.

▲ Introduction to vi Features

This section covers modes of operation, online help, the Work Buffer, emergency procedures, and other **vi** features.

▲▲ Modes of Operation

The **vi** editor is a part of the **ex** editor, which has five modes of operation:

- **ex** Command Mode
- **ex** Input Mode
- **vi** Command Mode
- **vi** Input Mode
- **vi** Last Line Mode

While you are using **vi**, you mostly use **vi** Command and Input Modes. On occasion you use Last Line Mode. While in Command Mode **vi** accepts keystrokes as commands, responding to each command as you enter it. In Command Mode **vi** does not display the characters you type. In Input Mode **vi** accepts keystrokes as text that it eventually puts into the file you are editing. It displays the text as you enter it. All commands that start with a colon (**:**) put **vi** in Last Line Mode. The colon moves the cursor to the bottom line of the screen, where you enter the rest of the command.

Watch the Caps Lock **Key and What Mode You Are In**

Almost anything you type in Command Mode means something to **vi**. If you think **vi** is in Input Mode when it is actually in Command Mode, the result of typing in text can be very confusing. When learning **vi**, you may want to set the **showmode** parameter (page 275) to help remind you which mode you are using. There is also **vedit**, which is an alias for **vi** that puts it in Beginner Mode by setting the **showmode** parameter (page 275) and turning off the **magic** parameter (page 275).

Also keep your eye on the Caps Lock key. In Command Mode uppercase letters have different effects than lowercase ones. It can be disorienting to give commands and have **vi** give the "wrong" responses.

In addition to the position of the cursor, there is another important difference between Last Line Mode and Command Mode. When you give a command in Command Mode, you do not terminate the command with a **RETURN**. However you must terminate all Last Line Mode commands with a **RETURN** (or **ESCAPE**).

You do not normally use the **ex** modes. When this chapter refers to Input and Command Modes, it means the **vi** modes, not the **ex** modes.

At the start of an editing session, **vi** is in Command Mode. There are several commands, such as Insert and Append, that put **vi** in Input Mode. When you press the **ESCAPE** key, **vi** always reverts to Command Mode.

The Change and Replace commands combine Command and Input Modes. The Change command deletes the text you want to change and puts **vi** in Input Mode so you can insert new text. The Replace command deletes the character(s) you overwrite and inserts the new one(s) you enter. Figure 8-3 on page 247 shows the modes as well as the methods for changing between them.

▲▲ The Display

The **vi** editor uses the status line and several special symbols to give information about what is happening during an editing session.

▲▲▲ The Status Line

The **vi** editor displays status information on the bottom line of the display area. This information includes error messages, information about the deletion or addition of blocks of text, and file status information. In addition **vi** displays Last Line Mode commands on the status line.

▲▲▲ Redrawing the Screen

You may want to redraw (refresh) the screen if it becomes garbled, overwritten (as when another user writes to you while you are in **vi**), or with some settings, when **vi** puts characters on the screen (sometimes it may leave @ on a line instead of deleting it). When your screen is overwritten by another user, the other user's message becomes intermixed with the display of the Work Buffer, and things can get confusing. The other user's message *does not* become part of the Work Buffer—it affects only the display. If this happens when you are in Input Mode, press ESCAPE to get into Command Mode, and then press CONTROL-L (or CONTROL-R) to redraw the screen.

Be sure to read the other user's message before redrawing the screen, because redrawing the screen causes the message to disappear. You can write back to the other user while in **vi** (page 280), quit **vi** and use the **write** utility from the shell, or open another window if you are using a GUI.

▲▲▲▲ The Tilde (~) Symbol

If the end of the file is displayed on the screen, **vi** marks lines that would appear past the end of the file with a tilde (~) at the left of the screen. When you start editing a new file, the **vi** editor marks every line on the screen, except for the first line, with these symbols.

▲▲ Correcting Text as You Insert It

While **vi** is in Input Mode, you can use the erase and line kill keys to back up over text that you are inserting so you can correct it. You can also use CONTROL-W to back up to the beginning of the word you are entering. Using these techniques, you cannot back up past the beginning of the line you are working on or past the beginning of the text you entered since you most recently put **vi** into Input Mode.

▲▲ Command Case

Be certain to observe the case of commands as this chapter describes them. The same letter serves as two different commands, depending on whether you enter it as an upper- or lowercase character.

If **vi** seems to be behaving strangely, make sure the terminal key SHIFTLOCK (on some terminals it is named CAPSLOCK) is off.

▲▲ The Work Buffer

The **vi** editor does all its work in the *Work Buffer*. At the start of an editing session, **vi** reads the file you are editing from the disk into the Work Buffer. During the editing session **vi** makes all changes to this copy of the file. It does not change the disk file until you write the contents of the Work Buffer back to the disk. Normally when you end an editing session, you command **vi** to write out the contents of the Work Buffer, which makes the changes to the text final. When you edit a new file, **vi** does not create the file until it writes the contents of the Work Buffer to the disk, usually at the end of the editing session.

Storing the text you are editing in the Work Buffer has advantages and disadvantages. If you accidentally end an editing session without writing out the contents of the Work Buffer, all your work is lost. However if you unintentionally make some major changes (such as deleting the entire contents of the Work Buffer), you can end the editing session without implementing the changes. The **vi** editor leaves the file as it was when you last wrote it out.

If you want to use the **vi** editor to look at a file but not to change it, you can use the **view** utility:

```
$ view filename
```

Calling the **view** utility actually calls the **vi** editor with the **−R** (readonly) option. Once you have invoked the editor in this way, you cannot write the contents of the Work Buffer back to the file whose name appeared on the command line. You can always write the Work Buffer out to a file with a different name.

▲▲ Line Length and File Size

The **vi** editor operates on any format file, provided the length of a single "line" (that is, the characters between two **NEWLINE** characters) can fit into available memory. The total length of the file is limited only by available disk space and memory.

▲▲ Abnormal Termination of an Editing Session

You can end an editing session in one of two ways: Either **vi** saves the changes you made during the editing session, or it does not save them. You can use the **ZZ** or **:wq** command from Command Mode to save your changes and exit from **vi** (page 250).

You can end an editing session without writing out the contents of the Work Buffer by giving the following command. (The **:** puts **vi** in Last Line Mode—you must press **RETURN** to execute the command.)

    :q!

When you use this command to end an editing session, **vi** does not preserve the contents of the Work Buffer; you lose all the work you did since the last time you wrote the Work Buffer to disk. The next time you edit or use the file, it appears as it did the last time you wrote the Work Buffer to disk. Use the **:q!** command cautiously.

When You Cannot Write Out a File

It may be necessary to write a file using **:w filename**, if you do not have write permission for the file you are editing. If you give the **ZZ** command and see the message `File is read only`, you do not have write permission for the file. Use the Write command with a temporary filename to write the file to disk under a different filename. If you do not have write permission to the working directory, **vi** may still not be able to write your file to the disk. Give the command again, using an absolute pathname of a dummy (nonexistent) file in your home directory in place of the filename. (For example Alex might give the command **:w /home/alex/temp**.)

If **vi** reports `File exists`, you will need to use **:w!** filename to overwrite the existing file (make sure this is what you want to do). See page 272.

You may run into a situation where you have created or edited a file, and **vi** will not let you exit. For example if you forgot to specify a filename when you first called **vi**, you get a message that the file cannot be written when you give the **ZZ** command. If **vi** does not let you exit normally, you can use the Write command (**:w**) to name the file and write it to disk before you quit using **vi**. To write the file give the following command, substituting the name of the file in place of *filename* (remember to follow the command with a **RETURN**):

    :w filename

After you give the Write command, you can use **:q** to quit using **vi**. You do not need to use the exclamation point (as in **q!**) because the exclamation point is necessary only when you have made changes since the last time you wrote the Work Buffer to disk. Refer to page 272 for more information about the Write command.

▲▲ Recovering Text after a Crash

If the system crashes while you are editing a file with **vi**, you can often recover text that would otherwise be lost. If the system saved a copy of your Work Buffer, it may send you mail telling you so. However even if you did not get mail when the system was brought up, give the following command to see if the system saved the contents of your Work Buffer:

```
$ vi -r
```

You will see a list of any Work Buffers that **vi** has saved (some may be old). If your work was saved, give the same command followed by a **SPACE** and the name of your file. After giving the command, you will be editing a recent copy of your Work Buffer. Use **:w** immediately to save the salvaged copy of the Work Buffer to disk, and then continue editing.

You Must Recover Files on the Machine You Were Using

The recovery feature of **vi** is specific to the machine you were using when the crash occurred. Because of this if you are running on a cluster, you must log in on the machine you were using before the crash in order to use the **–r** option.

▲ Command Mode—Moving the Cursor

While **vi** is in Command Mode, you can position the cursor over any character on the screen. You can also display a different portion of the Work Buffer on the screen. By manipulating the screen and cursor position, you can place the cursor on any character in the Work Buffer.

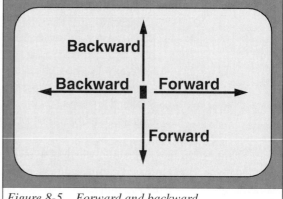

Figure 8-5   Forward and backward

You can move the cursor forward or backward through the text. As illustrated in Figure 8-5, *forward* always means toward the bottom of the screen and the end of the file. *Backward* means toward the top of the screen and the beginning of the file. When you use a command that moves the cursor forward past the end (right) of a line, the cursor generally moves to the beginning (left) of the next line. When you move it backward past the beginning of a line, it moves to the end of the previous line.

The length of a line in the Work Buffer may be too long to appear as a single line of the display area. When this happens, **vi** will wrap the current line onto the next line.

You can move the cursor through the text by any *Unit of Measure* (that is, character, word, line, sentence, paragraph, or screen). If you precede a cursor-movement command with a number, called a *Repeat Factor,* the cursor moves that number of units through the text. Refer to pages 281 and 283 at the end of this chapter for more precise definitions of these terms.

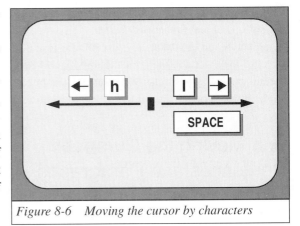

Figure 8-6   Moving the cursor by characters

▲▲ Moving the Cursor by Characters

The **SPACE** bar moves the cursor forward, one character at a time, toward the right side of the screen. The **l** (ell) key and the **RIGHT ARROW** key (Figure 8-6) do the same thing. The command **7 SPACE** or **7l** moves the cursor seven characters to the right. These keys *cannot* move the cursor past the end of the current line to the beginning of the next. The **h** and **LEFT ARROW** keys are similar to the **l** key but work in the opposite direction.

▲▲ Moving the Cursor by Words

The **w** (word) key moves the cursor forward to the first letter of the next word (Figure 8-7). Groups of punctuation count as words. This command goes to the next line if that is where the next word is. The command **15w** moves the cursor to the first character of the 15th subsequent word.

The **W** key is similar to the **w** key, except that it moves the cursor by blank-delimited words, including punctuation, as it skips forward. (Refer to "Blank-Delimited Word" on page 282.)

The **b** (back) key moves the cursor backward to the first letter of the previous word. The **B** key moves the cursor backward by blank-delimited words.

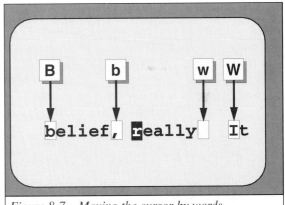

Figure 8-7   Moving the cursor by words

The **e** key moves the cursor to the end of the next word; **E** moves it to the end of the next blank-delimited word.

▲▲ Moving the Cursor by Lines

The **RETURN** key moves the cursor to the beginning of the next line (Figure 8-8), and the **j** and **DOWN ARROW** keys move it down one line to the character just below the current character. If there is no character immediately below the current character, the cursor moves to the end of the next line. The cursor will not move past the last line of text in the work buffer.

The **k** and **UP ARROW** keys are similar to the **j** key, but they work in the opposite direction. Also, the minus (–) key is similar to the **RETURN** key, but it works in the opposite direction.

▲▲ Moving the Cursor by Sentences and Paragraphs

The) and } keys move the cursor forward to the beginning of the next sentence or paragraph, respectively (Figure 8-9). The (and { keys move the cursor backward to the beginning of the current sentence or paragraph. See page 282 for more about sentences and paragraphs in **vi**.

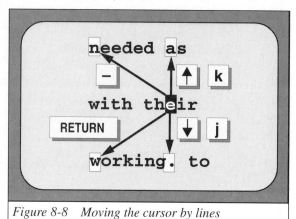

Figure 8-8   Moving the cursor by lines

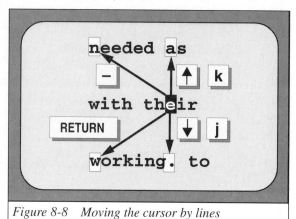

Figure 8-9   Moving the cursor by sentences, paragraphs, H, M, and L

▲▲ Moving the Cursor within the Screen

The **H** (Home) key positions the cursor at the left end of the top line of the screen. The **M** (Middle) key moves the cursor to the middle line, and **L** (Lower) moves it to the bottom line (Figure 8-9).

▲▲ Viewing Different Parts of the Work Buffer

The screen displays a portion of the text that is in the Work Buffer. You can display the text preceding or following the text on the screen by *scrolling* the display. You can also display a portion of the Work Buffer based on a line number.

Press **CONTROL-D** to scroll the screen Down (forward) through the file so that **vi** displays half a screenful of new text. Use **CONTROL-U** to scroll the screen Up (backward) the same amount. If you precede either of these commands with a number, **vi** will scroll that number of lines each time you use **CONTROL-D** or **CONTROL-U** for the rest of the session (unless you change the number of lines to scroll again). The **CONTROL-F** (forward) or **CONTROL-B** (backward) keys display almost a *whole* screenful of new text, leaving a couple of lines from the previous screen for continuity.

When you enter a line number followed by **G** (Goto), **vi** positions the cursor on that line in the Work Buffer. If you press **G** without a number, **vi** positions the cursor on the last line in the Work Buffer. Line numbers are implicit; your file does not need to have actual line numbers for you to use this command. Refer to "Line Numbers" on page 275 if you want **vi** to display line numbers.

▲ Input Mode

The Insert, Append, Open, Change, and Replace commands put **vi** in Input Mode. While **vi** is in Input Mode, you can put new text into the Work Buffer. Always press the **ESCAPE** key to return **vi** to Command Mode when you finish entering text. Refer to "Show Mode" on page 275 if you want **vi** to remind you when it is in Input Mode.

▲▲ The Insert Commands

The **i** (insert) command puts **vi** in Input Mode and places the text you enter *before* the character the cursor is on (the *current character*). The **I** command places text at the beginning of the current line (Figure 8-10). Although **i** and **I** commands sometimes overwrite text on the screen, the characters in the Work Buffer are not changed (only the display is affected). The overwritten text is redisplayed when you press **ESCAPE** and **vi** returns to Command Mode. Use **i** or **I** to insert a few characters or words into existing text or to insert text in a new file.

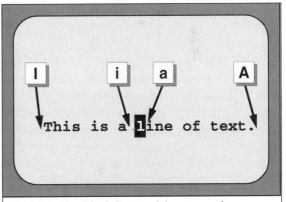

*Figure 8-10   The **i**, **I**, **a**, and **A** commands*

▲▲ The Append Commands

The **a** (append) command is similar to the **i** command, except that it places the text you enter *after* the current character (Figure 8-10). The **A** command places the text *after* the last character on the current line.

▲▲ The Open Commands

The **o** (open) and **O** commands open a blank line within existing text, place the cursor at the beginning of the new (blank) line, and put **vi** in Input Mode. The **O** command opens a line *above* the current line; **o** opens one below. Use the Open commands when entering several new lines within existing text.

▲▲ The Replace Commands

The **R** (replace) and **r** commands cause the new text you enter to overwrite (replace) existing text. The single character you enter following an **r** command overwrites the current character. After you enter that character, **vi** automatically returns to Command Mode. You do not need to press the **ESCAPE** key.

The **R** command causes *all* subsequent characters to overwrite existing text, until you press **ESCAPE** to return **vi** to Command Mode.

> ### Replacing TABs
>
> These commands may appear to behave strangely if you replace **TAB** characters. **TAB** characters can appear as several **SPACE**s—until you try to replace them. They are actually only one character and are replaced by a single character. Refer to "Invisible Characters" on page 276 for information on how to display **TAB**s as visible characters.

▲▲ The Quote Command

You can use the Quote command, **CONTROL-V**, while you are in Input Mode to enter any characters into your text, including characters that normally have special meaning to **vi**. Among these characters are **CONTROL-L** (or **CONTROL-R**), which redraws the screen; **CONTROL-W**, which backs the cursor up a word to the left; and **ESCAPE**, which ends Input Mode.

To insert one of these characters into your text, type **CONTROL-V** and then the character. **CONTROL-V** quotes the single character that follows it. For example to insert the sequence **ESCAPE[2J** into a file you are creating in **vi**, you type the character sequence **CONTROL-V ESCAPE[2J**. This is the character sequence that clears the screen of a DEC VT-100 terminal. Although you would not ordinarily want to type this sequence into a document, you might want to use it or another **ESCAPE** sequence in a shell script you are creating in **vi**. Refer to Chapters 11, 12, and 13 for information about writing shell scripts.

▲ Command Mode—Deleting and Changing Text

The commands in this section allow you to delete and replace, or change, text in the document you are editing. The Undo command is also covered because it allows you to restore deleted or changed text.

▲▲ The Undo Command

The Undo command, **u**, undoes what you just did. It restores text that you deleted or changed by mistake. The Undo command restores only the most recently deleted text. If you delete a line and then change a word, Undo restores only the changed word—not the deleted line. The **U** command restores the current line to the way it was before you started changing it, even after several changes. If you move up or down a line or lines, and then come back to a line, the **U** key will not work, but the **u** key will always undo the most recent change no matter what line you are on. The **U** key is only valid and will only undo all changes to a line if you do not leave that line.

▲▲ The Delete Character Command

The **x** command deletes the current character. You can precede the **x** command by a Repeat Factor (page 283) to delete several characters on the current line, starting with the current character. The **X** command deletes characters to the left of the cursor.

▲▲ The Delete Command

The **d** command removes text from the Work Buffer. The amount of text that **d** removes depends on the Repeat Factor and the Unit of Measure (page 281) you enter after the **d**. After the text is deleted, **vi** is still in Command Mode.

> ## Use **dd** to Delete a Single Line
>
> The command **d RETURN** deletes two lines: The current line and the following one. Use the **dd** command to delete just the current line, or precede **dd** by a Repeat Factor (page 283) to delete several lines.

You can delete from the current cursor position up to a specific character on the same line. To delete up to the next semicolon (;) give the command **dt;**. If you want to delete the remainder of the current line use **D** or **d$**. The following table lists of some Delete commands. Each command, except the last group that starts with **dd**, deletes *from* the current character.

Delete Command	Action
dl	Deletes current character (same as the **x** command)
d0	Deletes to beginning of line
d^	Deletes to the first character of the line (not including spaces or tabs)
dw	Deletes to end of word
d3w	Deletes to end of third word
db	Deletes to beginning of word

Delete Command	Action
dW	Deletes to end of blank-delimited word
dB	Deletes to beginning of blank-delimited word
d7B	Deletes to seventh previous beginning of blank-delimited word
d)	Deletes to end of sentence
d4)	Deletes to end of fourth sentence
d(	Deletes to beginning of sentence
d}	Deletes to end of paragraph
d{	Deletes to beginning of paragraph
d7{	Deletes to seventh paragraph preceding beginning of paragraph
dd	Deletes the current line
d/*text*	Deletes forward in text up to but not including the next occurrence of word ***text***
df*c*	Deletes forward on current line up to and including next occurrence of character *c*
dt*c*	Deletes on current line up to the next occurrence of *c*
D	Deletes to the end of line
d$	Deletes to the end of line
5dd	Deletes five lines starting with the current line
dL	Deletes through last line on screen
dH	Deletes through first line on screen
dG	Deletes through end of Work Buffer
d1G	Deletes through beginning of Work Buffer

Exchanging Characters

If two characters are out of order, position the cursor on the first character and give the command **xp**.

Exchanging Lines

If two lines are out of order, position the cursor on the first line and give the command **ddp**.

▲▲ The Change Command

The **c** command replaces existing text with new text. The new text does not have to occupy the same space as the existing text. You can change a word to several words, a line to several lines, or a paragraph to a single character.

The Change command deletes the amount of text specified by the Unit of Measure (page 281) that follows it and puts **vi** in Input Mode. When you finish entering the new text and press **ESCAPE**, the old word, line, sentence, or paragraph is changed to the new one. Pressing **ESCAPE** without entering new text has the effect of deleting the specified text.

When you change less than a line of text, **vi** does not delete the text immediately. Instead the **c** command places a dollar sign at the end of the text that is to be changed and leaves **vi** in Input Mode. You may appear to overwrite text, but only the text that precedes the dollar sign changes in the Work Buffer. Other text remains in the Work Buffer and is redisplayed when you press **ESCAPE**. When you change one or more lines, **vi** deletes the lines as soon as you give the Change command.

The **C** command replaces the text from the cursor position to the end of the line.

The following table lists some Change commands. Each command, except the last two, changes text *from* the current character.

Change Command	Action
cl	Changes the current character
cw	Changes to end of word
c3w	Changes to end of third word
cb	Changes to beginning of word
cW	Changes to end of blank-delimited word
cB	Changes to beginning of blank-delimited word
c7B	Changes to beginning of seventh previous blank-delimited word
c$	Changes to the beginning of the line
c0	Changes to the end of the line
c)	Changes to end of sentence
c4)	Changes to end of fourth sentence
c(	Changes to beginning of sentence
c}	Changes to end of paragraph
c{	Changes to beginning of paragraph
c7{	Changes to beginning of seventh preceding paragraph
ctc	Changes on current line up to the next occurrence of *c*
C	Changes to end of line
cc	Changes the current line
5cc	Changes five lines starting with the current line

dw Works Differently Than cw

The **dw** command deletes all the characters through (including) the **SPACE** at the end of a word, whereas the **cw** command changes only the characters in the word, leaving the trailing **SPACE** intact.

▲▲ The Substitute Command

The **s** and **S** commands also replace existing text with new text. The **s** command deletes the character the cursor is on and puts **vi** into Input mode. It has the effect of replacing the single character that the cursor is on with whatever you type until you press **ESCAPE**. The **S** command has the same effect as the **cc** command from the previous section. The **s** command will only replace characters on the current line. If you specify a Repeat Factor before an **s** command and this action would replace more characters than exist on the current line, **s** changes characters only to the end of the line (same as **C**, above).

Substitute Command	Action
s	Substitutes one or more characters for the current character
S	Substitutes one or more characters for current line
5s	Substitutes one or more characters for five characters starting with the current character

▲▲ The Case Command

The tilde (~) character changes the case of the character under the cursor from upper- to lowercase or vice versa. You can precede the tilde with a number to specify the number of characters you want the command to affect. For example **5~** will transpose the next five characters starting with the character under the cursor.

▲ Searching and Substituting

Searching for and replacing a character, an actual string of text, or a string that is matched by a regular expression is a key feature of any editor. The **vi** editor provides simple commands for searching for a character on the current line and more complex commands for searching for and optionally substituting for single and multiple occurrences of strings or regular expressions anywhere in the Work Buffer.

▲▲ Searching for a Character

You can search for and move the cursor to the next occurrence of a specified character on the current line by using the Find command. For example

```
fa
```

moves the cursor from the current position to the next occurrence of the character a, if one appears on the same line. You can also find the previous occurrence by using a capital **F**, so

`Fa`

moves the cursor to the position of the closest previous a in the current line.

The next two commands are used in the same manner as the preceding two. The **t** command places the cursor on the character before the next occurrence of the specified character, whereas the **T** command places it on the character after the previous occurrence of the specified character.

A semicolon (**;**) repeats the last **f**, **F**, **t**, or **T** command.

You can combine these search commands with other commands. For example the command **d2fq** deletes the text from the location of the cursor to the second occurrence of the letter q on the current line.

▲▲ Searching for a String

The forward and backward search commands just discussed are restricted to searches within the current line. The **vi** editor can also search backward or forward through the Work Buffer to find a specific string of text or a string that matches a regular expression (see Appendix A). To find the next occurrence of a string (forward), press the forward slash (**/**) key, enter the text you want to find (called the *search string*), and press **RETURN**. When you press the slash key, **vi** displays a slash on the status line. As you enter the string of text, it too is displayed on the status line. When you press **RETURN**, **vi** searches for the string. If **vi** finds the string, it positions the cursor on the first character of the string. If you use a question mark (**?**) in place of the forward slash, **vi** searches for the previous occurrence of the string. If you need to include a forward slash in a forward search or a question mark in a backward search, you must quote it by preceding it with a backslash (****).

The **N** and **n** keys repeat the last search without the need for you to enter the search string again. The **n** key repeats the original search exactly, and the **N** key repeats the search in the opposite direction of the original search.

Normally, if you are searching forward and **vi** does not find the search string before it gets to the end of the Work Buffer, it *wraps around* and continues the search at the beginning of the Work Buffer. During a backward search, **vi** wraps around from the beginning of the Work Buffer to the end. Also, **vi** normally performs case-sensitive searches. Refer to "Wrap Scan" (page 276) and "Ignore Case in Searches" (page 275) for information about how to change these search parameters.

▲▲▲ Special Characters in Search Strings

Because the search string is a regular expression, some characters take on a special meaning within the search string. The following paragraphs list some of these characters. The first two (^ and $) always have their special meanings within a search string (unless you quote them [page 258]), and the rest can have their special meanings within a search string turned off by a single command. Refer to "Allow Special Characters in Searches" on page 275.

^   **beginning-of-line indicator**   When the first character in a search string is a caret or circumflex, it matches the beginning of a line. The command **/^the** finds the next line that begins with the string the.

$ **end-of-line indicator**   Similarly a dollar sign matches the end of a line. The command **/!$** finds the next line that ends with an exclamation point.

. **any-character indicator**   A period matches *any* character, anywhere in the search string. The command **/l..e** finds **line, followed, like, included, all memory,** or any other word or character string that contains an **l** followed by any two characters and an **e**. To search for an actual period, use a backslash to quote the period (**\.**).

\> **end-of-word indicator**   This pair of characters matches the end of a word. The command **/s\>** finds the next word that ends with an s. Notice that whereas a backslash (\) is typically used to *turn off* the special meaning of a character, the character sequence \> has a special meaning, and > alone does not.

\< **beginning-of-word indicator**   This pair of characters matches the beginning of a word. The command **/\<The** finds the next word that begins with The. The beginning-of-word indicator uses the backslash in the same, atypical way as the end-of-word indicator.

\(...\) **save pattern**   These delimiters save whatever is between them into a special holding buffer. This buffer can then be referenced to call back up to nine previously saved patterns by using a backslash followed by a number (\1 through \9). See the search and replace examples below.

* **0 or more occurrences**   This character is a modifier that will match 0 or more occurrences of the character immediately preceding it. The command **/dis*m** will match the string di followed by 0 or more s characters followed by an m. Examples of successful matches would include dim or dism or dissm.

[ ] **character-class definition**   Square brackets surrounding two or more characters match any *single* character located between the brackets. The command **/dis[ck]** finds the next occurrence of *either* disk or disc.

There are two special characters you can use within a character-class definition. A caret (^) as the first character following the left bracket defines the character class to be *any but the following characters*. A hyphen between two characters indicates a range of characters. Refer to the examples in the table on the following page.

▲▲ Substituting One String for Another

A Substitute command is a combination of a Search command and a Change command. It searches for a string just as the **/** command does, allowing the same special characters that the previous section discussed. When it finds a string, the Substitute command changes it. The syntax of the Substitute command is

:*[g][address]*s/*search-string*/*replacement-string*[/*option*]

As with all commands that begin with a colon, **vi** executes a Substitute command from the status line.

Command	Result
/and	Finds the next occurrence of the string and **Examples:** sand and standard slander andiron
/\<and\\>	Finds the next occurrence of the word and **Example:** and
/^The	Finds the next line that starts with The **Examples:** The... There...
/^[0-9][0-9])	Finds the next line that starts with a two-digit number followed by a right parenthesis **Examples:** 77)... 01)... 15)...
/\<[adr]	Finds the next word that starts with an a, d, or r **Examples:** apple drive road argument right
/^[A-Za-z]	Finds the next line that starts with an upper- or lowercase letter **Examples:** This search will not find a line starting with the number 7... Dear Mr. Jones ... in the middle of a sentence like this ...

The next sections discuss the ***address***, **s** command, ***search-string***, ***replacement-string***, and ***option***.

▲▲▲ The Substitute Address

If you do not specify an ***address***, Substitute searches only the current line. If you use a single line number as the ***address***, Substitute searches that line. If the ***address*** is two line numbers separated by a comma, Substitute searches those lines and the lines between. Refer to "Line Numbers" on page 275 if you want **vi** to display line numbers. Any place a line number is allowed in the address, you may also use an ***address***-string enclosed between slashes. The **vi** editor operates on the next line that the ***address***-string matches. When you precede the first slash of the ***address***-string with the letter **g** (for global), **vi** operates on all lines in the file that the ***address***-string matches. (This **g** is not the same as the one that goes at the end of the Substitute command to cause multiple replacements on a single line—see "The Search and Replace Strings" following).

Within the ***address*** a period represents the current line, a dollar sign represents the last line in the Work Buffer, and a percent sign represents the entire Work Buffer. You can perform ***address*** arithmetic using plus and minus signs. Some examples of ***address***es are shown in the table on the following page.

▲▲▲ The Search and Replace Strings

An **s** comes after the ***address***, indicating that a Substitute command follows. A delimiter follows the **s** marking the beginning of the ***search-string***. Although the examples in this book use a forward slash, you can use any

Address	Portion of Work Buffer Addressed
5	Line **5**
77,100	Lines **77** through **100** inclusive
1,.	Beginning of Work Buffer through current line
.,$	Current line through end of Work Buffer
1,$	Entire Work Buffer
%	Entire Work Buffer
/pine/	The line containing the next occurrence of the word `pine`
g/pine/	All lines containing the word `pine`
.,.+10	Current line through tenth following line (eleven lines in all)

character that is not a letter, number, blank, or backslash as a delimiter. You must use the same delimiter at the end of the *search-string*.

Next comes the *search-string*. It has the same format as the search string in the **/** command and can include the same special characters. (The *search-string* is a regular expression—refer to Appendix A for more information.) Another delimiter marks the end of the *search-string* and the beginning of the *replace-string*.

The *replace-string* is the string that replaces the text matched by the *search-string*. The *replace-string* should be followed by the delimiter character. Some versions of **vi** allow you to omit the last delimiter when no option follows the *replace-string*, it is always required if an option is present. There are several characters that have special meaning in the *search-string* and other characters that have special meaning in the *replace-string*. For example an ampersand (**&**) in the *replace-string* represents the text that was matched by the *search-string*. A backslash in the *replace-string* quotes the character that follows it. Refer to the table on page 268 and Appendix A.

Normally the Substitute command replaces only the first occurrence of any text on a line that matches the *search-string*. If you want a global substitution—that is, if you want to replace all matching occurrences of text on a line—append the **g** (global) option after the delimiter that ends the *replace-string*. Another useful option is **c** (check). This option causes **vi** to ask if you would like to make the change each time it finds text that matches the *search-string*. Pressing **y** replaces the *search-string*, pressing **q** terminates the command, and pressing any other character simply continues the search without making that replacement.

The *address*-string need not be the same as the *search-string*. For example

```
:/candle/s/wick/flame/
```

will substitute `wick` for the first occurrence of `flame` on the next line that contains the string `candle` and

```
:g/candle/s/wick/flame/
```

will perform the same substitution on the first occurrence on each line of the file containing the string `candle`.

If the *search-string* is the same as the *address*-string, you can leave the *search-string* blank. For example `:/candle/s//lamp/` is equivalent to `:/candle/s/candle/lamp/`.

Using the following fraction of a poem,[1] you will see what damage the Substitute command can do:

```
$ tail -20 walrus
"But wait a bit," the Oysters cried,
"Before we have our chat;
For some of us are out of breath,
And all of us are fat!"
"No hurry!" said the Carpenter.
They thanked him much for that.

"A loaf of bread," the Walrus said,
"Is what we chiefly need:
Pepper and vinegar besides
Are very good indeed--
Now if you're ready, Oysters dear,
We can begin to feed."

"But not on us!" the Oysters cried,
Turning a little blue.
"After such kindness, that would be
A dismal thing to do!"
"The night is fine," the Walrus said.
"Do you admire the view?"
```

If you give the following Substitute commands while editing this file:

```
%s/Walrus/Penguin/g
%s/Oysters/Goldfish/g
```

you will end up with a file that looks like this:

```
$ tail -20 walrus
"But wait a bit," the Goldfish cried,
"Before we have our chat;
For some of us are out of breath,
And all of us are fat!"
"No hurry!" said the Carpenter.
They thanked him much for that.

"A loaf of bread," the Penguin said,
"Is what we chiefly need:
Pepper and vinegar besides
Are very good indeed--
Now if you're ready, Goldfish dear,
We can begin to feed."

"But not on us!" the Goldfish cried,
Turning a little blue.
"After such kindness, that would be
A dismal thing to do!"
"The night is fine," the Penguin said.
"Do you admire the view?"
```

---

1. With apologies to Lewis Carroll, from *Through the Looking-Glass and What Alice Found There*, 1872.

The following table shows some more examples of substitution.

Command	Result
:s/bigger/biggest/	Replaces the string `bigger` on the current line with `biggest` **Example:** `bigger` → `biggest`

:1,.s/Ch 1/Ch 2/g	Replaces every occurrence of the string `Ch 1`, before or on the current line, with the string `Ch 2`
	Examples:
	`Ch 1` → `Ch 2`
	`Ch 12` → `Ch 22`

:1,$s/ten/10/g	Replaces every occurrence of the string `ten` by the string `10`
	Examples:
	`ten` → `10`
	`often` → `of10`
	`tenant` → `10ant`

:g/chapter/s/ten/10/	Replaces the first occurrence of the string `ten` with the string `10` on all lines containing the word `chapter`
	Examples:
	`chapter ten` → `chapter 10`
	`chapters will often` → `chapters will of10`

:s/\(first\)\(last\)/\2\1/	Uses the pattern holding buffers to swap `first` and `last` on the current line **Example:** `firstlast` → `lastfirst`
:%s/\<ten\>/10/g	Replaces every occurrence of the word `ten` by the string `10` **Example:** `ten` → `10`

:.,.+10s/every/each/g	Replaces every occurrence of the string `every` by the string `each` on the current line through the tenth following line
	Examples:
	`every` → `each`
	`everything` → `eachthing`

:s/\<short\>/"&"/	Replaces the word `short` on the current line with `"short"` (enclosed within quotation marks) **Example:** `the shortest of the short` → `the shortest of the "short"`

▲ Miscellaneous Commands

Join

The Join command, **J**, joins the line below the current line to the end of the current line. It inserts a **SPACE** between what was previously two lines and leaves the cursor on this **SPACE**. If the current line ends with a period, **vi** inserts two **SPACE**s.

You can always "unjoin" (break) a line into two lines by replacing the **SPACE** or **SPACE**s where you want to break the line with a **RETURN**.

Status

The Status command, **CONTROL-G**, displays the name of the file you are editing, whether or not the file has been modified and/or locked, the line number of the current line, the total number of lines in the Work Buffer, and the percent of the Work Buffer preceding the current line.

. (period)

The **.** (period) command repeats the most recent command that made a change. If, for example, you had just given a **d2w** command (delete the next two words), the **.** command deletes the next two words. If you had just inserted text, the **.** command would repeat the insertion of the same text.

This command is useful if you want to change some, but not all, occurrences of a word or phrase in the Work Buffer. Search for the first occurrence of the word (use **/**), and then make the change you want (use **cw**). Following these two commands, you can use **n** to search for the next occurrence of the word and **.** to make the same change to it. If you do not want to make the change, use **n** again to find the next occurrence.

▲ The Yank, Put, and Delete Commands

The **vi** editor has a General-Purpose Buffer and 26 Named Buffers that can hold text during an editing session. These buffers are useful if you want to move or copy a portion of text to another location in the Work Buffer. A combination of the Delete and Put commands removes text from one location in the Work Buffer and places it in another. The Yank and Put commands copy text to another location in the Work Buffer without changing the original text.

▲▲ The General-Purpose Buffer

The **vi** editor stores the text that you most recently changed, deleted, or yanked (see the following) in the General-Purpose Buffer. The Undo command retrieves text from the General-Purpose Buffer when it restores text.

▲▲▲ The Yank Command

The Yank command (**y**) is identical to the Delete (**d**) command, except that Yank does not delete text from the Work Buffer. The **vi** editor places a *copy* of the yanked text in the General-Purpose Buffer, so that you can use Put (see below) to place another copy of it elsewhere in the Work Buffer. Use the Yank command just as you use **d**, the Delete command. The uppercase **Y** command yanks an entire line into the General-Purpose Buffer.

> ### Use **yy** to Yank One Line
>
> Just as **d** RETURN deletes two lines, **y** RETURN yanks two lines. Use the **yy** command to yank the current line.
>
> ### **D** Works Differently Than **Y**
>
> The **D** command (page 259) does not work in the same manner as the **Y** command: Whereas **D** deletes to the end of the line, **Y** yanks the entire line, regardless of the cursor position.

▲▲▲▲ The Put Commands

The Put commands, **P** and **p**, copy text from the General-Purpose Buffer into the Work Buffer.

If you delete or yank characters or words into the General-Purpose Buffer, **P** inserts them before the current *character,* and **p** inserts them after. If you delete or yank lines, sentences, or paragraphs, **P** inserts the contents of the General-Purpose Buffer before the *line* the cursor is on, and **p** inserts them after.

The Put commands do not destroy the contents of the General-Purpose Buffer, so it is possible to place the same text at several points within the file by using one Delete or Yank command and several Put commands.

Because **vi** has only one General-Purpose Buffer and **vi** changes the contents of this buffer each time you give a Change, Delete, or Yank command, *you can use only cursor-movement commands between a Delete or Yank command and the corresponding Put command.* Any other commands change the contents of the General-Purpose Buffer and therefore change the results of the Put command. If you do not plan to use the Put command immediately after a Delete or Yank, use a Named Buffer (see the following) rather than the General-Purpose Buffer.

▲▲▲ The Delete Commands

Any of the Delete commands that were described earlier in this chapter (page 258) automatically place the deleted text in the General-Purpose Buffer. Just as you can use the Undo command to put the deleted text back where it came from, you can use a Put command to put the deleted text at another location in the Work Buffer.

For example if you delete a word from the middle of a sentence using the **dw** command and then move the cursor to a SPACE between two words and give a **p** command, **vi** places the word you just deleted at the new location. Or if you delete a line using the **dd** command and then move the cursor to the line *below* the line where you want the deleted line to appear and give a **P** command, **vi** places the line at the new location.

Start Optional

▲▲ The Named Buffers

You can use a Named Buffer with any of the Delete, Yank, or Put commands. There are 26 Named Buffers, each named by a letter of the alphabet. Each Named Buffer can store a different block of text so that you can recall each block as needed. Unlike the General-Purpose Buffer, **vi** does not change the contents of a Named

Buffer unless you use a command that specifically overwrites that buffer. The **vi** editor maintains the contents of the Named Buffers throughout an editing session.

The **vi** editor stores text in a Named Buffer if you precede a Delete or Yank command with a double quotation mark (**"**) and a buffer name (for example **"kyy** yanks a copy of the current line into buffer **k**). You can use a Named Buffer in two ways. If you give the name of the buffer as a lowercase letter, **vi** overwrites the contents of the buffer when it deletes or yanks text into the buffer. If you use an uppercase letter, **vi** appends the newly deleted or yanked text to the end of the buffer. This feature enables you to collect blocks of text from various sections of a file and then deposit them at one place in the file with a single command. Named Buffers are also useful when you are moving a section of a file and do not want to use Put immediately after the corresponding Delete, and when you want to insert a paragraph, sentence, or phrase repeatedly in a document.

If you have one sentence that you use throughout a document, you can yank the sentence into a Named Buffer and put it wherever you need it by using the following procedure. After entering the first occurrence of the sentence and pressing **ESCAPE** to return to Command Mode, leave the cursor on the line containing the sentence. (The sentence must appear on a line or lines by itself for this procedure to work.) Then yank the sentence into Named Buffer **a** by giving the **"ayy** command (or **"a2yy** if the sentence takes up two lines). Now any time you need the sentence, you can return to Command Mode and give the command **"ap** to put a copy of the sentence below the line the cursor is on.

This technique provides a quick and easy way to insert text that you use frequently in a document. For example if you were editing a legal document, you might use a Named Buffer to store the phrase `The Plaintiff alleges that the Defendant` to save yourself the trouble of typing it every time you want to use it. Similarly if you were creating a letter that frequently used a long company name, such as `National Standards Institute`, you might put it into a Named Buffer.

▲▲ The Numbered Buffers

In addition to 26 Named Buffers and 1 General-Purpose Buffer, there are 9 Numbered Buffers. These are, in one sense, readonly buffers. The **vi** editor automatically fills them with the nine most recently deleted chunks of text that are at least one line long. The most recently deleted pattern is held in **"1**, the next most recent in **"2**, and so on. If you delete a block of text and then give some other **vi** commands so you cannot reclaim the deleted text with Undo, use **"1p** to paste the most recently deleted chunk of text below the location of the cursor. If you have deleted several blocks of text and want to reclaim a specific one, proceed as follows: Paste the contents of the first buffer with **"1p**. If the first buffer does not have the text you are looking for, undo the paste with **u** and then give the period (**.**) command to repeat the previous command. The Numbered Buffers work in a unique way with the period command: Instead of pasting the contents of buffer **"1**, the period command will paste the contents of the next buffer (**"2**). Another **u** and period replace the contents of buffer **"2** with that of buffer **"3**, and so on through the 9 buffers.

Stop Optional

▲ Reading and Writing Files

The **vi** editor reads a disk file into the Work Buffer when you call **vi** from the shell. The **ZZ** command that terminates the editing session writes the contents of the Work Buffer back to the disk file. This section discusses other ways of reading text into the Work Buffer and writing it out.

▲▲ The Read Command

The Read command reads a file into the Work Buffer. The new file does not overwrite any text in the Work Buffer but is positioned following the single address you specify (or the current line if you do not specify an address). You can use an address of 0 to read the file into the beginning of the Work Buffer. The format of the Read command is

>   *:[address]r [filename]*

As with other commands that begin with a colon, when you enter the colon, it appears on the status line. The *filename* is the pathname of the file that you want to read and must be terminated by RETURN. If you omit the *filename*, **vi** reads the file you are editing from the disk.

▲▲ The Write Command

The Write command writes part or all of the Work Buffer to a file. You can use an address to write out part of the Work Buffer and a filename to specify a file to receive the text. If you do not use an address or filename, **vi** writes the entire contents of the Work Buffer to the file you are editing, updating the file on the disk.

During a long editing session, it is a good idea to use the Write command occasionally. Then if a problem develops, a recent copy of the Work Buffer is safe on the disk. If you use a **:q!** command to exit from **vi**, the disk file reflects the version of the Work Buffer at the time you last used the Write command. The formats of the Write command are

>   *:[address]w[!] [filename]*
>   *:[address]w>> filename*

You can use the second format of the Write command to append text to an existing file. The following list covers the components of the Write command.

address   If you use an *address*, it specifies the portion of the Work Buffer that you want **vi** to write to the disk. The *address* follows the form of the *address* that the Substitute command uses. If you do not use an *address*, **vi** writes out the entire contents of the Work Buffer.

w!   Because Write can quickly destroy a large amount of work, **vi** demands that you enter an exclamation point following the **w** as a safeguard against accidentally overwriting a file. The only times you do not need an exclamation point are when you are writing out the entire contents of the Work Buffer to the file being edited (using no *address* and no filename) and when you are writing part or all of the Work Buffer to a new file. When you are writing part of the file to the file being edited, or when you are overwriting another file, you must use an exclamation point.

filename   The optional *filename* is the pathname of the file you are writing to. If you do not specify a *filename*, **vi** writes to the file you are editing.

▲▲ Identifying the Current File

The File command provides the same information as the Status command (**CONTROL-G**); it displays the name of the file you are editing, whether the file has been modified and/or locked, the line number of the current line, the total number of lines in the Work Buffer, and the percent of the Work Buffer preceding the current line. The filename the File command displays is the one the Write command uses if you give a **:w** command (rather than **:w filename**). The File command is

```
:f
```

An example of the display produced by the File command is

```
"practice" [Modified] line 11 of 35 --31%--
```

▲ Setting Parameters

You can adapt **vi** to your needs and habits by setting **vi** parameters. These parameters perform many functions, such as displaying line numbers, automatically inserting **RETURN**s for you, and establishing nonstandard searches.

You can set parameters in several different ways. You can set them while you are using **vi** to establish the environment for the current editing session. Alternatively you can set the parameters in your **.profile** ^{sh} or **.login** csh file or in a startup file that **vi** uses, **.exrc**. When you set the parameters in any of those files, each time you use **vi** the environment has been established, and you can begin editing immediately.

▲▲ Setting Parameters from vi

To set a parameter while you are using **vi**, enter a colon (**:**), the word **set**, a **SPACE**, and the parameter (see "Parameters" on page 274). The command appears on the status line as you type it and takes effect when you press **RETURN**.

▲▲ Setting Parameters in a Startup File

If you are using **sh** or **ksh**, you can put the following lines in the **.profile** file in your home directory:

EXINIT='set param1 param2 . . .'
export EXINIT

Replace *param1* and *param2* with parameters selected from the list in the next section. **EXINIT** is a shell variable that **vi** reads. An actual statement that ignores the case of characters in searches, displays line numbers, uses the C Shell to execute Solaris commands, and wraps text 15 characters from the right edge of the screen looks like this:

```
EXINIT='set autoindent numbers shell=/usr/bin/csh wrapmargin=15'
export EXINIT
```

Or if you use the parameter abbreviations it looks like this:

```
EXINIT='set ai nu sh=/usr/bin/csh wm=15'
export EXINIT
```

If you are using **csh**, put the following line in the **.login** file in your home directory:

setenv EXINIT 'set param1 param2 . . .'

Again, replace **param1** and **param2** with parameters from the following section. The values between the single quotation marks are the same as shown in the preceding example.

▲▲ Setting Parameters in the **.exrc** Startup File

Instead of setting **vi** parameters in your **.login** or **.profile** file, you can create a **.exrc** file and set them there. If you set the parameters in a **.exrc** file, use the following format:

set param1 param2 . . .

Following are examples of **.exrc** files that perform the same function as **EXINIT** described previously:

```
$ cat .exrc
set ignorecase
set number
set shell=/usr/bin/csh
set wrapmargin=15

$ cat .exrc
set ic
set nu
set sh=/usr/bin/csh
set wm=15
```

When you start **vi** it looks for a **.exrc** file that you own in your home directory and in your working directory. If it finds such a file, it uses the values that it contains. If you set parameters in your **.profile** or **.login** file, as well as in **.exrc**, the parameters in **.exrc** take precedence because **.exrc** is executed later than **.profile** and **.login**. Parameters set in **.exrc** also take precedence over those from the **EXINIT** shell variable.

▲▲ Parameters

This section contains a list of some of the most useful **vi** parameters. The **vi** editor displays a complete list of parameters and how they are currently set when you give the command **:set all** followed by a RETURN while using **vi**. The **ex man** page describes the parameters in detail; they are not in the **vi man** page. At the beginning of each parameter, in the right column, are the names of the parameters to use with **set**, followed by abbreviations you can use in place of the full names.

Line Numbers   **number (nu/nonu)**   The **vi** editor does not normally display the line number associated with each line. To display line numbers set the parameter **number**. To cause line numbers not to be displayed, set the parameter **nonumber**.

Line numbers, whether displayed or not, are not part of the file, are not stored with the file, and are not displayed when the file is printed. They appear on the screen only while you are using **vi**.

Line Wrap Margin   **wrapmargin (wm)**   The line wrap margin causes **vi** to break the text that you are inserting at approximately the specified number of characters from the right margin. The **vi** editor breaks the text by inserting a `NEWLINE` character at the closest blank-delimited word boundary. Setting the line wrap margin is handy if you want all your text lines to be about the same length. It relieves you of having to remember to press `RETURN` to end each line of input.

Set the parameter **wrapmargin=*nn*,** where *nn* is the number of characters *from the right side of the screen* where you want **vi** to break the text. This number is not the column width of the text but the distance from the end of the text to the right edge of the screen. Setting the wrap margin to 0 (zero) turns this feature off. By default, **vi** sets the wrap margin to 0.

Shell   **shell (sh)**   While you are in **vi**, you can cause **vi** to spawn a new shell. You can either create an interactive shell (if you want to run several commands) or run a single command. The **shell** parameter determines what shell **vi** invokes. By default **vi** sets the **shell** parameter to your login shell. To change it set the parameter **shell=*pathname*,** where *pathname* is the full pathname of the shell you want to use.

Show Mode   **showmode (smd/nosmd)**   The **vi** editor does not normally give you a visual cue to let you know when it is in Input Mode. On some versions of **vi**, however, you can set the parameter **showmode** to display the mode in the lower-right corner of the screen when **vi** is in Input or Command Mode. There are three types of Input Mode: OPEN, INSERT, and APPEND. Set **noshowmode** to cause **vi** not to display the message.

Flash   **flash (fl/nofl)**   The **vi** editor normally causes the terminal to beep when you give an invalid command or press `ESCAPE` when you are in Command Mode. Setting the parameter **flash** causes the terminal to flash instead of beep. Set **noflash** to cause it to beep. Not all terminals/emulators support this parameter.

Ignore Case in Searches   **ignorecase (ic/noic)**   The **vi** editor normally performs case-sensitive searches, differentiating between upper- and lowercase letters. It performs case-insensitive searches when you set the **ignorecase** parameter. Set **noignorecase** to restore case-sensitive searches.

Allow Special Characters in Searches   **magic**   The following characters have special meanings when used in a search string. Refer to "Special Characters in Search Strings" on page 263.

.   [   ]   *

When you set the **nomagic** parameter, these characters no longer have special meanings. The **magic** parameter gives them back their special meanings.

The ^ and $ characters always have a special meaning within search strings, regardless of how you set this parameter.

Invisible Characters   **list**   To cause **vi** to display each TAB as ^I and to mark the end of each line with a $, set the **list** parameter. To display TABs as white space and not mark ends of lines, set **nolist**.

Wrap Scan   **wrapscan (ws/nows)**   Normally when a search for the next occurrence of a search string reaches the end of the Work Buffer, **vi** continues the search at the beginning of the Work Buffer. The reverse is true of a search for the previous occurrence of a search string. The **nowrapscan** parameter stops the search at either end of the Work Buffer. Set the **wrapscan** parameter if you want searches to once again wrap around the ends of the Work Buffer.

Automatic Indention   **autoindent (ai/noai)**   The automatic indention feature works with the **shiftwidth** parameter to provide a regular set of indentions for programs or tabular material. This feature is normally off. You can turn it on by setting **autoindent** and turn it off by setting **noautoindent**.

When automatic indention is on and **vi** is in Input Mode, CONTROL-T moves the cursor from the left margin (or an indention) to the next indention position, RETURN moves the cursor to the left side of the next line under the first character of the previous line, and CONTROL-D backs up over indention positions. The CONTROL-T and CONTROL-D keys work only before text is placed on a line.

Auto Write   **autowrite (aw/noaw)**   By default **vi** asks you before writing out the Work Buffer when you have not explicitly told it to do so (as when you give a **:n** command to edit the next file). The **autowrite** option causes **vi** to automatically write the Work Buffer when you use commands such as **:n** to edit to another file. You can disable it by setting the **noautowrite** option.

Show Match   **showmatch (sm/nosm)**   This parameter is useful for programmers working in languages that use braces ({}) or parentheses as expression delimiters (Lisp, C, Tcl, and so on). When **showmatch** is set and you are entering code (in Input Mode), and you type a closing curly brace or parenthesis, the cursor will jump briefly to the matching opening brace or parenthesis (that is, the preceding corresponding element at the same nesting level). After the cursor highlights the matching element, it resumes its previous position. When you type a right brace or parenthesis that does not have a match, **vi** beeps. Use **noshowmatch** to turn off automatic matching.

Report   **report**   Causes **vi** to display a report on the status line whenever you make a change that affects at least *n* lines (**set report=n**). For example if **report** is set to 5, and you delete 5 lines, you will see the message 5 lines deleted. If you delete 4 or fewer lines, **vi** will not display a message. The default for **report** is 5.

Beautify	**beautify (bf/nobf)** Causes **vi** to ignore all control characters (except NEWLINE, TAB, and FORMFEED) while in Input Mode. Use **nobeautify** to turn this parameter off.
Shift Width	**shiftwidth (sw)** Controls the functioning of CONTROL-T and CONTROL-D in Input Mode when automatic indention is on. Set the parameter **shiftwidth=*nn***, where ***nn*** is the spacing of the indention positions. Setting the shift width is similar to setting the TAB stops on a typewriter; however with **shiftwidth** the distance between TAB stops is always constant.

▲ Advanced Editing Techniques

Start Optional

This section presents several commands that you may find useful once you have become comfortable using **vi**. While you are using **vi**, you can set and use markers to make addressing more convenient. Set a marker by giving the command **m***c*, where *c* is any character. (Letters are preferred because some characters, such as a single quotation mark, have special meanings when used as markers.)

▲▲ Using Markers

Once you have set a marker, you can use it in a manner similar to a line number. The **vi** editor does not preserve markers when you stop editing a file.

You can move the cursor to the beginning of a line that contains a marker by preceding the marker name with a single quotation mark. For example to set marker **t**, position the cursor on the line you want to mark, and give the command **mt**. Unless you reset marker **t** or delete the line it marks, during this editing session you can return to the beginning of the line you marked with the command **'t**.

You can delete all text from the current line through the line containing marker **r** with the following command:

```
d'r
```

You can use a grave accent (`—also called a grave mark, back tick, or reverse single quotation mark) to go to the exact position of the mark on the line. After setting marker **t**, you can move the cursor to the location of this marker (not the beginning of the line containing the marker) with the command **`t**. The following command deletes all the text from the current line up to the character where the mark **r** was placed; the rest of the line containing the marker remains intact.

```
d`r
```

You can use markers in addresses of commands in place of line numbers. The following command replaces all occurrences of The with THE on all lines from marker **m** to the current line (marker **m** must precede the current line):

```
:'m,.s/The/THE/g
```

▲▲ Editing Other Files

The following command causes **vi** to edit the file you specify with *filename*:

> *:e[!] [filename]*

If you want to save the contents of the Work Buffer, you must write it out (using **:w**) before you give this command. If you do not want to save the contents of the Work Buffer, **vi** insists that you use an exclamation point to show that you know that you will lose the work you did since the last time you wrote out the Work Buffer. If you do not supply a *filename*, **vi** edits the same file you are currently working on.

You can give the command **:e!** to start an editing session over again. This command returns the Work Buffer to the state it was in the last time you wrote it out, or, if you have not written it out, the state it was in when you started editing the file. This is useful when you make mistakes editing a file and decide that it would be easier to start over than to fix the mistakes.

Because this command does not destroy the contents of the Named Buffers, you can store text from one file in a Named Buffer, use a **:e** command to edit a second file, and put text from the Named Buffer in the second file. A **:e** command does destroy the contents of the General-Purpose Buffer and any markers you have set.

The command **:e#** attempts to close the current file and open the last file you were editing, placing the cursor on the line that it was on when you last closed the file. You must have **autowrite** (page 276) set in order for this feature to work without **vi** generating annoying prompts reminding you to save the file you are closing.

The **:e#** command can help you copy blocks of text from one file to another. Call **vi** with the names of several files as arguments. You can use **:n** to edit the next file, **:e#** to edit the file you just edited, and **:rew** to rewind the sequence of files so that you are editing the first file again. As you move between files, you can copy text from one file (into a named buffer [page 270]) and paste it into another. You can use **:n!** to force **vi** to close a file without writing out changes before it opens the next file.

▲▲ Macros and Shortcuts

The **vi** editor allows you to create your own macros and shortcuts. The **:map** command defines a key or sequence of keys that perform some action in Command Mode. The following command maps CONTROL-X to the commands that will find a left square bracket (**f[**), delete all characters from that square bracket to the next right square bracket (**f]**) on the same line, move the cursor down two lines (**2j**), and finally move the cursor to the beginning of the line (0).

```
:map ^X f[df]2j0
```

You can use ESCAPE and CONTROL sequences, but try to avoid remapping characters or sequences that are **vi** commands. Type **:map** by itself to see a list of the current mappings.

The **:abbrev** command is similar to **:map** but creates abbreviations you can use while in Input Mode. When you are in Input Mode and type a command you have defined with **:abbrev**, followed by a SPACE, **vi** replaces the command and the SPACE with the characters you specified when you defined the command. For ease of use, do not use common sequences of characters when creating abbreviations. The following command defines **ZZ** as an abbreviation for Mark G. Sobell.

```
:abbrev ZZ Mark G. Sobell
```

Stop Optional

▲▲ Executing Shell Commands from vi

You can execute shell commands in several ways while you are using **vi**. You can create a new interactive shell by giving the following command and pressing **RETURN**:

```
:sh
```

The **shell** parameter determines what kind of shell is created (usually **sh**, **csh**, or **ksh**). By default **shell** is the same as your login shell.

After you have done what you want to do in the shell, you can return to **vi** by exiting from the shell (press **CONTROL-D** or give the command exit).

You can execute a shell command line from **vi** by giving the following command, replacing *command* with the command line you want to execute. Terminate the command with a **RETURN**.

:!command

If :sh Does Not Work Right

It is possible for the **:sh** command to behave strangely, depending on how your shell has been configured. You may get warnings with the **:sh** command, or it may even hang. Experiment with the **:sh** command to be sure it works with your configuration. If it does not, then you might want to try using a different shell by setting the **vi shell** parameter to another shell before using **:sh**. For example

```
:set shell=/bin/sh
```

causes **vi** to use **sh** with the **:sh** command. You may need to change the **SHELL** environment variable after starting **:sh** to show the correct shell.

Edit Only One Copy of a File

When you create a new shell in this manner, you must remember that you are still using **vi**. A common mistake is to start editing the same file from the new shell, forgetting that **vi** is already editing the file from a different shell. Because each invocation of **vi** uses a different Work Buffer, you overwrite any work you did from the more recent invocation of **vi** when you finally get around to exiting from the original invocation of **vi** (assuming that you write the file to disk when you exit).

The **vi** editor spawns a new shell that executes the ***command***. When the command runs to completion, the newly spawned shell returns control to the editor.

Users frequently use this feature to carry on a dialog with the **write** utility. If Alex gets a message from Jenny while he is using **vi**, he can use the following command to write back to Jenny. After giving the command Alex can carry on a dialog with Jenny in the same way he would if he had invoked **write** from the shell.

```
:!write jenny
```

If Alex has modified the Work Buffer since he last wrote the file to disk, **vi** displays the following message before starting the **write** command:

```
File modified since last write.
```

When Alex finishes his dialog with Jenny, he presses CONTROL-D to terminate the **write** command. Then **vi** displays the following message:

```
Press any key to continue:
```

When Alex presses RETURN, he can continue his editing session in **vi**.

You can execute a command from **vi** and have **vi** replace the current line with the output from the command. If you do not want to replace any text, put the cursor on a blank line before giving the following command:

!!command

Nothing happens when you enter the first exclamation point. When you enter the second one, **vi** moves the cursor to the status line and allows you to enter the command you want to execute. Because this command puts **vi** in Last Line Mode, you must end the command with a RETURN.

Finally, you can execute a command from **vi** with standard input to the command coming from all or part of the file you are editing and standard output from the command replacing the input in the file you are editing. You can use this type of command to sort a list in place in a file you are working on.

To specify the block of text that is to become standard input for the command, move the cursor to one end of the block of text. Then enter an exclamation point followed by a command that would normally move the cursor to the other end of the block of text. For example if the cursor is at the beginning of the file and you want to specify the whole file, give the command **!G**. If you want to specify the part of the file between the cursor and marker **b**, give the command **! ' b**. After you give the cursor-movement command, **vi** displays an exclamation point on the status line and allows you to give a command.

For example to sort a list of names in a file, move the cursor to the beginning of the list and set marker **q** with an **mq** command. Then move the cursor to the end of the list and give the following command:

```
!'qsort
```

Press RETURN and wait. After a few seconds, you see the sorted list replace the original list on the screen. If the command did not do what you expected, you can usually undo the change with a **u** command.

! Can Destroy Your File

If you enter the wrong command or mistype a command, you can destroy your file (for example if the command you enter hangs). For this reason it is a good idea to save your file before using this command. The Undo command (page 259) can be a lifesaver. A **:e!** command (page 278) will get rid of your changes, bringing the buffer back to the state it was in last time you saved it.

Also, as with the **:sh** command, your default shell may not work properly with the **!** command. You may want to test your shell with a simple test file before relying on the use of the **!** command. If your usual shell doesn't work properly, change the **shell** parameter.

▲ Units of Measure

Many **vi** commands operate on a block of text—from a character to many paragraphs. You can specify the size of a block of text with a *Unit of Measure*. You can specify multiple Units of Measure by preceding a Unit of Measure with a Repeat Factor (page 283). This section defines the various Units of Measure.

▲▲ Character

A character is one character, visible or not, printable or not, including SPACEs and TABs. Some examples of characters are

```
a   q   A   .   5   R   -   >   TAB SPACE
```

▲▲ Word

A word is similar to an ordinary word in the English language. It is a string of one or more characters that is bounded on both sides by any combination of one or more of the following elements: A punctuation mark, SPACE, TAB, numeral, or NEWLINE. In addition **vi** considers each group of punctuation marks to be a word.

Word Count	Text
1	pear
2	pear!
2	pear!)
3	pear!) The
4	pear!) "The
11	This is a short, concise line (no frills).

▲▲ Blank-Delimited Word

A blank-delimited word is the same as a word, except that it includes adjacent punctuation. Blank-delimited words are separated from each other by one or more of the following elements: A **SPACE**, **TAB**, or **NEWLINE**.

Blank-Delimited Word Count	Text
1	pear
1	pear!
1	pear!)
2	pear!) The
2	pear!) "The
8	This is a short, concise line (no frills).

▲▲ Line

A line is a string of characters bounded by **NEWLINE**s. It is not necessarily a single, physical line on the terminal. You can enter a very long single (logical) line that wraps around (continues on the next physical line) several times, or disappears off the right edge of the display. It is a good idea, however, to avoid long logical lines by terminating lines with a **RETURN** before they reach the right side of the screen. Terminating lines in this manner ensures that each physical line contains one logical line and avoids confusion when you edit and format text. Some commands do not *appear* to work properly on physical lines that are longer than the width of the screen. For example with the cursor on a long logical line that wraps around several physical lines, pressing **RETURN** once appears to move the cursor down more than one line.

▲▲ Sentence

A sentence is an English sentence or the equivalent. A sentence starts at the end of the previous sentence and ends with a period, exclamation point, or question mark, followed by two **SPACE**s or a **NEWLINE**.

Sentence Count	Text
One: only 1 **SPACE** after the first period, **NEWLINE** after the second period	That's it. This is one sentence.
Two: 2 **SPACE**s after the first period, **NEWLINE** after the second period	That's it. This is two sentences.
Three: 2 **SPACE**s after the first two question marks, **NEWLINE** after the exclamation point	What? Three sentences? One line!

Sentence Count	Text
| *One*: NEWLINE after the period | ```
This sentence takes
up a total of
three lines.
``` |

▲▲ Paragraph

A paragraph is preceded and followed by one or more blank lines. A blank line is composed of two **NEWLINE** characters in a row.

Paragraph Count	Text
| *One*: blank line before and after text | ```
One paragraph
``` |
| *One*: blank line before and after text | ```
        This may appear to be
more than one paragraph.
        Just because there are
two indentions does not mean
it qualifies as two paragraphs.
``` |
| *Three*: 3 blocks of text separated by blank lines | ```
Even though in

English this is only
one sentence,

vi considers it to be
three paragraphs.
``` |

▲▲ Screen

The terminal screen is a window that opens onto part of the Work Buffer. You can position this window so that it shows different portions of the Work Buffer.

▲▲ Repeat Factor

A number that precedes a Unit of Measure (page 281) is a Repeat Factor. Just as the *5* in *5 inches* causes you to consider *5 inches* as a single Unit of Measure, a Repeat Factor causes **vi** to group more than one Unit of Measure and consider it as a single Unit of Measure. For example the command **w** moves the cursor forward

1 word. The command **5w** moves the cursor forward 5 words, and **250w** moves it forward 250 words. If you do not specify a Repeat Factor, **vi** assumes that you mean one Unit of Measure. If the Repeat Factor would move the cursor past the end of the file, it is left at the end of the file.

Summary

This summary of **vi** includes all the commands covered in this chapter, plus some additional ones.

▲▲ Starting vi

Command	Function
vi *filename*	Edits *filename* starting at line1
vi +*n filename*	Edits *filename* starting at line *n*
vi + *filename*	Edits *filename* starting at the last line
vi +/*pattern filename*	Edits *filename* starting at the first line containing *pattern*
vi –r *filename*	Recovers *filename* after a system crash
vi -R *filename*	Edits *filename* readonly
vedit *filename*	Edits *filename* in beginner mode

▲▲ Moving the Cursor by Units of Measure

You must be in Command Mode to use commands that move the cursor by Units of Measure. They are the Units of Measure that you can use in Change, Delete, and Yank commands. Each of these commands can be preceded with a Repeat Factor.

Command	Moves the Cursor
SPACE, **l,** *or* RIGHT ARROW	Space to the right
h *or* LEFT ARROW	Space to the left
w	Word to the right
W	Blank-delimited word to the right
b	Word to the left
B	Blank-delimited word to the left
$	End of line
e	End of word to the right

Command	Moves the Cursor
E	End of blank-delimited word to the right
0	Beginning of line (cannot be used with a Repeat Factor)
RETURN	Beginning of next line
j *or* DOWN ARROW	Down one line
–	Beginning of previous line
k *or* UP ARROW	Up one line
)	End of sentence
(	Beginning of sentence
}	End of paragraph
{	Beginning of paragraph
%	Move to matching brace of same type at same nesting level

▲▲ Viewing Different Parts of the Work Buffer

Command	Moves the Cursor
CONTROL-D	Forward one-half screenful
CONTROL-U	Backward one-half screenful
CONTROL-F	Forward one screenful
CONTROL-B	Backward one screenful
*n*G	To line *n* (without *n*, to the last line)
H	To top of screen
M	To middle of screen
L	To bottom of screen

▲▲ Adding Text

All the following commands (except **r**) leave **vi** in Input Mode. You must press **ESCAPE** to return it to Command Mode.

Command	Inserts Text
i	Before cursor
I	Before first nonblank character on line
a	After cursor

Command	Inserts Text
A	At end of line
o	Open a line below current line
O	Open a line above current line
r	Replace current character (no **ESCAPE** needed)
R	Replace characters, starting with current character (overwrite until **ESCAPE**)

▲▲ Deleting and Changing Text

In the following list M is a Unit of Measure that you can precede with a Repeat Factor, n is a Repeat Factor, and c is any character.

Command	Effect
nx	Deletes the number of characters specified by n, starting with the current character
nX	Deletes n characters before the current character, starting with the character preceding the current character
dM	Deletes text specified by M
$n$dd	Deletes the number of lines specified by n
dt$c$	Deletes to the next character c on the current line
D	Deletes to end of the line
n~	Change case of n

The following commands leave **vi** in Input Mode. You must press **ESCAPE** to return it to Command Mode.

Command	Effect
ns	Substitutes the number of characters specified by n
S	Substitutes for entire line
cM	Changes text specified by M
$n$cc	Changes the number of lines specified by n
ct$c$	Changes to the next character c on the current line
C	Changes to end of line

▲▲ Searching for a String

In the following list *rexp* is a regular expression that can be a simple string of characters.

Command	Effect
/*rexp* RETURN	Searches forward for *rexp*
?*rexp* RETURN	Searches backward for *rexp*
n	Repeats original search exactly
N	Repeats original search, opposite direction
/RETURN	Repeats original search forward
?RETURN	Repeats original search backward
f*c*	Positions the cursor on the next character *c* on the current line
F*c*	Positions the cursor on the previous character *c* on the current line
t*c*	Positions the cursor on the character before (to the left of) the next character *c* on the current line
T*c*	Positions the cursor on the character after (to the right of) the previous character *c* on the current line
;	Repeats the last **f**, **F**, **t**, or **T** command

▲▲ Substituting for a String

The format of a Substitute command is

> :*[address]s/search-string/replacement-string[/g]*

Element of Command	Contains
address	A search string, one line number, or two line numbers separated by a comma. A **.** represents the current line, **$** represents the last line, and **%** represents the entire file (some versions of **vi**). You can use a marker or a search string in place of a line number.
search-string	A regular expression that can be a simple string of characters
replacement-string	The replacement string
g	Indicates a global replacement (more than one replacement per line)

▲▲ Miscellaneous Commands

Command	Effect
J	Joins the current line and the following line
.	Repeats the most recent command that made a change
:w *filename*	Writes contents of Work Buffer to *filename* (or to current file if there is no *filename*)
:q	Quits **vi**
ZZ	Writes contents of Work Buffer to the current file and quits **vi**
:f *or* CONTROL-G	Displays the filename, status, current line number, number of lines in the Work Buffer, and percent of the Work Buffer preceding the current line
CONTROL-V	Inserts the next character literally even if it is a **vi** command (use in Input Mode)

▲▲ Yanking and Putting Text

In the following list *M* is a Unit of Measure that you can precede with a Repeat Factor, and *n* is a Repeat Factor. You can precede any of these commands with the name of a buffer in the form of **"x** where **x** is the name of the buffer (**a–z**).

Command	Effect
y*M*	Yanks text specified by *M*
nyy	Yanks the number of lines specified by *n*
Y	Yanks to end of line
P	Puts text before or above
p	Puts text after or below

▲▲ Advanced Commands

Command	Effect
m*x*	Sets marker *x*, where *x* is a letter from **a** to **z**
' '	Moves cursor back to its previous location
'*x*	Moves cursor to line with marker *x*
`*x*	Moves cursor to character with marker *x*
:e *filename*	Edits *filename*, requiring you to write out changes to the current file (with **:w** or **autowrite**) before editing the new file. Use **:e!** *filename* to discard changes to current file. Use **:e!** without a filename to discard changes to the current file and start editing the saved version of the current file.

Command	Effect
:n	Edits the next file when **vi** is started with multiple filename arguments. It requires you to write out changes to the current file (with **:w** or **autowrite**) before editing the next file. Use **:n!** to discard changes to current file and edit the next file.
:rew	Rewinds the filename list when **vi** is started with multiple filename arguments and starts editing with the first file. It requires you to write out changes to the current file (with **:w** or **autowrite**) before editing the first file. Use **:rew!** to discard changes to current file and edit the first file.
:sh	Starts a shell
:!*command*	Starts a shell and executes *command*
!!*command*	Starts a shell, executes *command*, places output in file replacing the current line

Review Exercises

1. How can you cause **vi** to enter Input Mode? How can you make it revert to Command Mode?

2. What is the Work Buffer? Name two ways of writing the contents of the Work Buffer to the disk.

3. If you are editing a file that contains the paragraph

```
The vi editor has a command, tilde (~),
that changes lowercase letters to
uppercase and vice versa.
The ~ command works with a Unit of Measure or
a Repeat Factor, so you can change
the case of more one character at a time.
```

   and the cursor is on the second tilde (~), how can you

   a. move the cursor to the end of the paragraph?

   b. move the cursor to the beginning of the word `Unit`?

   c. change the word `character` to `letter`?

4. In **vi**, with the cursor positioned on the first letter of a word, give the command **x** followed by **p**. Explain what happens.

5. What are the differences between the following commands?

   a. **i** and **I**

   b. **a** and **A**

   c. **o** and **O**

   d. **r** and **R**

   e. **u** and **U**

6. What command would you use to search backward through the Work Buffer for lines that start with the word `it`?

7. What command substitutes all occurrences of the phrase `this week` with the phrase `next week`?

8. Consider the following scenario: You start **vi** to edit an existing file. You make many changes to the file and then realize that you deleted a critical section of the file early in your editing session. You want to get that section back, but you do not want to lose all the other changes you made. What would you do?

9. Consider the following scenario: Alex puts the following line in his **.login** file:

   ```
   setenv EXINIT 'set number wrapmargin=10 showmode'
   ```

   Then Alex creates a **.exrc** file in the directory **/home/alex/literature** with the following line in it:

   ```
   set nonumber
   ```

   What will the parameter settings be when Alex runs **vi** while the working directory is **/home/alex/bin**? What will they be when he runs **vi** from the directory **/home/alex/literature**? What will they be when he edits the file **/home/alex/literature/promo**?

10. Use **vi** to create the **letter_e** file of e's used on page 49. Use as few **vi** commands as possible. What **vi** commands did you use?

Advanced Review Exercises

11. What commands can you use to take a paragraph from one file and insert it in a second file?

12. Create a file that contains the following list, and then execute commands from within **vi** to sort the list and display it in two columns. (*Hint:* Refer to page 860 in Part III for more information on **pr**.)

    ```
    Command Mode
    Input Mode
    Last Line Mode
    Work Buffer
    General-Purpose Buffer
    Named Buffer
    Regular Expression
    Search String
    Replacement String
    Startup File
    Repeat Factor
    ```

13. How do the Named Buffers differ from the General-Purpose Buffer?

14. Assuming your version of **vi** does not support multiple undo commands, if you delete a line of text, and then delete another line, and then delete a third line, what commands would you use to recover the first two lines that you deleted?

15. What command would you use to swap the words `hither` and `yon` on any line with any number of words between them (you need not worry about special punctuation, just upper- and lowercase letters and spaces)?

The emacs Editor

" **A**nd last (but most noisily not least), it's an issue that has been highly politicized. I mean, geez, who's seen this kind of polarization since the great **vi** vs. **emacs** war?"[1]

Except that the war goes on: Disciples, converts, zealots, and just plain fanatics battle on the fields of USENET groups, user groups, and so forth. Both are very good, solid software products, yet not many people learn both editors well. Each has its pluses and minuses. Choose one to start with, learn the other if you like.

In 1956 the Lisp (List processing) language was developed at MIT by John McCarthy. In its original conception, Lisp had only a few scalar (called *atomic*) data types and only one data structure, a list. Lists could contain atomic data or perhaps other lists. Lisp supported recursion and nonnumeric data (exciting concepts in those Fortran and COBOL days) and, in the Cambridge culture at least, was once the favored implementation language. Richard Stallman and Guy Steele were part of this MIT Lisp culture, and in 1975 they collaborated on **emacs**. This chapter discusses the **emacs** editor as implemented by the Free Software Foundation (GNU) and commonly provided with UNIX distributions. The **emacs** editor is not part of Solaris.

▲ About emacs

Initially **emacs** was prototyped as a series of editor commands or macros for the late 1960s text editor TECO (Text Editor and COrrector). The acronymic name, Editor MACroS, reflects these beginnings, although there have been many humorous reinterpretations, including ESCAPE META ALT CONTROL SHIFT, Emacs Makes All Computing Simple, and the unkind translation Eight Megabytes And Constantly Swapping.

Since then **emacs** has grown and evolved through more than 20 major revisions to the mainstream GNU version alone. The **emacs** editor is coded in C, and it contains a complete Lisp interpreter. It fully supports the X Window System and mouse interaction, and until recently was maintained by Stallman himself.

---

1. From a column on Net Computers by Michelle Murdock. Thanks to **www.ncworld.com**.

The original TECO macros are long gone, and **emacs** is a work still very much in progress. The Free Software Foundation has announced plans to add capabilities to **emacs**. There are plans to support variable-width fonts, wide character sets, and the world's major languages. In the long term they intend to move **emacs** in the direction of a WYSIWYG word processor and make it easier for beginners to use.

The **emacs** editor has always been considerably more than a text editor. Not having been developed originally in a UNIX environment, **emacs** does not adhere to the UNIX/Solaris philosophy. Whereas a UNIX/Solaris utility is typically designed to do one thing and to be used in conjunction with other utilities, **emacs** is designed to "do it all." Because there is a programming language (Lisp) underlying it, **emacs** users tend to customize and extend the editor rather than to use existing utilities or create new general-purpose tools. Instead they share their **.emacs** (customization) files.

Well before the X Window System, Stallman put a great deal of thought and effort into designing a window-oriented work environment, and he used **emacs** as his research vehicle. Over time he built facilities within **emacs** for reading and composing email messages, reading and posting netnews, giving shell commands, compiling programs and analyzing error messages, running and debugging these programs, and playing games. Eventually it became possible to enter the **emacs** environment and not come out all day, switching from window to window and from file to file. If you had only an ordinary serial, character-based terminal, **emacs** gave you tremendous leverage.

In an X Window System environment, **emacs** does not need to control the whole display, usually operating only one or two windows. However part or all of the original work environment is still available for those who want to use it.

As a *language-sensitive* editor, **emacs** has special features that you can turn on to help edit text, **nroff**, TeX, Lisp, C, Fortran, and so on. These feature sets are called *modes,* but they are not related in any way to the Command Mode and Input Mode found in **vi** and other editors. Because you never need to switch **emacs** between Input and Command Modes, **emacs** is called a *modeless* editor.

▲▲ emacs versus vi

Like **vi**, **emacs** is a display editor: It displays the text you are editing on the screen and changes the display as you type each command or insert new text. Unlike **vi**, **emacs** does not require you to keep track of whether you are in Command Mode or Insert Mode: Commands always use a **CONTROL** or other special key. The **emacs** editor always inserts ordinary characters, another trait of modeless editing. For many people this is convenient and natural.

As in **vi**, you edit a file in a work area, or *buffer,* and have the option of writing this buffer back to the file on the disk when you are finished. With **emacs**, however, you can have many work buffers, changing among them without having to write out and read back in. Furthermore you can display multiple buffers at one time, each in its own window. This is often helpful in cut-and-paste operations or to keep C declarations in one window while editing related code in another part of the file in another window.

Like **vi**, **emacs** has a rich, extensive command set for moving about in the buffer and altering text, but in **emacs** this command set is not "cast in concrete." You can change or customize commands at any time. Literally any key can be coupled, or *bound,* to any command, to better match a particular keyboard or just to fulfill a personal whim. Usually key bindings are set in the **.emacs** startup file, but they can also be changed interactively during a session. All the key bindings described in this chapter are standard on GNU **emacs** versions 19 and above. This version also supports many visual, mouse-oriented capabilities that are not covered here.

> ### Too Many Key Bindings
>
> If you change too many key bindings, you can easily produce a command set that you will not remember, or that will make it impossible for you to get back to the standard bindings again in the same session.

Finally, and *very* unlike **vi**, **emacs** allows you to use Lisp to write new commands or override old ones. Stallman calls this feature *online extensibility,* but it would take a gutsy Lisp guru to write and debug a new command while editing live text. It is much more common to add a few extra debugged commands to the **.emacs** file where they are loaded automatically when **emacs** starts up.

▲ Tutorial: Getting Started with emacs

The **emacs** editor has many, many features, and there are many ways to use it. Its complete manual had 29 chapters *before* the X Window System upgrade in version 19. However you can do a considerable amount of meaningful work with a relatively small subset of the commands. This section describes a simple editing session, explaining how to start and exit from **emacs** and how to move the cursor and delete text. It postpones or simplifies some issues in the interest of clarity. If you are using **emacs** in an X Window System environment, refer to "**emacs** and the X Window System" on page 329 as you read this section.

▲▲ Starting emacs

To edit a file named **sample**, type the shell command:

```
$ emacs -q sample
```

This command starts **emacs**, reads the file named **sample** into a buffer, and displays its contents on the screen. If this is the first time you have run **emacs** and there is no file with this name, **emacs** displays a blank screen with New File at the bottom. If you have run **emacs** already, then the New File message is displayed but quickly replaced with another message (Figure 9-1). The **–q** option tells **emacs** *not* to read the **.emacs** startup file from your home directory. This guarantees that you get standard uncustomized behavior and is sometimes useful for beginners or for other users wanting to bypass a **.emacs** file.

The screen starts out with a single window. At the bottom of this window is a reverse-video title bar called the *Mode Line*. The Mode Line, at a minimum, shows the name of the buffer that the window is view-

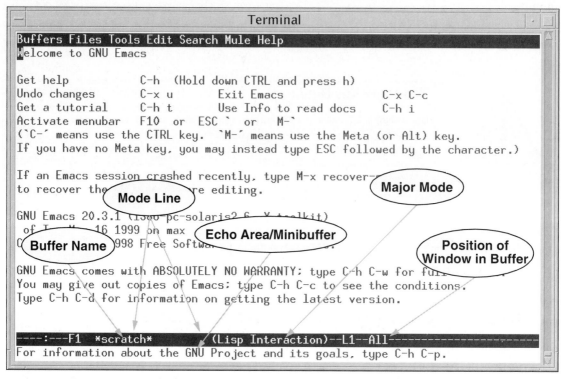

*Figure 9-1 The first **emacs** window you see*

ing, whether the buffer has been changed, what major and minor modes are in effect, and how far down the buffer the window is currently positioned. When you have more than one window, there is one Mode Line in each window. At the bottom of the screen, **emacs** leaves a single line open called the *Echo Area* or *Minibuffer*. This line is for short messages and special one-line commands.

There is a cursor in the window or Minibuffer. All the input and nearly all the editing takes place at the cursor. As you type ordinary characters, **emacs** inserts them at the cursor position. If there are characters under the cursor or to its right, they get pushed over as you type so no characters are lost.

▲▲ Stopping emacs

The command to exit from **emacs** is the two-key sequence CONTROL-X CONTROL-C. You can give this command at almost any time (in some modes you may have to first type CONTROL-G—see the next paragraph). It stops **emacs** gracefully, asking you to confirm changes if you made any during the editing session.

If you want to cancel a half-typed command or stop a running command before it is done, you can quit by typing CONTROL-G. The **emacs** editor displays Quit in the Echo Area and waits for your next command.

▲▲ Inserting Text

Typing an ordinary (printing) character pushes the cursor and any characters to the right of the cursor one position to the right and inserts the new character in the position just opened. Backspacing pulls the cursor and any characters to the right of the cursor one position to the left, erasing the character that was there before.

> ### Backspace Key
>
> With standard default key bindings, you backspace with the **CONTROL-D** key, whereas the **BACKSPACE** key (**CONTROL-H**) is bound to the online help function (page 303). For the moment it is easiest to backspace with **DELETE**.

The **RETURN** key inserts an invisible end-of-line character in the buffer and returns the cursor to the left margin, one line down.

Start **emacs** and type a few lines of text. If you make a mistake, back up using **DELETE**. It is possible to back up past the start of a line and up to the end of the line just above. Figure 9-2 shows a sample buffer.

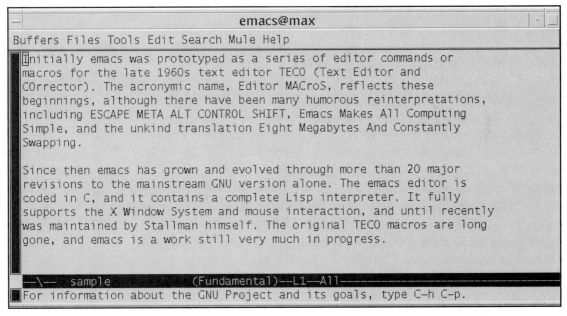

Figure 9-2   Sample buffer

▲▲ Moving the Cursor

You can position the cursor over any character in the **emacs** window and move the window so it displays any portion of the buffer. You can move the cursor forward or backward through the text (see Figure 8-5 on page 254) by various textual units (for example characters, words, sentences, lines, paragraphs). Any of the cursor-movement commands can be preceded by a repetition count (**CONTROL-U** followed by a numeric argument) that causes the cursor to move that number of textual units through the text. See page 300 for further discussion of numeric arguments.

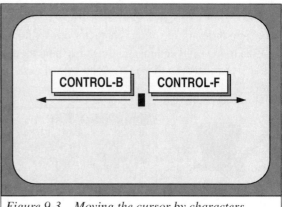

Figure 9-3   Moving the cursor by characters

▲▲▲ Moving the Cursor by Characters

Pressing **CONTROL-F** moves the cursor forward one character. If the cursor is at the end of a line, this command wraps it to the beginning of the next line. The command **CONTROL-U 7 CONTROL-F** moves the cursor seven characters forward (to the right).

Pressing **CONTROL-B** moves the cursor backward one character. The command **CONTROL-U 7 CONTROL-B** moves the cursor seven characters backward (to the left). **CONTROL-B** works in a manner similar to **CONTROL-F** (Figure 9-3).

▲▲▲ Moving the Cursor by Words

Pressing **META-f**[2] moves the cursor forward one word. To press **META-f** hold down the **META** or **ALT** key while you press **f**; if you do not have either of these keys, press **ESCAPE**, release it, and then press **f**. It leaves the cursor on the first character that is not part of the word the cursor started on. The command **CONTROL-U 4 META-f** moves the cursor forward one space past the end of the fourth word. See page 299 for more about keys.

Pressing **META-b** moves the cursor backward one word so the cursor is on the first letter of the word it started on. It works in a manner similar to **META-f** (Figure 9-4).

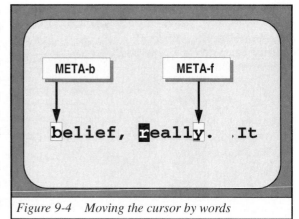

Figure 9-4   Moving the cursor by words

---

2. The **META** key is the diamond key on Sun keyboards and the **ALT** key on other keyboards.

▲▲▲ Moving the Cursor by Lines

Pressing **CONTROL-A** moves the cursor to the beginning of the line it is on; **CONTROL-E** moves it to the end. Pressing **CONTROL-P** moves the cursor up one line to the position directly above where the cursor started; **CONTROL-N** moves it down. As with the other cursor-movement keys, you can precede **CONTROL-P** and **CONTROL-N** with **CONTROL-U** and a numeric argument to move up or down multiple lines.

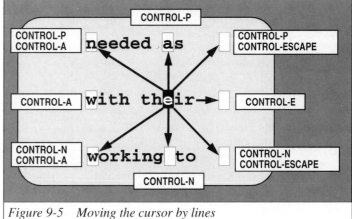

Figure 9-5   Moving the cursor by lines

You can use pairs of these commands to move the cursor up to the beginning of the previous line, down to the end of the following line, and so on (Figure 9-5).

▲▲▲ Moving the Cursor by Sentences, Paragraphs, and Window Position

Pressing **META-a** moves the cursor to the beginning of the sentence the cursor is on; **META-e** moves the cursor to the end. **META-{** moves the cursor to the beginning of the paragraph the cursor is on; **META-}** moves it to the end. You can precede any of these commands by a repetition count (**CONTROL-U** and a numeric argument) to move the cursor that many sentences or paragraphs.

Pressing **META-r** moves the cursor to the beginning of the middle line of the window. You can precede this command with a **CONTROL-U** and a line number (here **CONTROL-U** does not indicate a repetition count but a screen line number). The command **CONTROL-U 0 META-r** moves the cursor to the beginning of the top line (line zero) in the window. You can replace zero with the line number of the line you want to move the cursor to or a minus sign (–), in which case the cursor moves to the beginning of the last line of the window (Figure 9-6).

▲▲ Editing at the Cursor Position

You can type in new text and push the existing text to the right. Entering new text requires no special commands once the cursor is positioned. If you type in so much that the text in a line goes past the right edge of the window, **emacs** puts a backslash (\) in column 80 and then wraps the remainder of the text to the next line. The backslash appears on the screen but is never printed out. Although you can create an arbitrarily long line, some UNIX tools have problems with text files containing these very long lines. You can split a line at any point by positioning the cursor and pressing **RETURN**.

Pressing **DELETE** removes characters to the left of the cursor. The cursor and the remainder of the text on this line both move to the left each time you press **DELETE**. To join a line with the line above it, position the cursor on the first character of the second line and press **DELETE**.

Press **CONTROL-D** to delete the character under the cursor. The cursor remains stationary, and the remainder of the text on this line moves left to replace the deleted character.

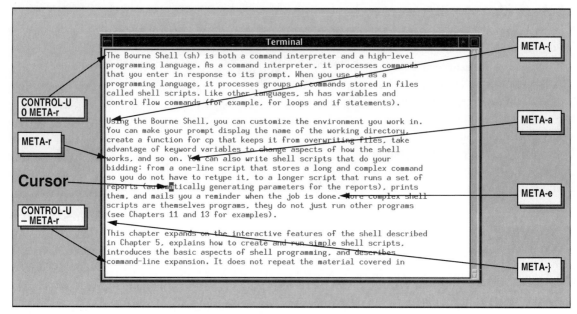

Figure 9-6   Moving the cursor by sentences, paragraphs, and window position

▲▲ Saving and Retrieving the Buffer

No matter what happens to a buffer during an **emacs** session, the associated file is not changed until you save the buffer. If you leave **emacs** without saving the buffer (this *is* possible if you are insistent enough), the file is not changed, and the session's work is discarded.

As mentioned previously, **emacs** prompts you about unsaved changes to the buffer contents. As **emacs** writes a buffer's edited contents back out to the file, it may optionally first make a backup of the original file contents. You can choose between no backups, one level (default), or an arbitrary number of levels. The one-level backup filenames are formed by appending the ~ character to the original filename. The multilevel backups append **.~n~** to the filename where **n** is the sequential backup number starting with 1.

The command **CONTROL-X CONTROL-S** saves the current buffer in its associated file. The **emacs** editor confirms a successful save with a message in the Echo Area.

If you are already editing a file with **emacs** and wish to begin editing another file (also called *visiting* a file), you can copy the new file into a new **emacs** buffer by giving the command **CONTROL-X CONTROL-F**. The **emacs** editor prompts you for a filename, reads that file into a new buffer, and displays that buffer in the current window. Having two files open in one editing session is more convenient than exiting from **emacs** and returning to the shell and then starting a new copy of **emacs** to edit a second file.

▲ Basic Editing Commands

This section takes a more detailed look at the fundamental **emacs** editing commands. It covers straightforward editing of a single file in a single window.

Visiting a File with CONTROL-X CONTROL-F

When using **CONTROL-X CONTROL-F**, **emacs** partially completes the path to the filename you are to enter. Normally this is the path to the working directory, but in some situations **emacs** may display a different path, such as the path to your home directory. You can edit this already-displayed path if it is not pointing to the directory you want.

▲▲ Keys: Notation and Use

Mainstream **emacs** uses 128-character ASCII codes. ASCII keyboards have the typewriter-style **SHIFT** key and a **CONTROL** key. In addition some keyboards have a **META** (diamond or **ALT**) key that controls the eighth bit (it takes seven bits to describe an ASCII character—the eighth bit of an eight-bit byte can be used to communicate other information). Because so much of the **emacs** command set is in the nonprinting **CONTROL** or **META** case, Stallman was one of the first to confront the problem of developing a notation for writing about keystrokes.

His solution, although not popular outside the **emacs** community, is clear and unambiguous (see the table below). It uses the capital letters **C** and **M** to denote holding down the **CONTROL** and **META** keys respectively, and a few simple acronyms for the most common special characters such as **RET** (this book uses **RETURN**), **LFD** (**LINEFEED**), **DEL** (**DELETE**), **ESC** (**ESCAPE**), **SPC** (**SPACE**), and **TAB**. Most **emacs** documentation, including the online help, uses this notation.

Character	Classic emacs Notation
(lowercase) a	a
(uppercase) SHIFT-a	A
CONTROL-a	C-a
CONTROL-A	C-a (do *not* use **SHIFT**), equivalent to **CONTROL-a**
META-a	M-a
META-a	M-A (*do* use **SHIFT**)
CONTROL-META-a	C-M-a
CONTROL-META-a	M-C-a (not used frequently)

There were some problems with this use of keys. Many keyboards had no **META** key, and some operating systems discarded the **META** bit. The **emacs** character set clashes with XON-XOFF flow control, which also uses **CONTROL-S** and **CONTROL-Q**, and continues to do so today.

Although the flow-control problem still exists, the **META** key issue was resolved by making it an optional two-key sequence starting with **ESCAPE**. For instance you can type **ESCAPE-a** in place of **META-a** or **ESCAPE CONTROL-A** to get **CONTROL-META-a**. If your keyboard does not have a **META** or **ALT** key, you can use the two-key **ESCAPE** sequence by pressing the **ESCAPE** key, releasing it, and then pressing the key following the **META** key in this book. For example if this book says "Press **META-r**", you can either press the **META** or **ALT** key while you press **r**, or you can press and release **ESCAPE** and then press **r**.

An aside on notation: This book uses an uppercase letter following the **CONTROL** key and a lowercase letter following the **META** key. In either case you *do not ever have to hold down the* **SHIFT** *key while entering a* **CONTROL** *or* **META** *character.* Although the **META** uppercase character (that is, **META-A**) is a different character, it is usually set up to cause no action or the same effect as its lowercase counterpart.

▲▲ Key Sequences and Commands

In **emacs** the relationship between key sequences (one or more keys that are pressed together or in sequence to issue an **emacs** command) and commands is very flexible, and there is considerable opportunity for exercising your personal preference. You can translate and remap key sequences to other commands and replace or reprogram commands themselves.

Although most **emacs** documentation glosses over all the details and talks about keystrokes as though they were the actual commands, it is important to know that the underlying machinery is separate from the key sequences and to understand that the behavior of the key sequences and the commands can be changed (page 325).

▲▲ Running a Command without a Key Binding: META-x

The **emacs** keymaps (the tables, or vectors, that **emacs** uses to translate key sequences to commands (page 326) are very crowded, and often it is not possible to bind every single command to a key sequence. You can execute any command by name by preceding it with **META-x**. The **emacs** editor prompts you for a command in the Echo Area and executes it after you enter the command name and press the **RETURN** key.

Sometimes, when there is no common key sequence for a command, it is described as **META-x** *command-name*. The **emacs** editor has a *smart completion* for most prompted answers, using **SPACE** or **TAB** to complete, if possible, to the end of the current word or the whole command, respectively. Forcing a completion past the last unambiguous point or typing **?** displays a list of alternatives. You can find more details on smart completion in the online **emacs** manual.

▲▲ Numeric Arguments

Some of the **emacs** editing commands take a numeric argument and interpret it as a repetition count. The argument immediately prefixes the key sequence for the command, and the most common case of no argument is almost always interpreted as a count of 1. Even an ordinary alphabetic character can have a numeric argument, which means "insert this many times." The two ways of giving a command a numeric argument are

- Press **META** with each digit (0–9) or the minus sign (–) (for example to insert 10 **z** characters, type **META-1 META-0 z**).

- Use **CONTROL-U** to begin a string of digits, including the minus sign (for example to move the cursor forward 20 words, type **CONTROL-U 20 META-f**).

For convenience **CONTROL-U** defaults to *multiply by four* when you do not follow it with a string of one or more digits. For example entering **CONTROL-U r** means insert **rrrr** (4 ∗ 1) while **CONTROL-U CONTROL-U r** means insert **rrrrrrrrrrrrrrrr** (4 ∗ 4 ∗ 1). For quick partial scrolling of a tall window, you may find it convenient to use repeated sequences of **CONTROL-U CONTROL-V** to scroll down four lines, **CONTROL-U META-v** to scroll up four lines, **CONTROL-U CONTROL-U CONTROL-V** to scroll down 16 lines, or **CONTROL-U CONTROL-U META-v** to scroll up 16 lines.

▲▲ Point and the Cursor

Point is the place in a buffer where editing takes place, and this is where the cursor is positioned. Strictly speaking, Point is the left edge of the cursor—it is thought of as always lying *between* two characters.

Each window has its own Point, but there is only one cursor. When the cursor is in a window, moving the cursor also moves Point. Switching the cursor out of a window does not change that window's Point; it is in the same place when you switch the cursor back to that window.

All of the cursor-movement commands previously described also move Point. In addition you can move the cursor to the beginning of the buffer with **META-<** or to the end of the buffer with **META->**.

▲▲ Scrolling through a Buffer

A buffer is likely to be much larger than the window through which it is viewed, so there has to be some way of moving the display of the buffer contents up or down to put the interesting part in the window. *Scrolling forward* refers to moving the text upward, with new lines entering at the bottom of the window. Use **CONTROL-V** to scroll forward one window (minus two lines for context). *Scrolling backward* refers to moving the text downward, with new lines entering at the top of the window. Use **META-v** to scroll backward one window (again leaving two lines for context). Pressing **CONTROL-L** clears the screen and repaints it, moving the current line to the center of the window. This command is useful if the screen display becomes garbled.

A numeric argument to **CONTROL-V** or **META-v** means "scroll that many lines"; thus **CONTROL-U 10 CONTROL-V** means scroll forward ten lines. A numeric argument to **CONTROL-L** means "scroll the text so the cursor is on that line of the window," where 0 means the top line and –1 means the bottom, just above the Mode Line. Scrolling occurs automatically if you exceed the window limits with **CONTROL-P** or **CONTROL-N**.

▲▲ Erasing Text

When text is erased, it can be discarded, or it can be moved into a holding area and optionally brought back later. The term *delete* means *permanent discard,* and the term *kill* means *move to a holding area.* The holding area, called the *Kill Ring,* can hold several pieces of killed text. You can use the text in the Kill Ring in many ways (see "Cutting and Pasting: Yanking Killed Text" on page 308).

The **DELETE** key deletes the character to the left of the cursor, while **CONTROL-D** deletes the character under the cursor. The **META-d** command kills from the cursor forward to the end of the current word, and the **META-DELETE** command kills the text from the cursor backward to the beginning of the previous word.

CONTROL-K kills forward to the end of the current line. It does *not* delete the line-ending **LINEFEED** character unless Point (and the cursor) are just to the left of the **LINEFEED**. This allows you to get to the left end of a line with **CONTROL-A**, kill the whole line with **CONTROL-K**, and then immediately type a replacement line without having to reopen a hole for the new line. Another consequence is that (from the beginning of the line) it takes **CONTROL-K CONTROL-K** (or **CONTROL-U 2 CONTROL-K**) to kill the text and close the hole.

▲▲ Searching

The **emacs** editor has several types of search commands. You can search in the following ways:

- incrementally for a character string
- incrementally for a regular expression (possible but very uncommon)
- for a complete character string
- for a complete full regular expression (Appendix A)

You can run each of the four subsequent searches either forward or backward in the buffer.

The *complete* string searches behave in the same manner as a search on other editors. Searching begins only when the search string is complete. In contrast an *incremental* search begins as you type the first character of the search string and keeps going as you enter additional characters. Initially this sounds confusing, but it is surprisingly useful and is the preferred search technique in **emacs**.

▲▲▲ Incremental Searches

A single command selects the direction of and starts an incremental search: **CONTROL-S** starts a forward incremental search, and **CONTROL-R** starts a reverse incremental search.

When you start an incremental search, **emacs** starts a special one-line dialog in the Echo Area. You are prompted with I-search: to enter some characters. When you enter a character, **emacs** begins searching for that character in the buffer. If it finds that character, it moves Point and cursor to that position so you can see the search progress.

After you enter each character of the search string, you can take any one of several actions:

- The search reaches your target in the buffer, and the cursor is positioned just to its right. In this case exit from the search and leave the cursor in its new position by entering **RETURN**. (Actually any **emacs** command not related to searching also takes you out, but remembering exactly which ones can be difficult. For a new user **RETURN** is safer.)

- The search reaches the current search string, but it's not yet at the target you want. Now you can refine the search string by adding another letter, reiterate your **CONTROL-R** or **CONTROL-S** to look for the next occurrence of this search string, or enter **RETURN** to stop the search and leave the cursor at its current position.

- The search hits the beginning or end of the buffer and reports Failing I-Search. You can proceed in several ways at this point:

  - If you mistyped the search string or reiterated **CONTROL-S** too often, press **DELETE** to back out some of the wrong characters or search reiterations. The text and cursor in the window jump backward in step with you.

- If you want to wrap past the beginning or end of the buffer and continue searching, you can force a wrap by entering **CONTROL-R** or **CONTROL-S** again.

- If the search has not found what you want but you want to stay at the current position, press **RETURN** to stop the search at that point.

- If the search has gone wrong and you just want to get back to where you started, press **CONTROL-G** (the quit character). From an unsuccessful search a single **CONTROL-G** backs out all the characters in the search string that could not be found. If this takes you back to a place you wish to continue searching from, you can add characters to the search string again. If you do not want to continue the search from here, a second **CONTROL-G** ends the search and leaves the cursor where it was to begin with.

▲▲▲ Nonincremental Searches

If you prefer that your searches just succeed or fail without showing all the intermediate results, you can give the nonincremental commands **CONTROL-S RETURN** to search forward or **CONTROL-R RETURN** to search backward. Searching does not begin until you enter a search string in response to the **emacs** prompt and press **RETURN** again. Neither of these commands wraps past the end of the buffer.

▲▲▲ Regular Expression Searches

You can perform both incremental and nonincremental regular expression searching in **emacs**. To begin a regular expression search, you can use the following commands:

META-CONTROL-X	Incrementally searches forward for regular expression; prompts for a regular expression one character at a time
META-x *isearch-backward-regexp*	Incrementally searches backward for regular expression; prompts for a regular expression one character at a time
META-CONTROL-S RETURN	Prompts for and then searches forward for a complete regular expression
META-x *isearch-backward-regexp* **RETURN**	Prompts for and then searches backward for a complete regular expression

▲ Online Help

The **emacs** help system is always available. With the default key bindings, you can start it with **CONTROL-H**. The help system then prompts you for a one-letter help command. If you do not know which help command you want, type **?** or **CONTROL-H**. This switches the current window to a list of help commands, each of them with a one-line description, and again requests a one-letter help command.

If, while still being prompted about what help you want, you decide you do not really want help after all, you can type **CONTROL-G** to cancel your help request and get back to your former buffer.

If the help output is only a single line, it appears in the Echo Area. If it is more, then the output appears in its own window. To scroll this output you can use **SPACE** to scroll forward and **DELETE** to scroll backward. When you are done with the help window, you can delete it by typing **q**. See page 314 for a discussion on working with multiple windows.

Some help commands such as **news** (CONTROL-H n for recent **emacs** changes) and tutorial (CONTROL-H t) have so much output that they give you a whole window right away. When you are done with this help window, you can delete it with CONTROL-X k, which deletes the **emacs** buffer holding the information. See page 313 for more information on using buffers.

On many terminals the BACKSPACE or LEFT ARROW key generates CONTROL-H. If you forget you are using **emacs** and try to back over a few characters, you may find yourself in the help system unintentionally. There is no danger to the buffer you are editing, but it can be unsettling to lose the window contents and not have a clear picture of how to restore it. In this case type CONTROL-G to return to editing the buffer. Some users elect to put help on a different key (page 326).

Following are some of the help commands:

CONTROL-H a	Prompts for *string* and then shows a list of commands whose names contain *string*.
CONTROL-H b	Shows a table (it is long) of all the key bindings now in effect.
CONTROL-H c *key-sequence*	Prints the name of the command bound to *key-sequence*. Multiple key sequences are allowed; however for a long key sequence where only the first part is recognized, the command describes the first part and quietly inserts the unrecognized part into your buffer. This can happen with three-character function keys (F1, F2, and so on, on the keyboard) that generate character sequences such as ESCAPE [SHIFT.
CONTROL-H k *key-sequence*	Prints the name and documentation of the command bound to *key-sequence.* (See the notes on the preceding command.)
CONTROL-H f	Prompts for the name of a Lisp function and prints the documentation for it. Because commands are Lisp functions, you can use a command name with this command.
CONTROL-H i	Takes you to the top menu of **info**, a documentation browser (not part of Solaris). Generally a complete **info** manual and **emacs** manual are kept online, and other GNU packages may have manuals here too. The **info** utility has its own help system. Type **?** for a summary or **h** for a tutorial.
CONTROL-H l (lowercase "ell")	Shows the last 100 characters typed. The record is kept *after* the first-stage keyboard translation. If you have customized the keyboard translation table, you must make a mental reverse translation.
CONTROL-H m	Shows the documentation and special key bindings for the current Major Mode (that is, Text, C, Fundamental, and so on).
CONTROL-H n	Shows the **emacs** news file (new changes made to **emacs**, ordered with most recent first).
CONTROL-H t	Runs an **emacs** tutorial session. When you are finished with the tutorial, you can reselect your original buffer with CONTROL-X b or kill the help buffer with CONTROL-X k (page 313).
CONTROL-H v	Prompts for a Lisp variable name and gives the documentation for that variable.
CONTROL-H w	Prompts for a command name and gives the key sequence, if any, bound to that command. Multiple key sequences are allowed. However for a long key sequence where only the first part is recognized, the command describes the first part and quietly

inserts the unrecognized part into your buffer. This can happen with three-character function keys (**F1**, **F2**, and so on, on the keyboard) that generate character sequences such as **ESCAPE [SHIFT**.

> ## Bug
>
> After a long **info** session, the **q** command (quit **info**) may take your window back to an **info** help buffer instead of your original buffer. This is a bug in some versions of **emacs**. You can reselect your original buffer with **CONTROL-X b**, or kill the help buffer with **CONTROL-X k**.

Even in this abridged presentation, it is clear that you can use the help system to browse through the **emacs** internal Lisp system. For the curious here is Stallman's suggested list of strings that match many names in the Lisp system:

char	line	word	sentence	paragraph	region	page
sexp	list	defun	buffer	screen	window	file
dir	register	mode	beginning	end	forward	backward
next	previous	up	down	search	goto	kill
delete	mark	insert	yank	fill	indent	case
change	set	what	list	find	view	describe

To get a view of the internal functionality of **emacs**, you can use any of the preceding strings with the following commands:

CONTROL-H a   This command is part of the help system; it prompts for a string and then displays the commands whose names contain that string.

META-x apropos   Prompts for a string and shows all the Lisp commands and variables whose names contain that string.

▲ Advanced Editing Topics

The basic **emacs** commands are sufficient for many editing tasks, but the serious user quickly finds the need for more power. This section presents some of the more advanced **emacs** capabilities.

▲▲ Undoing Changes

An editing session begins when you read a file into an **emacs** buffer. At that point the buffer content matches the file exactly. As you insert text and give editing commands, the buffer content becomes more and more different from the file. If you are satisfied with the changes, you write the altered buffer back out to the file and end the session.

A window's Mode Line has an indicator immediately to the left of emacs: that shows the modification state of the buffer in the window. Its three states are −− (not modified), ∗∗ (modified), and %% (readonly).

The **emacs** editor keeps a record of all the keys you have pressed (text and commands) since the beginning of the editing session, up to a limit currently set at 20,000 characters. If you are within the limit, it is possible to undo the entire session for this buffer, one change at a time. If you have multiple buffers (page 313), then each buffer has its own undo record.

Undoing is considered so important that it is given a backup key sequence, just in case some keyboards cannot easily handle the primary sequence. The two sequences are **CONTROL-_** (underscore, which on old ASR-33 TTY keyboards was **LEFT ARROW**) and **CONTROL-X u**. When you type **CONTROL-_**, **emacs** undoes the last command and moves the cursor to that position in the buffer, so you can see what happened. If you type **CONTROL-_** a second time, then the next to the last command is undone, and so on. If you keep on typing **CONTROL-_**, eventually you get the buffer back to its original unmodified state, and the ∗∗ Mode Line indicator changes to −−. This is in contrast to **vi**, where undo works only on the most recent commands.

When you break the string of Undo commands with *anything* (text or any command except Undo) then all the reverse changes you made during the string of undos become a part of the change record and can themselves be undone. This offers a way to redo some or all of the undos. If you decide you backed up too far, type a command (something innocuous like **CONTROL-F** that does not change the buffer), and begin undoing in reverse. The following table lists some examples.

Commands	Effect
CONTROL-_	Undoes the last change
CONTROL-_ CONTROL-F CONTROL-_	Undoes the last change, and changes it back again
CONTROL-_ CONTROL-_	Undoes the last two changes
CONTROL-_ CONTROL-_ CONTROL-F CONTROL-_ CONTROL-_	Undoes two changes, and changes them both back again
CONTROL-_ CONTROL-_ CONTROL-F CONTROL-_	Undoes two changes, and changes one of them back again

If you do not remember the last change you made, you can type **CONTROL-_** and undo it. If it was a change that you wanted to make, type **CONTROL-F CONTROL-_** and make it again. If you modified a buffer by accident, you can keep typing **CONTROL-_** until the Mode Line indicator shows −− once more.

If the buffer is completely ruined and you want to start over, issue the command **META-x revert-buffer** to discard the current buffer contents and reread from the associated file; **emacs** will ask you to confirm your command.

▲▲ Mark and Region

In a buffer Point is the current editing position, which you can move anywhere in the buffer by moving the cursor. It is also possible to set a Mark in the buffer. The contiguous characters between Point and Mark (either one may come first) are called the *Region*. There are many commands that operate on a buffer's current Region and not just on the characters near Point.

Mark is not as easy to move as Point. Once it is set it can be moved only by setting it somewhere else. Each buffer has only one Mark. The **CONTROL-@** command explicitly sets the Mark at the current cursor (and Point) position. Some keyboards generate **CONTROL-@** when you type **CONTROL-Q**. While this is not really a backup key binding, it is occasionally a convenient alternative. You can use **CONTROL-X CONTROL-X** to exchange Point and Mark.

To establish a Region you usually position Point at one end of the desired Region, set Mark with **CONTROL-@**, and then move Point to the other end of the Region. If you forget where you left the Mark, you can move the cursor back to it again with **CONTROL-X CONTROL-X**, or hop back and forth with repeated **CONTROL-X CONTROL-X** to show the Region more clearly.

If one Region boundary or the other is not to your liking, swap Point and Mark with **CONTROL-X CONTROL-X** to move the cursor from one end of the Region to the other, and move Point. Continue until you are satisfied with the Region.

There are many possibilities for operating on a Region. Some examples follow:

META-w	Copies the Region between Point and Mark nondestructively (without killing it) to the Kill Ring
CONTROL-W	Kills the Region
META-x print-region	Sends the Region between Point and Mark to the print spooler
META-x append-to-buffer	Prompts for a buffer and appends Region between Point and Mark to that buffer
META-x append-to-file	Prompts for a filename and appends Region between Point and Mark to that file
CONTROL-X CONTROL-U	Converts Region between Point and Mark to uppercase
CONTROL-X CONTROL-L	Converts Region between Point and Mark to lowercase

Each time you set the Mark in a buffer, you are also pushing the Mark's former location onto the buffer's *Mark Ring*. The Mark Ring is organized as a fifo (first in first out) list and holds the 16 most recent locations where the Mark was set. Each buffer has its own Mark Ring. This record of recent Mark history is useful because it often holds locations that you want to jump back to quickly. Jumping to a location pointed to by the Mark Ring can be faster and easier than scrolling or searching your way through the buffer to find the site of a previous change.

To work your way backward along the trail of former Mark locations, give the command **CONTROL-U CONTROL-@** one or more times. Each time you give the command, **emacs**

- moves Point (and the cursor) to the current Mark location
- saves the current Mark location at the *oldest* end of the Mark Ring
- pops off the *youngest* (most recent) Mark Ring entry and sets Mark

Each additional **CONTROL-U CONTROL-@** command causes **emacs** to move Point and the cursor to the previous entry on the Mark Ring.

Although this process may seem complex, it is really just a safe jump to a previous Mark location. It is safe because each jump's starting point is recirculated back through the Mark Ring where it is easy to find again. You can jump to all the previous locations on the Mark Ring (it may be fewer than 16) by giving the command **CONTROL-U CONTROL-@** again and again. You can go around the ring as many times as you like and stop whenever you want to.

Some commands set Mark automatically: The idea is to leave a bookmark before moving Point a long distance. One example is **META->**, which sets Mark before jumping to the end of the buffer. You can then go back to your starting position with **CONTROL-U CONTROL-@**. Searches behave similarly. To avoid surprises the message `Mark Set` appears in the Echo Area whenever Mark is set, either explicitly or implicitly.

▲▲ Cutting and Pasting: Yanking Killed Text

Recall that killed text is not actually discarded but kept in the Kill Ring. The Kill Ring holds the last 30 pieces of killed text and is visible from all buffers.

Retrieving text from the Kill Ring is called *yanking*. This terminology is opposite from **vi**'s; in **vi** *yanking* pulls text from the buffer, and *putting* puts text into the buffer. Killing and yanking are roughly analogous to cutting and pasting, and are **emacs**'s primary mechanisms for moving and copying text.

The following are the most common kill and yank commands:

META-d	Kills forward to the end of the current word
META-D	Kills backward to the beginning of the previous word
CONTROL-K	Kills to the end of the line, not including **LINEFEED**
CONTROL-U 1 CONTROL-K	Kills to the end of the line, including **LINEFEED**
CONTROL-U 0 CONTROL-K	Kills back to beginning of current line
META-w	Copies Region between Point and Mark to Kill Ring, but does *not* erase from the buffer
CONTROL-W	Kills Region from Point to Mark
META-z *char*	Kills up to but not including the next occurrence of *char*
CONTROL-Y	Yanks the most recently killed text into the current buffer at Point; sets Mark at the beginning of this text, and positions Point and cursor at the end
META-y	Erases the just-yanked text, rotates the Kill Ring, and yanks the next item (only after **CONTROL-Y** or **META-y**)

To move two lines of text, move Point to the beginning of the first line, and enter **CONTROL-U 2 CONTROL-K** to kill two lines. Then move Point to the destination position, and enter **CONTROL-Y**.

To copy two lines of text, move Point to the beginning of the first line, and type **CONTROL-U 2 CONTROL-K CONTROL-Y** to kill and then yank back immediately. Then move Point to the destination position and type **CONTROL-Y**.

To copy a larger piece, set the Region to cover this piece and then type **CONTROL-W CONTROL-Y** to kill and then yank back at once. Then move Point to the destination, and type **CONTROL-Y**. You can also set the Region and use **META-w** to copy the Region to the Kill Ring.

The Kill Ring is organized as a fixed-length fifo list, with each new entry causing the eldest to be discarded (once you build up to 30 entries in the Kill Ring). Simple cut-and-paste operations generally use only the newest entry. The older entries are kept to give you time to change your mind about a deletion. If you do change your mind, it is possible to "mine" the Kill Ring like an archaeological dig, working backward through time and down through the strata of killed material to copy a specific item back into your buffer.

To view every entry in the Kill Ring, begin a yanking session with **CONTROL-Y**. This copies the youngest entry to your buffer at the current cursor position. If this is not the item you want, continue the yanking session by typing **META-y**. This erases the previous yank and copies the next youngest entry to the buffer at the current cursor position. If this still is not the item you wanted back, type **META-y** again to erase it and retrieve a copy of the next entry, and so on. You can continue this all the way back to the very oldest entry. If you continue to type **META-y**, you wrap back to the youngest again. In this manner you can examine each entry as many times as you wish.

The sequence is **CONTROL-Y** followed by any mixture of **CONTROL-Y** and **META-y**. If you type any other command after **META-y**, the sequence is broken, and you must give the **CONTROL-Y** command again to start another yank session.

As you work backward in the Kill Ring, it is useful to think of advancing a Last Yank pointer back through history to older and older entries. This pointer is *not* reset to the youngest entry until you give a new kill command. Using this technique, you can work backward part way through the Kill Ring with **CONTROL-Y** and a few **META-y**'s, give some commands that do not kill, and then pick up where you left off with another **CONTROL-Y** and a succession of **META-y**'s.

It is also possible to position the Last Yank pointer with positive or negative numeric arguments to **META-y**. Refer to the online documentation for more information.

▲▲ Inserting Special Characters

As stated earlier, **emacs** inserts everything that is not a command into the buffer at the current cursor position. To insert characters that would ordinarily be **emacs** commands, you can use the **emacs** escape character, **CONTROL-Q**. There are two ways of using this escape character:

- **CONTROL-Q** followed by any other character inserts that character in the buffer, no matter what command interpretation it was supposed to have.

- **CONTROL-Q** followed by three octal digits inserts a byte with that value in the buffer.

> **CONTROL-Q**
>
> Depending on the way your terminal is set up, **CONTROL-Q** may clash with software flow control. If **CONTROL-Q** seems to have no effect, it is most likely being used for flow control. You must bind another key to insert special characters (page 326).

▲▲ Global Buffer Commands

The **vi** editor and its predecessors have global commands for bufferwide search and replacement. Their default operating Region was the entire buffer. The **emacs** editor has a similar family of commands. Their operating Region begins at Point and extends to the end of the buffer. If you wish to operate on the complete buffer, use **META-<** to set Point at the beginning of the buffer before issuing the command.

▲▲▲ Line-Oriented Operations

The following commands all take a regular expression and apply it to the lines between Point and the end of the buffer.

META-x occur	Prompts for a regular expression and lists each line with a match for the expression in a buffer named ✳**Occur**✳.
META-x delete-matching-lines	Prompts for a regular expression and then deletes each line with a match for the expression.
META-x delete-non-matching-lines	Prompts for a regular expression and deletes each line that does *not* have a match for that expression.

The **META-x occur** command puts its output in a special buffer named ✳**Occur**✳, which you can peruse and discard or use as a jump menu to reach each line quickly. To use the ✳Occur✳ buffer as a jump menu, switch to it (page 313), get the cursor on the copy of the desired destination line, and type **CONTROL-C CONTROL-C**. This switches to the buffer that was searched and positions the cursor on the line that the regular expression originally matched.

As with any buffer change, you can undo the deletion commands.

▲▲▲ Unconditional and Interactive Replacement

The following commands operate on the characters between Point and the end of the buffer, changing every string match or regular expression match. An unconditional replacement makes all replacements without question. An interactive replacement gives you the opportunity to see and approve each replacement before it is made.

META-x replace-string	Prompts for *string* and *newstring*. Then replaces every instance of *string* with *newstring*. Point is left at the site of the last replacement, but Mark is automatically set when you give the command, so you can return to it with **CONTROL-U CONTROL-@**.
META-x replace-regexp	Behaves similarly, replacing every *regexp* with *newstring*.
META-% string *or* **META-x query-replace**	Behaves similarly, replacing some of the matches of *string* with *newstring*.
META-x query-replace-regexp	Behaves similarly, replacing some of the matches for *regexp*.

If you perform an interactive replacement, **emacs** displays each instance of *string* or match of *regexp* and prompts you for an action to take. Following are some of the possible responses:

RETURN	Do not do any more replacements; quit now.
SPACE	Make this replacement and go on.
DELETE	Do *not* make this replacement. Skip over it and go on.

, (comma)	Make this replacement, display the result, and ask for another command. Any command is legal except that DELETE is treated like SPACE and does not undo the change.
. (period)	Make this replacement and quit searching.
! (exclamation point)	Replace this, and all remaining instances, without asking any more questions.

▲▲ Working with Files

When you *visit* (**emacs** terminology for calling up) a file, **emacs** reads it into an internal buffer (page 313), edits the buffer contents, and eventually saves the buffer back to the file. The commands discussed here relate to visiting and saving files.

Each **emacs** buffer keeps a record of its default directory (the directory the file was read from or the working directory, if it is a new file) that is prepended to any relative pathname you give it. This is a convenience to save some typing. Enter META-x **pwd** to print the default directory for the current buffer, or META-x **cd** to prompt for a new default directory and assign it to this buffer.

▲▲▲ Visiting Files

The following are the commands for visiting files:

CONTROL-X CONTROL-F	Prompts for a filename and reads its contents into a freshly created buffer. Assigns the file's final pathname component as the buffer name. Other buffers are unaffected. It is common and often useful to have several files simultaneously open for editing.
CONTROL-X CONTROL-V	Prompts for a filename and replaces the current buffer with a buffer containing the contents of the requested file. The current buffer is destroyed.
CONTROL-X 4 CONTROL-F	Prompts for a filename and reads its contents into a freshly created buffer. Assigns the file's final pathname component as the buffer name. Creates a new window for this buffer and selects that window. The window selected before the command still shows the buffer it was showing before, although the new window may cover up part of the old window.

The **emacs** editor deals well with visiting a file that has been already called up and whose image is now in a buffer. After a check of modification time to be sure the file has not been changed since it was last called up, **emacs** simply switches you to that buffer.

To create a nonexistent file, simply call it up. An empty buffer is created and properly named, so you can eventually save it. The message (New File) appears in the Echo Area, reflecting **emacs**'s understanding of the situation. Of course if this "new file" grew out of a typographical error, you probably want to issue CONTROL-X CONTROL-V with the correct name.

▲▲▲ Saving Files

You save a buffer by copying its contents back to the original file you called up. These are the relevant commands:

CONTROL-X CONTROL-S   This is the workhorse file-saving command. It saves the current buffer into its original file. If the current buffer is not modified, you get the message (No changes need to be saved).

CONTROL-X s   For each modified buffer, you are asked if you wish to save it. Answer **y** or **n**. This command is given automatically as you exit **emacs**, to save any buffers that have been modified but not yet written out. However if you want to save intermediate copies of your work, you can give it at any time.

What to Do If You Modify a Buffer by Mistake

It is usually during **CONTROL-X s** that you discover files whose buffers were modified by mistake, and now **emacs** wants to save the wrong changes back to the file. *Do not* answer **y** if you are not sure. First get done with the **CONTROL-X s** dialog by typing **n** to any saves you are not clear about. Then you have several options:

- Save the suspicious buffer into a temporary file with **CONTROL-X CONTROL-W**, and analyze it later.

- Undo the changes with a string of **CONTROL-_** until the ✱✱ indicator disappears from the buffer's Mode Line.

- If you are sure all the changes are wrong, use **META-x revert-buffer** to get a fresh copy of the file.

- Kill the buffer outright. Because it is modified, you are asked if you are sure.

- Give the **META-~** (tilde) command to clear the modified condition and ✱✱ indicator. A subsequent **CONTROL-X s** then believes that the buffer does not need to be written.

META-x set-visited-file-name   Prompts for a filename and sets this name as the current buffer's "original" name.

CONTROL-X CONTROL-W   Prompts for a filename, sets this name as the "original" file for the current buffer, and saves the current buffer into that file. This is equivalent to **META-x** *set-visited-file-name* followed by **CONTROL-X CONTROL-S**.

META-~ (tilde)   Clears modified flag from the current buffer. If you have mistakenly typed **META-~** against a buffer with changes you want to keep, you need to make sure the modified condition and its ✱✱ indicator are turned back on before leaving **emacs**, or all the changes will be lost. One easy way to do this is to insert a **SPACE** into the buffer and then remove it again with **DELETE**.

> ### Exit without First Getting a Warning
>
> Clearing the modified flag (**META-~**) allows you to exit without saving a modified buffer with no warning. Be careful if you choose to use this technique.

▲▲ Working with Buffers

An **emacs** buffer is a storage object that you can edit. It often holds the contents of a file but can also exist without being associated with any file. You can select only one buffer at a time, designated as the *current buffer*. Most commands operate only on the current buffer, even when multiple windows show two or more buffers on the screen. For the most part each buffer is its own world: It has its own name, its own modes, its own file associations, its own modified state, and indeed it may have its own special key bindings. You can use the following commands to create, select, list, and manipulate buffers:

CONTROL-X **b**	Prompts for a buffer name and selects it. If it does not exist, this command creates it first.
CONTROL-X 4 **b**	Prompts for a buffer name and selects it in another window. The existing window is not disturbed, although the new window may overlap it.
CONTROL-X CONTROL-B	Creates a buffer named ∗**Buffer List**∗ and displays it in another window. The existing window is not disturbed, although the new window may overlap it. The new buffer is not selected. In the ∗**Buffer List**∗ buffer, each buffer's data is shown, with name, size, mode(s), and original filename. A % appears for a readonly buffer, a ∗ indicates a modified buffer, and . appears for the selected buffer.
META-x **rename-buffer**	Prompts for a new buffer name and gives this new name to the current buffer.
CONTROL-X CONTROL-Q	Toggles the current buffer's readonly status and the associated %% Mode Line indicator. This can be useful to prevent accidental buffer modification or to allow modification of a buffer when visiting a readonly file.
META-x **append-to-buffer**	Prompts for a buffer name and appends the current Region between Point and Mark to the end of that buffer.
META-x **prepend-to-buffer**	Prompts for a buffer name and appends the current Region between Point and Mark to the beginning of that buffer.
META-x **copy-to-buffer**	Prompts for a buffer name and deletes the contents of the buffer before copying the current Region between Point and Mark into that buffer.
META-x **insert-buffer**	Prompts for a buffer name and inserts the entire contents of that buffer into the current buffer at Point.
CONTROL-X **k**	Prompts for a buffer name and deletes that buffer. If the buffer is modified but unsaved, you are asked to confirm.

META-x kill-some-buffers Goes through the entire buffer list and offers the chance to delete each buffer. As with **CONTROL-X k**, you are asked to confirm the kill order if a modified buffer is not yet saved.

▲▲ Working with Windows

An **emacs** *window* is a viewport that looks into a buffer. The **emacs** screen begins by displaying a single window, but this screen space can later be divided among two or more windows. On the screen the *current window* holds the cursor and views the *current buffer*.

A window views one buffer at a time. You can switch the buffer that a window views by giving the command **CONTROL-X b** *buffer-name* in the current window. Multiple windows can view one buffer; each window may view different parts of the same buffer, and each window carries its own value of Point. Any change to a buffer is reflected in all the windows viewing that buffer. Also, a buffer can exist without a window open on it.

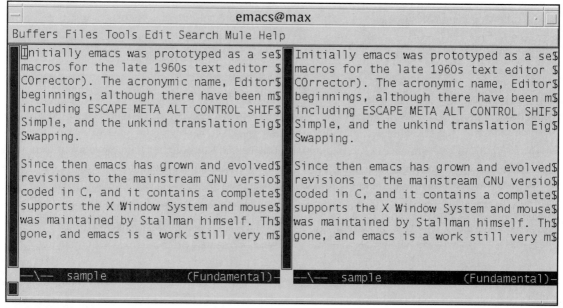

Figure 9-7   Splitting a window vertically

▲▲▲ Window Creation by Splitting

One way to divide the screen is to explicitly split the starting window into two or more pieces. The command **CONTROL-X 2** splits the current window in two, with one new window above the other. A numeric argument is taken as the size of the upper window in lines. The command **CONTROL-X 3** splits the current window in two, with the new windows arranged side by side (Figure 9-7). A numeric argument is taken as the number of columns to give the left window. For example **CONTROL-U CONTROL-X 2** splits the current window in two, and because of the special "times 4" interpretation of **CONTROL-U** standing alone, the upper window is to be given four lines (barely enough to be useful).

While these commands split the current window, both windows continue to view the same buffer. You can select a new buffer in either or both new windows, or you can scale each window to show different positions in the same buffer.

▲▲▲ Manipulating Windows

You can use **CONTROL-X o** (the letter "oh") to select the other window. If more than two windows are on the screen, a sequence of **CONTROL-X o** commands cycle through them all in top-to-bottom, left-to-right order. The **META-CONTROL-V** command scrolls the other window. If there are more than two, the command scrolls the window that **CONTROL-X o** would select next. You may use a positive or negative scrolling argument, just as with **CONTROL-V** scrolling in the current window.

▲▲▲ Other-Window Display

In normal **emacs** operation, explicit window splitting is not nearly so common as the implicit splitting done by the family of **CONTROL-X 4** commands. One of these commands is **CONTROL-X 4b**, which prompts for a *buffer name* and selects it in the other window. If there is no other window, it begins with a half-and-half split that arranges the windows one above the other. Another command, **CONTROL-X 4f**, prompts for a *filename,* calls it up in the other window, and selects the other window. If there is no other window, it begins with a half-and-half split that arranges the windows one above the other.

▲▲▲ Adjusting and Deleting Windows

Windows may be destroyed when they get in the way; no data is lost in the window's associated buffer, and you can make another window anytime you like. The **CONTROL-X 0** (zero) command deletes the current window and gives its space to its neighbors, while **CONTROL-X 1** deletes all windows except the current window.

It is also possible to adjust the dimensions of the current window, once again at the expense of its neighbors. You can make a window shorter with **META-x shrink-window**. Use **CONTROL-X ^** to increase the height of a window, **CONTROL-X }** to make the window wider (Figure 9-7), and **CONTROL-X {** to make the window narrower. Each of these commands adds or subtracts one line or column to or from the window, unless you precede the command with a numeric argument.

The **emacs** editor has its own guidelines for a window's minimum useful size and may destroy a window before you force one of its dimensions to zero. Although the window is gone, the buffer remains intact.

▲▲ Foreground Shell Commands

The **emacs** editor can run a subshell (a shell that is a child of the shell that is running **emacs**—see "Job Control" on page 357) to execute a single command line, optionally with input from a Region of the current buffer and optionally with command output replacing the Region contents. This is analogous to executing a shell command from the **vi** editor and having the input come from the file you are editing and the output go back into the same file (page 280). As with **vi**, how well this works depends in part on the capabilities of your shell.

META-! (exclamation point)   Prompts for a shell command, executes it, and displays the output.

CONTROL-U META-!   Prompts for a shell command, executes it, and inserts the output at Point.
(exclamation point)

META-| (vertical bar)   Prompts for a shell command, gives the Region contents as input, filters it through the command, and displays the output.

CONTROL-U META-| Prompts for a shell command, gives the Region contents as input, filters it through
(vertical bar)   the command, deletes the old Region contents, and inserts the output in that position.

The **emacs** editor can also start an interactive subshell, running continuously in its own buffer. See "Shell Mode" on page 324 for more information.

▲▲ Background Shell Commands

The **emacs** editor can run processes in the background, with output fed into a growing **emacs** buffer that does not have to remain in view. You can continue editing while the background process runs and look at its output later. Any shell command can be run, without any restrictions.

The growing output buffer is always named ∗**compilation**∗, and you can read it, copy from it, or edit it in any way, without waiting for the background process to finish. Most commonly this buffer is used to see the output of program compilation and then to correct any syntax errors found by the compiler.

To run a process in the background, give the command META-x **compile** to prompt for a shell command and begin executing it as a background process. The screen splits in half to show the ∗**compilation**∗ buffer.

You can switch to the ∗**compilation**∗ buffer and watch the execution, if you wish. To make the display scroll as you watch, position the cursor at the very end of the text with a META-> command. If you are not interested, just remove the window (with CONTROL-X 0 if you are in it or CONTROL-X 1 otherwise) and keep working. You can switch back to the ∗**compilation**∗ buffer later with CONTROL-X b.

You can kill the background process with META-x **kill-compilation**; **emacs** asks for confirmation and then kills the background process.

If standard format error messages appear in ∗**compilation**∗, you can automatically visit the line in the file where each one occurred. Give the command CONTROL-X ` (backquote or accent grave) to split the screen into two windows and visit the file and line of the next error message. Scroll the ∗**compilation**∗ buffer so that this error message appears at the top of its window. Use CONTROL-U CONTROL-X ` to start over with the first error message and visit that file and line.

▲ Language-Sensitive Editing

The **emacs** editor has a large collection of feature sets specific to a certain variety of text. The feature sets are called *Major Modes,* and a buffer may have only one Major Mode at a time.

A buffer's Major Mode is private to the buffer and does not affect editing in any other buffer. If you switch to a new buffer having a different mode, rules for the new mode are immediately in effect. To avoid confusion the name of a buffer's Major Mode appears in the Mode Line of any window viewing that buffer.

There are three classes of Major Modes:

- for editing human languages (for example text, **nroff**, TeX)

- for editing programming languages (for example C, Fortran, Lisp)

- for special purposes (for example shell, mail, dired, **ftp**)

In addition there is a Major Mode that does nothing special at all: Fundamental Mode. A Major Mode usually sets up the following:

- Special commands unique to the mode, possibly with their own key bindings. There may be just a few for languages, but special-purpose modes may have dozens.
- Mode-specific character syntax and regular expressions defining word constituent characters, delimiters, comments, whitespace, and so on. This conditions the behavior of commands oriented to syntactic units such as words, sentences, comments, or parenthesized expressions.

▲▲ Selecting a Major Mode

The **emacs** editor chooses and sets a mode when a file is called up by matching the filename against a set of regular expression patterns describing the filename and filename extension. The explicit command to enter a Major Mode is **META-x modename-mode**. This command is rarely used except to correct wrong guesses.

A file can define its own mode by having the text –*– **modename** –*– somewhere in the first nonblank line, possibly buried inside a comment suitable for that programming language.

▲▲ Human-Language Modes

A *human* language is meant eventually to be used by humans, possibly after being formatted by some text-formatting program. Human languages share many conventions about the structure of words, sentences, and paragraphs; with regard to these textual units, the major human language modes all behave the same.

Beyond the common region, each mode offers additional functionality oriented to a specific text formatter such as TeX, LaTeX, or **nroff**. Text-formatter extensions are beyond the scope of this presentation; the focus here is on the commands relating to human textual units (for example words, sentences, and paragraphs).

▲▲▲ Working with Words

As a mnemonic aid, the bindings are defined parallel to the character-oriented bindings **CONTROL-F**, **CONTROL-B**, **CONTROL-D**, **DELETE**, and **CONTROL-T**.

As discussed earlier, **META-f** and **META-b** move forward and backward over words, just as **CONTROL-F** and **CONTROL-B** move forward and backward over characters. They may start from a position inside or outside the word to be traversed, but in all cases Point finishes just beyond the word, adjacent to the last character skipped over. They accept a numeric argument specifying the number of words to be traversed.

The keys **META-d** and **META-DELETE** kill words forward and backward, just as **CONTROL-D** and **DELETE** delete characters forward and backward. They leave Point in exactly the same finishing position as **META-f** and **META-b**, but they kill the words they pass over. They also accept a numeric argument.

META-t transposes the word before Point with the word after Point.

▲▲▲ Working with Sentences

As a mnemonic aid, three of the bindings are defined parallel to the line-oriented bindings: **CONTROL-A**, **CONTROL-E**, and **CONTROL-K**.

As discussed earlier, **META-a** moves back to the beginning of a sentence and **META-e** moves forward to the end. In addition, **CONTROL-X DELETE** kills backward to the beginning of a sentence whereas **META-k** kills forward to the end of a sentence.

The **emacs** editor recognizes sentence ends with a regular expression kept in a variable named **sentence-end**. (If you are curious, give the command **CONTROL-H v sentence-end RETURN** to view this variable.) Briefly it looks for the characters **.**, **?**, or **!** followed by two **SPACE**s or an end-of-line marker, possibly with close quotation marks or close braces.

The **META-a** and **META-e** commands leave Point adjacent to the first or last nonblank character in the sentence. They accept a numeric argument specifying the number of sentences to traverse, and a negative argument runs them in reverse.

The **META-k** and **CONTROL-X DELETE** commands kill sentences forward and backward, in a manner analogous to **CONTROL-K** line kill. They leave Point in exactly the same finishing position as **META-a** and **META-e** but kill the sentences they pass over. They too accept a numeric argument. **CONTROL-X DELETE** is useful for quickly backing out of a half-finished sentence.

▲▲▲ Working with Paragraphs

As discussed earlier, **META-{** moves back to the most recent paragraph beginning, and **META-}** moves forward to the next paragraph ending. The **META-h** command marks the paragraph (that is, puts Point at the beginning and Mark at the end) that the cursor is currently on, or the next paragraph if it is in between.

The **META-}** and **META-{** commands leave Point at the beginning of a line, adjacent to the first character or last character of the paragraph. They accept a numeric argument specifying the number of paragraphs to traverse, and run in reverse if given a negative argument.

In human language modes paragraphs are separated by blank lines and text-formatter command lines, and an indented line starts a paragraph. Recognition is based on the regular expressions stored in the variables **paragraph-separate** and **paragraph-start**. A paragraph is composed of complete lines, including the final line terminator. If a paragraph starts following one or more blank lines, then the last blank line before the paragraph belongs to the paragraph.

▲▲▲ Filling

The **emacs** editor can *fill* a paragraph to fit a specified width. It breaks lines and rearranges them as necessary. Breaking takes place only between words, and there is no hyphenation. Filling can be done automatically as you type or in response to your explicit command.

META-x auto-fill-mode turns Auto Fill Mode on or off. Turn it off or on by giving the same command again. When Auto Fill Mode is on, **emacs** automatically breaks lines when you type **SPACE** or **RETURN** and are currently beyond the specified line width. This feature is useful when you are entering new text.

Auto Fill Mode does not automatically refill the entire paragraph you are currently working on. If you add new text in the middle of a paragraph, Auto Fill Mode breaks your new text as you type but does not refill the complete paragraph. To refill a complete paragraph or Region of paragraphs, either use **META-q** to refill the current paragraph or **META-x** *fill-region* to refill each paragraph in the Region between Point and Mark.

As before, paragraph boundaries are defined by the regular expressions stored in the **paragraph-separate** and **paragraph-start** variables.

You can change the filling width from its default value of 70 by setting the **fill-column** variable with either CONTROL-X f to set fill-column to the current cursor position, or CONTROL-U *nnn* CONTROL-X f to set fill-column to *nnn*, where 0 is the left margin.

▲▲▲ Case Conversion

The **emacs** editor can force words or Regions to all uppercase, all lowercase, or initial caps (that is, first letter of each word uppercase, balance lowercase). The commands are

META-l (lowercase "ell")	Converts word to the right of Point to lowercase
META-u	Converts word to the right of Point to uppercase
META-c	Converts word to the right of Point to initial caps
CONTROL-X CONTROL-L	Converts Region between Point and Mark to lowercase
CONTROL-X CONTROL-U	Converts Region between Point and Mark to uppercase

The word-oriented conversions move Point over the word just converted, the same as META-f, allowing you to walk through text, converting each word with META-l, META-u, or META-c, and skipping over words to be left alone with META-f.

A positive numeric argument converts that many words to the right of Point, moving Point as it goes. A negative numeric argument converts that many words to the left of Point but leaves Point stationary. This is useful for quickly changing the case of words you have just typed. Some examples appear in the following table.

These Characters and Commands	Produce These Results
HELLOMETA---META-l (lowercase "ell")	hello
helloMETA---META-u	HELLO
helloMETA---META-c	Hello

The word conversions are not picky about beginning in the middle of a word; in all cases they consider the first word constituent character to the right of Point as the beginning of the word to be converted.

▲▲▲ Text Mode

With very few exceptions, the commands for human-language text units such as words and sentences are always left turned on and available, even in the programming language modes. Text Mode adds very little to these basic commands but is still worth turning on just to get the TAB key. Use the command META-x **text-mode**.

In Text Mode TAB runs the function **tab-to-tab-stop**. By default TAB stops are set every eight columns. You can adjust them with META-x **edit-tab-stops**, which switches to a special ＊**Tab Stops**＊ buffer, where the current stops are laid out on a scale for you to edit. The new stops are installed when/if you type CONTROL-C CONTROL-C, but you are free to kill this buffer (CONTROL-X k) or switch away from it (CONTROL-X b) without ever changing the stops.

The tab stops you set here affect *only* the interpretation of TAB characters arriving from the keyboard. The **emacs** editor automatically inserts enough spaces to reach the TAB stop. This does *not* affect the interpretation of **TAB** characters already in the buffer or the underlying file. If you edit the **TAB** stops and then use them, you can still print your file, and the hard copy will look the same as the text on the screen.

▲▲ C Mode

Programming languages are read by humans but are interpreted by machines. Besides continuing to handle some of the human-language text units (for example words and sentences), the major programming language modes address the additional problems of dealing with

- "balanced expressions" enclosed by parentheses, brackets, or braces as textual units
- comments as textual units
- indention

In **emacs** there are Major Modes to support C, Fortran, and several variants of Lisp. In addition many users have contributed modes for their favorite languages. In these modes the commands for human textual units are still available, with occasional redefinitions: For example a paragraph is bounded only by blank lines, and indention does not signal a paragraph start. In addition each mode has custom coding to handle the language-specific conventions for balanced expressions, comments, and indention. This presentation discusses only C Mode.

▲▲▲ Working with Expressions

The **emacs** Major Modes are limited to lexical analysis. They can recognize most tokens (for example symbols, strings, numbers) and all matched sets of parentheses, brackets, and braces. This is enough for Lisp but not for C. The C Mode lacks a full-function syntax analyzer and is not prepared to recognize all of C's possible expressions.[3]

Following are the **emacs** editor commands applicable to parenthesized expressions and some tokens. By design the bindings run parallel to the **CONTROL** commands for characters and the **META** commands for words. All of these commands accept a numeric argument and run in reverse if that argument is negative.

CONTROL-META-f   Moves forward over an expression. The exact behavior for **CONTROL-META-f** depends on what character lies to the right of Point (or left of Point, depending on which direction you are moving Point):

  - If the first non whitespace is an opening delimiter (parenthesis, bracket, or brace), then Point is moved just past the matching closing delimiter.

---

3. In the **emacs** documentation the recurring term *sexp* refers to the historic Lisp term *S-expression.* Unfortunately it is sometimes used interchangeably with *expression,* even though the language might not be Lisp at all.

- If the first non whitespace is a token, then Point is moved just past the end of this token.

CONTROL-META-b Moves backward over an expression.

CONTROL-META-k Kills an expression forward. It leaves Point at the same finishing position as **CONTROL-META-f** but kills the expression it traverses.

CONTROL-META-@ Sets Mark at the position **CONTROL-META-f** would move to but does not change Point. To see the marked region clearly, you can look at both ends with a pair of **CONTROL-X CONTROL-X** commands to interchange Point and Mark.

▲▲▲ Function Definitions

In **emacs** a balanced expression at the outermost level is considered to be a function definition and is often called a *defun,* even though that term is specific to Lisp alone. Most generally it is understood to be a function definition in the language at hand.

In C Mode a function definition is understood to include the return data type, the function name, and the argument declarations appearing before the { character.

The following are the commands for operating on function definitions:

CONTROL-META-a Moves to the beginning of the most recent function definition. You can use this command to scan backward through a buffer one function at a time.

CONTROL-META-e Moves to the end of the next function definition. You can use this command to scan forward through a buffer one function at a time.

CONTROL-META-h Puts Point at the beginning and Mark at the end of the current (or next, if between) function definition. This command sets up an entire function definition for a Region-oriented operation such as kill.

Function Indention Style

The **emacs** editor now believes that an opening brace at the left margin is part of a function definition. This is a heuristic to speed up the reverse scan for a definition's leading edge. If your code has an indention style that puts that opening brace elsewhere, you may get unexpected results.

▲▲▲ Indention

The **emacs** C Mode has extensive logic to control the indention of C programs. Furthermore you can adjust the logic for many different styles of C indention.

Indention is called into action by the following commands:

TAB Adjusts the indention of the current line. **TAB** inserts or deletes whitespace at the beginning of the line until the indention conforms to the current context and rules in effect. Point is not moved at all unless it lies in the whitespace area; in that case it is moved to the end of that whitespace. **TAB** does not insert anything except leading whitespace, so you can hit it at any time and at any position in the line. If you really want to insert a tab in the text, you can use **META-i** or **CONTROL-Q TAB**.

LINEFEED   Shorthand for **RETURN** followed by **TAB**. The **LINEFEED** key is a convenience for entering new code, giving you an autoindent as you begin each line.

To indent multiple lines with a single command, there are two possibilities:

CONTROL-META-q   Re-indents all the lines inside the next pair of matched braces. **CONTROL-META-q** assumes the left brace is correctly indented and drives the indention from there. If the left brace itself needs help, type **TAB** on its line before giving this command. All the lines up to the matching brace are indented as if you had typed **TAB** on each one.

CONTROL-META-**   Re-indents all the lines in the current Region between Point and Mark. Put Point just to the left of a left brace and then give the command. All the lines up to the matching brace are indented as if you had typed **TAB on each one.

▲▲ Customizing Indention for Versions 19 and Above

Many styles of C programming have evolved, and **emacs** does its best to support automatic indention for all of them. The indention coding was completely rewritten for **emacs** version 19; now three times larger, it supports C, C++, Objective-C, and Java. The **emacs** syntactic analysis is much more precise and is able to classify each syntactic element of each line of program text into a single syntactic category (out of about 50) such as *statement, string, else-clause,* and so on.

With that analysis in hand, **emacs** goes to an offset table named **c-offsets-alist** and looks up how much this line should be indented from the preceding line.

In order to customize indention, you have to change the offset table. It is possible to define a completely new offset table for each customized style, but much more convenient to feed in a short list of exceptions to the standard rules. Each mainstream style (GNU, K&R [Kernighan and Ritchie], BSD, and so on) has such an exception list; all are collected in **c-style-alist**. Here is one entry from **c-style-alist**:

```
("gnu"
(c-basic-offset . 2)
(c-comment-only-line-offset . (0 . 0))
(c-offsets-alist . ((statement-block-intro . +)
    (knr-argdecl-intro . 5)
    (substatement-open . +)
    (label . 0)
    (statement-case-open . +)
    (statement-cont . +)
    (arglist-intro . c-lineup-arglist-intro-after-paren)
    (arglist-close . c-lineup-arglist)
    ))
)
```

Constructing one's own custom style is beyond the scope of this book; if you are curious, the long story is available in **emacs** online **info**, beginning at "Customizing C Indentation." The sample **.emacs** file adds a very simple custom style and arranges to use it on every **.c** file that is edited.

▲▲▲ Comment Handling

The following commands facilitate working with comments:

META-; (semicolon)   Inserts a comment on this line, or aligns an existing comment. This command inserts or aligns a comment. Its behavior differs according to the current situation on this line:

- If there is no comment on this line, an empty one is created at the value of **comment-column**.

- If text already on this line overlaps the position of **comment-column**, a comment is placed one **SPACE** after the end of the text.

- If there is already a comment on this line but not at the current value of **comment-column**, the command realigns the comment at that column. If text is in the way, it places the comment one **SPACE** after the end of the text.

Once an aligned (possibly empty) comment exists on the line, Point moves to the start of the comment text.

CONTROL-X ;   Sets **comment-column** to the column after Point. The left margin is column 0.

CONTROL-U – CONTROL-X ;   Kills the comment on the current line. This command sets **comment-column** from the first comment found above this line and then performs a **META-;** command to insert or align a comment at that position.

CONTROL-U CONTROL-X ;   Sets **comment-column** to the position of the first comment found above this line and then executes a **META-;** command to insert or align a comment on this line.

Each buffer has its own **comment-column** variable, which you can view with the **CONTROL-H v** **comment-column RETURN** help command.

▲▲ Special-Purpose Modes

The **emacs** editor has a third family of Major Modes that are not oriented toward a particular language or even oriented toward ordinary editing. Instead they perform some special function. They may define their own key bindings and commands to accomplish that function, for example

- Rmail: reads, archives, and composes email

- Dired: moves around in an **ls –l** display and operates on files

- VIP: simulates a complete **vi** environment

- Shell: runs an interactive subshell from inside an **emacs** buffer

This book only discusses Shell Mode.

▲▲▲ Shell Mode

One-time shell commands and Region filtering were discussed earlier. Refer to "Foreground Shell Commands" on page 315. Shell Mode differs: Each **emacs** buffer in Shell Mode has an underlying interactive shell permanently associated with it. This shell takes its input from the last line of the buffer and sends its output back to the buffer, advancing Point as it goes. The buffer, if not edited, is a record of the complete shell session.

The shell runs asynchronously, whether you have its buffer in view or not. The **emacs** editor uses idle time to read the shell's output and add it to the buffer.

Type **META-x shell** to create a buffer named ＊**shell**＊ and start a subshell. If a buffer named ＊**shell**＊ exists already, **emacs** just switches to that buffer.

The shell name to run is taken from one of these sources:

- the Lisp variable **explicit-shell-file-name**

- the environment variable **ESHELL**

- the environment variable **SHELL**

If you really want to start a second shell, then first use **META-x rename-buffer** to change the name of the existing shell's buffer. This process can be continued to create as many subshells and buffers as you want, all running in parallel.

In Shell Mode a special set of commands is defined. They are mostly bound to two-key sequences starting with **CONTROL-C**. Each sequence is meant to be similar to the ordinary control characters found in UNIX but with a leading **CONTROL-C**. Following are some of the Shell Mode commands:

RETURN	If Point is at the end of the buffer, **emacs** inserts the **RETURN** and sends this (the last) line to the shell. If Point is elsewhere, it copies this line to the end of the buffer, peeling off the old shell prompt (see the regular expression **shell-prompt-pattern**), if one existed. Then this copied line, now the last in the buffer, is sent to the shell.
CONTROL-C CONTROL-D	Sends **CONTROL-D** to the shell or its subshell.
CONTROL-C CONTROL-C	Sends **CONTROL-C** to the shell or its subshell.
CONTROL-C CONTROL-	Sends quit signal to the shell or its subshell.
CONTROL-C CONTROL-U	Kills the text on the current line not yet completed.
CONTROL-C CONTROL-R	Scrolls back to the beginning of the last shell output, putting the first line of output at the top of the window.
CONTROL-C CONTROL-O	Deletes the last batch of shell output.

Start Optional

▲ Customizing emacs

At the heart of **emacs** is a Lisp interpreter written in C. This version of Lisp is significantly extended with many special commands specifically oriented to editing. The interpreter's main task is to execute the Lisp-coded system that actually implements the "look and feel" of **emacs**.

Reduced to essentials, this system implements a continuous loop that watches keystrokes arrive, parses them into commands, executes those commands, and updates the screen.

There are a number of ways to customize this behavior.

- As single keystrokes come in, they are mapped immediately through a keyboard translation table. By changing the entries in this table, it is possible to swap keys. If you are used to **vi**, you can swap DELETE and CONTROL-H. Then CONTROL-H backspaces as it does in **vi**, and DELETE, which is not used by **vi**, is the help key. Of course if you use DELETE as an interrupt key, you may want to choose another key to swap with CONTROL-H.

- The mapped keystrokes are then gathered into small groups called *key sequences*. A key sequence may be only a single key, such as CONTROL-N, or may have two or more keys, such as CONTROL-X CONTROL-F. Once gathered the key sequences are used to select a particular procedure to be executed. The rules for gathering each key sequence and the specific procedure name to be executed when that sequence comes in are all codified in a series of tables called *keymaps*. By altering the keymaps you can change the gathering rules, or change which procedure is associated with which sequence. If you are used to **vi**'s use of CONTROL-W to back up over the word you are entering, you may want to change **emacs** CONTROL-W binding from its standard **kill-region** to **delete-word-backward**.

- The command behavior is often conditioned by one or more global variables or options. It may be possible to get the behavior you want by setting some of these variables.

- The command itself is usually a Lisp program that can be reprogrammed to make it behave as desired. Although this is not for beginners, the Lisp source to nearly all commands is available, and the internal Lisp system is fully documented. As mentioned before, it is common to load customized Lisp code at startup time even if you did not write it yourself.

Most **emacs** documentation glosses over all the translation, gathering, and procedure selection and talks about keystrokes as though they were the actual commands. However it is still important to know that the underlying machinery exists and to understand that its behavior can be changed.

▲▲ The .emacs Startup File

Each time you start **emacs**, it loads the file of Lisp code named **.emacs** from your home directory. This is the most common way to customize **emacs** for yourself. There are two command-line options controlling this:

–q	Ignores the **.emacs** file; just starts up without it. This is one way to get past a bad **.emacs** file.
–u *userid*	Uses the **.emacs** file from the home directory of *userid*.

This startup file is generally concerned only with key binding and option setting, and it is possible to write the Lisp statements in a fairly straightforward style.

Each parenthesized Lisp statement is a Lisp function call. Inside the parentheses the first symbol is the function name, and the rest of the **SPACE**-separated tokens are arguments to that function. The most common function in the **.emacs** file is simple assignment to a global variable, and it is named **setq**. The first argument is the name of a variable to be set, and the second argument is its new value. For example

```
(setq c-indent-level 8)
```

sets the variable named **c-indent-level** to 8.

To set the default value for a variable that is buffer-private, use the function name **setq-default**.

To set a specific element of a vector, use the function name **aset**. The first argument is the name of the vector, the second is the target offset, and the third is the new value of the target entry.

In the startup file the new value is usually a constant. Briefly the formats of these constants are as follows:

Numbers	Decimal integers, with an optional minus sign
Strings	Similar to C strings but with extensions for **CONTROL** and **META** characters: \C-s yields **CONTROL-S**, \M-s yields **META-s**, and \M-\C-s yields **CONTROL-META-s**
Characters	*Not* like C characters; start with ? and continue with a printing character or with a **BACKSLASH** escape sequence (for example ?a, ?\C-i, ?\033)
Booleans	*Not* **1** and **0**; use instead **t** for *true* and **nil** for *false*
Other Lisp Objects	Begin with a single quotation mark, and continue with the object's name

▲▲ Remapping Keys

The **emacs** command loop begins each cycle by translating incoming keystrokes into the name of the command to be executed. The basic translation operation uses the ASCII value of the current incoming character to index a 128-element vector called a *keymap*.

Sometimes a character's eighth bit is interpreted as the **META** *case*, but this cannot always be relied upon. At the point of translation, all **META** characters appear with the **ESCAPE** prefix, whether they were actually typed that way or not.

Each position in this vector is one of the following:

- Not defined at all. No translation possible in this map.
- The name of another keymap—switches to that keymap and waits for the next character to arrive.
- The name of a Lisp function to be called. Translation process is done; call this command.

Because keymaps can reference other keymaps, an arbitrarily complex recognition tree can be set up. However the mainstream **emacs** bindings use at most three keys, with a very small group of well-known *prefix keys,* each with its well-known keymap name.

Each buffer can have a *local keymap* that, if present, is used first for any keystrokes arriving while a window into that buffer is selected. This allows the regular mapping to be extended or overridden on a per-buffer basis and is most often used to add bindings for a Major Mode.

The basic translation flow runs as follows:

- Map the first character through the buffer's local keymap; if it is defined as a Lisp function name, then translation is done, and **emacs** executes that function. If not defined, then use this same character to index the global top-level keymap.
- Map the first character through the top-level global keymap **global-map**. At this stage and each following stage, the following conditions hold:
  - If the entry for this character is not defined, it is an error. Send a bell to the terminal, and discard all the characters entered in this key sequence.
  - If the entry for this character is defined as a Lisp function name, translation is done and the function is executed.
  - If the entry for this character is defined as the name of another keymap, then switch to that keymap and wait for another character to select one of its elements.

Everything must be a command or an error. Ordinary characters that are to be inserted in the buffer are usually bound to the command **self-insert-command**. The well-known prefix characters are each associated with a keymap. Some of these keymaps are

ctl-x-map   For characters following CONTROL-X

ctl-x-4-map   For characters following CONTROL-X **4**

help-map   For characters following CONTROL-H

esc-map   For characters following ESCAPE (including META characters)

mode-specific-map   For characters following CONTROL-C

To see the current state of the keymaps, type CONTROL-H **b**. They appear in the following order: First local, then global, and finally the shorter maps for each prefix key. Each line has the name of the Lisp function to be called; the documentation for that function can be retrieved with the commands CONTROL-H **f function-name** or CONTROL-H **k key-sequence**.

The most common sort of keymap customization is making small changes to the global command assignments without creating any new keymaps or commands. This is most easily done in the **.emacs** file, using the Lisp function **define-key**.

The **define-key** takes three arguments:

- keymap name
- single character defining a position in that map
- command to be executed when this character appears

For instance to bind the command **backward-kill-word** to CONTROL-W, use the statement

```
(define-key global-map "\C-w" 'backward-kill-word)
```

or to bind the command **kill-region** to CONTROL-X CONTROL-K, use the statement

```
(define-key ctl-x-map "\C-k" 'kill-region)
```

The \ character causes C-w to be interpreted as CONTROL-W instead of three letters (equivalent to \^w also). The unmatched single quotation mark in front of the command name is correct. It is a Lisp escape character to keep the name from being evaluated too soon.

▲▲ A Sample .emacs File for Versions 19 and Above

If executed, the following **.emacs** file produces a plain editing environment that minimizes surprises for **vi** users. Of course if any section or any line is inapplicable or not to your liking, you can edit it out or comment it with one or more **;** comment characters beginning in column 1.

```
;;; Preference Variables

(setq make-backup-files nil)          ;Do not make backup files
(setq backup-by-copying t)            ;If you do, at least do not destroy links
(setq delete-auto-save-files t)       ;Delete autosave files when writing orig
(setq blink-matching-paren nil)       ;Do not blink opening delim
(setq-default case-fold-search nil)   ;Do not fold cases in search
(setq require-final-newline 'ask)     ;Ask about missing final newline

;; Reverse mappings for C-h and DEL.
(keyboard-translate ?\C-h ?\177)
(keyboard-translate ?\177 ?\C-h))

;; reassigning C-w to keep on deleting words backward

;; C-w is supposed to be kill-region, but it's a great burden
;; for vi-trained fingers.  bind it instead to backward-kill-word
;; for more familiar, friendly behavior.
(define-key global-map "\^w" 'backward-kill-word)

;; for kill-region we use a two-key sequence c-x c-k.
(define-key ctl-x-map "\^k" 'kill-region)
```

```
;; C mode customization: set vanilla (8-space bsd) indentation style

(require 'cc-mode)                          ;kiss: be sure it's here

(c-add-style                                ;add indentation style
 "bsd8"                                     ;old bsd (8 spaces)
 '((c-basic-offset . 8)
   (c-hanging-comment-ender-p . nil)        ;isolated "*/" ends blk comments
   (c-comment-only-line-offset . 0)
   (c-offsets-alist . ((statement-block-intro . +)
                       (knr-argdecl-intro . +)
                       (substatement-open . 0)
                       (label . 0)
                       (statement-cont . +)
                       ))
   ))
(add-hook                                   ;this is our default style,
 'c-mode-hook                               ;set it always in c-mode-hook.
 (function
  (lambda ()
    (c-set-style "bsd8")))))

;; end of c mode style setup
```

Stop Optional

▲ emacs and the X Window System

With Version 19, GNU **emacs** fully embraced the X Window System environment. It can manage multiple X-level windows (called *frames* to avoid confusion with **emacs** windows), and each frame can contain multiple **emacs** windows as well as a menu bar. The first frame you see is similar to the non-X Window System version (Figure 9-8).

The usual mouse-oriented actions including cut and paste with other X clients are supported. Besides selecting a frame, the mouse can select, split, expand, or delete **emacs** windows within a frame. Each window can have its own scroll bar.

Mouse events have a notation similar to keyboard events—that is, M-Mouse-1 (**META**-Mouse-1 in this book) means hold the **META** key while giving a single click of the leftmost mouse button. As with keys, you can rebind mouse clicks to customize the look and feel of **emacs**.

You can select type fonts and foreground and background colors for each screen region.

▲▲ Mouse Commands for Cut and Paste

The cut-and-paste scheme that **emacs** uses works much like the scheme that mainstream X applications use, most notably **xterm**. You are assumed to be using a three-button mouse, but as usual on a two-button mouse,

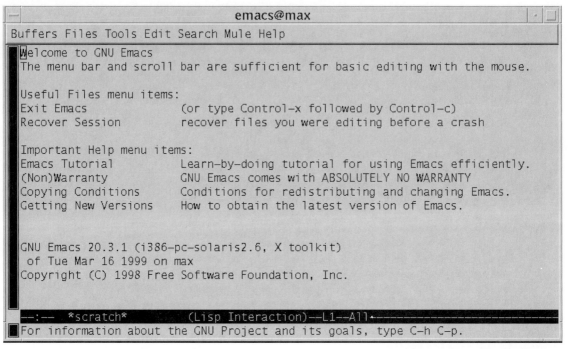

Figure 9-8   The first **emacs** *frame you see*

the center button may be simulated by pressing the left and right buttons at the same time. The **emacs** documentation numbers these buttons from left to right and calls them Mouse-1, Mouse-2, and Mouse-3.

As with **xterm**, regions are defined by dragging the left mouse button (Drag-Mouse-1) or by marking the endpoints with single clicks of Mouse-1 and Mouse-3. Once defined a region is pasted in **emacs** or another X application with a single click of Mouse-2.

In more detail:

Mouse-1   Selects the **emacs** window where the mouse is currently positioned and moves Point to that window at the location of the mouse pointer. This is the basic mouse-oriented technique for selecting an **emacs** frame and an **emacs** window within that frame. Within a specific window it is also the way to move Point without keyboard commands.

Drag-Mouse-1   First performs the Mouse-1 action to select frame, window, and initial Point, then sets Mark to the same position. Point follows the mouse as you drag but Mark remains at the initial position. The region between Point and Mark will be highlighted and also added to the **emacs** Kill Ring just as though you had typed **META-w**. However the region is not deleted and is made known to the X server (both as the primary selection and in the cut buffer) so that you can paste the highlighted region to other X applications.

Mouse-2	First performs the Mouse-1 action to select frame, window, and Point, then yanks the Kill Ring's most recent entry just as though you had typed **CONTROL-y**. Point is left at the end of the yanked material.
Mouse-3	Like **emacs** Mouse-3 is powerful and confusing, and its behavior depends on the current state of **emacs**.

- If no region is currently highlighted, Mouse-3 leaves Mark at the current Point and moves Point to the clicked position. The region between Point and Mark is highlighted, and its contents are added to the **emacs** Kill Ring. The net effect is precisely equivalent to Drag-Mouse-1. This is most often useful when you wish to define a large region that does not fit in one **emacs** window.

- If a region is currently highlighted, **emacs** extends or contracts the nearest boundary of the region so the clicked position becomes an edge. The region's Kill Ring entry and X definition are also extended or contracted so the contents remain in step.

- If a highlighted region exists and you have just clicked Mouse-3, a second consecutive click of Mouse-3 at the same position will kill this region from the buffer. It is already on the Kill Ring so **emacs** does not put it there a second time.

Double-Mouse-1	Selects and highlights a region around the clicked-on syntax unit specific to the current mode. (In text double-click inside a word to mark that word; in C double-click a double quotation to mark a string, and so on). Mouse-3 region adjustments will be made in syntax-unit granules.
Double-Drag-Mouse-1 ("dit-dahhhh")	Selects and highlights a contiguous region of syntax units for this mode.
Triple-Mouse-1	Selects and highlights the region around the clicked-on line. Mouse-3 region adjustments will be made in line granules.
Triple-Drag-Mouse-1 ("dit-dit-dahhhh")	Selects and highlights a contiguous region of complete lines.

The following are the suggested mouse-oriented methods (by no means the only methods) to accomplish some common editing actions:

Killing text	Click Mouse-1 at one end, Double-Mouse-3 at the other. To see the doomed region clearly, give just one Mouse-3 and the area will be highlighted. Then you can give a second Mouse-3 (don't move the mouse between clicks) and the highlighted area will disappear. The killed text can be pasted elsewhere in **emacs** with **CONTROL-y** or Mouse-2, or possibly in another X application (often, not always, using Mouse-2 at that end).

Marking a region Use Drag-Mouse-1 if the desired region is onscreen, otherwise Mouse-1 and Mouse-3. The highlighted region is on the Kill Ring just as though we had put it there with META-w and can be copied elsewhere in **emacs** with CONTROL-y or Mouse-2, or into another X application. Note this region is delimited by Point and Mark and is therefore accessible to all the region-oriented **emacs** commands.

Importing text Cut the text in some other X application, and switch to an **emacs** frame and window. CONTROL-y or Mouse-2 will insert the cut text at Point.

▲▲ Mouse-2 Selections

Yanking text is not common or even meaningful in every buffer (for example dired, **info**, compilation), and for these buffers highlighting and Mouse-2 are often managed differently in a mode-sensitive manner.

  Usually the scheme is to highlight some of the buffer objects by positioning the mouse over them, and then to operate on the object by clicking Mouse-2. The "operation" is package-specific; for dired the file is visited, for a compilation error message the source-code file is visited, and for an **info** menu that frame is visited.

  You can nearly always (except in the compilation buffer where each line is hot) spot objects that are Mouse-2-able; they will highlight as you sweep the mouse over them.

▲▲ Scroll Bars

Version 19 of **emacs** implemented optional scroll bars for each window; the scrolling scheme follows mainstream X applications, in particular **xterm**. The scroll bar appears at the right of each window, with a familiar rectangular box representing the window's current viewing position in the **emacs** buffer.

  Within the scroll-bar region the following mouse commands are active:

Mouse-2 Position (jump) the window to this point in the buffer.

Drag-Mouse-2 (On the rectangular box) Scroll the window to follow the mouse.

Mouse-1 Scroll the window contents upward toward end of file, moving the line at the clicked position up to the top of the screen. Often remembered as "here to top." NB: In this scheme it's irrelevant whether you are above or below the rectangular box.

Mouse-3 Scroll the window contents downward toward start of file, moving the line at the top of the screen down to the clicked position. Often remembered as "top to here."

▲▲ Manipulating Windows with the Mouse

Versions 19 and above accept mouse commands to adjust window boundaries and size. Within a window's mode line the following commands are active:

Mouse-1 Select this window (without moving Point).

Drag-Mouse-1 Adjust this window boundary upward or downward.

Mouse-2 Expand this window to fill the frame.

Mouse-3	Delete this window.
CONTROL-Mouse-2	Split this window into two side-by-side windows, with the boundary at the clicked position.

Within a window's scroll bar, this command is active:

CONTROL-Mouse-2	Split this window vertically, with the boundary at the clicked position.

▲▲ Frame Management

A single instantiation of **emacs** can drive any reasonable number of frames on the X display. Each frame has its own **emacs** window configuration. With a very few exceptions each frame is independent of the others. Often it is convenient to open a new frame, perhaps for reading mail or news, without disturbing the **emacs** window configuration in the current frame.

An **emacs** frame is just an X window and can be given input focus, resized, manipulated, killed, iconified, or restored with whatever mouse commands your window manager defines.

The **emacs** editor defines a family of keyboard commands for frame management, somewhat parallel to the commands for **emacs** window management. They mostly begin with **CONTROL-X 5** where the **emacs** window-oriented commands began with **CONTROL-X 4**.

▲▲▲ Manipulating Frames

CONTROL-X 5 o (lowercase "oh")	Selects the next frame and raises it to the top if necessary. Repeated use will cycle through all the frames of this **emacs** instantiation.
CONTROL-X 5 0 (number zero)	Delete the currently selected frame, unless it is the only frame. You cannot delete your only **emacs** frame this way. (Of course, you are always free to exit completely with **CONTROL-x CONTROL-c**.)
CONTROL-Z	Iconifies the currently selected frame. This command will also restore an **emacs** icon. This command suspends a non-X **emacs**.
CONTROL-X CONTROL-C	Exits from **emacs** and kills all the frames including the current one. This is usually the command that reminds you the hard way that frames are not fully independent, and is mentioned here only as a cautionary note. There is no standard command to "kill all the frames except this one."

▲▲▲ Switching to Another Frame

Just like windows, a frame may be *created* if it doesn't already exist, or just *selected* if it does exist. Some of the commands are:

CONTROL-X 5 2	Unconditionally creates a new frame that is a copy of the current frame. Each window in the new frame is viewing the same position in the same buffer as its counterpart, and editing changes to one will appear in the other. This is fun to look at for a few seconds, but, of course, you will probably select some other files and buffers for the second frame to view.

CONTROL-X **5b**
buffername RETURN

Prompts for a *buffername* and either creates a new frame for it or selects an existing frame with a window open on that buffer.

CONTROL-X **5f** *filename*
RETURN

Prompts for a *filename* and visits it in another frame. Creates a new frame for the visit if needed.

▲▲ Menu Bars

Any **emacs** command may be executed explicitly with META-x *command* RETURN or bound to a specific key sequence. Menu bars offer a third, mouse-oriented possibility. By default **emacs** versions 19 and above place a menu bar at the top of each frame, just below the window manager's title bar. Most commonly the bar appears as a line of reverse video with the menu headings:

```
Buffers Files Tools Edit Search Help
```

With the mouse cursor positioned on one of these headings, the mouse command Down-Mouse-1 (press and hold the left mouse button) pulls down a menu. You select a menu item by dragging the mouse pointer to that item. As the mouse points to each item, it is highlighted. Releasing Mouse-1 erases the menu and selects the highlighted item or selects nothing when no item was highlighted.

A menu item may be a buffer to switch to (in the Buffers menu) or perhaps an **emacs** command to execute. When a command is bound to a key sequence, that sequence is also shown in the menu item.

Some menu items bring up a submenu when selected; this secondary menu stays put even after you release Mouse-1. You select an item by highlighting it and clicking Mouse-1. To get out of the menu without doing anything, click Mouse-1 while nothing is highlighted.

Menu bar usage is optional. If you prefer not to use them, you can free up the menu line so you can display more buffer text. To turn menu bars on or off, execute the command:

```
META-x menu-bar-mode
```

▲ Resources for emacs

If you would like to try out **emacs**, but it is not available at your site, or after spending time with **emacs**, you want to try out more of its features and capabilities and wish to see more documentation, there is more material available in both paper and electronic form. GNU **emacs** itself is available in source form.

▲▲ USENET emacs FAQ (Frequently Asked Questions)

If you have access to USENET, many newsgroups now maintain a file of frequently asked questions (FAQ) and their answers. An excellent **emacs** FAQ file that addresses more than 125 common questions is available; copies of it can be found in the newsgroups **gnu.emacs.help**, **comp.emacs**, and **news.answers**. It has the most up-to-date information and is strongly recommended as a starting point.

▲▲ Access to emacs

If you have access to the Internet, you can use anonymous **ftp** to copy the current distribution from the host named **prep.ai.mit.edu**. There is no charge. Begin by retrieving the file **/pub/gnu/GNUinfo/FTP** for the most current instructions and list of alternative archive sites. In this same directory there is a file named **FAQ.emacs.README** which gives a pointer to the latest **emacs** FAQ file available for retrieval using **ftp**.

This same **ftp** file has some information about getting **emacs** via **uucp**, reproduced here for readers without **ftp**:

```
OSU is distributing via UUCP: most GNU software, MIT C Scheme,
Compress, News, RN, NNTP, Patch, some Appletalk stuff, some of the
Internet Requests For Comment (RFC) et al..  See their periodic
postings on the Usenet newsgroup comp.sources.d for informational
updates.  Current details from <staff@cis.ohio-state.edu> or
<...!osu-cis!staff>.



Information on how to uucp some GNU programs is available via
electronic mail from: uunet!hutch!barber, hqda-ai!merlin, acornrc!bob,
hao!scicom!qetzal!upba!ugn!nepa!denny, ncar!noao!asuvax!hrc!dan,
bigtex!james (aka james@bigtex.cactus.org), oli-stl!root,
src@contrib.de (Germany), toku@dit.co.jp (Japan) and info@ftp.uu.net.
```

If you have no electronic access to the Internet or **uucp**, you can order **emacs** on tape directly from the Free Software Foundation for about $200. Many different media and tape formats are available, and you can also buy typeset copies of the **emacs** User Manual, the **emacs** Lisp Manual, and an **emacs** Reference Card.

The Free Software Foundation can be reached at these addresses:

Mail: Free Software Foundation, Inc.
              675 Massachusetts Avenue
              Cambridge, MA 02139
              USA

Email: gnu@prep.ai.mit.edu

Phone: 617-876-3296

Summary

You can precede many of the following commands with a numeric argument to make the command repeat the number of times specified by the argument. Precede a numeric argument with **CONTROL-U** to keep **emacs** from entering the argument as text.

▲▲ Moving the Cursor

Key	Action—Moves Cursor
CONTROL-F	Forward by characters
CONTROL-B	Backward by characters
META-f	Forward by words
META-b	Backward by words
META-e	To end of sentence
META-a	To beginning of sentence
META-{	To end of paragraph
META-}	To beginning of paragraph
META->	Forward to end of buffer
META-<	Backward to beginning of buffer
CONTROL-ESCAPE	To end of line
CONTROL-A	To beginning of line
CONTROL-N	Down by lines
CONTROL-P	Up by lines
CONTROL-V	Forward (scroll) by windows
META-v	Backward (scroll) by windows
CONTROL-L	Clear and repaint screen, and scroll current line to center of window
META-r	To beginning of middle line
CONTROL-U *num* META-r	To beginning of line number *num* (**0** = top, **–** = bottom)

▲▲ Killing and Deleting

Key	Action
CONTROL-DELETE	Deletes characters under cursor.
DELETE	Deletes characters to the left of cursor.
META-d	Kills from cursor forward to the end of current word.
META-DELETE	Kills from cursor backward to beginning of previous word.
META-k	Kills forward to end of a sentence.
CONTROL-X DELETE	Kills backward to beginning of a sentence.
CONTROL-K	Kills text from cursor forward to (but not including) the line ending LINEFEED. If there is no text between the cursor and the LINEFEED, kills the LINEFEED itself.

Key	Action
CONTROL-U 1 CONTROL-K	Kills from cursor forward to and including LINEFEED.
CONTROL-U 0 CONTROL-K	Kills from cursor backward to beginning of this line.
META-z *char*	Kills up to but not including next occurrence of *char*.
META-w	Copies Region to Kill Ring; does not erase from buffer.
CONTROL-W	Kills Region.
CONTROL-Y	Yanks most recently killed text into current buffer at Point. Sets Mark at beginning of this text, Point and cursor at the end.
META-y	Erases just-yanked text, rotates Kill Ring, and yanks next item (only after CONTROL-Y or META-y).

▲▲ Searching

Key	Action
CONTROL-S	Incrementally prompts for a string and searches forward for a match
CONTROL-S RETURN	Prompts for a complete string and searches forward for a match
CONTROL-R	Incrementally prompts for a string and searches backward for a match
CONTROL-R RETURN	Prompts for a complete string and searches backward for a match
META-CONTROL-S	Incrementally prompts for a regular expression and searches forward for a match
META--CONTROL-S RETURN	Prompts for a complete regular expression and searches forward for a match
META-x isearch-backward-regexp	Incrementally prompts for a regular expression and searches backward for a match
META-x isearch-backward-regexp RETURN	Prompts for a complete regular expression and searches backward for a match

▲▲ Online Help

Key	Action
CONTROL-H a	Prompts for *string* and then shows a list of commands whose names contain *string*
CONTROL-H b	Shows a table (it is long) of all the key bindings now in effect
CONTROL-H c *key-sequence*	Prints the name of the command bound to this *key-sequence*
CONTROL-H k *key-sequence*	Prints the name and documentation of the command bound to this *key-sequence*

Key	Action
CONTROL-H f	Prompts for the name of a Lisp function and prints the documentation for that function
CONTROL-H i (lowercase "eye")	Takes you to the top menu of **info**, a documentation browser
CONTROL-H l (lowercase "ell")	Shows the last 100 characters typed
CONTROL-H m	Shows the documentation and special key bindings for the current Major Mode
CONTROL-H n	Shows the **emacs** news file
CONTROL-H t	Runs an **emacs** tutorial session
CONTROL-H v	Prompts for a Lisp variable name and gives the documentation for that variable
CONTROL-H w	Prompts for a command name and gives the key sequence, if any, bound to that command

▲▲ Region

Key	Action
META-W	Copies the Region nondestructively to the Kill Ring
CONTROL-W	Kills the Region
META-x print-region	Sends the Region to the print spooler
META-x append-to-buffer	Prompts for buffer name, and appends Region to that buffer
META-x append-to-file	Prompts for filename, and appends region to that file
CONTROL-X CONTROL-U	Converts Region to uppercase
CONTROL-X CONTROL-L	Converts Region to lowercase

▲▲ Working with Lines

Key	Action
META-x occur	Prompts for a regular expression and lists each line with a match for the expression in a buffer named *Occur*
META-x delete-matching-lines	Prompts for a regular expression and deletes each line with a match for that expression
META-x delete-nonmatching-lines	Prompts for a regular expression and deletes each line that does *not* match that expression

▲▲ Unconditional and Interactive Replacement

Key	Action
META-x replace-string	Prompts for *string* and *newstring*. Replaces every instance of *string* with *newstring*. Sets Mark at the start of the command.
META-% *or* META-x query-replace	As above, but queries for replacement of each instance of *string*. See table of responses below.
META-x replace-regexp	Prompts for a *regular expression* and *newstring*. Replaces every instance of the *regular expression* with *newstring*. Sets Mark at the start of the command.
META-x query-replace-regexp	As above, but queries for replacement of each instance of the *regular expression*. See table of responses below.

▲▲ Responses to Replacement Queries

Key	Action
RETURN	Does not do any more replacements; quits now
SPACE	Makes this replacement and goes on
DELETE	Does *not* make this replacement; skips over it and goes on
, (comma)	Makes this replacement, displays the result, and asks for another command
. (period)	Makes this replacement and quits searching
! (exclamation point)	Replaces this, and all remaining instances, without asking any more questions

▲▲ Working with Windows

Key	Action
CONTROL-X b	Switches buffer that window views
CONTROL-X 2	Splits current window vertically into two
CONTROL-X 3	Splits current window horizontally into two
CONTROL-X o (lowercase "oh")	Selects other window
META-CONTROL-V	Scrolls other window
CONTROL-X 4b	Prompts for buffer name, and selects it in other window
CONTROL-X 4f	Prompts for filename, and selects it in other window

Key	Action
CONTROL-X 0 (zero)	Deletes current window
CONTROL-X 1	Deletes all but current window
META-x shrink-window	Makes current window one line shorter
CONTROL-X ^	Makes current window one line taller
CONTROL-X }	Makes current window one character wider
CONTROL-X {	Makes current window one character narrower

▲▲ Working with Files

Key	Action
CONTROL-X CONTROL-F	Prompts for a filename and reads its contents into a freshly created buffer. Assigns the file's simple filename as the buffer name.
CONTROL-X CONTROL-V	Prompts for a filename, and reads its contents into the current buffer (overwriting the contents of the current buffer).
CONTROL-X 4 CONTROL-F	Prompts for a filename, and reads its contents into a freshly created buffer. Assigns the file's simple filename as the buffer name. Creates a new window for this buffer, and selects that window. This command splits the screen in half if you begin with only one window.
CONTROL-X CONTROL-S	Saves the current buffer to the original file.
CONTROL-X S	Prompts for whether or not to save each modified buffer (y/n).
META-x set-visited-file-name	Prompts for a filename and sets this name as the current buffer's "original" name.
CONTROL-X CONTROL-W	Prompts for a filename, sets this name as the "original" file for the current buffer, and saves the current buffer into that file.
META-~ (tilde)	Clears modified flag from the current buffer. Use with caution.

▲▲ Working with Buffers

Key	Action
CONTROL-X CONTROL-S	Saves the current buffer into its associated file.
CONTROL-X CONTROL-F	Prompts for a filename and visits that file.
CONTROL-X b	Prompts for a buffer name and selects it. If it does not exist, creates it first.

Key	Action
CONTROL-X **4b**	Prompts for a buffer name and selects it in another window. The existing window is not disturbed although the new window may overlap it.
CONTROL-X CONTROL-B	Creates a buffer named *Buffer List* and displays it in another window. The existing window is not disturbed although the new window may overlap it. The new buffer is not selected. In the *Buffer List* buffer each buffer's data is shown with name size mode(s) and original filename.
META-x **rename-buffer**	Prompts for a new buffer name and gives this new name to the current buffer.
CONTROL-X CONTROL-Q	Toggles the current buffer's readonly status and the associated %% Mode Line indicator.
META-x **append-to-buffer**	Prompts for buffer name and appends the current Region to the end of that buffer.
META-x **prepend-to-buffer**	Prompts for buffer name and appends the current Region to the end of that buffer.
META-x **copy-to-buffer**	Prompts for buffer name and deletes the contents of the buffer before copying the current Region into that buffer.
META-x **insert-buffer**	Prompts for buffer name and inserts the entire contents of that buffer into the current buffer at Point.
CONTROL-X **k**	Prompts for buffer name and deletes that buffer.
META-x **kill-some-buffers**	Goes through the entire buffer list and offers the chance to delete each buffer.

▲▲ Foreground Shell Commands

May not work with all shells.

Key	Action
META-! (exclamation point)	Prompts for a shell command, executes it, and displays the output
CONTROL-U META-! (exclamation point)	Prompts for a shell command, executes it, and inserts the output at Point
META-I (vertical bar)	Prompts for a shell command, gives the Region contents as input, filters it through the command, and displays the output
CONTROL-U META-I (vertical bar)	Prompts for a shell command, gives the Region contents as input, filters it through the command, deletes the old Region contents, and inserts the output in that position

▲▲ Background Shell Commands

Key	Action
META-x compile	Prompts for a shell command and runs it in the background, with output going to a buffer named *compilation*
META-x kill-compilation	Kills the background process

▲▲ Case Conversion

Key	Action
META-l (lowercase "ell")	Converts word to the right of Point to lowercase
META-u	Converts word to the right of Point to uppercase
META-c	Converts word to the right of Point to initial caps
CONTROL-X CONTROL-L	Converts Region between Point and Mark to lowercase
CONTROL-X CONTROL-U	Converts Region between Point and Mark to uppercase

▲▲ C Mode

Key	Action
CONTROL-META-f	Moves forward over an expression.
CONTROL-META-b	Moves backward over an expression.
CONTROL-META-k	Kills an expression forward. It leaves Point at the same finishing position as **CONTROL-Z f**, but kills the expression it traverses.
CONTROL-META-@	Sets Mark at the position **CONTROL-Z f** would move to, without changing Point.
CONTROL-META-a	Moves to the beginning of the most recent function definition.
CONTROL-META-e	Moves to the end of the next function definition.
CONTROL-META-h	Puts Point at the beginning and Mark at the end of the current (or next, if between) function definition.

▲▲ Shell Mode

Key	Action
RETURN	Sends the current line to the shell
CONTROL-C CONTROL-D	Sends **CONTROL-D** to shell or its subshell

Key	Action
CONTROL-C CONTROL-C	Sends **CONTROL-C** to shell or its subshell
CONTROL-C CONTROL-	Sends quit signal to shell or its subshell
CONTROL-C CONTROL-Ux	Kills the text on the current line not yet completed
CONTROL-C CONTROL-R	Scrolls back to beginning of last shell output, putting the first line of output at the top of the window
CONTROL-C CONTROL-O	Deletes the last batch of shell output

Review Exercises

1. Given a buffer full of English text, answer the following questions:

   a. How would you change every instance of his to hers?

   b. How would you do this only in the final paragraph?

   c. Is there a way to look at every usage in context before changing it?

   d. How would you deal with the possibility that His might begin a sentence?

2. What command moves the cursor to the end of the current paragraph? Can you use this command to skip through the buffer in one-paragraph steps?

3. Suppose you are typing a long sentence and get lost in the middle.

   a. Is there an easy way to kill the botched sentence and start over?

   b. What if it is just one word that is incorrect? Is there an alternative to backspacing one letter at a time?

4. After you have been working on a paragraph for a while, most likely some lines will have become too short and others too long. Is there a command to "neaten up" the paragraph without rebreaking all the lines by hand?

5. Is there a way to change the whole buffer to capital letters? Can you think of a way to change just one paragraph?

6. How would you reverse the order of two paragraphs?

7. How would you reverse two words?

8. Imagine that you saw a USENET posting with something particularly funny in it and saved the posting to a file. How would you incorporate this file into your own buffer? What if you wanted only a couple of paragraphs? How would you add > to the beginning of each included line?

9. On the keyboard alone **emacs** has always offered a very full set of editing possibilities. For any editing task there are generally several different techniques that will accomplish the same goal. In the X environment the choice is enlarged still further with a new group of mouse-oriented visual alternatives. From these options you must select the way that you like to solve a given editing puzzle best.

   Consider this Shakespeare fragment:

```
1. Full fathom five thy father lies;
2.    Of his bones are coral made;
3. Those are pearls that were his eyes:
4.    Nothing of him that doth fade,
5. But doth suffer a sea-change
6. Into something rich and strange.
7. Sea-nymphs hourly ring his knell:
8.            Ding-dong.
9. Hark! now I hear them--
10.     Ding-dong, bell!
```

that has been typed with some errors:

```
1. Full fathiom five tyy father lies;
2. These are pearls that were his eyes:
3.    Of his bones are coral made;
4.    Nothin of him that doth fade,
5. But doth susffer a sea-change
6. Into something rich and strange.
7. Sea-nymphs hourly ring his knell:
8.            Ding=dong.
9. Hard! now I hear them--
10.     Ding-dong, bell!
```

Using only the keyboard:

a. How many ways can you think of to move the cursor to the spelling errors?

b. Once the cursor is on or near the errors, how many ways can you think of to fix them?

c. Are there ways to fix errors without explicitly navigating/searching to them? How many can you think of?

d. Lines 2 and 3 are transposed. How many ways can you think of to correct this situation?

Using the mouse:

e. How do you navigate the cursor to a spelling error?

f. Once the cursor is on or near the errors, how many ways can you think of to fix them?

g. Lines 2 and 3 are transposed. Is there a visually oriented way to fix them?

h. Is there a visual way to correct multiple errors (similar to **META-%**)?

Advanced Review Exercises

10. Assume your buffer contains the C code shown here, with the Major Mode set for C and the cursor positioned at the end of the **while** line as shown by the black square

```
/*
 * Copy string s2 to s1.  s1 must be large enough
```

```
 * return s1
  */
char *
strcpy(s1, s2)
register char *s1, *s2;
{
     register char *os1;

     os1 = s1;
     while (*s1++ = *s2++)

     ;
return(os1);
}

/* Copy source into dest, stopping after '\0' is copied, and
   return a pointer to the '\0' at the end of dest.  Then our caller
   can concatenate to the dest string without another strlen call. */
char *
stpcpy (dest, source)
      char *dest;
      char *source;
{
   while ((*dest++ = *source++) != '\0') ■
      ; /* void loop body */
   return (dest - 1);
}
```

a. What command moves the cursor to the opening brace of **strcpy**? What command moves the cursor past the closing brace? Can you use these commands to skip through the buffer in one-procedure steps?

b. Assume the cursor is just past the closing parenthesis of the **while** condition. How do you move to the matching opening parenthesis? How do you move back to the matching close parenthesis again? Does the same command set work for matched [] and {}? How does this differ from the **vi** % command?

c. One procedure is indented in the Berkeley indention style; the other is indented in the GNU style. What command re-indents a line in accordance with the current indention style you have set up? How would you re-indent an entire procedure?

d. Suppose you want to write five string procedures and intend to use **strcpy** as a starting point for further editing. How would you make five duplicate copies of the **strcpy** procedure?

e. How would you compile the code without leaving **emacs**?

The Shell II (sh)

The Bourne Shell (**sh**), C Shell (**csh**), and Korn Shell (**ksh**) are command interpreters and high-level programming languages. As command interpreters, they process commands that you enter on the command line in response to a prompt. When you use a shell as a programming language, it processes groups of commands stored in files called *shell scripts*. Like other languages, shells have variables and control flow commands (for example **for** loops and **if** statements).

Using a shell, you can customize the environment you work in. You can make your prompt display the name of the working directory, create a function or alias for **cp** that keeps it from overwriting files, take advantage of keyword variables to change aspects of how the shell works, and so on. You can also write shell scripts that do your bidding: From a one-line script that stores a long and complex command so you do not have to retype it to a longer script that runs a set of reports (automatically generating parameters for the reports), prints them, and mails you a reminder when the job is done. More complex shell scripts are themselves programs; they do not just run other programs (see Chapters 11, 12, and 13 for examples).

Always make the Bourne Shell your primary root shell in single-user mode.[1] All system shell scripts are written to run under the Bourne Shell—if you will ever be working with your system in single-user mode (either in the process of booting it or to do system maintenance, administration, or repair work), it is a good idea to at least become familiar with this shell.

This chapter expands on the interactive features of the shell described in Chapter 5, explains how to create and run simple shell scripts, introduces the basic aspects of shell programming, and describes command-line expansion. It does not repeat the material covered in "Filename Generation/Pathname Expansion" on page 118 of Chapter 5. Chapter 11 explores control flow commands and more advanced aspects of Bourne and Korn Shell programming in detail. Chapter 12 covers interactive use of the C Shell and C Shell program-

---

1. You can use other shells, but it is not a good idea. The Bourne Shell is the only shell that is statically linked (**/sbin/sh**). If your machine crashes and the **/usr** filesystem is unavailable or some system libraries get corrupted, no other shell will work: You will not be able to boot your system and attempt to repair the damage because you will not have a shell to work with. If you want to use another shell, start it explicitly when the system is in single-user mode.

ming, and Chapter 13 explores some of the features of the Korn Shell that are absent from the Bourne Shell and also presents some more challenging shell programming problems.

All of the advanced shell chapters (10–13) discuss each of the different shells as appropriate, giving page references for more details of a topic within a specific shell. The $\frac{sh}{csh}$ 2 symbol indicates which shells a particular utility, builtin, or variable is a part of.

Which Shells Does This Chapter Cover?

This chapter is slanted toward the Bourne Shell, with notes and page references where the C or Korn Shells differ. Specifically the sections on "Creating a Simple Shell Script" (page 349), "Command Separation and Grouping" (page 351), and "Processes" (page 360), apply to both the C and Korn Shells as well as the Bourne Shell.

Job Control

The section on "Job Control" (page 357) does not apply to the Bourne Shell because **sh** does not support job control. The Job Shell (**jsh**) is *identical* to the Bourne Shell but supports a full implementation of job control. Make sure you are running **jsh** and not **sh** if you want to experiment with job-control commands. The **csh** and **ksh** Shells also support job control, and you can use them for experimentation too.

If You Are New to All This

You may want to postpone reading the "Job Control" section of this chapter (page 357) and the sections beyond it until you are comfortable creating and running simple shell scripts. However you should read "Parameters and Variables" (page 365). Besides user-created variables the shell maintains several keyword variables that control important characteristics of the shell.

Shell Programming

Because many users prefer the Bourne Shell's programming language to that of **csh** and because it shares many common features with the Korn Shell programming language, this and the following chapter describe **sh** (and **ksh**) programming in detail.

▲ Bourne Shell Background

The Bourne Shell is an early UNIX shell that was written by Steve Bourne of AT&T's Bell Laboratories. Over the years the Bourne Shell has been expanded and is still the basic shell provided with many commercial ver-

---

2. Refer to "Shell and Builtin and Variable Names" on page 17 for an explanation of the $\frac{sh}{csh}$ symbol.

sions of UNIX. Many shell scripts that help you manage and use Solaris have been written using the Bourne Shell because of its long and successful history.

▲▲ POSIX Shells

The POSIX standardization group has defined a standard for shell functionality (POSIX 1003.2). The Bourne Shell provides the features that match the requirements of this POSIX standard.

▲ Creating a Simple Shell Script

A *shell script* is a file that contains commands that the shell can execute. The commands in a shell script can be any commands you can enter in response to a shell prompt. For example a command in a shell script might run a Solaris utility, a compiled program you have written, or another shell script. As with commands you give on the command line, a command in a shell script can use ambiguous file references and can have its input or output redirected from/to a file or sent through a pipe (page 113). You can also use pipes and redirection with the input and output of the script itself.

In addition to the commands you would ordinarily use on the command line, there is a group of commands, the *control flow* commands (also called *control structures*), that finds most of its use in shell scripts. The control flow commands enable you to alter the order of execution of commands in a script as you would alter the order of execution of statements using a typical structured programming language. Refer to "Control Structures" on page 394 (**sh**), page 465 (**csh**), and page 493 (**ksh**) for specifics.

The easiest way to run a shell script is to give its filename on the command line. The shell then interprets and executes the commands in the script, one after another. By using a shell script, you can simply and quickly initiate a complex series of tasks or a repetitive procedure.

▲▲ chmod: Make a File Executable

To execute a shell script by giving its name as a command, you must have permission to read and execute the file that contains the script (see "Access Permissions" on page 88). Execute permission tells the shell and the system that the owner, group, or public has permission to execute the file. It also implies that the content of the file is executable.

When you create a shell script using an editor such as **vi**, the file does not typically have its execute permission set. The following example shows a file, **whoson**, that is a shell script containing three command lines. When you initially create a file such as **whoson**, you cannot execute it by giving its name as a command because you do not have execute permission.

```
$ cat whoson
date
echo Users Currently Logged In
who

$ whoson
whoson: execute permission denied
```

The shell does not recognize **whoson** as an executable file and issues an error message when you try to execute it. You can execute it by giving the filename as an argument to **sh** (sh whoson). When you do this **sh** takes the argument to be a shell script and executes it. In this case **sh** is executable and **whoson** is an argument that **sh** executes, so you do not need to have permission to execute **whoson**. You can do the same with **csh** and **ksh**.

    You can use **chmod** (pages 90 and 709) to change the access privileges associated with a file. Figure 10-1 shows **ls** with the **–l** option displaying the access privileges of **whoson** before and after **chmod** gives the owner execute permission.

```
$ ls -l whoson
-rw-rw-r--   1 alex      group            40 May 23 11:30 whoson

$ chmod u+x whoson                      No execute access
$ ls -l whoson
-rwxrw-r--   1 alex      group            40 May 23 11:30 whoson

$ whoson                                Execute access for owner
Sat May 23 11:40:49 PST 1997
Users Currently Logged In
jenny    pts/7    May 22 18:17
hls      pts/1    May 23 09:59
scott    pts/12   May 23 06:29 (bravo.tcorp.com)
alex     pts/4    May 23 09:08
```

*Figure 10-1   Using **chmod** to make a shell script executable*

    The first **ls** displays a hyphen (–) as the fourth character, indicating that the owner does not have permission to execute the file. Then **chmod** uses an argument to give the owner execute permission. The **u+x** causes **chmod** to add (**+**) execute permission (**x**) for the owner (**u**). (The **u** stands for *user*, although it actually refers to the owner of the file, who may be the user of the file at any given time.) The second argument is the name of the file. The second **ls** shows an **x** in the fourth position, indicating that the owner now has execute permission.

    If other users are going to execute the file, you must also change group and/or public access privileges. Any user must have execute access to a file to use the file's name as a command. If the file is a shell script (a shell command file), the user trying to execute the file must also have read access to the file. You do not need read access to execute a binary executable (compiled program).

    For more information refer to "Access Permissions" (page 88) and to **ls** and **chmod** in Part III.

    Finally the shell executes the file when its name is given as a command. If you try typing **whoson** in response to a shell prompt and you get an error message such as whoson: command not found., your login shell is not set up to search for executable files in the working directory. Try giving this command:

```
$ ./whoson
```

The **./** explicitly tells the shell to look for an executable file in the working directory. To change your environment so that the shell searches the working directory, refer to the **PATH** variable on page 372.

    Now you know how to write and execute simple shell scripts. The sections of this chapter titled "Command Separation and Grouping" (following) and "Redirecting Standard Error" (page 355) describe features that are useful when you are running commands either on a command line or from within a script. The section titled "Job Control" (page 357) explains the relationships between commands, shell scripts, and Solaris system processes. It also describes how a shell script is invoked and run and describes the environment in which it is run.

▲ Command Separation and Grouping

When you give the shell commands interactively or write a shell script, you must separate commands from one another. This section reviews the ways to do this that were covered in Chapter 5 and introduces a few new ones. This section applies to the Bourne, C, and Korn Shells.

▲▲ ; and NEWLINE: Separate Commands

The NEWLINE character is a unique command separator because it initiates execution of the command preceding it. You have seen this throughout this book each time you press the RETURN key at the end of a command line.

The semicolon (;) is a command separator that *does not* initiate execution of a command and *does not* change any aspect of how the command functions. You can execute a series of commands sequentially by entering them on a single command line and separating each from the next by a semicolon (;). To initiate execution of the sequence of commands, you must terminate the command line with a RETURN.

```
$ x ; y ; z
```

If **x**, **y**, and **z** are commands, the preceding command line yields the same results as the next three commands. The difference is that in the next example the shell issues a prompt after each of the commands (**x**, **y**, and **z**) finishes executing, while the preceding command line causes the shell to issue a prompt only after **z** is complete.

```
$ x
$ y
$ z
```

Although the whitespace around the semicolons in the earlier example makes the command line easier to read, it is not necessary. None of the command separators needs to be surrounded by SPACEs or TABs.

▲▲ \: Continue a Command

When you are entering a very long command line and you reach the right side of your display screen, you can use a backslash (\) character to continue the command on the next line. The backslash quotes, or escapes, the NEWLINE character that follows it so that the shell does not treat it as the command terminator (page 36).

▲▲ | and &: Separate Commands and Do Something Else

Other command separators are the pipe symbol (|) and the background task symbol (**&**). These command separators *do not* start execution of a command but *do* change some aspect of how the command functions. The pipe symbol alters the source of standard input or the destination of standard output, and the background task symbol causes the shell to execute the task in the background so you get a prompt back right away and can continue working on other things.

Each of the following command lines initiates a single job comprising three tasks:

```
$ x | y | z
$ ls -l | grep tmp | pg
```

In the first job the shell directs the output from task **x** to task **y** and directs **y**'s output to **z**. Because the shell runs the entire job in the foreground, you do not get a prompt back until task **z** runs to completion (and task **z** does not finish until task **y** finishes, and task **y** does not finish until task **x** finishes). In the second job task **x** is an **ls –l** command, task **y** is **grep tmp**, and task **z** is the paginator, **pg**. You end up with a long (wide) listing of the filenames of all of the files in the working directory that contain the string tmp, piped through **pg**.

The next command line executes tasks **d** and **e** in the background and task **f** in the foreground. The shell displays the job number between square brackets ^{jsh}_{csh}_{ksh} (see footnote 5 on page 357) and the PID (process identification) number for each process running in the background. You get a prompt back as soon as **f** finishes.

```
$ d & e & f
[1] 14271
[2] 14272
```

Before the shell displays a prompt for a new command, it checks to see if any background jobs have completed. For each job that has completed, the shell ^{jsh}_{ksh} displays its job number, the word Done, and the command line that invoked the job; then the shell displays the prompt. When the job numbers are listed, the number of the last job started is followed by a **+** character, and the job number of the previous job is followed by a **–** character. Any other jobs listed show a **SPACE** character. After running the last command, the shell displays the following before issuing a prompt:

```
[1]-   Done                d
[2]+   Done                e
$
```

The following command line executes all three tasks as background jobs. You get a shell prompt immediately.

```
$ d & e & f &
[1] 14290
[2] 14291
[3] 14292
$
```

You can use pipes to send the output from one task to the next and an ampersand (**&**) to run the whole job as a background task. Again the prompt comes back immediately. The shell regards the commands joined by a pipe as a single job. All pipes are treated as single jobs by the shell, no matter how many tasks are connected with the pipe (l) symbol and how complex they are. The C Shell shows three processes (all belonging to job 1) placed in the background. The Job and Korn Shells show only one process.

```
% x | y | z &
[1] 14302 14304 14306
%
```

Start Optional

You can demonstrate sequential and concurrent processes running in both the foreground and background. Create executable files named **a**, **b**, and **c**, and have each file **echo** sh csh ksh its name over and over as file **a** does.

```
$ cat a
echo "aaaaaaaaaaaaaaaaaaaaaaaaaa"
echo "aaaaaaaaaaaaaaaaaaaaaaaaaa"
echo "aaaaaaaaaaaaaaaaaaaaaaaaaa"
echo "aaaaaaaaaaaaaaaaaaaaaaaaaa"
echo "aaaaaaaaaaaaaaaaaaaaaaaaaa"
```

Execute the files sequentially and concurrently, using the example command lines from this section. When you execute two of these shell scripts sequentially, the output of the second file follows the output of the first file. When you execute the two files concurrently, their output is interspersed as control is passed back and forth between the tasks (multitasking).[3] The results are not always identical because Solaris schedules jobs slightly differently each time they run. Concurrent execution does not guarantee faster completion than sequential execution, and all background execution guarantees is a faster return of the prompt. Two sample runs are shown here:

```
$ a & b & c &
[1] 14717
[2] 14718
[3] 14719
$ aaaaaaaaaaaaaaaaaaaaaaaaaa
aaaaaaaaaaaaaaaaaaaaaaaaaa
aaaaaaaaaaaaaaaaaaaaaaaaaa
aaaaaaaaaaaaaaaaaaaaaaaaaa
bbbbbbbbbbbbbbbbbbbbbbbbbb
cccccccccccccccccccccccccc
aaaaaaaaaaaaaaaaaaaaaaaaaa
bbbbbbbbbbbbbbbbbbbbbbbbbb
bbbbbbbbbbbbbbbbbbbbbbbbbb
bbbbbbbbbbbbbbbbbbbbbbbbbb
bbbbbbbbbbbbbbbbbbbbbbbbbb
cccccccccccccccccccccccccc
cccccccccccccccccccccccccc
cccccccccccccccccccccccccc
cccccccccccccccccccccccccc
```

3. With faster computers and short programs, there may be no change of control back and forth: Each program may finish before it is time to change control. Try a similar script, with 1000 or more **echo** commands, to see the switch. The command **(a&b&c&) > hold** saves the output in the file named **hold** for easier viewing. See the next section for information on parentheses on the command line.

```
$ a & b & c &
[1] 14738
[2] 14739
[3] 14740
$ aaaaaaaaaaaaaaaaaaaaaaaaa
bbbbbbbbbbbbbbbbbbbbbbbbbbb
ccccccccccccccccccccccccc
bbbbbbbbbbbbbbbbbbbbbbbbbbb
bbbbbbbbbbbbbbbbbbbbbbbbbbb
bbbbbbbbbbbbbbbbbbbbbbbbbbb
ccccccccccccccccccccccccc
ccccccccccccccccccccccccc
ccccccccccccccccccccccccc
ccccccccccccccccccccccccc
aaaaaaaaaaaaaaaaaaaaaaaaa
aaaaaaaaaaaaaaaaaaaaaaaaa
aaaaaaaaaaaaaaaaaaaaaaaaa
aaaaaaaaaaaaaaaaaaaaaaaaa
bbbbbbbbbbbbbbbbbbbbbbbbbbb
```

▲▲ (): Group Commands

You can use parentheses to group commands. The shell creates a copy of itself, called a *subshell,* for each group, treating each group of commands as a job and creating a new process to execute each of the commands (see "Process Structure" on page 360 for more information on creating subshells). Each subshell (job) has its own environment—among other things, this means it has its own set of variables with values that can be different from other subshells.

The following command line executes commands **a** and **b** sequentially in the background while also executing **c** in the background. The shell prompt returns immediately.

```
$ (a ; b) & c &
15007
```

This example differs from the earlier example **a & b & c &** because tasks **a** and **b** are initiated sequentially, not concurrently.

Similarly the following command line executes **a** and **b** sequentially in the background and, at the same time, executes **c** and **d** sequentially in the background. The subshell running **a** and **b** and the subshell running **c** and **d** run concurrently. The prompt returns immediately.

```
$ (a ; b) & (c ; d) &
15020
15021
$
```

In the following shell script, the second pair of parentheses creates a subshell to run the commands following the pipe. Because of these parentheses the output of the first **tar** command is available for the second **tar** command, despite the intervening **cd** command. Without the parentheses the output of the first **tar** would be sent to **cd** and lost, because **cd** does not accept input from standard input. The **$1** and **$2** are shell variables that represent the first and second command-line arguments (page 376). The first pair of parentheses, which creates a subshell to run the first two commands, is necessary so that users can call **cpdir** with relative pathnames. Without these parentheses the first **cd** command would change the working directory of the script (and, consequently, the working directory of the second **cd** command), whereas with the parentheses only the working directory of the subshell is changed.

```
$ cat cpdir
(cd $1 ; tar -cf - . ) | (cd $2 ; tar -xvf - )
$ cpdir /home/alex/sources /home/alex/memo/biblio
```

The preceding command line copies the files and subdirectories included in the **/home/alex/sources** directory to the directory named **/home/alex/memo/biblio**. This shell script is almost the same as using **cp** with the **–r** option. For more information about subshells, see "Job Control" on page 357. Refer to Part III for more information on **cp** (page 719) and **tar** (page 912).

Stop Optional

▲ Redirecting Standard Error

Chapter 5 covered the concept of standard output and explained how to redirect a command's standard output. In addition to standard output, commands can send their output to another place: *standard error.* A command can send error messages to standard error to keep them from getting mixed up with the information it sends to standard output. Just as it does with standard output, the shell sends a command's standard error to the terminal unless you redirect it. Therefore unless you redirect one or the other you may not know the difference between the output a command sends to standard output and the output it sends to standard error. This section covers the syntax used by the Bourne and Korn Shells. In addition to this section, see page 452 if you are using **csh**.

When you execute a program, the process running the program opens three *file descriptors,* which are places the program sends its output to and gets its input from: 0 (standard input), 1 (standard output), and 2 (standard error). The redirect output symbol (> [page 109]) is shorthand for **1>**, which tells the shell to redirect standard output. Similarly < (page 110) is short for **<0**, which redirects standard input. The symbols **2>** redirect standard error. The program does not "know" where its input comes from nor where its output goes to; the shell takes care of that. For more information see "File Descriptors" on page 503.

The following examples demonstrate how to redirect standard output and standard error to different files and to the same file. When you run **cat** with the name of a file that does not exist and the name of a file that does exist, **cat** sends an error message to standard error and copies the file that does exist to standard output. Unless you redirect them, both messages appear on the terminal.

```
$ cat y
This is y.
$ cat x y
cat: cannot open x
This is y.
```

When you redirect standard output of a command using the greater than (>) symbol, the error output is not affected—it still appears on the screen.

```
$ cat x y > hold
cat: cannot open x
$ cat hold
This is y.
```

Similarly when you send standard output through a pipe, standard error is not affected. In the following example standard output of **cat** is sent through a pipe to **tr** (translate), which in this example converts lowercase characters to uppercase. The text that **cat** sends to standard error is not translated because it goes directly to the screen rather than through the pipe.

```
$ cat x y | tr "[a-z]" "[A-Z]"
cat: cannot open x
THIS IS Y.
```

The following example redirects standard output and standard error to different files. The notation **2>** tells the shell where to redirect standard error (file descriptor 2). The **1>** tells the shell where to redirect standard output (file descriptor 1). You can use **>** in place of **1>**.

```
$ cat x y 1> hold1 2> hold2
$ cat hold1
This is y.
$ cat hold2
cat: cannot open x
```

In the next example **1>** redirects standard output to **hold**. Then **2>&1** declares file descriptor 2 to be a duplicate of file descriptor 1. The result is that both standard output and standard error are redirected to **hold**.

```
$ cat x y 1> hold 2>&1
$ cat hold
cat: cannot open x
This is y.
```

In the preceding example **1> hold** precedes **2>&1**. If they had been listed in the opposite order, standard error would have been redirected to be a duplicate of standard output before standard output was redirected to **hold**. In that case only standard output would have been redirected to the file **hold**.

The next example declares file descriptor 2 to be a duplicate of file descriptor 1 and sends the output for file descriptor 1 through a pipe to the **tr** command:

```
$ cat x y 2>&1 | tr "[a-z]" "[A-Z]"
CAT: CANNOT OPEN X
THIS IS Y.
```

You can also use **1>&2** to redirect standard output of a command to standard error. This technique is often used in shell scripts to send the output of **echo** to standard error. In the following script standard output of the first **echo** is redirected to standard error:

```
$ cat message_demo
echo This is an error message. 1>&2
echo This is not an error message.
```

If you redirect standard output of **message_demo**, error messages such as the one produced by the first **echo** above still go to the screen (because you have not redirected standard error). Because (standard) output of a shell script is typically redirected to another file, this technique is often used so that error messages generated by the script are displayed on the screen. The **links** script (page 401) and several other scripts in the next chapter employ this technique.

You can also use the **exec** *builtin* csh^{sh4} to create additional file descriptors and redirect standard input, standard output, and standard error of a shell script from within the script (page 423).

▲ Job Control⁵

A job is a command pipeline. You run a simple job whenever you give Solaris a command (for example type **date** on the command line and press RETURN: You have run a job). You can also create several jobs with multiple commands on a single command line.

```
$ find . -print | sort | lp & grep -l alex /tmp/k > alexfiles &
[1] 18839
[2] 18876
request id is printer_1-1007 (standard input)
```

The portion of the command line up to the first **&** is one job. It consists of three processes [**find** (page 753), **sort** (page 45), and **lp** (page 43)] connected by pipes. The second job is a single process, running **grep**. Both jobs have been put into the background by the trailing **&** characters, so **sh** does not wait for them to complete before it gives you a prompt. Before the prompt the shell displays information about each background job: Its job number in square brackets followed by the PID of the last process in the job. The **lp** utility generates its regular informative output.

Using job control, you can move commands from the foreground to the background and vice versa, stop commands temporarily, and get a list of the commands that are currently running (or stopped). The Berkeley UNIX C Shell has supported job control for many years, though job-control features were often not implemented in the C Shell on computers running System V.

▲▲ jobs: List Jobs

The **jobs** builtin csh^{jsh}ksh lists all background jobs. The following sequence demonstrates what happens when you give the command **jobs** from the Bourne Shell and then from the Job Shell. There is a utility named **jobs**

---

4. A *builtin* (page 47) is a command that is built into and is part of the shells named within the shaded rectangle following its name (csh^{sh}ksh [page 17]). All builtins available in **sh** are also available in **jsh**. Give the command **man shell_builtins** to see a list of **sh** (and other) builtins.

5. The Bourne Shell does not support job control. The Job Shell (**jsh**) is identical to the Bourne Shell but supports a full implementation of job control. Make sure you are running **jsh** and not **sh** if you want to experiment with the commands in this section. The C and Korn Shells support job control.

(**/usr/bin/jobs**) that runs when you give a **jobs** command from the Bourne Shell. It does not generate any output, but neither does it generate an error. When you start the Job Shell, it adds some commands to the environment (similar to builtin commands) including **jobs**. Below, **sh** ensures that you are using the Bourne Shell, the **sleep** command run in the background creates a background job that **jobs** can report on, and **jobs** (**/usr/bin/jobs**) does not report on any jobs. Next the **jsh** command puts you in the Job Shell, **sleep** performs as above, and the **jobs** environment command displays job information.

```
$ sh
$ sleep 60 &
7807
$ jobs
$ jsh
$ sleep 60 &
[1] 7809
$ jobs
[1] + Running                    sleep 60
$
```

▲▲ fg: Bring a Job to the Foreground

As mentioned on page 352, the shell (other than the Bourne Shell) assigns a job number to any command that you run in the background. In the following example several jobs are started in the background. For each the Job Shell lists the job number and PID number immediately just before it issues a prompt.

```
$ xman &
[1] 1246
$ date &
[2] 1247
$ Sat Dec 7 11:44:40 PST 1998
[2]+ Done           date
$ find /usr -name ace -print > findout &
[2] 1269
$ jobs
[1]- Running           xman &
[2]+ Running           find /usr -name ace -print > findout &
```

The **jobs** command lists the first job, **xman**, as job 1. The **date** command does not appear in the jobs list because it completed before **jobs** was run. Because the **date** command completed before **find** was run, the **find** command became job 2.

To move a background job into the foreground, use the **fg** builtin ⌷ with a percent sign (**%**) followed by the job number as an argument. The following example moves job 2 into the foreground:

```
$ fg %2
```

You can also refer to a job by following the percent sign with a string that uniquely identifies the beginning of the command line used to start the job. Instead of the above command, for example, you could have used **fg %find** or **fg %f**, because either one uniquely identifies job 2. If you follow the percent sign with a question mark and a string, the string matches itself anywhere on the command line. In the above example **%?ace** also refers to job 2.

Often the job you wish to bring into the foreground is the only job running in the background or is the job that **jobs** lists with a plus (**+**). In these cases you can use **fg** without any arguments.

▲▲ bg: Put a Job into the Background

To put the current foreground job into the background, you must first press either **CONTROL-Z** or **CONTROL-Y**[6] to suspend the job. Pressing **CONTROL-Z** stops the job immediately; **CONTROL-Y** causes the job to continue to run until it tries to read input from the terminal, at which point it is suspended. Once the job is suspended, use the **bg** builtin ^jsh_dsh_ksh to resume execution of the job, putting it in the background.

```
$ bg
```

If a background job attempts to read from the terminal, the shell stops it (puts it to sleep [pages 106 and 362]) and notifies you that the job has been stopped and is waiting for input.[7] When this happens you must move the job into the foreground so that it can read from the terminal. The shell displays the command line as it moves the job into the foreground.

```
$ (sleep 5; cat > mytext) &
[1] 1343
$ date
Sat Dec 7 11:58:20 PST 1998
[1]+ Stopped (tty input)    ( sleep 5; cat >mytext )
$ fg
( sleep 5; cat >mytext )
Remember to let the cat out!
CONTROL-D
$
```

In this example the shell displays the job number and PID number of the background job as soon as it starts, followed by a prompt. At this point the user enters **date**, and its output appears on the screen. The shell waits until just before it issues a prompt (after **date** has finished) to notify you that job 1 is waiting for input. The reason for this delay is so that the notice does not disrupt your work—this is the default behavior of the shell. After the shell puts the job in the foreground, you can enter the input that the command was waiting for. Terminate the input with a **CONTROL-D** to signify EOF (end of file), and the shell displays another prompt.

The shell keeps you informed about changes in the status of a job: It notifies you when a background job starts, completes, or is waiting for input from the terminal. It also lets you know when a foreground job is suspended. Because notices about a job being run in the background can disrupt your work, the shell delays these until it is ready to display the next prompt.

---

6. The keys that activate these functions can be changed. For more information see "Job-Control Parameters" on page 904.

7. See "**tostop**" on page 904 if you want to change this default action.

If you try to leave a shell while there are stopped jobs, the shell gives you a warning and does not allow you to exit. If, after the warning, you use **jobs** to review the list of jobs or immediately try to leave the shell again, the shell allows you to leave and terminates your stopped jobs. Jobs that are running (not stopped) in the background continue to run. In the following example **find** (job 1) continues to run after the second **exit** terminates the shell but **cat** (job 2) is terminated.

```
$ find / -size +100k > $HOME/bigfiles 2>&1 &
[1] 1426
$ cat > mytest &
[2] 1428
$ exit
exit
There are stopped jobs.

[2]+ Stopped (tty input)    cat > mytext
$ exit


login:
```

▲ Processes

A *process* is the execution of a command by Solaris. The shell that starts up when you log in is a command, or a process, like any other. Whenever you give the name of a Solaris utility on the command line, a process is initiated. When you run a shell script, another shell process is started, and additional processes are created for each command in the script. Depending on how you invoke the shell script, the script is run either by a new shell or by a subshell of the current shell. A process is not started when you run a shell builtin such as **cd** sh csh ksh from the command line or within a script. The information in this section pertains to the Bourne, C, and Korn Shells.

▲▲ Process Structure

Like the file structure the process structure is hierarchical. It has parents, children, and even a *root*. A parent process *forks*[8] a child process, which in turn can fork other processes. (You can also use the term *spawn;* the words are interchangeable.) The operating system routine, or *system call,* that creates a new process is named **fork**. One of the first things Solaris does to begin execution when a machine is started up is to start **init**, a single process, called a *spontaneous process,* with PID number 1. This process holds the same position in the

---

8. The term *fork* is used to convey the fact that, as with a fork in the road, one process turns into two. Initially the two forks are identical except that one is identified as the parent and one as the child.

process structure as the root directory does in the file structure. It is the ancestor of all processes that each user works with. Among other things **init** runs a process named **ttymon**, which monitors all lines that someone can log in on and starts a **login** process when it detects activity on a line. After the user logs in, the login process becomes the user's shell process.

▲▲ Process Identification

Solaris assigns a unique PID number at the inception of each process. As long as a process is in existence, it keeps the same PID number. During one session the same process is always executing the login shell. When you fork a new process—for example when you use an editor—the new (child) process has a different PID number than its parent process. When you return to the login shell, you will find it is still being executed by the same process and has the same PID number as when you logged in.

The following interaction shows that the process running the shell forked (is the parent of) the process running **ps** (page 118). When you call **ps** with the **–l** option, it displays a long listing of information about each process. The line of the **ps** display with sh in the CMD column refers to the process running the shell. The column headed by PID lists the PID number. The column headed PPID lists the PID number of the *parent* of each of the processes. From the PID and PPID columns, you can see that the process running the shell (PID 18835) is the parent of the process running **sleep** (PID 18836). The parent PID number of **sleep** is the same as the PID number of the shell (18835). Refer to page 865 in Part III for more information on **ps** and all the columns it displays with the **–l** option.

```
$ sleep 10 &
18836
$ ps -l
F S   UID   PID  PPID  C PRI NI     ADDR     SZ    WCHAN TTY      TIME CMD
8 S   500 18836 18835  0  41 20  f6133748    167 f613393c pts/1   0:00 sleep
8 R   500 18835 18751  0  51 20  f5c172d0    187          pts/1   0:00 sh
```

When you give another **ps –l** command, you can see that the shell is still being run by the same process but that it forked another process to run **sleep**.

```
$ sleep 10 &
18838
$ ps -l
F S   UID   PID  PPID  C PRI NI     ADDR     SZ    WCHAN TTY      TIME CMD
8 S   500 18838 18835  0  40 20  f6167c30    167 f6167e24 pts/1   0:00 sleep
8 R   500 18835 18751  0  51 20  f5c172d0    187          pts/1   0:00 sh
```

Another tool you can use to see the parent/child relationship of processes is **ptree** (located in **/usr/proc/bin**). You can follow **ptree** on the command line with the name of a user or a PID number. The following example runs **ptree** three times, twice using jenny and once using 364 (the PID of Jenny's shell). The PID numbers of the processes that spawned Jenny's shell, as well as Jenny's shell itself, remain the same throughout. The PID number of the **ptree** process changes each time it is called as each invocation spawns a new process.

```
$ /usr/proc/bin/ptree jenny
152   /usr/sbin/inetd -s
  362   in.telnetd
    364   -csh
      383   ptree jenny

$ /usr/proc/bin/ptree jenny
152   /usr/sbin/inetd -s
  362   in.telnetd
    364   -csh
      384   ptree jenny

$ /usr/proc/bin/ptree 364
152   /usr/sbin/inetd -s
  362   in.telnetd
    364   -csh
      385   ptree 364
```

See "$$: PID Number" on page 380 for a description of how to instruct the shell to report on PID numbers. Refer to page 654 for more information on the **proc** file system.

▲▲ Executing a Command

When you give the shell a command, it usually forks (spawns) a child process to execute the command. While the child process is executing the command, the parent process *sleeps*. While a process is sleeping, it does not use any computer time; it remains inactive, waiting to wake up. When the child process finishes executing the command, it tells its parent of its success or failure via the exit status and dies. The parent process (which is running the shell) wakes up and prompts you for another command.

When you request that the shell run a process in the background by ending a command with an ampersand (**&**), the shell forks a child process without going to sleep and without waiting for the child process to run to completion. The parent process, executing the shell, reports the job number and PID number of the child and prompts you for another command. The child process runs in the background, independent of its parent.

Although the shell forks a process to run most of the commands you give it, some commands are built into the shell. The shell does not need to fork a process to run builtins. For a partial list of builtins, refer to page 428 or give the command **man shell_builtins**.

Within a given process, such as your login shell or a subshell, you can declare, initialize, read, and change variables. By default, however, a variable is local to a process. When a process forks a child process, the parent does not pass the value of a variable to the child. You can make the value of a variable available to child processes by using the **export** _{ksh}^{sh} builtin (page 368).

▲▲ Invoking a Shell Script

With the exception of the commands that are built into the shell (shell builtins), whenever you give the shell a command on the command line, the shell **fork**s, which creates a duplicate of the shell process (that is, a subshell). The new process attempts to **exec**, or execute, the command. Like **fork**, **exec** is a routine executed by the operating system (a system call). If the command is an executable program (such as a compiled C program), **exec** succeeds and the system overlays the newly created subshell with the executable program. If the command is a shell script, **exec** fails. When **exec** fails, the command is assumed to be a shell script, and the subshell runs the commands in the script. Unlike your login shell, which expects input from the command line, the subshell takes its input from a file, the shell script.

As discussed earlier, if you have a shell script in a file for which you do not have execute permission, you can run the commands in the script by using an **sh** command to **exec** a shell to run the script directly. In the following example **sh** creates a new shell that takes its input from the file named **whoson**:

```
$ sh whoson
```

Because the **sh** command expects to read a file containing commands, you do not need execute permission for **whoson**. (However you do need read permission.) Although **sh** reads and executes the commands in the file **whoson**, standard input, standard output, and standard error are still connected to the terminal. You can use **csh** and **ksh** in the same manner.

Although you can use **sh** to execute a shell script (and you do not need execute access to the file holding the script), this technique causes the script to run more slowly than giving yourself execute permission and directly invoking the script. Users typically prefer to make the file executable and run the script by typing its name on the command line. It is also easier just to type the name, and it is consistent with the way other kinds of programs are invoked (so you do not need to know whether you are running a shell script or another kind of program). However if **sh** is not your interactive shell or if you want to see how the script runs with different shells, you should give the **sh** (or the name of another shell) command followed by the name of the file containing the script, as shown earlier.

▲▲▲ #!: Specify a Shell

You can also put a special sequence of characters on the first line of a shell script to indicate to the operating system that it is a script or other type of file. Because the operating system checks the initial characters of a program before attempting to **exec** it, these characters save the system from making an unsuccessful attempt. They also tell the system which utility to use (usually **sh**, **csh**, or **ksh**). If the first two characters of a script are **#!**, the system interprets the characters that follow as the absolute pathname of the program that should execute the script. This can be the pathname of any program, not just a shell. The following example specifies that the current script should be run by **sh**:

```
$ cat sh_script
#!/usr/bin/sh
echo "This is a Bourne Shell script."
```

This feature is also useful if you have a script intended to be run with a shell other than the **sh** interactive shell. The following example shows a script that is intended to be executed by **csh**. It can be run from any shell, but **csh** must execute it. Because of the **#!** line, the operating system sees to it that **csh** executes it no matter which shell you run it from.

```
$ cat csh_script
#!/usr/bin/csh
echo "This is a csh script."
set person = jenny
echo "person is $person"
```

Following is a demonstration program that displays the name of the shell it was run under:

```
$ cat whichshell
#!/bin/csh
ps -f | grep $0
$ whichshell
    mark  2370  1933  0 16:36:45 pts/0    0:00 /bin/csh whichshell
```

The **–f** option causes **ps** to display the full command line that includes the name of the shell running the script. The **$0** variable ꜱʜ csh ksh holds the name of the calling program, so **grep** looks through the lines output by **ps –f** for the name of the program.

If you do not follow the **#!** with the name of an executable program, the shell reports that it cannot find the command that you asked it to run. You can optionally follow **#!** with SPACEs. If you omit the **#!** line and try to run, for example, a **csh** script from **sh**, the shell generates error messages or the script may just not run properly.

▲▲▲ #: Make a Comment

Comments make shell scripts (and all code) easier to read and maintain. If you put comments in your shell scripts, they will be easier to maintain by you or by others. The comment syntax is common to the Bourne, C, and Korn Shells.

If a pound sign (#) in the first character position of the first line of a script is not immediately followed by an exclamation point (!), or if a pound sign occurs in any location in a script other than the first character position, the shell interprets it as the beginning of a comment and ignores everything between the pound sign and the next NEWLINE character.

▲▲▲ Startup Files

When you log in on your system, the Bourne Shell looks for a file named **/etc/profile**. This file contains systemwide startup commands for the Bourne Shell, and only the system administrator can change it. After executing the commands in **/etc/profile**, the Bourne Shell looks for a file named **.profile** in your home directory. It executes the commands in **.profile** after those in **/etc/profile**. Because of this ordering you can override any systemwide commands given in **/etc/profile** with commands in **.profile**. If either file does not exist, the shell just skips it. The Korn Shell uses the same startup files as **sh**. See page 437 if you are using **csh**.

The following **.profile** file sets the **TERM**, **PATH**, **PS1**, and **CDPATH** variables (more on variables in the next section) and also sets the line kill key to CONTROL-U.

```
$ cat .profile
export TERM=vt100
export PATH=/usr/ucb:/usr/bin:/usr/sbin:/home/alex/bin:
export PS1="alex: "
export CDPATH=:$HOME
stty kill '^u'
```

▲ Parameters and Variables

Within the shell a *shell parameter* is associated with a value that is accessible to the user. There are several kinds of *shell parameters.* Parameters whose names consist of letters, digits, and underscores are often referred to as *shell variables,* or just *variables.* A variable name cannot start with a digit. Thus **A76**, **MY_CAT**, and **___X___** are valid variable names, whereas **69TH_STREET** (starts with a digit) and **MY–NAME** (contains a hyphen) are not. Shell variables that you can name and assign values to are *user-created variables*. One convention is to use only uppercase letters for names of global variables (*environment variables*), and to use mixed case or lowercase letters for other variables. You can change the values of user-created variables at any time, and you can make them *readonly,* so that their value cannot subsequently be changed. You can also make user-created variables global. A global variable is available to all shells and other programs you fork from the original shell.

When you want to assign a value to a variable in the Bourne and Korn Shells, use its name (no **SPACE**s on either side of the equal sign). Refer to the beginning of the C Shell chapter (page 435) if you are using **csh**.

```
$ myvar=abc
```

When you want to use the value of a variable in any shell, use its name preceded by a dollar sign (**$**).

```
$ echo $myvar
abc
```

Variables that have special meaning to the shell are called *keyword shell variables* (or just *keyword variables*) and usually have short, mnemonic names. When you start a shell (by logging in, for example), the shell inherits several keyword variables from the environment. Among these variables are **HOME**, which identifies your home directory, and **PATH**, which determines what directories the shell searches in what order to locate a command that you give the shell. The shell creates and initializes (with default values) other keyword variables when you start it; still other variables do not exist until you set them. You can change the values of most (but not all) of the keyword shell variables at any time although it is usually not necessary to change the values of keyword variables initialized in **/etc/profile**. If you need to change the value of a variable, do so in **.profile** $_{ksh}^{sh}$ or **.login** csh in your home directory. Just as you can make user-created variables global, you can make keyword variables global; this is often done automatically when the shell starts. You can also make a keyword variable readonly.

There is a group of parameters whose names do not resemble variable names. Most of these parameters have one-character names (for example **1**, **?**, and **#**) and are referenced (as are all variables) by preceding the name with a dollar sign (for example **$1**, **$?**, and **$#**). The values of these parameters reflect different aspects of your ongoing interaction with the shell. For example whenever you give a command on the command line, each argument on the command line becomes the value of a *positional parameter*. Positional parameters enable you to access command-line arguments, a capability that you will often require when you write sophisticated shell scripts. Other values frequently needed in shell scripts, such as the name of the last command executed, the number of command-line arguments, and the status of the most recently executed command, are available as *special parameters*. With the exception of the **set** builtin (page 378), you cannot assign values to positional and special parameters.

The following sections describe user-created variables, keyword variables, positional parameters, and special parameters.

▲▲ User-Created Variables

Again you can declare any sequence of letters, digits, and underscores as the name of a variable, as long as the first character is not a number. The first line in the following example declares the variable named **person** and initializes it with the value alex (use **set person = alex** in **csh**). When you assign a value to a variable in **sh** and **ksh**, *you must not precede or follow the equal sign with a* **SPACE** *or* **TAB**. Because the **echo** builtin copies its arguments to standard output, you can use it to display the values of variables.

```
$ person=alex
$ echo person
person
$ echo $person
alex
```

The second line shows that **person** does not represent alex. The string person is echoed as person. The shell only substitutes the value of a variable when you precede the name of the variable with a dollar sign (**$**). The command **echo $person** displays the value of the variable **person**. It does not display $person because the shell does not pass $person to **echo** as an argument. Because of the leading **$**, the shell recognizes that $person is the name of a variable, *substitutes* the value of the variable, and passes that value to **echo**. The **echo** builtin displays the value of the variable, not its name, never knowing that you called it with a variable. The final command (in the preceding example) displays the value of the variable **person**.

You can prevent the shell from substituting the value of a variable by quoting the leading **$**. Double quotation marks do not prevent the substitution; single quotation marks or a backslash (\) does.

```
$ echo $person
alex
$ echo "$person"
alex
$ echo '$person'
$person
$ echo \$person
$person
```

Because double quotation marks do not prevent variable substitution but do turn off the special meanings of most other characters, they are useful when you assign values to variables and when you use those values. To assign a value that contains **SPACE**s or **TAB**s to a variable, use double quotation marks around the value. Although double quotation marks may not be required, it is a good idea to place them around variables whose values you are using, as you can see from the second following example.

```
$ person="alex and jenny"
$ echo $person
alex and jenny
```

When you reference a variable that contains **TAB**s or multiple adjacent **SPACE**s, you need to use quotation marks to preserve the spacing. If you do not quote the variable, **echo** collapses each string of nonblank characters into a single **SPACE** when it copies them to standard output.

```
$ person="alex    and    jenny"
$ echo $person
```

```
alex and jenny
$ echo "$person"
alex    and    jenny
```

When you execute a command with a variable as an argument, the shell replaces the name of the variable with the value of the variable and passes that value to the program being executed. If the value of the variable contains a special character such as ✶ or **?**, the shell *may* expand that variable as described below.

The first line in the following sequence of commands assigns the string alex✶ to the variable **memo**. The Bourne Shell does *not expand the string* because **sh** does not perform pathname expansion (page 118) when assigning a value to a variable. All shells process a command line in a specific order. Within this order the Bourne Shell (but not **csh**) expands variables before it interprets commands. In the **echo** command line below, the double quotation marks quote the asterisk (✶) and prevent the Bourne Shell from expanding the **memo** variable before passing its value to the **echo** command:

```
$ memo=alex✶
$ echo "$memo"
alex✶
```

All shells interpret special characters as special when you reference a variable containing a special character that is not quoted. In the following example the shell expands the value of the **memo** variable because it is not quoted:

```
$ ls
alex.report
alex.summary
$ echo $memo
alex.report alex.summary
```

The preceding example shows that when you do not quote **memo**, the shell matches the value alex✶ to two files in the working directory, **alex.report** and **alex.summary**. When you quote the variable under **sh**, **echo** displays alex✶.

▲▲▲ unset: Remove a Variable

Unless you remove a variable (below), it exists as long as the shell in which it was created exists. To remove the *value* of a variable (but not the variable itself), set it to null. (Use **set person =** in **csh**.)

```
$ person=
$ echo $person

$
```

You can remove a variable with the **unset** builtin ^sh_csh_ksh^. To remove the variable **person**, give the following command:

```
$ unset person
```

▲▲▲ readonly: Make a Variable Permanent

You can use the **readonly** builtin ^sh_ksh^ to ensure that the value of a variable cannot be changed. The next example declares the variable **person** to be readonly. You must assign a value to a variable *before* you declare it to be readonly; you cannot change its value after the declaration. When you attempt to change the value of a readonly variable, the shell displays an error message.

```
$ person=jenny
$ echo $person
jenny
$ readonly person
$ person=helen
person: is read only
```

If you use the **readonly** builtin without an argument, it displays a list of all readonly shell variables. This list includes keyword variables that are automatically readonly, plus any keyword or user-created variables that you have declared as readonly.

▲▲▲ export: Make Variables Global

Variables are ordinarily local to the process in which they are declared: A shell script does not have access to variables declared in your login shell unless you explicitly make the variables available (global). You can use **export** _{sh}_{ksh} to make a variable available to a child process. Use **setenv** csh from the C Shell to replace the assignment *and* the **export**ing required by **sh** (page 454). The examples in this section will work with all shells as long as you use the proper syntax for assigning values to variables and for making them global.

Once you use the **export** builtin with a variable name as an argument, the shell places the value of the variable in the calling environment of child processes. This *call by value* gives each child process a copy of the variable for its own use.

Below, the **extest1** shell script assigns a value of american to the variable named **cheese**. Then it displays its filename (**extest1**) and the value of **cheese**. The **extest1** script then calls **subtest**, which attempts to display the same information. Then **subtest** declares a **cheese** variable and displays its value. When **subtest** finishes it returns control to the parent process, which is executing **extest1**. Then **extest1** again displays the value of the original **cheese** variable.

```
$ cat extest1
cheese=american
echo "extest1 1: $cheese"
subtest
echo "extest1 2: $cheese"
$ cat subtest
echo "subtest 1: $cheese"
cheese=swiss
echo "subtest 2: $cheese"
$ extest1
extest1 1: american
subtest 1:
subtest 2: swiss
extest1 2: american
```

The **subtest** script never receives the value of **cheese** from **extest1**, and **extest1** never loses the value. A child can never impact its parent's attributes. When a process attempts to display the value of a variable that has not been declared, as is the case with **subtest**, it displays nothing—the value of an undeclared variable is that of a null string.

The following script, **extest2**, is the same as **extest1** except that it uses **export** to make **cheese** available to the **subtest** script:

```
$ cat extest2
export cheese
cheese=american
echo "extest2 1: $cheese"
subtest
echo "extest2 2: $cheese"
$ extest2
extest2 1: american
subtest 1: american
subtest 2: swiss
extest2 2: american
```

Here the child process inherits the value of **cheese** as american and, after displaying this value, changes *its copy* to swiss. When control is returned to the parent, the parent's copy of **cheese** still retains its original value, american.

▲▲▲ read: Accept User Input

As you begin writing shell scripts, you soon realize that one of the most common uses of user-created variables is storing information a user enters in response to a prompt. Using **read** $^{sh}_{ksh}$, your scripts can accept input from the user and store the input in variables you create. (See page 460 for **csh**.) The **read** builtin reads one line from standard input and assigns the line to one or more variables. The following script shows how **read** works:

```
$ cat read1
echo "Go ahead: \c"
read firstline
echo "You entered: $firstline"
$ read1
Go ahead: This is a line.
You entered: This is a line.
```

The first line of the **read1** script uses **echo** to prompt the user to enter a line of text. The \c at the end of the string that **echo** displays suppresses the following NEWLINE, allowing you to enter a line of text on the same line as the prompt. The second line in **read1** reads the text into the variable **firstline**. The third line verifies the action of **read** by displaying the value of **firstline**. The variable is quoted (along with the text string) in this example because you, as the scriptwriter, cannot anticipate what characters the user might enter in response to the prompt. Consider what would happen if the variable were not quoted and the user entered ✳ in response to the prompt.

```
$ cat read1_no_quote
echo "Go ahead: \c"
read firstline
echo You entered: $firstline
$ read1_no_quote
Go ahead: ✳
You entered: read1 read1_no_quote script.1
$ ls
read1    read1_no_quote    script.1
```

The **ls** command demonstrates that the shell expands the asterisk into a list of all the files in the working directory. When the variable **$firstline** is surrounded by double quotation marks, the shell does not expand the asterisk. Thus the **read1** script behaves correctly.

```
$ read1
Go ahead: *
You entered: *
```

Of course if you want the shell to interpret the special meanings of special characters, you should not use quotation marks.

The **read2** script prompts for a command line and reads it into the variable **command**. The script then executes the command line by placing `$command` on a line by itself. When the shell executes the script, it replaces the variable with its value and executes the command line as part of the script.

```
$ cat read2
echo "Enter a command: \c"
read command
$command
echo Thanks
```

In the following example **read2** reads a command line that calls the **echo** builtin. The shell executes the command and then displays `Thanks`. Next **read2** reads a command line that executes the **who** utility.

```
$ read2
Enter a command: echo Please display this message.
Please display this message.
Thanks
$ read2
Enter a command: who
alex        pts/4         Jun 17 07:50   (:0.0)
scott       pts/12        Jun 17 11:54   (bravo.tcorp.com)
Thanks
```

The following **read3** script reads values into three variables. The **read** builtin assigns one word (a sequence of nonblank characters) to each variable.

```
$ cat read3
echo "Enter something: \c"
read word1 word2 word3
echo "Word 1 is: $word1"
echo "Word 2 is: $word2"
echo "Word 3 is: $word3"
$ read3
Enter something: this is something
Word 1 is: this
Word 2 is: is
Word 3 is: something
```

If you enter more words than **read** has variables, **read** assigns one word to each variable, with all the leftover words going to the last variable. Actually **read1** and **read2** both assigned the first word and all the leftover words to the one variable they each had to work with. Below **read** accepts five words into three variables. It assigns the first word to the first variable, the second word to the second variable, and the third through fifth words to the third variable.

```
$ read3
Enter something: this is something else, really.
Word 1 is:  this
Word 2 is:  is
Word 3 is:  something else, really.
```

▲▲▲ ` ... `: Substitute the Output of a Command

Command substitution replaces a command with the output of the command. You can use it to produce arguments for another command or assignment statement. The command you want to substitute for is enclosed between two backquotes, or grave accent marks. This technique works for all three shells; **ksh** has an additional method (page 383). Following, the shell executes **pwd** and substitutes the output of the command for the command and surrounding punctuation. Then the shell passes the output of the command, which is now an argument, to **echo**, which displays it.

```
$ echo `pwd`
/home/alex
```

The following shell script assigns the output of the **pwd** utility to the variable **where** and displays a message containing the value of this variable:

```
$ cat where
where=`pwd`
echo "You are using the $where directory."
$ where
You are using the /home/jenny directory.
```

Although this example illustrates how to assign the output of a command to a variable, it is not a realistic example. You can more directly display the output of **pwd** without using a variable.

```
$ cat where2
echo "You are using the `pwd` directory."
$ where2
You are using the /home/jenny directory.
```

The next chapter contains several scripts that make use of command substitution to assign values to variables (pages 401, 417, and 427).

▲▲ Keyword Variables

Most keyword variables are either inherited or declared and initialized by the shell when it is started. You can assign values to these variables from the command line or from the **.profile** ^sh_ksh or **.login** csh file in your home directory. Typically users want these variables to apply to any shells or subshells that they create, as well as to their login shell. Consequently for those variables not automatically exported by the shell, you must use **export** ^sh_ksh or **setenv** csh to make them available to descendants. They can be exported before or after they are set.

▲▲▲ **HOME**: Locate Your Home Directory

By default your home directory is your working directory when you first log in. Your home directory is determined when you establish your account and is stored in the **/etc/passwd** file. When you log in the shell inherits the pathname of your home directory and assigns it to the variable **HOME** sh csh ksh.

When you give a **cd** command without an argument, **cd** makes the directory whose name is stored in **HOME** the working directory.

```
$ pwd
/home/alex/laptop
$ echo $HOME
/home/alex
$ cd
$ pwd
/home/alex
```

This example shows the value of the **HOME** variable and the effect of the **cd** utility. After you execute **cd** without an argument, the pathname of the working directory is the same as the value of **HOME** (your home directory).

▲▲▲ **PATH**: Where to Find Programs

When you give the shell an absolute or relative pathname (not just a simple filename) as a command, it looks in the specified directory for an executable file with the appropriate filename. If the executable file does not have the exact pathname that you specify, the shell reports that it cannot find (or execute) the program. Alternatively if you give the shell a simple filename as a command, it searches through certain directories for the program you want to execute. The shell looks in several directories for a file that has the same name as the command and that you have execute permission for (a compiled program) or read and execute permission for (a shell script). The **PATH** sh csh ksh shell variable controls this search.

When you log in the shell assigns a default value to the **PATH** variable. The shell gets this value from the **/etc/profile** sh ksh or **/etc/.login** csh file. Normally the default specifies that the shell search your working directory and several system directories that are used to hold common commands. These system directories include **/bin** and **/usr/bin** as well as other directories that might be appropriate for your system. When you give a command, if the shell does not find the file named by the command in any of the directories listed in your **PATH** variable, it reports that it cannot find (or execute) the program.

The **PATH** variable specifies the directories in the order the shell is to search them. Each must be separated from the next by a colon. The following command causes the search for an executable file to start with the **/usr/local/bin** directory. If the shell does not find the file in this directory, it looks in **/bin** followed by **/usr/bin** and then **/usr/ucb**. If the search in those directories also fails, it looks in **/home/alex/bin**. It looks in the working directory last. A null value in the string indicates the working directory. There is a null value (nothing between the colon and the end of the line) as the last element of the string. The working directory is represented by a leading colon (not recommended— see the following security box), a trailing colon (as in the example), or two colons next to each other anywhere in the string. You can also represent the working directory explicitly with a period (**.**). The following command assigns a value to the variable **PATH**, and by exporting this value, makes the new value of **PATH** accessible to subshells and other shells you may invoke during the login session:

```
$ PATH=/usr/local/bin:/bin:/usr/bin:/usr/ucb:/home/alex/bin:
$ export PATH
```

See "**path**" in the list on page 461 for a **csh** example. Because Solaris stores many executable files in directories named **bin** (*binary*), users also typically put their executable files in their own **bin** directories. If you put your own **bin** directory at the end of your **PATH** as Alex has, the shell looks there for any commands that it cannot find in standard directories.

> ## **PATH** and Security
>
> Do not put the working directory first in your **PATH** when security is a concern. For example the first command most people type when entering a directory is **ls**. If the owner of the directory has an executable file named **ls** in this directory, then this file is executed instead of the system command **ls**, with possibly undesirable results. If you are running as Superuser, you should *never* put the working directory first in your **PATH**. In fact it is common for Superuser **PATH** to omit the working directory entirely. You can always execute a file in the working directory by prepending a **./** to the name, as in **./ls**.

If you want to add directories to your **PATH**, you can reference the old value of the **PATH** variable while you are setting **PATH** to a new value. The following command adds **/usr/openwin/bin** to the front of the current **PATH** and **/usr/ucb** to the end:

```
$ PATH=/usr/openwin/bin:$PATH:/usr/ucb:
```

▲▲▲ **MAIL**: Where Mail Is Kept

The **MAIL** variable _{csh}[sh/ksh] contains the pathname of the file that your mail is stored in (your *mailbox*). This pathname is usually **/var/mail/***name* or **/var/spool/mail/***name* where ***name*** is your login name).

The **MAILPATH** variable _{ksh}[sh] contains a list of filenames separated by colons. If this variable is set, the shell informs you when any one of the files is modified (for example when mail arrives). You can follow any of the filenames in the list with a percent sign (%) followed by a message. The message replaces the you have mail message when you get mail while you are logged in.

The **MAILCHECK** variable _{ksh}[sh] specifies how often, in seconds, the shell checks for new mail. The default is 600 seconds (10 minutes). If you set this variable to zero, the shell checks before each prompt. If you unset **MAILCHECK** as follows, the shell does not check for mail at all:

```
$ unset MAILCHECK
```

▲▲▲ **PS1**: Prompt the User (Primary)

The **PS1** _{ksh}[sh] or **prompt** csh (page 462) variable holds the shell prompt that lets you know that the shell is waiting for you to give it a command.The **sh** prompt used in the examples throughout this chapter is a $ followed by a SPACE; your prompt may differ. The shell stores the prompt as a string in the **PS1** (Prompt String 1) variable. When you change the value of this variable, you change the appearance of your prompt.

If you are working on more than one machine, it can be helpful to incorporate a machine name into your prompt. The following example shows how to change the prompt to the name of the machine you are using, followed by a colon and a SPACE (a SPACE at the end of the prompt makes the commands that you enter following the prompt easier to read):

```
$ PS1=" `hostname `: "
bravo: echo test
test
bravo:
```

▲▲▲ **PS2**: Prompt the User (Secondary)

Prompt String 2 is a secondary prompt that the shell stores in **PS2** $^{sh}_{ksh}$. On the first line of the following example, an unclosed quoted string follows **echo**. The shell assumes that the command is not finished and, on the
second line, gives the default secondary prompt (**>**). This prompt indicates that the shell is waiting for the user
to continue the command line. The shell waits until it receives the quotation mark that closes the string and
then executes the command.

```
$ echo "demonstration of prompt string
> 2"
demonstration of prompt string
2
$ PS2="secondary prompt: "
$ echo "this demonstrates
secondary prompt: prompt string 2"
this demonstrates
prompt string 2
$
```

The second command above changes the secondary prompt to secondary prompt: followed by a **SPACE**.
A multiline **echo** demonstrates the new prompt.

▲▲▲ **IFS**: Separate Input Fields

The **IFS** variable $^{sh}_{ksh}$ holds the Internal Field Separators. Refer to "Word Splitting" on page 383.

▲▲▲ **CDPATH**: Broaden the Scope of **cd**

The **CDPATH** variable $^{sh}_{ksh}$ allows you to use a simple filename as an argument to **cd** to change your working
directory to a directory that is not a child of your working directory. If you have several different directories
you like to work out of, this variable can speed things up and save you the tedium of constantly using **cd** with
longer pathnames to switch among them.

When **CDPATH** is not set and you specify a simple filename as an argument to **cd**, **cd** searches the
working directory for a subdirectory with the same name as the argument. If the subdirectory does not exist,
cd issues an error message. When **CDPATH** is set **cd** searches for an appropriately named subdirectory in
the directories in the **CDPATH** list. If it finds one, that directory becomes the working directory. With
CDPATH set you can use **cd** and a simple filename to change your working directory to a child of any of the
directories in the list stored in **CDPATH**.

The **CDPATH** variable takes on the value of a colon-separated list of directory pathnames (similar to
the **PATH** variable) and is usually set in **.profile** with command lines such as the following:

```
CDPATH=$HOME:$HOME/literature
export CDPATH
```

This setup causes **cd** to search your home directory, the **literature** directory, and then your working directory when you give a **cd** command. If you do not include your working directory in **CDPATH**, **cd** searches the working directory if the search of all other directories in **CDPATH** fails. If you want **cd** to search the working directory first (which you should never do when you are logged in as **root**—see "**PATH** and Security" on page 373), include a null string, represented by two colons (**::**), as the first entry in **CDPATH**.

```
CDPATH=::$HOME:$HOME/literature
export CDPATH
```

If the argument to the **cd** builtin ᶜˢ̣ʰ is an absolute filename—one starting with a slash (/)—the shell does not consult **CDPATH**.

▲▲▲ Running **.profile** with the **.** (Dot) Builtin

After you edit your **.profile** file ˢʰ to change the values of keyword shell variables, you do not have to wait until the next time you log in to put the changes into effect. You can run **.profile** with the **.** (dot) builtin ᶜˢ̣ʰ or run **.login** with the **source** builtin csh (page 474). As with all other commands, the **.** must be followed by a SPACE on the command line. Using the **.** builtin is similar to running a shell script, except that the **.** command runs the script as part of the current process. Consequently when you use **.** to run a script from your login shell, changes you make to the variables from within the script affect the login shell. You can use the **.** command to run any shell script, not just **.profile**, but there may be undesirable side effects (such as having the value of shell variables you rely on changed). If you ran **.profile** as a regular shell script and did not use the **.** builtin, the new variables would be in effect only in the subshell running the script. Refer to "export: Make Variables Global" on page 368.

In the following example **.profile** sets several variables and sets **PS1** to the machine name **bravo**. The **.** builtin puts the new values into effect.

```
$ cat .profile
PS1="bravo $"
.
.
$ . .profile
bravo $
```

▲▲ Positional Parameters

When you call a shell script, the command name and arguments are the positional parameters. They are called positional because you refer to them by their position on the command line. Although you can reference them, only the **set** builtin ˢʰ⁹ᶜˢ̣ʰ allows you to change the values of positional parameters (page 378).

▲▲▲ **$0**: Name of the Calling Program

The shell stores the name of the command you used to call a program in parameter **$0** ᶜˢ̣ʰ. It is parameter number zero because it appears before the first argument on the command line.

---

9. Although **set** is a **csh** builtin, it does not allow you to change the values of the positional parameters.

```
$ cat abc
echo The name of the command used
echo to execute this shell script was $0
$ abc
The name of the command used
to execute this shell script was abc
```

This shell script uses **echo** to verify the name of the script you are executing.

▲▲▲ $1–$9: Command-Line Arguments

The first argument on the command line is represented by the parameter **$1** _{sh csh ksh}, the second argument by the parameter **$2** _{sh csh ksh}, and so on up to **$9** _{sh csh ksh}. Although the other arguments are not thrown away, they must be promoted to one of the first nine positions before you can access them using one of these variables (see "**shift**: Promote Command-Line Arguments" on page 377). The following script shows positional parameters displaying command-line arguments.

```
$ cat display_5args
echo The first five command-line
echo arguments are $1 $2 $3 $4 $5
$ display_5args jenny alex helen
The first five command-line
arguments are jenny alex helen
```

The **display_5args** script displays the first five command-line arguments. The shell assigns a null value to each of the parameters that represents an argument that is not present on the command line. The **$4** and **$5** variables have a null value.

The **$*** variable _{sh csh ksh} represents all the command-line arguments (not just the first nine) as the **display_all** program demonstrates.

```
$ cat display_all
echo All the command-line arguments are:
echo $*
$ display_all a b c d e f g h i j k l m n o p
All the command-line arguments are:
a b c d e f g h i j k l m n o p
```

When you refer to a positional parameter, enclose the reference between double quotation marks. The quotation marks are particularly important when using positional parameters as arguments to commands, because without double quotation marks a positional parameter with a null value disappears.

```
$ cat showargs
echo "I was called with $# arguments, the first is :$1:."
$ showargs a b c
echo I was called with 3 arguments, the first is :a:.
$ echo $3

$ showargs $3 a b c
echo I was called with 3 arguments, the first is :a:.
$ showargs "$3" a b c
echo I was called with 4 arguments, the first is ::.
```

The preceding example first calls **showargs** with three simple arguments. The **showargs** script displays the number of arguments and the value of the first argument enclosed between colons. The shell stores the number of arguments that were passed to it in the $# special parameter $\frac{sh}{csh}$. Refer to "$* and $@: Value of Command-Line Arguments" on page 379.

The **echo** command demonstrates that the third positional parameter of the current shell ($3) has no value. In the final two calls to **showargs**, the first argument is $3. As shown, there is no value for this positional parameter so the shell replaces it with a null value. In the first case the command line becomes showargs a b c; the shell passes **showargs** three arguments. In the second case the command line becomes showargs " " a b c, which results in calling **showargs** with four arguments. The difference in the two calls to **showargs** illustrates a subtle problem that you must keep in mind when using positional parameters.

▲▲▲ shift: Promote Command-Line Arguments

The **shift** builtin $\frac{sh}{csh}$ promotes each of the command-line arguments. The first argument (which was **$1**) is discarded. The second argument (which was **$2**) becomes the first (now **$1**), the third becomes the second, the fourth becomes the third, and so on.

Using the command-line variables (**$1–$9**)[10] you can access only the first nine command-line arguments from a shell script. The **shift** builtin gives you access to the tenth command-line argument by making it the ninth. Successive shift commands make additional arguments available. The original first argument is discarded. Because there is no "unshift" command, it is not possible to bring back arguments that have been discarded.

```
$ cat demo_shift
echo "arg1= $1      arg2= $2      arg3= $3"
shift
echo "arg1= $1      arg2= $2      arg3= $3"
shift
echo "arg1= $1      arg2= $2      arg3= $3"
shift
echo "arg1= $1      arg2= $2      arg3= $3"
shift
$ demo_shift alice helen jenny
arg1= alice     arg2= helen     arg3= jenny
arg1= helen     arg2= jenny     arg3=
arg1= jenny     arg2=      arg3=
arg1=      arg2=      arg3=
demo_shift: cannot shift
```

The **demo_shift** program is called with three arguments. Double quotation marks around the arguments to **echo** preserve the spacing of the output display. The program displays the arguments and shifts them repeat-

---

10. **csh** and **ksh**: If you enclose the number in braces, you can address command-line arguments greater than nine. For example **${16}** represents the sixteenth command-line argument.

edly, until there are no more arguments to shift. The shell displays an error message when the script executes **shift** after it has run out of arguments.

Repeatedly using **shift** is a convenient way to loop over all the command-line arguments in shell scripts that expect an arbitrary number of arguments. See page 398 for a sample shell program that uses this technique.

▲▲▲ set: Initialize Command-Line Arguments

When you call the **set** builtin $\genfrac{}{}{0pt}{}{\text{sh}}{\genfrac{}{}{0pt}{}{\text{csh}}{\text{ksh}}}$ from **sh** or **ksh** with one or more arguments, it uses the arguments as values for positional parameters, starting with **$1** (for **csh** see footnote 9 on page 375). The following script uses **set** to assign values to the positional parameters **$1**, **$2**, and **$3**:

```
$ cat set_it
set this is it
echo $3 $2 $1
$ set_it
it is this
```

Combining the use of command substitution (page 371) with the **set** builtin is a convenient way to get standard output of a command in a form that can be easily manipulated in a shell script. The following script shows how to use **date** and **set** to provide the date in a useful format. The first command gives the output of **date**. Then **cat** displays the contents of the **dateset** script. The first command in the script uses command substitution to set the positional parameters to the output of the **date** utility. The next command, **echo $∗**, displays all of the positional parameters resulting from the previous **set**. Subsequent commands display the values of parameters **$1**, **$2**, **$3**, and **$4**. The final command displays the date in a format that you can use in a letter or report. You can also use the **format** argument to **date** to modify the format of its output. Refer to page 729 in Part III for more information on **date**.

```
$ cat dateset
set `date`
echo $∗
echo
echo "Argument 1: $1"
echo "Argument 2: $2"
echo "Argument 3: $3"
echo "Argument 6: $6"
echo
echo "$2 $3, $6"
$ date
Thu Dec 31 17:12:27 PST 1998
$ dateset
Thu Dec 31 17:12:30 PST 1998

Argument 1: Thu
Argument 2: Dec
Argument 3: 31
Argument 6: 1998

Dec 31, 1998
```

Without any arguments **set** displays a list of the shell variables that are set (all three shells). This includes user-created variables as well as keyword variables.

The Bourne and Korn Shell versions of the **set** builtin also accept a number of options that let you customize the behavior of the shell. When you replace the hyphen before the option with a plus sign, the option is turned off. The value of many of these options should be clear now; others are explained in the remainder of this chapter. Some of the more useful options and their effects are listed here. These options are not available with the C Shell version of **set**.

−a	**allexport**	Marks variables that you create or modify for automatic export.
−f	**noglob**	Stops **sh** from doing filename expansion (globbing).
−n	**noexec**	Causes **sh** to read and perform expansions on commands but not to execute them. This option is useful if you want to check a shell script for syntax errors; it is ignored for interactive shells.
−t	**exit**	Reads and executes a single command and then quits.
−u	**nounset**	Causes **sh** to return an error when you try to expand a variable that is not set. When this option is not set, the Bourne Shell expands variables that have not been set to a null string. When this option is set, shell scripts terminate when the shell attempts to expand an unset variable; interactive shells display `unbound variable` and do not execute the current command.

▲▲ Special Parameters

Special parameters make it possible to access useful values pertaining to command-line arguments and the execution of shell commands. You reference a shell special parameter by preceding a special character with a dollar sign (**$**). Like positional parameters it is not possible to modify the value of a special parameter.

▲▲▲ $* and $@: Value of Command-Line Arguments

The **$*** parameter _{csh}^{sh}_{ksh} represents all the command-line arguments, as the **display_all** script on page 376 showed.

The **$@** _{csh}^{sh}_{ksh} and **$*** parameters are the same except when they are enclosed within double quotation marks. Using **"$*"** treats the entire list of arguments as a single argument (with embedded spaces), whereas **"$@"** produces a list of separate arguments. This makes **$@** more useful than **$*** in shell scripts, as the **whos** script (page 406) demonstrates.

As the **showargs** script on page 376 and the following example demonstrate, the **$#** parameter contains the number of arguments on the command line. This string parameter represents a decimal number. You can use **test** _{ksh}^{sh} to perform logical tests on this number (page 395 and page 918 in Part III; for **csh** see "Numeric Variables" on page 456).

```
$ cat num_args
echo "This shell script was called
with $# arguments."
$ num_args helen alex jenny
This shell script was called
with 3 arguments.
```

In the preceding example the **echo** builtin displays a quoted string that spans two lines. Because the NEWLINE is quoted, the shell passes the entire string that is between the quotation marks, including the NEWLINE, to **echo** as an argument.

▲▲▲ $$: PID Number

The shell stores the PID number of the process that is executing it in the **$$** variable sh csh. In the following interaction **echo** displays the value of this variable, and the **ps** utility confirms its value (**ps** lists a lot more processes if you are running X). Both commands show that the shell has a PID number of 8232.

```
$ echo $$
8232
$ ps
  PID TTY      TIME CMD
 8232 pts/2    0:00 sh
```

The **echo** sh csh ksh builtin keeps the shell from having to create another process when you give an **echo** command. However the results are the same whether **echo** is a builtin or not, because the shell substitutes the value of **$$** *before* it forks a new process to run a command. In the following example the shell substitutes the value of **$$** and passes that value to **cp** as a prefix for a new filename. This technique is useful for creating unique filenames when the meanings of the names do not matter—it is often used in shell scripts for creating names of temporary files. When two people are running the same shell script, these unique filenames keep them from inadvertently sharing the same temporary file.

```
$ echo $$
8232
$ cp memo $$.memo
$ ls
8232.memo memo
```

The following example demonstrates that the shell creates a new shell process when it runs a shell script. The **id2** script displays the PID numbers of the process running it (not the process that called it—the substitution for **$$** is performed by the shell that is forked to run **id2**).

```
$ cat id2
echo "$0 PID= $$"
$ echo $$
8232
$ id2
id2 PID= 8362
$ echo $$
8232
```

The first **echo** in the preceding example displays the PID number of the login shell. Then **id2** displays its name (**$0**) and the PID of the subshell that it is running in. Finally the last **echo** shows that the current process is the login shell again.

The Bourne and Korn Shells store the value of the PID number of the last process that you ran in the background in **$!** sh ksh. The following example executes **sleep** as a background task and then uses **echo** to display the value of **$!**:

```
$ sleep 60 &
8376
$ echo $!
8376
```

▲▲▲ $?: Exit Status

When a process stops executing for any reason, it returns an *exit status* to its parent process. The exit status is also referred to as a *condition code* or *return code*. The **$?** ^sh_ksh or **$status** csh variable stores the exit status of the last command.

By convention a nonzero exit status represents a *false* value and means that the command failed. A zero is *true* and means that the command was successful. Below, the first **ls** command succeeds, whereas the second fails:

```
$ ls es
es
$ echo $?
0
$ ls xxx
xxx: No such file or directory
$ echo $?
2
```

You can specify the exit status that a shell script returns by using the **exit** builtin ^sh_csh_ksh, followed by a number, to terminate the script. If you do not use **exit** with a number to terminate a script, the exit status of the script is the exit status of the last command the script ran. The following example shows that the number following the word `exit` specifies the exit status:

```
$ cat es
echo This program returns an exit status of 7.
exit 7
$ es
This program returns an exit status of 7.
$ echo $?
7
$ echo $?
0
```

The **es** shell script displays a message and then terminates execution with an **exit** command that returns an exit status of 7, which is the user-defined exit status in this script. Then **echo** displays the value of the exit status of **es**. The second **echo** displays the value of the exit status of the first **echo**. The value is zero because the first **echo** was successful.

▲ Command-Line Expansion

Before the shell passes the command line to the program being called, it transforms the command line using a process named *command-line expansion*. The shell also uses this process on each line of a shell script as the shell is executing the script. You can use any of the shells without knowing much about command-line expansion, but you can make much better use of what they have to offer with an understanding of this topic.

Chapter 5 discussed one aspect of command-line expansion in "Filename Generation/Pathname Expansion" on page 118. This section reviews several types of command-line expansion you may be familiar with and introduces some new ones. It also discusses the order in which the shell performs the different expansions and provides some examples.

When the shell processes a command, it does not execute the command immediately. One of the first things that the shell does is to *parse* (isolate strings of characters in) the command line into *tokens* or *words*. The shell then proceeds to scan each token for the appearance of special characters and patterns that instruct the shell to take certain actions. These actions often involve substituting one or more filenames for a symbol. When the shell parses the following command line, it breaks it into three tokens: cp, $HOME/letter, and ..

```
$ cp $HOME/letter .
```

After separating tokens and before executing the command, the shell scans the tokens and performs command-line expansion.

▲▲ Parameter Expansion

When a single digit, optionally enclosed in braces, follows a dollar sign ($), the shell substitutes the value of the positional parameter corresponding to the integer for the token. This is called *parameter expansion*. Another type of parameter expansion occurs when a special character follows a dollar sign, in which case some aspect of the command or its arguments is substituted for the token (page 379).

▲▲ Braces

You can use braces to distinguish a variable from surrounding text without the use of a separator (for example a **SPACE**).

```
100 % prefix=Alex
101 % echo $prefix is short for ${prefix}ander.
Alex is short for Alexander.
```

Without braces **prefix** would have to be separated from **ander** with a **SPACE** so that the shell would recognize **prefix** as a variable. This change would cause Alexander to become Alex ander. Refer to the following Optional section and "{}: Brace Expansion" on page 447.

▲▲ Variable Expansion

Variable expansion takes place when the shell processes a token consisting of a dollar sign ($) followed by a variable name (user-defined or keyword), as in **$VARIABLE**. The shell replaces the token with the value of the variable.

Start Optional

The **$VARIABLE** syntax is a special case of the more general syntax **${VARIABLE}**, in which the variable name is enclosed by **${}**. The braces insulate the variable name from what surrounds it. Braces are necessary when catenating a variable value with a string.

```
$ PREF=counter
$ WAY=$PREFclockwise
$ FAKE=$PREFfeit
$ echo $WAY $FAKE

$
```

The preceding example does not work as planned. Only a blank line is output. The reason is that the symbols **PREFclockwise** and **PREFfeit** are valid variable names, but they are not set. By default **sh** and **ksh** evaluate an unset variable as an empty (null) string and display this value, whereas **csh** generates an error message. To achieve the intent of these statements, refer to the **PREF** variable using braces.

```
$ PREF=counter
$ WAY=${PREF}clockwise
$ FAKE=${PREF}feit
$ echo $WAY $FAKE
counterclockwise counterfeit
```

Stop Optional

▲▲ Command Substitution

Command substitution (page 371) allows you to use standard output of a command in-line within a shell script. (Another way of using standard output is to send it to a file and read it back in.) Command substitution is another type of command-line expansion that occurs after the tokens on the command line have been identified. The pattern the shell recognizes in this case is a token of the form

> ` *command* `

This notation instructs the shell to replace the token with standard output of *command*. To use standard output of *command,* the shell must first run *command* successfully.

▲▲ Word Splitting

The **IFS** (Internal Field Separators) shell variable ^{sh}_{ksh} specifies the characters you can use to separate arguments on a command line. It has the default value of **SPACE TAB NEWLINE**. Regardless of what **IFS** is set to, you can always use one or more **SPACE** or **TAB** characters to separate arguments on the command line, provided that these characters are not quoted or escaped. When you assign **IFS** the value of characters, these characters can also separate fields, but only in the event that they undergo some type of expansion. This type of interpretation of the command line is called *word splitting*. The following example demonstrates how setting **IFS** can affect the interpretation of a command line:

```
$ a=w:x:y:z
$ cat $a
cat: cannot open w:x:y:z
$ IFS=":"
$ cat $a
cat: cannot open w
cat: cannot open x
cat: cannot open y
cat: cannot open z
```

The first time **cat** is called, the shell expands the variable **a**, interpreting the string w:x:y:z as a single token to be used as the argument to **cat**. The **cat** utility cannot find a file named **w:x:y:z** and reports an error for that filename. After **IFS** is set to a colon (**:**), the shell expands the variable **a** into four words as separate arguments to **cat**. This causes the **cat** utility to report an error on four separate files: **w**, **x**, **y**, and **z**. Word splitting based on the colon (**:**) takes place only *after* the variable **a** is expanded.

The Bourne Shell splits all words on a command line according to the separating characters found in **IFS**. Consider the following commands:

```
$ IFS="p"
$ export IFS
```

The character p in the token export is a separator, so the effect of the command line is to start the **ex** editor with two filenames: **ort** and **IFS**.

You cannot unset the **IFS** shell variable.

Be Careful When Changing IFS

Although sequences of **SPACE** or **TAB** characters are treated as single separators, *each occurrence* of another field-separator character acts as a separator.

There are a variety of side effects of changing **IFS**, so change it cautiously. You may find it useful to first save the value of **IFS** before changing it; that way you can easily restore it if you get unexpected results. Or you can fork a new shell with an **sh** command before experimenting with **IFS**; if you get into trouble, you can simply exit back to your old shell where **IFS** is working properly.

▲▲ Pathname Expansion

The process of interpreting ambiguous file references and substituting the appropriate list of filenames is called *pathname expansion* (page 118). The shell performs this function when it encounters an ambiguous file reference—a token containing any of the characters *, ?, [, or]. If **sh** or **ksh** is unable to locate any files that match the specified pattern, the token with the ambiguous file reference is left alone; the shell does not delete the token nor replace it with a null string. An error message is generated by **csh**. In the first **echo** command in the following example, the shell expands the ambiguous file reference tmp* and passes three tokens (tmp1 tmp2 tmp3) to **echo**, which displays the three filenames it was passed by the shell. After **rm** removes the three tmp* files, the shell finds no filenames that match tmp* when it tries to expand it, so it passes the unexpanded string to the **echo** builtin, which displays the string it was passed. By default the same command causes the C Shell to display an error message: See "**noglob**" in the list on page 464.

```
$ ls
tmp1 tmp2 tmp3
$ echo tmp*
tmp1 tmp2 tmp3
$ rm tmp*
$ echo tmp*
tmp*
$ csh
% echo tmp*
echo: No match
```

Putting double quotation marks around an argument causes the shell to suppress pathname and all other expansions except parameter and variable expansions. Putting single quotation marks around an argument suppresses all types of expansion. In the following example when quoted with double quotation marks, the shell expands **$alex** to the value of the variable **alex** (sonar) because double quotation marks allow parameter expansion. This expansion does not occur when single quotation marks are used. Because neither single nor double quotation marks allow pathname expansion, the last two commands display the unexpanded argument tmp*.

```
$ echo tmp* $alex
tmp1 tmp2 tmp3 sonar
$ echo "tmp* $alex"
tmp* sonar
$ echo 'tmp* $alex'
tmp* $alex
```

The shell can distinguish the value of a variable from a reference to the variable and does not expand ambiguous file references if they occur in the value of a variable. This makes it possible for you to assign to a variable a value that includes special characters such as an asterisk (*).

In the next example the working directory has three files whose names begin with tmp. Even so, when you assign the value tmp* to the variable **var**, the shell does not expand the ambiguous file reference because it occurs in the value of a variable (in the assignment statement for the variable). There are no quotation marks around the string tmp*. Context alone prevents the expansion. After the assignment, the **set** builtin (with the help of **grep**) shows the value of **var** to be tmp*.

The three **echo** commands demonstrate three levels of expansion. When **$var** is quoted with single quotation marks, the shell performs no expansion and passes **echo** the character string $var, which **echo** displays. With double quotation marks the shell performs variable expansion only and substitutes the value of the **var** variable for its name preceded by a dollar sign. There is no filename expansion on this command because double quotation marks suppress it. In the final command the shell, without the limitations of quotation marks, performs variable substitution and then pathname expansion before passing the arguments on to **echo**.

```
$ ls tmp*
tmp1   tmp2   tmp3
$ var=tmp*
$ set | grep var
var=tmp*
$ echo '$var'
$var
$ echo "$var"
tmp*
$ echo $var
tmp1 tmp2 tmp3
```

Summary

The shell is both a command interpreter and a programming language. As a command interpreter, the shell executes commands you enter in response to its prompt. When you use it as a programming language, the shell executes commands from files called shell scripts.

You typically run a shell script by giving its name on the command line. To run a script in this manner you must have execute permission for the file holding the script. Otherwise the shell does not know that the script is executable. Alternatively you can execute the script by entering **sh**, **csh**, or **ksh** followed by the name of the file on the command line. Either way you need to have read permission for the file.

Job control is not part of the Bourne Shell but is included in the Job Shell, which is identical to the Bourne Shell in all other respects. A job is one or more commands connected by pipes. You can bring a job running in the background into the foreground with the **fg** builtin jsh/csh/ksh. A foreground job can be put into the background with the **bg** builtin jsh/csh/ksh, provided that it is first suspended by typing either CONTROL-Z or CONTROL-Y.

Each process has a unique identification, or PID, number and is the execution of a single Solaris command. When you give the shell a command, it forks a new (child) process to execute the command, unless the command is built into the shell (see page 428 for a partial list of builtins). While the child process is running, the shell is in a state called sleep. By ending a command line with an ampersand (**&**), you can run a child process in the background and bypass the sleep state so that the shell prompt returns immediately after you press RETURN. Each command in a shell script forks a separate process, each of which may fork other processes. When a process terminates it returns its exit status to its parent process: Zero signifies success, nonzero signifies failure.

The shell allows you to define variables. You can declare and initialize a variable by assigning a value to it; you can remove a variable declaration using **unset**. Variables are usually local to a process and must be exported, by using the **export** sh/ksh or **setenv** csh builtin, to make them available to child processes. The shell also defines some variables and parameters. The positional and special parameters are preceded with dollar signs in the following table to reflect the only manner in which you can reference them. Unlike the shell variables, you cannot assign values to them.

When the Bourne Shell processes a command line, it may replace some words with expanded text. There are a number of different types of command-line expansion; most are invoked by the appearance of some special character within a word (for example a leading dollar sign denotes a variable). The expansions take place in a specific order. The common expansions, in the order in which they occur, are: parameter expansion, variable expansion, command substitution, and pathname expansion. Surrounding a word with double quotation marks suppresses all but parameter and variable expansion. Single quotation marks suppress all types of expansion, as does quoting (escaping) a special character by preceding it with a backslash.

▲▲ Shell Parameters

Variable/ Parameter	Contents
CDPATH ^{sh} _{ksh}	List of directories for the shell to check when you give a **cd** builtin ^{sh} _{csh ksh} (page 374)
HOME ^{sh} _{csh ksh}	Pathname of your home directory (page 372)
IFS ^{sh} _{ksh}	Internal Field Separators (page 374)
MAIL ^{sh} _{csh ksh}	Name of the file where the system stores your mail (page 373)
MAILCHECK ^{sh} _{ksh}	How often (in seconds) the shell checks your mailbox for new mail (page 373)
MAILPATH ^{sh} _{ksh}	List of other potential mailboxes (page 373)
PATH ^{sh} _{csh ksh}	Search path for commands (page 372)
prompt csh	C Shell Prompt String (page 462)
PS1 ^{sh} _{ksh}	Bourne and Korn Shell Prompt String 1 (page 373)
PS2 ^{sh} _{ksh}	Bourne and Korn Shell Prompt String 2 (page 374)
SHELL ^{sh} _{csh ksh}	Name of the invoked shell
status csh	Exit status of the last task executed by the C Shell (page 381)
$0 ^{sh} _{csh ksh}	Name of the calling program (page 375)
$n ^{sh} _{csh ksh}	Value of the nth command-line argument (can be changed by **set**) (page 376)
$* ^{sh} _{csh ksh}	All command-line arguments (can be changed by **set** in **sh** and **csh**) (page 379)
$@ ^{sh} _{csh ksh}	All command-line arguments (can be changed by **set** in **sh** and **csh**) (page 379)
$# ^{sh} _{csh ksh}	Count of the command-line arguments (page 376)
$$ ^{sh} _{csh ksh}	PID number of the current process (page 380)
$! ^{sh} _{ksh}	PID number of the most recent background task (page 380)
$? ^{sh} _{ksh}	Exit status of the last task executed by the Bourne or Korn Shell (page 381)

▲▲ Special Characters

Special Character	Function
NEWLINE	Initiates execution of a command (page 351)
;	Separates commands (page 351)
( )	Groups commands for execution by a subshell or identifies a function (page 354)
&	Executes a command in the background (pages 116 and 351)
|	Pipe (page 351)
>	Redirects standard output (page 109)
>>	Appends standard output (page 112)
<	Redirects standard input (page 110)
<<	Here document (page 419)
*	Any string of characters in an ambiguous file reference (pages 120 and 351)
?	Any single character in an ambiguous file reference (page 119)
\	Quotes the following character (page 36)
'	Quotes a string, preventing all substitutions (page 36)
"	Quotes a string, allowing only variable and command substitution (pages 36 and 366)
`...`	Performs command substitution (page 383)
[ ]	Character class in an ambiguous file reference (page 121)
$	References a variable (page 365)
.	(dot builtin) Executes a command (only at the beginning of a line) (page 375)
#	Begins a comment (page 402)
{ }	Command grouping (used to surround the contents of a function) (page 429)
:	**null** builtin, returns *true* exit status (page 427)
&&	Logical AND: executes command on right only if command on left succeeds (returns a zero exit status [pages 468 and 519])
||	Logical OR: executes command on right only if command on left fails (returns a nonzero exit status [page 520])
!	Logical NOT: reverses exit status of command

Review Exercises

1. The following shell script adds entries to a file named **journal-file** in your home directory. It can help you keep track of phone conversations and meetings.

```
$ cat journal
# journal: add journal entries to the file
# $HOME/journal-file

file=$HOME/journal-file
date >> $file
echo "Enter name of person or group:  \c"
read name
echo "$name" >> $file
echo >> $file
cat >> $file
echo "------------------------------------------------------" >> $file
echo >> $file
```

   a. What do you have to do to the script in order to be able to execute it?

   b. Why does it use the **read** builtin the first time it accepts input from the terminal and the **cat** utility the second time?

2. What are two ways you can execute a shell script when you do not have execute access permission to the file containing the script? Can you execute a shell script if you do not have read access permission?

3. What is the purpose of the **PATH** variable?

   a. Set up your **PATH** variable so that it causes the shell to search the following directories in order:

   - **/usr/local/bin**
   - **/usr/bin/X11**
   - **/usr/bin**
   - **/bin**
   - **/usr/openwin/bin**
   - your own **bin** directory (usually **bin** or **.bin** in your home directory)
   - the working directory

   b. If there is a file named **whereis** in **/usr/bin** and also one in your own **bin**, which one is executed when you enter **whereis** on the command line? (Assume you have execute permission for both of the files.)

   c. If your **PATH** variable is not set to search the working directory, how can you execute a program located there?

   d. What command can you use to add the directory **/usr/games** to the end of the list of directories in **PATH**?

4. Assume that you have made the following assignment:

   ```
   $ person=jenny
   ```

   Give the output of each of the commands below.

   a. **echo $person**

   b. **echo '$person'**

   c. **echo "$person"**

5. Name two ways you can identify the PID of your login shell.

6. Explain the unexpected result below.

   ```
   $ whereis date
   date: /bin/date
   $ echo $PATH
   .:/usr/local/bin:/usr/bin:/bin
   $ cat > date
   echo "This is my own version of date."
   $ date
   Wed Mar 12 09:11:54 MST 1997
   ```

7. Assume that directories **/home/jenny/grants/biblios** and **/home/jenny/biblios** both exist. For both part a and b below, give Jenny's working directory after she executes the sequence of commands given. Explain.

   a.

   ```
   $ pwd
   /home/jenny/grants
   CDPATH=$(pwd)
   $ cd
   $ cd biblios
   ```

   b.

   ```
   $ pwd
   /home/jenny/grants
   CDPATH=$(pwd)
   $ cd $HOME/biblios
   ```

8. Try giving the following command:

   ```
   $ sleep 30 | cat /etc/motd
   ```

   Is there any output from **sleep**? Where does **cat** get its input from? What has to happen before you get a prompt back?

Advanced Review Exercises

9. Write a sequence of commands or a script that demonstrates that parameter expansion occurs before variable expansion and that variable expansion occurs before pathname expansion.

10. Type in the following shell scripts and run them:

```
$ cat report_dir
old_dir=$(pwd)
echo "Current working directory:  " $old_dir
go_home
echo "Current working directory:  " $(pwd)

$ cat go_home
cd
echo "New working directory:   " $(pwd)
echo "Last working directory: " $old_dir
```

What is wrong? Change them so that they work correctly.

11. The following is a modified version of the **read2** script from page 370. Explain why it behaves differently. For what type of input does it produce the same output of the original **read2** script?

```
$ cat read2
echo "Enter a command: \c"
read command
"$command"
echo "Thanks"
```

12. Explain the behavior of the following shell script:

```
$ cat quote_demo
twoliner="This is line 1.
This is line 2."
echo "$twoliner"
echo $twoliner
```

a. How many arguments does each **echo** command see in this script? Explain.

b. Redefine the **IFS** shell variable so that the output of the second **echo** is the same as the first.

13. Write a shell script that outputs the name of the shell that is executing it.

Bourne Shell Programming

C
hapter 10 explained more about the shells, particularly the Bourne Shell. This chapter introduces additional commands, builtins, and concepts that allow you to carry shell programming to a point where it can be useful. The first programming constructs covered are control structures, or control flow constructs. These structures allow you to write scripts that can loop over command-line arguments, make decisions based on the value of a variable, set up menus, and more. The Bourne Shell uses the same constructs found in high-level programming languages such as C.

This chapter goes on to explain how the Here document ^{sh}_{csh ksh} (page 419) makes it possible for you to redirect input to a script to come from the script itself, as opposed to the terminal or other file. The section titled "Expanding Null or Unset Variables" (page 422) shows you different ways to set default values for a variable. The section on the **exec** builtin ^{sh}_{csh ksh} explains how it provides a very efficient way to execute a command by completely replacing a process and how you can use it to redirect input and output from within a script. The next section covers the **trap** builtin ^{sh}_{ksh}, which provides a way to detect and respond to operating system signals (or interrupts, such as when you press **CONTROL-C**). Finally the section on functions ^{sh}_{ksh} gives you a clean way to execute code similar to scripts much more quickly and efficiently.

There are many examples of shell programs in this chapter. Although they illustrate certain concepts, most make use of information from earlier examples as well. This overlap reinforces your overall knowledge of shell programming, as well as demonstrating how commands can be combined to solve complex tasks. Running, modifying, and experimenting with the examples is a good way to become comfortable with the underlying concepts.

> ### Do Not Name Your Shell Script **test**
>
> You can create a problem for yourself if you give a shell script the name **test**. There is a Solaris utility with the same name. Depending on how you have your **PATH** variable set up and how you call the program, you may run your script or the utility, leading to confusing results.

This chapter illustrates concepts with simple examples that are followed by more complicated examples in sections marked "Optional." The more complex scripts illustrate traditional shell programming practices

393

and introduce some Solaris utilities often used in scripts. You can skip these sections the first time you read the chapter without loss of continuity. Return to them later when you feel comfortable with the basic concepts.

▲ Control Structures

The *control flow* commands alter the order of execution of commands within a shell script. The Bourne and Korn Shells share a common syntax, whereas the C Shell uses a different syntax (page 465). Control structures include the **if...then, for...in, while, until,** and **case** statements. In addition the **break** and **continue** statements work in conjunction with the control flow structures to alter the order of execution of commands within a script.

if...then

The syntax of the **if...then** _{ksh}^{sh} control structure is

> *if test-command*
>   *then*
>   *commands*
> *fi*

The **bold** words in the syntax description are the items you supply to cause the structure to have the desired effect. The *nonbold* words are the keywords the shell uses to identify the control structure.

Figure 11-1 shows that the **if** statement tests the status returned by the *test-command* and transfers control based on this status. When you spell *if* backward, it is *fi;* the **fi** statement marks the end of the **if** structure.

The following script prompts you for, and reads in, two words. Then it uses an **if** structure to evaluate the result returned by the **test** builtin _{ksh}^{sh} when it compares the two words. The **test** builtin returns a status of *true* if the two words are the same and *false* if they are not. Double quotation marks around **$word1** and **$word2** make sure that **test** works properly if you enter a string that contains a **SPACE** or other special character.

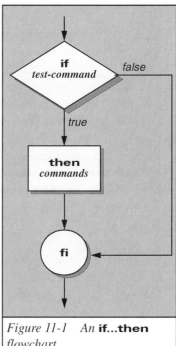

Figure 11-1   An **if...then** *flowchart*

```
$ cat if1
echo "word 1: \c"
read word1
echo "word 2: \c"
read word2

if test "$word1" = "$word2"
   then
       echo "Match"
fi
echo "End of program."
```

```
$ if1
word 1: peach
word 2: peach
Match
End of program.
```

In the preceding example the ***test-command*** is test "$word1" = "$word2". The **test** builtin returns a *true* status if its first and third arguments have the relationship specified by its second argument. If this command returns a *true* status (= 0), the shell executes the commands between the **then** and **fi** statements. If the command returns a *false* status (not = 0), the shell passes control to the statement after **fi** without executing the statements between **then** and **fi**. The effect of this **if** statement is to display Match if the two words match. The script always displays End of program.

In the Bourne and Korn Shells, **test** is a builtin—it is part of the shell. It is also a stand-alone utility usually kept in **/usr/bin/test**. This chapter discusses and demonstrates many Bourne Shell builtins. Each builtin may be a builtin in a given shell or not. You usually use the builtin version if it is available and the utility if it is not. Each version of a command may vary slightly from one shell to the next and from the utility to any of the shell builtins. To locate complete documentation first determine if you are using a builtin or a stand-alone utility. You can use the **type** builtin $\begin{smallmatrix}\text{sh}\\\text{ksh}\end{smallmatrix}$ for this purpose.

```
$ type test cat echo who
test is a shell builtin
cat is hashed (/bin/cat)
echo is a shell builtin
who is /bin/who
```

To get more information on a stand-alone utility, use the **man** command followed by the name of the utility. Use **man** followed by the name of the shell to look up a builtin. You can also refer to the utilities and builtins covered in Part III of this book.

The next program uses an **if** structure at the beginning of a script to check that you supplied at least one argument on the command line. The **–eq test** operator compares two integers. This structure displays a message and exits from the script if you do not supply an argument.

```
$ cat chkargs
if test $# -eq 0
   then
        echo "You must supply at least one argument."
        exit 1
fi
echo "Program running."
$ chkargs
You must supply at least one argument.
$ chkargs abc
Program running.
```

A test like the one in **chkargs** is a key component of any script that requires arguments. To prevent the user from receiving meaningless or confusing information from the script, the script needs to check to see whether the user has supplied the appropriate arguments. Sometimes the script simply tests to see whether arguments exist (as in **chkargs**). Other scripts test for a specific number of arguments or specific kinds of arguments.

Frequently **test** asks a question about the status of a file argument or the relationship between two file arguments. After verifying that at least one argument has been given on the command line, the following script tests the argument to see if it is the name of a regular file (not a directory or other type of file) in the working directory. The **test** builtin with the **–f** option and the command-line argument checks the file.

```
$ cat is_regfile
if test $# -eq 0
    then
        echo "You must supply at least one argument."
        exit 1
fi
if test -f "$1"
    then
        echo "$1 is a regular file in the working directory"
    else
        echo "$1 is NOT a regular file in the working directory"
fi
```

You can test many other characteristics of a file with **test** and various options. Some of the options are listed in the following table

Option	Test Performed on *file*
–d	Exists and is a directory file.
–e	Exists (not available in **sh**).
–f	Exists and is a regular file.
–r	Exists and is readable.
–s	Exists and has a length greater than 0.
–w	Exists and is writable.
–x	Exists and is executable.

Other options to **test** provide a way to test for a relationship between two files, such as whether one file is newer than another. Refer to later examples in this chapter, as well as **test** in Part III for more detailed information. (Although **test** is a builtin in **sh** and **ksh**, the **test** utility described in Part III on page 918 functions similarly.)

Always Test the Arguments

To keep the examples in this and subsequent chapters short and focused on specific concepts, the code to verify arguments is often omitted or abbreviated. It is a good practice to include tests for argument verification in your own shell programs. Doing so will result in scripts that are easier to run and debug.

The following example is another version of **chkargs** that checks for arguments in a way that is more traditional for Solaris shell scripts. The example uses the square bracket (**[]**) synonym for **test**. Rather than using the word **test** in scripts, you can surround the arguments to **test** with square brackets, as shown. The square brackets must be surrounded by whitespace (that is, **SPACE**s or **TAB**s).

```
$ cat chkargs
if [ $# -eq 0 ]
```

```
then
        echo "Usage: chkargs argument..." 1>&2
        exit 1
fi
echo "Program running."
exit 0
$ chkargs
Usage: chkargs arguments
$ chkargs abc
Program running.
```

The error message that **chkargs** displays is called a *usage message* and uses the 1>&2 notation to redirect its output to standard error (page 355). After issuing the usage message, **chkargs** exits with an exit status of 1, indicating that an error has occurred. The **exit 0** command at the end of the script causes **chkargs** to exit with a 0 status after the program runs without an error.

The usage message is a common notation to specify the type and number of arguments the script takes. Many Solaris utilities provide usage messages similar to the one in **chkargs**. When you call a utility or other program with the wrong number or kind of arguments, you often see a usage message. Following is the usage message that **cp** displays when you call it without any arguments.

```
$ cp
cp: Insufficient arguments (0)
Usage: cp [-f] [-i] [-p] f1 f2
       cp [-f] [-i] [-p] f1 ... fn d1
       cp -r|R [-f] [-i] [-p] d1 ... dn-1 dn
```

if...then...else

The introduction of the **else** statement turns the **if** structure into the two-way branch shown in Figure 11-2. The syntax of the **if...then...else** $^{sh}_{ksh}$ control structure is

> *if test-command*
> > *then*
> > > *commands*
> > *else*
> > > *commands*
> *fi*

Because a semicolon (**;**) ends a command the same way a NEWLINE does, you can place **then** on the same line as **if** by preceding it with a semicolon. (The **if** and **then** are separate builtins so they require a command separator between them; a semicolon and NEWLINE work equally well.) Some people prefer this notation for aesthetic reasons, others because it saves space.

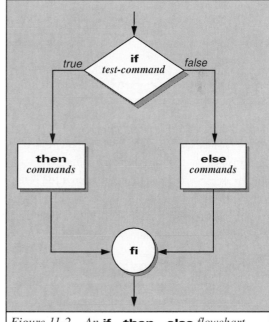

Figure 11-2   An **if...then...else** *flowchart*

> *if **test-command**; then*
>   ***commands***
> *else*
>   ***commands***
> *fi*

If the ***test-command*** returns a *true* status, the **if** structure executes the commands between the **then** and **else** statements and then diverts control to the statement following **fi**. If the ***test-command*** returns a *false* status, the **if** structure executes the commands following the **else** statement.

The next script builds on **chkargs**. When you run **out** with arguments that are filenames, it displays the files on the terminal. If the first argument is a **–v** (called an option in this case), **out** uses **pg** (similar to **more**, see page 35) to display the files. After determining that it was called with at least one argument, **out** tests its first argument to see if it is **–v**. If the result of the test is *true* (if the first argument is **–v**), **out** shifts the arguments to get rid of the **–v** and displays the files using **pg**. If the result of the test is *false* (if the first argument is *not* **–v**), the script uses **cat** to display the files.

```
$ cat out
if [ $# -eq 0 ]
   then
        echo "Usage: out [-v] filenames..." 1>&2
        exit 1
fi
if [ "$1" = "-v" ]
   then
        shift
        pg -- "$@"
   else
        cat -- "$@"
fi
```

Start Optional

In **out** the **––** argument to **cat** and **pg** tells the utility that no more options follow on the command line and not to consider leading hyphens (–) in the following list as indicating options. Thus **––** allows you to view a file with a name that starts with a hyphen. Though not common, filenames beginning with a hyphen do occasionally occur. (One way to create such a file is to use the command **cat > –fname**.) The **––** argument works with many other (but not all—it does not work with **more**) Solaris utilities. It is particularly useful with **rm** to remove a file whose name starts with a hyphen (**rm –– –fname**), including any that you create while experimenting with the **––** argument.

Stop Optional

if...then...elif

The format of the **if...then...elif** ^{sh}_{ksh} control structure is shown following.

> *if* **test-command**
> > *then*
> > > **commands**
> > *elif* **test-command**
> > > *then*
> > > > **commands**
> > > .
> > > .
> > > .
> > > .
> > > .
> > > *else*
> > > > **commands**
> *fi*

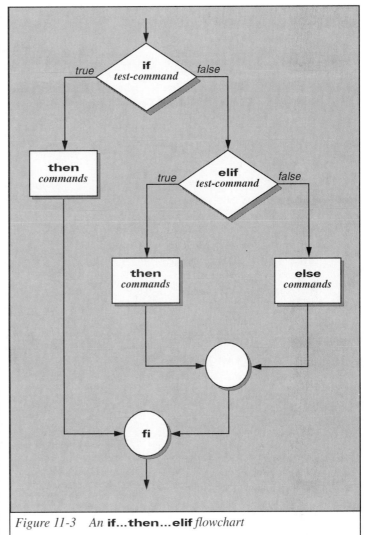

The **elif** statement combines the **else** statement and the **if** statement and allows you to construct a nested set of **if...then...else** structures (refer to Figure 11-3). The difference between the **else** statement and the **elif** statement is that each **else** statement must be paired with a **fi** statement, whereas multiple nested **elif** statements require only a single closing **fi** statement.

Figure 11-3   An **if...then...elif** *flowchart*

The following example shows an **if...then...elif** control structure. This shell script compares three words that the user enters. The first **if** statement uses the AND operator (**–a**) as an argument to **test**. The **test** builtin returns a *true* status only if the first and the second logical comparisons are true (that is, if **word1** matches **word2**, and **word2** matches **word3**). If **test** returns a *true* status, the program executes the command following the next **then** statement and passes control to the **fi** statement, and the script terminates.

```
$ cat if3
echo "word 1: \c"
read word1
echo "word 2: \c"
read word2
echo "word 3: \c"
read word3

if [ "$word1" = "$word2" -a "$word2" = "$word3" ]
   then
       echo "Match: words 1, 2, & 3"
   elif [ "$word1" = "$word2" ]
   then
       echo "Match: words 1 & 2"
   elif [ "$word1" = "$word3" ]
   then
       echo "Match: words 1 & 3"
   elif [ "$word2" = "$word3" ]
   then
       echo "Match: words 2 & 3"
   else
       echo "No match"
fi

$ if3
word 1: apple
word 2: orange
word 3: pear
No match
$ if3
word 1: apple
word 2: orange
word 3: apple
Match: words 1 & 3
$ if3
word 1: apple
word 2: apple
word 3: apple
Match: words 1, 2, & 3
```

If the three words are not the same, the structure passes control to the first **elif**, which begins a series of tests to see whether any pair of words is the same. As the nesting continues, if any one of the **if** statements is satisfied, the structure passes control to the next **then** statement and subsequently to the statement after **fi**. Each time an **elif** statement is not satisfied, the structure passes control to the next **elif** statement.

In the **if3** script the double quotation marks around the arguments to **echo** that contain ampersands (**&**) prevent the shell from interpreting them as special characters.

Start Optional

The following script, **links**, demonstrates the **if...then** and **if...then...elif** control structures. This script finds links to its first argument, a filename. If you provide a name of a directory as the second argument, **links** searches for links in that directory and all subdirectories. If you do not specify a directory, **links** searches the working directory and its subdirectories.

```sh
#!/bin/sh
# Identify links to a file
# Usage: links file [directory]

if [ $# -eq 0 -o $# -gt 2 ]; then
    echo "Usage: links file [directory]" 1>&2
    exit 1
fi
if [ -d "$1" ]; then
    echo "First argument cannot be a directory." 1>&2
    echo "Usage: links file [directory]" 1>&2
    exit 1
else
    file="$1"
fi
if [ $# -eq 1 ]; then
    directory="."
elif [ -d "$2" ]; then
    directory="$2"
else
    echo "Optional second argument must be a directory." 1>&2
    echo "Usage: links file [directory]" 1>&2
    exit 1
fi

# Check to make sure file exists and is a regular file:
if [ ! -f "$file" ]; then
    echo "links: $file not found or special file" 1>&2
    exit 1
fi
# Check link count on file
set -- `ls -l "$file"`
linkcnt=$2
if [ "$linkcnt" -eq 1 ]; then
    echo "links: no other links to $file" 1>&2
    exit 0
fi

# Get the inode of the given file
set `ls -i "$file"`
inode=$1

# Find and print the files with that inode number
echo "links: using find to search for links..." 1>&2
find "$directory" -local -inum $inode -print
```

In the following example Alex uses **links** while he is in his home directory to search for links to a file named **letter** in the working directory. The **links** script reports **/home/alex/letter** and **/home/jenny/draft** are links to the same file.

```
$ links letter /home
links: using find to search for links...
/home/alex/letter
/home/jenny/draft
```

In addition to the **if...then...elif** control structure, **links** introduces other features that are commonly used in shell programs. The following discussion describes **links** section by section.

The first line of the **links** script specifies the shell to execute the script. Refer to "#!: Specify a Shell" on page 363.

```
#!/bin/sh
```

In this chapter the **#!** notation appears in more complex examples only. It ensures that the proper shell executes the script, even if the user is currently running a different shell. It also works correctly if invoked within another shell script.

The second and third lines of **links** are comments—the shell ignores the text that follows pound signs up to the next NEWLINE character. These comments in **links** briefly identify what the file does and how to use it.

```
# Identify links to a file
# Usage: links file [directory]
```

The first **if** statement in **links** tests to see whether **links** was called with zero arguments or more than two arguments.

```
if [ $# -eq 0 -o $# -gt 2 ]; then
   echo "Usage: links file [directory]" 1>&2
   exit 1
fi
```

If either of these conditions is true, **links** sends a usage message to standard error and exits with a status of 1. The double quotation marks around the usage message prevent the shell from interpreting the square brackets as special characters. The square brackets in the usage message indicate to the user that the **directory** argument is optional.

The second **if** statement tests to see whether **$1** is a directory (the **–d** argument to **test** returns a *true* value if the file exists and is a directory).

```
if [ -d "$1" ]; then
   echo "First argument cannot be a directory." 1>&2
   echo "Usage: links file [directory]" 1>&2
   exit 1
else
   file="$1"
fi
```

If it is a directory, **links** presents a usage message and exits. If it is not a directory, **links** saves the value of **$1** in the **file** variable because later in the script **set** resets the command-line arguments. If the value of **$1** is not saved before the **set** command is issued, that value is lost.

The next section of **links** is an **if...then...elif** statement.

```
if [ $# -eq 1 ]; then
   directory="."
elif [ -d "$2" ]; then
   directory="$2"
else
      echo "Optional second argument must be a directory." 1>&2
      echo "Usage: links file [directory]" 1>&2
      exit 1
fi
```

The first *test-command* determines whether the user specified a single argument on the command line. If the *test-command* returns 0 (*true*), the user-created variable named **directory** is assigned the value of the working directory (**.**). If the *test-command* returns a *false* value, the **elif** statement is executed. The **elif** statement tests to see whether the second argument is a directory. If it is a directory, the **directory** variable is set equal to the second command-line argument, **$2**. If **$2** is not a directory, **links** sends a usage message to standard error and exits with a status of 1.

The next **if** statement in **links** tests to see if **$file** does not exist. This is an important inquiry because it would be pointless for **links** to spend time looking for links to a nonexistent file.

The **test** builtin with the three arguments **!**, **–f**, and **$file** evaluates to *true* if the file **$file** does *not* exist.

```
[ ! -f "$file"]
```

The **!** operator preceding the **–f** argument to **test** negates its result, yielding *false* if the file **$file** *does* exist and is a regular file.[1]

Next **links** uses **set** and **ls –l** to check the number of links **$file** has.

```
# Check link count on file
set -- `ls -l "$file"`
linkcnt=$2
if [ "$linkcnt" -eq 1 ]; then
    echo "links: no other links to $file" 1>&2
    exit 0
fi
```

The **set** builtin ᶜˢʰ uses command substitution to set the positional parameters to the output of **ls –l**. In the output of **ls –l**, the second field is the link count, so the user-created variable **linkcnt** is set equal to **$2**. The **--** is used with **set** to prevent it from interpreting as an option the first argument **ls –l** produces (the first argument is the access permissions for the file, and it is likely to begin with **–**). The **if** statement checks whether **$linkcnt** is equal to 1; if it is, **links** displays a message and exits. Although this message is not strictly speaking an error message, it is redirected to standard error. The way **links** has been written, all informational mes-

---

1. It would be preferable to use the **–e test** primitive here, but that is not available in the version of **test** built into **sh**. It is available from **/bin/sh** and the **test** builtin within **ksh**.

sages are sent to standard error. Only the final product of **links**, the pathnames of links to the specified file, is sent to standard output, so you can redirect the output as you please.

If the link count is greater than one, **links** goes on to identify the inode (page 619) for **$file**. As explained in Chapter 4 (page 95), comparing the inodes associated with filenames is a good way to determine whether the filenames are links to the same file. The **links** script uses **set** again to set the positional parameters to the output of **ls –i**. The first argument to **set** is the inode number for the file, so the user-created variable named **inode** is set to the value of **$1**.

```
# Get the inode of the given file
set `ls -i "$file"`
inode=$1
```

Finally **links** uses the **find** utility to search for filenames having inodes that match **$inode**.

```
# Find and print the files with that inode number
echo "links: using find to search for links..." 1>&2
find "$directory" -local -inum $inode -print
```

The **find** utility searches for files that meet the criteria specified by its arguments, beginning its search with the directory specified by its first argument (**$directory** in this case) and searching all subdirectories. The last three arguments to **find** specify that the filenames of files having inodes matching **$inode** should be sent to standard output. Because files in different filesystems may have the same inode number (yet they are not linked), **$directory** should be in the same filesystem as **$file** for accurate results. The **–local** argument to **find** prevents the search of subdirectories on other filesystems. Refer to page 92 and page 619 for more information about filesystems and links. Refer to page 753 in Part III for more information on **find**.

The **echo** above the **find** command in **links**, which tells the user that **find** is running, is included because **find** frequently takes a long time to run. Because **links** does not include a final exit statement, the exit status of **links** is that of the last command it runs, **find**.

▲▲▲ Debugging Shell Scripts

When you are writing a script like **links**, it is easy to make mistakes. While you are debugging a script, you can use the shell's **–x** option ^sh ^csh ^ksh, which causes the shell to display each command before it runs the command. This trace of a script's execution can give you a lot of information about where the bugs are.

Suppose that Alex wants to run **links** as in the previous example, while displaying each command before it is executed. He can either set the **–x** option for the current shell (**set –x**) so that all scripts display commands as they are run, or he can use the **–x** option to affect only the script he is currently executing.

```
$ sh -x links letter /home
```

Each command that the script executes is preceded by a plus sign (**+**) so that you can distinguish the output of the trace from any output that your script produces. You can also set the **–x** option of the shell running the script by putting the following **set** command at the top of the script.

```
set -x
```

You can turn off the debug option with a plus sign.

```
set +x
```

for...in

The **for...in** $_{ksh}^{sh}$ structure has the following format:

for loop-index in *argument-list*
do
    commands
done

This structure (Figure 11-4) assigns the value of the first argument in the *argument-list* to the *loop-index* and executes the *commands* between the **do** and **done** statements. The **do** and **done** statements mark the beginning and end of the **for** loop.

After the structure passes control to the **done** statement, it assigns the value of the second argument in the *argument-list* to the *loop-index* and repeats the *commands*. The structure repeats the *commands* between the **do** and **done** statements—once for each of the arguments in the *argument-list*. When the structure exhausts the *argument-list*, it passes control to the **done** statement, and the shell continues with the next command in the script.

The following **for...in** structure assigns apples to the user-created variable **fruit** and then displays the value of **fruit**, which is apples. Next it assigns oranges to **fruit** and repeats the process. When it exhausts the argument list, the structure transfers control to the statement following **done**, which displays a message.

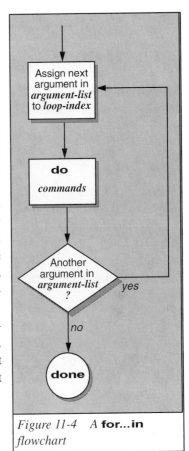

*Figure 11-4   A **for...in** flowchart*

```
$ cat fruit
for fruit in apples oranges pears bananas
do
   echo "$fruit"
done
echo "Task complete."

$ fruit
apples
oranges
pears
bananas
Task complete.
```

The next script lists the directory files in the working directory. This is done by looping over all files, using **test** to determine which are directory files.

```
$ cat dirfiles
for i in *
do
   if [ -d "$i" ]
       then
           echo "$i"
   fi
done
```

The ambiguous file reference character * stands for all files (except invisible files) in the working directory. Prior to executing the **for** loop, the shell expands the * and uses the resulting list to assign successive values to the index variable **i**.

for

The **for** $^{sh}_{ksh}$ control structure has the following format:

> *for loop-index*
> *do*
> > **commands**
>
> *done*

In the **for** structure the ***loop-index*** automatically takes on the value of each of the command-line arguments, one at a time. It performs a sequence of commands (usually) involving each argument in turn.

The following shell script shows a **for** structure displaying each of the command-line arguments. The first line of the shell script, **for arg**, implies **for arg in "$@"**, where the shell expands **"$@"** into a quoted list of command-line arguments. The balance of the script corresponds to the **for...in** structure.

```
$ cat for_test
for arg
do
    echo "$arg"
done
$ for_test candy gum chocolate
candy
gum
chocolate
```

Start Optional

The following script, **whos**, demonstrates the usefulness of the implied **"$@"** in the **for** structure. You give **whos** one or more **id**s for users as arguments (for example a user's name or login name), and **whos** displays information about the users. The information **whos** displays is taken from the first and fifth fields in the **/etc/passwd** file. The first field always contains a user's login name, and the fifth field typically contains the user's name. You can use a login name as an argument to **whos** to identify the user's name or use a name as an argument to identify the login name. The **whos** script is similar to the **finger** utility, although **whos** provides less information.

```
$ cat whos
#!/bin/sh
# adapted from finger.sh by Lee Sailer
# UNIX/WORLD, III:11, p. 67, Fig. 2

if [ $# -eq 0 ]
    then
        echo "Usage: whos id..." 1>&2
        exit 1
fi
```

```
for i
do
   nawk -F: '{print $1, $5}' /etc/passwd |
   grep -i "$i"
done
```

In the following script **whos** identifies the user whose login is chas and the user whose name is Marilou Smith:

```
$ whos chas "Marilou Smith"
chas Charles Casey
msmith Marilou Smith
```

This **whos** script uses a **for** statement to loop through the command-line arguments. The implied use of "**$@**" in the **for** loop is particularly useful in this script because it causes the **for** loop to treat an argument containing a space as a single argument. In this example the user quotes Marilou Smith, which causes the shell to pass it to the script as a single argument. Then the implied "**$@**" in the **for** statement causes the shell to regenerate the quoted argument Marilou Smith so that it is again treated as a single argument.

For each command-line argument, **whos** searches for **id** in the **/etc/passwd** file. Inside the **for** loop **nawk** extracts the first (**$1**) and fifth (**$5**) fields from the lines in **/etc/passwd** (which contain the user's login name and information about the user, respectively). The **$1** and **$5** are arguments that the **nawk** command sets and uses; they are included within single quotation marks and are not interpreted at all by the shell. (Do not confuse them with the positional parameters that correspond to the command-line arguments.) The first and fifth fields are sent, via a pipe, to **grep**. The **grep** utility searches for **$i** (which has taken on the value of a command-line argument) in its input. The **–i** option causes **grep** to ignore case as it searches. It displays each line in its input that contains **$i**.

An interesting syntactical exception that the shells $_{ksh}^{sh}$ give the pipe symbol (|) is shown on the line with the **nawk** command. You do not have to quote a NEWLINE that immediately follows a pipe symbol (that is, a pipe symbol that is the last thing on a line) to keep the NEWLINE from executing a command. You can see this if you give the command **who** | and press RETURN. The shell $_{ksh}^{sh}$ displays a secondary prompt. If you then enter **sort** followed by another RETURN, you see a sorted **who** list. The pipe works even though a NEWLINE followed the pipe symbol.

Because the **whos** script gets its information from the **/etc/passwd** file, information it displays is only as informative and accurate as the information in **/etc/passwd**. See page 613 for more information about **/etc/passwd**. Refer to Part III for more information on **nawk** (page 820) and **grep** (page 777).

Stop Optional

while

The **while** control structure $_{ksh}^{sh}$ (Figure 11-5) has the following syntax:

> *while **test-command***
> *do*
> > *commands*
> *done*

As long as the *test-command* returns a *true* exit status, the structure continues to execute the series of *commands* delimited by the **do** and **done** statements. Before each loop through the *commands*, the structure executes the *test-command*. When the exit status of the *test-command* is *false*, the structure passes control to the **done** statement, and the shell continues with the next command in the script.

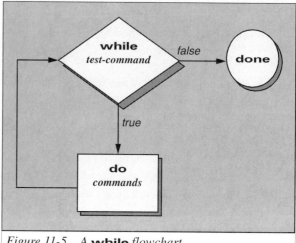

Figure 11-5   A **while** flowchart

The following shell script first initializes the **number** variable to a value of zero. The **test** builtin then determines if the value of **number** is less than 10. The script uses **test** with the **–lt** argument to perform a numerical test. You must use **–ne** (not equal), **–eq** (equal), **–gt** (greater than), **–ge** (greater than or equal), **–lt** (less than), or **–le** (less than or equal) for numerical comparisons, and **=** (equal) or **!=** (not equal) for string comparisons when you are working with **test**. The **test** builtin has an exit status of 0 (*true*) as long as **number** is less than 10. As long as **test** returns *true*, the structure executes the commands between the **do** and **done** statements.

```
$ cat count
#!/bin/sh
number=0
while [ "$number" -lt 10 ]
   do
       echo "$number\c"
       number=`expr $number + 1`
   done
echo
$ count
0123456789
$
```

The first command following **do** displays the string represented by **number**. The next command uses the **expr** utility to increment the value of **number** by one. Here **expr** converts its arguments to numbers, adds them, converts the result to characters, and echoes them to standard output. The backquotes cause the command that they enclose to be replaced by the output of the command (command substitution). This value is then assigned to the variable **number**. The first time through the loop, number has a value of zero, so **expr** converts the strings 0 and 1 to numbers, adds them, and converts the result back to a string (1). The shell then assigns this value to the variable **number**. The **done** statement closes the loop and returns control to the **while** statement to start the loop over again. The final **echo** causes **count** to send a NEWLINE character to standard output, so that the next prompt occurs in the leftmost column on the display (rather than immediately following 9).

Start Optional

The **spell** utility checks the words in a file against a dictionary of correctly spelled words. Input comes from a file named on the command line or from standard input. It displays each misspelled word on standard output. The following command produces a list of misspellings in the file **letter.txt**:

```
$ spell < letter.txt
```

The next shell script, **spell_check**, shows another use of a **while** structure. You can use **spell_check** to find the incorrect spellings in a file. It uses the **spell** utility to check your file against a system dictionary, but goes a step further: It enables you to specify your own list of correct words and removes these words from the output of **spell**. This script is useful for removing words that you use frequently, such as names and technical terms, that are not in a standard dictionary.

Although you can duplicate the functionality of the **spell_check** using **spell** with the + option (follow + with the name of a *personal dictionary* file), **spell_check** is included here for its instructive value.

The **spell_check** script requires two filename arguments: The first file contains your list of correctly spelled words, and the second file is the one you want to check. The first **if** statement verifies that the user specified two arguments, and the next two **if** statements verify that both arguments are readable files. (With the **–r** operator, **test** determines whether a file is readable, and the exclamation point negates the sense of the following operator.)

```
$ cat spell_check
#!/bin/sh
# remove correct spellings from spell output

if [ $# -ne 2 ]
    then
        echo "Usage: spell_check file1 file2" 1>&2
        echo "file1: list of correct spellings" 1>&2
        echo "file2: file to be checked" 1>&2
        exit 1
fi

if [ ! -r "$1" ]
    then
        echo "spell_check: $1 is not readable" 1>&2
        exit 1
fi

if [ ! -r "$2" ]
    then
        echo "spell_check: $2 is not readable" 1>&2
        exit 1
fi

spell < "$2" |
while read line
do
    if grep -v "^$line$" "$1" > /dev/null
        then
            echo $line
    fi
done
```

The **spell_check** script sends the output from **spell** through a pipe to standard input of a **while** structure, which reads one line at a time from standard input. The *test-command* (that is, **read line**) returns a *true* exit status as long as it receives a line from standard input. Inside the **while** loop an **if** statement[2] monitors the return value of **grep**, which determines whether the line that was read is in the user's list of correctly spelled words. The pattern that **grep** searches for (the value of **$line**) is preceded and followed by special characters that specify the beginning and end of a line (^ and $, respectively). These special characters are used so that **grep** finds a match only if the **$line** variable matches an entire line in the file of correctly spelled words. (Otherwise **grep** would match a string such as paul in the output of **spell** if the file of correctly spelled words contained the word paulson.) These special characters together with the value of the **$line** variable form a regular expression (page 953). The output of **grep** is redirected to **/dev/null** because the output is not needed, only the exit code is important (see "/dev/null" on page 113). The **if** statement checks the negated exit status of **grep** (the leading exclamation point negates, or changes the sense of the exit status— *true* becomes *false* and vice versa), which is 0 or *true* (*false* when negated) only if a matching line was found. If the exit status is *not* 0 or *false* (*true* when negated), the word was *not* in the file of correctly spelled words. The **echo** builtin sh csh ksh displays a list of words that are not in the file of correctly spelled words on standard output. Once the **read** builtin detects the EOF (end of file), it returns a *false* exit status, control is passed out of the **while** structure, and the script terminates.

Before you use **spell_check**, create a file of correct spellings containing words that you use frequently but that are not in a standard dictionary. For example if you work for a company named Blankenship and Klimowski, Attorneys, you would put Blankenship and Klimowski into the file. The following example shows how **spell_check** checks the spelling in a file named **memo** and removes Blankenship and Klimowski from the output list of incorrectly spelled words:

```
$ spell < memo
Blankenship
Klimowski
targat
hte
$ cat word_list
Blankenship
Klimowski
$ spell_check word_list memo
targat
hte
```

Refer to page 900 for more information on **spell**.

---

2. This **if** statement could also be written as:

```
if ! grep -qw "$line" "$1"
```

The **–q** option suppresses the output from **grep** so only an exit code is returned, and the **–w** option causes **grep** to match only a whole word.

Stop Optional

until

The **until** ^{sh}_{ksh} and **while** structures are very similar. They differ only in the sense of the test at the top of the loop. Figure 11-6 shows that **until** continues to loop *until* the ***test-command*** returns a *true* exit status. The **while** structure loops *while* the ***test-command*** continues to return a *true* or nonerror condition. The **until** structure is as follows:

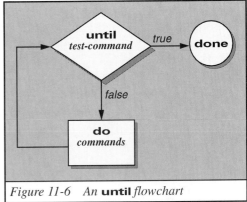

*Figure 11-6   An **until** flowchart*

> *until* ***test-command***
> *do*
> > ***commands***
> *done*

The following script demonstrates an **until** structure that includes **read**. When the user enters the correct string of characters, the ***test-command*** is satisfied, and the structure passes control out of the loop.

```
$ cat until1
secretname=jenny
name=noname
echo "Try to guess the secret name!"
echo
until [ "$name" = "$secretname" ]
do
   echo "Your guess: \c"
   read name
done
echo "Very good."
$ until1
Try to guess the secret name!

Your guess: helen
Your guess: barbara
Your guess: jenny
Very good
```

The following **locktty** script is similar to the **lock** command on Berkeley UNIX and the padlock icon on the CDE Front Panel. It prompts the user for a key (password), and then it uses an **until** control structure to "lock" the terminal. The **until** statement causes the system to ignore any characters typed at the keyboard until the user types in the original key on a line by itself, which unlocks the terminal. The **locktty** script can keep people from using your terminal while you are away from it for short periods of time. It saves you from having to log out if you are concerned about other users using your login.

```
$ cat locktty
#! /bin/sh
# adapted from lock.sh by Howard G. Port and
# Evelyn Siwakowsky
# UNIX/WORLD, III:4, p. 74, Fig. 3

trap '' 1 2 3 18
stty -echo
echo "Key: \c"
read key_1
echo
echo "Again: \c"
read key_2
echo
key_3=
if [ "$key_1" = "$key_2" ]
    then
        tput clear
        until [ "$key_3" = "$key_2" ]
        do
            read key_3
        done
    else
        echo "locktty: keys do not match" 1>&2
fi
stty echo
```

Forget Your Password?

If you forget your key (password), you will need to log in from another terminal and kill the process running **locktty**.

The **trap** builtin ^sh_ksh (page 425) at the beginning of the **locktty** script stops a user from being able to terminate the script by sending it a signal (for example by pressing the interrupt key, usually **DELETE** or **CONTROL-C**). Trapping signal 18 means that no one can use **CONTROL-Z** (job control, a stop from a tty) to defeat the lock. See the table on page 426 for a list of signals. The **stty –echo** command (page 902) causes the terminal not to display characters typed at the keyboard on the screen. This prevents the keys the user enters from appearing on the screen. After turning off echo, the script prompts the user for a key, reads the key into the user-created variable **key_1**, and then prompts the user to enter the same key again and saves it in the user-created variable **key_2**. The statement **key_3=** creates a variable with a **NULL** value. If **key_1** and **key_2** match, **locktty** clears the screen (with the **tput** command) and starts an **until** loop. The **until** loop keeps attempting to read from the terminal and assigning the input to the **key_3** variable. Once the user types in a string that matches one of the original keys (**key_2**), the **until** loop terminates, and **echo** is turned back on.

▲▲ break and continue

You can interrupt a **for, while,** or **until** loop with a **break** ^sh_ksh or **continue** ^sh_ksh statement. The **break** statement transfers control to the statement after the **done** statement, terminating execution of the loop. The **continue** command transfers control to the **done** statement, which continues execution of the loop.

The following script demonstrates the use of these two statements. The **for...in** structure loops through the values 1–10. The first **if** statement executes its commands when the value of the index is less than or equal to three (`$index -le 3`). The second **if** statement executes its commands when the value of the index is greater than or equal to 8 (`$index -ge 8`). In between the two **if**s, **echo** displays the value of the index. For all values up to and including 3, the first **if** displays `continue` and executes a **continue** statement that skips `echo $index` and the second **if** and continues with the next **for**. For the value of 8, the second **if** displays `break` and executes a **break** that exits from the **for** loop. The **echo** builtin displays the values of **index**.

```
$ cat brk
for index in 1 2 3 4 5 6 7 8 9 10
    do
        if [ $index -le 3 ] ; then
            echo "continue"
            continue
        fi
#
    echo $index
#
    if [ $index -ge 8 ] ; then
        echo "break"
        break
    fi
done

$ brk
continue
continue
continue
4
5
6
7
8
break
```

case

The **case** structure ^sh_ksh is

```
case test-string in
    pattern-1)
        commands-1
        ;;
    pattern-2)
        commands-2
        ;;
    pattern-3)
        commands-3
        ;;
    .
    .
    esac
```

Figure 11-7 shows that the **case** structure provides a multiple branch decision mechanism. The path that the structure takes depends on a match or lack of a match between the *test-string* and one of the *patterns*.

The following **case** structure uses the character that the user enters as the *test-string*. This value is represented by the variable **letter**. If the *test-string* has a value of A, the structure executes the command following the *pattern* A. The right parenthesis is part of the **case** control structure, not part of the *pattern*. If the *test-string* has a value of B or C, the structure executes the command following the matching *pattern*. The asterisk (✻) indicates *any string of characters* and serves as a catchall in case there is no match. If there is no *pattern* that matches the *test-string* and there is no catchall (✻) *pattern*, control passes to the command following the **esac** statement without the **case** structure taking any action. The second sample execution of **case1** shows the user entering a lowercase b. Because the *test-string* b does not match the uppercase B *pattern* (or any other *pattern* in the **case** statement), the program executes the commands following the catchall (✻) *pattern* and displays a message.

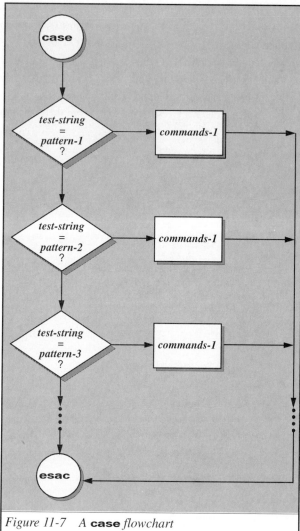

*Figure 11-7   A **case** flowchart*

```
$ cat case1
echo "Enter A, B, or C: \c"
read letter
case "$letter" in
  A)
      echo "You entered A"
      ;;
  B)
      echo "You entered B"
      ;;
  C)
      echo "You entered C"
      ;;
  ✻)
      echo "You did not enter A, B, or C"
      ;;
esac
```

```
$ case1
Enter A, B, or C: B
You entered B
$ case1
Enter A, B, or C: b
You did not enter A, B, or C
```

The *pattern* in the **case** structure is analogous to that of an ambiguous file reference. The *pattern* can include any of the special characters and strings shown in the following table.

Pattern	Matches
*	Matches any string of characters. Use it for the default case.
?	Matches any single character.
[...]	Defines a character class. Any characters enclosed within square brackets are tried, one at a time, in an attempt to match a single character. A hyphen between two characters specifies a range of characters.
|	Separates alternative choices that satisfy a particular branch of the **case** structure.

The next program is a variation of the previous one. This script accepts upper- and lowercase letters.

```
$ cat case2
echo "Enter A, B, or C: \c"
read letter
case "$letter" in
    a|A)
        echo "You entered A"
        ;;
    b|B)
        echo "You entered B"
        ;;
    c|C)
        echo "You entered C"
        ;;
    *)
        echo "You did not enter A, B, or C"
        ;;
esac
$ case2
Enter A, B, or C: b
You entered B
$
```

Start Optional

The following example shows how you can use the **case** structure to create a simple menu.[3] The **command_menu** script uses **echo** to present menu items and prompt the user for a selection. The **case** structure executes the appropriate utility, depending on the user's selection.

---

3. The Korn Shell has a menu control structure that automatically takes care of a lot of the work that this program does. See **select** on page 494.

```
$ cat command_menu
#!/bin/sh
# menu interface to simple commands

echo "\n        COMMAND MENU\n"
echo "  a.  Current date and time"
echo "  b.  Users currently logged in"
echo "  c.  Name of the working directory"
echo "  d.  Contents of the working directory\n"
echo "Enter a, b, c, or d:  \c"
read answer
echo
case "$answer" in
   a)
       date
       ;;
   b)
       who
       ;;
   c)
       pwd
       ;;
   d)
       ls
       ;;
   *)
       echo "There is no selection: $answer"
       ;;
esac

$ command_menu

        COMMAND MENU

  a.  Current date and time
  b.  Users currently logged in
  c.  Name of the working directory
  d.  Contents of the working directory

Enter a, b, c, or d: a

Mon Mar 30 16:33:07 PST 1998
```

The **echo** utility interprets the \n strings (toward the beginning of **command_menu**) as NEWLINE characters. If you do not include these characters, **echo** does not output the extra blank lines that make the menu easy to read. Following is a list of other backslash-quoted characters that **echo** interprets as useful printer control characters.

Quoted Character	Effect
\b	BACKSPACE
\c	Suppress trailing NEWLINE

Quoted Character	Effect
\f	FORMFEED
\n	NEWLINE
\r	RETURN
\t	Horizontal **TAB**
\v	Vertical **TAB**

You can also use the **case** control structure to take different actions in a script depending on how many arguments the script is called with. The script below, **safedit**, uses a **case** structure that branches based on the number of command-line arguments (**$#**). The **safedit** script saves a backup copy of a file you are editing with **vi**.

```
$ cat safedit
#!/bin/sh
# adapted from safedit.sh by Evan Kaminer
# UNIX/WORLD, IV:11, p. 129, Listing 2


PATH=/bin:/usr/bin
script=`basename $0`
case $# in

    0)
        vi
        exit 0
        ;;


    1)
        if [ ! -f "$1" ]
            then
                vi "$1"
                exit 0
            fi
        if [ ! -r "$1" -o ! -w "$1" ]
            then
                echo "$script: check permissions on $1" 1>&2
                exit 1
            else
                editfile=$1
            fi
```

```
            if [ ! -w "." ]
                then
                    echo "$script: backup cannot be " \
                        "created in the working directory" 1>&2
                    exit 1
                fi
            ;;
    *)
        echo "Usage: $script [file-to-edit]" 1>&2
        exit 1
        ;;
esac
tempfile=/tmp/$$.$script
cp $editfile $tempfile
if vi $editfile
    then
        mv $tempfile bak.`basename $editfile`
        echo "$script: backup file created"
    else
        mv $tempfile editerr
        echo "$script: edit error--copy of " \
            "original file is in editerr" 1>&2
fi
```

If you call **safedit** without any arguments, the **case** structure executes its first branch and calls **vi** without a filename argument. Because an existing file is not being edited, **safedit** does not create a backup file. (See the **:w** command on page 253 for an explanation of how to exit from **vi** when you have called it without a filename.) If the user calls **safedit** with one argument, **safedit** runs the commands in the second branch of the **case** structure and it verifies that the file specified by **$1** does not yet exist or is the name of a file for which the user has read and write permission. The **safedit** script also verifies that the user has write permission for the working directory. If the user calls **safedit** with more than one argument, the third branch of the **case** structure presents a usage message and exits with a status of 1.

In addition to the use of a **case** structure for branching based on the number of command-line arguments, the **safedit** script introduces several other features. First, at the beginning of the script, the **PATH** variable is set to search **/bin** and **/usr/bin**. This ensures that the commands executed by the script are standard utilities (which are kept in those directories). By setting **PATH** inside a script, you can avoid the problems that might occur if users have set up **PATH** to search their own directories first and have scripts or programs with the same names as utilities the script uses.

Second, the following line creates a variable named **script** and assigns the simple filename of the script to it:

```
script=`basename $0`
```

The **basename** utility sends the simple filename component of its argument to standard output, which is assigned to the **script** variable using command substitution. No matter which of the following commands the user calls the script with, the output of **basename** is the simple filename **safedit**:

```
$ /home/alex/bin/safedit memo
$ ./safedit memo
$ safedit memo
```

After the **script** variable is set, it is used in place of the filename of the script in usage and error messages. By using a variable that is derived from the command that invoked the script rather than a filename that is hardcoded (typed directly) into the script, you can create links to the script or rename it, and the usage and error messages will still provide accurate information.

A third significant feature of **safedit** is the use of the $$ variable in the name of a temporary file. The statement below the **esac** statement creates and assigns a value to the **tempfile** variable. This variable contains the name of a temporary file that is stored in the **/tmp** directory (as are many temporary files). The temporary filename begins with the PID number of the current shell and ends with the name of the script. The PID number is used because it ensures that the filename is unique, and **safedit** will not attempt to overwrite an existing file (as might happen if two people were using **safedit** at the same time and not using unique filenames). The name of the script is appended so that, should the file be left in **/tmp** for some reason, you can figure out where it came from. The PID is used in front of **$script** in the filename, rather than after it, because of the 14-character limit on filenames on some filesystems on older versions of UNIX. Current Solaris systems do not have this limitation. Because the PID is what ensures the uniqueness of the filename, it is placed first so that it cannot be truncated. (If the **$script** component is truncated, the filename is still unique.) For the same reason when a backup file is created inside the **if** control structure a few lines down in the script, the filename is composed of the string **bak.** followed by the name of the file being edited. On an older system if **bak** were used as a suffix rather than a prefix and the original filename was 14 characters, then **.bak** might be lost, and the original file would be overwritten. The **basename** utility extracts the simple filename of **$editfile** before it is prefixed with **bak.**.

Fourth, **safedit** uses an unusual *test-command* in the **if** structure: `vi $editfile`. The *test-command* calls **vi** to edit **$editfile**. When you finish editing the file and exit from **vi**, **vi** returns an exit code that is the basis for branching by the **if** control structure. If the editing session completed successfully, **vi** returns a 0, and the statements following the **then** statement are executed. If **vi** does not terminate normally (as would occur if the user used a **kill** command (page 785) from another terminal to kill the **vi** process), **vi** returns a nonzero exit status, and the script executes the statements following **else**.

Stop Optional

▲▲ The Here Document

A Here document sh4 csh ksh allows you to redirect input to a shell script from within the shell script itself. It is called a Here document because it is *here,* immediately accessible in the shell script, instead of *there,* perhaps in another file.

---

4. The name *Here document* is not used in the **man** pages for any of the shells. Search the **man** pages for << for more information.

The following script, **birthday**, contains a Here document. The two less than (<<) symbols in the first line indicate to the shell that a Here document follows. One or more characters that delimit the Here document follow the less than symbols—this example uses plus signs. Whereas the opening delimiter can occur adjacent to the less than symbols, the closing delimiter must occur on a line by itself. The shell sends everything between the two delimiters to the process as standard input. In the following example it is as though you had redirected standard input to **grep** from a file, except that the file is embedded in the shell script:

```
$ cat birthday
grep -i "$1" <<+
Alex      June 22
Barbara February 3
Darlene May 8
Helen     March 13
Jenny     January 23
Nancy     June 26
+
$ birthday Jenny
Jenny     January 23
$ birthday June
Alex      June 22
Nancy     June 26
```

When you run **birthday** it lists all the lines in the Here document that contain the argument you called it with. In the preceding example the first time **birthday** is run it displays Jenny's birthday, because it is called with an argument of **Jenny**. The second run displays all the birthdays in June.

Start Optional

The next script, **bundle**, includes a clever use of a Here document. The **bundle**[5] script is an elegant example of a script that creates a shell archive (or **shar**) file. The **bundle** program creates a file that is itself a shell script containing several other files as well as the code to recreate the original files.

Just as the shell does not treat special characters that occur in standard input of a shell script as special, the shell does not treat the special characters that occur between the delimiters in a Here document as special.

```
$ cat bundle
#!/bin/sh
# bundle:  group files into distribution package
```

---

5. Brian W. Kernighan and Rob Pike, *The Unix Programming Environment* (Englewood Cliffs, N.J.: Prentice Hall, 1984), 98. Reprinted with permission.

```
echo "# To unbundle, sh this file"
for i
do
    echo "echo $i 1>&2"
    echo "cat >$i <<'End of $i'"
    cat $i
    echo "End of $i"
done
```

As the following example shows, the output that **bundle** creates is a shell script, which is redirected to a file named **bothfiles**. It contains the contents of each file given as an argument to **bundle** (**file1** and **file2** in this case) inside a Here document. To extract the original files from **bothfiles**, the user simply runs it. Before each Here document is a **cat** command that causes the Here document to be written to a new file when **bothfiles** is run.

```
$ cat file1
This is a file.
It contains two lines.
$ cat file2
This is another file.
It contains
three lines.
$ bundle file1 file2 > bothfiles
$ cat bothfiles
# To unbundle, sh this file
echo file1 1>&2
cat >file1 <<'End of file1'
This is a file.
It contains two lines.
End of file1
echo file2 1>&2
cat >file2 <<'End of file2'
This is another file.
It contains
three lines.
End of file2
```

Following, **file1** and **file2** are removed before **bothfiles** is run. The **bothfiles** script echoes the names of the files it creates as it creates them. Finally the **ls** command shows that **bothfiles** has recreated **file1** and **file2**.

```
$ rm file1 file2
$ sh bothfiles
file1
file2
$ ls
bothfiles
file1
file2
```

▲ Expanding Null or Unset Variables

The expression **${name}** (or just **$name** if it is not ambiguous) expands to the value of the **name** variable (page 382). If **name** is null or not set, then **sh** and **ksh** expand **${name}** to a null string. The Bourne and Korn Shells provide the following alternatives to accepting the expanded null string as the value of the variable:

- Use a default value for the variable.
- Use a default value, and assign that value to the variable.
- Display an error.

You can choose one of these alternatives by using a modifier with the variable name.

▲▲ :–   Use a Default Value

The **:–** modifier `sh`/`ksh` uses a default value in place of a null or unset variable while allowing a nonnull variable to represent itself.

> *${name:–default}*

The shell interprets the **:–** as: "If *name* is null or unset, expand *default* and use the expanded value in place of *name,* else use *name*." The following command lists the contents of the directory named by the **LIT** variable; if **LIT** is null or unset, it lists the contents of **/home/alex/literature**.

```
ls ${LIT:-/home/alex/literature}
```

The default can itself have variable references that are expanded.

```
ls ${LIT:-$HOME/literature}
```

You can supply defaults for unset variables but leave null variables unchanged by omitting the colon:

```
ls ${LIT-$HOME/literature}
```

▲▲ :=   Assign a Default Value

The **:–** modifier `sh`/`ksh` does not change the value of a variable. In a script you may want to change the value of a null or unset variable to its default. You can do this with the **:=** modifier.

> *${name:=default}*

The shell expands the expression **${name:=default}** in the same manner as **${name:–default}** but also sets the value of *name* to the expanded value of *default*. When you omit the **:** from the **:=**, **sh** assigns values for unset variables but not for null ones. If your script contains a line such as the following and **LIT** is unset or null at the point where this line is executed, it is assigned the value **/home/alex/literature**:

```
ls ${LIT:=/home/alex/literature}
```

Shell scripts frequently start with the **:** (colon) builtin followed by this expansion modifier to set any variables that may be null or unset. The **:** builtin evaluates each token in the remainder of the command line but does not execute any commands. Without the leading **:** the shell evaluates and attempts to execute the "command" that results from the evaluation. The order of evaluation is such that if a variable is a command and you name that variable, it is executed. If it is not a valid command, the shell displays an error.

Use the following syntax to set a default for a null or unset variable (there is a **SPACE** following the colon):

: *${name:=default}*

If your script needs a directory for temporary files and uses the value of **TEMPDIR** for the name of this directory, the following line makes **TEMPDIR** default to **/tmp**:

```
: ${TEMPDIR:=/tmp}
```

▲▲ :?   Display an Error Message

Sometimes a script needs the value of a variable, and there is no reasonable default that you can supply at the time you write the script. In this case you can force the script to display an error message and terminate with an exit status of 1, if the variable is null or unset. The modifier for this purpose is **:?** $^{sh}_{ksh}$.

```
cd ${TESTDIR:?mesg}
```

If **TESTDIR** is null or unset, then the shell displays the expanded value of **mesg** on standard error and terminates the script. You must quote **mesg** if it contains blanks. If you omit **mesg**, then the default error message (`parameter not set`) is displayed. If you omit the **:**, then an error occurs only if the variable is unset; a null variable remains null. Interactive shells do not exit when you use **:?** .

Stop Optional

▲ Builtins

Commands that are built into a shell do not fork a new process when you execute them. The following sections discuss the **exec** and **trap** builtins and are followed by a table listing many of the shell builtins (page 428).

▲▲ exec: Execute a Command

The **exec** builtin $^{sh}_{csh\ ksh}$ has two primary purposes: To run a command without creating a new process and to redirect standard input, output, or error of a shell script from within the script.

When the shell executes a command that is not built into the shell, it typically creates a new process. The new process inherits environment (global or exported) variables from its parent but does not inherit variables that are not exported by the parent. Refer to "**export**: Make Variables Global" (page 368). In contrast **exec** executes a command in place of (overlays) the current process.

Insofar as **exec** runs a command in the environment of the original process, it is similar to the **.** (dot) command (page 375). However unlike the **.** command, which can run only scripts, **exec** can run both scripts and compiled programs. Also, whereas the **.** command returns control to the original script when it finishes running, **exec** does not. And finally whereas the **.** command gives the new program access to local variables, **exec** does not. The syntax of the **exec** builtin is

*exec **command arguments***

Because the shell does not create a new process when you run a command using **exec**, the command runs more quickly. However because **exec** does not return control to the original program, the **exec** builtin can be used only with the last command that you want to run in a script. The following script shows that control is not returned to the script:

```
$ cat exec_demo
who
exec date
echo This echo builtin is never executed.
$ exec_demo
jenny    pts/7    May 30  7:05 (bravo.tcorp.com)
hls      pts/1    May 30 06:59 (:0.0)
Sat May 30 08:20:51 PDT 1997
```

The next example is a modified version of the **out** script (page 398). It uses **exec** to execute the final command the script runs. Because the original **out** script runs either **cat** or **pg** and then terminates, the new version of **out** uses **exec** with both **cat** and **pg**.

```
$ cat out
if [ $# -eq 0 ]
   then
        echo "Usage: out [-v] filenames" 1>&2
        exit 1
fi
if [ "$1" = "-v" ]
   then
        shift
        exec pg "$@"
   else
        exec cat -- "$@"

fi
```

The second major use of **exec** is to redirect standard input, output, or error from within a script. After the following command in a script, all the input to the script is redirected to come from the file named **infile**:

```
exec < infile
```

Similarly the following command redirects standard output and error to **outfile** and **errfile**, respectively:

```
exec > outfile 2> errfile
```

When you use **exec** in this manner, the current process is not replaced with a new process, and **exec** can be followed by other commands in the script. When a script prompts the user for input, it is useful to redirect the output from within the script to go to the terminal. This redirection ensures that your prompt appears on the user's terminal, even if the user has redirected the output from the script. When redirecting the output in a script, you can use **/dev/tty** as a synonym for the user's terminal. The **/dev/tty** device is a pseudonym the system maintains for the terminal the user is logged in on. This pseudonym enables you to refer to the user's terminal without knowing which device it is. (The actual device appears in the second column of the output of **who**.) By redirecting the output from a script to **/dev/tty**, you ensure that prompts go to the user's terminal, regardless of which terminal the user is logged in on. The following command redirects the output from a script to the terminal the user is on:

```
exec > /dev/tty
```

Using **exec** to redirect the output to **/dev/tty** has one disadvantage—all subsequent output is redirected, unless you use **exec** again in the script. If you do not want to redirect the output from all subsequent commands in a script, you can redirect the individual **echo** commands that display prompts.

```
echo "Please enter your name: \c" > /dev/tty
```

You can also redirect the input to **read** to come from **/dev/tty**.

```
read name < /dev/tty
```

▲▲ trap: Catch a Signal

The **trap** builtin $_{\text{ksh}}^{\text{sh}}$ catches or traps a *signal*. A signal is a report to a process about a condition. Solaris uses signals to report interrupts generated by the user (for example by pressing the interrupt key) as well as bad system calls, broken pipes, illegal instructions, and other conditions. Using **trap**, you can direct the actions a script takes when it receives a signal.

This discussion covers the six signals that are significant when you work with shell scripts. The following table lists the signals, the signal numbers that systems often ascribe to them, and the conditions that usually generate each signal.

When a script traps a signal, it takes whatever action you specify. It can remove files or finish any other processing as needed, display a message, terminate execution immediately, or ignore the signal. If you do not use **trap** in a script, any of the six signals in the following table terminate the script while it is running in the foreground. Because you cannot trap the KILL signal, you can always use **kill -KILL** (or **kill –9**) to terminate a script (or any other process). Refer to page 785 in Part III for more information on **kill**. The format of **trap** is

> *trap ['commands'] [signal-numbers]*

The **trap** builtin does not require the single quotation marks shown above, but it is a good practice to use them. The single quotation marks cause shell variables within the *commands* to be expanded when the signal occurs, not when the shell evaluates the arguments to **trap**. Even if you do not use any shell variables in the *commands*, you need to enclose any command that takes arguments within either single or double quotation marks. Quoting the *commands* causes the shell to pass **trap** the entire command as a single argument.

Signal[a]			
Description	**Name**	**Number**	**Generating Condition**
Not a real signal		0	Exit because of exit command or reaching the end of the program (not an actual signal, but useful in **trap**).
Hang up	**SIGHUP**	1	Disconnect line.
Terminal interrupt	**SIGINT**	2	Press the interrupt key (usually CONTROL-C).
Quit	**SIGQUIT**	3	Press the quit key (usually CONTROL-SHIFT-l or CONTROL-SHIFT-\).
Kill	**SIGKILL**	9	The **kill** command with the **–9** option (cannot be trapped).
Software termination	**SIGTERM**	15	Default of the kill command.
Stop	**SIGTSTP**	24	Press the job-control stop key (usually CONTROL-Z).

a. Give the command **kill –l** for a list of signal names, or for a complete list of signal names and numbers, see **/usr/include/sys/signal.h**.

The *signal-numbers* are the numbers of the signals that **trap** catches. The *commands* part is optional. If it is not present, **trap** resets the trap to its initial condition, which is usually to exit from the script. If the *commands* part is present, the shell executes the *commands* when it catches one of the signals. After executing the *commands*, the shell resumes executing the script where it left off. If you want **trap** to prevent a script from exiting when it receives a signal but not to run any commands explicitly, you can use **trap** with a **null** (empty) builtin, as shown in the **locktty** script (page 412). The following command traps signal number 15, and the script continues:

```
trap '' 15
```

If you call **trap** without any arguments, the command displays a list of commands associated with each signal. The following script demonstrates the use of the **trap** builtin to trap signal number 2. It returns an exit status of 1.

```
$ cat inter
#!/bin/sh
trap 'echo PROGRAM INTERRUPTED; exit 1' 2
while true
do
   echo "Program running."
done

$ inter
Program running.
Program running.
Program running.
^CPROGRAM INTERRUPTED
$
```

The second line of **inter** sets up a trap for signal number 2. When the signal is caught, the shell executes the two commands between the single quotation marks in the **trap** command. The **echo** builtin displays the message PROGRAM INTERRUPTED. Then **exit** builtin csh/ksh/sh terminates this shell, and the parent shell displays a prompt. If **exit** were not there, the shell would return control to the **while** loop after displaying the message. The **while** loop repeats continuously until the script receives a signal, because the **true** utility always returns a *true* exit status. In place of **true** you can use the **null** builtin, which is written as a colon (**:**) and always returns a 0 or *true* status. The **while** statement would then be **while :** instead of **while true**.

The **trap** builtin frequently removes temporary files when a script is terminated prematurely, so the files are not left around, cluttering up the filesystem.

The following shell script, **addbanner**, uses two **trap**s to remove a temporary file when the script terminates normally or due to a hangup, software interrupt, quit, or software termination signal.

```
$ cat addbanner
#!/bin/sh
script=`basename $0`

if [ ! -r "$HOME/banner" ]
    then
        echo "$script: need readable $HOME/banner file" 1>&2
        exit 1
fi

trap 'exit 1' 1 2 3 15
trap 'rm /tmp/$$.$script 2> /dev/null' 0

for file
do
    if [ -r "$file" -a -w "$file" ]
        then
            cat $HOME/banner $file > /tmp/$$.$script
            cp /tmp/$$.$script $file
            echo "$script: banner added to $file" 1>&2
        else
            echo "$script: need read and write permission for $file" 1>&2
        fi
done
```

When called with one or more filename arguments, **addbanner** loops through the files, adding a header to the top of each. This script is useful when you use a standard format at the top of your documents, such as a standard layout for memos, or when you want to add a standard header to shell scripts. The header is kept in a file named **banner** in the user's home directory. The **HOME** variable contains the pathname of the user's home directory, so that **addbanner** can be used by several users without modification. If Alex had written the script with **/home/alex** in place of **$HOME** and then given the script to Jenny, either she would have had to change it or **addbanner** would have used Alex's **banner** file when Jenny ran it.

The first **trap** in **addbanner** causes it to exit with a status of 1 when it receives a hangup, software interrupt (terminal interrupt or quit signal), or software termination signal. The second **trap** uses a 0 in place of **signal-number**, which causes **trap** to execute its command argument *whenever* the script exits due to an **exit** command or due to reaching its end. Together these **trap**s remove a temporary file whether the script terminates either normally or prematurely. Standard error of the second **trap** is sent to **/dev/null** for cases in which **trap** attempts to remove a nonexistent temporary file. In those cases **rm** sends an error message to standard error. Because the standard error is redirected to **/dev/null**, the user does see the message.

▲▲ A Partial List of Builtins

A list of some of the shell builtins follows. Give the command **man shell_builtins** for a complete list.

Builtin	Action
:	**null** builtin (returns 0 or *true*) sh/csh/ksh (page 427).
.	Executes a program or shell script as part of the current process sh/ksh (page 375).
bg	Puts a job in the background jsh/csh/ksh (page 359).
break	Exits from **for, while,** or **until** loop sh/csh/ksh (page 412).
cd	Changes to another working directory sh/csh/ksh (page 79).
continue	Starts with next iteration of **for, while,** or **until** loop sh/csh/ksh (page 412).
echo	Displays arguments sh/csh/ksh (page 47).
eval	Scans and evaluates the command line sh/csh/ksh (page 431).
exec	Executes a program in place of the current process sh/csh/ksh (page 423).
exit	Exits from the current shell (usually the same as **CONTROL-D**) sh/csh/ksh (page 381).
export	Places the value of a variable in the calling environment (makes it global) sh/ksh (page 368).
fg	Brings a job into the foreground jsh/csh/ksh (page 358).
getopts	Parses arguments to a shell script sh/ksh (page 498).
jobs	Displays list of current jobs in the foreground and background jsh/csh/ksh (page 357).
kill	Sends a signal to a process or job sh/csh/ksh (page 785).
pwd	Prints the name of the working directory sh/ksh (page 79).
read	Reads a line from standard input sh/ksh (page 369).
readonly	Declares a variable to be readonly sh/ksh (page 367).
set	Sets shell flags or command-line argument variables; with no argument **set** lists all variables sh/csh/ksh (pages 378 and 454).
shift	Promotes each command-line argument sh/csh/ksh (page 377).
test	Compares arguments sh/ksh (pages 395, 918, and 456).

Builtin	Action
times	Displays total times for the current shell and its children ^{sh}_{ksh} (**times man** page).
trap	Traps a signal ^{sh}_{ksh} (page 425).
type	Displays how each argument would be interpreted as a command ^{sh}_{ksh} (page 395).
umask	File-creation mask ^{sh}_{csh ksh} (page 939).
unset	Removes a variable or function ^{sh}_{csh ksh} (page 367).
wait	Waits for a background process to terminate ^{sh}_{csh ksh} (page 475).

▲ Functions

A shell function ^{sh}_{ksh} is similar to a shell script: It stores a series of commands for execution at a later time. However because the shell stores a function in the computer's main memory instead of a file on disk, you can access it more quickly than you can access a script. Also, the shell preprocesses (parses) a function so that it starts up more quickly than a script. Finally the shell executes a shell function in the same shell that called it.

You can declare a shell function in your **.profile** file, in the script that uses it, or directly from the command line. You can remove functions with the **unset** builtin. The shell does not keep functions once you log out.

Removing Variables and Functions

If you have a shell variable and a function with the same name, then using **unset** removes the shell variable. If you then use **unset** again with the same name, it removes the function.

The syntax that declares a shell function is

function-name ( )
{
    commands
}

The *function-name* is the name you use to call the function. The *commands* comprise the list of commands the function executes when you call it. These *commands* can be anything you would include in a shell script, including calls to functions.

The next example shows how to create a simple function that displays the date, a header, and a list of the people who are using the system. This function runs the same commands as the **whoson** script described on page 349.

```
$ whoson ()
{
    date
    echo "Users Currently Logged On"
    who
}
$ whoson
Thu Jun 12 09:51:09 PDT 1997
Users Currently Logged On
hls       console      Jun 16 08:59   (:0)
alex      pts/4        Jun 16 09:33   (0.0)
jenny     pts/7        Jun 16 09:23   (bravo.tcorp.com)
```

If you want to have the **whoson** function always available without having to enter it each time you log in, put its definition in your **.profile** (page 81) file. After adding **whoson** to your **.profile** file, run **.profile** using the **.** (dot) command to put the changes into effect immediately.

```
$ cat .profile
TERM=vt100
export TERM
stty kill '^u'
whoson ()
{
    date
    echo "Users Currently Logged On"
    who
}
$ . .profile
```

You can specify arguments when you call a function. Within the function these arguments are available as positional parameters. The following example shows the **arg1** function entered from the keyboard. In this sequence the two greater than (**>**) signs are secondary shell prompts (**PS2**); do not enter them.

```
arg1() {
> echo "$1"
> }
$ arg1 my_first_arg
my_first_arg
```

Start Optional

The following function allows you to export variables using the syntax provided by the C Shell under the Bourne and Korn Shells. The **printenv** utility lists all environment variables and their values and verifies that **setenv** has worked correctly.

```
$ cat .profile
.
.
# setenv - keep csh users happy
setenv()
```

```
{
    if [ $# -eq 2 ]
        then
            eval $1=$2
            export $1
        else
            echo "Usage: setenv NAME VALUE" 1>&2
    fi
}
$ . .profile
$ setenv TCL_LIBRARY /usr/local/lib/tcl
$ set | grep TCL_LIBRARY
TCL_LIBRARY=/usr/local/lib/tcl
```

This function uses the **eval** builtin $\frac{sh}{csh}_{ksh}$ to force **sh** to scan the command **$1=$2** *twice*. Because **$1=$2** begins with a dollar sign (**$**), the shell treats the entire string as a single token—a command. With variable substitution performed, the command name becomes **TCL_LIBRARY=/usr/local/lib/tcl**, which results in an error. Using **eval**, a second scanning, which splits the string into the three desired tokens, is done and the correct assignment occurs.

Stop Optional

Summary

The shell is a programming language. Programs written in this language are called shell scripts, or just scripts. Shell scripts provide the decision and looping control structures present in high-level programming languages while allowing easy access to system utilities and user programs. Shell scripts can also use functions to modularize and simplify complex tasks.

The Bourne and Korn Shell control structures that use decisions to select alternatives are: **if...then**, **if...then...else**, and **if...then...elif**. The **case** control structure provides a multiway branch and can be used when you want to express alternatives using a simple pattern-matching syntax.

The **test** builtin can evaluate an expression in a shell script. The expression is often a comparison of two quantities or files, or an inquiry about the status of a file. As with all decisions within Solaris shell scripts, a *true* status is represented by the value zero, *false* by any nonzero value.

The looping control structures available in the Bourne and Korn Shells are: **for...in, for, until**, and **while**. These structures perform one or more tasks repetitively.

The **break** and **continue** control structures alter control within loops; **break** transfers control out of a loop, and **continue** transfers control immediately to the top of a loop.

The **trap** builtin $\frac{sh}{ksh}$ catches a signal sent by Solaris to the process running the script and allows you to specify actions to be taken upon receipt of one or more signals. The **trap** builtin might be used, for instance, to ignore the signal sent when the user presses the interrupt key.

The **exec** builtin $\frac{sh}{csh}_{ksh}$ executes a command without creating a new process. The new command overlays the current process, assuming the same environment and PID number of that process. This builtin executes user programs as well as other Solaris commands, when it is *not* necessary to return control to the calling process.

The Here document allows input to a command in a shell script to come from within the script itself.

A shell function is a series of commands that is parsed prior to its storage in main memory. Shell functions run faster than shell scripts and can be used repeatedly. A function can be defined on the command line, within a shell script, or, if you want the function definition to remain in effect across login sessions, you can define it in your **.profile** file. Like the functions of a programming language, a shell function is called by giving its name along with any arguments.

In addition to the use of control structures, builtins, functions, and the like, useful shell scripts generally employ Solaris utilities. The **find** utility, for instance, is commonplace in shell scripts that involve a search for files in the system hierarchy and can perform a vast range of tasks, from simple to very complex. A well-written shell script adheres to the use of standard techniques, such as specifying the shell to execute the script as the first line of the script, verifying the number and type of arguments, using a standard usage message to report command-line errors, and redirecting all informational messages to standard error.

Review Exercises

1. Rewrite the **journal** script of Chapter 10 (example 1, page 389) by adding commands to verify that the user has write permission for a file named **journal-file** in the user's home directory, if such a file exists. The script should take appropriate actions if **journal-file** exists and the user does not have write permission to the file. Verify that the modified script works.

2. The special parameter **$@** is referenced twice in the **out** script (page 398). Explain what would be different if the parameter **$*** were used in its place.

3. Write a filter that takes a list of files as input and outputs the basename (page 418) of each file in the list.

4. Write a function that takes a single filename as an argument and adds execute permission to the file for the user.

   a. When might such a function be useful?

   b. Revise the script so that it takes one or more filenames as arguments and adds execute permission for the user for each file argument.

   c. What can you do to make the function available every time you log in?

   d. What if, in addition to having the function available upon subsequent login sessions, you want to make the function available now in your current shell?

5. When might it be necessary or advisable to write a shell script instead of a shell function? Give as many reasons as you can think of.

6. Write a shell script that will display the names of all directory files, but no other types of files, in the working directory.

7. If your Solaris system runs the X Window System, open a small window on your screen and write a script to display the time in that window every 15 seconds. Read about the **date** utility (page 729) and

display the time using the **%r** field descriptor. Clear the window (using the **clear** command) each time before you display the time.

8. Using the **find** utility (page 753), perform the following steps.

   a. List all files in the working directory that have been modified within the last day.

   b. List all files on the system bigger than 1MB.

   c. Remove all files named **core** from the directory structure rooted at your home directory.

   d. List the inode numbers of all files in the working directory whose filenames end in **.c.**

   e. List all files on the root filesystem that have been modified in the last month.

9. Enter the following script named **savefiles** and give yourself execute permission to the file.

```
$ cat $HOME/bin/savefiles
#! /bin/sh
echo "Saving files in current directory in file savethem."
exec > savethem
for i in *
do
   echo "============================================================="
   echo "File: $i"
   echo "============================================================="
   cat "$i"
done
```

   a. What error message do you get when you execute this script? Rewrite the script so that the error does not occur, making sure the output still goes to **savethem**.

   b. What might be a problem with running this script twice in the same directory? Discuss a solution to this problem.

10. Write a short script that tells you whether the permissions for two files, whose names are given as arguments to the script, are identical. If the permissions for the two files are identical, output the common permission field. Otherwise output each filename followed by its permission field. (*Hint:* Try using the **cut** utility [page 727].)

11. Write a script that takes the name of a directory as an argument and searches the file hierarchy rooted at that directory for zero length files. Write the names of all zero length files to standard output. If there is no option on the command line, have the script delete the file after displaying its name, asking the user for confirmation, and receiving positive confirmation. A **–f** option on the command line indicates that the script should display the filename but not ask for confirmation before deleting the file.

Advanced Review Exercises

12. Write a function that takes a colon-separated list of items and outputs the items, one per line, to standard output (without the colons).

13. Generalize the function written in exercise 12 so that the character-separating list items is given as an argument to the function. If this argument is absent, the separator should default to a colon.

14. Write a function named **funload** that takes as its single argument the name of a file containing other functions. The purpose of **funload** is to make all functions in the named file available in the current shell (that is, **funload** loads the functions from the named file). To locate the file **funload** searches the colon-separated list of directories given by the environment variable **FUNPATH**. Assume that the format of **FUNPATH** is the same as **PATH** and that searching **FUNPATH** is similar to the shell's search of the **PATH** variable.

15. If your Solaris system runs X Windows, write a script that turns the root window a different color when the amount of free disk space in any filesystem reaches a certain threshold. (*Hint:* See **df** on page 736 in Part III.) Both the threshold and the color should be specified as arguments. Check disk usage every 30 minutes. Start the script executing when your X Windows session starts.

16. Enhance the **spell_check** script (page 409) to accept an optional third argument. If given, this argument specifies a list of words to be added to the output of **spell_check**. You can use a list of words like this to cull usages you do not want in your documents. For example if you decide you want to use disk rather than disc in your documents, you can add disc to the list of words, and **spell_check** will complain if you use disc in a document. Make sure that you include appropriate error checks and usage messages.

17. Rewrite **bundle** so that the script it creates takes an optional list of filenames as arguments. If one or more filenames are given on the command line, only those files should be recreated; otherwise all files in the shell archive should be recreated. For example suppose that all files with the filename extension **.c** are bundled into an archive named **srcshell** and you want to unbundle just the files **test1.c** and **test2.c**. The following command will unbundle just these two files:

```
$ sh srcshell test1.c test2.c
```

18. Using a single command line (pipes are all right) find all the unique shells in the **/etc/passwd** file, and

    a. print out two columns listing each shell followed by the username for every user who logs into that shell

    b. sort the columns by shell and then by username. (*Hint:* use **nawk**.)

The C Shell

The C Shell (**csh**) performs the same function as the Bourne Shell (**sh**), the Korn Shell (**ksh**), and other shells: It provides an interface between you and the Solaris operating system. It is an interactive command interpreter as well as a high-level programming language. Although you use only one shell at any given time, you should be able to switch back and forth comfortably between them as the need arises (for example you may run different shells in different windows). Because many of the concepts covered in Chapters 10 and 11 apply to **csh** as well as to **sh** and **ksh**, those chapters provide a good background for this chapter, as well as for shell use in general. This chapter highlights facets of **csh** that differ from those in **sh**, are absent from **sh** altogether, or are traditional **csh** features that have not taken a strong hold in **sh**.

The C Shell originated on Berkeley UNIX and is now included with Solaris; it comes with almost all UNIX systems. You can customize **csh** to make it more tolerant of mistakes and easier to use. By setting the proper shell variables, you can have **csh** warn you when you appear to be accidentally logging out or overwriting a file. Many popular features of the original C Shell are now shared by **sh, ksh**, and **csh**.

Although some of the functionality of **csh** is present in **sh** and **ksh**, there are differences in the syntax of some commands. For example the **csh** assignment statement has the following syntax:

*set **variable=value***

Having SPACEs on either side of the equal sign, though illegal in **sh**, is optional in **csh**. By convention shell variables in **csh** are generally named with lowercase letters, not uppercase (you can use either). If you reference an undeclared variable (one that has had no value assigned to it) **csh** will give you an error message, whereas **sh** and **ksh** will not. Finally the default **csh** prompt is the single % character, as you will see in the examples in this chapter.

Do Not Use csh as a Programming Language

If you have used UNIX and are comfortable with the C Shell, you may want to use **csh** as your login shell. The C Shell has a reputation as a poor programming language, and you might find **sh** or **ksh** easier to use for this purpose. If you are going to learn only one shell programming language, learn **sh**. The Bourne Shell is used throughout Solaris to program many system administration scripts including all of the scripts in **/etc/rc∗**.

▲ Shell Scripts

With **csh** you can execute files containing C Shell commands just as **sh** and **ksh** allow you to execute files containing Bourne and Korn Shell commands. The concepts of writing and executing scripts in the two shells are similar. However the methods of declaring and assigning values to variables and the syntax of control structures are different.

   You can run **sh**, **csh**, and **ksh** scripts while using any one of the shells as a command interpreter. There are several different methods for selecting the shell that runs a script. Refer to "#!: Specify a Shell" on page 363 for more information about ways to select a shell to run a script.

   If the first character of a shell script is a pound sign (#) and the following character is not an exclamation point (!), the C Shell executes the script under **csh**. If the first character is anything other than #, **csh** calls **sh** to execute the script.

Shell Game

When you are working with an interactive C Shell, if you run a script in which # is *not* the first character of the script and you call the script *directly* (without preceding its name with **csh**), **csh** calls **sh** to run the script. Things may look pretty strange. The example from "Reading User Input" on page 460 generates the following output. Although both examples are run from **csh**, the second one calls **csh** explicitly to run the script.

```
% cat user_in
echo -n "Enter input: "
set input_line = "$<"
echo $input_line
% user_in
-n Enter input:

% csh user_in
Enter input: here is some input
here is some input
```

echo: Getting Rid of the RETURN

The **csh echo** builtin uses a **–n** argument to get rid of a RETURN after **echo**, whereas the **sh** and **ksh echo** builtins use a trailing \c (see "read: Accept User Input" on page 369).

▲ Entering and Leaving the C Shell

You can execute **csh** by giving the command **csh**. If you are not sure which shell you are using, use the **ps** utility to find out. It shows whether you are running **csh**, **ksh**, **sh**, or possibly another shell. The **finger** command followed by your login name also displays the name of your login shell (which is stored in the **/etc/passwd** file). Tell your system administrator if you want to change your setup and login to the C Shell as a matter of course.

There are several ways to leave **csh**. The way you choose depends on two factors: Whether the shell variable **ignoreeof** csh is set and whether you are using the shell that you logged into (your login shell) or another shell that you created after you logged in. If you are not sure how to exit from **csh**, press CONTROL-D on a line by itself, with no leading SPACEs, just as you would to terminate standard input to another program. You will either exit or receive instructions on how to exit. If you have not set **ignoreeof** (page 464) and it has not been set for you in one of your startup files (see the next section), you can exit from any shell using CONTROL-D (the same procedure you use to exit from the Bourne and Korn Shells).

When **ignoreeof** is set CONTROL-D does not work. The **ignoreeof** variable causes the shell to display a message telling you how to exit. You can always exit from **csh** by giving an **exit** command. A **logout** command allows you to exit only from your login shell.

▲▲ Startup Files

When you log into the C Shell, it automatically executes a number of files. The first file is a system file named **/etc/.login**. This file contains systemwide configuration information such as your default **path**, checks for mail, and so on. After these files are executed, **csh** reads and executes the commands from the following files in your home directory:

.cshrc
Each time a **csh** process starts running, it executes this file (from your home directory). You can use the **.cshrc** file to establish variables and parameters that are local to a specific shell. Each time you create a new shell, **csh** reinitializes these variables for the new shell. In the following sample **.cshrc** file, the tildes (~) represent the pathname of your home directory. Refer to "~: Tilde Expansion" on page 448.

```
% cat ~/.cshrc
set noclobber
set dunique
set ignoreeof
set history=256
set path = (~/bin $path /usr/games)
alias h history
alias ll ls -l
```

This **.cshrc** file sets several shell variables, establishes two aliases (page 443), and adds two new directories to **$path**, one at the start of the list and one at the end.

.history
If **csh** is running as a login shell, after processing **.cshrc**, **csh** rebuilds the history list (next section) from the contents of the **.history** file (in your home directory—if it exists).

.login
If **csh** is running as a login shell, it next reads and executes the commands in **.login** in your home directory. This file should contain commands that you want to execute once, at the beginning of each session. You can use **setenv** (page 454) to declare environment variables here. You can also declare the type of terminal that you are using and set some terminal characteristics in your **.login** file. A sample follows:

```
% cat ~/.login
setenv history 20
setenv MAIL /usr/spool/mail/$user
if ( -z $DISPLAY ) then
    setenv TERM vt100
else
    setenv TERM xterm
endif
stty erase '^h' kill '^u' -lcase tab3
date '+Login on %A %B %d at %I:%M %p'
```

This file establishes the type of terminal that you are using by setting the **TERM** variable (the **if** statement [page 465] tries to figure out what value should be assigned to **TERM**). The sample **.login** then runs **stty** (page 902) to set terminal characteristics and **date** to display the time you logged on.

.logout   The shell runs this file (in your home directory) when you exit from your login shell. Following is a sample **.logout** file that uses **date** to display the time you logged out. The **sleep** command ensures that **echo** has time to display the message before the system logs you out. This is useful for dialup lines that may take some time to display the message.

```
% cat ~/.logout
date '+Logout on %A %B %d at %I:%M %p'
sleep 5
```

▲ History

The history mechanism maintains a list of recent command lines, also called *events.* It provides a shorthand for reexecuting any of the events in the list. The shorthand also enables you to execute variations of previous commands and to reuse arguments from them. The shorthand also makes it easy to replicate complicated commands and arguments that you used earlier in this login session or a previous one and to enter a series of commands that differ from one another in minor ways. The history list is also useful as a record of what you have done. It can be helpful when you want to keep a record of a procedure that involved a series of commands. The **history** builtin csh [1] displays your history list. If it does not, read on; you need to set some variables.

The value of the **history** variable csh determines the number of events preserved in the history list during a session. If you set the value of **history** too high, it can use too much memory. If it is unset, the shell saves only the most recent command.

---

1. A builtin is a command that is built into the shell. All builtins available in **sh** are also available in **jsh**. You can give the command **man shell_builtins** to see a complete list of **csh** (and other) builtins.

> ### history Can Help Track Down Mistakes
>
> When you have made a command-line mistake (not an error within a script or program), and you are not sure what you did wrong, you can look at the history list to review your recent commands. Sometimes this list can help you figure out what went wrong and how to fix things.

When you exit from the shell, the most recently executed commands are saved in the **~/.history** file. Next time you start the shell, this file initializes the history list. The value of the **savehist** variable csh determines the number of lines of history saved in **~/.history** (not necessarily the same as **history**). The **history** variable holds the number of events remembered during a session, **savehist** holds the number remembered between sessions.

The C Shell assigns a sequential *event number* to each command line. You can display this event number as part of the **csh** prompt (see "prompt" in the list on page 462). Examples in this section show numbered prompts when they help to illustrate the behavior of a command or group of commands.

Give the following command manually, or place it in your **.cshrc** startup file, to establish a history list of the 100 most recent events:

```
% set history = 100
```

The following command causes **csh** to save the 100 most recent events across login sessions:

```
% set savehist = 100
```

After you set **savehist**, you can log out and log in again, and the 100 most recent events from the previous login sessions appear in your history list. Set **savehist** in your **.cshrc** file if you want to maintain your event list from login to login.

Use the **history** builtin to display the events in your history list. The list of events is ordered with the oldest events at the top. The last event in the history list is the **history** command that displayed the list. The following history list includes a command to modify the **csh** prompt to display the history event number as well as the command number. To simplify the example **history** has been set to 10 and **savehist** to 20. (The event number is 20 greater than the command number because the list of events includes those events that were saved from the last login session—20 in this case.)

```
32 12 % history
   23   set prompt = "! % "
   24   ls -l
   25   cat temp
   26   rm temp
   27   vi memo
   28   lp memo
   29   vi memo
   30   lp memo
   31   rm memo
   32   history
```

As you run commands and your history list becomes longer, **history** produces a list that runs off the top of the screen. Use a pipe to send the output of **history** through **pg** (page 34) to browse through it or give the command **history 10** to look at your ten most recent commands.

▲▲ Reexecuting Events

You can reexecute any event in the history list. This feature can save you time, effort, and aggravation. Not having to reenter long command lines allows you to reexecute events more easily, quickly, and accurately than you could if you had to retype the entire command line. You can reference an event by:

1. its absolute event number

2. its number relative to the current event

3. the text it contains

All references to events begin with an exclamation point (!). One or more characters follow the exclamation point to specify an event.

▲▲ !!: Reexecute the Previous Event

You can always reexecute the previous event by giving the command !!. In the following example event 45 reexecutes event 44. This works whether or not your prompt displays an event number.

```
44 % ls -l text
-rw-rw-r--   1 alex      group          45 Apr 30 14:53 text
45 % !!
ls -l text
-rw-rw-r--   1 alex      group          45 Apr 30 14:53 text
```

As this example shows, when you use the history mechanism to reexecute an event, **csh** displays the command it is reexecuting.

▲▲ !*n*: Event Number

A number following an exclamation point refers to an event. If that event is in the history list, **csh** executes it. If it is not in the history list, the shell gives you an error message. A negative number following an exclamation point references an event relative to the current event. The command !–3 refers to the third preceding event. After you issue a command, the relative event number of a given event changes (event –3 becomes event –4). Both of the following commands reexecute event 44:

```
51 % !44
ls -l text
-rw-rw-r--   1 alex      group          45 Nov 30 14:53 text
52 % !-8
ls -l text
-rw-rw-r--   1 alex      group          45 Nov 30 14:53 text
```

▲▲ !*string*: Event Text

When a string of text follows an exclamation point, **csh** searches for and executes the most recent event that *began* with that string. If you enclose the string between question marks, **csh** executes the most recent event that *contained* that string. The final question mark is optional if a **RETURN** would immediately follow it.

```
68 % history
   59   ls -l text*
   60   tail text5
   61   cat text1 text5 > letter
   62   vi letter
   63   cat letter
   64   cat memo
   65   lp memo
   66   pine jenny
   67   ls -l
   68   history
69 % !l
ls -l
  .
  .
  .
70 % !lp
lp memo
request id is printer_1-1016 (1 file)
71 % !?letter?
cat letter
  .
  .
  .
```

▲▲ !*n*:*w*   Word within an Event

You can select any word or series of words from an event. The words are numbered starting with 0, representing the first word (usually the command) on the line, and continuing with 1, representing the first word following the command, through *n,* representing the last word on the line.

To specify a particular word from a previous event, follow the event designator (such as **!14**) with a colon and the number of the word in the previous event (for example use **!14:3** to specify the third word following the command from event 14). You can specify a range of words by separating two word designators with a hyphen. The first word following the command (word number 1) can be specified by a caret (**^**), and the last word by a dollar sign (**$**).

```
72 % echo apple grape orange pear
apple grape orange pear
73 % echo !72:2
echo grape
grape
74 % echo !72:^
echo apple
apple
75 % !72:0 !72:$
echo pear
pear
76 % echo !72:2-4
echo grape orange pear
grape orange pear
77 % !72:0-$
echo apple grape orange pear
apple grape orange pear
```

As the next example shows, **!$** refers to the last word of the previous event. You can use this shorthand to edit, for example, a file you just displayed with **cat**.

```
% cat report.718
.
.
.
% vi !$
vi report.718
.
.
.
```

If an event contains a single command, the word numbers correspond to the argument numbers. If an event contains more than one command, this correspondence is not true for commands after the first. Event 78, following, contains two commands separated by a semicolon so that the shell executes them sequentially. The semicolon is word number 5.

```
78 % !72 ; echo helen jenny barbara
echo apple grape orange pear ; echo helen jenny barbara
apple grape orange pear
helen jenny barbara
79 % echo !78:7
echo helen
helen
80 % echo !78:4-7
echo pear ; echo helen
pear
helen
```

▲▲ !!:s/*new*/*old*   Modify a Previous Event

On occasion you may want to change some aspect of an event you are reexecuting. Perhaps you entered a complex command line with a typo or incorrect pathname. Or you may want to specify a different argument in the reexecuted command. You can modify an event, or a word of an event, by following the event or word specifier with a colon and a modifier. The following example shows the substitute modifier correcting a typo in the previous event:

```
% car /home/jenny/memo.0507 /home/alex/letter.0507
car: Command not found
% !!:s/car/cat
cat /home/jenny/memo.0507 /home/alex/letter.0507
.
.
```

▲▲▲ ^*old*^*new*   Quick Substitution

The *quick substitution* is an abbreviated form of the substitute modifier. You can use it to reexecute the most recent event while changing some of the event text. The quick substitution character is the caret (^). For example this command

```
% ^old^new^
```

produces the same results as

```
% !!:s/old/new/
```

Thus substituting `cat` for `car` in the previous event could have been entered as

```
% ^car^cat
cat /home/jenny/memo.0507 /home/alex/letter.0507
.
.
.
```

As with other command-line substitutions, **csh** displays the command line as it appears after the substitution. You can leave off the final caret if it would be followed immediately by a **RETURN**.

The following table lists event modifiers and their effects.

Event Modifier	Effect
h	**head** Removes the last element of a pathname.
r	**root** Removes the filename extension.
e	**extension** Removes all but the filename extension.
t	**tail** Removes all elements of a pathname except the last.
p	**print** Does not execute the modified event, just prints it.
[g]s/*old*/*new*/	**substitute** Substitutes *new* for the first occurrence of *old*. With the **g** option, substitute all occurrences.[a]

a. The **s** modifier substitutes the *first* occurrence of the old string with the new one. Placing a **g** before the **s** (as in **gs**/*old*/*new*/) causes a global substitution, replacing *all* occurrences of the old string. The **/** is the delimiter in these examples; you can use any character that is not in either the old or the new string. The final delimiter is optional if a **RETURN** would immediately follow it. Like the **vi** Substitute command, the history mechanism replaces an ampersand (**&**) in the new string with the old string. The shell replaces a null old string (**s**//*new*/) with the previous old string or string within a command that you searched for with **?***string***?**.

Stop Optional

▲ Alias

The alias mechanism allows you to define new commands by letting you substitute any string for any command. The syntax of the **alias** builtin _{ksh} is

alias [name[=value]]

There should be no SPACEs around the equal sign. If *value* contains SPACEs or TABs, you must enclose *value* between quotation marks. The alias expansion feature is disabled for noninteractive shells (that is, shell scripts).

The *name* of the alias may not appear within the *value* of the alias, nor within the *value* of another alias that refers to the alias you are defining. You can nest aliases. To see a list of the current aliases, give the command **alias**. To view the alias for a particular name, use **alias** followed by the name and no value.

▲▲ Quotation Marks: Single versus Double

In the alias syntax use of either double or single quotation marks is significant. If you enclose *value* within double quotation marks, then any variables that appear in *value* are expanded when the alias is created. If you enclose *value* within single quotation marks, then variables are not expanded until the alias is used. The following example shows the difference:

```
% alias p1 "echo my prompt is $prompt"
% alias p2 'echo my prompt is $prompt'
% set prompt = ">>>>>>>>>>>>> "
>>>>>>>>>>>>> p1
my prompt is %
>>>>>>>>>>>>> p2
my prompt is >>>>>>>>>>>>>
```

▲▲ History Substitution in an Alias

You can substitute command-line arguments using the history mechanism, with a single exclamation point representing the input line containing the alias. Modifiers are the same as those used by **history** (page 438). The exclamation points are quoted in the following example so that the shell does not interpret them when building the aliases (which would produce incorrect results):

```
21% alias last echo \!:$
22% last this is just a test
test
23% alias fn2 echo \!:2:t
24% fn2 /home/jenny/test /home/alex/temp /home/barbara/new
temp
```

Event 21 defines an alias for **last** that displays the last argument. Event 23 defines an alias for **fn2** that displays the simple filename, or tail, of the second argument on the command line.

▲▲ Examples

You can use **alias** to create short names for commands that you use often. For example the following alias substitutes `ls -ltr` when you type **l**:

```
% alias l 'ls -ltr'
% l
total 41
-rw-r--r--  1 alex    group   30015 Mar  1 1994 flute.ps
```

```
-rw-r-----  1 alex    group     3089 Feb 11 1995 XTerm.ad
-rw-r--r--  1 alex    group      641 Apr  1 1995 fixtax.icn
-rw-r--r--  1 alex    group      484 Apr  9 1995 maptax.icn
drwxrwxr-x  2 alex    group     1024 Aug  9 17:41 Tiger/
drwxrwxr-x  2 alex    group     1024 Sep 10 11:32 testdir/
-rwxr-xr-x  1 alex    group      485 Oct 21 08:03 floor*
drwxrwxr-x  2 alex    group     1024 Oct 27 20:19 Test_Emacs/
```

Another common use of the **alias** mechanism is to protect yourself from mistakes. The following example substitutes the interactive version of **rm** when you give the command **zap**. (The **–i** option causes **rm** to ask you to verify each file that would be deleted, to protect you from accidentally deleting the wrong file.)

```
% alias zap 'rm -i'
% zap f*
rm: remove `fixtax.icn'? n
rm: remove `flute.ps'? n
rm: remove `floor'? n
```

In the next example **alias** causes **csh** to substitute ls −l every time you give an **ll** command and ls −F when you use **ls**. The **–F** option causes **ls** to print a slash (/) at the end of directory names and an asterisk (∗) at the end of the names of executable files.

```
% ls
Test_Emacs XTerm.ad  flute.ps  testdir
Tiger      fixtax.icn maptax.icn
% alias ls 'ls -F'
% alias ll 'ls -l'
% ll
total 41
drwxrwxr-x  2 alex    group     1024 Oct 27 20:19 Test_Emacs/
drwxrwxr-x  2 alex    group     1024 Aug 9 1997 Tiger/
-rw-r-----  1 alex    group     3089 Feb 11 08:03 XTerm.ad
-rw-r--r--  1 alex    group      641 Apr 1 08:03 fixtax.icn
-rw-r--r--  1 alex    group    30015 Mar 1 09:35 flute.ps
-rwxr-xr-x  1 alex    group      485 Oct 21 11:07 floor*
-rw-r--r--  1 alex    group      484 Apr 9 1997 maptax.icn
drwxrwxr-x  2 alex    group     1024 Sep 10 11:32 testdir/
```

In this example the string that replaces the alias **ll**, ls −l, itself contains an alias, **ls**. When the shell replaces an alias with its value, it looks at the first word of the replacement string to see if it is an alias. In the example just given, because the replacement string contains the alias **ls**, a second substitution occurs to produce the final command **ls –F –l**. (To avoid a *recursive plunge*, the ls in the replacement text, although an alias, is not expanded a second time.)

The **alias** builtin csh/ksh, when given a single alias without the **=** *value* field, responds by displaying the value of the alias. The **alias** builtin reports nothing if an alias has not been defined.

```
% alias ll
ls -l
% alias ls
ls -F
%alias wx
%
```

You can avoid alias substitution by preceding the aliased command with a backslash (\).

```
% \ls
Test_Emacs XTerm.ad  flute.ps  maptax.icn
Tiger      fixtax.icn floor     testdir
```

Because the replacement of an alias name with the alias value does not change the rest of the command line, any arguments are still received by the command that gets executed.

```
% ll f*
-rw-r--r--  1 alex   group      641 Apr  1 1995 fixtax.icn
-rw-r--r--  1 alex   group    30015 Mar  1 1994 flute.ps
-rwxr-xr-x  1 alex   group      485 Oct 21 08:03 floor*
```

When you give the **alias** builtin without any arguments, the shell displays a list of all the defined aliases.

```
% alias
alias ll='ls -l'
alias l='ls -ltr'
alias ls='ls -F'
alias zap='rm -i'
```

You can remove an alias with the **unalias** builtin csh/ksh. When the **zap** alias is removed, it is no longer displayed with the **alias** builtin, and its subsequent use results in an error message.

```
% unalias zap
% alias
ll ls -l
l ls -ltr
ls ls -F
% zap maptax.icn
zap: Command not found
```

▲ Command-Line Expansion

Command-line expansion is the transformation the shell makes to the command line before it passes it to the program that is being called. It is also the process that each line of a shell script undergoes as it is executed. You can use any of the shells without knowing much about command-line expansion, but you can make much better use of what they have to offer with an understanding of this topic.

Some types of expansion are present in some or all of the shells. Some are specific to a single shell. Refer to "Command-Line Expansion" on page 381 for an introduction to command-line expansion in the Bourne Shell, and see "Command Processing" on page 517 for information on the Korn Shell. The following sections review several types of command-line expansion you may be familiar with and introduce some new ones that are used by the C Shell. These sections also discuss the order in which the shell performs the different expansions and provide some examples.

Although **csh** provides history (page 438) and alias (page 443) expansion, they are not included in the following discussion because they are available only in interactive shells and, therefore, cannot be used in shell scripts.

When the shell processes a command, it does not execute the command immediately. One of the first things the shell does is to *parse* (isolate strings of characters in) the command line into tokens or words. The shell then proceeds to scan each token for the appearance of special characters and patterns that instruct the shell to take certain actions. These actions often involve substituting one word or words for another. When the shell parses the following command line, it breaks it into three tokens: cp, ~/letter, and ..

```
% cp ~/letter .
```

After separating tokens and before executing the command, the shell scans the tokens and performs *command-line expansion.* You have seen many examples of command-line expansion in this and previous chapters; a frequent one is the substitution of a list of actual filenames for an ambiguous file reference that includes any of the characters *, ?, [, and].

▲▲ {}: Brace Expansion

Brace expansion csh originated in the C Shell. It provides a convenient way to specify filenames when pathname expansion does not apply. Although brace expansion is almost always used to specify filenames, the mechanism can be used to generate arbitrary strings; the shell does not attempt to match the brace notation with a list of the names of existing files. The following example illustrates the way that brace expansion works:

```
% echo chap_{one,two,three}.txt
chap_one.txt chap_two.txt chap_three.txt
```

The shell expands the comma-separated strings inside the braces into a **SPACE**-separated list of strings. Each string from the list is prepended with the string chap_, called the *preamble,* and appended with the string .txt, called the *postamble.* Both preamble and postamble are optional, and the left-to-right order of the strings within the braces is preserved in the expansion. For the shell to treat the left and right braces specially and for brace expansion to occur, there must be at least one comma inside the braces and no unquoted whitespace characters. Brace expansions may be nested.

Brace expansion can be useful when there is a long preamble or postamble. The following copies the four files **main.c, f1.c, f2.c,** and **tmp.c,** located in the **/usr/local/src/C** directory, to the working directory:

```
% cp /usr/local/src/C/{main,f1,f2,tmp}.c .
```

Another use for brace expansion is to create directories with related names. Because the directories do not already exist, pathname expansion does not work in this case:

```
% ls -l
total 3
-rw-rw-r-- 1 alex    group      14 Jan 22 08:54 file1
-rw-rw-r-- 1 alex    group      14 Jan 22 08:54 file2
-rw-rw-r-- 1 alex    group      14 Jan 22 08:55 file3
% mkdir version{A,B,C,D,E}
% ls -l
total 8
```

```
-rw-rw-r--  1 alex    group       14 Jan 22 08:54 file1
-rw-rw-r--  1 alex    group       14 Jan 22 08:54 file2
-rw-rw-r--  1 alex    group       14 Jan 22 08:55 file3
drwxrwxr-x  2 alex    group     1024 Jan 25 13:27 versionA
drwxrwxr-x  2 alex    group     1024 Jan 25 13:27 versionB
drwxrwxr-x  2 alex    group     1024 Jan 25 13:27 versionC
drwxrwxr-x  2 alex    group     1024 Jan 25 13:27 versionD
drwxrwxr-x  2 alex    group     1024 Jan 25 13:27 versionE
```

If ambiguous file reference notation had been used to specify the directories instead of the notation above, there would be a very different (and undesired) result.

```
% ls -l
total 3
-rw-rw-r--  1 alex    group       14 Jan 22 08:54 file1
-rw-rw-r--  1 alex    group       14 Jan 22 08:54 file2
-rw-rw-r--  1 alex    group       14 Jan 22 08:55 file3
% mkdir version[A-E]
% ls -l
total 4
-rw-rw-r--  1 alex    group       14 Jan 22 08:54 file1
-rw-rw-r--  1 alex    group       14 Jan 22 08:54 file2
-rw-rw-r--  1 alex    group       14 Jan 22 08:55 file3
drwxrwxr-x  2 alex    group     1024 Jan 25 13:38 version[A-E]
```

Because the shell found no filenames matching version[A-E], it passed that string to **mkdir**, which created a directory with that name.

▲▲ ~: Tilde Expansion

Chapter 4 showed a shorthand notation to specify your home directory or the home directory of another user (page 87). This section provides a more detailed explanation of this notation, which is called a *tilde expansion*.

When the shell ᶜˢʰₖₛₕ scans the tokens in the previous example, it finds that one begins with a tilde (~), a special character when it appears at the start of a token. When the shell sees the tilde, it looks at the following string of characters, up to the first slash (/), or to the end of the word if there is no slash, as a possible login name. If this possible login name is null (that is, if the tilde appeared as a word by itself or if it was immediately followed by a slash), the shell substitutes the value of the **HOME** variable for the tilde. Or you can say that the shell expands the tilde into the value of **HOME**. The following example demonstrates this substitution or expansion. The last command copies the file named **letter** from Alex's home directory to the working directory.

```
% echo $HOME
/home/alex
% echo ~
/home/alex
% echo ~/letter
/home/alex/letter
% cp ~/letter .
```

If there is a string of characters and they form a valid login name, the shell substitutes the path of the home directory associated with that login name for the tilde and name. If it is not null and not a valid login name, the shell does not make any substitution.

```
% echo ~jenny
/home/jenny
% echo ~root
/root
% echo ~xx
~xx
```

▲▲ $n: Parameter Expansion

When a single digit follows a dollar sign ($), the shell _{csh} substitutes the value of the positional parameter corresponding to the integer for the token. This is called *parameter expansion.* The **$0** parameter refers to the name of the file that the current program was read from. A simple example follows:

```
$ cat paramexpan
echo "Name of the calling program is: " $0
echo "The third command line parameter (after the program name) is: $3

$ paramexpan apple orange banana pear grape
Name of the calling program is:  paramexpan
The third command line parameter (after the program name) is: banana
```

▲▲ $NAME: Variable Expansion

Another type of expansion, *variable expansion,* results when the shell _{csh} processes a token consisting of a dollar sign ($) followed by a variable name, as in **$VARIABLE**. The shell replaces the token with the value of the variable, whether user-defined or keyword.

There are many examples of parameter and variable expansion in this chapter. These expansions are suppressed when the token beginning with dollar sign ($) is enclosed in single quotation marks or is preceded with a backslash (\). However double quotation marks permit parameter and variable expansion to take place while suppressing other types of expansion. Double quotation marks override an enclosed backslash and cause the variable to be expanded (and the backslash to appear as itself). See page 382 for some examples.

▲▲ `cmd` Command Substitution

The process of command substitution (page 371) makes it possible to use standard output of a command in a shell script. The shell _{csh} performs command substitution, another type of command-line expansion, after it has identified the tokens on the command. The pattern the shell recognizes in this case is a token of the form[2]

`  command `

---

2. The Korn Shell adds another syntax, see page 521.

This notation instructs the shell to replace the token with standard output of ***command***. To use standard output of ***command***, the shell must first run ***command*** successfully.

▲▲ Job Control

There is not much difference between job control in **jsh** (page 357) and **csh**, and none between **jsh** and **ksh**. You can move commands between the foreground and background, suspend jobs temporarily, and get a list of the current jobs. The percent (%) character references a job when followed by a job number or a string prefix that uniquely identifies the job. You will see a minor difference between **jsh** and **csh** when you run a multiple-process command line in the background. Whereas **csh** displays the numbers for all the processes belonging to a job, **jsh** (and **ksh**) displays only the PID number of the last background process in each job.

```
% csh
% find . -print | sort | lp & grep -l alex /tmp/* > alexfiles &
[1] 18839 18840   18841
[2] 18876
request id is printer_1-1017 (standard input)

% jsh
$ find . -print | sort | lp & grep -l alex /tmp/* > alexfiles &
[1] 18901
[2] 18926
request id is printer_1-1018 (standard input)
```

▲ Directory Stack Manipulation

Using the C Shell, you can store a list of directories you are working with, enabling you to move easily among them. The list is referred to as a *stack*. You can think of it as a stack of dinner plates, where you typically add plates to and remove plates from the top of the stack (a first in last out, or filo stack).

▲▲ dirs: Display the Contents of the Stack

The **dirs** builtin csh displays the contents of the directory stack. If you call **dirs** when the directory stack is empty, it just displays the name of the working directory.

```
53 % dirs
~/literature
```

The **dirs** builtin uses a tilde (~) to represent the name of the user's home directory. The examples in the next several sections assume that you are referring to the directory structure that is shown in Figure 12-1.

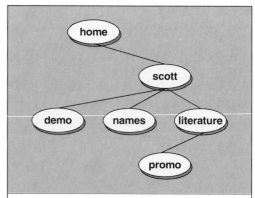

Figure 12-1   The directory structure in the examples

▲▲ pushd: Push a Directory onto the Stack

To change directories and, at the same time, add a new directory to the top of the stack, use the **pushd** (push directory) builtin `csh`. The **pushd** builtin also displays the contents of the stack. The following example is illustrated in Figure 12-2:

```
54 % pushd ../demo
~/demo ~/literature
55 % pwd
/home/scott/demo
56 % pushd ../names
~/names ~/demo ~/literature
57 % pwd
/home/scott/names
58 %
```

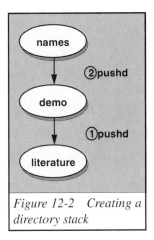

Figure 12-2   Creating a directory stack

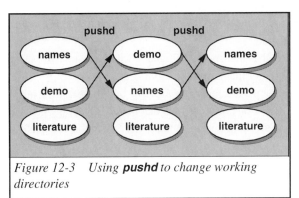

*Figure 12-3   Using **pushd** to change working directories*

When you use **pushd** without an argument, it swaps the top two directories on the stack and makes the new top directory (which was the second directory) the new working directory. This action is shown in Figure 12-3.

```
58 > pushd
~/demo ~/names ~/literature
59 > pwd
/home/scott/demo
```

Using **pushd** in this way you can easily move back and forth between two directories. To access another directory in the stack, call **pushd** with a numeric argument preceded by a plus sign. The directories in the stack are numbered starting with the top directory, which is number 0. The following **pushd** command changes the working directory to **literature** and moves it to the top of the stack:

```
60 > pushd +2
~/literature ~/demo ~/names
61 > pwd
/home/scott/literature
```

▲▲ popd: Remove a Directory from the Stack

To remove a directory from the stack, use the **popd** (pop directory) builtin `csh`. As Figure 12-4 shows, without an argument **popd** removes the top directory from the stack and changes the working directory to the new top directory.

*Figure 12-4   Using **popd** to remove a directory from the stack*

```
% popd
~/demo ~/names
% pwd
/home/scott/demo
```

To remove a directory other than the top one from the stack, use **popd** with a numeric argument preceded by a plus sign. If you remove a directory other than directory number 0 on the stack, this command does not change the working directory.

```
% popd +1
~/demo
% pwd
/home/scott/demo
```

▲▲ ✳ ? []: Filename Substitution

The shells csh/sh/ksh expand the characters ✳, ?, and [] in a pathname (page 118). Some shells csh/ksh expand command-line arguments that start with a tilde (~) into filenames with the ~ standing for the user's home directory or the home directory of the user whose name follows the tilde.

Brace expansion csh, like tilde expansion, is regarded as an aspect of filename substitution. This is true even though brace expansion can generate strings that are not the names of actual files.

The process of using patterns to match filenames is referred to as *globbing* csh/ksh, and the pattern itself is called a *globbing pattern*. If **csh** is unable to produce a list of one or more files that match a globbing pattern, it reports an error (unless the pattern contains a brace). If **ksh** cannot produce the list, it passes the unexpanded pattern to the command that will execute the command line.

Setting the **noglob** shell variable csh/ksh suppresses filename substitution, including both tilde and brace interpretation.

▲ Redirecting Standard Error

The Bourne and Korn Shells use a different syntax to combine and redirect standard output and standard error (page 355) than does the C Shell, which uses a greater than (>) symbol followed by an ampersand (**&**). The following examples, like the **sh** example (page 355), reference the file **x**, which does not exist, and the file **y**, which contains a single line:

```
% cat x
cat: No such file or directory
% cat y
This is y.
% cat x y >& hold
% cat hold
cat: Cannot open x
This is y.
```

Unlike both **sh** and **ksh**, **csh** does not provide a simple way to redirect standard error separately from standard output. There is a workaround that frequently provides a reasonable solution. With an argument of

y, **cat** sends a string to standard output, whereas an argument of **x** causes **cat** to send an error message to standard error. A subshell runs **cat** with both arguments and redirects standard output to a file named **outfile**. Error output is not touched by the subshell and is sent to the parent shell where both it and standard output are combined and sent to **errfile**. Because standard output has already been redirected, **errfile** contains only output sent to standard error.

```
% (cat x y > outfile) >& errfile
% cat outfile
This is y.
% cat errfile
cat: Cannot open x
```

It is useful to combine and redirect output when you want to run a slow command in the background and do not want its output cluttering up your terminal screen. For example because the **find** utility often takes a while to complete, it is a good idea to run it in the background.

The next command finds all the files in the filesystem hierarchy that are named **bibliography**. It runs in the background and sends its output to a file named **findout**. Because the **find** utility sends to standard error a report of directories that you do not have permission to search, you have a record in the **findout** file of any files named **bibliography** that are found, as well as a record of the directories that could not be searched.

```
% find / -name bibliography -print >& findout &
```

In this example if you did not combine standard error with standard output, the error messages would appear on your screen (and **findout** would contain only the list of files that were found).

While you are running a command in the background that has its output redirected to a file, you can look at the output by using **tail** with the **–f** option. The **–f** option causes **tail** to display new lines as they are written to the file.

```
% tail -f findout
```

To terminate the **tail** command, press the interrupt key (usually **CONTROL-C**). Refer to Part III for more information on **find** (page 753) and **tail** (page 909).

▲ Filename Completion

The C Shell can help you complete a filename[3] after you specify the first few letters. Filename completion is similar to filename generation, but the goal of filename completion is always to select a single file. Together, they make it practical to use long, descriptive filenames.

---

3. The Korn Shell also has filename completion, but it works differently than C Shell implementation. See "Pathname Completion" and "Pathname Expansion" on pages 512 and 513.

> ### Set **filec** for Filename Completion to Work
>
> You must set the **filec** variable in order for filename completion to work. It does not matter what you set it to:
>
> ```
> set filec xxx
> ```

To use **csh** filename completion when you are typing in a filename on the command line, type in a few letters of the name to identify the file in the directory and then press **CONTROL-D**; **csh** displays a list of all the files in the working directory that start with those characters. Pressing **ESCAPE** displays the longest unambiguous filename in the working directory that starts with the letters you entered. Sometimes this filename will be the one you were looking for. Both choices leave the cursor on the command line so you can finish typing. The following example shows the user typing the command **cat trig1A** and pressing **ESCAPE**. Because these letters uniquely identified the file, the shell fills in the rest of the filename:

```
42 % cat trig1A → ESCAPE → cat trig1A.302488
```

If two or more filenames match the prefix that you have typed, **csh** cannot complete the filename without more information from you. The C Shell attempts to maximize the length of the prefix by adding characters, if possible.

```
43 % ls h*
help.hist    help.text    help.trig01
44 % cat h → CONTROL-D
help.hist help.text help.trig01
44 % cat h (waits for more input)
```

You can fill in enough characters to resolve the ambiguity and then press **ESCAPE**.

In either case **csh** redraws the command line you have typed so that you can disambiguate the filename (and press **ESCAPE**) or finish typing the filename.

▲ Variables

While **csh** stores variable values as strings, you can work with these variables as numbers. Expressions in **csh** can use arithmetic, logical, and conditional operators. The **@** builtin can also evaluate arithmetic expressions but can only work with integers.

This section uses the term *numeric variable* to describe a string variable that contains a number that **csh** uses in arithmetic or logical-arithmetic computations. However no true numeric variables exist in **csh**.

A **csh** variable name consists of 1 to 20 characters, which can be letters, digits, and underscores (_) except that the first character cannot be a digit.

▲▲ Variable Substitution

Three builtins declare, display, and assign values to variables: **set** csh, **@** csh, and **setenv** csh. The **set** and **setenv** builtins both assume nonnumeric string variables. The **@** builtin works only with numeric variables. Both **set** and **@** declare local variables. The **setenv** builtin declares a variable *and* places it in the calling environment of all child processes. Using **setenv** is similar to assigning a value to a variable and then using **export** in the Bourne Shell. See "export: Make Variables Global" on page 368 for a discussion of local and environment variables.

Once the value—or merely the existence—of a variable has been established, **csh** substitutes the value of that variable when it sees the variable on a command line or in a shell script. Like **sh** and **ksh**, **csh** recognizes a word that begins with a dollar sign as a variable. If you quote the dollar sign by preceding it with a backslash (**\$**), the shell does not perform the substitution. When a variable is within double quotation marks, the substitution occurs even if you quote the dollar sign. If the variable is within single quotation marks, the substitution does not occur, regardless of whether you quote the dollar sign.

▲▲ String Variables

The C Shell treats string variables similarly to the way the Bourne and Korn Shells do. The major difference is in their declaration and assignment: **csh** uses an explicit command, **set** (or **setenv**), to declare and/or assign a value to a string variable.

```
% set name = fred
% echo $name
fred
% set
argv     ()
cwd      /home/alex
home     /home/alex
name     fred
path     (/usr/bin .)
prompt   %
shell    /bin/csh
status   0
term     vt100
user     alex
```

The first line above declares the variable **name** and assigns the string fred to it. (Unlike **sh** and **ksh**, **csh** allows SPACEs around the equal sign.) The next line displays this value. When you give a **set** command without any arguments, it displays a list of all the local shell variables and their values. When you give a **set** command with only the name of a variable and no value, it sets the value of the variable to a null string. Refer to the first two lines below. The next two lines show that the **unset** builtin removes a variable from the list of declared variables.

```
4 % set name
5 % echo $name
6 % unset name
7 % set
argv     ()
cwd      /home/alex
home     /home/alex
path     (/usr/bin .)
prompt   %
shell    /bin/csh
status   0
term     vt100
user     alex
```

When using **setenv** instead of **set**, the variable name is separated from the string being assigned to it by one or more SPACEs, and *no* equal sign.

```
% setenv SCRDIR /usr/local/src
% echo $SCRDIR
/usr/local/src
```

If you use **setenv** with no arguments, it displays a list of the environment variables—variables that are passed to any child processes of the shell. By convention environment variables are given uppercase names.

As with **set**, giving **setenv** a variable name without a value causes **setenv** to set the value of the variable to a null string. Although you can use **unset** to remove environment and local variables, **unsetenv** can remove *only* environment variables.

▲▲ Arrays of String Variables

Before you can access individual elements of an array csh, you must declare the entire array by assigning a value to each element of the array. The list of values must be enclosed in parentheses and separated by SPACEs.

```
 8 % set colors = (red green blue orange yellow)
 9 % echo $colors
red green blue orange yellow
10 % echo $colors[3]
blue
11 % echo $colors[2-4]
green blue orange
12 % set shapes = ('' '' '' '' '')
13 % echo $shapes
14 % set shapes[4] = square
15 % echo $shapes[4]
square
```

Event 8 declares the array of string variables named **colors** to have five elements and assigns values to each of these elements. If you do not know the values of the elements at the time you declare an array, you can declare an array containing the necessary number of null elements (event 12).

You can reference an entire array by preceding its name with a dollar sign (event 9). A number in square brackets following a reference to the array refers to an element of the array (events 10, 14, and 15). Two numbers in square brackets, separated by a hyphen, refer to two or more adjacent elements of the array (event 11). Refer to "Special Variable Forms" on page 460 for more information on arrays.

▲▲ Numeric Variables

The **@** builtin assigns a value to a numeric variable. You can declare single numeric variables with **@**, just as you can use **set** to declare nonnumeric variables. However if you give **@** a nonnumeric argument, it displays an error message. An **@** command without any arguments gives you a list of all shell variables, as the **set** command with no arguments does.

Many of the expressions that the **@** builtin can evaluate and the operators it recognizes are derived from the C programming language. The following is the format of a declaration or assignment using **@**. The SPACE after the **@** is required.

@ *variable-name operator expression*

The *variable-name* is the name of the variable that you are assigning a value to. The *operator* is one of the C assignment operators: =, +=, −=, *=, /=, or %=. (See page 824 for an explanation of these operators.) The *expression* is an arithmetic expression that can include most C operators; refer to "Expressions," following. You can use parentheses within the expression for clarity or to change the order of evaluation. Parentheses must surround parts of the expression that contain any of the following characters: <, >, **&**, or I.

Do Not Use a $ When Assigning a Value to a Variable

As with the other shells, variables having a value assigned to them (those on the left of the operator) must not be preceded by a dollar sign ($).

▲▲▲ Expressions

An expression can be composed of constants, variables, and the operators from the following table (listed in order of decreasing precedence). There is also a group of expressions that involve files rather than numeric variables or strings. These expressions are described on page 465.

Operator	Function
Parentheses	
()	Change the order of evaluation
Unary Operators	
−	Unary minus
~	One's complement
!	Logical negation
++	Postfix increment
−−	Postfix decrement
Arithmetic Operators	
%	Remainder
/	Divide
*	Multiply
−	Subtract
+	Add
Shift Operators	
>>	Right shift
<<	Left shift

Operator	Function
Relational Operators	
>	Greater than
<	Less than
>=	Greater than or equal to
<=	Less than or equal to
!=	Not equal to (compare strings)
==	Equal to (compare strings)
Bitwise Operators	
&	AND
^	Exclusive OR
|	Inclusive OR
Logical Operators	
&&	AND
||	OR

Expressions follow these rules:

1. The shell evaluates a missing or null argument as 0.

2. All results are decimal numbers.

3. Except for != and ==, the operators act on numeric arguments.

4. You must separate each element of an expression from adjacent elements by a **SPACE**, unless the adjacent element is an **&**, |, <, >, (, or).

Following are some examples that use **@**:

```
216 % @ count = 0
217 % echo $count
0
218 % @ count = ( 10 + 4 ) / 2
219 % echo $count
7
220 % @ result = ( $count < 5 )
221 % echo $result
0
222 % @ count += 5
223 % echo $count
12
224 % @ count++
225 % echo $count
13
```

Event 216 declares the variable **count** and assigns a value of 0 to it. Event 218 shows the result of an arithmetic operation being assigned to a variable. Event 220 uses **@** to assign the result of a logical operation involving a constant and a variable to **result**. The value of the operation is *false* (= 0) because the variable **count** is not less than 5. Event 222 is a compressed form of the following assignment statement:

```
% @ count = ( $count + 5 )
```

Event 224 uses a postfix operator to increment **count** by 1.

You can use the postfix increment (**++**) and decrement (**−−**) operators only in expressions containing a single variable name, as shown in the following example:

```
% @ count = 0
% @ count++
% echo $count
1
% @ next = $count++
@: Badly formed number
```

Unlike the C programming language, expressions in **csh** cannot use prefix increment and decrement operators.

▲▲▲ Arrays of Numeric Variables

You must use the **set** builtin to declare an array of numeric variables before you can use **@** to assign values to the elements of the array. The **set** builtin can assign any values to the elements of a numeric array, including zeros, other numbers, and null strings.

Assigning a value to an element of a numeric array is similar to assigning a value to a simple numeric variable. The only difference is that you must specify the element, or index, of the array. The format is

@ *variable-name[index] operator expression*

The *index* specifies the element of the array that is being addressed. The first element has an index of 1. The *index* must be either a numeric constant or a variable. It cannot be an expression. In the preceding syntax the square brackets around *index* are part of the syntax and do not indicate that *index* is optional. If you specify an *index* that is too large for the array you declared with **set**, **csh** displays @: Subscript out of range.

```
226 % set ages = (0 0 0 0 0)
227 % @ ages[2] = 15
228 % @ ages[3] = ($ages[2] + 4)
229 % echo $ages[3]
19
230 % echo $ages
0 15 19 0 0
231 % set index = 3
232 % echo $ages[$index]
19
233 % echo $ages[6]
Subscript out of range
```

Elements of a numeric array behave as though they were simple numeric variables. The difference is that you must use **set** to declare a numeric array. Event 226 above declares an array with five elements, each having a value of 0. Events 227 and 228 assign values to elements of the array, and event 229 displays the value of one of the elements. Event 230 displays all the elements of the array, 232 specifies an element by using a variable, and 233 demonstrates the out-of-range error message.

▲▲ Braces

As with **sh** and **ksh**, **csh** allows you to use braces to distinguish a variable from surrounding text without the use of a separator. For more information see "Braces" on page 382.

▲▲ Special Variable Forms

The special variable with the following syntax has the value of the number of elements in the ***variable-name*** array:

> *$#variable-name*

You can determine whether a variable has been set by looking at the value of the variable with the following syntax:

> *$?variable-name*

This variable has a value of 1 if ***variable-name*** has been set. Otherwise it has a value of 0.

```
% set days = (mon tues wed thurs fri)
% echo $#days
5
% echo $?days
1
% unset days
% echo $?days
0
```

▲▲▲ Reading User Input

Inside **csh** scripts you can use the **set** builtin csh to read a line from the terminal and assign it to a variable. The following portion of a shell script prompts the user and reads a line of input into the variable **input_line**:

```
echo -n "Enter input: "
set input_line = "$<"
```

The value of the shell variable **$<** is a line from standard input. The quotation marks around it are necessary to keep the shell from assigning only the first word of the line of input to the variable **input_line**.

▲▲ Shell Variables

This section lists some of the C Shell variables that are set by the shell, inherited by the shell from the environment, or set by the user and used by the shell. The section is divided into two parts: The first contains variables that take on significant values (for example the PID number of a background process). The second part lists variables that act as switches—*on* if they are declared, *off* if they are not.

Many of these variables are most often set from within one of **csh**'s two startup files: **.login** or **.cshrc** (page 437).

▲▲▲ Shell Variables That Take on Values

argv
csh This shell array variable contains the command-line arguments (also called positional parameters) from the command that invoked the shell. This array is indexed starting at 1, so **argv[1]** contains the first command-line argument. You can change any element of this array. Use **argv[∗]** to reference all the arguments together. You can abbreviate references to **argv** as **$∗** (short for **$argv[∗]**) and **$***n*** (short for **$argv[*n*]**). Refer to "Positional Parameters" on page 375, but note that **sh** does not use the **argv** form, only the abbreviated form. Use **$0** to reference the name of the calling program.

$#argv *or* **$#**
csh The shell sets this variable to the number of elements in the **argv** array. Refer to "Special Variable Forms" on page 460.

cdpath
csh The **cdpath** variable affects the operation of **cd** in the same way the Bourne and Korn Shells' **CDPATH** sh/ksh variable does (page 374). It takes on an array of absolute pathnames (see **path**, following) and is usually set in the **.login** file with a command line such as the following:

```
set cdpath = (/home/scott /home/scott/letters)
```

When you call **cd** with a simple filename, it searches the working directory for a subdirectory with that name. If one is not found, **cd** searches the directories listed in **cdpath** for the file.

cwd
csh The shell sets this variable to the name of the working directory. When you access a directory through a symbolic link, **csh** sets **cwd** to the name of the symbolic link. Refer to "Symbolic Links" on page 96.

filec
csh When set, enables filename completion. Refer to "Filename Completion" on page 453.

history
csh Controls the size of your history list. As a rule of thumb, its value should be kept around 100. Refer to "History" on page 438.

home *and* **HOME**
The **HOME** environment variable sh/csh is part of the shell's environment when it starts and is used to initialize the **home** local variable csh. **HOME** has the value of the pathname of the home directory of the user. The **cd** builtin refers to this variable, as does the filename expansion of ~. Refer to "~: Tilde Expansion" on page 448.

path *and* **PATH**
The **PATH** environment variable sh/ksh is part of the shell's environment when the shell is started. The **path** local variable csh is an array set by the shell from the value

of **PATH** (or to a default value if **PATH** is not set). The directories in the **path** array are searched for executable commands. If **path** is empty or unset, then you can execute commands only by giving their full pathname. You can set your **path** variable directly with a command such as the following:

```
% set path = ( /usr/bin /bin /usr/local/bin /usr/bin/X11 ~/bin . )
```

Refer to "PATH: Where to Find Programs" on page 372.

prompt   csh Holds the primary prompt, similar to the **PS1** variable sh ksh (page 373); if it is not set, the prompt is **%**, or **#** for **root** (Superuser). The shell expands an exclamation point in the prompt string to the current event number. (Just as the shell replaces a variable in a shell script with its value, the shell replaces an exclamation point in the prompt string with the current event number.) The following is a typical line from a **.cshrc** file that sets the value of **prompt**:

```
set prompt = '! % '
```

savehist   csh Specifies the number of commands that are saved from the history list when you log out. These events are saved in a file named **.history** in your home directory. The shell uses them as the initial history list when you log in again, causing your history list to continue across login sessions.

shell   csh Contains the pathname of the shell you are using.

status   csh Contains the exit status returned by the last command.

time   csh This variable provides two functions: (a) automatic timing of commands using the **time** builtin and (b) the format used by **time**. You can set it to either a single numeric value or to an array holding a numeric value and a string. The numeric value is used to control automatic timing; any command that takes more than that number of CPU seconds to run has **time** display the statistics on the command execution immediately after the command completes. A value of 0 results in statistics being displayed after every command. The string is used to control the formatting of the statistics, using special formatting sequences. These formatting sequences include the following:

Formatting Sequence	Result
%U	Time spent by the command running user code, in CPU seconds (user mode).
%S	Time spent by the command running system code, in CPU seconds (kernel mode).
%E	Wall clock time (total elapsed) taken by the command.
%P	Percent of time the CPU spent on this task during this period, computed as (%U+%S)/%E.

Formatting Sequence	Result
%W	Number of times the command's processes were swapped out to disk.
%X	Average amount of shared code memory used by the command, in kilobytes.
%D	Average amount of data memory used by the command, in kilobytes.
%K	Total memory used by the command (as %X+%D), in kilobytes.
%M	Maximum amount of memory used by the command, in kilobytes.
%F	Number of major page faults (pages of memory that had to be read off of the disk).
%I	Number of input operations.
%O	Number of output operations.

By default the **time** builtin uses the string: `"%Uu  %Ss  %E  %P%    %X+%Dk %I+%Oio %Fpf+%Ww"` which generates output in the following format:

```
% time
0.0u 1.0s 3:32:52 0% 0+0k 0+0io 0pf+0w
```

You can time commands when you are concerned about system performance. If many of your commands show a lot of page faults and swaps, your system is probably memory-starved and you should consider adding more memory to the system. You can use the information that **time** reports to compare performances of different system configurations and program algorithms.

user   csh The shell sets this variable to your login name.

$ sh csh ksh As in **sh** and **ksh**, this variable contains the PID number of the current shell.

▲▲▲ Shell Variables That Act as Switches

The following shell variables act as switches; their values are not significant. If the variable has been declared, the shell takes the specified action. If not, the action is not taken or is negated. You can set these variables in your **.cshrc** file, in a shell script, or from the command line.

echo   csh When you call **csh** with the **–x** option, it sets the **echo** variable. You can also set **echo** using **set**. In either case, when you declare **echo**, **csh** displays each command before it executes that command.

ignoreeof

csh When set, you cannot exit from the shell using CONTROL-D, so you cannot accidentally log out. When this variable is declared, you must use **exit** or **logout** to leave a shell.

noclobber

csh When set, prevents you from accidentally overwriting a file when you redirect output. It also prevents you from creating a file when you attempt to append output to a nonexistent file. To override **noclobber** add an exclamation point to the symbol you use for redirecting or appending output (for example >! and >>!). Refer to "–C" on page 539 for information on the equivalent **ksh** option.

Command Line	Effect When You _Do Not_ Declare noclobber	Effect When You _Do_ Declare noclobber
x > _fileout_	Redirects standard output from process **x** to _fileout_. Overwrites _fileout_ if it exists.	Redirects standard output from process **x** to _fileout_. The shell displays an error message if _fileout_ exists and it does not overwrite the file.
x >> _fileout_	Redirects standard output from process **x** to _fileout_. Appends new output to the end of _fileout_ if it exists. Creates _fileout_ if it does not exist.	Redirects standard output from process **x** to _fileout_. Appends new output to the end of _fileout_ if it exists. The shell displays an error message if _fileout_ does not exist. It does not create the file.

noglob

csh When you declare **noglob**, **csh** does not expand ambiguous filenames. You can use ∗, **?**, ~, and [] on the command line or in a shell script without quoting them. Refer to "–f" on page 539 for information on the equivalent **ksh** option.

nonomatch

csh When set, **csh** passes an ambiguous file reference that does not match a filename to the command that is being called. The shell does not expand the file reference. When you do not set **nonomatch**, **csh** generates a No match error message and does not execute the command.

```
% cat questions?
cat: No match
% set nonomatch
% cat questions?
No match
```

notify

csh When set, **csh** sends a message to your terminal whenever one of your background jobs completes. Ordinarily **csh** notifies you about a job completion immediately before the next prompt. Refer to "Job Control" on page 450.

verbose

csh The C Shell declares this variable when you call it with the **–v** option. You can also declare it using **set**. In either case **verbose** causes **csh** to display each command after a history substitution. Refer to "History" on page 438.

▲ Control Structures

The C Shell uses many of the same control structures as the Bourne Shell. In each case the syntax is different, but the effects are the same. This section summarizes the differences between the control structures in the two shells. For more information see "Control Structures" on page 394.

if

The syntax of the **if** control structure csh is

> *if (expression) simple-command*

The **if** control structure works only with simple commands, not with pipes or lists of commands. You can use the **if...then** control structure (page 467) to execute more complex commands.

```
% cat if_1
#!/bin/csh
# Routine to show the use of a simple if
# control structure.
#
if ( $#argv == 0 ) echo "if_1: there are no arguments"
```

This program checks to see if it was called with no arguments. If the expression (enclosed in parentheses) evaluates to *true*—that is, if there were zero arguments on the command line—the **if** structure displays a message to that effect.

In addition to the logical expressions described on page 457, you can use expressions that return a value based on the status of a file. The syntax of this type of expression is

> *–n filename*

where *n* is from the following list:

n	Meaning
d	The file is a directory file.
e	The file exists.
f	The file is an ordinary file.
o	The user owns the file.
r	The user has read access to the file.
w	The user has write access to the file.
x	The user has execute access to the file or search access to the directory.
z	The file is empty (has zero length).

If the specified file does not exist or is not accessible, **csh** evaluates the expression as 0. Otherwise if the result of the test is *true*, the expression has a value of 1; if it is *false*, the expression has a value of 0. The following example checks to see if the file specified on the command line is an ordinary file.

```
% cat if_2
#!/bin/csh
if -f $1 echo "Ordinary file"
```

goto

The syntax of a **goto** statement csh is

> goto *label*

A **goto** builtin transfers control to the statement beginning with *label:*. The following program fragment demonstrates the use of **goto**:

```
% cat goto_1
#!/bin/csh
#
# test for 2 arguments
#
if ($#argv == 2) goto goodargs
echo "Usage: goto_1 arg1 arg2"
exit 1
goodargs:
  .
  .
```

The **goto_1** script displays a standard usage message. Refer to page 397 for more information about usage messages.

▲▲ Interrupt Handling

The **onintr** statement csh transfers control when you interrupt a shell script. The format of an **onintr** statement is

> onintr *label*

When you press the interrupt key during execution of a shell script, the shell transfers control to the statement beginning with *label:*.

This statement allows you to terminate a script gracefully when it is interrupted. You can use it to ensure that when you interrupt a shell script, it removes temporary files before returning control to the parent shell.

The following script demonstrates **onintr**. It loops continuously until you press the interrupt key, at which time it displays a message and returns control to the shell.

```
% cat onintr_1
#!/bin/csh
# demonstration of onintr
onintr close
while ( 1 )
   echo "Program is running."
   sleep 2
end
close:
echo "End of program."
```

If a script creates temporary files, you can use **onintr** to remove them.

```
close:
rm -f /tmp/$$*
```

The ambiguous file reference **/tmp/$$*** matches all files in **/tmp** that begin with the PID of the current shell. Refer to page 380 for a description of this technique for naming temporary files.

if...then...else

The three forms of the **if...then...else** csh control structure are

Form 1

if (**expression**) *then*
    commands
endif

Form 2

if (**expression**) *then*
    commands
else
    commands
endif

Form 3

if (**expression**) *then*
    commands
else if (**expression**) *then*
    commands

    .

    .

    .

else
    commands
endif

   The first form is an extension of the simple **if** structure; it executes more complex **commands** or a series of **commands** if the **expression** is *true*. This form is still a one-way branch.

   The second form is a two-way branch. If the **expression** is true, the structure executes the first set of **commands**. If it is *false,* the set of **commands** following **else** is executed.

   The third form is similar to the **if...then...elif** structure of the Bourne Shell (page 399). It performs tests until it finds an **expression** that is *true* and then executes the corresponding **commands**.

```
% cat if_else_1
#!/bin/csh
# routine to categorize the first
# command-line argument
set class
set number = $argv[1]
#
if ($number < 0) then
    @ class = 0
else if (0 <= $number && $number < 100) then
    @ class = 1
else if (100 <= $number && $number < 200) then
    @ class = 2
else
    @ class = 3
endif
#
echo "The number $number is in class ${class}."
```

The preceding program assigns a value of 0, 1, 2, or 3 to the variable **class**, based on the value of the first command-line argument. The program declares the variable **class** at the beginning for clarity; you do not need to declare it before its first use. Again, for clarity, the script assigns the value of the first command-line argument to **number**. The first **if** statement tests to see if **number** is less than 0. If it is, the script assigns 0 to **class**. If it is not, the second **if** tests to see if the number is between 0 and 100. The **&&** is a logical AND, yielding a value of *true* if the expression on each side is true. If the number is between 0 and 100, 1 is assigned to **class**. A similar test determines whether the number is between 100 and 200. If it is not, the final **else** assigns 3 to **class**. The **endif** closes the **if** control structure. The final statement uses braces ({}) to isolate the variable **class** from the following period. Again, the braces isolate the period for clarity; the shell does not consider a punctuation mark as part of a variable name. The braces would be required if you wanted other characters to follow immediately after the variable.

foreach

The **foreach** builtin csh parallels the **for...in** structure of the Bourne Shell (page 405). The syntax is

> foreach *loop-index (argument-list)*
> > *commands*
> end

This structure loops through the *commands*. The first time through the loop, the structure assigns the value of the first argument in the *argument-list* to the *loop-index*. When control reaches the **end** statement, the shell assigns the value of the next argument from the *argument-list* to the *loop-index* and executes the commands again. The shell repeats this procedure until it exhausts the *argument-list*.

The following **csh** script uses a **foreach** structure to loop through the files in the working directory containing a specified string of characters in their filename and to change the string. For example you can use it to change the string **memo** in filenames to **letter**. The filenames **memo.1**, **dailymemo**, and **memories** would be changed to **letter.1**, **dailyletter**, and **letterries**. This script requires two arguments: The string to be changed and the new string. The *argument-list* of the **foreach** structure uses an ambiguous file reference to loop through all filenames that contain the first argument. For each filename that matches the regular expression, the **mv** utility changes the filename. The **echo** and **sed** commands appear within backprimes (` ) that indicate command substitution: The result of executing the commands within the backprimes replaces the backprimes and everything between them. Refer to " ` ... ` : Substitute the Output of a Command" on page 371 for more information. The **sed** utility substitutes the first argument for the second argument in the filename. The **$1** and **$2** are abbreviated forms of **$argv[1]** and **$argv[2]**. Refer to page 880 in Part III for more information on **sed**.

```
% cat rename
#!/bin/csh
# Usage:        rename arg1 arg2
#               changes the string arg1 in the names
#               of files in the working directory
#               into the string arg2
if ($#argv != 2) goto usage
foreach i ( *$1* )
   mv $i `echo $i | sed -n s/$1/$2/p`
end

exit 0

usage:
echo "Usage: rename arg1 arg2"
exit 1
```

Start Optional

The next script uses a **foreach** loop to assign the command-line arguments to the elements of an array named **buffer**.

```
% cat foreach_1
#!/bin/csh
# routine to zero-fill argv to 20 arguments
#
set buffer = (0 0 0 0 0 0 0 0 0 0 0 0 0 0 0 0 0 0 0 0)
set count = 1
#
if ($#argv > 20) goto toomany
#
foreach argument ($argv[*])
   set buffer[$count] = $argument
   @ count++
end
# REPLACE command ON THE NEXT LINE WITH THE PROGRAM
#   YOU WANT TO CALL.
exec command $buffer[*]
#
toomany:
echo "Too many arguments given."
echo "Usage: foreach_1 [up to 20 arguments]"
exit 1
```

This script calls another program named **command** with a command line guaranteed to contain 20 arguments. If **foreach_1** is called with fewer than 20 arguments, it fills the command line with zeros to complete the 20 arguments for **command**. More than 20 arguments cause it to display a usage message and exit with an error status.

The **foreach** structure loops through the commands one time for each of the command-line arguments. Each time through the loop, it assigns the value of the next argument from the command line to the variable **argument**. Then it assigns each of these values to an element of the array **buffer**. The variable **count** maintains the index for the **buffer** array. A postfix operator increments **count** using @ (@ **count++**). The **exec** builtin _{csh} (page 423), calls **program** so that a new process is not initiated. (Once **program** is called, the process running this routine is no longer needed, so there is no need for a new process.)

Stop Optional

while

The syntax of the **while** builtin csh is

> *while (**expression**)*
> > *commands*
>
> *end*

This structure continues to loop through the ***commands*** *while* the ***expression*** is true. If the ***expression*** is false the first time it is evaluated, the structure never executes the ***commands***.

```
% cat while_1
#!/bin/csh
# Demonstration of a While control structure.
# This routine sums the numbers between 1 and
# n, n being the first argument on the command
# line.
#
set limit = $argv[1]
set index = 1
set sum = 0
#
while ($index <= $limit)
    @ sum += $index
    @ index++
end
#
echo "The sum is $sum"
```

This program computes the sum of all the integers up to and including ***n***, where ***n*** is the first argument on the command line. The **+=** operator assigns the value of **sum + index** to **sum**.

▲▲ break and continue

You can interrupt a **foreach** or **while** structure with a **break** csh or **continue** csh statement. These statements execute the remaining commands on the line before they transfer control. The **break** statement transfers control to the statement after the **end** statement, terminating execution of the loop. The **continue** statement transfers control to the **end** statement, which continues execution of the loop.

switch

The **switch** structure csh is analogous to the **case** structure of the Bourne Shell (page 413).

> switch (***test-string***)
>
>> case ***pattern:***
>>> ***commands***
>> *breaksw*
>>
>> case ***pattern:***
>>> ***commands***
>> *breaksw*
>>
>> .
>>
>> .
>>
>> *default:*
>>> ***commands***
>> *breaksw*
>
> *endsw*

The **breaksw** statement causes execution to continue after the **endsw** statement. If you omit a **breaksw**, control falls through to the next command. See the table on page 415 for a list of special characters you can use within the ***pattern***s.

```
% cat switch_1
#!/bin/csh
# Demonstration of a switch control structure.
# This routine tests the first command-line argument
# for yes or no in any combination of upper- and
# lowercase letters.
#
# test that argv[1] exists
if ($#argv != 1) then
    echo "Usage: switch_1 [yes|no]"
    exit 1
else
# argv[1] exists, set up switch based on its value
    switch ($argv[1])
    # case of YES
        case [yY][eE][sS]:
        echo "Argument one is yes."
        breaksw
```

```
    #
    # case of NO
        case [nN][oO]:
        echo "Argument one is no."
    breaksw
    #
    # default case
        default:
        echo "Argument one is neither yes nor no."
        breaksw
    endsw
endif
```

▲ Builtins

Builtins are part of (built into) the shell. When you give a simple filename as a command, the shell first checks to see if it is the name of a builtin. If it is, the shell executes it as part of the calling process—the shell does not fork a new process to execute the builtin. It does not need to search the directory structure for the builtin program because the program is immediately available to the shell.

If the simple filename is not a builtin, the shell searches the directory structure for the program you want, using the **PATH** variable as a guide. When it finds the program, the shell forks a new process to execute it.

Although they are not listed below, all the control structure keywords (**if**, **foreach**, **endsw**, and so on) are builtins. The following list describes many of the **csh** builtins, some of which are also built into other shells.

% *job* `jsh csh ksh` A synonym for the **fg** builtin. The ***job*** is the job number of the job you want to bring into the foreground (page 358).

% *job* & `jsh csh ksh` A synonym for the **bg** builtin where ***job*** is the number of the job you want to put in the background (page 359).

@ `csh` Similar to the **set** builtin, but it evaluates numeric expressions. Refer to "Numeric Variables" on page 456.

alias `csh ksh` Creates and displays aliases. Refer to "Alias" on page 443.

bg `jsh csh ksh` Moves jobs into the background (page 359).

cd *or* chdir **cd** `sh csh ksh`, **chdir** `sh csh` Changes working directories. Refer to "**cd**: Change to Another Working Directory" on page 79.

dirs `csh` Displays the directory stack. Refer to "Directory Stack Manipulation" on page 450.

echo `sh csh ksh` Displays its arguments. In **csh** you prevent a RETURN after **echo** displays a line by using the **–n** option (see "Reading User Input" on page 460) whereas in **sh** and **ksh**

you use a trailing \c (see "**read**: Accept User Input" on page 369). Refer to page 747 in Part III for more information on **echo**.

eval   ^{sh csh ksh} Scans and evaluates the command line. When you put **eval** in front of a command, the command is scanned twice by the shell before it is executed. This is useful when you have a command that is generated as a result of command or variable substitution. Because of the order in which the shell processes a command line, it is sometimes necessary to repeat the scan in order to achieve the desired result (page 431).

exec   ^{sh csh ksh} Overlays the program that is currently being executed with another program in the same shell. The original program is lost. Refer to "**exec**: Execute a Command" on page 423 for more information; also refer to **source** later in this list.

exit   ^{sh csh ksh} You can use this builtin to exit from a C Shell. When you follow it with an argument that is a number, the number is the exit status that the shell returns to its parent process. Refer to "status" in the list on page 462.

fg   ^{jsh csh ksh} Moves jobs into the foreground. Refer to "Job Control" on page 450.

glob   ^{csh} Like **echo**, except it does not display SPACEs between its arguments and does not follow its display with a NEWLINE.

hashstat   ^{csh} Reports on the efficiency of **csh**'s hash mechanism. The hash mechanism speeds the process of searching through the directories in your search path. Also see the **rehash** and **unhash** builtins in this list.

history   ^{csh} Displays the history list of commands. Refer to "History" on page 438.

jobs   ^{jsh csh ksh} Identifies the current jobs, or commands. Refer to "Job Control" on page 450.

kill   ^{sh csh ksh} Terminates jobs or processes. Refer to "**kill**: Abort a Process" on page 508.

limit   ^{csh} Limits the computer resources that the current process and any processes it creates can use. You can put limits on the number of seconds of CPU time the process can use, the size of files that the process can create, and so forth.

login   ^{sh csh ksh} Logs in a user. Can be followed by a username.

logout   ^{sh csh ksh} Ends a session if you are using your original (login) shell.

nice   ^{csh} Lowers the processing priority of a command or a shell. It is useful if you want to run a command that makes large demands on the central processing unit and you do not need the output right away. If you are Superuser, you can use **nice** to raise the processing priority of a command. Refer to "Notes" on page 844 for more information on the **csh nice** builtin and to the same page in general for more information about the **nice** utility, which is available from **sh** and **ksh**.

nohup

csh Allows you to log out while processes are running in the background without terminating the processes. Some systems are set up to do this automatically. Refer to **nohup** on page 846 in Part III for information on both the **csh nohup** builtin and the **nohup** utility, which is available from **sh** and **ksh**.

notify

csh Causes the shell to notify you immediately when the status of one of your jobs changes. Refer to "Job Control" on page 450.

onintr

csh Controls what action an interrupt causes for a specific script. Refer to "Interrupt Handling" on page 466. Also see "trap: Catch a Signal" on page 425 for information on an equivalent command in **sh** and **ksh**.

popd

csh Removes a directory from the directory stack. Refer to "Directory Stack Manipulation" on page 450.

pushd

csh Changes the working directory and places the new directory at the top of the directory stack. Refer to "Directory Stack Manipulation," page 450.

rehash

csh Recreates the internal tables used by **csh**'s hash mechanism. Whenever a new instance of **csh** is invoked, the hash mechanism creates a sorted list of all commands available to the user, based on the value of **PATH**. After you add a command to one of the directories in **PATH**, use **rehash** to recreate the sorted list of commands. If you do not, **csh** may not be able to find the new command. Also refer to the **hash**, **hashstat**, and **unhash** builtins.

repeat

csh Takes two arguments, a count and simple command (no pipes or lists of commands), and repeats the command the number of times specified by the count.

set

sh csh ksh Declares, initializes, and displays the values of local variables. Refer to "Variables" on page 454.

setenv

csh Declares and initializes the values of environment variables. Refer to "Variables" on page 454.

shift

sh csh ksh Analogous to the Bourne Shell **shift** builtin (page 377). Without an argument **shift** promotes the indexes of the **argv** array. You can use it with an argument to perform the same operation on another array.

source

csh Executes the shell script given as its argument—it does not fork another process. It is similar to the **.** (dot) builtin in the Bourne Shell (page 375). The **source** builtin expects a C Shell script, so no leading pound sign is required in the script. The current shell executes **source** so that the script can contain commands, such as **set**, that affect the current shell. After you make changes to your **.cshrc** or **.login** file, you can use **source** to execute it from within the login shell in order to put the changes into effect without logging off and back on again. You can nest **source** builtins.

stop   _{jsh csh ksh} Stops jobs or processes that are running in the background. To stop a job identify it by following a **%** with a job number, string, or PID number. Refer to "Job Control" on page 450. The **stop** builtin accepts multiple arguments.

suspend   _{jsh csh ksh} Stops the current shell. It is similar to CONTROL-Z, which stops jobs running in the foreground.

time   _{csh} Executes the command that you give it as an argument. It displays a summary of time-related information about the executed command, according to the **time** shell variable (page 462). Without an argument **time** displays the times for the current shell and its children.

umask   _{sh csh ksh} Identifies or changes the access permissions that are assigned to files you create. Refer to page 939 in Part III for more information on **umask**.

unalias   _{csh ksh} Removes an alias. Refer to "Alias" on page 443.

unhash   _{csh} Turns off the hash mechanism. Also see the **hash**, **hashstat**, and **rehash** builtins in this list.

unlimit   _{csh} Removes limits on the current process. Refer to "limit" on page 473.

unset   _{sh csh ksh} Removes a variable declaration. Refer to "Variables" on page 454.

unsetenv   _{csh} Removes an environment variable declaration. Refer to "Variables" on page 454.

wait   _{sh csh ksh} Causes the shell to wait for all child processes to terminate. When you give a **wait** command in response to a C Shell prompt, **csh** does not display a prompt and does not accept a command until all background processes have finished execution. If you interrupt it with the interrupt key, **wait** displays a list of outstanding processes before returning control to the shell.

Summary

Like the Bourne and Korn Shells, the C Shell is both a command interpreter and a programming language. It was developed at the University of California at Berkeley. It has popular features, such as history, alias, and job control, that have been adapted by other shells.

You may prefer to use **csh** as a command interpreter, especially if you are used to the C Shell. In that case if your default login shell is **sh** or **ksh**, you can ask the system administrator to change your login shell to **csh**. The administrator will make the change in the **/etc/passwd** file, so the shell you requested remains in effect across login sessions. However this does *not* cause **csh** to run your shell scripts; they will continue to be run by **sh**, unless you explicitly specify another shell on the first line of the script, or invoke one on the command line. Specifying the shell on the first line of your shell scripts ensures the behavior you expect.

If you are used to **sh**, you will notice some differences between the two shells right away. For instance the syntax you use to assign a value to a variable differs and the SPACEs around the equal sign are optional. Both numeric and nonnumeric variables are created and given values using the **set** builtin. The **@** builtin can evaluate numeric expressions for assignment to existing numeric variables.

Because there is no **export** builtin in **csh**, you must use the **setenv** builtin to create an environment variable. You can also assign a value to the variable with the **setenv** command. The command **unset** removes both local and environment variables, whereas the command **unsetenv** removes only environment variables.

The syntax of the **csh alias** builtin is slightly different than **alias** in **sh**. Unlike **sh** the **csh alias** feature permits you to substitute command-line arguments using the syntax available with the history mechanism.

Most other **csh** features, such as history, word completion, and command-line editing, closely resemble their **sh** and **ksh** counterparts. The syntax of the **csh** control structures is slightly different but provides functionality equivalent to that found in **sh** and **ksh**.

The term *globbing*, a carryover from the Bourne Shell, refers to the matching of names containing special characters (such as * and ?) to filenames. If **csh** is unable to generate a list of filenames matching a globbing pattern, it displays an error message. This is in contrast to **sh**, which simply leaves the pattern alone.

Standard input and standard output can be redirected in **csh**, but there is no straightforward way to redirect them independently. To do so requires the creation of a subshell that redirects standard output to a file, while making standard error available to the parent process.

Review Exercises

1. Assume you are working with the following history list:

   ```
   37  pine alex
   38  cd /home/jenny/correspondence/business/cheese_co
   39  pg letter.0321
   40  vi letter.0321
   41  cp letter.0321 letter.0325
   42  grep hansen letter.0325
   43  vi letter.0325
   44  lp letter*
   45  cd ../milk_co
   46  pwd
   47  vi wilson.0321 wilson.0329
   ```

   Using the history mechanism, give commands to do each of the following:

   a. Send mail to Alex.

   b. Use **vi** to edit a file named **wilson.0329**.

   c. Send **wilson.0329** to the printer.

   d. Send both **wilson.0321** and **wilson.0329** to the printer.

2. How can you identify all the aliases currently in effect? Write an alias named **homedots** that lists the names (only) of all invisible files in your home directory.

3. How can you prevent a command from sending output to the terminal when you start it in the background? What can you do if you start a command in the foreground and later decide that it should run in the background?

4. What statement can you put in your **.cshrc** file to prevent yourself from accidentally overwriting a file when you redirect output? How can you override this feature?

5. Assume the working directory contains the following files:

```
adams.ltr.03
adams.brief
adams.ltr.07
abelson.09
abelson.brief
anthony.073
anthony.brief
azevedo.99
```

What happens if you press **TAB** after typing the following commands?

a. **pg adams.l**

b. **cat a**

c. **ls ant**

d. **file az**

What happens if you press **CONTROL-D** after typing these commands?

e. **ls ab**

f. **pg a**

6. Write an alias named **backup** that takes a filename as an argument and creates a copy of that file with the same name and a filename extension of **.bak**.

7. Write an alias named **qmake** (quiet make) that runs **make** with both standard output and standard error redirected to the file named **make.log**. The command **qmake** should accept the same options and arguments as **make**.

8. How can you make **csh** always display the pathname of the working directory as part of its prompt?

Advanced Review Exercises

9. What lines do you need to change in the Bourne Shell script **command_menu** (page 416) to make it a C Shell script? Make the changes and verify that it works.

10. Users often find **rm** (and even **rm –i**) too unforgiving because it removes files irrevocably. Create an alias named **delete** that moves files specified by its argument(s) into the **~/.trash** directory. Create a second alias named **undelete** that moves a file from the **~/.trash** directory into the working directory. Fi-

nally put the following line in your **.logout** file to remove any files that you deleted during the login session:

```
/bin/rm -f $HOME/.trash/* >& /dev/null
```

Explain what could be different if the following line were put in your **.logout** file instead.

```
rm $HOME/.trash/*
```

11. Modify the **foreach_1** program (page 469) so that it takes the command to **exec** as an argument.

12. Rewrite the program **while_1** (page 470) so that it runs faster. Use the **time** builtin to verify the improvement in execution time.

13. Write your own version of **find** named **myfind** that writes output to the file **findout**, but without the clutter of error messages (such as when you do not have permission to search a directory). The **myfind** command should accept the same options and arguments as **find**. Can you think of a situation in which **myfind** does not work as desired?

14. When the **foreach_1** script (page 469) is supplied with 20 or fewer arguments, why are the commands following toomany: not executed? (Why is there no **exit** command?)

The Korn Shell and Advanced Shell Programming

The Korn Shell (**ksh**) combines many features of the Bourne and C Shells. In addition **ksh** incorporates a number of new features. Because of the large number of features and configuration options available in **ksh**, you may find it easier to concentrate on the ones that you find most useful. If you have used **csh** before, then you can configure **ksh** to behave much the same way as **csh**.

This chapter builds on the material presented in the earlier chapters on shells and shell programming. If you read Chapters 10 through 12, you will recognize many of their features as they are presented in this chapter. You may find it useful to refer back to these chapters while reading this chapter. Even so not all of the features of **ksh** are presented here. Instead this chapter concentrates on the more useful features of **ksh** and how to customize **ksh** to suit your needs. For a complete description of the Korn Shell, refer to the **ksh man** page.

This chapter starts with a discussion of variables and the shell builtins. Next a discussion of command-line editing is followed by a section on command processing that describes the various steps the shell takes when processing a command line. Then an extensive section on shell programming guides you through the construction of two longer shell programs. Finally there is a list of Korn Shell options.

▲ Korn Shell Basics

If you want to use the Korn Shell as your login shell, Superuser can set up the **/etc/passwd** file so that you use the Korn Shell whenever you log in.

The basic behavior of the Korn Shell mimics that of the other shells: You type a command that names an executable program or script, optionally followed by arguments that are interpreted by the command. You can correct mistakes as described on page 23 before you press the **RETURN** key. You can also use the Korn Shell's powerful command-line editing (page 510) and history editing (page 514) facilities to create and modify command lines.

Like **sh** and **csh**, **ksh** evaluates variables, searches for aliases and functions, expands ambiguous file references, and handles redirection before executing a command. It is important to understand the precise sequence in which these steps are carried out, because it affects the meaning of a command line. Before describing the steps in command-line processing in detail, this chapter describes the various Korn Shell constructs that are involved in these steps, including aliases, functions, I/O redirection, variable expansion and evaluation, tilde expansion, and command substitution.

▲▲ Running Scripts

To execute a Korn Shell script, use the script name as an argument to **ksh**:

```
$ ksh script_name
```

This command calls **ksh** regardless of which shell you are working with. If you have execute permission for the file that contains the script, you can use the filename as a command:

```
$ script_name
```

If you start the first line of the script with **#!** followed by the path of **ksh** on your system, the Korn Shell runs the script, regardless of what shell you call the script from (page 363).

```
#!/bin/ksh
```

▲▲ Startup Files

The Korn Shell uses many of the same environment variables as the Bourne Shell and adds a few others. You can set these variables, along with commands that establish other characteristics of the Korn Shell environment, in the **/etc/profile** and **.profile** (in your home directory) Korn Shell startup files. Refer to "Startup Files" on page 364.

▲▲ Commands That Are Symbols

The Korn Shell uses the (,), [,], and $ symbols in various ways to identify builtin commands. To minimize confusion the following table lists the most common use of each of these commands even though some of the commands are not introduced until later in the chapter.

Builtin	Use
( )	subshell (page 354)
$( )	command substitution (page 521)
(( ))	assignment operator (use when the enclosed value contains an equal sign [page 489])
$(( ))	expression evaluation (not for use with an enclosed equal sign [page 490])
[ ]	**test** command (see the **chkargs** script on page 395)
[[ ]]	similar to **[ ]** but adds string comparisons (page 493)

▲ Variables

Like **sh** and **csh**, **ksh** allows you to create and use variables. The rules for naming and referring to variables are similar in all three shells (page 365). You assign values to variables as in the Bourne Shell with the following syntax:

VARIABLE=value

There must be no whitespace on either side of the equal (=) sign. If you want to include SPACEs in the value of the variable, put quotation marks around the value or quote the SPACEs.

In **ksh**, as in **sh** and **csh**, you reference the value of a variable by preceding the variable name with a dollar sign and enclosing it in braces, as in **${VARIABLE}**. The braces are optional unless the name of the variable is followed by a letter, digit, or underscore. Also, the Korn Shell refers to the arguments on its command line by position, using the special variables **$1**, **$2**, **$3**, and so forth up to **$9**. If you wish to refer to arguments past the ninth, you must use braces, as in **${10}**.

You can unset one or more variables with the **unset** builtin $\frac{sh}{csh}^1$:

```
$ unset PREF SUFF
```

This removes the variable's value and attributes.

▲▲ Variable Attributes

As in the Bourne Shell, in the Korn Shell you can set attributes for a variable that control the values it can take on. The **typeset** builtin sets attributes. The following example shows the variable **NAME** being assigned the uppercase (**–u**) attribute. A variable with this attribute translates all letters in its value to uppercase.

```
$ typeset -u NAME
$ NAME="Barbara Jackson"
$ echo $NAME
BARBARA JACKSON
```

Similarly you can assign a variable the lowercase attribute with **typeset –l**.

The integer attribute is very useful. By default the values of Korn Shell variables are stored as strings. However if you want to do arithmetic on a variable, the string variable is internally converted into a number, manipulated, and then converted back to a string. A variable with the integer attribute is stored as an integer. This makes arithmetic much faster. Assign the integer attribute as follows:

---

1. A *builtin* (page 47) is a command that is built into and is part of the shells named within the shaded rectangle following its name ($\frac{sh}{csh}$ [page 17]). All builtins available in **sh** are also available in **jsh**. Give the command **man shell_builtins** to see a list of **ksh** (and other) builtins.

```
$ typeset -i COUNT
```

The **integer** builtin_{ksh} is almost identical to **typeset –i**, so the above example is the same as

```
$ integer COUNT
```

You can assign a base other than 10 to an integer variable. The Korn Shell then uses this base to display the variable. The syntax is

*typeset -i **base variable***

where ***base*** is the base you want to use to display the value. If the base is not 10, the value is displayed as ***base*#*value***. (In base 2 the value 20 is written as 10100.)

```
$ COUNT=20
$ typeset -i2 BCOUNT
$ BCOUNT=$COUNT
$ echo $COUNT $BCOUNT
20 2#10100
```

The **export** attribute is similar to the **export** builtin_{sh ksh} (page 368). If a variable has this attribute, then a copy of it is inherited by all child processes. The Korn Shell supports the **export** builtin and also provides **typeset –x** to set the **export** attribute. You can set the **export** attribute for functions as well as variables; an exported function is available in all subshells.

The Korn Shell supports several variable attributes that are useful for formatting output. A variable can be assigned a particular width (number of columns) and can be left- or right-justified within that width. Leading zeros can be added or suppressed. The following table shows the corresponding options to the **typeset** builtin:

Option	Effect
–L *width*	Left-justifies within a width of *width*.
–R *width*	Right-justifies (blank filled) within a width of *width*.
–Z *width*	Right-justifies (zero filled if digits) within a width of *width*.

If you omit *width*, then **ksh** uses the width of the first value assigned to the variable. See the last few lines of the following example, where **MONTH** is first assigned a value of 11 without specifying a width (establishing a width of two characters) and then assigned a value of 8, which is displayed in a two-character field (with a trailing blank):

```
$ typeset -L8 FRUIT1 FRUIT2
$ FRUIT1=apple
$ FRUIT2=watermelon
$ echo $FRUIT1$FRUIT2
apple   watermel
$ echo $FRUIT2$FRUIT1
watermelapple
$ typeset -Z2 DAY
$ DAY=2; echo $DAY
02
```

```
$ typeset -L MONTH
$ MONTH=11; echo $MONTH/$DAY/97
11/02/97
$ MONTH=8; echo $MONTH/$DAY/97
8 /02/97
```

You can give the **readonly** attribute to a variable to prevent its value from being changed. Assign values to **readonly** variables before or at the same time that you give them this attribute:

```
$ PATH=/usr/ucb:/usr/bin:/usr/local/bin:/usr/games
$ typeset -r PATH FPATH=/usr/local/funcs
$ PATH=/usr/bin:/usr/ucb:/usr/local/bin:/usr/games
ksh: PATH: is read only
```

Here **PATH** and **FPATH** are given the **readonly** attribute. You can set the variable's value within the **typeset** builtin, as shown with **FPATH**.

You can use the **readonly** builtin $^{sh}_{ksh}$ in place of **typeset –r**.

```
$ readonly PATH FPATH=/usr/local/funcs
```

Without any arguments **typeset** displays a list of variables and their attributes. To see which attributes have been set for a given variable, use **typeset** and **grep**:

```
$ typeset | grep DAY
export 2 zerofill 2 rightjust 2 DAY
```

Use **typeset** followed by an option to see which variables have a certain attribute:

```
$ typeset -Z
DAY
```

▲▲ Locality of Variables

By default Korn Shell variables that you create and use in a shell script are *global:* They are recognized throughout the current shell session and all subshells. The Korn Shell also allows you to create variables that are *local* to a function. A variable that is local to a function is recognized only within that function. If a function has a local variable with the same name as a global variable, all references to that variable within the function refer to the local variable, whereas all references outside the function refer to the global variable.

Local variables are helpful in a function written for general use. Because the function is called by many scripts, perhaps written by different programmers, you need to make sure that names of the variables within the function do not interact with variables of the same name in the programs that call the function. Local variables eliminate this problem.

One of the uses of the **typeset** builtin is to declare a variable to be local to the function it is defined in. The following definition makes *varname* a local variable:

*typeset **varname***

The next example shows the use of a local variable in an interactive session. This is a function, not a shell script; if you put it in a file do not attempt to execute it. If you save this function in a file named **countd**, you can place it in your environment with the **.** (dot) builtin (for example **. countd**). Refer to "Running .profile with the . (Dot) Builtin" on page 375.

This example uses two variables named **count**. The first is declared and assigned a value of 10 in the login shell. Its value never changes as is verified by **echo** before and after running **count_down**. The other **count** is declared, via **typeset**, to be local to the function. Its value, which is unknown outside the function, ranges from 6 to 1, as the **echo** command within the function confirms.

The example shows the function being entered from the keyboard. The **>** characters at the left end of some of the lines are secondary prompts (**PS2**) provided by the shell.

```
$ count=10
$ function count_down {
typeset count
count=$1
while [ count -gt 0 ]; do
echo "$count..."
((count=count-1))
sleep 1
done
echo "Blast Off!"
return
}
$ echo $count
10
$ count_down 6
6...
5...
4...
3...
2...
1...
Blast Off!
$ echo $count
10
```

The `((count=count-1))` assignment is enclosed between double parentheses, which cause the shell to perform the enclosed assignment (page 489). Within the double parentheses you can reference shell variables without the leading dollar sign (**$**).

▲▲ Keyword Variables

The Korn Shell automatically defines and inherits a number of variables when you start a session. These variables include most of the keyword shell variables from **sh** (page 371) and **ksh**. Some of these variables have values that are set (and changed during your session). You cannot assign values to some of these variables. Others are variables you can assign values to and that have special meaning for the shell.

$# ^sh2_ksh The number of command-line arguments (page 379).

---

2. The names of the shells within the shaded box following the name of the keyword variable indicate which shells provide this variable.

*	**$*** ^sh_ksh All the command-line arguments as a single argument (page 379).	

$* ^sh_ksh All the command-line arguments as a single argument (page 379).

$@ ^sh_ksh All the command-line arguments, as individual arguments (page 379).

underscore ^ksh The last argument of the previous simple command in the current instance of the shell. This is similar, but not identical, to **csh**'s **!$** expression (page 441).

```
$ cat file1 file2 file3 > all3files
$ echo $_
file3
```

If you had issued these commands using **csh** and **!$** instead of **ksh** and **$_**, the output would have been all3files. The Korn Shell underscore argument specifically refers to arguments, not arbitrary symbols on the command line.

CDPATH ^sh_ksh The list of absolute pathnames of directories searched by **cd** (page 374).

FCEDIT ^ksh The name of the editor that the **fc** builtin uses (page 515).

FPATH *or* **fpath** ^ksh Contains a list of files that contain shell functions. See the discussion of shell functions and the **autoload** builtin on page 507.

HISTFILE ^ksh The name of the file that stores your history list (page 514).

HISTFILESIZE ^ksh The number of lines of history stored in **HISTFILE** (page 514).

HISTSIZE ^ksh The number of events stored in the history list during a session (page 514).

HOME ^sh_csh_ksh The pathname of your home directory (page 372).

IFS ^sh_ksh The Internal Field Separator (page 383).

LINENO ^ksh Before **ksh** executes a command from a script or function, it sets the value of **LINENO** to the line number of the command it is about to execute. The following script begins with the line **#!/bin/ksh** to ensure that the script runs under **ksh**:

```
$ cat showline
#!/bin/ksh
date
echo "Script $0: at line $LINENO"
$ showline
Thu Apr  2 06:07:56 PST 1998
Script showline: at line 3
```

MAIL ^sh_ksh The file where your mail is stored (page 373).

OPTARG *and* **OPTIND** ^sh_ksh These variables are set by the **getopts** builtin. Refer to "Builtins" on page 492.

PATH ^sh_csh_ksh The list of directories the shell searches for commands (page 372).

PPID

The value of the PID of the parent process (the process running the process that is evaluating this variable). [ksh]

PS1

The shell prompt string (page 373). [sh ksh]

PS2

The shell secondary prompt string (page 374). [sh ksh]

LINES *and* **COLUMNS** *and* **PS3**

Control the format of output generated by shell scripts using the **select** command (page 494). Refer to page 495 for more information on **LINES** and **COLUMNS**. [ksh]

PS4

The prompt string used in debugging mode. The Korn Shell has a trace facility that you turn on with **set –x**. The shell precedes each line of trace output by **PS4**, which is **+** by default. For example: [ksh]

```
$ MYNAME=alex
$ set -x
$ echo $MYNAME
+ echo alex
alex
$ PS4='DBG: '
+ PS4=DBG:
$ echo $MYNAME
DBG: echo alex
alex
```

OLDPWD *and* **PWD**

The shell stores the absolute pathname of the working directory, as set by the most recent **cd** command, in **PWD** [sh csh ksh], and the pathname of the previous working directory in **OLDPWD** [ksh]. You can toggle back and forth between directories by giving the command **cd $OLDPWD**.

The value of **PWD** is not necessarily the same as the value returned by the **/bin/pwd** command, because the **PWD** variable keeps track of the traversal of symbolic links. It keeps track of not only where you are, but how you got there.

```
$ cd
$ mkdir -p top/level2/level3
$ ln -s top/level2 symdir
$ cd symdir
$ /bin/pwd
/home/alex/top/level2
$ echo $PWD
/home/alex/symdir
$ pwd
/home/alex/symdir
```

The Korn Shell **pwd** builtin [ksh] keeps track of symbolic links, the C and Bourne Shell **pwd** builtins [csh sh] do not. The **pwd** utility (**/bin/pwd**) just tells you the name of the directory you are in, regardless of how you got there. The **–p** option to **mkdir** causes the command to create any missing intermediate directories (in this case **top** and **level2**) when creating the target directory.

RANDOM   _{ksh} Each time this variable is referenced, it is assigned a random integer value between 0 and 32767, inclusive. It is useful in several programming contexts, including test programs, generating dummy data, quizzes, and games.

SECONDS   _{ksh} When you reference it the value of this integer variable is the number of seconds that have elapsed since the start of the shell session. You can include it in your prompt, but it is more useful for timing events in scripts.

```
$ cat quiz_short
#!/bin/ksh
echo "What is the smallest prime number that is larger than 50? \c"
START=$SECONDS
read ANSWER
FINISH=$SECONDS
echo "You took $(($FINISH - $START)) seconds to answer"
if [ $ANSWER -ne 53 ]; then
    echo "   and you were incorrect; the answer is 53."
fi
```

The expression **$((FINISH – START))** is an example of the Korn Shell's built-in arithmetic capability (the dollar signs within the double parentheses are not required [page 489]).

TMOUT   If set and if **TMOUT** seconds elapse after a prompt is issued with no input, the shell exits. This automatic logout feature helps prevent someone who is not known to the system from coming up to an idle terminal, giving commands, and compromising system security. This is usually set as a **readonly** variable in a global startup file. If it is not **readonly**, you can set it to 0 to disable it.

Start Optional

▲▲ Expanding Shell Variables

Chapter 11 (page 422) discussed several alternatives to accepting a null value from an unset or null variable. The Korn Shell incorporates the expansions **sh** uses and adds a few of its own.

▲▲▲ String Pattern Matching

The Korn Shell provides a powerful set of string pattern-matching operators that allow you to manipulate pathnames and other strings. These operators can delete prefixes or suffixes that match patterns from strings. The four operators are listed in the following table:

String Operator	Meaning
#	Removes minimal matching prefixes.
##	Removes maximal matching prefixes.
%	Removes minimal matching suffixes.
%%	Removes maximal matching suffixes.

The syntax for these operators is:

${*varname op pattern*}

In this syntax **op** is one of the operators listed in the preceding table, and **pattern** is a match pattern similar to that used for filename generation. These operators are most commonly used to manipulate pathnames to extract or remove components or to change suffixes.

```
$ SOURCEFILE=/usr/local/src/prog.c
$ echo ${SOURCEFILE#/*/}
local/src/prog.c
$ echo ${SOURCEFILE##/*/}
prog.c
$ echo ${SOURCEFILE%/*}
/usr/local/src
$ echo ${SOURCEFILE%%/*}

$ echo ${SOURCEFILE%.c}
/usr/local/src/prog
$ CHOPFIRST=${SOURCEFILE#/*/}
$ echo $CHOPFIRST
local/src/prog.c
$ NEXT=${CHOPFIRST%%/*}
$ echo $NEXT
local
```

▲▲▲ Filename Generation

An important feature of most shells is the ability to refer to files by giving a pattern that describes one or more filenames. For example all the shells discussed in this book use ***.c** as a pattern describing all filenames that end in **.c**. The shells expand this pattern into a list of filenames that match the pattern. This process of matching filenames to a pattern is called *globbing*. Globbing is useful for specifying many files with a single pattern and long filenames with a short string.

Setting the **noglob** (**set –o noglob**) option turns off all pattern matching so that you will have to give filenames exactly: ***.c** will refer to only a file whose name consists of the three-character sequence *****, **.**, and **c**. See "Filename Generation/Pathname Expansion" on page 118.

▲▲ Array Variables

The Korn Shell supports one-dimensional array variables. Subscripts are integers, with zero-based subscripting (the first element of the array has the subscript 0). You assign an array of values to a variable using the **set** builtin (page 539) as follows:

set –A name element1 element2 ...

The following example demonstrates the use of an array variable:

```
$ set -A NAMES alex helen jenny scott
$ echo $NAMES
alex
$ echo ${NAMES[2]}
jenny
```

Because of the zero-based subscripting, the subscript 2 yields the third element of the array. You can display all the elements of the array using an asterisk:

```
$ echo ${NAMES[*]}
alex helen jenny scott
```

There are some special, noninteger subscripts as well. The subscripts [*] and [@] both extract the entire array but work differently when used within double quotation marks. An @ produces an array that is a duplicate of the original array, whereas a * produces a single element of an array (or a plain variable) that holds all the elements of the array separated by the first character in IFS (normally a **SPACE**). Below, the array A is filled with the elements of the NAMES variable using an * and B is filled using an @. The **set** builtin (without an argument) displays the values of the A and B arrays.

```
$ set -A A "${NAMES[*]}"
$ set -A B "${NAMES[@]}"
$ set | head -5
A[0]='alex helen jenny scott'
B[0]=alex
B[1]=helen
B[2]=jenny
B[3]=scott
```

You can use subscripts on the left side of an assignment statement to replace selected elements of the array.

```
$ NAMES[4]=william
$ echo ${NAMES[*]}
alex helen jenny william
```

▲▲ Arithmetic

The Korn Shell has the ability to perform assignments and evaluate many different types of arithmetic expressions. All arithmetic is done using integers, and you can represent numbers in any base from 2 to 36 using the *base#value* syntax (page 482).

▲▲▲ Assignments

There are a number of ways the shell can perform arithmetic assignments. One is with arguments of the **let** builtin [**ksh**]

```
$ let "VALUE=VALUE * 10 + NEW"
```

In this example the variables **VALUE** and **NEW** should contain integer values. Within a **let** statement dollar signs ($) do not need to precede variable names. Double quotation marks enclose the arguments to prevent the shell from attempting to expand the asterisk as a file pattern-matching operator—arguments that contain SPACEs must be quoted. Because many expressions that are arguments to **let** need to be quoted, the Korn Shell accepts ((expression)) as a synonym for let "expression", obviating the need for quotation marks and dollar signs ($).

```
$ ((VALUE=VALUE * 10 + NEW))
```

You can use either form any place a command is allowed. You can also get rid of SPACEs if you like. Each argument to **let** is evaluated as a separate expression so you can assign values to more than one variable on a single line.

```
$ let COUNT=COUNT+1 "VALUE=VALUE*10+NEW"
```

▲▲▲ Expressions

You can use arithmetic expressions as arguments to commands. You can use an arithmetic expression enclosed between **$((** and **))** in place of any numeric value.

```
$ echo "There are $((60*60*24*365)) seconds in a non-leap year."
There are 31536000 seconds in a non-leap year.
```

You do not need to enclose **$((expression))** within quotation marks as the Korn Shell does not perform filename expansion within the **$((** and **))**. This feature makes it easier for you to use an asterisk (*) for multiplication, as the previous example shows.

Fewer Dollar Signs ($)

When you use variables within double parentheses that are preceded by a dollar sign ($), the dollar sign that precedes individual variable references within the double parentheses is optional.

```
$ x=23
$ y=37
$ echo $((2*x + 3*y))
157
$ echo $((2*$x + 3*$y))
157
```

Start Optional

▲▲▲ Operators

An arithmetic expression in the Korn Shell uses the same syntax, precedence, and associativity of expressions as the C language. The Korn Shell supports all integral operators, with the exception of **++**, **––**, **?:**, and **,**. The following table lists all the operators you can use within arithmetic expressions in the Korn Shell.

Operator	Meaning
+	Unary plus
−	Unary minus
!	Logical NOT
~	Complement
&	Bitwise AND
^	Bitwise XOR
|	Bitwise OR
*	Multiplication
/	Division
%	Remainder
+	Addition
−	Subtraction
<<	Left shift
>>	Right shift
<	Less than
>	Greater than
<=	Less than or equal
>=	Greater than or equal
==	Equality
!=	Inequality
&&	Logical AND
||	Logical OR
=, +=, −=, *=, /=, %=, &=, ^=, |=	Assignments

The **&&** and **||** operators are called *short circuiting*. If the result of using one of these operators can be decided by looking only at the left operand, then the right operand is not evaluated.

```
$ ((N=10))
$ ((Z=0))
$ echo $((N || ((Z+=1)) ))
1
$ echo $Z
0
```

Here because the value of **N** is nonzero, the result of the **||** (OR) operation is 1 (*true*) no matter what the value of the right side is, so the **((Z+=1))** is never evaluated and **Z** keeps its original value.

The assignment operators such as **+=** are shorthand notations. For example **((N+=3))** is the same as **((N=N+3))**.

The remainder operator (**%**) gives the remainder when its first operand is divided by its second. Thus the expression **$((15%7))** has the value 1. The result of a logical operation is always either 0 (*false*) or 1 (*true*).

```
$ let "Var1=2#0101"
$ let "Var2=2#0110"
$ echo "$Var1 and $Var2"
5 and 6
$ echo $(( Var1 & Var2 ))
4
$ echo $(( Var1 && Var2 ))
1
$ echo $(( Var1 | Var2 ))
7
$ echo $(( Var1 || Var2 ))
1
$ echo $(( Var1 ^ Var2 ))
3
$ echo $(( !Var1 ))
0
$ echo $(( Var1 < Var2 ))
1
$ echo $(( Var1 > Var2 ))
0
```

The bitwise AND operator (**&**) selects the bits that are on in both 5 (0101 in binary) and 6 (0110 in binary); the result is binary 0100, which is 4 decimal. The logical AND operator (**&&**) produces a result of 1 if both of its operands are nonzero, and 0 otherwise. The bitwise inclusive OR operator (**|**) selects the bits that are on in either of 0101 and 0110, resulting in 0111, which is 7 decimal; it produces a result of 1 if either of its operands is nonzero, and 0 otherwise. The bitwise exclusive OR operator (**^**) selects the bits that are on in either, but not both, of the operands 0101 and 0110, giving 0011, which is 3 decimal. The logical NOT operator (**!**) produces a result of 1 if its operand is 0, and 0 otherwise. The comparison operators all produce a result of 1 if the comparison is *true,* and 0 otherwise.

Because the exclamation point in **((!Var1))** is enclosed within double parentheses, it does not need to be escaped to prevent the Korn Shell from interpreting the exclamation point as a history event (page 514).

Stop Optional

▲ Builtins

The Korn Shell provides a much richer set of builtins than either the Bourne or C Shells. They include builtins for option processing, I/O, control flow, and control of the user's environment. Some of these builtins have been mentioned previously; this section focuses on the builtins that have not been covered.

▲▲ Control Structures

Whereas this book refers to *control structure* or *control flow command,* the Korn Shell documentation refers to commands that are not simple commands. This chapter will stay with the term *control structure* or *control flow command* for consistency with the rest of the book. The control flow commands are primarily used for shell programming, although they can also be useful in interactive work. The Korn Shell control structures that control the process flow are **if...then, for...in, while, case, until, repeat,** and **select.** All of these except **repeat** are also present in **sh.**

The **if** (page 394), **while** (page 407), and **until** (page 411) structures have in common the use of a *test-command* (not the **test** builtin ^sh_ksh^). You can use the same syntax for Korn Shell *test-commands* that you use in the Bourne Shell. You can use the **test** builtin, the **[[** builtin (two left square brackets), or any other command as the *test-command*. The syntax of the **[[** builtin is

[[conditions]]

The result of executing this builtin, like the **test** builtin, is a return status. The **conditions** allowed within the brackets are almost a superset of those accepted by **test** (page 918). Where the **test** builtin uses **–a** to logically AND the result of two expressions, the Korn Shell uses **&&**. Similarly where **test** uses **–o** to logically OR two results, the Korn Shell uses ‖. The Korn Shell adds these tests:

Test	Result
–o *option*	True if the option named **option** is set or on.
(*expression*)	*True* if *expression* is *true.*
! *expression*	*True* if *expression* is *false.*
expression && *expression2*	*True* if *expression1* and *expression2* are both *true.*
expression ‖ *expression2*	*True* if either *expression1* or *expression2* is *true.*

You can use **test**'s numeric relational operators **–gt, –ge, –lt, –le, –eq,** and **–ne** with **[[.** The Korn Shell allows you to use arithmetic expressions, not just constants, as the operands.

```
$ [[ $(( ${#HOME} + 14 )) -lt ${#PWD} ]]
$ echo $?
1
```

In this example the condition is *false* (1). The condition would be *true* (0) if the length of the string represented by the variable **HOME** plus 14 was less than the length of the string represented by **PWD.** See the **es** script on page 381 for more about **$?** .

Start Optional

The **test** builtin ^sh_ksh^ tests to see if strings are equal or unequal. The **[[** builtin adds comparison tests for string operators: The > and < operators compare strings for order (so that, for example, `"aa" < "bbb"`). The = operator tests for pattern match, not just equality: *[[string = pattern]]* is *true* if *string* matches *pattern.* This operator is not symmetrical; the ***pattern*** must appear on the right side of the = sign. For example [[artist = a*]] is *true* (=0), whereas [[a* = artist]] is false (=1):

```
$ [[ artist = a* ]]
$ echo $?
0
$ [[ a* = artist ]]
$ echo $?
1
```

The next example has a command list that is started by a compound condition. The condition tests that the directory **bin** and the file **src/myscript.sh** exist. If this is true, then **cp** copies **src/myscript.sh** to **bin/myscript**. If the copy succeeds, then **chmod** makes **myscript** executable. If any of these steps fails, then **echo** displays a message.

```
$ [[ -d bin && -f src/myscript.sh ]] && cp src/myscript.sh \
bin/myscript && chmod +x bin/myscript || echo "Cannot make \
executable version of myscript"
```

Stop Optional

The **[[** builtin is useful by itself, but you will probably use it most as the test command for control structures. This builtin also allows an arithmetic test. This test appears inside double parentheses **(( ))** instead of square brackets. These double parentheses are not preceded by a **$** sign, and the value of this test is not a numeric value, only a *true* or *false* exit status. You can use all of the logical arithmetic operators shown on page 491. You can write either

```
if [[ $(( ${#HOME} + 14 )) -lt ${#PWD} ]]
then ...
```

or

```
if (( $(( ${#HOME} + 14 )) < ${#PWD} ))
then ...
```

or

```
if (( ${#HOME} + 14 < ${#PWD} ))
then ...
```

The final versions use comparison operators that are similar to arithmetic and thus may be more natural for you to use.

The Korn Shell recognizes the tokens **[[** and **((** and treats them as special symbols, not commands. Thus you need not follow **[[** or **((** with a SPACE.

select

The **select** control structure ksh displays a menu, assigns a value to a variable based on the user's choice of items, and executes a series of commands. The syntax of a **select** structure is

select **varname** *[in* **arg** *...]*
do
    commands
done

First **select** generates and displays a menu of the **arg** items. The menu is formatted with numbers before each item. For example a **select** structure that begins with

```
select fruit in apple banana blueberry kiwi orange watermelon STOP
```

would display the following menu:

```
1) apple
2) banana
3) blueberry
4) kiwi
5) orange
6) watermelon
7) STOP
```

You can have many items in the list of **args**. The **select** structure uses the values of the **LINES** and **COLUMNS** variables to determine the size of the display. (**LINES** has a default value of 24, and **COLUMNS** a default of 80.)

After displaying the menu, **select** displays the value of **PS3**, the special **select** prompt. The default value of **PS3** is the characters ?#, but typically you would set **PS3** to a more meaningful value.

If the user enters a valid number (one in the menu range), then **select** sets the value of **varname** to the argument corresponding to the number entered and executes the commands between **do** and **done**. The **select** structure then reissues the **PS3** prompt and waits for a user choice. It does this repeatedly until something causes it to exit from the statements between **do** and **done**, typically a **break**, **return**, or **exit** statement. The **break** statement exits from the loop. From within a function **return** returns control to the program that called the function. The **exit** statement exits from the current shell. The following script illustrates the use of **select**:

```
$ cat fruit
#!/bin/ksh
PS3="Choose your favorite fruit from these possibilities: "
select FRUIT in apple banana blueberry kiwi orange watermelon STOP
do
if [[ $FRUIT = STOP ]]; then

echo "Thanks for playing!"
break
fi
echo "You chose $FRUIT as your favorite."
echo "That is choice number $REPLY."
echo
done
```

```
$ fruit
1) apple
2) banana
3) blueberry
4) kiwi
5) orange
6) watermelon
7) STOP
Choose your favorite fruit from these possibilities: 3
You chose blueberry as your favorite.
That is choice number 3.

Choose your favorite fruit from these possibilities:
```

An invalid menu choice causes **ksh** to assign a null string to **varname** and to execute the ***commands*** between **do** and **done**. If the user presses RETURN without entering a choice, the Korn Shell redisplays the menu and the **PS3** prompt. The Korn Shell stores the user's response in the keyword variable **REPLY**.

As the syntax indicates, you can omit the keyword **in** and the list of arguments. If you do, **select** uses the current values of the positional parameters **$@**.

repeat

The **repeat** control structure ksh allows you to specify how many times a sequence of commands is to be executed. The syntax of **repeat** is

> repeat ***word***
> do
>   ***commands***
> done

Here ***word*** is expanded then evaluated as an arithmetic expression. The value of that expression determines how many times the ***commands*** are repeated.

```
$ repeat 3; do
>   echo "Bye"
>   done
Bye
Bye
Bye
$ read number
3
$ repeat $number; do
>   echo "Bye"
>   done
Bye
Bye
Bye
```

▲▲ Option Processing

The way that a utility interprets its command line is up to the specific utility. However there are conventions that most UNIX/Solaris utilities conform to. Refer to "The Command Line" on page 103. In particular any option the utility takes is indicated by a letter preceded by a hyphen.

```
$ ls -l -r -t
```

(See pages 792 and 794 for descriptions of these arguments to **ls**.) The options usually must precede other arguments such as filenames. Most utilities allow you to combine options behind a single hyphen. The previous command can also be written as

```
$ ls -lrt
```

Some utilities have options that themselves require arguments. The **cc** and **gcc** utilities have a **–o** option that must be followed by the name you want to give the executable file that is being generated. Typically an argument to an option is separated from its option letter by a **SPACE**.

```
$ cc -o prog prog.c
```

Another convention allows utilities to work with filenames that start with a hyphen. If you have a file whose name happens to be **–l**, then the following command is ambiguous:

```
$ ls -l
```

It could mean a long listing of all files in the working directory or a listing of the file named **–l**. It is interpreted as the former. Avoid creating files whose names begin with hyphens, but if you do create them, many utilities follow the convention that a **––** argument (two consecutive hyphens) indicates the end of options. You can type

```
$ ls -- -l
```

or

```
$ ls ./-l
```

to disambiguate the command.

These are conventions, not hard-and-fast rules, and there are a number of utilities that do not follow them (for example **find**), but following such conventions is a good idea; it makes it much easier for users to learn to use your program. When you write shell programs that require options, follow the Solaris option conventions.

GNU ––help Option

A convention followed by most GNU (page 12) utilities is to display a (sometimes extensive) help message when you call them with an argument of **––help**:

```
$ gzip --help
gzip 1.2.4 (18 Aug 93)
usage: gzip [-cdfhlLnNrtvV19] [-S suffix] [file ...]
 -c --stdout      write on standard output, keep original ...
 -d --decompress  decompress
 -f --force       force overwrite of output file and ...
 -h --help        give this help
 -l --list        list compressed file contents
 -L --license     display software license
 .
 .
 .
```

▲▲▲ getopts: Parse Options

The **getopts** builtin ^{sh}_{ksh} (also a stand-alone utility: **/usr/bin/getopts**) makes it easier for you to write programs that follow the UNIX/Solaris argument conventions. The syntax for **getopts** is

> *getopts **optstring** **varname** [arg ...]*

The *opstring* is a list of the valid option letters. If an option takes an argument, you indicate that fact by following the corresponding letter with a colon (:). The option string `dxo:lt:r` indicates that **getopts** should search for **–d**, **–x**, **–o**, **–l**, **–t**, and **–r** options and that the **–o** and **–t** options take arguments.

The **getopts** builtin checks an argument list for options in *optstring*. It stores the option letters it finds in *varname*. By default **getopts** uses the command-line arguments. If you supply a list of arguments (*arg*) after *varname*, they are used instead.

The **getopts** builtin uses the **OPTIND** and **OPTARG** variables to store option-related values. When a shell script starts, the value of **OPTIND** is 1. Each time **getopts** locates an argument, it increments **OPTIND** to be the index of the next argument to be processed. If the option takes an argument, then **ksh** assigns the value of the argument to **OPTARG**.

Consider the following problem: You have to write a program that can take three options.

- A **–b** option indicates that your program should ignore white space at the start of input lines.

- A **–t** option followed by the name of a directory indicates that your program should use that directory for temporary files. Otherwise it should use **/tmp**.

- A **–u** option indicates that your program should translate all its output to uppercase.

- A **––** ends option processing.

- Ignore all other options.

The problem is to write the portion of the program that determines which options the user has supplied. The following solution does not use **getopts**:

```
SKIPBLANKS=
TMPDIR=/tmp
CASE=lower
while [[ "$1" = -* ]] # Remember, [[ = ]] does pattern match
do
    case $1 in
        -b)     SKIPBLANKS=TRUE ;;
        -t)     if [ -d "$2" ]
                    then
                    TMPDIR=$2
                    shift
                else
                    print "$0: -t takes a directory argument." >&2
                    exit 1
                fi ;;
        -u)     CASE=upper ;;
        --)     break   ;;       # Stop processing options
          *)      print "$0: Invalid option $1 ignored." >&2 ;;
    esac
    shift
done
```

This program fragment uses a loop to check and **shift** arguments while the argument is not two hyphens (−−). As long as the argument is not two hyphens, the program continues to loop through a **case** statement that checks all the possible options. The **−− case** label breaks out of the **while** loop. The ✳ **case** label recognizes any option; it appears as the last **case** label to catch any unknown options. The ✳ **case** label prints an error message and allows processing to continue. On each pass through the loop, the program does a **shift** to get to the next argument. If an option takes an argument, the program does an extra **shift** to get past that argument. The following program fragment processes the same options using **getopts**:

```
SKIPBLANKS=
TMPDIR=/tmp
CASE=lower

while getopts :bt:u arg
do
   case $arg in
      b)      SKIPBLANKS=TRUE ;;
      t)      if [ -d "$OPTARG" ]
                 then
                     TMPDIR=$OPTARG
              else
                  print "$0: $OPTARG is not a directory." >&2
                  exit 1
              fi ;;
      u)      CASE=upper ;;
      :)      print "$0: Must supply an argument to -$OPTARG." >&2
              exit 1 ;;
      \?)     print "Invalid option -$OPTARG ignored." >&2 ;;
   esac
done
shift $((OPTIND-1))
```

In this version of the code, the **while** structure evaluates the **getopts** builtin each time it comes to the top of the loop. The **getopts** builtin uses the **OPTIND** variable to keep track of the index of the argument it is to process the next time it is called. Thus the second example calls **shift** only once, at the end, whereas the first example used **shift** to get each new argument. The **getopts** builtin returns a nonzero (*false*) status when it has handled all the arguments and control passes to the statement after **done**.

In the second example the **case** patterns do not start with a hyphen, because the value of **arg** is just the option letter (**getopts** strips off the hyphen). Also, **getopts** recognizes −− as the end of the options, so you do not have to specify it explicitly in the **case** statement.

Because you tell **getopts** which options are valid and which require arguments, it can detect errors in the command line. There are two ways that **getopts** can handle these errors. This example uses a leading colon in *optstring* to specify that you check for and handle errors in your code—when **getopts** finds an invalid option, it sets **varname** to ? and **OPTARG** to the option letter. When it finds an option that is missing an argument, it sets **varname** to : and **OPTARG** to the option lacking an argument.

The \? **case** pattern specifies the action to take when **getopts** detects an invalid option. The : **case** pattern specifies the action to take when **getopts** detects a missing option argument. In both cases **getopts** does not write any error message; it leaves that task to you.

If you omit the leading colon from **optstring**, both an invalid option and a missing option argument cause **varname** to be assigned the string ?. **OPTARG** is not set, and **getopts** writes its own diagnostic message to standard error. Generally this method is less desirable because you have less control over what the user sees when an error is made.

Using **getopts** will not necessarily make your programs shorter. Its principal advantages are that it provides a uniform programming interface and it enforces standard option handling.

▲▲ Input and Output

A programming language needs commands for input and output. In the Korn Shell the input command is **read** and the output command is **print**.

▲▲▲ read: Accept User Input

The syntax of **read** ^sh_ksh is similar to the Bourne Shell's **read** (page 369), but the Korn Shell **read** provides additional functionality.

> *read [–prs] [–un] [varname?prompt] [varname...]*

The variable names are optional. The following command is valid as it stands:

```
read
```

It reads an entire input line from standard input into the variable **REPLY**. When you supply arguments on the command line, **read** assumes they are variable names and splits the input line (using the characters in **IFS** as word separators) assigning each word sequentially to a *varname* argument. If there are not enough variables, the last variable is assigned a string equal to the remainder of the input line. If there are not enough words, the leftover variables are set to null (page 370).

The Korn Shell allows you to specify an input prompt by using the syntax *varname?prompt* for the first input variable name. For example if your script has a line of the form

```
read MON\?"Enter month, day and year separated by spaces: " DAY YR
```

then execution of this command causes the script to issue the prompt

```
Enter month, day and year separated by spaces:
```

and then pause while you type an input line. If you type three values, they are assigned to **MON**, **DAY**, and **YR**. The question mark (**?**) is escaped to prevent the Korn Shell from using it as a filename pattern-matching operator.

The **read** ksh builtin supports other options. Some of the more common ones are described in the following list.

–p coprocess The command

```
read -p...
```

reads its input line from standard output of the coprocess. For more information see "I/O Redirection and the Coprocess" on page 523.

–r   **raw input**   Ordinarily if the input line ends in a backslash character (\), the backslash and the **NEWLINE** following it are discarded, and the next line is treated as a continuation of the same line of input. This option causes a trailing backslash to be treated as a regular character. One application is for reading an input file that is itself a shell script containing backslashes that you want to reproduce.

–s   **save**   Saves input as a command line in the **history** file.

–u*n*   Use the integer *n* as the file descriptor that **read** takes its input from.

```
read -u4 arg1 arg2
```

is equivalent to

```
read arg1 arg2 <&4
```

For more information see "File Descriptors" on page 503.

The **read** builtin has exit status of 0 if it successfully reads any data. It has nonzero exit status when it reaches the EOF (end of file).

```
$ cat names
Alice Jones
Robert Smith
Alice Paulson
John Q. Public
$ while read First Rest
> do
>       print $Rest, $First
> done < names
Jones, Alice
Smith, Robert
Paulson, Alice
Q. Public, John
```

Start Optional

The placement of the redirection symbol (<) for the compound **while** structure is critical. It is important that you only place the redirection symbol at the **done** statement and not at the call to **read**. Each time you redirect input, the shell opens the file and repositions the read pointer at the start of the file.

```
$ read line1 < names; print $line1; read line2 < names; print $line2
Alice Jones
Alice Jones
$ (read line1; print $line1; read line2; print $line2) < names
Alice Jones
Robert Smith
```

In the first example each **read** opens **names** and starts at the beginning of the **names** file. In the second example **names** is opened once, as standard input of the subshell created by the parentheses. Each **read** then reads successive lines of standard input.

Another way to get the same effect is to open the input file with **exec** and hold it open, as shown below. (Refer to "File Descriptors" on page 503.)

```
$ exec 3< names
$ read -u3 line1; print $line1; read -u3 line2; print $line2
Alice Jones
Robert Smith
$ exec 3<&-
```

Stop Optional

▲▲▲ print: Display Output

The syntax for the **print** builtin ₖₛₕ, which is a replacement for **echo** $^{sh}_{csh}{}_{ksh}$, is

*print [–nRrps] [–un] **string...***

By default **print** writes the strings to standard output and recognizes both syntaxes (\c at the end of a string and the **–n** option) for suppressing the trailing NEWLINE.

Escape	Meaning
\a	The alert character (typically makes the display beep or flash)
\b	The backspace character
\c	Does not print, and suppresses a trailing NEWLINE
\e	ESCAPE character
\f	Form feed—puts a CONTROL-L character in the output stream
\n	NEWLINE—allows a single call to **print** to write multiple lines
\r	RETURN—puts a CONTROL-M character in the output stream
\t	TAB character
\v	The vertical tab character
\\	The backslash character
\0*nnn*	The ASCII character whose octal value is *nnn*—you can omit leading zeros
\x*nnn*	The ASCII character whose hexadecimal value is *nnn*

Remember that the backslash (\) character is a special character to the shell, and you must quote it or escape it to use it in any of the print escapes. Here is an example of the use of **print** escapes:

```
$ print "Columbus had 3 ships:\n\tThe Nina\n\tThe Pinta\n\tThe Santa Maria"
Columbus had 3 ships:
        The Nina
        The Pinta
        The Santa Maria
```

Some of the options to **print**_{ksh} have the same meaning as the corresponding options for **read**_{ksh}.

–p	The command

```
print -p...
```

directs its output line to standard input of the coprocess. Refer to "I/O Redirection and the Coprocess" (page 523).

–s   Directs output to the history file.

–u*n*   Sends output to file descriptor *n*. For more information see "File Descriptors" on page 503.

–n   **newline**   Suppresses trailing NEWLINEs.

–r   **raw input**   Ignores the special meaning of the escapes; displays them as ordinary characters.

–R   **raw input**   Ignores the special meaning of the escapes; displays them as ordinary characters. Also treats any following fields as string arguments, even if they start with a hyphen (except for **–n**).

The following example demonstrates the effect of several **print** options:

```
$ print -R -n -p "This NEWLINE \nwill not be recognized" ; echo " done"
-p This NEWLINE \nwill not be recognized done
$ print "This NEWLINE \nwill not be recognized" ; echo " done"
This NEWLINE
will not be recognized
 done
```

You must (almost) always use double quotation marks around the arguments to **print** (and **echo**). Without the quotation marks the \n would be displayed as n. In the preceding example the second command on the first command line displays done at the end of the output line because the **–n** option suppresses the trailing NEW-LINE. The **–R** option causes the **–p** and the \n not to be interpreted as options or special characters. The second command line shows what happens without these options.

▲▲ File Descriptors

As discussed on page 356, when a process wants to read from or write to a file, it must first open that file. When a process opens a file, Solaris associates a number (called a *file descriptor*) with the file. Each process has its own set of open files and its own file descriptors. After a process opens a file, it reads from and writes to that file by referring to it with the file descriptor. When the process no longer needs the file, it closes it, freeing the file descriptor.

A typical Solaris process starts with three open files: Standard input, which has file descriptor 0; standard output, with file descriptor 1; and standard error, with file descriptor 2. Often those are all the files the process needs. The Korn Shell allows you to redirect standard input, standard output, and standard error of all the commands you invoke, just as the Bourne Shell does. Recall that you can redirect standard output with the symbol **>** or the symbol **1>**, and that you redirect standard error with the symbol **2>**. You can redirect other file descriptors, but because file descriptors other than 0, 1, and 2 do not have any special conventional meaning, it's rarely useful to do so. The exception is in programs that you write yourself, in which case you control the meaning of the file descriptors and you can take advantage of redirection.

The Bourne and Korn Shells allow you to open files using the **exec** builtin as follows:

```
$ exec 3> outfile
$ exec 4< infile
```

The first of these commands opens **outfile** for output and holds it open, associating it with file descriptor 3. The second opens **infile** for input, associating it with file descriptor 4.

The token **<&** duplicates both input and output file descriptors. You can duplicate a file descriptor by making it refer to the same file as another open file descriptor, such as standard input or output. The following command opens or redirects file descriptor **n** as a duplicate of file descriptor **m**:

```
exec n<&m
```

Once you have opened a file, you can use it for input and output in two different ways. You can use I/O redirection on any command line, redirecting standard output to a file descriptor with **>&n**, or redirecting standard input from a file descriptor with **<&n**. You can also use the **read** (page 500) and **print** (page 502) builtins. If you invoke other commands, including functions (pages 429 and 506), they inherit these open files and file descriptors. When you have finished using a file, you can close it with

```
exec n<&-
```

When you invoke the next shell function with two arguments, it copies the file named by the first argument to the file named by the second argument: **mycp** copies **source** to **dest**. If you supply only one argument, the script interprets it as a **source** and copies **source** to standard output. If you invoke **mycp** with no arguments, it copies standard input to standard output.

```
function mycp
{
case $# in
0)     exec 3<&0 4<&1 ;;
1)     exec 3< $1 4<&1 ;;
2)     exec 3< $1 4> $2 ;;
*)     print "Usage: mycp [source [dest]]"
       exit 1 ;;
esac

cat <&3 >&4
exec 3<&- 4<&-
}
```

The real work of this function is done in the line that begins with `cat`. The rest of the script arranges for file descriptors 3 and 4, which are the input and output of the **cat** command, to be associated with the right file.

The next program takes two filenames on the command line and sorts both to temporary files. It then merges the sorted files to standard output, preceding each line by a number that indicates which file it came from.

The Korn Shell does not have *string* comparison operators for *less than or equal to* or *greater than or equal to*. You can use *not greater than*, as in this example (`[[ ! "$Line1" > "$Line2" ]]` in the **if** statement), as an equivalent for *less than or equal to*.

```
$ cat sortmerge
#!/bin/ksh
usage ()
{
if [[ $# -ne 2 ]]
then
print -u2 "Usage: $0 file1 file2"
exit 1
fi
}
# Default temporary directory
: ${TEMPDIR:=/tmp}
# Check argument count
usage "$@"
# Set up temporary files for sorting
file1=$TEMPDIR/file1.$$
file2=$TEMPDIR/file2.$$
# Sort
sort $1 > $file1
sort $2 > $file2
# Open files $file1 and $file2 for reading.  Use FD's 3 and 4.
exec 3<$file1
exec 4<$file2
# Read the first line of each file to figure out how to start.
read -u3 Line1
Status1=$?
read -u4 Line2
Status2=$?
# Strategy: while there's still input left in both files:
#        Output the lesser line.
#        Read a new line from the file that line came from.
while [[ $Status1 -eq 0 && $Status2 -eq 0 ]]
do
   if [[ ! "$Line1" > "$Line2" ]]
      then
      print "1.\t$Line1"
      read -u3 Line1
      Status1=$?
   else
      print "2.\t$Line2"
      read -u4 Line2
      Status2=$?
   fi
done
# Now one of the files is at end-of-file.
# Read from each file until the end.
# First file1:
while [[ $Status1 -eq 0 ]]
do
   print "1.\t$Line1"
   read -u3 Line1
   Status1=$?
done
```

```
# Next file2:
while [[ $Status2 -eq 0 ]]
do
   print "2.\t$Line2"
   read -u4 Line2
   Status2=$?
done
# Close and remove both input files
exec 3<&- 4<&-
rm -f $file1 $file2
exit 0
```

▲▲ Functions

The syntax for a shell function is (**ksh** accepts both formats, **sh** accepts only the first):

func_name()
{
commands
}

or

function func_name
{
commands
}

The first brace ({) can appear on the same line as the function name. If the function definition includes the names of aliases, they are expanded when the function is read, not when it is executed. You can use the **break** builtin inside a function to terminate its execution. The **functions** builtin _{ksh} lists all the defined functions.

Shell functions are useful both as a shorthand and to define special commands. The following function starts a process named **process** in the background, with the output normally displayed by **process** saved in **.process.out**:

```
start_process() {
process > .process.out 2>&1 &
}
```

There is no **setenv** builtin in **ksh**. The following function mimics the behavior of this command, which is available in **csh**:

```
$ setenv() {
if [ $# -eq 2 ]; then
eval $1="$2"
export $1
else
echo "Usage: setenv NAME VALUE" >&2
fi
}
```

This function checks to see that there are two arguments and displays a usage message if not. If there are two arguments, it assigns the value of the second argument to the name of the first and exports the first. (The Korn Shell **export** builtin is identical to **sh**'s [page 368]).

The **unfunction** builtin deletes a function definition:

unfunction func_name

The Korn Shell stores functions in memory so that they run more efficiently than shell scripts. The source for the functions is loaded into memory each time a shell or subshell is started. If you define too many functions, the overhead of starting a subshell (as when you run a script) becomes unacceptable.

You can also store functions in files so that they are read into memory the first time they are called. The **autoload**_{ksh} builtin notifies **ksh** that a function is stored in a file. When **autoload** is executed (normally when you start a new shell), the shell does not load the function into memory—it just keeps track of its name (it actually declares it as an undefined function). When a script first calls an **autoload** function, **ksh** searches through the directories listed in **FPATH** for a file with the same name as the function. (The syntax of **FPATH** is identical to that of **PATH** [page 372]). When it finds the file, it loads the function into memory and leaves it there. The syntax for **autoload** is

autoload func_name

It is your responsibility to ensure that the function definition and the file it is stored in have the same name. Typically you have one directory with many small files, each containing a single function definition. If you are working on several projects that make use of different shell functions, you may have several such directories.

▲▲ Built-in Commands

▲▲▲ Job Control

Job control under **ksh** is very similar to that of the C Shell (page 450).

▲▲▲ alias: Shortcut for a Command

Unlike the C Shell **alias** builtin (page 443), the Korn Shell **alias** builtin does not accept an argument. Use a **ksh** function—similar to **sh** functions (page 429)—when you need to use an argument. The syntax used to establish a **ksh alias** is

alias [–tx] [name[=command]]

where ***name*** is the name of the alias and ***command*** is the command line the alias is replaced with when it is called. The **–t** option produces a tracked alias and the **–x** option produces an exported alias. Establish aliases in your **.profile** file if you want them to be available each time you log in.

When you set up a *tracked* alias (**–t**) for a command, **alias** uses the absolute pathname of the command in its definition of the alias. Tracked aliases play a role in the Korn Shell similar to that of the hashing mechanism in the C Shell. When you call the alias, the shell uses the stored absolute pathname, avoiding an inefficient path search. When you change the **PATH** variable, all tracked aliases become undefined. The next time you use each undefined tracked alias, the Korn Shell reestablishes the pathname for the command in the alias. You cannot use the **–t** option to define a new, tracked alias; You must first define the alias, then establish it as a tracked alias using a second alias command.

The **trackall** option causes the Korn Shell to create a tracked alias for each command you enter (not just aliases you create). You can use this option in place of setting up tracked aliases for individual commands.

```
$ set -o trackall
```

The **–x** option causes **alias** to export an alias, so that it will be accessible to child processes (similar to an exported variable).

Without any options or arguments, **alias** lists active aliases (just as the C Shell **alias** does). With the **–t** option and no arguments **alias** lists tracked aliases, whereas the **–x** option lists exported aliases. To remove an alias use **unalias** with an argument of the alias name. The following example removes the alias named **deleteme**:

```
$ unalias deleteme
```

The following are some of the aliases that are built into the Korn Shell. You can unset or redefine them.

```
autoload='typeset -fu'
functions='typeset -f'
history='fc -l'
integer='typeset -i'
local=typeset
r='fc -e -'
stop='kill -STOP'
suspend='kill -STOP $$'
```

▲▲▲ kill: Abort a Process

The **kill** builtin _{sh csh ksh} sends a signal to a process or job. If you do not specify a signal, it sends a TERM (software termination, number 15) signal. For more information on signal names and numbers, see the table on page 426. In the following example the *n* is the signal number and *PID* is the identification number of the process that is to receive the signal.

kill –n PID

The shells also support named signals. To send a signal to a job, you can refer to the signal by name.

```
$ kill -TERM %1
```

This command sends the TERM signal to job number 1. Because TERM is the default signal for **kill**, you can also give the command as **kill %1**.

Generally any of these signals terminates a process. A program that is interrupted often has things in an unpredictable state: Temporary files may be left behind (when they are normally removed), and permissions may be changed. A well-written application traps, or detects, the arrival of signals and cleans up before exiting. Most carefully written applications trap the INT, QUIT, and TERM signals. Try INT first (press **CONTROL-C**, if the job is in the foreground). Because an application can be written to ignore these signals, you may need to use KILL. The KILL signal cannot be trapped or ignored; it is a "sure kill." Refer to page 785 in Part III for more information on **kill**.

▲▲▲ whence: Display the Absolute Pathname of a Utility

The **whence** builtin _{ksh} tells you the absolute pathname of a utility.

```
$ whence grep
/bin/grep
```

In this form **whence** reports only the pathnames of utilities that actually have a pathname; it does not tell you about aliases, functions, or builtins. With the **–v** option **whence** tells you the type of any command or reserved word that you can use in the Korn Shell.

```
$ whence pwd
pwd
$ whence -v pwd
pwd is a shell builtin
$ whence -v func
func is a function
$ whence -v if
if is a reserved shell keyword
```

The **type** builtin _{sh ksh} is a synonym for **whence –v**.

▲▲▲ trap: Catch a Signal

The **trap** builtin _{sh ksh} causes a shell script to execute a command when it receives an error or signal or upon exiting from a function or script. The syntax of **trap** is similar to the Bourne Shell's **trap** (page 425), including the ability to use signal names in place of numbers.

> *trap 'command' event*

Quote the ***command*** because it must be passed to **trap** as a single argument. The ***event*** arguments are names of signals (for example INT, TERM), the signal numbers, or one of the following:

Event	Occurrence
DEBUG	Occurs after every simple command. The following command causes your script to append the line number of the script and the pathname of the working directory to **/tmp/dir_trace** after each simple command: `trap 'echo $LINENO $PWD >> /tmp/dir_trace' DEBUG`
ERR	Occurs whenever a command completes with nonzero exit status. The following command causes your script to execute **cleanup** (a user-defined function) and then exit from the script with a status of 1. `trap 'cleanup ; exit 1' ERR`

Event	Occurrence
HUP, INT, or any signal name without the SIG prefix	Occurs when the named signal is received. See the table on page 426 for a more complete list.
EXIT or 0	Occurs whenever the script exits.

If *command* is a null string, then the corresponding signal or event is ignored. Any attempt to ignore or set a trap for the KILL (9) signal is ignored. If you have set the action for a signal or event using **trap** and you want to reset it to its default behavior, use a hyphen (–) as the action. Without any arguments the **trap** builtin lists all current traps in a form that can be saved and reread later by the shell.

The following script named **debug** demonstrates how **trap** works. Modify it and experiment with it to get a better feel for how to use **trap**: Look at the output in **dir_trace**; ERR is called when the script tries to run **rpcbind** (assuming you are not logged in as **root**); INT is called when you press CONTROL-C while the script is running.

```
$ cat debug
#!/bin/ksh
trap 'echo $LINENO $PWD >> dir_trace' DEBUG
trap 'echo ERROR' ERR
trap 'echo INTERRUPT;exit' INT
trap 'echo EXIT' EXIT
count=4

while [ count -gt 0 ]
do
   echo "hi there"
   /usr/sbin/rpcbind
   sleep 1
   echo $count
   ((count = count - 1))
done
```

By becoming familiar with the Korn Shell's large collection of builtins, you can take advantage of those that will help you in your day-to-day work with Solaris. Even if you do not use **ksh** on a regular basis, you will be able to use it when another shell cannot help you solve the problem at hand as easily.

▲ Command-Line Editing

The Korn Shell allows you to edit the current command line. If you make a mistake, you do not need to back up to the point of the mistake and reenter the command from there or press the line kill key and start over. You can use one of the command-line editors to modify the command line. You can also access and edit previous command lines stored in your history file (page 515).

The Korn Shell provides two command-line editors, one similar to **vi** (Chapter 8), and the other similar to **emacs** (Chapter 9). Depending on how the Korn Shell is set up on your system, you may be able to use one, both, or neither of the editors.

Use one of the following commands to set up your environment so that you can use the **vi** command-line editor:

    $ VISUAL=vi³

or

    $ set -o vi

Use one of the next commands to use the **emacs** command-line editor:

    $ VISUAL=emacs

or

    $ set -o emacs

▲▲ Using the vi Command-Line Editor

When you are entering Korn Shell commands with **vi** as your command-line editor, you are in Input Mode while you type commands.

As you are entering a command, if you discover an error before you press RETURN, you can press ESCAPE to switch to **vi** Command Mode. This is different from the **vi** editor's initial mode when you start to edit a file. You can then use many **vi** commands to edit the command line. It is as though you have a one-line window to edit the current command line as well as those for previous commands. You can use the **vi** cursor positioning commands, such as **h** and **l**, or **w** and **b**, optionally preceded by a Repeat Factor (page 283). You can use the arrow keys to position the cursor. You can also use the Search Forward (/) or Search Backward commands (**?**). You can modify the command line using **vi** Command Mode editing commands such as **x** (delete character), **r** (replace character), **~** (change case), and **.** (repeat last change). To change to Input Mode, use an Insert (**i**, **I**), Append (**a**, **A**), Replace (**R**), or Change (**c**, **C**) command. You do not have to return to Command Mode to run the command; just press RETURN, even if you are in the middle of the command line.

If you want to edit the command line using the full power of **vi**, you can press ESCAPE to enter Command Mode and type **v**. The Korn Shell then calls the stand-alone **vi** editor (not the Korn Shell's command-line **vi**) with a file containing a single line, the command line in its current state. When you exit from **vi** (**ZZ**), the Korn Shell executes the command or commands you edited. You can create a multiline sequence of commands in this manner.

---

3. If the **VISUAL** variable is not set, the shell will look at the **EDITOR** variable to select which editor to use.

▲▲▲ Pathname Operations

In Command Mode you can also use several commands that are not included in the stand-alone **vi** editor. These commands manipulate filenames and are called *Pathname Listing, Pathname Completion,* and *Pathname Expansion.* The commands in this section *will not work* unless you have set up your environment to use the **vi** command-line editor (page 510).

▲▲▲▲ **Pathname Listing:**   While the cursor is on a word, enter Command Mode (if you are not already in it) and type an equal sign (=). The **vi** command-line editor responds by listing all the pathnames that would match the current word if an asterisk were appended to it. For example suppose that the directory **films** contains the files **casablanca**, **city_lights**, **dark_passage**, **dark_victory**, and **modern_times**. You want to use **cat** to display one of the files, so you type

```
$ cat films/dar
```

At this point (before you have pressed RETURN), you realize that you are not sure what the full name of the file is. If you press ESCAPE and then =, the **vi** command-line editor lists the files and then reechos the partial command, including the prompt, like this:

```
1) dark_passage
2) dark_victory
$ cat films/dar
```

The cursor is on the letter **r**, where you left it, and you are in Command Mode. To finish typing a pathname, you must first type **a** to append.

▲▲▲▲ **Pathname Completion:**   This facility allows you to type a portion of a pathname and have the **vi** command-line editor supply the rest. You invoke Pathname Completion by pressing ESCAPE followed by a backslash (\). If the portion of the pathname that you have typed so far is sufficient to determine the entire pathname uniquely, then that pathname is displayed. If more than one pathname would match, then the command-line **vi** completes the pathname up to the point where there are choices and leaves you in Input Mode to type more. If you enter

```
$ cat films/dar
```

and press ESCAPE and then \, the shell extends the command line as far as it can.

```
$ cat films/dark_
```

Because every file in **films** that starts with **dar** has **k_** as the next characters, that's as far as **ksh** can extend the line without making a choice between files. You are left in Input Mode, with the cursor just past the _ character. If you add enough information to distinguish between the two possible files, Pathname Completion will yield the entire filename. Suppose that you now enter **p**, ESCAPE, and then \. The Korn Shell completes the command line. (The emacs in-line editor uses ESCAPE ESCAPE in place of ESCAPE \ for pathname completion.)

```
$ cat films/dark_passage
```

Because there is no further ambiguity, the shell appends a SPACE and leaves you in Input Mode to finish typing the command line. You can press RETURN to complete the **cat** command. If the complete filename is that of a directory, **ksh** will append a slash (/) in place of a SPACE.

▲▲▲▲ Pathname Expansion: This facility is like an interactive version of ordinary filename generation. You invoke Pathname Expansion by typing a pattern followed by an **ESCAPE** and an asterisk (✳), which causes the pattern to be replaced by all pathnames that match the pattern. If you enter

```
$ cat films/dar
```

and then press **ESCAPE** and ✳, the shell expands the command line to

```
$ cat films/dark_passage films/dark_victory
```

After it fills in the filenames, the **vi** command-line editor leaves you in Input Mode, with the cursor past the last character in the line. At this point you can continue to edit the line or press **RETURN** to execute the command. If no filenames match, the **vi** command-line editor causes your terminal to beep. (Some terminals flash rather than beep.)

The **vi** command-line editor commands are listed on page 541.

Pressing RETURN Executes the Command

Remember that pressing **RETURN** causes the Korn Shell to execute the command regardless of whether you are in Command Mode or Input Mode and regardless of where the cursor is on the command line. At the next prompt, you are back in Input Mode.

▲▲ Using the emacs Command-Line Editor

The **emacs** editor differs from the **vi** editor in that it is modeless. Thus you do not switch between Command Mode and Input Mode, as in **vi**. Like **vi** the **emacs** command-line editor provides commands for moving around in the command line as well as through your command history and for modifying part or all of the text. It also supports the Pathname Listing, Pathname Completion, and Pathname Expansion commands.

In **emacs** most commands are control characters. This allows **emacs** to distinguish between input and commands and thus to dispense with modes. The **ESCAPE** key also plays a special role in **emacs**, as do the erase and kill characters (page 299).

This discussion covers only Korn Shell **emacs** command-line editor commands, which differ, in a few cases, from the commands in the stand-alone **emacs** editor.

In **emacs** you perform cursor movement using both **CONTROL** and **ESCAPE** commands. To move the cursor one character backward in the command line, type **CONTROL-B**. Typing **CONTROL-F** moves it one character forward (page 296). As with **vi**, it is possible to precede these movements with counts. However to use a count you must first press **ESCAPE**, otherwise the numbers you type are entered on the command line.

Like **vi**, **emacs** also provides word motions and line motions. To move backward or forward one word in the command line, type **ESCAPE b** or **ESCAPE f** (page 296). To move several words use a count by pressing **ESCAPE** followed by the number. To get to the beginning of the line press **CONTROL-A**, to the end of the line press **CONTROL-E**, and to the next instance of the character *c* press **CONTROL-X CONTROL-F** followed by *c*.

You can add text to the command line by just moving the cursor to the correct place and typing the desired text. To delete text move the cursor just to the right of the characters that you want to delete, and then press the Erase key once for each character that you want to delete.

> **Using CONTROL-D**
>
> If you want to delete the character directly under the cursor, press **CONTROL-D**. If you enter **CONTROL-D** on an empty line or at the beginning of the line, it may terminate your shell session.

If you want to delete the entire command line, type the line kill character. This has the usual effect, except that you can type it while the cursor is anywhere in the command line. If you want to delete from the cursor to the end of the line, use **CONTROL-K**.

The **emacs** command-line editor commands are listed on page 543. The **emacs** pathname operation commands are identical to those in **vi** except that you use **ESCAPE ESCAPE** for pathname completion.

▲▲ History

The Korn Shell keeps a history of recently executed commands in a file, which means that the history can persist from one shell session to the next. You can select, edit, and reexecute any command in the history list from the current or a previous login session. The Korn Shell history remembers multiline commands in their entirety and allows you to edit them.

If it is set, the **HISTSIZE** variable determines the number of commands that are kept in the history list. The **HISTFILE** variable determines where the history list is saved when the Korn Shell exits. If any commands are saved in **HISTFILE**, the Korn Shell reads them back in when the shell starts, so the commands become part of the history list for your current session.

To access and edit any of the commands in the history file, you can use either the **vi** command-line editor, the **emacs** command-line editor, or the **fc** builtin _ksh_ (page 515).

▲▲▲ Using the vi Command-Line Editor on Previous Commands

When you are using the **vi** command-line editor and are in Command Mode (press **ESCAPE** to enter Command Mode), you can access previous commands using several **vi** commands that move the cursor up and down. It is as if you are using **vi** to edit a copy of the history file, with a screen that has room for only one command on it. When you use the **k** command to move up one line, you access the previous command. If you then use the **j** command to move down one line, you will be back to the original command.

While in Command Mode press the question mark (**?**) key followed by a search string to look back through your history list for the most recent command containing that string. If you have moved back into your history list, then use a forward slash (**/**) instead of the question mark to search forward toward your most recent command. Unlike the search strings in the **vi** utility, these search strings cannot contain regular expressions, but you can start the search string with a caret (**^**) to force the Korn Shell to locate only commands that start with the search string. As in the **vi** utility, pressing **n** after a successful search continues the search for the next occurrence of the search string.

You can also access events in the history list by using the event numbers. While you are in Command Mode, enter the event number followed by a **G** to go directly to the command with that event number.

When you initially move to the command, you are in Command Mode, not Input Mode. Now you can edit the command as you like or press **RETURN** to execute it.

▲▲▲ fc: Display, Edit, and Reexecute Commands

The **fc** (fix command) builtin ⃞ enables you to display the history file as well as to edit and reexecute previous commands. It provides many of the same capabilities as the command-line editors.

▲▲▲▲ Viewing the History List: When you call **fc** with the **–l** option, it displays commands from the history file on standard output. Without any arguments **fc –l** lists the 16 most recent commands (plus the **fc** command itself) in a numbered list. Because the Korn Shell sets up an alias, **history**, for the **fc –l** command, you can also use the **history** alias to display the history list. The list of events is ordered with the oldest events at the top (unless you use the **–r** option, which reverses the order).

```
$ fc -l
190   lp memor.0795
191   lp memo.0795
192   mv memo.0795 memo.071195
193   cd
194   view calendar
195   cd Work
196   vi letter.adams01
197   spell letter.adams01
198   nroff letter.admas01 > adams.out
199   nroff letter.adams01 > adams.out
200   page adams.out
201   lp adams.out
202   rm adams.out
203   cd ../memos
204   ls
205   rm *0486
206   fc -l
```

The **fc** builtin can take zero, one, or two arguments with the **–l** option. The arguments specify a part of the history list to be displayed. The syntax of this command is

fc –l [first [last]]

The **fc** builtin lists commands beginning with the most recent event that matches the *first* argument. The argument can be the number of the event, the first few characters of the command line, or a negative number (which is taken to be the *n*th previous command). Without a second argument **fc** displays the command lines from *first* through the most recent event. If you provide a second argument, **fc** displays all commands from the most recent event that matches the *first* argument through the most recent event that matches the *second*. The next command displays the history list from event 197 through event 205.

```
$ fc -l 197 205
 197   spell letter.adams01
 198   nroff letter.admas01 > adams.out
 199   nroff letter.adams01 > adams.out
 200   page adams.out
 201   lp adams.out
 202   rm adams.out
 203   cd ../memos
 204   ls
 205   rm *0486
```

The following command lists the most recent event that begins with the string view through the most recent event that begins with the string isp:

```
$ fc -l view isp
 194   view calendar
 195   cd Work
 196   vi letter.adams01
 197   spell letter.adams01
```

To list a single command from the history file, use the same identifier for the first and second arguments. The following command lists event 197:

```
$ fc -l 197 197
 197   spell letter.adams01
```

When you use the editor to change a series of commands or when you call the editor to work on one command and then add other commands, the Korn Shell treats the entire set of commands as one event. That is, if you edit a series of commands and execute them, they will be listed as a single new event in the history list. Following, 298 is a series of commands that were entered while **fc** was editing an event, and 301 is a semicolon-separated series of commands that were entered from the command line.

```
 297   ls -l
 298   ls
       who
       date
 299   fc -l
 300   history
 301   who;date;ls
```

▲▲▲▲▲ **Editing and Reexecuting Previous Commands:**   You can use **fc** to edit and reexecute previous commands.

fc [–e editor] [first [last]]

When you call **fc** with the **–e** option followed by the name of an editor, **fc** calls the editor with an event in the Work Buffer. Without first and last **fc** defaults to the most recent event. The next example invokes the **vi** editor to edit the most recent event:

```
$ fc -e vi
```

In this example the **fc** builtin uses the stand-alone **vi** editor. If you set the **FCEDIT** variable, you do not need to use the **–e** option to specify an editor on the command line. Because the value of **FCEDIT** has been changed to **/bin/vi** and **fc** has no arguments, the following command edits the most recent event with the **vi** editor.

```
$ export FCEDIT=/bin/vi
$ fc
```

If you call **fc** with a single argument, it invokes the editor to allow you to work on the specified command. The following example starts the editor with event 21 in the Work Buffer. When you exit from the editor, **sh** automatically executes the command.

```
$ fc 21
```

Again, you can identify commands with numbers or by specifying the first few characters of the command name. The following example calls the editor to work on events from the most recent event that begins with the letters `vi` through event number 206:

```
$ fc vi 206
```

> ### fc: The Shell Executes Whatever Is in the Buffer
>
> When you execute an **fc** command, whatever you leave in the editor buffer gets executed, possibly with unwanted results. If you decide you do not want to execute a command, delete everything from the buffer before you exit from the editor.

▲▲▲▲ **Reexecuting Previous Commands without Calling the Editor:**   You can reexecute previous commands without going into an editor. If you call **fc** with the **–e** option and an argument of **–**, it skips the editing phase and reexecutes the command. The following example reexecutes event 201:

```
$ fc -e - 201
lp adams.out
request id is printer_1-1019 (standard input)
```

whereas the next reexecutes the previous command:

```
$ fc -e -
```

Start Optional

▲ Command Processing

The Korn Shell always reads at least one line before processing a command. Some of the Korn Shell's builtins, such as **if** and **case**, span multiple lines. When the Korn Shell recognizes a command that covers more than one line, it reads the entire command before processing it. Commands can include many lines. In interactive sessions the Korn Shell prompts you with the secondary prompt, **PS2**, after you have typed the first line of a multiline command until it recognizes the end of the command. The default value for **PS2** is **>**, as it is in **sh**.

The Korn Shell carries out these basic steps, in this order, to process a command:

Token splitting	Divides the stream of input characters into words and recognizes I/O redirection operators (page 518).
Alias substitution	Recognizes aliases and expands them (page 521).
Filename expansion	Replaces words that begin with ~ by their expanded values (page 521).
Parameter expansion	Expands all variable expressions that are not quoted (page 522).
Command substitution	Evaluates commands inside backquotes ('...') or command substitution brackets [$()] and replaces the commands with their standard output (page 521).
Arithmetic expansion	Replaces arithmetic expressions with the resulting values (page 522).
Filename generation	Replaces pathnames that contain filename-matching patterns with their expanded lists of pathnames (page 522).
Quotation mark processing	Removes most quotation marks from the command line (page 522).
I/O redirection	Redirects standard input, output, error, and other file descriptors (page 523).
Command execution	Executes the resulting command line.

The order in which **ksh** carries out these steps affects the interpretation of the commands you enter. For example if you set a variable to a value that looks like the instruction for output redirection, and you enter a command using the variable's value to perform redirection, you might expect **ksh** to redirect the output.

```
$ SENDIT="> /tmp/saveit"
$ echo xxx $SENDIT
xxx > /tmp/saveit
$ cat /tmp/saveit
cat: cannot open /tmp/saveit
```

This does not work. The Korn Shell recognizes input and output redirection before it evaluates variables. When the Korn Shell executes the command line, it checks for redirection and, finding none, it goes on to evaluate the **SENDIT** variable. After **ksh** replaced the variable with > /tmp/saveit, it passes the arguments to **echo**, which dutifully copies its arguments to standard output. No **/tmp/saveit** file is created.

The following sections provide more detailed descriptions of each of the steps involved in command processing.

▲▲ Token Splitting

The Korn Shell first splits a command into tokens (words or symbols) so that it can determine whether the command is simple or compound and if there are any I/O redirection operators. The shell does not perform the redirection at this time. Korn Shell I/O redirection includes the familiar Bourne Shell operators for standard input (<), standard output (>), appending standard output (>>), standard error (**2>**), pipes (|), and Here documents (<<). Both shells can also duplicate or redirect any file descriptor if you precede the redirection operator with the file descriptor number. Thus the following command executes program **prog** with file descriptor 3 open for reading file **infile**, and file descriptor 4 open for writing file **outfile**:

```
$ prog 3< infile 4> outfile
```

In addition the Korn Shell supports the following redirection operators:

>| *filename*   Forces standard output to *filename*, even if the file exists and the **noclobber** option (page 539) is set. Normally **noclobber** prevents overwriting an existing file.

<&*n*   Duplicates standard input from file descriptor *n*.

>&*n*   Duplicates standard output from file descriptor *n*.

*[n]***<&–**   Closes standard input or file descriptor *n* if specified.

*[n]***>&–**   Closes standard output or file descriptor *n* if specified.

*[n]***<&p**   Transfers the input from the coprocess (page 523) to standard input or file descriptor *n* if specified.

*[n]***>&p**   Transfers the output to the coprocess (page 523) to standard output or file descriptor *n* if specified.

After the Korn Shell divides a command line into words or tokens, it looks at tokens starting from the left to determine what type of command it is. If the first token is a single left parenthesis, then the remainder of the input up to a matching right parenthesis is treated as a compound command (regardless of how many lines it spans) and executed in a subshell. If the first token is a double left parenthesis, then the input up to a matching double right parenthesis is treated as a single argument to a **let** builtin ₖₛₕ. Any other token that is not part of an I/O redirection or the start of a control structure (for example **for**, **case**) is taken to be the first token of a simple command. The remainder of the input up to a simple command terminator makes up the rest of the command. Most of the terminators are similar to those of the Bourne Shell (semicolon, pipe symbol, NEWLINE, **&&**, ||, and **&**).

The command separators **&&** and || provide a convenient form of conditional execution. They stand for AND and OR, respectively. You can combine commands into command lists separated by the **&&** and || operators.

The **&&** separator causes the Korn Shell to test the exit status of the command preceding it. If the command succeeds, **ksh** executes the next command; otherwise it skips the remaining commands on the command line. You can use this construct to execute commands conditionally.

```
$ mkdir backup && cp -r source backup
```

This compound command creates the directory **backup**. If **mkdir** succeeds, then the contents of directory **source** is copied recursively to **backup**.

The || separator also causes the Korn Shell to test the exit status of the first command but has the opposite effect: The remaining command(s) are executed only if the first one failed (that is, exited with nonzero status).

```
$ mkdir backup || echo "mkdir of backup failed" >> /tmp/log
```

The exit status of a command list is the exit status of the last command executed. You can group lists with parentheses. For example you could combine the previous two examples as follows:

```
$ (mkdir backup && cp -r source backup) || echo "mkdir of backup failed" >> /tmp/log
```

In the absence of parentheses, **&&** and || have equal precedence and are grouped left to right. The following two commands yield an exit status of 1 (*false*). See page 381 for a description of the **$?** variable.

```
$ true || false && false
echo $?
1
$ (true || false) && false
echo $?
1
```

Similarly the next two commands yield an exit status of 0 (*true*):

```
$ false && false || true
echo $?
0
$ (false && false) || true
echo $?
0
```

You can use pipes anywhere in a command that you can use simple commands. The pipe symbol has highest precedence of all operators. The command line

```
$ cmd1 | cmd2 || cmd3 | cmd4 && cmd5 | cmd6
```

is interpreted as if you had typed

```
$ ((cmd1 | cmd2) || (cmd3 | cmd4)) && (cmd5 | cmd6)
```

Do Not Rely on Rules of Precedence, Use Parentheses

Do not rely on the precedence rules when you use compound commands. Rather use parentheses to indicate the order in which you want the shell to interpret the commands.

You can put variable assignments on a command line. These assignments are local to the command shell and apply to the command only. The following command runs **my_script** with the value of **TEMPDIR** set to **~/temp**. The **TEMPDIR** variable is set only in the shell that is spawned to execute **my_script**. It is not set, or if it is already set, it is not changed, in the interactive shell you are running to execute the script.

```
$ TEMPDIR=~/temp my_script
```

In the Bourne Shell you can place these assignments anywhere on the command line. The Korn Shell requires you to place assignments at the beginning of the line.

▲▲ Alias Substitution

The Korn Shell next processes the command line by going through a series of expansions. The first expansion is alias substitution, in which the shell determines whether the first token is an alias and replaces it if it is. It does not replace an alias while processing the same alias. This prevents infinite recursion in handling an alias such as the following:

```
$ alias ls='ls -F'
```

▲▲ Filename Expansion

Next the Korn Shell performs filename (or tilde) expansion (page 448). The Korn Shell tilde (~) expansion feature replaces a ~ by itself on the command line with your home directory (**HOME**) and replaces a ~ followed by a user's login name with the home directory of that user.

Also, ~+ is a synonym for **PWD** and ~– is a synonym for **OLDPWD**.

▲▲ Command Substitution

After process substitution, the Korn Shell performs command substitution. A string within backquotes is treated as a command, which is executed within a subshell, and the text within and including the backquotes is replaced by standard output of the command. The Korn Shell also provides the newer **$(command)** syntax.

```
$ ls -l $(find . -name README -print)
```

This command uses **find** to find files under the working directory with the name **README**. The list of such files is standard output of **find** and becomes the list of arguments to **ls**. It is equivalent to

```
$ ls -l `find . -name README -print`
```

One advantage of the new syntax is that it avoids the rather arcane rules for token handling, quotation mark handling, and escaped backquotes within the old syntax. Another advantage of the new syntax is that it can be nested, where the old syntax cannot. For example you can do a long listing of all the **README** files whose size exceeds the size of **./README** with the following command:

```
$ ls -l $(find . -name README -size +$(echo $(cat ./README | wc -c)c ) -print )
```

Try giving this command after **set –x** to see how it is expanded. If there is no **README** file, you just get the output of **ls –l**.

$((versus $(

The symbols **$((** constitute a separate token; they introduce an arithmetic expression, not a command substitution. Thus if you want to use a parenthesized subshell within **$()**, you must have a space between the **$(** and the next **(**.

▲▲ Parameter Expansion

After the Korn Shell has performed command substitution on the command line, it performs all of the parameter expansions. Refer to "Expanding Shell Variables" on page 487. Variables are not expanded if they are enclosed within single quotation marks. If they are enclosed in double quotation marks, they are expanded, but the resulting text is not subject to filename generation (page 522).

Any string within double quotation marks is used as a single command-line argument, so variables that are expanded within double quotation marks are still treated as part of a single argument.

▲▲ Arithmetic Expansion

The shell replaces an argument of the form **$((expression))** by evaluating the expression for an integer value. Variable names within the expression do not need to be preceded by a dollar sign (**$**). In the following example an arithmetic expression is used to determine how many years are left until age 50:

```
$ cat age_check
#!/bin/ksh
read age\?"How old are you? "
if ((30 < age && age < 50)); then
echo "Wow, in $((50-age)) years, you'll be 50!"
fi
$ age_check
How old are you? 48
Wow, in 2 years, you'll be 50!
```

Arithmetic expansion does not take place if the argument is enclosed within single quotation marks.

▲▲ Filename Generation

After the shell expands variables and splits them into words, it looks for patterns in each word. If you have *not* set the **noglob** option, the shell uses these patterns to generate filenames for use as arguments to the command. Refer to "Filename Generation" on page 488. If no filenames match the pattern, the Korn Shell displays an error message.

▲▲ Processing Quotation Marks

With two exceptions, the Korn Shell next removes all single and double quotation marks. Escaped quotation marks and quotation marks that are the result of expanding variables are not removed but remain as part of the command line.

Stop Optional

▲▲ I/O Redirection and the Coprocess

Except for the Korn Shell's builtins, most commands you enter from the keyboard are executed in a new process. When an ordinary command is executed, any I/O redirection is performed on the new process before the command starts to run. If I/O redirection is applied to a builtin, the Korn Shell arranges for the redirection to apply only to that command, even though it executes in the same process as the shell. Shell functions also execute in the current process, although they have private sets of positional parameters, traps, and options. For example the command **set –x** within a function does not turn on the **xtrace** option for the parent shell.

The Korn Shell supports a feature known as the *coprocess,* which allows you to start a process that runs in the background and communicates directly with its parent shell (Figure 13-1). You invoke a process as the coprocess by ending the command line with **|&**.

The coprocess command must be a filter (reads from standard input and writes to standard output), and it must flush its output whenever it has accumulated a line, rather than saving several lines for output at once. To invoke the command as the coprocess, it is connected via a two-way pipe to the current shell. You can read its standard output by using **<&p**. You can write to the coprocess's standard input with **>&p**.

The coprocess allows a process to exchange information with a background process. It can be useful when you are working in a client-server environment or setting up an SQL (page 1045) front end/back end. The coprocess also serves as a tool to put a new interface on an interactive program—you can easily construct shell scripts to do this.

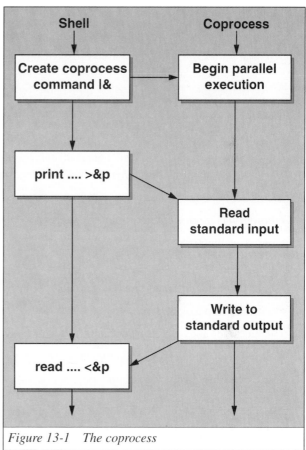

Figure 13-1   The coprocess

```
$ cat to_upper
#!/bin/ksh
while read arg; do
echo "$arg" | tr '[a-z]' '[A-Z]'
done
```

The Solaris **tr** utility does not flush its output after each line, but this "wrapper" script does. For each line read it writes the line translated to uppercase to standard output. The following script invokes **to_upper** as the coprocess:

```
$ cat coproc_script
#!/bin/ksh
to_upper |&
line_count=0
#coproc to_upper
while read pathname; do
   ((line_count=line_count+1))
   print "$pathname" >&p
   read newpath <&p
   print $line_count: "$newpath" | tr '/' '\\'
done
$ echo /home/alex | coproc_script
1: \HOME\ALEX
```

The value of the coprocess is manifest when it is a frequently used tool and the invoking script transforms the tool's input or output.

▲ Shell Programs

As an interactive shell, the Korn Shell's great advantages lie in its aliasing capacity and its command-line and history editing mechanisms. As a programming language, it has many features, some of which are not available in other shells:

- powerful control structures: **for...in**, **if...then**, **while**, **case**, **select**, and **until**

- recursive functions

- local variables

- built-in integer arithmetic and integer data types

- extended trap handling

- input (**read**) and output (**print**) facilities

- file control and I/O redirection for any file descriptor, including file descriptor duplication

- array variables and string manipulation operators

Earlier sections of this chapter discussed most of these features, many of which are useful both interactively and for shell programming. This section develops a complete shell program to show you how to combine some of these features effectively.

▲▲ Program Structures

The structures that the Korn Shell provides are not a random assortment. They have been carefully chosen to provide most of the structural features that are in other procedural languages such as C or Pascal. A procedural language must provide you with these capabilities:

- The ability to declare, assign, and manipulate variables and constant data. The Korn Shell provides string variables, together with powerful string operators, and integer variables, with a complete set of arithmetic operators.

- The ability to break large problems into small ones by creating subprograms. The Korn Shell allows you to create functions and call scripts from other scripts. Korn Shell functions can be called recursively; that is, a Korn Shell function can call itself. You may not need to use recursion often, but occasionally it allows you to solve apparently difficult problems with ease.

- The ability to execute statements conditionally, using statements such as **if**.

- The ability to execute statements iteratively, using statements such as **while** and **for**.

- The ability to transfer data to and from the program, communicating both with data files and with users.

Programming languages implement these capabilities in different ways but with the same ideas in mind. When you want to solve a problem using a program, you must first figure out a procedure that leads you to a solution. Such a procedure is called an *algorithm*. Typically you can implement the same algorithm in roughly the same way in different programming languages, and you use the same kinds of constructs in each language. Earlier in this chapter you saw examples of the use of all the Korn Shell programming structures except recursion. An example of a recursive Korn Shell function that proves useful is shown in the next section.

▲▲▲ Recursion

A recursive construct is one that is defined in terms of itself. This may seem circular, but it need not be. To avoid circularity a recursive definition must have a special case that is not self-referential. Recursive ideas occur in everyday life. For example you can define an ancestor as either your mother, your father, or one of their ancestors. This definition is not circular; it specifies unambiguously who your ancestors are (your mother or your father or your mother's mother or father or your father's mother or father, and so on).

A number of UNIX/Solaris system utilities can operate recursively. See the **–R** option to the **chmod** (page 709) and **chown** (page 713) utilities in Part III for examples.

Solve the following problem using a recursive shell function:

> Write a shell function named **makepath** that, given a pathname, creates all the components in that pathname as directories. For example the command **makepath a/b/c/d** should create directories **a**, **a/b**, **a/b/c**, and **a/b/c/d**. (The **mkdir** utility supports a **–p** option that does exactly this. Solve the problem without using **mkdir –p**.)

One algorithm for a recursive solution follows:

1. Examine this path argument. If it is a null string or if it names an already existing directory, do nothing and return.

2. If it is a simple path component, create it (using **mkdir**) and return.

3. Otherwise call **makepath** using the path prefix of the original argument. This (eventually) creates all the directories up to the last component, which you can then create with **mkdir**.

In general a recursive function must invoke itself with a simpler version of the problem than it was given, until finally it gets called with a simple case that does not need to call itself.

Here is one possible solution based on this algorithm:

```
# this is a function
# enter it at the keyboard, do not run it as a shell script
makepath()
{
    if [[ ${#1} -eq 0 || -d "$1" ]]
        then
            return 0         # Do nothing
    fi
    # Check if arg is a simple path component:
    if [[ "${1%/*}" = "$1" ]]
        then
            mkdir $1
            return $?
    fi
    makepath ${1%/*} || return 1
    mkdir $1
    return $?
}
```

In the test for a simple component (the **if** statement in the middle of the function), the left expression is the argument after the shortest suffix that starts with a / character has been stripped away (page 488). If there is no such character (for example if **$1** is alex) then nothing gets stripped off, and the two sides are equal. Suppose the argument is a simple filename preceded by a slash, such as **/usr**. In that case the expression **${1%/*}** evaluates to a null string. To make the function work in this case, you must take two precautions: Put the left expression within quotation marks as shown, and ensure that your recursive function behaves sensibly when passed a null string as an argument. In general good programs are robust: They are prepared for borderline, invalid, or meaningless input and behave appropriately.

By putting the following commands at the start of the function, you can turn on tracing and watch the recursion work.

```
setopt xtrace
if [[ -o xtrace ]]; then print "makepath $*"; fi
```

Because Korn Shell tracing does not show function calls, the second line above shows the function name and arguments each time it is executed while tracing is on.

```
$ makepath a/b/c
+ [[ -o xtrace ]]
+ print makepath a/b/c
makepath a/b/c
+ [{ 5 -eq 0 ]]
```

```
+ [[ -d a/b/c ]]
+ [[ a/b == a/b/c ]]
+ makepath a/b
+ [[ -o xtrace ]]
+ print makepath a/b
makepath a/b
+ [[ 3 -eq 0 ]]
+ [[ -d a/b ]]
+ [[ a == a/b ]]
+ makepath a
+ [[ -o xtrace ]]
+ print makepath a
makepath a
+ [[ 1 -eq 0 ]]
+ [[ -d a ]]
+ [[ a == a ]]
+ mkdir a
+ return 0
+ mkdir a/b
+ return 0
+ mkdir a/b/c
+ return 0
```

You can see the function work its way down the recursive path and back up again. It is instructive to invoke **makepath** with an invalid path, and see what happens. The following example shows what happens when you try to create the path **/a/b/c**, which requires that you create directory **a** in the root directory. Unless you have privileges, you are not permitted to do that.

```
$ makepath /a/b/c
+ [[ -o xtrace ]]
+ print makepath /a/b/c
makepath /a/b/c
+ [[ 6 -eq 0 ]]
+ [[ -d /a/b/c ]]
+ [[ /a/b == /a/b/c ]]
+ makepath /a/b
+ [[ -o xtrace ]]
+ print makepath /a/b
makepath /a/b
+ [[ 4 -eq 0 ]]
+ [[ -d /a/b ]]
+ [[ /a == /a/b ]]
+ makepath /a
+ [[ -o xtrace ]]
+ print makepath /a
makepath /a
+ [[ 2 -eq 0 ]]
+ [[ -d /a ]]
+ [[  == /a ]]
+ makepath
+ [[ -o xtrace ]]
+ print makepath
makepath
```

```
+ [[ 0 -eq 0 ]]
+ return 0
+ mkdir /a
mkdir: Failed to make directory "/a"; Permission denied
+ return 2
+ return 1
+ return 1
```

The recursion stops only when **makepath** is passed a null argument and the error return is passed all the way back, so the original **makepath** exits with nonzero status.

Use Local Variables with Recursive Functions

The example has glossed over a potential problem that you may encounter when you use a recursive function. By default Korn Shell variables are global. During the execution of a recursive function, many separate instances of that function may be simultaneously active. All but one of them are waiting for their child invocation to complete. If a recursive Korn Shell function uses variables, then unless you make the variables local, these functions all share a single copy of each variable. This can give rise to side effects that are rarely what you want. As a rule, you should use **typeset** (page 483) to make all the variables of a recursive function local.

▲▲ A Programming Problem: makesccs

This section combines some of the Korn Shell programming constructs into a complete program. The example uses **admin**, one of the Source Code Control System (SCCS) commands. If you are not familiar with SCCS, refer to page 579 for a description. The example also makes use of **find** (page 753). The specification for the program follows.

> Write a program, **makesccs**, that takes two directory names as arguments, **source** and **target**. The program should create a copy of the hierarchy rooted at **source** in **target**, except that each regular file under **source** should be checked in to a corresponding SCCS file under **target** using the **admin** command. If **target** does not exist, create it. The program should ensure that the pathname **source** is not a prefix of the pathname **target**, and vice versa. It should skip any file in **source** that is not a directory or regular file (such as a FIFO or socket).

The command

```
makesccs srcdir sccsdir
```

should create a hierarchy under **sccsdir** identical to the hierarchy under **srcdir**, except that if (for example) **srcdir/functions/func1.sh** is a regular file, then the command should create **sccsdir/functions/s.func1.sh**.

There are as many ways to solve a problem like this as there are programmers, so your **makesccs** program probably will not look like the one developed in this section.

Here is an algorithm for solving the problem:

- Check the command line for the correct number and type of arguments. If invalid, display usage message and exit.

- Traverse the source tree, using the **find** command to produce pathnames. For each pathname that **find** returns:

    - If the pathname refers to a directory, then make the corresponding path under the target.

    - If the pathname refers to a regular file, then

        * Construct the name of the SCCS file that would correspond to it.

        * Create that SCCS file using **admin**.

    - If the pathname refers to any other type of file, then write a message to a report file and skip the file.

    - At each stage, if an error occurs, write an appropriate message to an error file.

A few functions to manipulate pathnames are useful in solving the problem. The Solaris utility **dirname**, given a pathname, writes the path prefix to standard output. The **basename** utility does the opposite: The command **basename path** writes the last component of **path** to standard output.

If you have a file whose pathname is **a/b/c/d**, you want to create the pathname **a/b/c/s.d** as the corresponding SCCS filename.

```
sccsname()
{
        _dir=$(dirname $1)
        _base=$(basename $1)
        echo $_dir/s.$_base
}
```

The **sccsname** function picks the pathname apart and glues it back together again, inserting an **s.** at the appropriate place. The answer is written to standard output to enable you to use **sccsname** inside a command substitution statement such as

```
newname=$(sccsname oldname)
```

One function needs to check the command line arguments for validity. This function should ensure that exactly two arguments have been passed, that **$1** names an existing directory, that **$2** either does not exist or names an existing directory, and that neither argument is a prefix of the other.

```
checkargs()
{
        # Check argument count
        if [[ $# != 2 ]]
        then
                print -u2 "usage: checkin source dest"
                exit 1
        fi
        # Check first argument
        if [[ ! -d $1 ]]
        then
                print -u2 "$1: Not a directory"
                exit 1
        fi
        # Check second argument
        if [[ -a $2 && ! -d $2 ]]
        then
                print -u2 "$2: Not a directory"
                exit 1
        fi
        # Check that neither argument is a prefix of the other
        if [[ $1 = $2* || $2 = $1* ]]
        then
                print -u2 "Cannot create one hierarchy below \
or above the other"
                exit 1
        fi

        return 0
}
```

You can invoke this function with a command such as **checkargs "$@"**, which passes the command-line arguments directly to **checkargs**.

The main part of the program uses **find** to locate the files and directories. The command **find $source –print** will write the pathname of each file in the hierarchy rooted at **$source**, one per line, to standard output. If the script pipes this output into a loop and reads each pathname into a shell variable, it can manipulate that variable as follows:

- Determine whether the pathname names a directory, a regular file, or something else.

- Construct a corresponding pathname rooted in the target directory.

- Use **admin** to create the SCCS file at that pathname.

Thus the main body of the program can have the following structure:

find $source –print |
while read pathname
do
     commands
done

The program has to deal sensibly with errors and special conditions. It opens two files, one to report errors and one to log the names of files that were skipped.

Putting the various pieces together, and filling in the missing ones, here is a complete program to solve the problem:

```
$ cat makesccs
makepath()
{
        if [[ ${#1} -eq 0 || -d $1 ]]
        then
                return 0
        fi
        if [[ "${1%/*}" = "$1" ]]
        then
                mkdir $1
                return $?
        fi
        makepath ${1%/*} || return 1
        mkdir $1
        return $?
}
sccsname()
{
        _dir=$(dirname $1)
        _base=$(basename $1)
        echo $_dir/s.$_base
}
checkargs()
{
        if [[ $# != 2 ]]
        then
                print -u2 "usage: checkin <source> <dest>"
                exit 1
        fi
        if [[ ! -d $1 ]]
        then
                print -u2 "$1: Not a directory"
                exit 1
        fi
        # Check second argument
        if [[ -a $2 && ! -d $2 ]]
        then
                print -u2 "$2: Not a directory"
                exit 1
        fi
        # Check that neither argument is a prefix of the other
        if [[ $1 = $2* || $2 = $1* ]]
        then
                print -u2 "Cannot create one hierarchy below or above the other"
                exit 1
        fi
        return 0
}
ERRS=./err_file
REPORT=./report
```

```
checkargs "$@"
# Open error and report files
exec 3>$ERRS
exec 4>$REPORT
source=$1
dest=$2
find $source -print |
while read pathname
do
        target=$dest${pathname#$source}
        if [[ -d $pathname ]]
        then
                makepath $target || print -u3 "Cannot create $target"
        elif [[ -f $pathname ]]
        then
                target=$(sccsname $target)
                admin -i$pathname $target >&4 2>&3 || \
                        print -u3 "Cannot create $target"
        else
                print -u4 "$pathname not directory or regular file: skipped"
        fi
done
exec 3<&-
exec 4<&-
exit 0
```

There are a number of ways to improve this program. For example its exit status does not always reflect what happened. The exercises at the end of this chapter ask you to modify the program in various ways.

▲▲ Another Programming Problem: quiz

Here is another problem that you can solve with a Korn Shell program. This problem calls for interaction with the user, and consequently the solution will require different shell programming features. Following is the problem statement in general terms:

> Write a generic multiple-choice quiz program. The program should get its questions from data files, and present them to the user. It should keep track of the number of correct and incorrect answers. The user must be able to exit the program at any time with a summary of results to that point.

The detailed design of this program, and even the detailed description of the problem, depends on a number of choices: How will the program know which subjects are available for quizzes? How will the user choose a subject? How will the program know when the quiz is over? Should the program present the same questions (for a given subject) in the same order each time, or should it scramble them?

Of course there are many perfectly good choices that you can make in the specification of the problem. The following details narrow the problem specification:

- Each subject will correspond to a subdirectory of a master quiz directory. This directory will be named in the environment variable **QUIZDIR**, whose default will be **/usr/lib/quiz**.

- Each question in a particular subject corresponds to a file in the subject directory.

- The representation of the question is as follows. The first line of the file is the text of the question. If it takes more than one line, you must escape the **NEWLINE** with a backslash. (This choice makes it easy to read a single question with the built-in **read** command.) The second line of the file is an integer that is the number of choices. The next several lines are the choices themselves. The last line is the correct answer. For example here is a sample question file:

```
Who discovered the principle of the lever?
4
Euclid
Archimedes
Thomas Edison
The Lever Brothers
Archimedes
```

- The program will present all the questions in a subject directory. At any point, the user can interrupt the quiz with **CONTROL-C**, at which point the program will summarize the results so far and exit. If the user does not interrupt, then when the program has asked all the questions, it will summarize the results and exit.

- The program should scramble the questions in a subject before presenting them.

Following is a top-level design for this program:

1. Initialize. This involves a number of steps, such as setting counts of the number of questions asked so far, and the number correct and wrong, to zero.

2. Present the user with a choice of subject, and get the user's response.

3. Change to the corresponding subject directory.

4. Determine the questions to be asked (that is, the filenames in that directory). Rearrange them in random order.

5. Repeatedly present questions and ask for answers until the quiz is over or is interrupted by the user.

6. Present the results and exit.

Clearly some of these steps (such as step 3) are simple, whereas others (such as step 4) are complex and worthy of analysis on their own. Use shell functions for any complex step, and use the **trap** builtin to handle a user interrupt.

Here is a skeleton version of the program, with empty shell functions:

```
function initialize
{
# To be filled in.
}
```

```
function choose_subj
{
# To be filled in.  Will write choice to standard output.
}

function scramble
{
# To be filled in.  Will store names of question files, scrambled,
# in an array variable named questions.
}

function ask
{
# To be filled in.  Reads a question file, asks it, and checks the
# answer. Returns 1 if the answer was correct, 0 otherwise.  If it
# encounters an invalid question file, exit with status 2.
}

function summarize
{
# To be filled in.  Presents the user's score.
}

# Main program
initialize                          # Step 1 in top-level design
trap 'summarize ; exit 0' INT       # Handles user interrupts

subject=$(choose_subj)              # Step 2
[[ $? -eq 0 ]] || exit 2            # If no valid choice, exit

cd $subject || exit 2               # Step 3

echo                                # Skip a line
scramble                            # Step 4

for ques in ${questions[*]}         # Step 5
do
ask $ques
result=$?
((num_ques=num_ques+1))
if [[ $result == 1 ]]
then
((num_correct=num_correct+1))
fi
echo                                # skip a line between questions
   sleep ${QUIZDELAY:=1}
done

summarize                           Step 6
exit 0
```

To make reading the results a bit easier for the user, there is a **sleep** call inside the question loop. It delays **$QUIZDELAY** seconds (default = 1) between questions.

Now the task is to fill in the missing pieces of the program. In a sense this program is being written backwards. The details (the shell functions) come first in the file, but come last in the development process. This is a common programming practice. In this case it is an instance of top-down design. Fill in the broad outline of the program first and supply the details later. In this way you break the problem up into smaller problems, each of which you can work on independently. Shell functions are a great help in using the top-down approach.

One way to write the initialize function follows:

```
function initialize
{
num_ques=0                 # Number of questions asked so far
num_correct=0              # Number answered correctly so far
cd ${QUIZDIR:=/usr/games/lib/quiz} || exit 2
}
```

The next function, **choose_subj**, is a bit more complicated and is implemented using a **select** statement.

```
function choose_subj
{
subjects=$(\ls)
PS3="Choose a subject for the quiz from the following:  "
select Subject in $subjects
do
if [[ -z "$Subject" ]]
then
echo "No subject chosen.  Bye." >&2
exit 1
fi
echo $Subject
return 0
done
}
```

The function starts by getting a list of subject directories, using the **ls** command. The call to **ls** is escaped (by preceding the **ls** with a \) to ensure that if there is an alias or function named **ls** it will not be used. Next the **select** structure presents the user with a list of subjects (the directories found by **ls**), and places the chosen directory name in **Subject**. See page 494 for a description of **select**. Finally the function writes the subject directory to standard output, where (as shown in the skeleton program) it will be captured in a variable.

You must be prepared for the **cd** command to fail. The directory may be unsearchable, or conceivably another user may have removed the directory in between the **ls** command and the **cd** command.

The **scramble** function presents a number of difficulties. It uses an array variable to hold the names of the questions. You need an algorithm that can randomly scramble the various entries in an array and can make use of the Korn Shell's built-in **RANDOM** variable. Here is an implementation of the **scramble** function.

```
function scramble
{
set -A questions $(\ls)
quescount=${#questions[*]}        # Number of elements
((index=quescount-1))
while [[ $index > 0 ]]
do
((target=RANDOM % index))
exchange $target $index
((index=index-1))
done
```

This function initializes the array variable **questions** to the list of filenames (questions) in the current directory. The variable **quescount** is set to the number of such files. Then the following algorithm is used: Let the variable index count down from **quescount – 1** (the index of the last entry in the array variable). For each value of **index**, the function chooses a random value target between 0 and **index**, inclusive. The command

```
((target=RANDOM % index))
```

produces a random value between **0** and **index – 1** by taking the remainder (the **%** operator) when **$RANDOM** is divided by **index**. The function then exchanges the elements of **questions** at positions **target** and **index**. It is convenient to do this in another function, named **exchange**.

```
function exchange
{
temp_value=${questions[$1]}
questions[$1]=${questions[$2]}
questions[$2]=$temp_value
}
```

Function **ask** also makes use of the **select** structure. It must read the question file named in its argument and use the contents of that file to present the question, accept the answer, and see if it is right—see the code that follows.

This function makes use of file descriptor 3 to read successive lines from the question file, whose name was passed as an argument to the function. It reads the question into the variable named **ques**. It constructs the variable **choices** by initializing it to the null string, and then successively appending a colon followed by the next choice. (The purpose of this rather obscure code is discussed below.) Then it sets **PS3** to the value of **ques**, and uses the **select** structure, which has the effect of prompting the user with **ques**. The **select** structure places the user's answer in **answer**, and the function then checks it against the correct answer from the file. If the user has not made a valid choice, then **select** continues to issue the prompt and wait for a response.

The construction of the **choices** variable is done with an eye to avoiding a potential problem. Suppose that one of the answers has some whitespace in it. Then it might appear as two or more arguments in **choices**. To avoid this change the built-in **IFS** variable to recognize only the colon character as a separator, and set the function arguments to **$choices**. Be careful to remove the leading colon in **choices**. The **select** statement's default feature of using the positional arguments does the rest of the work.

```
function initialize
{
num_ques=0                    # Number of questions asked so far
num_correct=0                 # Number answered correctly so far
cd ${QUIZDIR:=/usr/games/lib/quiz} || exit 2
}

function choose_subj
{
subjects=$(\ls)
PS3="Choose a subject for the quiz from the following:  "
select Subject in $subjects
do
if [[ -z "$Subject" ]]
then
echo "No subject chosen.  Bye." >&2
exit 1
fi
echo $Subject
return 0
done
}

function exchange
{
temp_value=${questions[$1]}
questions[$1]=${questions[$2]}
questions[$2]=$temp_value
}

function scramble
{
set -A questions $(\ls)
quescount=${#questions[*]}        # Number of elements
((index=quescount-1))
while [[ $index > 0 ]]
do
((target=RANDOM % index))
exchange $target $index
((index=index-1))
done
}

function ask
{
exec 3<$1
read -u3 ques || exit 2
read -u3 num_opts || exit 2

index=0
choices=""
while [[ $index < $num_opts ]]
do
read -u3 next_choice || exit 2
choices="$choices:$next_choice"
((index=index+1))
done
```

```
read -u3 correct_answer || exit 2
exec 3<&-

SaveIFS="$IFS"
IFS=":"
choices=${choices#:}
set $choices

echo "You may press the Interrupt Key at any time to quit."
PS3=$ques"   "        # Make $ques the prompt for select, but...
# ...add some spaces for legibility.
select answer
do
IFS="$SaveIFS"
if [[ -z "$answer" ]]
then
echo  Not a valid choice. Please choose again.
elif [[ "$answer" = "$correct_answer" ]]
then
echo Correct!
return 1
else
echo No, the answer is $correct_answer.
return 0
fi
done
}

function summarize
{
if [[ $num_ques == 0 ]]
then
echo "You did not answer any questions"
exit 0
fi

((percent=num_correct*100/num_ques))
print "You answered $num_correct questions correctly, out of \
$num_ques total questions."
print "Your score is $percent percent."
}

# Main program
initialize                       # Step 1 in top-level design
trap 'summarize ; exit 0' INT    # Handles user interrupts

subject=$(choose_subj)           # Step 2
[[ $? -eq 0 ]] || exit 2         # If no valid choice, exit

cd $subject || exit 2            # Step 3

echo                             # Skip a line
scramble                         # Step 4

for ques in ${questions[*]}      # Step 5
do
ask $ques
```

```
result=$?
((num_ques=num_ques+1))
if [[ $result == 1 ]]
then
((num_correct=num_correct+1))
fi
echo                                    # skip a line between questions
    sleep ${QUIZDELAY:=1}
done

summarize                               Step 6
exit 0
```

▲ Korn Shell Options (set)

The following list describes many of the options you can use to alter the behavior of the Korn Shell. Refer to the **ksh man** page for a complete list. The **set** builtin ~~sh~~~~csh~~~~ksh~~ sets and unsets options. Use **set** as shown in the following examples:

$ **set −o vi** *(make* **vi** *the command-line editor)*
$ **set −C** *(turn on* **noclobber***)*

$ **set +o vi** *(turn off this option)*
$ **set +C** *(turn off this option)*

Option	Use
−A *name v1 v2...*	**array** Creates and assigns values to the elements of array *name*. The *v1*, *v2*, and so forth are values to be assigned to each element of the *name* (page 489).
−a	**automatic exporting** Causes all subsequently defined variables to be automatically exported.
−C	**noclobber** Prevents existing files from getting clobbered (overwritten) through the use of the redirect output operator (>). You can override this setting by using the >| operator for individual files (page 464).
−f	**no filename generation** Disables filename generation.
−o *arg*	**option** See the following list of *arg*s.
	bgnice Runs background jobs at a lower priority (default).
	emacs Sets the command-line editor to **emacs** (page 513).
	ignoreeof Prevents the shell from exiting when you give an EOF (**CONTROL-D**). Forces you to use **exit** to leave the shell (page 464).
	markdirs Appends a trailing slash (/) to the names of directories that were created using filename generation.
	monitor Same as **−m**.
	noclobber Same as **−C**.

Option	Use
	noglob Same as **–f**.
	nounset Same as **–u**.
	verbose Same as **–v**.
	vi Sets the command-line editor to **vi** (page 511).
	xtrace Same as **–x**.
–u	**unset** Generates an error when an unset parameter is used in a substitution.
–v	**verbose** Displays each shell input line as it is read.
–x	**debug** Displays commands and arguments as the commands are executed.

Summary

The Korn Shell implements nearly all of the features of the Bourne Shell as well as the most useful features of the C Shell. You can customize the Korn Shell to create a personal interactive environment by choosing settings for options and values for variables and by defining aliases and functions.

You assign attributes to Korn Shell variables with the **typeset** builtin. The Korn Shell provides operators to perform pattern matching on variables, provide default values for variables, and evaluate the length of the value of variables. The Korn Shell supports array variables and local variables for functions and provides built-in integer arithmetic capability using the **let** builtin and an expression syntax similar to the C programming language.

Condition testing is similar to that of the **test** utility, but the Korn Shell provides more testing primitives, including string ordering and pattern matching. The Korn Shell provides special syntax to allow you to use arithmetic and logical expressions as conditions.

The Korn Shell provides a rich set of control structures for conditional and iterative execution. The **select** control structure provides a simple method for creating menus in shell scripts and repeatedly prompting the user for responses. The **while, until**, and **if...then** structures have the same syntax as their Bourne Shell counterparts but can take advantage of the Korn Shell's more powerful logical and arithmetic condition testing. The **repeat** statement provides a convenient way to repeat a sequence of commands a number of times. Most Korn Shell control structures are also available with a C Shell syntax, for users that are more familiar with the C Shell.

The Korn Shell provides the ability to manipulate file descriptors. Coupled with powerful **read** and **print** builtins, this allows shell scripts to have as much control over input and output as programs written in lower-level languages. The Korn Shell provides all the I/O redirections of both **sh** and **csh** and more. A unique feature of the Korn Shell is its ability to launch a coprocess: A process that executes in parallel with the parent shell and whose standard input and output are connected via a two-way pipe to the parent shell. From the parent shell you can read standard output of the coprocess using **<&p**. You can write to standard input of the coprocess using **>&p**.

Functions are a powerful feature of the Korn Shell. You can call them from an interactive Korn Shell or from a shell script. Because they do not require a new process when they are called, Korn Shell functions are more efficient than shell scripts. As with functions in other modern programming languages such as C, Korn Shell functions may be recursive, which can lead to simpler solutions to some problems. The **autoload** builtin can load a function only if it is actually used, making functions more efficient and programming easier. The Korn Shell also provides some special functions that can be used to perform tasks periodically, to produce prompts that change dynamically, and to perform tasks when changing directories.

As with both the Bourne Shell and the C Shell, the Korn Shell includes the ability to start jobs as background tasks, to suspend jobs running in the foreground, and to move jobs between the background and foreground. Job control in the Korn Shell more closely matches that of the C Shell than the Bourne Shell.

Shell functions and the rich set of builtins and control structures are well suited to the use of the Korn Shell for both interactive and scripting purposes. The complete set of command-line substitutions and expansions are particularly useful during interactive use.

When using an interactive Korn Shell, you can edit your command line and commands from the history file using either of the Korn Shell's command-line editors (**vi** or **emacs**). If you use the **vi** command-line editor, you start in Input Mode, unlike the way you normally enter **vi**. You can switch between Command and Input Mode. The **emacs** editor is modeless and distinguishes commands from editor input by recognizing control characters as commands.

▲▲ Commands for the **vi** Command-Line Editor

Not all of the available **vi** command-line editor commands are given here. See the **ksh man** page for a complete list.

▲▲▲ Cursor-Movement Commands (**vi**)

In addition to the following commands, you may be able to use the arrow keys to move about. The arrow keys work regardless of mode.

Command	Action
l (lowercase "ell") *or* **SPACE**	Moves one character to the right.
h	Moves one character to the left.
w	Moves one word to the right.
b	Moves one word to the left.
W	Moves one space-delimited word to the right.
B	Moves one space-delimited word to the left.
0	Moves to beginning of line.
$	Moves to end of line.
e	Moves to end of word.
E	Moves to end of space-delimited word.

Command	Action
^	Moves to first nonblank position on line.
f*x*	Moves to next (right) occurrence of *x*.
F*x*	Moves to previous (left) occurrence of *x*.
; (semicolon)	Repeats last f or F command.
, (comma)	Repeats last f or F command, but in opposite direction.
*n*l	Moves to column *n*.

▲▲▲ Changing Text (vi)

Command	Action
i	Enters Insert Mode before current character.
a	Enters Insert Mode after current character.
I	Enters Insert Mode before first nonblank character.
A	Enters Insert Mode at end of line.
r*x*	Replaces current character with *x*.
R	Overwrites, starting at current character, until ESCAPE.
*n*x	Deletes *n* characters, starting at current character.
*n*X	Deletes *n* characters, starting just past current character.
D	Deletes from current character to end of line.
dd	Deletes entire command.
C	Changes from current character to end of line.

▲▲▲ History Editing Commands (vi)

Command	Action
j	Moves back one command in history.
k	Moves forward one command in history.
/*string* RETURN	Searches backward for command with *string* (not a regular expression except for ^ matching the start of a line).
?*string* RETURN	Searches forward for command with *string* (see previous note).
n	Repeats previous search.
N	Repeats previous search in opposite direction.
*n*v	Enters full-screen vi to edit command number *n*, or current command if *n* is omitted.
#	Inserts current command as a comment in history file.

▲▲▲ Miscellaneous Commands (vi)

Command	Action
ESCAPE=	Lists pathnames that match current word (pathname listing).
ESCAPE\	Completes current word to a unique or partial pathname (pathname completion).
ESCAPE✳	Expands current word to all matching pathnames (pathname expansion).
u	Undoes previous change.
~	Changes case of current character.
n.	Repeats, *n* times, the most recent command that caused a change; if *n* is omitted, it defaults to one.

▲▲ Commands for emacs Command-Line Editor

Not all of the **emacs** mode commands are given here. See the **ksh man** page for more details on using **emacs** editing mode in the Korn Shell.

▲▲▲ Cursor-Movement Commands (emacs)

In addition to the following commands, you may be able to use the arrow keys to position the cursor.

Command	Action
CONTROL-F	Moves one character to the right.
CONTROL-B	Moves one character to the left.
ESCAPE f	Moves one word to the right.
ESCAPE b	Moves one word to the left.
CONTROL-A	Moves to beginning of line.
CONTROL-E	Moves to end of line.
CONTROL-]*x*	Moves to next instance of *x*.

▲▲▲ Changing Text (emacs)

Command	Action
Erase	Deletes character to the right of current character.
CONTROL-D	Deletes current character.
CONTROL-K	Deletes to end of line.
Kill	Deletes entire line.
CONTROL-T	Transposes current and previous (to left) characters.
CONTROL-W	Deletes all characters from current character to Mark.
ESCAPE D	Deletes one word to right.

Command	Action
ESCAPE-h	Deletes one word to left.
ESCAPE l	Changes next word to all lowercase.
ESCAPE c	Changes first letter of next word to uppercase.
ESCAPE u	Changes next word to all uppercase.
ESCAPE .	Inserts last word from previous command line before current character.

▲▲▲ History Editing Commands (**emacs**)

Command	Action
CONTROL-P	Moves to previous line in history file.
CONTROL-N	Moves to next line in history file.
ESCAPE <	Moves to first line in history file.
ESCAPE >	Moves to last line in history file.
CONTROL-R *string*	Search backward for *string*.

▲▲▲ Miscellaneous Commands (**emacs**)

Command	Action
ESCAPE=	Lists pathnames that match current word (pathname listing).
ESCAPE ESCAPE	Completes current word to a unique or partial pathname (pathname completion).
ESCAPE*	Expands current word to all matching pathnames (pathname expansion).
CONTROL-U	Repeats next command four times.
CONTROL-V	Displays the current version of the Korn Shell.
CONTROL-L	Redisplays the current line.

Review Exercises

1. The **dirname** utility treats its argument as a pathname and writes to standard output the path prefix; that is, everything up to but not including the last component. Thus

```
dirname a/b/c/d
```

writes a/b/c to standard output. If path is a simple filename (has no / characters), then **dirname** writes a . to standard output.

Implement **dirname** as a Korn Shell function. Make sure that it behaves sensibly when given arguments such as /.

2. Implement the **basename** utility, which writes the last component of its pathname argument to standard output, as a Korn Shell function. For example

   ```
   $ basename a/b/c/d
   ```

   writes d to standard output.

3. The Solaris **basename** utility has an optional second argument. If you type

   basename path suffix

   then, after removing the prefix from *path*, **basename** removes the *suffix* from *path*. For example

   ```
   $ basename src/shellfiles/prog.sh .sh
   prog
   $ basename src/shellfiles/prog.sh .c
   prog.sh
   ```

   Add this feature to the function you wrote for exercise 2.

4. Write a Korn Shell function that takes a directory name as an argument and writes to standard output the maximum of the lengths of all filenames in that directory. If the function's argument is not a directory name, write an error message to standard output and exit with nonzero status.

5. Modify the function you wrote for exercise 4 to recursively descend all subdirectories of the named directory and find the maximum length of any filename in that hierarchy.

6. Write a Korn Shell function that lists the number of regular files, directories, block special files, character special files, fifos, and symbolic links in the working directory. Do this in two different ways:

   a. Use the first letter of the output of **ls –l** to determine a file's type.

   b. Use the file type condition tests of the **[[** builtin to determine a file's type.

7. The **makesccs** program (page 528) depends on the fact that **find** writes the pathname of a directory before it writes the pathname of any files in that directory. Suppose that this were not reliably true. Fix **makesccs**.

8. Change **makesccs** (page 528), so that if any call to **admin** fails, the program continues (as it does now) but eventually exits with nonzero status.

9. Modify the **quiz** program (page 532) so that the choices for a question are also randomly arranged.

Advanced Review Exercises

10. In the **makesccs** (page 528) program, file descriptors 3 and 4 are opened, and then during the loop, output is directed to these descriptors. An alternative method would be simply to append the output each time it occurs, using, for example

    ```
    print "Cannot create $target" >> $ERRS
    ```

    rather than

    ```
    print -u3 "Cannot create $target"
    ```

What is the difference? Why does it matter?

11. The check in **makesccs** (page 528) to prevent you from copying hierarchies on top of each other is simplistic. For example if you are in your home directory, the call **makesccs . ~/work/SCCS** will not detect that the source and target directories lie on the same path. Fix this check.

12. In principle recursion is never necessary. It can always be replaced by an iterative construct such as **while** or **until**. Rewrite **makepath** (page 525) as a nonrecursive function. Which version do you prefer? Why?

13. Lists are commonly stored in environment variables by putting a colon (:) between each of the list elements. (The value of the **PATH** variable is a good example.) You can add an element to such a list by catenating the new element to the front of the list, as in

```
PATH=/opt/bin:$PATH
```

If the element you add is already in the list, you now have two copies of it in the list. Write a Korn Shell function **addenv** that takes two arguments. The first is the name of a shell variable and the second is a string to prepend to the list that is the value of the shell variable only if that string is not already an element of the list. For example the call

```
addenv PATH /opt/bin
```

would add **/opt/bin** to **PATH** only if that pathname is not already in **PATH**. Be sure your solution works, even if the shell variable starts out empty. Also make sure you check the list elements carefully. If **/usr/opt/bin** is in **PATH** but **/opt/bin** is not, then the above example should still add **/opt/bin** to **PATH**. (*Hint:* You may find this easier to do if you first write a function **locate_field** that tells you whether a string is an element in the value of a variable.)

Programming Tools

The Solaris operating system provides an outstanding environment for programming, with a rich set of languages and development tools. C is the most popular programming language to use with Solaris, in part because the operating system itself is written mostly in C. Using C, programmers can easily access system services using function libraries and system calls. In addition there are a variety of tools for making the development and maintenance of programs easier.

There are two C compilers in common use on Solaris machines: The Sun WorkShop **cc** compiler that you can buy from Sun and the GNU **gcc** compiler that you can obtain for free over the Internet (page 984). This chapter applies to both compilers except as noted.

Before the introduction of Solaris2 (SunOS5), Sun included a UNIX C compiler with its operating system. Then Sun unbundled the C compiler from Solaris2. Although it was an extremely unpopular decision at the time, people have gradually begun to accept it as it has allowed Sun to develop a commercial C compiler that is better than the one it used to bundle with its operating system. SPARCWorks (the old name for the collection of compilers and related utilities) has gradually grown into an integrated development environment and is now part of WorkShop. It started out as separate tools that you could access from a button bar or the command line but gradually evolved into a more tightly integrated package that is normally run from a GUI. The compilers themselves are still accessible from the command line, and probably always will be. But there are certain tasks that you can only do from the GUI now, there are no command-line equivalents. The Solaris compilers that are available from Sun include: C, C++, FORTRAN 77, Fortran 90, Rational FORTRAN (**ratfor**), and Pascal. The WorkShop environment comes with a number of other tools.

There is a source browser (**sbrowser**), which acts as a cross-reference tool to help you identify programmatic constructs and search for code items such as functions, variables, and libraries. The source browser will also mark up your program graphically to show you function call graphs and C++ class hierarchies. There is an analyzer program (**analyzer**) that helps you tune your program for better performance. The analyzer uses a collector library to gather runtime data, then displays the data graphically in several different formats. The traditional **lint** command-line interface is also available, but with enhanced features. There are configuration management tools that let you keep and track different versions of your program. The different versions can be checked in and checked out for editing as needed. These tools are provided through an interface called TeamWare (**teamware**). As the name suggests, these tools are designed for use in a multideveloper environment where several people may be working on one project at the same time. There is a program (**filemerge**) that lets you merge different branches of a program back into common source. A command-line version of SCCS, called **rsccs**, lets you manage recursive trees of source code (like the free GNU **cvs** program—available from metalab, see page 984). There is a debugger (**debugger**, recently integrated into WorkShop), which provides capabilities that free debuggers do not, such as the ability to debug threads conveniently (page 576). One of the most useful features is the way that **debugger** handles forks in a program: You can stay with the parent, follow the child, stop and decide at each fork, or follow both the parent and the child in separate windows at the same time. Also, the traditional **dbx** debugger program is available and is able to debug all of the aforementioned programs and has other enhancements (such as thread debugging). The debugger also has the traditional notions of breakpoints, displaying and watching variables, structures, pointers, and classes. There is a distributed version of **make**, called **dmake**, which is like the free GNU version of **make**: It lets you exploit concurrency in your makefile across processors and across hosts automatically. There is a Motif user interface builder named **visu**, which uses a drag-and-drop code generator to allow rapid prototyping of Motif user interfaces.

In the latest version of WorkShop, you can take advantage of all this functionality by running the **workshop** program. It is the preferred front end for all the tools (including the compiler). Using **workshop** gives you an integrated environment including an editor (**emacs**, **xemacs**, **vi**, or other), **debugger**, code manager (**codemgr**), source browser (**sbrowser**), **analyzer**, compiler, and all of the other aforementioned tools all linked together. And one of the major advantages is that most of the tools will work with all of the different programming languages.

This chapter covers only a few of the tools that are part of WorkShop. It describes how to compile and link C programs, introduces the **dbx** debugger and tools that provide feedback about memory usage and CPU resources, and covers some of the most useful software development tools: The **make** utility and the Source Code Control System (**sccs**). The **make** utility helps you keep track of which modules of a program have been updated, and it helps to ensure that when you compile a program you use the latest versions of all program modules. Source code management systems track the versions of files involved in a project.

▲ Programming in C

One of the main reasons the Solaris system provides an excellent C programming environment is that C programs can easily access the services of the operating system. The system calls—the routines that make operating system services available to programmers—can be called from C programs. The system calls provide services such as creating files, reading from and writing to files, collecting information about files, allocating memory, and sending signals to processes. When you write a C program, you can use the system calls in the same way you use ordinary C program modules, or *functions,* that you have written.

A variety of *libraries* of functions have been developed to support programming in C. The libraries are collections of related functions that you can use just as you use your own functions and the system calls. Many of the library functions access basic operating system services through the system calls, providing the services in ways that are more suited to typical programming tasks. Other library functions serve special purposes (for example the math library functions).

This chapter describes the processes of writing and compiling C programs. However it will *not* teach you to program in C. If you want to learn C, there are many excellent texts on the market that will help you. These include *The New C Primer Plus,* by Waite and Prata, and *A Book on C: Programming in C,* by Kelley and Pohl. For those who already know some C, good choices are *The C Programming Language,* by Kernighan and Ritchie, and *C: A Reference Manual*, by Harbison and Steele. For learning C++ a book such as *C++ Primer,* by Lippman, or *C++ How to Program*, by H. M. Deitel and P. J. Deitel, should suit your needs. You can also look for tutorials on the Internet. For additional information about books, Web sites, and other sources of information on C and C++, consult the author's home page at **www.sobell.com**.

▲▲ Checking Your Compiler

First check to see that you have access to a compiler.[1] Give the following commands:

```
$ cc -version
/usr/ucb/cc:  language optional software package not installed
$ gcc --version
gcc: not found
```

If you get responses other than version information, neither compiler is installed or your **PATH** variable does not contain the necessary pathname. If you get version information from the **cc** command, then the Sun C compiler is installed; if you get version information from the **gcc** command, it means the GNU C compiler is installed.

Next make sure the compiler is functioning: As a simple test, create a file named **Makefile** with the lines:

```
$ cat Makefile
CC=cc
#CC=gcc
morning: morning.c
    $(CC) -o morning morning.c
```

If you are using the **gcc** compiler, remove the pound sign (#) from the front of the second line and put it in front of the first. Next create a source file named **morning.c** with the lines:

```
$ cat morning.c
#include <stdio.h>
int main(int argc, char** argv) {
  printf("Good Morning\n");
  return 0;
}
```

Compile the file with the command **make morning**. (Make sure that **/usr/ccs/bin** is in your **PATH**.) When it compiles successfully, run the program by giving the command **morning** or **./morning**. When you can get output from this program, you know you have a working C compiler. If you have the **gcc** compiler, always use cc in place of cc in the examples throughout this chapter.

---

1. No C compiler is included with the basic Solaris package. If you want a C compiler, you can either purchase one from Sun (**cc**) or you can download the GNU compiler (**gcc**) for free (page 984).

▲▲ A C Programming Example

You must use an editor, such as **vi**, to write or change a C program. The name of the C program file must end in **.c**. Typing the source code for a program is similar to typing a memo or shell script—the editor does not know whether your file is a C program, a shell script, or an ordinary text document. You are responsible for making the contents of the file syntactically suitable for the C compiler to process.

```
 1   /* convert tabs in standard input to spaces in */      Comments
 2   /* standard output while maintaining columns */
 3
 4   #include        <stdio.h>                               Preprocessor Directives
 5   #define         TABSIZE          8
 6
 7   /* prototype for function findstop */                   Function Prototype
 8   int findstop(int *);
 9
10   int main()
11   {                                                       Main Function
12   int c;            /* character read from stdin */
13   int posn = 0;     /* column position of character */
14   int inc;          /* column increment to tab stop */
15
16   while ((c = getchar()) != EOF)
17         switch(c)
18             {
19             case '\t':                 /* c is a tab */
20                     inc = findstop(&posn);
21                     for( ; inc > 0; inc-- )
22                             putchar(' ');
23                     break;
24             case '\n':                 /* c is a newline */
25                     putchar(c);
26                     posn = 0;
27                     break;
28             default:                   /* c is anything else */
29                     putchar(c);
30                     posn++;
31                     break;
32             }
33   return 0;
34   }
35
36   /* compute size of increment to next tab stop */        Function
37
38   int findstop(int *col)
39   {
40   int retval;
41   retval = (TABSIZE - (*col % TABSIZE));
42
43   /* increment argument (current column position) to next tabstop */
44   *col += retval;
45
46   return retval;           /* main gets how many blanks for filling */
47   }
```

*Figure 14-1   A simple C program (**tabs.c**—the line numbers are not part of the source code)*

Figure 14-1 illustrates the structure of a simple C program named **tabs.c**. The first two lines of the program are comments that describe what the program does. The string /∗ identifies the beginning of the comment, and the string ∗/ identifies the end—the C compiler ignores all the characters between them. Because a comment can span two or more lines, the ∗/ at the end of the first line and the /∗ at the beginning of the second are not necessary—they are included in **tabs.c** for clarity. As the comment explains, the program reads standard input, converts **TAB** characters into the appropriate number of spaces, and writes the transformed input to standard output. Like many Solaris utilities this program is a filter.

Following the comments at the top of **tabs.c** are *preprocessor directives;* these are instructions for the C preprocessor. During the initial phase of compilation, the C preprocessor expands the directives, making the program ready for the later stages of the compilation process. Preprocessor directives begin with the pound sign (#) and may optionally be preceded by **SPACE** and **TAB** characters.

You can use the **#define** preprocessor directive to define symbolic constants. *Symbolic constants* are names that you can use in your programs in place of constant values. For example **tabs.c** uses a **#define** preprocessor directive to associate the symbolic constant **TABSIZE** with the constant 8. **TABSIZE** is used in the program in place of the constant 8 as the distance between **TAB** stops. By convention the names of symbolic constants are composed of all uppercase letters.

By defining symbolic names for constant values, you can make your program easier to read and easier to modify. If you later decide to change a constant, you need to change only the preprocessor directive rather than changing the value everywhere it occurs in your program. If you replace the **#define** directive for **TAB-SIZE** in Figure 14-1 with the following directive, the program will place **TAB** stops every four columns rather than every eight:

```
#define    TABSIZE    4
```

The symbolic constants discussed above are one type of *macro*—the mapping of a symbolic name to *replacement text.* Macros are handy when the replacement text is needed at multiple points throughout the source code, or when the definition of the macro is subject to frequent change. The process of substituting the replacement text for the symbolic name is called *macro expansion.*

You can also use **#define** directives to define macros with arguments. Use of such a macro resembles a function call. However unlike C functions macros are replaced with C code rather than with function calls. The following macro computes the distance to the next **TAB** stop, given the current column position, **curcol**:

```
#define NEXTTAB(curcol) (TABSIZE - ((curcol) % TABSIZE))
```

The definition of this macro uses the macro TABSIZE, whose definition must appear prior to NEXTTAB in the source code. The macro NEXTTAB could be used in **tabs.c** to assign a value to **retval** in the function **findstop**.

```
retval = NEXTTAB(*col);
```

When several macro definitions are used in different modules of a program, they are typically collected together in a single file called a *header file* (or an *include file*). Although the C compiler does not put constraints on the names of header files, by convention they end in **.h**. The name of the header file is then listed in an **#include** preprocessor directive in each program source file that uses any of the macros. The program in Figure 14-1 uses **getchar** and **putchar**, which are macros defined in **stdio.h**. The **stdio.h** header file defines a variety of general-purpose macros and is used by many C library functions.

The angle brackets (< and >) that surround **stdio.h** in **tabs.c** instruct the C preprocessor to look for the header file in a standard list of directories (such as **/usr/include**). If you want to include a header file from some other directory, you can enclose its pathname between double quotation marks. You can specify an absolute pathname within the double quotation marks, or you can give a relative pathname. If you give a relative pathname, searching begins with the working directory and is followed by the same directories that are searched when the header file is surrounded by angle brackets.

Another way to specify directories to be searched for header files is to use the **–I** option to the C compiler. Assume that Alex wants to compile the program **deriv.c**, which contains the following preprocessor directive:

```
#include "eqns.h"
```

If the header file **eqns.h** is located in the subdirectory **myincludes**, Alex can compile **deriv.c** with the **–I** option to tell the C preprocessor to look for the file **eqns.h** there.

```
cc -I./myincludes deriv.c
```

With this command, when the C preprocessor encounters the **#include** directive in the file **deriv.c** file, it look for **eqns.h** in the subdirectory **myincludes** of the working directory.

Use Relative Pathnames for Include Files

Using absolute pathnames for include files does not work if the location of the header file within the filesystem changes. Using relative pathnames for header files works as long as the location of the header file relative to the working directory remains the same. Relative pathnames also work with the **–I** option on the **cc** command line and allow header files to be moved.

Prior to the definition of the function **main** is a *function prototype,* a declaration that tells the compiler what type a function returns, how many arguments a function expects, and what the types of those arguments are. In **tabs.c** the prototype for the function **findstop** informs the compiler that **findstop** returns type *int* and that it expects a single argument of type *pointer to int.* Once the compiler has seen this declaration, it can detect and flag inconsistencies in the definition and uses of the function. For example suppose that the reference to **findstop** in **tabs.c** was replaced with the following statement:

```
inc = findstop();
```

The prototype for **findstop** would cause the compiler to detect a missing argument and issue an error message. The programmer could then easily fix the problem. Without the prototype the compiler would not issue an error message, and the problem would manifest itself as unexpected behavior during execution. At this late point, finding the bug might be difficult and time-consuming.

Although you can call most C functions anything you want, each program must have exactly one function named **main**. The function **main** is the control module—your program begins execution with the function **main**. Typically **main** will call other functions in turn, which may call yet other functions, and so forth. By putting different operations into separate functions, you can make a program easier to read and maintain. The program in Figure 14-1 uses a function **findstop** to compute the distance to the next **TAB** stop. Although the few statements of **findstop** could easily have been included in the **main** function, isolating them in a separate function draws attention to a key computation.

Functions can make both development and maintenance of the program more efficient. By putting a frequently used code segment into a function, you avoid entering the same code over and over again into the program. Later when you want to make changes to the code, you need to change it only once.

If your program is long and involves several functions, you may want to split it into two or more files. Regardless of its size, you may want to place logically distinct parts of your program in separate files. A C program can be split into any number of different files; however each function must be wholly contained within a file.

> ## Use a Header File for Multiple Source Files
>
> When you are creating a program that takes advantage of multiple source files, put **#define** preprocessor directives into a header file and use an include statement with the name of the header file in any source file that uses the directives.

▲▲ Compiling and Linking a C Program

To compile **tabs.c**, give the following command[2]:

```
$ cc tabs.c
```

The **cc** (and **gcc**) utility calls the C preprocessor, the C compiler, the assembler, and the linker. The four components of the compilation process are shown in Figure 14-2. The C preprocessor expands macro definitions and also includes header files. The compilation phase creates assembly language code corresponding to the instructions in the source file. Then the assembler creates machine-readable object code. One object file is created for each source file. Each object file has the same name as the source file, except that the **.c** extension is replaced with a **.o**. The previous example creates a single object file, **tabs.o**. However after the C compiler successfully completes all phases of the compilation process for a program, it creates the executable file and then removes any **.o** files. If you successfully compile **tabs.c**, you will not see the **.o** file.

During the final phase of the compilation process, the linker searches specified libraries for functions your program uses and combines object modules for those functions with your program's object modules. By default the C compiler searches the standard C library, **libc.so**, which contains functions that handle input and output and provides many other general-purpose capabilities. If you want the linker to search other libraries, you must use the **–l** option to specify the libraries on the command line. Unlike most options to Solaris system utilities, the **–l** option does not come before all filenames on the command line—it comes after all the filenames of all modules that it applies to. In the next example the C compiler searches the math library, **libm.so**:

```
$ cc calc.c -lm
```

---

2. Use gcc in place of cc in the examples throughout this chapter if you are using the GNU C compiler—see "Checking Your Compiler" on page 549.

As you can see from the example the **–l** option uses abbreviations for library names, appending the letter following **–l** to **lib** and adding a **.so** or **.a** extension. The **m** in the example stands for **libm.so**.

Using the same naming mechanism, you can have a graphics library named **libgraphics.a**, which could be linked on the command line with

```
$ cc pgm.c -lgraphics
```

When this convention is used to name libraries, **cc** knows to search for them in **/usr/lib** and **/lib**. You can have **cc** also search other directories with the **–L** option.

```
$ cc pgm.c -L. -L/usr/X11R6/lib -lgraphics
```

The preceding command causes **cc** to search for the library file **libgraphics.a** in the working directory and in **/usr/X11R6/lib** before searching **/usr/lib** and **/lib**.

As the last step of the compilation process, by default the linker creates an executable file named **a.out**. Object files are deleted after the executable is created. In the next example the **–O** option causes **cc** to use the C compiler *optimizer*. The optimizer makes object code more efficient so that the executable program runs more quickly. The example also shows that the **.o** files are not present after **a.out** is created.

```
$ ls
acctspay.c  acctsrec.c  ledger.c
$ cc -O ledger.c acctspay.c acctsrec.c
$ ls
a.out        acctspay.c  acctsrec.c  ledger.c
```

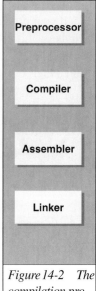

Figure 14-2   The compilation process

You can use the executable **a.out** in the same way you use shell scripts and other programs: By typing its name on the command line. The program in Figure 14-1 expects to read from standard input, so once you have created the executable, **a.out**, you can use a command such as the following to run it:

```
$ a.out < mymemo
```

If you want to save the **a.out** file, you should change the name to a more descriptive one. Otherwise you might accidentally overwrite it during a later compilation.

```
$ mv a.out tabs
```

To save the trouble of renaming **a.out** files, you can specify the name of the executable file when you use **cc**. If you use the **–o** option, the C compiler will give the executable the name of your choice rather than **a.out**. In the next example the executable is named **accounting**:

```
$ cc -o accounting ledger.c acctspay.c acctsrec.c
```

Assuming that **accounting** does not require arguments, you can run it with the following command:

```
$ accounting
```

You can suppress the linking phase of compilation by using the **–c** option with the **cc** command. The **–c** option is useful because it does not treat unresolved external references as errors; this capability enables you to compile and debug the syntax of the modules of a program as you create them. Once you have compiled and debugged all the modules, you can run **cc** again with the object files as arguments to produce an executable program. In the next example **cc** produces three object files but no executable:

```
$ cc -c ledger.c acctspay.c acctsrec.c
$ ls
acctspay.c  acctspay.o  acctsrec.c  acctsrec.o  ledger.c  ledger.o
```

If you then run **cc** again, naming the object files on the command line, **cc** will produce the executable. Because the C compiler recognizes the filename extension **.o**, it knows that the files need only to be linked. You can also include both **.c** and **.o** files on a single command line, as in this example:

```
$ cc -o accounting ledger.o acctspay.c acctsrec.o
```

The C compiler recognizes that the **.c** file needs to be preprocessed and compiled, whereas the **.o** files do not. The C compiler also accepts assembly language files ending in **.s**, and it treats them appropriately (that is, **cc** assembles and links them). This feature makes it easy to modify and recompile a program.

Refer to page 769 in Part III for more information on **gcc**.

▲ Using Shared Libraries

Most modern operating systems use shared libraries, also called dynamic libraries, because they are loaded and linked into the program at runtime. On Solaris, as on other UNIX systems, the names of files housing shared libraries end with the filename extension **.so** (shared object). Usually **libaaa.so** is a symbolic link to **libaaa.so.*x***, where *x* is a (small) number representing the version of the library. Many of these libraries are kept in **/usr/lib**: Solaris 2.6 has more than 70 shared libraries in **/usr/lib**, more than 30 in **/usr/openwin/lib**, and more than a dozen in **/usr/dt/lib**. Applications can have their own shared libraries; for example the Sun compiler keeps its libraries in **/opt/SUNWspro/lib**.

The **ldd** (list dynamic dependencies) utility tells you which shared libraries a program needs. For example:

```
$ ldd /bin/cp
libc.so.1 =>     /usr/lib/libc.so.1
libdl.so.1 =>    /usr/lib/libdl.so.1
```

shows that **cp** uses only the C library, **libc**, and the dynamic link library **libdl**. Running **ldd** on **dtcm** (the CDE Calendar Manager) lists 18 libraries from **/usr/lib**, **/usr/openwin/lib**, and **/usr/dt/lib**. Using the **–s** (search) option tells you how the runtime loader will search for the needed libraries:

```
$ ldd -s /usr/dt/bin/dtcm | head

    find library=libDtWidget.so.1; required by /usr/dt/bin/dtcm
     search path=/usr/dt/lib:/usr/openwin/lib  (RPATH from file /usr/dt/bin/dtcm)
     trying path=/usr/dt/lib/libDtWidget.so.1
        libDtWidget.so.1 =>      /usr/dt/lib/libDtWidget.so.1

    find library=libcsa.so.0; required by /usr/dt/bin/dtcm
     search path=/usr/dt/lib:/usr/openwin/lib  (RPATH from file /usr/dt/bin/dtcm)
     trying path=/usr/dt/lib/libcsa.so.0
        libcsa.so.0 =>   /usr/dt/lib/libcsa.so.0
```

The program that does the dynamic linking is named **ld.so.1** (yes, that is a utility name with two embedded periods) and by default it looks only in **/usr/lib** for shared libraries. The notion of a search path extends the list of directories that **ld.so.1** will look in to find the shared libraries. You can only use absolute pathnames in the search path. A search path is specified at compile time (actually link time) by using the **–R** option followed by a colon-separated list of directories to search. The **dtcm** calendar manager was likely linked with a command such as the following:

> *cc flags* *-o dtcm* **objects** *-R /usr/openwin/lib:/usr/dt/lib* **libraries**

This command line allows **ld.so.1** (and **ldd**) to search **/usr/openwin/lib** and **/usr/dt/lib** for the X and CDE libraries the executable needs.

The compiler needs to see the shared libraries at link time to make sure the needed functions and procedures are there as promised by the header (**.h**) files. Use the **–L** option to tell the compiler to look in the directory **mylib** for shared or static libraries: **–L mylib**. Unlike the search path **–L** can use relative pathnames such as **–L ../lib**. This is handy when a program builds its own shared library. The library can be at one location at build time (**–L**) but in another location (that is, after it is installed) at runtime (**–R**). (The **SPACE** after the **–L** is optional and is usually omitted. You can repeat the **–L** and the **–R** options multiple times on the link line.)

▲▲ Fixing Broken Binaries

The command-line search path is a fairly new idea. The old way to create the search path was using the **LD_LIBRARY_PATH** and, more recently, **LD_RUN_PATH** environment variables. These variables have the same format as **PATH** (page 372). The directories in **LD_LIBRARY_PATH** are normally searched before the usual library locations. Some of the newer releases of Solaris have extended the function of **LD_LIBRARY_PATH** to allow you to specify directories to be searched either before or after the normal locations. See the **ld man** page for details. **LD_RUN_PATH** behaves similarly to **LD_LIBRARY_PATH**, but if **–R** is used, it supersedes anything in **LD_RUN_PATH**.

There are several problems with the use of **LD_LIBRARY_PATH**: Because there is only one environment variable, it has to be shared among all programs. If two programs have the same name for a library or use different incompatible versions of the same library, only the first will be found and one of the programs will not run.

> **LD_LIBRARY_PATH Caution**
>
> A malicious user can create a Trojan horse named **libc.so** and place it in a directory that is searched before /usr/lib (any directory in **LD_LIBRARY_PATH** that appears before /usr/lib). The fake **libc** will then be used instead of the real **libc**.

LD_LIBRARY_PATH still has its place in scripts used to fix broken binaries. Suppose the broken binary **bb** uses the shared library **libbb.so**, which you want to put in **/opt/bb/lib** and not **/usr/lib** as the **bb** programmer requested. The command **ldd bb** will tell you which libraries are missing. Not a problem; rename **bb** to **bb.broken** and create a **/bin/sh** wrapper named **bb**:

```
#!/bin/sh
LD_LIBRARY_PATH=/opt/bb/lib
export LD_LIBRARY_PATH
exec bb.broken "$@"
```

(The **$@** rather than **$*** preserves SPACEs in the parameters.) This wrapper can also be used to install programs in arbitrary locations.

> ### Runtime Linker
>
> The System 7 runtime linker permits programs to find shared libraries without having to set **LD_LIBRARY_PATH** and makes the loading of shared libraries even more efficient. Shared objects can now be loaded at runtime relative to where the requesting object is located.

▲▲ Creating Shared Libraries

Shared libraries can save both disk space and memory space when multiple programs use the same library. To make a shared library, first compile the source files with the **–KPIC** option (position-independent code) to **cc** or the **–fPIC** option to **gcc**. Second, link these object files into the **lib.so** file using the **–G** option to the linker. You can either give the command **ld –G** or put **–G** on the link line of the makefile). C++ files have special needs, and libraries (shared or not) often have to be made by the compiler rather than **ld** or **ar**. Shared libraries can depend on other shared libraries and have their own search path. If you set **LD_LIBRARY_PATH**, add the **–i** flag to the link phase when compiling to ignore the current **LD_LIBRARY_PATH** or you may have unexpected results. Ideally you would not have **LD_LIBRARY_PATH** set at all on a global level, but only use it in wrappers as needed.

▲▲ Using **LD_PRELOAD**

LD_PRELOAD environment variable contains a SPACE-separated list of shared modules that the linker is to preload. These modules can hide functions inside the system libraries. For example the program **snoop** always looks up machine names, and sometimes one just wants IP numbers. It uses the system call **gethostbyaddr** to find names. You can override this function by preloading a dumb version of **gethostbyaddr**. Let **preload.c** be

```
void *gethostbyaddr(void) { return 0 };
/* for output to a pipe */
int isatty(int dummy) { return 1 };
int _isatty(int dummy) { return 1 };
```

Compile with **cc –G –KPIC preload.c –o preload.so**. Then run **snoop** with the command **LD_PRELOAD=/opt/sbin/preload.so snoop** *options*. Now only IP addresses will be shown. **LD_PRELOAD** has restrictions when used with setuid or setgid executables. See the **ld man** page for details.

▲ make: Keep a Set of Programs Current

When you have a large program with many source and header files, the files typically depend on one another in complex ways. When you change a file that other files depend on, you *must* recompile all dependent files. For example you might have several source files, all of which use a single header file. When you make a change to the header file, each of the source files must be recompiled. The header file might depend on other header files, and so forth. Figure 14-3 shows a simple example of dependency relationships. Each arrow in this figure points from a file to another file that depends on it. Also see **make** on page 803 in Part III.

When you are working on a large program, it can be difficult, time-consuming, and tedious to determine which modules need to be recompiled due to their dependency relationships. The **make** utility automates this process.

In its simplest use **make** looks at *dependency lines* in a file named **Makefile** or **makefile** in the working directory. The dependency lines indicate relationships among files, specifying a *target file* that depends on one or more *prerequisite files.* If you have modified any of the prerequisite files more recently than their target file, **make** updates the target file based on construction commands that follow the dependency line. The **make** utility normally stops if it encounters an error during the construction process.

The file containing the updating information for the **make** utility is called a *makefile.* See page 549 for a trivial example. A simple makefile has the following syntax:

> *target: prerequisite-list*
> TAB *construction-commands*

The dependency line is composed of the *target* and the *prerequisite-list*, separated by a colon. Each *construction-commands* line (you may have more than one) must start with a TAB and must follow the dependency line. Long lines can be continued with a BACKSLASH (\) as the last character on the line.

The *target* is the name of the file that depends on the files in the *prerequisite-list.* The *construction-commands* are regular commands to the shell that construct (usually compile and/or link) the target file. The **make** utility executes the *construction-commands* when the modification time of one or more of the files in the *prerequisite-list* is more recent than that of the target file.

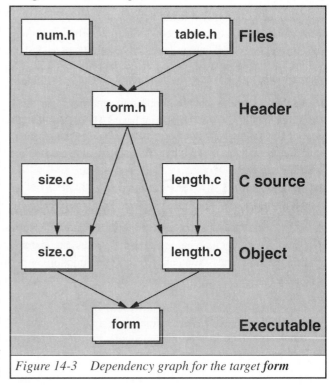

*Figure 14-3   Dependency graph for the target **form***

The following example shows the dependency line and construction commands for the file named **form** in Figure 14-3. It depends on the prerequisites **size.o** and **length.o**. An appropriate **cc** command constructs the **target**.

```
form: size.o length.o
        cc -o form size.o length.o
```

Each of the prerequisites on one dependency line can be a target on another dependency line. For example both **size.o** and **length.o** are targets on other dependency lines. Although the example in Figure 14-3 is simple, the nesting of dependency specifications can create a complex hierarchy that specifies relationships among many files.

The following makefile (named **Makefile**) corresponds to the complete dependency graph shown in Figure 14-3. The executable file **form** depends on two object files, and the object files each depend on their respective source files and a header file, **form.h**. In turn **form.h** depends on two other header files.

```
$ cat Makefile
form:size.o length.o
   cc -o form size.o length.o
size.o:size.c form.h
   cc -c size.c
length.o:length.c form.h
   cc -c length.c
form.h:num.h table.h
   cat num.h table.h > form.h
```

Although the last line would not normally be seen in a makefile, it serves to illustrate the fact that you can put any shell command on a construction line. Because makefiles are processed by the shell, the command line should be one that you could input in response to a shell prompt.

Make sure that **/usr/ccs/bin** is in your **PATH** before giving the command

```
$ make
```

which builds the default target **form** if its prerequisites are more recent or if the target does not exist. Thus if the file **form** has been deleted, **make** will rebuild it, regardless of the modification dates of its prerequisite files. The first target in a makefile is the default and is built when you call **make** without any arguments.

If you want **make** to rebuild a target other than the first in the makefile, you must provide the target as an argument to **make**. The following command rebuilds only **form.h** if it does not exist or if its prerequisites are more recent.

```
$ make form.h
```

▲▲ Implied Dependencies

You can rely on *implied* dependencies and construction commands to make your job of writing a makefile easier. For instance if you do not include a dependency line for an object file, **make** assumes that it depends on a compiler or assembler source code file. Thus if a prerequisite for a target file is **xxx.o** and there is no dependency line with **xxx.o** as a target, **make** looks at the extension to try to determine how to build the .o file. If it finds an appropriate source file, **make** provides a default construction command line that calls the proper compiler or the assembler to create the object file. The following table lists some of the filename extensions that **make** recognizes and the type of file that corresponds to the suffix.

Filename Extension	Corresponding Type of File
xxx.c	C source code
xxx.C, xxx.cc, xxx.cxx, xxx.c++, xxx.cpp	C++ source code
xxx.f	FORTRAN source code
xxx.h	Header file
xxx.l	**lex** or **flex** source code
xxx.s	Assembler code
xxx.sh	Shell scripts
xxx.y	**yacc** or **bison** source code

The next example shows a makefile that keeps a file named **compute** up to date. The **make** utility ignores any line that begins with a pound sign (**#**). Thus the first three lines of the following makefile are comment lines. The first dependency line shows that **compute** depends on two object files: **compute.o** and **calc.o**. The corresponding construction line gives the command **make** needs to produce **compute**. The next dependency line shows that **compute.o** depends not only on its C source file but also on a header file, **compute.h**. The construction line for **compute.o** uses the C compiler optimizer (**−O** option). The third set of dependency and construction lines is not required. In their absence **make** infers that **calc.o** depends on **calc.c** and produces the command line needed for the compilation.

```
$ cat Makefile
#
# Makefile for compute
#
compute:compute.o calc.o
      cc -o compute compute.o calc.o

compute.o:compute.c compute.h
      cc -c -O compute.c

calc.o:calc.c
      cc -c calc.c

clean:
   rm *.o
```

There are no prerequisites for the last target, **clean**, in the makefile above. This target is commonly used to get rid of extraneous files that may be out of date or no longer needed, such as **.o** files.

The following are some sample executions of **make**, based on the previous makefile. As the **ls** command that follows shows, **compute.o**, **calc.o**, and **compute** are not up to date. Consequently the **make** command runs the construction commands that re-create them.

```
$ ls -ltr
total 22
-rw-rw----   1 alex   pubs    311 Jun 21 15:56 makefile
-rw-rw----   1 alex   pubs    354 Jun 21 16:02 calc.o
-rwxrwx---   1 alex   pubs   6337 Jun 21 16:04 compute
-rw-rw----   1 alex   pubs     49 Jun 21 16:04 compute.h
-rw-rw----   1 alex   pubs    880 Jun 21 16:04 compute.o
-rw-rw----   1 alex   pubs    780 Jun 21 18:20 compute.c
-rw-rw----   1 alex   pubs    179 Jun 21 18:20 calc.c

$ make
cc -c -O compute.c
cc -c calc.c
cc -o compute compute.o calc.o
```

If you run **make** once and then run it again without making any changes to the prerequisite files, **make** indicates that the program is up to date and does not execute any commands.

```
$ make
make: 'compute' is up to date.
```

The following example uses the **touch** utility to change the modification time of a prerequisite file. This simulation shows what would happen if you were to make a change to the file. The **make** utility executes only the commands necessary to make the out-of-date targets up to date.

```
$ touch calc.c
$ make
cc -c calc.c
cc -o compute compute.o calc.o
```

In the next example **touch** changes the modification time of **compute.h**. The **make** utility re-creates **compute.o** because it depends on **compute.h** and recreates the executable because it depends on **compute.o**.

```
$ touch compute.h
$ make
cc -c -O compute.c
cc -o compute compute.o calc.o
```

As these examples illustrate, **touch** is useful when you want to fool **make** into recompiling programs or into *not* recompiling them. You can use it to update the modification times of all the source files so that **make** considers that nothing is up to date. The **make** utility will then recompile everything. Alternatively you can use **touch** or the **–t** option to **make** to touch all relevant files so that **make** considers everything to be up to date. This is useful if the modification times of files have changed, yet the files are all up to date. (As happens when you copy a set of files from one directory to another.) If you want to see what **make** *would* do if you ran it, run **make** with the **–n** option. The **–n** option shows the commands that **make** would execute, but it does not execute them.

Once you are satisfied with the program you have created, you can use the makefile to clean out the files you no longer need. It is useful to keep intermediate files around while you are writing and debugging your program, so that you need rebuild only the ones that change. If you will not be working on the program again for a while, though, you should release the disk space. The advantage of using a **clean** target in your makefile is that you do not have to remember all the little pieces that can safely be deleted. The example that follows simply removes all the object (**.o**) files:

```
$ make clean
rm *.o
```

Start Optional

▲▲ Macros

The **make** utility has a macro facility that enables you to create and use macros within a makefile. The syntax of a macro definition is

ID = *list*

Replace *ID* with an identifying name, and replace *list* with a list of filenames. After this macro definition, **$(ID)** represents *list* in the makefile.

You can use a macro so that you can compile a program with any of several C compilers (for example the Sun **cc** compiler or the GNU **gcc** compiler) with only a minor change to the makefile. By using the **CC** macro and replacing all occurrences of cc in the makefile on page 560 with $(CC), you only need to assign a value to **CC** to use the compiler of your choice. The following example uses the **cc** compiler, but by replacing the CC=cc assignment with CC=gcc it could use the **gcc** compiler. If you do not assign a value to the **CC** macro it defaults to **cc**. You can override the value of **CC** assigned in the makefile by setting the **CC** environment variable or by assigning a value to **CC** on the **make** command line (**make CC=gcc**).

```
$ cat Makefile
#
# Makefile for compute
#
CC=cc
compute:compute.o calc.o
        $(CC) -o compute compute.o calc.o

compute.o:compute.c compute.h
        $(CC) -c -O compute.c

calc.o:calc.c
        $(CC) -c calc.c

clean:
        rm *.o
```

The **CC** macro invokes the C compiler with only the options that you specify.

There are additional macro definitions that are commonly used in programs. The **CFLAGS** macro sends arguments to the C compiler. The **LDFLAGS** macro sends arguments to the linker (**ld**, or **cc –o**). The **COMPILE.c** macro expands to **$(CC) $(CFLAGS) $(CPPFLAGS) –c**. The **LINK.c** macro expands to **$(CC) $(CFLAGS) $(CPPFLAGS) $(LDFLAGS)**.

The following makefile uses macros, as well as implied dependencies and constructions.

```
# makefile: report, print, printf, printh
#
CC=cc
CFLAGS = -fast
# comment out the two lines above, uncomment the two
# below if you are using the GNU gcc compiler
#CC=gcc
#CFLAGS = -O
FILES = in.c out.c ratio.c process.c tally.c
OBJECTS = in.o out.o ratio.o process.o tally.o
HEADERS = names.h companies.h conventions.h

report:         $(OBJECTS)
                $(LINK.c) -o report $(OBJECTS)

ratio.o:        $(HEADERS)

process.o:      $(HEADERS)

tally.o:        $(HEADERS)

print:
        pr $(FILES) $(HEADERS) | lp

printf:
        pr $(FILES) | lp

printh:
        pr $(HEADERS) | lp
```

Following the comment lines and the definition of the **CC** macro, the makefile uses the **CFLAGS** macro to make sure that **make** always selects the optimal compilation options (**–fast** option) when it invokes the C compiler as the result of an implied construction. (The **CC** and **CFLAGS** definitions for the **gcc** C compiler perform the same functions when they are uncommented and you are using the **gcc** compiler [except that you would use **–O4** with **gcc** instead of **–fast**].) Whenever you put a construction line in a makefile, the construction line overrides the corresponding implied construction line, if one exists. If you want to apply a macro to a construction command, you must include the macro in that command. This was done, for example with **OBJECTS** in the construction command for the **report** target. Following **CFLAGS** the makefile defines the **FILES**, **OBJECTS**, and **HEADERS** macros. Each of these macros defines a list of files.

The first dependency line shows that **report** depends on the list of files that **OBJECTS** defines. The corresponding construction line links the **OBJECTS** and creates an executable file named **report**.

The next three dependency lines show that three object files depend on the list of files that **HEADERS** defines. There are no construction lines, so when it is necessary, **make** looks for a source code file corresponding to each of the object files and compiles it. These three dependency lines ensure that the object files are recompiled if any of the header files are changed.

Finally, the **LINK.c** macro is invoked to link the executable file. If you specify any **LDFLAGS** they are used in this step. For example if your program used networking code such as sockets or DNS calls, you would assign a value to **LDFLAGS** as shown below.

```
LDFLAGS = -lsocket -lnsl
```

You can combine several targets on one dependency line, so these three dependency lines could have been combined into one line as follows:

```
ratio.o process.o tally.o: $(HEADERS)
```

The three final dependency lines send source and header files to the printer. They have nothing to do with compiling the **report** file. None of these targets (**print**, **printf**, and **printh**) depends on anything. When you call one of these targets from the command line, **make** executes the construction line following it. As an example the following command prints all the source files that **FILES** defines:

```
$ make printf
```

Stop Optional

▲ Debugging C Programs

The C compiler is liberal about the kinds of constructs it allows in programs. In keeping with the UNIX philosophy that "no news is good news" and that the user knows what is best, **cc**, like many other Solaris utilities, accepts almost anything that is logically possible according to the definition of the language. Although this approach gives the programmer a great deal of flexibility and control, it can make debugging difficult.

The program **badtabs.c** in Figure 14-4 is a flawed version of the program **tabs.c** discussed earlier. It contains some errors and does not run properly but serves to illustrate some debugging techniques.

In the following example **badtabs.c** is compiled and then run with input from the **testtabs** file. Inspection of the output shows that the TAB character has not been replaced with the proper number of SPACEs.

```
$ cc -o badtabs badtabs.c
$ cat testtabs
abcTABxyz
$ badtabs < testtabs
abc    xyz
```

One way to debug a C program is to insert print statements at critical points throughout the source code. To learn more about the behavior of **badtabs.c** when it runs, you can add the following calls to the **fprintf()** function:

```
case '\t':              /* c is a tab */
    fprintf(stderr, "before call to findstop, posn is %d\n", posn);
    inc = findstop(&posn);
    fprintf(stderr, "after call to findstop, posn is %d\n", posn);
    for( ; inc > 0; inc-- )
        putchar(' ');
    break;
case '\n':              /* c is a newline */
    fprintf(stderr, "got a newline\n");
    putchar(c);
    posn = 0;
    break;
default:                /* c is anything else */
    fprintf(stderr, "got another character\n");
    putchar(c);
    posn++;
    break;
```

```
1    /* convert tabs in standard input to spaces in */
2    /* standard output while maintaining columns */
3
4    #include        <stdio.h>
5    #define         TABSIZE         8
6
7    /* prototype for function findstop */
8    int findstop(int *);
9
10   main()
11   {
12   int c;          /* character read from stdin */
13   int posn = 0;   /* column position of character */
14   int inc;        /* column increment to tab stop */
15
16   while ((c = getchar()) != EOF)
17         switch(c)
18             {
19             case '\t':                  /* c is a tab */
20                     inc = findstop(&posn);
21                     for( ; inc > 0; inc-- )
22                             putchar(' ');
23                     break;
24             case '\n':                  /* c is a newline */
25                     putchar(c);
26                     posn = 0;
27                     break;
28             default:                    /* c is anything else */
29                     putchar(c);
30                     posn++;
31                     break;
32             }
33
34   }
35
36   /* compute size of increment to next tab stop */
37
38   int findstop(int *col)
39   {
40   int colindex, retval;
41   retval = (TABSIZE - (*col % TABSIZE));
42
43   /* increment argument (current column position) to next tabstop * /
44   *col += retval;
45
46   return retval;            /* main gets how many blanks for filling */
47   }
```

	Comments
	Preprocessor Directives
	Function Prototype
	Main Function
	Function

*Figure 14-4   The **badtabs.c** program (the line numbers are not part of the source code; the arrows point to errors in the program)*

The **fprintf** statements in this code send their messages to standard error, so if you redirect standard output of this program, it will not be interspersed with the error output. Following is an example that demonstrates the operation of this program on the input file **testtabs**:

```
$ cc -o badtabs badtabs.c
$ badtabs < testtabs > testspaces
got another character
got another character
got another character
before call to findstop, posn is 3
```

```
after call to findstop, posn is 3
got another character
got another character
got another character
got a newline
$ cat testspaces
abc    xyz
```

The **fprintf** statements provide additional information about the execution **of tabs.c**; in particular they show that the value of the variable **posn** is not incremented in **findstop**, as it should be. This might be enough to lead you to the cause of the bug in the program. If not, you might attempt to "corner" the offending code by inserting **fprintf** statements in **findstop**.

For simple programs, or in cases where you may have some idea of what is wrong with your program, adding print statements that trace the execution of the code can often help you solve the problem quickly. A better strategy may be to switch to one of the tools that Solaris provides to help you debug programs.

▲▲ lint: Find Errors in a Program

If you are using the **cc** compiler, the C program verifier, **lint**,[3] is one of the most useful debugging tools. It checks programs for potential bugs and portability problems. Unlike the C compiler **lint** is very strict. It detects and reports on a wide variety of problems and potential problems, including variables that are used before they are set, arguments to functions that are not used, and functions that use return values that were never returned.

The **lint** utility uncovers two problems with the sample program **tabs.c**:

```
$ lint tabs.c
function returns value which is always ignored
  putchar

declared global, could be static
  findstop tabs.c(38)
```

The first warning from **lint** points out that the return codes from the calls to **putchar** are never checked. If **putchar** fails, the error will not be detected and the output of the **tabs** program will be incorrect. The second warning says that you could have declared **findstop** to be static instead of global.

Although you are free to ignore **lint**'s warnings and go ahead and compile your program, a warning typically means that the program has a bug or a nonportable construct or that you have violated a standard of good programming. Paying attention to **lint**'s warnings is a good way to debug your programs and to hone your programming skills.

---

3. The **lint** utility does not come with the basic Solaris system but is included when you buy a C compiler from Sun.

▲▲ gcc: Compiler Warning Options
Find Errors in a Program

The **gcc** compiler has many of the features of **lint** built into it and then some. It is able to identify many constructs in C programs that pose potential problems, even for programs that conform to the syntax rules of the language. For instance, if you request, the compiler can report if a variable is declared but not used, if a comment is not properly terminated, or if a function returns a type not permitted in older versions of C. Options that enable this stricter compiler behavior all begin with the uppercase letter **W** (for *Warning*).

Among the **–W** options is a class of warnings that typically result from programmer carelessness or inexperience. The constructs causing these warnings are generally easy to fix and easy to avoid. A partial list of such options follows.

–W Option	Report Errors
–Wimplicit	When a function or parameter is not explicitly declared.
–Wreturn-type	When a function that is not void does not return a value, or when the type of a function defaults to **int**.
–Wunused	When a variable is declared but not used.
–Wcomment	When the characters /∗, which normally begin a comment, are seen within a comment.
–Wformat	When certain input/output statements contain format specifications that do not match the arguments.

To get warnings about all of the preceding errors, along with others in this class, use the **–Wall** option.

The program **badtabs.c** is syntactically correct. However if you compile (**–c** causes **gcc** to compile but not to link) it with the **–Wall** option, you will see several problems.

```
$ gcc -c -Wall badtabs.c
badtabs.c:47: warning: '/*' within comment
badtabs.c:11: warning: return-type defaults to 'int'
badtabs.c: In function 'main':
badtabs.c:34: warning: control reaches end of non-void function
badtabs.c: In function 'findstop':
badtabs.c:40: warning: unused variable 'colindex'
badtabs.c:49: warning: control reaches end of non-void function
```

The first warning error message references line 47. Inspection of the code for **badtabs.c** around that line reveals a comment that is not properly terminated. The compiler sees the string /∗ in the following line as the beginning of a comment:

```
/* increment argument (current column position) to next tabstop * /
```

However because the characters ∗ and / at the end of the line are separated by a **SPACE**, they do not signify the end of the comment to the compiler. Instead the compiler interprets all the statements, including the statement that increments the argument, through the string ∗/ at the very end of the **findstop** function as part of the comment.

Compiling with the **–Wall** option can be very helpful when debugging a program. By removing the SPACE between the characters * and /, **badtabs** produces the correct output.

The next few paragraphs discuss the remaining warning messages. Although most do not cause problems in the execution of **badtabs**, programs can generally be improved by rewriting parts of the code that produce warnings.

Because the definition of the function **main** does not include an explicit type, the compiler assumes type **int**, the default. This results in the warning error message referencing line 11 in **badtabs.c**, the top of the function **main**. An additional warning is given when the compiler encounters the end of the function **main** (line 34) without seeing a value returned.

By convention if a program runs successfully, it should return a zero value; if no value is returned, the exit code is undefined. Although it is common to see C programs that do not return a value, the oversight can cause problems when the program executes. When you add the following statement at the end of the function **main** in **badtabs.c**, the warning referencing line 34 disappears:

```
return 0;
```

Line 40 of **badtabs.c** contains a declaration for the local variable **colindex** in the function **findstop**. The error message referencing that line occurs because **colindex** is never used. Removing its declaration gets rid of the error message.

The final error message, referencing line 49, results from the improperly terminated comment discussed above. The compiler issues the error message because it never sees a return statement in **findstop**. (The compiler ignores commented text.) Because the function **findstop** is type **int**, the compiler expects a return statement before reaching the end of the function. The warning disappears when the comment is properly terminated.

There are many other **–W** options available with the **gcc** compiler. The ones not covered in the **–Wall** class often involve portability differences; modifying the code causing the warnings may not be appropriate. The warnings tend to result from programs written in different C dialects as well as from constructs that may not work well with other (especially older) C compilers. To learn more about these and other warning options, see **gcc** on page 769 in Part III and the **gcc man** page.

▲▲ Symbolic Debuggers

Solaris provides debuggers, including **dbx**,[4] for tackling problems that evade the simpler methods involving print statements, **lint**, and compiler warning options. Other debuggers, including **gdb**, **xxgdb**, and **ups**, are available from the Internet (refer to Appendix B). All are high-level symbolic debuggers—they enable you to analyze the execution of a program in terms of C language statements. They also provide a lower-level view for analyzing the execution of a program in terms of the machine instructions. Except for **dbx**, each of the debuggers mentioned in this paragraph provides a graphical user interface.

---

4. Supplied with the C compiler but not part of the basic Solaris package.

A debugger enables you to monitor and control the execution of a program. You can step through a program line by line while you examine the state of the execution environment. It also allows you to examine *core* files. (Core files are named **core**.) When a serious error occurs during the execution of a program, the operating system can create a core file containing information about the state of the program and the system when the error occurred. This file is a dump of the computer's memory (it used to be called *core memory*, thus the term *core dump*) that was being used by the program. To conserve disk space your system may be set up so that core files are not saved. You can use the **ulimit** _{sh}_{ksh} or **limit** csh builtin to enable core files to be saved. If you are running **sh**, the following command allows core files of unlimited size to be saved to disk.

```
$ ulimit -c unlimited
```

The operating system will advise you when it has dumped core. You can use a symbolic debugger to read information from the core file to identify the line in the program where the error occurred, to check the values of variables at that point, and so forth. Because core files tend to be large and take up disk space, be sure to remove them when you are done.

▲▲▲▲ Starting a Symbolic Debugger

The following examples demonstrate the use of the Sun **dbx** (next) and GNU **gdb** (page 573) debuggers. The GNU debugger uses many of the same commands that **dbx** uses. There are some differences in the more complex features (such as threads management), but most of the basic functionality is identical (breakpoints, variable watching, and so on). Other symbolic debuggers offer a different command interface but operate in a similar manner.

To make full use of a symbolic debugger with a program, it is necessary to compile the program with the **–g** option. The **–g** option causes **cc** and **gcc** to generate additional information that the debugger uses. This information includes a *symbol table*—a list of variable names used in the program and associated values. Without the symbol table information, the debugger is unable to display the values and types of variables. If a program is compiled without the **–g** option, **dbx** (and **gdb**) is unable to identify source code lines by number, as many **dbx** commands require. The following example uses the **–g** option when creating the executable file **tabs** from the C program **tabs.c**, discussed at the beginning of this chapter:

```
$ cc -g tabs.c -o tabs
```

Input for **tabs** is contained in the file **testtabs**, which consists of a single line.

```
$ cat testtabs
xyzTABabc
```

If you are using **gdb**, go to page 573.

▲▲▲▲ The **dbx** Debugger: You cannot specify the input file to **tabs** until you have called the debugger and started execution with the **run** command. To run the debugger on the sample executable, give the name of the executable file on the command line when you run **dbx**. You will see introductory statements about **dbx**, including instructions on bypassing the introductory statements next time you run **dbx**, followed by the **dbx** prompt (**dbx**). The debugger is now ready to accept commands. The **list** command displays the first ten executable lines of source code. A subsequent **list** command displays the next ten lines of code.

```
$ dbx tabs
The major new features of this release relative to 3.2 are:


o The Collector now supports MT applications (see 'help collectormt')
o Runtime checking (RTC) is supported with fork/exec/attach (see 'help
  rtc attach' for details)
o RTC has an API for allocators (see 'help rtc api')
o New command 'regs' to print current value of registers (see 'help regs')
o New command 'showblock' to give details about heap block (see 'help showblock')
o Enhanced 'pathmap' command (see 'help pathmap')
o New dbxenv variable 'language_mode' (see 'help dbxenv' under 'language_mode')
o New dbxenv variable 'output_inherited_members' (ee 'help dbxenv' under
  'output_inherited_members')
o Two new dbx read-only variables: $helpfile and $helpfile_html (see 'help help')
o New -v (verbose) flag to the 'module' and 'modules' commands
  (see 'help module' and 'help modules')
o New +r flag to print and display commands (see 'help print')
  .
  .
  .
To suppress this message, add the following line to your .dbxrc file:
        dbxenv suppress_startup_message 4.0

Reading symbolic information for tabs
Reading symbolic information for rtld /usr/lib/ld.so.1
Reading symbolic information for libc.so.1
Reading symbolic information for libdl.so.1
Reading symbolic information for libc_psr.so.1

(dbx) list
   13    int posn = 0;    /* column position of character */
   14    int inc;         /* column increment to tab stop */
   15
   16    while ((c = getchar()) != EOF)
   17         switch(c)
   18         {
   19         case '\t':              /* c is a tab */
   20             inc = findstop(&posn);
   21             for( ; inc > 0; inc-- )
   22                 putchar(' ');
(dbx) list
   23             break;
   24         case '\n':              /* c is a newline */
   25             putchar(c);
   26             posn = 0;
   27             break;
   28         default:                /* c is anything else */
   29             putchar(c);
   30             posn++;
   31             break;
   32         }
```

One of the most important features of a debugger is the ability to run a program in a controlled environment. You can stop the program from running whenever you want. While it is stopped you can check on the state of an argument or variable. The **stop** command can be given a source code line number, an actual memory address, or a function name as an argument. The following command tells **dbx** to stop the process whenever the function **findstop** is called:

```
(dbx) stop in findstop
(2) stop in findstop
```

Having set a breakpoint, you can issue a **run** command to start execution of **tabs** under the control of the debugger. The **run** command syntax allows you to use angle brackets to redirect input and output (just as the shells do). The following **run** command specifies **testtabs** as input. When the process stops (at the breakpoint), you can use the **print** command to check the value of ***col**. The **where** command displays the function stack. The example shows that the currently active function has been assigned the number 1. The function that is called **findstop** (**main**) has been assigned the number 2.

```
(dbx) run < testtabs
Running: tabs < testtabs
(process id 19780)
stopped in findstop at line 41 in file "tabs.c"
   41   retval = (TABSIZE - (*col % TABSIZE));

(dbx) print *col
*col = 3

(dbx) where
=>[1] findstop(col = 0xeffff89c), line 41 in "tabs.c"
  [2] main(), line 20 in "tabs.c"
```

Variables and arguments can be checked only in the active function. The following example shows that the request to examine the value of the variable **posn** at breakpoint 1 results in an error. The error results because the variable **posn** is declared in the function **main**, not in the function **findstop**.

```
(dbx) print posn
dbx: "posn" is not defined in the scope 'tabs'tabs.c'findstop'
dbx: see 'help scope' for details
```

The **up** command changes the active function to the caller of the currently active function. Because **main** calls the function **findstop**, the function **main** becomes the active function when the **up** command is given. (The **down** command does the inverse.) The **up** command may be given an integer argument, which specifies the number of levels in the function stack to backtrack, with **up 1** meaning the same as **up**. (You can use the **where** command to determine the argument to use with **up**.)

```
(dbx) up
Current function is main
20 inc = findstop(&posn);
(dbx) print posn
posn = 3
(dbx) print *col
dbx: "col" is not defined in the scope 'tabs'tabs.c'main'
```

The **cont** (continue) command causes the process to continue running from where it left off. The **testtabs** file contains only one line; the process finishes executing, and the results appear on the screen. The debugger reports the exit code of the program. A **cont** command given after a program has finished executing reminds you that execution of the program has completed. Below, the debugging session is then ended with a **quit** command:

```
(dbx) cont
xyz     abc
execution completed, exit code is 0
(dbx) cont
dbx: can't continue execution -- no active process
(dbx) quit
$
```

The **dbx** utility has many commands that are designed to make debugging easier. To learn more about **dbx**, type **help** to get a list of the command classes available under **dbx**.

```
(dbx) help
Command Summary
   Use 'commands' to see a command summary consisting of one-line
   descriptions of each dbx command.

Execution and Tracing
   cancel       catch       clear        cont        delete
   fix          fixed       handler      ignore      intercept
   next         pop         replay       rerun       restore
   run          runargs     save         status      step
   stop         trace       unintercept  when        whocatches

Displaying and Naming Data
   assign       call        dis          display     down
   dump         examine     exists       frame       hide
   print        undisplay   unhide       up          whatis
   where        whereami    whereis      which

Accessing Source Files
   bsearch      cd          edit         file        files
   func         funcs       line         list        loadobject
   loadobjects  module      modules      pathmap     pwd
   .
   .
The command 'help <cmdname>' provides additional
help for each command or topic.  For new and changed features,
see 'help changes', and 'help FAQ' for
answers to frequently asked questions about dbx.
```

As given in the instructions following the list, entering **help** followed by the name of a command or command class will give more information. The following lists information about the **where** command:

```
(dbx) help where
where               # Print a procedure traceback
where <num>         # Print the <num> top frames in the traceback
where -f <num>      # Start traceback from frame <num>
where -h            # Include hidden frames
where -q            # Quick traceback (only function names)
```

```
where -v                    # Verbose traceback (include function args and line info)
```

Any of the above forms may be followed by a thread or LWP ID to obtain the traceback for the specified entity.

▲▲▲▲▲ **The gdb Debugger:**   You cannot specify the name of the input file when you first call the debugger; you must wait until you start running the program you are debugging from within **gdb**. To debug a program give the name of the executable file on the command line as an argument to **gdb**. You will see introductory statements about **gdb**, followed by the **gdb** prompt [**(gdb)**]. When you see the prompt, **gdb** is ready to accept commands. The **list** command displays the first ten lines of source code. A subsequent **list** command displays the next ten lines of source code.

```
$ gdb tabs
GNU gdb 4.17
Copyright 1998 Free Software Foundation, Inc.
GDB is free software, covered by the GNU General Public License, and you are
welcome to change it and/or distribute copies of it under certain conditions.
Type "show copying" to see the conditions.
There is absolutely no warranty for GDB.  Type "show warranty" for details.
This GDB was configured as "i386-pc-solaris2.6"...
(gdb) list
4       #include        <stdio.h>
5       #define         TABSIZE         8
6
7       /* prototype for function findstop */
8       int findstop(int *);
9
10      int main()
11      {
12      int c;          /* character read from stdin */
13      int posn = 0;   /* column position of character */
(gdb) list
14      int inc;        /* column increment to tab stop */
15
16      while ((c = getchar()) != EOF)
17              switch(c)
18              {
19                      case '\t':               /* c is a tab */
20                              inc = findstop(&posn);
21                              for( ; inc > 0; inc-- )
22                                      putchar(' ');
23                              break;
```

One of the most important features of a debugger is the ability to run a program in a controlled environment. You can stop the program from running whenever you want. While it is stopped you can check on the state of an argument or variable. The **break** command accepts a source code line number or a function name as an argument. The following command tells **gdb** to stop the process whenever the function **findstop** is called:

```
(gdb) break findstop
Breakpoint 1 at 0x8048b4b: file tabs.c, line 41.
```

The debugger acknowledges the request by displaying the breakpoint number, the hexadecimal memory address of the breakpoint, and the corresponding source code line number (41). The debugger numbers breakpoints in ascending order as you create them, starting with 1.

Having set a breakpoint, you can issue a **run** command to start execution of **tabs** under the control of the debugger. The **run** command syntax allows you to use angle brackets to redirect input and output (just as the shells do). Below, the **testtabs** file is specified as input. When the process stops (at the breakpoint), you can use the **print** command to check the value of ***col**. The **backtrace** (or **bt**) command displays the function stack. The example shows that the currently active function has been assigned the number 0. The function that is called **findstop** (**main**) has been assigned the number 1.

```
(gdb) run < testtabs
Starting program: /home/jenny/c/tabs < testtabs

Breakpoint 1, findstop (col=0x8047c84) at tabs.c:41
41          retval = (TABSIZE - (*col % TABSIZE));
(gdb) print *col
$1 = 3
(gdb) backtrace
#0  findstop (col=0x8047c84) at tabs.c:41
#1  0x8048a6d in main () at tabs.c:20
```

Variables and arguments can be checked only in the active function. The request to examine the value of the variable **posn** at breakpoint 1 results in an error because the variable **posn** is declared in the function **main**, not **findstop**.

```
(gdb) print posn
No symbol "posn" in current context.
```

The **up** command changes the active function to the caller of the currently active function. Because **main** calls the function **findstop**, the function **main** becomes the active function when you give the **up** command. (The **down** command does the inverse.) The **up** command may be given an integer argument, which specifies the number of levels in the function stack to backtrack, with **up 1** meaning the same as **up**. (You can use **backtrace** to determine the argument to use with **up**.)

```
(gdb) up
#1  0x8048a6d in main () at tabs.c:20
20                              inc = findstop(&posn);
(gdb) print posn
$2 = 3
(gdb) print *col
No symbol "col" in current context.
```

The **cont** (continue) command causes the process to continue running from where it left off. The **testtabs** file contains only one line; the process finishes executing, and the result appears on the screen. The debugger reports the exit code of the program. A **cont** command given after a program has finished executing reminds you that the program has finished executing. Below, the debugging session is ended with a **quit** command:

```
(gdb) cont
Continuing.
xyz     abc

Program exited normally.
(gdb) cont
The program is not being run.
(gdb) quit
$
```

If your program takes different command-line arguments, it is a good idea to test each of the arguments with the debugger. To perform this testing you can use the **set args** command to specify the command-line arguments to use when the program is run. For instance if a program has a **–d** flag for debugging and a **–v** flag for verbose output, you would give the command **set args –v –d** before executing the program.

The **gdb** utility supports many commands that are designed to make debugging easier. To learn more about **gdb**, use the **help** command (from the **(gdb)** prompt) to display a list of command classes.

```
(gdb) help
List of classes of commands:

aliases -- Aliases of other commands
breakpoints -- Making program stop at certain points
data -- Examining data
files -- Specifying and examining files
internals -- Maintenance commands
obscure -- Obscure features
running -- Running the program
stack -- Examining the stack
status -- Status inquiries
support -- Support facilities
tracepoints -- Tracing of program execution without stopping the program
user-defined -- User-defined commands

Type "help" followed by a class name for a list of commands in that class.
Type "help" followed by command name for full documentation.
Command name abbreviations are allowed if unambiguous.
```

As given in the instructions following the list (above), enter `help` followed by the name of a command class or command name to display more information. The following command lists the commands in the class **data**:

```
(gdb) help data
Examining data.

List of commands:

call -- Call a function in the program
delete display -- Cancel some expressions to be displayed when program stops
disable display -- Disable some expressions to be displayed when program stops
disassemble -- Disassemble a specified section of memory
display -- Print value of expression EXP each time the program stops
enable display -- Enable some expressions to be displayed when program stops
```

```
inspect -- Same as "print" command
output -- Like "print" but don't put in value history and don't print newline
print -- Print value of expression EXP
printf -- Printf "printf format string"
ptype -- Print definition of type TYPE
set -- Evaluate expression EXP and assign result to variable VAR
set variable -- Evaluate expression EXP and assign result to variable VAR
undisplay -- Cancel some expressions to be displayed when program stops
whatis -- Print data type of expression EXP
x -- Examine memory: x/FMT ADDRESS

Type "help" followed by command name for full documentation.
Command name abbreviations are allowed if unambiguous.
```

The next command requests information on **whatis**, which takes a variable name or other expression as an argument.

```
(gdb) help whatis
Print data type of expression EXP.
```

▲▲▲ Graphical Symbolic Debuggers

There are several graphical user interfaces to **gdb**. Two interfaces that are similar are **xxgdb** and **mxgdb** (a Motif-based interface). These graphical versions of **gdb** provide you with a number of windows, including a Source Listing window, a Command window that contains a set of commonly used commands, and a Display window for viewing the values of variables. The left mouse button selects commands from the Command window. You can click on the desired line in the Source Listing Window to set a breakpoint and you can select variables by clicking on them in the Source Listing window. Selecting a variable and clicking on **print** in the Command window displays the value of the variable in the Display window. You can view lines of source code by scrolling (and resizing) the Source Listing window.

The **ddd** debugger also provides a graphical user interface to **gdb**. Unlike **xxgdb** and **mxgdb**, **ddd** can graphically display complex C structures and the links between them. This display makes it easier to see errors in these structures. Otherwise the **ddd** interface is very similar to that of **xxgdb** and **mxgdb**.

Unlike **xxgdb** and **mxgdb**, **ups** was designed from the ground up to work as a debugger with a graphical user interface; the graphical interface was not added on after the debugger was complete. The result is an interface that is easier to use. For example **ups** automatically displays the value of a variable when you click on it. It also has a built-in C interpreter that allows you to attach C code to the program you are debugging. Because this attached code has access to the variables and values in the program, you can use it to perform sophisticated checks, such as following and displaying the links in a complex data structure.

▲ Threads

A *thread* is a single sequential flow of control within a process. Threads are the basis for multithreaded programs, which allow a single program to control concurrently running threads, each performing a different task. Multithreaded programs generally use *reentrant* code (code that multiple threads can use simultaneously) and are most valuable when run on multiple-CPU machines. There are other reasons for writing multithreaded programs: On Solaris the NFS server is multithreaded partly because it provides a cleaner interface and is easier to write than multiple server processes. Multithreading, when applied judiciously, can also serve as a lower-overhead replacement for the traditional fork-exec idiom for spawning processes.

Multiple Threads Are Not Always Better

If you write a multithreaded program with no clear goal or division of effort for a single CPU machine (for example a parallel server process), you are likely to end up with a program that runs more slowly than a nonthreaded program on the same machine.

Sun's **cc** compiler has an option, **–xautopar** (automatic parallelization), that causes the compiler to determine what parts of your program are suitable for multithreading. This can save you the time and trouble of learning and programming threads but may not be as good as if you were able to do your own thread management. It can, however, provide a noticeable speedup for parallel loops on multiprocessor machines. Do not use this option on single-processor machines as it frequently slows down execution speed—the overhead of threads and context switching outweighs any marginal gains that **–xautopar** may provide. The Sun Fortran compiler provides an equivalent option: **–autopar**. The GNU **gcc** compiler has no equivalent option.

Solaris2 supports two types of threads: Proprietary Solaris threads (older) and POSIX threads. The basic features and capabilities of the two types of threads are similar. If your primary goal is source code portability between operating systems, POSIX threads will serve you best. If your goal is compatibility with older versions of Solaris, choose Solaris threads. Solaris threads also provide some capabilities that POSIX threads lack because of tighter integration with the operating system. Look at both types of threads when deciding how to write your program.

▲ System Calls

Three fundamental responsibilities of the Solaris kernel are to control processes, to manage the filesystem, and to operate peripheral devices. As a programmer, you have access to these kernel operations through system calls and library functions. This section discusses system calls at a general level; a detailed treatment is beyond the scope of this book.

A system call, as the name implies, instructs the system (kernel) to carry out an operation directly on your behalf. A library routine is indirect; it issues system calls for you. The advantages of a library routine are that it may insulate you from the low-level details of kernel operations and that it has been written carefully to make sure it performs efficiently.

For example it is straightforward to use the standard I/O library function **fprintf**() to send text to standard output or standard error. Without this function you would need to issue several system calls to achieve the same result. The calls to the library routines **putchar**() and **getchar**() in Figure 14-1 ultimately use the **write**() and **read**() system calls to perform the I/O operations.

▲▲ **truss**: Trace System Calls

The **truss** utility (trace system calls and signals) runs a program and generates a trace of:

- system calls
- signals
- machine faults

A line of **truss** output shows the name of the system call made by the program, the name of the signal received by the program, or the fault incurred by the program together with the corresponding arguments and return values. Refer to page 926, the **truss man** page, or AnswerBook2 for more information.

▲▲ Controlling Processes

When you enter a command line at a shell prompt, the shell process calls the **fork** system call to create a copy of itself (spawn a child) and then uses an **exec** system call to overlay that copy in memory with a different program (the command you asked it to run). The following table lists system calls that affect processes.

System Call	Effect
fork()	Creates a copy of a process.
exec()	Overlays a program in memory with another.
wait()	Causes the parent process to wait for the child to finish running before it resumes execution.
exit()	Causes a process to exit.
nice()	Changes the priority of a process.
kill()	Sends a signal to a process.

▲▲ Accessing the Filesystem

Many operations take place when a program reads from or writes to a file. The program needs to know where the file is located; the filename must be converted to an inode number on the correct filesystem. Your access permissions must be checked, not only for the file itself but also for all the intervening directories in the path to the file. The file is not stored in one continuous piece on the disk; all the disk blocks that contain pieces of the file must be located. The appropriate kernel device driver must be called to control the actual operation of the disk. Finally once the file has been found, the program may need to find a particular location within the file, rather than working with it sequentially from beginning to end.

The following table lists some of the most common system calls in filesystem operations:

System Call	Effect
stat()	Gets status information from an inode, such as the inode number, the device on which it is located, owner and group information, and the size of the file.

System Call	Effect
lseek()	Moves to a position in the file.
creat()	Creates a new file.
open()	Opens an existing file.
read()	Reads a file.
write()	Writes a file.
close()	Closes a file.
unlink()	Unlinks a file (deletes a name reference to the inode).
chmod()	Changes file access permissions.
chown()	Changes file ownership.

Access to peripheral devices on a UNIX/Solaris system is handled through the filesystem interface. Each peripheral device is represented by one or more special files, usually located under **/dev**. When you read or write to one of these special files, the kernel passes your requests to the appropriate kernel device driver. As a result, you can use the standard system calls and library routines to interact with these devices—you do not need to learn a new set of specialized functions. This is one of the most powerful features of a UNIX/Solaris system because it allows users to use the same basic utilities on a wide range of devices.

The availability of standard system calls and library routines is the key to the portability of Solaris tools. For example as an applications programmer, you can rely on the read and write system calls working the same way on different versions of the Solaris system and on different types of computers. The systems programmer who writes a device driver or ports the kernel to run on a new computer, however, must understand the details at their lowest level.

▲ Source Code Management

When you work on a project involving many files that evolve over long periods of time, it can be hard to keep track of the versions of the files, especially if several people are updating them. This problem occurs particularly in large software development projects. Source code and documentation files change frequently as you fix bugs, enhance programs, and release new versions of the software. It becomes even more complex when there is more than one active version of each file. Frequently customers are using one version of a file while a newer version is being modified. You can easily lose track of the versions and accidentally undo changes that were already made or duplicate earlier work.

To help avoid these kinds of problems, Solaris includes utilities for managing and tracking changes to files. This book covers SCCS, the Source Code Control System. Although it can be used on any text file, SCCS is most often used to manage source code and software documentation.

SCCS can control who is allowed to update files. For each update it records who made the changes and includes notes about why the changes were made. Because it stores the original version of a file as well as changes to the file as they are made, it is possible to regenerate any version of a file. Saving the changes that are made to a file rather than a complete new version conserves disk space; however the SCCS files themselves consume a lot of space because of all the information they store about each update. Whether these tools actually save disk space or not depends on the sizes of the files and the nature of the changes that are made to them.

The following sections provide overviews of SCCS. The SCCS utilities are described in more detail in Part III, where they are listed under their individual names.

▲▲ Evolution of an SCCS File

When you change an SCCS file and record the changes in SCCS, the set of changes is referred to as a *delta*. Each delta has an associated version number, or SCCS Identification String (called SID), consisting of either two or four components. The first two, which are always used, are the *release* and *level* numbers. When an SCCS file is created, by default SCCS assigns a release number of 1 and a level number of 1, which corresponds to Version 1.1 (or delta 1.1). Also by default, SCCS assigns subsequent version numbers of 1.2, 1.3, and so on. However you have control over the version numbers and can skip level numbers or change the release number. You should ordinarily only change the release number when the file has undergone a major revision.

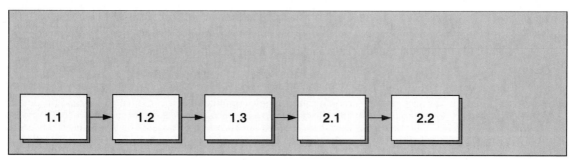

Figure 14-5   The history of an SCCS file

Usually files undergo a sequential development, where each delta includes all previous deltas. This kind of development is depicted in Figure 14-5. However there are cases when changes are made to an intermediate version of a file. For example if you were working on the source code file shown in Figure 14-5, and you had to make an emergency bug fix to Version 2.1 to deliver to customers prior to delivering Version 2.2, you would want to record a delta that reflected that fix but that excluded the changes involved in Version 2.2. In that case you would create the *branch* delta shown in Figure 14-6.

It is possible that you would work on the two deltas to Version 2.1 concurrently or that you would work on one while someone else worked on the other. However because SCCS was designed to avoid the problems of coordination that occur when changes are made independently on the same file, SCCS normally prohibits concurrent deltas to the same version. Although you ordinarily would not want to, you can override this restriction if necessary.

Unlike the earlier, sequentially applied deltas, the branch delta in Figure 14-6 has four components to its version number: *release*, *level*, *branch*, and *sequence number*. Version 2.1.1.1 is the first delta to the first branch on Release 2, Level 1. Successive deltas on that branch would be 2.1.1.2, 2.1.1.3, and so forth. Successive branches on Version 2.1 would start with deltas 2.1.2.1, 2.1.3.1, and so forth.

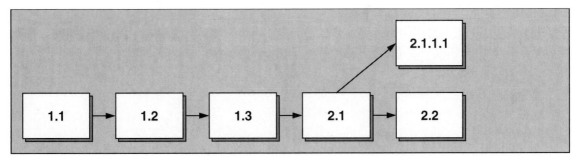

Figure 14-6   A branch in the evolution of an SCCS file

The evolution of an SCCS file can become complicated when there are many branch deltas. When you record changes to a file, try to keep the evolution of the versions as simple as you can. You should make a delta to a file only when you are sure that the changes you have made are complete. For example when you are fixing a collection of bugs in a file, you should fix each one and completely test it before recording the changes in a delta. This technique saves you from having deltas that reflect incomplete, transitional stages in the history of a file.

▲▲ Creating an SCCS File

The **admin** utility is one of the most important parts of SCCS—you can use it to create SCCS files as well as to change characteristics of existing SCCS files. If you have a Bourne Shell script called **blitz**, you can use **admin** to create an SCCS-encoded version.

Making SCCS a Little More Friendly

All the examples in this section use the **sccs** front end to the SCCS utilities. The front end automatically puts and expects to find encoded files in the **SCCS** directory within your working directory. It also takes care of adding and removing the leading **s.** on the filenames you work with. You can use this front end by giving the command **sccs** on the same line before the SCCS utility. See the following examples.

The **sccs admin** command at the bottom of Figure 14-7 creates the initial version of the SCCS-encoded file **s.blitz**, Version 1.1. This file includes the contents of the file **blitz** as well as the control information SCCS adds. Because the example uses the **sccs** front end, **admin** creates the file in the SCCS directory (which you must first create) and gives it a prefix of **s.**. The statement **admin** presents, No id keywords (cm7), is a warning message. The string in parentheses, cm7, is a code for a help message. If you give the command **help** followed by the code, the **help** utility will produce an explanation of the message.

```
$ cat blitz
:
# A script that noisily but cautiously
# empties the working directory

echo "The working directory is ` pwd ` "
echo "Delete all files in ` pwd ` ? \c"
read answer
case $answer in
        y|Y|[yY]es)
                    echo "OUCH!!!  BANG!!!  SPLAT!!!"
                    rm *
                    echo "We got 'em boss!"
                    ;;
        *)          echo "Files remain untouched"
                    ;;
esac
$ mkdir SCCS
$ sccs admin -iblitz blitz
No id keywords (cm7)
$ ls SCCS
s.blitz
```

*Figure 14-7   Contents of the **blitz** file*

```
$ help cm7
cm7:
'No id keywords'
No SCCS identification keywords were substituted for.
You may not have any keywords in the file,
in which case you can ignore this warning.
    .
    .
```

As the **help** utility explains, the message in Figure 14-7 indicates that there are no SCCS keywords in the encoded file. Keywords are SCCS codes you can use to insert information about the SCCS file into the text retrieved from the encoded file. For example you can use keywords to identify the SCCS filename, the version number, and the date and time the text was retrieved from the encoded file.

The %W% SCCS keyword inserts a string @(#) in a file that the **what** command recognizes. (Try putting %W% somewhere in your SCCS file when you are editing it.)

The **what** command is an SCCS utility that sends to the standard output the text that follows the string @(#). Many standard Solaris utilities include these strings to identify the version number of the program. You can use **what** to identify the version of the Korn Shell on a system.

```
$ what /usr/bin/ksh
/usr/bin/ksh:
        Version M-11/16/88i
        SunOS 5.6 Generic August 1997
```

Because keywords are not used in the examples in this book, you can safely ignore warning messages about keywords when they occur in the examples.

Although you can call the **admin** utility with many other arguments, in the form shown in Figure 14-7 its format is:

sccs admin –iname filename

The *name* is the name of the file SCCS will encode. The *filename* is the name of the SCCS-encoded file. The **sccs** front end will give it an **s.** prefix.

After you use **admin** to create an SCCS-encoded file, move the original file to a backup directory. If you leave the original file in the working directory, SCCS will not allow you to retrieve the file from the encoded version while you are working in that directory. If you could retrieve the file, you would overwrite the version in your working directory.

▲▲ Retrieving an SCCS File

Do not edit an SCCS-encoded file such as **s.blitz**—editing the file defeats the purpose of using SCCS. Use the **get** utility with the **–e** option to create an unencoded, writable version of the file. The **–e** option indicates to SCCS that you intend to edit the file and make a delta. In other words, it indicates to SCCS that you plan to make changes and record the changes using SCCS. If you call **get** without the **–e** option, SCCS creates an unencoded version of the file that is not writable. The following command recreates the file **blitz** for editing:

```
$ sccs get -e blitz
1.1
new delta 1.2
16 lines
```

The **get** utility displays the version number of the retrieved delta, the version number that will be applied when the new changes are recorded in SCCS, and the number of lines in the file. If you forget to move the original **blitz** file to another directory after you create it, **get** displays the following error message. (Again you can give the command **help ge4** to find out more about the error message.)

```
$ sccs get -e blitz
ERROR [SCCS/s.blitz]: writable 'blitz' exists (ge4)
```

Give the following command to put **blitz** away without making any changes (so you can **get** it again):

```
$ sccs unget blitz
1.2
```

By default the **get** command retrieves the most recent delta to the file. In the case of the file **s.blitz**, that delta is Version 1.1. You can also use **get** with the **–r** option to retrieve a specific delta or to change the number of the new delta.

```
$ sccs get -e -r2 blitz
1.1
new delta 2.1
16 lines
```

Because there are no existing versions with a release number of 2, this command retrieves the latest delta prior to Release 2, and it changes the new version number to 2.1. If versions with a release number of 2 already existed, this command would have retrieved the most recent one.

If you retrieve a version that is earlier than the most recent version, SCCS will create a branch delta. For example if a version number higher than 1.2 exists for **s.blitz**, retrieving Version 1.2 creates a branch delta.

```
$ cat blitz
:
# A script that cautiously
# empties the working directory

echo "The working directory is ` pwd ` "
echo "Delete all files in ` pwd ` ? \c"
read answer
case "$answer" in
        y|Y|[yY]es)
                echo "Files being removed"
                rm *
                echo "Done"
                ;;
        *)      echo "Files remain untouched"
                ;;
esac
$ sccs delta blitz
comments? frivolous statements replaced \
with serious ones
No id keywords (cm7)
1.2
3 inserted
3 deleted
13 unchanged
```

*Figure 14-8   Modified **blitz** file*

```
$ sccs get -e -r1.2 blitz
1.2
new delta 1.2.1.1
16 lines
```

It is easiest to keep track of the evolution of your SCCS files if only one **get** is active for a specific file at a time. However SCCS allows you to simultaneously update different versions of a file as long as you put the retrieved files in different directories. If you try to retrieve a version while the working directory contains a previously retrieved version that is editable, SCCS displays an error message.

By default SCCS prevents you from simultaneously working on two deltas to the same version of a file. If you want to have more than one **get** active against a single version of a file, you must use the **admin** utility to add the **j** flag to the SCCS file (SCCS distinguishes between *options,* which are used on the command line, and *flags,* which are added to a file as control information). Refer to **admin** in Part III for more information.

▲▲ Recording Changes to an SCCS File

After you have edited the retrieved file and are ready to record the changes in SCCS, use the **delta** utility to record your changes. The user who retrieves a file must be the one who gives the **delta** command. Consequently you can use **delta** only if you were the one who executed the corresponding **get**.

```
$ sccs delta blitz
comments?
```

The **delta** utility prompts you for comments. In response enter the reason for the changes. Assuming you had changed the **echo** commands inside the **case** control structure in **blitz** as shown in Figure 14-8, you might enter the comment shown. Most versions of SCCS use a NEWLINE to terminate a comment, so to continue a comment from one line to the next, you must escape the NEWLINE character (that is, precede the NEWLINE with a backslash). Other versions of SCCS expect comments to span multiple lines, and they terminate a comment when you use CONTROL-D on a line by itself. If your version of SCCS uses CONTROL-D to terminate a comment, do not escape the NEWLINEs that occur within comments.

In the example in Figure 14-8, **delta** displays a warning message followed by the version number and a summary of the changes that were made to the file after you enter your comments.

If you make a delta and later decide to remove it, you can use the **rmdel** utility to delete it. The following command removes Version 1.2 of **s.blitz**:

```
$ sccs rmdel -r1.2 blitz
```

The **rmdel** utility removes only the latest version, or the latest version on a branch. After using **rmdel** to remove the latest version, you can remove the next most recent version, and so forth.

Although you would not want to edit it, you can look at an SCCS-encoded file to get a better idea of how SCCS works. Figure 14-9 shows the **s.blitz** file. To look at an encoded file, use **cat** with the **–v** option and pipe the output through **more**. The **–v** option causes **cat** to display visible representations of nonprinting characters. The characters ^A at the start of some lines represent CONTROL-A, which SCCS uses to identify lines that contain control information.

```
$ cat -v s.blitz
^Ah52551
^As 00004/00004/00012
^Ad D 1.2 98/07/10 13:21:36 alex 2 1
^Ac frivolous statements replaced
^Ac with serious ones
^Ae
^As 00016/00000/00000
^Ad D 1.1 98/07/10 13:13:32 alex 1 0
^Ac date and time created 98/07/10 13:13:32 by alex
^Ae
^Au
^AU
^Af e 0
^At
^AT
^AI 1
:
^AD 2
# A script that noisily but cautiously
^AE 2
^AI 2
# A script that cautiously
^AE 2
# empties the working directory

echo "The working directory is ` pwd` "
echo "Delete all files in ` pwd` ? \c"
read answer
case $answer in
        y|Y|[yY]es)
^AD 2
                echo "OUCH!!!  BANG!!!  SPLAT!!!"
                rm ✳
                echo "We got 'em boss!"
^AE 2
^AI 2
                echo "Files being removed"
                rm ✳
                echo "Done"
^AE 2

                ;;
✳)      echo "Files remain untouched"
                ;;
esac
^AE 1
```

Figure 14-9   Contents of an encoded SCCS file

▲▲ Obtaining the History of an SCCS File

The **prs** utility prints information about the history of an SCCS file. Although you can call **prs** with a variety of arguments that specify what information it reports and the format of the report, when it is called without any arguments, **prs** prints summary information about all deltas.

Figure 14-10 shows the following information about each delta: The date and time of creation, the user who made the delta, the sequence number of the delta and its predecessor, and the number of lines inserted, deleted, and unchanged. After the MRs: label would be a list of any modification request (MR) numbers for

```
$ sccs prs blitz
SCCS/s.blitz:

D 1.2 98/07/10 13:21:36 alex 2 1        00004/00004/00012
MRs:
COMMENTS:
frivolous statements replaced
with serious ones

D 1.1 98/07/10 13:13:32 alex 1 0        00016/00000/00000
MRs:
COMMENTS:
date and time created 98/07/10 13:13:32 by alex
```

*Figure 14-10   The **prs** utility*

the delta. A *modification request* is a bug report against a program or software document. There is no information after the modification request label in Figure 14-10 because the examples do not use MR numbers. If you use the **v** flag and the **–m** option with **admin, delta** prompts you for MR numbers each time you use it. See **admin** in Part III for more information.

▲▲ Restricting Access to SCCS Files

You can use the **admin** utility to establish a list of users who are allowed to make deltas to an SCCS file. By default the list of users who can make changes to a file is empty, which means that anyone can make a delta. The following command gives permission to Alex and Jenny and implicitly denies permission to everyone else. After this command is executed, only Alex and Jenny will be able to make deltas:

```
$ sccs admin -aalex -ajenny blitz
```

The **–e** (erase) option removes a user from the list, denying him or her permission to make deltas. The following command removes Jenny from the list of authorized users.

```
$ sccs admin -ejenny blitz
```

In addition to allowing you to restrict access to a list of users, SCCS allows you to *lock* releases of a file so that no one can change them. The following command uses the **–f** option to set the **l** flag to lock Release 1 of **s.blitz**:

```
$ sccs admin -fl1 blitz
```

After executing this command, if you try to retrieve a Release 1 delta for editing, **get** will give you an error message. Use the following command to lock all releases of the **s.blitz** file:

```
$ sccs admin -fla blitz
```

Summary

The operating system interface to C and a variety of software development tools make Solaris well suited to programming in C. The C libraries provide general-purpose C functions that make operating system services and other functionality available to C programmers. The standard C library, **libc**, is always accessible to C programs, and you can use other libraries by including them in an option to the **cc** or **gcc** command.

You can write a C program using a text editor, such as **vi**. C programs always have a function named **main** and often have other functions. Preprocessor directives define symbolic constants and macros, and instruct the preprocessor to include header files.

When you use **cc** or **gcc**, it calls the C preprocessor, followed by the C compiler and the assembler. The compiler creates assembly language code, which the assembler uses to create object modules. Finally the linker combines the object modules into an executable file. You can use the C program verifier, **lint**, and a debugger (such as **dbx**) to aid in the process of debugging a program. You can use the **gcc** compiler's built-in verifier by using the **–Wall** option.

The **make** utility uses a file named **Makefile** (or **makefile**) that documents the relationships among files. It keeps track of which modules of a program are out of date and compiles files in order to keep all modules up to date. The dependency line which specifies the exact dependency relationship between target and prerequisite files is the key to the operation of a makefile. Not only does a dependency line specify a relationship, but it gives the construction commands that bring the target up to date. Implied dependencies and construction commands, as well as the **make** macro facility, simplify writing a complex makefile.

Several utility programs comprise the Source Code Control System, SCCS, used to track changes to files involved in larger software projects. SCCS stores the original files as well as each set of changes that was made to the originals so that you can regenerate any version (delta) of a file at any time. SCCS also documents the history of a file by recording who made each delta and when and why they made it.

Review Exercises

1. What function does every C program have? Why should you split large programs into several functions?

2. What command could you use to compile **prog.c** and **func.c** into an executable named **cprog**?

3. Show two ways to instruct the C preprocessor to include the header file **/usr/include/math.h** in your C program. Assuming that the **declar.h** header file is located in the subdirectory named **headers** of your home directory, describe two ways to instruct the C preprocessor to include this header file in your C program.

4. Both C functions **getchar** and **putchar** appear in the standard C library **libc.so**. Show that **getchar** and **putchar** are also macros on your system. Can you think of more than one way to show this?

5. How are the names of system libraries abbreviated on the **cc** command line? Where does **cc** search for libraries named in this manner? Describe how to specify your own library on the **cc** command line.

6. What command can you use to create an SCCS-encoded version of a file named **answers**? What command can you use to retrieve an editable version of **answers**?

7. Write a **makefile** that reflects the following relationships:

    a. The C source files **transactions.c** and **reports.c** are compiled to produce an executable **accts**.

    b. **transactions.c** and **reports.c** include a header file **accts.h**.

   c. The header file **accts.h** is composed of two other header files: **trans.h** and **reps.h**.

8. How can you restrict the SCCS-encoded file **s.answers** so that:

   a. Only Barbara and hls can make changes.

   b. No one can make changes to Release 2.

9. If you retrieve Version 4.1 of the file **s.answers** for editing and then attempt to retrieve the same version again, what will SCCS do? Why is SCCS set up this way?

10. Modify the **tabs.c** program so that it exits cleanly (with a specific return value). Compile the program, and run it using the **dbx** or another debugger. What values does the debugger report when the program finishes executing?

11. In **Makefile** below identify:

   a. targets

   b. construction commands

   c. prerequisites

```
$ cat Makefile
leads:      menu.o users.o resellers.o prospects.o
            cc -o leads menu.o users.o resellers.o prospects.o

menu.o:     menu.h dialog.h inquiry.h

users.o:    menu.h dialog.h

prospects.o:dialog.h
```

12. Refer to **Makefile** in exercise 11 to answer the following questions:

   a. If the target **leads** is up to date and you then change **users.c**, what happens when you run **make** again? Be specific.

   b. Rewrite the makefile using the following macros:

```
OBJECTS = menu.o users.o resellers.o prospects.o
HFILES = menu.h dialog.h
```

13. Read about **make** on page 803 in Part III and the **make man** page to answer the following questions:

   a. What does the **–t** option do?

   b. If you have files in the working directory named **makefile** and **Makefile**, how can you instruct **make** to use **Makefile**?

   c. Give two ways to define a variable so that you can use it inside a makefile.

14. Suppose that the file named **synchr.c** has four revisions numbered 1.1 through 1.4. Show how to:

   a. Check out the latest revision for editing.

   b. Check out the latest revision for compiling only.

c. Check in a new revision after editing the latest revision. Allow editing of the working file to continue.

d. Check out revision 1.2 for editing.

e. Delete revision 1.2.

Advanced Review Exercises

15. Refer to the makefile for **compute** on page 560. Suppose that there is a file in the working directory named **clean**. What is the effect of giving the following command. Explain.

    ```
    $ make clean
    ```

16. The discussion of the makefile on page 559 states that the command

    ```
    cat num.h table.h > form.h
    ```

    is not normally seen in makefiles.

    a. Discuss the effect of removing this construction command from the makefile while retaining the dependency line.

    b. The construction command above works only because the file **form.h** is made up of **num.h** and **table.h**. More often **#include** directives in the target define the dependencies. Suggest a more general technique that updates **form.h** whenever **num.h** or **table.h** has a more recent modification date.

System Administration

T
he system administrator is responsible for setting up new users, installing and removing terminals and workstations, maintaining and upgrading the network and network connections, making sure there is enough space on the disk, backing up files, installing and upgrading software, bringing up and shutting down the system, monitoring system and network activity, helping users when they have problems, keeping the system secure, and performing many other network and computer housekeeping tasks. This chapter provides you with the basic knowledge you need to administer a Solaris2 system. It describes the location of files, utilities, and directories in a Solaris2 system. You will find subtle differences between Solaris2 and SVR4 UNIX. If you are familiar with SVR4, you will be comfortable on a Solaris2 system. If you are familiar with Solaris2, this chapter provides you with additional, version-specific information about Solaris 2.6 and Solaris 7 (also called Solaris 2.7). Except as noted, this chapter applies to all versions of Solaris2 (Solaris 2.x [see page 16]).

Because Solaris2 is so configurable and runs on different platforms (Sun SPARC and Intel x86), this chapter cannot discuss every system configuration or every action you will have to take as a system administrator. This chapter complements the administration sections of the manuals and the AnswerBook2[1] documentation. In addition there are many good books dedicated to system administration. This chapter assumes you are familiar with the following terms. Refer to the Glossary on page 1025 for definitions.

block	daemon	device	device filename
disk partition	environment	filesystem	fork
kernel	login shell	mount (a device)	process
root filesystem	run level	signal	spawn
system console	X server		

---

1. AnswerBook2 (pages 26 and 643) is an excellent administration and user resource. It is included on the Documentation CDROM with some Solaris licenses; you need to purchase it separately from SunSoft with other licenses. If you do not have AnswerBook2 installed on your network, use your browser to go to **docs.sun.com**, where Sun maintains an expanded and up-to-date version of AnswerBook2.

591

Solaris2 provides a filesystem structure that is very similar to UNIX SVR4. This organization makes it easy for other computers running compatible software to share certain identical files, such as utilities and manual pages. At the same time, each system must maintain private areas for files that differ from system to system, such as databases, system log files, and spooling areas.

▲▲ Product Name

The name of the latest version of the Solaris operating system is **Solaris 7**. Code, path, and package names may use **Solaris 2.7** or **SunOS 5.7**. If you are using a different version of Solaris your version will have a different name. There is no "Solaris 6," only **Solaris 2.6** and **SunOS 5.6**. For more information see "Name and Version of the Operating System" on page 16.

▲ The System Administrator and Superuser

One person is often designated as the system administrator. On large systems this can be a full-time job. On smaller systems a user of the system may be assigned to do system administration in addition to his or her other work.

The system administrator has access to certain systemwide powers that are beyond those of ordinary users.

- Some commands, such as commands that halt the system, can be executed only by the system administrator.

- Read, write, and execute file-access and directory-access permissions do not affect the system administrator.

- The system administrator can search any directory and create a file in or remove a file from any directory. The system administrator can also read from, write to, or execute any file.

- Some restrictions and safeguards that are built into some commands do not apply to the system administrator. For example the system administrator can change any user's password without knowing the old password.

There are a number of ways to become Superuser:

1. When you bring up the system, if it comes up in single-user mode (page 603) and you supply the proper password, you log on as Superuser.

2. Once the system is up and running in multiuser mode (page 605), you can log in as **root**, and if you supply the proper password, you will be Superuser.

3. You can give an **su** (substitute user) command while you are logged in as yourself, and, with the proper password, you will have Superuser privileges. To be sure that you are using the system's official version of **su** (and not one planted on your system by someone trying to break in), you should always specify **su**'s absolute pathname (that is, **/usr/bin/su**) when you use it.

4. You can use a freely available program such as **sudo** or **priv** to selectively give users Superuser privileges on a per user and per command basis. These programs are not included with Solaris2 but are widely ported and available at archives sites. For more information see "How Do I Find the Program I Want on the Internet?" on page 967.

Superuser and Security

Because the powers listed above affect the security of all users' files as well as the security of the entire system, there is a special login name and password for the user who logs in on the system to perform these functions. The login name is ***root***. Although you can set up a Solaris system with any name in place of **root**, it is not advisable to do so: Many programs depend on this name being **root**. There is a special name for a user who is logged in as **root**: *Superuser*.

Because of the extensive powers of destruction you have when you are Superuser, it is a good idea to become Superuser only when necessary. If you are just doing your ordinary day-to-day work, log in as yourself. That way you will not erase someone else's files or bring down the machine by mistake.

5.   While you are running as Superuser, you can use **chmod** with a **u+s** argument to change a file's mode to *setuid* (set user ID). Setuid programs run on behalf of **root** and have all the access privileges that **root** has. You, as an ordinary user, can run a setuid program (assuming you have permission to execute it). While the setuid program is running, it has full **root** privileges. Your privileges do not change. When the program finishes running, all privileges are back to the way they were before the program was started. Setuid programs are extremely powerful, and also extremely dangerous, which is why there are very few of them on the system. Examples of setuid programs include **at**, **crontab**, and **ps**. The following example shows two ways for Superuser to give a program setuid privileges.

```
# ls -l my*
-rwxr-xr-x   1 root      other      24152 Apr 29 16:30 myprog
-rwxr-xr-x   1 root      other      24152 Apr 29 16:31 myprog2
# chmod 4755 myprog
# chmod u+s myprog2
# ls -l my*
-rwsr-xr-x   1 root      other      24152 Apr 29 16:30 myprog
-rwsr-xr-x   1 root      other      24152 Apr 29 16:31 myprog2
```

Refer to **chmod** (page 709) and **ls** (the **–l** option, page 792) in Part III for more details on creating and identifying programs that are setuid.

When you give an **su** command to become Superuser, you spawn a new shell. To remind you of your special powers, this shell displays a different prompt (# by default). You return to your normal status (and your former shell) by terminating the shell (by pressing CONTROL-D or giving an **exit** command).

▲▲ System Administration Tools

Many of the commands Superuser uses are kept in the **/usr/sbin** directory.[2] They are kept there (rather than in **/usr/bin**) to lessen the chance that a user other than Superuser will try to use them by mistake. (Many of

---

2. There are additional utilities and startup scripts in **/sbin**. These files are used by the system in single-user mode and to change between run levels and are not generally run directly by Superuser.

the commands can be run by ordinary users.) You can execute these commands by giving their full pathnames on the command line (that is, **/usr/sbin/mkfs**) or by including the **/usr/sbin** directory in your **PATH** when you are logged in as Superuser.

You can control where **root** is allowed to log in directly (as **root**) by making changes to the CONSOLE line in the **/etc/default/login** file. Regardless of what is in this file, you can always log in on the machine as an ordinary user and then use **su** to become **root**.

The first example shows a good setup for publicly accessible machines. With no **root** login on the console, you can place your machine in an untrusted environment without fear of someone logging in directly to the **root** account from the console. It means you have to have a valid account on the machine before you can attempt to obtain Superuser privileges. Change the line that begins with the word CONSOLE to read:

```
# root cannot login directly on any device
CONSOLE=
```

To enable **root** to log in directly on the console, edit the **/etc/default/login** file and make sure the line that begins with CONSOLE is not commented out and reads as follows:

```
# root can log in on console
CONSOLE=/dev/console
```

This kind of access is good for machines in a server room, for example where the general user population does not have access to it. Machines that do allow **root** to log in on the console should have extra physical security, such as locked doors or other restricted access.

In a trusted environment place a # at the left end of the CONSOLE line (comment it out) to allow **root** to log in from anywhere.

```
# root can log in remotely or on console
#CONSOLE=
```

Do Not Allow **root** Access over the Internet

When you comment out the CONSOLE line in the **/etc/default/login** file, you allow **root** to log in on the machine *directly over the network* (using **telnet** for example). It is *not a good idea* to allow this kind of **root** access to any machine connected to the Internet.

Finally to limit root login to a single port, use the following CONSOLE line.

```
# root can only login on /dev/term/a serial port only
CONSOLE=/dev/term/a
```

▲▲ Avoiding a Trojan Horse

A *Trojan horse* is a program that does something destructive or disruptive to your system while appearing to be benign. As an example, you could store the following program in a file named **mkfs**:

```
while true
  do
  echo 'Good Morning Mr. Jones. How are you today? Ha Ha Ha.' > /dev/console
  done
```

If you were running as Superuser and ran this command, it would continuously write a message to the console. If the programmer were malicious, it could do worse. The only thing missing in this plot is access permissions.

When you use **su** to become Superuser, your **PATH** is set up as

```
PATH=/usr/sbin:/usr/bin
```

A malicious user could implement this Trojan horse by changing Superuser's **PATH** variable to include a publicly writable directory at the start of the **PATH** string.[3] Then you would need to put the bogus **mkfs** program file in that directory. Because the fraudulent version appears in a directory mentioned earlier than the real one in **PATH**, the shell runs it. The next time Superuser tried to run **mkfs**, the fraudulent version would run.

▲▲ Changing the Default PATH

When you use **su** to become **root**, the shell reads the **/etc/default/su** script.[4] When you log in as **root**, the shell uses **/etc/default/login**. Within each of these scripts is a line defining the variable named **SUPATH**, which controls the value of **PATH** when you become Superuser (**SUPATH** controls **PATH**). Uncomment the line that begins with #SUPATH and change the value assigned to **SUPATH** there. Do not add **.** (dot) to **SUPATH** because you may set up the Trojan horse just described.

On a system with NIS+ installed, the following variable initialization may be appropriate:

```
SUPATH=/usr/sbin:/usr/bin:/usr/lib/nis
```

Superuser, **PATH**, and Security

The fewer directories you keep in your **PATH** when you are **root**, the less likely that you will execute an untrusted program as **root**. If possible, keep only the default **/usr/sbin** and **/usr/bin** directories. Never include the working directory (as **.** or **::** or a colon [**:**]) at the beginning or end of the **PATH** string.

▲▲ kill: Terminate a Process

The **kill** builtin does just what its name says it does: It kills a process. It is not the first method you (a user or system administrator) should try when you need to abort a process. See **kill** on page 785 in Part III for information about different options and arguments to kill.

---

3. The catch is that you need to be able to write to **/etc/default/login**—where the **PATH** variable is set for **root**—and only **root** can do that. See the next section for more information.

4. Except if you use **su –** or **su – root**, in which case the shell $_{ksh}^{sh}$ reads **/etc/profile** as it does when you log in as root.

kill: A Method of Last Resort

Because of its inherent dangers, using **kill** is a method of last resort, especially for a system administrator or anyone running as Superuser. One **kill** command, if issued by **root**, can bring the system down.

Usually a user can kill a process from another window or by logging in on another terminal. Sometimes you may have to log in as **root** (or use **su**) to kill a process for a user. To kill a process you need to know the PID of the process. You can use **ps** to get this information. You also need to know the name of the program the user is running and/or the login name of the user. You can usually make do without the name of the program, and, if you are on a small system, you may not need either.

In the following example a user is complaining that Netscape is stuck and he cannot do anything from his terminal. A more experienced user could open another window and kill the process himself, but in this case you will kill it for him. First you use **ps** with the **–u** option followed by the name of the user to view all the processes associated with that user.

```
$ ps -u fred
PID TTY        TIME CMD
26770 ?        0:00 dtexec
26761 pts/3    0:00 dtfile
26719 ??       0:00 dtterm
26658 ?        0:00 fbconsol
26748 pts/8    0:00 csh
26756 ?        0:00 cat
26757 pts/3    0:00 sh
26718 ?        0:01 dtwm
26788 pts/1    0:00 script
26773 pts/8    0:02 netscape
26711 pts/3    0:00 ttsessio
26727 ?        0:00 sdtvolch
26789 pts/4    0:00 csh
25171 pts/1    0:00 csh
26712 pts/3    0:00 dtsessio
26774 pts/8    0:00 netscape
26648 ?        0:00 Xsession
26787 pts/1    0:00 script
26695 ?        0:00 dsdm
26771 ?        0:01 dtmail
25223 ?        0:00 sh
26629 vt01     0:04 Xsun
26762 pts/1    0:00 sh
26694 pts/3    0:00 sdt_shel
26697 pts/3    0:00 csh
26758 pts/3    0:01 dtfile
```

This is a fairly short list and the process running Netscape is easy to find. Another way to go about searching is to produce a long list of all the processes using **ps** and use **grep** to find all those running Netscape:

```
$ ps -ef | grep netscape
fred 26773 26748  2 11:40:40 pts/8    0:03 netscape
fred 26795 26789  0 11:42:03 pts/4    0:00 grep netscape
```

There may be many people running Netscape, and you may need to look in the left column to find the name of the user so that you can kill the right one. Of course you can combine the two commands and use **ps –u fred | grep netscape**.

Now that you know the PID of Fred's process running Netscape (26773), you can use **kill** to terminate it. The safest way to do this is to log in as fred (or **su** to fred [**su fred**] if you are logged in as root) and give the command:

```
$ kill -9 26773
```

You can give the same command while you are logged in as root, but a typing mistake can have much more far-reaching consequences than if you make the mistake while you are logged in as a user. A user can only kill his or her own processes whereas Superuser can kill any process (including system processes).

Concept of Least Privilege

When you are working on the computer, especially when you are working as the system administrator, always perform any task using the least privilege possible. If you can perform a task logged in as an ordinary user, do so. If you must be logged in as Superuser, do as much as you can as an ordinary user, log in or **su** so you are Superuser, do as much of the task as has to be done as Superuser, and revert to being an ordinary user as soon as you can.

Because you are more likely to make a mistake when you are rushing, this concept becomes more important when you have less time to apply it.

▲ Detailed Description of System Operation

This section covers the following topics:

- booting the system
- single-user mode and maintenance
- the transition from single-user to multiuser mode
- multiuser mode
- logging in
- bringing the system down
- crashes

It covers these topics so that you understand the basics of how the system functions and can make intelligent decisions as a system administrator. It does not cover every aspect of system administration in the depth necessary to set up or modify all system functions. It provides a guide to bringing a system up and keeping it running from day to day.

Subsequent sections of this chapter and Part III of this book describe many of the system administration files and utilities in detail.

▲▲ SPARC PROM Mode

On a SPARC system the most basic operating level is PROM (or firmware) mode. You can set system startup options, boot the system, run diagnostic utilities, configure security, and check on the status of connected hardware components from this mode.[5] PROM mode is indicated by one of the following prompts:

```
press b (boot), c (continue), or n (new command mode)
>
```

or

```
OK
```

When you shut down a system, you will see one of these prompts. The **>** prompt is often referred to as old mode. The **OK** prompt is referred to as new mode. To get from the **>** to the **OK** prompt, type **n** and press RETURN. At this point you may be prompted for a PROM password (see below). To get from the **OK** prompt to the **>** prompt, you can type **old-mode**. UltraSPARC class machines do not have the **old-mode** command. On an Ultra you will see a prompt that looks like this:

```
Type boot, go (continue), or login (command mode)
>
```

Though it appears very similar to the old-mode **>** prompt above, it behaves like new command mode. The difference is that for every new-mode command that you type, you are prompted for the PROM password if it is set. A PROM password is very similar to the concept of a BIOS password on an Intel machine. If you type **login** at the Ultra **>** prompt, you can type as many PROM commands as you wish without having to type the PROM password again. If there is no PROM password set, then you do not have to type **login**. You can set a PROM password for most modern SPARC machines by issuing the following two commands:

```
OK setenv security-mode command
OK setenv security-password PromPW
```

The first command sets the security mode for the PROM. Replace PromPW with the PROM password you wish to set. The security mode can be one of three different levels. The security mode can be **none** (default), **command**, or **full**. When security mode is set to **none**, then no PROM password is needed to get to new command mode or to boot the system to single-user mode. If the security mode is **command**, then a

---

5. There is no equivalent to the SPARC PROM mode on an Intel x86 machine. For more information see "Solaris x86 Configuration Assistant" on page 600.

PROM password is required to get to new command mode, to boot single user, or to use any other flags to the **b** or **boot** commands; but you can still reboot the machine from multiuser mode without a PROM password. When security mode is set to **full**, all of the restrictions of **command** apply, and in addition, rebooting the machine requires that you issue the PROM password; also, if the machine crashes, it will not automatically reboot but will require the PROM password to continue.

Keep your PROM password in a safe place. If you set your security mode to **full** and forget your PROM password, you will not be able to boot the machine! There is no way to recover your PROM password. However a person familiar with the hardware of your machine can put in a new PROM from another machine and thus cause all PROM options to be set to factory defaults. Also, if the PROM is set to **command** security mode, you can bring the machine up multiuser, log in as **root**, and use the **eeprom** utility to reset the PROM password to some other value, or set security mode to **none**.

Loose Keyboard Connection?

If the > prompt appears spontaneously on the console screen and a large white area appears that disrupts or overwrites portions of your display, you probably have a loose keyboard connection. To fix this problem make sure that the keyboard is firmly plugged in at both ends and press **c** to continue, followed by **RETURN**. Then refresh your display by using **xrefresh** (OpenLook) or the **Workspace** menu (CDE) to redraw the screen.

The rest of this section covers the **OK** prompt (new command) mode, the more significant and feature-rich of the two modes. Diagnostics are only available at the **OK** prompt. The types of diagnostics available vary depending on the revision of the PROM installed in your machine. The subset listed here is always available.[6]

PROM Command	Effect
printenv	Displays a list of all startup hardware options on the SPARC machine (use from **OK** prompt).[a]
setenv	Changes an option. This command works in the same manner as the C shell function of the same name.[a]
set-defaults	Restores factory defaults.
help	Lists diagnostic commands. The most useful of these are **test-network**, **test-memory**, and **probe-scsi**.

a. These options are also available to **root** in single- or multiuser mode by using the **eeprom** utility. Refer to the **eeprom man** page for details.

---

6. It is also possible to program the PROM using the Forth language: You enter a Forth program in place of a command. For a complete reference to PROM programming, diagnostics, and booting, see AnswerBook2.

PROM Command	Effect
test-network	Tells you if your network interface controller is working properly.
test-memory	Performs a self-test of system RAM.
probe-scsi	Displays a list of all SCSI devices connected to the internal SCSI system bus.
probe-scsi-all	Displays all SCSI devices on all buses. Useful if your system is equipped with multiple SCSI controllers.
b	Boots from PROM mode. Use with the **>** prompt.
boot	Boots from PROM mode. Use with the **OK** boot prompt.

▲▲▲ Booting the Machine

Use **boot** (from the **OK** prompt) or **b** (from the **>** prompt) to boot the machine. There are three main options that work with the **b** and **boot** commands: **−s** (single user), **−r** (reconfigure), and **−a** (ask).

If you add the **−s** flag, the machine will come up in single-user mode (page 603). For example:

```
OK boot -s
```

will bring your machine up in single-user mode from the **OK** prompt and

```
> b -s
```

will bring your machine up in single-user mode from the **>** prompt.

The **−r** option performs a reconfigure reboot (page 634). It tells the system to check all devices plugged into all expansion slots[7] and configure the system accordingly. It will add and remove the appropriate links from the **/devices** and **/dev** directories.

The **−a** option tells the machine to ask for certain system parameters. Normally when you boot your system, Solaris2 uses a special file, **/etc/system**, to configure the kernel. This file controls things such as which device drivers are to be loaded at boot time and how much shared memory is to be configured for databases. It also allows the system administrator to give the system performance tuning parameters for virtual memory and other system resources. If you make a mistake in the **/etc/system** file, you can set up a situation where you cannot boot your machine. The **−a** option tells the system to ask where the **system** file is, where the kernel is, and where to mount the **root** filesystem. It displays default values in square brackets ([ ]).

▲▲ Solaris x86 Configuration Assistant

On Intel machines there is no direct equivalent to the PROM mode on SPARC machines. Instead the PROM-like features are divided into two stages.

---

7. SBUS is the internal expansion bus for most of the SPARC line and is an IEEE standard. Newer UltraSPARC machines use the PCI bus just as most Intel-based machines do.

 Stage I

When you turn on the machine, the BIOS loads the first sector from your boot device (typically a hard disk). This sector contains information about where to go to load information about any peripherals that the BIOS does not recognize. It is capable of reading and loading the operating system from a UFS filesystem. The boot sector secondary boot loads the Solaris Configuration Assistant, which is the first PROM-like division of the x86 machine. Your screen will display something similar to the following:

```
Solaris Intel Platform Edition Booting System



Running Configuration Assistant...
Autobooting from bootpath: /isa/ata@1,1f0/cmdk@0,0:a

If the system hardware has changed, or to boot from a difference device,
interrupt the autoboot process by pressing ESC.

Press ESCape to interrupt boot in 5 seconds
```

If you press **ESCAPE** within 5 seconds, you will see the Device Configuration Assistant. Otherwise the boot process will continue. See "Stage II" following.

▲▲▲ Device Configuration Assistant

You can use the Device Configuration Assistant to control new devices or peripherals. When you install a new device, you will need to use this mode to add the driver for the device so that Solaris will recognize it.

The Device Configuration Assistant also allows you to boot your machine from the Solaris CDROM or from the network (if you have network booting enabled—see AnswerBook2). After hitting **ESCAPE** to enter this mode, keep pressing the appropriate Continue key (for example **F2**), labeled at the bottom of each screen, until it asks you if you want to boot from network, local disk, or CDROM. Reply appropriately.

▲▲▲ Stage II

The second stage of the SPARC PROM-like mode (which you get to whether you use the Device Configuration Assistant or not) allows you to change the boot options and flags, probe devices and buses, and run diagnostics. The Stage II screen will look like the following:

```
<<< Current Boot Parameters >>>
Boot path: /isa/ata@1,1f0/cmdk@0,0:a
Boot args: kernel/unix

Type    b [file-name] [boot-flags] <ENTER>        to boot with options
or      i <ENTER>                                 to enter boot interpreter
or      <ENTER>                                   to boot with defaults

              <<< timeout in 5 seconds >>>


Select (b)oot or (i)nterpreter: i
Entering boot interpreter - type ctrl-d to resume boot

> help
```

In this example the system will be booted from the first disk on the first EIDE bus, using the first slice of the disk (**:a**). If you do not press **b** or **i** within 5 seconds, the system will continue to boot. The user presses the **i** key to enter the interactive boot interpreter and then enters **help** to see a list of commands.

To bring the system up in single-user mode (page 603), give the command **b –s** instead of **i** before the 5 seconds are up. If you want to do a reconfigure reboot (page 634), give the command **b –r**.

▲▲ Booting the System

Booting a system is the process of reading the Solaris system kernel into the system memory and starting it running. (The kernel is the heart of the Solaris system; the non-platform-specific part of it is stored in **/kernel/genunix**.)

As the last step of the boot procedure, Solaris runs the **init** program as PID number 1. The **init** program is the first genuine process to run after booting, and it becomes the parent of all the login shells that will eventually run on the system.

On Solaris2 the **init** process has several *run levels,* although you will typically use only two: **s**, or single-user, and **3**, or extended multiuser. The first thing that **init** does is to read the **/etc/default/init** file to set the appropriate environment variables. What **init** does at each run level is controlled by a file named **/etc/inittab**. The **init** program is responsible for running the **rc** shell scripts that perform various startup and maintenance functions. On older versions of System V, **init** also forked a **getty** process for each line that someone could log in on. In SVR4 and Solaris2 one process named **ttymon** monitors all lines on the system and starts up the appropriate login process when it detects activity on a line. If the **/etc/inittab** file does not exist, **init** will prompt you for a run level.

The **initdefault** entry in the **/etc/inittab** file determines whether the system comes up in single-user or multiuser mode. This entry specifies the run level Solaris boots up to. The default is extended multiuser mode (run level 3). In Solaris 2.6 the CDE login environment is invoked after booting is complete, whereas in earlier versions an **xdm**[8] or normal terminal login (default) process was invoked.

The **rc** (run command) scripts handle the tasks that need to be taken care of when you first bring the system up and subsequently when the system goes from single-user to multiuser mode. The **rc** scripts are shell scripts that have the letters **rc** in their filenames and are located in the **/sbin** directory. The **/sbin** directory also stores other system initialization routines including programs to configure the system interfaces, set the hostname, and mount applicable filesystems.

The **/sbin/rc∗** files are scripts that run other scripts in the **/etc/rc∗.d** directories. For example **/sbin/rc2** executes the scripts in the **/etc/rc2.d** directory. The **/etc/rc2.d** directory contains a few scripts whose names begin with K, and more scripts beginning with S. The **/sbin/rc2** script first executes all of the **K∗** scripts with an argument of **stop** and then executes all of the **S∗** scripts with an argument of **start**. This setup allows the system to control which processes are stopped and which are started whenever it enters a given run level. Occasion-

---

8. **xdm** is the X Display Manager. It provides a login box and starts up your environment based on profiles stored in your home directory. See the manual pages or AnswerBook2 for more information.

ally you may see a file in an **rc?.d** directory with a name ending in **.sh**. This suffix indicates that the system is to execute the file using the Bourne Shell dot (**.**) command. For example the system runs the **/etc/rcS.d/S50drvconfig** script with an argument of **start** and uses the dot command to execute **/etc/rcS.d/S40standardmounts.sh**. Avoid creating **∗.sh** files yourself. Using scripts with **start** and **stop** arguments is more flexible because it allows you to write one script that can both execute or kill a process, depending on how it is called. For instance the files named **/etc/rc3.d/S15nfs.server**, **/etc/rc2.d/K60nfs.server**, and **/etc/init.d/nfs.server** are all links to the same file that the system uses to start or stop NFS file service daemons depending on the run level.

The **/etc/init.d** directory is a common place for all startup, shutdown, or other command scripts. Every script in **/etc/rc∗.d** should have a link in **/etc/init.d**. As mentioned above, **/etc/rc3.d/S15nfs.server** has a link in **/etc/init.d** named **nfs.server**. The names of files in the **/etc/init.d** directory are functional. That is, if you want to turn NFS services on or off, you use the **nfs.server** script. If you want to turn **syslog** on or off, run the **syslog** script. Because each of these files is a link to a script, you must call the file with a **start** or **stop** argument. This directory allows you to find the script you want without digging through a number of directories and scripts, some of which have names that may not be intuitive. The numbers that are part of the filenames in the **/etc/rc∗.d** directories may change from one OS release to the next but the files in **/etc/init.d** will always have the same names. Following are two examples of calls to these scripts:

```
# sh /etc/init.d/nfs.server stop
# sh /etc/init.d/syslog start
```

The first example stops all processes related to serving filesystems over the network using NFS. The second example starts all processes related to the system logging utility **syslog**.

▲▲▲ Single-User Mode

When the system is in single-user mode, only the system console is enabled. You can run programs from the console in single-user mode as you would from any terminal in multiuser mode. The differences are that not all filesystems may be mounted, and few of the system daemons will be running. You cannot access a file on a filesystem that is not mounted. The **root** filesystem and the **/usr** and **/var** filesystems are always mounted in single-user mode. When it is part of the **root** filesystem, **/usr** is always mounted implicitly when **root** is mounted; on a separate filesystem Solaris2 mounts **/usr** explicitly anytime **root** is mounted. As part of single-user initialization, **/sbin/rcS** runs the system scripts in **/etc/rcS.d**.

▲▲▲ Maintenance

With the system in single-user mode, you can perform system maintenance that requires filesystems unmounted or just a quiet system—no one except you using it, so that no user programs interfere with disk maintenance and backup programs. The classical UNIX term for this state is *quiescent*.

See "Backing Up Files" on page 631 for a discussion of one of the most important and often neglected areas of system administration.

▲▲▲▲ Checking Filesystem Integrity: The **fsck** (filesystem check) utility verifies the integrity of a filesystem and, if possible, repairs any problems it finds. A filesystem (except **root**) must not be mounted while **fsck** is checking it. If you do not specify a device when you run **fsck**, it will check all devices listed in the **/etc/vfstab** (virtual filesystem table) file.

Because many filesystem repairs destroy data, **fsck** asks you before making each repair. Two options cause **fsck** to run without asking you questions. The **–y** option assumes a *yes* response to all questions, and a **–n** assumes *no*.

During a normal reboot cycle, **fsck** is run on every filesystem automatically before it is mounted. In most cases it sees that the filesystem is marked as clean, skips it, and continues on with the next filesystem. If your system crashes or goes down as the result of a power failure or other non-planned shutdown, always run **fsck** on a filesystem before it is mounted. The **fsck** utility should be run on *all* filesystems before Solaris is brought up in multiuser mode after it has been down for any reason. When your system enters single-user mode, the **rcS** script runs **fsck** (typically with the **–o p** option—for check, fix noninteractively, and quit if there is a problem that requires your input) on all filesystems that are to be mounted. The **fsck** utility uses **vfstab** to specify the files to be checked. Refer to **fsck** in Part III for more information.

If **fsck** cannot automatically repair a filesystem while the system is booting, the system will enter an intermediate state resembling single-user mode. It will identify filesystems that are damaged and instruct you to run **fsck** by hand to fix them. No further system initialization will take place until you complete the requested repairs. After making the repairs, give the command **exit** (or press CONTROL-D) and let the system resume initialization.

▲▲▲ Going to Multiuser Mode

After you have determined that all is well with all filesystems, you can bring the operating system up to multiuser mode. An entry in the **inittab** file determines which run level number represents the multiuser state. Giving the command

```
# telinit 3
```

or

```
# exit
```

in response to the Superuser prompt (when the system is in single-user mode) brings the system up to multiuser mode. The **telinit** utility (**/etc/telinit**) tells **init** what run state to enter. The **telinit** executable is just a symbolic link to the **init** executable, but by convention running **telinit** is preferred to running **init** directly.

When the system goes from single-user to multiuser mode, the **/sbin/rc2** and **/sbin/rc3** scripts mount filesystems and start daemons. These scripts in turn execute the **K∗** and **S∗** scripts in the **/etc/rc2.d** and **/etc/rc3.d** directories. To customize your system initialization, add or remove shell scripts to/from the **/etc/rc2.d** and **/etc/rc3.d** directories.

Many of the system initializations and critical system processes are started from **/etc/rc2.d**. The only major stock system function that is started in **/etc/rc3.d** is NFS. If your machine is on a network and running NFS (run level 3), you should be able to share local filesystems with remote machines and remote filesystems with the local machine. Add scripts that start processes such as a Web server or a database to **/etc/rc3.d**. In general run level 3 is used to provide services to other users on a network. Run level 2 is referred to as multiuser mode, and run level 3 is extended multiuser mode; but because run level 2 is rarely used by itself, this chapter uses the term *multiuser* to refer to run level 3.

▲▲ Multiuser Mode

Multiuser mode is the normal state for a Solaris system. All appropriate filesystems are mounted, and users can log in from all connected terminals and dial-in lines. All support services and daemons are enabled and running. Once the system is in multiuser mode, you will see a login screen or prompt.

▲▲▲ Logging In

When you bring a system up in multiuser mode, the Service Access Controller (**sac**) starts up the appropriate port monitors, such as **ttymon**, to monitor the lines users can use to log in. (For more information on the Service Access Facility and **ttymon**, see the **ttymon man** page and AnswerBook2.) The **ttymon** process displays a login: prompt on a terminal connected to the machine and waits for someone to try to log in. When you enter your login name, **ttymon** establishes the characteristics of your terminal and then overlays itself with a **login** process and passes to the **login** process whatever you entered in response to the login: prompt. The **login** program consults the **/etc/passwd** file to see if there is a username associated with the login name you entered. It then consults the **/etc/shadow** file to see if there is a password associated with the login name. If there is, **login** prompts you for a password; if not, it continues without requiring a password. If your login name requires a password, **login** verifies the password you enter by checking the **/etc/shadow** file again. If either your login name or password is not correct, **login** displays Login incorrect. and prompts you to log in again. When you log in on the console of your machine using XDM or CDE (as opposed to a terminal), the **xdm** or CDE process verifies your login directly without using **sac** or **ttymon**.

All passwords in the **/etc/shadow** file are encrypted through a one-way hash. It is not possible to recover an encrypted password. When you log in the **login** process encrypts the password you type in at the prompt and compares it to the encrypted password in **/etc/shadow**. If it matches, you are authenticated.

With NIS or NIS+, **login** compares your login name and password with the information in the appropriate naming service instead of (or in addition to) the **passwd** and **shadow** files. If your system is configured to use more than one of these methods (**/etc/passwd**, NIS, or NIS+), it checks the **/etc/nsswitch.conf** file to see what order to consult them in. For example the following line in **/etc/nsswitch.conf** indicates that the system should check the **/etc/passwd** file first, followed by NIS and then by NIS+.

```
passwd:      files nis nisplus
```

For more information on the **/etc/nsswitch.conf** file and the services that it affects, refer to page 612 and the **nsswitch.conf man** page.

Solaris 2.6 introduced PAM, a Pluggable Authentication Module facility, which allows you greater control over user logins than do the **/etc/passwd** and **/etc/shadow** files. Using PAM, you can specify multiple levels of authentication, mutually exclusive authentication methods, or parallel methods that are each in themselves sufficient to grant access to the system. For example you can have a different authentication method for console logins versus **telnet** logins. And you can require that modem users authenticate themselves via two or more methods (such as a smartcard or badge reader). PAM modules also provide security technology vendors with a more convenient way to interface their hardware or software products with your system. The **/etc/pam.conf** file configures this service (see the **pam.conf man** page). The features of the Solaris implementation of the PAM facility are similar to those of Linux.

If the login name and password are correct, **login** consults the appropriate service to initialize your user and group IDs, establish your home directory, and determine what shell you will be working with.

The **login** utility assigns values to the **HOME, PATH, LOGNAME, SHELL, TZ**, and **MAIL** variables. It looks in the **/etc/group** file to identify all the groups the user belongs to (page 610). When **login** has finished its work, it overlays itself with the login shell, which inherits the variables **login** has set.

The login shell $^{sh9}_{ksh}$ assigns values to the **IFS, MAILCHECK, PS1**, and **PS2** shell variables (Chapter 10 covers these variables) and then executes the commands in the **/etc/profile** shell script. Exactly what this script does is system-dependent. It usually displays the contents of the **/etc/motd** (message of the day) and **/etc/issue** files, lets you know if you have any mail, and sets **umask** (page 939), the file-creation mask.

After executing the commands in **/etc/profile**, the shell $^{sh}_{ksh}$ executes the commands from the **.profile** shell script in your home directory. Because the shell executes a user's **.profile** script *after* the **/etc/profile** script, a sophisticated user can override any variables or conventions that were established by the system whereas a new user can remain uninvolved in these complications.

The login shell csh runs **/etc/.login** to set several shell variables and then reads and executes the commands in the user's **.cshrc** and **.login** files. None of the messages are printed if the **.hushlogin** file exists in the user's home directory.

▲▲▲ Running a Program and Logging Out

When you see a shell prompt, you can execute a program or log off the system. When you log off the process running the shell dies. Either the parent process (in the case of CDE or **xdm**) or **init** receives the operating system signal that one of its children has died. When **init** receives one of these signals, it takes action based on the contents of the **/etc/inittab** file. In the case of a process controlling a line for a terminal, it informs **ttymon** that the line is free for another user.

When you exit from a remote or terminal login, **init** takes over and displays a new login prompt. In the case of CDE, when you exit all of your windows will die and the **dtlogin** daemon takes care of initiating a new login display. For **xdm** either **init** or **xdm** itself, depending on your configuration, will bring up a new login display.

▲▲ Bringing the System Down

The **shutdown** script (**/usr/sbin/shutdown**) performs all the tasks involved in bringing the system down. Use this script to bring the system down to single-user mode or all the way to PROM mode; refer to AnswerBook2 or your system manual for more information. The next section describes the actions you can take to perform the key steps of **shutdown** manually, if necessary.

▲▲▲ Going to Single-User Mode

Because going from multiuser to single-user mode can affect other users, you must be Superuser to make this change. Make sure you give other users enough warning before going to single-user mode; otherwise they may lose whatever they were working on.

---

9. The preceding entry is specific to the shells named in the shaded box. A reference to **sh** implies **jsh**.

Following are a number of ways to bring down the system.

When you need to shut down the machine relatively quickly, you can use the following procedure in place of **shutdown**:

1. Log in as **root** or use **su** to become Superuser.

2. Use **wall** (write all) to warn everyone who is using the system to log off.

3. If you are sharing files via NFS, use **unshare** to disable network access to the shared filesystems. (Use **share** without an argument to see what filesystems are being shared.)

4. Use **umount** to unmount all mounted devices. (Use **mount** without an argument to see what devices are mounted.)

5. Give the command **telinit s** to bring the system down to single-user mode or **telinit 0** to bring the system down to PROM mode.

Be Very Careful with halt

In an emergency you can bring the system down very quickly with the following procedure. **This procedure will have a *significant impact* on users on the system.**

1. Log in as **root** or use **su** to become Superuser.

2. Use the **halt** utility to **sync** all filesystems immediately and take the system down to PROM mode.

On SPARC LX class machines and above you can use **poweroff** to halt the machine and then turn the power off. These machines have power supplies that can be controlled by software. Intel and SPARC2 and below class machines do not have this capability.

▲▲▲▲ Turning the Power Off: Once the system is in single-user mode, shutting it down is quite straightforward. Give the command **init 0** (preferred) or **halt** to bring the system down to PROM (SPARC) or BIOS/CMOS Setup (x86) mode. When the appropriate prompt[10] appears or the system starts rebooting, it is safe to turn the power off.

▲▲ Crashes

A *crash* is the system stopping when you do not intend it to. After a crash, you must carefully bring up the operating system to minimize possible damage to the filesystems. Frequently there will be little or no damage.

---

10. For SPARC systems the prompt will be the OK or > prompt. An x86 machine will tell you to Press Any key to continue. When you press a key, the machine reboots.

Although the filesystems are checked automatically during the boot process if needed, you will have to check them manually if there is a problem that cannot be repaired automatically. To check the filesystems manually after a crash, boot the system up to single-user mode. *Do not* mount any devices other than the **root** (which the Solaris system mounts automatically). If you have **/** and **/usr** on different filesystems, Solaris2 automatically mounts **/usr** at this time. Solaris2 automatically runs **fsck** on **root** (and **/usr** if separate), repairing it as needed. If **fsck** cannot repair the **root** filesystem automatically, the system will enter an intermediate mode resembling single-user mode where you must perform the **fsck** on **root** manually (see "Checking Filesystem Integrity" on page 603); then type **exit** to resume the single-user initialization process. Now run **fsck** on all the other filesystems and repair them as needed *before* mounting them. Make note of any ordinary files or directories that you repair (and can identify), and inform their owners that they may not be complete or correct. Look in the **lost+found** directory in each filesystem for missing files. For more information see "Notes" on page 762.

If files are not correct or are missing altogether, you may have to recreate them from a backup copy of the filesystem. For more information see "Backing Up Files" on page 631.

As Solaris crashes, it attempts to save information on its pre-crash state that you can use to debug the cause of the crash. Solaris keeps a complete copy of the data in memory along with a core dump containing a traceback of the current *call stack* (the nested level of subroutine calls made up to the time when the program crashed). All of this information is stored at the end of the system's swap space (page 618) as a crash dump. You can configure the system so that when it reboots it looks for a crash dump and transfers it to a file under **/var/crash/***hostname*, where *hostname* is the name of your system. The command line that runs **savecore** in **/etc/init.d/sysetup** determines whether the system saves crash information. By default this function is disabled (commented out), but you can edit **/etc/init.d/sysetup** and enable crash dumps by removing the **#** from the appropriate lines at the end of the file. For each crash Solaris stores two files: A copy of the version of Solaris that was running at the time of the crash and a copy of the contents of the system's memory. These files are named **unix.N** and **vmcore.N**, where **N** represents a sequence number (so you know which files are related). Using these files to debug the Solaris kernel is beyond the scope of this book; refer to AnswerBook2 or the **crash man** page for more information.

Start Optional

▲ Important Files and Directories

This section details the most common files that are used to administer the system. Also see "Important Standard Directories and Files" on page 83. Some of these files may be shared across multiple hosts using the Network Information Service (NIS [page 218]).

/dev/null   Any output you redirect to this file will disappear. You can send error messages from shell scripts here when you do not want the user to see them. Also called the *bit bucket*.

If you redirect input to come from this file, it will appear as a null (empty) file. You can create an empty file named **nothing** by giving the following command. You can also use this technique to truncate an existing file to zero length without changing its permissions. Also see **touch** on pages 561 and 922.

```
$ cat /dev/null > nothing
```

or

```
$ cp /dev/null nothing
```

/etc/aliases   Used by the mail delivery system (**sendmail**) to construct **aliases** for users. Edit this file to suit your local preferences. There are a number of good examples in this file showing how you can create **aliases** for users, create mailing lists, and direct email to files. After editing this file, run **newaliases** to inform **sendmail** that the **aliases** file has changed. The **/etc/aliases** file is a symbolic link to **/etc/mail/aliases**.

/etc/cron.d   By default users can use the **at** and **crontab** utilities to schedule jobs. This directory includes the **at.allow** and **cron.allow** files that list the login names of users who are permitted to use these utilities. The **at.deny** and **cron.deny** files in this directory specify users who are not permitted to use the corresponding utilities. If you wish to allow everyone to use them, create empty **at.deny** and **cron.deny** files, and do not create **at.allow** or **cron.allow**. Conversely if no one is to use **at** and/or **crontab**, remove **at.allow**, **at.deny**, **cron.allow**, and **cron.deny**. This will not prevent Super-user from using either **at** or **cron**.

/etc/dumpdates   Contains information about the last execution of **ufsdump**. For each filesystem it stores the time of the last dump at a given dump level. The **ufsdump** utility uses this information to determine which files to back up when executing at a particular dump level. Refer to "Backing Up Files" on page 631 or **ufsdump** in Part III for more information. Following is a sample **/etc/dumpdates** file from a machine with four filesystems and a backup schedule that uses three dump levels:

```
/dev/rdsk/c0t0d0s7          5 Thu Apr 23 03:53:55 1998
/dev/rdsk/c0t0d0s7          2 Sun Apr 19 08:25:24 1998
/dev/rdsk/c0t0d0s4          2 Sun Apr 19 08:57:32 1998
/dev/rdsk/c0t0d0s6          2 Sun Apr 19 08:58:06 1998
/dev/rdsk/c0t0d0s0          2 Sun Apr 19 09:02:27 1998
/dev/rdsk/c0t0d0s7          0 Sun Mar 22 22:08:35 1998
/dev/rdsk/c0t0d0s4          0 Sun Mar 22 22:33:40 1998
/dev/rdsk/c0t0d0s6          0 Sun Mar 22 22:35:22 1998
/dev/rdsk/c0t0d0s0          0 Sun Mar 22 22:43:45 1998
```

The first column contains the raw device name of the dumped filesystem. The second column contains the dump level and the date of the dump.

/etc/group

Groups allow users to share files or programs without allowing all system users access to them. This scheme is useful if several users are working with files that are not public. Also see "ACL (Access Control List)" on page 674.

An entry in the **/etc/group** file has the four fields shown below. If an entry is too long to fit on one line, end the line with a backslash (\), which quotes the following RETURN, and continue the entry on the next line.

group-name:password:group-ID:login-name-list

The *group-name* is from one to six characters, the first being alphabetic and none being uppercase. The *password* is an optional encrypted password. Because there is no good way to enter a password into the **group** file, group passwords are not very useful and should be avoided. The **group-ID** is a number between 0 and 2,147,483,647. To maintain compatibility with other operating systems and versions of Solaris prior to 2.5, assign group numbers in the range 100–60,000. The **login-name-list** is a comma-separated list of users who belong to the group. A sample entry in a **group** file is shown below. The group is named **pubs**, has no password, and has a group ID of 100.

```
pubs::100:alex,jenny,scott,hls,barbara
```

The **/etc/group** file does not define groups. Groups come into existence when a user is assigned a group ID number in the **/etc/passwd** file. The **/etc/group** file associates a name with each group (number).

Each user has a primary group, which is the group that user is assigned in the **/etc/passwd** file. In addition you may belong to other groups, depending on what **login-name-lists** you are included on in the **/etc/group** file. In effect you simultaneously belong to both your primary group and to any groups you are assigned to in **/etc/group**. When you attempt to access a file you do not own, the operating system checks to see whether you are a member of the group that has access to the file. If you are, your access permissions are controlled by the group access permissions for the file. If you are not a member of the group that has access to the file (and you do not own the file), you are subject to the public access permissions for the file.

When you create a new file, it is assigned to the group that is associated with the directory the file is being written into, assuming that you belong to the group. If you do not belong to the group that has access to the directory, the file is assigned to your primary group.

Older releases of UNIX/Solaris required you to use the **newgrp** utility to change your group ID number to another group, assuming you are listed in the **login-name-list** of that group. The **newgrp** command takes an argument, which is the name of the group you want to change to. (You can always use **newgrp** without an argument or type **exit** to change your group ID back to what it was when you first logged in.)

/etc/inittab　　　**initialization table**　　Controls how the **init** process behaves. Each line in **inittab** has four colon-separated fields:

id:run-level:action:process

The *id* uniquely identifies an entry in the **inittab** file. The *run-level* is the system run level(s) at which *process* is executed. The *run-level(s)* are zero or more characters chosen from 0123456s. If there is more than one run level listed, the associated *process* is executed at each of the specified run levels. When you do not specify a run level, **init** executes *process* at all run levels. When the system changes run levels, all entries in **inittab** that do not include the new run-level are sent the SIGTERM signal to allow them to terminate gracefully. After 5 seconds, *process* is killed if it is still running.

　　The *process* is any valid system command. The command is executed using the Bourne Shell, so you can use any valid Bourne Shell syntax.

　　The *action* is one of the following keywords: **respawn**, **wait**, **once**, **boot**, **bootwait**, **powerfail**, **powerwait**, **off**, **ondemand**, **initdefault**, or **sysinit**. This keyword controls how the *process* is treated when it is executed. The most commonly used keywords are **wait** and **respawn**.

　　The **wait** keyword instructs **init** to start *process* and wait for it to terminate. All subsequent scans of **inittab** ignore this **wait** entry. Because a **wait** entry is started only once (upon entering *run-level*) and not executed again while the system remains at *run-level*, it is often used to redirect **init** output to the console.

　　The **respawn** entry tells **init** to start *process* if it does not exist but not to wait for it to terminate. If *process* does exist, **init** goes on to the next entry in the **inittab**. The **init** utility continues to rescan **inittab** looking for processes that have died. When a *process* dies a **respawn** entry makes **init** restart it automatically.

　　All of the *actions* are documented in the **inittab man** page.

/etc/magic　　　Most files begin with a unique identifier called a *magic number*. The **/etc/magic** file is a text database containing the list of all known magic numbers on the system. When you use the **file** utility to determine the type of a file, it consults the **/etc/magic** file. Occasionally you will acquire a new tool that creates a new type of file that is unrecognized by the **file** command. When this happens you need to update the **/etc/magic** file; refer to the **magic man** page for details.

/etc/mnttab　　　**mount table**　　Contains a list of all currently mounted devices. When you call **mount** without any arguments, it consults this file and displays a list of mounted devices. Each time you (or an **rc** script) call **mount** or **umount**, these programs make the necessary changes to **mnttab**. Although this is an ASCII text file, you should not edit it.

> ### Fixing mnttab
>
> The operating system maintains its own internal mount table, which may, on rare occasions, differ from this file. To bring the **mnttab** file in line with the operating system's mount table, reboot the system.

/etc/motd

Contains the message of the day, which is displayed each time someone logs in. The file should be kept short because users tend to see the message many times. Being repeatedly subjected to a long message of the day can be tedious.

/etc/nsswitch.conf

Solaris keeps databases containing information on, among others, hosts and users. The data to populate these databases can come from many sources. For example hostnames and addresses can come from the local **/etc/hosts** file, DNS, NIS, and more. The **nsswitch.conf** file controls the order in which the various sources are consulted to populate the database and ultimately to fulfill a request from the system. Each line in this file contains a database name followed by a colon, whitespace, and zero or more sources separated by spaces. A very basic line from **nsswitch.conf** follows:

```
hosts:      files
```

This line tells the system that all requests to the **hosts** database should be filled by local files such as **/etc/hosts**. Valid options for sources are files, nis, nisplus (NIS+), and dns (**hosts** only). In Solaris 2.5 and above there is also an XFN source for accessing FNS (federated naming service—seeAnswerbook2 for more information).

If you want to consult DNS when your request for a host is not resolved by local files, add dns (another source) to the **hosts** line as follows:

```
hosts:      files dns
```

The following line contains another example of how the **hosts** database can be configured.

```
hosts:      xfn nis [NOTFOUND=return] files
```

The square brackets ([]) specify criteria that modify how the search is performed. This example first consults the xfn source. If xfn has the answer, no further searching takes place. If xfn does not provide an answer, then nis is checked. If nis returns an answer saying it could not find an answer, the process stops ([NOTFOUND=return]) and no answer is returned. Only if nis does not return an answer *and* does not return NOTFOUND are the local files (**/etc/hosts**) consulted. In other words NIS provides an authoritative answer; only if NIS is not available should local files be consulted.

/etc/pam.conf	Specifies the authentication methods used by PAM (Pluggable Authentication Module) applications. Unless you thoroughly understand how to configure PAM, *avoid changing the contents of* **/etc/pam.conf**. Mistakes in the configuration of PAM can quickly make your system unusable. Available starting with Solaris 2.6.
/etc/passwd	Describes users to the system. Each line in **passwd** has seven colon-separated fields and describes one user.

> ### *login-name:dummy-password:user-ID:group-ID:info:directory:program*

The *login-name* is the user's login name—the name that the user enters in response to the `login:` prompt or GUI login screen. The value of the *dummy-password* is the character x. Older versions of UNIX/Solaris included an encrypted password in this field. Beginning with SVR4, the encrypted password is stored in a file named **/etc/shadow** (page 616). Although it is optional, for security every account should have a password. By convention disabled accounts have an asterisk (∗) in this field.

The *user-ID* is a number from 0 to 2,147,483,647, with 0 indicating Superuser, and 0–99 reserved by convention. The *group-ID* identifies the user as a member of a group. It is also a number between 0 and 2,147,483,647, with 0–99 being reserved. Even though Solaris 2.6 and above can support more than two billion different user and group IDs, it is recommend that you stay within the range 100–60,000 to maintain compatibility with other versions of UNIX/Solaris.

The *info* is information that various programs, such as accounting programs and email, use to further identify the user. Normally it contains at least the first and last name of the user.

The *directory* is the absolute pathname of the user's home directory. The *program* is the program that will run once the user logs in. If *program* is not present, **/usr/bin/sh** is assumed. You can put **/usr/bin/csh** here to log in to the C Shell, or **/usr/bin/ksh** to log in using the Korn Shell.

A brief sample **passwd** file follows. The *info* field stores telephone extension numbers.

```
# cat /etc/passwd
bill:x:1102:10:ext 123:/home/bill:
roy:x:1104:10:ext 475:/home/roy:/usr/bin/csh
tom:x:1105:10:ext 476:/home/tom:
lynn:x:1166:10:ext 500:/home/lynn:
mark:x:1107:10:ext 112:/home/mark:/usr/bin/ksh
sales:x:1108:10:ext 102:/home/sales:
anne:x:1109:10:ext 355:/home/anne:
toni:x:1164:10:ext 357:/home/toni:/usr/bin/csh
ginny:x:1115:10:ext 109:/home/ginny:/usr/bin/csh
```

The *program* specified in the right-hand field of each line in the **passwd** file is usually a shell, but as shown below, it can be any program. The following line in the **passwd** file will create a "user" whose only purpose is to execute the **who** utility:

```
who:x:1000:1000:execute who:/usr:/usr/bin/who
```

Using **who** as a login name causes the system to log you in, execute the **who** utility, and log you out. This entry in the **passwd** file does not provide a shell—there is no way for you to stay logged in after **who** is finished executing.

This is a useful technique for providing special accounts that may only do one thing. For instance sites may create an **ftp** (page 765) account so that they can enable anonymous **ftp** access to their systems. Because nobody actually logs in to this account, the shell might be set to an invalid program, or to a program that just displays This account is not valid for login.

Do Not Replace a Login Shell with a Shell Script

Be careful when using special shells in place of login shells in **/etc/passwd**. Do not use shell scripts as replacements for shells. A user may be able to interrupt a shell script, giving him or her full shell access when you did not intend to do so. When installing a dummy shell, use a compiled program, not a shell script.

/etc/power.conf　　Used by the power management facilities to control power to the monitor, CPU, CDROM, and other components. Each entry in **power.conf** occupies one line comprising three whitespace-separated fields that specify the device name, the number of seconds after which an idle device will be powered down, and any dependent devices.

```
$ cat /etc/power.conf
/dev/kbd                300
/dev/mouse              300
/dev/fb                 0 0             /dev/kbd /dev/mouse
```

This example shows a configuration that will turn off a monitor after 5 minutes (300 seconds) of inactivity on both the keyboard (**/dev/kbd**) and the mouse (**/dev/mouse**). The video board driver (**/dev/fb**)[11] depends on the keyboard and the mouse registering as idle. The zeros in the third entry tell the power management facility to power down the video as soon as both the keyboard and the mouse are registered as idle (in this case after they have both been inactive for 300 seconds). If you replace the zeros in this entry, you would add additional time to the 300 seconds specified in the keyboard and mouse entries.

---

11. The fb stands for frame buffer. See footnote 13 on page 629.

/etc/printers.conf   Controls the printer subsystem on Solaris 2.6 and above. This file is similar in appearance to the **/etc/printcap** file on BSD UNIX but has subtle differences. The Solaris print client subsystem uses it to enable easy access and setup of remote printers (local printers are still handled in the traditional way). To convert a BSD-style **printcap** file to **/etc/printers.conf**, run **/usr/lib/print/conv_lpd** on the existing **printcap** file. To convert a UNIX System V **/etc/lp** hierarchy to a **/etc/printers.conf** file, run **/usr/lib/lp/conv_lp** with no arguments. To avoid having to learn the syntax of this file, use **lpadmin** to add and remove printers (page 639).

/etc/profile   Contains a systemwide login shell $^{sh}_{ksh}$ initialization script. When you log in the first thing the shell does is to execute the commands in this file in the same environment as the shell. (For more information on executing a shell script in this manner, refer to the discussion of the **.** [dot] command on page 375.) This file allows the system administrator to establish systemwide environment parameters that individual users can override. Using this file, you can set shell variables, execute utilities, and take care of other housekeeping tasks.

Following is an example of an **/etc/profile** file that displays the message of the day (the **/etc/motd** file), sets the file-creation mask (**umask**), and displays all the recent **news** items (files in **/var/news**):

```
# cat /etc/profile
cat /etc/motd
umask 022
news
```

/etc/.login   Contains a systemwide login shell csh initialization script; similar to **/etc/profile** (above).

.profile   The shell $^{sh}_{ksh}$ executes the commands in this file in the same environment as the shell each time a user logs in; it must be located in a user's home directory.

It usually specifies a terminal type (for **vi** and other programs), runs **stty** to establish terminal characteristics desired by the user, and performs other housekeeping functions when a user logs in.

A typical **.profile** file specifying a vt100 terminal and **CONTROL-H** as the erase key is as follows:

```
$ cat .profile
TERM=vt100
export TERM
stty erase '^h'
```

If you log in from more than one type of terminal, you may want to construct a more elaborate routine, such as the following one, which asks you for the terminal type each time you log in:

```
$ cat .profile
echo 'Terminal type: \c'
read TERM
export TERM
stty erase '^h'
```

.cshrc

The shell csh executes the commands in this file in the same environment as the shell each time a user logs in; it is similar to **.profile** (above) and must be located in your home directory.

The C Shell executes the programs and scripts in this file whenever a user or program starts a new shell. When you start a **cmdtool**, **shelltool**, **xterm**, or launch a remote command (using **rsh** for example), the shell invokes **.cshrc** before displaying the prompt.

.login

This file performs a similar function to the **.cshrc** file (above) in the user's home directory, but it is only executed by the shell csh during a login process. Opening a new shell window will usually not invoke this script, but using **telnet** to log in on a machine, or running **xterm** with the **–ls** (login shell) flag will invoke it.

Run Command (rc) Files

The **init** program executes a run command (**rc**) file each time it changes state or run level. The run command scripts perform tasks such as mounting filesystems (when the system goes multiuser), removing temporary files (after the filesystems are mounted), and unmounting filesystems (when the system is returned to single-user mode). The run command scripts are named **/sbin/rc0**, **/sbin/rc1**, **/sbin/rc2**, **/sbin/rc3**, **/sbin/rc5**, **/sbin/rc6**, and **/sbin/rcS**. The **/sbin/rc4** script is not present and the **/sbin/rc5** (not typically used) and **/sbin/rc6** scripts are links to **/sbin/rc0** as Solaris is shipped. The rest of the **rc** scripts have corresponding directories in **/etc**. For example **/sbin/rc3** has **/etc/rc3.d**. The scripts within the **rc✷.d** directories are executed by their corresponding scripts in **/sbin**.

/etc/shadow

Contains encrypted user passwords. Each entry occupies one line composed of nine fields, separated by colons:

login-name:password:last-mod:min:max:warn:inactive:expire:flag

The *login-name* is the name the user enters in response to the login: prompt. The *password* is an encrypted password that the **passwd** utility puts into this file. If unauthorized access is not a problem, the password field can initially be null (::). When the user first logs in, he or she can run **passwd** to select a password. Otherwise you can run **passwd** while you are Superuser to assign a password to the user. Or if you are using **admintool**, you can assign a password when you create the account.

The *last-mod* field indicates when the password was last modified. The *min* is the minimum number of days that must elapse before the password can be changed; *max* is the maximum number of days before the password must be changed. The *warn* specifies how much advance warning (in days) to give the user before the password expires. The account will be invalidated if the number of days between login sessions exceeds the number of days specified in the ***inactive*** field. The account will also be invalid as of the date specified in the **expire** field. The last field in an entry, *flag*, is reserved for future use.

The **shadow** password file should not be publicly readable (or writable) and should be owned by **root** in order to make it more difficult for someone to break into your system by identifying accounts without passwords or by using specialized programs that try to match encrypted passwords.

A number of conventions exist that should be followed when making special **shadow** entries. An entry of *LK* or NP in the ***password*** field indicates *locked* and *no password*, respectively. *No password* is different than an empty password in that it implies that this is an administrative account that nobody ever actually logs in on directly. Occasionally programs will run with the privileges of this account for system maintenance functions. These accounts are set up under the principle of least privilege.

Entries in the **shadow** file must appear in the same order as they do in the **passwd** file, and there must be one and only one **shadow** entry for every **passwd** entry.

/etc/vfstab   **virtual filesystem table**   Contains the list of device filenames that **fsck** checks by default. This list should be the same as the list of devices that the run command (**rc**) script mounts when you bring the system up to multiuser mode. A sample file follows.

```
# cat /etc/vfstab
#device            device            mount        FS      fsck    mount     mount
#to mount          to fsck           point        type    pass    at boot   options
#
#/dev/dsk/c1d0s2 /dev/rdsk/c1d0s2 /usr            ufs     1       yes       -
fd                 -                /dev/fd      fd      -       no        -
/proc              -                /proc        proc    -       no        -
/dev/dsk/c0t0d0s1 -                 -            swap    -       no        -
/dev/dsk/c0t0d0s0 /dev/rdsk/c0t0d0s0 /           ufs     1       no        -
/dev/dsk/c0t0d0s6 /dev/rdsk/c0t0d0s6 /usr        ufs     1       no        -
/dev/dsk/c0t0d0s7 /dev/rdsk/c0t0d0s7 /export     ufs     2       yes       nosuid
swap               -                /tmp         tmpfs   -       yes       -
```

The **/etc/vfstab** file includes seven fields separated by SPACEs. They specify:

- the block device name (page 622)
- the character device name that **fsck** should check (page 622)
- the directory the filesystem is mounted on (the *mount point*)
- the filesystem type
- a number used by **fsck** to decide when to check the filesystem
- whether the filesystem should be mounted automatically at boot time
- options, such as whether the filesystem is mounted for reading and writing (default), or just for reading

If there is no entry for a particular field, a hyphen serves as a placeholder. The **/export** entry above uses the **nosuid** option to indicate that setuid executables are not to have their effective user ID changed when they are executed from this filesystem. Any setuid programs become equivalent to standard executable files when this option is used.

/kernel/genunix   **generic UNIX**   This file contains the generic portion of the Solaris system kernel that is loaded when you boot the system. The platform-specific part of the kernel is kept in **/platform/***platform-name***/kernel/unix**. Different values of *platform-name* represent different hardware classes of machines (for example **i86pc**, **sun4c**, **sun4m**, **sun4d**, **sun4u**, or **sun4u2**).

/usr/lib/cron   A link to **/etc/cron.d** (page 609).

/usr/sbin/shutdown   A shell script that brings the system down properly (page 606).

/var/adm/messages   Contains messages from daemons, the kernel, and security programs. For example you will find filesystem full warning messages, error messages from system daemons (NFS, syslog, printer daemons), SCSI and IDE disk error messages, messages from security-related programs such as **su**, and more. Check **/var/adm/messages** periodically to keep informed about important system events. Much of the information that is displayed on the system console is also sent to **messages**. If you have a system problem and do not have access to the console, check this file for messages about the problem.

/var/sadm   This directory houses directories that store information about software packages that are installed on the system and patches that have been applied to the system.

swap   Even though **swap** is not actually a file, swap space can be added and deleted from the system dynamically. Swap space is used by the virtual memory subsystem. When your machine runs low on real memory (RAM), it writes memory pages from RAM to the swap space on your disk. Which pages are written and when is controlled by finely tuned algorithms in the kernel. When these pages are needed by running programs, they are brought back into RAM. This technique is called *paging*. When a system is running very short on memory, an entire process may be paged out to disk. This technique is called *swapping* and is very rare on Solaris releases above 2.4.

By convention swap space is put on slice 1 of your hard disk (page 635). However if you run out of swap space or underestimated the amount of swap space needed when you installed Solaris, you can use **mkfile** to create a new swap file and **swap** to enable it. Running an application that requires a large amount of virtual memory may result in the need for additional swap space. You can temporarily expand the swap space into the filesystem; see **mkfile** (page 814), **swap** (page 907), and the corresponding **man** pages.

Keep Track of Swap Space Usage

By default Solaris mounts **/tmp** using the TMPFS virtual memory filesystem over the swap space. You can check the status of your swap space with the command **df –k /tmp**. If you see less space available than you expected, you may be running low on swap space; use **ps** to search for memory hogs.

    If you find yourself running low on virtual memory, check your **/tmp** filesystem. If you have a lot of files in **/tmp** consuming space or several large files, clean them up; doing so may alleviate your problems.

Stop Optional

Start Optional

▲ Types of Files

The Solaris system supports several types of files: Ordinary, directory, block special, character special, fifo special, sockets, doors, and symbolic links. Ordinary files hold user data; directories hold directory information. Special files represent routines in the kernel that provide access to some feature of the operating system. Block and character special files represent device drivers that let you communicate with peripheral devices such as terminals, printers, and disk drives. Fifo (first in, first out) special files, also called *named pipes,* allow unrelated programs to exchange information. Sockets allow unrelated processes on the same or different computers to exchange information. One type of socket, the UNIX domain socket, is a special file. Symbolic links allow you to link files that are in different filesystems. (Plain links, also called hard links, work only within a single filesystem, see "Symbolic Links" on page 96.)

▲▲ Ordinary Files, Directories, Links, and Inodes

An *ordinary* file stores user data, such as textual information, programs, or an image such as a **jpeg** or **tiff** file. A *directory* is a disk file with a standard format that stores a list of names of ordinary and directory files.

    A directory relates each of its filenames to a specific inode, which is identified by an inode number. An *inode* is a data structure that defines the file's existence. It contains critical information such as the name of the owner of the file, where it is physically located on the disk, and how many links point to it.

    When you move (**mv**) a file within a filesystem, you change the filename portion of the directory entry that is associated with the inode that describes the file. You do not create a new inode. If you move a file to another filesystem, **mv** first creates a new inode on the destination filesystem, and then it deletes the original inode. You can also use **mv** to move a directory recursively, in which case all the objects are copied and deleted as above.

When you make an additional hard link (**ln**) to a file, you create another reference (an additional file-name) to the inode that describes the file. You do not create a new inode.

When you remove (**rm**) a file, you remove the entry in the directory that describes the file. When you remove the last link to a file, the operating system puts all the blocks the inode pointed to back in the *free list* (the list of blocks on the disk that are available for use).

Every directory always has at least two entries (**.** and **..**). The **.** entry is a link to the directory itself. The **..** entry is a link to the parent directory. In the case of the **root** directory, where there is no parent, the **..** entry is a link to the **root** directory itself. It is not possible to create hard links to directories.

▲▲ Symbolic Links

Because each filesystem has a separate set of inodes, you only can create hard links to a file from within the filesystem that holds that file. To get around this limitation, Solaris provides symbolic links. Files that are linked by a symbolic link do not share an inode: You can create a symbolic link to a file from any filesystem. You can also create a symbolic link to a directory, device, or other special file. For more information see "Symbolic Links" on page 96.

▲▲ Special Files

By convention special files appear in the **/dev** and **/devices** directories and their subdirectories. The **/dev** directory contains symbolic links to the actual device in the **/devices** directory. When you give a **boot –r** command (see "Add/Remove Devices: Reconfigure Reboot" on page 634), Solaris creates the special files for each device attached to the system in **/devices** and links to these special files in **/dev**. Look at the following command to see why **/dev** is useful:

```
$ ls -l /dev/term/a
lrwxrwxrwx   1 root     root       29 Apr 23 16:20 /dev/term/a -> ../../devices/isa/asy@1,3f8:a
```

The hardware device referred to by **/dev/term/a** has a long and complicated pathname. You can use the entry in **/devices** just as effectively as the one in **/dev**, but the simple entry in **/dev** insulates you from having to see, know, or enter this unwieldy pathname.

Each special file represents a device or file: You read from and write to the file to read from and write to the device it represents. Although you will not normally read directly from or write directly to device files, the kernel and many system utilities do.

The following example shows part of the output an **ls –lL** command produces for the **/dev** directory. The **–L** option causes **ls** to display the names of the files in **/dev**, rather than showing them as symbolic links to the **/devices** directory:

```
$ ls -lL /dev
crw-------   1 root     sys       11,   5 Mar 26 04:56 rawip
crw-rw-rw-   1 root     sys       36,   2 Mar 26 05:15 rdiskette
crw-rw-rw-   1 root     sys       36,   2 Mar 26 05:15 rdiskette0
drwxrwxr-x   2 root     sys          1024 Mar 26 05:15 rdsk
crw-rw-rw-   1 root     sys       36,   2 Mar 26 05:15 rfd0
```

```
drwxrwxr-x   2 root     sys          512 Mar 26 04:56 rmt
drwxrwxr-x   2 root     sys          512 Mar 26 04:56 sad
crw-------   1 root     sys       11,103 Mar 26 04:56 smc
drwxr-xr-x   2 root     root         512 Mar 26 05:17 sound
crw-rw-rw-   1 root     sys       11, 10 Mar 26 05:15 spx
crw-rw-rw-   1 root     root     166,  2 Apr 13 05:13 stderr
crw-rw-rw-   1 root     root     166,  0 Apr 13 05:13 stdin
crw-rw-rw-   1 root     root     166,  1 Apr 13 05:13 stdout
drwxrwxr-x   2 root     sys          512 Mar 26 04:56 swap
crw--w----   1 root     tty        0,  0 Mar 26 17:12 syscon
crw--w----   1 root     tty        0,  0 Mar 26 04:56 systty
crw-rw-rw-   1 root     sys       26,  0 Apr 23 16:20 ttyp0
crw-rw-rw-   1 root     sys       26,  1 Apr 23 16:20 ttyp1
crw-rw-rw-   1 root     sys       26,  2 Apr 23 16:20 ttyp2
crw-rw-rw-   1 root     sys       26,  3 Apr 23 16:20 ttyp3
crw-rw-rw-   1 root     sys       26,  4 Apr 23 16:20 ttyp4
crw-rw-rw-   1 root     sys       26,  5 Apr 23 16:20 ttyp5
```

The first character of each line is always **b**, **c**, **d**, **l**, or **p** for block, character, directory, symbolic link, or named pipe (see following section). Solaris 2.6 added two new file types: **D** for door, and **s** for AF-UNIX style socket. Doors are a new interprocess communication mechanism. The next nine characters represent the permissions for the file, followed by the number of hard links and the names of the owner and group. Where the number of bytes in a file would appear for an ordinary or directory file, a device file shows its *major* and *minor device numbers* separated by a comma (see below). The rest of the line is the same as any other **ls –l** listing.

Some devices are stored in subdirectories of **/dev**. The **/dev/dsk** and **/dev/rdsk** subdirectories contain entries that represent hard disk drives. The **/dev/rmt** subdirectory contains entries that represent magnetic tape drives. Many of the device files in these subdirectories also appear as symbolic links in the parent directory, **/dev**.

▲▲▲ Fifo Special Files (Named Pipes)

The *fifo special* files, also called *named pipes,* represent pipes: You read from and write to the file to read from and write to the pipe. The term *fifo* stands for *first in, first out*—the way any pipe works. The first information that you put in one end is the first information that comes out the other end. When you use a pipe on a command line to send the output of a program to the printer, the printer prints the information in the same order that the program produced it and sent it into the pipe.

Unless you are writing sophisticated programs, you will not be working with fifo special files. However many of the programs that you use on Solaris, including the windowing system and file manager, use named pipes for interprocess communication. The following list shows **X0**, a named pipe.

```
# ls -l /var/X/.X11-pipe
-rw-rw-rw-   1 root            0 Mar 19 16:38 X0
```

The X Window System display uses this pipe. Programs that are X clients such as **xterm** and **mailtool** use this file to communicate with the X server (your display).

The UNIX/Solaris system has had pipes for many generations. Without named pipes, however, only processes that were children of the same ancestor could exchange information using pipes. Using named pipes, *any* two processes on a single machine can exchange information. One program writes to a fifo special file. Another program reads from the same file. The programs do not have to run at the same time or be aware of each other's activity. The operating system handles all buffering and information storage. The term *asynchronous* (*async*) applies to this type of communication because the programs on the two ends of the pipe do not have to be synchronized.

▲▲▲ Sockets

Like fifo special files, sockets allow asynchronous processes that are not children of the same ancestor to exchange information. Sockets are the central mechanism of the interprocess communication that is the basis of the networking facility. When you use networking utilities, pairs of cooperating sockets manage the communication between the processes on your computer and the remote computer. Sockets form the basis of utilities such as **rlogin** (remote login) and **rcp** (remote copy).

Solaris 2.6 separated UNIX domain sockets (marked with an **s** [for socket] in an **ls –l** listing) from fifos (marked with a **p** [for pipe]) as types of special files. In previous versions of Solaris, sockets and fifos shared the same kernel implementation and were both designated with a **p**.

▲▲▲ Major and Minor Device Numbers

A *major device number* represents a class of hardware devices: A terminal, printer, tape drive, disk drive, and so on. In the preceding list of the **/dev** directory, all the terminals have a major device number of 26.

A *minor device number* represents a particular piece of hardware within a class. Although all the terminals are grouped together by their major device number, each has a different minor device number (**ttyp0** is 0, **ttyp1** is 1, and so on). This setup allows one piece of software (the device driver) to service all similar hardware, while being able to distinguish among different physical units.

▲▲▲ Block and Character Devices

This section describes typical device drivers. Because device drivers can be changed to suit a particular purpose, the descriptions in this section may not pertain to every system.

A *block device* is an I/O (input/output) device that is characterized by

- the ability to perform random-access reads

- a specific block size

- handling only single blocks of data at a time

- accepting only transactions that involve whole blocks of data

- being able to have a filesystem mounted on it

- having the kernel buffer its input and output

- appearing to the operating system as a series of blocks numbered from 0 through $n - 1$, where n is the number of blocks on the device

The standard block devices on a Solaris system are disk media such as hard and floppy disks and CDROM drives.

A *character device* is any device that is not a block device. Some examples of character devices are printers, terminals, tape drives, and modems.

The device driver for a character device determines how a program reads from and writes to the device. For example the device driver for a terminal allows a program to read the information you type on the terminal in two ways. A program can read single characters from a terminal in *raw* mode (that is, without the driver doing any interpretation of the characters). This mode has nothing to do with the *raw device* described in the following section. Alternatively a program can read a line at a time. When a program reads a line at a time, the driver handles the erase and kill characters, so that the program never sees typing mistakes and corrections. In this case the program reads everything from the beginning of a line to the RETURN that ends a line; the number of characters in a line can vary.

▲▲▲ Raw Devices

Device driver programs for block devices usually have two entry points so that they can be used in two ways: As block devices *or* as character devices. The character device form of a block device is called a *raw* device. A raw device is characterized by

- direct I/O (no buffering through the kernel)

- a one-to-one correspondence between system calls and hardware requests

- device-dependent restrictions on I/O

An example of a utility that uses a raw device is **fsck**. It is more efficient for **fsck** to operate on the disk as a raw device, not restricted by the fixed size of blocks in the block device interface. Because **fsck** has full knowledge of the underlying filesystem structure, it can operate on the raw device using the largest possible units. When a filesystem is mounted, processes normally access the disk through the block device interface. This explains why it is important to allow **fsck** to modify only an unmounted filesystem. Otherwise there would be the danger that another process would change a disk block using the block device, while **fsck** was rearranging the underlying structure through the raw device, resulting in a corrupted filesystem.

▲ Volume Management

The Solaris volume management daemon is named **vold**. This daemon runs in the background when your system is in multiuser mode and handles removable media such as floppy drives and CDROMs. Although not available yet, the framework is in place for future support of ZIP and/or JAZZ drives.

▲▲ CDROM

When you insert a CDROM into a Solaris machine, **vold** recognizes the event and mounts the CDROM in the **/cdrom** directory.[12]

When **vold** sees that a new disk is available, it creates a subdirectory under **/cdrom** named with the volume name of the CDROM. For instance when you insert the Solaris Documentation CDROM, **vold** creates a new mount point in **/cdrom** named **solaris_2_6_documentation**. All of the CDROM files are available under this directory. Also, **vold** creates a link to this directory named **/cdrom/cdrom0** (a second drive would create a link named **/cdrom/cdrom1**). A link with a known name is useful when you want to access the CDROM from an automated process such as a shell script.

Give the following command when you are done with a CDROM.

```
$ eject cdrom
```

If you have multiple CDROM drives attached to your machine, specify cdrom0 or cdrom1 as the CDROM to be ejected.

▲▲ Floppy Disk

Currently, PC and Sparc floppy drives cannot tell when you insert a disk and you must inform **vold** when a floppy has been inserted into the drive: Choose the **File** menu from the **File Manager** window and select **Check for Floppy** (OpenWindows) or **Open Floppy** (CDE). Or choose **Open Floppy** from the **Front Panel File Manager** Control (CDE). When **vold** detects the new floppy, it opens a **File Manager** window that displays and allows you to work with the files on the floppy. You can also give **volcheck** from the command line.

Just as **vold** mounts CDROMs in **/cdrom** (preceding section), it mounts floppy disks in **/floppy**. You can work with MS Windows/DOS or Solaris floppies. However you can run only Solaris executables (not MS Windows/DOS programs). You can even store Solaris executable files on a DOS diskette.

When you are done with the floppy, you can type **eject** in a shell window or choose the **File** menu from the **File Manager** window and select Eject (CDE). If you are running OpenWindows, click on the Eject Floppy button within the **File Manager** window.

To format a floppy disk, insert the disk into the floppy drive and give the following command:

```
$ fdformat
```

Use a **–d** option if you want an MS Windows/DOS format floppy (equivalent to the MS Windows/DOS **format** command. Once you have formatted your floppy for DOS, you can use the **File Manager** to mount the disk.

---

12. The **vold** daemon recognizes both UFS and HSFS (High Sierra filesystem) format, allowing you to read standard CDROMs that are readable on DOS and MS Windows platforms.

Disable Volume Management

If you need to access a floppy or CDROM as a raw device, you must first disable volume management. For instance if you have a CDROM writer attached to a Solaris system, you must tell volume management not to use this device, or you will not be able to write CDROMs with it. One solution to this problem is to disable volume management by giving the following command while you are logged in as root:

```
# sh /etc/init.d/volmgt stop
```

The other solution is to modify **/etc/vold.conf** and restart the volume management daemon (**vold**).

If your CDROM writer is SCSI ID 5, and your **vold.conf** has an entry that looks like this:

```
use cdrom drive /dev/rdsk/c*s2 dev_cdrom.so cdrom%d
```

change the above entry to ignore the CD writer by changing the entry to this:

```
use cdrom drive /dev/rdsk/c*[0-46]s2 dev_cdrom.so cdrom%d
```

Then restart **vold** by running:

```
# sh /etc/init.d/volmgt stop; sh /etc/init.d/volmgt start
```

Occasionally you will need to disable volume management when you get a floppy disk that holds a **tar** file or **cpio** archive, or is a non-DOS, non-UFS diskette. Proceed to stop volume management as described above. When you are finished working with the floppy, enable volume management again with the following command:

```
# sh /etc/init.d/volmgt start
```

▲ Day-to-Day System Administration

In addition to bringing up and shutting down the system, you have other responsibilities as the system administrator. This section covers the most important of these responsibilities.

▲▲ Adding and Removing Users

More than a login name is required for a user to be able to log in and use the system. A user must have the necessary files, directories, permissions, and optionally a password in order to log in. Minimally a user must have an entry in the **/etc/passwd** and **/etc/shadow** files and a home directory. Refer to the system manuals if you want to run a Network Information Service (NIS or NIS+) to manage the **passwd** database.

▲▲▲ Add a New User

The **useradd** utility makes it easy to add new user accounts to your system. By default **useradd** assigns the next highest unused user ID to a new account and specifies the Bourne Shell as the user's login shell. The following example also creates the user's home directory (in **/usr/home**), specifies the user's group ID, and puts the user's full name in the comment field.

```
# useradd -m -d /usr/home -g 100 -c "Alex Watson" alex
```

To give the user a password, use the **passwd** utility with the user's login name as an argument. Because you are logged in as Superuser, **passwd** does not ask you for the old password, even if there is one. Because of this special treatment, you can give a user a new password if the old one is forgotten.

```
# passwd alex
Changing password for alex.
New password:
Type new password again:
```

To test the new setup, log in as the new user, and create an appropriate **.profile** or **.login** and **.cshrc** file in the new user's home directory. (You may have to manually assign a value to and export the **TERM** shell variable if you want to use **vi** to create this file [see page 987].) It is a common practice to have a default **.login** or **.profile** file that you can copy into each new user's home directory. If there are default copies of these files in a directory named **/etc/skel**, **useradd** will copy them to the new user's home directory automatically if you use the **–m** option; the path **/etc/skel** is a default which can be changed with the **–k** option. The following command modifies the home directory and shell for the **passwd** entry that you added with **useradd**:

```
# passmgmt -m -h /home/alex -s /bin/ksh alex
```

For more information on adding and modifying **passwd** file entries, see the **useradd**, **passmgmt**, and **usermod man** pages.

▲▲▲ Remove a User

If appropriate, make a backup copy of all the files belonging to the user before deleting them.

The **userdel** utility makes it easy to delete old user accounts from your system. The following command will remove **alex**'s account, his home directory, and all his files.

```
# userdel -r alex
```

To turn off a user's account temporarily, you can use **usermod** to change the expiration date for the account. The following command line will prevent **alex** from logging in, because it specifies that his account expired in the past (December 31, 1989).

```
# usermod -e "12/31/89" alex
```

▲▲▲ Add a Group

Just as **useradd** adds a new user to the system, **groupadd** adds a new group by adding an entry to **/etc/group**. The first example below demonstrates creating a new group named **rtfm** for users who are allowed to update the online manual pages.

```
# groupadd -g 1024 rtfm
```

Unless you use the **–g** option to assign a group ID, the system picks the next available sequential number greater than 100. The **–o** option allows the group ID to be non-unique if you want to have multiple names for the same group ID.

The analogue of **userdel** for groups is **groupdel**, which takes a group name as an argument. You can also use **groupmod** to change the name or group id of a group as in the following examples:

```
# groupmod -g 1025 rtfm
# groupmod -n manuals rtfm
```

The first example gives the previously created **rtfm** group a new group ID. The second example renames the **rtfm** group **manuals**.

Group ID Cautions

The **groupmod** utility does not change group numbers in **/etc/passwd** when you renumber a group. You must edit **/etc/passwd** and change the entries yourself. If you change the number of a group, files that belonged to the group will no longer belong to the group. They may belong to no group or to another group with the old group ID.

▲▲▲ admintool

Sun provides **admintool**, a graphical user interface that allows you to add, remove, and modify users, groups, hosts, printers, serial ports, and software. It is intended for local administration, not a distributed environment. Start **admintool** by giving the command **admintool** on a terminal emulation window or by selecting System_Admin from the Application Manager window and then selecting Admintool. The **admintool** utility includes a comprehensive help system that is available by clicking on help in the upper-right corner of the window. Refer to "Add a Printer Using admintool" on page 641.

▲▲ Adding and Removing Software Packages

A package is the collection of scripts, files, and directories required to run a software application. Using packages makes it easier to transfer, install, and uninstall applications. Solaris has a set of *core,* or required, packages and a set of optional packages. The core packages include the core root (SUNWcsr), the core usr (SUNWcsu), and the core devices (SUNWcsd) packages. Optional packages include the X imaging library (SUNWxil), the X graphics library (SUNWxgl), and many of the internationalization packages for multibyte character sets such as Chinese (ASCII uses a single byte to represent each character).

During the initial installation of Solaris, you were given the option of installing the entire distribution, developer system support, end-user system support, or basic core system support. The entire distribution includes all packages from the CDROM and requires a lot of disk space. You can also customize which packages you want installed, and add or remove packages after the install is complete. Use **pkginfo** to get a list of one-line summaries of all packages installed on your system (any user can run this utility). Use **pkginfo** followed by the name of the package to get information about a particular package. For instance **pkginfo SUNWcsr** will give you information about the core Solaris2 root package. To get more detailed information, such as the date the package was installed, number, type and size of files in the package, and the package version, use the **–l** flag. Here is an example of issuing **pkginfo** on a typical SPARC machine:

```
$ pkinfo -l SUNWcsr
PKGINST:  SUNWcsr
NAME:  Core Solaris, (Root)
CATEGORY:  system
ARCH:  sparc
VERSION:  11.6.0,REV=1997.07.15.21.46
BASEDIR:  /
VENDOR:  Sun Microsystems, Inc.
DESC:  core software for a specific instruction-set architecture
PSTAMP:  on297m15214751
INSTDATE:  Mar 24 1998 12:44
HOTLINE:  Please contact your local service provider
STATUS:  completely installed
FILES:     506 installed pathnames
50 shared pathnames
55 linked files
78 directories
166 executables
21308 blocks used (approx)
```

If you find that there is a package that you forgot to install, or did not anticipate needing, you can install it with the **pkgadd** utility. Use the **–d** flag to point to the directory where all of the packages are located (usually on the CDROM). For example while logged in as **root**, use the following command to add the Sun automated security enhancement tools (ASET) from the CDROM for the SPARC version of Solaris 7:

```
# pkgadd -d /cdrom/sol_7_sparc_sun_srvr/s0/Solaris_2.7/Product SUNWast
```

Refer to the **pkgadd man** page for other options you can use to customize placement of a package. To remove the same package (if you are running short of disk space), log in as **root** and give the following command:

```
# pkgrm SUNWast
```

You do not have to tell **pkgrm** where the package is installed, it queries the system to find out the information it needs to uninstall the package. The **pkgrm** utility removes links, unloads device drivers, and stops daemons as necessary.

▲▲ Web Start

Web Start (Figure 15-1), which has a graphical user interface, makes it easier to install software, including the Solaris software group, Solstice utilities, and

Figure 15-1   The Web Start logo

other copackaged software. It allows you to tailor the software selection to meet your needs, or, if you prefer, you can use default values throughout. It runs in local mode from the computer you are installing the software on, or in Client-Server mode from any desktop on your LAN. Because Web Start requires bitmapped graphics and a frame buffer,[13] the Client-Server mode is useful when you want to install software on a machine without these features, such as a *headless server* (a machine without a display).

To use Web Start to install software on an existing system, put the CDROM in the drive and reboot the system from the CDROM (or just run the appropriate program if you are not installing from scratch). The Web Start window should appear, giving you further instructions.

One of the functions of Web Start is setting up a new system. First it creates root and swap partitions, in a size you can choose, on the system disk and then sets up the system and other disks, allowing you to lay out the partitions/filesystems as you wish (Customized installation option). By default Web Start creates a **/opt** partition; you cannot store copackaged software anywhere else.[14] Although it allows you to install localized (various language) versions of Solaris, you cannot remove the English version. Web Start does not install system upgrades.

Web Start Can Destroy All of Your Data

Web Start will install Solaris over a previous version. Doing so destroys everything on the system disk and potentially data on other disks.

▲▲ Patches

As operating system bugs (problems or errors in the source code) are found and fixed by Sun Microsystems, Sun generates files, called patches, that you can use to fix the problems on your system.[15] Installing a patch is much simpler than installing a new version of the operating system. Patches make it possible for Sun to release fixes to Solaris between versions. Some of these problems that patches fix are security holes that may compromise the security of the system and some are bugs that could cause the system to crash or just cause programs not to run correctly. Most of the important patches are publicly available via anonymous **ftp** from **sunsolve.sun.com**. Log in to this **ftp** site as **anonymous** and give your email address as your password. Refer to "How Do I Use ftp?" on page 974. Once you are logged on, **cd** to the **pub/patches** directory. Display a list of files that pertains to your version of the operating system and hardware (SPARC or Intel). The following example shows how to get a list of files for Solaris 2.6. Files that start with **2.6_** are for SPARC machines and those that start with **2.6_x86_** are for Intel machines. Substitute the version number of your operating system in place of 2.6.

---

13. A frame buffer is memory that temporarily stores a full frame of picture data coupled with hardware that drives a monitor.

14. The **/opt** directory is your only choice according to the Sun documentation. However by using symbolic links or automounted filesystems, you can fool Web Start into thinking it is installing in **/opt** while actually installing elsewhere.

15. This discussion is limited to Operating System patches and does not cover patches that are applied to other programs. Refer to page 851 in Part III for more information on **patch**, the utility that applies patches to programs other than the Operating System.

```
ftp> cd pub/patches
250 CWD command successful.
ftp> ls 2.6*
200 PORT command successful.
150 Opening ASCII mode data connection for file list.
2.6_Recommended.README
2.6_Recommended.tar.Z
2.6_x86_Recommended.README
2.6_x86_Recommended.tar.Z
226 Transfer complete.
remote: 2.6*
102 bytes received in 0.015 seconds (6.45 Kbytes/s)
ftp>
```

Download and read the **README** file for your OS and architecture. This file includes background and instructions on installing the recommended patches. If you decide to install the patches, download the **tar.z** file that corresponds to the **README** file you just downloaded and follow the instructions in the **README** file.

If you want to install a single patch, download the patch file, uncompress it, and read the **README** file included in the archive you just downloaded. The **README** file has information about which hardware the patch should be applied to, which patches must be applied simultaneously, and which are mutually exclusive or conflicting.

Which Patch Program to Use?

The **installpatch** utility is being phased out. Starting with Solaris 2.6 use **patchadd** to install patches instead of any included **installpatch** script. A patch for **patchadd** is available as patch number 106125 for SPARC and 106126 for Intel platforms. Apply this patch before all others as it will significantly increase the speed of installing all other patches.

Continue to use **installpatch** on versions earlier than 2.6. Use the following instructions, substituting **patchadd** for **installpatch**.

The **patchadd** utility cross-references the patch information with the packages that are installed on your system. If **patchadd** determines that this patch is for a package or packages that are not installed, it will terminate installation. Following is an example of installing patch 106126-06 and then removing it:

```
# uncompress 106126-06.tar.Z
# tar xf 106126-06.tar
# cd 106126-06
# more README.106126-06
  .
  .
# /usr/sbin/patchadd .

Checking installed patches...
Verifying sufficient filesystem capacity (dry run method)...
Installing patch packages...
```

```
Patch number 106126-06 has been successfully installed.
See /var/sadm/patch/106126-06/log for details

Patch packages installed:
SUNWswmt
```

/usr/sbin/patchrm 106126-06

```
Checking installed packages and patches...

Backing out patch 106126-06...

Patch 106126-06 has been backed out.
```

Check the patch list regularly to see if your system is up to date. Alternatively you can join one or more of the security-related mailing lists to stay informed about new patch releases as they become available. Refer to "What Are Some Useful Mailing Lists?" on page 966.

Sun provides a different patch area for contract customers. The public area has most, but not all, of the recommended system patches. An example of a patch that may not be available in the public area is a patch that contains encryption software, which is prohibited by U.S. law from leaving North America.

▲▲ Backing Up Files

One of the most neglected tasks of the system administrator is making backup copies of files on a regular basis. The backup copies are vital in two instances: When the system malfunctions and files are lost, and when a user (or the system administrator) deletes or corrupts a file by accident. Even if you set up RAID striping with parity, or a mirror, you still need to maintain a backup. Although mirrors and RAID are useful for fault tolerance (disk failure), they will not help in the event of catastrophic system failure (fire, flood, and so on) or accidental removal or corruption of a file. It is a good idea to have a written backup policy and to keep copies of backups offsite (in another building, at home, or at a completely different facility or campus if possible).

You must back up the filesystems on a regular basis. Backup files are usually kept on magnetic tape or other removable media. Exactly how often you should back up which files depends on your system and needs. The criterion is, "If the system crashes, how much work are you willing to lose?" Ideally you would back up all the files on the system every few minutes so that you would never lose more than a few minutes of work.

The trade-off is, "How often are you willing to back up the files?" The backup procedure typically slows down the machine for other users, takes a certain amount of your time, and requires that you have and store the media (tape or disk) that you keep the backup on. Avoid backing up an active filesystem; the results may be inconsistent and restoring from the backup may be impossible. This requirement is a function of the backup program and the filesystem you are backing up.

Another question is when to run the backup? Unless you kick the users off and bring the machine down to single-user mode (not a very user-friendly practice), you want to do it when the machine is its quietest. Depending on the use of the machine, sometime in the middle of the night can work well. Then the backup is least likely to impact the users and the files are not likely to change as they are being read for backup.

UFS (UNIX Filesystem) is the default Solaris filesystem and **ufsdump** is the default backup program. There are many programs available that let you back up active filesystems. Two such programs are *Legato Networker* (which comes with Solaris when you buy a server license) and the *Veritas FileSystem (VxFS)*, which Sun sells as a direct replacement for UFS. VxFS has a utility program that lets you back up an active filesystem without any special third-party backup program.

A *full* backup makes copies of all files, regardless of when they were created or accessed. An *incremental* backup makes copies of the files that have been created or modified since the last (usually full) backup.

The more people using the machine, the more often you should back up the filesystems. A common schedule might have you perform an incremental backup one or two times a day and a full backup one or two times a week.

▲▲▲ ufsdump, ufsrestore: Backup and Restore Files

The **ufsdump** utility backs up an entire filesystem, or it backs up only those files that have changed since the last **ufsdump**. The **ufsrestore** utility restores either an entire filesystem, an individual file, or piece of the filesystem hierarchy (a directory and its descendents). You will get the best results if you perform a backup on a quiet (the classic UNIX term is *quiescent*) system so that the files are not changing as you make the backup.

The following command performs a complete backup of all files (including directories and special files) on the **root** (/) partition:

```
# ufsdump 0uf /dev/rmt/0 /
```

The option specifies that the whole filesystem is to be backed up (a full backup). There are ten dump levels: 0–9. Zero is the highest (most complete) level and always backs up the entire filesystem. Each additional level is incremental with respect to the level above it. For example 1 is incremental to 0 and only backs up files that have changed since the last level 0 dump. Level 2 is incremental to 1 and only backs up files that have changed since the last level 1 dump, and so on. You can construct a very flexible schedule using this scheme. Also, you do not need to use sequential numbers for backup levels. It is all right to perform a level 0 dump, followed by level 2 and 5 dumps.

The **u** indicates that the **/etc/dumpdates** file (page 609) will be updated with filesystem, date, and dump level information for use by the next incremental dump. The **f** option and its argument (**/dev/rmt/0**) specify that the backup will be written to a file named **/dev/rmt/0** (a tape drive).

The following command makes a partial backup containing all files that have changed since the last level 0 dump. The first argument is a 1 specifying a level 1 dump.

```
# ufsdump 1uf /dev/rmt/0 /
```

To restore an entire filesystem from a tape, first restore the most recent complete (level 0) backup. Do this carefully, because **ufsrestore** can overwrite the existing filesystem. When you are logged in as Superuser, **cd** to the directory the filesystem is mounted on, and give the following command:

```
# ufsrestore if /dev/rmt/0
```

The **i** option invokes an interactive mode that allows you to choose which files and directories you would like to restore. As with **ufsdump**, the **f** option specifies the name of the device that the backup tape is mounted on. When **ufsrestore** finishes load the next lower level (higher number) dump tape and issue the same **ufsrestore** command. If you have multiple incremental dumps at a particular level, always restore with the most recent one. You do not need to invoke **ufsrestore** with any special arguments to restore an incremental dump; it will restore whatever is on the tape.

You can also use **ufsrestore** to extract individual files from a tape by using the **x** option and specifying the filenames on the command line. Whenever you restore a file, the restored file will be in your working directory. Make sure you are in the right directory before restoring files. The following commands restore the **etc/inetd.conf** file from the tape in **/dev/rmt/0**. The filename of the dumped file does not begin with a **/** because all dumped pathnames are relative to the filesystem that you dumped—in this case **/**. Because the restore command is given from the **/** directory, the file will be restored to its original location: **/etc/inetd.conf**.

```
# cd /
# ufsrestore xf /dev/rmt/0 etc/inetd.conf
```

If you use the **x** option without specifying a file or directory name to extract, the entire dumped filesystem is extracted. Use the **r** option to restore an entire filesystem without having to go through the interactive interface. The following command restores the filesystem from the tape on **/dev/rmt/0** into the working directory without interaction.

```
# ufsrestore rf /dev/rmt/0
```

You can also use **ufsdump** and **ufsrestore** to access a tape drive on another system over the network. There are detailed examples of backing up and restoring across a network in the **ufsdump** and **ufsrestore** **man** pages.

Occasionally **ufsrestore** will prompt you with:

```
You have not read any volumes yet.
Unless you know which volume your file(s) are on you should start
with the last volume and work towards the first.
Specify next volume #:
```

Enter **1** (one) in response to this prompt. If the filesystem spans more than one tape or disk, this prompt allows you to switch tapes.

At the end of the dump, you will receive another prompt:

```
set owner/mode for '.'? [yn]
```

Answer **y** to this prompt when restoring entire filesystems or files that have been accidentally removed. Doing so will restore the appropriate permissions to the files and directories being restored. Answer **n** if you are restoring a dump to a directory other than the one it was dumped from; the working directory permissions and owner will be set to those of the person doing the restore (typically **root**).

After you have completed a dump, the tape drive automatically rewinds to the beginning of the tape. If you do not want the tape drive to rewind, use the non-rewinding tape device **/dev/rmt/0n**. This device allows you to back up multiple filesystems to one volume. Following is an example of backing up a system where the **root**, **/usr**, and **/var** directories are on different filesystems.

```
# ufsdump 0uf /dev/rmt/0n /
# ufsdump 0uf /dev/rmt/0n /usr
# ufsdump 0uf /dev/rmt/0 /var
```

The **/dev/rmt** directory has 24 different device names that can access the **/dev/rmt/0** device. Each name accesses a different minor device number that controls some aspect of how the tape drive is used. The most useful device names are **/dev/rmt//0n** for non-rewinding and **/dev/rmt//0c** (or **/dev/rmt//0cn**) for compression (if your drive supports hardware compression). The preceding example uses the non-rewinding device for the first two dumps. If you use the rewinding device, the tape will rewind after each dump and you will only be left with the last dump on the tape. For a complete list of options and parameters and what they mean, consult the **mtio man** page. This **man** page documents the magnetic tape I/O interfaces and options.

You can use the **mt** (magnetic tape) utility to manipulate files on a multivolume dump tape. The following commands position (**mt**) and restore (**ufsrestore**) the **/var** filesystem from the previous example.

```
# mt -f /dev/rmt/0 fsf 2
# ufsrestore rf /dev/rmt/0
```

▲▲ Add/Remove Devices: Reconfigure Reboot

On occasion you will need to add or remove hardware devices from the system. For many devices, such as external modems and printers, you need only plug in the device and set up the appropriate software. In some cases, such as when you install or remove SCSI or IDE devices, video boards, or interface boards, you need to tell your system that you have added or removed a component.

To allow the system to probe the new configuration, bring the system down, turn it off, unplug it, add or remove the device, plug it back in, turn it on, and do one of the following.

1. *From a SPARC platform:* Bring the system up to the PROM mode (to stop the normal boot progression, press and hold the Stop key on your keyboard and then press the **a** key after the RAM selftest has completed). Then from the **OK** prompt type:

   ```
   OK boot -r
   ```

2. *From an Intel or SPARC platform:* From the > prompt on a SPARC machine or the Select boot (b) or interpreter (i) prompt on an x86 machine, type:

   ```
   > b -r
   ```

In both cases the **–r** flag tells the system to reconfigure as it reboots. It will probe all devices on internal and external buses to see what is attached to the system. Based on its findings the system dynamically rebuilds the **/devices** and **/dev** directories.

Another way to add or remove a controller on either a SPARC or Intel machine is to create a file named **reconfigure** in the **/** directory and reboot. You can use the following command to create the file:

```
# touch /reconfigure
```

With the file in place, bring the system down and back up as usual. Booting with the **/reconfigure** file in place is equivalent to booting with the **b –r** command (above). With either method Solaris displays messages as it comes up telling you it is rebuilding the **/devices** and **/dev** directories.

▲▲ Add/Remove Drivers

There are several ways to install/uninstall drivers. You can perform a reconfigure reboot (preceding section), or you can bring your system up after you have added or removed the device, log in as **root**, and issue the following commands (skip the **disks** command if you just added a tape or jukebox and skip **tapes** if you just added a disk):

```
# drvconfig
# disks
# tapes
# devlinks
```

This sequence of commands will only work if you are adding an additional device (such as a hard disk) to an existing controller, not when you are adding a new controller board (such as a hard disk controller—ISA, PCI, or SBUS) to the system.

> ### Reboot after Removing a Device
>
> It is important to perform a reconfigure reboot when you remove a device from the system. Although your system will continue to function without a reconfigure reboot, it is poor house-keeping and can lead to confusion, particularly if there is more than one administrator.
>
> Before removing a hard disk from the system and reconfiguring, remove the **/etc/vfstab** entry for that disk.

▲▲ Disk Capacity Planning/Partitioning

A *partition* (also called a *slice*) is a section of a (hard) disk that has a name so you can address it separately from other sections. Under DOS/MS Windows partitions (and sometimes whole disks) were labeled with **C:**, **D:**, and so on. This section discusses how to set up partitions under UNIX/Solaris.

Before you use a new disk or install Solaris on a disk for the first time, the disk must be formatted and labeled. In practice any disk you get will already be formatted by the manufacturer; you may need to label it with a Solaris disk label. To label a disk run **format** (next section); you will see a message telling you that the disk does not have a valid label and asking if you would like to label it. Answer **yes** and **format** will label the disk.

It can be difficult to plan your partition sizes appropriately if you are new to Solaris. For this reason many people choose to have only two partitions. Slice 1 is reserved for the swap partition, which can be any size, from 0 up to many hundreds of megabytes or, rarely, gigabytes, and slice 0 is designated as **root** and contains the remainder of the disk space. This makes managing space much easier. But if a program runs amok, the entire disk can fill up and system accounting and logging information (which may contain data that can tell you what went wrong) may be lost. For this reason you may want to make **/var** a separate slice.

Because it holds the bulk of system logs, package information, and accounting data, having **/var** in a separate partition can be advantageous. If a user runs a job that uses up all the disk space, the logs will not be affected. A good size for the **/var** partition is anything from about 30MB up to 150MB for extremely active systems with many verbose daemons. Systems serving as license servers for licensed software often fall into this category.

It is also common strategy to put user home directories into their own, separate partition. If you do not have a separate disk for the home directories, then putting them in their own partition can avoid some problems. Common partition names are **/export/home** and **/usr/home**.

Some sites choose to separate the **root** and **/usr** partitions. This can be useful if you want to export **/usr** to another machine and want the extra security that separate partitions can give. By itself the root partition usually consumes less than 30MB of disk space. On occasions you may install a special program that has many kernel drivers that consume a lot of space in the root partition. If you run into this situation, you need to adjust the space allotted to the root partition accordingly. The size of **/usr** will depend greatly on the number of OS packages you install. If you chose to install all packages from the CDROM, you will need about 600MB of disk space.

Finally **/opt** is another candidate for separation. If you plan to install a large number of software packages in addition to Solaris, you may want to keep them in a separate partition. If you install the additional software in the same partition as the users, for example it may start to encroach user's home directories. Many sites keep all the **/opt** software on one server and export it to others. If you choose to create a **/opt** partition, its size should be appropriate to the software you plan to install.

▲▲▲ format: Partitioning a Disk

Many times when you add a new disk, simply getting the system to recognize the disk is not enough. In order for the disk to be useful, it must be labeled and partitioned appropriately. Solaris will normally get the disk configuration information (number of cylinders, tracks, sectors/track, and more) automatically by querying the disk.

When you log in as **root** and start the **format** utility, it displays a numbered list of disks, starting with zero. Each disk entry includes its device representation and its absolute hardware path and instance. Choose the number of the disk you want to work with. Most disks come from the manufacturer with a suitable label; if the disk you select lacks a suitable label, **format** asks if you want to label it (answer *yes*). If the disk you want to work with is not in the list, it may be that you did not perform a reconfigure reboot to update the list of attached devices.

The **format** program has many options for analyzing, repairing, and partitioning a disk. Although formatting and repairing are sometimes necessary, you will use **format** mostly to partition disks. Partitioning allows you divide a disk into a maximum of eight separate *partitions* or subdisks. You can use each partition independently for swap devices, filesystems, databases, or other functions. When you select the disk you want to work with, you will see the `format>` prompt. To get to the partitioning submenu, enter **partition, part,** or just **p**.[16] You will see the `partition>` prompt. To see a list of all currently defined partitions, enter **print** or **p** from this submenu. The format utility will display something like the following:

---

16. The `partition` prompt is for SCSI disks. See "**fdisk**: Partitioning a Disk" on page 638 if you are working with an IDE disk.

```
partition> p
Current partition table (original):
Total disk cylinders available: 4824 + 2 (reserved cylinders)

Part      Tag    Flag    Cylinders        Size           Blocks
  0       root    wm      0 -  187      40.02MB    (188/0/0)     81968
  1       swap    wu    188 - 1597     300.18MB    (1410/0/0)   614760
  2       backup  wm      0 - 4823       1.00GB    (4824/0/0)  2103264
  3    unassigned wm      0                  0     (0/0/0)           0
  4        var    wm   1598 - 1950      75.15MB    (353/0/0)    153908
  5    unassigned wm      0                  0     (0/0/0)           0
  6        usr    wm   1951 - 3712     375.11MB    (1762/0/0)  `768232
  7    unassigned wm   3713 - 4823     236.52MB    (1111/0/0)   484396

partition>
```

Notice that partition 2 defines the entire disk. This is a convention. It is a good idea to leave partition 2 alone as a reference point. Some people also use partition 2 to make a filesystem if they wish to use the entire disk as one filesystem. Following are guidelines to remember when defining a partition table for a disk. For more information see "Disk Capacity Planning/Partitioning" on page 635.

1. Do not modify partition 2. This partition is called the **backup** or **overlap** partition.

2. Do not overlap partitions that contain data. If the first partition ends at cylinder 187, then the second one should begin at cylinder 188. If you overlap partitions, the filesystem will become corrupt as data for overlapping files is written to the disk. Because partition 2 contains no data or filesystem, it is safe to have other partitions overlapping it.

3. There are only a few tags that are defined. The tags are relatively meaningless at this time. When you are asked to choose a tag, you may choose one of the predefined tags (see below) or leave it unassigned as the default.

4. Older disks used a constant number of sectors per track. This made positioning the disk head easier but resulted in a lot of wasted space on the outer tracks. Newer disks use an encoding called ZBR, which stands for Zone-Bit Recording. This means that the sector size of the disk stays constant, which means that the outer cylinders have more sectors, and consequently more information passes under the disk head per disk revolution and data access is faster on these sectors. These outer cylinders correspond to the lower cylinders (cylinders starting at zero). Put your speed-critical data on the lower-numbered cylinders.

5. Never put a raw partition on cylinder 0. A few sectors on cylinder 0 are reserved for things like the disk label, bad block, and partition tables. A filesystem will preserve this information. But if you use this area for a raw partition, this information will be deleted and the disk may become unusable. An example of a raw partition is a raw database partition such as is used for a Sybase or Oracle database. Except for swap space, start all raw partitions at cylinder 1 or greater. For more information see "swap" on page 618.

6. By convention **root** is kept on partition 0, **swap** on partition 1, **/var** on partition 3 or 4, and **/usr** on partition 6. Often **/export** or **/opt** is kept on partition 5 or 7. Many people choose to combine **root**, **/var**, and **/usr** into partition 0, which generally results in less wasted space.

7. When using megabytes to specify the size of a partition, remember to check how many cylinders have been allocated so that you know where to begin the next partition.

Following is the sequence of commands necessary to define partition 1 (shown above) on a clean disk:

```
partition> 1
Part      Tag     Flag    Cylinders       Size            Blocks
  5 unassigned    wm        0             0          (0/0/0)              0

Enter partition id tag[unassigned]: swap
Enter partition permission flags[wm]:
Enter new starting cyl[0]: 188
Enter partition size[0b, 0c, 0.00mb, 0.00gb]: 300m
partition> p
```

The **wm** flags entry means that the partition is writable and mountable—you will probably never need to modify the **flags**. After defining a partition using **m** or **g** to specify megabytes or gigabytes, always run **print** to check for the ending cylinder. Do this before defining the next contiguous partition so that you do not waste space or have any overlap.

Once you are done defining partitions, label the disk using the **label** command from the `format>` or `partition>` prompt. Then quit **format** and run **newfs** on each partition that is to hold a filesystem. Refer to AnswerBook2 for more information.

▲▲▲ fdisk: Partitioning a Disk

The **fdisk** utility can modify a fixed disk partition table on an IDE disk (Intel machine). If you are familiar with the DOS/MS Windows **fdisk** program, the Solaris utility of the same name should be a welcome improvement. It offers interactive and batch modes for updating disk partitions and allows you to set up a disk to handle both DOS/MS Windows and UNIX partitions simultaneously. When you call **fdisk** directly, you need to figure out and specify the name of the raw device you want to work with. You can call **fdisk** from the **format** utility, which figures out which disks are available and allows you to choose one (see previous section). See the **fdisk** and **format man** pages for details.

fdisk Can Destroy Everything

Be as careful with **fdisk** as you would be with a utility that formats a hard drive. Changes you make with **fdisk** can easily result in the loss of large amounts of data. If you are using **fdisk** and have any question about what you are doing, back out with Cancel—your changes do not take effect until you leave **fdisk**.

▲▲ Add/Remove Printers

Unlike Microsoft operating systems UNIX/Solaris takes a very simplistic approach to printers. There are no special drivers to load into the operating system core to manage a printer. Printers are simply attached to a serial or parallel port (or directly to the network). Applications are responsible for generating output that will properly drive the printer. This choice makes operating system support for printers very easy (at the expense of the application developer).

The table below lists the packages you need for local or remote printing according to the version of Solaris you are running.

Operating System	Printer Type	Packages
< 2.6	local and remote	SUNWlpr, SUNWlps, SUNWlpu
>= 2.6	remote	SUNWpcr, SUNWpcu
>= 2.6	local	SUNWpsr, SUNWpsu

If you are using a local PostScript printer, make sure the SUNWpsf package is installed: It contains a number of important filters (Solaris 2.6 and above). If you prefer BSD syntax for submitting (**lpr**) and removing (**lprm**) print jobs and for controlling the queue (**lpc**), add the SUNWscplp package (Solaris 2.6 and above).

The **lpadmin** utility adds and removes local and remote printers from a system and will work on any version of Solaris. It also has the capability of supporting forms and printer classes; refer to the **lpadmin man** page for more information. The following sections discuss basic **lpadmin** functionality.

▲▲▲ Add a Local Printer

A *local printer* is one that is attached directly to your machine via the serial or parallel port. Following is an example of how to use **lpadmin** to install a local printer named **argon** attached to serial port A and set to transfer data at 38,400 bps. Certain local printers, such as network printers and SPARC printers, do not follow these installation instructions but generally have their own installation programs.

```
# lpadmin -p argon -D "printer 1" -I any -o nobanner -v /dev/term/a -o stty=38400
```

The **–p** option specifies the printer name and creates a directory in **/etc/lp/printers** named **argon** that holds the configuration information for this printer.

The **–D** option specifies the printer description, which is displayed when you use **lpstat** to display the printer status.

The **–I any** option indicates that this printer accepts all content types. Other content types include **simple** (plain text) and **postscript** (PostScript).

The **–o nobanner** option indicates that banner pages are not required. The **lp** command also has a **–o nobanner** option that you can use to eliminate a banner from a given print job. If you specify the **–o banner** option to **lpadmin**, users cannot turn off banner pages.

The **–v /dev/term/a** option sets up serial port A to communicate with the printer. Serial port B is represented by **/dev/term/b** and the parallel port by **/dev/bpp0**.

The **–o stty=38400** option sets the communication rate (expressed in bits per second) between the computer and printer. On many older SPARC machines, the serial port hardware is not capable of supporting speeds above 38,400 bps. SPARC Ultras are capable of supporting 76,800 bps and above depending on the model. The speed of the serial ports on a Solaris x86 machine depends on the hardware, but is frequently 115,200 bps. At this speed the limiting factor can be the printer.

After you have added a printer with **lpadmin**, you need to tell the system that the printer is ready to accept print jobs. Issue the following two commands to complete the setup:

```
# enable argon
# accept argon
```

The **enable** command specifies that the printer is now able to print. The **accept** command enables the printer queue so that it can start collecting jobs. If you run only **accept**, then jobs will queue up but nothing will print. If you run only **enable**, then jobs currently in the queue will print, but nothing further will be allowed in the queue.

▲▲▲ Add a Remote Printer for Solaris 2.5 and Earlier

You need to use both **lpadmin** and **lpsystem** to add a remote printer to a system running any version of Solaris up to and including 2.5.1. The **lpsystem** utility informs local printer daemons of the existence of a remote machine with an attached printer. The following commands add to the local system a printer named **xenon**, which is attached to a machine named **newton**:

```
# lpsystem -t s5 newton
# lpadmin -p xenon -s newton!xenon
```

The first command informs local printer daemons that a remote system named **newton** is running a UNIX System V type print spooler that will be used locally. The **–s newton!argon lpadmin** option makes the printer available locally. (Quote the exclamation point if you are using the C Shell.) If **xenon** were running a BSD-based **lpr/lpd** print system (for example a Linux or SunOS4 machine), you would use **bsd** in place of **s5** in the **lpsystem** options.

▲▲▲ Add a Remote Printer for Solaris 2.6 and Above

Solaris 2.6 simplified the task of installing a remote printer and is capable of interfacing directly with network printers such as the HP4M+ and HP5M without vendor-supplied software (although this software will give you additional capabilities). Solaris 2.6 and above is capable of communicating directly with many network printers. For easier centralized administration it also integrates with the NIS and NIS+ network services to allow you to define and use printer network maps. See AnswerBook2 for more details on central administration and network information service integration.

To add a printer named **krypton** on **kepler**, issue the following command (you no longer need **lpsystem**):

```
# lpadmin -p krypton -s kepler
```

Starting with Solaris 2.6 you do not need to specify the name of the remote printer as long as it is the same as the same as the local printer name you are using. Use the following commands to install an HP5M printer named **helium** that is attached to the network:

```
# mkdir /var/printers
# touch /var/printers/helium
# lpadmin -v /var/printers/helium -p helium -o dest=helium:9100
```

You must be able to lock the **/var/printers/helium** file but it has no other requirements. The **9100** is the standard TCP/IP port on which HP printers listen for network connections. Using this port number is an HP convention, other manufacturers may use different port numbers. Consult your printer documentation for details.

You do not need to issue **enable** and **accept** commands when you install a remote printer.

Printer Output Stair-Stepping off the Page

A common problem with printing plain text manifests itself as text gradually stepping off the page to the right:

```
Does your plain text
                    look like this
                                  when you print it?
                                                    Does
```

it eventually scroll off the page? is the last part of the preceding message. This problem is most prevalent with HP printers. To correct this problem set the remote printer name to text as in the following example:

```
# lpadmin -p helium -s helium!text
```

▲▲▲ Add a Printer Using admintool

The **admintool** utility runs under CDE and OpenWindows. To run it and change a printer setup, you need to be Superuser or a member of the **sysadmin** group (group 14).

If you are adding a printer to a serial port, you need to set up the port before you can install the printer. By default Solaris serial ports are set up for terminal control so that you can plug a terminal into the port and log in on the machine. After you start **admintool**, choose the Browse pull-down menu and select Serial Ports. Click on the serial port you want to use to select it. Choose the Edit pull-down menu and select Modify.... Set the Baud Rate to match the communication rate of the printer you are installing. Set the Template to be Initialize Only - No Connection. Then deselect the Service Enable checkbox and click on OK.[17]

Go to the Browse menu and select Printers. Click on the Edit menu and select Add. Choose Access to Printer if you want to add access to a remote printer or Local Printer if you want to add a local printer.

If you choose Access to Printer, **admintool** displays the Add Access To Printer window. The space next to the Print Client label should be filled in with the name of your local machine. The Printer Name is the name of the printer on the remote system, the Print Server is the name of the remote system, and the Description is an optional description of the printer for use from only the local machine. Mark the Default Printer checkbox if you want this printer to be the default printer for the local machine.

---

17. Although these steps are not required, they allow you to use the Serial Port part of **admintool** as a log to keep track of how things are supposed to be set up.

If you are installing a local printer, you will see the **Local Printer** window. Here the local machine is the **Print Server**. The **Name**, **Description**, and **Default Printer** are as just described. The default **User Access List** is `all`; change this only if you want to limit the users who can use the printer you are setting up. Make appropriate selections from the remaining items. Use **admintool** help, available from the main **admintool** window, if you have any questions. When you are finished click on **OK**. After adding a local printer using **admintool**, issue **enable** and **accept** commands. Refer to "Add a Local Printer" on page 639.

▲▲▲ Remove a Printer

Before physically removing a local printer from the system or turning off access to a remote printer, use **lpadmin** to remove the printer from the **lp** print service to prevent files from accumulating in the printer queue and consuming system resources. The following example removes the printer named **argon** (either a local or remote printer) and is valid on all versions of Solaris:

```
# lpadmin -x argon
```

If you are using Solaris 2.5 or earlier, use **lpsystem** to remove the host reference from the **lp** system. Do not remove a remote host reference until all printers using that host are removed or those printers will become unusable. Use the following command to delete the local reference to a remote machine named **newton**:

```
# lpsystem -r newton
```

You can also remove a printer using **admintool**: Click on the **Browse** menu and select **Printers** as before. Select the printer you want to remove by clicking on it. Under the **Edit** menu select **Delete** and click on **OK**.

▲▲ Check Your Mail and Log Files

Users frequently email **root** and **postmaster** to communicate with the system administrator. If you do not forward **root**'s mail to yourself (a good practice, see page 661), remember to check **root**'s mail periodically.

You will not receive reminders about mail that arrives for **root** if you always use **su** to perform system administration tasks. However after using **su** to become **root**, you can give the command **mailx –u root** to look at Superuser's mail. You should also look at the system log files regularly for evidence of problems. Two important files are **/var/adm/messages**, where the operating system and some applications record errors, and the files in the **/var/log** directory, which include errors from the mail system (syslog files).

▲▲ Schedule Routine Tasks

It is a good practice to schedule certain routine tasks to run automatically. For example you may want to remove old core files once a week, summarize accounting data daily, and rotate system log files monthly. The **cron** utility runs commands at regularly scheduled times. Using **crontab**, you can submit a list of commands in a format that can be read and executed by **cron**. Refer to **crontab** in Part III and **/etc/cron.d** on page 609 for more information.

Like the **cron** utility the **at** utility allows you to run a job some time in the future. Unlike the **cron** utility the **at** utility will only run a job once. For instance you can schedule an **at** job that will reboot your system at

3 AM (when all users are logged off—see the following example). It is also possible to run an **at** job from within an **at** job. For instance you could have an **at** job that would check for new patches every 18 days, something that would be very difficult with **cron**. Refer to **at** in Part III for more information.

```
# at 3am
at> reboot
at> CONTROL-D
commands will be executed using /bin/sh
job 910170000.a at Wed Nov  4 03:00:00 1998
```

▲▲ Install New Software

Most manufacturers provide detailed instructions to guide you through the process of installing new software or system upgrades; some even provide special tools or menu-driven user interfaces to simplify the task. Many software vendors supply software for Solaris as packages. Refer to "Adding and Removing Software Packages" on page 627. As you acquire local software, particularly free (public-domain) software, you should install it on your system in a consistent, predictable manner. For example you might create a directory tree under **/usr/local** for binaries (**/usr/local/bin**), manual pages (**/usr/local/man**), and so forth. You should avoid installing nonstandard software in the standard system directories (such as **/usr/bin**) to prevent confusion later and to avoid overwriting or losing the software when you install standard software upgrades in the future. Make sure that the users on your system know where to find the local software, and remember to make an announcement whenever you install, change, or remove local tools.

By convention most software that Sun distributes is installed in the **/opt** directory. This directory can be on your local disk as a separate partition, on your local disk as a part of **root**, or it can exist on a network mounted filesystem. If you plan to have a lot of third-party software on your system, plan your **/opt** partition size properly.

▲▲ Install AnswerBook2

AnswerBook2 comes on the Solaris Documentation CDROM that comes with your operating system CDROM. Follow these steps to install AnswerBook2 under Solaris 2.6. See the next section if you are running Solaris 7.

1. Insert the Documentation CDROM into the CDROM drive and wait about 10 seconds for **vold** to mount the CDROM (or give the command **volcheck** if you are in a hurry).

2. Log in as Superuser.

3. If you are on a SPARC machine:

    ```
    # cd /cdrom/solaris_2_6_documentation/Solaris_2.6_Doc/sparc/Product
    ```

    If you are on an Intel machine:

    ```
    # cd /cdrom/solaris_2_6_documentation/Solaris_2.6_Doc/i386/Product
    ```

4. Give the command:

```
pkgadd -d . *
```

and answer **y** to various questions as necessary. Near the end of the installation **pkgadd** displays `Document server started as process dwhttpd` as it adds the **ab2mgr** startup script to **/etc/init.d** with a link in **/etc/rc2.d**.

5. Give the command:

```
# /usr/dt/bin/anwerbook2
```

which launches a browser that connects to **http://*yourhost*:8888**. You can also set the **AB2_DEFAULTSERVER** environment variable to this URL so that no matter what machine you log in on, it will connect to the correct URL. Replace *yourhost* with the name of your machine.

6. Review the AnswerBook2 documentation displayed by the previous step. Specifically select the first item on the list (Help/*Accessing Online Documentation*) and then *Installing Document Server Software*. Review *Installing Software* and *Administering an AnswerBook2 Server/Administering the Document Server*.

7. Give the command:

```
# /usr/dt/bin/answerbook2_admin
```

This program adds other material to your AnswerBook2 collection and configures the AnswerBook2 server. The first time you run this program, it will tell you that you need to run

```
# /usr/lib/ab2/bin/ab2admin -o add_admin -u id
```

while logged in as Superuser. Pick an account name that you will use to administer AnswerBook2. Any name will do as it will only be used within AnswerBook2. Then give the preceding command, replacing *id* with the account name you have chosen. The **ab2admin** utility then asks you to enter a password for this account. Keep this password in a safe place. If you forget it, you will not be able to modify your AnswerBook2 configuration easily.

8. To add the rest of the document collections and packages from the Documentation CDROM, give the following command:

```
# pkgadd -d /cdrom/solaris_2_6_documentation/Solaris_2.6_Doc/common/Product/
```

The **pkgadd** utility presents a list of packages with a query at the end of the list. Respond with **all** to install all of the documentation. For each package you will see a prompt similar to the following (produced by SUNWaman package):

```
The installation options are as follows:
Option: Description:
------------------------------------------
1. nil:    less than 1 Megabyte disk space required [slowest performance].
2. heavy:  117.68 Megabytes disk space required [best performance].

Note: If the install option which you choose below fails
      due to lack of space, try another location, or
      choose a lower install option number.
```

If you have a lot of spare disk space, choose option 2. If you will not need AnswerBook2 frequently and do not mind inserting the CDROM and waiting a bit when you do need it, choose option 1. (Are you going to be near the CDROM drive when you need AnswerBook2?) You can also store some packages on the disk and not others.

When you install each package, **pkgadd** prompts you with:

```
Specify the parent of the AnswerBook home directory:
```

Respond with **/export/answerbook**, **/opt/answerbook**, or another shared directory (if you want to be an AnswerBook2 server for other machines).

9. Bring up AnswerBook2 again by giving the command **answerbook2**, clicking an AnswerBook2 icon, pointing your browser to **http://*yourhost*:8888** (replace *yourhost* with the name of your machine), or pressing the reload button on your browser if AnswerBook2 is still displayed. You will see all of the AnswerBook2 collections from your Documentation CDROM in an easy-to-browse-and-search hypertext format.

10. Give the following command to add new collections of information to AnswerBook2 using a GUI interface:

```
/usr/dt/bin/answerbook2_admin
```

Select the **add collections** option, and type in the pathname to the directory where the AnswerBook2 data is stored. For example

```
/cdrom/solaris2_6_documentation/Solaris_2.6_Doc/common/Product/SUNWaadm
```

Or use the command-line interface:

```
/usr/lib/ab2/bin/ab2admin
```

and type **add_coll –d *path***, where *path* is the location where the AnswerBook2 data is stored.

You will then be asked to log in with the AnswerBook2 administrator id and password. Extensive help is available in both the GUI and command-line versions.

▲▲ Install AnswerBook2 under Solaris 7

Under Solaris 7 you can use **pkgadd** (as just described) or Web Start to install AnswerBook2. Web Start, a GUI utility that is packaged with Solaris 7, makes the job of installing and removing packages such as AnswerBook2 much easier. To use Web Start insert the 2.7 Documentation CDROM and double-click on the installer icon when it appears. Follow the instructions on the screen.

You can also configure AnswerBook2 to run directly from the CDROM by logging in as **root** and giving the following command from the top level of the Documentation CDROM (that is where the **ab2cd** script is located):

```
# ./ab2cd
```

If you get a message saying that the AnswerBook2 server is already running, stop it with the following command before giving the same command again.

```
# /usr/lib/ab2/bin/ab2admin -o stop
```

As with the conventional setup, you can access AnswerBook2 by using a browser with the address **http://***server***:8888**, where *server* is the name of the host containing the CDROM.

▲▲ Share Files with Other Machines

Sharing local files with other machines saves disk space and creates a single place to change data (such as application software) instead of having to change it on multiple machines. By convention shared filesystems are stored under the **/export** or **/usr/export** directory, with each subdirectory housing a shared filesystem. You can keep a shared filesystem under any directory you please.

> **Sharing** /home
>
> You need to make special provisions in order to share the **/home** directory. Because **/home** is usually under the control of the **automountd** daemon, you need to disable **automountd** or remove **/home** from **/etc/auto_master** (page 649) in order to share it. Refer to the second paragraph of the Tip on page 653 for more information.

To share a filesystem you need to enable NFS by editing **/etc/dfs/dfstab**. This file is run by the **/etc/rc3.d/S15nfs.server** script when the system enters run level 3. Here is a sample **dfstab** file with three shared filesystems.

```
# cat /etc/dfs/dfstab
#       Place share(1M) commands here for automatic execution
#       on entering init state 3.
#
#       Issue the command '/etc/init.d/nfs.server start' to run the NFS
#       daemon processes and the share commands, after adding the very
#       first entry to this file.
#
#       share [-F fstype] [ -o options] [-d "<text>"] <pathname> [resource]
#       .e.g,
#       share  -F nfs  -o rw=engineering  -d "home dirs"  /export/home2
share -F nfs -o ro=huey,rw=dewey:louie,root=dewey -d "home directories" /export/home
share -F nfs -o ro,rw=dewy,root=dewy -d "applications" /export/apps
share -F nfs -o ro -d "Oracle" /export/apps/oracle
```

The **–F** option specifies the filesystem type. On a freshly installed Solaris machine, NFS (Network Filesystem) is the only relevant choice. Add-on network filesystems such as AFS (Andrew Filesystem) and DFS (Distributed Filesystem) are also available. See the table on page 653 for a list of other common filesystem types.

The **–o** option is followed by a comma-separated list of arguments. The **ro** argument takes 0 or more colon-separated values. With no values readonly access is given to all machines. The **rw** argument is similar to **ro** but gives read-write access. The **root** argument must be followed by one or more hostnames in a colon-separated list.

Do Not Share **root** Files Unless You Must

Use the **root** argument with extreme caution. By default files owned by **root** are not writable by **root** from another machine, even if you export the filesystem with read-write privileges. The **root**=*host* syntax allows a remote machine to create, change, and delete files owned by **root**. *Do not* use the **root** option unless it is absolutely necessary. If you use this option, remove it when it is no longer needed.

The same warning applies to using the **anon=0** flag. This will effectively give root access to hosts that have **rw** access.

You can use the **–d** argument to provide a description of the resource being shared. The argument (following the options) is the name of the filesystem that is to be shared.

A filesystem that is mounted on a directory within an exported filesystem will not be exported automatically with the exported filesystem. You need to individually export each filesystem that you want exported even if it resides within an already-exported filesystem. Looking at the preceding **/etc/dfstab** file, you see that both **/export/apps** and **/export/apps/oracle** are exported, even though **oracle** is a subdirectory of **apps**. Most other subdirectories and files are automatically exported.

Exporting Symbolic Links and Device Files

When you export a symbolic link, make sure the object of the link is available on the client (remote) machine. The object of the link must either exist on a client machine or you must export and mount it along with the exported link or it will not point to the file it points to on the server.

A device file refers to a kernel interface. When you export a device file, you export that interface. If the client machine does not have the same type of device, the exported device will not work.

▲▲▲ Share Filesystems

When you first edit the **/etc/dfs/dfstab** file, the NFS service daemons are not running. When the **/etc/rc3.d/S15nfs.server** script runs and sees **/etc/dfs/dfstab** with only comments in it, it does not start the NFS service daemons. There are a number of ways you can start these daemons after you have created the file.

1. Reboot the machine. This will automatically start all the right services.

2. Run the **/etc/rc3.d/S15nfs.server** (or **/etc/init.d/nfs.server**) script:

    ```
    # sh /etc/init.d/nfs.server start
    ```

3. (Not recommended) Start the daemons by hand. If you are an experienced administrator you can consult the startup scripts to see how they work.

Once NFS services have been started, if you change the **/etc/dfs/dfstab** file, use **shareall** to run **/etc/dfs/dfstab** and share the filesystems as specified in **dfstab**. You can also execute individual **share** commands by hand. An easy method of doing this is to copy and paste directly from the file into a window running a **root** shell. You cannot unshare a filesystem by deleting a file from **dfstab** and running **shareall**. See the following section.

▲▲▲ Unshare Filesystems

If you want to remove access to a filesystem so that other machines can no longer mount it, you must use an **unshare** command such as the following:

```
# unshare -F nfs /export/home
```

Use **unshare** without any arguments to unshare all exported filesystems, for example when preparing to bring the system down. When you use **unshare** on a filesystem others are using remotely, they will get messages in their windows and on their console saying server not responding, Stale NFS file handle, or something similar. The analogue of **shareall** is **unshareall**.

▲▲▲ Mount Remote Filesystems

In order to use a remote filesystem on your local machine, it must be mounted. The following examples show three ways to mount a remote filesystem, assuming that a machine named **donald** is on the same network as your local machine and is sharing its **/export/home**, **/export/apps**, and **/export/apps/oracle** filesystems.

1. You can **mount** the filesystem by hand:

   ```
   # mkdir /myhome /apps

   # mount donald:/export/home /myhome
   # mount -o ro,nosuid donald:/export/apps /apps
   # mount -o ro donald:/export/apps/oracle /apps/oracle
   ```

   Use **mkdir** to make directories to mount the filesystems on and **mount** to mount the filesystems. By default filesystems are mounted read-write (assuming the NFS server is exporting with read-write permissions). The first mount line above mounts the **/export/home** directory from the machine named **donald** on the local directory **/myhome**. The second and third mount lines use the **–o ro** option to force a read-only mount. The second **mount** line also adds the **–o nosuid** option by using the multiple option form of the **–o** option. The **nosuid** option forces mounted setuid executables to be run with regular Solaris permissions.

2. You can mount the filesystems by using entries in **/etc/vfstab**. The following entry will mount the **/var/mail** directory from the server named **mailhost** whenever the machine is booted.

   ```
   mailhost:/var/mail     -      /var/mail    nfs     -     yes   intr,hard,bg,noac
   ```

   The significant differences between this and a local **vfstab** entry are that there is no raw device to check, the filesystem type is NFS instead of UFS, it is not **fsck**'d at boot, and the options for an NFS filesystem differ from those of a UFS filesystem. The preceding example options are designed for mounting a mail spool directory from a mail server. These and other common NFS options are explained in the following table. See the **mount_nfs man** page for a complete list of options.

Option	Meaning
actimeo=n	Set the attribute cache for files to expire in n seconds.
bg	If the first mount attempt fails, continue trying to mount in the background.
fg	If the first mount attempt fails, continue trying to mount in the foreground.
intr (nointr)	Allow (do not allow) **CONTROL-C** to interrupt applications waiting for a remote mount.
hard	Continue retrying a request until the server responds. Use this option on all filesystems mounted with read-write permissions.
noac	Do not cache file attributes for this filesystem (by default options like size and access time are cached and reused).
ro	Mount filesystem with readonly access.
rw	Mount filesystem with read-write access (default).
soft	Give an error if the server does not respond. Do not use this option on writable filesystems.
vers=n	Between Solaris2 systems, this defaults to 3. You may need to force it to 2 for systems that do not support NFSv3.

3. You can use the **automount** facility to mount filesystems on demand. The **automount** utility is particularly useful when there are a large number of servers or a large number of filesystems. It also helps to remove server-server dependencies. If you have two servers that each mount filesystems from the other, then if both machines are down, both may hang on the way up as each tries to mount a filesystem from the other when using traditional **vfstab**-based mounts. The **automount** facility gets around this by only mounting a filesystem from another machine when a process tries to access it.

▲▲▲▲▲ Automatically Mount Filesystems: An autofs filesystem is like any other filesystem except it remains unmounted until it is needed, at which time the system mounts it automatically (called *demand mounting*). It is unmounted once again when it is no longer needed (5 minutes of no activity by default). The **automountd** daemon, which is started by the **/etc/rc2.d/S74autofs** script when the system enters run level 2, creates autofs mount points, which appear to the user as though the underlying autofs filesystem is mounted.[18] When a process attempts to access one of the directories of the unmounted autofs filesystem, the filesystem notifies the **automountd** daemon, which mounts the autofs filesystem.

---

18. If this feature is turned off, or if you are using a version of Solaris prior to 2.6, you have to give a command, such as **ls /home/alex**, that accesses one of the subdirectories of the autofs mount point (in this case **/home**) in order to create the demand that causes **automountd** to mount the autofs filesystem so you can see it. Before you issue the **ls** command, **/home/alex** does not appear to be in **/home**.

The main file that controls the behavior of **automountd** is **/etc/auto_master** (Figure 15-2). The +auto_master line indicates that any **auto_master** map in NIS or NIS+ should be automatically incorporated.

The rest of the entries are presented in three columns. The first column holds the name of the autofs *mount point*—the location where the autofs filesystem is mounted. The second column contains the name of

```
# cat /etc/auto_master
# Master map for automounter
#
+auto_master
```

Mount Point	Map	Options
/net	-hosts	-nosuid,nobrowse
/home	auto_home	-nobrowse
/xfn	-xfn	

Figure 15-2   The /etc/auto_master file

the map to use with the mount point, and the third column (optional) holds mount options for map entries that do not explicitly specify any options.

There are two types of maps that tell **automountd** where to look for a filesystem to mount on the mount point. An *indirect map,* which does not start with a hyphen, names a file in **/etc** that contains names of filesystems to mount under the mount point and the (remote) machine and pathname of the filesystem (Figure 15-3). A special map, also called a built-in map, handles a remote filesystem in a specific way.

There are three special maps: **–hosts**, **–xfn**, and **–null**. By default the **–hosts** special map works with the **/net** autofs mount point. When you access **/net/***hostname, hostname* is automatically expanded to a list of all filesystems exported from server ***hostname***, and these filesystems are mounted under **/net/***hostname*. The **–xfn** special map works in conjunction with Sun's Federated Naming Service (FNS). These directories are mounted under **/xfn**. Refer to AnswerBook2 for more information on setting up FNS. The **–null** map disables entries that are inherited from NIS or NIS+. Any **–null** entries must precede the **+***auto_master* entry to be effective.

automount and Putting Users in /home

Adding a new user named Bob with a home directory in **/home/bob** will fail because **/home** is under the control of **automountd**. Putting Bob's home directory in **/export/home/bob** will work once you change the **passwd** file entry to **/export/home/bob** and put an entry into **/etc/auto_home** (following).

The **/home** line in **auto_master** (Figure 15-2) indicates that **/home** is an autofs filesystem that is under the control of **automount**. The map for **/home** is in a file named **/etc/auto_home** (an indirect map, Figure 15-3). The use of indirect maps allows you to set up separate maps for different administrative domains. You can then modify the map (typically in NIS or NIS+, but it can be replicated in files as well) and all the changes will automatically be propagated to all hosts.

The first column of an indirect map holds the relative autofs mount point. This mount point is prepended with the corresponding autofs mount point from column one of the **auto_master** file (Fig-

```
# cat /etc/auto_home
```

Mount Point	Options	Location
marketing	-nosuid,noquota	aristotle:/export/marketing
graphics	-nosuid,noquota	davinci:/export/graphics
engineering	-nosuid,noquota	archimedes:/export/engineering

Figure 15-3   The /etc/auto_home file

ure 15-3) to create the absolute autofs mount point. In this example **marketing** (from **auto_home**) would be prepended with **/home** (from **auto_master**) to make **/home/marketing**. The second column holds the options, and the third column shows the server and filesystem that is to be mounted.

In the preceding example all home directories have quotas and setuid executables disabled. A user that has **/home/marketing/sheila** as her home directory will automatically have it mounted from **aristotle** when she logs in; a user in **/home/graphics/paul** will have his home directory mounted from **davinci**.

There are also a number of other special characters and techniques that you can use when employing indirect maps. For example if the following is an entry in **/etc/auto_master**:

```
/opt        auto_opt            -nosuid,ro
```

then by default all **/opt** mounted filesystems will have setuid disabled on all executables and will be mounted readonly. The **/etc/auto_opt** file looks like this:

```
# cat /etc/auto_opt
wordperfect  -suid                  achilles:/export/opt/wordperfect
mail         -rw,noac,intr,fg       achilles:/var/mail
*                                   aristotle,plato,socrates(1):/export/opt/&
```

The first line mounts a directory as **/opt/wordperfect** from the server **achilles**. Because there are setuid executables in this directory that control printing (unfortunate, but a real-life example), the **auto_opt** file sets the **–suid** option, which overrides the global **–nosuid** option set in **auto_master**.

The second line uses **automount** to mount the mail directory, also from **achilles**. The **intr** option indicates that you can interrupt this command with CONTROL-C, **fg** says that repeated mount requests, if needed, are to be performed in the foreground, and the **noac** option tells Solaris that no data or attribute caching is to be used on this directory. Because cached attributes are not necessarily current and because mail clients and **sendmail** rely on attributes of the mail file (and its lock file) to determine if the mail file can be updated, the **noac** option lessens the risk of accessing your mail file at the same time that new mail is being delivered, which could corrupt the mail folder.

In the last line the asterisk (∗) matches whatever else the system is trying to mount on **/opt** (a wildcard). As with a regular expression, the ampersand (**&**) is replaced with whatever the asterisk matched. This entry uses multiple servers and priorities. The servers' names are separated by commas and a number in parentheses following a server name specifies a priority. The higher the number, the lower the priority, with a default of 0 (the highest priority). Using the preceding example, if you attempt to mount **/opt/oracle**, **automountd** would first try to mount **/export/opt/oracle** from **aristotle** or **plato** (**automount** will first try to determine which host is on a closer network, failing that, the choice is random). If neither one of these mounts succeeds, **socrates** would be tried next. In Solaris 2.6 automatic failover was added. For readonly filesystems if you have multiple servers specified, as in the example above, and one goes down, **automount** will automatically mount one of the other replicated entries. You will get an error message if you attempt replicated mounts with a read-write filesystem.

When you add a new user with home directory **/export/home/bill**, and you want his home directory to appear as **/home/bill**, add an appropriate entry to **/etc/auto_home** that includes the server name, and update Bill's **passwd** entry.

The **automount** utility is an important part of administering a large collection of machines in a consistent way. The **automountd** daemon has provisions for mounting other types of filesystems besides NFS. It has variables that let you mount filesystems based on architecture, operating system version, CPU type, hostname, and other criteria. This daemon also recognizes executable maps so you can run a program or script that determines what is to be mounted. Consult the appropriate **man** pages and AnswerBook2 for more information.

▲▲▲ Unmount Remote Filesystems

Consider the **vfstab** entry for **/var/mail** given on page 648. Either of the following commands causes **/var/mail** directory to be unmounted.

```
# umount mailhost:/var/mail
# umount /var/mail
```

The first command explicitly unmounts the server and filesystem. The second command asks **umount** to consult the **/etc/vfstab** to get the necessary information and then unmount the appropriate filesystem from the appropriate server.

You can also unmount all remote filesystems with a single command: **umountall**. With the **–F** option this command unmounts all NFS filesystems from all remote hosts:

```
# umountall -F nfs
```

If you are using a filesystem **umount** is trying to unmount, it will display a message such as:

```
nfs umount: /opt/oracle: is busy
```

You can try the same command with the **–k** option. The **–k** option is valid only for **umountall** (not **umount**); it causes **umountall** to find processes that are using the filesystem that it is trying to unmount, kill them, and attempt to unmount the filesystem again. If that does not work, ask all users to log off the system, kill any processes that may be using the filesystem you want to unmount (oracle daemons or client programs such as editors or other applications), and try again. If all else fails, reboot the system.

Because the **–F** option specifies the type of filesystem to unmount, you can also use **umountall** to unmount all filesystems mounted by **automount**, UFS filesystems, or any other type of filesystem. For example:

```
# umountall -F -k nfs
# umountall -F autofs
# umountall -F ufs
# umountall -F lofs
```

The third example will unmount all local UFS filesystems that are not being used. It will fail on the **root** filesystem (and **/usr** and **/var** if they are mounted separately from **root**) because the bulk of the system daemons are started from the **root** hierarchy.

The fourth example will unmount all loopback filesystems (LOFS). A LOFS is created by **automountd** when the **automount** map indicates that the mount point is on the local machine. Rather than creating an inefficient network connection to itself, a loopback mount point is created and a link is made from the mount point to the actual location of the filesystem.

Loopback Filesystem and automount

If a LOFS is mounted via **automount**, you will not be able to unmount the UFS filesystem housing the mounted LOFS until the LOFS filesystem is unmounted. For example if **/home/bill** (a LOFS) is mounted, you need to unmount it before unmounting **/export/bill** (the underlying filesystem).

▲▲▲ Miscellaneous Filesystem Commands

If you give a **dfmounts** command with the argument of a hostname, it displays the resources that are mounted from that server. Refer to page 738 for more information on **dfmounts**.

automount Controlled by nsswitch.conf

As with many Solaris2 services, the behavior of **automount** can be controlled with the **/etc/nsswitch.conf** file (page 612). The order of the entries in the **/etc/nsswitch.conf** file controls which service is consulted first when resolving a mount point (files, NIS, or NIS+).

Disappearing /home

Once a directory has been assigned as an autofs mount point, it is under the control of the **automountd** daemon. You cannot have the same directory (such as **/home** or **/opt**) as an autofs mount point and an entry mounted using **/etc/vfstab**. Do not put a **/home** entry in **/etc/vfstab**. Because automounting is enabled by default, and because the **/etc/auto_master** file has an entry for **/home**, the **vfstab** version of **/home** will disappear each time you reboot the system.

    To disable automounting of **/home**, delete or comment out the **/home** entry from the **/etc/auto_master** file (by starting the line with a #). To disable automounting completely, use **mv** to rename **/etc/rc2.d/S74autofs** as **/etc/rc2.d/.S74autofs** and reboot. (Giving this file an invisible filename keeps it from being seen and executed yet it is still there if you want to resurrect it.)

The following table lists some of the different types of filesystems you may encounter.

Filesystem	Brief Description
UFS	**Unix filesystem** The default filesystem.
s5	**System V filesystem** Deprecated.
UFS+	A version of UFS available with SDS (Solstice DiskSuite) and Solaris 7 that can log and dynamically grow a filesystem.
PCFS	**PC filesystem** Gives you the ability to read from and write to DOS format floppies.

Filesystem	Brief Description
HSFS	**High Sierra filesystem** Gives you the ability to read from DOS/MS Windows ISO-9660 CDROMs.
LOFS	**Loopback filesystem** Used when **automount** is running and the client and server are on the same machine (page 652).
CACHEFS	**Caching filesystem** Used in conjunction with **AUTOFS** to permit local caching of frequently accessed files. You can specify file sizes and space parameters.
AUTOFS	**Automount filesystem** (page 649).
NFS	**Network filesystem**
VxFS	**Veritas filesystem** A journaling filesystem similar to NTFS. VxFS is sold by Sun under license by Veritas Corporation.
AFS	**Andrew filesystem** Developed by Carnege Mellon to be able to support wide area networks over slow links, provide a global naming structure, and more.
DFS	**Distributed filesystem** Based on AFS, but not to be confused with the Windows NT filesystem of the same name.
VOLFS	**Volume management filesystem** Used by **vold** to mount CDROM and floppy disks on **/cdrom** or **/floppy**, respectively.
PROCFS	**Process filesystem** A window into the kernel used by utilities such as **ps** to display process information. The **/proc** filesystem is the only PROCFS filesystem. See the following section.
TMPFS	**Temporary filesystem** Uses **/tmp** as a RAM disk by sharing the virtual memory and swap partition.
WEBNFS	Provides a means whereby filesystems can be accessed through the Web using NFS.

▲▲ Procfs

The **/proc** directory is a special kind of filesystem that provides a window into the kernel. With **/proc** you can obtain information on any process running on your computer including its current state, memory usage, CPU usage, terminal, parent, group, and more. You can retrieve this information using a simple C program:

```
/* Given a process ID, this program will print its parent using procfs */
#include <stdio.h>
#include <sys/types.h>
#include <sys/fcntl.h>
#include <sys/procfs.h>

main(int argc, char *argv[]) {
struct prstatus pstat;
char procfile[30]="/proc/";
int fd;

if (argc < 2) {
fprintf(stderr, "You must supply an argument\n");
exit(1);
}
```

```
strcat(procfile, argv[1]);

if ((fd = open(procfile, O_RDONLY)) < 0) {
fprintf(stderr, "Error opening %s", procfile);
perror(" ");
exit(1);
}

/* Grab process information/status */
if (ioctl(fd, PIOCSTATUS, (void *) &pstat) < 0) {
perror("getting process status");
exit(1);
}

printf("%d\n", pstat.pr_ppid);
exit(0);
}
```

For more information refer to the **proc man** page in section 4 of the system manuals (**man –s4 proc**).

Another way to obtain this information is by running the utilities in **/usr/proc/bin** (see following table and the **proc man** page in section 1). Except as noted, each of these utilities requires an argument of a PID number and displays information about the process you specified. Starting with Solaris 2.6, **/proc/***pid* is a directory holding lots of individual files containing process information for PID *pid*. The information is in binary format, so viewing it with **cat** or **pg** will not reveal much.

Program (in /usr/proc/bin)	Function
pcred	Displays real and effective uid and gid.
pfiles	Shows information about open files (inode, device major, minor, and so on).
pflags	Displays thread status information, signals, and tracing flags.
pgrep	Displays the process numbers of processes that match the argument (2.7 only).
pkill	Kills the processes that match the argument (2.7 only).
pldd	Shows shared objects loaded and libraries linked with this process.
pmap	Displays the address space of the process.
prun	Sets a process to running state (see **pstop**).
psig	Shows actions to be performed on receipt of signals.
pstack	Shows the stack for all threads of a process.
pstop	Sets a process to stopped state (stops it from running—see **prun**).
ptime	Times a process to completion. Similar to the **time** builtin, but with better resolution. Takes a command as an argument instead of a PID.
ptree	Displays the process tree (parents and children) for a process, can take a username as an argument.
pwait	Waits for the process to terminate.
pwdx	Displays the current working directory.

The next example uses **ptree** to show the process tree of a **sleep** command that is run in the background. The user is logged in via **telnet** and is running a C Shell.

```
kudos% /usr/proc/bin/ptree 2746
152   /usr/sbin/inetd -s
  2668  in.telnetd
    2670  -csh
      2746  sleep 500
```

▲▲ Network Services

A network can be as big as the Internet, connecting millions of machines with backbones running around the globe, or as small as a home network connecting two machines in the same room. There are two ways to set up the software to connect a Solaris machine to a network.

The easiest way is to run the **sys-unconfig** utility and reboot the machine. When the machine comes up it will prompt you for system configuration information: Hostname, (NIS) domain name, timezone, IP address, IP subnet mask, and **root** password. The other way to set up the networking software requires you to edit a few files.

▲▲▲ Set Up Network Files

This section contains information about how to set up four important files: **hosts**, **netmasks**, **defaultrouter**, and **hostname.***interface*.

▲▲▲▲ hosts: List of Machines:

First edit the **/etc/hosts** file. This file stores the name and IP address of the other machines that your machine knows about. At the very least, it must have the hostname and IP address that you have chosen for your local machine and a special entry for **localhost**. This entry is for a *loopback service,* which allows the local machine to talk to itself (for example for **automount** and RPC services). The IP address of the loopback service is always 127.0.0.1. Following is a minimal **/etc/hosts** file for a machine named **achilles**.

```
# cat /etc/hosts
#
# Internet host table
#
127.0.0.1       localhost
199.188.177.5   achilles
```

If you are not using NIS, NIS+, or DNS to look up hostnames (called *hostname resolution*), then you must include in **/etc/hosts** all of the hosts that you want your machine to be able to contact. The order in which hostname resolution services are checked is controlled by the **hosts** entry in the **/etc/nsswitch.conf** file (page 612).

▲▲▲▲ netmasks: For a Subnetted Network:

You need a **/etc/netmasks** file if you are setting up a subnetted network (page 195). Refer to the **netmasks man** page and the example in the **/etc/netmasks** file.

▲▲▲▲ **defaultrouter**: Specify a Default Router: On some networks you will need the **/etc/defaultrouter** file to point to the default router. It must contain the IP address or hostname of one or more default routers. If you use a hostname, that hostname must be in the **/etc/hosts** file.

▲▲▲▲ **hostname.*interface***: Specify Network Hardware: You will need a **/etc/hostname.*interface*** file. The *interface* portion of the filename depends on the kind of network hardware your machine uses. Solaris sets up this file automatically when you perform a reconfigure reboot (page 634). Common examples of *interfaces* are: **hme0** (100 Mbit:SPARC), **le0** (10 Mbit:SPARC), **dnet0** (PC with Digital ethernet board), and **elx0** (PC with 3COM ethernet board). The single line in this file contains either the IP address or name of the local machine exactly as listed in **/etc/hosts**. For the previous example on an Ultra-SPARC machine with a 100 Mbit interface card, there would be a file named **/etc/hostname.hme0** containing the word `achilles`. The **0** in **hme0** indicates that this is the first **hme** board in the machine (most likely built-in). A second **hme** board would be indicated by a file named **/etc/hostname.hme1**. A machine with both an **hme** and **le** board in it would have **hostname.hme0** and **hostname.le0** files in the **/etc** directory. You must perform a reconfigure reboot when you add a new board to your Solaris machine. Refer to "Add/Remove Devices: Reconfigure Reboot" on page 634.

Start Optional

You can add additional addresses on each interface by using files named **/etc/hostname.*interface*:*n***, where *n* is the ID of the additional address. For example you can use **/etc/hostname.hme0:1** for an additional IP address that is listened to on **hme0**.

Stop Optional

▲▲▲ NIS

Solaris 2.6 and above also support native NIS network services as a package. Previous versions of Solaris supplied NIS services by running the NIS+ software in compatibility mode. In order to set up NIS, you will need to install the SUNWnisr and SUNWnisu software packages. See AnswerBook2 or a separate book such as *Managing NFS and NIS* by Hal Stern for information on setting up and maintaining NIS servers for your network. NIS is most commonly used to provide a central means of distributing passwords, groups, service names and ids (through **/etc/services**), aliases, automount maps, and a few other less frequently used tables. For more information see "Network Information Service (NIS)" on page 218.

The easiest way to make a new configuration take effect is to reboot the system. (You can do this without rebooting if you like; refer to the **ifconfig man** page for details.)

▲▲▲▲ DNS: Domain Name Service

If you are using DNS (page 217) for hostname resolution, you will need to create a file named **/etc/resolv.conf** and edit **/etc/nsswitch.conf**.

▲▲▲▲ resolv.conf: How to Resolve Hostnames:

The following **/etc/resolv.conf** is a sample file for the **tcorp.com** domain. A **resolv.conf** file usually has at least two lines: A domain line and a nameserver line.

```
# cat /etc/resolv.conf
domain tcorp.com
nameserver 199.198.197.196
nameserver 199.198.197.195
```

The first line (optional) specifies the **domain** name. This domain name is appended to all hostnames that are not fully qualified (do not end in a period). So if you **ping** a machine named **achilles**, the resolver function of your machine will first look for **achilles.tcorp.com**.

The **nameserver** line(s) indicate which machines the local machine should query to resolve hostnames to IP addresses and vice versa. These machines are consulted in the order they appear with a 10-second timeout between queries. The sample file causes this machine to query 199.198.197.196 followed by 199.198.197.195 if the first machine does not answer within 10 seconds.

▲▲▲▲▲ nsswitch.conf: Specify Order to Consult Services:

The **/etc/nsswitch.conf** file determines the order in which services are consulted. Valid entries for the `hosts:` line in this file are `files` (**/etc/hosts**, **/etc/passwd**, and so on), `nis`, `xfn` (for Solaris 2.5 and above), `nisplus` (NIS+), and `dns`. The following `hosts:` line causes the local files to be consulted before the system queries a DNS machine.

```
hosts:      files dns
```

▲▲▲ PPP

If you have two machines running Solaris at two different locations, PPP (Point-to-Point Protocol) allows you to connect the machines together and run **telnet** (or any other network application) just as if they were on the same network. Over the years the PPP packages included with Solaris have undergone steady improvement. There are PPP packages included on the Solaris CDROM, and in 2.6 there are separate and improved PPP packages on the Intranet Extensions CDROM. There are also various free PPP implementations for Solaris, such as the PPP package that comes with Linux, and the **dp** program. The Solaris-bundled PPP packages are documented in the **man** pages and in AnswerBook2. If you did not perform a full install when you set up Solaris, make sure that SUNWapppr, SUNWapppu, and SUNWpppk packages are installed in order to use PPP. See page 627 for more information on how to add and remove packages from the system.

▲▲ sendmail: Set Up Mail

The Internet mail protocol is called SMTP (simple mail transfer protocol). Mail programs are divided into two categories: MUAs (mail user agents) and MTAs (mail transfer agents). The MUAs that come with Solaris are

/usr/bin/mail, **/usr/bin/mailx**, **mailtool**, and **dtmail**. If you are running Solaris 2.5 or above and CDE, you will probably be using **dtmail**; most other versions of Solaris use **mailtool**. The MTA that comes with Solaris is **sendmail**. MUAs are covered in earlier chapters, this section covers **sendmail**.

The de facto Internet standard UNIX daemon for transferring mail between machines is **sendmail**. It takes care of queuing messages, transmitting messages, handing off to a local delivery agent, relaying messages, and other necessary housekeeping. The original version of **sendmail** came from the University of California at Berkeley. You can download it from **ftp.sendmail.org**. The version of **sendmail** included with Solaris has been adapted by Sun and includes several Sun-specific features and customizations. Complete details are available in AnswerBook2.

When you are setting up a system to send and receive mail, check the following:

1. Does the partition that holds **/var/mail** have enough space for the amount of mail you expect to receive? All incoming mail for all users is stored in **/var/mail**. If your users do not regularly delete mail and clean their mailboxes, the space used in this directory may fill the partition. Some administrators keep **/var/mail** on a separate partition for this reason.

2. Does the partition that holds **/var/spool/mqueue** have enough space? The **/var/spool/mqueue** directory holds outgoing and incoming mail that has been queued for delivery. Outgoing mail may be queued because a host is temporarily unavailable. Incoming mail may be temporarily queued because a user's mailbox is too full, or because the mail server is too busy to process the connection at this moment. The partition that holds **/var/spool/mqueue** must have enough space to queue the largest mail message that you would expect to receive or send. Typically the requirements for such a partition are not more than a few tens of megabytes, but some people send large attachments and may require substantially more space.

3. Is your system to be a stand-alone mail server system, or a client of another mail system? Many sites have one central machine where all mail is stored and delivered. If Tcorp uses a stand-alone mail server, Bill might receive email as **bill@socrates.tcorp.com**, **bill@tcorp.com**, or **bill@plato.tcorp.com**; all his email will go to one place. Making the decision about whether your machine is to be a client of a central server or a server by itself determines how you need to proceed.

▲▲▲ sendmail: Mail Client

It is easier to set up **sendmail** on a client machine than on a server. By default **sendmail** configuration files are configured for client setup. There are only a few things you need to do to make **sendmail** a fully operational client.

A client machine needs to know the name of the mail server or mail host. If you are running DNS, add a machine named **mailhost** to your DNS domain. If you are running NIS or NIS+, you can add an entry for **mailhost** to your name service. How you perform each of these tasks is very site-dependent. If neither of the above applies to you, add an entry for **mailhost** in **/etc/hosts**. Do not add a separate entry, just add the word `mailhost` as the third column to the line referencing the mail server. The following line from **/etc/hosts** identifies the machine *achilles* as the server where mail is delivered and relayed (the **mailhost**):

```
199.188.177.5   achilles mailhost
```

The `mailhost` entry indicates to **sendmail** that this machine is the mail server and that it knows how to contact hosts, about special hosts, about relays and domains, and how to deliver and queue to these hosts. The local client machine sends all mail that it does not know how to deliver to **mailhost**.

Because your machine will queue its mail to the server, and because remote hosts will deliver mail to this server, you either need to **rlogin** to the mail server to read your mail (tedious and inefficient), or mount the **/var/mail** spool directory on your machine. To mount the file you can add an entry to **/etc/vfstab** (not recommended because you may not be able to boot the system if the mail server is down) or you can use **automount** (page 649). To use **automount** add a mail entry to one of the indirect **automount** maps such as the following line from **/etc/auto_opt** (page 651):

```
mail        -rw,noac,intr     achilles:/var/mail
```

Next remove the existing **/var/mail** directory and make it a link to this new **automount** point.

```
# rm -rf /var/mail
# ln -s /opt/mail /var/mail
```

Now whenever you launch a mail reader, it will attempt to access your mailbox in **/var/mail/$USER**, which will trigger an automatic mount from **achilles** with the appropriate options.

If the mail server is not responding, perhaps because it is too busy, then queue files will accumulate. Running **sendmail** periodically will scan the queue and deliver any accumulated files. Adjust the following **cron** entry (page 642) to check the queue as frequently as you like:

```
45 * * * * /usr/lib/sendmail -q
```

▲▲▲ sendmail: Mail Server

Configuring **sendmail** as a mail server requires more work than configuring it as a client. Some of the configuration files are quite complex and some are written in the **m4** macro language. Discussing all of the rules, macros, and variables and what they do is enough to fill a large book. This section provides the minimum amount of information that you need to get **sendmail** configured to send mail to and receive mail from remote hosts on the Internet.

To get started configure your local machine as a primary mail server by replacing the default configuration file (**/etc/mail/sendmail.cf**). The following commands save a copy of the default file and copy in the server version.

```
# cp /etc/mail/sendmail.cf /etc/mail/client.cf
# cp /etc/mail/main.cf /etc/mail/sendmail.cf
```

Open the new **/etc/mail/sendmail.cf** in an editor. Add a line just below the one that says `my official hostname`. The new line should begin with `Dm` followed by your domain name and should not contain any **SPACE**s. If your domain is **tcorp.com**, then the line should read `Dmtcorp.com`. This line instructs **sendmail** to take mail that is for *user@tcorp.com* and deliver it to *user* on the local machine. If your machine is part of an already existing domain that has a primary mail server, but you would like to receive mail at **socrates.tcorp.org** separately, then add a line to **/etc/mail/sendmail.cf** that says `Dmsocrates.tcorp.com`. The following commands stop **sendmail** and start it up again, rereading the configuration files in the process.

```
# sh /etc/init.d/sendmail stop
# sh /etc/init.d/sendmail start
```

At this point you should be able to send and receive mail. There are many options you can change: You can receive email for multiple domains or multiple hosts, set up special delivery agents, forward email, and so on. See the system **man** pages, AnswerBook2, and other books specifically on **sendmail** for more information.

▲▲▲▲▲ Aliases: Rather than setting up several accounts for a user, you can use aliases to allow a user to receive email under several different names. Frequently a system administrator, postmaster, or web-master will want to receive email sent to names other than the ones they log in under. Users frequently send mail to **root**, postmaster, www, and webmaster without knowing the login names of the people who will receive the email. Using an alias, the user does not have to log in to a specific account or use **su** to check email; it ends up in his or her mailbox automatically. Also, if the system administrator is on vacation, it is a simple matter to send the mail to someone else for the duration. The following excerpt is a sample of an **/etc/aliases** file:

```
# Following alias is required by the mail protocol, RFC 822
# Set it to the address of a HUMAN who deals with this system's mail problems.
Postmaster: root

# Alias for mailer daemon; returned messages from our MAILER-DAEMON
# should be routed to root.
MAILER-DAEMON: root

# Aliases to handle mail to programs or files, eg news or vacation
# decode: "|/usr/bin/uudecode"
nobody: /dev/null
#
# all mail to webmaster should be forwarded to root and a copy
# saved to an archive file
webmaster: root,/var/mail/webmaster.archive
#
# all mail to root should go to alex
# replace alex with jenny when he is on vacation.
root: alex
```

Whenever you edit **/etc/aliases**, you must run the **newaliases** utility to rebuild the **aliases** database. Rather than having to scan the **aliases** text file by hand every time an email message is received, **sendmail** consults a hash file in dbm format.[19] The **newaliases** utility rebuilds this database and informs **sendmail** that

---

19. Each dbm (a primitive, internal database format) database record consists of a unique key and a value. On a call to the database, the key is looked up in a hash table and the value is updated or returned. The value is typically made up of multiple fields that the application knows how to parse but are meaningless to the dbm database. The most common versions of the dbm database are dbm, ndbm, and gdbm.

the database has been rebuilt so that it can deliver incoming messages to the appropriate mailbox or file. In addition to user's names, you can use filenames as aliases (see the previous example). You can also specify multiple files, or multiple local or remote users. See the **aliases man** page for more details.

▲▲ System Reports

There are many utilities that report on one thing or another. The **who, finger, ls, ps**, and other utilities generate simple end-user reports. The report utilities described in this section all come with Solaris and generate reports that can help you with system administration issues.

A complete analysis and breakdown of these statistics and what they mean is beyond the scope of this book. Consult a performance-tuning book such as Cockcroft and Pettit, *Sun Performance and Tuning,* one of Sun's white papers on the subject (from their Web page), or AnswerBook2 for more information.

▲▲▲ sar: Report on System Activity

The **sar** (system activity reporter) utility reports on system activity. It has two modes, one where it collects data continuously and reports on it as you request (give the command **man –s 1m sar** for information) and the other where it collects data on your command and reports on it immediately. This section discusses the second mode. With the argument(s) discussed below, but no options, or the **–u** option, **sar** reports on the following:

- **%usr** the percent of time the system is in *user mode* (running user or application code)
- **%sys** *system mode* (running system programs or system calls from a user program)
- **%wio** waiting for I/O (but otherwise idle)
- **%idle** completely idle

The two arguments to **sar** in the following example instruct it to take five samples, at 5-second intervals. The example shows a busy system with very little time spent waiting for I/O. Significantly higher **%wio** numbers could indicate that measures need to be taken to speed up disk throughput, or rearrange or add I/O bus capacity (perhaps by adding another SCSI controller).

```
$ sar 5 5

SunOS max 5.6 Generic_105182-03 i86pc     10/02/98

15:33:44    %usr    %sys    %wio    %idle
15:33:49      50      42       5        2
15:33:54      55      40       5        0
15:33:59      52      37      11        0
15:34:04      62      30       8        0
15:34:09      60      31       9        0

Average       56      36       8        0
```

Experience and system history will help you to interpret **sar** results for your system. It is not uncommon for a system with a slow tape drive to experience a very high **%wio** percentage but otherwise be in excellent health while you are backing up the system. A high **%sys** may mean that you have a process that is making numerous, inefficient system calls inside a tight loop, that there is a network bottleneck, or that the system is processing a large number of NFS operations.

The **–d** option reports on block devices (generally disks and tapes). The columns indicate:

- **time**   the time

- **device**   name of the device

- **%busy**   percentage of the time the device was busy

- **avque**   average queue length

- **r+w/s**   reads plus writes per second

- **blks/s**   number of 512-byte blocks transferred

- **avwait**   average time a request had to wait in milliseconds

- **avserv**   average time to service a request in milliseconds

(**fd** = floppy drives, **nfs** = remotely mounted filesystems, **st** = tape devices, and **sd** = local disks)

```
$ sar -d 5 5

SunOS max 5.6 Generic_105182-03 i86pc    10/02/98

15:34:13   device        %busy   avque   r+w/s   blks/s   avwait   avserv

15:34:18   fd0              0     0.0       0       0       0.0      0.0
           nfs1             0     0.0       0       0       0.0      0.0
           nfs2             0     0.0       0       0       0.0      0.0
           sd0             45     0.9      66     832       3.2      9.8
           sd1              2     0.0       2       0       1.7     11.5
           st0              0     0.0       0       0       0.0      0.0

15:34:23   fd0              0     0.0       0       0       0.0      0.0
           nfs1             0     0.0       0       0       0.0      0.0
           nfs2             0     0.0       0       0       0.0      0.0
           sd0             86    23.1      91    1109     238.9     15.8
           sd1              1     0.0       1       0       0.0      7.5
           st0              0     0.0       0       0       0.0      0.0
  .
  .
  .
Average    fd0              0     0.0       0       0       0.0      0.0
           nfs1             0     0.0       0       0       0.0      0.0
           nfs2             0     0.0       0       0       0.0      0.0
           sd0             64     7.3      90    1019      71.0      9.8
           sd1              1     0.0       2       0       0.4      6.5
           st0              0     0.0       0       0       0.0      0.0
```

▲▲▲ iostat: Report I/O Statistics

The **iostat** utility can report CPU, terminal, disk, and tape I/O activity. The following example uses the **–x** option, which is one of three options that reports on disk activity. It uses arguments of **5** and **3**, which instruct **iostat** to run three reports at 5-second intervals. The first report covers the time since the system was last booted; the following reports cover the period since the last report (the preceding 5 seconds in this case).

```
$ iostat -x 5 3
                              extended device statistics
    device    r/s   w/s    kr/s    kw/s wait actv   svc_t  %w   %b
    fd0       0.0   0.0     0.0     0.0  0.0  0.0     0.0    0    0
    sd0       0.1   0.2     1.6     1.4  0.0  0.0    23.2    0    0
    sd1       0.0   1.7     0.0     0.0  0.0  0.0     1.7    0    0
    nfs1      0.0   0.0     0.0     0.0  0.0  0.0     0.0    0    0
    nfs2      0.0   0.0     0.0     0.0  0.0  0.0   438.0    0    0
                              extended device statistics
    device    r/s   w/s    kr/s    kw/s wait actv   svc_t  %w   %b
    fd0       0.0   0.0     0.0     0.0  0.0  0.0     0.0    0    0
    sd0      15.8  76.4    39.8   524.8  2.6  1.0    39.0   20   67
    sd1       0.0   2.0     0.0     0.0  0.0  0.1    30.8    0    4
    nfs1      0.0   0.0     0.0     0.0  0.0  0.0     0.0    0    0
    nfs2      0.0   0.0     0.0     0.0  0.0  0.0     0.0    0    0
                              extended device statistics
    device    r/s   w/s    kr/s    kw/s wait actv   svc_t  %w   %b
    fd0       0.0   0.0     0.0     0.0  0.0  0.0     0.0    0    0
    sd0      36.2  49.2   201.8   364.2  1.7  1.6    38.4   45   89
    sd1       0.0   1.2     0.0     0.0  0.0  0.0    13.6    0    1
    nfs1      0.0   0.0     0.0     0.0  0.0  0.0     0.0    0    0
    nfs2      0.0   0.0     0.0     0.0  0.0  0.0     0.0    0    0
```

The report contains the following columns:

- **device**   name of the device

- **r/s**   reads per second

- **w/s**   writes per second

- **kr/s**   kilobytes read per second

- **kw/s**   kilobytes written per second

- **wait**   average number of transactions waiting in the queue

- **actv**   average number of active transactions

- **svc_t**   average time for service in milliseconds

- **%w**   percent of time transactions are waiting

- **%b**   percent of time the disk is busy

The **iostat** summary mode (**–D** option) reports on:

- **rps**   reads/second
- **wps**   writes/second
- **util**   percent utilization

for each disk on one line. With the **–c** option **iostat** reports the percentage of time the system has spent

- **us**   in user mode
- **sy**   in system mode
- **wt**   waiting for I/O
- **id**   idling

The following command uses one argument, the interval between reports. Without a second argument **iostat** runs until you kill it. Use this setup with a long polling interval, such as 5, 10, or 20 minutes, to get trend analysis of disk and CPU usage over long periods of time (days, months, or even years). You can then use a graphing program such as **gnuplot**, **xmgr**, or **sas** to plot the results over time. On the downside, as you increase your polling interval, you increase the chances that you will miss important peaks as the data is averaged over longer periods of time.

```
$ iostat -Dc 300
            sd0            sd1            sd11           cpu
  rps wps util   rps wps util   rps wps util   us sy wt id
    0   0  0.5     0   0  0.0     0   0  0.0     1  1  0 97
    0   7  6.2     0   2  2.5     0   8  8.0     4  4  6 86
    0   1  1.0     0   0  0.0     0   0  0.0     1  1  0 98
    0   0  0.3     0   0  0.0     0   0  0.0     0  2  0 98
    0   0  0.7     0   2  2.3     0   7  5.1     2  3  6 89
    0   1  0.7     0  14 19.3     0  88 81.4    10 17 63 11
    0   0  0.2     0   7 11.2     0  87 77.3     5  9 71 15
    0   1  0.9     0   0  0.0     0  51 50.4     3  4 48 45
    0   6  5.4     0   2  1.9     7   7 14.3     0  4  5 90
    0   0  0.6     0   5  8.2     0   2  1.2    10  8  8 74
    0   0  1.0     0   0  0.0     0   0  0.1     2  1  0 97
```

This system has periodic strenuous requirements on one disk **sd11**, which correlate with high CPU wait usage (equivalent to **%wio** in **sar**). There is definitely a disk bottleneck.

To map disk names given by **sar** and **iostat** into physical disk devices, you can use the **/etc/path_to_inst** file together with the **format** utility. Following is a shell script that simplifies the process:

```
$ cat diskname
#!/bin/sh
#
# map a block of raw device to iostat/sar equivalent
# e.g. diskname /dev/dsk/c0t3d0s2
#
```

```
if [ $# -ne 1 ]; then
echo "Usage: $0 disk-block|raw-device-name"
exit 1
fi

device=`/bin/ls -l $1 | nawk '{print $NF}' | nawk -F'/' '{for (i=4; i<NF; i++)
{printf("%s/", $i);}; split($NF,last,":"); print last[1];}'

if [ -z "${device}" ]; then
echo "$0: No such device."
exit 1
fi

/usr/ucb/echo -n "$1 = "
nawk -v dev=$device '$1 ~ dev {gsub("cmdk", "sd"); print $3 $2}' /etc/path_to_inst |
tr -d '"'
```

▲▲▲ vmstat: Report Virtual Memory Statistics

With output similar to **iostat**, **vmstat** generates virtual memory information along with (limited) disk and CPU activity. The following example shows virtual memory statistics in 3-second intervals for seven iterations. As with **iostat**, the first line covers the time since the system was last booted; the rest of the lines cover the period since the previous line.

```
$ vmstat 3 7
 procs     memory            page            disk          faults      cpu
 r b w   swap  free  re  mf pi po fr de sr f0 s3 -- --   in   sy   cs us sy id
 0 0 0 106904 1924   0   7  0  0  0  0  0  0  0  0  0  167  939  155  8  3 89
 0 0 0 106936 1956   0   0  0  0  0  0  0  0  0  0  0  117  650  105  2  1 97
 0 0 0 106696 1704   0 227  5  2  2 880  0  0  2  0  0  101  295  165 21 10 68
 0 0 0 104480 1440   0 359 220 280 498 632 232 0  4  0  0  376  741  348 41 25 34
 0 0 0 104460 2272   0   0  0 176 176 392  0  0  2  0  0  254  515   97  1  3 96
 0 0 0 106868 3356  10  12  1  0  0 152  0  0  0  0  0   44  261   91  1  1 98
 0 0 0 106840 3288   0   0  0  0  0  0  0  0  0  0  0   46  643  104  2  1 97
```

- **procs**   three columns of process information

  - **r**   number of runnable processes

  - **b**   number of blocked processes

  - **w**   number of swapped processes

- **memory**   two columns of memory information in kilobytes

  - **swap**   available swap space

  - **fre**   size of the free list

- **page**   seven columns of system paging activity

  - **re**   reclaimed pages

  - **mf**   minor page faults

  - **pi**   page ins

- **po**   page outs

- **fr**   pages freed

- **de**   memory deficit pages (indicating extreme memory shortage)

- **sr**   scanned pages

- **disk**   the number of disk operations per second per disk for up to four disks

- **faults**   trap/interrupt rates per second for

  - **in**   device interrupts

  - **sy**   system calls

  - **cs**   CPU context switches

- **cpu**   percentage of CPU time spent in each of these states

  - **us**   user

  - **sy**   system

  - **id**   idle

If **de** is greater than zero, or **po** gets quite large (>100–200/second), your machine probably needs more memory. The **vmstat** summary mode (**–s** option) reports on raw system counters since the machine's last reboot including the `total name lookups` and `cache hits`. For a server it is best to keep the cache hits at 80% or higher. If it gets below this level, you probably need to add more memory or tune your kernel:

```
$ vmstat -s | grep name
  1328764 total name lookups (cache hits 90%)
```

▲▲▲ netstat: Report Network Statistics

The **netstat** utility displays network statistics for your machine. It can also dump the routing table, display network socket usage, display multicast membership, and display ARP tables. The following example shows **netstat** in its role as network statistics reporter. Unlike **vmstat** and **iostat** you cannot tell it how many reports you want it to generate; you can only tell it what polling interval you want to use. Like **vmstat** and **iostat** the first report line is averaged over system uptime and should generally be ignored.

```
# netstat -I le0 -i 3
      input    le0          output            input   (Total)     output
  packets errs  packets errs  colls  packets errs  packets errs  colls
  19210554 2605  14587803 1       62743  151930872 2605  168208762 1      62743
  30       0     23      0     0      290      0     199     0     0
  299      0     271     0     0      606      0     610     0     0
  29       0     27      0     0      213      0     196     0     0
  43       0     17      0     0      263      0     244     0     0
  69       0     34      0     0      410      0     400     0     0
  80       0     86      0     0      1065     0     872     0     0
```

The **–I** option specifies that interface **le0** is to be examined, and the **–i** option specifies the polling interval. Each of the columns represents network packets over a polling interval. Other common interfaces are

hme0 (100 Mbit), **dnet0** (x86 card with Digital chips), and **fddi0**. You can use **ifconfig –a** to get a list of interfaces configured on your machine.

- **input le0**
  - **packets**   number of network packets received
  - **errs**   number of errors that occurred while receiving **packets**
- **output le0**
  - **packets**   number of network packets sent
  - **errs**   number of errors that occurred while sending **packets**
- **colls**   number of packets that were blocked by network collisions. If you have a full-duplex Ethernet card and hub, this number will always be 0; on a shared Ethernet medium, you will occasionally experience collisions.

The 6th through 10th columns show the same types of stats as the 1st through 5th, except they cover all packets on all network interfaces (including the loopback interface).

▲▲▲ mpstat: Report Multiple Processor Statistics

The **mpstat** utility shows per-processor usage statistics. On a single CPU system, **vmstat** information is usually sufficient, but if you have more than one CPU, you may want to use **mpstat** to give you additional information. The only two arguments for **mpstat** are a polling interval and an optional count. The following example shows **mpstat** information for a two-CPU compute-server machine with the polling interval set to 4 seconds for five intervals.

```
$ mpstat 4 5

CPU minf mjf xcal  intr ithr  csw icsw migr smtx  srw syscl  usr sys  wt idl
  0    1   0  184   220    8   73   19    5    2    0    78   61   1    0  38
  1    1   0  179    35   20   73   17    5    3    0    77   65   1    0  34
CPU minf mjf xcal  intr ithr  csw icsw migr smtx  srw syscl  usr sys  wt idl
  0    0   0   86   326    9  298  137    7    1    0   364   98   2    0   0
  1    1   0   70   198  103  283  128    7    1    0   163   97   3    0   0
CPU minf mjf xcal  intr ithr  csw icsw migr smtx  srw syscl  usr sys  wt idl
  0    0   0  136   331    4  319  143    6    1    0   367   98   2    0   0
  1    9   0   10   189   90  219  107    6    1    0    90   98   2    0   1
CPU minf mjf xcal  intr ithr  csw icsw migr smtx  srw syscl  usr sys  wt idl
  0    0   0  113   325    6  301  137    7    0    0   298   98   2    0   0
  1    0   0   41   182   95  248  120    6    0    0   180   98   2    0   0
CPU minf mjf xcal  intr ithr  csw icsw migr smtx  srw syscl  usr sys  wt idl
  0    0   0   44   304    6  251  115    9    0    0   154   98   1    0   1
  1    0   0   78   166   91  283  134    9    1    0   283   98   2    0   0
```

The **mpstat** utility displays the following 16 columns of information about each processor (including the processor number—**CPU**):

- **CPU**   CPU number

- **minf**   minor faults

- **mjf**   major faults

- **xcal**   cross CPU calls

- **intr**   interrupts

- **ithr**   interrupts as threads

- **csw**   context switches

- **icsw**   involuntary context switches

- **migr**   thread migrations across processors

- **smtx**   spins acquiring kernel mutex locks

- **srw**   spins on acquiring read/write locks

- **syscl**   system calls

- **usr**   time spent executing on behalf of user

- **sys**   time spent executing on behalf of system

- **wt**   time spent waiting for I/O

- **idl**   idle time

▲▲▲ top: Report on Processes Using the Most Resources

The **top** utility (not supplied with Solaris, see page 969) is a useful supplement to **ps**. At its simplest, you give a **top** command and it displays the most resource intensive processes and updates itself periodically.

▲ Problems

It is your responsibility as the system administrator to keep the system secure and running smoothly. If a user is having a problem, it usually falls to the administrator to help the user get back on the right track. This section presents some suggestions on ways to keep users happy and the system functioning at its peak.

▲▲ When a User Cannot Log In

When a user has trouble logging in on the system, the problem may be a user error or a problem with the system software or hardware. These steps may help you determine where the problem is.

- Determine if just that one user has a problem, just that one user's terminal/workstation has a problem, or if the problem is more widespread.

- If just that user has a problem, it may be that the user does not know how to log in. The user's terminal will respond when you press **RETURN**, and you will be able to log in as yourself. Make sure the user has a valid login name and password; then show the user how to log in.

- Make sure the user's home directory exists and corresponds to the entry in the **/etc/passwd** file. Check the user's startup files (**.profile** or **.login** and **.cshrc**) for errors. Verify that the user owns his or her home directory and startup files and that they are readable (and, in the case of the home directory, executable). Confirm that the entry for the user's login shell in the **/etc/passwd** file is valid (that is, that the entry is accurate and that the shell exists exactly as specified).

- Change the user's password, if there is a chance that he or she has forgotten the correct password.

- If just that one user's terminal has a problem, other users will be using the system, but that user's terminal will not respond when you press **RETURN**. For a serial terminal try pressing the **BREAK** and **RETURN** keys alternately to reestablish the proper connection rate and make sure the terminal is set for a legal connection rate such as 9600 bps. For any terminal/workstation try pressing the keys listed below:

Key	What It Does
CONTROL-Q	This key "unsticks" the terminal if someone pressed CONTROL-S.
interrupt	This key stops a runaway process that has hung up the terminal. The interrupt key is usually CONTROL-C.
ESC	This key can help if the user is in Input Mode in **vi**.
CONTROL-L	This key redraws the screen if the user was using **vi**.
CONTROL-R	This key is an alternate for CONTROL-L.
:q!RETURN	This sequence will get the user out of **ex** or **vi**.

- Check the terminal or monitor cable from where it plugs into the terminal to where it plugs into the computer (or as far as you can follow it). Check the **/etc/ttydefs** entry for that line. Finally try turning the terminal or monitor off and then turning it back on again.

- If the problem appears to be widespread, check to see if you can log in from the system console. If you can, make sure the system is in multiuser mode. If you cannot, the system may have crashed—reboot it and perform any necessary recovery.

- Check the **/etc/inittab** file to see that it is starting the appropriate login service (for example **ttymon**).

- Check the **/var/adm/messages** file. This file accumulates system errors, messages from daemon processes, and other important information. It may indicate the cause or more symptoms of a problem. Also, check the console of the machine. Occasionally messages get printed to the console about system problems that do not get written to **/var/adm/messages** (for instance if the disk is full).

- If the user is logging in over a network connection, check **/etc/inetd.conf** to make sure the service the user is trying to use is enabled. If the user is using **telnet** or **rlogin**, make sure that the corresponding entry in **/etc/inetd.conf** is not commented out (there should be no # at the beginning of the line). If it is commented out, delete the #, save the changes to the file, and then kill the **inetd** process. Killing **inetd** causes it to reread **/etc/inetd.conf**. Refer to page 785 in Part III for more information on **kill**.

- Check for full filesystems. Sometimes if the **/tmp** filesystem or the user's home directory is full, the login will fail in unexpected ways. If applications that start when the user logs in cannot create temporary files or cannot update files in the user's home directory, then the login process itself may terminate.

- If you are running CDE, check the **/var/dt/Xerrors** file and the **.dt/errorlog** file in the user's home directory. Also, check that the **dtlogin** process is running. Sometimes the following commands will get things working again:

```
# sh /etc/init.d/dtlogin stop
# sh /etc/init.d/dtlogin start
```

- If you are running XDM, check the **/var/tmp/xdm-errors** file. This is the default file used by **xdm** to log any errors. Make sure that **xdm** and the X server are running. Sometimes you can get things going again by killing the **Xsun** processes to force **xdm** to start a new X server.

- Use the **truss** utility (page 926) to follow all the system calls of the login process. To do this you can run **truss** on **inetd** if the user is attempting to log in over a network, **ttymon** if the user is trying to use a local terminal, **dtlogin** if the machine is running CDE, or **xdm** if the machine is using XDM. The latter two are particularly verbose. Use the **–o** flag to redirect the output to a temporary file so that you can peruse it at your leisure. For example if the process id of **inetd** is 167, then the following command will start a system call trace on **inetd** and any subprocesses that it spawns.

```
# truss -o /tmp/inetd.tr -faep 167
```

The **–f** option tells **truss** to follow all forks, **–a** says to show all arguments passed to each **exec** system call, **–e** says to show all environment variables that are passed in each **exec** system call, and **–p 167** says to attach to the process that is running as PID 167.

▲▲ When the System is Slow

When the system is running slowly for no apparent reason, there may be a process that did not exit when a user logged out. Symptoms include poor response time and a system load, as shown by **w** or **uptime**, that is greater than 1.0. Use **ps –ef** or **/usr/ucb/ps –aux** to list all processes. The **top** (page 969), **proctool** (page 968), and **qps** (page 968) programs are also excellent for quickly finding rogue processes. Things to look for in **ps –ef** output include a large number in the TIME field. For example if you find a Netscape process that has a TIME field over 100.0, there is a good chance that this process has run amok. However if the user is doing a lot of Java work and has not logged out for a long period of time, this may be normal. Look at the START field to see when the process was started. If the process has been running for longer than the user has been logged in, then it is a good candidate to be killed.

The BSD version of **ps** (**/usr/ucb/ps**) with the **–aux** flags shows processes along with the percentage of the CPU and system memory that they are consuming:

```
$ /usr/ucb/ps -aux
USER       PID %CPU %MEM   SZ  RSS TT        S    START   TIME COMMAND
alex      7370 25.0  0.6 1960 1444 pts/0     O    Aug 31 4303:27 ./rc5des-sp20
william   8935  1.5  9.12811223052 pts/21    S    Sep 02 69:16 netscape4_exe
root     11330  0.6  0.6 2880 1452 ?         S 20:45:06  0:00 in.rshd
doug     11331  0.5  0.4 1124  896 ?         S 20:45:08  0:00 tcsh -c /usr/ucb/p
root       143  0.3  1.0 3992 2508 ?         S    Jul 19 82:42 /usr/lib/autofs/au
root         3  0.2  0.0    0    0 ?         S    Jul 19 440:57 fsflush
root     11332  0.2  0.4 1052  900 ?         O 20:45:09  0:00 /usr/ucb/ps -aux
root        97  0.1  0.4 1972 1036 ?         S    Jul 19 13:31 /usr/sbin/rpcbind
root       168  0.1  0.8 2860 2044 ?         S    Jul 19  4:08 /usr/sbin/nscd -S
root       116  0.0  0.5 1840 1220 ?         S    Jul 19  0:36 /usr/sbin/inetd -s
casey     2403  0.0  1.0 5500 2432 ?         S    Aug 09 12:47 /opt/java1.2.b2/bi
root         0  0.0  0.0    0    0 ?         T    Jul 19  0:00 sched
root         1  0.0  0.2 1572  488 ?         S    Jul 19  1:07 /etc/init -
root         2  0.0  0.0    0    0 ?         S    Jul 19  0:01 pageout
```

The output is truncated at 80 columns to fit on a typical terminal window. You can use the **–w** option to **/usr/ucb/ps** to adjust the width of the output and the **–ww** option to display all characters no matter how wide the line is.

There are several processes that are more prone to running amok than others. These include Netscape, Matlab (if installed), **textedit** (on older versions of Solaris), **rpc.ttdbserverd** (particularly on X server machines), and in some cases **dsdm** (the CDE drag-and-drop handler). If the system gets slow and you notice one of these processes consuming a lot of CPU time, check to be sure that the user/owner of the process is not active, and then kill the process or contact the user. Then check to make sure you have all the appropriate system patches installed (page 629).

When a user gets stuck and leaves his or her terminal unattended without notifying anyone, it is convenient to **kill** all processes owned by that user. If the user is running a window system such as CDE or Open-Windows on the console, kill the window manager process. Managers to look for include **twm**, **dtwm**, **olwm**, and **mwm** (the names of most window managers end in wm). Usually the window manager is either the first (see **/usr/openwin/lib/Xinitrc** for an example) or last thing to be run, and exiting from the window manager logs the user out. If killing the window manager does not work, try killing the X server process itself. This process is typically listed as **/usr/openwin/bin/X** or **/usr/openwin/bin/Xsun**. If that fails, you can kill all processes owned by a user by running **kill –1 –1**, or equivalently **kill –HUP –1** as the user. Using **–1** (one) in place of the process ID tells **kill** that it should send the signal to all processes that are owned by that user. For example as root you could type:

```
# su jenny -c 'kill -HUP -1'
```

If this does not kill all processes (sometimes HUP will not kill a process), then you can use the KILL signal. The following line will definitely **kill** all processes owned by Jenny, and it will not be friendly about it. (If you do not use **su jenny**, it will bring the machine down.)

```
# su jenny -c 'kill -9 -1'
```

▲▲ lsof: Find Large, Open Files

The **lsof** utility (not supplied with Solaris, see page 968) can help you locate large files. The name **lsof** is short for **ls** open files. This utility has options that let you look at just certain processes, look only at certain file descriptors of a process, or show certain network connections (network connections use file descriptors just as normal files do and **lsof** can show them as well). Once you have identified a suspect process using **ps –ef**, run the following command:

```
# lsof -s -p n
```

Replace *n* with the process id of the suspect process; **lsof** displays a list of all file descriptors that process *n* has open. The **–s** option displays the size of all open files. The size information may be helpful in determining if the process has a very large file open. If it does, contact the owner of the process, or, if necessary, kill the process. The **–r***n* option redisplays the output of **lsof** every *n* seconds.

▲▲ Keeping a Machine Log

A machine log that includes the following information may be helpful in finding and fixing problems with the system. Note the time and date for each entry in the log. Avoid the temptation of keeping the log *only* on the computer, because it will be most useful to you at times when the machine is down. Another good idea is

Condition	Action
Hardware modifications	Keep track of all modifications to the hardware—even those installed by factory representatives.
System software modifications	Keep track of any modification that anyone makes to the operating system software, whether it is a patch or a new version of a program.
Hardware malfunctions	Keep as accurate a list as possible of any problems with the system. Make note of any error messages or numbers that the system displays on the system console and what users were doing when the problem occurred.
User complaints	Make a list of all reasonable complaints made by knowledgeable users (for example "machine is abnormally slow").

to keep a record of all email regarding user problems. One way to do this is to just save all of this mail to a separate file as you read it. Another way would be to set up a special mail alias that users can mail to when they have problems. This alias can then forward mail to you and also store a copy in a archive file. Following is an example of an entry in the **/etc/aliases** file that sets up this type of alias:

```
trouble: admin,/var/mail/admin.archive
```

Email sent to the **trouble** alias will be forwarded to the **admin** user and also stored in the file **/var/mail/admin.archive**. Remember that when you edit the **/etc/aliases** file, you need to run the **newaliases** command to inform the mail daemon (**sendmail**) to rebuild the **alias** database.

▲▲ Keeping the System Secure

No system with dial-in lines or public access to terminals is absolutely secure. You can make your system as secure as possible by changing the Superuser password frequently, setting a PROM password (page 598), and choosing passwords that are hard to guess. Do not tell anyone who does not *absolutely* need to know what the Superuser password is. You can also encourage system users to choose difficult passwords and to change them periodically.

A password that is hard to guess is one that someone else would not be likely to think that you would have chosen. Do not use words from the dictionary (spelled forwards or backwards), names of relatives, pets, or friends, or words from a foreign language. A good strategy is to choose a couple of short words, include some punctuation (for example put a ^ between them), mix the case, and replace a couple of the letters in the words with numbers. Remember that only the first eight characters of a password are significant. An example of a good password would be C&yGram5 (candygrams) if it were not printed in this book. There are several very good password-cracking programs that you can use to find users who have chosen poor passwords. These programs work by repeatedly encrypting words from dictionaries, phrases, names, and other sources. If the encrypted password matches the output of the program, then the program has found the password of the user. Two programs that crack passwords are **crack** and **cops** (both on page 969).

Make sure that no one (except Superuser) can write to files containing programs that are owned by **root** and run in the setuid mode (for example **mailx** and **su**). Also make sure that users do not transfer programs that run in the set user ID mode and are owned by **root** onto the system by means of mounting tapes or disks. These programs can be used to circumvent system security. Refer to **chmod** in Part III for more information about the set user ID mode. One technique that prevents users from having set user ID files is to use the **–nosuid** flag to **mount**. It is a good idea to add this option to the flags section in the **vfstab** file (page 617).

Some versions of Solaris come with many critical directories set with group write permission. This will make the system less secure. There is a free utility named **fix-modes** that was developed by a Sun engineer (in addition to the built-in ASET tools package, discussed below), which sets all directories to more reasonable permissions. Running this program will cause many Sun patches and new packages to report that these directories have improper permissions because they expect the Sun defaults. These programs will ask you if you wish to reset the permissions. Answer *no* to leave the permissions in the modified, more secure state. If the **/etc** directory on your machine is writable by group, you need to run **fix-modes**. Here is an example of adding a package (SUNWlicsw) after you have run **fix-modes**:

```
The following files are already installed on the system and are being
used by another package:
/usr <attribute change only>
/usr/bin <attribute change only>
/usr/lib <attribute change only>
Do you want to install these conflicting files [y,n,?,q] n
Do you want to continue with the installation of <SUNWlicsw> [y,n,?] y
```

▲▲▲ ACL (Access Control List)

ACLs (access control lists) were introduced in Solaris 2.5 and changed slightly in 2.6. They are designed to augment standard Solaris file permissions, which for example do not allow you to give file access to more than one group of people nor to everybody in one group except one person. To overcome these shortcomings

ACLs give you complete control over who can access a file or directory on an individual basis. You can give as many users or groups read, write, or execute access as needed.

You can use ACLs to augment your capabilities for controlling system files. To delegate editing **/etc/motd** to Jenny, use **setfacl** to give Jenny write access without having to set up a special group or give write access to everybody. Use these capabilities carefully and only as needed. Keep a log of your ACL permission assignments. ACLs may or may not work over a network filesystem depending on your OS level, the remote host support for ACLs, and the type and support for ACLs in the filesystem. They will work over NFS with Solaris releases 2.5 and above.

By default an ACL gives everyone read access to a file (**chmod** permissions will override ACL permissions if the **chmod** permissions are more restrictive). Below, Alex uses **touch** (page 561) to create the **report** file and **ls** to show its permissions. Next the **getfacl** utility lists the ACL permissions (which in this case give the same access as the traditional permissions).

```
$ touch report
$ ls -l report
-rw-r--r--   1 alex      alex          0 Jun 26 14:52 report
$ getfacl report

# file: report
# owner: alex
# group: alex
user::rw-
group::r--              #effective:r--
mask:r--
other:r--
```

Next Alex uses **setfacl** to give Jenny read and write permission to the file. The **–m** option modifies an existing ACL or creates a new one if one does not exist. Because the file is owned by Alex and is associated with the group **alex**, giving Jenny these permissions would not be possible with **chmod** unless Alex gave everyone read and write access to **report**. The output of **ls** shows nothing different except for the plus sign (following the permissions) that indicates that the file has an ACL. The output of **getfacl** shows that Jenny now has read and write access to the file.

```
$ setfacl -m u:jenny:rw- report
$ ls -l report
-rw-r--r--+ 1 alex      alex          0 Jun 26 14:52 report
$ getfacl report

# file: report
# owner: alex
# group: alex
user::rw-
user:jenny:rw-          #effective:r--
group::r--              #effective:r--
mask:r--
other:r--
```

The argument to **setfacl** consists of a comma-separated list of colon-separated entries. All of the possible entries are not covered here; refer to the **setfacl man** page for the complete specification. Each entry specifies the type of entity being given permission: user (u), group (g), or other (o); the specific instance of that entity (for example bill, sales, or default—indicated by : :); and the permissions (for example r--, ---, r-x, or rwx). The following examples show some ways of setting the ACLs for a file named **report**.

```
# setfacl -m u:bill:rw- report
# setfacl -m g:pubs:rw-,g:sales:r--,g::--- report
# setfacl -s u::rwx,u:jenny:r--,g::r--,g:sales:rw-,m:r--,o:--- report
```

The first line modifies (**–m**) the ACL for **report**, giving user **bill** read and write permissions. The second line gives group **pubs** read and write access, group **sales** read access, and the default group no access at all.

The **–s** flag in the third line replaces any existing ACLs for the file with a new one. When you use the **–s** option, you *must,* at a minimum, specify the permissions for the default user (you, unless you are working as **root**), the default group, and other. If you wish to specify additional user or group entries in your ACL, you must also (at a minimum) specify a mask entry (limits permissions for group and users except the owner), and there must be no duplicate user or group entries in the ACL. The third line gives the default user (owner) all permissions (u::rwx), Jenny read permission (u:jenny:r--), the default group read permission (g::r--), and the **sales** group read and write permissions (g:sales:rw-). The mask (m:r--) is set to read, and everybody else has no access at all (o:---). There are additional rules for what must be specified if you are setting up an ACL for a directory.

For the third example **getfacl** returns the following:

```
# file: new
# owner: alex
# group: pubs
user::rwx
user:jenny:r--          #effective:r--
group::r--              #effective:r--
group:sales:rw-         #effective:r--
mask:r--
other:---
```

▲▲▲ Automated Security Enhancement Tools

The ASET (automated security enhancement tools) auditing mechanism can help you maintain the security of your system. It allows you to audit and restrict access to system files, providing three levels of security (**low**, **med**, **high**) that are controlled by the **–l** command-line flag or the **ASETSECLEVEL** environment variable.

The **low** level does not alter the system in any way but does perform routine checks and report potential problems. The **med** level may change permissions on some system setup files; it causes **aset** to report all alterations made as well as any other problems that were found. The **med** level does not change any system services. The **high** level changes permissions on many system files. It attempts to give all files the least exposure possible. At **high**, security is of the most importance. There are a few system commands that may have different behavior because of the security restrictions. Start by using **low** or **med** security until you are familiar with how **aset** works.

The **/usr/aset** directory contains all the **aset** support files. The **asetenv** and **asetmasters** files control the behavior of **aset** at each level. Do not modify these files unless you are very familiar with how **aset** works. Refer to the **aset, asetenv,** and **asetmasters man** pages for details.

▲▲ Monitoring Disk Usage

Sooner or later, you will probably start to run out of disk space. Do not fill up a disk—Solaris runs best with at least 5 to 30 percent of the disk space free in each filesystem. When the filesystem becomes full, it can become fragmented. This is similar to the DOS concept of fragmentation, but not nearly as pronounced, and typically rare on modern Solaris filesystems such as UFS. UNIX filesystems are resistant to fragmentation by design. If you keep your filesystems from running near full capacity for long periods of time, you may never need to worry about fragmentation at all. Using more than the maximum optimal disk space in a filesystem also degrades system performance. If there is no space on a filesystem, you cannot write to it at all.

To check on fragmentation you can unmount the filesystem and use **fsck** on it. As part of **fsck** execution, fragmentation is computed and displayed. You can defragment a filesystem by backing it up, using **newfs** to make a clean empty image, and then doing a restore. The utility that you use to do your backup and restore is irrelevant and completely up to you. You can use **ufsdump/ufsrestore, tar, cpio,** or a third-party backup program.

Solaris provides several programs that you can use to determine who is using how much disk space on what filesystems. Refer to the **du, quot,** and **df** utilities and the **–size** option of the **find** utility in Part III. In addition to these utilities, you can use the disk quota system to manage disk space, as described below.

The main ways to increase the amount of free space on a filesystem are to compress files, delete files, grow filesystems, and condense directories. This section contains some ideas on ways to maintain a filesystem so that it does not get overloaded.

▲▲▲ Growing Files

Some files, such as log files and temporary files, grow automatically over time. Core dump files take up space and are rarely needed. Also, users occasionally run programs that accidentally generate huge files. As the system administrator, you must review these files periodically so that they do not get out of hand.

If a filesystem is running out of space quickly (that is, over the period of an hour rather than weeks or months), the first thing to do is to figure out why it is running out of space. Use a **ps –ef** command to determine whether a user has created a runaway process that is creating a huge file. In evaluating the output of **ps**, look for a process that has used a large amount of CPU time. If such a process is running and creating a large file, the file will continue to grow as you free up space. If you remove the huge file, the space it occupied will not be freed until the process terminates, so you need to kill the process. Try to contact the user running the process and ask the user to kill it. If you cannot contact the user, log in as **root** and kill the process. Refer to **kill** in Part III for more information.

You can also truncate a large log file rather than removing it. For example if the **/var/adm/messages** file has gotten very large because a system daemon is misconfigured, you can use **/dev/null** to truncate it:

```
# cp /dev/null /var/adm/messages
```

If you were to remove the **/var/adm/messages** file, you would have to remember to restart the **syslogd** daemon. Without restarting **syslogd** the space on the filesystem would not be released.

If no single process is consuming the disk space, but it has instead been used up gradually, locate unneeded files and delete them. You can archive them using **cpio**, **ufsdump**, or **tar** before you delete them. You can safely remove any files named **core** that have not been accessed for several days. The following command performs this function:

```
# find / -name core -atime +3 -exec rm {} \;
```

Look through the **/tmp** and **/var/tmp** directories for old temporary files and remove them. The **/var/adm/spellhist** file keeps track of all the misspelled words that **spell** finds—make sure it does not get too big. Keep track of disk usage in **/var/mail**, **/var/spool**, **/var/adm**, and **/var/news**.

Start Optional

▲▲▲ Disk Quota System

The disk quota system limits the disk space and number of files owned by individual users. You can choose to limit each user's disk space or the number of files each user can own or both. For each resource that is limited, there are actually two limits. The lower limit, or *quota*, can be exceeded by the user, although a warning is presented each time the user logs in when he or she is above the quota. After a certain number of warnings (set by the system administrator), the system will behave as if the user has reached the upper limit. Once the upper limit is reached or the user has received the specified number of warnings, the user will not be allowed to create any more files or use any more disk space. The user's only recourse at that point is to remove some files.

Users can review their usage and limits with the **quota** command. Superuser can use **quota** to obtain information about any user.

First you must decide which filesystems to limit and how to allocate space among users. Typically, only filesystems that contain users' home directories, such as **/home**, are limited. Use the **edquota** command to set the quotas and then **quotaon** to start the quota system. You will probably want to put the **quotaon** command into the appropriate run command script, so that the quota system will be enabled when you bring up the system (page 616). The quota system is automatically disabled when the filesystems are unmounted.

Stop Optional

▲▲▲ Removing Unused Space from a Directory

A directory with too many filenames in it is inefficient. The point at which a directory on a UFS filesystem becomes inefficient varies, depending partly on the length of the filenames it contains. Keep your directories relatively small. Having fewer than a few hundred files (or directories) in a directory is generally a good idea, and having more than a few thousand is generally a bad idea. Additionally Solaris uses a caching mechanism for frequently accessed files to speed the process of locating an inode from a filename. This caching mechanism only works on filenames of up to 30 characters in length, so avoid extremely long filenames for frequently accessed files.

If you find a directory that is too large, you can usually break it into several smaller directories by moving its contents into new directories. Make sure you remove the original directory once you have moved its contents.

Because Solaris directories do not shrink automatically, removing a file from a directory will not shrink the directory, even though it will make more space on the disk. To remove unused space and make a directory smaller, you must copy or move all the files into a new directory and remove the original directory.

The following procedure removes unused directory space. First remove all unneeded files from the large directory. Then create a new empty directory. Next move or copy all remaining files from the old large directory to the new empty directory. Finally delete the old directory and rename the new directory.

```
# mkdir /home/alex/new
# mv /home/alex/large/* /home/alex/new
# rmdir /home/alex/large
# mv /home/alex/new /home/alex/large
```

▲ Getting Information to Users

As the system administrator, one of your primary responsibilities is communicating with the system users. You need to make announcements, such as when the system will be down for maintenance, when a class on some new software will be held, and how users can access the new system printer. You can even start to fill the role of a small local newspaper, letting users know about new employees, births, the company picnic, and so on.

Different items you want to communicate will have different priorities. Information about the company picnic in two months is not as time-sensitive as the fact that you are bringing the system down in five minutes. To meet these differing needs, Solaris provides different ways of communicating. The most common methods are described and contrasted below. All of these methods are generally available to everyone, except for **motd** (the message of the day), which is typically reserved for Superuser.

write
Use the **write** utility to communicate with any individual user who is logged in. You might use it to ask a user to stop running a program that is bogging down the system. Users can also use **write** to ask you, for example, to mount a tape or restore a file.

wall
The **wall** (write all) utility is most effective for communicating immediately with everyone who is logged in. It works similarly to **write**, but it sends a message to everyone who is logged in. Use it if you are about to bring the system down or you are in another crisis situation. Users who are not logged in will not get the message.

Use **wall** while you are Superuser *only* in crisis situations—it will interrupt anything anyone is doing.

rwall
The **rwall** utility is used in a similar way to **wall**. The difference is that **rwall** can be used to communicate to users on other machines. You would use this utility instead of **wall**, for instance, if your machine was serving filesystems via NFS to other machines on the network. The same caveats apply to usage of this utility in place of **wall**.

mail
Mail is useful for communicating less urgent information to one or more system users. When you send mail, you have to be willing to wait for each user to read it. The mail utilities are useful for reminding users that they are forgetting to log out, bills are past due, or they are using too much disk space.

Users can easily make permanent records of messages they receive via mail, as opposed to messages received via **write**, so that they can keep track of important details. It would be appropriate to use mail to inform users about a new, complex procedure, so that each user could keep a copy of the information for reference.

Message of the Day
All users see the message of the day each time they log in. You can edit the **/etc/motd** file to change the message. The message of the day can alert users to upcoming periodic maintenance, new system features, or a change in procedures.

news
The **news** utility displays news: Meeting announcements, new hardware or software on the system, new employees, parties, and so on.

Summary

The system administrator is responsible for backing up files, adding and removing users, helping users who have problems logging in, and keeping track of disk usage and system security.

This chapter explains many of the files and programs you will have to work with to maintain a Solaris system. Much of the work you do as the system administrator requires you to log in as Superuser. The login name for Superuser is **root**. When you are logged in as Superuser, you have extensive systemwide powers that you do not normally have. You can read from and write to any file and execute programs that ordinary users are not permitted to execute.

A series of programs and files control how the system appears at any given time. Many of the files you work with as the system administrator are located in the **/etc** directory.

When you bring up the system, it is sometimes in single-user mode. In this mode only the system console is functional, and not all the filesystems are mounted. When the system is in single-user mode, you can back up files and use **fsck** to check the integrity of filesystems before you mount them. The **telinit** utility brings the system to its normal multiuser state.

With the system running in multiuser mode, you can still perform many administration tasks, such as adding users and printers.

Review Exercises

1. What option should you use with **fsck** if you just want to review the status of your filesystems without making any changes to them? How does **fsck** determine what devices to check if you do not specify one on the command line?

2. How does single-user mode differ from multiuser mode?

3. How would you communicate each of the following messages?

   a. The system is coming down tomorrow at 6:00 in the evening for periodic maintenance.

   b. The system is coming down in 5 minutes.

   c. Jenny's jobs are slowing the system down drastically, and she should postpone them.

   d. Alex's wife just had a baby girl.

4. If Alex belongs to five groups—**inhouse**, **pubs**, **sys**, **other**, and **supers**—how would his group memberships be represented? Assume that inhouse is his primary group. How would Alex create a file that belongs to the group **pubs**?

5. How can you identify the user ID of another user on your system? What is the user ID of **root**?

6. How can you redirect the output of the **find** command so that whatever it sends to the standard error disappears?

7. How many inodes does a file have? What happens when you add a hard link to a file? What happens when you add a symbolic link?

8. How would you add a printer named **quark** that is on a remote machine named **physics**? How would you add a printer named **greens** if it was attached to the local machine on serial port B at 19,200 bps?

9. What are the differences between a character device and a block device?

10. What is a named pipe? Give an example of how one is used.

11. How would you mount the **/export/apps** filesystem from a server named **achilles** to a client named **perseus**. Give the commands for the client and the server machines.

Advanced Review Exercises

12. A process is using 100% of the CPU time. How do you identify the process and determine if you should kill it?

13. What are the differences between a fifo and a socket?

14. Develop a strategy for coming up with a password that an intruder would not be likely to guess but that you will be able to remember.

15. Develop a backup strategy that is executed by **cron** and includes the follow components:

    a. A level 0 backup is done once per month.

    b. A level 2 dump is performed one day per week.

    c. A level 5 dump is performed every day that neither a level 0 nor a level 2 is performed.

    d. In the worst case how many restores would you have to perform to recover a file that was dumped using the above schedule?

16. How would you restrict access to a tape drive on your system so that only certain users could read and write tapes?

17. Design and implement a job that runs every night at 11:30 and removes all files named **core** that are more than a week old from the **/home** filesystem.

18. When **fsck** puts files in a **lost+found** directory, it has lost the directory information for the files (and thus has lost the names of the files). Each file is given a new name, which is the same as the inode number for the file:

    ```
    $ ls -lg lost+found
    -rw-r--r-- 1 alex pubs    110 Jun 10 10:55 51262
    ```

    What can you do to identify these files and restore them?

19. What do the letters of the **su** command stand for? (*Hint:* It is not Superuser.) What can you do with **su** besides give yourself Superuser privileges? How would you log in as Alex if you did not know his password but knew the **root** password? How would you establish the same environment that Alex has when he first logs on?

20. How would you allow a user to execute privileged commands without giving the user the Superuser password?

21. Why are setuid shell scripts inherently unsafe?

22. Use **at** to reboot the system

    a. at 3A.M. the following morning

    b. next Friday at 1 minute past midnight friday morning

    c. two weeks from tomorrow at the current time

    d. in 30 minutes, using the C Shell

23. Give a command that will make a level 0 dump of the **/usr** filesystem to the first tape device on the system. What command would you use to take advantage of a drive that supports compression? What command would place a level 3 dump of the **/var** filesystem immediately after the level 0 dump on the tape?

24. Use an ACL to create a new directory **/home/shared/billken** so that users Bill and Kendra can create files in the directory. Any new files or subdirectories that either user creates should automatically be writable by either user. No one else should have access to this directory or the files within it. Modify this directory so that the group **spiffy** has read-only access to all files and directories within **billken**.

25. A utility named **/usr/bin/netclk** accepts a connection over the network and quits once the connection is dropped. How can you use the built-in functionality of Solaris to make this program run so that it restarts automatically (without modifying **netclk**)? (*Hint:* It should only run in multiuser mode)

26. A process is consuming a great deal of memory. How do you determine how much physical memory it is using and what percentage this is of the total memory?

27. When a user logs in, you would like the system to check for a login name in the local **/etc/passwd** file first and then to check NIS. How do you implement this strategy?

PART

III

The Solaris Utility
Programs

The following tables list the utilities grouped by function. Although most of these are true utilities (programs that are separate from the shell), some are built into the shells (builtins). The utilities in this section are sorted alphabetically.

Utilities That Display and Manipulate Files

Utility	Function
cat	Joins or displays files—page 698
catman	Preformats and indexes man pages—page 700
cmp	Checks two files to see if they differ—page 714
comm	Compares sorted files—page 716
compress	Compresses or decompresses files—page 717
cp	Copies one or more files—page 719
cpio	Creates an archive or restores files from an archive—page 721
cut	Selects characters or fields from input lines—page 727
dd	Copies a file from one device to another—page 731
diff	Displays the differences between two files—page 739
dircmp	Displays the differences between two directories—page 742
find	Finds files based on various criteria—page 753
fmt	Formats text very simply—page 760
grep	Searches for a pattern in files—page 777
gzip	Compresses or decompresses files—page 781
head	Displays the beginning of a file—page 784
ln	Makes a link to a file—page 787
lp	Prints files—page 789
ls	Displays information about one or more files—page 791
man	Displays documentation for commands—page 809
mkdir	Makes a directory—page 813
more	Displays a file, one screenful at a time—page 815
mv	Moves (renames) a file—page 818
nawk	Searches for and processes patterns in a file—page 820
od	Dumps the contents of a file—page 847
paste	Joins corresponding lines from files—page 849

Utility	Function
pg	Displays a file, one screenful at a time—page 857
pr	Paginates files for printing—page 860
rm	Removes a file (deletes a link)—page 873
rmdir	Removes a directory—page 876
sed	Edits a file (not interactively)—page 880
sort	Sorts and/or merges files—page 891
spell	Checks a file for spelling errors—page 900
tail	Displays the last part of a file—page 909
tar	Stores or retrieves files to/from an archive file—page 912
touch	Updates access and modification time for a file—page 922
ufsdump	Backs up files or filesystems—page 933
ufsrestore	Restores files from a ufsdump archive—page 936
uniq	Displays lines of a file that are unique—page 940
wc	Displays the number of lines, words, and characters in a file—page 944

Network Utilities

Utility	Function
ftp	Transfers files over a network—page 765
rcp	Copies one or more files to or from a remote computer—page 870
rlogin	Logs in on a remote computer—page 872
rsh	Executes commands on a remote computer—page 877
rwho	Displays names of users on computers attached to a network—page 879
telnet	Connects to a remote computer over a network—page 916

Communication Utilities

Utility	Function
mailx	Sends and receives electronic mail—page 797
mesg	Enables/disables reception of messages—page 812
write	Sends a message to another user—page 948

Utilities That Display and Alter Status

Utility	Function
cd	Changes to another working directory—page 707
chgrp	Changes the group associated with a file—page 708
chmod	Changes the access mode of a file—page 709
chown	Changes the owner of a file—page 713
date	Displays or sets the time and date—page 729
df	Displays the amount of available disk space—page 736
dfmounts	Lists remotely mounted filesystems—page 738
du	Displays information on disk usage—page 745
file	Displays the classification of a file—page 752
finger	Displays detailed information on users—page 758
kill	Terminates a process—page 785
nice	Changes the priority of a command—page 844
nohup	Runs a command that keeps running after you log out—page 846
ps	Displays process status—page 865
quot	Summarizes filesystem ownership information—page 868
sleep	Creates a process that sleeps for a specified interval—page 890
stty	Displays or sets terminal/emulator parameters—page 902
truss	Traces a process—page 926
umask	Establishes or displays the file-creation permissions mask—page 939
w	Displays information on system users—page 942
which	Shows where a command is located in your path—page 945
who	Displays names of users—page 946

Utilities That Are Programming Tools

Utility	Function
cc	Compiles C programs—page 702
gcc	Compiles gcc, g++, C, and C++ programs—page 769
make	Keeps a set of programs current—page 803
patch	Updates source code—page 851

Source Code Management (SCCS) Utilities

Utility	Function
admin	Creates or changes the characteristics of an SCCS file—page 691
delta	Records changes in an SCCS-encoded file—page 734
get	Creates an unencoded version of an SCCS file—page 773
prs	Prints a summary of the history of an SCCS file—page 862
rmdel	Removes a delta from an SCCS file—page 875

Miscellaneous Utilities

Utility	Function
at	Executes a shell script at a time you specify—page 694
cal	Displays a calendar—page 697
crontab	Schedules a command to run regularly at a specified time—page 725
echo	Displays a message—page 747
expr	Evaluates an expression—page 749
fsck	Checks and repairs a filesystem—page 761
mkfile	Creates a file/swap area—page 814
swap	Administrates swap space—page 907
tee	Copies standard input to standard output and zero or more files—page 915
test	Evaluates an expression—page 918
tr	Replaces specified characters—page 924
tty	Displays the pathname of the login device—page 932
xargs	Converts standard output of one command into arguments for another—page 949

The following sample command shows the format that is used throughout Part III. These descriptions of the commands are similar to the **man** page descriptions (pages 27 and 809); however most users find the descriptions in this book easier to read and understand. These descriptions emphasize the most useful features of the commands and often leave out the more obscure ones. For information about the less commonly used features, refer to the **man** pages and AnswerBook2.

sample Very brief description of what the command does

Syntax: *sample [options] arguments*

This section includes syntax descriptions like the one above that show you how to run the command. Options and arguments enclosed in square brackets ([]) are not required. Words that you make substitutions for when you actually type the command appear in ***this bold italic typeface***. Hyphenated words listed as arguments to a command identify single arguments (for example ***source-file***) or groups of similar arguments (for example ***directory-list***). As an example, the term ***file-list*** means a list of one or more files.

Summary

Unless stated otherwise, the output from a command goes to standard output. The section on "Standard Input and Standard Output" on page 106 explains how to redirect output so that it goes to a file other than the display.

The statement that a command "takes its input from files you specify on the command line or from standard input" indicates that the command is a member of the class of UNIX/Solaris commands that takes input from files specified on the command line or, if you do not specify a filename, from standard input. It also means that the command can receive input redirected from a file or sent through a pipe (page 113).

Arguments

This section describes the arguments that you use when you run the command. The argument itself, as shown in the preceding "Syntax" section, is printed in ***bold italic type***.

Options

This section lists the common options you can use with the command. Unless otherwise specified, you must precede all options with a hyphen. Most commands accept a single hyphen before multiple options (page 104). The following are some sample options:

–t **toc** This is an example of a simple option preceded by a single dash and not followed with any arguments. The **toc** appearing as the first word of the description is a cue, a suggestion of what the option letter stands for. In this case **t** stands for **toc** or table of contents.

–f ***program-file*** Includes an argument. The argument is set in ***bold italic type*** in both the heading to the left and the description to the right. You substitute another word (filename, string of characters, or other value) for any arguments you see in ***this typeface***.

Notes

This section contains miscellaneous notes, some important and others merely interesting. POSIX-compliance information is also located here.

Discussion

This optional section contains a discussion about how to use the utility and any quirks it may have.

Examples

This section contains examples of how to use the command. It is tutorial in nature and is more casual than the preceding sections of the command description.

admin

Creates or changes the characteristics of an SCCS file

Syntax:

admin [options] –iname filename
admin [options] –n file-list
admin [options] file-list

Summary

The **admin** utility is part of SCCS (page 579). The **admin** utility creates and changes characteristics of SCCS files.

Use the first syntax shown above to create an SCCS-encoded version of an existing file, or use the second syntax to create one or more new SCCS-encoded files that are not based on existing files. The third syntax changes the characteristics of SCCS files.

Arguments

In the first format *filename* is the name that will be given to the newly encoded SCCS file. Like the names of all SCCS files, the *filename* must begin with the characters **s.**. In the second format *file-list* is a list of SCCS filenames to be assigned to the newly created files. Each of the files in the *file-list* must also begin with **s.**. The first format creates a single SCCS-encoded file based on an existing file. The second format creates any number of new SCCS-encoded files based on null deltas.

The *file-list* in the third format is a list of existing SCCS files. If you include a directory in *file-list*, **admin** processes all of the SCCS-encoded files in the directory.

Options

–a*login*   **authorize**   Adds *login* to the list of users who are allowed to make deltas to the files. Replace *login* with the user's login name or a numerical group ID. Before any users are added to the list of authorized users, the list is assumed to be empty, and any user can make a delta. You can use any number of **–a** options on a command line. If you use a numerical group ID in place of *login*, all users belonging to the group can make deltas to the file. If you precede *login* with an exclamation point, **!***login*, the user will not be able to make deltas.

–d*flag*   **delete**   Removes *flag* from an SCCS file. You can use multiple **–d** options on a single command line to remove multiple flags. See "Flags," below.

–e*login*   **erase**   Removes a user from the list of authorized users; syntax is the same as **–a**.

–f*flag*[*value*]   **flag**   Inserts *flag* with a value of *value* in the SCCS file. Flags override default characteristics of SCCS files. You may specify any number of flags on a single command line. See the next section for information about flags and their values.

–i*name*   **initialize**   Uses the file *name* as the initial delta for a new SCCS file.

691

–m[*mrlist*]

modify   Lists the modification requests that are the reason for an initial delta. Replace *mrlist* with a comma-separated list of modification request numbers. You can use the **–m** option only if the **v** flag is set, and only on an initial delta. See "Flags," below.

–n

new   Creates a new SCCS-encoded file. When it is used without the **–i** option, **admin** creates a new SCCS file based on a null delta (an empty file). When you use the **–i** option, you do not need to use **–n**, as it is redundant.

–r*x*

release   Identifies the version number **admin** will associate with an initial delta. Replace *x* with the version number (page 580). If you specify only the release component of the version number, SCCS inserts the delta into the first level of the release. For example if you use **–r3**, SCCS inserts the delta into Version 3.1. If the release is not specified on the command line, **admin** inserts the initial delta into Version 1.1. You can use the **–r** option only with **–i**.

–y*comment*

Inserts *comment* as the comment for the initial delta in a new SCCS file. Replace *comment* with the text of your comment. You must surround your comment with quotation marks if it contains spaces. If you do not use **–y** when creating an initial delta, SCCS inserts a standard comment, including the date and time of creation and the login of the user who created it. The **admin** utility ignores the **–y** option if you are not creating an initial delta.

Flags

The **admin** utility can insert flags in SCCS files to change default characteristics of the files. Each **flag** must be preceded by the **–f** option on the command line.

b

branch   Creates branch deltas for the highest-numbered trunk delta. Use the **–b** option with **get** (page 773) to make these branches. You can always make branch deltas for trunk deltas that have successors on the trunk (that is, regardless of whether the **b** flag is set).

j

joint edit   This flag allows multiple concurrent updates to the same version of an SCCS file. This flag is rarely used, because one of the purposes of SCCS is to prevent different people from making changes to the same file at the same time. If this flag is not set, once you have used **get** with the **–e** option on a version of an SCCS file, you must use **delta** to record the changes before anyone can again use **get** with the **–e** option on that version.

***l*list**

lock (starts with the letter "ell")   Identifies releases that users are not allowed to make deltas against. The ***list*** may include a single release number, several release numbers separated by commas, or **a**, which locks all releases.

Examples

The following command creates a new SCCS-encoded file named **s.menu1** that includes the file **menu1** as its first delta.[1]

```
$ admin -imenu1 s.menu1
No id keywords (cm7)
```

The **admin** utility displays the message No id keywords, indicating that there are no SCCS keywords in the new file. When keywords are included in an SCCS file, information about the SCCS file is inserted in the corresponding text file retrieved by **get**. Keywords are beyond the scope of this book—you can ignore the warning message when it occurs in the examples.

The next command creates three new SCCS-encoded files. These files are not created from existing files, and consequently the initial version of each is empty.

```
$ admin -n s.menu_mon s.menu_tues s.menu_wed s.menus_march
```

The next example locks Release 2 of **s.menus_march**, the SCCS-encoded file. It also adds Alex and Barbara to the list of users who are authorized to make deltas. Of course Alex and Barbara cannot make deltas to Release 2. The first option is dash "eff" "ell" 2.

```
$ admin -fl2 -aalex -abarbara s.menus_march
```

Any time after you execute the above command, you can remove Barbara from the list with the following command. This command also uses the **–d** option to remove the lock on Release 2. The first option is dash "dee" "ell" 2.

```
$ admin -dl2 -ebarbara s.menus_march
```

---

1. See the tip named "Making SCCS a Little More Friendly," page 581 and the following examples for information about using the **sccs** front end to help with file naming and placement.

at

Syntax: *at [options] time [date] [+increment]*

Summary

The **at** utility causes the operating system to execute commands it receives from standard input. It executes them as a shell script in the working directory at the time you specify.

When the operating system executes commands using **at**, it sends you standard output and standard error of the resulting processes via email. You can redirect the output to avoid getting mail.

The **atq** utility displays a list of **at** jobs you have queued. It is the same as **at** with the **–l** option. If you run **atq** as Superuser, it displays *all* **at** jobs scheduled by all users on the system.

The **atrm** utility allows you to cancel **at** jobs that you have queued. It is the same as running **at** with the **–r** option.

Arguments

The *time* is the time of day you want **at** to execute the job. You can specify the *time* as a one-, two-, or four-digit number. One- and two-digit numbers specify an hour, and four-digit numbers specify an hour and minute. You can also give the time in the form **hh:mm**. The **at** utility assumes a 24-hour clock unless you place **am**, **pm**, **midnight**, or **noon** immediately after the number, in which case **at** uses a 12-hour clock. You can use the word **now** in place of *time*. All of the times, dates, days, and months **at** uses are from the LC_TIME locale category discussed on page 1010.

The *date* is the day of the week or date of the month on which you want **at** to execute the job. If you do not specify a day, **at** executes the job today if the hour you specify in *time* is greater than the current hour. If the hour is less than the current hour, **at** executes the job tomorrow.

To specify a day of the week, you can spell it out or abbreviate it to three letters. You can also use the days **today** and **tomorrow**.

Use the name of a month followed by the number of the day in the month to specify a date. You can follow the month and day number with a year.

The *increment* is a number followed by one of the following (plural or singular is allowed): **minutes**, **hours**, **days**, or **weeks**. The **at** utility adds the *increment* to the *time* you specify. You cannot give an increment if you have already given a date.

Options

–c   **csh**   Runs the commands under the C Shell.

–f *file*   **file**   Typing commands for **at** from the keyboard is risky, as it is difficult to correct mistakes. This option gives **at** the name of a *file* that contains a list of commands you want to execute at the specified time.

–k	**ksh** Runs the commands under the Korn Shell.	

–l *job-list*

list (the letter "ell")   Displays information about jobs specified with *job-list*. If you omit *job-list*, **at** reports on all jobs in the queue. Using this option with **at** is the same as running **atq**.

–m

mail   Sends you mail telling you that the job ran. Without this option **at** does not provide any confirmation that the job was run (except for mailing you the job's standard output and standard error that you do not redirect).

–r *job-list*

delete   Cancels jobs that you previously submitted with **at**. The *job-list* argument is a list of one or more job numbers of the jobs you want to cancel. Using this option with **at** is the same as running **atrm**. If you do not remember the job number, use the –l option to list your jobs and their numbers.

–s

sh   Runs the commands under the Bourne Shell.

–t *time*

touch   Submits the job at *time*, where time format is similar to that used by **touch** (page 922) for submitting the job.

Notes

The shell saves the environment variables and the working directory that are in effect at the time you submit an **at** job, so that they are available when it executes the commands. The –l and –r options are not for use when you initiate a job with **at**. Use them only to determine the status of a job or cancel one. If you do not specify a shell for **at** to use (with one of the **–c**, **–k**, or **–s** options), it will default to the shell specified by the **SHELL** environment variable.

Superuser must put your login name in the **/usr/lib/cron/at.allow** file (one name per line) for you to be able to use **at**. Superuser can also prevent you from using **at** by putting your login name in the **/usr/lib/cron/at.deny** file. If **at.deny** exists and is empty, then all users on your system can use the **at** commands. If neither **/usr/lib/cron/at.allow** nor **/usr/lib/cron/at.deny** exists, then only Superuser can use **at**. For more information see "/etc/cron.d" in the list on page 609.

Jobs you submit to **at** are run by **cron** via **crontab**, the **crontab** file, and a program named **atrun**. The frequency with which **cron** executes **atrun** is based on the **atrun** entry in **crontab** and is normally every five minutes. If you want to run **at** with finer granularity, you must change the entry in **crontab** (page 725).

Examples

You can use any of the following techniques to paginate and print **long_file** at two o'clock tomorrow morning. The first example executes the command directly from the command line, whereas the last two examples use a file containing the necessary command (**pr_tonight**) and execute it using **at**. If you execute the command directly from the command line, you must signal the end of the list of commands by pressing CONTROL-D at the beginning of a line.

The line that begins with Job contains the job number and the time **at** will execute the job.

```
$ at 2am
at> pr long_file | lp
at> CONTROL-D
at> <EOT>
commands will be executed using /bin/sh
job 892198800.a at Fri Apr 10 02:00:00 1998

$ cat pr_tonight
#!/bin/sh
pr long_file | lp

$ at -f pr_tonight 2am
commands will be executed using /bin/sh
job 892198801.a at Fri Apr 10 02:00:00 1998

$ at 2am < pr_tonight
commands will be executed using /bin/sh
job 892198802.a at Fri Apr 10 02:00:00 1998
```

If you run **at –l** after the preceding commands, it displays a list of jobs in its queue.

```
$ at -l
892198800.a     Fri Apr 10 02:00:00 1998
892198801.a     Fri Apr 10 02:00:01 1998
892198802.a     Fri Apr 10 02:00:02 1998
```

The following command removes one of the jobs from the queue:

```
$ at -r 892198801.a
$ at -l
892198800.a     Fri Apr 10 02:00:00 1998
892198802.a     Fri Apr 10 02:00:02 1998
```

The next example executes **cmdfile** at 3:30 PM (1530 hours) a week from today:

```
$ at -f cmdfile 1530 +1 week
commands will be executed using /bin/sh
job 892765800.a at Thu Apr 16 15:30:00 1998
```

The final example executes a **find** job at 7 PM on Friday. It creates an intermediate file, redirects the error output, and prints the file. The technique used in the example for separating standard output from standard error will only work from the Bourne and Korn Shells. See page 452 if you are using the C Shell.

```
$ at 7pm Friday
at> find / -name "core" -print > report.out 2> report.err
at> lp report.out
at> CONTROL-D
at> <EOT>
commands will be executed using /bin/sh
job 892260000.a at Fri Apr 10 19:00:00 1998
```

cal

Displays a calendar

Syntax:

cal [[month] year]

Summary

The **cal** utility displays a calendar for a month or year.

Arguments

The arguments specify the month and year for which **cal** displays a calendar. The *month* is a decimal integer from 1 to 12, and the *year* is a decimal integer. If you do not specify any arguments, **cal** displays a calendar for the current month. If you specify a single argument, it is taken to be the year.

Notes

Do not abbreviate the year. The year 99 does not represent the same year as 1999.

Examples

The following command displays a calendar for August 1999:

```
$ cal 8 1999

    August 1999
 S  M Tu  W Th  F  S
 1  2  3  4  5  6  7
 8  9 10 11 12 13 14
15 16 17 18 19 20 21
22 23 24 25 26 27 28
29 30 31
```

The next command displays a calendar for all of 1949 (only the first six months are shown):

```
$ cal 1949
                          1949

        Jan                   Feb                   Mar
 S  M Tu  W Th  F  S    S  M Tu  W Th  F  S    S  M Tu  W Th  F  S
                   1             1  2  3  4  5             1  2  3  4  5
 2  3  4  5  6  7  8    6  7  8  9 10 11 12    6  7  8  9 10 11 12
 9 10 11 12 13 14 15   13 14 15 16 17 18 19   13 14 15 16 17 18 19
16 17 18 19 20 21 22   20 21 22 23 24 25 26   20 21 22 23 24 25 26
23 24 25 26 27 28 29   27 28                  27 28 29 30 31
30 31
        Apr                   May                   Jun
 S  M Tu  W Th  F  S    S  M Tu  W Th  F  S    S  M Tu  W Th  F  S
                1  2    1  2  3  4  5  6  7             1  2  3  4
 3  4  5  6  7  8  9    8  9 10 11 12 13 14    5  6  7  8  9 10 11
10 11 12 13 14 15 16   15 16 17 18 19 20 21   12 13 14 15 16 17 18
17 18 19 20 21 22 23   22 23 24 25 26 27 28   19 20 21 22 23 24 25
24 25 26 27 28 29 30   29 30 31               26 27 28 29 30
```

697

cat

Joins or displays files

Syntax: *cat [options] [file-list]*

Summary

The **cat** utility joins files end to end. It takes its input from files you specify on the command line or from standard input. You can use **cat** to display the contents of one or more text files on the screen.

Argument

The *file-list* is composed of pathnames of one or more files that **cat** displays. You can use a hyphen in place of a filename to cause **cat** to read standard input (for example **cat a – b** gets its input from file **a**, standard input [terminated by a **CONTROL-D**, if you enter it at the keyboard] and then file **b**).

Options

–b	**blank** Numbers the lines of output except for blank lines.
–e	**end of line** Marks the ends of lines with dollar signs. This option will only work with **–v**.
–n	**number** Numbers the lines of output.
–s	**silent** Does not complain about nonexistent files.
–t	**tab** Marks each **TAB** with a ^I and **FORMFEED** with a ^L. This option will only work with **–v**.
–u	**unbuffered** Does not buffer the output—the default is buffered.
–v	**visual** Displays **CONTROL** characters with the caret notation (^M) and characters that have the high bit set (**META** characters) with the M– notation. It does not convert **TABs** and **LINEFEEDs**. Use **–t** if you want to display **TABs**. Use **–e** to mark the ends of lines. **LINEFEEDs** cannot be displayed as anything but themselves or else the line would be too long.

Notes

The **–e** and **–t** options are ignored by **cat** if you do not specify the **–v** option. The name **cat** is derived from one of the functions of this utility, *catenate,* which means to join together sequentially, or end to end.

Use the **od** utility (page 847) to display the contents of a file that does not contain text (for example an executable program file).

> ## cat **Can Destroy Files**
>
> Despite **cat**'s warning message, the shell destroys the input file (**letter**) before invoking **cat** in the following example.
>
> ```
> $ cat memo letter > letter
> cat: input/output files 'letter' identical
> ```
>
> You can prevent this from happening by setting the **noclobber** variable from **csh** (page 464) and **ksh** (page 539).

Examples

The following command line displays the contents of the text file named **memo** on the screen:

```
$ cat memo
.
.
```

The next example catenates three files and redirects the output to a file named **all**:

```
$ cat page1 letter memo > all
```

The following **cat** command appends a fourth file to **all** using the append standard output symbol (**>>**).

```
$ cat index >> all
```

You can use **cat** to create short text files without using an editor. Enter the command line shown below, type the text that you want in the file, and then press **CONTROL-D** on a line by itself. The **cat** utility takes its input from standard input (the keyboard), and the shell redirects standard output (a copy of the input) to the file you specify. The **CONTROL-D** signals the EOF and causes **cat** to return control to the shell (page 108).

```
$ cat > new_file
.
.
(text)
.
.
CONTROL-D
```

Below, a pipe sends the output from **who** to standard input of **cat**. The **cat** utility creates the **output** file that contains the contents of the **header** file, the output of **who**, and finally, **footer**. The hyphen on the command line causes **cat** to read standard input after reading **header** and before reading **footer**.

```
$ who | cat header - footer > output
```

catman

Preformats and indexes man pages

Syntax: *catman [options] [sections]*

Summary

The **catman** utility converts (preformats) **man** pages, with their imbedded formatting codes, to a ready-to-display format. It also creates an index file named **windex** that **apropos** (**man –k** [page 54]) uses in its search for a manual page that matches a keyword.

Argument

The *sections* argument restricts the manual sections that **catman** operates on to the sections you specify in the SPACE-separated list (see examples).

Options

–M *dir*   **manual directory**   Uses *dir* as the manual page directory instead of the default **/usr/share/man**.

–n   **no reindex**   Causes **catman** not to create an index (**windex**) file.

–p   **print**   Displays what would be done instead of actually doing it.

–w   **windex**   Only creates the **windex** file, does no preformatting.

–T *macro*   **macros**   Uses the *macro* macro package to reformat the manual pages instead of the default **man** macro package. Some utilities are distributed using the **mandoc**, **me**, or in rare cases **ms** macro packages.

Discussion

The **catman** utility acts as a front end for the **makewhatis** script. In Solaris, **makewhatis** is provided as an undocumented utility in **/usr/lib**. The **whatis** file has been renamed **windex**.

Constructing an up-to-date **windex** file is essential for **man** to function properly. There must be a **windex** file located in the top directory of every manual page collection in your **MANPATH**. Without a **windex** file entry, **man** will not show you a **man** page unless you use the **–F** flag. Whenever you add a new **man** page to a **MANPATH**, reconstruct the **windex** file by using a command such as:

```
# catman -M /new/manpath -w
```

When you use **catman** to preformat manual pages, subsequent use of **man** will give you the manual page immediately (as if typing **more** on a file) instead of giving you the message: `"Reformatting page. Wait... done"`, which is displayed as **nroff** formats the manual page on the fly. The preformatted manual page directories are constructed by replacing the **man** prefix of the directory name with **cat**. For example preformatted versions of the **man** pages in **man1**, **man1m**, and **man4** are in **cat1**, **cat1m**, and **cat4**.

Examples

The following example preformats all of the **man** pages in sections **1**, **1m**, and **4** of the default **man** directory (**/usr/share/man**) and rebuilds the **windex** file:

```
# catman 1 1m 4
```

The next command preformats all of the manual pages in the default directory without rebuilding the windex file:

```
# catman -n
```

The final command rebuilds the manual pages only in the **1** and **n** directories in **/usr/local/man** and then rebuilds the **windex** file automatically.

```
# catman -M /usr/local/man 1 n
```

cc

Compiles C programs

Syntax: *cc [options] file-list [–larg]*

Summary

The C compiler preprocesses, compiles, assembles, and links C language source files.[2] See Chapter 14 for a discussion of using C and related utilities under Solaris.

The conventions used by the C compiler for assigning and recognizing filename extensions are summarized in the following table:

Filename Extension	Meaning
.c	C language source file
.i	Preprocessed C language source file
.ii	Preprocessed C++ language source file
.s	Assembly language source file
.o	Object file
.a	Static library of object modules
.so	Shared library of object modules

The **cc** utility takes its input from files you specify on the command line. Unless you use the **–o** option, **cc** saves the executable program it produces in **a.out**.

Argument

The *file-list* contains the pathnames of the files that **cc** is to compile, assemble, and/or link.

---

2. In a software package named *Sun Professional C,* sold separately from Solaris, Sun provides a development environment that includes a C compiler to preprocess, compile, assemble, and link C language source files. The C compiler also assembles and links assembly language source files, links object files only, and builds object files for use in shared libraries. The base Solaris system does include **as** and **ld** so you can assemble and link programs without having to buy the C package. A no-cost alternative is the **gcc** compiler (page 769) and related tools available from GNU. (See page 976 for download information.)

Options

Without any options **cc** accepts C language source files, assembly language source files, and object files that follow the naming conventions outlined above. The **cc** utility preprocesses, compiles, assembles, and links these files as appropriate, producing an executable file named **a.out**. If you use **cc** to create object files without linking them (to produce an executable file), each object file is named by adding the extension **.o** to the basename of the corresponding source file. If **cc** creates an executable file, it deletes any intermediate object files that it created.

      The meaning of some of the most commonly used options are given below. When certain filename extensions are associated with an option, you can assume that the extension is added to the basename of the source file.

–c
: **compile** Suppresses the linking step of compilation. The **cc** utility compiles and/or assembles source code files and leaves the object code in files with the extension **.o**.

–D_name_[**=**_value_]
: **define** Usually #define preprocessor directives are given in header, or include, files. You can use this option to define symbolic names on the command line instead. For example **–DUNIX** is equivalent to having the line #define UNIX in an include file, and **–DMACH=i586** is the same as #define MACH i586.

–E
: **everything** Suppresses all steps of compilation on C or C++ source code files _except_ preprocessing and writes the result to standard output. By convention the extension **.i** is used for preprocessed C source and **.ii** for preprocessed C++ source.

–fast
: **fast** Uses the maximum optimization for the hardware that the compiler is being run on. It turns on all optimizer flags that are appropriate for a hardware platform. If the code is executed on a different platform, it will run correctly but will probably run more slowly as software emulation traps will have to be executed instead. Other optimization arguments used after **–fast** will override implicitly defined optimizations.

–g
: **debug** Embeds additional symbol table information in the object files. Symbolic debuggers such as **gdb** or **dbx** use this information. Although this option is necessary only if you later use a debugger, it is a good practice to include it as a matter of course.

–H
: **header hierarchy** Displays the hierarchy of all included files during compilation.

–I_directory_
: **include** Looks for include files in _directory_ before looking in the standard locations. Give this option multiple times to look in more than one directory.

–Kpic
: Causes **cc** to produce _position-independent_ code, which is suitable for building a shared library.

–KPIC
: Similar to **–Kpic** but used for large shared object libraries. When there are a large number of object modules, offsets between modules may be large, and **–KPIC** should be used.

−larg   library   Searches the directories **/lib** and **/usr/lib** for a library file named **lib**arg**.so** (and then for **lib**arg**.a**). If this library is found, **cc** then searches this library for any required functions. You must replace *arg* with the name of the library you want to search. For example the **−lm** option normally links the standard math library **libm.so**. The position of this option is significant; it generally needs to go at the end of the command line but can be repeated multiple times to search different libraries. Libraries are searched in the order in which they appear on the command line. The linker uses the library only to resolve undefined symbols from modules that *precede* the library option on the command line. You can add other directories to search through using the **−L** option.

−Ldirectory   library   Adds *directory* to the list of directories to search for libraries given with the **−l** option. Directories that are added to the list with **−L** are searched before looking in the standard locations for libraries.

−O   Equivalent to **−xO2**, turns on standard compiler optimizations.

−o *file*   output   Places the executable program that results from linking into *file* instead of **a.out**. When used with the **−c** flag, the compiled object module is put in *file* instead of a *file***.o**.

−p   profile   Provides additional code in the executable that generates a file at runtime that can be used to profile the executable using the **prof** utility. Also see these options: **−xF**, **−xpg**, **−xsb**.

−Rdirectory   runtime   Adds *directory* to the list of directories that the runtime linker searches (**/lib** and **/usr/lib** by default) when it looks for shared object libraries that are required by the executable at runtime. You can use more than one **−R** flag or you can separate multiple directories following a single **−R** flag with colons.

 In place of using the **−R** option, you can put *directory* in the environment variable **LD_LIBRARY_PATH** at runtime. This practice is discouraged as different executables frequently require different library paths, and you may not be able to specify an **LD_LIBRARY_PATH** that will satisfy all executables.

−S   stop   Stops the assembling and linking steps of compilation on C or C++ source code files. The resulting assembly language files use the **.s** filename extension.

−s   strip   Removes all debugging information from the object file or executable.

−Uname   undefine   Similar to the **−D** option, this is equivalent to having an #undef argument in an include file for the symbol *name*.

−v   verify   Runs **lint**-like checks on the source file.

−w   no warnings   Inhibits all warning messages.

–x486	Generates optimizations specific to the Intel 80486 family of processors. (Only available on the compiler that runs on x86 machines.) Also available: **–xpentium**, **–x386**.
–xautopar	**automatic parallel** On SPARC platforms, generates code that is suited for running on multiprocessor machines. This option performs dependence analysis and restructures loops where necessary. When you use this flag, optimization is automatically raised to **–xO3** if the current optimization is below this level. When the **PARALLEL** environment variable is set, the executable will only use **PARALLEL** number of processors when run.
–xCC	Allows C++ style comments (// this is a comment).
–xF	Turns on additional debugging information that can be used by the SparcWorks **analyzer** program
–xOn	**optimize** Attempts to improve the object code produced by the compiler. The value of **n** may be 0,1, 2, 4, or 5. The default value of **n** is 2. Larger values of **n** result in better optimization but may increase both the size of the object file and the time it takes **cc** to run. There are many related options that allow you to control precisely the types of optimizations attempted by **cc** when you use **–O**. (See the **cc man** page.)
–xpg	Generates a **gmon.out** file that contains profiling data after normal program completion. Similar to **–p** but **gmon.out** is for use with the **gprof** utility.
–Xsb	Generates additional information for use by the SparcWorks source manager utility.
–Xt	**transition** Causes **cc** to accept C programming language features that existed in the traditional Kernighan and Ritchie C programming language. This option allows you to correctly compile older programs written using the traditional C language that existed before the ANSI standard C language was defined. Where K&R features are in conflict with the ANSI standard, warnings are issued detailing the conflict.

Notes

The preceding is only a small fraction of the full set of options available with the Sun C compiler. See the **cc man** page for a complete list.

Although the **–o** option is generally used to specify a filename to store object code, this option can also be used to name files resulting from other compilation steps. In the following example the **–o** option causes **cc** to store the executable file in **acode** instead of **a.out** (the default):

```
$ cc -o acode pgm.c
```

For more information see "Programming in C" on page 548.

Examples

The first example compiles, assembles, and links a single C program, **compute.c**. The executable output is put in **a.out**. The **cc** utility deletes the object file.

```
$ cc compute.c
```

The next example compiles the same program, using the C optimizer (**–O** option). It assembles and then links the optimized code. The **–o** option causes **cc** to put the executable output in **compute**.

```
$ cc -O -o compute compute.c
```

The next command assembles and links a C source file, an assembly language file, and an object file. The **–o** option saves the executable program in **progo**.

```
$ cc -o progo procom.c profast.s proout.o
```

In the next example **cc** searches the standard math library **/usr/lib/libm.so** when it is linking the **himath** program. It places the executable output in **a.out**.

```
$ cc himath.c -lm
```

In the next example the C compiler compiles **badtabs.c** (page 565) with an option that checks the code for questionable source code practices (**–v**). The **–g** option embeds debugging support in the executable file, which is saved in **badtabs** with the **–o badtabs** option. Full hardware-specific optimization is enabled with the **–fast** option.

The warnings produced by the C compiler are displayed on standard output.

```
% cc -v -g -fast -o badtabs badtab.sc
cc: Warning: -g conflicts with auto-inlining, auto-inlining turned off
"tab.c", line 34: warning: Function has no return statement : main
IROPT changed opt level from -O5 to -O4 for routine main
IROPT changed opt level from -O5 to -O4 for routine findstop
```

When compiling programs that use the X11 include files and libraries, you may need to use the **–I** and **–L** options to tell **cc** where to locate those include files and libraries. The **–R** flag tells the runtime linker where to look for **libX11.so**. The final example uses those options and also instructs **cc** to link the program with the basic X11 library:

```
$ cc -I/usr/openwin/include plot.c -L/usr/openwin/lib -R/usr/openwin/lib -lX11
```

cd

Changes to another working directory

Syntax: *cd [directory]*

Summary

When you call **cd** and specify a directory, that directory becomes the working directory. If you do not specify a directory, **cd** uses the value of **HOME** (your home directory).

Argument

The *directory* is the pathname of the directory that you want to become the working directory.

Notes

Although **cd** is a stand-alone utility, it is also a builtin csh/sh/ksh. Refer to the discussions of the **HOME** shell variable on pages 372 and 461. Chapter 4 contains a discussion of **cd** on page 79. Also refer to the **cd man** page for more detailed information.

Each of the three shells has a variable, **CPATH** sh/ksh or **cdpath** csh, that affects the operation of **cd**. Each of these variables contains a list of directories **cd** searches in addition to the working directory. If **CDPATH/cdpath** is not set, **cd** searches only the working directory. If it is set, **cd** searches each of the directories listed in **CDPATH/cdpath**. For more information refer to page 374 (**CDPATH** under **sh**), page 461 (**cdpath** under **csh**), or page 485 (**CDPATH** under **ksh**).

Examples

The following command makes your home directory become the working directory:

```
$ cd
```

The next command makes the **/home/alex/literature** directory the working directory. The **pwd** builtin verifies the change.

```
$ cd /home/alex/literature
$ pwd
/home/alex/literature
```

Next **cd** makes a subdirectory of the working directory the new working directory:

```
$ cd memos
$ pwd
/home/alex/literature/memos
```

Finally **cd** uses the **..** reference to the parent of the working directory to make the parent the new working directory:

```
$ cd ..
$ pwd
/home/alex/literature
```

chgrp

Changes the group associated with a file

Syntax: *chgrp [options] group file-list*

Summary

The **chgrp** utility changes the group associated with a file.

Arguments

The ***group*** is the name or numeric group ID of the new group. The ***file-list*** is a list of pathnames of the files and directories whose group association you want to change.

Options

–f   **force**   Does not report errors.

–h   When you include a symbolic link in the ***file-list***, this option changes the group of the symbolic link, not the linked-to file. Without this option **chgrp** changes the group of the linked-to file and not that of the symbolic link.

–R   **recursive**   When you include a directory in the ***file-list***, this option descends the directory hierarchy, setting the group ID on all files it encounters.

Notes

To change the group association of a file, you must be Superuser or you must both own the file and belong to the ***group*** that the file currently is associated with (the group shown by **ls –l**).

This utility does not create new groups but allows you to change the group association to one of the groups in the **/etc/group** file (page 610). Use the **groups** utility to list the groups you belong to.

Usually when you change the group of a symbolically linked file, you want to change the link, not the linked-to file. If you are working as Superuser and you use **chgrp** with the **–R** option, it is a good idea to include the **–h** option for safety so you do not change the group of files you do not mean to touch.

Example

The following command changes the group that the **manuals** file is associated with. The new group is **pubs**.

```
$ chgrp pubs manuals
```

chmod

Changes the access mode of a file

Syntax:

chmod [options] who operation permission file-list   (symbolic)
chmod [options] mode file-list   (absolute)

Summary

The **chmod** utility changes the ways in which a file can be accessed. Only the owner of a file or Superuser can change the access mode, or permissions, of a file. For more information see "Access Permissions" on page 88.

You can specify the new access mode absolutely or symbolically.

Arguments

Arguments give **chmod** information about what permissions to apply to which files.

Symbolic

The **chmod** utility changes the access permission for the class of user specified by *who*. The class of user is designated by one or more of the following letters:

who		
Letter	**User Class**	**Meaning**
u	User	Owner of the file.
g	Group	Group to which the owner belongs.
o	Other	All other users.
a	All	Can be used in place of (replaces) **ugo**.

The *operation* to be performed is defined by the following list:

operation	
Operator	**Meaning**
+	Adds permission for the specified user class.
−	Removes permission for the specified user class.
=	Sets permission for the specified user—resets all other permissions for that user class.

In the following table, which defines access ***permission***, *setuid* is short for *set user ID* and *setgid* is short for *set group ID*. For more information see "Setuid and Setgid Permissions" on page 90.

permission	
Letter	**Meaning**
r	Sets read permission.
w	Sets write permission.
x	Sets execute permission.
l	Enables mandatory locking.
s	Setuid/setgid—depending on the *who* argument—to that of the owner/group of the file while the file is being executed (pages 90 and 593).
t	Sets the sticky bit (only Superuser can set the sticky bit, and it can be used only with **u**) (page 1046).
u	Makes the permissions you are setting match those already present for the owner.
g	Makes the permissions you are setting match those already present for the group.
o	Makes the permissions you are setting match those already present for others.

Absolute

In place of the symbolic method of changing the access permissions for a file, you can use an octal number to represent the mode. Construct the number by ORing the appropriate values from the following table. (To OR two octal numbers from the following table, you can just add them. Refer to the second table following for examples.)

Number	Meaning
4000	Setuid (pages 90 and 593) when the program is executed.
20n0	Setgid (pages 90 and 593) when the program is executed with $n = 7$, 5, 3, or 1, else enables mandatory locking.
1000	Sticky bit (page 1046).
0400	Owner can read the file.
0200	Owner can write to the file.
0100	Owner can execute the file.
0040	Group can read the file.
0020	Group can write to the file.
0010	Group can execute the file.
0004	Others can read the file.
0002	Others can write to the file.
0001	Others can execute the file.

The following table lists some typical modes:

Mode	Meaning
0777	Owner, group, and public can read, write, and execute file.
0755	Owner can read, write, and execute; group and public can read and execute file.
0711	Owner can read, write, and execute; group and public can execute file.
0644	Owner can read and write; group and public can read file.
0640	Owner can read and write, group can read, and public has no access to file.

Options

–f   **force**   Does not report errors.

–R   **recursive**   When you include a directory in the *file-list*, this option descends the directory hierarchy, setting the permissions on all files it encounters.

Notes

Because directories have different characteristics than regular files (you cannot execute a directory), access permissions are redefined for directories. For more information see "Directory Access Permissions" on page 91.

You can use the **ls** utility (with the **–l** option) to display file access privileges (page 792).

When you are using symbolic arguments, the only time you can omit the *permission* from the command line is when the *operation* is =. This omission takes away all permissions.

Examples

The following examples show how to use the **chmod** utility to change permissions on a file named **temp**. The initial access mode of **temp** is shown by **ls**.

```
$ ls -l temp
-rw-rw-r-- 1 alex  pubs     57  Jul 12 16:47 temp
```

The command line below removes all access permissions for the group and all other users, so that only the owner has access to the file. When you do not follow an equal sign with a permission, **chmod** removes all permissions for the specified user class. The **ls** utility verifies the change.

```
$ chmod go= temp
$ ls -l temp
-rw------- 1 alex  pubs     57  Jul 12 16:47 temp
```

The next command changes the access modes for all users (owner, group, and all others) to read and write. Now anyone can read from or write to the file. Again **ls** verifies the change.

```
$ chmod a=rw temp
$ ls -l temp
-rw-rw-rw- 1 alex   pubs      57  Jul 12 16:47 temp
```

Using an absolute argument, the **a=rw** becomes **666**. The next command performs the same function as the previous **chmod** command:

```
$ chmod 666 temp
```

The following command removes the write access privilege for other users. This change means that members of the **pubs** group can still read from and write to the file, but other users can only read from the file.

```
$ chmod o-w temp
$ ls -l temp
-rw-rw-r-- 1 alex   pubs      57  Jul 12 16:47 temp
```

The following command yields the same result using an absolute argument:

```
$ chmod 664 temp
```

The next command adds execute access privilege for all users. If **temp** is a shell script or other executable file, all users can now execute it.

```
$ chmod a+x temp
$ ls -l temp
-rwxrwxr-x 1 alex   pubs      57  Jul 12 16:47 temp
```

Again the absolute command that yields the same result is

```
$ chmod 775 temp
```

The following commands turn on the set user id (setuid) bit and the sticky bit (only works for Superuser):

```
# chmod 4755 temp
# ls -l temp
-rwsr-xr-x 1 alex   pubs      57  Jul 12 16:47 temp
# chmod 1755 temp
# ls -l temp
-rwxr-xr-t 1 alex   pubs      57  Jul 12 16:47 temp
```

See the tips on page 91 for security cautions regarding setuid.

chown

Changes the owner of a file

Syntax: *chown [**options**] owner file-list*

Summary

The **chown** utility changes the ownership of a file.

Arguments

The *owner* is the name or numeric user ID of the new owner. The *file-list* is a list of pathnames of the files whose ownership you want to change.

Options

–f **force** Does not report errors.

–h Changes the owner of a symbolic link. Without this option the owner of the file referenced by the symbolic link is changed.

–R **recursive** When you include a directory in the *file-list*, this option descends the directory hierarchy, setting the ownership on all files it encounters.

Notes

Only Superuser can change the ownership of a file.

Usually when you change the owner of a symbolically linked file, you want to change the link, not the linked-to file. If you are working as Superuser and you use **chown** with the **–R** option, it is a good idea to include the **–h** option for safety so you do not change the owner of files you do not mean to touch.

Examples

The following command changes the owner of the **chapter1** file in the **manuals** directory. The new owner is Jenny.

```
# chown jenny manuals/chapter1
```

The command below makes Alex the owner of all files in the **/home/alex/literature** directory and in all of its subdirectories:

```
# chown -R alex /home/alex/literature
```

713

cmp

Checks two files to see if they differ

Syntax: *cmp [options] file1 [file2]*

Summary

The **cmp** utility does a byte-by-byte comparison of *file1* and *file2*. If the files differ, **cmp** outputs the byte (character) and line number of the first difference and stops. Unlike **diff** (page 739) **cmp** works with binary as well as ASCII files.

The **cmp** utility returns an exit status of 0 if the files are the same and an exit status of 1 if they are different. An exit status of 2 indicates an error.

Arguments

The *file1* and *file2* arguments identify the two files to compare. Using a filename of – for either *file1* or *file2* causes **cmp** to read standard input in place of that file.

Options

–l   **long**   Displays the byte number in decimal and the differing bytes in octal for each difference. This option causes **cmp** to show all the differences in the files, not just the first.

–s   **suppress**   Suppresses output from **cmp**. Use this option when you are interested only in the exit status resulting from the comparison.

Notes

The **cmp** utility only sets the exit status and does not display any output if the files are identical.

When **cmp** displays the bytes that are different in the two files (with the –l option), the byte from *file1* is shown first, followed by the byte from *file2*.

Examples

The following examples use the files **a** and **b** shown below. These files have two differences. The first is that the word lazy in file **a** appears as lasy in file **b**. The second difference is more subtle; there is a TAB character just before the NEWLINE character in file **b**.

```
$ cat a
The quick brown fox jumped over the lazy dog's back.
$ cat b
The quick brown fox jumped over the lasy dog's back.TAB
```

The first example uses **cmp** without any options to compare the two files. The **cmp** utility reports that the files are different and identifies the offset from the start of the files of the first difference.

```
$ cmp a b
a b differ: char 39, line 1
```

The **–l** option displays all the bytes that differ in the two files. (Because this option creates a lot of output if the files have many differences, you may want to redirect the output to a file.) The following example shows the two differences between **a** and **b**.

```
$ cmp -l a b
    39 172 163
    53  12  11
cmp: EOF on a
```

The left-hand number in the first line of output above is the decimal byte (character) offset of the first difference as in the previous example. To its right is 172, the ASCII octal value for z and then the value of s. You can read the second line of output similarly: 12 is ASCII **NEWLINE** and 11 is a **TAB**.

comm

Compares sorted files

Syntax: *comm [options] file1 file2*

Summary

The **comm** utility displays a three-column, line-by-line comparison of two sorted files. (If the files have not been sorted, **comm** will not work properly.) The first column lists all lines found only in *file1*, the second column lists lines found only in *file2*, and the third lists those common to both files. Lines in the second column are preceded by one TAB, and those in the third column are preceded by two TABs.

Arguments

The *file1* and *file2* are pathnames of the files that **comm** compares. You can use a hyphen in place of either *file1* or *file2* (but not both) to cause **comm** to read standard input.

Options

You can use the options **–1**, **–2**, and **–3** individually or in combination.

–1	**comm** does not display column 1 (does not display lines it finds only in *file1*).
–2	**comm** does not display column 2 (does not display lines it finds only in *file2*).
–3	**comm** does not display column 3 (does not display lines it finds in both files).

Examples

The following examples use two files, **c** and **d**, that are in the working directory. The contents of these files is shown below. As with all input to **comm**, the files are in sorted order (see **sort** on page 891).

File c	File d
bbbbb	aaaaa
ccccc	ddddd
ddddd	eeeee
eeeee	ggggg
fffff	hhhhh

The first command below calls **comm** without any options, so it displays three columns. The first column lists those lines found only in file **c**, the second column lists those found in **d**, and the third lists the lines found in both **c** and **d**.

```
$ comm c d
            aaaaa
bbbbb
ccccc
                    ddddd
                    eeeee
fffff
        ggggg
        hhhhh
```

The next example shows the use of options to prevent **comm** from displaying columns 1 and 2. The result is column 3, a list of the lines common to files **c** and **d**.

```
$ comm -12 c d
ddddd
eeeee
```

compress   Compresses or decompresses files

Syntax: *compress [options] [file-list]*
         uncompress [options] [file-list]
         zcat [file-list]

Summary

The **compress** utility compacts files, reducing disk space requirements and the time needed to transmit files between computers. A **compress**ed file has a filename extension of **.Z**; compressing the file **fname** creates the file **fname.Z** and deletes the original file. To restore **fname**, use **uncompress** with an argument of **fname.Z** (you can omit the **.Z**). The **zcat** utility decompresses a compressed file and, without changing the file, sends the output to standard output.

Arguments

The *file-list* is a list of one or more files that are to be **compress**ed or **uncompress**ed. If *file-list* is empty, **compress/uncompress** reads from standard input and sends the compressed/uncompressed output to standard output. The information in this section applies to both **compress** and **uncompress** (which are both links to the same file).

Options

–c   Sends a file to standard output. When compressing a file, no **.Z** file is created and no files are changed. When uncompressing a file, no files are changed and the uncompressed output is displayed on the screen (unless you redirect it). Usually you will need to pipe the output through **pg**. The command **uncompress –c** is identical to **zcat**.

–f   **force**   Forces compression even if the size of the file is not reduced, the **.Z** file already exists (and will be overwritten), or standard input comes from the keyboard. When running **uncompress** this option overwrites files without prompting.

–v   **verbose**   For each file, displays the name of the file, the name of the compressed file, and the amount of compression (no value is given for expansion).

Notes

To see an example of a file that gets larger when compressed, compare the size of a file that has been compressed once with the same file compressed again. Because **compress** complains if you give it an argument with the extension **.Z**, you need to rename the file before compressing it a second time. Other files that may get larger when you compress them are **.gif** and **.jpeg** graphics files, which are already compressed.

Just as **cat** allows you to view files that are not compressed, **zcat** allows you to view compressed files. It does not change the files that it works on.

Also refer to the GNU **gzip** and **gunzip** utilities on page 781.

Discussion

Almost all files become much smaller when compressed with **compress**. Once in a while a file may become larger, and then only by a small amount. The type of a file and its contents determine how much reduction is actually done; text files are often reduced by 60 to 70 percent.

The **compress** utility does not change the attributes of a file including owner, permissions, modification time, and access times.

If the compressed version of a file already exists, **compress** reports that fact and asks for your confirmation before overwriting the existing file. The **–f** option overrides this default behavior.

Examples

In the first example **compress** compacts two files. Next **uncompress** decompresses one of the files. When a file is compressed and decompressed, its size changes, but its modification time remains the same.

```
$ ls -l
total 175
-rw-rw-r-- 1 alex group  33557 Jul 20 17:32 loans
-rw-rw-r-- 1 alex group 143258 Jul 20 17:32 mortgages
$ compress *
$ ls -l
total 51
-rw-rw-r-- 1 alex group  9693 Jul 20 17:32 loans.Z
-rw-rw-r-- 1 alex group 40426 Jul 20 17:32 mortgages.Z
$ uncompress loans.Z
$ ls -l
total 75
-rw-rw-r-- 1 alex group 33557 Jul 20 17:32 loans
-rw-rw-r-- 1 alex group 40426 Jul 20 17:32 mortgages.Z
```

In the next example the files in Jenny's home directory are archived using the **cpio** utility. The archive is compacted with **compress** before it is written to tape. See page 721 for more information on using **cpio**.

```
$ find /home/jenny -depth -print | cpio -oBm | compress >/dev/rmt/0
```

cp
Copies one or more files

Syntax:

    cp [options] source-file destination-file
    cp [options] source-file-list destination-directory
    cp [options] source-directory-list destination-directory

Summary

The **cp** utility copies one or more ordinary files, including text and executable program files. It has two modes of operation: The first copies one file to another, and the second copies one or more files to a directory.

Arguments

The *source-file* is the pathname of the ordinary file that **cp** copies. The *destination-file* is the pathname that **cp** assigns to the resulting copy of the file.

    The *source-file-list* is one or more pathnames of ordinary files that **cp** is going to copy. When you use the **–r** option, the *source-file-list* can also contain directories. The *destination-directory* is the pathname of the directory in which **cp** places the resulting copied files.

    When you specify a *destination-directory* on the command line, **cp** gives each of the copied files the same simple filename as its *source-file*. If, for example, you copy the text file **/home/jenny/memo.416** to the **/home/jenny/archives** directory, the copy has the simple filename **memo.416**, but the new pathname that **cp** gives it is **/home/jenny/archives/memo.416**.

Options

–i   **interactive**   Prompts the user whenever **cp** would overwrite an existing file. If you enter **y**, **cp** continues. If you enter anything other than **y**, **cp** does not make the copy.

–p   **preserve**   Preserves each file's owner, group, permissions, and modification dates when copying it.

–r   **recursive**   Causes **cp** to recursively copy all subdirectories and their contents into the *destination-directory*. Use this option only with the third syntax form of **cp**, above.

Notes

The **/usr/xpg4/bin/cp** utility is a POSIX-compliant version of **cp**.

    If the *destination-file* exists before you execute **cp**, **cp** overwrites the file, destroying the contents but leaving the access privileges, owner, and group associated with the file as they were.

    If the *destination-file* does not exist, **cp** uses the access privileges of the *source-file*. The user becomes the owner of the *destination-file,* and the user's group becomes the group associated with the *destination-file*.

With the **–p** option **cp** always sets the access privileges, owner, and group to match those of the *source-file*.

Examples

The first command makes a copy of the file **letter** in the working directory. The name of the copy is **letter.sav**.

```
$ cp letter letter.sav
```

The next command copies all the files with filenames ending in **.c** into the **archives** directory, a subdirectory of the working directory. Each copied file retains its simple filename but has a new absolute pathname.

```
$ cp *.c archives
```

The next example copies **memo** from the **/home/jenny** directory to the working directory:

```
$ cp /home/jenny/memo .
```

The final command copies the files named **memo** and **letter** from the working directory into **/home/jenny**. The copies have the same simple filenames as the source files (**memo** and **letter**) but have the absolute pathnames: **/home/jenny/memo** and **/home/jenny/letter**.

```
$ cp memo letter /home/jenny
```

cpio

Creates an archive or restores files from an archive

Syntax:

cpio –o [options]
cpio –i [options] [patterns]
cpio –p [options] directory

Summary

The **cpio** utility has three modes of operation. It allows you to place multiple files into a single archive file, to restore files from an archive, and to copy a directory hierarchy to another location. The archive file used by **cpio** may be a file on disk, on tape or other removable media, or on a remote system.

In the first form above, **cpio** reads a list of ordinary or directory filenames from standard input and writes the archive of these files to standard output. Use this form to create an archive. In the second form **cpio** reads the name of an archive from standard input and extracts files from the archive. You can decide to restore all the files from the archive or only those whose names match specific *patterns*. In the final form **cpio** reads ordinary or directory filenames from standard input and copies the files to a *directory*.

Arguments

The default action of **cpio** when extracting files from an archive (**–i** option) is to extract all the files found in the archive. You can choose to extract files selectively by supplying one or more *patterns* to **cpio**. Each *pattern* is treated as a separate regular expression. If the name of a file in the archive matches one of the *patterns*, that file is extracted; otherwise the file is ignored.

When using **cpio** to copy files into a *directory*, you must give the name of the target *directory* as an argument to **cpio**.

Options

Major Options

There are three options that determine the mode in which **cpio** operates. You must include exactly one of these options whenever you use **cpio**.

–o   **copy-out mode**   Constructs an archive from the ordinary and/or directory files named on standard input (one per line). The archive is written to standard output as it is built. The **find** utility frequently generates the filenames for a **cpio** archive. The following command builds an archive of your entire system:

```
$ find / -depth -print | cpio -o >/dev/rmt/0
```

The **–depth** option causes **find** to search for files in a depth-first search. This reduces the likelihood of a problem occurring because of permission problems on some file or directory. See the discussion of this option on page 723.

–i

copy-in mode   Reads a **cpio** archive from standard input and extracts files. Without any *patterns* on the command line, **cpio** extracts all files from the archive. With *patterns*, **cpio** extracts only files whose names match the *patterns* (similar to those used in filename generation). The following example extracts only files with names that end in **.c**:

```
$ cpio -i \*.c </dev/rmt/0
```

The backslash prevents the shell from expanding the ∗ before passing the argument to **cpio**.

–p

pass-through mode   Copies files from one place on your system to another. Instead of constructing an archive file containing the files named on standard input, **cpio** copies the files into the *directory* (the last argument given to **cpio**). The effect is the same as if you had created an archive with copy-out mode and then extracted the files with copy-in mode, except that using the pass-through mode avoids creating an actual archive. The following example maintains modification times (**–m**) while copying the working directory and all subdirectories (**–d**) to the **code** directory in Alex's home directory.

```
$ find . -depth -print | cpio -pdm ~alex/code
```

Other Options

The remaining options alter the behavior of **cpio**. These options work with one or more of the above major options.

–a

access   Resets the access times of input files after copying them.

–B

block   Forces the block size to 5120 bytes instead of the default 512 bytes.

–c

compatible   Writes header information in ASCII so that older (incompatible) **cpio** utilities on other machines can read the file. This option is rarely needed.

–C *blocksize*

Sets the block size used for input and output to *blocksize* bytes. Do not use with the **–p** option.

–d

directory   Creates directories as needed when it is copying files. For example you need this option when extracting files from an archive with a file list generated by **find** with the **–depth** option. This option only works in copy-in and pass-through modes.

–f

Reverses the sense of the *patterns* when extracting files from an archive. Files are extracted from the archive only if they do not match any of the *patterns*.

–k

corrupt   Skips past corrupted file headers and I/O errors if possible. Use only with the **–i** option.

–L	**link** Follows symbolic links. By default **cpio** does not follow symbolic links. Always use this criterion when you use **cpio** with **find** and the **–follow** instruction.
–l	**link** Links files when possible instead of copying them. Use only with the **–p** option.
–m	**modification** Preserves the modification times of files that are extracted from the archive. Without this option the files show the time that they were extracted. With this option the created files show the same time that they showed when they were copied to the archive. Does not work when copying a directory.
–r	**rename** Allows you to rename files as **cpio** copies them. When **cpio** prompts you with the name of a file, you can respond with a new name to give the copied file a new name, a period to give the copied file the same name as the original, or a RETURN to not copy the file.
–t	**table of contents** Displays a table of contents of the archive. This option works only when you use the **–i** option, although no files are actually read in from the archive. With **–v** this option causes **cpio** to display the same information as **ls –l**.
–u	**unconditionally** Overwrites existing files regardless of their modification times. Without this option **cpio** will not overwrite a more recently modified file with an older one; it just displays a warning message.
–v	**verbose** Lists all the files as they are processed. With the **–t** option it displays a detailed table of contents in a format similar to that used by **ls –l**.

Discussion

You can use both ordinary and directory filenames as input when you create an archive. If the name of an ordinary file appears in the input list before the name of its parent directory, the ordinary file appears before its parent directory in the archive as well. This can lead to an avoidable error: When you extract files from the archive, the child has nowhere to go in the file structure if its parent has not yet been extracted.

Making sure that files appear after their parent directories in the archive is not always a solution. One problem occurs if you use the **–m** option when extracting files. Because the modification time of a parent directory is updated each time a file is created within the directory, the original modification time of the parent directory is lost when the first file is written to it.

The solution to this potential problem is to make sure all the files appear *before* their parent directories when creating an archive *and* to create directories as needed when extracting files from an archive. When you use this technique, directories are extracted only after all the files have been written to them, and their modification times will be preserved.

With the **–depth** option the **find** utility generates a list of files with all children appearing in the list before their parent directories. Using this list as input to **cpio** when you are creating an archive gives you just what you need. (Refer to the first example below.) The **–d** option causes **cpio** to create parent directories as needed while it is extracting files from an archive. The **–m** option preserves the modification times of the copied files. Using this combination of utilities and options preserves directory modification times through a create/extract sequence.

This way of doing things solves another potential problem. Sometimes a parent directory may not have permissions set so you can extract files into it. When **cpio** automatically creates the directory with **–d**, you can be assured of write permission to the directory. When the directory is extracted from the archive (after all the files are written into the directory), it is extracted with its original permissions.

Examples

The first example creates an archive of all the files in Jenny's account, writing the archive to a tape drive:

```
$ find /home/jenny -depth -print | cpio -oB >/dev/rmt/0
```

The **find** utility produces the filenames that **cpio** uses to build the archive. The **–depth** option to **find** causes all entries in a directory to be listed before listing the directory name itself. This makes it possible for **cpio** to preserve the original modification times of directories. Use the **–d** (make-directories) and the **–m** (modification-time) when you extract files from this archive (see the following examples). The **–B** option blocks the tape at 5120 bytes/block.

To check the contents of the archive file and get a detailed listing of all the files it contains, use

```
$ cpio -itv < /dev/rmt/0
```

To restore the files that formerly were in the memo subdirectory in Jenny's account, use the following command:

```
$ cpio -idm /home/jenny/memo/\* < /dev/rmt/0
```

The **–d** option is used with **cpio** in the above example to make sure that any subdirectories that were in the memo directory are recreated as needed, and the **–m** (preserve-modification-time) option preserves the modification times of files and directories. The asterisk in the regular expression is escaped to keep the shell from attempting to expand it.

The final example uses the **–f** option to restore all the files in the archive except those that were formerly in the **memo** subdirectory:

```
$ cpio -ivmdf /home/jenny/memo/\* < /dev/rmt/0
```

The **–v** option lists the extracted files as **cpio** processes the archive. This option allows you to verify that the correct files are extracted.

crontab   Schedules a command to run regularly at a specified time

Syntax: *crontab **filename***
               *crontab **options** [**user-name**]*

Summary

The **crontab** utility allows you to submit a list of jobs that the system will run at the times you specify. The commands are stored in files that are referred to as **crontab** files. The system utility named **cron** reads the **crontab** files and runs the commands. If a command line in your **crontab** file does not redirect its output, standard and error output are mailed to you.

Arguments

In the first format *filename* is the name of a file that contains the **crontab** commands. If you use a hyphen as the *filename*, **crontab** reads commands from standard input as you type them; end with CONTROL-D.

The *user-name* in the second format can be specified by Superuser to change the **crontab** file for a particular user.

Options

−e   **edit**   Runs the text editor specified by the **EDITOR** shell variable on your **crontab** file (or creates a new file if one does not exist), enabling you to add, change, or delete entries. After creating/editing **crontab**, this option installs it.

−l   **list**   Displays the contents of your **crontab** file.

−r   **remove**   Deletes your **crontab** file.

Notes

Each **crontab** entry begins with five SPACE-separated fields that specify when the command should run:

- minute (0–59)
- hour (0–23)
- day of the month (1–31)
- month of the year (1–12)
- day of the week (0–6 with 0 = Sunday)

An asterisk represents all possible values. Refer to **/etc/cron.d** in the list on page 609 for more information about setting up **crontab**.

Examples

In the example below the **root** user sets up a command to be run by **cron** every Saturday (day six) morning at 2:05 AM that removes all **core** files on the system that have not been accessed in the previous five days. The **root** user enters the command directly from the console.

```
# crontab
5 2 ** 6      /usr/bin/find / -name core -atime +5 -exec rm {} \;
CONTROL-D
```

To add an entry to your **crontab** file, run **crontab** with the **–e** (edit) option. The **–l** (list) option displays a copy of your **crontab** file.

```
# crontab -l
5 2 ** 6  /usr/bin/find / -name core -atime +5 -exec rm {} \;
```

cut

Selects characters or fields from input lines

Syntax: *cut [options] [file-list]*

Summary

The **cut** utility selects characters or TAB-separated fields from lines of input and writes them to standard output. Characters and fields are numbered starting with 1.

Argument

The *file-list* is a list of ordinary files. If omitted, **cut** reads from standard input.

Options

−c *clist*   **character**   Selects the characters specified by the column numbers in *clist*. The value of *clist* is one or more comma-separated column numbers and/or hyphen-separated column ranges.

−d *dchar*   **delimeter**   Uses *dchar* as the field delimiter when you use the **−f** option to select fields from the input. The default delimiter is the TAB character. Quote characters as necessary to protect them from shell expansion. If you use this option and select more than one field from the input lines, **cut** uses *dchar* to separate the output fields.

−f *flist*   **field**   Selects the TAB-separated fields given by the field number in *flist*. The value of *flist* is one or more comma-separated field numbers and/or hyphen-separated field ranges. Also see the **−d** option.

Notes

Although limited in functionality, **cut** is easy to learn and use and is a good choice when columns and fields can be selected without pattern matching. It is sometimes used with **paste** (page 849).

Examples

For the following two examples, assume that the **ls** command with the **−l** option produces the following output in the working directory:

```
$ ls -l
total 148
-rwxrwxrwx  1 alex     group         123 Jan 31  1997 countout
-rwxrw-r--  1 alex     group        2065 Aug 16 14:48 headers
-rw-rw-r--  1 root     root           72 May 24 11:44 memo
-rwxrw-r--  1 alex     group         715 Mar  2 16:30 memos_save
-rw-rw-rw-  1 alex     group          14 Jan  8  1997 tmp1
-rw-rw-rw-  1 alex     group          14 Jan  8  1997 tmp2
-rw-rw-r--  1 alex     group         218 Nov 27  1996 typescript
```

The first command outputs the permissions of the files in the working directory. The **cut** utility with the **–c** option selects characters 2 through 10 from each input line. The characters in this range are written to standard output.

```
$ ls -l | cut -c2-10
total 148
rwxrwxrwx
rwxrw-r--
rw-rw-r--
rwxrw-r--
rw-rw-rw-
rw-rw-rw-
rw-rw-r--
```

The next command outputs the size and name of each file in the working directory. This time the **–f** option causes **cut** to select the fifth and ninth fields from the input lines. The **–d** option tells **cut** that SPACEs, not TABs, delimit fields in the input. When **cut** encounters multiple delimiters, it counts each delimiter as a separate field. The **tr** utility (page 924) with the **–s** option compresses multiple SPACEs into a single SPACE so that **cut** counts the fields properly.

```
$ ls -l | tr -s ' ' ' ' | cut -f5,9 -d ' '
123 countout
2065 headers
72 memo
715 memos_save
14 tmp1
14 tmp2
218 typescript
```

The last example uses **cut** to display a list of full names as stored in the fifth field of the **/etc/passwd** file. The **–d** option specifies the colon character as the field delimiter.

```
$ cat /etc/passwd
root:x:0:0:Root:/:/bin/sh
jenny:x:401:50:Jenny Chen:/home/jenny:/bin/ksh
alex:x:402:50:Alex Watson:/home/alex:/bin/sh
scott:x:504:500:Scott Adams:/home/scott:/bin/csh
hls:x:505:500:Helen Simpson:/home/hls:/bin/sh
$ cut -d: -f5 /etc/passwd
Root
Jenny Chen
Alex Watson
Scott Adams
Helen Simpson
```

date

Displays or sets the time and date

Syntax: *date [options] [+format]*
date [options] newdate

Summary

The **date** utility displays the time and date. Superuser can use it to change the system time and date.

Arguments

When Superuser specifies a *newdate*, the system clock changes to reflect the new date. The *newdate* argument has one of the following formats:

    nnddhhmm[cc[yy]][.ss]

or

    [nndd]hhmm

The *nn* is the number of the month (01–12), *dd* is the day of the month (01–31), *hh* is the hour based on a 24-hour clock (00–23), and *mm* is the minutes (00–59). The last four digits are optional; if you do not specify a year, **date** assumes the year has not changed. The optional *cc* specifies the first two digits of the year (the value of the century minus 1), and *yy* specifies the last two digits of the year.

You can use the *+format* argument to specify the format of the output of **date**. Following the + sign, you can specify a format string consisting of field descriptors and text. The field descriptors are preceded by percent signs, and each one is replaced by its value in the output. See the following table for a list of the field descriptors.

Field Descriptor	Meaning
%a	Abbreviated weekday—Sun to Sat.
%A	Full weekday—Sunday to Saturday.
%b	Abbreviated month—Jan to Dec.
%B	Full month—January to December.
%c	Date and time in default format used by **date**.
%d	Day of the month—01 to 31.
%D	Date in mm/dd/yy format.
%H	Hour—00 to 23.
%j	Day of the year (Julian)—001 to 366.
%m	Month of the year—01 to 12.
%M	Minutes—00 to 59.
%n	NEWLINE character.

Field Descriptor	Meaning
%p	AM or PM.
%r	Time in AM/PM notation.
%S	Seconds—00 to 59.
%t	TAB character.
%T	Time in **hh:mm:ss** format.
%w	Day of the week—0 to 6 (0 = Sunday).
%y	Last two digits of the year—00 to 99.
%Y	Year in four-digit format (for example 1997).
%Z	Time zone (for example PDT).

Any character in a format string that is neither a percent sign (%) nor a field descriptor is assumed to be ordinary text and is copied to the output. You can use ordinary text to add punctuation to the date and to add labels (for example you can put the word DATE: in front of the date). Surround the format argument with single quotation marks if it contains SPACEs or other characters that have a special meaning to the shell.

Options

–a [–]*sss.fff*   **adjust**   Slowly adjusts the system clock by the number of seconds and fractions of a second specified by *sss.fff*. Use the minus sign to adjust the time backward.

–u   **universal**   Displays or sets the date in Greenwich Mean Time (GMT—also called Universal Coordinated Time [UTC]). The system operates in GMT, and **date** converts it to and from the local standard time or daylight saving time.

Notes

The **/usr/xpg4/bin/date** utility is a POSIX-compliant version of **date**.

Examples

The first example below shows how to set the date for 2:22 PM on January 26:

```
# date 01261422
Tue Jan 26 14:22:00 PST 1999
```

The next example shows the *format* argument. It causes **date** to display the date in a commonly used format.

```
$ date '+%h %d, 19%y'
Jan 26, 1999
```

dd

Copies a file from one device to another

Syntax: *dd [arguments]*

Summary

The **dd** (device-to-device copy) utility copies a file from one place to another. The primary use of **dd** is to copy files to and from devices such as tape drives. Often **dd** can handle the transfer of information to and from other operating systems when other methods fail. A rich set of arguments gives you precise control over the characteristics of the transfer.

Arguments

Without any arguments **dd** copies standard input to standard output.

bs=*n*　　　**block size**　Reads and writes *n* bytes at a time. This argument overrides the **ibs** and **obs** arguments.

cbs=*n*　　　**conversion block size**　When performing data conversion during the copy, converts *n* bytes at a time. Use only with the **ascii** or **ebcdic** option to the **conv** argument.

conv=*type*[,*type*...]　　Converts the data that is being copied by applying conversion *type*s in the order given on the command line. The *type*s of conversions are shown in the following table:

type	Meaning
ascii	Converts EBCDIC-encoded characters to ASCII, allowing you to read tapes written on IBM mainframe (and similar) computers.
asciib	Converts EBCDIC-encoded characters to ASCII using BSD-compatible character translations.
block	Each time a line of input is read (that is, a sequence of characters terminated with a NEWLINE character), outputs a block of text without the NEWLINE. Each output block has the size given in the **obs** or **bs** argument and is created by adding trailing SPACE characters to the text until it is the proper size.
ebcdic	Converts ASCII-encoded characters to EBCDIC, allowing you to write tapes for use on IBM mainframe (and similar) computers.
ebcdicb	Converts ASCII-encoded characters to EBCDIC using BSD-compatible character translations.
lcase	Converts uppercase letters to lowercase while copying data.

type	Meaning
noerror	When a read error occurs, **dd** normally terminates. This argument allows **dd** to continue processing data. This is useful when trying to recover data from bad media.
ucase	Converts lowercase letters to uppercase while copying data.
unblock	Performs the opposite of the block conversion discussed above.
swab	Swap pairs of input bytes. Copy an odd byte if it exists. This conversion is good for big/little endian[a] conversions.

a. *Endian* refers to the ordering of bytes in a multibyte number.

count=*numblocks* — Copies *numblocks* input blocks. The size of each block is the number of bytes given in the **ibs** argument.

ibs=*n* — **input block size**   Reads *n* bytes at a time.

if=*filename* — **input file**   Reads from *filename* instead of from standard input. You can use a device name for *filename* to read directly from that device.

iseek=*numblocks* — Seeks *numblocks* blocks of input before starting to copy. The size of each block is the number of bytes given in the **ibs** argument. May be faster than **skip** on a disk.

obs=*n* — **output block size**   Writes *n* bytes at a time.

of=*filename* — **output file**   Writes to *filename* instead of to standard output. You can use a device name for *filename* to write directly to that device.

oseek=*numblocks* — Seeks *numblocks* blocks of output before starting to copy and writing any output. The size of each block is the number of bytes given in the **obs** argument.

skip=*numblocks* — Skips *numblocks* blocks of input before starting to copy. The size of each block is the number of bytes given in the **ibs** argument.

Notes

The **dd** utility allows you to use a shorthand notation to give large numbers as arguments. Appending a **b** to a number indicates that the number is multiplied by 512; and appending a **k** multiplies the number by 1024.

Examples

The first example shows how to use the **dd** utility to make an exact copy of a floppy disk by first copying the disk's contents to a file on a hard drive and then, after inserting a fresh disk into the floppy disk drive, copying that file to the floppy disk. This works regardless of what is on the floppy disk. In this case it is a DOS-formatted disk. The copy that results from the second call to **dd** is also a DOS-formatted disk, after the copy.

The **floppy.copy** file that this example creates is an exact copy of the original floppy diskette in drive A. When you copy the file to another floppy in drive A, the new floppy becomes an exact copy of the original diskette. The initial command disables volume management so you can access the floppy directly. The final command reenables it.

```
# sh /etc/init.d/volmgt stop
# dd if=/dev/diskette of=floppy.copy
2880+0 records in
2880+0 records out
```

Insert a new, formatted floppy.

```
# dd if=floppy.copy of=/dev/diskette
2880+0 records in
2880+0 records out
# sh /etc/init.d/volmgt start
```

The second example shows a simple shell script to do a full system backup to a remote system. The shell script uses the **rsh** utility to run **dd** on the remote system.

```
#!/bin/sh
# Do a full backup to remote tape drive on bravo

machine=bravo
device=/dev/rmt/0

echo "Backing up to $machine using device $device...(be patient)...\c"
cd /
tar -cf - . | rsh -l hls $machine dd obs=256k of=$device
echo "Full backup to $machine ($device) done on " `date` >/etc/last.backup
echo "done."
```

delta

Records changes in an SCCS-encoded file

Syntax: *delta [options] file-list*

Summary

The **delta** utility is part of SCCS (page 579); it records the changes made to a file previously retrieved by **get** with the **–e** option.

Argument

The *file-list* is a list of SCCS-encoded files (that start with **s.**). If the list includes directory names, all files that begin with **s.** in the named directory are added to *file-list*. Any files in *file-list* that do not begin with **s.** or that are unreadable are ignored.

Options

–m[*mrlist*]   **modification requests**   If the **v** flag has been set with the **admin** utility, you can use this option to input a list of modification requests. These requests are used as the reason for the delta. If you do not use this option and the **v** flag has been set, **delta** prompts you with MRs? when standard input is attached to your keyboard. Respond with the list of modification requests terminated by a **RETURN**. (Escape one or more **RETURN**s by preceding them with backslashes if the list occupies more than one line). You can enter a null list of modification requests either by using the **–m** option with no **mrlist**, or by pressing **RETURN** immediately after the MRs? prompt.

–p   **print**   Runs **diff** to compare the versions of the file before and after the delta is performed. The results are displayed on standard output.

–r*version-number*   **release**   Use this option only when you have two or more outstanding **get**s on the same SCCS file. The **–r** option identifies the **get** that the current **delta** corresponds to. You can specify the version number that was used for the **get** or the version number that will be used for the **delta**.

–y[*comments*]   Allows you to enter text that will be used as the reason for making the delta. If you do not use the **–y** option and standard input comes from a keyboard, **delta** prompts you for comments with comments?. You can enter a null comment either by using the **–y** option with no **comments**, or by pressing **RETURN** immediately after the comments? prompt.

Notes

The **/usr/xpg4/bin/delta** utility is a POSIX-compliant version of **delta**.

Examples

These examples illustrate the use of the **delta** utility after **get** has been used with the **−e** option to retrieve the highest trunk delta.[3]

In the first example the **v** flag is set on **s.memo**. In the subsequent **delta** the user is prompted for a list of modification requests. The user inputs a list of numbers followed by RETURN.

```
$ admin −fv s.memo
$ delta s.memo
MRs? 19539 74A 13704
comments?
  .
  .
```

In the next example the **−m** option is used to enter the same list of modification requests.

```
$ delta −m"19539 74A 13704" s.memo
comments? changes based on reviews
  .
  .
```

Below, the user enters comments directly on the command line following the **−y** option.

```
$ delta −y"changes based on reviews" s.memo
MRs?
  .
  .
```

The final example illustrates what happens when you have multiple **get**s outstanding on different versions of a file.

```
$ delta s.memo
  .
  .
ERROR [s.memo]: missing −r argument (de1)
```

You must use the **−r** option to identify the version associated with the delta.

```
$ delta −r2.2 s.memo
  .
  .
```

---

3. See the tip named "Making SCCS a Little More Friendly," page 581, and the following examples for information about using the **sccs** front end to help with file naming and placement.

df

Displays the amount of available disk space

Syntax: *df [options] [filesystem-list]*

Summary

The **df** (disk free) utility reports how much free space remains on any mounted device or directory.

Argument

When you call **df** without an argument, it reports on the free space remaining on each mounted device.

The *filesystem-list* is an optional list of one or more pathnames that specify the filesystems you want a report on. The **df** utility permits you to refer to a mounted filesystem by its device pathname *or* by the pathname of its mount point.

Options

When you call **df** without any options, it reports on the free space, in blocks, remaining on each device. There are 512 bytes per block on a UFS filesystem.

−a   **all**   Reports on all filesystems, probably including some you do not care about.

−k   **kilobyte**   For each filesystem, reports the name, size in kilobytes, amount of used and available space, percent of capacity the filesystem is filled to, and mount point. This option yields a clean list with a header at the top that makes it easy to read. See the example.

−l   **local**   Reports only on local filesystems.

−o i   Displays the number of inodes that are being used and that are free for a filesystem. You can run out of inodes (usually by having a lot of smaller files) even though **df −k** says there is plenty of space. If this happens, you will not be able to create any new files on that filesystem.

Notes

The **/usr/xpg4/bin/df** utility is a POSIX-compliant version of **df**.

Examples

With the **−k** option **df** displays information in an easy-to-read format with a header and with all sizes in kilobytes (1K or 1024 bytes). The **−l** option limits the display to locally mounted filesystems.

736

```
$ df -kl
Filesystem            kbytes     used    avail capacity  Mounted on
/dev/dsk/c0d0s0        59827    52532     1313    98%    /
/dev/dsk/c0d0s6       542995   463857    24839    95%    /usr
/proc                     0        0        0     0%    /proc
fd                        0        0        0     0%    /dev/fd
/dev/dsk/c0d0s1        29905    17585     9330    66%    /var
/dev/dsk/c0d0s7       694813   577098    62130    91%    /export/home
swap                  89920      428    89492     1%    /tmp
```

Without the **–k** option **df** displays values in blocks and files, which is usually not as useful. Also, there is no indication of how much space is available on each device.

```
$ df -l
/                 (/dev/dsk/c0d0s0  ):   14590 blocks    33052 files
/usr              (/dev/dsk/c0d0s6  ):  158276 blocks   246236 files
/proc             (/proc            ):       0 blocks      940 files
/dev/fd           (fd               ):       0 blocks        0 files
/var              (/dev/dsk/c0d0s1  ):   24640 blocks    15396 files
/export/home      (/dev/dsk/c0d0s7  ):  235430 blocks   335807 files
/tmp              (swap             ):  178984 blocks     9688 files
```

dfmounts   Lists remotely mounted filesystems

Syntax: *dfmounts [options] [hostname]*

Summary

The **dfmounts** utility lists all exported local filesystems along with remote hosts that have mounted them.

Argument

Without *hostname*, **dfmounts** reports on local filesystems that are exported and can be mounted by remote hosts. With *hostname*, **dfmounts** reports on filesystems that are local to *hostname* and are exported.

Options

–F *fstype*   **file system type**   Shows only shared filesystems of type *fstype* (for example **nfs**).

–h   **no header**   Omits the header.

Notes

This command is a more flexible and informative replacement for the **showmount** command.

Discussion

The **dfmounts** utility displays a single header line followed by lines containing the following fields:

- **RESOURCE**   the resource name used by **mount**
- **SERVER**   the server that is sharing this resource
- **PATHNAME**   the pathname used by **share**
- **CLIENTS**   machines that are using this resource

Null fields are indicated with a hyphen (–) and fields containing only whitespace are enclosed in double quotation marks ("). This utility generates an error if there are no exported filesystems.

Example

This example queries the server **bravo** for its currently shared resources and which hosts are using them:

```
# dfmounts bravo
RESOURCE     SERVER PATHNAME                CLIENTS
    -        bravo /export/home1/jennifer   delta,kudos,hurrah
    -        bravo /export/home2/alex        kudos
    -        bravo /export/home2/conner      delta, kudos
    -        bravo /export/home2/zeke         delta
```

diff

Displays the differences between two files

Syntax: *diff [options] file1 file2*
diff [options] file1 directory
diff [options] directory file2
diff [options] directory1 directory2

Summary

The **diff** utility displays the differences between two files on a line-by-line basis. It displays the differences as instructions that you can use to edit one of the files to make it the same as the other.

Arguments

The *file1* and *file2* are pathnames of the files that **diff** works on. When the *directory2* argument is used in place of *file2*, **diff** looks for a file in *directory2* with the same name as *file1*. Similarly when the directory argument is used in place of *file1*, **diff** looks for a file in *directory1* with the same name as *file2*. You can use a hyphen in place of *file1* or *file2* to cause **diff** to use standard input. When you specify two directory arguments, **diff** compares all files in *directory1* with files in *directory2* that have the same names.

Options

–b   **blanks**   Ignores blanks (SPACEs and TABs) at the ends of lines and considers other strings of blanks equal.

–c   **context**   Displays the sections of the two files that differ, including three lines around each line that differs to show the context. Each line in *file1* that is missing from *file2* is preceded by –; each extra line in *file2* is preceded by +; and lines that have different versions in the two files are marked with **!**. When lines that differ are within three lines of each other, they are grouped together in the output.

–C *lines*   **context**   Displays lines just as **–c** does except that it uses *lines* lines around each line that differs to show context.

–e   **edit**   Creates a script for the **ed** editor that will edit *file1* to make it the same as *file2* and sends it to standard output. You must add **w** (write) and **q** (quit) instructions to the end of the script if you are going to redirect input to **ed** from the script.

–i   **ignore case**   Ignores differences in case when comparing files.

–r   **recursive**   When using **diff** to compare the files in two directories, this option causes the comparisons to extend through common subdirectories as well.

Notes

The **sdiff** utility is similar to **diff**, but the output may be easier to read. If you experiment with **sdiff**, make sure you use the **–w *n*** option, which sets the page width to *n* characters (the default is 130). Refer to the **sdiff man** page for more information.

Discussion

When you use **diff** without any options, it produces a series of lines containing Add (**a**), Delete (**d**), and Change (**c**) instructions. Each of these lines is followed by the lines from the file that you need to add, delete, or change. A *less than* symbol (**<**) precedes lines from **file1**. A *greater than* symbol (**>**) precedes lines from **file2**. The **diff** output is in the format shown below. A pair of line numbers separated by a comma represents a range of lines; **diff** uses a single line number to represent a single line.

Instruction	Meaning (to change file1 to file2)
line1 a line2,line3 > lines from file2	Appends lines from **file2** after line1 in **file1**.
line1,line2 d line3 < lines from file1	Deletes line1 through line2 from **file1**.
line1,line2 c line3,line4 < lines from file1 --- > lines from file 2	Changes line1 through line2 in **file1** to lines from **file2**.

The **diff** utility assumes that you are going to convert *file1* to *file2*. The line numbers to the left of each of the **a**, **c**, or **d** instructions always pertain to *file1*; numbers to the right of the instructions apply to *file2*. To convert *file1* to *file2*, ignore the line numbers to the right of the instructions. (To convert *file2* to *file1*, run **diff** again, reversing the order of the arguments.)

Examples

The first example shows how **diff** displays the differences between two short, similar files:

```
$ cat m
aaaaa
bbbbb
ccccc
$ cat n
aaaaa
ccccc
$ diff m n
2d1
< bbbbb
```

The difference between files **m** and **n** is that the second line from file **m** (bbbbb) is missing from file **n**. The first line that **diff** displays (2d1) indicates that you need to delete the second line from file 1 (**m**) to make it the same as file 2 (**n**). Ignore the numbers following the letters on the instruction lines. (They would apply if you were converting **file2** to **file1**.) The next line **diff** displays starts with a *less than* symbol (**<**), indicating that this line of text is from **file1**. In this example you do not need this information—all you need to know is the line number so that you can delete the line.

The next example uses the same **m** file and a new file, **p**, to show **diff** issuing an **a** (append) instruction.

```
$ cat p
aaaaa
bbbbb
rrrrr
ccccc
$ diff m p
2a3
> rrrrr
```

In this example **diff** issues the instruction 2a3 to indicate that you must append a line to file **m**, after line 2, to make it the same as file **p**. The second line that **diff** displays indicates that the line is from file **p** (the line begins with >, indicating **file2**). In this example you need the information on this line; the appended line must contain the text rrrrr.

The next example uses **m** again, this time with file **r**, to show how **diff** indicates a line that needs to be changed:

```
$ cat r
aaaaa
-q
ccccc
$ diff m r
2c2
< bbbbb
---
> -q
```

The difference between the two files is in line 2: File **m** contains bbbbb, and file **r** contains -q. Above, **diff** displays 2c2 to indicate that you need to change line 2. After indicating that a change is needed, **diff** shows that you must change line 2 in file **m** (bbbbb) to line 2 in file **r** (-q) to make the files the same. The three hyphens indicate the end of the text in file **m** that needs to be changed and the start of the text in file **r** that is to replace it.

Next a *group* of lines in file **m** needs to be changed to make it the same as file **t**:

```
$ cat t
aaaaa
11111
hhhhh
nnnnn
$ diff m t
2,3c2,4
< bbbbb
< ccccc
---
> 11111
> hhhhh
> nnnnn
```

Here **diff** indicates that you need to change lines 2 through 3 (2,3) in file **m** from bbbbb and ccccc to 11111, hhhhh, and nnnnn.

dircmp

Displays the differences between two directories

Syntax: *dircmp [options] directory1 directory2*

Summary

The **dircmp** utility displays the differences between two directories and optionally, between the contents of ASCII files in each directory with the same relative pathnames.

Arguments

The *directory1* and *directory2* are the pathnames of the directories you want to compare.

Options

–d   **diff** Uses **diff** to compare the contents of text files with the same filename in each directory. By default **dircmp** prints only the word `same` or `different` followed by the filename.

–s   **suppress** Suppresses messages about identical files.

–w *n*   **width** Changes the output line width to *n* characters (default is 72).

Discussion

The **dircmp** utility generates two reports: The first lists all files only in *directory1* (left column) and all files only in *directory2* (right column). The second lists all files in both directories and indicates `same` or `different` for each filename.

You can use **dircmp** to assist in many system administration functions. When you are upgrading to a new version of Solaris you may want to compare the **/etc/rc*** trees on a new install to the machine you are about to upgrade. Mount the partition containing **/etc** from the old OS on the new machine. Then use **dircmp** to find exactly which files have been customized, how they have been customized, and if those customizations are applicable to the new version of Solaris.

You can also use **dircmp** to compare software trees. If you have two different trees of software undergoing separate development and you need to do a top-level comparison of each to see what modifications may have been made, **dircmp** can compare the directories and print out a list of all the files that have changed.

Examples

Assume you are working with the two directories shown below. All of the files are ASCII (text) files except for **myprog**.

```
$ ls *

dir1:
five    four    myprog   one     three   two

dir2:
five    myprog  one      seven   six     three   two
```

When you compare these directories, **dircmp** displays two pages. The first page shows the names of the files that are not present in both directories (those present in **dir1** but not in **dir2** on the left, those from **dir2** but not **dir1** on the right). The second page shows the names of the files that are common to the two directories and whether their contents are the same or different (**dir1/five** differs from **dir2/five**, **dir1/three** differs from **dir2/three**, and **dir1/myprog** differs from **dir2/myprog**). The report covers both ASCII and binary files.

```
$ dircmp dir1 dir2

Jul 17 15:39 1998  dir1 only and dir2 only Page 1

./four                                      ./seven
./six
.
.
.
.
Jul 17 15:39 1998  Comparison of dir1 dir2 Page 1

directory       .
different       ./five
different       ./myprog
same            ./one
different       ./three
same            ./two
```

With the **–d** option **dircmp** displays the same two pages it did without the option and adds one more page for each pair of files that differ. The additional pages show the output of **diff** (page 739) run on each pair of files that differ.

```
$ dircmp -d dir1 dir2

Jul 17 15:39 1998  dir1 only and dir2 only Page 1

./four                                      ./seven
./six
.
.
.
.
Jul 17 15:39 1998  Comparison of dir1 dir2 Page 1

directory       .
different       ./five
different       ./myprog
same            ./one
different       ./three
same            ./two
.
.
.
```

```
Jul 17 15:39 1998  diff of ./five in dir1 and dir2 Page 1

1c1
< new text for dir1 file five
---
> new text for dir2 file five
.
.
.
Jul 17 15:39 1998  diff of ./myprog in dir1 and dir2 Page 1

dir1/myprog is an object file
.
.
.
Jul 17 15:39 1998  diff of ./myprog in dir1 and dir2 Page 1

dir2/myprog is an object file
.
.
.
Jul 17 15:39 1998  diff of ./three in dir1 and dir2 Page 1

1c1
< new text for three in dir1
---
> this is file three, version one
```

The report does not tell you how the binary files differ. The message `myprog is an object file` comes from **diff**, which cannot compare binary files. When you run **dircmp** on non-ASCII files, the **diff** and **pr** utilities, both of which are used by **dircmp**, send messages to standard error. Using the **–s** option in either of the preceding examples suppresses the information about files that are the same.

du

Displays information on disk usage

Syntax: *du [options] [pathname-list]*

Summary

The **du** (disk usage) utility reports how many 512-byte blocks a file or directory (along with all its subdirectories and files) occupies. It displays the number of blocks that the directory or file occupies.

Argument

Without an argument **du** displays information only about the working directory and its subdirectories. The *pathname-list* specifies the directories and files you want information about.

Options

Without any options **du** displays the total storage used for each argument in *pathname-list*. For directories **du** displays this total only after recursively listing the totals for each subdirectory.

–a   **all**   Displays the space used by all ordinary files along with the totals for each directory. Even without this option, **du** will report on all plain files in *pathname-list*.

–d   Reports only on files and directories on the same filesystem as that of the argument being processed.

–k   **kilobyte**   Displays sizes in 1024-byte blocks in place of the 512-byte default.

–r   **report**   Displays error messages instead of being silent about directories without read permission, files that cannot be read, and so on.

–s   **summary**   Displays only the total for each directory or file you specify on the command line; subdirectory totals are not included in the display.

Notes

The **/usr/xpg4/bin/du** utility is a POSIX-compliant version of **du**.

Examples

The following use of **du** displays size information about subdirectories in the working directory. The last line contains the grand total for the working directory and its subdirectories.

```
$ du
26      ./Postscript
4       ./SCCS
47      ./XIcon
4       ./Printer/SCCS
12      ./Printer
105     .
```

The total (105) is the number of blocks occupied by all the plain files and directories under the working directory. All files are counted, even though **du** displays only the sizes of directories.

Next **du** displays only the grand total for the working directory:

```
$ du -s
105        .
```

If you use the **−r** option and you do not have read permission to a file or directory that **du** encounters, **du** sends a warning message (instead of the default silence) to standard error and skips that file or directory.

```
$ du -r /var/spool/lp
4          /var/spool/lp/admins
du: /var/spool/lp/fifos/private: Permission denied
du: /var/spool/lp/fifos/public: Permission denied
2          /var/spool/lp/fifos
du: /var/spool/lp/requests/max: Permission denied
2          /var/spool/lp/requests
2          /var/spool/lp/system
du: /var/spool/lp/tmp: Permission denied
20         /var/spool/lp
```

The last examples show the effect of the **−k** command. The first **du** command shows the results in 512-byte blocks, whereas the second shows 1-kilobyte blocks (1K, or 1024 bytes).

```
$ du -s /usr/dt
132442  /usr/dt
$ du -sk /usr/dt
66221   /usr/dt
```

echo

Displays a message

Syntax: *echo [option] [message]*

Summary

The **echo** command copies its arguments, followed by a NEWLINE, to standard output.

Argument

The optional *message* is one or more arguments. These arguments can include quoted strings, ambiguous file references, and shell variables. A SPACE or the value of **IFS** (page 383) separates each argument from adjacent arguments. The shell recognizes an unquoted special character in an argument (for example the shell expands an asterisk into a list of filenames in the working directory).

In addition to the standard **echo** utility (**/usr/bin/echo**) and the Berkeley version of **echo** (**/usr/ucb/echo**), each shell has a slightly different version of an **echo** builtin `sh csh ksh`.

The **echo** utility or builtin allows you to terminate the *message* with a \c (`sh ksh` and **/usr/bin/echo**) or use the **–n** argument (`csh` and **/usr/ucb/echo**) to prevent **echo** from displaying the NEWLINE that normally ends a *message*. To prevent the shell from interpreting the backslash in \c as a special character, you must quote it. The examples below show the three ways you can quote an escape sequence.

Option

–n   Suppresses the NEWLINE terminating the message (`csh` and **/usr/ucb/echo**). Refer to the preceding discussion.

Notes

You can use **echo** to send messages to the screen from a shell script (Chapter 10). For other uses of **echo**, refer to the discussion of **echo** starting on page 120.

If you want shell-independent results from **echo**, specify the absolute pathname of **echo** (**/usr/bin/echo**).

From the Bourne and Korn Shells you can produce a multiline echo using only apostrophes.

```
$ echo 'Hi
> there.'
Hi
there.
$
```

From the C Shell you must quote the NEWLINE that ends each line in addition to using apostrophes.

```
% echo 'Hi\
there.
Hi
there.
%
```

The **echo** utility (sh ksh and **/usr/bin/echo** only) provides an escape notation to represent certain nonprinting characters in *message*. A partial list of the backslash-escaped characters recognized by **echo** follows:

Escape Sequence	Meaning (sh, ksh, and /usr/bin/echo only)
\a	Bell (alert) (not with **sh**)
\b	BACKSPACE
\c	Suppress trailing NEWLINE (**sh**, **ksh**, and **/usr/bin/echo** only)
\n	NEWLINE
\t	HORIZONTAL TAB
\v	VERTICAL TAB
\\	BACKSLASH

Examples

The following examples show how you can use **echo** under the Bourne Shell. The first example uses double quotation marks to quote the single quotation mark (escaping its special meaning) while allowing the dollar signs to keep their special meaning and mark the start of the variables. The **USER** and **HOME** variables are set by the shell. The second example quotes the backslash that precedes the octal number 07, which rings the bell.

```
$ echo "$USER's home directory is $HOME"
alex's home directory is /home/alex

$ echo "Display this line and ring the bell\07"
Display this line.
```

The following examples contain messages with the escape sequence \c. In the first example the shell processes the arguments before calling **echo**. When the shell sees the \c, it replaces the \c with the character c. The last three examples show how to quote the \c so that it is passed to **echo** to prevent **echo** from appending a NEWLINE to the end of the message. All examples are from the Bourne Shell.

```
$ echo There is a newline after this.\c
There is a newline after this.c

$ echo 'There is no newline after this.\c'
There is no newline after this.$

$ echo "There is no newline after this.\c"
There is no newline after this.$

$ echo There is no newline after this.\\c
There is no newline after this.$
```

The next example shows how to suppress a NEWLINE from the C Shell. Because the suppress NEWLINE instruction is an option (and not part of the argument), you can quote the argument(s) in any manner you please.

```
% echo -n There is no newline after this.
There is no newline after this.%
```

expr

Evaluates an expression

Syntax: *expr **expression***

Summary

The **expr** utility evaluates an expression and displays the result. It evaluates character strings that represent either numeric or nonnumeric values. Operators are used with the strings to form expressions.

Argument

The ***expression*** is composed of strings with operators in between. Each string and each operator constitute a distinct argument that you must separate from other arguments with a **SPACE** (or **IFS** [page 383]). You must also quote operators that have special meanings to the shell (for example the multiplication operator **∗**).

The following list of **expr** operators is in order of decreasing precedence. You can change the order of evaluation by using parentheses.

:	**comparison** Compares two strings, starting with the first character in each string and ending with the last character in the second string. The second string is a regular expression with an implied caret (**^** [matches the beginning of the line]) as its first character. If there is a match, it displays the number of characters in the second string. If there is no match, it displays a zero.
∗	**multiplication**
/	**division**
%	**remainder** Works only on strings that contain the numerals 0 through 9 and optionally a leading minus sign. They convert the strings to integer numbers, perform the specified arithmetic operation on numbers, and convert the result back to a string before displaying it.
+	**addition**
–	**subtraction** Functions in the same manner as the operators described above.
<	**less than**
<=	**less than or equal to**
= *or* ==	**equal to**
!=	**not equal to**
>=	**greater than or equal to**
>	**greater than** Relational operators work on both numeric and nonnumeric arguments. If one or both of the arguments is nonnumeric, the comparison is nonnumeric, using the locale-specific collating sequence (frequently ASCII). If both arguments are numeric, the comparison is numeric. The **expr** utility displays a 1 (one) if the comparison is *true* and a 0 (zero) if it is *false*.
&	**AND** Evaluates both of its arguments. If neither is 0 or a null string, it displays the value of the first argument. Otherwise it displays a 0. You must quote this operator.

749

| **OR** Evaluates the first argument. If it is neither 0 nor a null string, it displays the value of the first argument. Otherwise it displays the value of the second argument. You must quote this operator.

Notes

The **/usr/xpg4/bin/expr** utility is a POSIX-compliant version of **expr**.

The **expr** utility returns an exit status of 0 (zero) if the expression is neither a null string nor the number 0, a status of 1 if the expression is null or 0, and a status of 2 if the expression is invalid.

The **expr** utility is useful in Bourne Shell scripts. Because **csh** and **ksh** have the equivalent of **expr** built in, **csh** and **ksh** scripts do not normally use **expr**.

Although **expr** and this discussion distinguish between numeric and nonnumeric arguments, all arguments to **expr** are actually nonnumeric (character strings). When applicable **expr** attempts to convert an argument to a number (for example when using the + operator). If a string contains characters other than 0 through 9 with an optional leading minus sign, **expr** cannot convert it. Specifically if a string contains a plus sign or a decimal point, **expr** considers it to be nonnumeric.

Examples

The following examples show command lines that call **expr** to evaluate constants. You can also use **expr** to evaluate variables in a shell script. In the fourth example **expr** displays an error message because of the illegal decimal point in 5.3.

```
$ expr 17 + 40
57
$ expr 10 - 24
-14
$ expr -17 + 20
3
$ expr 5.3 \* 4
expr: non-numeric argument
```

The multiplication (*), division (/), and remainder (%) operators provide additional arithmetic power, as the examples below show. You must quote the multiplication operator (precede it with a backslash) so that the shell does not treat it as a special character (an ambiguous file reference). You cannot put quotation marks around the entire expression because each string and operator must be a separate argument.

```
$ expr 5 \* 4
20
$ expr 21 / 7
3
$ expr 23 % 7
2
```

The next two examples show how you can use parentheses to change the order of evaluation. You must quote each parenthesis and surround the backslash/parenthesis combination with SPACEs.

```
$ expr 2 \* 3 + 4
10
$ expr 2 \* \( 3 + 4 \)
14
```

You can use relational operators to determine the relationship between numeric or nonnumeric arguments. The command below compares two strings to see if they are equal. The **expr** utility displays a 0 when the relationship is *false* and a 1 when it is *true*.

```
$ expr fred == mark
0
$ expr mark == mark
1
```

The relational operators in the following examples, which must be quoted, can establish order between numeric or nonnumeric arguments. Again, if a relationship is *true,* **expr** displays a 1.

```
$ expr fred \> mark
0
$ expr fred \< mark
1
$ expr 5 \< 7
1
```

The next command compares **5** with **m**. When one of the arguments **expr** is comparing with a relational operator is nonnumeric, **expr** considers the other to be nonnumeric. In this case because **m** is nonnumeric **expr** treats **5** as a nonnumeric argument. The comparison shown below is between the ASCII values of **m** and **5**. The ASCII value of **m** is 109, and **5** is 53, so **expr** evaluates the relationship as *true*.

```
$ expr 5 \< m
1
```

The next example shows the matching operator determining that the four characters in the second string match four characters in the first string. The **expr** utility displays a 4.

```
$ expr abcdefghijkl : abcd
4
```

The **&** operator displays a 0 if one or both of its arguments are 0 or a null string. Otherwise it displays the first argument.

```
$ expr '' \& book
0
$ expr magazine \& book
magazine
$ expr 5 \& 0
0
$ expr 5 \& 6
5
```

The l operator displays the first argument if it is not 0 or a null string. Otherwise it displays the second argument.

```
$ expr '' \| book
book
$ expr magazine \| book
magazine
$ expr 5 \| 0
5
$ expr 0 \| 5
5
$ expr 5 \| 6
5
```

file

Displays the classification of a file

file

Syntax: *file [option] file-list*

Summary

The **file** utility classifies files according to their contents.

Argument

The *file-list* contains the pathnames of one or more files that **file** classifies. You can specify any type of file, including ordinary, directory, and special files, in the *file-list*.

Option

–f *file*

file   Takes the names of files to be examined from *file* (where the files are listed one per line) rather than from the command line.

Notes

The **file** utility works by checking the access permissions associated with a file and examining the first part of a file, looking for keywords and a magic number that the linker and other programs use. The list of magic numbers and keywords is stored in the file named **/usr/lib/locale/*lang*/LC_MESSAGES/magic** or, if that file does not exist, **/etc/magic** (page 611). See the footnote on page 161 for information on *lang*.

The results of **file** are not always correct.

Examples

Some examples of file identification follow:

```
$ file memo proc new
memo: English text
proc: commands text
new:  empty file
```

There are many different file types that **file** can classify. Some of the more common file types found on UNIX/Solaris systems, as displayed by **file**, are

English text	ELF 32-bit LSB executable 80386...	archive	ascii text
c program text	commands text	core file	cpio archive
data	directory	empty file	executable

find

Finds files based on various criteria

Syntax: *find [directory-list] [expression]*

Summary

The **find** utility selects files that are located in specified directories and are described by an expression.

Arguments

The *directory-list* contains the pathnames of directories that **find** is to search. When **find** searches a directory, it searches all subdirectories, to all levels.

The *expression* contains criteria, as described in "Criteria" below. The **find** utility tests each of the files in each of the directories in the *directory-list* to see if it meets the criteria described by the *expression*.

A SPACE separating two criteria is a logical AND operator: The file must meet *both* criteria to be selected. A **–o** separating the criteria is a logical OR operator: The file must meet one or the other (or both) of the criteria to be selected.

You can negate any criterion by preceding it with an exclamation point. The **find** utility evaluates criteria from left to right unless you group them using parentheses.

Within the *expression* you must quote special characters so that the shell does not interpret them but passes them to **find**. Special characters that you may frequently use with **find** are parentheses, square brackets, question marks, and asterisks.

Each element within the *expression* is a separate argument. You must separate arguments from each other with a field separator: A SPACE or **IFS** (page 383). There must be a separator on both sides of each parenthesis, exclamation point, criterion, or other element. When you use a backslash to quote a special character, the separators go on each side of the pair of characters (for example " \ [").

Criteria

The following is a list of criteria that you can use within the *expression*. As used in this list, ±*n* is a decimal integer that can be expressed as +*n* (more than *n*), –*n* (less than *n*), or *n* (exactly *n*).

–atime ±*n*   A file meets this criterion if it was last accessed the number of days ago specified by ±*n* (+*n* means "more than *n* days ago" and –*n* means "fewer than *n* days ago"). When you use this option, **find** changes the access times of directories it searches.

–cpio *dev*   A file always meets this action criterion. It writes the file on device *dev* in **cpio** format.

–depth   A file always meets this action criterion. It causes **find** to take action on entries in a directory before it acts on the directory itself. When you use **find** to send files to the **cpio** utility, the **–depth** criterion enables **cpio** to preserve modification times of directories (assuming you use the **–m** option to **cpio**). See "Discussion" and "Examples" under **cpio** on pages 723 and 724.

–exec *command* **\;**   A file meets this action criterion if the *command* returns a zero (*true*) exit status. You must terminate the *command* with a quoted semicolon. A pair of braces ({ }) within the *command* represents the name of the file being evaluated. You can use the **–exec** action criterion at the end of a group of other criteria to execute the *command* if the preceding criteria are met. Refer to "Discussion." See **xargs** on page 949 for a more efficient way of doing what this option does.

–follow   This criterion causes **find** to follow a symbolic link pointing to a directory file. Always use this criterion when you use **find** with **cpio** with the **–L** option.

–group *name*   A file meets this criterion if it belongs to the group named *name*. You can use a numeric group ID in place of *name*.

–inum *n*   A file meets this criterion if its inode number is *n*.

–links ±*n*   A file meets this criterion if it has the number of links specified by ±*n*.

–mount   A file always meets this action criterion. It causes **find** not to search directories in filesystems other than the one in which the directory being searched (from the *directory-list* argument) resides.

–mtime ±*n*   A file meets this criterion if it was last modified ±*n* days ago (**+n** means "more than *n* days ago" and **–n** means "fewer than *n* days ago").

–name *filename*   A file meets this criterion if *filename* matches its name. You can use ambiguous file references but must quote them.

–newer *filename*   A file meets this criterion if it was modified more recently than *filename*.

–nogroup   A file meets this criterion if it belongs to a group that is not listed in the **/etc/group** file.

–nouser   A file meets this criterion if it belongs to a user who is not in the **/etc/passwd** file (that is, the user ID associated with the file does not correspond to a known user of the system).

–ok *command* **\;**   This action criterion is the same as **–exec**, except that it displays each *command* to be executed, enclosed in angle brackets, and executes the *command* only if it receives a y from standard input.

–print   A file always meets this action criterion. When evaluation of the *expression* reaches this criterion, **find** displays the pathname of the file it is evaluating. If this is the only criterion in the *expression*, **find** displays the names of all the files in the *directory-list*. If this criterion appears with other criteria, **find** displays the name only if the preceding criteria are met. If no action criteria appear in the expression, **–print** is assumed by default. Refer to the following "Discussion" and "Notes" sections.

–size ±*n*[**c**]   A file meets this criterion if it is the size specified by ±*n*, measured in 512-byte blocks. Follow *n* with the letter c to measure files in characters (bytes).

–type *filetype*   A file meets this criterion if its file type is the specified *filetype*. Select *filetype* from the following list:

filetype	Description
b	Block special file
c	Character special file
d	Directory file
f	Ordinary file
l	Symbolic link
p	Fifo (named pipe)
s	Socket

–user *name*   A file meets this criterion if it belongs to the user with the login name *name*. You can use a numeric user ID in place of *name*.

Discussion

Assume that **x** and **y** are criteria. The following command line never tests to see if the file meets criterion **y** if it does not meet criterion **x**. Because the criteria are separated by a **SPACE** (the logical AND operator), once **find** determines that criterion **x** is not met, the file cannot meet the criteria, so **find** does not continue testing. You can read the expression as "(test to see) if the file meets criterion **x** *and* (**SPACE** means *and*) criterion **y**."

```
$ find dir x y
```

The next command line tests the file against criterion **y** if criterion **x** is not met. The file can still meet the criteria, so **find** continues the evaluation. It is read as "(test to see) if criterion **x** *or* criterion **y** is met." If the file meets criterion **x**, **find** does not evaluate criterion **y**, as there is no need.

```
$ find dir x -o y
```

Certain "criteria" do not select files but cause **find** to take action. The action is triggered when **find** evaluates one of these *action criteria*. Therefore the position of an action criterion on the command line, and not the result of its evaluation, determines whether **find** takes the action.

The **–print** action criterion causes **find** to display the pathname of the file it is testing. The following command line displays the names of *all* the files in the **dir** directory (and all its subdirectories), whether they meet the criterion **x** or not:

```
$ find dir -print x
```

The following command line displays only the names of the files in the **dir** directory that meet criterion **x**:

```
$ find dir x -print
```

Examples

The following command line finds all the files in the working directory, and all subdirectories, that have filenames that begin with a. The command uses a period to designate the working directory. The ambiguous file reference is enclosed within quotation marks to prevent the shell from interpreting it. The command does not instruct **find** to do anything with these files—not even display their names. However if you give **find** no instructions or simple instructions, it will implicitly append a **–print** instruction to the command. Even though there is no explicit print instruction in the next command line, **find** displays the appropriate output.

```
$ find . -name 'a*'
.
.
.
```

The next command line finds and explicitly displays the filenames of all the files in the working directory, and all subdirectories, that have filenames that begin with a. This is the same program (with the same output) as shown above, except that it has an explicit print instruction:

```
$ find . -name 'a*' -print
.
.
.
```

The following command line sends a list of selected filenames to the **cpio** utility, which writes them to tape. You can read this **find** command as, "find, in the root directory and all subdirectories (/), all files that are ordinary files (**–type f**) that have been modified within the past day (**–mtime –1**), with the exception of files whose names are suffixed with **.o** (**! –name** '*.o'). (An object file carries a **.o** suffix and usually does not need to be preserved, as it can be recreated from the corresponding program source code.)

```
$ find / -type f -mtime -1 ! -name '*.o' -print | cpio -oB > /dev/rmt/0
```

Using **find**'s built-in **cpio** instruction, the preceding command can be written as

```
$ find / -type f -mtime -1 ! -name '*.o' -cpio /dev/rmt/0
```

The command line below finds, displays the filenames of, and deletes all the files in the working directory, and all subdirectories, that are named **core** or **junk**. The parentheses and the semicolon following **–exec** are quoted so that the shell does not treat them as special characters. **SPACE**s separate the quoted parentheses from other elements on the command line. You can read this **find** command as, "find, in the working directory and all subdirectories (**.**), all files that are named **core** (**–name core**) *or* (**–o**) are named **junk** (**–name junk**) [if a file meets these criteria, continue with] *and* (**SPACE**) print (**–print**) the name of the file *and* (**SPACE**) delete the file (**–exec rm** { })."

```
$ find . \( -name core -o -name junk \) -print -exec rm {} \;
.
.
```

The shell script below uses **find** with the **grep** command to identify files that contain a particular string. This script enables you to look for a file when you remember its contents but cannot remember what its filename is. The **finder** script below locates files in the working directory and all subdirectories that contain the string specified on the command line. The **–type f** criterion is necessary so that **find** passes **grep** only the names of ordinary files, not directory files.

```
$ cat finder
find . -type f -exec grep -l "$1" {} \;
$ finder "Executive Meeting"
./january/memo.0102
./april/memo.0415
```

When **finder** is called with the string Executive Meeting, it locates two files containing that string, **./january/memo.0102** and **./april/memo.0415**. The period (**.**) in the pathnames represents the working directory (that is, **january** and **april** are subdirectories of the working directory).

The next command finds all files in two user directories that are larger than 100 blocks (**–size +100**) and have only been accessed more than five days ago—that is, have not been accessed within the past five days (**–atime +5**). This **find** command then asks whether you want to delete the file (**–ok rm {}**). You must respond to each of these queries with a **y** (for *yes*) or **n** (for *no*). The **rm** command works only if you have execute and write access permission to the directory.

```
$ find /home/alex /home/barbara -size +100 -atime +5 -ok rm {} \;
< rm ... /home/alex/notes >? y
< rm ... /home/alex/letter >? n
.
.
```

In the next example **/home/alex/memos** is a symbolic link to Jenny's directory named **/home/jenny/memos**. When the **–follow** option is used with **find**, the symbolic link is followed, and the contents of that directory are found.

```
$ ls -l /home/alex
lrwxrwxrwx  1 alex    pubs      17 Aug 19 17:07 memos -> /home/jenny/memos
-rw-r--r--  1 alex    pubs    5119 Aug 19 17:08 report

$ find /home/alex -print
/home/alex
/home/alex/memos
/home/alex/report
/home/alex/.profile

$ find /home/alex -follow -print
/home/alex
/home/alex/memos
/home/alex/memos/memo.817
/home/alex/memos/memo.710
/home/alex/report
/home/alex/.profile
```

finger

Displays detailed information on users

Syntax: *finger [options] [user-list]*

Summary

The **finger** utility displays the login names of users, together with their full names, device numbers, the times they logged in, and other information.

The **finger** utility understands network address notation. If your system is attached to a network, you can use **finger** to display information about users on remote systems that you can reach over the network.

finger May Be a Security Risk

The **finger** utility may pose a security risk. Some sites do not run the **fingerd** daemon for this reason.

Arguments

If you do not specify a *user-list*, **finger** provides a short (**–s**) report on every user who is currently logged in on the local system. If you specify one or more usernames, **finger** provides a long (**–l**) report for each of these users.

If the *user-list* includes an at sign (@), the **finger** utility interprets the name following the @ sign as the name of a remote host to contact over the network. If there is also a name in front of the @ sign, **finger** provides information on that particular user on the remote system. Only the **–l** option will work with a *user-list* that includes an @ sign.

Options

–l	**long** Displays detailed information about a user.
–m	**match** If a *user-list* is specified, displays entries only for those users whose *login* names match the names given in *user-list*. Without this option the *user-list* names match *login* and *full* names.
–p	**plan** Does not display the contents of **.plan** file for users. Because it is possible for this file to contain escape sequences that can change the behavior of your display, you may not wish to view it. Normally the long listing of **finger** shows you the contents of this file if it exists in the user's home directory.
–s	**short** Provides a short report about a user.

Notes

When you specify a network address, the **finger** utility works by querying a standard network service (**fingerd**) that runs on the remote system. Although this service is supplied with most UNIX systems today, some sites choose not to run it (to minimize load on their systems, as well as possible security risks, or simply to maintain privacy). If you try to use **finger** to get information on someone at such a site, the result may be an error message or nothing at all. The remote system determines how much information to share with your system and in what format. As a result, the report displayed for any given system may differ from the examples shown.

Discussion

The long report provided by the **finger** utility includes the user's login name, full name, home directory location, and login shell, followed by information about when the user last logged in on the system and how long it has been since the user last typed on the keyboard or received and read electronic mail. After extracting this information from various system files, the **finger** utility then displays the first line of the **.project** file and the whole of the **.plan** file from the user's home directory. It is up to each user to create these files, which are usually used to provide more information about the user (such as telephone number, postal mail address, schedule, interests, and so forth).

The short report generated by **finger** is similar to that provided by the **w** utility; it includes the user's login name, full name, the number of the device the user is logged in on, how much time has elapsed since the user last typed on the keyboard, the time the user logged in, and where the user logged in from. If the user has logged in over the network, the name of the remote system is identified as the user's location.

Examples

The first example displays information on all the users currently logged in on the system.

```
$ finger
Login      Name              TTY        Idle    When        Where
alex     Alex Watson       console    5:55 Tue 07:52   :0
hls      Helen Simpson     pts/2           Mon 05:12   :0.0
jenny    Jenny Chen        pts/11          Mon 05:12   bravo.tcorp.com
```

The next two examples cause **finger** to contact the remote system named **kudos** over the network for information:

```
$ finger @kudos
[kudos]
Login      Name              TTY        Idle    When        Where
alex     Alex Watson       pts/5      5:55 Tue 07:52   :0
roy      Roy Wong          pts/7           Mon 05:12   :0.0
```

```
$ finger watson@kudos
[kudos]
Login name: alex                     In real life: Alex Watson
Directory: /home/alex                Shell: /bin/sh
On since Apr 14 07:52:20 on console from :0
6 hours 12 minutes Idle Time
Mail last read Mon Apr 13 05:12:25 1998
Plan:
For appointments contact Jenny Chen, x1693.
```

fmt

Formats text very simply

Syntax: *fmt [options] [file-list]*

Summary

The **fmt** utility does simple text formatting by attempting to make all nonblank lines nearly the same length.

Argument

The **fmt** utility reads all the files in *file-list* and prints a formatted version of their contents to standard output. If you do not give any filenames, **fmt** reads standard input.

Options

−s   **split**   Only splits lines to make them shorter; does not catenate lines to make longer lines. This option is useful when formatting a document that contains short lines of code that you do not want joined together.

−w *n*   **width**   Changes the output line width to *n* characters. Without this option **fmt** tries to keep output lines close to 72 characters wide. Also *−n*.

Notes

The **fmt** utility works by moving NEWLINE characters. The indention of lines, as well as the spacing between words, is left intact.

This utility is often used to format text while you are using an editor such as **vi**. For example you can format a paragraph in the **vi** editor's command mode by positioning the cursor at the top of the paragraph, then entering **!}fmt**. This replaces the paragraph with the result of feeding it through **fmt** (press **u** before you press any other key if you do not like the change).

Example

The following example shows how **fmt** attempts to make all the lines the same length. The **−50** option gives a target line length of 50 characters.

```
$ cat memo
One factor that is important to remember while administering the dietary
intake of Carcharodon carcharias is that there is, at least from
the point of view of the subject,
very little
differentiating the prepared morsels being proffered from your digits.

In other words, don't feed the sharks!
$ fmt -50 memo
One factor that is important to remember while
administering the dietary intake of Carcharodon
carcharias is that there is, at least from the
point of view of the subject, very little
differentiating the prepared morsels being
proffered from your digits.

In other words, don't feed the sharks!
```

fsck

Checks and repairs a filesystem

Syntax: *fsck [options] filesystem-list*

Summary

The **fsck** utility verifies the integrity of a filesystem and reports on any problems it finds. For each problem it finds, **fsck** asks you if you want it to attempt to fix the problem or ignore it. If you repair the problem, you may lose some data; however that is often the most reasonable alternative. When you specify more than one filesystem, **fsck** attempts to check filesystems in parallel (checking several at the same time as opposed to one after another).

The person responsible for the upkeep of the system should run **fsck** while logged in as Superuser. The filesystem that **fsck** is run on should be unmounted. The root filesystem, which cannot be unmounted, must be quiescent. The best way to ensure quiescence is to bring the system down to single-user mode. Normally you should run **fsck** while the system is in single-user mode. Most startup scripts include commands to run **fsck** on all the filesystems listed in **/etc/vfstab** before bringing the system into multiuser operation. The **/etc/rc2.d/S01MOUNTFSYS** script runs **mountall**, which runs **fsck** before mounting a file.

Argument

The *filesystem-list* is an optional list of filesystems you want to check. If you do not specify a list, **fsck** checks the filesystems listed in the **/etc/vfstab** file. When specifying filesystems, use the character special device (also called a raw device [page 623]) name of the device that holds the filesystem (for example **/dev/rdsk/c0t0d0s6**).

Options

You can separate the options to **fsck** into two groups. The first group consists of those options that affect the overall behavior of **fsck**; these options should precede all other types of options and arguments:

–F *fstype*   **filesystem type**   Only checks filesystems of type *fstype*. The most common type of filesystem under Solaris is UFS.

–m   **mountable**   Check that a filesystem can be mounted; return an exit status and brief message.

–n   **no**   Assumes a *no* response to any questions that arise while checking a filesystem.

–o   **options**   One or more of the following suboptions can appear following **–o**. If you use more than one suboption, separate the options with commas and no SPACEs.

Suboption	Description
b=*block*	Uses block number *block* as the superblock of the filesystem. Check for the location of superblocks with the command **newfs –N** *device*, where *device* is the name of the filesystem as shown by **mount**. If the machine crashes while the superblock is being updated, the superblock may become corrupt. This option allows you to specify an alternate superblock. Block 32 is always an alternate superblock, but others are available depending on size of disk and **newfs** options.
c	**convert** Convert old filesystem type to new. This can be used to convert an old SunOS4 UFS filesystem to be used on Solaris2.
f	**force** The **fsck** utility keeps track of whether a filesystem is *clean*. (A clean filesystem is one that was either just successfully checked with **fsck** or successfully unmounted and has not been mounted since.) Clean filesystems are skipped by **fsck**, which greatly speeds up system booting under normal conditions. This suboption forces **fsck** to check the filesystems even if they are marked as clean.
p	**preen** Attempts automatic repair of any problems found while processing a filesystem. With this option **fsck** quits if it finds a problem that requires your input. Required for parallel processing.
w	Only checks a filesystem if you have write access to it.

–V   **validate**   Displays the command to be run and validates it, but does not execute it.

–y   **yes**   Assumes a *yes* response to any questions that arise while checking a filesystem.

Notes

When a filesystem is consistent, you see a report such as the following:

```
# fsck /dev/dsk/c0t0d0s0
** /dev/dsk/c0t0d0s0
** Last Mounted on /
** Phase 1 - Check Blocks and Sizes
** Phase 2 - Check Pathnames
** Phase 3 - Check Connectivity
** Phase 4 - Check Reference Counts
** Phase 5 - Check Cyl groups
3691 files, 28225 used, 83413 free (157 frags, 10407 blocks,  0.1% fragmentation)
```

If **fsck** finds problems with a filesystem, it reports each problem, allowing you to choose whether to repair or ignore it.

Under Solaris, **fsck** is a front end that calls other utilities to handle different types of filesystems. For example **fsck** calls **fsck_ufs** to check the widely used UFS filesystem type. By splitting **fsck** in this manner, filesystem developers can provide programs to check their filesystems without impacting the development of other filesystems or changing how system administrators use **fsck**.

Run **fsck** on filesystems that are unmounted or mounted readonly. If you run **fsck** on a mounted filesystem by mistake, use CONTROL-C to stop immediately. Continuing may cause the filesystem to become corrupted beyond repair.

Back Up Your Files

Although it is technically feasible to repair files that are damaged and that **fsck** says you should remove, it is usually not practical. The best insurance against significant loss of data is frequent backups. Refer to page 627 for more information on backing up the system.

When **fsck** encounters a file that has lost its link to its filename, **fsck** asks you whether you want to reconnect it. If you choose to reconnect it and fix the problem, the file is put in a directory named **lost+found**, and it is given its inode number as a name. In order for **fsck** to restore files in this way, there should be a **lost+found** directory in the root directory of each filesystem. For example if your filesystems are **/**, **/usr**, and **/var**, you should have the following three **lost+found** directories: **/lost+found**, **/usr/lost+found**, and **/var/lost+found**. If the necessary **lost+found** directory does not exist in a UFS filesystem, **fsck** creates it. If it does exist but does not have enough room, **fsck** attempts to make it larger.

Messages

This section explains **fsck**'s standard messages. It does not explain every message that **fsck** produces. In general **fsck** suggests the most logical way of dealing with a problem in the file structure. Unless you have information that suggests another response, respond to its prompts with **yes**. Use the system backup tapes or disks to restore any data that is lost as a result of this process.

Phase	What Is Checked
Phase 1–Check Blocks and Sizes	Inode information.
Phase 2–Check Pathnames	Directories that point to bad inodes it found in Phase 1.
Phase 3–Check Connectivity	Unreferenced directories and a nonexistent or full **lost+found** directory.
Phase 4–Check Reference Counts	Unreferenced files, a nonexistent or full **lost+found** directory, bad link counts, bad blocks, duplicated blocks, and incorrect inode counts.
Phase 5–Check Cyl Groups	Free list and other filesystem structures. If any problems are found with the free list, then Phase 6 is run.
Phase 6–Salvage Free List	Fixes problems found in Phase 5.

The last line of the **fsck** display is a summary of filesystem usage (below):

```
3691 files, 28225 used, 83413 free (157 frags, 10407 blocks,  0.1% fragmentation)
```

Each block on a filesystem is broken into fragments, or parts, so that when a file needs only a portion of a block, the remainder of the block can be allocated to another file. The preceding message lets you know that the filesystem holds 3,691 files that occupy 28,225 blocks. In addition the system has 83,413 free blocks, of which 157 are fragmented and 10,407 are complete. For convenience the percent of fragmentation is also displayed (0.1%).

ftp

Transfers files over a network

ftp [options] [remote-computer]

Summary

The **ftp** utility uses the standard file transfer protocol to transfer files between different systems that can communicate over a network. The *remote-computer* is the name or network address of the remote system. To use **ftp** you must have an account (or access to a guest or anonymous account) on the remote system.

Argument

If you specify a *remote-computer* on the command line, **ftp** tries to establish a connection to that system. Without an argument **ftp** presents an ftp> prompt and waits for a command.

Options

–g   **no globbing**   Disable filename generation.

–i   **no interactive**   Turn off prompting for each file when transferring multiple files.

–n   **no auto login**   You can configure **ftp** so that it automatically logs in on some remote computers. If you have set **ftp** to do automatic logins, this option disables that behavior. A discussion on configuring **ftp** for automatic logins follows.

–v   **verbose**   Tells you more about how **ftp** is working. Responses from the remote computer are displayed, and **ftp** reports information on how fast files are transferred.

Notes

Many computers, including non-UNIX systems, support file transfer protocol. The **ftp** utility is an implementation of this protocol for UNIX/Solaris systems, allowing you to exchange files with many different types of systems.

By convention many sites offer archives of free information on a system named **ftp** (for example **ftp.uu.net**). You can use the guest account **anonymous** on many systems. When you log in as **anonymous**, you are prompted to enter a password. Although any password is frequently accepted, by convention you should supply your email address (for example **alex@tcorp.com**). This information helps the remote site to know who uses its services. Most systems that support anonymous logins allow you to use the name **ftp** as an easier-to-spell and quicker-to-type synonym for **anonymous**. On many machines that permit **anonymous ftp** access, the interesting files are in a directory named **pub**. For more information see "How Do I Download gzip?" on page 976.

If there are sites that you visit regularly with **ftp**, you can set up your local account so you can log in on those machines automatically. The **ftp** utility reads the **.netrc** file in your home directory to determine if you have an automatic login set up for a remote machine. The following is a typical **.netrc** file:

```
$ cat .netrc
machine bravo login alex password mypassword
default login anonymous password alex@tcorp.com
```

Each line identifies a remote machine. The keywords `machine`, `login`, and `password` precede the corresponding login elements. The last line in this example replaces the word `machine` with `default`. When you connect to a remote system that is not mentioned in **.netrc**, **ftp** uses the information on this line to try to log in.

The .netrc File Can Be a Security Hole

Make the file **.netrc** unreadable by everyone except yourself to protect the account information (passwords) that is kept in it. Use the command **chmod 600 .netrc** to effect this change.

Discussion

The **ftp** utility is interactive; after you start it up, it prompts you to enter commands to transfer files or set parameters. There are a number of commands you can use in response to the `ftp>` prompt. The following are the ones more commonly used:

! [*command*] Runs *command* on the local system. Without *command* the ! escapes to a shell on the local system (use CONTROL-D or **exit** to return to **ftp** when you are through).

ascii Sets the file transfer type for ASCII files. This command allows you to transfer text files from systems that end lines with a RETURN/LINEFEED combination and automatically strips off the RETURN. This command is useful when the remote computer is a DOS or MS Windows machine.

binary Sets the file transfer type so that you can transfer files that contain non-ASCII (unprintable) characters correctly.

bye Closes any connection to a remote computer and terminates **ftp**. Same as **quit** or an EOF.

cd *directory* Changes to a working directory named *directory* on the remote system.

close Closes the connection with the remote system without exiting from **ftp**.

dir [*directory*] [*local-file*] Displays a directory listing from the remote system. If you do not specify a directory name, the working directory is displayed. If you specify *local-file*, the listing is saved on the local system in a file named *local-file*; if not, it is sent to standard output.

get *remote-file* [*local-file*] Picks up a copy of the file named *remote-file* and stores it on the local system. If you do not provide the name of a *local-file*, **ftp** tries to use the remote system's name for the file on the local system. You can provide a file's pathname as a valid *remote-file* or *local-file* name.

glob Toggles filename expansion for the **mget** and **mput** commands.

help Displays a list of commands recognized by the **ftp** utility on the local system.

lcd *[local_directory]*	Changes your working directory to *local_directory* on your local machine. Without an argument, this command changes your working directory on your local machine to your home directory (just as **cd** does without an argument).
ls *[directory] [local-file]*	Similar to **dir** (above) but produces a more concise listing on some remote computers.
mget *remote-file-list*	**multiple get** Unlike the **get** command the **mget** command can retrieve multiple files from the remote system. You can name the remote files literally or use wildcards.
mput *local-file-list*	**multiple put** The **mput** command can put multiple files from the local system onto the remote system. You can name the local files literally or use wildcards.
open *[remote-name]*	If you did not specify a remote system on the command line or if the attempt to connect to the system failed, you can specify the name of the system you want to connect to using **open** with *remote-name*. If you do not specify *remote-name*, **ftp** prompts you for a name.
prompt	When using **mget** or **mput** to receive or send multiple files, or **mdel** to delete multiple files, **ftp** asks for verification (by default) before transferring or deleting each file. This command *toggles* that behavior: If **ftp** is asking for verification, then **prompt** causes it to stop asking; if **ftp** is not asking, **prompt** causes it to ask.
put *local-file [remote-file]*	Deposits a copy of the file named *local-file* from the local system on the remote system. If you do not provide the name of a *remote-file*, **ftp** tries to use the local system's name for the file on the remote system. You can provide a file's pathname as a valid *remote-file* or *local-file* name.
pwd	Causes **ftp** to display the pathname of the working directory on the remote computer. You can use **!pwd** to see your local working directory.
quit	Quits the **ftp** session. Same as **bye**.
user *name [password]*	If the **ftp** utility did not log you in automatically, you can specify your user *name* and *password* on the remote system with the **user** command.

Example

The **ftp** utility displays various messages to let you know how your requests are proceeding. To keep the example below clear and brief, the progress messages from **ftp** are not shown.

In the following example Alex connects to the remote system **bravo** and changes directories to **pub**. After listing the contents of the directory on the remote system, Alex transfers a **clibs.tgz** from the working directory on the remote system to the **src** directory on the local system. Next Alex opens a local shell and uses **ls** to list the contents of the working directory on the local system, changes the working directory on the remote system, and then transfers all the ***.txt** files from the working directory on the local machine to the remote system. The **prompt** command allows Alex to send all the files without **ftp** requesting verification for each file as it is transferred.

```
$ ftp bravo
Connected to bravo.
220 bravo FTP server (Version wu-2.4(1) Sun Jul 31 21:15:56 CDT 1994)
ready.
331 Password required for alex.
230 User alex logged in.
Remote system type is UNIX.
Using binary mode to transfer files.
ftp> cd pub
250 CWD command successful.
ftp> dir
200 PORT command successful.
150 Opening ASCII mode data connection for /bin/ls.
total 681
drwxr-xr-x    2 ftp       ftp            2048 Jul 19 10:11 .
drwxr-xr-x   12 ftp       ftp            1024 Jul 16 13:58 ..
-rw-r--r--    1 ftp       ftp           71801 Jul 19 10:11 clibs.tgz
-rw-r--r--    1 ftp       ftp          611342 Jul 19 10:11 GNUchess.4.0.79.SPARC.32bit...
226 Transfer complete.
ftp> get clibs.tgz src/clibs.tgz
200 PORT command successful.
150 Opening BINARY mode data connection for clibs.tgz (71801 bytes).
226 Transfer complete.
71801 bytes received in 0.455 secs (1.5e+02 Kbytes/sec)
ftp> !
->ls
379a.txt    381a.txt    383.txt
-> ^D
ftp> cd ../incoming
250 CWD command successful.
ftp> prompt
Interactive mode off.
ftp> mput *.txt
local: ./379a.txt remote: ./379a.txt
200 PORT command successful.
150 Opening BINARY mode data connection for ./379a.txt.
226 Transfer complete.
442 bytes sent in 0.0698 secs (6.2 Kbytes/sec)
local: ./381a.txt remote: ./381a.txt
200 PORT command successful.
150 Opening BINARY mode data connection for ./381a.txt.
226 Transfer complete.
285 bytes sent in 0.0319 secs (8.7 Kbytes/sec)
local: ./383.txt remote: ./383.txt
200 PORT command successful.
150 Opening BINARY mode data connection for ./383.txt.
226 Transfer complete.
1071 bytes sent in 0.00201 secs (5.2e+02 Kbytes/sec)
ftp> quit
221 Goodbye.
```

See pages 207 and 976 for additional information on using **ftp**.

gcc   Compiles gcc, g++, C, and C++ programs

Syntax:

gcc [options] file-list [–larg]

g++ [options] file-list [–larg]

Summary

This GNU utility is not included with Solaris. (See page 976 for download information.) The GNU C compiler preprocesses, compiles, assembles, and links C language source files. This compiler is also capable of processing C++ source code when called as **g++**. The name **g++** is a synonym for the **gcc** command, but the compiler makes different assumptions about some input files when called as **g++**. The name **gcc** is used in this description.

The GNU C compiler can also be used to assemble and link assembly language source files, link object files only, or build object files for use in shared libraries. See Chapter 14 for a discussion of using C and related utilities under Solaris.

The conventions used by the C compiler for assigning filename extensions are summarized in the following table:

Filename Extension	Meaning
.a	Static library of object modules.
.c	C language source file.
.C, .cc, or .cxx	C++ language source file.
.i	Preprocessed C language source file.
.ii	Preprocessed C++ language source file.
.o	Object file.
.s	Assembly language source file.
.S	Assembly language source file that needs preprocessing.
.so	Shared library of object modules.

The **gcc** utility takes its input from files you specify on the command line. Unless you use the **–o** option, **gcc** stores the executable program it produces in **a.out**.

Argument

The *file-list* contains the pathnames of the files that **gcc** is to compile, assemble, and/or link.

Notes

For more information see "Programming in C" on page 548.

Options

Without any options, **gcc** accepts C and C++ language source files, assembly language source files, and object files that follow the naming conventions outlined above. The **gcc** utility preprocesses, compiles, assembles, and links these files as appropriate, producing an executable file named **a.out**. If you use **gcc** to create object files without linking them to produce an executable file, each object file is named by adding the extension **.o** to the basename of the corresponding source file. When **gcc** creates an executable file, it deletes any temporary object files it created.

The meaning of some of the most commonly used options are given below. When certain filename extensions are associated with an option, you can assume that the extension is added to the basename of the source file.

–c	**compile**　Suppresses the linking step of compilation. The **gcc** utility compiles and/or assembles source code files and leaves the object code in files with the extension **.o**.
–D_name_[=_value_]	**define**　Usually #define preprocessor directives are given in header, or include, files. You can use this option to define symbolic names on the command line instead. For example **–DUNIX** is equivalent to having the line #define UNIX in an include file, and **–DMACH=i586** is the same as #define MACH i586.
–E	**everything**　Suppresses all steps of compilation on C or C++ source code files _except_ preprocessing and writes the result to standard output. By convention the extension **.i** is used for preprocessed C source and **.ii** for preprocessed C++ source.
–fpic	Causes **gcc** to produce _position-independent_ code, which is suitable for installing into a shared library.
–fPIC	Similar to **–fpic** but used for large shared object libraries. When there are a large number of object modules, offsets between modules may be large and you should use **–fPIC**.
–fwritable-strings	By default the GNU C compiler places string constants into _protected memory,_ where they cannot be changed. Some (usually older) programs assume that you can modify string constants. This option changes the behavior of **gcc** so string constants can be modified. Also see **–traditional**.
–g	**gdb**　Embeds diagnostic information in the object files. This information is used by symbolic debuggers such as **gdb**. Although it is necessary only if you later use a debugger, it is a good practice to include this option as a matter of course.
–I_directory_	**include**　Looks for include files in _directory_ after looking in the standard locations. You can give this option multiple times to look in more than one directory.
–l_arg_	Searches the directories **/lib** and **/usr/lib** for a library file named **lib**_arg_**.so** (and then for **lib**_arg_**.a**). If **gcc** finds this library, it then searches this library for required functions. You must replace _arg_ with the name of the library you want to search. For example the **–lm** option normally links the standard math library **–libm.so**. The position of this option is significant; it generally needs to go at the end of the command line but can be repeated multiple times to search different libraries. Libraries are searched in the order in which they appear on the command line. The linker uses the library only to resolve undefined symbols from modules that _precede_ the library option on the command line. You can add other directories to search through using the **–L** option.

–L*directory*	**library** Adds *directory* to the list of directories to search for libraries given with the **–l** option. The compiler searches directories that you add to the list with **–L** before looking in the standard locations for libraries.
–o *file*	**output** Places the output in *file* instead of *source.suffix*. When you are generating an executable file, places the output in *file* instead of **a.out**. With the **–c** flag the compiled object module is put in *file* instead of *file*.**o**.

> ### A Lot of Options: The –o Option
>
> This list of options is only a small fraction of the full set of options available with the GNU C compiler. See the **gcc man** page for a complete list.
>
> Although the **–o** option is generally used to specify a filename to store object code, this option can also be used to name files resulting from other compilation steps. In the following example the **–o** option causes the assembly language produced by the following **gcc** command to be stored in the file **acode** instead of **pgm.s**, the default:
>
> ```
> $ gcc -S -o acode pgm.c
> ```

–O*n*	**optimize** Attempts to improve the object code produced by the compiler. The value of *n* may be 0, 1, 2, or 3, with a default of 1. Larger values of *n* result in better optimization but may increase both the size of the object file and the time it takes **gcc** to run. Using **–O0** turns off optimization. There are many related options that allow you to control precisely the types of optimizations attempted by **gcc** when you use **–O** (refer to the **gcc man** page).
–p	**profile** Provides additional code in the executable that generates a file at runtime that can be used to profile the executable using the **prof** utility.
–pedantic	The C language accepted by the GNU C compiler includes features that are not part of the ANSI standard for the C language. Using this option forces **gcc** to reject these *language extensions* and accept only standard C programming language features.
–pg	**gnu profile** Provides profiling code specifically for the **gprof** profiler.
–pipe	Uses pipes to connect compilation stages together. By default **gcc** will generate temporary files (typically in **/tmp**) to hold preliminary phases of compilation, assembly, or linking. This flags tells the compiler to not use the temporary files but instead to build a command pipeline linking together the various phases of compiling. Although this option speeds up compilation time, it also uses more memory; use it carefully on machines where memory is limited.
–S	**stop** Stops the assembling and linking steps of compilation on C or C++ source code files. The resulting assembly language files use the **.s** filename extension.
–traditional	Causes **gcc** to accept only C programming language features that existed in the traditional Kernighan and Ritchie C programming language. This option allows you to

compile correctly older programs written using the traditional C language that existed before the ANSI standard C language was defined. Also see **–fwritable-strings**.

–W   **warning**   Provides extra warning messages.

–w   **no warning**   Inhibits all warning messages.

–Wall   **warning all**   Turns on all extra warning messages.

Examples

The first example compiles, assembles, and links a single C program, **compute.c**. The **gcc** utility places the output in **a.out** and deletes the object file.

```
$ gcc compute.c
```

The next example compiles the same program, using the optimizer (**–O** option). It assembles and then links the optimized code. The **–o** option causes **gcc** to put the executable output in **compute**.

```
$ gcc -O -o compute compute.c
```

Next a C source file, an assembly language file, and an object file are compiled, assembled, and linked. The executable output goes to **progo**.

```
$ gcc -o progo procom.c profast.s proout.o
```

In the next example **gcc** searches the standard math library stored in **/lib/libm.so** when it is linking the **himath** program. It places the executable output in **a.out**.

```
$ gcc himath.c -lm
```

In the final example the C compiler compiles **topo.c** with options that check the code for questionable source code practices (the **–Wall** option) and violations of the ANSI C standard (the **–pedantic** option). The **–g** option embeds debugging support in the executable file, which is saved in **topo** with the **–o topo** option. Maximum optimization is enabled with the **–O3** option.

The warnings produced by the C compiler are displayed on standard output. In this example the first and last warnings result from the **–pedantic** option. The other warnings result from the **–Wall** option.

```
$ gcc -Wall -g -O3 -pedantic -o topo topo.c
In file included from topo.c:2:
/usr/include/ctype.h:65: warning: comma at end of enumerator list
topo.c:13: warning: return-type defaults to 'int'
topo.c: In function 'main':
topo.c:14: warning: unused variable 'c'
topo.c: In function 'getline':
topo.c:44: warning: 'c' might be used uninitialized in this function
```

When compiling programs that use the X11 include files and libraries, you may need to use the **–I** and **–L** options to tell **gcc** where to locate those include files and libraries. The next example uses those options and also instructs **gcc** to link the program with the basic X11 library:

```
$ gcc -I/usr/openwin/include plot.c -L/usr/openwin/lib -lX11
```

get
Creates an unencoded version of an SCCS file

Syntax: *get [options] file-list*

Summary
The **get** utility, part of SCCS (page 579), retrieves files from their SCCS-encoded versions. The retrieved files are given the same names as their encoded counterparts, except that the leading **s.** is removed. The options determine characteristics of the retrieved files.

Argument
The *file-list* is a list of SCCS-encoded files (which start with **s.**). If the list includes directory names, all files that begin with **s.** in the named directories are added to *file-list*. Any files in *file-list* that do not begin with **s.** or that are unreadable are ignored. The **get** utility will not create an unencoded version of a file if a file with the same name exists in the working directory.

Options
Without any options **get** retrieves the most recent version of the SCCS file. The file is not writable. To create an editable version of an SCCS file, you must use the **−e** option.

−b   **branch**   With **−e** this option creates a branch delta for a trunk delta that has no successors on the trunk. To use the **−b** option, you must have set the **b** flag using the **admin** utility. If the **b** flag has not been set or if the retrieved delta has a successor delta, the **−b** option is ignored.

−c*date-time*   **cutoff**   Causes deltas made after *date-time* to be excluded from the retrieved file. The *date-time* argument has the format:

>   *YY[MM[DD[HH[MM[SS]]]]]*

The brackets indicate that all components of *date-time* may be omitted except *YY*, starting from the right. The maximum possible values will be substituted for any omitted values (for example 59 is used if *SS* is omitted). The two-digit components may be separated by any number of nonnumeric characters. For example a colon (**:**) may be used between the components (for example 94:02:25:03:36).

−e   **edit**   Use this option to indicate to SCCS that you intend to edit the retrieved file and then to use **delta** to create a new SCCS-encoded version. The version of the encoded file that **get** retrieves depends on the other options you use. If you do not use options to specify characteristics of the retrieved file, the most recent version of the encoded file will be retrieved. Once you have used **get** with the **−e** option on a particular version, you cannot use it again on the same version until after you have used **delta** to complete the first cycle of editing, unless you have set the **j** flag (see **admin** on page 691). You can always use **get** with the **−e** option on another version of the file;

however you must give the command from a different directory. If you try to use **get** with the **–e** option twice in the same directory, the second **get** will fail, because a writable file with the unencoded filename already exists in that directory.

–k   **keyword**   You can use this option to recreate an editable file if you accidentally remove or ruin a file that you previously retrieved with **get**. The keywords in the new copy will be preserved, so they will not be lost when you finish editing the file and run **delta**.

–r*version-number*   **release**   Identifies a particular version of the SCCS-encoded file to be retrieved. If you use the **–e** option with **–r**, **–r** also determines the version number of the associated delta. The version number specified with the **–r** option may include up to four components: release, level, branch, and sequence number. The version retrieved depends on the version number components you specify with the **–r** option and on what versions already exist. Similarly if you use **–e**, the version number of the created delta depends both on the number you specify and on what versions already exist. See "Version Numbers," below, for further information.

Version Numbers

Following is a summary of how the **get** utility identifies what version to retrieve when you use the **–r** option and what version number to assign to the new delta. For each type of version number that you can specify with the **–r** option, and each set of conditions, the list describes the version that will be retrieved and the delta that will be created.

The summary on the next page describes the cases when you do not use the **–b** option. When you use the **–b** option, a new branch is always created.

The following descriptions refer to *trunk deltas* and *branch deltas*. Trunk deltas always have two-component version numbers (release.level), whereas branch version numbers always have four components (release.level.branch.sequence).

Component
Specified: Release

Condition: Release specified is the highest existing release.
Version retrieved: Highest existing level in the specified release.
Delta created: Next level for the specified release.

Condition: Release number is higher than the highest existing release.
Version retrieved: Highest existing level in the highest existing release.
Delta created: First level of the specified release number.

Condition: Release number is less than the highest existing release, and release number is nonexistent.
Version retrieved: Highest existing level in the highest release that is less than the specified release.
Delta created: A new branch for the retrieved delta.

Condition: Release number is less than the highest existing release, and release number exists.
Version retrieved: Highest existing trunk delta in the specified release.
Delta created: A new branch for the retrieved delta.

    Component
      Specified: Release.Level

      Condition: No trunk successor exists.
  Version retrieved: Specified trunk delta.
    Delta created: Next trunk delta (that is, level + 1).

      Condition: Trunk successor exists.
  Version retrieved: Specified trunk delta (that is, release.level).
    Delta created: New branch for the retrieved trunk delta.

    Component
      Specified: Release.Level.Branch
  Version retrieved: Highest sequence number on the specified branch.
    Delta created: Next sequence number on the specified branch.

    Component
      Specified: Release.Level.Branch.Sequence

      Condition: Branch corresponds to highest existing branch for the specified release.level.
  Version retrieved: Specified release.level.branch.sequence.
    Delta created: Next sequence number.

      Condition: Branch number is less than the highest existing branch.
  Version retrieved: Specified release.level.branch.sequence.
    Delta created: New branch for the specified release.level.

Examples

The first command retrieves the highest numbered trunk delta. This file will not be editable.[4]

```
$ get s.thesis
 3.1
 .
 .
```

    The next command includes in the retrieved file only deltas created on or before 2 PM (1400 hours) on March 4, 1999.

```
$ get -c99:03:04:14:00:00 s.thesis
.3.1
 .
 .
 .
 .
 .
```

---

4. See the tip named "Making SCCS a Little More Friendly," page 581 and the following examples for information about using the **sccs** front end to help with file naming and placement.

The following command retrieves the highest numbered trunk delta for editing. The new delta will have the same release number and the next level number.

```
$ get -e s.thesis
3.1
new delta 3.2
.
.
```

Below, the highest existing trunk delta will be retrieved (because the specified release, 4, is higher than any existing release). The new delta will be Version 4.1.

```
$ get -e -r4 s.thesis
3.1
new delta 4.1
.
.
```

grep

Searches for a pattern in files

Syntax: *grep [options] pattern [file-list]*

Summary

The **grep** utility searches one or more files, line by line, for a *pattern*. The *pattern* can be a simple string or another form of a regular expression (Appendix A). The **grep** utility takes various actions, specified by options, each time it finds a line that contains a match for the *pattern*.

    The **grep** utility takes its input from files you specify on the command line or from standard input.

Arguments

The *pattern* is a regular expression, as defined in Appendix A. You must quote regular expressions that contain special characters, SPACEs, or TABs. An easy way to quote these characters is to enclose the entire expression within single quotation marks.

    The *file-list* contains pathnames of ordinary text files that **grep** searches.

Options

If you do not specify an option, **grep** sends lines that contain a match for *pattern* to standard output. If you specify more than one file on the command line, **grep** precedes each line that it displays with the name of the file that it came from followed by a colon.

–c	**count**	Displays only the number of lines that contain a match in each file.
–h	**no header**	When *file-list* contains more than one file, omits the name of the file from each line of output.
–i	**ignore case**	Causes lowercase letters in the pattern to match uppercase letters in the file, and vice versa. Use this option when searching for a word that may be at the beginning of a sentence (that is, may or may not start with an uppercase letter).
–l	**list**	Displays only the name of each file that contains one or more matches. It displays each filename only once, even if the file contains more than one match. The output is delimited by NEWLINEs.
–n	**number**	Precedes each line by its line number in the file. The file does not need to contain line numbers. This number represents the number of lines in the file up to and including the displayed line.
–s	**suppress**	Does not display an error message if a file in *file-list* does not exist or is not readable.

777

–v
    reverse sense of test   Causes lines *not* containing a match to satisfy the search. When you use this option by itself, **grep** displays all lines that do not contain a match for the *pattern*.

–w
    word   With this option the *pattern* must match a whole word. This is helpful if you are searching for a specific word that may also appear as a substring of another word in the file. (Search for the regular expression \<pattern\>.)

Notes

The **/usr/xpg4/bin/grep** utility is a POSIX-compliant version of **grep**.

The **grep** utility returns an exit status of 0 if it finds a match, 1 if it does not find a match, and 2 if the file is not accessible or there is a syntax error.

Two utilities perform functions similar to that of **grep**. The **egrep** utility allows you to use *extended regular expressions,* which include a different set of special characters than do basic regular expressions (page 959). The **fgrep** utility is fast and compact but processes only simple strings, not regular expressions.

Examples

The following examples assume that the working directory contains three files: **testa**, **testb**, and **testc**. The contents of each file are

File testa	**File testb**	**File testc**
aaabb	aaaaa	AAAAA
bbbcc	bbbbb	BBBBB
ff-ff	ccccc	CCCCC
cccdd	ddddd	DDDDD
dddaa		

The **grep** utility can search for a pattern that is a simple string of characters. The following command line searches **testa** for, and displays each line containing, the string bb:

```
$ grep bb testa
aaabb
bbbcc
```

The **–v** option reverses the sense of the test. The following example displays all the lines *without* bb:

```
$ grep -v bb testa
ff-ff
cccdd
dddaa
```

The **–n** option displays the line number of each displayed line.

```
$ grep -n bb testa
1:aaabb
2:bbbcc
```

The **grep** utility can search through more than one file. Following, **grep** searches through each file in the working directory. The name of the file containing the string precedes each line of output.

```
$ grep bb *
testa:aaabb
testa:bbbcc
testb:bbbbb
```

When the search for the string bb is done with the **–w** option, **grep** produces no output because none of the files contains the string bb as a separate word.

```
$ grep -w bb *
$
```

The search that **grep** performs is case sensitive. Because the previous examples specified lowercase bb, **grep** did not find the uppercase string BBBBB in **testc**. The **–i** option causes both upper- *and* lowercase letters to match either case of letter in the pattern.

```
$ grep -i bb *
testa:aaabb
testa:bbbcc
testb:bbbbb
testc:BBBBB
$ grep -i BB *
testa:aaabb
testa:bbbcc
testb:bbbbb
testc:BBBBB
```

The **–c** option displays the number of lines in each file that contain a match.

```
$ grep -c bb *
testa:2
testb:1
testc:0
```

The following command line displays lines from the file **text2** that contain a string of characters starting with st, followed by zero or more characters (. * represents zero or more characters in a regular expression—see Appendix A), and ending in ing.

```
$ grep 'st.*ing' text2
.
.
.
```

You can use the ^ regular expression alone, which matches the beginning of a line, to match every line in a file. Together with the **–n** option, it displays the lines in a file, preceded by their line numbers.

```
$ grep -n '^' testa
1:aaabb
2:bbbcc
3:ff-ff
4:cccdd
5:dddaa
```

The next command line counts the number of times different #include statements appear in C source files in the working directory. The **–h** option causes **grep** to suppress the filenames from its output. The input to **sort** is all lines from ***.c** that contain a match for `#include`. The output from **sort** is an ordered list of lines that contains many duplicates. When **uniq** with the **–c** option processes this list, it outputs repeated lines only once, along with a count of the number of repetitions in its input.

```
$ grep -h '^#include' *.c | sort | uniq -c
9 #include "buff.h"
2 #include "poly.h"
1 #include "screen.h"
6 #include "window.h"
2 #include "x2.h"
2 #include "x3.h"
2 #include <math.h>
3 #include <stdio.h>
```

The final command line calls the **vi** editor with a list of files in the working directory that contain the string `Sampson`. The backquotes (page 371) cause the shell to execute the **grep** command in place and supply **vi** with a list of filenames that you want to edit. (The single quotation marks are not necessary in this example, but they are required if the string you are searching for contains special characters or **SPACE**s. It is generally a good habit to quote the pattern so the shell does not interpret any special characters it may contain.)

```
$ vi `grep -l 'Sampson' *`
.
.
```

gzip

Compresses or decompresses files

Syntax:

*gzip [**options**] [**file-list**]*
*gunzip [**options**] [**file-list**]*

Summary

This GNU utility is not included with Solaris. (See page 976 for download information.) The **gzip** utility compresses files, reducing disk space requirements and the time needed to transmit files between computers. When **gzip** compresses a file, it adds the extension **.gz** to the filename; compressing the file **fname** creates the file **fname.gz** and deletes the original file. To restore **fname** use the command **gunzip** with the argument **fname.gz**. You can omit the **.gz** extension when you restore a file.

Argument

The *file-list* is a list of one or more files that are to be compressed or decompressed. If a directory appears in *file-list* with no **--recursive** option, **gzip** issues an error message and ignores the directory. With a **--recursive** option **gzip** recursively compresses all files within the directory (and subdirectories to any level).

Options

If *file-list* is empty or if the special option **–** is present, **gzip** reads from standard input. Using the **--force** option permits standard input to come from the keyboard and causes **gzip** to write to standard output. Options in parentheses are short versions of the options.

--decompress *or*   (**–d**)   Decompresses a file compressed with **gzip**. This option with **gzip** is equiva-
--uncompress   lent to **gunzip**.

--fast *or*   (**–n**)   Gives you control over the trade-off between the speed of compression and
--best   the amount of compression. In the form **–n**, **n** is a digit from 1 to 9; level 1 is the fast-
                          est compression, level 9 the best. The default level employed by **gzip** is 6. The
                          options **--fast** and **--best** are synonyms for –1 and –9, respectively.

--force   (**–f**)   Forces compression even if a file already exists, has multiple links, or comes
                          from the keyboard. The option has a similar effect with **gunzip**.

--recursive   (**–r**)   For directories in *file-list*, descends tree rooted at the directory, compressing
                          all files recursively. Used with **gunzip**, recursively decompresses files.

--stdout   (**–c**)   Writes the results of compression or decompression to standard output instead
                          of overwriting the original file.

--verbose   (**–v**)   For each file, displays the name of the file, the name of the compressed file,
                          and the amount of compression. Displays similar information with **gunzip**.

Notes

Refer to "How Do I Download gzip?" on page 976 for information about obtaining a copy of **gzip**.

In addition to the **gzip** format, **gunzip** recognizes several other compressed file formats, enabling **gunzip** properly to decompress a file compressed with **compress**.

The GNU **tar** (and not the Solaris version) utility calls **gzip** when you call it with the **−z** option.

Discussion

Almost all files become much smaller when compressed with **gzip**. Rarely a file becomes larger, but only by a slight amount. The type of a file and its contents (as well as the **−n** option) determine how much reduction is actually done; text files are often reduced by 60 to 70 percent.

To see an example of a file that gets larger when compressed with **gzip**, compare the size of a file that has been compressed once with the same file compressed with **gzip** again. Because **gzip** complains if you give it an argument with the extension **.gz**, you need to rename the file before compressing it a second time.

The file attributes such as owner, permissions, and modification and access times are left intact when compression by **gzip** takes place.

If the compressed version of a file already exists, **gzip** reports that fact and asks for your confirmation before overwriting the existing file. If a file has multiple links to it, **gzip** issues an error message and terminates. The **−−force** option overrides the default behavior in both of these situations.

Related Utilities

Following is a list of related utilities that allow you to view and manipulate compressed files. None of these utilities changes the files that it works on. (See page 976 for download information.)

zcat *file-list*
Works like **cat** except that *file-list* contains compressed files that are decompressed with **gunzip** as each is output. If you have installed **gzip** on your system, you will have two versions of **zcat**. The Solaris version (**/usr/bin/zcat**) works with files created by **compress**, and the GNU version (frequently in **/usr/local/bin/zcat**) works with both **compress** *and* **gzip** files.

zdiff *[options] file1 [file2]*
A GNU utility. Works like **diff** except that *file1* and *file2* are decompressed with **gunzip** as needed. The **zdiff** utility accepts many of the same options as **diff** (page 739). If you omit *file2*, **zdiff** compares *file1* with the compressed version of *file1* (assuming it exists).

zmore *file-list*
A GNU utility. Works like **more** except that *file-list* contains compressed files that are decompressed with **gunzip** as each is displayed.

Examples

In the first example **gzip** compresses two files. Next **gunzip** decompresses one of the files. When a file is compressed and decompressed, its size changes, but its modification time remains the same.

```
$ ls -l
total 175
-rw-rw-r-- 1 alex group 33557 Jul 20 17:32 patch-27
-rw-rw-r-- 1 alex group 143258 Jul 20 17:32 patch-28
```

```
$ gzip *
$ ls -l
total 51
-rw-rw-r-- 1 alex group 9693 Jul 20 17:32 patch-27.gz
-rw-rw-r-- 1 alex group 40426 Jul 20 17:32 patch-28.gz
$ gunzip patch-27.gz
$ ls -l
total 75
-rw-rw-r-- 1 alex group 33557 Jul 20 17:32 patch-27
-rw-rw-r-- 1 alex group 40426 Jul 20 17:32 patch-28.gz
```

In the next example the files in Jenny's home directory are archived using the **cpio** utility. The archive is compressed with **gzip** before it is written to tape. See page 721 for more information on using **cpio**.

```
$ find /home/jenny -depth -print | cpio -oBm | gzip >/dev/ftape
```

head

Displays the beginning of a file

Syntax: *head [option] [file-list]*

Summary

The **head** utility displays the beginning (head) of a file. It takes its input from one or more files you specify on the command line or from standard input.

Argument

The *file-list* contains pathnames of the files that **head** displays. If you specify more than one file, **head** displays the filename of each file before it displays the first few lines. If you do not specify any files, **head** takes its input from standard input.

Option

–n or **–n** *n*   Displays *n* lines.

Notes

The **head** utility displays ten lines by default.

Examples

The examples are based on a file named **eleven**, which contains eleven lines numbered one through eleven. In the first example **head** displays the first ten lines of the **eleven** file (no arguments):

```
$ head eleven
line one
line two
line three
line four
line five
line six
line seven
line eight
line nine
line ten
```

The next example displays the first three lines (**–3**) of the file:

```
$ head -3 eleven
line one
line two
line three
```

kill

Terminates a process

Syntax: *kill [options] [PID-list]*

Summary

The **kill** utility terminates one or more processes by sending them signals. By default **kill** sends a software termination signal (SIGTERM, signal number 15), although you can specify a different signal. The process must belong to the user executing **kill**, except that Superuser can terminate any process. The shells have **kill** builtins _{ksh}, which work exactly like the **kill** utility.

Argument

The **PID-list** contains process identification (PID) _{ksh} or job _{ksh} numbers of processes **kill** is to terminate. You must precede a job number with a percent sign (**%**). In place of a job number, you can use a string that uniquely identifies the job (also preceded by a **%**).

Options

–l   list ("ell")   Lists all signal names. For a complete list of signal names and numbers, see **/usr/include/sys/signal.h**.

–signal   **signal**   Sends the *signal* signal to the specified processes. Signal can be the name or number of a signal. See the table on page 426 for a list of common signals. If you do not specify a signal, **kill** sends the software termination signal (TERM).

Notes

The shell displays the PID number of a background process when you initiate the process. You can also use **ps** to determine PID numbers.

If the (TERM) does not terminate a process, try using a KILL (9) signal. A process can choose to ignore any signal except KILL.

To terminate all processes that the current login process initiated and have the operating system log you out, give the command **kill –KILL 0**.

> ### Superuser + kill Can Bring the System Down
>
> If you run the command **kill –9 0** or **kill –KILL 0** while you are logged in as Superuser, you will bring the system down.

Examples

The first example shows a command line executing the file **compute** as a background process and the **kill** utility terminating it:

```
$ compute &
[2] 259
$ kill 259
$
[2] + Terminated                     compute
```

The next example shows the **ps** utility determining the PID number of the background process running a program named **xprog** and the **kill** utility terminating **xprog** with the KILL signal:

```
$ ps -u alex
PID TTY        TIME CMD
  2619 vt01     0:04 Xsun
  2717 ?        0:00 sdtvolch
  2701 pts/2    0:00 ttsessio
  2648 ?        0:00 fbconsol
  2709 ??       0:00 dtterm
  2687 pts/2    0:00 csh
  2746 ?        0:00 xprog
  2684 pts/2    0:00 sdt_shel
  2638 ?        0:00 Xsession
  2702 pts/2    0:00 dtsessio
  2685 ?        0:00 dsdm
  2708 ?        0:01 dtwm
  2751 pts/2    0:00 dtfile
  2718 ?        0:00 ksh
  2747 pts/2    0:00 sh
  2715 ??       0:00 xterm
$ kill -KILL 2746
$
[1] + Terminated                  xprog
```

For more information see "kill: Terminate a Process" on page 595.

ln

Makes a link to a file

Syntax:
   ln [options] existing-file new-link
   ln [options] existing-file-list directory

Summary

The **ln** (link) utility creates a hard link (page 94) to a file or a symbolic link (page 96) to a file or directory.

Arguments

The *existing-file* is the pathname of the file you want to make a link to. The *new-link* is the pathname of the new link. The *existing-file* must be a regular file when you are creating a hard link and can be a regular file or a directory for a symbolic link.

Using the second syntax format, the *existing-file-list* contains the pathnames of the ordinary files you want to make links to. The **ln** utility establishes the new links so that they appear in the *directory*. The simple filenames of the entries in the *directory* are the same as the simple filenames of the files in the *existing-file-list*.

Options

When you do not specify the **–s** option, **ln** creates a hard link.

–f
   force Completes a link regardless of file access permissions. Refer to "Notes" following.

–s
   symbolic Creates a symbolic link. When you use this option, the *existing-file* and *new-link* may be directories, and they may be on different filesystems. Refer to "Symbolic Links" on page 96.

Notes

The **/usr/xpg4/bin/ln** utility is a POSIX-compliant version of **ln**.

A hard link is an entry in a directory that points to a file. The operating system makes the first link to a file when you create the file using an editor, a program, or redirected output. You can make additional links using **ln** and remove links with **rm**. The **ls** utility with the **–l** option shows you how many links a file has. Refer to "Links" on page 92.

If *new-link* is the name of an existing file that you do not have write access permission to, **ln** displays your access permission and waits for your response (unless you use the **–f** option).

You can use symbolic links to link across filesystems and to create links to directories. When you use the **ls –l** command to list information about a symbolic link, **ls** displays –> and the name of the linked-to file after the name of the link.

Examples

The first command makes a hard link between **memo2** in the **/home/alex/literature** directory and the working directory. The file appears as **memo2** (the simple filename of the existing file) in the working directory.

```
$ ln /home/alex/literature/memo2 .
```

The next command makes another link to the same file. This time the file appears as **new_memo** in the working directory.

```
$ ln /home/alex/literature/memo2 new_memo
```

The following command makes a link that causes the file to appear in another user's directory. You must have write and execute access permission to the other user's directory for this command to work. If you own the file, you can use **chmod** to give the other user write access permission to the file.

```
$ ln /home/alex/literature/memo2 /home/jenny/new_memo
```

The next command makes a symbolic link to an existing file, **memo3**, in the directory **/home/alex/literature**. The symbolic link is in a different filesystem, **/tmp**. The **ls –l** command shows the linked-to filename.

```
$ pwd
/home/alex/literature
$ ln -s memo3 /tmp/memo
$ ls -l /tmp/memo
lrwxrwxrwx 1 alex  pubs 5  Jul 13 11:44 /tmp/memo -> memo3
```

The final example attempts to make a symbolic link named **memo1** to the file **memo2**. Because the file **memo1** exists, **ln** refuses to make the link.

```
$ ls -l memo?
-rw-rw-r--   1 alex      group          224 Jul 31 14:48 memo1
-rw-rw-r--   1 alex      group          753 Jul 31 14:49 memo2
$ ln -s memo2 memo1
ln: cannot create memo1: File exists
```

lp

Prints files

Syntax: *lp [options] [file-list]*
lpstat
*cancel **job-number***

Summary
The **lp** (line printer) utility places one or more files in the printer queue. It provides orderly access to the printer for several users or processes. You can use the **cancel** utility to remove files from the queue and the **lpstat** utility to check the status of files in the queue. Refer to "Notes" below.

The **lp** utility takes its input from files you specify on the command line or from standard input. It sends a unique identification number to standard output and the specified files to the printer. You can use the identification number with the **cancel** utility to cancel a print job.

Arguments
The *file-list* is a list of one or more pathnames of files that **lp** prints. The *job-number* argument to **cancel** is the identifier that **lp** assigned to the job. It is displayed by **lp** and **lpstat**.

Options
Check with the system administrator about installation-dependent options.

–c   **copy file** Copies a file before placing it in the printer queue so that it cannot be changed. If you do not use this option, the printed copy will reflect any changes you make before it is printed.

–d *printer*   **destination** Sends the *file-list* to the printer named *printer*. Without this option **lp** uses the default printer.

–m   **mail** Sends mail to report when the file has finished printing.

–n*n*   **number of copies** Causes **lp** to print *n* copies.

–s   **suppress** Suppresses the request id message you would otherwise get when you submit a print job.

–w   **write** Uses **write** to report when the file has finished printing. If you are not logged in, **lp** uses **mail** instead.

Notes
There are many options for **lp**. Refer to the **lp man** page for a complete list.

The **lpstat** utility displays the job identification number and status of jobs in the printer queue. Without any options or arguments, **lpstat** displays information about all printing jobs you started.

The **cancel** utility aborts a job that you started with **lp**. You must call it with the job identification number of the job you want to cancel.

The next section includes examples showing typical uses of **lpstat** and **cancel**. Refer to the **man** pages for a complete list of the options and arguments to **lpstat** and **cancel**.

See page 639 for information on adding and removing printers to/from the system.

Examples

The following command line prints the file named **memo2**. The message following the command is from **lp**. It tells you the job number (printer_1-496) in case you want to use **cancel** to end the job. The `printer_1` portion of the job number is the name of the printer.

```
$ lp memo2
request id is printer_1-496 (1 file)
```

Below, a pipe sends the output of **ls** to the printer.

```
$ ls | lp
request id is printer_1-497 (standard input)
```

Next **nawk** uses the commands in **a1** to process **report7** and sends the output to the printer, using a pipe and **lp**. The job runs in the background.

```
$ nawk -f a1 report7 | lp &
12345
12346
request id is printer_1-498 (standard input)
```

The next examples use two different methods to paginate and send the **memo** file to the printer. Refer to **pr** (page 860) for more information.

```
$ cat memo | pr | lp
request id is printer_1-499 (standard input)
$ pr memo | lp
request id is printer_1-500 (standard input)
```

The example below shows that job printer_1-500 is waiting to be printed. It was submitted by Alex at 11:59 AM on July 13.

```
$ lpstat
printer_1-500 alex 5721 Jul 13 11:59
```

The following command cancels job number 500 on printer_1.

```
$ cancel printer_1-500
```

ls

Displays information about one or more files

Syntax: *ls [options] [file-list]*

Summary

The **ls** utility displays information about one or more files. It lists the information alphabetically by filename unless you use an option to change the order.

Arguments

When you do not use an argument, **ls** displays the names of the files in the working directory. Without the **–a** option, **ls** does not list invisible files (files whose names start with a period).

    The *file-list* contains one or more pathnames of files. You can use the pathname of any ordinary, directory, or device file. These pathnames can include ambiguous file references.

    When you specify a directory, **ls** displays the contents of the directory (unless you use the **–d** option). The **ls** utility displays the name of the directory only when it is needed to avoid ambiguity, such as when more than one directory is included in the listing. If you specify an ordinary file, **ls** displays information about just that file.

Options

The options determine the type of information **ls** displays, how it displays it, and the order in which it displays it.

    Without any options **ls** displays a short list that contains only filenames.

–a   **all**   Without a *file-list* (no arguments on the command line), this option displays information about all the files in the working directory, including invisible files (those with filenames that begin with a period). When you do not use this option, **ls** does not list information about invisible files, unless you explicitly include the name of an invisible file in *file-list*.

                In a similar manner when you use this option with a *file-list* that includes an appropriate ambiguous file reference, **ls** displays information about invisible files. (The ✳ ambiguous file reference does not match a leading period in a filename—see page 120.)

–A   **all**   Works as the **–a** option does except that it does not display **.** (the working directory) and **..** (the parent of the working directory).

–b   Displays nonprinting characters in a filename by using the octal notation of a backslash followed by three octal digits (**\ddd**).

–c   **change**   With **–t** this option sorts by the last time the inode for each file was changed (file status change). When you use it with **–l**, **ls** displays these times rather than file modification times.

–C

column   Lists files in vertically sorted columns. When output is going to the screen, the –C option is the default.

–d

directory   Displays the names of directories without displaying their contents. When you give this option without an argument, **ls** displays information about the working directory. This option displays ordinary files normally.

–F

Displays a slash after each directory, an asterisk after each executable file, and an at sign (@) after symbolic links.

–i

inode   Displays the inode number of each file. With **–l** this option displays the inode number in column 1 and shifts all other items one column to the right.

–l

long ("ell")   Displays the seven columns shown in Figure III-1. The first column, which contains 11 characters, is divided as described in the following paragraphs. The first character describes the type of file, as shown in the following table:

First Character	Type of File
–	Ordinary
b	Block special device
c	Character special device
d	Directory
D	Door
l	Symbolic link
p	Fifo (named pipe) special file
s	AF_UNIX address family socket

Refer to pages 76 and 619 for more information on types of files.

The next nine characters of the first column represent access permissions associated with the file. These nine characters are divided into three sets of three characters each.

The first three characters represent the owner's access permissions. If the owner has read access permission to the file, an **r** appears in the first character position. If the owner is not permitted to read the file, a hyphen appears in this position. The next two positions represent the owner's write and execute access permissions. A **w** appears in the second position if the owner is permitted to write to the file, and an **x** appears in the third position if the owner is permitted to execute the file. An **s** in the third position indicates that the file has setuid permission (page 90) and execute permission. An **S** indicates setuid without execute permission. A hyphen indicates the owner does not have the access permission associated with the character position.

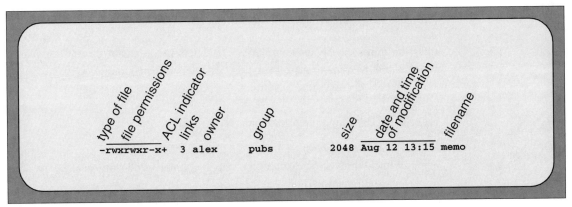

*Figure III-1   The columns of the **ls –l** command*

In a similar manner the second and third sets of three characters represent the access permissions of the user's group and other users. An **s** in the third position of the second set of characters indicates that the file has setgid permission with execute permission, and an **S** indicates setgid without execute permission.

The last character is **t** if the sticky bit is set with execute permission and **T** if it is set without execute permission. Refer to **chmod** on page 709 for information on changing access permissions.

A plus sign (**+**) just after the last permission position indicates that the file has ACL permissions in addition to those shown. Refer to "ACL (Access Control List)" on page 674.

The second column indicates the number of hard links to the file. Refer to page 92 for more information on links.

The third and fourth columns display the name of the owner of the file and the name of the group the file belongs to.

The fifth column indicates the size of the file in bytes or, if information about a device file is being displayed, the major and minor device numbers. In the case of a directory, this number is the size of the actual directory file, not the size of the files that are entries within the directory. (Use **du** to display the size of all the files in a directory.)

The last two columns display the date and time the file was last modified, and the filename.

A symbolic link shows an arrow and the pathname of the file that it is linked to at the right end of the line. The **/usr/man** symbolic link to **/usr/share/man** is displayed as:

```
$ ls -l /usr/man
lrwxrwxrwx   1 root      root        11 Apr 23 16:05 /usr/man -> ./share/man
```

–L **link** Lists information about the file referenced by a symbolic link rather than information about the link itself.

–q **question mark** Displays nonprinting characters in a filename as question marks. When output is going to the screen, this is the default behavior.

–r **reverse** Displays the list of filenames in reverse sorted order.

–R **recursive** Lists subdirectories recursively.

–s **size** Displays the size of each file in 512-byte blocks. The size precedes the filename. With **–l** this option displays the size in column 1 and shifts each of the other items one column to the right.

–t **time modified** Displays the list of filenames in order by the time of last modification. It displays the files that were modified most recently first.

–u **time accessed** When you use this option with the **–t** option, it sorts by the last time each file was accessed. When you use it with **–l**, it displays access times rather than modification times.

–x Lists files in horizontally sorted columns.

–1 **one column** (one) Causes **ls** to list one filename per line. This is the default when output is not sent to the screen.

Notes

The **/usr/xpg4/bin/ls** utility is a POSIX-compliant version of **ls**.

Refer to page 118 for examples of using **ls** with ambiguous file references.

Examples

All of the following examples assume that the user does not change to another working directory.

The first command line shows the **ls** utility with the **–x** option. You see a horizontally sorted alphabetical list of the names of the files in the working directory.

```
$ ls -x
bin          c            calendar
execute      letters      shell
```

The **–F** option appends a slash (/) to files that are directories, an asterisk to files that are executable, and an at sign (@) after symbolic links.

```
$ ls -Fx
bin/         c/           calendar
execute*     letters/     shell@
```

Next the **–l** (**long**) option displays a long list. The files are still in alphabetical order.

```
$ ls -l
total 8
drwxrwxr-x  2 jenny    pubs    80  May 20 09:17 bin
drwxrwxr-x  2 jenny    pubs   144  Mar 26 11:59 c
-rw-rw-r--  1 jenny    pubs   104  May 28 11:44 calendar
-rwxrw-r--  1 jenny    pubs    85  May  6 08:27 execute
drwxrwxr-x  2 jenny    pubs    32  Oct  6 22:56 letters
drwxrwxr-x 16 jenny    pubs  1296  Jun  6 17:33 shell
```

The **–a** (**all**) option lists all files, including invisible ones.

```
$ ls -a
.               .profile    c           execute     shell
..              bin         calendar    letters
```

Combining the **–a** and **–l** options displays a long list of all the files, including invisible files, in the working directory. This list is still in alphabetical order.

```
$ ls -al
total 12
drwxrwxr-x  6 jenny    pubs   480  Jun  6 17:42 .
drwxrwx--- 26 root     root   816  Jun  6 14:45 ..
-rw-rw-r--  1 jenny    pubs   161  Jun  6 17:15 .profile
drwxrwxr-x  2 jenny    pubs    80  May 20 09:17 bin
drwxrwxr-x  2 jenny    pubs   144  Mar 26 11:59 c
-rw-rw-r--  1 jenny    pubs   104  May 28 11:44 calendar
-rwxrw-r--  1 jenny    pubs    85  May  6 08:27 execute
drwxrwxr-x  2 jenny    pubs    32  Oct  6 22:56 letters
drwxrwxr-x 16 jenny    pubs  1296  Jun  6 17:33 shell
```

If you add the **–r** (reverse) option to the command line, **ls** produces a list in reverse alphabetical order.

```
$ ls -ral
total 12
drwxrwxr-x 16 jenny    pubs  1296  Jun  6 17:33 shell
drwxrwxr-x  2 jenny    pubs    32  Oct  6 22:56 letters
-rwxrw-r--  1 jenny    pubs    85  May  6 08:27 execute
-rw-rw-r--  1 jenny    pubs   104  May 28 11:44 calendar
drwxrwxr-x  2 jenny    pubs   144  Mar 26 11:59 c
drwxrwxr-x  2 jenny    pubs    80  May 20 09:17 bin
-rw-rw-r--  1 jenny    pubs   161  Jun  6 17:15 .profile
drwxrwx--- 26 root     root   816  Jun  6 14:45 ..
drwxrwxr-x  6 jenny    pubs   480  Jun  6 17:42 .
```

Use the **–t** and **–l** options to list files so that the most recently modified file appears at the top of the list.

```
$ ls -tl
total 8
drwxrwxr-x 16 jenny    pubs  1296  Jun  6 17:33 shell
-rw-rw-r--  1 jenny    pubs   104  May 28 11:44 calendar
drwxrwxr-x  2 jenny    pubs    80  May 20 09:17 bin
-rwxrw-r--  1 jenny    pubs    85  May  6 08:27 execute
drwxrwxr-x  2 jenny    pubs   144  Mar 26 11:59 c
drwxrwxr-x  2 jenny    pubs    32  Oct  6 22:56 letters
```

Together the **–r** and **–t** options cause **ls** to list files with the file you modified least recently at the top of the list.

```
$ ls -trl
total 8
drwxrwxr-x  2 jenny    pubs    32 Oct  6 22:56 letters
drwxrwxr-x  2 jenny    pubs   144 Mar 26 11:59 c
-rwxrw-r--  1 jenny    pubs    85 May  6 08:27 execute
drwxrwxr-x  2 jenny    pubs    80 May 20 09:17 bin
-rw-rw-r--  1 jenny    pubs   104 May 28 11:44 calendar
drwxrwxr-x 16 jenny    pubs  1296 Jun  6 17:33 shell
```

The next example shows **ls** with a directory filename as an argument. The **ls** utility lists the contents of the directory in alphabetical order.

```
$ ls bin
c       e       lsdir
```

To display information about the directory file itself, use the **–d** (**directory**) option. This option lists information only about a directory and not about its contents.

```
$ ls -dl bin
drwxrwxr-x 2 jenny    pubs        80 May 20 09:17 bin
```

You can use the following command to display a list of all the invisible filenames (those starting with a period) in the working directory. This is a convenient way to list all the initialization files in your home directory.

```
$ ls -Ad .*
```

The final example lists three executable files. The file named **executable.1** has its setgid bit on (s in place of x in the group permissions), **executable.2** has its sticky bit on (t in place of x in the other permissions), and **executable.3** has its setuid bit on (s in place of x in the owner permissions). Refer to pages 90 and 593 for information on the setgid and setuid bits; see page 1046 for a definition of the sticky bit.

```
$ ls -l ex*
-rwxr-s---  1 root     pubs     23341 Aug 26 14:58 executable.1
-rwxr-xr-t  1 root     pubs     47371 Aug 26 14:58 executable.2
-rwsr-xr-x  1 root     pubs     23805 Aug 26 14:58 executable.3
```

mailx

Sends and receives electronic mail

Syntax:

mailx [–s subject] user-list
mailx –f [filename]

Summary

The **mailx** utility sends and receives electronic mail to/from a nongraphical environment (a terminal or terminal emulator).

When you use **mailx** to send someone a message, the system puts the message in that user's mailbox, which is typically a file with the name **/var/mail/name**, where **name** is the login name of the user you are sending the message to. When you use **mailx** to read messages that other people have sent you, **mailx** normally reads from your mailbox and then stores the messages after you read them in a file named **mbox** in your home directory.

The way **mailx** appears and functions depends to a large extent on the **mailx** *environment*. When you call **mailx**, it establishes an environment based on variables that are set in two files: The **/etc/mail/mailx.rc** file and the **.mailrc** file in your home directory. Superuser sets up the first file if needed (nice in a multiuser environment). You can change any aspect of your **mailx** environment that is established by **/etc/mail/mailx.rc** by setting variables in your **.mailrc** file. Or if you are satisfied with the environment set up by the **/etc/mail/mailx.rc** file, you do not need a **.mailrc** file at all.

Arguments

Without any arguments **mailx** displays any messages that are waiting for you. With one or more arguments, **mailx** sends messages. The *user-list* is a list of the users you are sending a message to.

Options

–f *[filename]*   Reads messages from *filename* instead of from your system mailbox. Without *filename*, **mailx** reads the **mbox** file in your home directory.

–s *subject*   Sets the subject field to *subject* when you are sending messages. If *subject* contains SPACEs, enclose it within quotation marks.

Sending Messages

To send a message give the command **mailx** followed by the login names of the people you want to send the message to. If you use the **–s** option to enter a subject in the command line, that line appears in the header when the recipients read the message. If you do not use the **–s** option, you are prompted for a subject line, provided that your environment is set up to do so. Entering a subject line in response to this prompt causes that line to appear in the header. At this point **mailx** is in Input Mode and you can enter the text of your message. When you are done enter CONTROL-D on a line by itself to terminate your message. Depending on your **mailx** environment, you may then be given a prompt to enter the names of users who are to receive copies of your message. The **mailx** utility then sends your message to the appropriate recipients.

Refer to page 70 for information on network addresses.

You can run **mailx** commands while **mailx** is in Input Mode. All Input Mode commands start with a tilde (~). They are called *tilde escapes* because they temporarily allow you to escape from Input Mode so that you can give a command. The tilde must appear as the first character on a line.

The following list describes some of the more important tilde escapes.

~! *command*	Gives a shell command while you are composing a message. Replace *command* with a shell command line.
~?	Displays a list of all tilde escapes.
~| *command*	Replaces the message you are composing with the result of piping the message through *command* (**fmt** for example).
~b *name-list*	**blind** Sends blind carbon copies (Bcc) to *name-list*. The people who receive blind carbon copies are not listed on the copy of the message that goes to the addressee; the people who receive regular carbon copies (Cc) are listed—see **~c** below.
~c *name-list*	**copy** Sends copies (Cc) to *name-list*.
~d	**dead letter** Retrieves the **dead.letter** file from your home directory so you can continue writing it or modify it. This file is created when you quit **mailx** while composing a message.
~h	**header** Prompts you for the Subject, To, Cc, and Bcc fields. Each prompt includes the current entries for that field; you can use the erase and line kill keys to back up and edit the entries or you can just add new ones.
~m [*msg-list*]	**message** Includes the messages specified by the *msg-list* in a message you are composing, placing a TAB at the beginning of each line. (Refer to "Reading Messages," which follows, for a description of *msg-list*.) You can use **~m** only when you are sending a message while reading your messages (see the **m** and **r** commands, also in "Reading Messages").
~p	**print** Displays the entire message you are currently composing.
~q	**quit** Quits, saving the message you are composing in the file **dead.letter** in your home directory. See **~d** to retrieve this file.
~r *filename*	**read** Reads *filename* into the message you are composing.
~s *subject*	**subject** Sets the subject field for the message you are composing to *subject*, replacing the current subject if there is one.
~t *name-list*	**to** Adds the users in the *name-list* to the list of people who receive the message.
~v	**vi** Calls the **vi** editor so that you can edit the message you are composing.

Reading Messages

When you have mail you want to read, call **mailx** without any arguments. The **mailx** utility displays a list of headers of messages waiting for you. Each line of the display has the following format:

[>] status message-# from-name date lines/characters [subject]

The **>** indicates that the message is the *current message*. The **status** is N if the message is new or U (for unread) if the message is not new (that is, you have seen its header before) but you have not read it yet. The status is O for old messages you have already read. The **message-#** is the sequential number of the message in your mailbox. The **from-name** is the name of the person who sent you the message. The **date** and **lines/characters** are the date the message was sent and its size. The **subject** is the optional subject field for the message.

After the list of headers, **mailx** displays its prompt, a question mark (**?**). The **mailx** utility is in Command Mode, waiting for you to give it a command. The easiest way to read your messages is to press RETURN. After each message, **mailx** prompts you. Pressing RETURN is a shorthand for displaying the next message. Keep pressing RETURN to read each message in turn. The characters **+** and **–** can also be used to move forward and backward among the messages. If you want to read a message out of sequence, you can enter a number followed by RETURN. Usually you give **mailx** commands to manipulate and respond to a message before reading another.

In the following summary of commands, *msg-list* is a message number or a range of message numbers (use a hyphen to indicate a range as in **a–b**). In *msg-list* an asterisk (✳) stands for all messages and a dollar sign ($) stands for the last message.

If you do not specify a *msg-list* where one is called for, **mailx** responds as though you had specified the current message (the one preceded by a **>** in the header list).

Most of the following commands can appear in your **.mailrc** file; however it usually makes sense to use only **alias** and **set** there.

!command	Allows you to run a shell command while you are reading messages. Replace *command* with a shell command line.
| command	Pipe the current message through *command*. This command works only when you are composing a message, not when you are reading one.
?	Displays a list of all **mailx** commands.
a [alias] [name-list]	**alias** You can declare *alias* (alias name) to represent all the login names in *name-list*. When you want to send a message to everyone in *name-list*, just send a message to *alias*. The **mailx** utility expands *alias* into the *name-list*. Without any arguments this command displays the currently defined aliases. With just an *alias* the command displays the corresponding alias.
d [msg-list]	**delete** Deletes the messages in the *msg-list* from your mailbox. Without *msg-list* it deletes the current message.
ex *or* **x**	**exit** Exits from **mailx** without changing your mailbox. If you deleted any messages during this session with **mailx**, they are not removed from your mailbox.
h	**header** Displays a list of headers. Refer to the **z** command that follows if you want to scroll the list of headers.
m *name*	**mailx** Sends a message to *name*. Using this command is similar to calling **mailx** with *name* from the command line.

p *[msg-list]* **print** Displays the messages in the *msg-list*.

pre *[msg-list]* **preserve** Preserves messages in the *msg-list* in your mailbox. Use this command after you have read a message but do not want to remove it from your system mailbox. Refer to the **q** command.

q **quit** Exits from **mailx**, saving in your **mbox** file messages that you read and did not delete and leaving messages that you have not read in your system mailbox. You can use the **pre** command to force **mailx** to leave a message in your system mailbox even though you have read it.

R *[message]* **reply** Replies to a *message*. This command copies the subject line of the *message* and addresses a reply message to the person who sent you the *message*. Everyone who got a copy of the original *message* also gets a copy of the new message. The **R** command puts **mailx** in Input Mode so you can compose a message.

r *[message]* **reply** Replies to a *message*. This command is like the **R** command, except that it sends a reply to only the person who sent you the message.

s *[msg-list] filename* **save** Saves the messages in *msg-list* in file *filename*. When you save a message in a file by using this command, **mailx** does *not* save the message in your **mbox** file when you exit from **mailx** with the **q** command. This command appends to *filename* if it already exists; otherwise it creates it.

set See the introduction to the following section, "The **mailx** Environment," for a description of this command. Although you can give the **set** command in response to a **mailx** prompt, it is typically used in a **.mailrc** file.

top *[msg-list]* Displays the top few lines of the specified messages.

u *[msg-list]* **undelete** Restores the specified messages. You can restore a deleted message only if you have not quit from **mailx** since you deleted the message.

unset Like the command **set**, this command modifies the **mailx** environment. It can be given in response to the **mailx** prompt to remove the value of an environment variable, but it is usually given in **.mailrc**. See the following section for a discussion.

v *[msg-list]* **vi** Edits the specified messages with **vi**.

z$\pm$ Scrolls the list of headers (see the **h** command) forward (**+**) or backward (**–**).

The mailx *Environment*

You can establish the **mailx** environment by assigning values to **mailx** variables using the **set** command in the **.mailrc** file in your home directory. The **set** command has the following format:

> *set [name[=value]]*

The *name* is the name of the **mailx** variable that you are setting, and the *value* is the optional value you are assigning to the variable. The *value* may be either a string or a number. If you use **set** without a *value*, **mailx** assigns the variable a null value (the values of some **mailx** variables are not relevant; it is only important that they are set).

The following is a list of some of the more important **mailx** variables:

askcc	If set, **mailx** prompts you for the names of people to receive copies of messages you send.
asksub	If set, **mailx** prompts you for the subject of each message.
crt=*number*	Assign *number* to this variable if you want messages containing *number* or more lines to be piped through the utility named by the **PAGER** variable (below). If you are using a standard ASCII terminal or emulator, set *number* to 24.
dot	If set, you can terminate **mailx** messages by entering a period (**.**) on a line by itself. Unless **ignoreeof** is also set (see below), entering CONTROL-D on a line by itself still serves to terminate **mailx** messages.
ignore	If set, **mailx** ignores interrupts while you are composing and sending messages. Setting **ignore** can make your job easier if you are working over a noisy telephone line.
ignoreeof	If set, CONTROL-D does not terminate **mailx** messages.
PAGER=*pathname*	If set, *pathname* is the location of the pager you want **mailx** to use for messages that do not fit on your screen. The default pager is usually **pg**.
record=*filename*	If set, **mailx** puts a copy of all your outgoing messages in *filename*.
VISUAL=*editor*	If set, *editor* is the location of the editor you want **mailx** to use when you give the **~v** command while composing a message. The default editor is **vi**.

Notes

By default the Bourne Shell checks every 60 seconds for new mail. If mail has arrived, it presents a message before the next prompt. You can change the frequency of the checks by setting the **MAILCHECK** variable in your shell environment (page 373). The shell does not check for new mail if **MAILCHECK** is not set.

Examples

The following example shows Alex using **mailx** to read his messages. After calling **mailx** and seeing that he has two messages, he gives the command **p 2** (just **2** is enough) followed by RETURN to display the second message. After displaying the message, **mailx** displays a prompt, and Alex deletes the message with a **d** command.

```
$ mailx
mailx version 5.0 Tue Jul 15 23:42:53 PDT 1997  Type ? for help.
"/var/mail/alex": 2 messages 2 new 2 unread
 N  1 hls                Wed Sep 11 00:15  14/327  your trip
>N  2 jenny              Tue Sep 10 06:32  22/614  our meeting
 (text of message 2)
 .
 .
 .
 & d
```

After reading his second message, Alex tries to read his first message by pressing **RETURN** (following). The **mailx** utility tells him he is at the end of his mailbox (At EOF), so he gives the command **p 1** (or just **1**) followed by **RETURN** to view his first piece of mail. After reading it, he chooses to save a copy in the file **hls_msgs**. Because the file already exists, the message is appended to it. Finally he decides he did not really want to delete his second message and that he wants to read both messages again later, so he exits from **mailx** with an **x** command, leaving both messages in his system mailbox.

```
& RETURN
At EOF
& p 1
(text of message 1)
 .
 .
 .
& s hls_msgs
"hls_msgs" [Appended] 14/327
& x
$
```

make

Syntax: *make [options] [target-files] [arguments]*

Summary

The **make** utility keeps a set of executable programs current, based on differences in the modification times of the programs and the source files that each is dependent on. The executable programs, or *target-files*, are dependent on one or more *prerequisite files*. The relationships between *target-files* and prerequisites are specified on *dependency lines* in a makefile. Construction commands follow the dependency line, specifying how **make** can update the *target-files*. Also refer to page 558 for more information on **make**.

Arguments

The *target-files* refer to targets on dependency lines in the makefile. If you do not specify a *target-file* on the command line, **make** updates the target on the first dependency line in the makefile. Arguments of the form **name=value** set the variable **name** to **value** inside the makefile. See "Discussion" for more information.

Options

If you do not use the **–f** option, **make** takes its input from a file named **makefile** or **Makefile** (**make** looks for a file in that order) in the working directory.[5] Many users prefer the name **Makefile** because it shows up at the top of directory listings. Most free UNIX software comes with a **Makefile**, whereas many programs that will compile on both DOS and UNIX come with **makefile** instead (for example **ghostscript**).

–d	**display dependencies** When rebuilding a target, displays all dependencies that are newer to show why **make** is rebuilding the target.
–D	**display text** Displays the **makefile** text as it is processed.
–dd	**detailed dependencies** Displays dependency checking in great detail.
–DD	**detailed text** Displays the **makefile** text, hidden dependency reports, state reports, and the **make.rules** file. This option generates a lot of output.
–e	**environment** Causes environment variables to override variables assigned in the makefile (for example **CC**).
–f *file*	**input file** Uses *file* as input in place of **makefile**.

---

5. The GNU **make** utility looks for a file named **GNUmakefile** before looking for these files.

–i   **ignore error codes**   Ignores error codes returned by commands. This option is equivalent to the special **.IGNORE:** target in a makefile.

–k   **keep going**   When a construction command fails, discontinues work on the current target, but continues with the next target from the list of *target-files* instead of quitting.

–K *statefile*   **keep state**   Uses *statefile* instead of **make**'s implicit set of internal rules. If you use more than one **–K** option, **make** catenates the *statefiles* together. Also see the **.KEEP_STATE:** and **.KEEP_STATE_FILE:** special targets.

–n   **no execution**   Displays, but does not execute, the commands **make** would use to bring the *target-files* up to date.

–p   **print dependencies**   Shows all macro definitions and target dependencies.

–P   **print dependencies**   Shows dependencies without building them.

–q   **query**   Returns a zero status code if *target-files* are up to date, nonzero otherwise.

–r   **rules**   Does not read in the default **/usr/share/lib/make/make.rules** file.

–s   **silent**   Works silently without displaying the names of the commands being executed.

–S   **stop processing**   The opposite of the **–k** option. Stops processing upon receipt of nonzero exist status from command.

–t   **touch**   Updates modification times of target files but does not execute any construction commands. Refer to **touch** on page 922.

–V   **sysV mode**   Puts **make** into sysV mode. See the **sysV-make man** page for details. Rarely used.

Notes

The **/usr/xpg4/bin/make** utility is a POSIX-compliant version of **make**.

Discussion

Although the most common use of **make** is to build programs from source code, its use is not restricted to this single activity; it is also a general-purpose build utility that is suitable for a wide range of uses including documentation control.

     Much of the power of **make** comes from the features that you can use inside a makefile. For example you can define and assign values to macros. For more information see "Macros" on page 562. Under Solaris2 the Bourne Shell executes all **make** commands by default; if you want **make** to use another shell, you must set the **SHELL** macro within the makefile. To define the **SHELL** macro and assign a value to it, place the following line near the top of your makefile:

```
SHELL=/bin/sh
```

Using this assignment makes your makefile more portable, allowing you to use it on other systems that may not default to the Bourne Shell. Some versions of **make** use the value of the **SHELL** environment variable if you do not set the **SHELL** macro inside the makefile.

The following table lists some of the macros that you can use in a makefile. These macros allow others to customize your makefile for their environment by changing an environment variable or editing the Makefile and changing a macro assignment.

Macro	Meaning
CC	C Compiler to use (defaults to **cc**, though **gcc** is also common).
CFLAGS	C Compiler flags to use when compiling and linking. Examples include **–O**, **–g**.
COMPILE.c	A useful macro equivalent to **$(CC) $(CFLAGS) $(CPPFLAGS) –c**.
CPPFLAGS	C Compiler flags to use only when compiling. Examples include **–DSYSV**, **–K PIC** (or **–fPIC**).
LDFLAGS	Flags to pass to the linker. Examples include **–lsocket**, **–lnsl**, **–lposix4**.
LINK.c	Equivalent to **$(CC) $(CFLAGS) $(CPPFLAGS) $(LDFLAGS)**.

Other features allow you to perform the following tasks:

- Run specific construction commands silently (by preceding them with the @ sign). For example the following lines will display a short help message when you run the command **make help**:

```
help:
    @echo "You may make the following:"
    @echo " "
    @echo "libbuf.a    -- the buffer library"
    @echo "Bufdisplay  -- display any-format buffer"
    @echo "Buf2ppm     -- convert buffer to pixmap"
```

This technique works because there is no file named **help** in the working directory, so **make** runs the construction commands in an attempt to build this file. Because the construction commands only display messages and do not, in fact, build the file **help**, you can run **make help** repeatedly with the same result.

- Ignore the exit status of specific commands by preceding them with a hyphen (–). For example the following line allows **make** to continue whether or not the call to **/bin/rm** is successful (the call to **/bin/rm** fails if **libbuf.a** does not exist):

```
-/bin/rm libbuf.a
```

- Use special variables to refer to information that might change from one use of **make** to the next. Such information might include the files that need updating, the files that are newer than the target, or the files that match a pattern. For example you can use the variable **$?** in a construction command to identify all prerequisite files that are newer than the target file. This special variable allows you to print files that have changed since the last time you printed files:

```
list:           .list
.list:          Makefile buf.h xtbuff_ad.h buff.c buf_print.c xtbuff.c
    pr $? | lp
    date >.list
```

In this example the target list depends on the source files that might be printed. The construction command **pr $? I lp** prints only those source files that are newer than the file **.list**. Finally the line **date > .list** modifies **.list** so that it is newer than any of the source files (so that the next time you run the command **make list**, only the files that have been changed again are printed).

- Include other makefiles as if they were part of the current makefile. The following line causes **make** to read **Make.config** and treat the contents of that file as though it were part of the current makefile. This allows you to put information common to more than one makefile in a single place.

```
include Make.config
```

Examples

The first example causes **make** to bring the *target-file* named **analysis** up to date by issuing the three **cc** commands shown below. It uses a file named **makefile** or **Makefile** in the working directory.

```
$ make analysis
cc -c analy.c
cc -c stats.c
cc -o analysis analy.o stats.o
```

The next example also updates **analysis**, but it uses a **makefile** named **analysis.mk** in the working directory.

```
$ make -f analysis.mk analysis
'analysis' is up to date.
```

The following example lists the commands **make** would execute to bring the *target-file* named **credit** up to date. Because of the **–n** option, **make** does not actually execute the commands.

```
$ make -n credit
cc -c -O credit.c
cc -c -O accounts.c
cc -c -O terms.c
cc -o credit credit.c accounts.c terms.c
```

The next example uses the **–t** option to update the modification time of the *target-file* named **credit**. After you use the **–t** option, **make** thinks that **credit** is up to date.

```
$ make -t credit
$ make credit
'credit' is up to date.
```

Following is a simple makefile for building a utility named **ff**. Because the **cc** command needed to build **ff** is complex, using a makefile allows you to rebuild **ff** easily without having to retype (let alone remember) the **cc** command.

```
$ cat Makefile
# Build the ff command from the fastfind.c source
SHELL=/bin/sh
CC=cc

ff:
  $(CC) -traditional -O3 -m486 -g -DBIG=5120 -o ff fastfind.c myClib.a
$ make ff
cc -traditional -O3 -m486 -g -DBIG=5120 -o ff fastfind.c myClib.a
```

The final example shows a much more sophisticated makefile. Some of the features used in this makefile are not discussed here. See the **make man** page for information about these and other advanced features.

```
$ cat Makefile
#####################################################################
## build and maintain the buffer library
#####################################################################
#
SHELL=/bin/sh

#####################################################################
## Flags and libraries for compiling. The XLDLIBS are needed
#  whenever you build a program using the library. The CFLAGS
#  give maximum optimization.
#
# For the Solaris C Compiler, change these two lines:
#  CC = cc
#  CFLAGS = -O
#
CC = gcc
CPPFLAGS= -I/usr/openwin/include -I.
CFLAGS = -O3
XLDLIBS = -L/usr/openwin/lib -R/usr/openwin/lib -lXaw -lXt -lXmu -lXext -lX11 -lm
BUFLIB = libbuf.a

#####################################################################
## Miscellaneous
INCLUDES=buf.h
XINCLUDES=xtbuff_ad.h
OBJS=buff.o buf_print.o xtbuff.o

#####################################################################
## Just a 'make' generates a help message
help Help:
@echo "You may make the following:"
@echo " "
@echo " libbuf.a -- the buffer library"
@echo " bufdisplay -- display any-format buffer"
@echo " buf2ppm -- convert buffer to pixmap"
```

```
########################################################################
## The main target is the library
libbuf.a: $(OBJS)
rm libbuf.a
$(AR) $(ARFLAGS) libbuf.a $(OBJS)

########################################################################
## Secondary targets -- utilities built from the library
bufdisplay: bufdisplay.c $(BUFLIB)
$(LINK.c) bufdisplay.c -o bufdisplay $(BUFLIB) $(XLDLIBS)

buf2ppm: buf2ppm.c $(BUFLIB)
$(LINK.c) buf2ppm.c -o buf2ppm $(BUFLIB)


########################################################################
## Build the individual object units
buff.o: $(INCLUDES) buff.c
$(COMPILE.c) buff.c

buf_print.o: $(INCLUDES) buf_print.c
$(COMPILE.c) buf_print.c

xtbuff.o: $(INCLUDES) $(XINCLUDES) xtbuff.c
$(COMPILE.c) xtbuff.c
```

man

Displays documentation for commands

Syntax: *man [options] command*

Summary

The **man** utility provides online documentation for the commands available on the Solaris system. In addition to user commands, documentation is available for many other commands and details that relate to use of Solaris.

A one-line header is associated with each manual page. This header consists of a command name, the section of the manual in which the command is found, and a brief description of what the command does. These headers are stored in a database so that you can perform quick searches on keywords associated with each **man** page.

Argument

The argument tells **man** to display the reference manual pages for the command named *command*.

Options

–a   **all**   Displays manual pages for all sections. Use this option when you are not sure which section contains the information you are looking for.

–k *keyword*   **keyword**   Searches for *keyword* in the database of manual page headers and displays the list of headers that contain matches. You can scan this list for commands of interest. The **apropos** command (page 54) is an alias for **man –k**. Refer to **catman** on page 700 for information about how to create the database of headers that **man** uses.

–M *path*   Looks in the directory given by *path* instead of looking in the default locations for manual pages. The *path* has the same syntax as the **PATH** shell variable.

–s *section*   Limits the search to *section*. You can specify multiple sections by separating the section numbers with commas. Refer to page 29 for a list of manual sections. Without this option **man** searches through all sections in numerical order, stopping when it finds a match.

Notes

The argument to **man** is not always a command name. For example the command **man ascii** lists all of the ASCII characters and their various representations, and **man shell_builtins** gives you a list of builtins and which shells use each.

Some utilities described in the manual pages have the same name as shell builtin commands. The behavior of the shell builtin may be slightly different than the behavior of the utility as described in the manual page. Look at the shell manual page for more informations about builtins (for example **man sh**).

Discussion

The manual pages are organized as a set of sections, each pertaining to a separate aspect of the UNIX system. Section 1 contains user-callable commands and is the section most likely to be accessed by users who are not system administrators or programmers. Other sections of the manual contain system calls, library functions, and commands used only by the system administrator. See page 29 for a complete listing of the manual sections.

The **more** utility displays manual pages that fill more than one screen. You can change to another pager by setting the environment variable **PAGER** to the name of the pager you want to use. If, for example, you are using the Bourne Shell, adding the following line to your **.profile** file allows you to use **pg** in place of **more**:

```
PAGER=/bin/pg
export PAGER
```

You can tell **man** where to look for **man** pages by setting the environment variable **MANPATH** to a colon-separated list of directories. If you are using the Bourne Shell, you can add the following lines to **.profile** in your home directory to cause **man** to search the several different directories that contain **man** files:

```
MANPATH=/usr/openwin/share/man:/usr/openwin/man:/usr/share/man:/usr/dt/share/man:/usr/dt/man:/usr/local/man
export MANPATH
```

Examples

The following example uses **man** to display the documentation for the command **write**, which sends messages to another user's screen.

```
$ man write

User Commands                                                    write(1)

NAME
     write - write to another user

SYNOPSIS
     write user [ terminal ]

DESCRIPTION
     The write utility reads lines from the user's standard input
     and writes them to the terminal of another user.  When first
     invoked, it writes the message:

          Message   from   sender-login-id   (sending-terminal)
          [date]...

     to user.  When it has successfully completed the connection,
     the sender's terminal will be alerted twice to indicate that
     what  the  sender  is  typing  is  being  written  to   the
     recipient's terminal.

--More--(10%)
```

The next example displays the **man** page for another command—the **man** command itself. This is a good starting place for someone learning about the system.

```
$ man man

User Commands                                                   man(1)

NAME
     man - find and display reference manual pages

SYNOPSIS
     man [ - ] [ -adFlrt ] [ -M path ] [ -T macro-package ]
         [-s section ] name ...
     man [ -M path ] -k keyword ...
     man [ -M path ] -f file ...

DESCRIPTION
     The man command  displays  information  from  the  reference
     manuals.   It displays complete manual pages that you select
     by name, or one-line summaries selected  either  by  keyword
     (-k),  or  by  the  name  of an associated file (-f).  If no
     manual page is located, man prints an error message.

  Source Format
     Reference Manual pages are marked up with nroff(1).

--More--(5%)
```

The next example shows how the **man** utility can be used to find the **man** pages that pertain to a certain topic. In this case all of the **man** page headers containing the string printer are displayed. Many of these **man** pages are from section 1.

```
$ man -k printer | tail
lpc             lpc (1b)        - line printer control program
lpset           lpset (1m)      - set printing configuration in /etc/printers.conf...
lptest          lptest (1b)     - generate line printer ripple pattern
mcpp            mcpp (7d)       - ALM-2 Parallel Printer port driver
nroff           nroff (1)       - format documents for display or line-printer
postio          postio (1)      - serial interface for PostScript printers
postmd          postmd (1)      - matrix display program for PostScript printers
printers        printers (4)    - user-configurable printer alias database
printers.conf   printers.conf (4)  - system printing configuration database
terminfo        terminfo (4)    - terminal and printer capability database
```

The search for the keyword entered with the **–k** option is not case sensitive. The **apropos** command is an alias for **man –k** (page 54).

mesg

Enables/disables reception of messages

Syntax: *mesg [options]*

Summary

The **mesg** utility enables or disables reception of messages sent by someone using the **write** or **talk** utility. When you call **mesg** without an argument, it tells you whether messages are enabled or disabled.

Options

–n	**no**	Disables reception of messages.
–y	**yes**	Enables reception of messages.

Notes

On most systems when you first log in, messages are enabled. Some utilities, such as **pr**, automatically disable messages while they are sending output to the screen.

Examples

The following example demonstrates how to disable messages:

```
$ mesg -n
```

The next example calls **mesg** without an option and verifies that you disabled messages:

```
$ mesg
is n
```

mkdir

Makes a directory

Syntax: *mkdir [option] directory-list*

Summary
The **mkdir** utility creates one or more directories.

Argument
The *directory-list* contains one or more pathnames of directories that **mkdir** creates.

Options

–m *mode*   **mode** Sets the file access permissions of the new directory to *mode*. You may use either the symbolic form or an octal number to represent the mode (page 709).

–p   **parent** Creates any parent directories that do not exist in the path to the directory you are creating.

Notes
You must have permission to write to and search (execute permission) the parent directory of the directory you are creating. The **mkdir** utility creates directories that contain the standard invisible entries **.** (representing the directory itself) and **..** (representing the parent directory). The permissions of the new directory are 777 (read, write, search for everyone) but may be altered by the file creation mask: **umask** (page 939).

Examples
The following command creates a directory named **accounts** as a subdirectory of the working directory and a directory named **prospective** as a subdirectory of **accounts**:

```
$ mkdir -p accounts/prospective
```

Below, without changing working directories, the same user creates another subdirectory within the **accounts** directory:

```
$ mkdir accounts/existing
```

Next the user changes the working directory to the **accounts** directory and creates one more subdirectory:

```
$ cd accounts
$ mkdir closed
```

The last example shows the user creating another subdirectory. This time the **–m** option removes all access permissions for group and others.

```
$ mkdir -m go= accounts/past_due
```

mkfile

Creates a file/swap area

Syntax: *mkfile [options] size file-list*

Summary

The **mkfile** utility creates local or NFS-mounted files that you can use as swap areas.

Arguments

The *size* is the size of the file you are creating and can be expressed as *n***k**, *n***b**, or *n***m**, where *n* is a number and **k**, **b**, and **m** stand for kilobytes (1,024 or 2^{10} bytes), blocks (512 or 2^9 bytes), and megabytes (1,048,576 or 2^{20} bytes), respectively. The *file-list* is a list of one or more names of files that you want to create. You must create these files on filesystems that have enough free space to hold them.

Options

–n   **no allocate**   Creates the file, but leaves it sparse (empty). Disk blocks are allocated as needed. You can use this option to create NFS-mounted swap areas for diskless clients. See AnswerBook2 for information on setting up diskless clients.

–v   **verbose**   Causes **mkfile** to display filenames and sizes as it creates files.

Discussion

You can use **mkfile** (together with **swap** [page 907]) to create a new swap area for your system. The **swap** utility specifies whether to use the swap file as a supplement to or replacement for an existing swap file. Do not create a swap file in **/tmp** as this is already a virtual memory filesystem. For more information see the Tip named "Keep Track of Swap Space Usage" on page 619.

Example

The following example creates a 60MB **swap** file named **swap1** on the **/export** filesystem (which must have enough space to hold it):

```
# mkfile 60m /export/swap1
```

more

Displays a file, one screenful at a time

Syntax:

more [options] [file-list]
page [options] [file-list]

Summary

The **more** utility displays a text file on a screen or in a window. It is similar to **cat** but pauses each time it fills the screen. In response to the **more** prompt, you can press the **SPACE** bar to view another screenful, or use any of the other **more** commands to skip forward or backward in the file, display the current line number, invoke the **vi** editor, or display a list of the available commands. The **more** commands are described below. The **page** utility (another way of calling **more**) clears the screen before another screenful is displayed so that the text does not appear to scroll.

The number followed by a percent sign that **more** displays as part of its prompt represents the portion of the file that has already been displayed. If **more** receives input from standard input, this number may not be accurate (nor reasonable).

This utility takes its input from files you specify on the command line or from standard input.

Argument

The *file-list* is the list of files that you want to view. If you do not specify any files, **more** reads from standard input.

Options

–d
display   Displays an explanatory message after each screenful (Press space to continue, 'q' to quit.) and after the user enters an illegal command (Press 'h' for instructions). This option makes **more** easier for beginners to use.

–n
number of lines   Specifies the number of lines **more** displays in a screenful. Replace *n* with the number of lines your screen or window displays. If you do not use this option, **more** uses the **TERM** variable and the information in the Terminfo database to determine the size of the screen.

+n
Displays the file starting at line number *n*.

+/pattern
Displays the file starting two lines above the line containing *pattern*. Do not put a slash after *pattern*.

–s
squeeze   Presents multiple, adjacent blank lines as a single blank line. When you use **more** to display paginated text, such as **nroff** output, this option cuts out blank page headers and footers.

Notes

The **/usr/xpg4/bin/more** utility is a POSIX-compliant version of **more**.

The **pg** utility described on page 857 performs the same function as **more**.

You can set the options to **more** either from the command line when you call **more** or by setting a variable named **MORE**. For example to use **more** with the **–d** option, you can use the following commands from the Bourne Shell.

```
$ MORE=-d; export MORE
```

Bourne and Korn Shell users typically set **MORE** from their **.profile** file, and C Shell users set it from their **.cshrc** file. Once you have set the **MORE** variable, **more** is invoked with the specified option each time you call it. The **MORE** variable applies whether you invoke **more** from the command line, or whether another utility (such as **man** or **mailx**) calls it.

Commands

Whenever **more** pauses, you can use one of the following commands. The *n* is an optional numeric argument that defaults to 1. You do not need to follow these commands with RETURN.

Command	Effect
*n*SPACE	Displays *n*[a] more lines; without *n*, it displays the next screenful.
*n*RETURN	Displays *n*[a] more lines.
*n*d	Displays half a screenful or *n*[a] more lines.
*n*f	Skips *n*[a] screenfuls and displays a screenful.
*n*b	Skips back *n*[a] screenfuls and displays a screenful.
q or :q	Exits from **more**.
=	Displays the current line number.
v	Starts the **vi** editor on the current file, at the current line.
h	Displays a list of all the **more** commands.
n/*rexp*	Searches for the *n*th occurrence of the regular expression *rexp*.[a]
*n*n	Searches for the *n*th occurrence of the last regular expression entered.[a]
!*command*	Invokes a shell and runs *command*.
n:n	Skips to the *n*th next file listed on the command line.[a]
n:p	Skips to the *n*th previous file listed on the command line.[a]
:f	Displays the current filename and line number.
.	Repeats the previous command.

a. *n* is optional and defaults to 1 if not specified.

Examples

The following command line displays the file **letter**. To view more of **letter**, the user presses the SPACE bar in response to the **more** prompt.

```
$ more letter
.
.
--More--(71%) SPACE bar
.
.
$
```

Instead of pressing SPACE, the user could have pressed **h** to display a list of the **more** commands, pressed **v** to cause **more** to invoke the **vi** editor on the current line, or given any one of the other **more** commands.

In the next example **more** starts displaying **letter** two lines above the line containing the word receive.

```
$ more +/receive letter
  ...skipping
When we last spoke (January 14, 1994), I agreed that
we would ship your order within one week of
the date we receive it into our warehouse.
.
.
--More--(92%)q
.
.
```

mv   Moves (renames) a file

Syntax: *mv [options] existing-file new-filename*
mv [options] existing-file-list new-directory

Summary

The **mv** utility moves and/or renames one or more files. It has two forms. The first moves/renames a single file with a new filename that you supply. The second moves one or more files so that they appear in an existing, specified directory.

The **mv** utility physically moves the file if it is not possible to rename it (that is, if you move it from one filesystem to another).

Arguments

In the first form the ***existing-file*** is a pathname that specifies the ordinary file that you want to rename. The ***new-filename*** is the new pathname of the file. The ***new-filename*** can appear in the same or a different directory as the ***existing-file*** with a new simple filename, or it can appear in a different directory with the same simple filename (but a different absolute pathname).

In the second form the ***existing-file-list*** contains the pathnames of the files that you want to move, and the ***new-directory*** specifies the new parent directory for the files. The files you rename will have the same simple filenames as the files in the ***existing-file-list*** but new absolute pathnames.

Options

–f   **force**   Causes **mv** *not* to prompt you if a move would overwrite an existing file that you do not have write permission for. You must have write permission for the directory holding the target file.

–i   **interactive**   Prompts you for confirmation if a move/rename would overwrite an existing file. If your response begins with a **y** or **Y**, then the move/rename proceeds; otherwise the file is not moved/renamed.

Notes

The **/usr/xpg4/bin/mv** utility is a POSIX-compliant version of **mv**.

Solaris implements **mv** as **ln** and **rm**. When you execute the **mv** utility, it first makes a link (**ln**) to the ***new-file*** and then deletes (**rm**) the ***existing-file***. If the ***new-file*** already exists, **mv** deletes it before creating the link.

As with **rm**, you must have write and execute access permission to the parent directory of the ***existing-file***, but you do not need read or write access permission to the file itself. If the move would overwrite an existing file that you do not have write permission for, **mv** displays the access permission and waits for a response. If you enter **y** or **yes**, **mv** renames the file; otherwise it does not. If you use the **–f** option, **mv** does not prompt you for a response—it goes ahead and overwrites the file.

If the *existing-file* and the *new-file* or *directory* are on different filesystems, Solaris implements **mv** as **cp** and **rm**. In this case **mv** actually moves the file instead of just renaming it.

After you move a file, you become the owner of the file. The **mv** utility will not move a file onto itself.

Examples

The first command line renames **letter**, a file in the working directory, as **letter.1201**:

```
$ mv letter letter.1201
```

The next command line renames the file so that it appears, with the same simple filename, in the **/usr/archives** directory:

```
$ mv letter.1201 /usr/archives
```

The following command line renames all the files in the working directory whose names begin with **memo** so they appear in the **/usr/backup** directory:

```
$ mv memo* /usr/backup
```

nawk

Searches for and processes patterns in a file

Syntax: *nawk [options] [program] [file-list]*

Summary

The **nawk** (new **awk**) utility is a pattern-scanning and processing language. It searches one or more files to see if they contain records (usually lines) that match specified patterns and then performs actions, such as writing the record to standard output or incrementing a counter, each time it finds a match.

You can use **nawk** to generate reports or filter text. It works equally well with numbers and text; when you mix the two, **nawk** almost always comes up with the right answer.

The authors of the original **awk** (Alfred V. Aho, Peter J. Weinberger, and Brian W. Kernighan) program designed it to be easy to use, and to this end they sacrificed execution speed.

The **nawk** utility takes many of its constructs from the C programming language. It includes the following features:

- flexible format
- conditional execution
- looping statements
- numeric variables
- string variables
- regular expressions
- relational expressions
- C's **printf**

The **nawk** utility takes its input from files you specify on the command line or from standard input.

Arguments

The ***program*** is a **nawk** program that can be literally included on the command line or with the **–f** option in a file. Putting the program on the command line allows you to write simple, short **nawk** programs without having to create a separate program file. To prevent the shell from interpreting the **nawk** commands as shell commands, it is a good idea to enclose the ***program*** within single quotation marks. Putting the program in a file reduces typing when you are going to give the same **nawk** command over and over again. It also is helpful when the program is long or complex. See the **–f** option below and "Discussion" on the next page.

The ***file-list*** contains pathnames of the ordinary files that you want **nawk** to process; these are the input files.

Options

–F *c*   Uses *c*, an extended regular expression that can be a single character (page 959), as the input field separator (**FS** [page 822 has more about **nawk** variables]).

–f *program-file*   Reads its program from *program-file*. You can use this option multiple times on the command line.

–v *var=value*   Assigns *value* to the variable *var*. This assignment takes place in the order that **nawk** comes to it on the command line or in the program file and can be included between filenames for greater flexibility. It is not available within a **BEGIN** pattern (see the next section).

Notes

The **/usr/xpg4/bin/awk** utility is a POSIX-compliant version of **nawk**.

See page 842 for examples of **nawk** error messages.

Discussion

A **nawk** program consists of one or more program lines containing a *pattern* and/or *action* in the following format:

> *pattern { action }*

The *pattern* selects records (usually lines) from the input file. The **nawk** utility performs the *action* on all records that the *pattern* selects. You must enclose the *action* within braces so that **nawk** can differentiate it from the *pattern*. If a program line does not contain a *pattern*, **nawk** selects all records in the input file. If a program line does not contain an *action*, **nawk** copies the selected records to standard output.

To start **nawk** compares the first record in the input file (from the *file-list*) with each *pattern* in the *program-file* or *program*. If a *pattern* selects the record (if there is a match), **nawk** takes the *action* associated with the *pattern*. If the record is not selected, **nawk** takes no *action*. When **nawk** has completed its comparisons for the first record of the input file, it repeats the process for the next record of input. It continues this process, comparing subsequent records in the input file, until it has read the entire *file-list*.

If several *patterns* select the same record, **nawk** takes the *actions* associated with each of the *patterns* in the order in which they appear. It is possible for **nawk** to send a single record from the input file to standard output more than once.

Patterns

You can use a regular expression (Appendix A), enclosed within slashes, as a *pattern*. The ~ operator tests to see if a field or variable matches a regular expression. The !~ operator tests for no match.

You can perform both numeric and string comparisons using the following relational operators:

Operator	Meaning
<	Less than
<=	Less than or equal to
==	Equal to
!=	Not equal to
>=	Greater than or equal to
>	Greater than

You can combine any of the *patterns* described above using the Boolean operators || (OR) or **&&** (AND).

The comma is the range operator. If you separate two *patterns* with a comma on a single **nawk** program line, **nawk** selects the range of records beginning with the first record that contains the first *pattern*. The last record **nawk** selects is the next subsequent record that contains the second *pattern*. After **nawk** finds the second *pattern*, it starts the process over by looking for the first *pattern* again.

Two unique *patterns*, **BEGIN** and **END**, do not actually match lines of input. The **nawk** utility executes the *actions* associated with the **BEGIN** *pattern* before, and with the **END** *pattern* after, it processes all the files in the *file-list*.

Actions

The *action* portion of a **nawk** command causes **nawk** to take an *action* once it matches a *pattern*. If you do not specify an *action*, **nawk** performs the default *action*, which is the Print command (explicitly represented as {print}). This *action* copies the record from the input file to standard output.

You can follow a Print command with arguments, causing **nawk** to print just the arguments you specify. The arguments can be variables or string constants. Using **nawk**, you can send the output from a Print command to a file (>), append it to a file (>>), or pipe it to the input of another program (|).

Unless you separate items in a Print command with commas, **nawk** catenates them. Commas cause **nawk** to separate the items with the output field separator (normally a SPACE—see "Variables," following).

You can include several *actions* on one line within a set of braces by separating them with semicolons.

Comments

The **nawk** utility disregards anything on a program line following a pound sign (#). You can document a **nawk** program by preceding comments with this symbol.

Variables

Variables in **nawk** are not declared prior to their use. You can optionally give a variable an initial value. Numeric variables that you do not initialize are automatically initialized to 0, string variables to the null string. In addition to user variables, **nawk** maintains program variables for your use. You can use both user and program variables in the *pattern* and in the *action* portion of a **nawk** program. The following is a list of some of the **nawk** program variables:

Variable	Represents
$0	The current record (as a single variable).
$1–$n	Fields in the current record.
ARGC	The number of command line arguments, excluding options and the program name.
ARGV	An array of the command line arguments, excluding options and the program name. The first element of the array is numbered zero.
FILENAME	Name of the current input file.
FNR	Ordinal record number of the current record within the current file.

Variable	Represents
FS	Input field separator (default: SPACE or TAB).
NF	Number of fields in the current record.
NR	Ordinal record number of the current record within all files.
OFS	Output field separator (default: SPACE).
ORS	Output record separator (default: NEWLINE).
RS	Input record separator (default: NEWLINE).

In addition to initializing variables within your **nawk** program, you can use the **–v** option to initialize variables on the command line. Initializing variables in this manner can be useful if the value of a variable changes from one run of **nawk** to the next.

The input and output record separators are, by default, NEWLINE characters. Thus **nawk** takes each line in the input file to be a separate record and appends a NEWLINE to the end of each record that it outputs. The input field separators are, by default, SPACEs and TABs. The output field separator is a SPACE. You can change the value of any of the separators at any time by assigning a new value to its associated variable. This assignment can be done either within a **nawk** program or on the command line using the **–v** option.

Functions

A list of some of the functions that **nawk** provides for manipulating numbers and strings follows:

Name	Function
close(*expression*)	Closes the file whose name matches *expression*.
cos(*x*)	Returns cosine of *x*, where *x* is in radians.
exp(*x*)	Returns the exponential function of *x*.
getline	Reads the next input record (as though **nawk** had reached the bottom of the program) and sets **$0** and **NF**, **NR**, and **FNR**.
getline *var*	Reads the next input record (as though **nawk** had reached the bottom of the program), sets *var* to the value of the input record, and sets **NR** and **FNR**.
getline [*var*] < *expression*	Opens and reads a record from the file whose name matches *expression*. As long as the file remains opened, subsequent calls with an *expression* that matches the same file get additional records.
gsub(*search,replacement*[,*str*])	Replaces all occurrences of the extended regular expression *search* (can be a string) in *str* with the string *replacement* and returns the number of replacements. Works on **$0** if *str* is not specified.
index(*str1,str2*)	Returns the (one-based) index of *str2* in *str1* or 0 if *str2* is not present.
int(*num*)	Returns the integer portion of *num*.

Name	Function
length(*str*)	Returns the number of characters in *str;* if you do not supply an argument, it returns the number of characters in the current input record.
log(*x*)	Returns the natural logarithm of *x*.
match(*str, search*)	Returns the (one-based) index of *search* (an extended regular expression) in *str* or **0** if *str* is not present.
sin(*x*)	Returns sine of *x*, where *x* is in radians.
split(*str,arr,del*)	Places elements of *str*, delimited by *del*, in the array *arr[1]...arr[n];* returns the number of elements in the array.
sprintf(*fmt,args*)	Formats *args* according to *fmt* and returns the formatted string; mimics the C programming language function of the same name.
sqrt(*x*)	Returns the square root of *x*.
sub(*search,replacement[,str]*)	Replaces the first occurrence of the extended regular expression *search* (can be a string) in *str* with the string *replacement*. Works on **$0** if *str* is not specified.
substr(*str,pos,len*)	Returns a substring of *str* that begins at *pos* and is *len* characters long.
system(expression)	Issues the shell command given by *expression* and returns the exit status for the command. See the **man** page for the **system(3S)** function.
tolower(*str*)	Converts string *str* to lowercase.
toupper(*str*)	Converts string *str* to uppercase.

Operators

The following **nawk** arithmetic operators are from the C programming language:

Operator	Function
*	Multiplies the expression preceding the operator by the expression following it.
/	Divides the expression preceding the operator by the expression following it.
%	Takes the remainder after dividing the expression preceding the operator by the expression following it.
+	Adds the expression preceding the operator to the expression following it.
−	Subtracts the expression following the operator from the expression preceding it.
=	Assigns the value of the expression following the operator to the variable preceding it.
++	Increments the variable preceding the operator.
−−	Decrements the variable preceding the operator.
+=	Adds the expression following the operator to the variable preceding it and assigns the result to the variable preceding the operator.

Operator	Function
-=	Subtracts the expression following the operator from the variable preceding it and assigns the result to the variable preceding the operator.
*=	Multiplies the variable preceding the operator by the expression following it and assigns the result to the variable preceding the operator.
/=	Divides the variable preceding the operator by the expression following it and assigns the result to the variable preceding the operator.
%=	Takes the remainder, after dividing the variable preceding the operator by the expression following it, and assigns it to the variable preceding the operator.

Associative Arrays

An associative array is one of **nawk**'s most powerful features. An associative array uses strings as its indexes. Using an associative array, you can mimic a traditional array by using numeric strings as indexes.

You assign a value to an element of an associative array just as you would assign a value to any other **nawk** variable. The syntax is

array[string] = value

The *array* is the name of the array, *string* is the index of the element of the array you are assigning a value to, and *value* is the value you are assigning to the element of the array.

There is a special **for** structure you can use with a **nawk** array. The syntax is

for (elem in array) action

The *elem* is a variable that takes on the values of each of the elements in the array as the **for** structure loops through them, *array* is the name of the array, and *action* is the action that **nawk** takes for each element in the array. You can use the *elem* variable in this *action*.

The "Examples" section contains programs that use associative arrays (pages 835 and 838).

printf

You can use the **printf** command in place of Print to control the format of the output that **nawk** generates. The **nawk** version of **printf** is similar to that of the C language. A **printf** command takes the following syntax:

printf "control-string", arg1, arg2, ..., argn

The *control-string* determines how **printf** formats *arg1–n*. The *arg1–n* can be variables or other expressions. Within the *control-string* you can use \n to indicate a NEWLINE and \t to indicate a TAB.

The *control-string* contains conversion specifications, one for each argument (*arg1–n*). A conversion specification has the following syntax:

%[–][x[.y]]conv

The – causes **printf** to left justify the argument. The *x* is the minimum field width, and the *.y* is the number of places to the right of a decimal point in a number. The *conv* is a letter from the following list:

Refer to the following "Examples" section for examples of how to use **printf** (page 832 and following).

conv	Conversion
d	Decimal
e	Exponential notation
f	Floating-point number
g	Use **f** or **e**, whichever is shorter
o	Unsigned octal
s	String of characters
x	Unsigned hexadecimal

Examples

A simple **nawk** program is

```
{ print }
```

This program consists of one program line that is an *action*. It uses no *pattern*. Because the *pattern* is missing, **nawk** selects all records in the input file. Without any arguments the **print** command prints each selected record in its entirety. This program copies the input file to standard output.

The following program has a *pattern* part without an explicit *action*.

```
/jenny/
```

In this case **nawk** selects all records from the input file that contain the string jenny. When you do not specify an *action*, **nawk** assumes the *action* to be Print. This program copies all the records in the input file that contain jenny to standard output.

The following examples work with the **cars** data file. From left to right, the columns in the file contain each car's make, model, year of manufacture, mileage in thousands, and price. All whitespace in this file is composed of single **TABs** (there are no **SPACEs** in the file).

```
$ cat cars
plym    fury     97    73     2500
chevy   nova     99    60     3000
ford    mustang  75    45     10000
volvo   gl       88    102    9850
ford    ltd      93    15     10500
chevy   nova     90    50     3500
fiat    600      75    115    450
honda   accord   91    30     6000
ford    thundbd  94    10     17000
toyota  tercel   92    180    750
chevy   impala   75    85     1550
ford    bronco   93    25     9500
```

The first example below selects all records that contain the string chevy. The slashes indicate that chevy is a regular expression. This example has no *action* part.

Although neither **nawk** nor shell syntax requires single quotation marks on the command line, it is a good idea to use them because they can prevent problems. If the **nawk** program you create on the command line includes SPACEs or any special characters that the shell interprets, you must quote them. Always enclosing the program in single quotation marks is the easiest way of making sure you have quoted any characters that need to be quoted.

```
$ nawk '/chevy/' cars
chevy    nova     99      60       3000
chevy    nova     90      50       3500
chevy    impala   75      85       1550
```

The next example selects all records from the file (it has no *pattern* part). The braces enclose the *action* part—you must always use braces to delimit the *action* part so that **nawk** can distinguish it from the *pattern* part. This example prints the third field (**$3**), a SPACE (the output field separator, indicated by the comma), and the first field (**$1**) of each selected record.

```
$ nawk '{print $3, $1}' cars
97 plym
99 chevy
75 ford
88 volvo
93 ford
90 chevy
75 fiat
91 honda
94 ford
92 toyota
75 chevy
93 ford
```

The next example includes both a *pattern* and an *action* part. It selects all records that contain the string chevy and prints the third and first fields from the records it selects.

```
$ nawk '/chevy/ {print $3, $1}' cars
99 chevy
90 chevy
75 chevy
```

The next example selects records that contain a match for the regular expression h. Because there is no explicit action, it prints all the records it selects.

```
$ nawk '/h/' cars
chevy    nova     99      60       3000
chevy    nova     90      50       3500
honda    accord   91      30       6000
ford     thundbd  94      10       17000
chevy    impala   75      85       1550
```

The next *pattern* uses the matches operator (~) to select all records that contain the letter h in the first field:

```
$ nawk '$1 ~ /h/' cars
chevy    nova     99      60       3000
chevy    nova     90      50       3500
honda    accord   91      30       6000
chevy    impala   75      85       1550
```

The caret (^) in a regular expression forces a match at the beginning of the record or, in this case, the beginning of the first field:

```
$ nawk '$1 ~ /^h/' cars
honda    accord  91      30      6000
```

A pair of brackets surrounds a character-class definition (page 954). Next **nawk** selects all records that have a second field that begins with t or m. Then it prints the third and second fields, a dollar sign, and the fifth field. You must quote the dollar sign to keep **nawk** from interpreting it as a special character. It is a literal character that you want sent to the output.

```
$ nawk '$2 ~ /^[tm]/ {print $3, $2, "$"  $5}' cars
75 mustang $10000
94 thundbd $17000
92 tercel $750
```

The next example shows three roles that a dollar sign can play in a **nawk** program. A dollar sign followed by a number forms the name of a field. Within a regular expression a dollar sign forces a match at the end of a record or field (5$). Within a string you can use a dollar sign as itself (but you must quote it).

```
$ nawk '$3 ~ /5$/ {print $3, $1, "$"  $5}' cars
75 ford $10000
75 fiat $450
75 chevy $1550
```

Below, the equal to relational operator (==) causes **nawk** to perform a numeric comparison between the third field in each record and the number 75. The **nawk** command takes the default *action*, Print, on each record that matches.

```
$ nawk '$3 == 75' cars
ford     mustang 75      45      10000
fiat     600     75      115     450
chevy    impala  75      85      1550
```

The next example finds all cars priced at or under $3,000:

```
$ nawk '$5 <= 3000' cars
plym     fury    97      73      2500
chevy    nova    99      60      3000
fiat     600     75      115     450
toyota   tercel  92      180     750
chevy    impala  75      85      1550
```

Next the **–v** option assigns values to the **make** and **model** variables on the command line. The **awk** program then finds all cars that are of the specified make (ford) and are not of the specified model (thundbd):

```
$ nawk -v make=ford -v model=thundbd '$1 == make && $2 != model {print $0}' cars
ford     mustang 75      45      10000
ford     ltd     93      15      10500
ford     bronco  93      25      9500
```

When you use double quotation marks, **nawk** performs textual comparisons, using the ASCII collating sequence as the basis of the comparison. Below, **nawk** shows that the *strings* 450 and 750 fall in the range that lies between the *strings* 2000 and 9000.

```
$ nawk '$5 >= "2000" && $5 < "9000"' cars
plym     fury      97       73       2500
chevy    nova      99       60       3000
chevy    nova      90       50       3500
fiat     600       75       115      450
honda    accord    91       30       6000
toyota   tercel    92       180      750
```

When you need a numeric comparison, do not use quotation marks. The next example gives the correct results. It is the same as the previous example but omits the double quotation marks.

```
$ nawk '$5 >= 2000 && $5 < 9000' cars
plym     fury      97       73       2500
chevy    nova      99       60       3000
chevy    nova      90       50       3500
honda    accord    91       30       6000
```

Next the range operator (**,**) selects a group of records. The first record it selects is the one specified by the *pattern* before the comma. The last record is the one selected by the *pattern* after the comma. If there is no record that matches the *pattern* after the comma, **nawk** selects every record up to the end of the file. The next example selects all records starting with the record that contains volvo and concluding with the record that contains fiat:

```
$ nawk '/volvo/ , /fiat/' cars
volvo    gl        88       102      9850
ford     ltd       93       15       10500
chevy    nova      90       50       3500
fiat     600       75       115      450
```

After the range operator finds its first group of records, it starts the process over, looking for a record that matches the *pattern* before the comma. In the following example **nawk** finds three groups of records that fall between chevy and ford. Although the fifth record in the file contains ford, **nawk** does not select it because, at the time it is processing the fifth record, it is searching for chevy.

```
$ nawk '/chevy/ , /ford/' cars
chevy    nova      99       60       3000
ford     mustang   75       45       10000
chevy    nova      90       50       3500
fiat     600       75       115      450
honda    accord    91       30       6000
ford     thundbd   94       10       17000
chevy    impala    75       85       1550
ford     bronco    93       25       9500
```

When you are writing a longer **nawk** program, it is convenient to put the program in a file and reference the file on the command line. Use the **–f** option, followed by the name of the file containing the **nawk** program.

The following **nawk** program named **pr_header** has two *actions* and uses the **BEGIN** *pattern*. The **nawk** utility performs the *action* associated with **BEGIN** before it processes any of the records of the data file: It prints a header. The second *action*, **{print}**, has no *pattern* part and prints all the records in the file.

```
$ cat pr_header
BEGIN   {print "Make    Model   Year    Miles   Price"}
        {print}

$ nawk -f pr_header cars
Make    Model   Year    Miles   Price
plym    fury    97      73      2500
chevy   nova    99      60      3000
ford    mustang 75      45      10000
volvo   gl      88      102     9850
ford    ltd     93      15      10500
chevy   nova    90      50      3500
fiat    600     75      115     450
honda   accord  91      30      6000
ford    thundbd 94      10      17000
toyota  tercel  92      180     750
chevy   impala  75      85      1550
ford    bronco  93      25      9500
```

In the previous and following examples, the whitespace in the headers is composed of single TABs, so that the titles line up with the columns of data.

```
$ cat pr_header2
BEGIN {
print "Make    Model   Year    Miles   Price"
print "--------------------------------------"
}
        {print}

$ nawk -f pr_header2 cars
Make    Model   Year    Miles   Price
--------------------------------------
plym    fury    97      73      2500
chevy   nova    99      60      3000
ford    mustang 75      45      10000
volvo   gl      88      102     9850
ford    ltd     93      15      10500
chevy   nova    90      50      3500
fiat    600     75      115     450
honda   accord  91      30      6000
ford    thundbd 94      10      17000
toyota  tercel  92      180     750
chevy   impala  75      85      1550
ford    bronco  93      25      9500
```

When you call the **length** function without an argument, it returns the number of characters in the current record, including field separators. The **$0** variable always contains the value of the current record. In the next example **nawk** prepends the length to each record, and then a pipe sends the output from **nawk** to **sort**, so that the records of the **cars** file appear in order of length. The formatting of this report depends on TABs for horizontal alignment. The three extra characters at the beginning of each record throw off the format of several records, including the last. A remedy for this situation is covered shortly.

```
$ nawk '{print length, $0}' cars | sort
19 fiat 600      75      115      450
20 ford ltd      93      15       10500
20 plym fury     97      73       2500
20 volvo         gl      88       102      9850
21 chevy         nova    90       50       3500
21 chevy         nova    99       60       3000
22 ford bronco   93      25       9500
23 chevy         impala  75       85       1550
23 honda         accord  91       30       6000
24 ford mustang  75      45       10000
24 ford thundbd  94      10       17000
24 toyota        tercel  92       180      750
```

The **NR** variable contains the record number of the current record. The following **pattern** selects all records that contain more than 23 characters. The **action** prints the record number of all the selected records.

```
$ nawk 'length > 23 {print NR}' cars
3
9
10
```

You can combine the range operator (**,**) and the **NR** variable to display a group of records of a file based on their record numbers. The next example displays records 2 through 4.

```
$ nawk 'NR == 2 , NR == 4' cars
chevy    nova     99      60      3000
ford     mustang  75      45      10000
volvo    gl       88      102     9850
```

The **END** *pattern* works in a manner similar to the **BEGIN** *pattern*, except that **nawk** takes the *actions* associated with it after it has processed the last of its input records. The following report displays information only after it has processed the entire data file. The **NR** variable retains its value after **nawk** has finished processing the data file, so that an *action* associated with an **END** *pattern* can use it.

```
$ nawk 'END {print NR, "cars for sale." }' cars
12 cars for sale.
```

The next example uses **if** commands to change the values of some of the first fields. As long as **nawk** does not make any changes to a record, it leaves the entire record, including separators, intact. Once it makes a change to a record, it changes all separators in that record to the value of the output field separator. The default output field separator is a **SPACE**.

```
$ cat separ_demo
        {
        if ($1 ~ /ply/)  $1 = "plymouth"
        if ($1 ~ /chev/) $1 = "chevrolet"
        print
        }
```

```
$ nawk -f separ_demo cars
plymouth fury 97 73 2500
chevrolet nova 99 60 3000
ford      mustang 75       45       10000
volvo     gl        88      102      9850
ford      ltd       93       15      10500
chevrolet nova 90 50 3500
fiat      600       75      115       450
honda     accord 91         30      6000
ford      thundbd 94        10      17000
toyota    tercel  92        180      750
chevrolet impala 75 85 1550
ford      bronco  93        25      9500
```

You can change the default value of the output field separator by assigning a value to the **OFS** variable. The example below assigns a **TAB** character to **OFS** using a common escape sequence notation. This fix improves the appearance of the report but does not properly line up the columns.

```
$ cat ofs_demo
BEGIN {OFS = "\t"}
        {
        if ($1 ~ /ply/)  $1 = "plymouth"
        if ($1 ~ /chev/) $1 = "chevrolet"
        print
        }
```

```
$ nawk -f ofs_demo cars
plymouth              fury    97       73       2500
chevrolet             nova    99       60       3000
ford      mustang 75          45       10000
volvo     gl        88        102      9850
ford      ltd       93        15       10500
chevrolet             nova    90       50       3500
fiat      600       75        115      450
honda     accord 91           30       6000
ford      thundbd 94          10       17000
toyota    tercel  92          180      750
chevrolet             impala  75       85       1550
ford      bronco  93          25       9500
```

You can use **printf** (page 825) to refine the output format. The following example uses a backslash at the end of a program line to mask the following **NEWLINE** from **nawk**. You can use this technique to continue a long line over one or more records without affecting the outcome of the program.

```
$ cat printf_demo
BEGIN {
   print "                                        Miles"
   print "Make        Model        Year    (000)        Price"
   print \
    "------------------------------------------------------"
   }
   {
```

```
    if ($1 ~ /ply/)  $1 = "plymouth"
    if ($1 ~ /chev/) $1 = "chevrolet"
    printf "%-10s %-8s    19%2d    %5d     $ %8.2f\n",\
        $1, $2, $3, $4, $5
    }
```

```
$ nawk -f printf_demo cars
                              Miles
Make        Model     Year    (000)        Price
-------------------------------------------------
plymouth    fury      1997      73    $  2500.00
chevrolet   nova      1999      60    $  3000.00
ford        mustang   1975      45    $ 10000.00
volvo       gl        1988     102    $  9850.00
ford        ltd       1993      15    $ 10500.00
chevrolet   nova      1990      50    $  3500.00
fiat        600       1975     115    $   450.00
honda       accord    1991      30    $  6000.00
ford        thundbd   1994      10    $ 17000.00
toyota      tercel    1992     180    $   750.00
chevrolet   impala    1975      85    $  1550.00
ford        bronco    1993      25    $  9500.00
```

The next example creates two new files, one with all the records that contain chevy and the other with records containing ford:

```
$ cat redirect_out
/chevy/   {print > "chevfile"}
/ford/    {print > "fordfile"}
END       {print "done."}
$ nawk -f redirect_out cars
done.
$ cat chevfile
chevy    nova     99      60      3000
chevy    nova     90      50      3500
chevy    impala   75      85      1550
```

The **summary** program produces a summary report on all cars and newer cars. The first two records of declarations are not required; **nawk** automatically declares and initializes variables as you use them. After **nawk** reads all the input data, it computes and displays averages. What happens to this program when you process a car made in the year 2000? How would you fix it?

```
$ cat summary
BEGIN           {
                yearsum = 0 ; costsum = 0
                newcostsum = 0 ; newcount = 0
                }
                {
                yearsum += $3
                costsum += $5
                }
$3 > 90 {newcostsum += $5 ; newcount ++}
END             {
```

```
                    printf "Average age of cars is %4.1f years\n",\
                           99 - (yearsum/NR)
                    printf "Average cost of cars is $%7.2f\n",\
                           costsum/NR
                       printf "Average cost of newer cars is $%7.2f\n",\
                              newcostsum/newcount

              }
$ nawk -f summary cars
Average age of cars is 10.5 years
Average cost of cars is $6216.67
Average cost of newer cars is $7035.71
```

Following, **grep** shows the format of a record from the **passwd** file that the next example uses:

```
$ grep 'jenny' /etc/passwd
jenny:x:1001:10:Jenny Chin:/home/jenny:/bin/csh
```

The next example demonstrates a technique for finding the largest number in a field. Because it works with the **passwd** file, which delimits fields with colons (**:**), it changes the input field separator (**FS**) before reading any data. (Alternatively the assignment to **FS** could be made on the command line using the **–v** option.) This example reads the **passwd** file and determines the next available user ID number (field 3). The numbers do not have to be in order in the **passwd** file for this program to work.

The *pattern* causes **nawk** to select records that contain a user ID number greater than any previous user ID number that it has processed and less than 60,000. (The system administrator does not want any user IDs greater than 59,999.) The program selects records with user IDs greater than the value of **saveit** and less than 60,000. Each time it selects a record, **nawk** assigns the value of the new user ID number to the **saveit** variable. Then **nawk** uses the new value of **saveit** to test the user ID of all subsequent records.

Finally **nawk** adds 1 to the value of **saveit** and displays the result.

```
$ cat find_uid
BEGIN                       {FS = ":"
                             saveit = 0}
$3 > saveit && $3 < 60000    {saveit = $3}
END                          {print "Next available UID is " saveit + 1}
```

```
$ nawk -f find_uid /etc/passwd
Next available UID is 1092
```

The next example shows another report based on the **cars** file. This report uses nested **if else** statements to substitute values based on the contents of the price field. The program has no *pattern* part—it processes every record.

```
$ cat price_range
{
if ($5 <= 5000) $5 = "inexpensive"
else if ($5 > 5000 && $5 < 10000) $5 = "please ask"
else if ($5 >= 10000) $5 = "expensive"
printf "%-10s %-8s    19%2d     %5d      %-12s\n",\
   $1, $2, $3, $4, $5
}
```

```
$ nawk -f price_range cars
plym        fury        1997        73      inexpensive
chevy       nova        1999        60      inexpensive
ford        mustang     1975        45      expensive
volvo       gl          1988        102     please ask
ford        ltd         1993        15      expensive
chevy       nova        1990        50      inexpensive
fiat        600         1975        115     inexpensive
honda       accord      1991        30      please ask
ford        thundbd     1994        10      expensive
toyota      tercel      1992        180     inexpensive
chevy       impala      1975        85      inexpensive
ford        bronco      1993        25      please ask
```

Below, the **manuf** associative array (page 825) uses the contents of the first field of each record in the **cars** file as an index. The array is composed of the elements **manuf[plym]**, **manuf[chevy]**, **manuf[ford]**, and so on. The **++** C language operator increments the variable that it follows.

The *action* following the **END** *pattern* is the special **for** structure that loops through the elements of an associative array. A pipe sends the output through **sort** to produce an alphabetical list of cars and the quantities in stock.

```
$ cat manuf
nawk ' {manuf[$1]++}
END   {for (name in manuf) print name, manuf[name]}
' cars |
sort

$ manuf
chevy 3
fiat 1
ford 4
honda 1
plym 1
toyota 1
volvo 1
```

The **manuf.sh** program is a more complete shell script that includes error checking. This script lists and counts the contents of a column in a file, with both the column number and the name of the file specified on the command line.

The first **nawk** *action* (the one that starts with {count) uses the shell variable **$1** in the middle of the **nawk** program to specify an array index. Because of the way the single quotation marks are paired, the **$1** that appears to be within single quotation marks is actually not quoted: The two quoted strings in the **nawk** program surround, but do not include, the **$1**. Because the **$1** is not quoted, the shell substitutes the value of the first command line argument in place of **$1**, so that **$1** is interpreted before the **nawk** command is invoked. The leading dollar sign (the one before the first single quotation mark on that line) causes **nawk** to interpret what the shell substitutes as a field number. Refer to Chapters 11 through 13 for more information on shell scripts.

```
$ cat manuf.sh
if [ $# != 2 ]
   then
        echo "Usage: manuf.sh field file"
        exit 1
fi
nawk < $2 '
        {count[$'$1']++}
END     {for (item in count) printf "%-20s%-20s\n",\
           item, count[item]}' |
sort

$  manuf.sh
Usage: manuf.sh field file


$  manuf.sh 1 cars
chevy               3
fiat                1
ford                4
honda               1
plym                1
toyota              1
volvo               1


$ manuf.sh 3 cars
75                  3
88                  1
90                  1
91                  1
92                  1
93                  2
94                  1
97                  1
99                  1
```

The **word_usage** script displays a word usage list for a file you specify on the command line. The **tr** utility lists the words from standard input, one to a record. The **sort** utility orders the file with the most frequently used words at the top of the list. It sorts groups of words that are used the same number of times in alphabetical order. Refer to **sort** (page 891) and **tr** (page 924) for more information.

```
$ cat word_usage
tr -cs 'a-zA-Z' '[\n*]' < $1 |
nawk    '
        {count[$1]++}
END     {for (item in count) printf "%-15s%3s\n", item, count[item]}' |
sort +1nr +0f -1

$ word_usage textfile
the              42
file             29
fsck             27
```

```
system          22
you             22
to              21
it              17
SIZE            14
and             13
MODE            13
  .
  .
  .
  .
```

Below is a similar program in a different format. The style mimics that of a C program and may be easier to read and work with for more complex **nawk** programs.

```
$ cat word_count
tr -cs 'a-zA-Z' '[\n*]' < $1 |
nawk ' {
      count[$1]++
}
END    {
      for (item in count)
          {
          if (count[item] > 4)
              {
              printf "%-15s%3s\n", item, count[item]
              }
          }
} ' |
sort +1nr +0f -1
```

The **tail** utility displays the last ten records of output, illustrating that words occurring fewer than five times are not listed.

```
$ word_count textfile | tail
directories      5
if               5
information      5
INODE            5
more             5
no               5
on               5
response         5
this             5
will             5
```

The following example generates a list of characters that appear as the first character in a record in the **cars** file and counts the number of records that begin with that letter.

It uses the **substr** function to extract the first character of every record and stores this character in an associative array named **char**. This technique can be useful to find the distribution of user accounts starting with the same letter. As a system administrator, you could use this information to divide and balance accounts across multiple hosts or directories.

```
$ nawk '{char[substr($1,1,1)]++;}; END {for (var in char) {print var, char[var]}}' cars
f 5
h 1
p 1
t 1
v 1
c 3
```

The next example shows one way to put a date on a report. The first record of input to the **nawk** program comes from **date**. The **nawk** program reads this record as record number 1 (NR == 1) and processes it accordingly. It processes all subsequent records with the **action** associated with the next **pattern** (NR > 1).

```
$ cat report
if (test $# = 0) then
    echo "You must supply a filename."
    exit 1
fi
(date; cat $1) |
nawk '
NR == 1    {print "Report for", $1, $2, $3 ",", " $6}
NR >  1    {print $5 "      " $1}'

$ report cars
Report for Thu Apr 9, 1998
2500      plym
3000      chevy
10000      ford
9850      volvo
10500      ford
3500      chevy
450      fiat
6000      honda
17000      ford
750      toyota
1550      chevy
9500      ford
```

The next example uses the **numbers** file and sums each of the columns in a file you specify on the command line. It performs error checking, reporting on and discarding rows that contain nonnumeric entries. The **next** command (13th line) causes **nawk** to skip the rest of the commands for the current record and to read in another. At the end of the program, **nawk** displays a grand total for the file.

```
$ cat numbers
10      20      30.3      40.5
20      30      45.7      66.1
30      xyz      50      70
40      75      107.2      55.6
50      20      30.3      40.5
60      30      45.0      66.1
70      1134.7  50      70
80      75      107.2      55.6
90      176      30.3      40.5
100      1027.45 45.7      66.1
110      123      50      57a.5
120      75      107.2      55.6
```

```
$ cat tally
nawk 'BEGIN   {
              ORS = ""
              }

NR == 1{
  nfields = NF
  }
  {
  if ($0 ~ /[^0-9. \t]/)
      {
      print "\nRecord " NR " skipped:\n\t"
      print $0 "\n"
      next
      }
  else
      {
      for (count = 1; count <= nfields; count++)
         {
         printf "%10.2f", $count > "tally.out"
         sum[count] += $count
         gtotal += $count
         }
      print "\n" > "tally.out"
      }
  }

END   {
  for (count = 1; count <= nfields; count++)
      {
      print "   -------" > "tally.out"
      }
  print "\n" > "tally.out"
  for (count = 1; count <= nfields; count++)
      {
      printf "%10.2f", sum[count] > "tally.out"
      }
  print "\n\n        Grand Total " gtotal "\n" > "tally.out"
} ' < numbers


$ tally
Record 3 skipped:
      30      xyz     50      70

Record 6 skipped:
      60      30      45.O    66.1

Record 11 skipped:
      110     123     50      57a.5
```

```
$ cat tally.out
    10.00     20.00     30.30     40.50
    20.00     30.00     45.70     66.10
    40.00     75.00    107.20     55.60
    50.00     20.00     30.30     40.50
    70.00   1134.70     50.00     70.00
    80.00     75.00    107.20     55.60
    90.00    176.00     30.30     40.50
   100.00   1027.45     45.70     66.10
   120.00     75.00    107.20     55.60
   -------   -------   -------   -------
   580.00   2633.15    553.90    490.50

        Grand Total 4257.55
```

The next **nawk** example reads the **passwd** file. It lists users who do not have passwords and users who have duplicate user ID numbers. (The **pwck** utility also performs these checks, as well as a few more.)

```
$ cat /etc/passwd
bill::1102:10:ext 123:/home/bill:/bin/sh
roy:x:1104:10:ext 475:/home/roy:/bin/sh
tom:x:1105:10:ext 476:/home/tom:/bin/sh
lynn:x:1166:10:ext 500:/home/lynn:/bin/sh
mark:x:1107:10:ext 112:/home/mark:/bin/sh
sales:x:1108:10:ext 102:/m/market:/bin/sh
anne:x:1109:10:ext 355:/home/anne:/bin/sh
toni::1164:10:ext 357:/home/toni:/bin/sh
ginny:x:1115:10:ext 109:/home/ginny:/bin/sh
chuck:x:1116:10:ext 146:/home/chuck:/bin/sh
neil:x:1164:10:ext 159:/home/neil:/bin/sh
rmi:x:1118:10:ext 178:/home/rmi:/bin/sh
vern:x:1119:10:ext 201:/home/vern:/bin/sh
bob:x:1120:10:ext 227:/home/bob:/bin/sh
janet:x:1122:10:ext 229:/home/janet:/bin/sh
maggie:x:1124:10:ext 244:/home/maggie:/bin/sh
dan::1126:10::/home/dan:/bin/sh
dave:x:1108:10:ext 427:/home/dave:/bin/sh
mary:x:1129:10:ext 303:/home/mary:/bin/sh
```

```
$ cat passwd_check
nawk < /etc/passwd '    BEGIN   {
  uid[void] = ""              # tell nawk that uid is an array
  }
  {                           # no pattern indicates process all records
  dup = 0                     # initialize duplicate flag
  split($0, field, ":")       # split into fields delimited by ":"
  if (field[2] == "")         # check for null password field
    {
    if (field[5] == "")     # check for null info field
      {
      print field[1] " has no password."
      }
    else
      {
      print field[1] " ("field[5]") has no password."
      }
    }
```

```
    for (name in uid)            # loop through uid array
        {
        if (uid[name] == field[3])    # check for 2nd use of UID
            {
            print field[1] " has the same UID as " name " : UID = " uid[name]
            dup = 1  # set duplicate flag
            }
        }
    if (!dup)   # same as: if (dup == 0)
            # assign UID and login name to uid array
        {
        uid[field[1]] = field[3]
        }
    }'
```

```
$ passwd_check
bill (ext 123) has no password.
toni (ext 357) has no password.
neil has the same UID as toni : UID = 1164
dan has no password.
dave has the same UID as sales : UID = 1108
```

The final example shows a complete interactive shell script that uses **nawk** to generate a report.

```
$ cat list_cars
trap 'rm -f $$.tem > /dev/null;echo $0 aborted.;exit 1' 1 2 15
echo "Price range (for example 5000 7500): \c"
read lowrange hirange

echo '
                                Miles
Make        Model       Year    (000)       Price
-------------------------------------------------' > $$.tem
nawk < cars '
$5 >= '$lowrange' && $5 <= '$hirange' {
   if ($1 ~ /ply/)   $1 = "plymouth"
   if ($1 ~ /chev/)  $1 = "chevrolet"
   printf "%-10s %-8s    19%2d    %5d    $ %8.2f\n", $1, $2, $3, $4, $5
   }' | sort -n +5 >> $$.tem
cat $$.tem
rm $$.tem
```

```
$ list_cars
Price range (for example 5000 7500): 3000 8000

                                Miles
Make        Model       Year    (000)       Price
-------------------------------------------------
chevrolet   nova        1979      60     $  3000.00
chevrolet   nova        1980      50     $  3500.00
honda       accord      1981      30     $  6000.00
```

```
$ list_cars
Price range (for example 5000 7500): 0 2000

Make        Model      Year      (000)        Price
-----------------------------------------------------
fiat        600        1965       115     $    450.00
toyota      tercel     1982       180     $    750.00
chevrolet   impala     1965        85     $   1550.00

$ list_cars
Price range (for example 5000 7500): 15000 100000

                                 Miles
Make        Model      Year      (000)        Price
-----------------------------------------------------
ford        thundbd    1984        10     $ 17000.00
```

Error Messages

The following examples show some of the more common causes of **nawk**'s infamous error messages (and nonmessages). Although **nawk**'s messages are a great improvement over those of **awk**, some are still quite challenging. The examples are run under **sh**. (When using **nawk** with other shells, the error message you get may be different.)

The first example leaves the single quotation marks off the command line, so the shell interprets **$3** and **$1** as shell variables. Another problem is that because there are no single quotation marks, the shell passes **nawk** four arguments instead of two.

```
$ nawk {print $3, $1} cars
Missing }
```

The next command line includes a typo that **nawk** does not catch (`prinnt`). Instead of issuing an error message, **nawk** just does not do anything useful.

```
$ nawk '$3 >= 83 {prinnt $1}' cars
```

The next example has no braces around the *action*:

```
$ nawk '/chevy/ print $3, $1' cars
nawk: syntax error at source line 1
 context is
        /chevy/ >>>  print <<<  $3, $1
nawk: bailing out at source line 1
```

There is no problem with the next example—**nawk** did just what you asked it to. (None of the records in the file contain a z).

```
$ nawk '/z/' cars
```

The following program contains a useless *action* (the Print command is probably missing):

```
$ nawk '{$3}' cars
nawk: illegal statement
 input record number 1, file cars
 source line number 1
```

The next example shows an improper *action* for which **nawk** does not issue an error message:

```
$ nawk '{$3  " made by "  $1}' cars
```

The heading in the following example is not displayed because there is no backslash after the print command in the **BEGIN** block. The backslash is needed to quote the following NEWLINE so that the line can be continued. Without it **nawk** sees two separate statements and displays an error.

```
$ cat print_cars
BEGIN   {print
"Model  Year     Price"}
/chevy/ {printf "%5s\t%4d\t%5d\n", $2, $3, $5}

$ nawk -f print_cars cars

nawk: illegal statement
 source line number 2
```

After placing the missing backslash at the end of the first line, the program works fine.

```
$ nawk -f print_cars cars
nova   99      3000
nova   90      3500
impala 75      1550
```

You must use double quotation marks, not single quotation marks, to delimit strings.

```
$ cat print_cars2
BEGIN {OFS='\t'}
$3 ~ /5$/ {print $3, $1, "$" $5}

$ nawk -f print_cars2 cars
nawk: syntax error at source line 1
 context is
          BEGIN >>>   {OFS=' <<<
nawk: illegal statement at source line 1   1
```

nice

Changes the priority of a command

Syntax: *nice [option] command-line*

Summary

The **nice** utility changes the execution priority of a command line. You can specify a decrement in the range of 1–19, which decreases the priority of the command. Superuser can use **nice** to increase the priority of a command by using a negative decrement.

The **nice** builtin csh has a different syntax from the **nice** utility. Refer to "Notes" below. If you want to change the priority of a running job, use **renice**, also described in "Notes."

Argument

The *command-line* is the command line you want to execute at a different priority.

Option

With no option **nice** defaults to an adjustment of 10, lowering the priority of the command by 10.

–value or –n value   Changes the priority by an adjustment of *value*. A positive *value* lowers the priority, whereas a negative *value* raises the priority. Only Superuser can use a negative *value*. The range of priorities is from –20 (the highest priority) to 19 (the lowest priority). If you specify a value past either end of this range, the priority is set to the limit of the range. Using the first form, entering a negative *value* results in a number preceded by two hyphens (for example **––12**, a high priority that only Superuser can use).

Notes

The **/usr/xpg4/bin/nice** utility is a POSIX-compliant version of **nice**.

The **nice** builtin csh requires you to precede the **nice** value with a single minus sign (**–**) to decrement it and raise the priority (Superuser only). Use a single plus sign (**+**) to increment it and lower the priority. If you do not specify a value, **nice** sets the priority to 4.

One difficulty with understanding how priorities are used in UNIX comes from the fact that higher priority values mean a lower priority is used by the operating system to schedule the job for execution. So positive entries for value result in the job being scheduled less often, whereas negative entries cause the job to be scheduled more often.

High Priority Can Yield a Slow System

If Superuser schedules a job to run at the highest priority, system performance can suffer. All other jobs, including the operating system, can be affected. To avoid a slow system, use **nice** with negative values carefully (Superuser only).

Another utility, **renice**, allows you to change the priority of a running job (**nice** only lets you change the priority of a job before you start it). It can work similarly to **nice**, except that in place of the command line you need to supply the PID number of the process whose priority you want to change. For example:

```
$ renice 19 31454
```

decreases the priority of the job with PID 31454 as much as possible. Unless you are Superuser you can only change the priority of your own jobs and you can only use positive priority numbers.

If you want more control over viewing and changing priorities, refer to the **priocntl man** page.

Example

The following command executes **find** in the background at the lowest possible priority:

```
$ nice -19 find / -name core -print > corefiles.out &
[1] 24135
```

nohup

Runs a command that keeps running after you log out

Syntax: *nohup command-line*

Summary

The **nohup** utility executes a command line so that it keeps running after you log out. Normally when you log out, the system kills all of your processes.[6] Refer to "Notes" below for information on the **nohup** builtin csh.

Argument

The ***command-line*** is the command line you want to execute.

Notes

The **/usr/xpg4/bin/nohup** utility is a POSIX-compliant version of **nohup**.

When you log out the system normally sends all of your processes a SIGHUP (hangup) signal, which kills them. The **nohup** utility works by arranging for your processes to ignore SIGHUP and SIGQUIT (quit) signals. Ignoring these signals ensures that the process will not be killed when you log out.

The **nohup** utility automatically lowers the priority of the command it executes by 5. See **nice** (page 844) for information about priorities.

If you do not redirect the output from a process that you execute with **nohup**, both standard output *and* standard error are sent to the file named **nohup.out** in the working directory. If you do not have write permission for the working directory, **nohup** opens a **nohup.out** file in your home directory.

Unlike the **nohup** utility the **nohup** builtin csh does not send output to **nohup.out**.

Example

The following command executes **find** using **nohup**:

```
$ nohup find / -name core -print > corefiles.out
```

---

6. The C Shell is an exception. Jobs that you run in the background (with **&**) under **csh** are implicitly run with **nohup**.

846

od

Dumps the contents of a file

Syntax: *od [options] [file-list]*

Summary

The **od** (octal dump) utility dumps the contents of a file. It is useful for viewing executable (object) files and text files with embedded nonprinting characters.

This utility takes its input from the files you specify on the command line or from standard input.

Argument

The *file-list* specifies the pathnames of the files that **od** displays. If you do not specify a *file-list*, **od** reads from standard input.

Options

If you do not specify an option, the dump is in octal.

−c   **character**   Produces a character dump with certain nonprinting characters displayed as printing characters preceded by a backslash. The **od** utility displays nonprinting characters that are not in the following list as three-digit octal numbers.

Symbol	Character
\0	null
\b	BACKSPACE
\f	FORMFEED
\n	NEWLINE
\r	RETURN
\t	TAB

−d   **decimal**   Produces a decimal dump. Same as **−t u2**.

−o   **octal**   Produces an octal dump. This is the default and is the same as **−t o2**.

−t *xn*   **type**   Takes any one of several arguments, *x*. With an argument of **a**, produces a dump in which nonprinting characters are displayed by name (see second example). Other arguments are **c**, (character), **d** (signed decimal), **o** (octal—the default), **u** (unsigned decimal), **x** (hexadecimal), and **f** (float). You can follow each of the arguments, except for **a** and **c**, with a number, *n,* which specifies the number of bytes that make up each number.

−x   **hexadecimal**   Produces a hexadecimal dump. Same as **−t x2**.

847

Notes
The **/usr/xpg4/bin/od** utility is a POSIX-compliant version of **od**.

Examples
The file **ac**, used in the following examples, contains all the ASCII characters (printing and nonprinting). The first example displays each byte as a named character, escape (see the preceding **–c** option), or an octal number. The first column shows the offset of each byte from the start of the file. The offsets are given as octal values.

```
$ od -c ac
0000000  \0 001 002 003 004 005 006 007  \b  \t  \n 013  \f  \r 016 017
0000020 020 021 022 023 024 025 026 027 030 031 032 033 034 035 036 037
0000040      !   "   #   $   %   &   '   (   )   *   +   ,   -   .   /
0000060   0   1   2   3   4   5   6   7   8   9   :   ;   <   =   >   ?
0000100   @   A   B   C   D   E   F   G   H   I   J   K   L   M   N   O
0000120   P   Q   R   S   T   U   V   W   X   Y   Z   [   \   ]   ^   _
0000140   `   a   b   c   d   e   f   g   h   i   j   k   l   m   n   o
0000160   p   q   r   s   t   u   v   w   x   y   z   {   |   }   ~ 177
0000200
```

The next example shows the nonprinting bytes displayed as names:

```
$ od -t a ac
0000000 nul soh stx etx eot enq ack bel  bs  ht  lf  vt  ff  cr  so  si
0000020 dle dc1 dc2 dc3 dc4 nak syn etb can  em sub esc  fs  gs  rs  us
0000040  sp   !   "   #   $   %   &   '   (   )   *   +   ,   -   .   /
0000060   0   1   2   3   4   5   6   7   8   9   :   ;   <   =   >   ?
0000100   @   A   B   C   D   E   F   G   H   I   J   K   L   M   N   O
0000120   P   Q   R   S   T   U   V   W   X   Y   Z   [   \   ]   ^   _
0000140   `   a   b   c   d   e   f   g   h   i   j   k   l   m   n   o
0000160   p   q   r   s   t   u   v   w   x   y   z   {   |   }   ~ del
0000200
```

paste   Joins corresponding lines from files

Syntax: *paste [option] [file-list]*

Summary

The **paste** utility reads lines from the *file-list* and joins corresponding lines in its output. By default output lines are separated by a **TAB** character.

Argument

The *file-list* is a list of ordinary files. If omitted, **paste** reads from standard input.

Option

–d *dlist*   **delimiter**   The *dlist* holds the delimiter that separates each line of input from the next on a single line of output. If *dlist* contains a single character, **paste** uses that character as the delimiter instead of the default **TAB** character. If *dlist* contains more than one character, the characters are used, each in turn, to delimit output lines. If **paste** comes to the end of the characters in the *dlist* string and needs another delimiter, it starts over again with the first character in the string. Following is a list of symbols that you can use to represent special characters in *dlist*.

Symbol	Character
\n	NEWLINE
\t	TAB
\\	BACKSLASH
\0	Empty string (not null)

Notes

A common use of **paste** is to rearrange the columns of a table. A utility such as **cut** (page 727) can get the desired columns in separate files, and then **paste** can join them in any order.

Examples

The following example uses the files **fnames** and **accntinfo**. You can create these files by processing **/etc/passwd** with **cut**. The **paste** command puts the full name field first, followed by the remaining user account information. A **TAB** character separates the two output fields.

```
$ cat fnames
Jenny Chen
Alex Watson
Scott Adams
Helen Simpson
```

```
$ cat accntinfo
jenny:KcDO6q8DsjJjs:401:50:/home/jenny:/bin/ksh
alex:edJigJPVhGS5k:402:50:/home/alex:/bin/sh
scott:mdieDnvImaG.M:504:500:/home/scott:/bin/csh
hls:Ud2Ih6OBN1crk:505:500:/home/hls:/bin/sh

$ paste fnames accntinfo
Jenny Chen      jenny:KcDO6q8DsjJjs:401:50:/home/jenny:/bin/ksh
Alex Watson     alex:edJigJPVhGS5k:402:50:/home/alex:/bin/sh
Scott Adams     scott:mdieDnvImaG.M:504:500:/home/scott:/bin/csh
Helen Simpson   hls:Ud2Ih6OBN1crk:505:500:/home/hls:/bin/sh
```

The next examples use the files **p1**, **p2**, **p3**, and **p4**. The last example uses the **−d** option to give **paste** a list of characters to use to separate output fields.

```
$ cat p1
1
one
ONE
$ cat p2
2
two
TWO
$ cat p3
3
three
THREE
$ cat p4
4
four
FOUR

$ paste p1 p2 p3 p4
1       2       3       4
one     two     three   four
ONE     TWO     THREE   FOUR

$ paste p4 p3 p2 p1
4       3       2       1
four    three   two     one
FOUR    THREE   TWO     ONE

$ paste -d "+-=" p3 p2 p1 p4
3+2-1=4
three+two-one=four
THREE+TWO-ONE=FOUR
```

patch

Updates source code

Syntax: *patch [options]*

Summary

The **patch** utility attempts to update a file from a file of change information, or a patch, created by **diff**. The **patch** utility can read many different forms of **diff** output, including context **diff**s, **ed** scripts, and the default **diff** output. See the **diff man** page for more information on these and other output forms. Most patches for free software are distributed as context **diff**s, which are created by using **diff** with the **–c** option.

      The **patch** utility is useful when making changes to large software applications, because it allows one version of the application source to be changed into another simply by applying patches. The presence of the utility is often assumed by software developers, who email patches so users can install updates.

Arguments

The **patch** utility reads the change information from standard input (unless you use the **–i** option), usually redirected from a file or a pipe, and attempts to identify the file to be updated from the change information. If **patch** cannot determine which file is to be updated from the patch instructions, it prompts you for a file-name. If there are changes to multiple files in the change information, then **patch** updates all of the files.

Options

–b   **backup**   Saves a copy of the original file before applying the patch as *file*.**orig**. Using this option, you can restore the *target-file* if necessary. It is a good idea always to use this option.

–c   **context**   Interprets the patch file as a context-sensitive patch (generated with **diff –c** or **–C**).

–d *directory*   **directory**   Makes *directory* the working directory before further processing.

–e   **ed**   Interprets the patch file as an **ed** script.

–i *patchfile*   **input**   Takes the patch from the file named *patchfile* rather than standard input.

–l   **loose** ("ell")   Performs *loose* pattern matching when trying to locate where patches should go in *target-file*. With this option any sequence of whitespace in the patch instructions matches any sequence of whitespace in *target-file*. All other matches must be exact.

–n   **normal**   Interprets the patch file as a normal **diff**.

–N   **ignore**   Ignores the patch hunk if it has already been applied to a file. Without this option the hunk is appended to the **.rej** file.

851

–o *outfile*   **output**   Directs all output from **patch** to *outfile* instead of modifying each file as it is processed. Results in an *outfile* that contains the appended output of one or more patch runs, depending on the number of files processed.

–p*n*   **prefixes**   Strips prefixes from the paths of files to be patched. The value *n* is the number of slashes to remove from the start of pathnames (any directory names between these slashes are also removed). Setting *n* to 0 causes **patch** to use full path-names. Using **–p** without *n* causes the pathnames to be unchanged. If you omit this option entirely, then the entire pathname up to the simple filename is removed. The **–p** option makes it possible for you to **patch** files that you have in a location that is different than the location used by the person who built the *patch-file*.

–r *rejectfile*   **reject**   Changes the suffix for reject files from the default **.rej** to *.rejectfile*.

–R   **reverse**   Attempts to apply the patch in reverse. See "Discussion" below.

Notes

You can create a **patch** file by keeping a directory holding the previous version of an application and making your changes to a copy of that application in another directory. The **–r** option of **diff** builds a **patch** file containing all the differences between the old and new versions. See "Examples," following.

If you are a distributor of software source code, you can help your users by maintaining a file named **patchlevel.h** that holds the current version number and patch number of your software.

If you are building a **patch** file and want to add a file, you need to create an empty file with the same name as the new file to serve as the source file before comparing with **diff**.

The Solaris version of **patch** lacks some of the features found in the free version of **patch**, including *fuzz factors*. It also does not report on hunk success under normal circumstances (only reporting done) and is very picky about the format of context **diff** patches. See "How Do I Use ftp?" (page 974), and download, compile, and install **patch-2.5.tar.gz** (or the current version) from the GNU site.

Discussion

The **patch** utility is designed to simplify the task of keeping the source code for large software applications up to date. If you are a software developer, this makes it easier for you to provide updates to users. If you are a user, **patch** makes it easier for you to obtain and install updates.

The **patch** utility works by reading the patch file and locating *hunks*. Each hunk describes the changes needed to change part of a file into the new version. When **patch** finds a hunk, it locates the affected portion of the target file and performs the changes that are indicated in the hunk. The **patch** utility is able to extract hunks that are embedded in mail messages and other text, making it easy to apply patches: Just feed the mail message as standard input to the **patch** program.

If **patch** finds a hunk that cannot be applied to the target file, that hunk is rejected. All rejected hunks are saved in a file named by adding the filename extension **.rej** to the name of the target file. When **patch** is successful in making changes to a file (and you have used the **–b** option), a copy of the original target file is kept with the extension **.orig**. This makes it possible for you to compare the original and changed versions to examine the changes that were made.

While locating the place where a hunk applies to the target file, **patch** checks to see if the change has already been made. If the change has been made, it may be because the person who built the patch file accidently reversed the old and new files when building the **patch**. In this case **patch** asks if you would like to apply the **patch** in reverse. If you know that a patch file contains reversed patches, then you can give **patch** the **–R** option to apply patches in reverse automatically. The **–R** flag is not applicable to patches that use **ed** script **diff**s. There is not enough information in these patches to reverse the patch.

If the patch is generated from a software development tree that includes version control markers from SCCS or **cvs**, the **patch** script may have extra directory components such as **SCCS/s.filename.c** or **RCS/filename.c,v**. Use the **–p** flag to strip off these extra directory components.

Examples

In the following example the distributor is building a **patch** file for a small software application. The new version of the application source code is in the directory **pi**, whereas the directory **Old_pi** holds the previous version.

```
$ ls -l Old_pi
total 8
-rw-rw-r--  1 alex     group         204 Jul  3 14:13 Makefile
-rw-r--r--  1 alex     group           0 Aug  4 08:10 patchlevel.h
-rw-r--r--  1 alex     group        7516 Jul 14 09:43 pi.c
$ ls -l pi
total 9
-rw-rw-r--  1 alex     group         226 Aug  4 08:12 Makefile
-rw-r--r--  1 alex     group          39 Aug  4 08:10 patchlevel.h
-rw-r--r--  1 alex     group        7396 Aug  4 08:09 pi.c
```

The developer uses the following command to build a patch file using the context (**–c**) option to **diff** (page 739). In this example the **–r** option is not needed because there are no subdirectories in **pi** and **Old_pi**, but the developer included it anyway.

```
$ diff -r -c Old_pi pi >patch.1.7
```

The **patch.1.7** patch file contains all the information needed to change the old version of the **pi** application into the new version. If you are using the Solaris version of **patch**, you must comment out the lines of the patch file that begin with the word diff. Use ✳✳✳ at the beginning of the line to comment them out.

```
$ cat patch.1.7
diff -c -r Old_pi/Makefile pi/Makefile
*** Old_pi/Makefile     Wed May 20 19:41:43 1998
--- pi/Makefile Wed May 20 19:40:39 1998
***************
*** 6,12 ****
  all:  pi

  pi:   pi.c
!         gcc -O3 -m486 pi.c -o pi

  piform:       piform.icn
          icont piform
```

```
--- 6,13 ----
  all:  pi

  pi:   pi.c
! #     gcc -O3 -m486 pi.c -o pi
!       cc -fast -o pi pi.c

  piform:          piform.icn
         icont piform
diff -c -r Old_pi/patchlevel.h pi/patchlevel.h
*** Old_pi/patchlevel.h Wed May 20 19:52:39 1998
--- pi/patchlevel.h     Wed May 20 19:51:52 1998
****************
*** 0 ****
--- 1,2 ----
+ #define VERSION 1
+ #define PATCHLEVEL 7
diff -c -r Old_pi/pi.c pi/pi.c
*** Old_pi/pi.c Wed May 20 19:40:50 1998
--- pi/pi.c     Wed May 20 19:41:33 1998
****************
*** 67,77 ****
            }
        nwd    = places/NDS + 2;  /* 1 for error accumulation, 1 for '3.' */

-       unit(r,0);               /* initialize the result number */
-

                                 /* compute the arctangent terms and combine */
!       arctan(24, 8, at);
!       addmm(0, r, at, r);
        arctan(8, 57, at);
        addmm(0, r, at, r);
        arctan(4, 239, at);
--- 67,74 ----
            }
        nwd    = places/NDS + 2;  /* 1 for error accumulation, 1 for '3.' */

                                 /* compute the arctangent terms and combine */
!       arctan(24, 8, r);
        arctan(8, 57, at);
        addmm(0, r, at, r);
        arctan(4, 239, at);
****************
*** 89,96 ****
        int positive;            /* switches sign of arctangent term */
        long d2;                 /* d squared */
        int i;                   /* loop control */
!       int nt;                  /* number of zero terms on left */
!       int nextT;

        d2 = (long)d*(long)d;    /* d squared */

--- 86,92 ----
        int positive;            /* switches sign of arctangent term */
```

```
        long d2;                       /* d squared */
        int i;                         /* loop control */
!       int nextT;                           /* number of unchanged 'digits' on left */

        d2 = (long)d*(long)d;     /* d squared */

***************
*** 105,113 ****
            if ((nextT = findNextTerm(nextT, t)) < nwd) {
                divms(nextT, t, (long)((i<<1)-1), s);
                positive = !positive;
!               nt = findNextTerm(0, s);
!               if (positive) addmm(nt, at, s, at);
!               else          submm(nt, at, s, at);
                }
            }
        }
--- 101,108 ----
            if ((nextT = findNextTerm(nextT, t)) < nwd) {
                divms(nextT, t, (long)((i<<1)-1), s);
                positive = !positive;
!               if (positive) addmm(nextT, at, s, at);
!               else          submm(nextT, at, s, at);
                }
            }
        }
```

After creating the patch file the developer mails it to all users.

```
$ mail pi-users
To: pi_users
Subject: New version of pi available


Hi - Here are the patches you need to upgrade to version 1.7
of the pi program:

~r patch.1.7
patch.1.7: 92 lines
(continue editing letter)
CONTROL-D
```

If you receive this mail, you can save the message to a file and then change directories to the directory immediately above the old version of **pi** and run **patch** to upgrade your source code (remembering to comment out the diff lines with *** first). There is no need to extract the patches from the mail file. Some mail programs allow you to pipe the message directly into **patch** without having to save it to a file. Other times the patch may be an attachment to a piece of mail. Save the attachment to a file and proceed as above. While running, **patch** shows you some of the processing that is taking place. Two hunks are successfully processed.

```
$ patch -c -p 0 -b <../mail.pi
  Looks like a new-style context diff.
  The next patch looks like a new-style context diff.
File to patch:
```

```
No file found -- skip this patch? [no] yes
Skipping patch...
, The next patch looks like a new-style context diff.
done
```

Another shortcoming of the Solaris2 **patch** is that it does not indicate which hunk is having a problem. In the preceding example **patch** is having a problem with the **patchlevel.h** file, but you would never know it from the output.

For more information see "Patches" on page 629.

pg

Displays a file, one screenful at a time

Syntax: *pg [options] [file-list]*

Summary

The **pg** utility displays a text file on a screen or in a window. It is similar to **cat** but pauses each time it fills the screen. In response to the **pg** prompt, you can press RETURN to view another screenful, press the interrupt key (usually CONTROL-C) to terminate the program, or give one of the commands discussed below.

This utility takes its input from files you specify on the command line or from standard input.

Argument

The *file-list* is the list of files that you want to view. If you do not specify any files, **pg** reads from standard input.

Options

–c	**clear** Clears the screen and places the cursor in the upper-left corner before displaying each screenful.
–e	**end** Causes **pg** *not* to pause at the end of each file.
–f	**force** Keeps **pg** from splitting long lines. This option is useful for displaying files that contain lines with nonprinting characters. (When a line containing many nonprinting characters is displayed, the line may be more than twice its original length.) These characters appear in files to underline or display characters in reverse video.
–*lines*	Specifies the screen size. Replace *lines* with the number of lines you want **pg** to use as a screen size. If you do not use this option, **pg** uses one line fewer than the height of the screen as described in the Terminfo description for the terminal or emulator you are using.
+*n*	Starts displaying the file at line *n*.
–n	**no newline** Causes **pg** commands to take effect as soon as you enter them without waiting for you to press RETURN.
+/*pattern*/	Starts displaying the file at the first line that contains a string that matches *pattern*. Replace *pattern* with the string or other regular expression you want to match.
–p *prompt*	Changes the prompt from the default (**:**) to one you specify. Replace *prompt* with the prompt you want **pg** to use. If you include the string %d in the *prompt*, **pg** replaces it with the number of the page it is displaying each time it issues the prompt.

–s   **standout**   Causes **pg** to display all its messages and prompts in standout mode. Standout mode is usually reverse video and is dependent on the Terminfo name that describes your terminal or emulator.

Notes

Also refer to the **more** utility described on page 815.

Commands

While you are viewing a file, you can give **pg** commands that affect what it displays next or how it displays it. Always give a command in response to the **pg** prompt [a colon (**:**) unless you change it with the **–p** option], and terminate it with a RETURN (unless you use the **–n** option). The **pg** utility displays a list of available commands when you give the command **h**.

Searching for a Pattern

You can search forward or backward for a pattern using one of the following command formats:

[n]/pattern/[tmb]
[n]?pattern?[tmb]

The *n* is an optional number that searches for the *n*th occurrence of the pattern. If you do not specify *n*, **pg** searches for the first occurrence. The **/** delimiter causes **pg** to search forward, and **?** causes it to search backward. [Some very old terminals cannot handle question marks properly, so **pg** allows you to use carets (^) in place of the question marks.]

The *pattern* is a string or other regular expression that you are searching for. Refer to Appendix A for more information on regular expressions.

The optional character that follows the final delimiter (**/** or **?**) indicates where you want **pg** to position the line containing the pattern on the screen. Normally **pg** positions the pattern at the top of the screen (*t*). You can select the middle (*m*) or bottom (*b*) of the screen if you prefer. Once you select a position, **pg** uses that position until you specify a new position.

Displaying Text by Its Position in the File

In response to the **pg** prompt, you can display a portion of the file based on its location in reference to the beginning of the file or to the portion of the file you are currently viewing.

You can precede each of the following commands with an address. The **pg** utility interprets an address that you precede with a plus or minus sign as a relative address—an address that is relative to the portion of the file you are currently viewing. A plus indicates forward, toward the end of the file, and a minus indicates backward, toward the beginning of the file. Without a sign **pg** assumes the address specifies a distance *from* the beginning of the file. The address is in units of lines or pages, as is appropriate to the command.

SPACE   Displays the next page. You can enter a number of pages as an address before the SPACE command. (Unless you use the **–n** option, you must terminate this, and all commands, with a RETURN.)

l   **lines** ("ell")   With a relative address an **l** scrolls the screen the number of lines you specify (the default is one line). With an absolute address **l** causes **pg** to display the line you specify at the top of the screen.

Displaying Other Files
Use the following commands when you have specified more than one file on the command line and you want to look at a file other than the one you are currently viewing.

in   **next**   Give the command **n** to view the next file. Precede the **n** with a number *i* to view the *i*th subsequent file.

ip   **previous**   Use the **p** command like the **n** command to view the previous file from the *file-list*.

Example
The following example shows **pg** displaying the file named **memo**. The user just presses RETURN in response to **pg**'s prompts. In the final prompt EOF stands for *end of file*.

```
$ pg memo
.
.
: RETURN
.
.
: RETURN
.
.
(EOF): RETURN
```

pr

Paginates files for printing

Syntax: *pr [options] [file-list]*

Summary

The **pr** utility breaks files into pages, usually in preparation for printing. By default each page has a header with the name of the file, date, time, and page number.

The **pr** utility takes its input from files you specify on the command line or from standard input. The output from **pr** goes to standard output and is frequently redirected by a pipe to **lp** for printing.

Argument

The *file-list* contains the pathnames of ordinary text files you want **pr** to paginate. If you do not specify any files, **pr** reads standard input.

Options

You can embed options within the *file-list*. An embedded option affects only files following it on the command line.

–c   **control**   Uses a caret (^) to represent control characters. For example a **BACKSPACE** is represented as ^H.

–*column*   Displays output in the number of ***columns*** specified. Do not use this option with **–m**.

–d   **double space**   Double-spaces the output.

–f   **formfeed**   Uses a **FORMFEED** character to skip to the next page, rather than fill the current page with **NEWLINE** characters.

–h *header*   **header**   The **pr** utility displays ***header*** at the top of each page in place of the filename. If ***header*** contains **SPACE**s, you must enclose it within quotation marks.

–l *lines*   **length**   Changes the page length from the standard 66 lines to ***lines*** lines.

–m   **multiple columns**   Displays all specified files simultaneously in multiple columns. Do not use this option with **–columns**.

–n[*ck*]   **number**   Numbers the lines of the file. The *c* and *k* arguments are optional. The *c* is a character that **pr** appends to the number to separate it from the contents of the file. If you do not specify *c*, **TAB** is used. The *k* argument specifies the number of digits in each line number. By default *k* is five. Do not put any **SPACE**s between the **–n** and the *c*, or the *c* and the *k*.

−o *offset*

offset   Specifies the number of SPACEs to skip before displaying the first character of each output line. Replace *offset* with the number of columns of indention you want. Without this option **pr** displays an offset of zero.

+*page*

Causes output to begin with the specified *page*. This option begins with a *plus sign,* not a hyphen.

−s[*x*]

separate   Separates columns with the single character *x* instead of SPACEs (the default). If you do not specify *x,* **pr** uses TABs as separation characters.

−t

no header or trailer   Causes **pr** not to display its header and trailer. The header that **pr** normally displays is five lines long and includes the name of the file, the date, the time, and the page number. The trailer is five blank lines.

−w *n*

width   Changes the page width from standard 72 columns to *n* columns. This option is effective only with multicolumn output (the −**m** and −**columns** options).

Notes

The **/usr/xpg4/bin/pr** utility is a POSIX-compliant version of **pr**.

When you use the −**columns** option to display the output in multiple columns, **pr** displays the same number of lines in each column (with the possible exception of the last).

The **write** utility cannot send messages to your screen while you are running **pr** with its output going to the screen. The **pr** utility disables messages to prevent another user from sending you a message and disrupting **pr**'s output to your screen.

Examples

The first command line shows **pr** paginating a file named **memo** and sending its output through a pipe to **lp** for printing:

```
$ pr memo | lp
request id is printer_1-600 (standard input)
```

Next **memo** is sent to the printer again, this time with a special heading at the top of each page. The job is run in the background.

```
$ pr -h 'MEMO RE: BOOK' memo | lp&
[1] 4904 4905
request id is printer_1-601 (standard input)
```

Below, **pr** displays the **memo** file on the screen, without any header, starting with page 3:

```
$ pr -t +3 memo
.
.
```

prs

Prints a summary of the history of an SCCS file

Syntax: *prs [options] file-list*

Summary

The **prs** utility, a part of SCCS (page 579), displays a summary of one or more deltas to an SCCS file. Without any options it displays a standard summary of every delta in the history of a file. With options **prs** displays a summary of selected deltas. You can also use a data specification (**–d**) to select the information that will be displayed about each delta and to select the format it will be displayed in.

Argument

The *file-list* is a list of SCCS-encoded files, all of which start with **s.**. If the list includes directory names, all files that begin with **s.** in the named directory are added to *file-list*. The **prs** utility reports on all files listed in *file-list*. Any files in *file-list* that do not begin with **s.** or that are unreadable are ignored.

Options

–a

    all Causes **prs** to display information about deltas that have been removed as well as about existing deltas. Without this option **prs** reports on only existing deltas.

–c*date-time*

    cutoff Selects the deltas made before or after a cutoff *date-time*. Use with either **–e** or **–l**. The *date-time* argument has the format:

    YY[MM[DD[HH[MM[SS]]]]]

    The brackets indicate that all components of *date-time* may be omitted except *YY*, starting from the right. The maximum possible values will be substituted for any omitted values (for example 59 is used if *SS* is omitted). The two-digit components may be separated by any number of nonnumeric characters. For example a colon (**:**) may be used between the components (for example 94:02:25:03:36).

–d*data-spec*

    data-specification Specifies the data that is included in the display and the format of the display. You can put labels into the display by including text in the *data-spec* string. Refer to "Data Specifications," following, for more information.

–e

    earlier With **–r** this option causes **prs** to print information about all the deltas created earlier than the specified delta as well as about the specified delta. With **–c** it causes **prs** to print information about all deltas created prior to the specified *date-time*.

–l

    later With **–r** this option causes **prs** to print information about all the deltas created later than the specified delta, as well as about the specified delta. With **–c** it causes **prs** to print information about all deltas created after the specified *date-time*.

–r[*version-number*] **release**   Selects the delta you want information about. Without a version number **–r** displays information about the most recent delta.

Data Specifications

You can use the following keywords after the **–d** option to tell **prs** what information to display and how to display it. In the data specification following **–d**, you can use \t to specify a TAB, or \n to specify a NEWLINE. Text in the data specification that is not a keyword is displayed in the output as it appears in the data specification. A typical data specification includes several keywords separated by SPACEs, TABs, or NEWLINEs. By default **prs** uses the following specification if you do not include one on the command line:

```
":Dt:\t:DL:\nMRs:\n:MR:COMMENTS:\n:C:"
```

The strings MRs: and COMMENTS: are labels, and the \t and \n represent TAB and NEWLINE, respectively. All the other characters inside the double quotation marks are keywords. The following table lists the most useful keywords.

Keyword	Explanation
:DT:	Delta type (D for delta, R for removed delta).
:DL:	Number of lines inserted, deleted, and unchanged.
:I:	Version number (SCCS Identification String).
:D:	Date delta was created.
:T:	Time delta was created.
:P:	Creator of the delta.
:DS:	Sequence number of the delta.
:DP:	Sequence number of the preceding delta.
:MR:	Modification request numbers for the delta.
:C:	Comments for the delta.
:Dt:	The same as :DT :I: :D: :T: :P: :DS: :DP:.

Examples

The first example prints standard information about every delta that has been made to the SCCS-encoded file **s.dissertation**.[7]

---

7. See the tip named "Making SCCS a Little More Friendly," page 581 and the following examples for information about using the **sccs** front end to help with file naming and placement.

```
$ prs s.dissertation
s.dissertation:

D 1.3 94/07/22 14:10:45 alex 3 2    00018/00005/04046
MRs:
COMMENTS:
edits

D 1.2 94/07/21 11:07:32 alex 2 1    00080/00000/04051
MRs:
COMMENTS:
added abstract for chapter 4

D 1.1 94/07/20 14:06:14 alex 1 0    04051/00000/00000
MRs:
COMMENTS:
date and time created 94/07/20 14:06:14 by alex
```

The next example prints information only about Version 1.3.

```
$ prs -r1.3 s.dissertation
s.dissertation:

D 1.3 94/07/22 14:10:45 alex 3 2    00018/00005/04046
MRs:
COMMENTS:
edits
```

Below, the comments are printed out for each delta that was created prior to 1:00 PM on July 22, 1994.

```
$ prs -d :C:  -c94:07:22:12 -e s.dissertation
added abstract for chapter 4

date and time created 94/07/20 14:06:14 by alex
```

The next command prints out the following information for the most recent delta: The type of the delta, the date and time of creation, and the creator of the delta. **SPACE**s are used to separate the data items.

```
$ prs -d :DT: :D: :T: :P:  s.dissertation
D 94/07/22 14:10:45 alex
```

ps

Displays process status

Syntax: *ps [options] [process-list]*

Summary

The **ps** utility displays status information about active processes. When you run **ps** without any options, it displays the status of all active processes that your login device (terminal) controls. There are four columns, each with one of the following headings:

Heading	Meaning
PID	The identification number of the process.
TTY	**terminal** The device that controls the process.
TIME	The number of minutes and seconds the process has been running.
CMD	The command line the process was called with. The command is truncated to fit on one line.

Options

–a   **all**   Reports on most processes including some system processes. Normally **ps** reports only on your processes. Use the **–e** option to get a report on all processes.

–e   **every process**   Reports on all running processes.

–f   **full**   Generates a full listing. See the "Discussion" section for a description of all the columns that this option displays.

–l   **long**   Generates a long listing showing more information about each process. See the "Discussion" section for a description of all the columns that this option displays.

–o *format*   **output**   Formats list according to *format*. Refer to "DISPLAY FORMATS" in the **ps man** page for a discussion of this option.

–p *process-list*   Lists only information for processes named in the *process-list*, a comma- or SPACE-separated list of PID numbers.

–u *uid-list*   **username**   Lists only information for users listed in *uid-list* (as numerical user IDs or login names). With the **–f** option **ps** displays the login name to identify the user in the list; otherwise it uses the numerical User ID.

Notes

The Berkeley version of **ps** is available as **/usr/ucb/ps**. See page 672 for an example of Berkeley **ps**.

Discussion

The columns that **ps** displays depend on your choice of options. Except as noted, all of the columns in the following table are displayed by the **–f** and **–l** options.

Column Title	Meaning
F	**flags** The flags associated with the process. For historical purposes only (**–l** only).
S	**state** The state of the process as specified by one or more letters from the following list (**–l** only): **O** Running **R** Runnable: Available for execution (in the run queue) **S** Sleeping **T** Stopped: Either by a job control signal or being traced **Z** Zombie: process terminated without a waiting parent
UID	**user ID** The user ID of the person who owns the process. The **–f** option causes **ps** to display the user name in place of the numeric UID.
PID	**process ID** The process identification number of the process.
PPID	**parent PID** The process identification number of the parent process.
C	Obsolete.
STIME	The time the process started (**–f** only).
PRI	**priority** The priority of the process (**–l** only).
NI	**nice** Nice value. Used to figure out the priority of the process (**–l** only).
ADDR	**address** The memory address of the process (**–l** only).
SZ	The size of the process in virtual memory (in pages) (**–l** only).
WCHAN	**wait** If this process is sleeping, the address of the event that this process is waiting for. Blank if the process is running (**–l** only).
TTY	**terminal** The name of the device controlling the process.
TIME	The number of minutes and seconds that the process has been running.
CMD	The command line that started the process. This column is always displayed last on a line.

Examples

The first example shows **ps**, without any options, displaying the user's active processes (just the shell).

```
$ ps
   PID TTY      TIME CMD
   572 pts/5    0:00 sh
```

The **–f** (full) option shows more information about the processes, including the user's name, parent process ID, and the start time.

```
$ ps -f
    UID   PID  PPID  C     STIME TTY       TIME CMD
   alex   572   570  0 16:37:59 pts/5      0:00 -sh
```

With the **–l** (long) option, **ps** displays even more information about each of the processes substituting the user ID for the username and not including the start time.

```
$ ps -l
 F S   UID   PID  PPID  C PRI NI     ADDR    SZ  WCHAN TTY       TIME CMD
 8 R  1017   572   570  0  51 20 f5eee710   187        pts/5     0:00 sh
```

The next sequence of commands shows how to use **ps** to determine the process number of a process running in the background and how to terminate that process using **kill**. In this case it is not necessary to use **ps**, because the shell displays the process number of the background processes. The **ps** utility verifies the PID number.

The first command executes **find** in the background. The shell displays the job and PID number of the process, followed by a prompt.

```
$ find /home/alex -name memo -print >memo.out &
[1]     1715
$
```

Next **ps** confirms the PID number of the background task. If you did not already know this number, using **ps** would be the only way to find it out:

```
$ ps
  PID TTY       TIME CMD
  572 pts/5     0:00 ksh
 1715 pts/5     0:00 find
```

Finally **kill** (page 785) terminates the process:

```
$ kill 1715
$
[1]  + Terminated       find /home/alex --name memo -print >memo.out &
$
```

quot

Summarizes filesystem ownership information

Syntax: *quot [options] [filesystem]*

Summary

The **quot** utility reports who owns how many 1024-byte blocks of a given filesystem.

Argument

The *filesystem* is the name of the filesystem to report on. You must always use this argument except when you use the **–a** option.

Options

–a   **all**   Shows information on all mounted filesystems (do not use the *filesystem* argument with this option).

–c   **columns**   Lists all file sizes in order, starting with 0 blocks, 1 block, 2 blocks, and so on. Each line shows the number of blocks, the number of files that are that size, and the total number of blocks containing files that are that size or smaller (cumulative total). This option is mutually exclusive with **–f** and **–v**.

–f   **files**   Adds the number of files to the standard **quot** report.

–v   **verbose**   Gives three columns in addition to the usual output. The columns contain the number of blocks not accessed in the last 30, 60, and 90 days, respectively.

Notes

The **quot** utility is a supplement to **df** and a primitive disk accounting tool. Use it to find out which users are hogging disk space on your system. Files larger than 2048 blocks will be treated as 2048-block files, but the total block count will be correct. This utility can only be run by Superuser.

Examples

The following example shows the users in a medium-sized home directory filesystem. You can pipe this output through **sort –n** to get the listing sorted by number of blocks.

```
# /usr/sbin/quot /export/home1
/export/home1:
832210  bill
590836  bob
588069  hls
402867  juan
94479   jenny
55554   art
55186   alex
```

The next command lists the numbers of blocks and the number of files in the ten largest groups reported with the **–c** option.

```
# /usr/sbin/quot -c /export/home1 | tail
1864    1        1450530
1872    1        1452402
1888    2        1456178
1904    1        1458082
1928    2        1461938
1936    1        1463874
1960    8        1479554
1976    1        1481530
2016    1        1483546
2047    141      2943378
```

rcp

Copies one or more files to or from a remote computer

Syntax: *rcp [options] source-file destination-file*
rcp [options] source-file-list destination-directory

Summary

The **rcp** utility copies one or more ordinary files, including text and executable program files, between two computers that can communicate over a network. As with **cp**, **rcp** has two modes of operation: The first copies one file to another, and the second copies one or more files to a directory.

Arguments

The *source-file* is the pathname of the ordinary file that **rcp** will copy. To copy a file *from* a remote computer, precede *source-file* with the name of the remote computer system followed by a colon (**:**). The *destination-file* is the pathname that **rcp** assigns to the resulting copy of the file. To copy a file *to* a remote computer, precede *destination-file* with the name of the remote computer system followed by a colon (**:**).

The *source-file-list* is one or more pathnames of ordinary files that **rcp** will copy. When you use the **–r** option, the *source-file-list* can also contain directories. To copy files *from* a remote computer, precede each file's pathname in *source-file-list* with the name of the remote computer system followed by a colon (**:**). The *destination-directory* is the pathname of the directory in which **rcp** places the resulting copied files. To copy files *to* a remote computer, precede *destination-directory* with the name of the remote computer system followed by a colon (**:**).

Options

–p **preserve** Sets the modification times and file access permissions of each copied file to match those of the original *source-file*. Without this option **rcp** uses the current file-creation mask (**umask** on page 939) to modify the access permissions.

–r **recursive** Use this option only when the destination is a directory. If any of the files in the *source-file-list* is a directory, this option copies the contents of that directory and its subdirectories into the *destination-directory*. The subdirectories themselves are copied, as well as the files they contain.

Notes

You must have a login account on the remote computer to copy files to or from it using **rcp**. If the name of the *source-file* or *destination-file* does not include a full pathname, **rcp** assumes that the pathname is relative to your home directory on the remote machine.

The **rcp** utility does not prompt for a password; there are several alternative methods that **rcp** uses to verify that you have the authority to read or write files on the remote system. One common method requires that the name of your local computer be specified in a file named **/etc/hosts.equiv** on the remote computer. If the name of your computer is there, **rcp** allows you to copy files *if* your login names are the same on both

870

computers and your account on the remote computer has the necessary permissions to access files there. Another common way to authorize copying files to or from a remote computer is on a per-user basis. Each user's home directory can contain a file named **.rhosts** that lists trusted remote systems and users. With the second method your local and remote usernames do not have to match, but your local username must appear on the line in the remote **.rhosts** file that starts with the name of your local machine. See **rsh** on page 877 for details.

If you use a wildcard (such as ✻) in a remote filename, you must quote the pathname, so that the wildcard is interpreted by the shell on the remote computer (and not by the local shell). As with **cp**, if the *destination-file* exists before you execute **rcp**, **rcp** overwrites the file.

> ### .rhosts Is a Security Risk
>
> There is a security risk inherent in allowing users to make their own **.rhosts** files. Also, all data sent by **rcp** is sent cleartext across the network and can be intercepted easily.

Examples

The first example copies all the files with filenames ending in **.c** into the **archives** directory on the remote computer named **bravo**. Because the command does not specify the full pathname of the **archives** directory, **rcp** assumes that it is a subdirectory of the user's home directory on **bravo**. The copied files retain their simple filenames.

```
$ rcp ✻.c bravo:archives
```

The next example copies **memo** from the **/home/jenny** directory on **bravo** to the working directory on the local computer:

```
$ rcp bravo:/home/jenny/memo .
```

The next command copies two files named **memo.new** and **letter** to Jenny's home directory on the remote computer **bravo**. The absolute pathnames of the copied files on **bravo** are **/home/jenny/memo.new** and **/home/jenny/letter**.

```
$ rcp memo.new letter bravo:/home/jenny
```

The final command copies all the files in Jenny's **reports** directory, which is just under her home directory on **bravo,** to the **oldreports** directory on the local computer, preserving the original modification dates and file access permissions on the copies:

```
$ rcp -p 'jenny@bravo:reports/✻' oldreports
```

rlogin   Logs in on a remote computer

Syntax: *rlogin [option] hostname*

Summary

The **rlogin** utility establishes a login session on a remote computer over a network.

Argument

The *hostname* is the name of a computer that your system can reach over a network. The *hostname* can be the official name of the host or a nickname.

Option

−l *login-name*   **login** Logs you in on the remote computer as the user specified by *login-name* rather than as yourself.

Notes

A list of *hostnames* is stored in the hosts database, which is contained in one or more of the following locations: The **/etc/hosts** file, the Network Information Service (NIS) hosts map, and the Internet DNS (domain name server).

If the file named **/etc/hosts.equiv** located on the remote computer specifies the name of your local computer, the remote computer will not prompt you to enter your password. Computer systems that are listed in this file are considered as secure as your local machine.

An alternative way to specify a trusted relationship is on a per-user basis. Each user's home directory can contain a file named **.rhosts** that contains a list of trusted remote systems and users.

You can use **~.** at the beginning of a line to disconnect from the remote computer.

> ### .rhosts Is a Security Risk
>
> There is a security risk inherent in allowing users to make their own **.rhosts** files. Also, all data sent by **rlogin** is sent cleartext across the network and can be intercepted easily.

Examples

The following example illustrates the use of **rlogin**. On the local system Alex's login name is **alex**, but on the remote computer **bravo**, his login name is **watson**. The remote system prompts Alex to enter a password because he is logging in using a different username than the one he uses on the local system.

```
$ who am i
alex        tty06        Sep 14 13:26
$ rlogin -l watson bravo
Password:
```

If the local computer is named **hurrah**, a **.rhosts** file on **bravo** like the one below allows the user **alex** to log in as the user **watson** without entering a password:

```
$ cat /home/watson/.rhosts
hurrah alex
```

872

rm

Removes a file (deletes a link)

Syntax: *rm [options] file-list*

Summary

The **rm** utility removes both hard and symbolic links to one or more files. When you remove the last hard link to a file, you can no longer access the file, and the system releases the space the file occupied on the disk for use by another file (the file is deleted). For more information see "Links" on page 92.

    To delete a file you must have execute and write access permission to the parent directory of the file, but you do not need read or write access permission to the file itself.[8] If you are running **rm** interactively (that is, **rm**'s standard input is coming from your keyboard) and you do not have write access permission to the file, **rm** displays your access permission and waits for you to respond. If you enter **y**, **rm** deletes the file; otherwise it does not. If standard input is not coming from your keyboard, **rm** deletes the file without question.

> ### Be Careful When Using rm
>
> The **rm** utility is powerful: Make sure you know what you are deleting before giving an **rm** command. Each of the following options as well as the use of ambiguous file references in an **rm** command line can be deadly. When combined, the results can be catastrophic. The **–r** and **–f** options (see below) recursively force removal of files. The command **rm –rf** *, given from your home directory, can quickly remove *all* but your invisible files in and below your home directory. The results can be even worse if you are logged in as **root**. Be very careful when using this utility: Always review the command line before you press RETURN.

Argument

The *file-list* contains the list of files that **rm** deletes. The list can include ambiguous file references. Because you can remove a large number of files with a single command, use **rm** cautiously, especially when you are using an ambiguous file reference. If you are in doubt as to the effect of an **rm** command with an ambiguous file reference, use the **echo** utility with the same file reference first to evaluate the list of files the reference generates.

Options

–f   **force**   Removes files for which you do not have write access permission without asking for your consent. It also suppresses informative output if a file does not exist.

---

8. Subdirectories are an exception. You cannot use an **rm –r** command to remove a subdirectory that you do not own, even if you do own the parent directory.

–i	**interactive** Asks before removing each file. If you use **–r** with this option, **rm** also asks you before examining each directory.
–r	**recursive** Deletes the contents of the specified directory, including all its subdirectories, and the directory itself. Use this option cautiously.

Notes

The **/usr/xpg4/bin/rm** utility is a POSIX-compliant version of **rm**. Refer to "rm: Remove a Link" on page 98 for information about removing links. Refer to the **rmdir** utility (page 876) if you need to remove an empty directory. You can always use **rm –r** to remove an empty or populated directory.

When you want to remove a file that begins with a hyphen, you must prevent **rm** from interpreting the filename as an option. One way to do this is to give the special option **––** before the name of the file. The special option tells **rm** that no more options follow—arguments that come after it are filenames, even if they look like options.

Examples

The following command lines delete files, both in the working directory and in another directory:

```
$ rm memo
$ rm letter memo1 memo2
$ rm /home/jenny/temp
```

The next example asks the user before removing each file in the working directory and its subdirectories. This command is useful for removing filenames that contain special characters, especially SPACEs, TABs, and NEWLINEs. (You should never create filenames containing these characters on purpose, but it may happen accidentally.)

```
$ rm -ir .
```

rmdel

Removes a delta from an SCCS file

Syntax: *rmdel –rversion-number file-list*

Summary

The **rmdel** utility, part of SCCS (page 579), removes changes that were previously recorded in an SCCS file using **delta**. The **rmdel** utility will not remove a delta if there is an outstanding **get** (that is, a **get** for which the corresponding **delta** has not been done) on the specified delta. Also, **rmdel** will not remove a delta if it has a successor (that is, **rmdel** will only remove the newest delta on the trunk or on a branch).

To use **rmdel** you must be the owner of the SCCS file and the directory it is in, or the one who created the delta.

Argument

The *file-list* is a list of SCCS-encoded files, all of which start with **s.**. If the list includes directories, all files that begin with **s.** in the named directories are added to *file-list*. The **rmdel** utility removes the specified delta from all files in *file-list*. Any files in *file-list* that do not begin with **s.** or that are unreadable are ignored.

Option

–rversion-number **release** Mandatory. Specifies the full version number of the delta you want to remove. If the delta is a trunk delta, the version number contains two components (release.level). If the delta is a branch delta, it contains four components (release.level.branch.sequence).

Examples

The following command is applied to an SCCS file named **s.memo**. These deltas to the **s.memo** file exist:

```
1.1
1.2
2.1
2.1.1.1
2.2
2.2.1.1
2.2.1.2
3.1
```

The only deltas that can be removed using **rmdel** are 3.1 (the only trunk delta with no successors), 2.1.1.1, and 2.2.1.2. To use **rmdel** to remove branch delta 2.1.1.1, give the following command:[9]

```
$ rmdel -r2.1.1.1 s.memo
```

---

9. See the tip named "Making SCCS a Little More Friendly," page 581 and the following examples for information about using the **sccs** front end to help with file naming and placement.

rmdir

Removes a directory

Syntax: *rmdir **directory-list***

Summary

The **rmdir** utility deletes empty directories from the filesystem by removing links to those directories.

Argument

The ***directory-list*** contains pathnames of empty directories that **rmdir** removes.

Notes

Refer to the **rm** utility with the **–r** option if you need to remove directories that are not empty, together with their contents.

Examples

The following command line deletes the empty **literature** directory from the working directory:

```
$ rmdir literature
```

The next command line removes the **letters** directory using an absolute pathname:

```
$ rmdir /home/jenny/letters
```

Here is the message you get when you try to remove a directory that has files in it:

```
$ rmdir /home/jenny/notes
rmdir: notes: Directory not empty
```

rsh

Executes commands on a remote computer

Syntax: *rsh [option] hostname [command-line]*

Summary
The **rsh** utility runs *command-line* on *hostname* by starting a shell on the remote system and running the program you specify. If you omit *command-line*, **rsh** calls **rlogin**, which logs you in on the remote computer.

Arguments
The *hostname* is the name of the remote computer. Any arguments following *hostname* are part of *command-line*, which is run on the remote system. You must quote or escape shell special characters in *command-line* if you do not want them expanded by the local shell prior to passing them to **rsh**.

Option

–l *login-name*   If your login name on the remote computer is different than your local login name, you can use this option to give the remote login name.

Notes
See "Notes" on page 872 and the following "Examples" for a discussion of how to set up a remote login.

Examples
In the first example Alex uses **rsh** to obtain a list of the files in his home directory on **bravo**:

```
$ rsh bravo ls
Cost-of-living
Info
Work
preferences
```

In the second example the output of the previous command is redirected into the file **bravo.ls**. Because the redirection character **>** is not escaped, it is interpreted by the local shell, and the file **bravo.ls** is created on the local machine.

```
$ rsh bravo ls > bravo.ls
$ cat bravo.ls
Cost-of-living
Info
Work
preferences
```

The next example quotes the redirection character **>**. The file **bravo.ls** is created on the remote computer (**bravo**), as shown by **ls** run on **bravo**.

```
$ rsh bravo ls ">" bravo.ls
$ rsh bravo ls
Cost-of-living
Info
Work
bravo.ls
preferences
```

In the final example **rsh** without *command-line* logs in on the remote computer. Here Alex has used the **−l watson** option to log in on **bravo** as **watson**. The **/home/watson/.rhosts** file must be configured to allow Alex to log in on the account in this manner.

```
$ rsh -l watson bravo
Last login: Sat Jul 27 16:13:53 from :0.0
UNIX 2.0.18. (POSIX).
$ hostname
bravo
$ exit
rlogin: connection closed.
```

rwho

Displays names of users on computers attached to a network

Syntax: *rwho [option]*

Summary

The **rwho** utility displays the names of users currently logged in on computers attached to a local network, together with their device numbers, the times they logged in, and how much time has passed since they typed on their keyboards. By default **rwho** displays only the names of users who have typed on their keyboards in the past hour.

Option

−a   **all**   Displays the names of all users who are currently logged in, even if they have been idle for more than one hour.

Notes

The information displayed by **rwho** is broadcast on the network by the **rwhod** daemon, which is typically started by a run command script when the system is brought up. The **rwhod** daemon can create a lot of traffic on the network and may not be running at your site. If **rwho** displays no information, it is likely that **rwhod** is not running.

Example

The following example illustrates the use of **rwho**. The username appears in column 1, followed by the name of the computer and the device the user logged in from, and the time at which the user logged in. If the fourth column is blank, the user is actively typing at the keyboard; otherwise the fourth column indicates how many hours and minutes have passed since the user last typed on the keyboard.

```
$ rwho -a
watson    bravo:tty01     Sep 14 10:19
barbara   tcorp:pts/17    Sep 13 10:54   2:33
jenny     tcorp:pts/7     Sep 14 14:24    :01
```

879

sed

Edits a file (not interactively)

Syntax:

*sed [–n] –f **script-file** [file-list]*
*sed [–n] **script** [file-list]*

Summary

The **sed** (stream editor) utility is a batch (not interactive) text editor. The **sed** commands are usually stored in a *script-file* (first format), although you can give simple **sed** commands from the command line (second format). By default **sed** copies lines from the *file-list* to standard output, editing the lines in the process. It selects lines to be edited by position within the file (line number) or context (pattern matching).

The **sed** utility takes its input from files you specify on the command line or from standard input. Unless you redirect output from **sed**, it goes to standard output.

Arguments

The *script-file* is the pathname of a file containing a **sed** script (see "Discussion," below).

The *script* is a **sed** script, included on the command line. This format allows you to write simple, short **sed** scripts without creating a separate *script-file*.

The *file-list* contains pathnames of the ordinary files that **sed** processes. These are the input files. If you do not specify any files, **sed** takes its input from standard input.

Options

If you do not use the **–f** option, **sed** uses the first command-line argument as its script.

–f   **file**   Causes **sed** to read its script from the *script-file* given as the first command-line argument.

–n   **no print**   Causes **sed** not to copy lines to standard output except as specified by the Print (**p**) instruction or flag.

Notes

The **/usr/xpg4/bin/sed** utility is a POSIX-compliant version of **sed**.

Discussion

A **sed** script consists of one or more lines in the following format:

> *[address[, address]] instruction [argument-list]*

If you omit the *addresses,* **sed** processes all lines from the input file. The *addresses* select the line(s) the *instruction* part of the command operates on. The *instruction* is the editing instruction that modifies the text. The number and kinds of arguments in the *argument-list* depend on the instruction.

The **sed** utility processes an input file as follows:

1. **sed** reads one line from the input file (*file-list*).

2. **sed** reads the first command from the *script-file* (or command line), and, if the address selects the input line, **sed** acts on the input line as the *instruction* specifies.

3. **sed** reads the next command from the *script-file*. If the address selects the input line, **sed** acts on the input line (as possibly modified by the previous instruction) as the new *instruction* specifies.

4. **sed** repeats step 3 until it has executed all of the commands in the *script-file*.

5. If there is another line in the input file, **sed** starts over again with step 1; otherwise it is finished.

Addresses

A line number is an address that selects a line. As a special case, the line number **$** represents the last line of the last file in *file-list*.

A regular expression (refer to Appendix A) is an address that selects the lines that contain a string that the expression matches. Although slashes are often used to delimit regular expressions, **sed** permits you to use any character (you must quote those with special meaning to the shell).

Except as noted, zero, one, or two addresses (either line numbers or regular expressions) can precede an instruction. If you do not use an address, **sed** selects all lines, causing the instruction to act on every input line. One address causes the instruction to act on each input line that the address selects. Two addresses cause the instruction to act on groups of lines. The first address selects the first line in the first group. The second address selects the next subsequent line that it matches; this line is the last line in the first group. After **sed** selects the last line in a group, it starts the selection process over again, looking for the next line that the first address matches. This line is the first line in the next group. The **sed** utility continues this process until it has finished going through *file-list*.

Instructions

a   **append** The Append instruction appends one or more lines to the currently selected line. If you do not precede the Append command with an address, it appends to each input line from *file-list*. You cannot precede an Append instruction with two addresses. An Append command has the following format:

> *[address] a*\
> *text* \
> *text* \
> .
> .
> .
> *text*

You must end each line of appended text, except the last, with a backslash (the backslash quotes the following NEWLINE). The appended text concludes with a line that does not end with a backslash. The **sed** utility *always* writes out appended text, regardless of whether you set the **–n** flag on the command line. It even writes out the text if you delete the line to which you appended the text.

c   **change**   The Change instruction is similar to Append and Insert, except that it changes the selected lines so that they contain the new text. You can use this command with two addresses. If you specify an address range, Change replaces the entire range of lines with a single occurrence of the new text.

d   **delete**   The Delete instruction causes **sed** not to write out the lines it selects. It also causes **sed** not to finish processing the lines. After **sed** executes a Delete instruction, it reads the next input line from the *file-list* and begins over again with the first command in the *script-file*.

i   **insert**   The Insert instruction is identical to the Append instruction, except that it places the new text *before* the selected line.

n   **next**   The Next instruction reads the next input line from the *file-list*. It writes out the currently selected line, if appropriate, and starts processing the new line with the next command in the *script-file*.

p   **print**   The Print instruction writes the selected lines to standard output. It writes the lines immediately and does not reflect the effects of subsequent instructions. This instruction overrides the **–n** option on the command line.

q   **quit**   The Quit instruction causes **sed** to stop processing.

r *file*   **read**   The Read instruction reads the contents of *file* and appends it to the selected line. You cannot precede a Read instruction with two addresses. A single **SPACE** and the name of a file must follow a Read instruction.

s   **substitute**   The Substitute instruction is akin to that of **vi**. It has the following format:

> *[address[,address]]* **s**/*pattern*/*replacement-string*/[**g**][**p**][**w** *file*]

The *pattern* is a regular expression that is delimited by any character (quote characters with a special meaning to the shell); however slash (/) is traditionally used. The *replacement-string* starts immediately following the second delimiter and must be terminated by the same delimiter. The final (third) delimiter is required. The *replacement-string* can contain an ampersand (**&**), which **sed** replaces with the matched *pattern*. Unless you use the **g** flag, the Substitute instruction replaces only the first occurrence of the *pattern* on each selected line.

The **g** (global) flag causes the Substitute instruction to replace all nonoverlapping occurrences of the *pattern* on the selected lines.

The **p** (print) flag causes **sed** to send all lines on which it makes substitutions to standard output. This flag overrides the **–n** option on the command line.

The **w** (**write**) flag is similar to the **p** flag, except that it sends the output to a specified file. A single **SPACE** and the name of a file (*file*) must follow the write flag.

w *file*   **write**   This instruction is similar to the **p** instruction, except that it sends the output to a specified file. A single **SPACE** and the name of a file (*file*) must follow the Write instruction.

Control Structures

!   **NOT**   The NOT structure causes **sed** to apply the following instruction, located on the same line, to each of the lines *not* selected by the address portion of the command.

{ }   **group instructions**   When you enclose a group of instructions within a pair of braces, a single address (or address pair) selects the lines on which the group of instructions operates.

Examples

The following examples use the input file **new**:

```
$ cat new
Line one.
The second line.
The third.
This is line four.
Five.
This is the sixth sentence.
This is line seven.
Eighth and last.
```

Unless you instruct it not to, **sed** copies all lines, selected or not, to standard output. When you use the **–n** option on the command line, **sed** copies only selected lines.

The command line that follows displays all the lines in the **new** file that contain the word line (all lowercase). The command uses the address /line/, a regular expression. The **sed** utility selects each of the lines that contains a match for that pattern. The Print (**p**) instruction displays each of the selected lines.

```
$ sed '/line/ p' new
Line one.
The second line.
The second line.
The third.
This is line four.
This is line four.
Five.
This is the sixth sentence.
This is line seven.
This is line seven.
Eighth and last.
```

The preceding command does not use the **–n** option, so it displays all the lines in the input file at least once. It displays the selected lines an additional time because of the Print instruction.

The following command uses the **–n** option so that **sed** displays only the selected lines:

```
$ sed -n '/line/ p' new
The second line.
This is line four.
This is line seven.
```

Below, **sed** copies part of a file based on line numbers. The Print instruction selects and displays lines 3 through 6.

```
$ sed -n '3,6 p' new
The third.
This is line four.
Five.
This is the sixth sentence.
```

The command line below uses the Quit instruction to cause **sed** to display only the top of a file, in this case the first five lines of **new**. This enables you to look at the top of a file in the same way the **head** utility does.

```
$ sed '5 q' new
Line one.
The second line.
The third.
This is line four.
Five.
```

When you need to give **sed** more complex or lengthy commands, you can use a script file. The following script file (**print3_6**) and command line perform the same function as the command line in a previous example (**sed -n '3,6 p' new**):

```
$ cat print3_6
3,6 p

$ sed -n -f print3_6 new
The third.
This is line four.
Five.
This is the sixth sentence.
```

The following **sed** script, **append_demo**, demonstrates the Append instruction. The command in the script file selects line 2 and appends a NEWLINE and the text AFTER. to the selected line. Because the command line does not include the **–n** option, **sed** copies all the lines from the input file **new**.

```
$ cat append_demo
2 a\
AFTER.

$ sed -f append_demo new
Line one.
The second line.
AFTER.
The third.
This is line four.
Five.
This is the sixth sentence.
This is line seven.
Eighth and last.
```

The **insert_demo** script selects all the lines containing the string This and inserts a NEWLINE and the text BEFORE. before the selected lines.

```
$ cat insert_demo
/This/ i\
BEFORE.

$ sed -f insert_demo new
Line one.
The second line.
The third.
BEFORE.
This is line four.
Five.
BEFORE.
This is the sixth sentence.
BEFORE.
This is line seven.
Eighth and last.
```

The next example demonstrates a Change instruction with an address range. When you give a Change instruction a range of lines, it does not change each line within the range but changes the block of text to a single occurrence of the new text.

```
$ cat change_demo
2,4 c\
SED WILL INSERT THESE\
THREE LINES IN PLACE\
OF THE SELECTED LINES.

$ sed -f change_demo new
Line one.
SED WILL INSERT THESE
THREE LINES IN PLACE
OF THE SELECTED LINES.
Five.
This is the sixth sentence.
This is line seven.
Eighth and last.
```

The next example demonstrates a Substitute command. The **sed** utility selects all lines, because the command has no address. It replaces the first occurrence on each line of the string line with sentence and displays the resulting line. The **p** flag displays each line where a substitution occurs. The command line calls **sed** with the **–n** option, so **sed** only displays the lines that the script explicitly requests it to display. You can combine the **–n** and **–f** options following a single hyphen.

```
$ cat subs_demo
s/line/sentence/p

$ sed -nf subs_demo new
The second sentence.
This is sentence four.
This is sentence seven.
```

The next example is similar to the preceding one, except a **w** flag and filename (**temp**) at the end of the Substitute command cause **sed** to create the file **temp**. The command line does not include the **–n** option, so it displays all lines, including those that **sed** changes. The **cat** utility displays the contents of the file **temp**. The word Line (starting with an uppercase L) is not changed.

```
$ cat write_demo1
s/line/sentence/w temp

$ sed -f write_demo1 new
Line one.
The second sentence.
The third.
This is sentence four.
Five.
This is the sixth sentence.
This is sentence seven.
Eighth and last.

$ cat temp
The second sentence.
This is sentence four.
This is sentence seven.
```

The following is a Bourne Shell script named **sub** that changes all occurrences of REPORT to report, FILE to file, and PROCESS to process in a group of files. The **For** structure loops through the list of files supplied on the command line. (See page 405 for more information on the **For** structure.) As it processes each file, **sub** displays the filename before running **sed** on the file. This script uses a multiline embedded **sed** command—as long as the NEWLINEs within the command are quoted (that is, placed between single quotation marks), **sed** accepts the multiline command as though it appeared on a single command line. Each Substitute command includes a **g** (global) flag to take care of the case where one of the strings occurs more than one time on a line.

```
$ cat sub
for file
do
        echo $file
        mv $file $$.subhld
        sed 's/REPORT/report/g
            s/FILE/file/g
            s/PROCESS/process/g' $$.subhld > $file
done
rm $$.subhld

$ sub file1 file2 file3
file1
file2
file3
```

Following, **sed** uses the Write command to copy part of a file to another file (**temp2**). The line numbers 2 and 4, separated by a comma, select the range of lines **sed** is to copy. This script does not alter the lines.

```
$ cat write_demo2
2,4 w temp2

$ sed -n -f write_demo2 new

$ cat temp2
The second line.
The third.
This is line four.
```

The script **write_demo3** is very similar to **write_demo2**, except that it precedes the Write command with the NOT operator (!), causing **sed** to write to the file the lines *not* selected by the address.

```
$ cat write_demo3
2,4 !w temp3

$ sed -n -f write_demo3 new

$ cat temp3
Line one.
Five.
This is the sixth sentence.
This is line seven.
Eighth and last.
```

Following, **next_demo1** demonstrates the Next instruction. When **sed** processes the selected line (line 3), it immediately starts processing the next line, without printing line 3. Thus it does not display line 3.

```
$ cat next_demo1
3 n
p

$ sed -n -f next_demo1 new
Line one.
The second line.
This is line four.g
Five.
This is the sixth sentence.
This is line seven.
Eighth and last.
```

The next example uses a textual address. The sixth line contains the string the, so the Next command causes **sed** not to display it.

```
$ cat next_demo2
/the/ n
p

$ sed -n -f next_demo2 new
Line one.
The second line.
The third.
This is line four.
Five.
This is line seven.
Eighth and last.
```

The next set of examples uses the **compound.in** file to demonstrate how **sed** instructions work together:

```
$ cat compound.in
1. The words on this page...
2. The words on this page...
3. The words on this page...
4. The words on this page...
```

The first example that uses **compound.in** instructs **sed** to substitute the string `words` with `text` on lines 1, 2, and 3, and the string `text` with `TEXT` on lines 2, 3, and 4. It also selects and deletes line 3. The result is `text` on line 1, `TEXT` on line 2, no line 3, and `words` on line 4. The **sed** utility made two substitutions on lines 2 and 3: It substituted `text` for `words` and `TEXT` for `text`. Then it deleted line 3.

```
$ cat compound
1,3 s/words/text/
2,4 s/text/TEXT/
3 d
$ sed -f compound compound.in
1. The text on this page...
2. The TEXT on this page...
4. The words on this page...
```

The next example shows that the ordering of instructions within a **sed** script is critical. Both Substitute commands are applied to the second line, as in the previous example, but the order in which the substitutions occur changes the result.

```
$ cat compound2
2,4 s/text/TEXT/
1,3 s/words/text/
3 d

$ sed -f compound2 compound.in
1. The text on this page...
2. The text on this page...
4. The words on this page...
```

Below, **compound3** appends two lines to line 2. The **sed** utility displays all the lines from the file once, because no **–n** option appears on the command line. The Print instruction at the end of the script file displays line 3 an additional time.

```
$ cat compound3
2 a\
This is line 2a.\
This is line 2b.
3 p

$ sed -f compound3 compound.in
1. The words on this page...
2. The words on this page...
This is line 2a.
This is line 2b.
3. The words on this page...
3. The words on this page...
4. The words on this page...
```

The next example shows that **sed** always displays appended text. Here line 2 is deleted, but the Append instruction still displays the two lines that were appended to it. Appended lines are displayed even if you use the **–n** option on the command line.

```
$ cat compound4
2 a\
This is line 2a.\
This is line 2b.
2 d

$ sed -f compound4 compound.in
1. The words on this page...
This is line 2a.
This is line 2b.
3. The words on this page...
4. The words on this page...
```

The final examples use regular expressions in addresses. The regular expression in the command below (**^.**) matches one character at the beginning of a line (that is, it matches every line that is not empty). The replacement string (between the second and third slashes) contains a **TAB** character followed by an ampersand (**&**). The ampersand takes on the value of whatever the regular expression matched. This type of substitution is useful for indenting a file to create a left margin. See Appendix A for more information on regular expressions.

```
$ sed 's/^./    &/' new
        Line one.
        The second line.
        The third.
    .
    .
```

You may want to put the above **sed** command into a shell script so that you do not have to remember it (and retype it) every time you want to indent a file.

```
$ cat indent
sed 's/^./    &/' $*
$ chmod u+x indent
$ indent new
        Line one.
        The second line.
        The third.
    .
    .
    .
```

Generally when you create a **sed** command that you think you may want to use again, it is a good idea to put it into a shell script or a *script-file* to save yourself the effort of trying to reconstruct it.

In the following shell script, the regular expression (two **SPACE**s followed by an *∗$*) matches one or more spaces at the end of a line. It removes trailing spaces at the end of a line, which is useful for cleaning up files that you created using **vi**.

```
$ cat cleanup
sed 's/  *$//' $*
```

sleep

Creates a process that sleeps for a specified interval

Syntax: *sleep* ***time***

Summary

The **sleep** utility causes the process executing it to go to sleep for the specified number of seconds.

Argument

The *time* is the integer number of seconds you want the process to sleep for.

Examples

You can use **sleep** from the command line to execute a command after a period of time. The example below executes a process in the background that reminds you to make a phone call in 20 minutes (1200 seconds):

```
$ (sleep 1200; echo "Remember to make call.") &
[1] 4660
```

You can also use **sleep** within a shell script to execute a command at regular intervals. The following **per** shell script executes a program named **update** every 90 seconds:

```
$ cat per
#!/bin/sh
while true
do
    update
    sleep 90
done
```

If you execute a shell script such as **per** in the background, you can only terminate it with a **kill** command.

The final example shows a shell script that accepts the name of a file as an argument and waits for that file to appear on the disk. If the file does not exist, the script sleeps for 105 seconds before checking for the file again.

```
$ cat wait_for_file
#!/bin/sh

if [ $# != 1 ]; then
echo "Use: wait_for_file filename"
exit 1
fi

while true
do
if [ -f "$1" ]; then
echo "$1 is here now"
exit 0
fi
sleep 105
done
```

sort

Sorts and/or merges files

Syntax: *sort [options] [field-specifier-list] [file-list]*

Summary

The **sort** utility sorts and/or merges the lines of one or more text files based on sort fields you specify.

The **sort** utility takes its input from files you specify on the command line or from standard input. Unless you use the **–o** option, output from **sort** goes to standard output.

Arguments

The *field-specifier-list* specifies one or more sort fields within each line. The **sort** utility uses the sort fields to order the lines from the *file-list*, which contains pathnames of one or more ordinary files that hold the text to be sorted. The **sort** utility sorts and merges multiple files unless you use the **–m** option, in which case **sort** assumes the files are sorted and only merges the files. If you specify only one filename, it just sorts that file.

Options

If you do not specify an option, **sort** orders the file in the machine collating (frequently ASCII) sequence. (This is the internal order in which the computer sorts letters, numbers, and other characters. If the **LC_COLLATE** POSIX shell variable is present, it controls the order in which the computer sorts characters.) You can embed options within the *field-specifier-list* by following a field specifier with an option without a leading hyphen; see *sopt* and *eopt* in "Discussion," following.

–b   **blanks** Blanks (**TAB** and **SPACE** characters) are normally field delimiters in the input file. Unless you use this option, **sort** *also* considers leading blanks to be part of the field they precede. This option considers multiple blanks as single field delimiters with no intrinsic value, so **sort** does not consider these characters in sort comparisons.

–c   **check only** Checks to see that the file is sorted according to the specified options. The **sort** utility does not display anything if everything is in order. It displays a message and returns an exit status of 1 if the file is not in sorted order.

–d   **dictionary order** Ignores all characters that are not alphanumeric characters or blanks. For example with this option **sort** does not consider punctuation.

–f   **fold lowercase into uppercase** Considers all lowercase letters to be uppercase letters. Use this option when you are sorting a file that contains both upper- and lowercase text.

–i   **ignore** Ignores nonprinting characters when you perform a nonnumeric sort.

–k *sort-key*   **key** Defines a single field specifier. When you use more than one field specifier, you must precede each with **–k**. See "Discussion," following.

–m   **merge** Assumes that multiple input files are in sorted order and merges them without verifying that they are sorted.

–n	**numeric sort** When you use this option, minus signs and decimal points take on their arithmetic meaning and **sort** orders sort fields in arithmetic order. Without this option **sort** orders sort fields in the machine collating sequence.
–o *filename*	**output** Sends output to *filename* instead of standard output. Replace *filename* with a filename of your choice—it can be the same as one of the names in the *file-list.*
–r	**reverse** Reverses the sense of the sort (for example **z** precedes **a**).
–t *x*	**delimiter** Replaces *x* with the character that is the field delimiter in the input file. This character replaces SPACEs, which become regular (nondelimiting) characters.
–u	**unique** Outputs repeated lines only once. When you use the **–c** and **–u** options together, **sort** displays a message if the same line appears more than once in the input file, even if the file is in sorted order.

Notes

The **/usr/xpg4/bin/sort** utility is a POSIX-compliant version of **sort**.

Discussion

In the following description, a *field* is a sequence of characters on a line in an input file. These sequences are bounded by blanks (or other delimiter set with the **–t** option) and/or the beginning or end of the line. These fields are used to define sort fields.

A *sort field* is a sequence of characters that **sort** uses to put lines in order. A sort field can contain part or all of one or more fields in the input file. Refer to Figure III-2.

The *field-specifier-list* contains pairs of pointers that define subsections of each line (sort fields) for comparison. Each *field-specifier* is a set of argu-

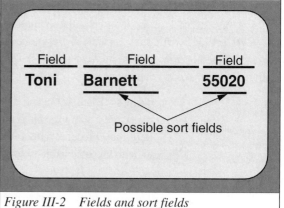

Figure III-2   *Fields and sort fields*

ments to a **–k** option on the command line and has the following syntax:

   –k start-field[.first-char] [sopt] [,stop-field[.last-char] [eopt]]

where *start-field* specifies the starting sort field with 1 being the first column, 2 the second, and so forth. A *start-field* of 1 (one) tells **sort** to start the comparison at the beginning of the line. The field separator is a SPACE character unless you use the **–t** option.

The *first-char* specifies the first character of the *start-field* to use for the comparison. Without a *first-char*, **sort** starts at the beginning of the *start-field*. A *first-char* of 3 tells **sort** to start with the third character of the *sort-field*.

The *sopt* is one or more options chosen from **b, d, f, i, n,** or **r**. Except for **b**, these options perform the same functions as their hyphen-preceded counterparts whether they appear in the *sopt, eopt,* or both positions. The **b** option applies to the *start-* or *stop-field* element it is adjacent to.

The *stop-field*, *last-char*, and *eopt* specifiers perform analogous functions in specifying the ending of the sort field: The *stop-field* and *last-char* specify the end of the sort comparison field, whereas the *eopt* performs as described above.

The **–b** option (and the **b** *sopt*/*eopt*) causes **sort** to count multiple leading blanks as a *single* field delimiter character. If you do not use this option, **sort** considers each leading blank to be a character in the sort field and includes it in the sort comparison.

If you specify more than one sort field, **sort** examines them in the order you specify them on the command line. If the first sort field of two lines is the same, **sort** examines the second sort field. If these are again the same, **sort** looks at the third field. This process continues for all the sort fields you specify. If all the sort fields are the same, **sort** examines the entire line.

If you do not use any options or arguments, the sort is based on entire lines.

Start Optional

Older versions of **sort** used a different scheme to specify sort fields. The version of **sort** included with Solaris 2.6 and later supports this older scheme although it is obsolete. This optional section describes the older scheme.

Instead of a *field-specifier* following a **–k** option, it is formed by a pair of pointers that stand as arguments on the command line. A pointer is in the form ±**f.c**. The first of each pair of pointers begins with a plus sign, and the second begins with a hyphen or minus sign.

You can make a pointer point to any character on a line. Pointers having the form ±**f.c** skip **f** fields plus an additional **c** characters. The plus sign that precedes the first of each pair of pointers indicates that all characters to the right of the pointer, up to the other pointer in the pair, are to be included in the sort field. If there is no second pointer in the pair, all characters up to the end of the line are included. The hyphen or minus sign that precedes the second pointer in the pair indicates that all characters to the left of the pointer, back to the first pointer in the pair, are to be included in the sort field.

You can specify options that pertain only to a given sort field by immediately following the field specifier by one of the options **b**, **d**, **f**, **i**, **n**, or **r** *not* preceded with a hyphen.

Stop Optional

Examples

The examples in this section demonstrate some of the features and uses of the **sort** utility. The examples assume that a file named **list**, shown on the following page, is in the working directory. This file contains a list of names and zip codes. Each line of the file contains three fields: The first name field, the last name field, and the zip code field. For the examples to work, make sure all the blanks in the file are SPACEs, and not TABs.

```
$ cat list
Tom Winstrom       94201
Janet Dempsey      94111
Alice MacLeod      94114
David Mack         94114
Toni Barnett       95020
Jack Cooper        94072
Richard MacDonald  95510
```

The first example demonstrates **sort** without any options or arguments other than a filename. Below, **sort** sorts the file on a line-by-line basis. If the first characters on two lines are the same, **sort** looks at the second characters to determine the proper sorted order. If the second characters are the same, **sort** looks at the third characters. This process continues until **sort** finds a character that differs between the lines. If the lines are identical, it does not matter which one **sort** puts first. In this example **sort** needs to examine only the first three letters (at most) of each line. The **sort** utility displays a list that is in alphabetical order by first name.

```
$ sort list
Alice MacLeod        94114
David Mack           94114
Jack Cooper          94072
Janet Dempsey        94111
Richard MacDonald    95510
Tom Winstrom         94201
Toni Barnett         95020
```

You can instruct **sort** to perform its comparison on any field and character on a line. Blanks normally separate one field from another. The next example sorts the same list by last name, the second field. The **–k 2** argument indicates that **sort** is to begin its comparison with the second field. Because there is no *stop-field*, the sort field extends to the end of the line. Now the list is almost in last-name order, but there is a problem with Mac.

```
$ sort -k 2 list
Toni Barnett         95020
Jack Cooper          94072
Janet Dempsey        94111
Richard MacDonald    95510
Alice MacLeod        94114
David Mack           94114
Tom Winstrom         94201
```

In the example above, MacLeod comes before Mack. After finding that the sort fields of these two lines are the same through the third letter (Mac), **sort** put L before k, because it arranges lines in the order of character codes. In the ASCII codes, uppercase letters come before lowercase.

The **f** option makes **sort** treat upper- and lowercase letters as equals and thus fixes the problem with MacLeod and Mack.

```
$ sort -k 2f list
Toni Barnett         95020
Jack Cooper          94072
Janet Dempsey        94111
Richard MacDonald    95510
David Mack           94114
Alice MacLeod        94114
Tom Winstrom         94201
```

The next example attempts to sort list on the third field, the zip code. Following, **sort** does not put the numbers in order but puts the shortest name first and the longest name last. With the argument of **–k 3**, **sort** compares the third field of each line. The third field starts just after the first delimiter (**SPACE**) following the second field. Thus **sort** counts the SPACEs after the second field (last name) as part of the sort field. The ASCII value of a SPACE character is less than that of any other printable character, so **sort** puts the zip code that is preceded by the greatest number of SPACEs first and the zip code that is preceded by the fewest SPACEs last.

```
$ sort -k 3 list
David Mack            94114
Jack Cooper           94072
Tom Winstrom          94201
Toni Barnett          95020
Janet Dempsey         94111
Alice MacLeod         94114
Richard MacDonald     95510
```

The **b** option causes **sort** to ignore leading SPACEs. With the **b** option the zip codes come out in the proper order, as shown below. When **sort** determines that MacLeod and Mack have the same zip codes, it compares the entire lines, putting Alice MacLeod before David Mack (because A comes before D).

```
$ sort -k 3b list
Jack Cooper           94072
Janet Dempsey         94111
Alice MacLeod         94114
David Mack            94114
Tom Winstrom          94201
Toni Barnett          95020
Richard MacDonald     95510
```

To sort alphabetically by last name when zip codes are the same, **sort** needs to make a second pass that sorts on the last name field. The next example shows how to make this second pass by specifying a second sort field and uses the **f** option to keep the Mack/MacLeod problem from cropping up again.

```
$ sort -k 3b -k 2f list
Jack Cooper           94072
Janet Dempsey         94111
David Mack            94114
Alice MacLeod         94114
Tom Winstrom          94201
Toni Barnett          95020
Richard MacDonald     95510
```

The next example shows a **sort** command that not only skips fields but skips characters as well. The **3.4** causes **sort** to start its comparison on the fourth character of the third field. Because the command does not specify an end to the sort field, **sort** assumes that it is the end of the line. The sort field is the last two digits in the zip code.

```
$ sort -k 3.4fb list
Tom Winstrom          94201
Richard MacDonald     95510
Janet Dempsey         94111
Alice MacLeod         94114
David Mack            94114
Toni Barnett          95020
Jack Cooper           94072
```

The problem of how to sort by last name within zip code is solved by a second pass covering the last name field. Although the second element in the pair of pointers for the second pass is not necessary (you already know that the zip codes match from the first pass) it is included for its instructional value. A third pass, in case zip code and last names are the same, is not required and not included. If the second pass does not yield a difference between compared fields, **sort** compares entire lines so it automatically sorts on first name within last name.

```
$ sort -k 3.4b -k 2,2f list
Tom Winstrom          94201
Richard MacDonald     95510
Janet Dempsey         94111
David Mack            94114
Alice MacLeod         94114
Toni Barnett          95020
Jack Cooper           94072
```

The next set of examples uses the **cars** data file. From left to right the columns in the file contain each car's make, model, year of manufacture, mileage, and price.

```
$ cat cars
plym     fury     97     73      2500
chevy    nova     99     60      3000
ford     mustang  75     45      10000
volvo    gl       88     102     9850
ford     ltd      93     15      10500
chevy    nova     90     50      3500
fiat     600      75     115     450
honda    accord   91     30      6000
ford     thundbd  94     10      17000
toyota   tercel   92     180     750
chevy    impala   75     85      1550
ford     bronco   93     25      9500
```

Without any options **sort** displays a sorted copy of the file.

```
$ sort cars
chevy    impala   75     85      1550
chevy    nova     90     50      3500
chevy    nova     99     60      3000
fiat     600      75     115     450
ford     bronco   93     25      9500
ford     ltd      93     15      10500
ford     mustang  75     45      10000
ford     thundbd  94     10      17000
honda    accord   91     30      6000
plym     fury     97     73      2500
toyota   tercel   92     180     750
volvo    gl       88     102     9850
```

Unless you specify otherwise, a sort field extends to the end of the line. To sort from the beginning of the line (and start with the first field), use a **–k 1** sort field specifier as shown in the next example. The next example also shows one problem to avoid when you are using **sort**. In this example the objective is to sort by manufacturer and then by price within manufacturer. The command line instructs **sort** to sort on the entire line (**–k 1**) and then make a second pass, sorting on the fifth field (price) all lines whose first-pass sort fields were the same (**–k 5**). Because no two lines are the same, **sort** makes only one pass, sorting on each entire line. (If two lines differed only in the fifth field, they would be sorted properly on the first pass anyway, so the second pass would be unnecessary.) Look at the lines with the ltd and mustang. They are sorted by the second field rather than the fifth, demonstrating that **sort** never made a second pass and never sorted by the fifth field.

```
$ sort -k 1 -k 5 cars
chevy    impala   75       85       1550
chevy    nova     90       50       3500
chevy    nova     99       60       3000
fiat     600      75       115      450
ford     bronco   93       25       9500
ford     ltd      93       15       10500
ford     mustang 75       45       10000
ford     thundbd 94       10       17000
honda    accord   91       30       6000
plym     fury     97       73       2500
toyota   tercel   92       180      750
volvo    gl       88       102      9850
```

The next example forces the first-pass sort to stop just before the second field by defining the end of the first sort field (**,1**). Now the ltd and mustang are properly sorted by price. But look at the bronco. It is less expensive than the other Fords, but **sort** has it positioned as the most expensive. The **sort** utility put the list in ASCII collating sequence order, not numeric order: 9500 comes after 17000 because 9 comes after 1.

```
$ sort -k 1,1 -k 5 cars
chevy    impala   75       85       1550
chevy    nova     99       60       3000
chevy    nova     90       50       3500
fiat     600      75       115      450
ford     mustang 75       45       10000
ford     ltd      93       15       10500
ford     thundbd 94       10       17000
ford     bronco   93       25       9500
honda    accord   91       30       6000
plym     fury     97       73       2500
toyota   tercel   92       180      750
volvo    gl       88       102      9850
```

The **n** (numeric) option on the second pass puts the list in the proper order.

```
$ sort -k 1,1 -k 5n cars
chevy    impala   75        85       1550
chevy    nova     99        60       3000
chevy    nova     90        50       3500
fiat     600      75        115      450
ford     bronco   93        25       9500
ford     mustang  75        45       10000
ford     ltd      93        15       10500
ford     thundbd  94        10       17000
honda    accord   91        30       6000
plym     fury     97        73       2500
toyota   tercel   92        180      750
volvo    gl       88        102      9850
```

The next example again shows that, unless you instruct it otherwise, **sort** orders a file starting with the field you specify and continuing to the end of the line. It does not make a second pass unless two of the first sort fields are the same. Although this example sorts the cars by years, it does not sort the cars by manufacturer within years.

```
$ sort -k 3 -k 1 cars
fiat     600      75        115      450
ford     mustang  75        45       10000
chevy    impala   75        85       1550
volvo    gl       88        102      9850
chevy    nova     90        50       3500
honda    accord   91        30       6000
toyota   tercel   92        180      750
ford     ltd      93        15       10500
ford     bronco   93        25       9500
ford     thundbd  94        10       17000
plym     fury     97        73       2500
chevy    nova     99        60       3000
```

Specifying an end to the sort field for the first pass allows **sort** to perform its secondary sort properly.

```
$ sort -k 3,3 -k 1 cars
chevy    impala   75        85       1550
fiat     600      75        115      450
ford     mustang  75        45       10000
volvo    gl       88        102      9850
chevy    nova     90        50       3500
honda    accord   91        30       6000
toyota   tercel   92        180      750
ford     bronco   93        25       9500
ford     ltd      93        15       10500
ford     thundbd  94        10       17000
plym     fury     97        73       2500
chevy    nova     99        60       3000
```

The next examples demonstrate an important sorting technique: Putting a list in alphabetical order, merging upper- and lowercase entries, and eliminating duplicates. The unsorted list is

```
$ cat short
Pear
Pear
apple
pear
Apple
```

The following is a plain sort:

```
$ sort short
Apple
Pear
Pear
apple
pear
```

The following folded sort is a good start, but it does not eliminate duplicates:

```
$ sort -f short
Apple
apple
Pear
Pear
pear
```

The **–u** (unique) option eliminates duplicates but causes all the uppercase entries to come first.

```
$ sort -u short
Apple
Pear
apple
pear
```

When you attempt to use both **–u** and **–f**, some entries get lost.

```
$ sort -uf short
Apple
pear
```

Two passes is the answer. Both passes are unique sorts, and the first folds uppercase letters onto lowercase ones.

```
$ sort -u -k 1f -k 1 short
Apple
apple
Pear
pear
```

spell

Checks a file for spelling errors

Syntax: *spell [options] [+local-file] [file-list]*

Summary

The **spell** utility checks the words in a file against a dictionary file. It displays a list of words that it cannot either find in the dictionary or derive from one of the words in the dictionary. This utility takes its input from files you specify on the command line or from standard input. You can set up an auxiliary custom dictionary.

Arguments

The *file-list* is a list of files that **spell** checks. If you specify more than one file, **spell** generates one list of words for all the files.

The *+local-file* is a file containing a sorted list of words, one word per line. The **spell** utility removes the words in *local-file* from its output. The *local-file* supplements the standard dictionary with additional words that are correctly spelled. It is useful for removing proper names and technical terms from the output of **spell**.

Options

–b   **British**   Accepts British spellings.

–v   Displays all words that are not literally in the dictionary. As the example on the next page shows, it gives a proposed derivation for any word **spell** would normally accept.

Notes

The **spell** utility is not a foolproof way of finding spelling errors. It also does not check for misused but properly spelled words (for example *read* instead of *red*). The spell utility uses a list of only about 25,000 words (**/usr/share/lib/dict/words**) and is therefore of limited use.

Examples

The following examples use **spell** to check the spelling in the **check** file. The **–v** option causes **spell** to display all words that are not actually in its dictionary.

```
$ cat check
Here's a sampel document that is tobe
used with th Spell utilitey.
It obviously needs proofing quite badly.

$ spell check
sampel
```

```
th
tobe
utilitey

$ spell -v check
sampel
th
tobe
utilitey
+ly     badly
+'s     Here's
+s      needs
+ly     obviously
+ing    proofing
+d      used
```

stty
Displays or sets terminal/emulator parameters

Syntax: *stty [options] [arguments]*

Summary

Without any arguments **stty** displays certain parameters affecting the operation of the terminal/emulator. For a list of some of these parameters and an explanation of each, see "Arguments," below. The arguments establish or change the parameter(s) you specify.

Arguments

The arguments to **stty** specify which parameters **stty** is to alter. You can turn on each of the parameters that is preceded by an optional hyphen (indicated in the following list as [–]) by specifying the parameter without the hyphen. You can turn it off by specifying it with the hyphen. Unless specified otherwise, this section describes the parameters in their *on* states.

Special Keys and Characteristics

columns *n*	Sets the line (window) width to *n* columns.
ek	**erase & kill** Sets the erase and line kill keys to their default values (**DELETE** and **CONTROL-U**).
erase *x*	Sets the erase key to *x*.[10]
intr *x*	Sets the interrupt key to *x*.[10]
kill *x*	Sets the kill key to *x*.[10]
rows *n*	Sets the number of rows on the screen (window) to *n*.
sane	Sets the parameters to values that are usually acceptable. The **sane** argument is useful when several **stty** parameters have changed, making it difficult to use the terminal/emulator even to run **stty** to set things right. If **sane** does not appear to work, try entering
	`CONTROL-J stty sane CONTROL-J`
werase *x*	Sets the word erase key to *x*. See footnote 10 on page 902.

---

10. To specify a control character, just type the control character. If you want to make the **BACKSPACE** key the erase key, give the command **stty erase** and then press the **BACKSPACE** key. To make **CONTROL-C** the interrupt key, give the command **stty intr** and then press **CONTROL-C**. To make **CONTROL-U** the kill key, give the command **stty kill** and then press **CONTROL-U**. If the **CONTROL** key you want to use already has a function (other than the one you are trying to use it for), give a command such as **stty erase '^h'** where ^h is two characters: A caret and an h. The quotation marks are required.

Modes of Data Transmission

[–]cstopb Selects two stop bits (**–cstopb** specifies one stop bit).

[–]parenb **parity enable** Turns parity on. When you specify **–parenb**, the system does not use or expect a parity bit when communicating with a device.

[–]parodd Selects odd parity (**–parodd** selects even parity).

[–]raw The normal state is **–raw**. When the system reads input in its raw form, it does not interpret the following special characters: Erase (usually **DELETE**), line kill (usually **CONTROL-U**), interrupt execution (**CONTROL-C**), and EOF (**CONTROL-D**). In addition it does not use parity bits. With humor typical of UNIX's heritage, you can specify **–raw** as **cooked**.

Treatment of Characters

[–]echo Echoes characters as they are typed (full duplex operation). If a device is half duplex and displays two characters for each one it should display, turn the **echo** parameter off (**–echo**).

[–]echoe The normal setting is **echoe**, which causes Solaris to send the character sequence **BACKSPACE SPACE BACKSPACE** when you use the erase key to delete a character. The effect is to move the cursor backwards across the line, removing characters as you delete them.

[–]echoke The normal setting is **echoke**. When you use the kill character to delete a line while this option is set, all characters back to the prompt are erased on the current line. If this option is cleared, then pressing the kill key moves the cursor to the beginning of the next line instead.

[–]echoprt The normal setting is **–echoprt**, meaning erased characters are not echoed. If you set **echoprt**, characters that you erase are shown between a backslash (\) and a slash (/) as you erase them. For example if you type the word `sort` and then erase it by pressing **BACKSPACE** four times, you see `sort\tros/` when **echoprt** is set. Also, if you use the kill character to delete the entire line, having **echoprt** set causes the entire line to be displayed as if you had **BACKSPAC**ed to the beginning of the line.

[–]lcase For uppercase-only terminals, translates all uppercase characters into lowercase as they are entered (also [–]**LCASE**). A throwback to the old days.

[–]nl Accepts only a **NEWLINE** character as a line terminator. With **–nl** in effect the system accepts a **RETURN** character from the keyboard as a **NEWLINE**, while it sends a **RETURN** followed by a **NEWLINE** to the screen in place of a **NEWLINE**.

[–]tabs Transmits each **TAB** character to the screen as a **TAB** character. When **tabs** is turned off (**–tabs**), the system translates each **TAB** character into the appropriate number of **SPACE**s and transmits these **SPACE**s to the screen (also [–]**tab3**).

Job-Control Parameters

dsusp *x*   Sets the suspend-when-job-requests-input key to *x*. See footnote 10 on page 902.

susp *x*   Sets the suspend key to *x*. See footnote 10 on page 902.

[–]tostop   Stops background jobs if they attempt to send output to the screen (**–tostop** allows background jobs to send output to the screen).

Options

Without an option or argument, **stty** displays a summary report that includes only a few of its parameters.

–a   **all**   Reports on all parameters.

–g   **generate report**   Generates a report of the current settings in a format you can use as arguments to another **stty** command.

Notes

The **/usr/xpg4/bin/stty** utility is a POSIX-compliant version of **stty**.

The **sh**, **csh**, and **ksh** shells all retain some control over standard input if you are using the shell interactively (for example with your login shell). This control means that a number of the options available with **stty** appear to have no effect. For example the command **stty –echo** appears to have no effect under **ksh**.

```
% stty -echo
% date
Tue Jul 15 15:36 PDT 1997
```

Also, although **stty –echo** does work when using **sh** interactively, **stty –echoe** does not. You can, however, still use these options to affect scripts and other utilities.

```
$ cat testit
#!/bin/ksh
stty -echo
echo "Enter a value: \c"
read a
echo "You entered: $a"
stty echo
$ testit
Enter a value: You entered: this is a value
```

In the above example the input typed at the Enter a value: prompt is not displayed as it is typed. The value is, however, retained by the **a** variable and is displayed by the echo "You entered: $a" statement.

You can always change the values of the special characters, such as kill and erase.

The **stty** utility affects the keyboard attached to standard input. You can view or change the characteristics of a device other than the one you are using by redirecting the input to **stty**:

*stty [**arguments**] < /dev/**ttyxx***

The *ttyxx* is the filename of the target device. You can change the characteristics of a device only if you own its device file or if you are Superuser.

Examples

The first example shows **stty** without any arguments, displaying several display parameters. (Your system may display more or different parameters.) The character following the erase = is the erase key. A ^ preceding a character indicates a **CONTROL** key. In the example the erase key is set to **CONTROL-H**.

If **stty** does not display the erase character, it is set to its default value, **DELETE**. If you do not see a kill character, it is set to its default, ^U.

```
$ stty
speed 38400 baud; -parity
rows = 24; columns = 80; ypixels = 0; xpixels = 0;
erase = ^h; swtch = <undef>;
brkint -inpck -istrip icrnl -ixany imaxbel onlcr tab3
echo echoe echok echoctl iexten
```

Next **ek** returns the erase and line kill keys to their default values:

```
$ stty ek
```

The next display verifies the change. The **stty** utility does not display either the erase character or the line kill character, indicating that they are both set to their default values.

```
$ stty
speed 38400 baud; -parity
rows = 24; columns = 80; ypixels = 0; xpixels = 0;
swtch = <undef>;
brkint -inpck -istrip icrnl -ixany imaxbel onlcr tab3
echo echoe echok echoctl iexten
```

The next example uses a **CONTROL-H** character to set the erase key. See footnote 10 on page 902.

```
$ stty erase '^H'
$ stty
speed 38400 baud; -parity
rows = 24; columns = 80; ypixels = 0; xpixels = 0;
erase = ^h; swtch = <undef>;
brkint -inpck -istrip icrnl -ixany imaxbel onlcr tab3
echo echoe echok echoctl iexten
```

Below, **stty** sets the line kill key to **CONTROL-X**. This time the user entered a caret (^) followed by an **x** to represent **CONTROL-X**. You can use either a lower- or uppercase letter and must include the quotation marks.

```
$ stty kill '^x'
$ stty
speed 38400 baud; -parity
rows = 24; columns = 80; ypixels = 0; xpixels = 0;
erase = ^h; kill = ^x; swtch = <undef>;
brkint -inpck -istrip icrnl -ixany imaxbel onlcr tab3
echo echoe echok echoctl iexten
```

Below, **stty** turns off TABs so the appropriate number of SPACEs is sent to the screen in place of a TAB. Use this command if a terminal/emulator does not automatically expand TABs.

```
$ stty -tabs
```

If you log in and everything that appears on the screen is in uppercase letters, give the following command and then check the CAPS LOCK key. If it is set, turn it off.

```
$ STTY -LCASE
```

swap   Administrates swap space

Syntax: *swap [options] [swapname] [swaplow] [swaplen]*

Summary
The **swap** utility adds to, deletes from, lists the status of, and summarizes the use of swap space.

Arguments
The *swapname* specifies the name of a swapfile created by **mkfile**, or the path of a raw disk partition to be used as swap space. The *swaplow* argument is the offset from the beginning of the file in 512-byte blocks where swapping is to start (**–a**) or end (**–d**). The *swaplen* argument specifies the length of the swap area in 512-byte blocks. The *swaplen + swaplow* must be less than or equal to the size of the file or partition. If neither *swaplen* nor *swaplow* are specified, the entire file or partition is used except for the first page (see "Discussion" following).

Options

–a *name*   **add**   Adds the *name* file or partition to the system swap area.

–d *name*   **delete**   Deletes the *name* file or partition from the system swap area. Pages currently in use are moved to other swap areas. It is safe to delete the *name* file when **swap** finishes executing.

–l   **list**   Displays all system swap areas currently in use in a five-column tabular format. The columns are:

Column Heading	Meaning
swapfile	Location of the swap area.
dev	Major and minor numbers of the raw device (not used for files).
swaplow	Swaplow value for the swap area.
blocks	Swaplen value for the swap area.
free	Unallocated 512-byte blocks in the swap area.

–s   **summary**   Displays summary information about system swap space. The following table clarifies the summary results:

Label	Meaning
allocated	The number of 1024-byte blocks of swap space that are currently in use on all swap areas.
reserved	The number of 1024-byte blocks of swap space that is not currently allocated but that have been reserved by processes for future allocation.

Label	Meaning
used	The sum of the allocated and reserved values.
available	The number of 1024-byte blocks of swap space that is neither allocated nor reserved.

Discussion

The first page[11] of the swap area is never used, making it safe to have a swap area that starts at cylinder 0 of a disk. Although the partition table and other housekeeping data is kept in this cylinder, the virtual memory subsystem (page 618) will not overwrite this important data because it skips the first page.

Examples

The following example adds a file, **/scratch/swap1**, to the system swap space. This file was previously created with **mkfile** (page 814).

```
# swap -a /scratch/swap1
```

The next example lists three swap areas: Two on local hard drives and one on a file (created when memory becomes short).

```
# swap -l
swapfile              dev   swaplo blocks    free
/dev/dsk/c0t0d0s1     32,1      16 410384  366016
/dev/dsk/c0t1d0s1     32,9      16 307424  264192
/export/swap1          -        16 102384  102384
```

The next example deletes the **/export/swap1** swap area and then deletes the file:

```
# swap -d /export/swap1
# rm /export/swap1
```

The final example summarizes current swap information:

```
# swap -s
total: 62952k bytes allocated + 14376k reserved = 77328k used, 812632k available
```

---

11. The size of this page depends on the hardware you are using. It is typically in the 2K to 4K range.

tail

Displays the last part of a file

Syntax: *tail [options] [file-list]*

Summary

The **tail** utility displays the last part, or end, of a file. It takes its input from one or more files you specify on the command line or from standard input.

Argument

The *file-list* contains pathnames of the files that **tail** displays. If you specify more than one file, **tail** displays the filename of each file before it displays the lines of the file. If you do not specify any files, **tail** takes its input from standard input.

Options

±n[x]   Specifies units and direction of counting. If you omit *x*, the unit of counting is lines. The unit, represented by *x*, can be b (blocks), c (characters), or l (lines—the default). Although it is not a unit, you can replace *x* with r for a listing in reverse order. The *n* is the number of units you want tail to count. You can put a plus sign (+) in front of *n* to cause **tail** to count from the start of the file instead of the end. You will get an error message if you do not include a sign. You cannot use this form of **tail** with any other options.

−b   **blocks**   Counts by blocks.

−c   **characters**   Counts by bytes (characters).

−f   **follow**   After copying the last line of the file, **tail** enters an endless loop. It waits and copies additional lines from the file if it grows. This option is useful for tracking the progress of a process that is running in the background and sending its output to a file. The **tail** utility waits indefinitely; you must use the interrupt key or **kill** command to terminate it.

−l   **lines**   Counts by lines

−r   **reverse**   Displays lines in reverse order from the starting point you specify. By default this option displays the entire file in reverse order.

Notes

The **/usr/xpg4/bin/tail** utility is a POSIX-compliant version of **tail**. The **tail** utility displays ten lines by default.

Examples

The examples are based on the following **eleven** file:

```
$ cat eleven
line one
line two
line three
line four
line five
line six
line seven
line eight
line nine
line ten
line eleven
```

First **tail** displays the last ten lines of the **eleven** file (no options):

```
$ tail eleven
line two
line three
line four
line five
line six
line seven
line eight
line nine
line ten
line eleven
```

The next example displays the last three lines (**−3**) of the file:

```
$ tail -3 eleven
line nine
line ten
line eleven
```

The example below displays the file, starting at line eight (**+8**):

```
$ tail +8 eleven
line eight
line nine
line ten
line eleven
```

The next example displays the last six characters in the file (**−c6**). Only five characters are evident (leven); the sixth is a **NEWLINE**.

```
$ tail -6c eleven
leven
```

The final example demonstrates the **–f** option. Below, **tail** tracks the output of a **make** command, which is going to **accounts.out**:

```
$ make accounts > accounts.out &
$ tail -f accounts.out
       cc -c trans.c
       cc -c reports.c
 .
 .
 .
CONTROL-C
$
```

In the example above, using **tail** with **–f** has the same effect as running **make** in the foreground and letting its output go to the screen; however using **tail** has some advantages. First the output of **make** is saved in a file. (The output would not be saved if you simply let it go to the screen.) Also, if you decide to do something else while **make** is running, you can kill **tail**, and the screen will be free for you to use while **make** continues in the background. When you are running a large job, such as compiling a large program, you can use **tail** with the **–f** option to check on its progress periodically or in a separate window.

tar

Stores or retrieves files to/from an archive file

Syntax: *tar option [modifiers] [file-list]*

Summary

The **tar** (tape archive) utility creates, adds to, lists, and retrieves files from an archive file. The archive is often stored on tape.

Options

Use only one of the following options to indicate what type of action you want **tar** to take. You can affect the action of the option by following it with one or more modifiers. Refer to "Notes," following, for a discussion of the location/device that the archive is read from or written to.

–c **create**   Stores the files named in *file-list* in a new archive. This option destroys any existing archive on the target file. If a *file-list* argument is a directory, **tar** recursively copies the files within the directory into the archive.

–r **replace**   Writes the *file-list* to the end of the archive. It leaves files that are already in the archive intact, so there may be duplicate copies of files in the archive after **tar** finishes. When **tar** extracts the files, the last copy of a file in the archive is the one that ends up on the disk.

–t **table of contents**   Without a *file-list* this option produces a table of contents of all the files in an archive. With a *file-list* it displays the name of each of the files in the *file-list* each time it occurs in the archive. You can use this option with the –v option (see following) to display detailed information about each file in the archive.

–u **update**   Adds the files from *file-list*, if they are not already in the archive or if they have been modified since they were last written to the archive. Because of the additional checking that this requires, **tar** runs more slowly when you use this option.

–x **extract**   Restores the *file-list* from the archive and writes it to the disk. Any existing files with the same name are overwritten. Without a *file-list* all the files in the archive are extracted. If the *file-list* includes a directory, **tar** extracts that directory and all the files below it. The **tar** utility attempts to keep the owner, modification time, and access privileges the same as those of the original file. If **tar** reads the same file more than once, the later versions of the file overwrite any previous versions.

Modifiers

You can specify one or more modifiers following an option. A leading hyphen is not required. However it is good practice to use the hyphen to maintain consistency with other utilities.

If a modifier takes an argument, that modifier must be the last one in a group. For example the arguments are arranged legally in the following **tar** command:

```
$ tar -cb 10 -f /dev/rmt/0
```

On the other hand the following **tar** command generates an error:

```
$ tar -cbf 10 /dev/rmt/0
tar: Invalid value for blocksize
```

The error is generated because the **–b** modifier takes an argument but is not the last modifier in a group. This is different from the original version of **tar**, used with many UNIX systems, that allowed this construct.

–b [*n*] block Uses *n* as the blocking factor for creating an archive. Use this option only when **tar** is creating an archive directly to a tape. (When **tar** reads a tape archive, it automatically determines the blocking factor.) The value of *n* is the number of 512-byte blocks to write as a single block on the tape. If you do not specify *n*, it defaults to 20.

–f *filename* file Uses *filename* as the name of the file (device) to hold the archive. Refer to "Notes," following, for additional information about how **tar** decides where to read or write a file from/to. The *filename* can be the name of an ordinary file or a device (such as a tape drive).

You can use a hyphen (–) in place of a filename as a way to refer to standard input when creating an archive and standard output when extracting files from an archive.

–h Follows symbolic links and includes the linked-to files as if they were normal files and directories.

–m modify Sets the modification time to the time of extraction. Without this option **tar** attempts to maintain the modification time of the original file. This option only works with the **–x** function.

–v verbose Lists each file as **tar** reads or writes it. When combined with the **–t** option, **–v** causes **tar** to display a more detailed list of the files, showing ownership, permissions, size, and other useful information for files in the archive.

–w what Asks you for confirmation before reading or writing each file. Respond with **y** if you want **tar** to take the action. Any other response causes **tar** not to take the action.

–X *filename* exclude Does not process the files listed in *filename*, a file that contains a list of filenames, one per line, to exclude from processing. If *filename* contains a directory name, then no files or directories within that directory are processed.

Notes

When you use the **–f**, **–b**, and/or **–X** options, the first arguments following the options must correspond to the options you use. Following these arguments is the *file-list*.

The **tar** utility looks for the name of a file or device to read from/write to in the following sequence: First it looks for a **–f** option on the command line, next it looks at the **TAPE** variable, and finally it looks in the **/etc/default/tar** file. When it finds a name to use, **tar** stops looking.

You can use ambiguous file references when you write files to the archive but not when you read them.

The name of a directory file within the *file-list* references all files and subdirectories within that directory.

If you write a file using a simple filename, the file appears in the working directory when you read it back. If you write a file using a relative pathname, it appears with that relative pathname, starting from the working directory when you read it back. When restoring a file, make sure the filename you specify is the same as the one on the tape. If you are not sure of the exact filename on the tape, run **tar** with the **–tv** options, passing the output through **grep** or **pg** to find the file you are looking for.

As you read and write files, **tar** attempts to preserve links between files. Unless you use the **–h** option, **tar** does not inform you when it fails to maintain a link.

See the **cpdir** shell script on page 355 for an example that uses **tar** to copy a directory to another location on a disk.

Solaris **tar** has a pathname length limit of 255 characters and cannot copy device entries (such as those in **/dev**). If these or other limitations create a problem for you, you may wish to look into the GNU **tar** utility, which is superior to Solaris **tar** in many respects. (See page 976 for download information.)

Examples

The following example makes a copy of the **/home/alex** directory and all files and subdirectories within that directory on a tape device. The **–v** modifier causes the command to list all the files it writes to the tape as it proceeds. This command erases anything that was already on the tape.

```
$ tar -cvf /dev/rmt/0 /home/alex
/home/alex/
/home/alex/.login
/home/alex/.profile
.
.
```

In the next example the same directory is saved on the tape device **/dev/rmt/1** with a blocking factor of 100. Without the **–v** modifier **tar** does not display the list of files it is writing to the tape. The command runs in the background and displays any messages after the shell issues a new prompt.

```
$ tar -cb 100 -f /dev/rmt/1 /home/alex &
[1] 4298
```

The next command displays the table of contents of the archive on tape device **/dev/rmt/0**:

```
$ tar -tvf /dev/rmt/0
drwxrwxrwx alex/group        0 Jun 30 21:39 1999 /home/alex/
-rw-r--r-- alex/group      678 Aug  6 14:12 1998 /home/alex/.login
-rw-r--r-- alex/group      571 Aug  6 14:06 1998 /home/alex/.profile
drwx------ alex/group        0 Nov  6 22:34 1998 /home/alex/mail/
-rw------- alex/group     2799 Nov  6 22:34 1998 /home/alex/mail/sent-mail
-rw------- alex/group        0 Aug 10 18:27 1998 /home/alex/mail/saved-messages
```

tee

Copies standard input to standard output and zero or more files

Syntax: *tee [options] file-list*

Summary

The **tee** utility copies standard input to standard output *and* to zero or more files you specify on the command line.

Argument

The *file-list* contains the pathnames of files that receive output from **tee**.

Options

Without any options **tee** overwrites the output files if they exist and responds to interrupts. If a file in *file-list* does not exist, **tee** creates it.

–a   **append**   Appends output to existing files rather than overwriting them.

–i   **ignore**   Causes **tee** not to respond to interrupts.

Example

In the following example a pipe sends the output from **make** to **tee**, which copies it to standard output and the file **accounts.out**. The copy that goes to standard output appears on the screen. The **cat** utility displays the copy that was sent to the file.

```
$ make accounts | tee accounts.out
        cc -c trans.c
        cc -c reports.c
  .
  .
  .
$ cat accounts.out
        cc -c trans.c
        cc -c reports.c
  .
  .
```

Refer to page 911 for a similar example that uses **tail –f** rather than **tee**.

telnet

Connects to a remote computer over a network

Syntax:

*telnet [**options**] [**hostname** [**port**]]*

Summary

The **telnet** utility uses the standard telnet protocol to connect to a remote system over a network. The ***hostname*** is the name or network address of the remote system. The **telnet** utility is commonly used to establish a login session on a remote system, provided you have an account there.

Arguments

If you specify a ***hostname*** on the command line, **telnet** tries to establish a connection to that system. If you do not specify the name of a remote computer, **telnet** performs interactively, prompting you to enter one of the commands described in "Discussion," below. If you do not specify a ***port***, **telnet** uses the default ***port***.

> ### telnet Does Not Encrypt Your Password (Or Anything Else)
>
> All data is sent cleartext across the network, including passwords; **telnet** is a very *insecure* way of logging in on a computer.

Options

−e *c*

    escape   Changes the escape character from **CONTROL-]** to the *c*.

−l *login-name*

    login   Attempts an automatic login to the remote computer using ***login-name***. If the remote computer understands how to handle automatic login with **telnet**, you are prompted for that user's password.

Notes

Many computers, including non-UNIX systems, support the telnet protocol. The **telnet** command is an implementation of this protocol for UNIX systems, allowing you to connect to many different types of systems. Although you typically use **telnet** to log in, the remote computer may offer other services through **telnet**, such as access to special databases.

Discussion

You can put **telnet** into command mode after you are connected to a remote computer by typing the escape character. On UNIX/Solaris systems the escape character is usually **CONTROL-]**. When you connect to a remote system, it should report the escape character it recognizes. To leave command mode, type a **RETURN** on a line by itself.

In response to a `telnet>` prompt, you can use the following commands:

?

    help   Displays a list of commands recognized by the **telnet** utility on the local system.

close

    Closes the connection to the remote system. If you specified the name of a system on the command line when you started **telnet**, close has the same effect as quit—the

telnet program quits, and you are returned to the shell. If you used the **open** command instead of specifying a remote system on the command line, close returns **telnet** to command mode.

open *hostname*   If you did not specify a hostname on the command line or if the attempt to connect to the system failed, you can specify the name of a remote system interactively with the **open** command.

quit   Quits the **telnet** session (similar to **close**).

z   If you were using a shell that supports job control when you started **telnet**, you can suspend your session with the remote system by using the **z** command. When you suspend a session, you return to your login shell on your local system. To resume your **telnet** session with the remote system, type **fg** at a shell prompt.

Example

In the following example the user connects to a remote system named **bravo**. After running a few commands, the user escapes to command mode (by pressing **CONTROL-]**) and uses the **z** command to suspend the **telnet** session to be able to run a few commands on the local system. The user gives the Job Shell **fg** command to resume using **telnet**. Finally the Job Shell **logout** command on the remote system ends the **telnet** session. The local system displays a prompt.

```
kudos% telnet bravo
Trying 130.128.52.2 ...
Connected to bravo.
Escape character is '^]'.

SunOS 5.6

login: watson
Password:
Last login: Sat Apr 18 06:03:47 from kudos
Sun Microsystems Inc.   SunOS 5.6      Generic August 1997

bravo%
.

.
bravo% CONTROL-]
telnet> z

Stopped (user)
kudos%
.

.
kudos% fg
telnet bravo

bravo$ logout
Connection closed by foreign host.
kudos%
```

test

Evaluates an expression

Syntax:

    *test **expression***
    *[**expression**]*

Summary

The **test** command evaluates an expression and returns a condition code indicating that the expression is either *true* (0) or *false* (not 0).

As the second format above shows, instead of using the word `test` when you use the **test** command, you can use square brackets around the expression (**[ ]**) as long as you leave a **SPACE** after the leading bracket and before the trailing bracket.

Argument

The ***expression*** contains one or more criteria (see the following list) that **test** evaluates. A **–a** separating two criteria is a logical AND operator: Both criteria must be true for **test** to return a condition code of *true*. A **–o** is a logical OR operator. When **–o** separates two criteria, one or the other (or both) of the criteria must be true in order for **test** to return a condition code of *true*.

You can negate any criterion by preceding it with an exclamation point (**!**). You can group criteria with parentheses. If there are no parentheses, **–a** takes precedence over **–o**, and **test** evaluates operators of equal precedence from left to right.

Within the ***expression*** you must quote special characters, such as parentheses, so that the shell does not interpret them but passes them on to **test**.

Because each element (such as a criterion, string, or variable) within the **expression** is a separate argument, you must separate each element from other elements with a **SPACE**.

You can use the following criteria within the ***expression:***

Criteria	Meaning
string	True if *string* is not the null string.
–n *string*	True if *string* has a length greater than zero.
–z *string*	True if *string* has a length of zero.
string1 = string2	True if *string1* is equal to *string2*.
string1 != *string2*	True if *string1* is not equal to *string2*.
int1 relop int2	True if integer *int1* has the specified algebraic relationship to integer *int2*. The *relop* is a relational operator from the list following this table. As a special case, **–l** *string*, which gives the length of *string*, may be used for *int1* or *int2*.
file1 **–nt** *file2*	True if *file1* exists and was modified after *file2* (the modification time of *file1* is newer than that of *file2*).

Criteria	Meaning
file1 −ot *file2*	True if *file1* exists and was modified before *file2* (the modification time of *file1* is older than that of *file2*).
−e *filename*	True if the file named *filename* exists. Not available from **sh**.
−b *filename*	True if the file named *filename* exists and is a block special file.
−c *filename*	True if the file named *filename* exists and is a character special file.
−d *filename*	True if the file named *filename* exists and is a directory.
−f *filename*	True if the file named *filename* exists and is a regular (ordinary) file.
−g *filename*	True if the file named *filename* exists and its set group ID bit is set.
−k *filename*	True if the file named *filename* exists and its sticky bit is set.
−L *filename*	True if the file named *filename* exists and is a symbolic link.
−p *filename*	True if the file named *filename* exists and is a named pipe (Fifo).
−r *filename*	True if the file named *filename* exists and you have read access permission to it.
−s *filename*	True if the file named *filename* exists and contains information (has a size greater than 0 bytes).
−t *file-descriptor*	True if the file represented by *file-descriptor* is open and associated with the screen. The *file-descriptor* for standard input is 0, for standard output is 1, and for standard error is 2.
−u *filename*	True if the file named *filename* exists and its setuid bit is set (page 90).
−w *filename*	True if the file named *filename* exists and you have write access permission to it. This test does not check to see that you have write access permission to the directory or the filesystem containing *filename*.
−x *filename*	True if the file named *filename* exists and you have execute access permission to it. For a file this permission indicates you can execute the file, whereas for a directory it indicates that you have search permission to the directory.

Relop	Description
−gt	Greater than
−ge	Greater than or equal to
−eq	Equal to
−ne	Not equal to
−le	Less than or equal to
−lt	Less than

Notes

The **test** command is built into **sh** and **ksh**. The **−e** criterion is not available from **sh**.

To avoid problems when a user enters a value that **test** could confuse with an operator (such as **!**) or a criterion (such as *string*) and to increase portability of the code you are writing, write this code:

```
[ "$1" -a "$2" ]
```

as:

```
[ "$1" ] && [ "$2" ]
```

Examples

The following examples show how to use the **test** utility in Bourne Shell scripts. Although **test** works from a command line, it is more commonly used in shell scripts to test input or verify access to a file.

The first two examples show incomplete shell scripts. They are not complete because they do not test for upper- as well as lowercase input or inappropriate responses and do not acknowledge more than one response.

The first example prompts the user, reads a line of input into the user variable **user_input**, and uses **test** to see if the user variable **user_input** matches the quoted string yes. Refer to Chapters 10 and 11 for more information on variables, **read**, and **if**.

```
$ cat user_in
echo "Input yes or no: \c"
read user_input
if [ "$user_input" = yes ]
    then
        echo You input yes.
fi
```

The next example prompts the user for a filename and then uses **test** to see if the user has read access permission (**−r**) for the file *and* (**−a**) if the file contains information (**−s**).

```
$ cat validate
echo "Enter filename: \c"
read filename
if [ -r "$filename" -a -s "$filename" ]
    then
        echo File $filename exists and contains information.
        echo You have read access permission to the file.
fi
```

The **−t 1** criterion checks to see if the process running **test** is sending output to the screen. If it is, the **test** utility returns a value of *true* (0). Following is a listing of the shell script **term** that runs **test**.

```
$ cat term
test -t 1
echo "This program is (=0) or is not (=1)
sending its output to the screen:" $?
```

First **term** is run with the output going to the screen; that is, the output is not redirected to a file. The **test** utility returns a 0. The shell stores this value in the shell variable that records the condition code of the last process, **$?**. The **echo** utility displays this value.

```
$ term
This program is (=0) or is not (=1)
sending its output to a screen: 0
```

The next example runs **term** and redirects the output to a file. The contents of the file **temp** show that **test** returned a 1, indicating that its output was not going to the screen.

```
$ term > temp
$ cat temp
This program is (=0) or is not (=1)
sending its output to a screen: 1
```

touch
Updates access and modification time for a file

Syntax: *touch [options] file-list*

Summary

The **touch** utility updates the time a file was last accessed and the time it was last modified. You can set the times to the current time or to any other time with command-line arguments. This utility is frequently used with **make**.

Argument

The *file-list* contains the pathnames of the files **touch** is to update.

Options

When you do not use the **–c** option, **touch** creates files if they do not exist. Without the **–t** option **touch** uses the current date and time.

–a   **access time**   Updates the access time only, leaving the modification time unchanged.

–c   **do not create**   Does not create a file when a file in *file-list* does not exist.

–m   **modify time**   Updates the modification time only, leaving the access time unchanged.

–r *filename*   **reference**   Updates with the access and modification times from the file named *filename*.

–t *time*   **time**   Uses *time* in place of the current time when changing or setting one of the times associated with a file. Give *time* in the following format:

$$[CC[YY]]MMDDhhmm[.SS]$$

The year, *YY*, is optional and specifies the last two digits of the year. If you specify *YY*, you can also give the century, *CC*, which specifies the first two digits of the year. The *MM* is the number of the month (01–12), *DD* is the day of the month (01–31), *hh* is the hour based on a 24-hour clock (00–23), and *mm* is the minutes (00–59). The optional portion, *.SS*, gives seconds (.00–.59); the number of seconds must be preceded by a period. Any optional portion missing from the time specification is assumed to be unchanged.

Notes

One of the most frequent uses for **touch** is creating an empty file. The following commands show two ways to create an empty file (where none existed before):

```
$ cat /dev/null > newfile1
$ touch newfile2
```

Examples

The following commands demonstrate how **touch** functions. The first commands show **touch** updating an existing file. The **ls** utility with the **–l** option displays the modification time of the file. The last three command lines show **touch** creating and verifying the existence of a file.

```
$ ls -l program.c
-rw-r--r--   1 alex      group        5860 Apr 21 09:54 program.c
$ touch program.c
$ ls -l program.c
-rw-r--r--   1 alex      group        5860 Aug 13 19:01 program.c
$ ls -l read.c
read.c: No such file or directory
$ touch read.c
$ ls -l read.c
-rw-rw-r--   1 alex      group           0 Aug 13 19:01 read.c
```

The next example demonstrates the use of the **–a** option to change access time only, and the **–t** option to specify a date for **touch** to use instead of the current date and time.

The first **ls** command displays the file *modification* times, whereas the second **ls** (with the **–u** option) displays file *access* times. The **touch** command changes the access time associated with each file to April 20 of the current year at 7:44 AM. The final two **ls** commands show the results.

```
$ ls -l
total 46
-rw-r--r--   1 alex      group        9828 Apr 15 16:55 cases
-rw-r--r--   1 alex      group       12529 Apr 12 08:14 excerpts
$ ls -lu
total 46
-rw-r--r--   1 alex      group        9828 Apr 18 17:02 cases
-rw-r--r--   1 alex      group       12529 Apr 21 13:54 excerpts
$ touch -at 04200744 cases excerpts
$ ls -l
total 46
-rw-r--r--   1 alex      group        9828 Apr 15 16:55 cases
-rw-r--r--   1 alex      group       12529 Apr 12 08:14 excerpts
$ ls -lu
total 46
-rw-r--r--   1 alex      group        9828 Apr 20 07:44 cases
-rw-r--r--   1 alex      group       12529 Apr 20 07:44 excerpts
```

tr   Replaces specified characters

Syntax: *tr [options] string1 [string2]*

Summary

The **tr** utility reads standard input and, for each input character, maps it to an alternate character, deletes the character, or leaves the character unchanged. The result goes to standard output.

Arguments

The **tr** utility is typically used with two arguments, *string1* and *string2*. The position of each character in the two strings is important; **tr** replaces each character from *string1* with the corresponding character in *string2*.

With one argument, *string1*, and the option **–d**, **tr** deletes the characters specified in *string1*. The option **–s** replaces multiple sequential occurrences of characters in *string1* with single occurrences (for example abbc becomes abc).

You can use several specifiers other than plain strings within *string1* and *string2*. See "Notes" and "Examples," following, for information on the range specifier.

Options

–c   **complement**   Complements *string1* with respect to the ASCII collating sequence. This causes **tr** to match all characters *except* those in *string1*.

–d   **delete**   Deletes characters that match those specified in *string1*. If used with the **–s** option, both *string1* and *string2* must be given (see "Notes," below).

–s   **squeeze**   When you call **tr** with one argument, it replaces multiple sequential occurrences of each character in *string1* with a single occurrence of that character. If you use both *string1* and *string2*, **tr** first translates the characters in *string1* to those in *string2* and then replaces multiple sequential occurrences as with a single argument.

Notes

The **/usr/xpg4/bin/tr** utility is a POSIX-compliant version of **tr**. When *string1* is longer than *string2*, the results are unspecified.

If you use the **–d** and **–s** options at the same time, **tr** deletes the characters in *string1* and then reduces multiple sequential occurrences of characters in *string2*.

In addition to using plain strings in *string1* and *string2*, you can use arguments that specify a range of characters. You specify a range of characters as the first character in the range followed by a hyphen and the last character (for example you can specify all lowercase characters in alphabetic order as "a-z"). See the first example.

924

You can use a class specifier in place of *string1* or *string2* as " [*class*] ", where *class* is one of the following: **alnum** (alphanumeric), **alpha** (alphabetic), **blank** (SPACE), **cntrl** (CONTROL), **digit** (0–9), **graph** (graphical), **lower** (lowercase), **print** (printing), **punct** (punctuation), **space** (SPACE), **upper** (uppercase), or **xdigit** (not a digit).

Examples

You can use a hyphen to represent a range of characters in *string1* or *string2*. The two command lines in the following example produce the same result:

```
$ echo abcdef | tr 'abcdef' 'xyzabc'
xyzabc
$ echo abcdef | tr 'a-f' 'x-za-c'
xyzabc
```

The next example demonstrates a popular method for disguising text, often called *rotate 13* because it replaces the first letter of the alphabet with the 13th, the second with the 14th, and so forth:

```
$ echo The punchline of the joke is ... |
> tr '[A-M][N-Z][a-m][n-z]' '[N-Z][A-M][n-z][a-m]'
Gur chapuyvar bs gur wbxr vf ...
```

To make the text intelligible again, reverse the order of the arguments to **tr**.

```
$ echo Gur chapuyvar bs gur wbxr vf ... |
> tr '[N-Z][A-M][n-z][a-m]' '[A-M][N-Z][a-m][n-z]'
The punchline of the joke is ...
```

The **–d** option causes **tr** to delete selected characters.

```
$ echo If you can read this, you can spot the missing vowels! |
> tr -d 'aeiou'
If y cn rd ths, y cn spt th mssng vwls!
```

In the following example **tr** replaces characters and reduces pairs of identical characters to single characters:

```
$ echo tennessee | tr -s 'tnse' 'srne'
serene
```

The following examples replace each sequence of nonalphabetic characters (the complement of all the alphabetic characters as specified by 'a-zA-Z') in the file **draft1** with a single NEWLINE character. Both examples extend *string2* to the length of *string1* so that all 52 characters specified by *string1* are replaced by \n. The first command specifies that the NEWLINE be repeated 52 times—the length of *string1*. The second command extends *string2* with as many NEWLINEs as necessary to make it the length of *string1*. The square brackets are required. The output is a list of words, one per line.

```
$ tr -cs a-zA-Z '[\n*52]' < draft1
$ tr -cs a-zA-Z '[\n*]' < draft1
```

truss

Traces a process

Syntax:

*truss [**options**] **command** [**args**]*
*truss [**options**] –p **pid***

Summary

The **truss** utility traces a process, displaying system calls made by, signals received by, and machine faults incurred by the process.

Arguments

The first syntax executes **command** and traces it. The second syntax uses the **–p** option to specify one or more running processes separated by commas; **truss** attaches to and reports on the specified running process(es).

Options

When you use an optional exclamation point ([**!**]), it negates the specified action. For example **–t !open,close** causes **open** and **close** system calls not to be displayed.

–a	**args** Displays all arguments passed to an **exec** call after a fork.
–c	**count** Counts system calls, faults, and signals instead of displaying them, and generates a summary report.
–e	**environment** Shows all environment variables in use at the time of an **exec**.
–f	**fork** Traces all child processes.
–o *outfile*	**output** Sends all output to *outfile* instead of standard output.
–r *fd*	**read** Shows the contents of buffers for read calls to file descriptor *fd*. Shows calls to other file descriptors and write calls to *fd* as usual.
–s [**!**]*signal-list*	**signals** Displays only signals that appear in the comma-separated *signal-list*.
–t [**!**]*call-list*	**trace** Displays only system calls that appear in the comma-separated *call-list*.
–v [**!**]*call-list*	**verbose** Displays the contents of structures for system calls that appear in the comma-separated *call-list*.
–x [**!**]*call-list*	**hex** Displays data passed only to system calls that appear in the comma-separated *call-list*, in raw (usually hexadecimal) format.
–w *fd*	**write** Shows the contents of buffers for write calls to file descriptor *fd*. Shows calls to other file descriptors and read calls to *fd* as usual.

926

<u>**Solaris 7 only**</u>

–d   **date**   Displays time stamps preceding each line of output. Time stamps are relative
                                              to the beginning of the trace.

–D   **delta**   Displays time stamps preceding each line of output. Time stamps are relative
                                              to the beginning of the process or thread.

–T [!] *call-list*   **stop**   Causes all system calls that appear in the comma-separated *call-list* to stop the
                                              process (send it a STOP signal). When these system calls are traced, the process is
                                              stopped and **truss** exits. The process is left in a suitable state for attaching a debug-
                                              ger.

–u [!]*lib-list* [:][!]*func-list*   **user trace**   Traces and displays user-level function calls and/or library accesses.
                                              The *lib-list* is one or more comma-separated shared object libraries, and *func-list* is
                                              one or more comma-separated function names.

–U [!]*lib-list* [:][!]*func-list*   **user stop**   Traces functions and libraries in the same manner as **–u**, but stops in the
                                              same manner as **–T**.

Note
The **truss** utility is an example of an excellent tool that is designed to exploit the **procfs** (page 654).

Examples
The first example shows how to find out which open files correspond to which file descriptors. This example
only traces open and close system calls made by a process (**finger**), which allows you to see when each file
descriptor is in use. The number to the right is the status code returned by each call. When a file descriptor is
successfully opened, the status code is equal to the file descriptor number, otherwise an error is displayed. When
finger tries to open **/etc/default/finger**, the call generates an error (ENOENT) because the file does not exist.

```
$ truss -t open,close finger
open("/dev/zero", O_RDONLY)                  = 3
open("/usr/lib/libsocket.so.1", O_RDONLY)    = 4
close(4)                                     = 0
open("/usr/lib/libnsl.so.1", O_RDONLY)       = 4
close(4)                                     = 0
   .
   .
close(3)                                     = 0
open("/etc/default/finger", O_RDONLY)        Err#2 ENOENT.
   .
   .
```

After obtaining the number of the file descriptor you are interested in (file descriptor 4 in this case, some
versions of **finger** use 3), you can use **truss** to get more information. The following example uses **truss** to run
finger and generates a verbose report on all read and write access to file descriptor 4. Standard output appears
on the screen, whereas standard error (the output of **truss**) is redirected with the **–o** option to **truss.out**.

```
$ truss -o truss.out -t open,close,read,write -r 4 -w 4 finger
Login       Name          TTY      Idle   When    Where
alex        Alex Watson   pts/4           Fri 12:23  :0.0
```

The next example shows **truss** reporting on a **fork**ed process; it shows some of the functionality of **truss** as it relates to forking and **exec**ing subprocesses.

Because **xargs** reads data from standard input, **ls** pipes data to **xargs** via the **truss** command. The command **truss ls | xargs** would have the effect of running **truss** on the **ls** command, not the point of this example. The **xargs** output appears on the screen. Without the **–o** option, **xargs** output would be interleaved with the **truss** output.

```
# ls | truss -fae -t fork,exec,exit -o /tmp/xargs.tr xargs -n 1 file
```

After running this command, **/tmp/xargs.tr** shows that each of the **exec** system calls displays all of the environment variables (**–e** option), and each fork displays all of the arguments that are passed by the **exec** call (**–a** option).

The **–n 1** argument to **xargs** is inefficient because it tells **xargs** to invoke **file** with only one argument from **ls** at a time (**file** can take many arguments at a time). Of course the entire example is artificial because there is no need to run **ls** and pipe the output to **file** in the first place; **file** can do it all. This is still a useful illustration of the capabilities of **truss**. The first line that **truss** generates shows the program it is executing (**xargs**). The next line shows the command-line arguments for **xargs** (labeled `argv:` below) followed by the environment variables and their values. This information is repeated for each call to **xargs**. The left column displays the process ID of each child.

```
399:    execve("/usr/bin/xargs", 0x08047CAC, 0x08047CC0)  argc = 4
399:     argv: xargs -n 1 file
399:     envp: HOME=/home/jenny HZ=100 LOGNAME=jenny
399:      MAIL=/var/mail/jenny
399:      MANPATH=/usr/openwin/share/man:/usr/openwin/man:/usr/share/man
399:      PATH=/usr/bin:/usr/dt/bin:/usr/openwin/bin:/usr/ucb:/usr/ccs/bin::
399:      PWD=/home/jenny SHELL=/bin/csh TERM=vt100 TZ=US/Pacific
399:      USER=jenny
```

For each call to **xargs** (one call is made for each filename that **ls** pipes to **xargs**), **truss** displays each **fork** call twice (once for each fork of the running process): The first instance is **fork**'s return code to the parent (the child process ID), and the second instance is **fork**'s return code to the child (the parent process ID). After the output shown above, **truss** generates the following, showing the fork system call where 399 is the parent and 402 is the child. The third and fourth lines show the execution of file with the argument **jenny.mem** (the name of the file that **ls** passed to **xargs**:

```
399:    fork()                                      = 402
402:    fork()              (returning as child ...)  = 399
402:    execve("/usr/bin/file", 0x0804CD48, 0x08047CF0)  argc = 2
402:     argv: file jenny.mem
```

Following is a simplistic C program that uses signals. The system libraries translate the old-style **signal** call in the program to the more modern **sigaction** call. (The example uses the **signal** call because it is easier to code than **sigaction** and makes the example clearer.)

```
/*sigtest.c*/
#include <sys/signal.h>
main() { signal(SIGTSTP, SIG_IGN); while(1) sleep(1000);}
```

After compiling the program, the following command shows the behavior of the **sigaction** system call and its structures:

```
$ truss -v sigaction -t sigaction sigtest
sigaction(SIGTSTP, 0x08047C18, 0x08047C74)      = 0
    new: hand = 0x00000001 mask = 0 0 0 0 flags = 0x0016
    old: hand = 0x00000000 mask = 0 0 0 0 flags = 0x0000
sigaction(SIGALRM, 0x08047BD4, 0x08047C60)      = 0
    new: hand = 0xDFF875E8 mask = 0 0 0 0 flags = 0x0000
    old: hand = 0x00000000 mask = 0 0 0 0 flags = 0x0000
```

The `old` line shows the signal mask at the time of the cal; `new` is the one that is replacing it. Each field enumerates the values of a structure passed to **sigaction** telling it what to do (again, behind the scenes). The SIGALRM signal is used by the **sleep** call to wake the program up when 1000 seconds have passed.

The next example shows the default output of **truss** (with no options). All of the **kill** commands are given from a second window so you can leave **truss** running in the foreground and see its output immediately.

```
% truss sigtest
execve("sigtest", 0x080474B4, 0x080474BC)  argc = 1
open("/dev/zero", O_RDONLY)                     = 3
.
.
.
alarm(1000)                                     = 0
sigsuspend(0x08047404)             (sleeping...)
```

The following commands (*italics*) are given from a second window. First **ps** determines the PID of **sigtest**, then **kill** sends a TSTP signal to that process. The **truss** utility reports that the signal was received and ignored. (That is all **sigtest** does: It ignores the TSTP signal.) Without any arguments, **truss** reports on all signals received by the program it is tracing. Next **kill** sends a HUP signal to **sigtest** and **truss** reports that is was received and that the default action was taken (the process was killed).

```
% ps -ef | grep sigtest
    alex  1657  1656  0 21:46:40 pts/9    0:00 sigtest
    alex  1656  1652  0 21:46:40 pts/9    0:00 truss sigtest
    alex  1680  1675  0 21:48:22 pts/10   0:00 grep sigtest
% kill -TSTP 1657

    Received signal #24, SIGTSTP, in sigsuspend() [ignored]
      siginfo: SIGTSTP pid=1675 uid=500
sigsuspend(0x08047404)             (sleeping...)

% kill -HUP 1657

    Received signal #1, SIGHUP, in sigsuspend() [default]
      siginfo: SIGHUP pid=1675 uid=500
sigsuspend(0x08047404)                      Err#4 EINTR
         *** process killed ***
```

The next **truss** command narrows the scope of the trace and shows only the TSTP signal (and no others). While **truss** reports on a TSTP signal, it does not report on a CONT signal (which does not affect **sigtest**) and does not report on a HUP signal (which kills the **sigtest** process). The output following the **kill –HUP** command is the report of a system call by **truss**, not a signal.

```
% truss -s TSTP sigtest
execve("sigtest", 0x080474AC, 0x080474B4)  argc = 1
open("/dev/zero", O_RDONLY)                       = 3
sigsuspend(0x08047404)                            Err#4 EINTR
    .

    .
alarm(1000)                                       = 0
sigsuspend(0x08047404)            (sleeping...)
```

*(commands in **italics** given from a second window)*

```
% ps -ef | grep sigtest
   alex  1688  1652  0 21:51:57 pts/9    0:00 truss -s TSTP sigtest
   alex  1689  1688  0 21:51:57 pts/9    0:00 sigtest
   alex  1691  1675  0 21:52:14 pts/10   0:00 grep sigtest
% kill -TSTP 1689

   Received signal #24, SIGTSTP, in sigsuspend() [ignored]
      siginfo: SIGTSTP pid=1675 uid=500
sigsuspend(0x08047404)            (sleeping...)

% kill -CONT 1689
(no output)
% kill -HUP 1689

sigsuspend(0x08047404)                            Err#4 EINTR
         *** process killed ***
```

The final **truss** command reports on all signals that are not TSTP. Because this command is run under the C Shell, the exclamation point must be quoted (in this example it is preceded by a backslash). Here the TSTP signal does not generate any output, but the HUP signal does (the first two lines after the **kill –HUP** command report on the signal, the next two report on the system call).

```
% truss -s \!TSTP sigtest
execve("sigtest", 0x080474A8, 0x080474B0)  argc = 1
open("/dev/zero", O_RDONLY)                       = 3
    .

    .
alarm(1000)                                       = 0
sigsuspend(0x08047404)            (sleeping...)
```

*(commands in **italics** given from a second window)*

```
% ps -ef | grep sigtest
   alex  1695  1652  0 21:54:21 pts/9    0:00 truss -s !TSTP sigtest
   alex  1696  1695  0 21:54:21 pts/9    0:00 sigtest
   alex  1699  1675  0 21:54:41 pts/10   0:00 grep sigtest
```

```
% kill -TSTP 1696
(no output)
% kill -HUP 1696
```

```
    Received signal #1, SIGHUP, in sigsuspend() [default]
        siginfo: SIGHUP pid=1675 uid=500
sigsuspend(0x08047404)                              Err#4 EINTR
            *** process killed ***
```

Using truss to Debug the /etc/inetd.conf File

Assume the **inetd** daemon is process 169. You can use the following command to show only **fork**, **exec**, and **open** calls at first to make sure that configuration files are being read properly and daemons are being launched properly. Any new daemon launched from **inetd** (for example **telnetd**) will immediately be visible on your screen as it runs. You will see it opening its configuration files, and you will be able to tell by the return codes if they are successful or not (see ENOENT on page 927). You can expand arguments to **truss** from there as necessary. The output is stored in the file **/tmp/inetd.tr**.

```
# truss -fa -o /tmp/inetd.tr -t open,fork,exec -p 169
```

There are many more useful examples in the **truss man** page.

tty

Displays the pathname of the login device

Syntax:　　　　　　*tty [option]*

Summary

The **tty** utility displays the pathname of standard input if it is a terminal, window, or monitor. The exit status of **tty** is 0 if standard input is a keyboard and 1 if it is not.

Option

−s　　　　　　**silent**　Causes **tty** to set its exit status and not to display anything.

Notes

If standard input is not a screen, **tty** displays the message not a tty.

Example

The following example illustrates the use of **tty** and shows that it sets a return code:

```
$ tty
/dev/pts/1
$ echo $?
0
$ tty < memo
not a tty
$ echo $?
1
```

ufsdump Backs up files or filesystems

Syntax: *ufsdump [options] file-list*

Summary

The **ufsdump** utility creates a backup copy of files or a filesystem.

Argument

The *file-list* is a single filesystem or list of files or directories residing in a single filesystem. The **ufsdump** utility will not back up files from multiple filesystems.

Options

Unlike most other commands, **ufsdump** does not look for a dash (–) preceding options. When you do not specify any options, **ufsdump** uses **9uf /dev/rmt/0**.

0–9	**dump level** The most comprehensive dump level is 0, which means dump all files in the filesystem. Each dump level from 1 to 9 is incremental with respect to the previous dump level. That is, 1 will only back up files changed since the last level 0 dump, 2 will only back up files changed since the last level 1 dump, and so forth.
a *file*	**archive file** Keeps a table of contents for use by **ufsrestore** in *file*.
b *n*	**blocking factor** Sets the blocking factor for writing to a tape device to *n* 512-byte blocks. For tapes where the density is less than 6250 BPI (bytes per inch), the default blocking factor is 20. For tapes where the density is greater than 6250 BPI, the default blocking factor is 64. For cartridge tapes (**c** option) the default blocking factor is 126 (highest available for most tape drives).
c	**cartridge** Sets the defaults for a cartridge tape instead of half-inch reel-to-reel tape; sets the tape density to 1000 BPI and the blocking factor to 126.
d *n*	**density** Sets the tape density to *n* BPI. Because **ufsdump** can automatically detect the end of media, this parameter only serves to have the **ufsdump** screen output properly display how much tape has been used so far.
f *file*	**dump file** Sends dump output to *file*, which is generally a tape device in the **/dev/rmt** directory. If – is used instead of a file, the dump is sent to standard output. The *file* can also be **machine:/device** or **user@machine:/device**, in which case a network dump will be performed as the indicated user, on the indicated machine, to the indicated device or file. This dump is performed using **rsh**, so **.rhosts** and **hosts.equiv** permissions must be set appropriately.
n	**notify** Sends a message to all members of the **sys** group who are logged in when a dump requires attention. Without this option messages are sent only to standard output.

o   **offline**   Takes the drive offline when end of media is reached. For most 4mm and 8mm devices, this also ejects the tape from the drive.

s *n*   **size**   Sets the length in feet for tapes and cartridges, and the number of 1024-byte blocks for diskettes. Because **ufsdump** can automatically detect the end of media, this parameter only serves to have the **ufsdump** screen output properly display what percent of a tape has been used so far.

S   **size estimate**   Estimates the amount of space that will be needed for a dump without actually performing a dump.

u   **update**   Updates the dump record in **/etc/dumpdates** (page 609). Each record in this file contains the filesystem name, date and time of dump, and dump level.

v   **verify**   Verifies the contents of the tape against the filesystem being dumped. If the contents of the tape after the dump is not identical to the contents of the filesystem, **ufsdump** prompts for new media and repeats the entire process. (This option will not work when the dump is sent to standard output using the **f** option with an argument of **–**.)

W   **WARNING**   Lists all filesystems in **/etc/dumpdates**, when they were last backed up, and at what level. Filesystems that have not been backed up in the last 24 hours are highlighted.

Notes

The **ufsdump** utility usually backs up to a tape device. Although it is possible to back up to a file or another disk, utilities such as **tar** are generally used for this task so that the archive is more portable. As with any backup, the specified files or filesystems should be inactive or quiescent. For more information see "Backing Up Files" on page 631.

Besides backups, **ufsdump** is sometimes also used as a means of transferring directories from one filesystem to another, or filesystems from one host to another. For example the following commands transfer the **reports** directory from **/export/vol1** to **/export/vol2**:

```
# cd /export/vol1
# ufsdump 0f - reports | (cd /export/vol2; ufsrestore xf -)
```

There is a section of the **ufsdump man** page titled "Suggested Dump Schedule" that provides a useful starting point for developing your own dump schedule.

Examples

The following example shows how to dump three filesystems: The root filesystem (**/**, which contains **/usr**), **/var**, and **/export**. Alex performs a level 0 dump to the first tape device installed on the system. The device is **/dev/rmt/0cn**, where the **c** indicates that the device supports compression and the **n** indicates a no-rewind device (the tape will not automatically rewind after it has been written to).

```
# ufsdump 0uf /dev/rmt/0cn /
DUMP: Writing 63 Kilobyte records
DUMP: Date of this level 0 dump: Sat Sep 05 17:45:53 1998
DUMP: Date of last level 0 dump: the epoch
```

```
DUMP: Dumping /dev/rdsk/c0t3d0s0 (bravo:/var) to /dev/rmt/0cn.
DUMP: Mapping (Pass I) [regular files]
DUMP: Mapping (Pass II) [directories]
DUMP: Estimated 133470 blocks (65.17MB) on 0.02 tapes.
DUMP: Dumping (Pass III) [directories]
DUMP: Dumping (Pass IV) [regular files]
DUMP: 133432 blocks (65.15MB) on 1 volume at 330 KB/sec
DUMP: DUMP IS DONE
DUMP: Level 0 dump on Sat Sep 05 17:49:33 1998

# ufsdump 0uf /dev/rmt/0cn /var
DUMP: Writing 63 Kilobyte records
DUMP: Date of this level 0 dump: Sat Sep 05 17:49:33 1998
DUMP: Date of last level 0 dump: the epoch
DUMP: Dumping /dev/rdsk/c0t3d0s4 (bravo:/var) to /dev/rmt/0cn.
DUMP: Mapping (Pass I) [regular files]
DUMP: Mapping (Pass II) [directories]
DUMP: Estimated 66735 blocks (30.57MB) on 0.01 tapes.
DUMP: Dumping (Pass III) [directories]
DUMP: Dumping (Pass IV) [regular files]
DUMP: 66720 blocks (30.57MB) on 1 volume at 330 KB/sec
DUMP: DUMP IS DONE
DUMP: Level 0 dump on Sat Sep 05 17:50:00 1998

# ufsdump 0uof /dev/rmt/0c /export
DUMP: Writing 63 Kilobyte records
DUMP: Date of this level 0 dump: Sat Sep 05 17:50:00 1998
DUMP: Date of last level 0 dump: the epoch
DUMP: Dumping /dev/rdsk/c0t3d0s7 (bravo:/export) to /dev/rmt/0c.
DUMP: Mapping (Pass I) [regular files]
DUMP: Mapping (Pass II) [directories]
DUMP: Estimated 2117632 blocks (1034MB) on 0.21 tapes.
DUMP: Dumping (Pass III) [directories]
DUMP: Dumping (Pass IV) [regular files]
DUMP: 2117618 blocks (1034MB) on 1 volume at 330 KB/sec
DUMP: DUMP IS DONE
DUMP: Level 0 dump on Sat Sep 05 18:47:53 1998
```

The last command rewinds the tape (because it uses the rewinding tape device **/dev/rmt/0c** versus **/dev/rmt/0cn**) and ejects it (because of the **o** option).

A couple of days later, to back up files that have changed since the level 0 dump, Alex performs an incremental dump of the **/export** filesystem. The following example shows an incremental level 1 dump on **/export** two days later when about 30MB worth of files have changed since the previous level 0 dump.

```
# ufsdump 1uf /dev/rmt/0cn /export
DUMP: Writing 63 Kilobyte records
DUMP: Date of this level 1 dump: Mon Sep 07 19:00:00 1998
DUMP: Date of last level 1 dump: Sun Sep 06 19:00:00 1998
DUMP: Dumping /dev/rdsk/c0t3d0s7 (bravo:/export) to /dev/rmt/0cn.
DUMP: Mapping (Pass I) [regular files]
DUMP: Mapping (Pass II) [directories]
DUMP: Estimated 66735 blocks (30.21MB) on 0.01 tapes.
DUMP: Dumping (Pass III) [directories]
DUMP: Dumping (Pass IV) [regular files]
DUMP: 66720 blocks (30.21MB) on 1 volume at 330 KB/sec
DUMP: DUMP IS DONE
DUMP: Level 0 dump on Sat Sep 05 19:01:30 1998
```

ufsrestore   Restores files from a ufsdump archive

Syntax: *ufsrestore function [options] [file-list]*

Summary

The **ufsrestore** utility restores files from a dump archive that was previously created by **ufsdump**. You can use it interactively or in batch mode to restore all files and directories recursively or restore selected files.

Argument

The *file-list* is a list of files and/or directories that you want to restore. If you do not specify a *file-list*, **ufsrestore** restores all files in the archive.

Functions

Choose only one function from the following list:

i
: **interactive**   Uses the interactive interface to allow you to select the files you want to restore. Refer to "Interactive Commands" on page 937.

r
: **recursive**   Restores everything on the tape into the working directory (which is normally the root of the filesystem you are restoring to). This option is useful for recovering a corrupted filesystem. First restore the level 0, then restore each subsequent incremental dump until all files are recovered.

R
: **resume**   When **ufsrestore** is interrupted it keeps a checkpoint of where it was. This option prompts you for the volume **ufsrestore** needs to continue restoring.

t
: **table of contents**   Displays the table of contents from the dump archive. Without a *file-list* **ufsrestore** lists the archive recursively. The **h** option modifies the output.

x
: **extract**   Extracts *file-list* from the archive. Without a *file-list* **ufsrestore** extracts the entire archive. If a file that is being extracted already exists on the disk, **ufsrestore** issues a warning. The **h** option changes the behavior of this function.

Options

Unlike most other utilities, a hyphen (–) does not precede **ufsrestore** options. You can use one or more of the following options to modify the behavior of the functions listed above.

a *file*
: **archive file**   Reads the table of contents from *file* instead of from the dump itself. With the **x** or **i** function this option causes **ufsrestore** to prompt for the volume that has the files before extracting them.

b *n*   **blocking factor**   Sets the blocking factor for reading from a tape device. Use the same blocking factor that you used to write the tape. See the **ufsdump b** option on page 933.

f *file*   **dump file**   Uses *file* as the dump archive instead of **/dev/rmt/0** (default). If *file* is a dash (–), then reads from standard input.

h   **no hierarchical**   Extracts (**x**) or lists (**t**) the directory itself rather than its contents.

s *n*   **skip**   Skips to *n*th file on a tape containing more than one dump.

v   **verbose**   Displays the file type, name, and inode for each restored file.

y   **yes**   Assumes you want to skip over bad tape blocks and continue without being prompted.

Interactive Commands
The following commands are available for use in interactive mode (**i** function).

add *file-list*   Adds the named files or directories to the list of files to extract. If *file-list* is a directory, then the directory is expanded recursively unless the **h** option is specified.

cd *directory*   Changes to the indicated directory in the dump archive.

delete *file-list*   Deletes the named files or directories from the list of files to extract. If *file-list* is a directory, then the directory is expanded recursively unless the **h** option is specified.

extract   Extracts all files and directories in the current list.

help   Displays usage information.

ls *[directory]*   Shows all files in *directory*, or, without an argument, in the working directory. Files and directories that are in the current extract list are prefixed with *.

pwd   Displays the name of the working directory in the archive.

quit   Quits without extracting.

setmodes   Gives you the prompt:

```
Set owner mode for '.'
```

Answer **y** if you want to set permissions, owner, and times of the working directory to be those of the original dumped filesystem; use when you are restoring an entire filesystem or files from a dump to their original locations. Answer **n** if you are restoring part of a dump to a location that is other than its original location; this leaves the working directory permissions unchanged.

verbose   Toggles verbose mode. When **verbose** is on, inode numbers are displayed by **ls** and information about each file is displayed as it is extracted.

what   Reads and displays the dump header from the archive.

Notes

After you perform a full restore, you must perform a full (level 0) dump for consistency or future incremental dumps will not work. Refer to the **ufsrestore man** page for information about the meaning of **ufsrestore** messages.

Examples

The following command restores the **/var** filesystem (the second dump archive on the tape) in batch mode and without rewinding the tape, from a tape drive that supports compression.

```
# ufsrestore rfs /dev/rmt/0cn 2
```

You can use the following commands to use **ufsrestore** interactive mode to restore the files named **adm** and **cron** from a dump stored in **/tmp/dumpfile**:

```
# ufsrestore if /tmp/dumpfile
ufsrestore > ls
.:
 adm/           lost+found/    ntp/           saf/           yp/
 audit/         mail           opt/           spool/
 cron/          news/          preserve/      statmon/
 log/           nis/           sadm/          tmp/

ufsrestore > add adm cron
ufsrestore > ls
.:
*adm/           lost+found/    ntp/           saf/           yp/
 audit/         mail           opt/           spool/
*cron/          news/          preserve/      statmon/
 log/           nis/           sadm/          tmp/

ufsrestore > extract
You have not read any volumes yet.
Unless you know which volume your file(s) are on you should start
with the last volume and work towards the first.
Specify next volume #: 1
set owner/mode for '.'? [yn] y
ufsrestore >  quit
```

When you run **ufsrestore** to read a dump archive, it will often prompt you for a volume number. Enter **1** unless your dump is stored on multiple volumes. The next command runs in batch mode to perform the same tasks as the previous example.

```
# ufsrestore xf /tmp/dumpfile adm cron
```

The next command displays the table of contents of the first dump archive on the media in the default tape drive (**/dev/rmt/0**):

```
# ufsrestore t
```

umask

Establishes or displays the file-creation permissions mask

Syntax: *umask [**mask**]*

Summary

The **umask** builtin specifies a mask that the system uses to set up access permissions when you create a file.

Argument

The *mask* is a three-digit octal number, with each digit corresponding to permissions for the owner of the file, members of the group the file is associated with, and everyone else. When you create a file, the system subtracts these numbers from the numbers corresponding to the access permissions the system would otherwise assign to the file. The result is three octal numbers that specify the access permissions for the file. (Refer to **chmod** on page 709 for a complete description and examples of these numbers.)

   Without any arguments **umask** displays the file-creation permissions mask.

Notes

The **umask** builtin ^{sh} csh _{ksh} generally goes in the initialization file for your shell (**.profile** for **sh** and **ksh**, and **.cshrc** for **csh**). The **umask** builtin _{ksh} accepts symbolic arguments matching those allowed by **chmod**. For example the argument **o+w** turns *off* the write bit in the mask for other users, causing files to be created with that bit set *on* in the permissions. Refer to **chmod** on page 709 for more information on symbolic permissions. The **umask** builtin ^{sh} csh does not allow symbolic arguments; you must always use the three-digit octal form as shown below.

   The mask is initially set from the **/etc/default/login** file when the system is booted. It is inherited by new shells as they are created. Users may change the mask in their startup files; shells that are spawned from that login shell will inherit the value of the mask from the login shell.

Examples

The following command sets the file-creation permissions mask to **066**. The command has the effect of removing read and write permission for members of the group the file is associated with and everyone else. It leaves the owner's permissions as the system specifies. If the system would otherwise create a file with a permission value of 777 (read, write, and execute access for owner, group, and everyone else), it will now create the file with 711 (all permissions for the owner and only execute permission for group and everyone else).

```
$ umask 066
```

The next example shows how the **ksh** version of **umask** allows you to specify a mask value symbolically:

```
$ umask
02
$ umask g+rw,o+rw
$ umask
00
$ umask g-rw,o-rw
$ umask
066
```

939

uniq

Displays lines of a file that are unique

Syntax: *uniq [options] [input-file] [output-file]*

Summary

The **uniq** utility displays a file, removing all but one copy of successive repeated lines. If the file has been sorted (page 891), **uniq** ensures that no two lines that it displays are the same.

Arguments

If you do not specify the *input-file* on the command line, **uniq** uses standard input. If you do not specify the *output-file* on the command line, **uniq** uses standard output.

Options

In the following description a *field* is any sequence of characters not containing whitespace (any combination of SPACEs and TABs). Fields are bounded by whitespace or the beginning or end of a line.

–c　**count**　Precedes each line with the number of occurrences of the line in the input file.

–d　**duplicates**　Displays only lines that are repeated.

–f *nfield* or **–***nfield*　**field**　Ignores the first *nfield* fields of each line. The **uniq** utility bases its comparison on the remainder of the line, including the leading blanks of the next field on the line (see **–s** above). An abbreviated form of this option, **–***nfield*, is also recognized by **uniq**.

–s *nchar* or **+***nchar*　**skip characters**　Ignores the first *nchar* characters of each line. If you also use the **–f** option (following), **uniq** ignores the first *nfield* fields followed by *nchar* characters. This option can be used to skip over the leading blanks of a field. An abbreviated form of this option, **+***nchar*, is also recognized by **uniq**.

–u　**unique**　Displays only lines that are *not* repeated.

Examples

These examples assume the file named **test** in the working directory contains the following text:

```
$ cat test
boy took bat home
boy took bat home
girl took bat home
dog brought hat home
dog brought hat home
dog brought hat home
```

Without any options **uniq** displays only one copy of successive repeated lines.

```
$ uniq test
boy took bat home
girl took bat home
dog brought hat home
```

The **–c** option displays the number of consecutive occurrences of each line in the file.

```
$ uniq -c test
    2 boy took bat home
    1 girl took bat home
    3 dog brought hat home
```

The **–d** option displays only lines that are consecutively repeated in the file.

```
$ uniq -d test
boy took bat home
dog brought hat home
```

Below, the **–f** argument skips the first field in each line, causing the lines that begin with boy and the one that begins with girl to appear to be consecutive repeated lines. The **uniq** utility displays only one occurrence of these lines.

```
$ uniq -f 1 test
boy took bat home
dog brought hat home
```

The **–u** option displays only lines that are *not* consecutively repeated in the file.

```
$ uniq -u test
girl took bat home
```

The next example uses both the **–f** and **–s** arguments (2 and 2) first to skip two fields and then to skip two characters. The two characters this command skips include the **SPACE** that separates the second and third fields and the first character of the third field. Ignoring these characters, all the lines appear to be consecutive repeated lines containing the string at home. The **uniq** utility displays only the first of these lines.

```
$ uniq -f 2 -s 2 test
boy took bat home
```

The following example is equivalent to the previous one but uses the abbreviated form of the **–f** *nfields* and **–s** *nchars* options:

```
$ uniq -2 +2 test
boy took bat home
```

w

Displays information on system users

Syntax: *w [options] [login-name]*

Summary

The **w** utility displays the names of users who are currently logged in, together with the number of the device they used to log in, the times they logged in, which commands they are running, and other information.

Argument

If a *login-name* is supplied as an argument to the **w** utility, the display is restricted to information about that user.

Options

–h   **no header**   Suppresses the header line that is normally displayed by **w**.

–s   **short**   Displays only the username, login device, idle time, and the command names.

w Is Not Always Right

If a user is running several processes on the same terminal/monitor, the **w** utility tries to determine which one is the current (foreground) process; sometimes it does not pick the right one.

Discussion

The first line that the **w** utility displays is the same as that provided by the **uptime** command. This report includes the time of day, how long the computer has been running (in days, hours, and minutes), and how many users are logged in. The report also indicates how busy the system is (load average). From left to right, the load averages indicate the number of processes that have been waiting to run (in the run queue) in the past minute, 5 minutes, and 15 minutes.

The columns of information that **w** displays for each user are:

User tty login@ idle JCPU PCPU what

The *User* is the login name of the user. The *tty* is the device name for the line the user is logged in on. The *login@* is the date and time the user logged in. The *idle* column indicates how long the person has been idle (how many minutes have elapsed since the last key was pressed on the keyboard). The next two columns, *JCPU* and *PCPU*, give measures of how much computer processor time the person has used during the cur-

942

rent login session and on the task shown in the *what* column. The *what* column displays what command that person is currently running.

Examples

The first example shows the full list produced by the **w** utility:

```
$ w
  8:20am  up 4 days,  2:28,  6 users,  load average: 0.04, 0.04, 0.00
User     tty            login@ idle   JCPU    PCPU   what
alex     pts/4          5:55am 13:45                 w
alex     pts/5          5:55am    27   2:55      1   -ksh
jenny    pts/7          5:56am 13:44                 vi 36tmp.txt
scott    pts/12         7:17pm           1          run_budget
```

The next example shows the use of the **–s** option to produce an abbreviated list:

```
$ w -s
  8:20am  up 4 days,  2:28,  6 users,  load average: 0.04, 0.04, 0.00
User     tty          idle  what
alex     pts/4       13:45  w
alex     pts/5          27  -ksh
jenny    pts/7       13:44  vi 36tmp.txt
scott    pts/12             run_budget
```

The final example requests information about Alex:

```
$ w alex
  8:20am  up 4 days,  2:28,  6 users,  load average: 0.04, 0.04, 0.00
User     tty            login@ idle   JCPU    PCPU   what
alex     pts/4          5:55am 13:45                 w
alex     pts/5          5:55am    27   2:55      1   -ksh
```

WC

Displays the number of lines, words, and characters in a file

Syntax: *wc [options] [file-list]*

Summary

The **wc** (word count) utility displays the number of lines, words, and characters contained in one or more files. If you specify more than one file on the command line, **wc** displays totals for each file and totals for the group of files. The **wc** utility takes its input from files you specify on the command line or from standard input.

Argument

The *file-list* contains the pathnames of one or more files that **wc** analyzes.

Options

If you do not specify an option, **wc** assumes the **−l**, **−w**, and **−c** options (lines, words, and bytes).

−c   Displays only the number of bytes in the file.

−l   **lines** ("ell")   Displays only the number of lines (that is, **NEWLINE** characters) in the file.

−m   Displays only the number of characters in the file (frequently yields the same output as **−c**).

−w   **words**   Displays only the number of words in the file.

Notes

A word is a sequence of characters bounded by **SPACE**s, **TAB**s, **NEWLINE**s, or a combination of these.

Examples

The following command line displays an analysis of the file named **memo**. The output is the number of lines, words, and characters in the file.

```
$ wc memo
      5      31      146 memo
```

The next command displays the number of lines and words in three files. The line at the bottom, with the word `total` in the right column, contains the sum of each column.

```
$ wc -lw memo1 memo2 memo3
     10      62 memo1
     12      74 memo2
     12      68 memo3
     34     204 total
```

which

Shows where a command is located in your path

Syntax: *which **command-list***

Summary

The **which** utility takes each command name in ***command-list*** and locates the file that contains it.

Argument

Each argument to **which** is assumed to be the name of a command. For each command name the **which** utility searches all the directories listed in your **PATH** environment variable, in order, until it locates the command. At that point **which** displays the full pathname of the command.

If **which** does not locate the command in your search path, it displays an error message.

Notes

The **which** utility cannot locate aliases, functions, and shell builtins because these do not appear in your search path. The **which** utility stops searching for a command as soon as it finds the first occurrence of that command in your search path.

Examples

The first example locates the commands **vi**, **cc**, and **which**:

```
$ which vi cc which
/bin/vi
/usr/ucb/cc
/bin/which
```

The second example shows the error that **which** displays when it cannot find a file.

```
$ which qqqq
no qqqq in /usr/dt/bin /usr/openwin/bin /bin /usr/bin /usr/ucb /usr/ccs/bin .
```

who

Displays names of users

Syntax: *who [options]*
              who am i

Summary

The **who** utility displays the names of users currently logged in, together with their login device numbers, the times they logged in, and other information.

Arguments

When given the two arguments **am i**, **who** displays information about the user who is logged in on the device the command is given on—the same as running **who** with the **–m** option.[12]

Options

–b   **boot**   Displays the date and time the system was last booted.

–H   **header**   Displays a header.

–l   **login**   Lists lines waiting for a user to log in.

–m   Displays information about the user who is giving the command—the same as running **who** with the two arguments am i.

–q   **quick**   Lists only the usernames, followed by the number of users logged in on the system.

–T   Adds the State, Idle, PID, and Comments columns to the output. The State column is located just to the left of the LINE column. It indicates whether you can write to a screen; that is, does that user have messages enabled? A plus (**+**) means that messages are enabled, whereas a hyphen (**–**) means they are disabled. A question mark (**?**) indicates **who** cannot determine the access state. If messages are enabled, you can use **write** to communicate with the user. Refer to "**mesg**: Deny or Accept Messages" on page 60.

Notes

The **/usr/xpg4/bin/who** utility is a POSIX-compliant version of **who**.

The **finger** utility (page 758) provides information similar to the information **who** provides.

---

12. Also see the Berkeley **whoami** command: **/usr/ucb/whoami**.

Discussion

The syntax of the line that **who** displays is

name [state] line time [idle] [pid] [comments] [exit]

Field	Contents
name	Login name of the user.
state	Indicates whether messages are enabled or disabled (see the **–T** option).
line	The device name (in **/dev**) associated with the line the user is logged in on.
time	Time that the user logged in.
idle	Length of time since the keyboard was last used.
pid	The user's process ID number.
comments	Comment line from **/etc/inittab**.
exit	Exit status for a dead process.

Examples

The following examples demonstrate the use of the **who** utility:

```
$ who
hls        pts/11    Jul 30 06:01   (bravo.tcorp.com)
jenny      pts/7     Jul 30 06:02   (bravo.tcorp.com)
alex       pts/4     Jul 30 14:56   (:0.0)

$ who am i
alex       pts/7     Jul 30 14:56  (alex.bravo.com)

$ who -TH
NAME          LINE        TIME          IDLE    PID  COMMENTS
hls        -  tty1        Jul 30 06:01  03:53  12115     (bravo.tcorp.com)
jenny      +  tty2        Jul 30 06:02  14:47  12123     (bravo.tcorp.com)
alex       +  ttyp3       Jul 30 14:56   .     24128     (:0.0)
```

write

Sends a message to another user

Syntax: write *destination-user [tty-name]*

Summary

You and another user can use **write** to establish two-way communication. Both of you must execute the **write** utility, each specifying the other user's login name as the ***destination-user***. The **write** utility then copies text, line by line, from each keyboard to the other user's screen.

When you execute the **write** utility, a message appears on the ***destination-user***'s screen indicating that you are about to transmit a message.

When you want to stop communicating with the other user, press **CONTROL-D** once at the start of a line to return to the shell. The other user must do the same.

Arguments

The ***destination-user*** is the login name of the user you are sending a message to. The ***tty-name*** can be used after the ***destination-user***, to resolve ambiguities if the ***destination-user*** is logged in on more than one device. If you do not use the ***tty-name*** argument and the other user is logged in several times, **write** automatically chooses the login session with the least amount of idle time.

Notes

It may be helpful to set up a protocol for carrying on communication when you use **write**. Try ending each message with **o** for "over" and ending the transmission with **oo** for "over and out." This gives each user time to think and enter a complete message without the other user wondering whether the first user is finished.

The **write** utility passes any line that you begin with an exclamation point (minus the exclamation point) to the shell for execution. The other user does not see the command line or the shell output.

Each user controls permission to write to his or her own screen. Refer to **mesg** on page 812.

Another utility, **talk** (page 59), also allows you to have a two-way conversation with another user. The **talk** utility divides the users' screens into two windows and displays the statements of the two users in different windows on both screens. Both users can type simultaneously. Users generally find it easier to hold a conversation with **talk** than with **write**. You can also use **talk** to communicate with a user on a remote system over a network.

Example

Refer to page 58 for a tutorial example of **write**.

xargs

Converts standard output of one command into arguments for another

Syntax: *xargs [options] [command]*

Summary

The **xargs** utility is a convenient, efficient way to convert standard output of one command into arguments for another command. It reads from standard input, keeps track of the maximum allowable length and number of arguments in a command line, and avoids exceeding these limits by repeating *command* (and iterating through the arguments) as necessary.

Argument

You can give **xargs** a command line as the argument *command*. If any arguments to *command* should precede the arguments from standard input, they must be included as part of *command*. By default, **xargs** assumes that standard input is to be appended to *command* to form a complete command line. If you omit *command*, it defaults to **echo**.

Options

–irepl-string	**insert** Uses lines from standard input as arguments to *command*. All occurrences of *repl_string* in *command* are replaced by the arguments generated from standard input of **xargs**. If you omit *repl_string*, it defaults to the string { }, which matches the syntax used in the **find** command's **–exec** option (page 754). With this option *command* is executed for each input line. The **–l** option is ignored when you use **–i**.
–lmaxlines	**lines** ("ell") Executes *command* once for every *maxlines* of input. The final iteration may contain fewer than *maxlines* lines of input. If *maxlines* is omitted, it defaults to 1.
–nmaxargs	**number** Executes *command* once for every *maxargs* arguments in the input. Or put another way, for each iteration **xargs** calls *command* with *maxargs* arguments. The final iteration may contain fewer than *maxargs* arguments.
–p	**prompt** Prompts the user prior to each execution of *command*.
–ssizeargs	**size** Executes *command* using as many arguments as possible but not exceeding a command line of *sizeargs* bytes. The final iteration may contain fewer than *sizeargs* bytes.

Notes

The most common use of **xargs** is as an efficient alternative to using the **–exec** option of **find** (see **–exec command \;** on page 754). If you call **find** with the **–exec** option to run a command, it runs each command individually, once for each file that is processed. This is often inefficient, because every execution of a command requires the creation of a new process. By accumulating as many arguments as possible, **xargs** can greatly reduce the number of processes needed. The first example below shows how to use **xargs** with **find**.

Using **xargs** is safer than using command substitution—the `command` feature in any of the shells. When you use command substitution to build an argument list for another command, you may exceed the command length limit imposed by Solaris. When you exceed this limit, Solaris issues an error message and does not run the command. Because **xargs** avoids exceeding this limit by splitting up the list of arguments and repeating *command* as many times as necessary, you are assured that Solaris will always run *command*.

The **–i** option changes how **xargs** handles whitespace that is present in standard input. Without this option **xargs** treats sequences of SPACEs, TABs, and NEWLINEs as equivalent. With this option **xargs** treats NEWLINE characters specially. If a NEWLINE is encountered in standard input when using the **–i** option, **xargs** runs *command* using the argument list that has been built up to that point.

Discussion

As **xargs** reads standard input, it assumes the strings separated by sequences of SPACEs, TABs, and NEWLINEs are to be used as arguments to *command*. The **xargs** utility constructs a new command line from *command* and as many strings read from standard input as it can. If *command* line would exceed the maximum command line length, **xargs** runs *command* with the command line that has been built. If there is more standard input, **xargs** repeats this process of building up as long a command line as possible before running *command*. This process continues until all the input has been read.

Examples

If you want to locate and remove all the files whose names end in **.o** from the working directory and its subdirectories, you can do so with the **–exec** option of **find** (page 753).

```
$ find . -name \*.o -exec rm -f {} \;
```

This approach calls the **rm** utility once for each **.o** file that **find** locates. Each invocation of **rm** requires a new process. If there are a lot of **.o** files, then a significant amount of time is spent creating, starting, and then cleaning up these processes. You can greatly reduce the number of processes by allowing **xargs** to accumulate as many filenames as possible before calling **rm**. The **–f** option to **rm** prevents **rm** from asking any questions.

```
$ find . -name \*.o -print | xargs rm -f
```

In the next example the contents of all the ***.txt** files located by **find** are searched for lines containing the word `login`. The names of all files that contain `login` are displayed by **grep**.

```
$ find . -name \*.txt -print | xargs grep -w -l login
```

The next example shows how you can use the **–i** option to have **xargs** embed standard input within *command* instead of appending it to *command*. This option also causes *command* to be executed each time a **NEWLINE** character is encountered in standard input; the **–l** option cannot be used to override this behavior.

```
$ cat names
Tom,
Dick,
and Harry
$ xargs echo "Hello," < names
Hello, Tom, Dick, and Harry
$ xargs -i echo "Hello {}.  Join me for lunch?" < names
Hello Tom,. Join me for lunch?
Hello Dick,. Join me for lunch?
Hello and Harry. Join me for lunch?
```

The final example uses the same input file as the previous example and also uses the **–n** and **–l** ("ell") options:

```
$ xargs echo "Hi there" < names
Hi there Tom, Dick, and Harry
$ xargs -n1 echo "Hi there" < names
Hi there Tom,
Hi there Dick,
Hi there and
Hi there Harry
$ xargs -l2 echo "Hi there" < names
Hi there Tom, Dick,
Hi there and Harry
```

Regular Expressions

A regular expression defines a set of one or more strings of characters. Several utilities, including **vi, emacs, grep, nawk,** and **sed,** use regular expressions to make it easier to search for and replace strings. A simple string of characters is a regular expression that defines one string of characters: Itself. A more complex regular expression uses letters, numbers, and special characters to define many different strings of characters. A regular expression is said to *match* any string it defines.

This appendix describes the regular expressions used by **ed, vi, emacs, grep, nawk, sed,** and other utilities. The regular expressions used in ambiguous file references with the shell are somewhat different and are described in Chapter 5.

▲ Characters

As used in this appendix, a *character* is any character *except* a NEWLINE. Most characters represent themselves within a regular expression. A *special character* is one that does not represent itself. If you need to use a special character to represent itself, you must quote it. Refer to "Quoting Special Characters" on page 956.

▲ Delimiters

A character, called a *delimiter,* usually marks the beginning and end of a regular expression. The delimiter is always a special character for the regular expression it delimits (that is, it does not represent itself but marks the beginning and end of the expression). Although **vi** permits the use of other characters as a delimiter and **grep** does not use delimiters at all, the regular expressions in this appendix use a forward slash (/) as a delimiter. In some unambiguous cases the second delimiter is not required. For example you can sometimes omit the second delimiter when it would be followed immediately by RETURN.

▲ Simple Strings

The most basic regular expression is a simple string that contains no special characters except delimiters. A simple string matches only itself.

In the following examples the strings that are matched **look like this**.

Regular Expression	Matches	Examples
/ring/	**ring**	**ring**, sp**ring**, **ring**ing, st**ring**ing
/Thursday/	**Thursday**	**Thursday**, **Thursday**'s
/or not/	**or not**	**or not**, po**or not**hing

▲ Special Characters

You can use special characters within a regular expression to cause the regular expression to match more than one string.

▲▲ Period

A period (.) matches any character.

Regular Expression	Matches	Examples
/ .alk/	All strings consisting of a **SPACE** followed by any character followed by **alk**	will **talk**, may **balk**
/.ing/	All strings consisting of any character preceding **ing**	s**ing**ing, **ping**, before **ing**lenook

▲▲ Square Brackets

Square brackets ([]) define a *character class* that matches any single character within the brackets. If the first character following the left square bracket is a caret (^), the square brackets define a character class that matches any single character not within the brackets. You can use a hyphen to indicate a range of characters. Within a character class definition, backslashes and asterisks (described in the following sections) lose their special meanings. A right square bracket (appearing as a member of the character class) can appear only as the first character following the left square bracket. A caret is special only if it is the first character following the left bracket.

Regular Expression	Matches	Examples
/[bB]ill/	Member of the character class **b** and **B** followed by **ill**	**bill**, **Bill**, **bill**ed
/t[aeiou].k/	**t** followed by a lowercase vowel, any character, and a **k**	**talk**ative, s**tink**, **teak**, **tank**er
/number [6–9]/	**number** followed by a SPACE and a member of the character class **6** through **9**	**number 6**0, **number 8**:, get **number 9**
/[^a–zA–Z]/	Any character that is not a letter	**1**, **7**, **@**, **.**, **}**, Stop**!**

▲▲ Asterisk

An asterisk (∗) can follow a regular expression that represents a single character. The asterisk represents *zero or more* occurrences of a match of the regular expression. An asterisk following a period matches any string of characters. (A period matches any character, and an asterisk matches zero or more occurrences of the preceding regular expression.) A character class definition followed by an asterisk matches any string of characters that are members of the character class.

A regular expression that includes a special character always matches the longest possible string, starting as far toward the beginning (left) of the line as possible.

Regular Expression	Matches	Examples
/ab∗c/	**a** followed by zero or more **b**'s followed by a **c**	**ac**, **abc**, **abbc**, debbca**abbc**
/ab.∗c/	**ab** followed by zero or more characters followed by **c**	**abc**, **abxc**, **ab45c**, x**ab 756.345 x c**at
/t.∗ing/	**t** followed by zero or more characters followed by **ing**	**thing**, **ting**, I **thought of going**
/[a–zA–Z]∗/	A string composed only of letters and SPACEs	1. **any string without numbers or punctuation**!
/(.∗)/	As long a string as possible between **(** and **)**	Get **(this) and (that)**;
/([^)]∗)/	The shortest string possible that starts with **(** and ends with **)**	**(this)**, Get **(this and that)**

▲▲ Caret and Dollar Sign

A regular expression that begins with a caret (^) can match a string only at the beginning of a line. In a similar manner a dollar sign at the end of a regular expression matches the end of a line.

Regular Expression	Matches	Examples
/^T/	A **T** at the beginning of a line	**T**his line..., **T**hat Time..., In Time
/^+[0–9]/	A plus sign followed by a digit at the beginning of a line	**+5** +45.72, **+7**59 Keep this...
/:$/	A colon that ends a line	...below**:**

▲▲ Quoting Special Characters

You can quote any special character (but not a digit or a parenthesis) by preceding it with a backslash. Quoting a special character makes it represent itself.

Regular Expression	Matches	Examples
/end\./	All strings that contain **end** followed by a period	The **end.**, s**end.**, pret**end.**mail
/ \\/	A single backslash	\
/ */	An asterisk	*****.c, an asterisk (*****)
/ \[5\]/	**[5]**	it was five **[5]**
/and \/or/	**and/or**	**and/or**

▲ Rules

The following rules govern the application of regular expressions.

▲▲ Longest Match Possible

As stated previously, a regular expression always matches the longest possible string, starting as far toward the beginning of the line as possible. For example given the following string,

```
This (rug) is not what it once was (a long time ago), is it?
```

the expression /Th.*is/ matches

```
This (rug) is not what it once was (a long time ago), is
```

and /(.*)/ matches

        (rug) is not what it once was (a long time ago)

however, /([^)]*)/ matches

        (rug)

        Given the following string,

        singing songs, singing more and more

the expression /s.*ing/ matches

        singing songs, singing

and /s.*ing song/ matches

        singing song

▲▲ Empty Regular Expressions

Within some utilities such as **vi** and **less**, and not in **grep**, an empty regular expression always represents the regular expression that you used most recently. For example if you give **vi** the following Substitute command

        :s/mike/robert/

and then you want to make the same substitution again, you can use the following command:

        :s//robert/

        Alternatively you can use the following commands to search for the string mike and then make the substitution:

        /mike/
        :s//robert/

The empty regular expression (*//*) represents the regular expression that you used most recently (/mike/).

▲ Bracketing Expressions

You can use quoted parentheses, \(and \), to *bracket* a regular expression. The string that the bracketed regular expression matches can subsequently be used, as explained in "Quoted Digit," following. A regular expression does not attempt to match quoted parentheses. Thus a regular expression enclosed within quoted parentheses matches what the same regular expression without the parentheses would match. The expression /\(rexp\)/ matches what /rexp/ would match, and /a\(b*\)c/ matches what /ab*c/ would match.

        You can nest quoted parentheses. The bracketed expressions are identified only by the opening \(, so there is no ambiguity in identifying them. The expression /\([a-z]\([A-Z]*\)x\)/ consists of two bracketed expressions, one within the other. In the string 3 t dMNORx7 1 u, the preceding regular expression matches dMNORx, with the first bracketed expression matching dMNORx and the second matching MNORx.

▲ The Replacement String

The **vi** and **sed** editors use regular expressions as search strings within Substitute commands. You can use the ampersand (**&**) and quoted digits (**\n**) special characters to represent the matched strings within the corresponding replacement string.

▲▲ Ampersand

Within a replacement string, an ampersand (**&**) takes on the value of the string that the search string (regular expression) matched. For example the following **vi** Substitute command surrounds a string of one or more digits with **NN**. The ampersand in the replacement string matches whatever string of digits the regular expression (search string) matched.

```
:s/[0-9][0-9]*/NN&NN/
```

Two character class definitions are required because the regular expression **[0–9]*** matches *zero* or more occurrences of a digit, and *any* character string is zero or more occurrences of a digit.

▲▲ Quoted Digit

Within the search string, a quoted regular expression (**\(xxx\)**) matches what the regular expression would have matched without the quotes.

Within the replacement string, a quoted digit (**\n**) represents the string that the bracketed regular expression (portion of the search string) beginning with the *n*th **\(** matched.

For example you can take a list of people in the form

> *last-name, first-name initial*

and put it in the following form:

> *first-name initial last-name*

with the following **vi** command:

```
:1,$s/\([^,]*\), \(.*\)/\2 \1/
```

This command addresses all the lines in the file (`1`, `$`). The Substitute command (`s`) uses a search string and a replacement string delimited by forward slashes. The first bracketed regular expression within the search string, `\([^,]*\)`, matches what the same unbracketed regular expression, `[^,]*`, would match. This regular expression matches a string of zero or more characters not containing a comma (the ***last-name***). Following the first bracketed regular expression are a comma and a **SPACE** that match themselves. The second bracketed expression, `\(.*\)`, matches any string of characters (the ***first-name*** and ***initial***).

The replacement string consists of what the second bracketed regular expression matched (`\2`) followed by a **SPACE** and what the first bracketed regular expression matched (`\1`).

▲ Extended Regular Expressions

The **egrep** utility, **grep** when run with the **–E** option (similar to **egrep**), and **nawk** provide all the special characters that are included in ordinary regular expressions [but not \(and \)] as well as several others. Patterns using the extended set of special characters are called *full regular expressions* or *extended regular expressions*.

Two of the additional special characters are the plus sign (**+**) and question mark (**?**). They are similar to the *****, which matches *zero* or more occurrences of the previous character. The plus sign matches *one* or more occurrences of the previous character, whereas the question mark matches *zero* or *one* occurrence. You can use all three of these special characters *****, **+**, and **?** with parentheses, causing the special character to apply to the string surrounded by the parentheses. Unlike the parentheses in bracketed regular expressions, these parentheses are not quoted.

Regular Expression	Matches	Examples
/ab+c/	**a** followed by one or more **b**'s followed by a **c**	y**abc**w, **abbc**57
/ab?c/	**a** followed by zero or one **b** followed by **c**	b**ac**k, **abc**def
/(ab)+c/	One or more occurrences of the string **ab** followed by **c**	z**abc**d, **ababc**!
/(ab)?c/	Zero or one occurrences of the string **ab** followed by **c**	x**c**, **abc**c

In full regular expressions the vertical bar (|) special character is the OR operator. A vertical bar between two regular expressions causes a match with strings that match either the first expression or the second or both. You can use the vertical bar with parentheses to separate from the rest of the regular expression the two expressions that are being ORed.

Regular Expression	Meaning	Examples
/ab|ac/	Either **ab** or **ac**	**ab**, **ac**, **ab**ac
/^Exit|^Quit/	Lines that begin with **Exit** or **Quit**	**Exit**, **Quit**, No Exit
/(D|N)\. Jones/	**D. Jones** or **N. Jones**	P.**D. Jones**, **N. Jones**

Summary

A regular expression defines a set of one or more strings of characters. A regular expression is said to match any string it defines. The following characters are special within a regular expression:

Special Character	Function
.	Matches any single character.
*	Matches zero or more occurrences of a match of the preceding character.
^	Forces a match to the beginning of a line.
$	Matches the end of a line.
\	Quotes a special character.
\<	Forces a match to the beginning of a word.
\>	Forces a match to the end of a word.

The following strings are special forms of regular expressions that match classes of characters and bracket regular expressions:

Regular Expression	Function
[xyz]	Defines a character class that matches *x*, *y*, or *z*.
[^xyz]	Defines a character class that matches any character except *x*, *y*, or *z*.
[x–z]	Defines a character class that matches any character *x* through *z*, inclusive.
\(xyz\)	Matches what **xyz** matches (a bracketed regular expression).

In addition to the above special characters and strings (excluding quoted parentheses), the following characters are special within extended regular expressions:

Extended Regular Expressions	
Special Character/ Regular Expression	**Matches**
+	One or more occurrences of the preceding character.
?	Zero or one occurrence of the preceding character.
(xyz)+	One or more occurrences of what **xyz** matches.
(xyz)?	Zero or one occurrence of what **xyz** matches.

Extended Regular Expressions	
Special Character/ Regular Expression	**Matches**
(*xyz*)*	Zero or more occurrences of what *xyz* matches.
xyz|*abc*	Either what *xyz* or what *abc* matches.
(*xy*|*ab*)*c*	Either what *xyc* or what *abc* matches.

Refer to page 263 for a description of regular expressions in **vi**. The following characters are special within a replacement string in **sed** and **vi**:

Character	Function
&	Represents what the regular expression (search string) matched.
n	A quoted number, *n*, represents the *n*th bracketed regular expression in the search string.

Help!

There is a lot of help available for Solaris users and would-be users. Besides this book there is help on your machine, on the Internet, and in other books and periodicals. This book is a starting place, not by any means an ending place.

The Internet is much bigger than most people realize. An abundance of help for Solaris users and system administrators is available on the Internet; you just have to find it and read it or download it. That is what the first part of this appendix is about: Finding and downloading Solaris information, documentation, source code, and compiled code. The author's home page (**www.sobell.com**) contains an up-to-date version of the tables in this appendix, corrections to this book, as well as pointers to many other Solaris sites.

The latter part of this appendix (page 987 and following) helps you get started with your own system: How to use the printer, which keys are what, and information about a graphical user interface and its components (mouse, window, and so on).

▲ System Documentation and Information

Distributions of Solaris come with reference manual pages stored online. You can read these documents, referred to as **man** pages, using the **man** or **xman** utility (give the command **man man**, or see page 27). You can read **man** pages to get more information about specific topics while reading this book or to determine what features are available with Solaris. You can search for topics using the **apropos** utility (see page 54, or give the command **apropos apropos** or **man apropos**).

In addition to the **man** utility, Solaris offers other online information. AnswerBook2 provides queriable, hypertext-linked access to additional information on utilities, hardware, software, and system features (page 26).

▲▲ Where Can I Find More Documentation?

There are quite a few good books available on different aspects of using and administrating UNIX systems in general and Solaris systems in specific. In addition you may find the following documents useful:[1]

---

1. The right-hand columns of most of the tables in this chapter show Internet addresses. All sites have an implicit **http://** prefix unless **ftp://** is shown. You do not need to specify the prefix, but you cannot use **ftp** to access a pure **http** site (some sites are set up to work with either **http** or **ftp** access).

Documentation		
Tool	**What It Does**	**Where to Get It**
Solaris2 FAQ	A thorough FAQ maintained by Casper Dik and broken into groups: General/Sources of Information/System Administration/ Networking/Troubleshooting/ Software Development/Kernel Parameters.	**www.wins.uva.nl/pub/solaris/solaris2**
FAQs	Frequently Asked (Answered) Questions of all types.	**ftp://rtfm.mit.edu/pub/** (Get **index-byname** and search for `solaris`. This index is large [300K+] as it covers all news groups.) **metalab.unc.edu/pub/solaris/FAQS**
RFCs	Request for Comments (page 198).	**ftp://ftp.uu.net/inet/rfc** (download **rfc-index** for a list of RFCs)
Sun Security Bulletin Archive	A list of almost all of the security bulletins sent out by Sun.	**sunsolve.sun.com/pub-cgi/secbul.pl**

▲▲ Where Can I Look Up a Word?

There are many online dictionaries on the Web. The following list shows a few of them.

Dictionaries		
Name	**Specialty**	**Where to Get It**
whatis?com	knowledge exploration tool	**whatis.com**
Tech Encyclopedia	computer terms	**www.techweb.com/encyclopedia/defineterm.cgi**
The Free On-line Dictionary of Computing	computer terms	**www.foldoc.doc.ic.ac.uk/foldoc**
Military Maritime Command and Control System (MCCIS): Project Documentation	security	**cliffie.nosc.mil/~NAPDOC/docprj/security/ glossary-of-compusec-terms/index.html**
Sun Glossary	general and Solaris specific computer terms	**www.sun.com/glossary/glossary.html**
Merriam-Webster	English language	**www.m-w.com/netdict.htm**

▲▲ What Are Some Useful Solaris Internet Sites?

Often these particular sites are so busy that you cannot log in. When this happens you are usually given a list of alternative, or *mirror,* sites to try. For a more current list of sites that have Solaris-related information, use a browser to visit **www.sobell.com** and choose **Solaris**. Also see the Tip on page 985 for the location of some FAQs that contain a lot of useful information.

Location	What It Does	Where to Get It
Sun	(USA) Sun's Solaris home page. Links to downloads, drivers, articles, and more.	**www.sun.com/solaris**
UNC	(USA) The browser and **ftp** entry into the University of North Carolina's Metalab (formerly named **sunsite**), which contains a lot of Solaris source, binary, and documentation files.	**metalab.unc.edu/pub/solaris**
Sun	(USA) Sun provides compiled free software for Solaris 2.5, 2.6, and System 7 on x86 and SPARC platforms.	**sunfreeware.com**
Sun	(USA) Sun provides all AnswerBook2 documentation ever produced on CD.	**docs.sun.com**
Sun	(USA) Sun provides a searchable index of white papers, bug reports, problem issues, patches, FAQs, and more (*registered users only*).	**sunsolve1.sun.com**
Sun (Canada)	(CA) The Sun Canadian groups put up a lot of freeware in the **pub** directory tree both as source and as precompiled binaries ready to install.	**opcom.sun.ca**
Sun	(USA) A list of Solaris links.	**sunfreeware.com/othersites.html**
GNU	(USA) Central site for Free Software Foundation (GNU) software.	**ftp://ftp.gnu.org:/pub/gnu** (**html**: see instructions on page 984; **ftp**: **cd** to **pub/gnu**. See page 976 for information on obtaining **gzip**.) Also see **www.gnu.org**.
Network Associates	Pretty Good Privacy (PGP) information.	**www.pgp.com** (commercial site, has free software)

Location	What It Does	Where to Get It
X Consortium	(USA) Central site for X Window System software.	**ftp://ftp.x.org:contrib**
Doug	(USA) Source code, security, and intrusion detection tools, **lpd** information, and more.	**www.eng.auburn.edu/~doug/second.html**

▲▲ What Are the Names of Some Solaris Newsgroups?

One of the best ways of getting specific information is through a newsgroup (pages 229 and 236). Frequently you can find the answer to your question just by reading postings to the newsgroup. Try using **dejanews** power search to look through newsgroups (**www.dejanews.com**) to see if your question has already been asked and answered. If necessary, you can post your question for someone to answer. Make sure your question has not been answered before you post it.

alt.solaris.x86	Intel group
alt.sys.sun	Small general Solaris newsgroup
comp.sys.sun.admin	Administrators
comp.sys.sun.apps	Applications
comp.sys.sun.hardware	Hardware
comp.sys.sun.misc	Miscellaneous
comp.sys.sun.wanted	Sun hardware and software wanted to buy
comp.unix.solaris	Main Solaris newsgroup

▲▲ What Are Some Useful Mailing Lists?

Subscribing to a mailing list (page 201) allows you to participate in an electronic discussion. With most lists, you can send email to and receive email from a group of users that is dedicated to a specific topic. Moderated lists do not tend to stray as much as unmoderated lists, assuming the list has a good moderator. The disadvantage of a moderated list is that some discussions may be cut off when they get interesting if the moderator deems the discussion has gone on for too long. Mail lists described as bulletins are strictly unidirectional: You cannot post information to these lists but can only receive periodic bulletins. If you have the subscription address for a mailing list but are not sure how to subscribe, put the word `help` in the body and/or header of email that you send to the address. You will usually receive instructions via email.

List Name	Subscription Address	Type	Description
bugtraq	**listserv@netspace.org**	moderated	Full disclosure mailing list on operating system, program bugs, and security holes. Tendency for tangential discussions.
CERT	**cert-advisory-request@cert.org**	bulletins	Security advisories.

List Name	Subscription Address	Type	Description
CIAC	**majordomo@rumpole.llnl.gov** body: `subscribe ciac-bulletin`	bulletins	Announcements about viruses and vendor security holes.
firewalls	**majordomo@gnac.com** body: `subscribe firewalls`	open	Discussions about firewall policy and implementation issues. Discussions can be off track.
firewall wizards	**firewall-wizards@nfr.net**	moderated	Moderated doppelgänger for firewalls.
freefire	**freefire-l-request@inka.de**	bulletins	Announcements of free firewalls and toolkits.
ssa-managers	**majordomo@eng.auburn.edu** body: `subscribe ssa-managers`	open	Issues relating to SPARCStorage devices and the controlling software (A1000, D1000, SPARCStorage array, A5000, Veritas Volume Manager, Solstice DiskSuite, and so on).
sun-managers	**majordomo@ sunmanagers.ececs.uc.edu** body: `subscribe sun-managers`	open	Mail list cross-posted to **comp.sys.sun.admin** for discussions about Sun operating systems and SPARC-based computers.
SunSolve Early Notifier	**SunSolve-EarlyNotifier@ Sun.COM**	bulletin	Early notification of the release of OS patches.
Best of Security	**best-of-security-request@ cyber.com.au**	bulletin	A digested form of bugtraq.
COAST Security archive	**coast-request@cs.purdue.edu**	bulletin	Periodic updates and announcements from the COAST team.
WWW Security	**majordomo@nsmx.rutgers.edu**	open	Discussions of WWW security issues and their solutions.

▲ How Do I Find the Program I Want on the Internet?

There are many ways to learn of interesting software packages and where they are available on the Internet. The following tables list many free packages and sites. Many of these sites have additional packages available; you just have to look around for them (click on various directories from your browser or use **cd** and **ls** from **ftp**—see the following sections).

Another way to learn about a package is through a newsgroup (page 966). If your newsreader can use HTML links in the messages to download the software directly, it will locate the package and run **ftp** automatically. If not, you will have to use the steps outlined in the following sections and use **ftp** or your browser to download the software.

▲▲ Utility Programs

Following are just a few of the many sites on the Internet from which you can obtain utility programs that run on Solaris systems.

Tool	What It Does	Where to Get It
cdrecord	A CDROM burner that works with most available CDROM and CDRW devices.	ftp://ftp.fokus.gmd.de/pub/unix/cdrecord
Subnet mask calculator	For more information see "Subnets" on page 195.	www.ccci.com/tools/subcalc/index.html
patch (GNU)	Similar to the Solaris-supplied **patch**, but better (page 851).	ftp://ftp.gnu.org/gnu/patch/patch-2.5.tar.gz
fastpatch	For applying Sun OS patches to Solaris 2.5.1 or lower. Much faster than **installpatch**, but cannot be backed out.	ftp://ftp.wins.uva.nl/pub/solaris/auto-install/
fix-modes	Sets system file and directory permissions to more reasonable defaults (page 674).	ftp://ftp.wins.uva.nl/pub/solaris
lsof	For more information see "lsof: Find Large, Open Files" on page 673.	ftp://vic.cc.purdue.edu/pub/tools/unix/lsof
lynx	A free text-only character-based Web browser.	www.crl.com/~subir/lynx.html
memconf	Shows what kinds of SIMMs are in which slots in a SPARC station.	www.rkdltd.demon.co.uk
proctool	For more information see "When the System is Slow" on page 671.	ftp://opcom.sun.ca/pub/freeware/sparc/*
procmail	Email filtering software.	www.procmail.org ftp://ftp.procmail.org/pub/procmail/
qps	For more information see "When the System is Slow" on page 671.	ftp://ftp.eng.auburn.edu/pub/doug
sformat	An improved, free replacement disk analyzer and formatter for UNIX (requires **scg**).	ftp://ftp.fokus.gmd.de/pub/unix/sformat ftp://ftp.fokus.gmd.de/pub/unix/kernel/scg

Tool	What It Does	Where to Get It
star	Free, faster, POSIX-compliant replacement for Solaris **tar**.	**ftp://ftp.fokus.gmd.de/pub/unix/star**
top	A utility that gives continual reports about the state of a system, including a list of which processes are using most of the CPU's resources. For more information see "When the System is Slow" on page 671.	**ftp://ftp.groupsys.com/pub/top**

▲▲ Security Programs

There are many sites that contain many programs dedicated to system security. In addition to the following, refer to the tables on page 1000 for more programs and sites.

Tool	What It Does	Where to Get It
COAST/ CERIAS	COAST/CERIAS Security Archives at Purdue.	**ftp://coast.cs.purdue.edu/pub/tools/unix** **www.cs.purdue.edu/coast/archive** **www.cerias.purdue.edu**
CERT	Carnegie Mellon Software Engineering Institute Computer Emergency Response Team coordination center.	**www.cert.org**
cops	Finds bad passwords and audits your system.	**ftp://coast.cs.purdue.edu/pub/tools/unix/cops**
crack	Finds bad passwords.	**ftp://coast.cs.purdue.edu/pub/tools/unix/sudo**
sudo	Restricts and audits **su** usage.	**www.courtesan.com/sudo**
priv	Restricts and audits **su** usage.	**ftp://ftp.ucdavis.edu/pub/unix**
des	File encryption.	**ftp://ftp.hacktic.nl/pub/crypto/applied-crypto**
Sun Security Bulletins	Sun Security Bulletins.	**sunsolve.sun.com/pub-cgi/secbul.pl**
Sun Security Patches	Sun Security Patches.	**sunsolve.sun.com/sunsolve/pubpatches/ patches.html**
privtool	A free mail user agent that is a look-alike for Sun's OpenLook **mailtool**, but which provides an interface to PGP.	**http://www.netspace.net.au/~ggt/privtool.html**

Tool	What It Does	Where to Get It
PGP	Software, information, and related products.	**www.pgp.com or www.nai.com** **ftp://ftp.hacktic.nl/pub/replay/pgp**
PGPelm	A PGP-enabled version of the popular UNIX email client Elm.	**ftp://ftp.sunet.se/pub/security/pgp/utils/elm**
RIPEM	An encryption routine that has received more widespread use than PEM, but still lacks the broad base of PGP. Current versions are available outside the United States without restrictions.	**ftp://utopia.hacktic.nl/pub/replay/crypto/** **APPS/ripem**
PGP and PEM sendmail	Encryption routines. There are PGP and PEM extended versions of **sendmail**. Also see RIPEM.	**ftp://ftp.ox.ac.uk/pub/crypto/pgp/utils** (PGP **sendmail** extensions and other PGP enabled programs) **comp.mail.sendmail newsgroup-FAQ**
SKIP	Encrypts all traffic between two machines at the session level.	**www.skip.org**
IPSec	Secures machine-to-machine communications (notes).	**www.ietf.org/html.charters/ipsec-charter.html**
cfs	Cryptographic filesystem by Matt Blaze.	**www.cryptography.org** **comp.security.firewalls** newsgroup
tripwire	Checks your host for possible signs of intruder activity.	**ftp://coast.cs.purdue.edu/pub/COAST/Tripwire** **www.tripwiresecurity.com**
satan	Scans your host and network for known vulnerabilities (showing its age).	**ftp://ciac.llnl.gov/pub/ciac/sectools/unix/satan** **ftp://coast.cs.purdue.edu/pub/COAST/tools/** **SATAN_Extensions.tar.Z**
SecurID card	Security Dynamics Technologies, Inc.	**www.securid.com**
Miscellaneous security	Miscellaneous security.	Also check **www.hacktic.nl** (Hack-Tic Magazine Archive [in Dutch]) and **www.cryptography.com** (U.S. and Canada only).

▲▲ Communication Programs

Tool	What It Does	Where to Get It
BIND	The original domain name services source code.	**ftp://ftp.isc.org/isc/bind**
cyrus	An IMAP mail server.	**ftp://ftp.andrew.cmu.edu/pub/cyrus-mail**
dp	A free PPP replacement.	**www.ces.purdue.edu/dp**
majordomo	Free mailing list software.	**ftp://ftp.greatcircle.com/pub/majordomo**

Tool	What It Does	Where to Get It
smartlist	Free mailing list software.	**www.procmail.org** **ftp://ftp.procmail.org/pub/procmail/**
mailman	GNU mailing list manager.	**www.list.org**
listserv	Free mailing list software.	**www.l-soft.com**
ppp	A free PPP replacement.	**ftp://cs.anu.edu.au/pub/software/ppp**
Everything serial	Serial port utilities, resources, programming tips, PPP, and modem settings.	**www.stokely.com**
pine	A popular cross-platform mail client.	**ftp://ftp.cac.washington.edu/pine** **www.cac.washington.edu/pine**
sendmail	The original version of **sendmail** from the University of California at Berkeley.	**ftp://ftp.sendmail.org/pub/sendmail/**

▲▲ Miscellaneous Programs

Tool	What It Does	Where to Get It
Acroread	The Adobe Acrobat PDF reader.	**www.adobe.com** (click on Free Plug-ins and Updates, UNIX adjacent to Acrobat Reader, and then on Solaris.)
apache	The most popular Web server in the world.	**www.apache.org**
inn	The most popular USENET news server source.	**ftp://ftp.isc.org/isc/inn**
bootpd	A Bootp server for UNIX (also answers DHCP requests).	**ftp://ftp.eng.auburn.edu/pub/doug**
dhcp	A DHCP server for UNIX.	**ftp://ftp.isc.org/isc/dhcp**
gnuplot	A GNU X plotting program.	**ftp://ftp.dartmouth.edu/pub/gnuplot**
change-sun-hostid	A suite of utilities for manipulating system hostid and other NVRAM properties on SPARC stations.	**ftp://ftp.mindlink.net/pub/crypto/sun-stuff**
ImageMagick	A suite of image manipulation, display, and conversion programs.	**ftp://ftp.x.org**
GIMP	GNU Image Manipulation Program (similar to PhotoShop).	**www.gimp.org**
perl	A popular general-purpose language, frequently used for WWW CGI scripting.	**www.perl.org**

Tool	What It Does	Where to Get It
CPAN	Comprehensive Perl Archive Network.	**www.cpan.org**
Tcl/Tk	Popular extension language and GUI toolkit.	**www.scriptics.com**
neosoft	Tcl/Tk archive.	**www.neosoft.com/tcl**
ups	A graphical debugger.	**ftp://ftp.x.org/contrib/utilities**
sysinfo	Query system information, configuration, and devices.	**http://www.magnicomp.com/**
xmgr	An X plotting/graphing program.	**ftp://ftp.x.org/contrib/applications**
tgif	X-based drawing program.	**ftp://ftp.x.org/contrib/applications/tgif**
xfig	X-based drawing program.	**ftp://ftp.x.org/contrib/applications/drawing_tools/xfig/**
transfig	Translates **xfig** files to other formats.	**ftp://ftp.x.org/contrib/applications/drawing_tools/transfig**
xv	X-based image display, manipulation, and conversion program.	**www.trilon.com/xv**
RAPS/toptool	Software performance monitoring tool for Solaris.	**www.foglight.com/product/toptool.html**
sas	Commercial program from SAS Inc. For more information see "Patches" on page 629.	**www.sas.com**
samba	Turns your UNIX workstation into a CIFS/SMB file server that looks like an NT server.	**samba.anu.edu.au**
netatalk	Turns your UNIX workstation into an Appletalk server for Macs.	**ftp://terminator.rs.itd.umich.edu/unix/netatalk**
xview	An OpenLook GUI toolkit.	**ftp://ftp.x.org**
proctool	A GUI that gives enhanced **ps**-like functionality.	**http://sunfreeware.com**
SE	The system engineer's toolkit. This is a suite of utilities for diagnosing system performance problems and finding bottlenecks.	**www.sun.com/sun-on-net/performance/se3**
xpdf	A PDF document viewer.	**www.foolabs.com/xpdf**
mxgdb	A GUI front end to **gdb** debugger.	**ftp://ftp.x.org/contrib/applications**
System patches	For more information see "Patches" on page 629.	**sunsolve.Sun.COM/pub-cgi/us/pubpatchpage.pl**

▲ Downloading, Installing, and Running Software

The following sections discuss the differences between a binary and source file, how to use **ftp** to download a file, how to download and install the **gzip** compression utility, how to use **tar** and **gzip** to unpack an archive file, and how to compile, link, and install a binary file. The final section in this part shows how to download a file using the Netscape browser.

▲▲ What Is the Difference Between Installing a Binary and a Source Software File?

A source file contains all the source code (written in C for example) that makes up a program. You can read and edit source code with an editor such as **vi** or **dtpad**. The source code for the **gcc** compiler is almost 9MB. Not only does it contain all the instructions for the compiler, but it includes all of the programmer's comments. When you download source code, you need to compile it before you can install and run it. Because you compile the source code, you can generally compile it to run on your machine (that is, SPARC or x86). Compiling source code can take quite a while and may require some experience. For more information see "How Do I Compile and Link the Software?" on page 981.

A binary (also called executable) file is the product of compiling (and assembling and linking) the source code, frequently with a C compiler. There are no comments and no long variable names (usually), just ones and zeros, so it does not take up as much space. The binary file for the **gcc** compiler is about 6MB. When you are looking for a binary file to run on your machine, make sure it was compiled for your machine (SPARC versus x86). After you download a binary file, you just need to install it by copying it into the right location and you are ready to run the program. Installing a binary file takes less time and experience than compiling and installing source code.

▲▲ How Do I Get a Program Off the Internet and Run It on My Computer?

Follow steps 1 and 2 *or* steps 1 and 3 below to get software off the Internet and run it on your machine.

1. **Download and install gzip**[2]

    You usually need **gzip** to decompress a free software file (page 976).

---

2. If you do not have the **gzip** utility on your system (it is a GNU product and Sun does not supply it), you must get it before you can continue installing **gcc**. Refer to "How Do I Download gzip?" on page 976.

2. **Binary or executable code**
   Get software already compiled for your platform and version of Solaris (page 974 or 984).

   a. Decompress
      Most files that you download are compressed using **compress** (Sun files) or **gzip** (most free software files). One notable exception is the **gzip** utility itself: It is not usually compressed. For more information see "How Do I Unpack the Software Source Code?" on page 981. Although you are not unpacking source code, the steps are the same for unpacking executable code. Page 981 covers the use of **gzip** and **tar** (next step). If the filename ends in **.Z**, it was compressed with **compress** (page 49). Even though the file was compressed with **compress**, you can decompress it with **gzip** as shown in the example.

   b. Extract files from the decompressed archive
      Most files that you download are archived in **tar** format so that you only have to download one file. Before you can use the file, you must unarchive it (extract the files from it) using **tar** (page 977).

   c. Install
      You can install many binary files using the **pkgadd** utility (page 978).

3. **Source code**
   Get software that you must compile before you can install it.

   a. Decompress
      See 2a.

   b. Extract files from archive
      See 2b.

   c. Compile and link
      You must compile and link source code (frequently using **gcc** or **cc**) before you can install it. Normally there is a makefile that simplifies this task (page 981).

   d. Install
      Usually the makefile also installs the software (page 984).

▲▲▲ How Do I Use ftp?

To install a new software package or a new version of software you already have, you need to get a copy of the software. A common way to get software for Solaris, especially free software, is to obtain the distribution package from the Internet. Use the **ftp** utility to connect to a remote site that has the distribution package and transfer, or download, a copy to your machine.

The following example shows how to connect to the remote system on the Internet named **metalab.unc.edu** as the anonymous user.

Traditionally any password was acceptable for anonymous **ftp**; by convention you were expected to give your email address. Today some sites reject your connection if they cannot identify the name of your computer.

Before you start downloading, figure out where you are going to work (typically in the **/var/tmp** or **/tmp** directory). Working as yourself (not Superuser), use **cd** to change to the **/var/tmp** directory. Then use **ftp** to connect to **metalab.unc.edu**. Log in as **anonymous** or **ftp** and give your email address as a password.

> ## Only Become Superuser When You Must
>
> Because mistakes you make as Superuser can have a larger impact than mistakes you make while logged in as yourself, it is a good idea to become Superuser only when you absolutely must.

```
$ cd /var/tmp
$ ftp metalab.unc.edu
Connected to metalab.unc.edu.
220-               Welcome to UNC's MetaLab ftp archives!
220-          (at the site formerly known as sunsite.unc.edu)
220-
220-You can access this archive via http with the same URL.
220-
220-example:   ftp://metalab.unc.edu/pub/Linux/ becomes
220-           http://metalab.unc.edu/pub/Linux/
220-
220-For more information about services offered by MetaLab,
220-go to http://metalab.unc.edu
220-
220-WE'RE BACK TO USING WUFTPD.
220-You can still get tarred directories if you issue the following command:
220-    get dirname.tar
220-You can also get gzipped or compressed tarred directories by following
220-the .tar with .gz or .Z, respectively.
220-
220-Have any suggestions or questions? Email ftpkeeper@metalab.unc.edu.
220-
220 helios.oit.unc.edu FTP server (Version wu-2.4.2-academ[BETA-13](7) Wed Feb 10
02:22:09 EST 1999) ready.
Name (metalab.unc.edu:jenny): ftp
331 Guest login ok, send your complete e-mail address as password.
Password:
230 Guest login ok, access restrictions apply.
ftp>
```

If you need to transfer a file containing non-ASCII data, such as a binary program or a compressed file, you need to set **ftp** accordingly:

```
ftp> binary
```

If you fail to specify a binary transfer, you will not get the results you expect. The transfer may take a long time to complete, and the size and contents of the file will not be correct. This is the most common mistake that is made when using **ftp**. To correct it turn on the binary option (above) and transfer the file again.

Although not required for a file transfer, you can put **ftp** back into ASCII mode with this command:

```
ftp> ascii
```

While using **ftp** you can type **help** at any ftp> prompt to see a list of commands. Refer to pages 207 and 765 for more information on **ftp**.

▲▲▲ How Do I Download gzip?

Many free software packages are available for Solaris. Some of these packages are in the Solaris software package format so that they are easy to install. Most of these packages come in a file compressed by the free GNU **gzip** utility (not provided with Solaris [pages 50 and 781]). If you do not have **gzip**, you cannot use the software you download that has been compressed with **gzip**.

This section explains how to download the **gzip** package for several versions of Solaris running on either an Intel x86 or SPARC machine. The **gzip** package is not usually compressed because it is assumed that if you are downloading it, you do not have it, and therefore could not use it to decompress the file that you are downloading (itself). The techniques shown here will work on any software in the Solaris software package format. You must decompress most files that you download before using **tar** to extract the files from the archive: Not decompressing **gzip** before using **tar** is an exception. Files compressed with **gzip** (or with **compress**) can be decompressed with a **gunzip** or **gzip –d** command.

After logging in on **metalab.unc.edu** (page 974), use **cd** to change directories to **pub/solaris** and **ls** to list the contents of the **solaris** directory.

```
ftp> cd pub/solaris
250 CWD command successful.
ftp> ls
200 PORT command successful.
150 Opening ASCII mode data connection for file list.
freeware
FAQS
i86pc
sparc
X11R6.4.SPARC.Solaris.2.4.pkg.tgz
X11R6.4.SPARC.Solaris.2.5.1.pkg.tgz
X11R6.4.SPARC.Solaris.2.5.pkg.tgz
226 Transfer complete.
137 bytes received in 0.024 seconds (5.63 Kbytes/s)
```

To download an x86 (Intel) version of **gzip**, **cd** to **i86pc**; for a SPARC version, **cd** to **sparc**. Then list all the versions of **GNUzip** that are available. Although the example shows how to download and install an x86 version of **gzip**, you work with a SPARC file the same way: Only the filename will be different.

```
ftp> cd i86pc
250 CWD command successful.
ftp> ls GNUzip*
200 PORT command successful.
150 Opening ASCII mode data connection for file list.
GNUzip.1.2.4.i86pc.Solaris.2.5.1.pkg.tar
GNUzip.1.2.4.i86pc.Solaris.2.6.pkg.tar
226 Transfer complete.
remote: GNUzip*
82 bytes received in 0.031 seconds (2.57 Kbytes/s)
```

If you had given this **ls** command in the **sparc** directory, you would have seen:

```
GNUzip.1.2.4.SPARC.Solaris.2.4.pkg.tar
GNUzip.1.2.4.SPARC.Solaris.2.5.1.pkg.tar
GNUzip.1.2.4.SPARC.Solaris.2.5.pkg.tar
GNUzip.1.2.4.SPARC.Solaris.2.6.pkg.tar
```

Pick the version of **GNUzip** that corresponds to the version of Solaris you are using. Give a **bin** command to make sure **ftp** is in binary mode, and use **get** to download the file. Wait until you see the message Transfer complete and get an ftp> prompt before giving a **quit** command to leave **ftp**.

```
ftp> bin
200 Type set to I.
ftp> get GNUzip.1.2.4.i86pc.Solaris.2.6.pkg.tar
200 PORT command successful.
150 Opening BINARY mode data connection for GNUzip.1.2.4.i86pc.Solaris.2.6.pkg.tar
(153600 bytes).
226 Transfer complete.
local: GNUzip.1.2.4.i86pc.Solaris.2.6.pkg.tar remote:
GNUzip.1.2.4.i86pc.Solaris.2.6.pkg.tar
153600 bytes received in 15 seconds (10.13 Kbytes/s)
ftp> quit
221 Goodbye.
```

▲▲▲ How Do I Install gzip?

Once you have downloaded the **gzip** archive file, you are ready to install it. Following, **ls** ensures that the file that you just downloaded (**GNUzip.1.2.4.i86pc.Solaris.2.6.pkg.tar**) is in your working directory. The **umask** command ensures that the files will be installed with the proper permissions. The **tar** utility extracts the files from the **tar** archive.

```
$ ls
GNUzip.1.2.4.i86pc.Solaris.2.6.pkg.tar   wsconAAA0gNAQG:0.0
wsconAAA03c9mF:0.0
$ umask 0
$ /usr/bin/tar -xvf GNUzip.1.2.4.i86pc.Solaris.2.6.pkg.tar
x GNUzip, 0 bytes, 0 tape blocks
x GNUzip/pkgmap, 1656 bytes, 4 tape blocks
x GNUzip/pkginfo, 214 bytes, 1 tape blocks
x GNUzip/root, 0 bytes, 0 tape blocks
x GNUzip/root/usr, 0 bytes, 0 tape blocks
x GNUzip/root/usr/local, 0 bytes, 0 tape blocks
x GNUzip/root/usr/local/bin, 0 bytes, 0 tape blocks
x GNUzip/root/usr/local/bin/gzexe, 3858 bytes, 8 tape blocks
x GNUzip/root/usr/local/bin/gzip, 61440 bytes, 120 tape blocks
.
.
.
.
.
x GNUzip/root/usr/local/man/man1/znew.1, 999 bytes, 2 tape blocks
x GNUzip/install, 0 bytes, 0 tape blocks
x GNUzip/install/preinstall, 504 bytes, 1 tape blocks
$
```

Now when you are ready to install the **gzip** utility and need to write to the protected parts of the file-system, you need to work as Superuser. Give the **su** command, then use **ls** to make sure the **GNUzip** directory is in the working directory. To install the utility run **pkgadd**, specifying the working directory (**–d .**) as the location of the software package named **GNUzip**. Answer **y** when you are asked about running as Superuser and give the command **exit** when you are told that all went well and you see a prompt. That is the only time you have to be Superuser for this whole process; **exit** gets you back to being you. You can check that **gzip** is working by giving the command **gzip --help**.

```
$ su
Password:
# ls
GNUzip                                    wsconAAA03c9mF:0.0
GNUzip.1.2.4.i86pc.Solaris.2.6.pkg.tar    wsconAAA0gNAQG:0.0
#
# pkgadd -d . GNUzip

Processing package instance <GNUzip> from </var/tmp>

GNUzip 1.2.4 i86pc Solaris 2.6
(i86pc) 1.2.4
GNU
## Processing package information.
## Processing system information.
   5 package pathnames are already properly installed.
## Verifying disk space requirements.
## Checking for conflicts with packages already installed.
## Checking for setuid/setgid programs.

This package contains scripts which will be executed with super-user
permission during the process of installing this package.

Do you want to continue with the installation of <GNUzip> [y,n,?] y

Installing GNUzip 1.2.4 i86pc Solaris 2.6 as <GNUzip>

## Executing preinstall script.
## Installing part 1 of 1.
/usr/local/bin/gzexe
/usr/local/bin/gzip
.
.
.
/usr/local/man/man1/znew.1
[ verifying class <none> ]
/usr/local/bin/gunzip <linked pathname>
/usr/local/bin/zcat <linked pathname>
/usr/local/bin/zcmp <linked pathname>
/usr/local/man/man1/gunzip.1 <linked pathname>
/usr/local/man/man1/zcat.1 <linked pathname>
/usr/local/man/man1/zcmp.1 <linked pathname>
```

```
Installation of <GNUzip> was successful.
# exit

$ gzip --help
gzip 1.2.4 (18 Aug 93)
usage: gzip [-cdfhlLnNrtvV19] [-S suffix] [file ...]
 -c --stdout      write on standard output, keep original files unchanged
 -d --decompress  decompress
 -f --force       force overwrite of output file and compress links
 -h --help        give this help
 -l --list        list compressed file contents
 -L --license     display software license
 -n --no-name     do not save or restore the original name and time stamp
 -N --name        save or restore the original name and time stamp
 -q --quiet       suppress all warnings
 -r --recursive   operate recursively on directories
 -S .suf --suffix .suf     use suffix .suf on compressed files
 -t --test        test compressed file integrity
 -v --verbose     verbose mode
 -V --version     display version number
 -1 --fast        compress faster
 -9 --best        compress better
 file...          files to (de)compress. If none given, use standard input.
$
```

▲▲▲ Downloading (Using **ftp**), Compiling, and Installing GNU **make**

This example shows you how to download (following), compile (page 981), and install (page 984) a source code version of GNU **make**. Most software distributions consist of one or more **tar** (pages 50 and 977) archives that have been compressed with **gzip** (page 976) to save disk space and transfer time. Such files typically have the filename extension **.tar.gz** or **.tgz**. Refer to page 974 and following if you need to download and install **gzip**.

This example downloads **make** from **prep.ai.mit.edu** (the primary GNU site) and works in the **/tmp** directory. First **cd** to **/tmp** and give the **ftp** command to connect to the remote site. Then log in as the anonymous user (**ftp**), give your email address as a password, **cd** to the directory that holds the distributions for GNU (**/pub/gnu**), and list the versions of **make** in that directory. Use the **ftp binary** command to make sure the file is downloaded in binary mode. Although some remote systems do this automatically, it never hurts to use the **binary** command, even if the transfer involves only ASCII files. Then download the most recent version of **make** as well as a file named **makeinfo.README** in case it has any pertinent information.

```
% cd /tmp
% ftp prep.ai.mit.edu
Connected to prep.ai.mit.edu.
220 aeneas.MIT.EDU FTP server (Version wu-2.4.2-academ[BETA-15](1) Tue May 19
10:40:47 EDT 1998) ready.
Name (prep.ai.mit.edu:jenny): ftp
331 Guest login ok, send your complete e-mail address as password.
Password:
```

```
230-Welcome, archive user!
230-
230-If you have problems downloading and are seeing "Access denied" or
230-"Permission denied", please make sure that you started your FTP client in
230-a directory to which you have write permission.
230-
 .

 .
230 Guest login ok, access restrictions apply.

ftp> cd /pub/gnu
250-If you have problems downloading and are seeing "Access denied" or
 .

 .
250-Please read the file README-about-.gz-files
250-  it was last modified on Tue Jul  9 17:18:11 1996 - 800 days ago
250 CWD command successful.

ftp> ls make*
200 PORT command successful.
150 Opening ASCII mode data connection for file list.
make-3.55-3.56.diff.gz
make-3.56-3.57.diff.gz
 .

 .
make-3.75.tar.gz
make-3.76-3.76.1.diff.gz
make-3.76.1-3.77.diff.gz
make-3.76.1.tar.gz
make-3.77.tar.gz
makeinfo.README
226 Transfer complete.
remote: make*
635 bytes received in 0.16 seconds (3.97 Kbytes/s)

ftp> binary
200 Type set to I.
ftp> get makeinfo.README
200 PORT command successful.
150 Opening BINARY mode data connection for makeinfo.README (1095 bytes).
226 Transfer complete.
local: makeinfo.README remote: makeinfo.README
1095 bytes received in 0.24 seconds (4.46 Kbytes/s)

ftp> get make-3.77.tar.gz
200 PORT command successful.
150 Opening BINARY mode data connection for make-3.77.tar.gz (668524 bytes).
226 Transfer complete.
local: make-3.77.tar.gz remote: make-3.77.tar.gz
668524 bytes received in 80 seconds (8.13 Kbytes/s)
ftp> quit
221 Goodbye.
%
```

▲▲▲▲▲ How Do I Unpack the Software Source Code?   After downloading the distribution package—the single **gzip**-ed **tar** archive file, **make-3.77.tar.gz**—you need to decompress and extract the files. This distribution creates the **make-3.77** subdirectory and places all the extracted files there:

```
% cd /tmp
% ls mak*
make-3.77.tar.gz  makeinfo.README

% gzip -d make*gz
% tar xvf make-*
x make-3.77, 0 bytes, 0 tape blocks
x make-3.77/Makefile.in, 22736 bytes, 45 tape blocks
x make-3.77/AUTHORS, 1368 bytes, 3 tape blocks
x make-3.77/COPYING, 18043 bytes, 36 tape blocks
x make-3.77/ChangeLog, 170168 bytes, 333 tape blocks
x make-3.77/INSTALL, 8110 bytes, 16 tape blocks
x make-3.77/Makefile.am, 4223 bytes, 9 tape blocks
.

.
x make-3.77/w32/subproc/sub_proc.c, 27656 bytes, 55 tape blocks
x make-3.77/w32/subproc/w32err.c, 1264 bytes, 3 tape blocks
% ls mak*
make-3.77.tar    makeinfo.README

make-3.77:
AUTHORS          alloca.c          dosbuild.bat      make.info-10      remote-stub.c
COPYING          amiga.c           expand.c          make.info-2       rule.c
ChangeLog        amiga.h           file.c            make.info-3       rule.h
INSTALL          ar.c              filedef.h         make.info-4       signame.c
Makefile.DOS     arscan.c          function.c        make.info-5       signame.h
Makefile.am      build.sh.in       getloadavg.c      make.info-6       stamp-h.in
Makefile.ami     build_w32.bat     getopt.c          make.info-7       subproc.bat
Makefile.in      commands.c        getopt.h          make.info-8       texinfo.tex
NEWS             commands.h        getopt1.c         make.info-9       variable.c
NMakefile        config.ami        glob              make.lnk          variable.h
README           config.h-vms      implicit.c        make.texinfo      version.c
README.Amiga     config.h.W32      install-sh        makefile.com      vmsdir.h
README.DOS       config.h.in       job.c             makefile.vms      vmsfunctions.c
README.W32       confih.dos        job.h             misc.c            vmsify.c
README.customs   configure         main.c            missing           vpath.c
SCOPTIONS        configure.bat     make-stds.texi    mkinstalldirs     w32
SMakefile        configure.in      make.1            read.c
acconfig.h       default.c         make.h            readme.vms
acinclude.m4     dep.h             make.info         remake.c
aclocal.m4       dir.c             make.info-1       remote-cstms.c
```

▲▲▲▲▲ How Do I Compile and Link the Software?   Before you start to build the software, *read the instructions*. The majority of problems people have when installing software come from failing to read all of the instructions or failing to follow the instructions carefully. Most software packages come with a file that you should read first, commonly named **README** or **readme**. The listing of **make-3.77** shows a file named **README**. This file contains useful information about FAQs, bugs, documentation, compilation, and so on. Its second paragraph instructs you to read the **INSTALL** file.

```
% pg INSTALL
Basic Installation
==================

The 'configure' shell script attempts to guess correct values for
various system-dependent variables used during compilation.  It uses
those values to create a 'Makefile' in each directory of the package.
It may also create one or more '.h' files containing system-dependent
definitions.  Finally, it creates a shell script 'config.status' that
you can run in the future to recreate the current configuration, a file
'config.cache' that saves the results of its tests to speed up
reconfiguring, and a file 'config.log' containing compiler output
(useful mainly for debugging 'configure').

If you need to do unusual things to compile the package, please try
to figure out how 'configure' could check whether to do them, and mail
diffs or instructions to the address given in the 'README' so they can
be considered for the next release.  If at some point 'config.cache'
contains results you don't want to keep, you may remove or edit it.

The file 'configure.in' is used to create 'configure' by a program
called 'autoconf'.  You only need 'configure.in' if you want to change
it or regenerate 'configure' using a newer version of 'autoconf'.

The simplest way to compile this package is:

1. 'cd' to the directory containing the package's source code and type
'./configure' to configure the package for your system.  If you're
using 'csh' on an old version of System V, you might need to type
'sh ./configure' instead to prevent 'csh' from trying to execute
'configure' itself.

Running 'configure' takes awhile.  While running, it prints some
messages telling which features it is checking for.
.
.
.
.
```

Like many software packages, **make** uses the GNU **configure** utility to look at your system and determine the capabilities and features found there. Instructions for running **configure** are given in the **INSTALL** file. Run **configure** to prepare for compilation. If you are running the C Shell, give the command shown following to make sure **configure** runs under the Bourne Shell. If you are running the Bourne Shell, you can give the command **configure** or **./configure** if necessary.

```
% cd make-3.77
% sh configure
creating cache ./config.cache
checking for a BSD compatible install... ./install-sh -c
```

```
checking whether build environment is sane... yes
checking whether make sets ${MAKE}... yes
checking for working aclocal... missing
checking for working autoconf... missing
checking for working automake... missing
.
.
.
.
checking for working alloca.h... (cached) yes
checking for alloca... (cached) yes
checking for working strcoll... (cached) yes
updating cache ../.config.cache
creating ./config.status
creating Makefile
creating config.h
```

After running **configure** to configure the software, you can build GNU **make** by running Solaris **make** (step 2 of **INSTALL**). It is a good idea to save the output of **make** in a file so you can check it for problems. Using either **tee** or **tail** allows you to watch the progress of the compilation. Refer to page 909 in Part III for more information on **tail** and the **–f** option.

```
% make
make all-recursive
Making all in glob
gcc -DHAVE_CONFIG_H -I. -I. -I.    -g -O2 -c glob.c
gcc -DHAVE_CONFIG_H -I. -I. -I.    -g -O2 -c fnmatch.c
rm -f libglob.a
ar cru libglob.a glob.o fnmatch.o
ranlib libglob.a
gcc -DHAVE_CONFIG_H -I. -I. -I. -I./glob -DLIBDIR=\"/usr/local/lib\"
DINCLUDEDIR=\"/usr/local/include\" -D_LARGEFILE_SOURCE -D_FILE_OFFSET_BITS=64 -g -O2
-c main.c
.
.
.
gcc -DHAVE_CONFIG_H -I. -I. -I. -I./glob -DLIBDIR=\"/usr/local/lib\"
DINCLUDEDIR=\"/usr/local/include\" -D_LARGEFILE_SOURCE -D_FILE_OFFSET_BITS=64 -g -O2
-c getloadavg.c
gcc -g -O2    -o make  main.o commands.o job.o dir.o file.o misc.o read.o  remake.o
rule.o implicit.o default.o variable.o expand.o function.o  vpath.o version.o ar.o
arscan.o remote-stub.o signame.o getopt.o  getopt1.o getloadavg.o  glob/libglob.a
lkstat -L/usr/local/lib -lkvm -lelf
```

The Imake System

Software written for the X Window System is often distributed with a different method of configuring the source code. Instead of providing the GNU **configure** utility, these packages use the **Imake** system provided with X. The instructions for a package that uses **Imake** usually instruct you to run the **xmkmf** utility to configure the software.

▲▲▲▲ How Do I Install the Compiled Software?   Many software packages include tests
that you can run on the software before you install it. Information on conducting these tests is given with the
instructions that come with the software. If you will be overwriting an older version of the program you are
installing, it is a good idea to make a copy of the older version first.

Because there were no problems found while building **make** and because this version of **make** goes in
/usr/local/bin and does not overwrite the Solaris version of make in **/usr/ccs/bin**, you can simply become
Superuser and install **make**.

```
% su
Passwd:
# make install
Making install in glob
/bin/sh ./mkinstalldirs /usr/local/bin
./install-sh -c make /usr/local/bin/make
chgrp sys /usr/local/bin/make && chmod g+s /usr/local/bin/make
/bin/sh ./mkinstalldirs /usr/local/info
./install-sh -c -m 644 ./make.info /usr/local/info/make.info
./install-sh -c -m 644 ./make.info-1 /usr/local/info/make.info-1
./install-sh -c -m 644 ./make.info-2 /usr/local/info/make.info-2
./install-sh -c -m 644 ./make.info-3 /usr/local/info/make.info-3
./install-sh -c -m 644 ./make.info-4 /usr/local/info/make.info-4
./install-sh -c -m 644 ./make.info-5 /usr/local/info/make.info-5
./install-sh -c -m 644 ./make.info-6 /usr/local/info/make.info-6
./install-sh -c -m 644 ./make.info-7 /usr/local/info/make.info-7
./install-sh -c -m 644 ./make.info-8 /usr/local/info/make.info-8
./install-sh -c -m 644 ./make.info-9 /usr/local/info/make.info-9
./install-sh -c -m 644 ./make.info-10 /usr/local/info/make.info-10
make install-man1
/bin/sh ./mkinstalldirs /usr/local/man/man1
./install-sh -c -m 644 ./make.1 /usr/local/man/man1/make.1
# exit
%
```

You have built and installed a new version of **make**.
Installing a new software package onto your Solaris system
is not difficult if you carefully read and follow the instructions that come with the software. Most software distributions install in a manner similar to **make**.

▲▲▲ Downloading a File Using a Browser (and Installing It)

You can use a browser such as Netscape in place of **ftp** to
download a file from an **ftp** site as well as a Web (http) site.
This example downloads the **gcc** compiler from Metalab
using the Netscape browser. After starting Netscape, enter
metalab.unc.edu/pub/solaris in the Location Toolbar
(Figure 7-9, page 233), press **RETURN**, and Netscape displays
the window shown in Figure B-1.

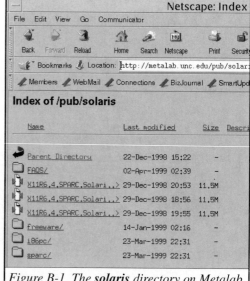

*Figure B-1 The **solaris** directory on Metalab*

> ## Source of a Lot of Useful Information
>
> The **FAQS** directory (**metalab.unc.edu/pub/solaris/FAQS**) contains a number of files filled with useful information about Solaris.

In this case you know that the file containing the **gcc** compiler is somewhere below the **/pub/solaris** directory on Metalab. If you did not have this information, you could have gone to the Metalab home page (**metalab.unc.edu**) and clicked on **FTP Archive** and then on **solaris** to get to the same window.

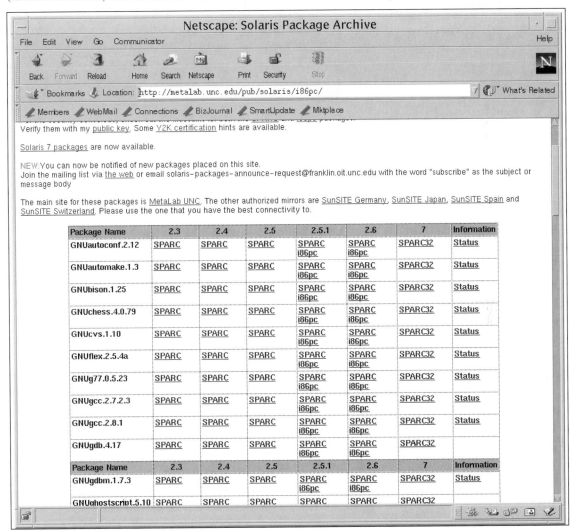

Figure B-2   The Solaris Package Archive at Metalab

The **i86pc** and **sparc** directories contain tools and binary applications compiled for Intel and SPARC machines, respectively. The **freeware** directory contains free software, some of which duplicates files in the other two groups and much of which is in source, not binary, format (page 973).

Assume you are running Solaris on an Intel machine, and click on **i86pc** (click on the filename, not the folder). The screen shown in Figure B-2 appears.

Suppose you want the latest version of **gcc** (listed as **GNUgcc**) running under Solaris 2.6 for an Intel machine. Look in the 2.6 column and you can see that GNUgcc.2.8.1 is available for the i86pc. When you click on i86pc in that box, Netscape displays the Save As window shown in Figure B-3. It is a good practice to save downloaded programs in **/tmp** or **/var/tmp**. Change the Selection window so that the file is stored in **/var/tmp** and click on OK.

While downloading, Netscape displays a Download window that keeps you informed about the progress of the file transfer. When the Download window closes, the file you downloaded is ready for you to work with. Exit from Netscape or choose another window.

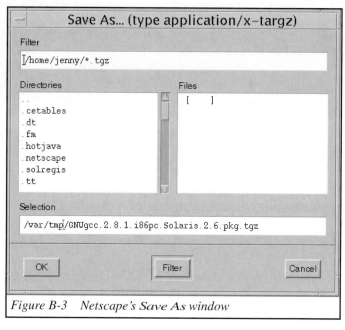

Figure B-3   Netscape's Save As window

▲▲▲ Installing the File

There are still a couple of things you can do before you require the powers of Superuser. The file you downloaded is archived with **tar** and compressed with **gzip** (indicated by the **.tgz** filename extension). Use **cd** to change to the **/var/tmp** directory, set the **umask** so the file permissions are correct, decompress the archive, and extract the files with the following commands. The **–c** option causes **gunzip** to send the decompressed file to standard output. You can use two steps to decompress and extract the files, using an intermediate file, if you like (do not use the **–c** option).

```
$ cd /var/tmp
$ umask 0
$ gunzip -c GNUgcc.2.8.1.i86pc.Solaris.2.6.pkg.tgz | /usr/bin/tar -xvf -
.
.
```

In order to install the **gcc** compiler, you must write to directories that only Superuser can write to. Become Superuser and run **pkgadd**.

```
$ su
Password:
# pkgadd -d . GNUgcc
.

Installation of <GNUgcc> was successful.
# exit
$
```

When the **pkgadd** utility checks if it can run as Superuser, reply with a **y**. When you get the shell prompt back, exit so you are no longer Superuser, and the installation is complete.

▲ Getting Started with Solaris

▲▲ How Do I Specify the Terminal I Am Using?

Because **vi**, **emacs**, **dtterm**, and a number of other programs take advantage of features that are specific to various kinds of terminals (and terminal emulators), you must tell them what type of terminal or terminal emulator you are using. On many systems your terminal type may be set for you automatically. If your terminal type is not specified, or not specified correctly, your screen will look strange or you will get a message when you start a program that requires this information. If this happens, you need to specify your terminal type.

Refer to "What Is the Termcap or Terminfo Name for My Terminal?" on page 988 for help in determining your terminal type.

When you log in you may be prompted to identify the type of terminal you are using:

```
TERM = (vt100)
```

There are two ways to respond to this prompt: You can press **RETURN** to set your terminal type to the name in parentheses. If that name does not describe the terminal you are using, you can enter the correct name before you press **RETURN**.

```
TERM = (vt100) dtterm
```

You can also receive the following prompt:

```
TERM = (unknown)
```

This prompt indicates that the system does not know what type of terminal you are using. If you are going to be running programs that require this information, enter the name of your terminal or terminal emulator before you press **RETURN**.

If you do not receive a prompt such as the one above, you can check whether your terminal type has been set by giving the command:

```
$ echo $TERM
```

If the system responds with the wrong name, a blank line, or an error message, set or change the terminal name. If you are using the Bourne or Korn Shell, enter commands similar to the following to identify the type of terminal you are using:

TERM=name
export TERM

Replace ***name*** with the terminal name for your terminal, making sure you do not put a **SPACE** before or after the equal sign. If you always use the same type of terminal, you can place this command in your **.profile** file. This causes the Solaris system to set the terminal type each time you log in (page 81).

The C Shell requires the following command syntax:

*setenv TERM **name***

You can place a command such as this one in your **.login** file for automatic execution. Again, replace **name** with the appropriate name for your terminal. For example give the following command to set your terminal type if you are using the console, CDE, and **csh** (the **csh** prompt is **%**):

```
% setenv TERM dtterm
```

▲▲ How Do I Send Files to a Printer?

Most Solaris systems have at least one printer for producing hardcopy. Typically you will be able to use the **lp** utility to send output to a printer. If your system has more than one printer, you will need to use the **–d** option with **lp** to request a specific printer. Refer to "**lp**: Print a File" on page 43.

▲▲ What Is the Name of the Machine I Will Log In On?

This question applies only to networked machines. If you log in on the console or in on a terminal or PC connected directly to your computer, you can ignore this question. If you log in on a group of networked machines, you will be asked to specify or choose the machine you want to log in on. Usually you will be able to log in on only one or a few machines; you must find out which machines your name and password combination will work on. Check with your system administrator.

▲▲ What Is My Login Name?

This is the name that you use to identify yourself to Solaris. It is also the name that other users use to send you electronic mail. If you are logging in on your own personal Solaris system for the first time, you will log in as **root** and create a login for yourself. Refer to "Adding and Removing Users" on page 625. Make sure you log in under your own name as soon as possible and become **root** or Superuser only as needed. There are many dangers to running as **root**. Refer to "The System Administrator and Superuser" on page 592.

▲▲ What Is My Password?

On systems that have several users or that are connected to a network, passwords can prevent others from accessing your files. To start with the system administrator assigns you a password. On your own system you assign yourself a password when you set up your account. You can change your password at any time (page 24).

▲▲ What Is the Termcap or Terminfo Name for My Terminal?

Terminal names describe the functional characteristics of your terminal (or terminal emulator) to programs that require this information, such as the **vi** editor. While terminal names are referred to as Terminfo names on System V and as Termcap names on BSD, the difference is in the method the two systems use to store the terminal characteristics internally, not in the manner that you specify the name of your terminal. Solaris provides support for both Terminfo and Termcap names, making it easier to use applications from either System

V or BSD. Five terminal names that are often used with Solaris are **dtterm** (running CDE from the console), **sun-cmd** (running OpenLook from the console), **vt100** if you are dialing into the Solaris system or using a terminal emulator, and **xterm** or **vs100** if you are running **xterm**.

If you do not know which name to use, you can try **vt100**. Many types of terminals and terminal emulators support the features found on a DEC VT-100 terminal, which provides sufficient capability to run many programs.

If you are running a terminal emulator from a PC or Macintosh, you probably have the ability to choose the type of terminal you want to emulate. Set the emulator to either **vt100** or **vt220** and set **TERM** to the same value. For more help see "How Do I Specify the Terminal I Am Using?" on page 987.

▲▲ Which Shell Will I Be Using?

The shell interprets the commands you enter from the keyboard. You will probably be using Bourne Shell (**sh**), C Shell (**csh**), or Korn Shell (**ksh**). They are similar in many respects because they have a common origin. For the most part the examples in this book use the Bourne Shell but are generally applicable to any of these shells and other shells available on Solaris. Chapters 5, 10, 11, 12, and 13 describe the three shells and the differences between them in detail.

▲ How Do I Get Started with a Graphical User Interface (GUI)?

A graphical user interface typically runs on a *bit-mapped display,* a device that allows the system to draw each dot or *pixel* on the screen independently, frequently in any one of a wide range of colors. A *character-based display* (also called an ASCII terminal) is equipped to draw only a set of specific symbols on the screen (such as alphanumeric characters), using fixed combinations of pixels. With a bit-mapped display you can plot lines and draw pictures, as well as form many styles and sizes of alphanumeric characters.

A typewriter-style keyboard is an effective way to enter numbers and letters, but an awkward interface for drawing lines or selecting a particular point on a display screen. It is much easier to use a *mouse.* In addition to the cursor associated with your keyboard, which determines where the next character you type on the keyboard appears on the screen, the mouse controls a separate cursor, called the *mouse pointer,* that points to some location on the screen. As you slide a mouse around on your tabletop the mouse pointer moves on the screen relative to the movement of the mouse.

A mouse is equipped with one, two, or three buttons that you use to carry out certain operations. To *click* a mouse button, press and release it (you hear an audible click); to *double-click,* press and release the mouse button twice in quick succession without moving the mouse. You often select something pictured on your screen by moving the mouse pointer on top of it and clicking a particular mouse button. Sometimes you need to specify an area of the window or highlight a section of text by *dragging* the mouse pointer. Press and hold down one of the buttons while you drag (move) the mouse pointer to a new location, and then release the button. This text assumes you are using a right-handed three-button mouse. If you are left-handed, see "Remapping Mouse Buttons" on page 159. If you have a two-button mouse, pressing both buttons at the same time has the same effect as pressing the middle button of a three-button mouse. If you have another type of mouse, you must specify its type when you set up the X Window System.

▲▲ What Is a Window?

When you use a *Window System,* you may work with several windows on your screen, each running a different program. A common window on Solaris systems is a *terminal emulator* such as **xterm**, which can provide the familiar shell command-line interface to the system. Other windows may run more specialized utilities, such as a text previewer (for example **pageview**), an icon editor (such as **dticon**), or multimedia tools such as an audio/video playback program. Figure B-4 shows a mix of standard Solaris utilities and other applications programs running in different windows, including a terminal emulator, clock, the Style Manager and the Application Managers. Regardless of the program running in a particular window, most windows operate using a set of common features. Each of these features, or properties, of the window system is described in the following paragraphs.

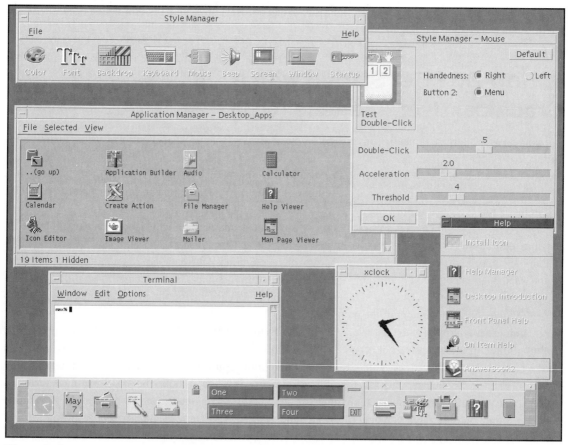

Figure B-4   A graphical user interface

▲▲▲ What Is the Root Window?

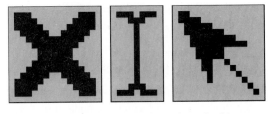

The background area that fills in the screen between the application windows is called the *root window*. As you move the mouse pointer around the screen, the shape of the pointer changes. These changes serve as cues to the operations you can perform with the mouse. When it is positioned over the root window, the pointer is shaped like the letter *X*. If you move the pointer inside a terminal window, the pointer changes to an arrow or a large *I* shape called an *I-beam*. The I-beam pointer is easy to position between individual characters on your screen. When you move it to a title bar button, the mouse pointer often changes to a shape, such as an arrow, that points at that object.

▲▲ What Is a Title Bar?

The *title bar* appears at the top of the window and usually contains the name of the program that controls the window, along with a few buttons. See "Title Bar" on page 138 for information on using title bars and buttons.

▲▲ What Is a Button?

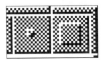

Buttons are usually shown as small squares or rectangles, meant to be pressed to carry out some operation. To press a button on your screen, move the mouse pointer on top of it and click the left mouse button. Although you typically find some buttons on a title bar, they appear in many other contexts as well. Buttons are commonly used to turn simple attributes on or off or to make other simple yes/no choices.

▲▲ What Is a Slider?

A *slider* is a type of bar that lets you adjust some attribute within a range, like the sliding controls on a stereo system's graphic equalizer that allow you to minimize or boost certain audio frequencies. A button within the slider marks the current setting on the bar and allows you to change the setting. There are two common ways to use a slider on the screen. You can position the mouse pointer on the slider button, hold down the left or middle mouse button, and drag the button to the position you want. Or you can click the left or middle mouse button in the empty space on one side of the slider button or the other. The slider will move toward the mouse pointer each time you click the mouse button. The embedded figure has a slider that allows you to adjust characteristics of the mouse.

▲▲ What Is a Scroll Bar?

A *scroll bar* is a type of slider that appears along the side or bottom of a window. When a window is too small to display a complete body of text or a graphic, you can use the scroll bar(s) to browse through the portion of the text or image that is hidden from view. A scroll bar that appears vertically along one side of a window allows you to move up and down through the text or picture; a horizontal scroll bar usually appears across the bottom and allows you to scroll a wide page left and right. Embedded in this paragraph is a vertical scroll bar. For more information see "Scrolling Text" on page 142.

▲▲ What Is an Icon?

If you are working with several windows, you may find it handy to put one or more of them aside temporarily, to clear some space on your screen. It would also be convenient if you could restart the application quickly, at the point where you left it. An *icon* is a small picture that represents a window. Embedded in this paragraph are icons for **dtbuilder** (left) and the Style Manager (right). When you *iconify* a window, you can no longer see the contents of the window; instead an icon represents it somewhere on the screen. The method you use to iconify a window varies from one window system to another; usually you select the operation from a menu or click on a button on the title bar. To restore an application from the icon, position the mouse pointer over the icon and double-click on it.

Security

There are many dimensions to system security: The security of your system as a whole depends on the security of your email, files, network, login and remote access policies, as well as the physical security of the host itself. These dimensions overlap and their borders are not always clear. For instance email security is affected by the security of files and your network. If the medium over which you transport your email (the network) is not secure, then you must take extra steps to ensure the security of your messages. If you save your secure email into a file, you rely on the file system for file security. A failure in any one of these areas can lead to a domino effect, compromising security in other areas, and potentially compromising system security as a whole.

This short appendix cannot cover all the facets of system security; it just gives you an overview of the complexity of setting up and maintaining a secure system. This appendix provides some specifics, some concepts, and some paths to follow. Depending on how important system security is to you, you may want to purchase one or more of the books that is dedicated to the subject, read from some of the Internet sites that are dedicated to security (page 969), or hire someone who is an expert in the field. Do not rely on this appendix as your sole source of information on system security.

Many of the products and programs mentioned in this appendix are listed in the tables on pages 969 and 1000.

▲ Encryption

One of the building blocks of security is encryption. Encryption provides a way for you to scramble data with a *key* (a password or phrase) so that only someone who knows the key can decrypt (unscramble) it. There are many different encryption algorithms. Almost all algorithms theoretically can be broken; some just take longer than others. Some (in theory) would take so many years to break that it becomes impractical.[1]

Developing and analyzing strong encryption software is extremely difficult; there are many nuances to encryption algorithms and a good background in mathematics is requisite. Also, unless an algorithm has undergone public scrutiny for a significant period of time, it is generally not considered secure. It is often

---

1. There is an exception to this statement. The one-time pad algorithm (discussed shortly) can never be broken.

993

impossible to know that an algorithm is completely secure, but it is possible to know that one is not secure. Time is the test of a good algorithm.

An encryption algorithm uses a key that is a certain number of bits long. Each bit you add to the length of a key effectively doubles the *key space* (the number of combinations allowed by the number of bits in the key—two to the power of the length of the key in bits[2]) and means it will take twice as long for an attacker to decrypt your message (assuming there are no inherent weaknesses or shortcuts to exploit). However it is meaningless to compare algorithms based only on the number of bits used. An algorithm that uses a 64-bit key can be more secure than an algorithm that uses a 128-bit key.

The two types of encryption you are likely to see are *public key encryption* and *private key encryption.* Public key encryption, also called *asymmetric encryption,* uses two different keys. Private (or secret) key encryption, also called *symmetric encryption,* uses one key that you and the person you are communicating with (hereafter referred to as your *friend*) share as a secret. Typically public key algorithm keys are in the 512- to 2048-bit range, whereas private key algorithms use keys in the 64- to 512-bit range. There is a unique kind of encryption algorithm called a *one-time pad* where the key is the same length as the text to be encrypted. However, because of the extreme difficulties in generating a truly random key and storing or distributing it, the one-time pad has very limited application in practical use. The key of a one time pad is a true random number that is mathematically mixed with the text by means of an exclusive OR operation. This makes it impossible for an attacker to guess the key or exploit any algorithmic shortcuts or deficiencies.[3]

▲▲ Public Key Encryption

To use public key encryption, you must generate two keys. You keep one of the keys for yourself (the private key), and give the other key away to the world (the public key). Likewise your friends will generate a pair of keys and give you their public keys. Public key encryption has two very useful properties:

1. When you encrypt something with somebody's public key, only that person can decrypt it using his or her private key.

2. When you encrypt something with your private key, anybody else can decrypt it with your public key.

You may wonder why the second point is useful at all: Why would you want everybody else to be able to decrypt something you just encrypted? The answer is: Because your encryption serves as a digital signature. If the message decrypts properly with your public key, then *only* you could have encrypted it with your private key: The message is authentic. Combining these two modes of operation yields privacy and authenticity. You can sign something with your private key so that it is verified as authentic, and then you can encrypt it with your friend's public key so that only he or she can decrypt it.

There are three major shortcomings to public key encryption:

---

2. A 2-bit key would have a key space of 4 (2^2), a 3-bit key would have a key space of 8 (2^3), and so on.

3. For further reading, consult a book such as Bruce Schneier's, *Applied Cryptography: Protocols, Algorithms, and Source Code in C* (John Wiley & Sons, 1995).

1. Public key encryption algorithms are generally much slower than secret key algorithms.

2. Public key encryption usually requires a much larger key size and a way to generate large prime numbers to use as components for your key. This is why public key algorithms tend to be slow.

3. It is difficult to authenticate the key, that is, to prove who it came from. This is known as the key distribution problem and is the raison d'être for companies such as Verisign.

Algorithms such as RSA, Diffie-Hellman, and El-Gamal implement public key encryption methodology. Today a 512-bit key is considered the low end for RSA encryption and offers marginal protection; 1024-bit keys are expected to withhold determined attackers for several more years.

▲▲ Secret Key Encryption

Secret key encryption is generally fast. First you and your friend agree on which algorithm to use and a key that you will share. Then either of you can decrypt or encrypt a file with the same key. Behind the scenes, secret key encryption algorithms are most often implemented as a network of black boxes (these can be hardware, software, or a combination thereof). Each box computes some reversible transform on the input data and passes it on to the next box. The security of secret key encryption relies on the difficulty of determining which box was used and the number of passes through all of the boxes. A good algorithm will pass the data through all of the boxes many times before yielding a result, and there will be no obvious mapping from input data to output data.

The disadvantage of secret key encryption is that you need a secure channel over which to share your key. For example you would not send your key using email; if your email is intercepted, then your encryption is useless. You could use the phone, but your phone might be tapped. Commonly used implementations of secret key encryption algorithms are DES (data encryption standard), 3DES (triple DES), IDEA, RC5, and Blowfish.

None of these have undergone more scrutiny than DES, which has been around for a very long time. Yet there are a couple of drawbacks to the use of DES. It is only available with the North American (U.S., Canada, and Mexico) Solaris distribution because of U.S. export restrictions that classify encryption software as a munition. These laws, however, have not kept people from reimplementing the DES algorithm overseas by reading the published papers and writing the corresponding code.

Also, with advances in computing power and speed since DES was developed, its relatively small 56-bit key renders it inadequate for operations requiring more than basic security for relatively short periods of time. However DES is probably more than adequate for tasks such as sending email to a friend when you only need it to be confidential, or secure, for a few days (for instance to give the time and place for a meeting to take place in a few hours). For a large sum of money, you can build a specialized machine that can crack DES keys in a matter of hours to days. It is unlikely that anybody is interested enough in your email to invest a large sum of money in decrypting it.

▲▲ Implementation

In practice most commercial software packages make use of both private and public key encryption algorithms, taking advantage of the strengths of each and avoiding the weaknesses. The public key algorithm is used first, as a means of negotiating a randomly generated secret key, and providing for message authenticity. Then a secret key algorithm such as 3DES, IDEA, or Blowfish is used to encrypt and decrypt the data on both ends for speed.

▲▲ File Security

From an end user's perspective, file security is one of the most critical areas of security. On operating systems such as DOS or MS Windows, there is minimal to no file security. Everybody is the equivalent of Superuser. On UNIX, including Solaris, some file security is built into the operating system. You have basic security control with commands such as **chmod** (pages 90 and 709), and more extensive options with access control lists (ACLs [page 674]) to give others (limited) access to files that you own. However even these tools are insufficient if your account is compromised (for example by someone watching your fingers on the keyboard as you type in your password). To provide maximum file security, you must encrypt your files. Then even if someone knows your password, they cannot read your files.

A utility named **crypt** comes with Solaris, but its algorithm is based on World War II know-how. Methods to break this type of encryption have been available for quite a while; **crypt** is a poor choice for an encryption tool. There is also a program named **des** (not a part of Solaris) that uses DES encryption (a part of Solaris).

▲▲ PGP

The most popular personal encryption package available today is PGP (Pretty Good Privacy). PGP, originally developed and distributed for free, is now maintained by Network Associates Inc. (**www.pgp.com**) as a commercial product, but the free version is still available. PGP provides a common interface to several encryption algorithms that have undergone public scrutiny. The default algorithm, IDEA, uses a 128-bit key and is generally thought to be very secure.

PGP has the notion of a ring of trust so that if you trust somebody, and they trust somebody else, the person that you trust can serve as a means of providing an introduction to the third party. When you trust somebody, you perform an operation called *key signing*. By signing somebody else's key, you are providing PGP with a means of verifying that that person's public key is authentic and safe for you to use to send him or her email. When you sign a key, PGP will ask you whether you trust this person to introduce other person's keys to you. You can assign trust based on your personal knowledge of a person's character. It is recommended that you only sign somebody's key after you have met face to face to avert any possible chance of a "person in the middle"[4] scenario.

---

4. Person in the middle: If Alex and Jenny try to carry on a secure email exchange over a network, Alex first sends Jenny his public key. However suppose that Mr. X sits in between Alex and Jenny on the network and intercepts Alex's public key. Mr. X then sends *his own* public key to Jenny. Jenny then sends her public key to Alex, but once again Mr. X intercepts it and substitutes *his* public key and sends that to Alex. Without some kind of active protection (a piece of shared information), Mr. X, the *person in the middle,* can decrypt all traffic between Alex and Jenny, reencrypt it, and send it on to the other party.

▲ Email Security

Email security overlaps file security and, as discussed later, network security. PGP is the most frequently used tool for email security. You can also use PEM (privacy enhanced mail), a standard rather than an algorithm. There are several implementations of PEM available both inside and outside the United States.

RIPEM (Riordan's Internet Privacy Enhanced Mail) provides similar functionality to PEM and uses the RSA public key encryption toolkit, mandating a license for use in North America (with exemptions for personal use). RIPEM is used more than PEM, but not as much as PGP. Current versions are available outside the United States without restrictions.

▲▲ Mail Transfer Agents

There are PGP and PEM extended versions of the popular **sendmail** package. You can check the **comp.mail.sendmail** newsgroup FAQ for further information.

▲▲ Mail User Agents

There are a number of free mail user agents that have hooks for encryption programs. The **privtool** utility looks like Sun's **mailtool** but has an interface to PGP. There are PGP-extended versions of the **elm** mailer; see the **comp.mail.elm** newsgroup for more information. There are also PGP macros available that allow you to use the **emacs** mail agent to send and receive encrypted email from **emacs**.

▲ Network Security

Network security is vital to the security of a computing site. However without the right infrastructure, providing network security is difficult to impossible. For example if you run a shared network topology[5] such as Ethernet and have network jacks in public locations so that anyone can plug into the network at will, how can you prevent someone from plugging a machine in and capturing all the packets[6] that traverse the network? You cannot, so you have a potential security hole. Another common security hole is the use of **telnet** for logins. Because **telnet** sends and receives clear (unencoded) text, anyone "listening in" on the line can easily capture login names and passwords, compromising security.

---

5. Shared network topology: A network in which each packet may be seen by machines other than its destination. "Shared" means that the 100Mbs bandwidth is shared by all users.

6. A *packet* is a block of data that is transmited over a network. Also called a *frame* or *datagram*.

Do not allow unauthenticated PCs (any PC that you can use without giving a name and password [to the PC]) on your network. With an authenticated PC, you may have a log of a malicious user. Any PC user on the network is effectively Superuser because:

- There is no concept of root on a PC—all users are effectively Superuser and can watch the network, capture packets, send packets, and so on.

- On UNIX/Solaris only Superuser can put the network interface in promiscuous mode and collect packets. On UNIX/Solaris ports under 1024^7 are privileged. That is, normal user protocols cannot bind to these ports. This is an important (but regrettable) means of security for some protocols such as NIS, NFS, **rsh**, and **lpd**. A PC user can write a program that binds to any port.

Normally a data switch on your LAN automatically protects your machines from people snooping on your network for data. In high load situations switches have been known to behave unpredictably, directing packets to the wrong ports. A security-enabled hub is designed so that only packets that should go to a machine are visible to that machine; other packets are scrambled. Even security-enabled hubs are not foolproof. For example if someone plugs a shared mini-hub into a security hub, then all the machines plugged into the mini-hub may be able to see each other's packets depending on the hub's configuration and security policies.

▲▲ Network Security Solutions

One solution to the shared network problems is to encrypt messages that travel between machines. SKIP[8] provides just such a technology: All packets traveling between the machines are encrypted before being transmitted and decrypted when they are received. SKIP requires extensive setup and lowers network performance by 10 to 20%, but it provides a solution between two Internet hosts running Solaris (also available for Sun's PCNFS and MS Windows). Sun performed an innovative end-run around U.S. cryptography laws by shipping the SKIP specification to a partner in Russia, who in turn implemented SKIP outside of U.S. jurisdiction and made it available worldwide.

The solution that has become the Internet standard is called IPSec (Internet Protocol Security protocol). IPSec is a framework that defines how hosts can communicate securely. It provides integrity, confidentiality, authenticity, vendor interoperability, and flexibility of implementation.

IPv6 (page 198) also has provisions for encryption. However it may be quite some time before IPv6 is implemented widely.

---

7. The term *port* has many meanings. Here it is a number assigned to a program. The number links incoming data with a specific service. For example port 21 is used by **ftp** traffic and port 23 is used by **telnet**.

8. Simple Key Management for Internet: Sun developed SKIP and placed the technology into the public domain to ensure interoperability between multiple implementations, including Sun's.

▲▲ Network Security Guidelines

The following list contains some very general guidelines for establishing and maintaining a secure system. The list is not complete; it is intended only as a guide.

- Fiberoptic cable is more secure than copper cable. Copper is subject to active and passive eavesdropping. With access to your copper cable, all a data thief needs to monitor your network traffic is a passive device for measuring magnetic fields. It is extremely difficult to tap a fiberoptic cable without interrupting the signal. Sites requiring top security keep fiberoptic cable in pressurized conduits: A pressure change signals that security has been breached.

- Avoid inactive ports in public areas. If a malicious user can plug a laptop into the network without being detected, you may have a serious security problem.

- Install switches or secure hubs. Switched network gear has dramatically fallen in price, and the slightly higher cost is well worth it for the extra security that you get. Some switches have provisions for locking a hardware address to a port for enhanced security.

- UNIX/Solaris systems contain a huge number of programs that, while useful, significantly reduce the security of the host. Install the smallest Solaris operating system that meets your needs. For Web and **ftp** servers, install only the "Core System Support" image. Users usually require additional packages.

- Do not allow NFS or NIS access outside of your network. If you allow NIS access outside your network, it only requires a little bit of work for a malicious user to steal your entire password map. NFS security is marginal to nonexistent and should not be allowed outside your network to machines that you do not trust. A common joke is that NFS stands for No File Security. Use SKIP, IPSec, or firewalls to provide access outside your domain. Virtual private networks (VPNs) are often built into new firewalls or provided as separate products to join you with customers or partners. If you must allow business partners to access your files, consider using a secure filesystem such as NFS with Kerberos (page 224), secure NFS (encrypts authentication, not traffic), or cfs (cryptographic filesystem).

- Mount **/usr** readonly (`ro`) in **/etc/vfstab**. For example:

```
/dev/dsk/c0t3d0s4 /dev/rdsk/c0t3d0s4 /usr   ufs 1 no  ro
```

- Mount UFS filesystems other than **root** `nosuid` to prevent setuid programs executing on this filesystem. For example:

```
/dev/dsk/c0t3d0s5 /dev/rdsk/c0t3d0s5 /var   ufs 1 no  nosuid
/dev/dsk/c0t3d0s6 /dev/rdsk/c0t3d0s6 /local ufs 2 yes nosuid
```

- Add the following line to **/etc/syslog.conf** to cause Solaris to record unsuccessful login attempts, all **su** attempts, reboots, and more in **/var/log/authlog**.

```
auth.info         /var/log/authlog
```

- Then create and secure the **/var/log/authlog** file with the following commands. Truncate or rotate the log on a regular basis (so it does not get too large).

```
touch /var/log/authlog
chown root /var/log/authlog
chmod 600 /var/log/authlog
```

- Use some sort of barrier or firewall product between your network and the Internet. There are several valuable mailing lists including firewalls, and also the **comp.security.firewalls** newsgroup.

Several of the preceding suggestions are courtesy of Hal Pomeranz and appear in the comprehensive SANS Institute (**www.sans.org**) publication, *Solaris Security: Step-by-Step.*

▲ Host Security

Your host must be secure. Simple security steps include preventing remote logins and leaving the **/etc/hosts.equiv** and individual users' **.rhosts** files empty (or not having them at all). Complex security steps include installing products such as SKIP or IPSec. There are many common security measures that are between these two extremes.

Solaris2 provides a number of packages and utilities for auditing host security setup. One of these is the ASET (Automated Security Enhancement Tool) package, which can be set to one of three levels for security auditing and detection. Refer to the **aset man** page for more information. Another is PAM (Pluggable Authentication Module), which allows you to set up different methods of authentication (page 605).

Although it decreases performance, process accounting is a good supplement to system security. It can provide a continuous record of user actions on your system. See the **turnacct man** page for more information.

The **syslog** facility can direct information generated by system daemons to specific files. On larger groups of machines, you may want to send all important **syslog** information to a secure host where that host's only function is to store **syslog** data where it cannot be tampered with. See the **syslogd man** page.

There are many free programs that can enhance system security. Some of these are summarized in the table on page 969 and in the following table:

Tool	What It Does	Where to Get It
cops	Checks password file for bad passwords as well as other vulnerabilities.	**ftp://coast.cs.purdue.edu/pub/tools/unix**
courtney	Identifies signatures of network attacks (requires Perl, **tcpdump**, and **libpcap**).	libpcap-0.0 **ftp.ee.lbl.gov:/libpcap∗** tcpdump-3.0 **ftp.ee.lbl.gov:/tcdump∗** perl5 **ftp.uu.net:/sysems/gnu/perl∗** courtney **coast.cs.purdue.edu/pub/tools/unix** courtney **ftp.sunet.se:pub/security/tools/audit**
fix-modes	Sets directory permissions to more reasonable defaults; removes write access by group to many system directories (page 674).	**ftp.sunet.se/pub/security/tools/admin** **ftp.fwi.uva.nl/pub/solaris**

Tool	What It Does	Where to Get It
gabriel	Designed to detect SATAN scans without **tcpdump**, **perl**, or **libpcap**.	**ftp.sunet.se:pub/security/tools/audit**
kerberos	Complete, secure network authentication system.	**athena-dist.mit.edu/pub/ATHENA**
klaxon	Launches out of **inetd** and allows you to put alarms on unused services.	**coast.cs.purdue.edu/pub/tools/unix**
logdaemon	Has portable, secure replacements for **telnetd**, **login**, **ftpd**, **rexecd**. Requires **tcp_wrappers**.	**ftp://coast.cs.purdue.edu/pub/tools/unix/ logdaemon**
OPIE	Provides one-time passwords for system access.	**ftp://ftp.hacktic.nl/pub/crypto/crypto/APPS/opie**
rpcbind	Replaces Solaris2 **rpcbind** with a more secure version.	**ftp://coast.cs.purdue.edu/pub/tools/unix/rpcbind**
satan	Scans your host and network for vulnerabilities. This program is starting to show its age.	**ftp://coast.cs.purdue.edu/pub/tools/unix/satan**
sfingerd	A secure, configurable replacement for the **finger** daemon.	**ftp://coast.cs.purdue.edu/pub/tools/unix/sfingerd**
skey	One-time disposable passwords for login.	**ftp://coast.cs.purdue.edu/pub/tools/unix/skey**
ssh	A secure **rsh**, **rdist**, **rlogin** replacement with encrypted sessions and other options.	**www.ssh.org** **ftp://coast.cs.purdue.edu/pub/tools/unix/ssh**
SSLtelnet	A **telnetd** replacement that uses secure socket layer.	**ftp://ftp.psy.uq.oz.au:/pub/Crypto/SSLapps**
ssyslog	A cryptographically secure replacement for **syslog**.	**www.core-sdi.com/ssyslog**
STel	A secure, encrypted **telnet** replacement.	**ftp://ftp.hacktic.nl/pub/crypto/crypto/APPS/stel**
sudo	Gives very limited Superuser capabilities on an as-needed basis to system operators.	**ftp://coast.cs.purdue.edu/pub/tools/unix/sudo** **ftp://ftp.courtesan.com/pub/sudo**

Tool	What It Does	Where to Get It
swatch	A Perl-based log parser and analyzer.	**ftp://coast.cs.purdue.edu/pub/tools/unix/swatch**
tcp_wrappers	Monitor, filter, and log incoming requests for the **systat, finger, ftp, telnet, rlogin, rsh, exec, tftp, talk**, and other network services by wrapping system daemons.	**ftp://coast.cs.purdue.edu/pub/tools/unix/ tcp_wrappers** **ftp://ftp.porcupine.org/pub/security/index.html**
tklogger	A log visualization tool. Requires Tcl/Tk.	**ftp://coast.cs.purdue.edu/pub/tools/unix/tklogger**
tocsin	Like **klaxon**, but watches the network directly and catches more alarms than **klaxon**. It is able to detect stealth scans.[a]	**ftp://coast.cs.purdue.edu/pub/tools/unix/tocsin**
tripwire	Checks for possible signs of intruder activity.	**ftp://coast.cs.purdue.edu/pub/COAST/Tripwire/**
xinetd	A secure and configurable replacement for **inetd**.	**ftp://coast.cs.purdue.edu/pub/tools/unix/xinetd**

a. A *stealth scan* is one in which unique properties of a host IP stack are used to scan a host for services while trying to avoid detection.

▲▲ Login Security

Without a secure host, good login security cannot add much protection. The preceding table and the table on page 969 list some of the best login security tools, including replacement daemons for **telnetd**, **rlogind**, and **rshd**. The current choice of most sites is **ssh**, which comes as both freeware and as a commercially supported package that works on UNIX/Solaris, MS Windows, and Macintosh platforms. However for UNIX/Solaris-only solutions, **STel** is a good choice—unlike **ssh** it has never displayed a security hole.

The PAM facility (page 605) allows you to set up multiple authentication methods for users in series or in parallel. In series PAM requires multiple methods of authentication for a user. In parallel PAM uses any one of a number of methods for authentication.

Although not a frequent choice, you can configure your system to take advantage of one-time passwords. S/Key is the original implementation of one-time passwords by Bellcore. OPIE (one-time passwords in everything), developed by the U.S. Naval Research Labs, is an improvement over the original Bellcore system. With this system, the user gets a piece of paper listing a set of one-time passwords. Each time a user logs in, the user enters a password from the piece of paper. Once used, a password becomes obsolete and the next password in the list is the only one that will work. Even if a malicious user compromises the network and sees your password, it will be of no use because the password can only be used one time. This setup makes it very difficult for someone to log in as you but does nothing about protecting the data you type at the keyboard. One-time passwords are a good solution if you are at a site where there is no encrypted **telnet** software. A truly secure (or paranoid) site will combine one-time passwords and encrypted logins.

Another type of secure login that is becoming more common is facilitated by a *smart card*. Smart cards are credit-card-like devices that use a challenge-response method of authentication. Smart card authentication relies on something you have (the card) and something you know (a pass phrase, userid, or pin). For example you might type in your login name in response to the Solaris prompt and get a challenge from Solaris. After you enter the challenge on the smart card, the smart card displays a response. You copy this response back to the Solaris system to finish your authentication. The most popular smart card in use today is the SecurID card from Security Dynamics Technologies, Inc. (**www.securid.com**).

▲▲ Remote Access Security

Issues and solutions surrounding remote access security overlap those pertaining to login security.

Local logins may be secure with just a login name and password, whereas remote logins (and all remote access) should be made more secure. Many breakins can be traced back to reusable passwords. It is a good idea to use an encrypted authentication client such as **ssh**, **STel**, or **kerberos**. Smart cards can also be used for remote access authentication.

Modem pools can also be an entry point. Most people are aware of the ease with which a network line can be monitored. But people take for granted the security of the public switched telephone network (PSTN). You may want to set up an encrypted channel after dialing into a modem pool. One way to do this is by running **ssh** over PPP.

There are ways to provide stringent modem authentication policies so that unauthorized users are not able to use your modems. The most common ones are PAP (password authentication protocol), CHAP (challenge handshake authentication protocol), and Radius. PAP and CHAP are relatively weak when compared with Radius, so the latter has rapidly gained in popularity. Cisco also provides a method of authentication called TACACS (more recently TACACS+).

One or more of these authentication techniques are available in an RAS (remote access server—a computer in a network that provides network access to remote users via modem). Before purchasing an RAS, check what kind of security it provides and decide if that level of security meets your needs.

Two other techniques for remote access security may be built into a modem (or RAS if it has integrated modems). One is callback: After you dial in, you get a password prompt. Once you type in your password, the modem hangs up and calls you back at a phone number it has stored internally. This technique is not foolproof. Some modems have a built-in callback table with about 10 entries. This works for small sites with only a few modems. If you use more modems, you will need to have callback provided by the RAS software.

The second technique is to use CLID (caller ID) or ANI (automatic number identification) to decide whether to answer the call. Depending on your wiring and the local phone company, you may or may not be able to use ANI. ANI information is provided before the call, while CLID information is provided along with the call.

▲▲ Viruses and Worms

There are no known UNIX/Solaris viruses or worms at large on the Internet. Techniques to generate rather limited viruses are said to be available in certain labs, but UNIX is generally virus resistant. There is no way to infect the equivalent of the DOS master boot record. MS Windows machines and Macs have no concept of a privileged user. All users have access to all files. UNIX file permissions serve as an inoculation against viruses. Windows NT is resistant for similar reasons. You can easily protect your system against many viruses and worms by keeping your system patches up to date. You can prevent a disaster in case of a virus by making periodic system backups.

Just after 5 PM on November 2, 1988, Robert T. Morris Jr., a graduate student at Cornell University, released the first big virus onto the Internet. This virus was called an Internet worm and was designed to propagate copies of itself over many machines on the Internet.

The worm was a piece of code that exploited four vulnerabilities, including one in **finger**, to get a buffer to overflow on a system. Once the buffer overflowed, the code was able to get a shell, and then to recompile itself on the remote machine. It spread around the Internet very quickly and was not disabled, despite many people's efforts, for 36 hours. While still technically possible today, the UNIX security community has been actively fixing security holes, making such a wide-scale attack much less likely.

▲▲ Physical Security

Physical security is often overlooked; it covers access to the computer itself and to the console or terminal attached to the machine. If the machine is unprotected in an unlocked room, then you have very little hope for physical security. (As a simple example of its vulnerability, someone could walk in, remove the hard drive from the computer, take it home, and analyze it.) There are certain steps you can take to improve the physical security of your computer:

1. Keep servers in a locked room with limited access. Either a key, a combination, or swipe card should be required to gain access. Protect windows as well as doors.

2. Use a security system for public machines such as a fiberoptic security system, which can secure an entire lab full of machines. This system requires you to run a fiberoptic cable through each of the machines such that the machine cannot be removed (or opened) without cutting the cable. When the cable is cut, an alarm goes off. Some machines are much harder to secure than others. PCs with plastic cases are difficult to secure. Sun SPARC stations often have a little screw on the back with a hard plastic cover that you can run the cable through. In this position the cable prevents access to the screw and thereby prevents anyone from opening the top of the machine. Although this is not a perfect solution, it may improve your security enough to cause a would-be thief to go somewhere else.

3. On a SPARC machine use a PROM password (page 598) to prevent anyone from booting the machine in single-user mode or from the CDROM. Most modern PCs also have a BIOS password, which allows much the same functionality. You can set the order in which a PC searches for a boot device, preventing the PC from being booted from a floppy disk or CDROM. The password protects the BIOS from unauthorized modification.

4. Run only fiberoptic cable between buildings. Not only is this more secure, it is safer in the event of lightning strikes, and it is required by many commercial building codes.

Summary

There is a new old adage: Security is inversely proportional to usability. There must be a balance between the requirements that your users have to get their work done and the amount of security that is implemented. It is often unnecessary to provide top security if you just have a small business with only a few people. On the other hand, if you work for a government military contractor, you are bound to have extreme security constraints and an official audit policy to determine if your security policies are being implemented correctly.

Review your own security requirements periodically. Several of the tools mentioned in this appendix are designed to help you do this. Tools like COPS, tripwire, ASET, and SATAN all provide some type of auditing mechanism. You can also hire external auditors. There are companies that specialize in security and auditing. Hiring one of them to examine your site can be costly but may result in specific recommendations for areas that you may have overlooked in your initial setup. When you hire somebody to audit your security, you may be giving them both physical and Superuser access to your systems. Make sure that the company that you use has a good solid history, has been in business for several years, and has impeccable references. Check on them periodically: Things change over time.

Your total security package is based on your risk assessment of your vulnerabilities. Strengthen those areas that are most important for your business. For example many sites will rely on a firewall to completely protect them from the Internet, whereas internal hosts receive little or no security attention. Crackers refer to this as, "the crunchy outside surrounding the soft chewy middle." Yet this is entirely sufficient to protect some sites. Perform your own risk assessment and address your needs accordingly. If need be, hire a full-time security administrator whose job it is to design and audit your security policies.

If you are interested in war stories and security issues, you may want to read Clifford Stoll's *The Cuckoo's Egg: Tracking a Spy Through the Maze of Computer Espionage* (Pocket Books, 1990).

The POSIX Standards

The existence of different versions of the UNIX system has been a very fruitful source of creative and innovative software. However it has also been a persistent source of frustration for users and programmers. Users who moved between different versions of the system (such as BSD and System V) would discover that commands that worked on one system did not work, or worked differently, on the other. Programmers found a similar phenomenon: Programs that worked on one system would behave differently, or even fail to compile, on the other. In 1984 the user's group **/usr/group** (which is now called UniForum) started an effort to specify a "standard UNIX." This effort has expanded beyond the wildest dreams of its initiators as the POSIX series of standards.

POSIX standards specify interfaces for application programs. They say nothing about how the interfaces are to be implemented. Thus a wide variety of systems, including most varieties of UNIX and many systems that are unrelated to UNIX, now supply versions of these interfaces. UNIX has included many of these features since its inception, and more features appear with each release. As a consequence, UNIX can support more and more application programs that run on other POSIX systems.

Solaris2 supports IEEE Std 1003.1 and IEEE Std 1003.2, commonly known as POSIX.1 and POSIX.2. Give the command **man posix** for more information.

POSIX is the name for a collection of software standards, based on but not limited to the UNIX system. (POSIX is almost an acronym for Portable Operating System Interface.) The standards are developed by working groups of the Institute for Electrical and Electronics Engineering (IEEE); participation in these groups is open to everyone. For this and other reasons, the POSIX standards are referred to as Open Systems Standards.

The explicit goal of the POSIX effort is to promote application portability. Thus the standards specify both program and user interfaces but not implementations. At this writing there are 7 adopted POSIX standards (see the following table) and more than 20 draft standards and profiles under development.

▲ POSIX.1

POSIX.1 (POSIX 1003.1) is the original POSIX standard. It was adopted in 1988 and revised in 1990. POSIX.1 is a C programming language interface standard. In its original form it specified the syntax and semantics of 203 C language functions and the contents of various data structures. Subsequent revisions have greatly expanded its scope. In 1993 interfaces for supporting real-time programming were added, and in 1995 interfaces for supporting multithreaded application programs were added.

POSIX.1 specifies the abstract structure of a filesystem. For example a system that conforms to POSIX.1 must have a hierarchical filesystem with directories, fifo files, and regular files. Each file must have attributes typical of UNIX system files, such as permission bits, owner and group IDs, and link counts. The programming interfaces refer to filenames using familiar UNIX-style pathnames such as **/home/alex/src/load.c**.

Name	Description
POSIX 1003.1	(POSIX.1) Base system interfaces in the C language. Adopted in 1988, modified several times since. Includes real-time extensions (1003.1b) and threads (1003.1c). These were adopted separately but are published as a single document.
POSIX 1003.2	(POSIX.2) Shell and utilities, including interactive utilities and a few C interfaces (which will be moved to POSIX 1003.1 in the next revision). Adopted in 1992. Amended in 1994 to include batch processing (1003.2d).
POSIX 2003	(POSIX.3) Test methods for measuring conformance to POSIX standards. Adopted in 1991, currently being revised.
POSIX 2003.1	(POSIX.3.1) Test methods for POSIX 1003.1. Adopted in 1992.
POSIX 2003.2	(POSIX.3.2) Test methods for POSIX 1003.2. Adopted in 1996.
POSIX 1003.5	(POSIX.5) Ada language binding to 1990 version of 1003.1. Updated in 1996 to include Ada binding to 1003.1 real-time features.
POSIX 1003.9	(POSIX.9) FORTRAN binding to 1990 version of 1003.1. Approved in 1992.
POSIX 1003.17	(POSIX.17) Standard for X.500 Directory Services, a protocol that allows multiple distributed directories to be searched as a single entity. The word *directory* does not refer to a Solaris filesystem directory, but to a generic data base. Approved in 1993. Note: This includes several standards whose IEEE project numbers used to be 1224.2, 1326.2, 1327.2, and 1328.2.
POSIX 1387.2	System administration: Software management (principally a software installation standard). Adopted in 1995.

Issues related to system administration are specifically excluded from POSIX.1, as are implementation details. After all, an application program does not need to know how to create a new device special file and does not care how the **open()** function (which opens a file) works internally. By avoiding implementation issues, the standard allows systems that are not based on UNIX to conform to POSIX.1.

The POSIX.1 committee was responsible for codifying existing practice, not engineering a new version of the UNIX system. During the development of the POSIX.1 standard, partisans of BSD and System V were forced to try to reconcile their differences. In some cases this meant standardizing on behavior from one or the other version. In a few cases the working group decided that both the BSD and System V implementations of some features were deficient, and it created new interfaces (such as terminal control) based on existing practice but with new syntax and semantics. Where no compromise seemed to be reachable, the working group adopted optional behavior. For example BSD has had job control at least since release 4.1, whereas SVR3 does not support job control. POSIX.1 makes job control an option.

One compromise took a unique form. POSIX.1 specifies formats for file archives. On UNIX System V the preferred archive format is **cpio** (page 721). On BSD the preferred format is **tar** (page 912). POSIX.1 requires that both formats be supported, in slightly modified forms. Because the specification of utilities is outside the scope of POSIX.1, neither the **cpio** nor the **tar** utility is mentioned; only the file formats for the archives are part of the standard. POSIX.1 requires that the implementation provide unnamed archive creation and archive reading utilities. See page 1018 for a discussion of the **pax** utility specified by POSIX.2.

The POSIX standards, like all IEEE standards, are subject to periodic revision. POSIX.1 was revised in 1990, and the real-time and threads standards were adopted as amendments in 1993 and 1996, respectively. A further set of amendments that includes symbolic links (page 96) is currently in ballot. Under the new IEEE numbering guidelines, many C language interface standards that were originally conceived as separate standards will be treated as amendments to POSIX.1. Current efforts in this area include security (1003.1e) and networking (1003.1f, related to NFS, and 1003.1g, related to sockets).

The POSIX.1 standard is available from the American National Standards Institute (ANSI) or from the IEEE. In addition it has been adopted as an international standard by the International Standards Organization (ISO) and the International Electrotechnical Commission (IEC), which jointly coordinate international computing standards. The formal name for POSIX.1 is ISO/IEC IS 9945-1:1990. For a detailed description of the standard from a programmer's point of view, see *The POSIX.1 Standard: A Programmer's Guide,* by Fred Zlotnick (Benjamin/Cummings, 1991).

▲▲ The POSIX.1 FIPS

POSIX.1 is a widely referenced standard. In particular it is the subject of a Federal Information Processing Standard (FIPS) published by the U.S. government. A FIPS specifies conformance requirements for computing systems procured by federal government agencies. FIPS 151-2 requires conformance to the 1990 version of the POSIX.1 standard and some of its optional features (such as job control and supplementary groups). The practical consequence is that just about every vendor who implements a POSIX.1 conforming system also implements the FIPS-required options. Thus FIPS 151-2 has become a de facto extended POSIX.1 standard.

The National Institute of Standards and Technology, which published the FIPS, has developed a conformance test suite. At this writing more than 100 systems have been certified as conforming to FIPS 151-2 or to its predecessor, FIPS 151-1. Most of these are UNIX systems, but versions of DEC's VMS and Unisys's CTOS operating system, which are not UNIX based, have also been certified.

▲ POSIX.2

POSIX.2, the shell and utilities standard, was formally approved as an IEEE standard in September 1992 and as an international standard in June 1993. For users, as opposed to application developers, POSIX.2 is the most important POSIX standard. Its principal purpose is to specify the semantics of a shell (based on the Korn Shell) and a collection of utilities that you can use to develop portable shell scripts. A secondary purpose is to promote user portability. This term refers to a standard specification for utilities such as **vi, man,** and **who** that are not very useful for scripts but are typically used interactively.

POSIX.2 is independent of POSIX.1, and a system can claim conformance to POSIX.2 without claiming conformance to POSIX.1. This is not true of most of the other POSIX standards, which take POSIX.1 as a base. In practice you can expect virtually all UNIX systems to comply with both POSIX.1 and POSIX.2 within a few years. Many non-UNIX systems will also comply, making them "UNIX-like," at least on the outside. Solaris2 supports POSIX.2.

▲▲ Localization

One of the most important features of POSIX.2 is that it is fully localized. That is, it describes the behavior of the shell and utilities in the context of different character sets and locale-specific information (such as date and time formats). For example the **grep** utility has a **–i** option that causes **grep** to ignore case in determining matches. POSIX.2 specifies what this means for alphabets in which the uppercase to lowercase mapping is either not defined or not one-to-one.

The general idea behind localization is that every process executes in a particular locale. The POSIX.2 standard defines a locale as "the definition of the subset of the environment of a user that depends on language and cultural conventions." The locale describes how the process should display or interpret information that depends on the language and culture, including character set and the method of writing times, dates, numbers, and currency amounts. Localization is not unique to POSIX.2; both the C standard and POSIX.1 support it to a limited degree. However POSIX.2 is much more specific in its description of how locale-specific information is provided to the system and how it affects the system's operation.

An important feature of POSIX.2 locales is that they are fragmented into categories. The standard specifies six locale categories and defines six environment variables corresponding to these categories.

Environment Variable	Locale Category
LC_CTYPE	Describes which characters are considered alphabetic, numeric, punctuation, blank, and so on, and describes the mapping of uppercase to lowercase, and vice versa.
LC_COLLATE	Describes the order of characters for sorting. Used by **sort**, **uniq**, regular expressions, and more.
LC_TIME	Describes abbreviated and full names for months and days of the week, local equivalents of AM and PM, appropriate date representation, appropriate 12- and 24-hour time representation, and time and date formatting. Used by **date** and more.
LC_NUMERIC	Describes the rules and symbols for displaying non-monetary numeric data: The character to use as a decimal point, the character to separate groups of digits (such as the comma in 65,536), and the number of digits in a group.

Environment Variable	Locale Category
LC_MONETARY	Describes the rules and symbols for displaying monetary numeric data: The currency symbol, where it is positioned, how negative values are written, the currency decimal point character, the thousands separator, the number of fractional digits, and other details of how currency values are written.
LC_MESSAGES	Describes the formats of informative and diagnostic messages and interactive responses, and expressions to be interpreted as yes and no responses for those utilities that query the user.

Two more environment variables, **LC_ALL** and **LANG**, interact with these six to provide overrides and defaults. If **LC_ALL** is set, then its value is used in place of the value of any of the other six **LC_*** variables. If **LANG** is set, then its value is used in place of any **LC_*** variable that is not set.

Each of these environment variables can be set to a value that is the name of a locale and that will cause features of the shell and some utilities to change behavior. For example here is a fragment of a shell session on a system with POSIX.2 internationalization (your system may behave differently). In this and the following example assume that **LANG** and the **LC_*** variables have been exported. They must be exported because they affect the standard utilities only when they are in the environment of those utilities.

```
$ LC_TIME=POSIX
$ date
Thu Aug 25 21:21:03 1994
$ LC_TIME=Fr_FR # French
$ date
Jeu 25 Ao 21:21:12 PDT 1994
```

There are two standard locale names: POSIX and C. They describe the identical locale, which is a generic UNIX locale; setting all the locale environment variables to **POSIX** will result in traditional UNIX system behavior. Other locale names are implementation defined. There is no standard format. Common conventions include the abbreviated language and country in the locale name. Thus **En_US** and **Fr_CA** might be locale names for locales describing English in the United States and French in Canada.

An example that was actually run on a system that supports POSIX.2 style localization shows the results of mixing locales:

```
$ LC_TIME=Fr_FR
$ LANG=De_DE
$ cal 1 1995

        Janvier 1995
 Dim Lun Mar Mer Jeu Ven Sam
   1   2   3   4   5   6   7
   8   9  10  11  12  13  14
  15  16  17  18  19  20  21
  22  23  24  25  26  27  28
  29  30  31
```

```
$ rm NoSuchFile
rm: NoSuchFile: Verzeichnis/Datei im Pfadnamen existiert nicht.
```

On some POSIX.2 systems it is possible for users to define their own locales in addition to those provided by the system; see the definition of the **localedef** utility on page 1017.

Give the command **man –s 5 locale** for more information.

▲▲ The POSIX Shell

POSIX.2 specifies the syntax and semantics of a shell command language. The POSIX Shell is generically named **sh**, but it is most closely based on the Korn Shell, **ksh**. The POSIX Shell is actually almost a subset of the 1988 version of **ksh**. The newer versions of **ksh** have been designed as supersets of the POSIX Shell. If you want to write shell scripts that are portable across all POSIX Shell implementations, you should try to avoid using constructs that are not supported by the POSIX Shell. Here is a brief description of some of the differences between the POSIX Shell and its relative, **ksh**:

- The POSIX Shell does not support the **typeset** keyword.

- The POSIX Shell does not support the Select command.

- The POSIX Shell does not support the two-argument form of the **cd** command.

- The POSIX Shell does not automatically define and maintain the value of the **PWD** environment variable.

- The POSIX Shell has a different syntax for doing integer arithmetic. It does not use the **let** keyword. Arithmetic expressions are initiated by the symbols **$((** and terminated by **))**. Within the parentheses you must refer to shell variables by using a $ sign. For example the following brief POSIX Shell dialogue displays 7 (because Solaris **ksh** is POSIX-compliant, this works with **ksh** also):

  ```
  $ x=3;y=4
  $ z=$(($x + $y))
  $ echo $z
  7
  ```

  The equivalent **ksh** sequence is:

  ```
  $ x=3;y=4
  $ let z="x + y"
  $ echo $z
  7
  ```

- In **ksh** you can also use double parentheses for arithmetic instead of **let**, but the syntax is different. Two ways to write the **let** statement in **ksh** are:

  ```
  $ x=3;y=4
  $ z=$((x + y))
  $ echo $z
  7
  ```

  and

  ```
  $ echo $((z=x+y))
  7
  ```

- You can define shell functions in the POSIX Shell, just as you can in **ksh**. However **ksh** supports multiple syntaxes to define functions. The POSIX Shell supports only one of these; it does not support the **function** keyword, and it requires braces ({}) even if the function body is a single command. The following function definition style is valid in the POSIX Shell and in **ksh**:

```
parent()
{
_dir=$(dirname $1)
echo $(basename $_dir)
}
```

The preceding function displays the name of the parent (last-but-one) component of the pathname given as an argument.

```
$ parent /home/alex/literature/moby_dick
literature
```

- In the POSIX Shell, functions execute in the caller's environment. This is largely but not entirely true for **ksh**. For example consider the following shell dialogue:

```
$ side_effect()
> {
> trap "rm /tmp/foo" 0 # on exit, remove it
> }
$ trap - 0                # on exit, no action
$ trap
$ side_effect
$ trap
trap -- 'rm /tmp/foo' EXIT
```

The **trap – 0** command resets the traps in effect, and the subsequent **trap** command shows that no traps are set. When the POSIX Shell executes the **side_effect** function and returns from the function, the trap has been set for when the calling shell exits. The subsequent **trap** command shows that the trap that was set in **side_effect** is also in effect in the calling shell. In the 1988 **ksh** the trap is set for execution of the function and occurs when the function exits. (The 1993 version of **ksh** follows the POSIX semantics.)

▲▲ Utilities for Portable Shell Applications

POSIX.2 specifies 72 required utilities, referred to as Execution Environment Utilities. Most of them are familiar from SVR3 or Berkeley UNIX or are derived from UNIX utilities. A few, such as **pathchk** and **printf** (see the following table), are inventions of the POSIX.2 committee. These were created to satisfy requirements that specifically relate to portability. Other utilities are adopted from the UNIX system but have changed semantics, to resolve conflicts between SVR3 and Berkeley UNIX, to remove behavior that does not make sense in an internationalized context, or to fix inconsistencies (especially with the syntax of options).

Sun has taken measures to make sure that each user has what he or she needs: If the historical behavior of a utility differs from the POSIX.1 behavior, Solaris keeps the historical utility in place and puts a

POSIX.1-compliant version in the **/usr/xpg4/bin** directory. (The directory is named for the X/Open Common Applications Environment (CAE) Portability Guide Issue 4, a superset of POSIX.1 and POSIX.2[1]). If you want to take advantage of the POSIX or XPG4 features, set your **PATH** (**sh** or **ksh**) or **path** (**csh**) environment variable so that the **/usr/xpg4/bin** directory precedes all other directories in the search path. Refer to page 372 (Bourne Shell), page 461 (C Shell), or page 485 (Korn Shell) for more information on the **PATH** variable.

The Execution Environment Utilities are shown below. Utilities that are not described in the main part of this text are marked with an asterisk (*****). Utilities that have significant differences from their traditional UNIX semantics are marked with a dagger (**†**). Utilities that are new (that is, inventions of the POSIX.2 working group) are marked with a double dagger (**‡**) and are described following the table.

The Execution Environment Utilities			
awk	basename	bc*	cat
cd	chgrp	chmod	chown
cksum*‡	cmp*	comm	command*‡
cp	cut*	date	dd*
diff	dirname*	echo†	ed
env*	expr	false	find
fold*	getconf*‡	getopts	grep†
head	id*	join*	kill†
ln	locale*‡	localedef*‡	logger*‡
logname*	lp*	ls	mailx*
mkdir	mkfifo*‡	mv	nohup
od†	paste	pathchk*‡	pax*‡
pr	printf*‡	pwd	read
rm	rmdir	sed	sh
sleep	sort	stty	tail
tee	test	touch	tr
true	tty	umask	uname*
uniq	wait	wc	xargs

---

1. Solaris supports the X/Open Common Applications Environment (CAE) Portability Guide Issue 3 (XPG3), Issue 4 (XPG4), Issue 4 Version 2 (XPG4v2), and Networking Services Issue 4 (XNET4). Give the command **man posix** for more information.

 cksum

The **cksum** utility computes a checksum for a file. It is useful when you are sending or receiving a file and want to ensure that it was not corrupted in transmission. The **cksum** utility replaces a utility named **sum** that was present in both BSD and SVR4. The POSIX.2 committee did not use **sum**, because BSD and System V had differing, incompatible implementations. The algorithm used by **cksum** is based on a cyclic redundancy check from the Ethernet standard ISO 8802-3.

The syntax is

*cksum [**file...**]*

You can name zero or more files on the command line. If you do not specify a filename, **cksum** computes a checksum for standard input. For each input file **cksum** writes to standard output the file's checksum, byte count, and name. (Actually it is not a byte count but an octet count. On those rare systems where a byte is not 8 bits, these will differ.)

▲▲▲ command

The **command** utility executes any command line in a manner designed to guarantee that you are executing the version of the command that you would expect. If you type

*command **command_name** [arguments...]*

the shell executes ***command_name*** without looking for a shell function of that name. If you use the **–p** option, as in

*command –p **command_name** [arguments...]*

the shell searches for **command_name** using a special value for **PATH**, one that is guaranteed to find all the standard utilities. This protects you from accidentally invoking local utilities or functions with the same names as standard utilities.

If the system supports POSIX.2's User Portability Utilities Option (page 1018), then **command** has two more option flags. With the **–v** option, **command** reports the absolute pathname of *command_name* without running it, using your **PATH** variable for the search. If *command_name* is a built-in shell utility, a reserved word, or a function, just its name is written. If *command_name* is an alias, the command line representing its alias definition is written. The **–V** option is similar but distinguishes between functions, reserved words, and built-in utilities.

▲▲▲ getconf

The **getconf** utility lets you determine the values of various options and configuration-dependent parameters, such as whether the system supports the User Portability Utilities Option or what maximum length filename the system supports. Some of these parameters may vary depending on where you are in the filesystem. For example a UNIX system might support both traditional System V filesystems (in which filenames are limited to 14 characters) and BSD filesystems (in which filenames can be as long as 255 characters).

You invoke **getconf** in any of the following ways:

*getconf **system_var***

getconf **path_var pathname**

getconf –a

The first syntax is used for systemwide variables. For example you can determine the maximum number of simultaneous processes that any one user ID can own with the call

```
$ getconf CHILD_MAX
40
```

The second syntax is used to determine the values of variables that may vary from place to place in the file hierarchy. For example you can determine the maximum permissible length of a filename in the **/tmp** directory with the command

```
$ getconf NAME_MAX /tmp
255
```

The third syntax displays all variables, which is the same as the set of symbols that you can query. You can also find this list in the POSIX.2 standard (which refers directly to POSIX.1 for some of these symbols). The following table lists some of the more useful symbols:

Symbol (argument to getconf)	Meaning
PATH	Reports a value of the **PATH** variable that will find all standard utilities.
LINE_MAX	Reports the maximum length of an input line that you can reliably pass to a standard utility that processes text files. It must be at least 2048.
POSIX2_UPE	Displays 1 if the system supports the User Portability Utilities Option (page 1018).
POSIX2_LOCALEDEF	Displays 1 if the system supports the ability to define new locales using the **localedef** utility (page 1017).
PATH_MAX *dir*	Reports the length of the longest pathname that you can reliably use, relative to directory *dir*. This may vary from place to place in the filesystem.
NAME_MAX *dir*	Reports the length of the longest filename that you can use in *dir*. This may vary from place to place in the filesystem.

▲▲▲ locale

The **locale** utility is part of POSIX.2's internationalization of the UNIX environment. The **locale** utility exports information about the current locale. If invoked with no arguments or options, **locale** writes to standard output the values of the **LANG** and **LC_*** environment variables. This utility can also take options or arguments that allow you to write information about all available public locales or the names and values of selected keywords used in defining locales. The description of these keywords is beyond the scope of this book, but an example will illustrate their use. Suppose a user has typed a response to a question, and you want to determine, in a localized way, whether the response is affirmative or negative. The definition of the **LC_MESSAGES** locale category contains the keyword **yesexpr**. The value associated with this keyword is a regular expression describing the responses that should be treated as yes in the current locale. If the user's response is in a shell variable named **response**, then the following shell fragment will work:

```
yes=`locale yesexpr`
echo $response | grep "$yes" > /dev/null
if [ $? -eq 0 ]
then
echo "Answer was yes"
else
echo "Answer was no"
fi
```

▲▲▲ localedef

The Solaris **localedef** utility allows you to define a locale. Such support is an option in POSIX.2. The information required to define a locale is voluminous, and its description is beyond the scope of this book. You can find a sample set of locale definition files, provided by the Danish Standards Association, in Annex G of the POSIX.2 standard.

▲▲▲ logger

The **logger** utility provides a means for scripts to write messages to an unspecified system log file. The format and method of reading these messages are unspecified by POSIX.2 and will vary from one system to another. The syntax of **logger** is

logger **string** ...

The intended purpose of the **logger** utility is for noninteractive scripts that encounter errors to record these errors in a place where system administrators can later examine them.

▲▲▲ mkfifo

POSIX.1 includes a **mkfifo()** function that allows programs to create fifo special files (named pipes that persist in the filesystem even when not in use). This utility provides the same functionality at the shell level. The syntax is

mkfifo [–m **mode**] *file* ...

By default the mode of the created fifos is 660 (rw-rw----), modified by the caller's **umask**. The **–m** option allows you to include a **mode** argument (in the same format as that used by **chmod**) to specify the mode of the new fifo.

▲▲▲ pathchk

The **pathchk** utility allows portable shell scripts to determine if a given pathname is valid on a given system. The problem arises because the character set used in the pathname may not be supported on the system, or the pathname may be longer than the maximum **PATH_MAX** for this filesystem or may have components (filenames) longer than the maximum **FILE_MAX** for this filesystem. The syntax of **pathchk** is

> *pathchk [–p] pathname ...*

For each pathname argument **pathchk** checks that the length is no greater than **PATH_MAX**, that the length of each component is no greater than **NAME_MAX**, that each existing directory in the path is searchable, and that every character in the pathname is valid in its parent directory. If any of these fail, **pathchk** writes a diagnostic message to standard error. If you use the **–p** option, then **pathchk** performs a more stringent portability check: Pathnames are checked against a maximum length of 255 bytes, filenames against a maximum length of 14 bytes, and characters against the portable filename character set (which consists of the lowercase and uppercase letters of the Roman alphabet, the digits 0–9, period, underscore, and hyphen). The limits of 255 for **PATH_MAX** and 14 for **NAME_MAX** are the minimum that any POSIX-conforming system can support.

▲▲▲ pax

The name **pax** is ostensibly an acronym for Portable Archive eXchange, but it is also a bilingual pun. The disputes between the advocates of the **tar** and **cpio** formats were referred to as the tar wars (in which 3-cpio did battle with tar-2-d-2), and **pax** is the peace treaty. The **pax** utility can read and write archives in several formats. These specifically include, but are not limited to, the POSIX.1 **tar** and **cpio** formats. Other formats are implementation defined. It is the stated intent of the POSIX.2 committee to define a new archive format in a future revision of the standard. That format will become the default for **pax**.

The syntax of the **pax** command is too complex to describe here (as you might expect from looking at all the options available to **tar** and **cpio**). If it exists in your system, consult the manual pages. The USENIX Association funded the development of a portable implementation of **pax** and placed it in the public domain, so this utility is now widely available.

▲▲▲ printf

The **printf** utility was invented largely to deal with the incompatibility between the BSD and System V versions of **echo** (page 747). BSD **echo** treats a first argument of **–n** in a special fashion, whereas System V displays it. System V **echo** treats certain strings starting with \ in a special fashion, whereas BSD displays them. POSIX.2 states that any **echo** command line in which **–n** is the first argument or in which any argument starts with \ will have implementation defined behavior. To display any but the simplest strings in a portable manner, use **printf**.

The *f* in **printf** stands for formatted, and the **printf** utility allows you to send strings to standard output under the control of a formatting argument. The syntax is

> *printf format [string ...]*

Both the name **printf** and the syntax of the format string are borrowed from C.

▲▲ The User Portability Utilities Option (UPE)

The UPE is a collection of 37 utilities and shell built-in commands for interactive use. This portion of the standard is an option; that is, a system can conform to POSIX.2 without providing these. Their purpose is to promote user portability by creating a uniform interactive command environment. All of the UPE utilities are listed in the following table. Those that are not described in the main part of this text are marked with an asterisk (*).

UPE Utilities			
alias	at	batch*	bg
crontab	csplit*	ctags*	df
du	ex	expand*	fc
fg	file	jobs	man
mesg	more	newgrp	nice
nm*	patch	ps	renice*
split*	strings*	tabs*	talk
time	tput*	unalias	unexpand*
uudecode*	uuencode*	vi	who
write			

Three of these utilities, **bg, fg,** and **jobs,** need be supported only if the system also supports job control. Two others, **ctags** and **nm**, need be supported only if the system also supports the Software Development Utilities option.

Many of the UPE utilities are affected by localization. For example the **at** utility can accept names of days of the week as part of its time specification. The way one writes these names depends on the value of **LC_TIME**.

▲▲ Software Development Utilities

As an option, POSIX.2 specifies the behavior of some utilities useful to software developers, such as **make, lex,** and **yacc.** In fact there are three separate options in POSIX.2 that cover three sets of development tools:

- The Software Development Utilities Option specifies the behavior of the **ar, make,** and **strip** utilities. These utilities are useful for software development in any programming language.

- The C Language Development Utilities Option specifies the behavior of the **c89, lex,** and **yacc** utilities. The **c89** command invokes a C compiler that conforms to the 1989 C standard (ANSI X3.159-1989, also ISO/IEC 9899-1990.) The **lex** and **yacc** utilities are useful high-level tools that parse input streams into tokens and take actions when a particular token is recognized. They have historically been available on UNIX systems.

- The FORTRAN Development and Runtime Utilities Option specifies the behavior of the **asa** and **fort77** utilities. The **asa** utility converts between FORTRAN's arcane printer control commands and ASCII output. The **fort77** command invokes a FORTRAN compiler that conforms to the FORTRAN 77 standard (ANSI X3.9-1978).

▲ POSIX.3

Developers of the POSIX standards recognized early in the process that testing systems for conformance to the standards was going to be essential. In the past other standards efforts have suffered from lack of appropriately specified conformance tests or from conflicting conformance tests with different measures of conformance. The POSIX.3 standard specifies general principles for test suites that measure conformance to POSIX standards. For each standard a set of assertions (individual items to be tested) is developed. For POSIX.1 a test methods standard with more than 2400 assertions has been adopted as POSIX.3.1. For POSIX.2 there is a draft test methods standard under development at this writing. It contains almost 10,000 assertions.

Users who are involved in testing or procuring systems that must conform to standards need to be familiar with POSIX.3 and its associated test methods standards. For other users these standards have little importance.

▲ POSIX.4

The POSIX.4 standard is an addition to and modification of the POSIX.1 standard that describes C language interfaces for real-time applications. The standard defines real-time as "the ability of the operating system to provide a required level of service in a bounded response time." Real-time systems have historically been implemented as stand-alone systems controlling processes or machines, or as embedded systems (such as inside a microwave oven). However there has always been a need for combined interactive and real-time systems, and the UNIX system has served as the base for many implementations of real-time facilities.

POSIX.4 was adopted in September 1993. The facilities specified in POSIX.4 are those commonly used by real-time applications such as semaphores, timers, interprocess communication, shared memory, and so on. Although there have been quite a few implementations of these and related facilities in various UNIX systems, there was no well-established and widely accepted set of UNIX real-time interfaces. Thus the routines specified in POSIX.4 are largely the invention of the POSIX.4 committee. They have already been implemented on a number of UNIX systems.

POSIX.4 is structured as a collection of optional extensions to POSIX.1. Thus a system can claim conformance to some parts of the standard and not others. However it must claim conformance to POSIX.1. This has been a subject of some controversy, because many real-time applications, particularly for embedded systems, do not need the support of an operating system with all of the POSIX.1 machinery.

Most real-time applications have traditionally been implemented as sets of cooperating, closely coordinated processes. In many cases this cooperation extends to the use of shared data, and one convenient way to do this is to use multiple threads of control in a single process. Support for threads allows a single process to have multiple execution paths active at once, and—on hardware with multiple processors—to actually execute those paths simultaneously. The original POSIX real-time project included an attempt at standardizing threads interfaces. It was soon recognized that this was sufficiently complicated to be a separate standard, and a new committee was formed. The resulting POSIX threads standard, POSIX.1c, was adopted in 1995.

It is possible to implement POSIX threads in a user-level library or in the kernel or in some combination.

▲ POSIX.5

POSIX.5 is an Ada language version of POSIX.1. It specifies Ada routines that provide essentially the same functionality as the C routines of POSIX.1. The UNIX/Solaris system itself is written in C, and C has always been the most widely used programming language on UNIX systems, but the Ada community has always been interested in the UNIX system and in providing a standard way for Ada programs to access UNIX system services. POSIX.5 provides that standard. In principle POSIX.5 provides the exact functionality provided by POSIX.1. This does not mean that there is a precise one-to-one correlation between the interfaces in POSIX.1 and POSIX.5, because differences in the languages make that impossible.

The POSIX.5 working group is tracking changes to POSIX.1 and will keep the Ada version of the standard synchronized with the C version. The POSIX.20 working group, which works in concert with POSIX.5, is developing an Ada language version of POSIX.4 and POSIX.4a; this will provide Ada programmers with the ability to use standard interfaces for real-time applications on the UNIX system and UNIX-like systems. This is important to the Ada community, because Ada has from its inception been used heavily in the development of real-time systems.

▲ POSIX.9

POSIX.9 is a FORTRAN version of POSIX.1. It specifies routines in the FORTRAN 77 language that provide the same functionality as POSIX.1. FORTRAN was the "second language" on UNIX systems, in the sense that FORTRAN compilers have been available and widely used on UNIX systems almost as long as the UNIX system has been available. Nevertheless there has not been a widely supported set of FORTRAN interfaces to UNIX system services. Thus there is no widespread existing practice to codify. The interfaces in POSIX.9 are essentially all inventions of the POSIX.9 working group. They correspond fairly closely to the C interfaces.

There is a new and more powerful version of the FORTRAN language, Fortran 90. (The name FORTRAN is properly written with all uppercase letters for versions of the language up through FORTRAN 77. Starting with Fortran 90, the name is spelled with an initial uppercase letter.) There was some discussion about using Fortran 90 as the basis for POSIX.9. The consensus of the working group was that there was currently insufficient experience with Fortran 90. It would not be surprising to see POSIX.9 modified in a few years to use a more modern version of the FORTRAN language.

▲▲ System Administration

System administration was explicitly omitted from the scope of POSIX.1. In part this was because so many UNIX variants had developed incompatible tools, file hierarchies, and interfaces for system administration that there was little chance for quick agreement. Indeed when the POSIX System Administration committee first started work, it chose not to use any existing practice but rather to invent a new approach. That effort did not advance far. The committee reorganized itself and selected three areas of system administration to be standardized separately, by three subcommittees:

POSIX 1387.2 **Software distribution** This includes standards for packaging applications and for the installation, rollback, and maintenance of these packages.

POSIX 1387.3 **User/group administration** This includes standards for adding new users and groups to systems, deleting users and groups from systems, and administering mail accounts and quotas.

POSIX 1387.4 **Printer administration** This is intended to standardize application interfaces to print facilities. (POSIX 1387.1 is an overview document rather than a standard.) At this writing only POSIX 1387.2 is an official IEEE standard; it was adopted in June 1995. Few systems currently support 1387.2.

▲ Draft POSIX Standards

The remaining POSIX standards committees are in various stages of preparing drafts of standards or of profiles. If you are interested in a particular standard or draft standard, you can contact the IEEE Computer Society in Washington, D.C., for more information.

▲▲ Security

One area of current standards development is system security. Since early in its development, the UNIX system has had a simple and relatively effective security paradigm. File access permissions are assigned according to three levels of granularity (owner, group, and other [page 88]), and certain actions require privileges. The privileges are monolithic; that is, either a process has all the privileges that the system supports (such as adding users, changing the ownership of files, changing its user ID), or it has none. One user ID is reserved for a privileged user, Superuser.

For most ordinary purposes this paradigm works well, particularly in organizations where small groups cooperate on projects. However it does not provide the level of security that some users need. The Department of Defense has defined several different levels of security in a document commonly referred to as the *Orange Book*. Some vendors have layered additional security features on top of UNIX systems to conform to the more secure levels of the *Orange Book*.

An important feature of all the POSIX standards is that they support an abstract privilege model in which privileges are discrete. Each time a POSIX standard describes an action that requires some privilege, the phrase *appropriate privileges* is used. Thus POSIX.2 states that **chmod** can be used to change the mode of a file by the owner of the file or by a process with appropriate privileges. One model of these privileges is the Superuser model, but there can be others. Thus POSIX allows many security paradigms.

The POSIX.1e committee is developing user interfaces, program interfaces, and structures to define higher levels of security. They include the following general areas:

Least Privilege This is the idea that a process should only have the privileges that are absolutely necessary for its function. The monolithic nature of traditional UNIX system privileges is considered a security hazard. You may recall that in 1988, a worm program traveled across the Internet, crippling computers around the world (page 1004). The worm exploited a feature of the **sendmail** program. Because **sendmail** has to write to all users' mail files, it must have some privileges. On a classical UNIX system, this means it has all privileges, and the worm used this fact to acquire all privileges itself.

Discretionary Access Controls (DACs)

These are additional access restrictions under the control of the creator of an object (such as a file). A typical DAC is an Access Control List (ACL), a list of user IDs permitted access to the file. This acts as an additional restriction to that imposed by the file's mode.

Mandatory Access Controls (MACs)

These are similar to two security levels. An object is created at some level, not under the control of its creator, and can be accessed only by processes at the same or a higher level. The level can be determined by the process's user or group ID or by the nature of the process itself.

Auditability Mechanism

This covers which types of objects or actions need to be audited and the mechanisms for keeping track of the audit trail.

In all of these areas there is existing practice for UNIX systems; that is, you can find DACs, MACs, partitioned privilege, and audit mechanisms on secure UNIX systems today. The goal of POSIX.1e is to standardize the practices.

The POSIX.22 committee is addressing similar issues in a distributed environment. Clearly network security adds its own layer of difficulties, including file access on remotely mounted systems.

▲▲ Networks

There are a number of POSIX groups working on different standards related to networks. The areas that need to be standardized occur at many different levels. Some are visible to users, some to application programs, and some only to the operating system.

The most visible network feature to a user is the availability of remote filesystems. There is a well-established existing practice for this on UNIX systems, via packages such as NFS (page 219) and RFS. The purpose of remote filesystems is to enable file hierarchies on remote hosts to behave, to the extent possible, as if they are mounted on the local host. That is, the presence of the network should be transparent to the user and the user's programs. The POSIX.1f committee is charged with standardizing transparent file access.

There is also existing practice for allowing programs on two different hosts to communicate with each other, much as pipes or fifos allow programs on the same host to communicate. In fact there are at least two competing approaches: Berkeley sockets and the XTI interface from X/Open. The POSIX.1g committee is trying to resolve the differences between these approaches. Sockets and XTI are referred to as protocol-independent interfaces, because they are above the level of the network protocol, the convention that describes precisely how hosts on the network communicate.

That protocol is also the subject of considerable standards effort. There is already an international standard for network protocols, the ISO OSI. However most UNIX systems have historically used a different protocol, TCP/IP. Trying to resolve the differences between OSI, TCP/IP, and other network protocols will be difficult. The IEEE 1238 committee is working on part of this problem.

▲ Profiles and POSIX Standards

An important concept in the POSIX lexicon is that of a profile. As the number of standards grows, the number of combinations of standards grows exponentially. However the number of sensible, coherent combinations is much smaller. Many of the POSIX committees are developing AEPs, or application environment profiles, rather than standards. An AEP is a "standard collection of standards" suitable for a particular application area. For example the POSIX.10 committee is developing a supercomputing AEP. This profile references a number of standards that would be useful for applications that run on supercomputers. These include POSIX.1, POSIX.2, the ISO Fortran (Fortran 90) standard, and the C standard. A user who needs the resources of a supercomputer will typically also need the features provided by most or all of these standards.

Profiles are most useful as tools for procurements, particularly by large organizations such as government agencies. Typically such organizations find that requiring conformance to one or two standards does not adequately specify their needs. For example although the POSIX.1 standard is quite useful and widely referenced, knowing that your system conforms to POSIX.1 does not, by itself, guarantee you much; most complex applications require facilities well outside the scope of POSIX.1. In fact the NIST POSIX FIPS is really a profile. It requires conformance to POSIX.1, support for certain POSIX.1 options, and conformance to the C standard.

If you are going to ask hardware vendors to propose systems to satisfy a complex set of requirements, using a profile makes your job much simpler. Thus it is not surprising that the U.S. government and the European commission are actively involved in the development of POSIX profiles and also develop profiles for their own purposes. As the number of POSIX standards grows, these standards are taking a more central place in government profiles.

Summary

The IEEE POSIX committees have developed standards for programming and user interfaces based on historical UNIX practice, and new standards are under development. Most of the standards are compromises between versions of System V and versions of BSD, with a few innovations where compromise was not possible or was technically inadvisable. The standards have met with broad acceptance from government bodies and industry organizations.

POSIX.1 standardizes C language interfaces to the core UNIX system facilities; Ada and FORTRAN versions of these interfaces are specified by POSIX.5 and POSIX.9. POSIX.2 standardizes a shell and a collection of utilities useful for scripts and interactive use. It specifies how these tools should behave in international environments, where character sets and local conventions differ from those in the original UNIX environment. POSIX.4 specifies interfaces for real-time programs executing in UNIX-like environments.

Standards under development will cover parts of system administration, extended system security, networks, and user interfaces. Existing UNIX system practice in all of these areas will form the basis of the new standards. In turn innovations from these standards will find their way into future UNIX systems.

Glossary

All entries marked with FOD are courtesy of the Free Online Dictionary of Computing (**wombat.doc.ic.ac.uk** or **www.instantweb.com/foldoc**), Denis Howe, editor. Used with permission.

Absolute pathname	A pathname that starts with the root directory (*/*). An absolute pathname locates a file without regard to the working directory.
Access	In computer jargon, a verb to mean use, read from, or write to. To access a file means to read from or write to the file.
Access permission	Permission to read from, write to, or execute a file. If you have "write access permission to a file," you can write to the file. Also, *access privilege.*
Alias	A mechanism in the C and Korn Shells that enables you to define new commands.
Alphanumeric character	One of the characters, either upper- or lowercase, from A to Z and 0 to 9, inclusive.
Ambiguous file reference	A reference to a file that does not necessarily specify any one file but can be used to specify a group of files. The shell expands an ambiguous file reference into a list of filenames. Special characters represent single characters (**?**), strings of zero or more characters (*****), and character classes (**[ ]**) within ambiguous file references. An ambiguous file reference is a type of *regular expression.*
Angle bracket	There is a left angle bracket (**<**) and a right angle bracket (**>**). The shell uses **<** to redirect a command's standard input to come from a file and **>** to redirect the standard output. Also, the shell uses the characters **<<** to signify the start of a here document and **>>** to append output to a file.
Append	To add something to the end of something else. To append text to a file means to add the text to the end of the file. The shell uses **>>** to append a command's output to a file.
Argument	A number, letter, filename, or another string that gives some information to a command and is passed to the command at the time it is called. A command line argument is anything on a command line following the command name that is passed to the command.

Arithmetic expression	A group of numbers, operators, and parentheses that can be evaluated. When you evaluate an arithmetic expression, you end up with a number. The Bourne Shell uses the **expr** command to evaluate arithmetic expressions; the C Shell uses @, and the Korn Shell uses **let**.
Array	An arrangement of elements (numbers or strings of characters) in one or more dimensions. The C and Korn Shells and **nawk** can store and process arrays.
ASCII	American Standard Code for Information Interchange. A code that uses seven bits to represent both graphic (letters, numbers, and punctuation) and CONTROL characters. You can represent textual information, including program source code and English text, in ASCII code. Because it is a standard, it is frequently used when exchanging information between computers. See the file **/usr/pub/ascii** or give the command **man ascii** to see a list of ASCII codes.
	There are extensions of the ASCII character set that make use of eight bits. The seven-bit set is common; the eight-bit extensions are still coming into popular use. The eighth bit is sometimes referred to as the meta bit.
Asynchronous event	An event that does not occur regularly or synchronously with another event. Solaris system signals are asynchronous; they can occur at any time, because they can be initiated by any number of nonregular events.
Automatic mounting	A way of demand mounting directories from remote hosts without having them hard-configured into **/etc/vfstab**. Also, called *automounting*.
Back door	A hole in the security of a system deliberately left in place by designers or maintainers. The motivation for such holes is not always sinister; some operating systems, for example come out of the box with privileged accounts intended for use by field service technicians or the vendor's maintenance programmers.
	Ken Thompson's 1983 Turing Award lecture to the ACM revealed the existence of a back door in early UNIX versions that may be the most fiendishly clever security hack of all time. The C compiler contained code that would recognize when the `login` command was being recompiled and insert some code recognizing a password chosen by Thompson, giving him entry to the system whether or not an account had been created for him.
	Normally such a back door could be removed by removing it from the source code for the compiler and recompiling the compiler. But to recompile the compiler, you have to *use* the compiler—so Thompson also arranged that the compiler would *recognize when it was compiling a version of itself* and insert into the recompiled compiler the code to insert into the recompiled `login` the code to allow Thompson entry, and, of course, the code to recognize itself and do the whole thing again the next time around. And having done this once, he was then able to recompile the compiler from the original sources; the hack perpetuated itself invisibly, leaving the back door in place and active but with no trace in the sources. Sometimes called a worm-hole. Also, *trap door*.[FOD]

Background process A process that is not run in the foreground. Also, called a *detached process,* a background process is initiated by a command line that ends with an ampersand (**&**). You do not have to wait for a background process to run to completion before giving the shell additional commands. If you have job control, you can move background processes to the foreground, and vice versa.

Basename The name of a file which, in contrast to a pathname, does not mention any of the directories containing the file (and therefore does not contain any slashes [/]). For example **hosts** is the basename of **/etc/hosts**.^{FOD}

Baud The maximum information-carrying capacity of a communication channel in symbols (state-transitions or level-transitions) per second. This coincides with bits per second only for two-level modulation with no framing or stop bits. A symbol is a unique state of the communication channel, distinguishable by the receiver from all other possible states. For example it may be one of two voltage levels on a wire for a direct digital connection or it might be the phase or frequency of a carrier.^{FOD}

Baud is often mistakenly used as a synonym for bits per second.

Baud rate Transmission speed. Usually used to measure terminal or modem speed. Common baud rates range from 110 to 19,200 baud. See *baud.*

Berkeley UNIX One of the two major versions of the UNIX operating system. Berkeley UNIX was developed at the University of California at Berkeley by the Computer Systems Research Group. It is often referred to as *BSD* (Berkeley Software Distribution).

Bit The smallest piece of information a computer can handle. A *bit* is a **b**inary dig**it**, either a 1 or 0 (on or off).

Bit-mapped display A graphical display device in which each pixel on the screen is controlled by an underlying representation of zeros and ones.

Blank character Either a **SPACE** or a **TAB** character, also called *white space.* Also, in some contexts, **NEWLINE**s are considered blank characters.

Block A section of a disk or tape (usually 1024 bytes long, but shorter or longer on some systems) that is written at one time.

Block device A disk or tape drive. A block device stores information in blocks of characters. A block device is represented by a block device (block special) file. Contrast with *Character device.*

Blocking factor The number of logical blocks that make up a physical block on a tape or disk. When you write 1K logical blocks to a tape with a physical block size of 30K, the blocking factor is 30.

Block number Disk and tape blocks (see *Block*) are numbered, so that Solaris can keep track of the data on the device. These numbers are block numbers.

Boot To load the Solaris system kernel into memory and start it running. Also, *bootstrap.*

Bourne Shell A UNIX/Solaris command processor. It was developed by Steve Bourne at AT&T Bell Laboratories. See *Shell*.

Brace There is a left brace ({) and a right brace (}). Braces have special meanings to the shell.

Bracket Either a square ([) or angle bracket (<). See *Square bracket* and *Angle bracket*.

Branch In a tree structure a branch connects nodes, leaves, and the root. The UNIX/Solaris filesystem hierarchy is often conceptualized as an upside-down tree. The branches connect files and directories. In a source code control system such as SCCS or RCS, a branch occurs when a revision is made to a file and is not included in other, subsequent revisions to the file.

Broadcast A transmission to multiple, unspecified recipients. On Ethernet, a broadcast packet is a special type of multicast packet, which all nodes on the network are always willing to receive.[FOD]

Broadcast address The last address on a subnet (usually 255), reserved as a shorthand to mean all hosts.

Broadcast network A type of network, such as Ethernet, in which any system can transmit information at any time, and all systems receive every message.

BSD See *Berkeley UNIX*.

Buffer An area of memory that stores data until it can be used. When you write information to a file on a disk, Solaris stores the information in a disk buffer until there is enough to write to the disk or until the disk is ready to receive the information.

Builtin (command) A command that is built into a shell. Each of the three major shells—the Bourne, C, and Korn Shells—has its own set of builtins. When the shell runs a builtin, it does not fork a new process. Consequently builtins run more quickly and can affect the environment of the current shell. Because builtins are used in the same way utilities are used, you will not typically be aware of whether a command is built into the shell or is a utility.

Byte A component in the machine data hierarchy usually larger than a bit and smaller than a word; now most often eight bits and the smallest addressable unit of storage. A byte typically holds one character.[FOD]

C programming language A modern systems language that has high-level features for efficient, modular programming as well as lower-level features that make it suitable as a systems programming language. It is machine-independent, so that carefully written C programs can be easily transported to run on different machines. Most of the UNIX/Solaris operating system is written in C, and UNIX/Solaris provides an ideal environment for programming in C.

C Shell The C Shell is a UNIX/Solaris command processor. It was originally developed by Bill Joy for Berkeley UNIX. It was named for the C programming language because its programming constructs are similar to those of C. See *Shell*.

Calling environment A list of variables and their values that is made available to a called program. See "Executing a Command" in Chapter 10 and "Variable Substitution" in Chapter 12.

Cache A small fast memory holding recently accessed data, designed to speed up subsequent access to the same data. Most often applied to processor-memory access but also used for a local copy of data accessible over a network, from a hard disk, and so on.^{FOLDOC}

Case-sensitive Able to distinguish between upper- and lowercase characters. Unless you set the **ignorecase** parameter, **vi** performs case-sensitive searches. The **grep** utility performs case-sensitive searches unless you use the **–i** option.

Catenate To join sequentially or end to end. The Solaris **cat** utility catenates files—it displays them one after the other. Also, *concatenate*.

Character class A group of characters in a regular expression that defines which characters can occupy a single character position. A character class definition is usually surrounded by square brackets. The character class defined by **[abcr]** represents a character position that can be occupied by **a**, **b**, **c**, or **r**.

Character device A terminal, printer, or modem. A character device stores or displays characters one at a time. A character device is represented by a character device (character special) file. Contrast with *Block device*.

Child process A process that was created by another process, the parent process. Every process is a child process except for the first process, which is started when Solaris begins execution. When you run a command from the shell, the shell spawns a child process to run the command. See *Process*.

Ciphertext Text that is encrypted. Contrast with *Plaintext*.

Cleartext Text that is not encrypted. Also, *plaintext*. Contrast with *Ciphertext*.

Client A computer (or program) that requests one or more services from a server.

Command What you give the shell in response to a prompt. When you give the shell a command, it executes a utility, another program, a built-in command, or a shell script. Utilities are often referred to as commands. When you are using an interactive utility such as **vi** or **mail**, you use commands that are appropriate to that utility.

Command line A line of instructions and arguments that executes a command. This term usually refers to a line that you enter in response to a shell prompt.

Command substitution What the shell does when you surround a command with backquotes or grave accent marks. The shell replaces the command, including the backquotes, with the output of the command.

Concatenate See *Catenate*.

Condition code See *Exit status*.

Console terminal The main system terminal, usually the one that receives system error messages. Also, *console*.

CONTROL character A character that is not a graphic character such as a letter, number, or punctuation mark. Such characters are called **CONTROL** characters because they frequently act to control a peripheral device. **RETURN** and **FORMFEED** are **CONTROL** characters that control a terminal or printer.

The word **CONTROL** is shown in this book in **THIS FONT** because it is a key that appears on most terminal keyboards. **CONTROL** characters are represented by ASCII codes less than 32 (decimal). Also, *nonprinting character*.

Control flow commands Commands that alter the order of execution of commands within a shell script or other program. Each one of the shells provides control structures, such as **If** and **While**, as well as other commands that alter the order of execution (for example **exec**).

Control structure A statement used to change the order of execution of commands in a shell script or other program. Control structures are among the commands referred to as control flow commands. See *Control flow commands*.

Cookie Data stored on a client system by a server. The client system browser sends the cookie back to the server each time it accesses that server. For example a catalog shopping service may store a cookie on your system when you place your first order. When you return to the site, it knows who you are and can supply your name and address for subsequent orders.

Cracker An individual who attempts to gain unauthorized access to a computer system. These individuals are often malicious and have many means at their disposal for breaking into a system.[FOD]

Crash The system stops unexpectedly. Derived from the action of the hard disk heads upon the surface of the disk when the air gap between the two collapses.

.cshrc file A file in your home directory that the C Shell executes each time you invoke a new C Shell. You can use this file to establish variables and aliases.

Current (process, line, character, directory, event, and so on) The item that is immediately available, working, or being used. The current process is the process that is controlling the program you are running; the current line or character is the one the cursor is on; the current directory is the working directory.

Cursor A small lighted rectangle or underscore that appears on the terminal screen and indicates where the next character is going to appear.

Daemon (From the mythological meaning, later rationalized as the acronym "Disk And Execution MONitor.") A program that is not invoked explicitly but lies dormant waiting for some condition(s) to occur. The idea is that the perpetrator of the condition need not be aware that a daemon is lurking (though often a program will commit an action only because it knows that it will implicitly invoke a daemon).[FOD]

Datagram	A self-contained, independent entity of data carrying sufficient information to be routed from the source to the destination computer without reliance on earlier exchanges between this source and destination computer and the transporting network.ᶠᴼᴰ
Dataless	A computer, usually a workstation, that uses a local disk to boot a copy of the operating system and access system files but does not use a local disk to store user files.
Debug	To correct a program by removing its bugs (that is, errors).
Default	Something that is selected without being explicitly specified. For example when used without an argument, **ls** displays a list of the files in the working directory by default.
Delta	A set of changes made to a file that has been encoded by the Source Code Control System (SCCS).
Denial of Service	An attack on a host or network that attempts to make the target unusable.
Detached process	See *Background process.*
Device	A disk drive, printer, terminal, plotter, or other input/output unit that can be attached to the computer.
Device driver	Part of the Solaris kernel that controls a device such as a terminal, disk drive, or printer.
Device file	A file that represents a device. Also, *special file.*
Device filename	The pathname of a device file. All UNIX/Solaris systems have two kinds of device files—block and character device files. Solaris and many versions of UNIX also have fifos (named pipes) and sockets. Device files are traditionally located in the **/dev** directory. Solaris stores easy-to-use names in **/dev** that point to the **/devices** directory.
Device number	See *Major device number* and *Minor device number.*
Directory	Short for *directory file.* A file that contains a list of other files.
Disk partition	See, *Partition.*
Diskless	A computer, usually a workstation, that has no disk and must contact another computer (a server) to boot a copy of the operating system and access the necessary system files.
Distributed computing	A style of computing in which tasks or services are performed by a network of cooperating systems, some of which may be specialized.
DNS	Domain Name Service. A distributed service that manages the correspondence of full hostnames (those that include a domain name) to IP addresses and other system characteristics.

Domain	A name associated with an organization, or part of an organization, to help identify systems uniquely. Domain names are assigned hierarchically; the domain Berkeley.EDU refers to the University of California at Berkeley, for example (part of the higher-level education domain).
Domain Name Service	See *DNS*.
Door	An evolving filesystem-based RPC mechanism.
Drag	To move an icon from one position or application to another, usually in the context of a window manager. The motion part of drag and drop.
Editor	A utility that creates and modifies text files. Solaris provides **dtpad**, **textedit**, **vi**, and others. A popular editor that is not supplied with Solaris is **emacs**. You can obtain the **emacs** text editor from GNU (Appendix B).
Effective user ID	The user ID that a process appears to have; usually the same as the user ID. For example while you are running a setuid program, the effective user ID of the process running the program is that of the owner of the program.
Element	One thing, usually a basic part of a group of things. An element of a numeric array is one of the numbers that are stored in the array.
Environment	See *Calling environment*.
EOF	End of File.
Escape	See *Quote*.
Ethernet	A type of local area network originally designed to transport data at rates up to 10 million bits per second over coaxial cable.
Event	An occurrence or happening of significance to a task or program, such as the completion of an asynchronous input/output operation such as a keypress or mouse click.[FOD]
Exit status	The status returned by a process; either successful (usually 0) or unsuccessful (usually 1).
Expression	See *Logical expression* and *Arithmetic expression*.
Failsafe session	A session that allows you to log in on a minimal desktop in case your standard login does not work well enough to allow you to log in to fix a login problem.
FDDI	Fiber Distributed Data Interface. A type of local area network designed to transport data at the rate of 100 million bits per second over fiberoptic cable.
File	A collection of related information, referred to by a filename. The UNIX/Solaris system views peripheral devices as files, allowing a program to read from or write to a device, just as it would read from or write to an ordinary file.

Filesystem	A data structure that usually resides on part of a disk. All UNIX/Solaris systems have a root filesystem, and most have at least a few other filesystems. Each filesystem is composed of some number of blocks, depending on the size of the disk partition that has been assigned to the filesystem. Each filesystem has a control block, named the superblock, that contains information about the filesystem. The other blocks in a filesystem are inodes, which contain control information about individual files, and data blocks, which contain the information in the files.
Filename	The name of a file. A filename is used to refer to a file.
Filename completion	Automatic completion of a filename after you specify a unique prefix.
Filename extension	The part of a filename following a period.
Filename generation	What occurs when the shell expands ambiguous file references. See *Ambiguous file-reference.*
Filter	A command that can take its input from standard input and send its output to standard output. A filter transforms the input stream of data and sends it to standard output. A pipe usually connects a filter's input to standard output of one command, and a second pipe connects the filter's output to standard input of another command. The **grep** and **sort** utilities are commonly used as filters.
Firewall	A method for keeping a network secure. It can be implemented in a single router that filters out unwanted packets, or it can use a combination of routers, proxy servers, and other devices. Firewalls are widely used to give users access to the Internet in a secure fashion as well as to separate a company's public WWW server from its internal network. They are also used to keep internal network segments more secure. See also, *proxy server.*
Footer	The part of a format that goes at the bottom (or foot) of a page. Contrast with *Header.*
Foreground process	When you run a command in the foreground, the shell waits for the command to finish before giving you another prompt. You must wait for a foreground process to run to completion before you can give the shell another command. If you have job control, you can move background processes to the foreground, and vice versa. See *Job control.* Contrast with *Background process.*
Fork	To create a process. When one process creates another process, it forks a process. Also, *spawn.*
Frame	A data link layer packet that contains the header and trailer information required by the physical medium. Network layer packets are encapsulated to become frames.[FOD]
Free list	The list of blocks in a filesystem that are available for use. Information about the free list is kept in the superblock of the filesystem.
Function	See *Shell function.*

Gateway

A device, often a computer, that is connected to more than one dissimilar type of network to pass data between them. Unlike a router, a gateway often must convert the information into a different format before passing it on.

Graphical User Interface

See *GUI.*

Group

A collection of users. Groups are used as a basis for determining file access permissions. If you are not the owner of a file and you belong to the group the file is assigned to, you are subject to the group access permissions for the file. On Solaris 2, a user may simultaneously belong to several groups. On older versions of UNIX/Solaris, each user belongs to only one group at a time, although a user may temporarily change group affiliation with the **newgrp** command.

Group ID

A unique number that identifies a set of users. It is stored in the password and group databases (**/etc/passwd** and **/etc/group** files or their NIS equivalents). The group database associates group IDs with group names.

GUI

Graphical User Interface. A GUI provides a way to interact with a computer system by choosing items from menus or manipulating pictures drawn on a display screen, instead of by typing command lines.

Hacker

A person who enjoys exploring the details of programmable systems and how to stretch their capabilities, as opposed to users who prefer to learn only the minimum necessary. One who programs enthusiastically (even obsessively) or who enjoys programming rather than just theorizing about programming.[FOD]

Hard link

A directory entry that contains the filename and inode number for a file. The inode number identifies the location of control information for the file on the disk, which in turn identifies the location of the file's contents on the disk. Every file has at least one hard link, which locates the file in a directory. When you remove the last hard link to a file, you can no longer access the file. See *Link* and *Symbolic link.*

Header

When you are formatting a document, the header goes at the top (or head) of a page. In electronic mail the header identifies who sent the message, when it was sent, the subject of the message, and so forth.

Here document

A shell script that takes its input from the file that contains the script.

Hexadecimal number

A base 16 number. Hexadecimal (or *hex*) numbers are composed of the hexadecimal digits 0–9 and A–F. Refer to the following table.

Decimal	Octal	Hex	Decimal	Octal	Hex
1	1	1	17	21	11
2	2	2	18	22	12
3	3	3	19	23	13
4	4	4	20	24	14

Decimal	Octal	Hex	Decimal	Octal	Hex
5	5	5	21	25	15
6	6	6	31	37	1F
7	7	7	32	40	20
8	10	8	33	41	21
9	11	9	64	100	40
10	12	A	96	140	60
11	13	B	100	144	64
12	14	C	128	200	80
13	15	D	254	376	FE
14	16	E	255	377	FF
15	17	F	256	400	100
16	20	10	257	401	101

Hidden file   See *Invisible file*.

History   A mechanism provided by the C and Korn Shells that enables you to modify and reexecute recent commands.

Home directory   The directory that is your working directory when you first log in. The pathname of this directory is stored in the **HOME** shell variable.

Hub   The central connecting device in networks (primarily ethernet) that are arranged with a *star* topology (as opposed to a *ring*). A generic term for a layer-2 shared-media networking device.

Icon   A small picture drawn on a display screen as a placeholder for a larger window.

Iconify   The process of changing a window into an icon. Contrast with *Restore*.

Indentation   See *Indention*.

Indention   The blank space between the margin and the beginning of a line that is set in from the margin.

Inode   A data structure that contains information about a file. An inode for a file contains the file's length, the times the file was last accessed and modified, the time the inode was last modified, owner and group IDs, access privileges, number of links, and pointers to the data blocks that contain the file itself. Each directory entry associates a filename with an inode. Although a single file may have several filenames (one for each link), it has only one inode.

Internet   The Internet (capital I) is the largest internet in the world. It is a multilevel hierarchy composed of backbone networks (e.g., ARPAnet, NSFNet, MILNET), mid-level networks, and stub networks. These include commercial (**.com** or **.co**), university (**.ac**

or **.edu**), research (**.org** or **.net**), and military (**.mil**) networks and span many different physical networks around the world with various protocols including the Internet Protocol (IP). Outside the United States country code domains are popular (**.us**, **.es**, **.mx**, **.de**, and so forth) although you will see them used within the United States too.

Input Information that is fed to a program from a terminal or other file. See *Standard input*.

Installation A computer at a specific location. Some aspects of the Solaris system are installation-dependent. Also, *site*.

Interactive A program that allows ongoing dialogue with the user. When you give commands in response to shell prompts, you are using the shell interactively. Also, when you give commands to utilities such as **vi** and **mail**, you are using the utilities interactively.

Interface The meeting point of two subsystems. When two programs work together in some way, their interface includes every aspect of either program that the other deals with. The *user interface* of a program includes every aspect of the program the user comes into contact with—the syntax and semantics involved in invoking the program, the input and output of the program, and its error and informational messages. The shell and each of the utilities and built-in commands has a user interface.

Invisible file A file whose filename starts with a period. These files are called invisible because the **ls** utility does not normally list them. Use the **–a** option of **ls** to list all files, including invisible ones. Also, the shell does not expand a leading asterisk (∗) in an ambiguous file reference to match the filename of an invisible file. Also, *hidden file*.

I/O device Short for Input/Output device. See *Device*.

IP address A four-part address associated with a particular network connection for a system using the Internet Protocol (IP). A system that is attached to multiple networks that use the IP will have a different IP address for each network interface.

IP multicast Transmitting data to a group of selected users at the same time on a network. IP multicast reduces network traffic by transmitting a packet one time, with the router at the end of the path breaking it apart as needed for multiple recipients.

Job control A facility that enables you to move commands from the foreground to the background, and vice versa. C and Korn Shell job control enables you to stop commands temporarily.

jpeg Joint Photographic Experts Group. The original name of the committee that designed the standard image compression algorithm. JPEG is designed for compressing either full-color or grey-scale digital images of natural, real-world scenes. It does not work as well on non-realistic images, such as cartoons or line drawings. Filename extensions: **.jpg**, **.jpeg**.^{FOD}

Jumpstart This Solaris service allows rapid installation of a new system simply by plugging it into the network and turning it on.

Justify	To expand a line of type to the right margin in the process of formatting text. A line is justified by increasing the space between words and sometimes between letters on the line.
Kerberos	A security system developed at MIT that authenticates users and machines. It does not provide authorization to services or databases; it establishes identity at logon, which is used throughout the session. Once you are authenticated you can open as many terminals, windows, services, or other network accesses until your session expires.
Kernel	The essential part of UNIX/Solaris, responsible for resource allocation, low-level hardware interfaces, security, and so on.^{FOD}
Korn Shell	A command processor developed by David Korn at AT&T Bell Laboratories. It is compatible with the Bourne Shell but includes many extensions. See *Shell*.
Keyboard	A hardware input device consisting of a number of mechanical buttons (keys) that the user presses to input characters to a computer. By default a keyboard is connected to standard input of a shell.^{FOD}
LAN	See *Local Area Network*.
Leaf	In a tree structure, the end of a branch that cannot support other branches. When the Solaris filesystem hierarchy is conceptualized as a tree, files that are not directories are leaves. See *Node*.
Least privilege, concept of	Mistakes that Superuser makes can be much more devastating than those made by an ordinary user. When you are working on the computer, especially when you are working as the system administrator, always perform any task using the least privilege possible. If you can perform a task logged in as an ordinary user, do so. If you must be logged in as Superuser, do as much as you can as an ordinary user, log in or **su** so you are Superuser, do as much of the task as has to be done as Superuser, and revert to being an ordinary user as soon as you can. Because you are more likely to make a mistake when you are rushing, this concept becomes more important when you have less time to apply it.
Link	A pointer to a file. There are two kinds of links—hard links and symbolic (soft) links. A hard link associates a filename with a place on the disk where the contents of the file is located. A symbolic link associates a filename with the pathname of a hard link to a file. See *Hard link* and *Symbolic link*.
Local Area Network	A network that connects computers within a localized area (such as a single site, building, or department).
Log in	To gain access to a computer system by responding correctly to the `login:` and `Password:` prompts. Also, *log on*.
Log out	To end your session by exiting from your login shell. Also, *log off*.

Logical expression   A collection of strings separated by logical operators (>, >=, =, !=, <=, and <) that can be evaluated as true or false.

.login file   A file the C Shell executes when you log in. You can use it to set environment variables and to run commands that you want executed at the beginning of each session.

Login name   The name you enter in response to the login: prompt. Other users use your login name when they send you mail or write to you. Each login name has a corresponding user ID, which is the numeric identifier for the user. Both the login name and the user ID are stored in the password database (**/etc/passwd** or the NIS equivalent).

Login shell   The shell that you are using when you first log in. The login shell can fork other processes that can run other shells, utilities, and programs.

.logout file   A file the C Shell executes when you log off, assuming the C Shell is your login shell. You can put commands in the **.logout** file that you want run each time you log off.

Machine collating sequence   The sequence in which the computer orders characters. The machine collating sequence affects the outcome of sorts and other procedures that put lists in alphabetical order. Many computers use ASCII codes, and so their machine collating sequences correspond to the ordering of the ASCII codes for characters.

Macro   A single instruction that a program replaces by several (usually more complex) instructions. The C compiler recognizes macros, which are defined using a **#define** instruction to the preprocessor.

Magic number   The magic number occurs in the first 512 bytes of a program and is the numeric or character string that uniquely identifies the type of file (much like a DOS 3-character filename extension). See the magic **man** page (4) for more information.

Main memory   Random Access Memory (RAM) that is an integral part of the computer. It is contrasted with disk storage. Although disk storage is sometimes referred to as memory, it is never referred to as main memory.

Major device number   A number assigned to a class of devices such as terminals, printers, or disk drives. Using the **ls** utility with the **–l** option to list the contents of the **/devices** directory displays the major and minor device numbers of many devices (as *major, minor*).

MAN   See *Metropolitan Area Network*.

Menu   A list from which the user may select an operation to be performed. This is often done with a mouse or other pointing device under a Graphical User Interface but may also be controlled from the keyboard. Menus are very convenient for beginners because they show what commands are available and make experimenting with a new program easy, often reducing the need for user documentation. Experienced users, however, usually prefer keyboard commands, especially for frequently used operations, because they are faster to use.[FOD]

Metropolitan Area Network	A network that connects computers and local area networks at multiple sites in a small regional area, such as a city.
Merge	To combine two ordered lists so that the resulting list is still in order. The **sort** utility can merge files.
Metacharacter	A character that has a special meaning to the shell or another program in a particular context. Metacharacters are used in the ambiguous file references recognized by the shell and in the regular expressions recognized by several utilities. You must quote a metacharacter if you want to use it without invoking its special meaning. See *Regular character* and *Special character*.
META key	A key on the keyboard that is labeled META or ALT. Use this key as you would the SHIFT key. While holding it down, press another key. The **emacs** editor makes extensive use of the META key.
Minimize	See *Iconify*.
Minor device number	A number assigned to a specific device within a class of devices. See *Major device number*.
Mount	To make a filesystem accessible to system users. When a filesystem is not mounted, you cannot read from or write to files it contains.
Mount point	A directory that you mount a local or remote filesystem on.
Mouse	A mouse is a device that you use to point to a particular location on a display screen, typically so you can choose a menu item, draw a line, or highlight some text. You control a pointer on the screen by sliding a mouse around on a flat surface; the position of the pointer moves relative to the movement of the mouse. You select items by pressing one or more buttons on the mouse.
Multitasking	A computer system that allows a user to run more than one job at a time. One way you can tell that Solaris is multitasking is that it allows you to run a job in the background while running a job in the foreground.
Multiuser system	A computer system that can be used by more than one person at a time. Solaris is a multiuser operating system. Contrast with *Single-user system*.
Netiquette	The conventions of politeness recognized on USENET and in mailing lists, such as not (cross-)posting to inappropriate groups and refraining from commercial advertising outside the business groups. The most important rule of netiquette is "Think before you post." If what you intend to post will not make a positive contribution to the newsgroup and be of interest to several readers, do not post it. Personal messages to one or two individuals should not be posted to newsgroups, use private e-mail instead.ᶠᴼᴰ
Netmask	A 32-bit mask (for IPv4), which shows how an Internet address is to be divided into network, subnet, and host parts. The netmask has ones in the bit positions in the

32-bit address, which are to be used for the network and subnet parts, and zeros for the host part. The mask should contain at least the standard network portion (as determined by the address class), and the subnet field should be contiguous with the network portion.^{FOD}

Network address The network portion (**netid**) of an IP address. For a class A network, this is the first byte or segment of the IP address, for class B it is the first two bytes, and for class C it is the first three bytes. In each case the balance of the IP address is the host address (**hostid**). Assigned network addresses are globally unique within the Internet. Also, *network number*.

Network File System See *NFS*.

Network Information Service See *NIS*.

NFS Network File System. A remote filesystem designed by Sun Microsystems, available on computers from most UNIX system vendors.

NIS Network Information Service. A distributed service built on a shared database to manage system-independent information (such as login names and passwords).

Network segment A part of an Ethernet or other network, on which all message traffic is common to all nodes, that is, it is broadcast from one node on the segment and received by all others. This is normally because the segment is a single continuous conductor. Communication between nodes on different segments is via one or more routers.^{FOD}

Network switch A connecting device in networks. Switches are increasingly replacing shared media hubs in order to increase bandwidth. For example a 16-port 10BaseT hub shares the total 10Mbps bandwidth with all 16 attached nodes. By replacing the hub with a switch, each sender and receiver has the full 10Mbps capacity. Each port on the switch can give full bandwidth to a single server or client station or to a hub with several stations.

Node In a tree structure, the end of a branch that can support other branches. When the Solaris filesystem hierarchy is conceptualized as a tree, directories are nodes. See *Leaf*.

Nonprinting character See **CONTROL** *character*. Also, *nonprintable character*.

Null string A string that could contain characters but does not. A string of zero length.

Octal number A base 8 number. Octal numbers are composed of the digits 0–7, inclusive. Refer to the table under *Hexadecimal number*.

Operating system A control program for a computer that allocates computer resources, schedules tasks, and provides the user with a way to access resources.

Option	A command line argument that modifies the effects of a command. Options are usually preceded by hyphens on the command line, and they usually have single character names (such as **–h**, **–n**). Some commands allow you to group options following a single hyphen (for example **–hn**).
Ordinary file	A file that is used to store a program, text, or other user data. See *Directory* and *Device file*.
Output	Information that a program sends to the terminal or another file. See *Standard output*.
Packet	A unit of data sent across a network. *Packet* is a generic term used to describe a unit of data at any layer of the OSI protocol stack, but it is most correctly used to describe application layer data units ("application protocol data unit," APDU).[FOD]
Paging	The process by which virtual memory is maintained by the operating system. The contents of process memory is moved (paged out) to the swap area as needed to make room for other processes.
Parent process	A process that forks other processes. See *Process* and *Child process*.
Partition	A section of a (hard) disk that has a name so you can address it separately from other sections. A disk partition can hold a filesystem or another structure, such as the swap area. Under DOS/MS Windows partitions (and sometimes whole disks) are labeled **C:**, **D:**, and so on. Also, *slice* and *disk partition*.
Pathname	A list of directories separated by slashes (/) and ending with the name of a file which can be a directory or not. A pathname is used to trace a path through the file structure to locate or identify a file.
Pathname element	One of the filenames that form a pathname.
Pathname, last element of a	The part of a pathname following the final /, or the whole filename if there is no /. A simple filename. Also, *basename*.
Peripheral device	See *Device*.
Persistent	Data that is stored on nonvolatile media such as a hard disk.
Physical device	A tangible device, such as a disk drive, that is physically separate from other similar devices.
PID	Process IDentification, usually followed by the word *number*. Solaris assigns a unique PID number as each process is initiated.
Pipe	A connection between programs such that standard output of one is connected to standard input of the next. Also, *pipeline*.
Pixel	The smallest element of a picture, typically a single dot on a display screen.
Plaintext	Text that is not encrypted. Contrast *Ciphertext*.

Point-to-point link A connection limited to two endpoints, such as the connection between a pair of modems.

Port The number assigned to an application program running on a TCP/IP-based network such as the Internet. The number links incoming data to the correct service (program). Standard, well-known ports are used by everyone: Port 80 is used for HTTP (Web) traffic.

Printable character One of the graphic characters: A letter, number, or punctuation mark; contrasted with a nonprintable or CONTROL character. Also, *printing character.*

Process The execution of a program.

.profile file A startup file that a Bourne or Korn login shell executes when you log in. The C Shell executes **.login** instead. You can use the **.profile** file to run commands, set variables, and define functions.

Program A sequence of executable computer instructions contained in a file. Solaris utilities, applications, and shell scripts are all programs. Whenever you run a command that is not built into a shell, you are executing a program.

Prompt A cue from a program, usually displayed on the screen, indicating that it is waiting for input. The shell displays a prompt, as do some of the interactive utilities, such as **Mail**. By default the Bourne and Korn Shells use a dollar sign ($) as a prompt and the C Shell uses a percent sign (%).

Proxy server An application that serves as a firewall by breaking the connection between the sender and receiver. All input is forwarded out a different port, closing a straight path between two networks and preventing a cracker from obtaining internal addresses and details about a private network.

Proxy servers are available for common Internet services such as HTTP, FTP, and SNMP. For example an HTTP proxy is used for Web access and presents only one organization-wide address (IP address) to the Internet. It funnels all user requests to the Internet and keeps track of them. When the responses come back, it fans them back out to the appropriate users, using their unique IP addresses. Proxy servers are generally just one part of an overall firewall strategy to prevent intruders from stealing information or damaging an internal network. Other functions, which may be combined with or be separate from the proxy application are packet filtering, which blocks traffic based on origin and type, and user activity reporting, which helps management learn how the Internet is being used. Finally, the proxy server may cache frequently used Web pages so that the next request for that page is available locally. Also, *proxy.*

Quote When you quote a character, you take away any special meaning that it has in the current context. You can quote a character by preceding it with a backslash. When you are interacting with the shell, you can also quote a character by surrounding it with single quotation marks. For example the command **echo *** or **echo '*'** displays *.

The command **echo** ✳ displays a list of the files in the working directory. Also, *Escape.* See *Ambiguous file reference, Metacharacter, Regular character, Regular expression,* and *Special character.*

RAS See *Remote Access Server.*

Redirection The process of directing standard input for a program to come from a file rather than from the keyboard. Also, directing standard output or standard error to go to a file rather than to the screen.

Reentrant Code that can have multiple simultaneous, interleaved, or nested invocations that do not interfere with each other. Non interference is important for parallel processing, recursive programming, and interrupt handling.

It is usually easy to arrange for multiple invocations (that is, calls to a subroutine) to share one copy of the code and any readonly data, but, for the code to be reentrant, each invocation must use its own copy of any modifiable data (or synchronized access to shared data). This is most often achieved using a stack and allocating local variables in a new stack frame for each invocation. Alternatively the caller may pass in a pointer to a block of memory which that invocation can use (usually for outputting the result) or the code may allocate some memory on a heap, especially if the data must survive after the routine returns.

Reentrant code is often found in system software, such as operating systems and teleprocessing monitors. It is also a crucial component of multithreaded programs where the term *thread-safe* is often used instead of reentrant.^{FOD}

Regular character A character that always represents itself in an ambiguous file reference or another type of regular expression. Contrast with *Special character.*

Regular expression A string—composed of letters, numbers, and special symbols—that defines one or more strings. See Appendix A.

Relative pathname A pathname that starts from the working directory. Contrast with *Absolute pathname.*

Remote access server A computer in a network that provides access to remote users via analog modem or ISDN connections. It includes the dialup protocols and access control (authentication) and may be a regular file server with remote access software or a proprietary system such as Shiva's LANRover. The modems may be internal or external to the device. Also, *RAS.*

Remote filesystem A filesystem on a remote computer that has been set up so that you can access (usually over a network) its files as though they were stored on your local computer's disks. An example of a remote filesystem is NFS.

Restore The process of turning an icon into a window. Contrast with *Iconify.*

Return code See *Exit status.*

Root directory   The ancestor of all directories and the start of all absolute pathnames. The name of the root directory is /.

Root filesystem   The filesystem that is available when the system is brought up in single-user mode. The name of this filesystem is always /. You cannot unmount or mount the root filesystem.

Root login   Usually the login name of Superuser. See *Superuser*.

Router   A device, often a computer, that is connected to more than one similar type of network to pass data between them. See *Gateway*.

Run   To execute a program.

Scroll   To move lines on a terminal or window up and down or left and right.

Server   A powerful, centralized computer (or program) designed to provide information to clients (smaller computers or programs) on request.

Session   The lifetime of a process. For a desktop it is the desktop session manager. For a character-based terminal it is the user's login shell process. In the CDE it is launched by **dtlogin**. Or the sequence of events between when you start using a program, such as an editor, and when you finish.

Setgid   When you execute a file that has setgid (set group ID) permission, the process executing the file takes on the privileges of the group the file belongs to. The **ls** utility shows setgid permission as an s in the group's executable position. See *Setuid*.

Setuid   When you execute a file that has setuid (set user ID) permission, the process executing the file takes on the privileges of the owner of the file. As an example if you run a setuid program that removes all the files in a directory, you can remove files in any of the file owner's directories even if you do not normally have permission to do so. The **ls** utility shows setuid permission as an s in the owner's executable position. See *Setgid*.

Shell   A UNIX/Solaris system command processor. There are three major shells: The Bourne Shell, the C Shell, and the Korn Shell. See *Bourne Shell*, *C Shell*, and *Korn Shell*.

Shell function   A series of commands that the shell stores for execution at a later time. Shell functions are like shell scripts, but they run more quickly because they are stored in the computer's main memory rather than in files. Also, a shell function is run in the environment of the shell that calls it (unlike a shell script, which is typically run in a subshell).

Shell script   A program composed of shell commands. Also, *shell program*.

Signal   A very brief message that the UNIX system can send to a process, apart from the process's standard input.

Simple filename	A single filename, containing no slashes (/). A simple filename is the simplest form of a pathname. Also, the last element of a pathname. Also, *basename*.
Single-user system	A computer system that only one person can use at a time. Contrast with *Multiuser system*.
Sort	To put in a specified order, usually alphabetic or numeric.
SPACE character	A character that appears as the absence of a visible character. Even though you cannot see it, a **SPACE** is a printable character. It is represented by the ASCII code 32 (decimal). A **SPACE** character is considered a *blank* or *white space*.
Spam	(From the Monty Python *Spam* song.) To post irrelevant or inappropriate messages to one or more USENET newsgroups or mailing lists in deliberate or accidental violation of netiquette (see also). Also, to send large amounts of unsolicited email indiscriminately. This email usually promotes a product or service. Spam is the electronic equivalent of junk mail.^{FOD}
Sparse file	A file that is large but takes up little disk space. The data in a sparse file is not dense (thus its name). Examples of sparse files are core files, dbm files, and **/etc/utmp** (→ **/var/adm/utmp**).
Spawn	See *Fork*.
Special character	A character that has a special meaning when it occurs in an ambiguous file reference or another type of regular expression, unless it is quoted. The special characters most commonly used with the shell are * and ?. Also, *metacharacter* and *wild card*.
Special file	See *Device file*.
Spool	To place items in a queue, each waiting its turn for some action. Often used when speaking about the **lp** utility and the printer; that is, **lp** spools files for the printer.
SQL	Structured Query Language. A language that provides a user interface to relational database management systems (RDBMS). SQL is the de facto standard, as well as being an ISO and ANSI standard. It is often embedded in other programming languages.^{FOD}
Square bracket	There is a left square bracket ([) and a right square bracket (]). They are special characters that define character classes in ambiguous file references and other regular expressions.
Standard error	A file to which a program can send output. Usually only error messages are sent to this file. Unless you instruct the shell otherwise, it directs this output to the screen (that is, to the device file that represents the screen).
Standard input	A file from which a program can receive input. Unless you instruct the shell otherwise, it directs this input so that it comes from the keyboard (that is, from the device file that represents the keyboard).

Standard output   A file to which a program can send output. Unless you instruct the shell otherwise, it directs this output to the screen (that is, to the device file that represents the screen).

Startup file   A file that the login shell runs when you log in. The Bourne and Korn Shells run **.pro-file**, and the C Shell runs **.login**. The C Shell also runs **.cshrc** whenever a new C Shell or a subshell is invoked. The Korn Shell runs an analogous file whose name is identified by the **ENV** variable.

Status line   The bottom (usually the 24th) line of the terminal. The **vi** editor uses the status line to display information about what is happening during an editing session.

Sticky bit   An access permission bit that causes an executable program to remain on the swap area of the disk. It takes less time to load a program that has its sticky bit set than one that does not. Only Superuser can set the sticky bit. If the sticky bit is set on a directory that is publicly writable, only the owner of a file in that directory can remove the file.

Streaming tape   A tape that moves at a constant speed past the read/write heads rather than speeding up and slowing down, which can slow the process of writing to or reading from the tape. A proper blocking factor helps ensure that the tape device will be kept streaming.

String   A sequence of characters.

Subdirectory   A directory that is located within another directory. Every directory except the root directory is a subdirectory.

Subnet   A portion of a network, which may be a physically independent network segment, which shares a network address with other portions of the network and is distinguished by a subnet number. A subnet is to a network what a network is to an internet.

Subnet address   The subnet portion of an IP address. In a subnetted network the host portion of an IP address is split into a subnet portion and a host portion using an address mask (the subnet mask).

Subnet mask   A bit mask used to identify which bits in an IP address correspond to the network address and subnet portions of the address. This mask is often referred to as the *subnet mask* because the network portion of the address can be determined by the class inherent in an IP address. The address mask has ones in positions corresponding to the network and subnet numbers and zeros in the host number positions. Also, *address mask*.

Subnet number   The subnet portion of an IP address. In a subnetted network the host portion of an IP address is split into a subnet portion and a host portion using an address mask (the subnet mask).

     If a plus sign (**+**) appears where the netmask should be in the **/etc/netmasks** file, it indicates that the network number is in the NIS **netmasks.byaddr** map.

Subshell   A shell that is forked as a duplicate of its parent shell. When you run an executable file that contains a shell script by using its filename on the command line, the shell forks a subshell to run the script. Also, commands surrounded with parentheses are run in a subshell.

Superblock   A block that contains control information for a filesystem. The superblock contains housekeeping information, such as the number of inodes in the filesystem and free list information.

Superuser   A privileged user who has access to anything any other system user has access to and more. The system administrator must be able to become Superuser in order to establish new accounts, change passwords, and perform other administrative tasks. The login name of Superuser is typically **root**.

Swap   What occurs when the operating system moves a process from main memory to a disk, or vice versa. Swapping a process to the disk allows another process to begin or continue execution.

Swap space   An area of a disk (that is, a swap file) used to store the portion of a processes' memory that has been paged out. Under a virtual memory system, it is the amount of swap space rather than the amount of physical memory that determines the maximum size of a single process and the maximum total size of all active processes. Also, *swap area* or *swapping area*.[FOD]

Switch   See *Network switch*.

Symbolic link   A directory entry that points to the pathname of another file. In most cases a symbolic link to a file can be used in the same ways a hard link can be used. Unlike a hard link, a symbolic link can span filesystems and can connect to a directory.

System administrator   The person who is responsible for the upkeep of the system. The system administrator has the ability to log in as Superuser. See *Superuser*.

System console   See *Console terminal*.

System mode   The designation for the state of the system while it is doing system work. Some examples are: Making system calls, running NFS and autofs, processing network traffic, and performing kernel operations on behalf of system. Contrast with *User mode*.

System V   One of the two major versions of the UNIX system.

Tape, streaming   See *Streaming tape*.

Termcap   Terminal capability. The **termcap** file contains a list of various types of terminals and their characteristics. System V replaced the function of this file with **terminfo**.

Terminfo   Terminal information. The **/usr/lib/terminfo** directory contains many subdirectories, each containing several files. Each of these files is named for, and contains a summary of the functional characteristics of, a particular terminal. Visually oriented programs, such as **vi**, make use of these files. An alternative to the **termcap** file.

Thicknet	A type of coaxial cable (thick) used for an Ethernet network. Devices are attached to thicknet by tapping the cable at certain fixed points.
Thinnet	A type of coaxial cable (thin) used for an Ethernet network. Thinnet cable is smaller in diameter and more flexible than thicknet cable. Each device is typically attached to two separate cable segments using a T-shaped connector; one segment leads to the device ahead of it on the network and one to the device that precedes it.
Thread-safe	See *Reentrant.*
tiff	Tagged Image File Format. A file format used for still-image bitmaps, stored in tagged fields. Application programs can use the tags to accept or ignore fields, depending on their capabilities.ᶠᴼᴰ
Token ring	A type of local area network in which computers are attached to a ring of cable. A token packet circulates continuously around the ring; a computer can transmit information only when it holds the token.
ToolTalk	A Solaris service that allows applications to communicate with each other without knowing about each other's presence. Applications create and send ToolTalk messages, and the ToolTalk service forwards them to the correct applications.
Trojan horse	A program that does something destructive or disruptive to your system. Its action is not documented and the system administrator would not approve of it if he or she were aware of it. See "Avoiding a Trojan Horse" (page 594).
	(Coined by MIT-hacker-turned-NSA-spook Dan Edwards.) A malicious security-breaking program that is disguised as something benign, such as a directory lister, archive utility, game, or (in one notorious 1990 case on the Mac) a program to find and destroy viruses. Similar to *back door.*ᶠᴼᴰ
TTY	Teletypewriter. A terminal.
Usage message	A message displayed by a command when you call the command using incorrect command line arguments.
User ID	A number that the password database associates with a login name. Also, *UID.*
User interface	See *Interface.*
User mode	The designation for the state of the system while it is doing user work such as running a user program (but not the system calls made by the program). Contrast with *System mode.*
Utility	A program included as a standard part of Solaris. You typically invoke a utility either by giving a command in response to a shell prompt or by calling it from within a shell script. Utilities are often referred to as commands. Contrast with *Built-in command.*
Variable	A name and an associated value. The shell allows you to create variables and use them in shell scripts. Also, the shell inherits several variables when it is invoked, and

it maintains those and other variables while it is running. Some shell variables establish characteristics of the shell environment, whereas others have values that reflect different aspects of your ongoing interaction with the shell.

Virus   (By analogy with biological viruses.) A cracker program that searches out other programs and "infects" them by embedding a copy of itself in them, so that they become Trojan horses (see also). When these programs are executed, the embedded virus is executed too, propagating the "infection," usually without the user's knowledge.[FOD]

WAN   See *Wide Area Network*.

Whitespace   A collective name for SPACEs and/or TABs and occasionally NEWLINEs. Also, *white space*.

Wide Area Network   A network that interconnects LANs and MANs, spanning a large geographic area (typically in different states or countries).

Wild card   See *Metacharacter*.

Window   A region on a display screen that runs, or is controlled by, some particular program.

Window manager   A program that controls how windows appear on a display screen and how you manipulate them.

Word   A sequence of one or more nonblank characters separated from other words by TABs, SPACEs, or NEWLINEs. Used to refer to individual command line arguments. In **vi** a word is similar to a word in the English language—a string of one or more characters that is bounded by a punctuation mark, a numeral, a TAB, a SPACE, or a NEWLINE.

Work Buffer   A location where **vi** stores text while it is being edited. The information in the Work Buffer is not written to the file on the disk until you command the editor to write it.

Working directory   The directory that you are associated with at any given time. The relative pathnames you use are *relative to* the working directory. Also, *current directory*.

Workstation   A small computer, typically designed to fit in an office and be used by one person. It is usually equipped with a bit-mapped graphical display, keyboard, and mouse.

Worm   (From *Tapeworm* in John Brunner's novel *The Shockwave Rider*, Ballantine Books, 1990. [via XEROX PARC]) A program that propagates itself over a network, reproducing itself as it goes. Nowadays the term has negative connotations, as it is assumed that only crackers write worms. Compare *Virus, Trojan horse*.[FOD]

XDMCP   X Display Manager Control Protocol. XDMCP allows the login server to accept requests from network displays. XDMCP is built into many X terminals.

X terminal   A graphics terminal designed to run the X Window System.

X Window System   A design and set of tools for writing flexible, portable windowing applications, created jointly by researchers at the MIT and several leading computer manufacturers.

Index

Symbols

Trademark Acknowledgments

Alpha, VMS: Digital Equipment Corporation (DEC)

CDE is a product of the Open Group and ported by Xi Graphics

CTOS: Unisys

emacs: Free Software Foundation

Excel, DOS, MS-DOS, Word, Windows, Windows 95, Windows NT: Microsoft, Inc.

HP Deskjet: Hewlett Packard, Inc.

Infoseek: Infoseek Corporation

Macintosh, PowerMacintosh: Apple Computer, Inc.

Netscape: Netscape Communications Corporation

PostScript: Adobe Software, Inc.

Power PC: International Business Machines Corporation

Quicken, TurboTax Deluxe for Windows, TurboTax for DOS: Intuit, Inc.

Solaris, Sun, and SunOS: Sun Microsystems, Inc.

UNIX is a registered trademark in the United States and other countries, licensed exclusively through X/Open Company, Ltd.

X Window System: MIT